WHERE to SKI
AND Snowboard 2007

Published in Great Britain by
NortonWood Publishing
The Old Forge
Norton St Philip
Bath BA2 7LW
United Kingdom

tel 01373 835208
e-mail w11@wtss.co.uk

Editors Chris Gill and Dave Watts
Assistant editors Mandy Crook,
Catherine Weakley, Leigh Thompson,
Henry Druce, Wendy-Jane King,
Sheila Reid, Rebecca Miles
Pacific editor Bronwen Gora
Contributors Chris Allan,
Minty Clinch, Alan Coulson,
Nicky Holford, James Hooke,
Eric Jackson, Tim Perry, Ian Porter,
Adam Ruck, Helena Wiesner,
Fraser Wilkin
Admin assistant Sian Blackmar
Research assistant Alex Gill

Advertising managers
Richard Luscombe, Dave Ashmore

Design by Val Fox
Production by Guide Editors
Contents photos generally
by Snowpix.com / Chris Gill
Production manager Ian Stratford
Proof-readers Sally Vince,
Robin Campbell
Printed and bound in Italy
by Officine Grafiche Calderini SpA

This edition published 2006
Copyright (text and illustrations)
© Chris Gill and Dave Watts 2006

The right of Chris Gill and Dave Watts
to be identified as Authors of this
Work has been asserted by them in
accordance with the Copyright,
Design and Patents Act 1988.

Although every care has been taken in
compiling this publication, using the
most up-to-date information available
at the time of going to press, all details
are liable to change and cannot be
guaranteed. Neither NortonWood
Publishing nor the editors accept any
liability whatsoever arising from errors
or omissions, however caused.

10 9 8 7 6 5 4 3 2 1

ISBN-10:   0–9536371–8–2
ISBN-13:   978–0–9536371–8–8

A CIP catalogue entry for this book is
available from the British Library.

Book trade sales are handled by
Portfolio Books Ltd
Unit 5, Perivale Industrial Park
Horsenden Lane South
Greenford UB6 7RL
tel 020 8997 9000
fax 020 8997 9097
e-mail sales@portfoliobooks.com

**Individual copies of the book can be
bought by calling: 01373 835208**

**You can buy the book online at
amazon.co.uk by using a link from our
website at www.wtss.co.uk**

WHERE *to* SKI
AND *Snowboard* 2007

The 1,000 Best Winter Sports Resorts in the World

Edited by
Chris Gill
and
Dave Watts

NortonWood

fascinates YOU.

Stubai Facts

- Stubai Glacier - Austria's largest glacier area
- absolutely snow-guaranteed from October until June
- Family-friendly: children under 10 ride the cablecars free of charge
- Child care at Mickey Mouse Ski Club
- Family hotels
- Easily reachable - just 20 minutes transfer from Innsbruck Airport to your hotel
- Winter diversity: 4 ski areas, 147 km of ski runs, 67 km of sledding runs, 130 km of cross country ski trails

Tourist Association Stubai Tyrol
Dorf 3 | 6167 Neustift | Austria
Tel. +43 5226 2228 | Fax +43 5226 2529
info@stubai.at | **www.stubai.at**

Contents

Resort chapters

About this book

It's simply the best

Where to Ski and Snowboard is the best guide to winter sports resorts that you can buy. Here's why:

- With every new edition we aim to take a step forward. This year, we have **new chapters** on areas in Austria, Italy, Switzerland and the US, and coverage for the first time of Japan and South America. We have yet again added 32 pages to the book – since the first edition we have expanded it by 50 per cent, from 512 to 768 pages. Many of these extra pages this year are devoted to expanding our coverage of the 20 most important resorts.

- By making the most of technology we are able to publish at the right time while going to press very late by conventional book publishing standards – so we can include the late-breaking news that makes the book **up to date for the season ahead**. When we started in the early 1990s, we went to press in June; this year, it's 6 August, only a month ahead of publication day.

- We work hard to make our information **reader-friendly**, with clearly structured text, comparative ratings and no-nonsense verdicts for the main aspects of each resort. This year we have introduced double-page piste maps with helpful annotations.

- We don't hesitate to express **critical views**. We learned our craft at Consumers' Association, where Chris became editor of *Holiday Which?* magazine and Dave became editor of *Which?* itself – so a consumerist attitude comes naturally to us.

- Our resort chapters give an **unrivalled level of detail** – including scale plans of each major resort, so that you get a clear idea of size, and all the facts you need.

- The book benefits enormously from the **hundreds of reports** that readers send in on the resorts they visit. (Every year, the 100 best reports are rewarded by a free copy of the book, and many of our best regular reporters get a free week's lift pass; prove your worth by sending us useful reports, and you too could ski for free.)

- We use **colour printing** fully – we include not only piste maps for every major resort but also scores of photographs, chosen to allow you to see for yourself what the resorts are like.

Our ability to keep on investing in *Where to Ski and Snowboard* is largely due to the support of our advertisers – many of whom have been with us since the first edition in 1994. We are grateful for that support, and hope you will in turn support our advertisers (and tell them that you saw their ads in these pages).

We are absolutely committed to helping you, our readers, to make an informed choice; and we're confident that you'll find this edition the best yet. Enjoy your skiing and riding this season.

Chris Gill and Dave Watts
Norton St Philip, 6 August 2006

GET YOUR MONEY BACK
when you book a holiday

You can reclaim the price of Where to Ski and Snowboard when you book a winter sports holiday for the 2006/07 or 2007/08 seasons. All you have to do is book the holiday through the specialist ski travel agency Ski Solutions.

Ski Solutions is Britain's original and leading ski travel agency. You can buy whatever kind of holiday you want through them.

Ski Solutions sells the package holidays offered by all the bonded tour operators in Britain (apart from the very few who are direct-sell only). And if that isn't enough choice, they can tailor-make a holiday, based on any form of travel and any kind of accommodation. No one is better placed to find you what you want than Ski Solutions.

Making a claim
Claiming your refund could not be easier. When you make your definite booking, tell Ski Solutions that you want to take up this offer and claim the refund. They will deduct the price of the book from your bill.

Phone Ski Solutions on
020 7471 7700

Get next year's edition free
by reporting on your holiday

There are too many resorts for us to visit them all every year, and too many hotels, bars and mountain restaurants for us to see. So we are very keen to encourage more readers to send in reports on their holiday experiences. As usual, we'll be giving 100 copies of the next edition to the writers of the best reports.

There are five main kinds of feedback we need:

- what you particularly **liked and disliked** about the resort
- what aspects of the resort came as a **surprise** to you
- your other suggestions for **changes to our evaluation** of the resort – changes we should make to the ratings, verdicts, descriptions etc
- your experience of **queues** and other weaknesses in the lift system, and the **ski school** and associated childcare arrangements
- your feedback on **individual facilities** in the resort – the hotels, bars, restaurants (including mountain restaurants), nightspots, equipment shops, sports facilities etc.

You can send your reports to us in two ways. In order of preference, they are:

- by e-mail to: reports@wtss.co.uk (don't forget to give us your postal address)
- word-processed and printed on paper.

Consistently helpful reporters are invited to become 'resort observers', which means that when possible we'll arrange free lift passes in your holiday resorts, in exchange for detailed reports on those resorts.

Our postal address is:
Where to Ski and Snowboard, FREEPOST SN815, The Old Forge, Norton St Philip, Bath BA2 7ZZ

The editorial

SIZE MATTERS, AT LEAST TO US

One day, we'll devise a method of gauging the size of ski areas that is reliable, meaningful and easily applicable both to American resorts and to European ones. Until then, we continue to rely on the figures the resorts produce – in Europe, the total length of the marked and patrolled pistes, in America, the total 'skiable acres' within the resort boundary. (We bridge the gap between the two by occasionally comparing the overall physical size of different areas – for example, Val-d'Isère/Tignes is about six times the size of Mammoth.)

We are often sceptical of the claimed figures. For example, we can't see that Courmayeur has 100km of separately identifiable pistes; that Les Deux Alpes offers 220km; or that St Moritz can muster 350km. But until we come up with the magic method, we muddle through using those figures.

So we're pleased, in a way, to report the fact that another wild claim has been greatly moderated: amazingly, Cervinia seems to have reduced the claimed size of its ski area from 200km to 130km. But wait a minute: didn't they increase it only a few years ago? Sure enough, a rummage through the files reveals that in the mid 1990s the resort claimed 96km; in the late 1990s, it went up to 120km; the increase to 200km came in 2001. 'We're very sceptical of this hike,' we said at the time. We would write to ask what on earth is going on, but the chances of a sensible reply are rather slim.

SWISS SKI SCHOOL MALAISE

As we note in our introduction to Switzerland, competition between ski schools there is much less common than in other Alpine countries. Not that we are claiming a causal relationship, but it happened to be in the Swiss resort of St Moritz that we bagged this picture , showing an instructor helping his class down a steep pitch on a run that gave the class 'a bit of an adventure'. He probably went home thinking he had done a good day's work; the class probably went home thinking they had had enough.

ITALIAN LEGISLATION FEVER

Italy seems to have gone legislation crazy at present – sometimes to good effect, sometimes not. We approve wholeheartedly of Italy's completely effective ban on smoking in bars and restaurants, noted last year, and the requirement for children to wear crash-hats.

But they seem to over-react to events without thinking things through. A few years ago, for example, after some major crashes between skiers and snowboarders, they set about rushing through a

VIETATO SCIARE FUORI PISTA !
FORBIDDEN SKIING OFF-SLOPE !
CI/IE ALIDEM ALICCEDHALD DED DICTE VEDDOTEM

law saying that boarders and skiers should be segregated, on different mountains. That one never got through to the statute book. But more recently, some regions have reacted to avalanches by banning off-piste skiing close to lifts and pistes, on the grounds that you might trigger avalanches on to the innocents below. We understand that this is now generally the case in Alto Adige (Südtirol) – and we certainly saws signs piste-side to this effect when we visited last season – as shown above. Major off-piste routes, well away from civilisation, are apparently not affected.

This makes no sense to us. The slopes around pistes and lifts are where all of us get our first taste of skiing off-piste. Often, these slopes are too gentle to avalanche. Where slopes are steep enough to slide, and if that slide might hit lifts or pistes, the resort authorities should not allow snow to build up to dangerous levels. Off-piste skiers don't 'cause' avalanches, they trigger them; if a slope presents a risk of avalanche, other factors might trigger it.

CARRY ON SKIING, WHILE THE SUN SHINES

A persistent complaint of ours about North America and Austria is that the skiing day is too short, especially in spring. So we're pleased to recognise examples of mountains elsewhere offering a skiing day that reflects, at least vaguely, the hours of daylight. The sign shown on the left, found at Lagalb outside St Moritz, would give the average Colorado ski patroller a heart attack: a cable-car in high Alpine terrain running until 5.30pm, with the last piste patrol at 5.40. That's about two hours after they would have closed everything down in the average Colorado resort, and a good 90 minutes after shutdown in many Austrian resorts. Let's have more of this, we say.

Betriebszeiten / Orario d'esercizio

Betriebszeit ab Prima corsa	9.00
Letzte Fahrt Ultima corsa	17.30
Letzte Pistenkontrolle Ultimo controllo piste	17.40

LEARNING FROM UNCLE SAM

On the other hand, our annual trips across the pond always have us drawing up a wish-list for the Alps. What it often includes is:
Grooming maps It's standard practice in North America to issue maps each morning showing which runs were groomed last night – very valuable for intermediates wanting to avoid cruddy or bumpy runs and for good skiers who love warp-speed cruising down groomed blacks. Courchevel and Méribel do it; why not other resorts that like to think they are competing internationally?
Free guided tours Again, these are standard in North America – and really popular with our reporters, who find it helps them get their bearings. But Alpine resorts are so paranoid about losing ski school business that they refuse to do this.
Safe off-piste areas One of the few European resorts that has got this right is Avoriaz – not a resort renowned for its steeps or off-piste. But it has created 'snow-cross' runs which are effectively off-piste or free-ride areas, but which are controlled for avalanches, closed if conditions are dangerous and patrolled at the end of the day. Many Alpine resorts have actually moved in the wrong direction, by declaring runs that were pistes to be unpatrolled ski-routes.

INFORMATION, PLEASE

We've often moaned about the 'relative' nature of piste classification, which means that in Val-d'Isère a green run can be a testing mogul-field while in Gstaad a black can be a novice cruise. So we're delighted to see any attempt to give objective information about the steepness of runs. Last season in the tiny Brenta Dolomite resort of Pinzolo we came across signs like this at the top of several runs, showing the average and maximum gradients. A maximum gradient of 43% might not mean much to you now, but it would if this approach became more common. (It translates into an angle to the horizontal of about 23°, which is about right for a red run.)

WHAT'S YOUR POSITION ON THIS?

Ever wondered how far you've skied in a day? Or how fast? Or how much vertical you've racked up? Of course you have! Barometric altimeters will track your vertical reasonably efficiently. But they can't match the versatility of the latest generation of GPS (Global Positioning System) devices – astonishing gadgets that work out your position and altitude by processing signals from a number of satellites in stationary orbit above the Earth.

In some resorts – Keystone for example – you can now rent GPS devices, and have your data entered into comparative tables posted at the foot of the slopes, showing who has skied the most vertical in a day, or whatever. Leaving aside this dreadful competitive stuff, you can track your travels on skis with a common-or-garden GPS, as sold in the shops here. We tried out one of these on a trip to Courchevel in March. A round trip from Le Praz to Cîme de Caron in Val-Thorens and back logged a vertical of around 8000m – about what we would expect for a big day touring a well equipped area. What did quite surprise us was that we travelled a distance of 78km.

The real fun starts, though, back at your PC. Download the stored data on to your computer, upload your tracks to GoogleEarth (earth.google.com) and you can see your route in 3D, superimposed on Google's amazing photo-based imagery of the planet; our 3V day is shown below. Fascinating, although useless. Or is it? The GPS unit can also display a digital map with information like contour lines, roads and other features to help make navigation easy. We can imagine that in bad visibility that could be quite handy – for the technically competent, at least.

The editorial

AUF WIEDERSEHN, GLETSCHERS

If there is anyone who doubts that the world is getting warmer, they will learn a lot by taking a quick look at what is happening to the glaciers of the Alps. For years, they have been shrinking. Increasingly, they are not viable summer skiing areas because the winter snowfall that persists through the summer is not sufficient to produce the safe skiing surface that they need.

Every year, the roll of glacier resorts that are abandoning summer skiing grows. Among

largest **ski paradise!**

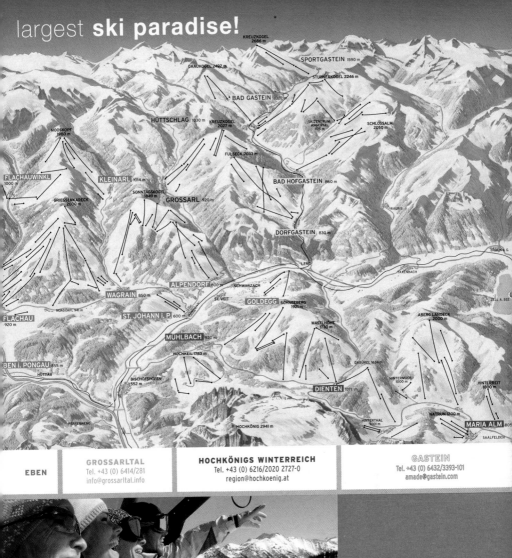

| EBEN | **GROSSARLTAL**
Tel. +43 (0) 6414/281
info@grossarltal.info | **HOCHKÖNIGS WINTERREICH**
Tel. +43 (0) 6216/2020 2727-0
region@hochkoenig.at | **GASTEIN**
Tel. +43 (0) 6432/3393-101
amade@gastein.com |

Hugely attractive for …

… everyone who can't get enough of endless slopes, inviting ski chalets, value-for-money packages and the unique feeling of live action. Each of the five ski regions in the alliance is fantastic in itself - together they provide the added value so typical of Ski amadé. And with only one ticket you can join in the live action! In no other alpine region will you find such a wide range of facilities within such a small area. And it's so convenient - you can get to Austria's largest ski paradise quickly and easily from Salzburg, the popular airport among the British. Information on package deals, snow reports and live cams at:

1 TICKET FOR:

- **860 KILOMETRES OF RUNS**
  (280 km blue, 483 km red
  and 97 km black)

- **270 LIFTS**

- Slopes **UP TO AN ALTITUDE OF 2,700 M**

- **120 MODERN PISTE BASHERS**

- **75% RUNS SERVED
  BY SNOW MACHINES**

www.skiamade.co.uk

the glaciers that abandoned summer opening this year or last are Austria's Pitztal, France's Alpe-d'Huez and Italy's Marmolada. Many other glaciers now operate appreciably smaller areas than they once did. We're not great fans of summer skiing, so we're not too concerned about this from the point of view of losing the opportunity to cut a few more turns. But the message these developments convey about global warming is a gloomy one.

The shrinking of the glaciers is taking place at a really alarming pace. The picture below shows what the Swiss resort of Andermatt now has to do to get skiers down from the top station of its cable-car on to the ever-lower surface of the glacier: build a snow ramp, and then in summer cover it with a white reflective blanket to help preserve it for the next winter.

ANOTHER BUMPER SNOW SEASON

Last year we published a comprehensive review of snowfall patterns. This year we have asked the author, Fraser Wilkin, to bring us up to date on last season. Here is his report.

The 2005–2006 season was average or better-than-average for the Alps, despite the slow start in many resorts that has become typical in recent years. Early season in the Tarentaise resorts of France was grim, with early-season favourites such as Val-d'Isère relying on artificial help to lay their base (not very effectively, judging by our Christmas visit). But in the end resorts here fared well – Tignes received 618cm of snow over the season compared with a long-term average of 605cm. Arc 2000 had 640cm of snow compared with just 340cm the previous season and an average of 690cm. La Rosière received 676cm compared with an average of 614cm. Much of this, however, was due to bumper March snowfalls. This has been the pattern of several recent seasons. The moral? Take a holiday in March or April rather than in December or early January.

The exceptions to lack of early snow were Austria and the northern fringes of the Swiss and French Alps, where resorts as diverse as Lech, Engelberg and Avoriaz had good snow from the start.

Rain and snow affected many regions over the New Year holiday, before cold and settled conditions established themselves over the Alps for the first half of January. This left southern resorts fearing a repeat of the 2004–2005 snow drought. Conditions were much better further north and east, with most of Austria remaining in good shape. The weather became more unsettled later in January, bringing yet more fresh snow to Austria, and then to other areas including the southern resorts of Serre-Chevalier and Sestriere.

After a quiet start to February, powerful Atlantic storms (a rarity in recent seasons) swept heavy snow across the Alps, with some rain at lower levels. Colder weather returned later in the month with further snow for the Southern Alps. March was very unsettled, and a series of potent storms saw huge snowfalls across the northern French Alps (Chamonix, Val-d'Isère) and western and central Switzerland (Crans-Montana, Verbier). This

time the east and south missed the heaviest snowfalls, but there remained excellent cover across the Alps despite a dramatic increase in temperature at the end of the month. These unsettled conditions continued into April, when the northern Alps saw further heavy snow at altitude. The weather settled down later in the month, with some great spring skiing on upper slopes. Overall, snowfall during the season was most consistent in Austria.

Rarely has North America seen such a successful season across such a wide area. After an indifferent start, most of California had an outstanding season. The pattern in Utah was not dissimilar, although it enjoyed a stronger early season. Much of Colorado got off to an excellent start, with most resorts fully operational by Christmas. The only problems were in the southern Rockies (eg Taos, which received less than 60% of its long-term average) and parts of the east (eg Killington, which received only 77% of average). Just about everywhere else enjoyed above-average snowfall, including most of western Canada, which suffered so badly in the previous season. For example, Mammoth in California got 178% of its long-term average snowfall, Jackson Hole in Wyoming 122%, Alta in Utah 120%, Vail in Colorado 112%. In Canada, Sunshine Village near Banff got 122% of its average yearly snowfall and Whistler near Vancouver 116%.

PICTURE THIS
Last year we again invited readers to submit resort pictures for publication in the book, and offered 'some sort of prize' for the best picture submitted. We were not inundated, but we did get some worthwhile contributions: the following have pictures published in this edition: David Maxwell-Lees (Alpbach, Söll); Peter Gillett (Mayrhofen), Amanda McCormick (St Anton), Ed Chester (Chamonix), Arpad Palfi (Val-d'Isère). Many thanks to all who sent in contributions. We reckon the best of these came from Arpad Palfi, who wins a sailing day on a splendid yacht in the Solent provided by our associated enterprise Yacht Ventures, worth £145.

If you'd like to see your digital photos in print, send the best ones to photos@wtss.co.uk. There will again be some sort of prize for the best picture submitted.

OUR ANNUAL AWARDS
Last year we introduced two annual awards to recognise the most important new resort developments. Here are this year's winners.

Best European Resort Development 2006 – Zermatt
At long last, Zermatt's separate mountains are due to be fully linked. For the 2006/07 season, a new gondola is planned from Furi to Riffelberg, linking the Glacier area with Gornergrat; as a result, you no longer have to go back to the village (and then cross it) to get from the Glacier area to the other main sectors.

Best North American Resort Development 2006 – Big Sky/Moonlight
The biggest linked ski area in the US is no longer Vail, but the combined slopes of these little-known resorts in deepest Montana. What's more, the trails are delightfully deserted – they get perhaps one-tenth the number of visitors that Vail gets – and the snowfall is heavier than practically anywhere in Colorado. The resorts have been physically linked for some time, but didn't have a shared lift pass until 2005/06, when they ended an ongoing dispute.

Adelboden – no wonder people keep coming back

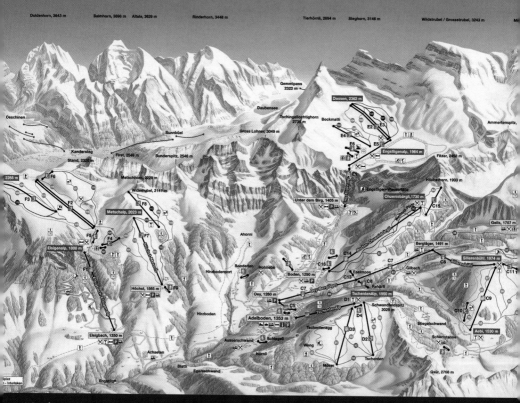

- 185 km pistes
- 58 lift facilities
- 36 ski huts and après-ski bars
- Host of the FIS Ski World Cup 06/07.01.2007
- Family-friendly
- Snow secure from December to April with ski mountains up to 8000 ft. in height

- First accredited Alpine Wellness Holiday destination in Switzerland
- 1 hour drive from Berne airport
- Direct flights to Berne airport from Birmingham, London City, London Gatwick, London Stansted, Manchester, Southampton

(subject to schedule changes)

Further information: **www.adelboden.ch**

Adelboden
Frutigen

Wildstrubel, 3244 m
Rohrbachstein, 2950 m
Weisshorn, 2948 m
Wildhorn, 3246 m
Gletscherhorn, 2943 m
Laufbodenhorn, 2701 m
Mittaghorn, 2686 m
Rawilpass
Plaine Morte
Ammertenhorn, 2666 m
Iffighorn, 2378 m
Hohberg
Regenboldshorn, 2193 m
Metschstand, 2100 m
Luegli, 2138 m
Oberlaubhorn, 1999 m
Leiterli, 2001 m
Steinsto
Blatti
Guetfläck
Metschhorn, 1901 m
Agismatte
C3
Brenggen
Leiterli, 1943 m
A8
B6
B4
Iffigfeld
Betelberg
A2
Hahnenmoos, 1957 m
B3
Simmenfälle
A9
Stoss-Leiterli
Mülkerblatten, 1936 m
Lauenen
Haslerberg
C1
B2
Metsch, 1470 m
A5
Stoss, 1634 m
Tschä
C2
Lavey, 2200 m
B5
Balmen
A6
Hasler
B1
Rothenbach, 1072 m
Oey
A1
A4
e Boden
Seewlehorn, 2487 m
B7
Bühlberg, 1664 m
Blatti
Wallegg, 1585 m
Brandegg
Tannenbühl
Stand
Hubel
A3
Albristhorn, 2762 m
Lenk, 1068 m
Wistätthorn, 2362 m
A7
Mauren
A10
Seiten
Zweisimmen - Spiez
Thun - Bern
Aegerten
Flöschhorn, 2079 m
Powered by
visiorama

Adelboden Tourismus, Dorfstrasse 23, 3715 Adelboden, Switzerland
Tel. +41 (0)33 673 80 80, Fax +41 (0)33 673 80 92, info@adelboden.ch

Berner Oberland

What's new?

New lifts and other major developments in top resorts

In this chapter we summarise major developments in ski resorts last season and those planned for 2006/07. Each major resort chapter has a 'News' panel near the start; you'll find many more news items in those panels. If you want to keep up to date with resort developments in the run-up to the season, go to our website at www.wtss.co.uk; you'll find a constant flow of news on the opening page, and an archive of past items.

ANDORRA

SOLDEU RENEWAL
A six-pack will replace the oldest chair-lift in Soldeu, the Espiolets 2, which runs parallel to the main gondola from the village.

AUSTRIA

ALPBACH'S QUAD
A fixed quad will replace the Galtenberglift drag from Inneralpbach, ending at Böglalm and easing queues at the bottom.

ELLMAU WARMS UP
The Tanzboden drag-lift below Hartkaiser and Brandstadl will be replaced by a six-pack with heated seats.

MUTTERS RE-OPENED AT INNSBRUCK
The Mutters ski area, closed for several years, re-opened last season with three new lifts: an eight-seat gondola, a fast quad chair and a drag. And a fast quad opened on the slopes above Igls.

KAPRUN'S MAISKOGEL UPGRADE
For 2006/07 a six-pack with covers is to replace the Almbahn double chair at Maiskogel, extending to the top of the mountain.

SIX-PACKS FOR KITZBÜHEL
The triple chair at Ehrenbachhöhe and the Hanglalm T-bar in the Resterhöhe area will both be replaced by six-packs this season.

MAYRHOFEN'S MEGA-CABLE-CAR
A new 160-person cable-car (Austria's largest) will go from Mayrhofen to Ahorn in 2006/07.

NEW SCHATTBERG GONDOLA FOR SAALBACH/HINTERGLEMM
An eight-seat gondola takes over from the double chair linking Schattberg Ost and Schattberg West. A six-pack with heated seats and covers will replace the two drag-lifts on Wildenkarkogel's slopes.

NEW ACCESS TO SCHLADMING'S SLOPES
A new gondola with mid-station will replace the bottom Planai West chair, going to Lärchkogel in the heart of the Planai slopes.

SOLL'S SIX-PACK
The Tanzboden drag-lift below Hartkaiser and Brandstadl will become a six-pack with heated seats.

ANNIVERSARY GONDOLA AT ST ANTON
St Anton's 70th birthday as a resort sees the opening of a jumbo gondola to replace the queue-prone cable-car to Galzig.

WESTENDORF'S ISOLATION ENDED BY LINK WITH KITZBÜHEL
Last season a new piste and gondola linked Westendorf to the fringes of the Kitzbühel slopes near Aschau.

FRANCE

ARC 2000 BOTTLENECK REMOVED

Above Arc 2000 a fast six-seat covered chair will move 3,000 people an hour, replacing the queue-prone Plagnettes chair to Col de la Chal, which will be shortened, starting higher up the hill.

IMPROVED ACCESS FROM AVORIAZ TO CHATEL

For 2006/07 the old Chaux Fleurie chair (a key link from Avoriaz to Châtel and a long-standing bottleneck) is to be replaced by a six-pack.

A SIX-PACK FOR CHAMONIX

For 2006/07 the slow Col Cornu quad from Les Vioz at Le Brévent will become a fast six-pack.

AND TWO FOR CHATEL

The triple chair from Les Combes to the top of Linga becomes a six-pack, as does the slow Chaux Fleurie chair (see Avoriaz).

IMPROVEMENTS AT COURCHEVEL

Last season the Chapelets six-pack replaced the Signal and Bel Air drags in 1650.

DECONGESTING LES DEUX-ALPES

Last season two old chair-lifts from the central slope area to just below Tête Moute were replaced by the fast Bellecombes six-pack. And the bottleneck Grand Nord piste was widened.

LES MENUIRES' NEW GONDOLA TO BE COMPLETED

For 2006/07 the second stage of the new gondola up to Roc des 3 Marches will open.

BETTER SNOW-PARK ACCESS AT MÉRIBEL

A six-pack will replace the Chatelet chair serving the impressive Plattières snow-park.

A QUAD FOR MORZINE

For 2006/07 a new quad chair will replace two drag-lifts on the Nyon plateau.

LA PLAGNE – SIX-PACKS ALL ROUND

The Charmettes and Bouclet drag-lifts from La Roche to Aime-la-Plagne will become six-packs. In Les Coches, the Orgere drag and the Plan Bois chair will also be replaced by a six-pack.

SERRE-CHEVALIER UPGRADES

Last season three much-needed fast six-seat chairs replaced the Forêt and Rouge drags above L'Aravet, the Clôt Gauthier chair above Fréjus and the Grand Serre chair above Grand Alpe.

SIX-PACK FOR STE-FOY-TARENTAISE

A fast new six-pack (the resort's first fast lift) to the east of the resort's bowl is scheduled for 2006/07 along with two new pistes.

TIGNES' PALAFOUR IMPROVEMENTS

The two Palafour chairs from Tignes-le-Lac towards l'Aiguille Percée will be replaced by a fast six-seat chair.

NEW LIFT BASE IN VAL-D'ISERE

Last season Le Laisinant, between the town and Le Fornet, became a fourth way into the Val-d'Isère slopes, with the opening of a six-pack going up over wooded lower slopes – a great asset in bad weather.

BETTER LINKS BETWEEN VALMOREL AND ST-FRANÇOIS-LONGCHAMP

Links with the Longchamp ski area are greatly improved. For 2006/07 the outward Madeleine chair is to be upgraded; for 2005/06 the return Frêne drag lifts were replaced by a six-pack.

ITALY

FIVE NEW CHAIR-LIFTS FOR CERVINIA/VALTOURNENCHE
Two chairs from the bottom of the Cervinia nursery slopes will replace four drag-lifts; one is a six-pack that will get you well on the way to Plan Maison. Above Valtournenche, a six-pack and two quads will replace three successive drag-lifts.

COURMAYEUR PROVIDES NEW SLOPES ACCESS
A new eight-person gondola is due to open between Dolonne and Plan Checrouit. The old Pra Neyron chair at the top of the gondola will be replaced by a six-pack.

MONTEROSA IMPROVEMENTS
In Alagna, the ancient cable-car to Punta Indren (closed last season) is expected to re-open for one last season. Its replacement is to run from Passo dei Salati, hopefully from 2007/08. For 2005/06 a new eight-seat gondola above Champoluc replaced two chairs from Crest to Ostafa.

PASSO TONALE LINK WITH PONTEDILEGNO BECOMES TWO-WAY
A new gondola will go up to Passo Tonale from Pontedilegno (their slopes were linked by a new piste last year).

SAUZE D'OULX – BETTER SLOPE ACCESS FROM JOUVENCEAUX
For 2006/07 a new chair will replace the old double accessing the slopes from the Jouvenceaux sector. It will go directly to Sportinia.

SELLA RONDA: CORVARA'S NEW GONDOLA
A gondola will replace the Col Alto chair out of Corvara.

FAST QUADS FOR SELVA/VAL GARDENA
For 2006/07 fast quads are due to replace the Sotsaslonch drag above Plan de Gralba and the Sochers lift at Ciampinoi.

SKI SOLUTIONS

Britain's original and largest specialist ski travel agency

- the first and only place you need to call to book your ski holiday

Call SKI SOLUTIONS first, rather than ringing round lots of tour operators - it's an instant short cut to your ideal ski holiday. Start the snowball rolling by giving us a rough idea of what you're looking for:

- *How many in your party?*
- *Are there any children? What ages?*
- *What levels of skier?*
- *Traditional or modern resort?*
- *Which departure airport?*
- *What standard of accommodation?*

Our experienced staff will gently "cross-examine" you to reveal any personal preferences. We will then research a shortlist of suitable holidays and e-mail you with accommodation descriptions, pictures and prices for both hotels and chalets alike.

Or, if you are looking for the ideal chalet for your party, visit our chalet-search service at www.skisolutions.com. Here you will be able to browse through hundreds of chalets in Europe and North America, compile a shortlist and, if you like, e-mail this to your group. Once you've made your final selection, contact us by e-mail or phone.

We save you time, effort and money by costing each option exactly, taking into account all the various supplements and discounts. (We spend our lives immersed in brochures, so we are experts on the small print.) Without any obligation on your part, we can "hold" the holidays that interest you for a couple of days, while you make up your mind.

After further discussions with you we will then book the holiday of your choice. The price of the holiday will be exactly as in the brochure: our service is absolutely FREE.

Between us, the 25 staff of SKI SOLUTIONS have skied over 100 resorts on both sides of the Atlantic and we have a first-hand up-to-date knowledge of the hotels, chalets and apartments offered by most of the operators in these places.

We are a ski travel agency as opposed to a ski tour operator.
When you call us you immediately place at your disposal
a choice of thousands of holidays offered by a wide
variety of different reputable, fully bonded tour
operators, both large and small.

The human ski-holiday search engine

SKI SOLUTIONS.com 020 7471 7700

84 Pembroke Road, Kensington, London W8 6NX fax 020 7471 7701 www.skisolutions.com

SWITZERLAND

ADELBODEN/LENK LINK UPGRADE

Bühlberg's drag-lift (above Lenk) will be replaced by a six-pack.

IMPROVEMENTS AT MÜRREN

A fast quad chair will replace the Engetal drag-lift up to Birg. A cable-car will replace the venerable funicular from Lauterbrunnen in the valley to Grütschalp, for access to the mountain railway leading to the village.

SECOND SIX-PACK FOR SAAS-FEE

For 2006/07 a new six-pack (only the resort's second chair-lift) is planned for the Morenia area.

FURTHER IMPROVEMENT AT VERBIER

A six-pack with covers will go from La Combe (near Les Ruinettes) to Attelas. Last season a 'chondola' – a mix of eight-seat gondola cabins and six-seat chairs on the same lift – was installed between Les Ruinettes and La Chaux via the ridge at Côte de Brunet. A new fast quad from Siviez to Cambatzeline, en route to Greppon Blanc, replaced the Novelli double chair. And the quad chair from Veysonnaz to above Thyon was replaced by an eight-seat gondola.

BIGGER, FASTER GONDOLA FOR VILLARS

For 2006/07 a faster eight-seat gondola will replace the old four-seat one from the village to Roc d'Orsay.

AT LAST! ZERMATT'S RIFFELBERG GONDOLA

A new eight-seat gondola will run from Furi up to Riffelberg, with a mid-station at Schweigmatten; this will be a great improvement, meaning that you will be able to move from Klein Matterhorn to the other sectors of Zermatt's slopes without having to walk or ride through the village to the Sunnegga funicular.

UNITED STATES

MORE TERRAIN AT ASPEN

There will be 20 to 30 more acres of terrain for the Deep Temerity sector at Aspen Highlands, following the opening of a triple chair there last season. Aspen Mountain's Silver Queen gondola cabins will be upgraded.

BEAVER CREEK EXPANDS

A new area, Stone Creek Chutes, is to open to the east of Rose Bowl, providing 180 acres of expert glades.

BIG SKY GETS BIGGER

Big Sky will open another 212 acres of terrain on Lone Mountain this season, accessed by the Tram.

NEW GONDOLA FOR BRECKENRIDGE

A new eight-seat gondola is due this season, going from the Transportation Centre on the outskirts of town via the base of Peak 7 to the base of Peak 8.

NEW TERRAIN, LIFT FOR THE CANYONS

There will be a new quad chair to the north-east of the Dreamscape area, with an extra 200 acres of terrain.

ANOTHER QUAD FOR DEER VALLEY
Bald Mountain will get a third fast quad (replacing the Sterling triple) this season.

KEYSTONE UNGROOMED
For 2006/07 Keystone plans to add another 300 acres of ungroomed terrain served by snowcats.

JACKSON HOLE MAKES DO
Jackson's infamous little cable-car is being demolished, and the replacement (with twice the capacity) won't be ready until 2008. For the next two seasons, access to the Rendezvous summit will be provided by a chair-lift running from the top of the Sublette chair.

PARK CITY TRIPLE
There will be a new triple chair this season from Resort Center to a blue run going down to the King Con fast chair.

SNOWBIRD'S MINERAL BASIN ACCESS
A fast quad will replace the old Peruvian chair from the base this season, going almost to the top of the mountain. A tunnel with a moving carpet at the top will access Mineral Basin on the back of the mountain.

FAST STEAMBOAT
A fast quad is due to replace the Sunshine triple chair.

WINTER PARK UPGRADES
A new triple chair is planned for the back side of Parsenn Bowl, returning you to Parsenn Bowl quicker after skiing Backside Parsenn or Vasquez Cirque.

CANADA

BIG WHITE CLAIMS RECORD
What is claimed to be Canada's longest six-pack, the Snow Ghost Express, is due this season, running parallel to the Ridge Rocket fast quad to alleviate peak-time queues.

SUN PEAKS GETS A GRIP
For 2006/07 a new fixed-grip quad chair on Tod Mountain will take you from mid-mountain to near the top of the Sunburst Express.

WHISTLER'S PICCOLO
The Piccolo Express, a new fast quad, is to be built near the top of Whistler Mountain, running from the bottom of Flute Bowl to Piccolo peak. It will access expert terrain, a new intermediate gladed area and two new trails for early intermediates, and eliminate the need to hike out of Flute Bowl.

SPAIN

BAQUEIRA'S BEGINNER GONDOLA GROWS
A lower stage will be added to last year's new gondola out of the village to the main beginner area.

NORWAY

HEMSEDAL IMPROVEMENTS FOR CHILDREN
There will be a new drag and slope area for the children's area.

SWEDEN

ÅRE'S CHONDOLA
The Olympia fast chair will be replaced by a new 'chondola' with eight-seat chairs and eight-seat gondola cabins.

winter

RESCHENPASS

Skiparadies

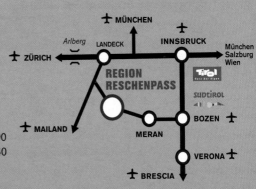

Lift pass bargains

Some of us don't have to pay full-fare

by **Mandy Crook**

We revealed last year that lift pass prices in most resorts have lagged behind the rate of inflation in recent years – and that the cost of a pass in some of the top Swiss and Austrian resorts had actually gone down since 1995, largely thanks to exchange rate movements. But your pass is still a large part of the cost of a winter sports holiday – a very large part in North America, where lift passes can be twice the cost of European ones if you pay the full rate.

So ways of saving on the cost are well worth knowing about, and as your editors approach qualifying age for some of these discounts they seem to be getting more interested in them. So we've studied the lift passes offered by all the resorts that merit a long chapter in this book. We look here at the special lift pass deals on offer for the older skier, for the younger skier and for those of any age who are beginners and therefore don't need access to the full lift network. And we take a quick look at special family deals, too.

34

FREE SKIING FOR INFANTS

Very young children can expect to ski for free. Most of the areas we surveyed offer free passes to children up to the age of five, six, seven or eight. There is no clear national pattern to the picture, but most of the resorts with a relatively mean qualifying age of five are French. Uniquely, Chamonix offers free passes only to children under four. At the other end of the spectrum are the resorts of the Milky Way (Sauze d'Oulx, Sestriere, for example), which offer free six-day passes until the age of ten.

The only resorts we found that do not offer any free passes at all are those covered by the Arlberg pass – Lech and St Anton – but even there it costs only 10 euros to buy a whole season's pass for a child under eight years old.

When obtaining free passes for your tiny tots, expect to provide identity and proof of age. Generally – and not surprisingly – free passes for tinies are available only when purchasing a ticket for an accompanying adult.

DISCOUNTS FOR JUNIORS

All the passes we surveyed offer some sort of discount for pre-teenage children – usually, children under aged 13, but in a few cases under 12 and in lots of cases under a higher limit of 15 or 16. Some resorts are much more generous than others with the level of discount. The best deals we found were in Davos and St Moritz (Switzerland) and in Fernie (Canada), which all offer a lift pass for children aged under 13 at about one-third of the price of an adult pass.

Otherwise the best you are likely to be offered is a half-price ticket. Of the other 43 lift passes, the discounts were pretty evenly spread in the range 25 per cent to 55 per cent, except that three resorts came in under 25 per cent – Megève, Montgenèvre, Soldeu,

Looking at the variations between countries, it was noticeable that none of the French resorts is particularly generous to its junior skiers: the best discount we found in France was 33 per cent (offered by the Portes du Soleil resorts) and the worst were Montgenèvre, which offers a mere 19 per cent, and Megève, which offers 20 per cent.

TEENAGERS

✔ Discounts of 40 per cent or more in Winter Park, Ischgl and Saas Fee

✔ Discounts available to under-20s in a few resorts, and under-22s in Jackson Hole

✘ French resorts give no discounts beyond age 16

DISCOUNTS FOR TEENAGERS

The position for teenagers is much more varied. For 14 of the 46 lift passes we looked at (ie nearly a third), no discounts at all are offered for teenagers. These include five lift passes in France (the Three Valleys pass being one of them), four in Italy, three in the US and one each in Austria (Obergurgl) and Andorra (Soldeu). On the other hand, all the lift passes we surveyed in Switzerland and Canada offered some discount.

The maximum age at which the teenage discount is on offer also varied greatly: the most common age limit for the discount is 16, but good numbers of resorts draw the line at 18, 19 or even 20 – this last group containing the Jungfrau area (Grindelwald/Mürren/Wengen), Verbier and Zermatt in Switzerland, and the Ski Welt (Ellmau and Söll), the Arlberg (Lech/St Anton) and Schladming in Austria. Top of the league was Jackson Hole, which offers discounts to people under 22 – an astonishingly high figure. It was noticeable that no lift pass among the French resorts we surveyed offer a discount once you're over the age of 16.

Naturally, the size of the discount offered varies too. Of the 32 resorts offering discounts, the majority were in the range 15 per cent to 35 per cent, with just a few higher and a few lower.

The three offering the most discount – Winter Park in Colorado, Ischgl in Austria and Saas Fee Switzerland – offer these discounts only to under-14s (Winter Park) or under-16s. The best all-round deal we found was that of Davos/Klosters in Switzerland, which offers a 33 per cent discount to teenagers who are under 19.

SPECIAL DEALS FOR FAMILIES

Some resorts recognise that the cost of lift passes is a particular obstacle for families wanting to take ski holidays. Of course, free passes for infants and discounts for juniors and teenagers are a key way for families to save on their lift pass costs. But some resorts go further, and give discounts specially for families. Verbier, for example, treats family groups of at least three specially by discounting the lift pass of the second parent by 30 per cent and increasing the discounts it normally gives for juniors and teenagers.

DISCOUNTS FOR OLDER SKIERS

The good news is that more than three-quarters of lift passes offer some sort of discount to the over-60s or the over-65s. However, there are marked country variations: all the French and Canadian lift passes and all but one of the US and Italian lift passes offer a discount; but only four of the ten Austrian passes and three of the six Swiss passes.

Where discounts are on offer, the minimum age for a discount varies quite a bit too. The minimum ages are:

- 65 for American and Canadian resorts
- 60 for French resorts (except Serre-Chevalier, where it's 65)
- 60 for the four Austrian resorts that offer discounts – though in the Arlberg (Lech/St Anton), it's 60 for women and 65 for men
- a mix of 60, 62 or 65 for the Italian and Swiss resorts that offer discounts.

And the amount of discount varies from an impressive 50 per cent or so in Mammoth, Jackson and Soldeu down to under 10 per cent in Megève, Aspen and Banff/Lake Louise, but with the majority offering a discount in the range 15-25 per cent.

Lift pass bargains

35

✔ Discounts universal in France, with a low qualifying age of 60

✔ Serious discounts of around 50 per cent in Mammoth, Jackson Hole and Soldeu

✘ No discounts in most Austrian resorts

✘ Disgraceful discrimination against men in Lech/St Anton

✘ Affluent Megève has France's lowest discount for older skiers (10 per cent), and a uniquely high qualifying age for a free pass: 80

FREE PASSES FOR THE VERY OLDEST …

A few resorts in France allow the very oldest skiers to ski absolutely free. So does the main Grandvalira area in Andorra. None of the resorts we surveyed in Austria, Italy, Switzerland, the US or Canada seem to make such an offer. Publicly owned Winter Park in Colorado does offer free skiing to the over 70s Monday to Thursday. And the Arlberg (Lech/St Anton) in Austria makes skiing almost free for the over 75s – it charges a mere 10 euros for the whole season.

In the French resorts that offer free skiing, the minimum qualifying ages are as follows:

72+ The Three Valleys (Courchevel, Méribel, Menuires, St-Martin, Val-Thorens), Paradiski area, Alpe-d'Huez, Les Deux-Alpes

75+ Flaine, Montgenèvre, Serre-Chevalier, Val-d'Isère/Tignes

80+ Megève

Note there are no free tickets for the oldest skiers in Chamonix or in the Portes de Soleil resorts (Morzine-Avoriaz, Châtel, Les Gets, Champéry), although the Morzine-Les Gets pass (part of the Portes du Soleil) is free to over 75s.

DEALS FOR BEGINNERS

If you are a total beginner, you are unlikely to make good use of a full area pass, and many resorts recognise this by offering beginners a deal. This does not come in the form of a discount like the age-related deals already described. Instead, you might be offered one of the following:

- the free use of a few lifts on the nursery slopes
- a cheap pass covering just a few lifts
- a points cards – essentially a system of paying by the ride using a different currency (you get points removed for each ride)
- a lift, lesson and equipment hire package – a very common deal in North America.

But in some resorts you get no deal at all. Often these are resorts where the beginner slopes are up the mountain, and the lift company doesn't see why it should let you ride up its major lifts without paying fully for the privilege. Such resorts are best avoided by beginners, who can save substantial amounts by heading to a resort that recognises their modest needs. Read the resort chapters of the book to find resorts offering a deal to suit you.

White weddings

Why not tie the knot on the snow?

by **Dave Watts**

As the cost of getting married in the UK rises, more keen skiers and boarders are choosing to tie the knot in ski resorts, inviting their family and friends to join them. If you are tempted, using a tour operator that specialises in weddings can make things a lot simpler; they'll help you through the local legal system, paperwork and language, and advise on the venue and details for both the ceremony and the reception.

JON SIMS

Jon, Liz and guests outside the mountain hut where their drinks reception was held ↘

One of *Where to Ski and Snowboard*'s best regular reporters got married in 2006 – in the Italian Alps. And in a resort the book had brought to his attention. Jon Sims says: 'My wife, Liz, and I looked at the options offered for getting married in the sun but decided that the prospect of getting married in the mountains, surrounded by snow for a real White Wedding, was much more appealing. We had already been skiing a number of times in the Monterosa Ski area and had been impressed by the service of Ski 2 during our holidays. So we asked them about their wedding package. This costs about £1,000 and consists of the whole wedding service including the hire of the Commune (where you get married), legal documents, fees and a local (English) translator to make sure everyone knows what is going on. They did a great job and we and all our guests had a wonderful time.

'For the wedding we were blessed with great weather, a beautiful blue-sky day following snow the previous day. So a few of us nipped out for a couple of hours' skiing in perfect conditions before heading back to get ready. The service at the Commune went exactly as planned and my wife looked beautiful in her dress (carefully packed and carried as hand luggage from the UK). The drinks reception at 2400m gave fantastic views down the valley and lots of photo opportunities, and our four-course wedding breakfast in Lo Bistrot in the valley turned out to be a seven-course Italian wedding banquet.

'A perfect day! Followed by a couple more skiing with our best mates and chatting with our non-skiing ones.'

Jobs in the mountains

Is it time to do that season on snow you hanker for?

by **Wendy King**

You enjoy the holidays, but they're not enough. You pine for the pistes on your return, drool over the latest snowy webcam shots and are getting to think that maybe it's time to ditch the daily grind back home and seek out the ultimate winter tonic: a season in the Alps. After all, your chalet host and resort rep seemed to be having a wonderful time, so why shouldn't you? Good question.

Every winter, seasonal workers head for ski resorts in Europe and North America expecting to have a great time on the slopes, with a little work thrown in to pay for it. Having persuaded a first-time season-worker to confess all, we have tried to outline answers to some of the questions you might ask.

IS IT ONLY FOR YOUNG SINGLES?

The work generally attracts the 18-35 age group – many are gap-year students. But anyone in a position to take the time out, or willing to rearrange their lives to pursue their dream, can find something suitable. Even if you are in serious employment, you might be able to negotiate a sabbatical. You don't need to go alone either. Some employers seek couples to run their chalets (Silver Ski, for example).

FIRST STEPS?

Start by reflecting on what type of work you enjoy, what specialist skills you possess and where you would like to be based. When on holiday, chat to those already employed in the resort to find out what their jobs involve. Your host/rep may be able to put you in touch with their employer – and working for an outfit you were happy to travel with has a certain logic.

WHAT'S THE TIMETABLE?

Recruitment takes place between July and October, with a second intake in November to fill remaining vacancies. Apply early, though, if you want to pick and choose, and have some preparation time. You'll normally head out to the resort in early December. But you don't have to do a full season: some employers need cover during peak weeks, such as school holidays, or when vacancies arise due to staff drop-out, illness or injury. School specialists such as PGL and TOPS have part-time placements for reps and instructors.

WHAT JOBS CAN I DO?

Many vacancies are for chalet hosts or for resort reps. But there are other possibilities. Resorts need staff for administration and reception roles. Most companies need maintenance people. Plongeurs (or 'washers-up' to you and me) usually work late shifts, so often get a lot of time on the mountain, as do bar staff – but you'll need to sleep sometime.

WHERE CAN I WORK?

Matching the type of job you want with where you want to go could
be tricky. If you are hoping for chalet work, then the major French
resorts are the obvious starting point. Verbier in Switzerland has
chalets galore. But Austrian and North American resorts are generally
better suited to hotel, leisure or rep work. In North America one
company usually runs the whole resort infrastructure, so it can be
simpler to look for casual work; especially if you plan to head out
independently.

TOUR OP OR NOT?

You will need to decide whether you want a 'packaged' job with a
tour operator, or to look for a job with a resort business.

Heading out independently means you have to find both
accommodation and employment in the resort, and sort out such
things as your lift pass and insurance. It is wise to have enough
savings to support your adventure should the search end fruitlessly.
Some returning seasonnaires like the flexibility it can bring, but for
first-timers a tour operator package has clear attractions.

You could apply to tour operators directly. Major companies
generally have the most vacancies to fill and will appeal if you aren't
fussy over destination or want a broader choice of job. Smaller
businesses can offer a more individual and personal approach.

There are also web-based agencies, whose sites are a great source of
information and advice. This market has grown rapidly since 2000
when the first ski recruitment site with online CV registration started
– First Tracks (now Voovs.com). Most agencies are run by ex-season
workers with first-hand knowledge to answer your questions. Signing
up to the database is usually free; although a couple charge a small
fee (Ski Connections charges £10). Some mediate between you and a
potential employer.

WHAT ABOUT QUALIFICATIONS AND TRAINING?

Previous experience and/or relevant qualifications will almost
certainly be required in some form. Some posts necessitate a formal
qualification: an NNEB certificate to work with children, for example.
Instructors must also be certified. There are ways you can obtain the
bare necessities, though. Natives, for example, runs a four-day
cookery workshop and Voovs.com has an online food hygiene
course.

Even if you don't need or get skills training, there is likely to be
training designed to impart company standards in certain areas,
whether in hygiene or customer service. Most courses are held just
before the season begins.

DO I NEED TO SPEAK THE LINGO?

Foreign language skills are helpful, but essential only for resort reps. Of course, being able to communicate effectively will make settling into resort life easier and help you to establish a better rapport with the locals. If you are hoping to improve your French, make sure you go to a resort where English doesn't dominate.

WHAT WILL I EARN?

You don't take a job in the mountains for the money. Tour operators who are providing your accommodation, season lift pass and insurance are likely to pay £50 to £60 a week (which some employers pay on a monthly basis – if that bothers you, it's best to ask at the interview).

DOES THE DREAM MATCH REALITY?

Seasonal work is tough, but reports suggest 30-40 per cent of workers return for more. You will be expected to juggle early starts and late nights over a six-day week. Key factors seem to be development of a sensible routine, and maintaining the right attitude – keeping your expectations realistic. Go expecting a full-on party and not much work and you are likely to be disappointed. Go with an open mind, a strong work ethic and the determination to enjoy the experience, and you are likely to end the season planning the next. Mid-season is crunch time, when the novelty is over and there is little scope for rest and play. This period generally sees the highest drop-out rate.

Last word goes to our first-timer: 'Better than I thought it would be. Waking up in the mountains and walking to work in knee-deep snow are things I will never forget.'

Gap-year courses

How to qualify as a ski or snowboard instructor

by **Rebecca Miles**

Growing numbers of 18-year-olds, career-breakers and even early retirees are going on gap-year instructor courses. Many want to become instructors. But many simply want to spend 10 weeks on the slopes and feel they've had a good time and achieved something, as well as improving their skiing or snowboarding by the end of it. We've looked at what's on offer and what it qualifies you to do.

Ski Le Gap was the first company to offer gap-year instructor courses to the British in 1994. But now there are lots of course providers and there has been a burst of new companies particularly since 2002. Previously it took years to qualify as an instructor, slowly working your way through the levels. Now, if you've got the cash, you can get the first stage in the bag in a season. And there's the catch – courses cost in the region of £6,000. But that's not putting people off.

In 2004/05, 900 Brits took instructor exams as part of a gap course with the British (BASI), Canadian (CSIA) or New Zealand (NZSI) governing bodies, the three most popular in the UK. Course directors estimate that between 25 and 50 per cent of their pupils go on to work in the snowsports industry – the rest return to their job, make a career change or go to university. Mark Jones, a director of ICE (International Centre for Excellence) in Val-d'Isère, said, 'About 25 per cent of people on our courses are having career breaks, and really want to kick-start some adventure into their lives.' Tom Saxlund, a

MORE DETAILS

A fuller version of this feature than we have room for here, plus a table giving basic details of the main gap-year course providers, their fees, the qualifications they offer and the resorts they offer courses in, appears on our website: www.wtss.co.uk.

Some of the providers mentioned there also offer much shorter courses (eg four weeks) which typically include three weeks of intensive training and the week-long BASI instructor level course and exam.

director of New Generation, said 'Our gappers really like skiing, want to improve and want to devote more time to doing it.'

On most courses around two-thirds of pupils will be either pre- or immediately post-university but the other third will be made up of late 20s, 30-, 40- and 50-somethings, taking sabbaticals, giving themselves an early retirement present, or a taking the opportunity to change their career thanks to, say, a redundancy payment. On the gap course run by BASI in Nendaz, Switzerland in 2005/06, for example, there was a 50-year-old doctor taking a sabbatical and a 61-year-old early retiree, alongside four 18-year-olds.

Course providers are often very proud to state that there is no maximum age to join their course; as long as you are fit and able you'll find a place. Youngsters have to wait until they are over 16.

WHAT DO YOU DO AFTERWARDS?

How easy is it to work as an instructor after having done a gap-year course? The snowsports instruction industry is a political minefield and, despite valiant efforts by BASI and others to make it possible for Brits to work in, say, France, it's just not that easy.

Thirty-seven countries are members of the International Ski Instructors Association (ISIA), a political body that recognises national qualifications and sets minimum standards that must be met for its members to be accredited. The theory is that if you have an ISIA qualification then you can teach in any of the ISIA member countries. In practice, this isn't possible because some countries specify further qualifications to reach the top level within their governing body. So, for example, to be a fully qualified ski instructor in France, you do need to pass the notorious speed test.

BASI has a three-level system starting at instructor and progressing to ski teacher ISIA and then international ski teacher diploma. If you pass at the end of a 10-week course, you qualify as an instructor (formerly BASI 3). This entitles you to teach in the UK (eg at dry slopes, snowdomes and in Scotland), Canada, USA, Germany, Austria, Italy, Andorra, Spain, eastern Europe, Australia and New Zealand. For some countries you will need a work visa, but in New Zealand, for example, it is fairly easy for a Brit to get a temporary working visa.

The Canadian system has four levels, one being the lowest, four the highest. On a gap-year course, you could expect to pass level one and some reach level two. With level one, you would be able to teach beginners, with level two, up to blue runs. With a level one you can teach in Canada, USA, New Zealand, Australia and South America. To teach in most European countries, you would need to be level four.

New Zealand also has four stages. On a typical gap course, you would work towards the first two: the certificate in ski or snowboard instruction (CSI), which allows you to teach advanced beginners, and stage one, which allows you to teach advanced intermediates. A CSI certificate entitles you to teach in New Zealand, stage one in USA, Canada, Australia, Japan, Andorra, Switzerland, Austria and Italy.

HOW MUCH DOES IT COST?

The average 10-week gap-year instructor course is £6,000, which includes full-time tuition (the norm is five days a week), accommodation (the norm is with five or six evening meals a week, but it may be self-catering) and lift pass for the season. Lunches aren't included and spending money of approximately £100 a week is recommended. Gap courses typically start in January and go through to March.

Off-piste adventures

Escape the crowds and experience skiing at its best

by **Chris Gill**

There's no doubt about it: the pleasure of skiing on the pistes of Europe's mountains is being eroded. Lift systems are continually upgraded to cope with the ever-growing numbers of visitor beds installed in the resorts. But the piste networks can't be expanded to match. As the crowding gets worse, the attraction grows of getting away into the wilds and making fresh tracks through virgin snow.

Crowds aside, skiing off-piste also has its own rewards, of course: when it all comes together, the satisfaction of skiing soft, deep snow is intense – and modern equipment means that it can all come together much more easily than it did in the days of long, skinny skis. But if you're a beginner, where and how do you start? If you have already got a taste for the steep and deep, where and how can you develop and exploit your skills? Read on.

SAFETY FIRST

Once you have some experience of skiing off-piste, you may feel competent to judge what is safe and what is not, but as a beginner you have a lot to learn.

There are two key differences between pistes and non-pistes. On a piste, in principle, you can expect to be safe from avalanches – the devastating slides of compacted snow that crush everything in their path, from trees to houses. And on a piste you can be confident that you are not going to suddenly come upon a cliff or a crevasse.

Of course, there are lots of off-piste slopes that are entirely safe; the problem is identifying them. Quite small slopes can hold enough snow to bury you. Even a slope that is itself too gentle to slide may have slopes above that are pregnant with snow waiting to avalanche. Quite close to the pistes there can be holes and cliffs where a fall could be serious.

But there are off-piste slopes where the risk of avalanche is clearly minimal. There are lots of places in the Alps, for example, where a blue or red run zig-zags down an open mountainside, and the steeper slope between the zigs and the zags is off-piste. Because the whole slope is criss-crossed by pistes, you know that it is (or should be) essentially safe from the avalanche point of view. Inspecting the slope as you ride a lift over it is one way to assess other hazards.

SPECIAL OFF-PISTE KIT

'Fat' skis make deep snow skiing a whole lot easier; for some of us, in fact, it's wide skis that make deep snow skiing possible. You can get skis specially made for skiing powder, but most of us need to ski on the

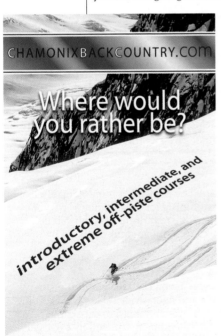

same skis in all conditions, and modern 'free-ride' skis fit the bill beautifully. Read the equipment chapter on page 55 for more.

Whenever you embark on a serious off-piste adventure your guide should ensure that everyone is wearing an avalanche transceiver and knows how to use it. Your transceiver is normally transmitting a radio signal; if one of your group is buried, you switch to receive mode, and 'sweep' the snow looking for the strongest signal.

It also makes sense to wear Recco reflectors – tiny electronic devices that reflect radio signals coming from a matching Recco detector unit, which in turn detects the reflected signal, and can pinpoint the reflector. Many major resorts have Recco detectors. Adhesive reflector strips can be attached to your boots, and they are built in to some brands of ski clothing.

DOING IT BY THE DAY

Most resorts have off-piste terrain that is worth exploring, and instructors or guides who can be hired to help you explore it. But some resorts have ski schools or specialist guiding outfits that regularly operate off-piste groups, which makes the whole business much more accessible. In some resort chapters in this book you will find special feature panels compiled with the help of such outfits.

Start by looking at the chapters on St Anton (Austria); Les Arcs, Chamonix, Courchevel, Les Deux-Alpes, Méribel, Morzine, Serre-Chevalier, Val-d'Isère, Val-Thorens (France); Courmayeur, Monterosa (Italy); Andermatt, Verbier (Switzerland). Chamonix attracts many of the best skiers and most accomplished guides in the business, and Val-d'Isère has an unrivalled range of teaching and guiding businesses specialising in off-piste and powder skiing.

'OFF-PISTE' IN NORTH AMERICA

American and Canadian resorts are great places to develop deep snow technique. To quote from our introductory chapter to the USA: 'Many Europeans have the idea that American resorts don't have off-piste terrain. It's true that resorts practically always have a boundary, and that venturing beyond it may be discouraged or forbidden. But within the boundary there is often very challenging terrain that is very much like off-piste terrain in an Alpine resort, but with the important advantage that it is patrolled and avalanche-controlled – so you don't need to hire a guide. We rate this as one of the great attractions of American resorts.'

PACKAGED COURSES

If you are keen on getting started by going on a proper organised course, rather than just trying off-piste for the odd day as part of a largely piste-based holiday, there are tour operators who can help. The best-known is the Ski Freshtracks programme operated by the Ski Club of Great Britain, which has a wide range of different holidays.

ABOVE AND BEYOND THE LIFTS

There are three main ways in which you can take your off-piste skiing to another level, literally and figuratively. There is ski-touring – climbing on skis with special hinged bindings; or cat-skiing (pretty much confined to North America) – riding up the hill in a tracked vehicle like a piste groomer; or heli-skiing, where a helicopter replaces the snowcat. They offer different rewards for different investments of effort and cash. But all are well worth trying.

Smart apartments

The transformation of French self-catering holidays

by **Dave Watts**

Apartment holidays used to be the budget option for most people – shoe-horn six people into a studio advertised for six and you'd have a cheap, but not very comfortable time. Now things have changed, particularly in France, home of the cramped apartment: smart apartments are increasingly available where you have room to swing several cats. Some even have comfortable furniture to relax in, and a pool, sauna, steam room and gym to add to the pampering. Sure, the budget option still exists but now you can have a comfortable apartment holiday with all the other advantages that it brings. We've highlighted smart apartments for the first time in this edition – look for the `SMART APARTMENTS – SEE FEATURE` label in the resort chapters. Later in this chapter is a table summarising some of what's on offer in which resorts.

I've been taking my annual ski holiday with my wife and a couple of friends in apartments ever since 1992. That's because we value the freedom an apartment gives you. You don't have to stick to meal times (and meals) dictated by the hotel or chalet staff, you can slob around in whatever clothes you want, you can go out and come back in whenever you want. And, crucially, you are free to have a big lunch up the mountain without having to worry about eating the huge meal your chalet staff or hotel have prepared for you; if you lack the appetite for a full meal in the evening you can buy some snacks like oysters, smoked salmon, paté and local cheeses along with a good bottle of wine or two from the supermarket. If you are hungry you can go out to a restaurant to eat. Staying in an apartment doesn't mean having to cook big meals or wash up – not for us anyway. But it does mean you need to book a place with a dishwasher! On recent holidays to Zermatt a couple of us have regularly left the apartment at 7.40am to catch the 8am train up the mountain – if breakfast didn't start till 8am we'd have had to skip that. Instead one of us (not me) is an early riser and nips down to the bakery for fresh bread and croissants every morning – delicious.

So it's the independence we value. When we started this

ERNA LOW

Many of the smart new apartment buildings have plush reception areas and good leisure facilities
↓

apartment lark, we couldn't find the sort of thing we were looking for in tour operators' brochures – all the apartments there were, were of the cram-em-in and make-it-cheap variety. So we ended up booking independently, through agents in resorts and direct with apartment owners. But it was hard work doing the research – especially because it was before the internet took off.

Now, in France at least – the country that used to have the smallest, most sordid apartments – a few tour operators offer some really smart and spacious places. The smart French apartment concept was kick-started by French construction company MGM. Now they've been joined by other brands such as Montagnettes, Lagrange Prestige and Canadian developer Intrawest. Many properties constructed by MGM are now operated by another company, CGH.

What can you expect in one of the **SMART APARTMENTS – SEE FEATURE** places we feature in selected chapters and in the table opposite? First, you get more space than in your average French apartment – but not as much as you'd get as standard in North America. (Note that we haven't flagged any Canadian or US apartments as smart because, in our experience, they nearly all are.) You still need to check the space is enough to meet your expectations – I always reckon an apartment for four adults needs to be at least 50m^2 – and check whether the number it's advertised for involves anyone sleeping in the living room, in bunk beds or on a mezzanine, which might not suit you. You might also be disappointed by the amount of hanging and storage space, especially for wet ski gear and storing suitcases. Second, you get a modern design with smartish furniture (but we're often disappointed by the lack of really comfy sofas and easy chairs

LUXURY APARTMENTS MENTIONED IN THE CHAPTERS

Alpe-d'Huez	**Oz-en-Oisans**: Chalet des Neiges
Les Arcs	Arc 1950, Chalet des Neiges, Chalet Altitude, Alpages de Chantal **Peisey-Vallandry**: L'Orée des Cimes
Chamonix	Balcons du Savoy, Ginabelle
Courchevel	Chalets les Montagnettes, Chalets du Forum
Les Deux-Alpes	Cortina, Alpina Lodge
Flaine	**Les Carroz**: Les Fermes du Soleil
Les Menuires	Residence Montalys, Chalets les Montagnettes, Les Alpages, Chalets du Soleil, Les Chalets de l'Adonis
Méribel	Les Fermes de Méribel
La Plagne	Chalets les Montagnettes, Les Hauts Bois, Pelvoux **Montalbert**: Chalets de Montalbert, Les Granges **Champagny-en-Vanoise**: Les Alpages de Champagny
Puy-St-Vincent	Gentianes
La Rosière	Cimes Blanche, Balcons
Samoëns	Fermes de Samoëns
Serre-Chevalier	Hameau du Rocher Blanche
Ste-Foy-Tarentaise	See resort chapter, page 371
St-Martin	Les Chalets du Gypse, Les Chalets de St-Martin
Tignes	L'Ecrin des Neiges, Residence Village Montana, Ferme du Val-Claret, Chalets d'Ercule
Val-d'Isère	Chalets du Jardin Alpin, Chalets du Laisinant
Val-Thorens	Too many to list – see resort chapter, page 416

Smart apartments

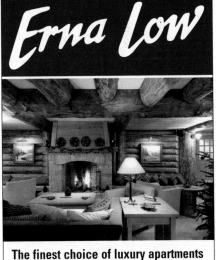

↑ A few smart places even have an outdoor pool (right). And you can expect a higher standard of furnishing than in a 'normal' apartment (left) but ...

ERNA LOW

ERNA LOW

... you may not get really comfy sofas and easy chairs you can sink into (left). Intrawest has built its first smart village in the Alps – Arc 1950 (right) – and is starting work on another in Flaine ↓

you can sink into and relax – often because sofas are designed as sofa-beds and are more comfortable to sleep in than sit on). Third, many smart new apartments now include leisure facilities such as a pool, sauna, steam room and gym (but check whether there will be a charge for using these, and if so how much). Fourth, a lot of them also have comfortable reception areas with comfy furniture and log fires. Personally, we think this is a bit of a waste of space; we'd prefer more space and more comfortable furniture in the living rooms. Fifth, many of them come with dishwashers (check, if this is important to you); but separate kitchens are relatively rare – most new apartments we've seen have very limited open-plan kitchen areas forming part of the living room.

You'll gather from the above that these places aren't perfect. We'd prefer to stay in a smart North American condo with loads of space, comfortable furniture and a private hot-tub on your own balcony. But these smart apartments in Europe are a vast improvement on what was on offer ten years ago. And if you quiz the tour operator you are booking through and tell them what you want and don't want, they will point you towards the best places for you – the ones featured in this chapter don't pretend everything is perfect and they don't want dissatisfied clients.

Luxury chalets

The ultimate ski holiday?

by **Chris Gill**

The catered chalet concept (explained for the benefit of newcomers in the panel below) goes from strength to strength, with ever-expanding programmes from the established operators and ever-increasing numbers of competitors. So, not surprisingly, in compiling this annual review of the top of the market – chalets that rival good hotels for comfort and quality of cuisine – we've found more choice than ever: more companies offering more chalets in more resorts. But there is no immediate threat to the ruling trio of Méribel and Val-d'Isère in France, and Verbier in Switzerland.

You can find isolated luxury chalets in all sorts of places, from Austria to Aspen, but the breed in general is still not widespread: most are concentrated in the more upmarket French mega-resorts.

The greatest concentration is found in **Méribel**. Long-time local specialist Meriski, more than any other operator, illustrates the transformation of the chalet business over the last two decades. In the 1980s it was a run-of-the-mill operation, but then it successfully repositioned itself upmarket. It hasn't all been plain sailing for the company, which has changed hands a couple of times recently, but it still has a wide range of impressively comfortable chalets.

Descent International now has an enviable portfolio of properties in the secluded Brames area of the resort. The famously luxurious chalet Brames is the grandest property I have visited in Méribel, with a two-storey living room and a glorious view up the valley towards Mont Vallon. Nearby, the company has the equally desirable 10-bed chalets Aurore and Boréale, and at Belvédère it has chalet Génépi.

VIP has six impressive chalets, including Indiana Lodge – right on the slopes, with great views over the town and an outdoor hot-tub – and Kublai Lodge – with Indonesian artefacts, steam room, gym and cinema. Sister company Snowline operates at a slightly more modest

THE EVOLUTION OF THE CHALET HOLIDAY

The catered chalet holiday is a uniquely British idea. Tour operators install their own cooks and housekeepers in private chalets that they take over for the season. They package them with travel from the UK, normally offering half-board. Dinner is a no-choice affair at a communal table, including wine unlimited in quantity but often severely limited in quality. You can either book a whole chalet (the smallest typically sleep six or eight) or book space in a larger chalet that you share with whoever else turns up.

In the early days of the chalet, in the 1960s and 1970s, the catered chalet business didn't do luxury. Taking a chalet holiday meant roughing it in creaky old buildings, putting up with spartan furniture and paper-thin walls, and with six or more people sharing a bathroom. And the chalet girl – always a girl, back then – was often straight out of college or finishing school, and more intent on having a fun season on the slopes than preparing gourmet meals.

It was only in the late 1980s that one or two companies realised that people would pay a lot more for comfortable and stylish accommodation, good food and wine, and a little bit of personal service – just enough to make the customer feel the staff are there to do something other than have a good time. The new formula worked, probably better than anyone would have expected.

level but still has some very desirable properties. Their top chalet, Isba, has an outdoor hot-tub and a cinema.

Scott Dunn Ski has three properties here – in terms of luxury, towards the lower end of this company's increasingly impressive range of properties. Supertravel's programme now has The Lodge in the Belvédère area, as well as the 20-bed Cardamines. Purple Ski has impressive places in every part of the resort, including the lovely Iamato in Village. Several of Total's properties here deserve to be included in the luxury category, particularly Phoebe.

If you like the idea of luxury but want to keep the cost down, consider staying with Bonne Neige down in the old village of Les Allues. Les Allodis is a converted barn that makes a real change from the modern properties that dominate in Méribel – all beams and antique furniture, but with mod cons including outdoor hot-tub.

Courchevel is well established as the smartest resort in France, and at last has a growing number of smart chalets on the UK package market. The resort is at the heart of the Supertravel programme; it has 10 desirable properties here – some apartments but some proper chalets. Kaluma has two swanky properties.

Flexiski has a rustic 10-bed chalet off the Bellecôte piste – Anemone, one of Courchevel's originals. But this is now rather eclipsed by the cute little eight-bed chalet Chinchilla in the exclusive Hameau du Cospillot. The 10-bed Hermine, nearby, is now in the Descent portfolio. Scott Dunn Ski has nine properties in Courchevel.

La Tania, not far away on the road towards Méribel, has developed quite a range of comfortable chalet properties, including the best of the Ski Amis range, the 14-bed Balkiss. Ski Power and Le Ski have some neat-looking properties with en suite rooms here.

Val-d'Isère is the great rival to Méribel in the French chalet business. The local specialist, YSE, doesn't operate at the very top of the market, but the company's ancient Mountain Lodges are old favourites, offering no picture windows but atmospheric and comfortable living rooms, with stone walls and ample leather sofas. The newly built Chalet des Pistes is their top property, part of a small cluster of chalets in a great on-slope location at La Daille. Scott Dunn's impressive portfolio here is dominated by the 12-bed Eagle's Nest – an extraordinary place, with an indoor jet-stream pool.

The grand enclave of four modern chalets at the southern extremity of the resort – Bergerie, Mistral, Lafitenia and Le Chardon – that once were operated by The Ski Company Ltd have passed through the hands of Scott Dunn into those of Le Chardon Mountain Lodges, apparently a sister company of Ski Activity. Descent has added to its portfolio the chalet du Crêt, a renovated farmhouse well known to many Brits in its previous incarnation as a restaurant.

VIP has some very smart places, including 12 spacious, stylish chalet-apartments in Aspen Lodge on the main street – a novel concept in chalets, with a reception desk, lounge area and coffee bar. Their 200-year-old Farmhouse, by the church, is something else – a beautifully converted, er, farmhouse. Sister company Snowline has several properties, though the best are apartments.

Luxury places in next-door **Tignes** are thin on the ground. Total has the best properties here, including some striking modern places with pool and outdoor hot-tub.

The other great French mega-area, Paradiski, offers lots of chalets in **La Plagne** and growing numbers at **Peisey-Vallandry**, on the

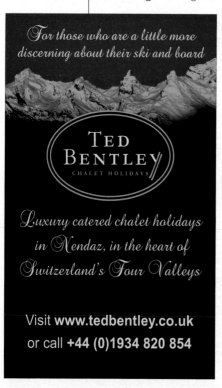

Les Arcs side of the cable-car link from La Plagne. Few deserve a mention here; start with the Ski Amis and Ski Beat brochures.

Chamonix isn't known for luxury chalets, but Flexiski has a gem in the wood-built eight-bed chalet Bornian, with a particularly welcoming beamed living room. Locally based Collineige has secured an enviable range of very individual properties.

Morzine is known mainly for cheap-and-cheerful properties, but Snowline has an impressive cluster of 'town house' properties right in the centre, while in the nearby backwater of Essert-Romand is the deeply comfortable Chalet Gueret, rebuilt with all mod cons a few years back after the all-wood original burned down. Up at **Les Gets** are two seductive alternatives. Descent has the Ferme de Moudon, as seen on Channel 4's *Grand Designs Abroad*: a chic interior in a 17th-century chalet. And there is the Ferme de Montagne – a beautifully renovated old chalet with eight rooms that operates as a small hotel rather than a tour-operator catered chalet, with lots of services.

In Switzerland, **Verbier** is the chalet capital. Chalet Goodwood is much the best I have visited here – fabulously comfortable and stylish, in a central position. It is now run by Descent International, whose equally swanky Septième Ciel could scarcely be in a more different location – high on the Savoleyres side of Verbier. Ski Verbier's portfolio includes several glorious properties. At the top of

Luxury chalets

53

Luxury chalets

54

the range are the recently built Attelas and Sorojasa. Flexiski's Bouvreuil is a richly furnished apartment.

Ted Bentley is a new operation, at present offering a single property in **Nendaz** – chalet Merri, newly built with a grand two-storey living room, but with only half of the four bedrooms en suite.

Zermatt, curiously, has never been a great chalet resort. Scott Dunn has long been the main source, and went up a gear when it acquired two central, spacious and stylish 10-bed apartments that were briefly offered by the Ski Company – Saphir and Louise. I'm not convinced about the antique furnishings of Descent's chalet Zen, but its facilities and position are excellent. VIP now has two apartment-based chalets here – the very central Haus Glacier and radically modern Haus Bor. Total's handful of properties here includes the Génépy, stylishly created within a lovely old wooden building.

Elsewhere in Switzerland, Descent's chalet Eugenia in **Klosters** is a fabulous place – even the bathrooms are remarkable. Possibly even more remarkable is the company's palatial Chesa Albertini in **St Moritz** – 'more a mansion than a chalet', as they say, and with 1000m^2 of floor space they are apparently not exaggerating.

In Austria, luxury chalets are curiously rare. In **St Anton** the good news is that Flexiski's absolutely central Amalian Haus is getting a makeover this summer, with slick new bathrooms and a restyle for the sitting/dining room. Supertravel has the minimalist Chiara, plus a couple of more traditional places, and Total has properties both here and over the hill in **Lech**.

Selected luxury chalet

Good gear guide

The latest kit means more fun for less effort

by **Dave Watts**

The most interesting innovation for 2007: the Rossignol Radical R11 Mutix allows you to personalise the skis' performance to your own taste. Left: with short arms (for quick, short turns); right: with long arms (for longer GS-style turns) ↓

Skis just keep on getting shorter, wider and more fun – and high-performance women-specific models are helping the ladies outperform the men. Boots are becoming comfier and more responsive to help get the best performance out of the radical sidecuts of the latest skis. Snowboard boots are going from black to white and boards are getting more colourful. And sales of helmets and protective gear is on the up.

Skis have changed beyond recognition in the last few years, with the changes being ushered in by the carving revolution, which started in the early 1990s. Skis are now around 20cm or more shorter than those we'd have chosen 10 years ago. They are also wider, meaning more surface area, and they have hourglass shapes. This means that skis now perform much better in return for less effort: they carve more easily and turn more quickly (making skiing on-piste much more fun) and they float much better (making off-piste more enjoyable for a wider range of people).

So if you are still skiing on skis that you've had for a few years, you are unlikely to be getting as much fun and excitement out of your holiday as you could. Consider investing in a new pair for 2007.

Last March I went on a week-long test of all the new skis for the 2006/07 season, organised by the Snowsports Industries of Great Britain (a trade body of ski distributors and retailers). Out of 600 skis from 15 different manufacturers, there wasn't a poor ski to be seen.

Prices for buying in the UK have become much more competitive in recent years and value for money has increased. Even in the last 12 months some prices have improved. For example, Snow+Rock was selling the Rossignol Bandit B3 for £520 last season. This season it will be charging just £499 with a higher performance binding. And last year the Salomon Scrambler Hot cost £499; this season, its much-improved successor the Salomon X-Wing Fury will be on sale for the same price with new technology and a new binding system. Snow+Rock will also have a bargain package aimed at first-time ski buyers for the coming season. They'll be offering Head boots, skis, bindings, poles and a ski bag for a total of just £279.

GREAT NEW SKIS FOR 2007

Both the Salomon and Rossignol skis mentioned above are free-ride skis, designed for skiing off-piste as well as on. And I loved both of them on the test. They floated through the powder, powered through the crud and carved very easily on the piste. One of them would be my ski of choice for the coming season. But most of the other manufacturers also offer good free-ride skis, including for example, the K2 Apache Recon, Scott Aztec Pro, Head Monster and the Volkl Unlimited ranges.

↑
Atomic Metron 11 B5
Head Monster i.M77
Scott Aztec Pro
Volkl Supersport
 Limited Edition
Salomon X-Wing Fury
Rossignol Bandit B3
K2 Public Enemy

Twin-tip skis (where the tails as well as the tips curve upwards) are growing in popularity. The concept was invented to allow freestylers to make jumps in the terrain-park, half-pipe or just off natural hits in the snow and land or take-off backwards (aka 'fakie'). But now many younger skiers ('mainly 15 to 35' say Snow+Rock) are buying them as their main or only pair of skis because they work just as well on- or off-piste as many 'normal' skis as well as being good for jumps and tricks and having graphics that look cool and funky. The Rossignol Scratch FS, K2 Public Enemy and Salomon Foil are likely best sellers.

With on-piste skis, the most interesting innovation for 2007 is the brand new Rossignol Mutix. This comes complete with a tool kit and the choice of using long or short arms which you attach to the ski; you get eight of each when you buy the skis (two in front of each binding and two behind). The idea is that the short arms make the ski lively, quick to turn and snappy and ideal for short radius 'slalom' turns. The long arms give the ski extra power and stability at speed and make the ski ideal for fast cruising and long 'giant slalom' turns. I have to say that I was sceptical at first but I tried them for one run with the short arms on and then immediately after with the long arms on and noticed a huge difference. Personally I preferred the short arms even though I enjoy fast cruising and long GS turns – but I found they worked well for that too. You can try any combination of long and short arms you like and 'personalise' the ski to your own particular preference – there are lots of possible permutations.

As well as the Rossignol Mutix, there are lots of other good skis aimed at those who want to ski primarily on-piste. But the craze for skier-cross skis which began a few years ago is now over and skis that might have been classed as skier-cross then are being sold as on-piste performance/prestige skis by Snow+Rock.

WOMEN'S SKIS: A GROWING MARKET

For years ski manufacturers have made skis aimed specifically at women. In the old days, many of these were simply lighter with 'girly' graphics and colours (such as pink). Often they were aimed at the lower intermediate end of the market rather than catering for advanced and expert skiers too. But now all that has changed: nearly every manufacturer is taking the women's market very seriously and producing a range of skis designed specifically for women (even experts), taking account of their different physical make-up to men. In general, women tend to be lighter and less powerful than men and manufacturers adjust for this by giving their women's skis a different construction and designing the flex and shape specifically for women. All this makes for skis that are easier to turn.

In the ski test, as many as one in five skis were made specifically

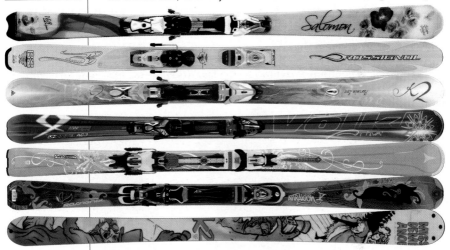

↑ Women's skis:
Salomon Siam
Rossignol Bandit B3W
K2 Burnin Luv
Volkl Attiva
 Unlimited AC3
Atomic Balanze 7.4
Rossignol Attraxion
K2 Missdemeanour

for women. And our women testers found that nearly all the skis they tried compared with the unisex equivalent worked very well for them. These included the K2 T:Nine, Volkl Attiva, Salomon Siam and Rush, Dynastar Exclusive, Atomic Balanze and Rossignol Attraxion and Bandit Women ranges. There are even special women's twin-tip skis such as the K2 Missdemeanour, Rossignol Scratch Girl FS and Salomon Temptress and Minx.

BOOTS GET LIGHTER, MORE CONVENIENT AND COMFIER

Ski boots are your most important purchase. Set aside enough time for a bootfitter to find the right pair for you and fit them properly. This will enhance your skiing pleasure and performance as well as comfort. The main development with boots recently has been to make them fit your feet better by all sorts of anatomical improvements. The use of different softer plastics in key areas of the boot gives a better fit and makes them easier to get on and off. They have also

Salomon Falcon 10
Salomon 1080 SPK
Nordica
 Olympia SM 10
↓

become much lighter and more dynamically flexible, making it easier to flex the boot to adapt to terrain and control your skis.

Almost all boots today have heat mouldable liners to mirror image your foot for comfort as well as performance; and improvements in boot design have allowed these thermal liners to become thinner, giving greater power and control between foot and ski. Always use footbeds in your boots, especially custom-built footbeds made to the shape of your particular feet. These will support your foot and distribute pressure evenly under the whole foot, improving comfort and control and reducing muscle cramps and foot fatigue. For the ultimate performance, consider personalising your boots with a custom fit liner from Zipfit or from Conform'able with foam injection. Boots can be fitted with a Booster strap, which makes the flex more progressive, gives a closer fit and better transmission from foot to ski.

Salomon this year has a new Falcon range of high-performance boots with a special 'Second Skin' outer shell allowing the boot to be a better fit and give better transmission from foot to ski by having different thickness of plastic material in different parts of the boot. This has been designed to work well with its new Smartrak binding mounting system which replaces its Pilot system. They also have a two-buckle SPK freestyle boot designed specifically for park and pipe.

↑ Salomon Smartrak binding on Salomon Equipe 3V

Women-specific boots are developing all the time, too. This year, for example, Head has a new Dream range with an all-round cuff specially designed to fit women's calves. Boot makers have also become more conscious of the cold feet problem that many (especially women) skiers have and are coming up with solutions such as fleece linings and built-in boot heaters. You should dry your boots out every night – consider investing in a pair of boot dryers.

↑ Icebreaker Sport 320 Coronet top, in the coco colour

RED Tantrum Audex helmet Salomon Relay binding ↓

SOCKS AND STUFF ....

Always wear a clean pair of technical ski socks when you are out on the mountain (and when you are trying out boots in a shop); I wore Falke socks for much of last season and loved their silky feel; Smartwool and Wigwam Ultimax are other great brands. Smartwool socks are just one of a range of great products made from Merino wool, which wicks away moisture, is non-allergenic and non-bacterial (ie it doesn't smell even when worn for days on end). I've been wearing a mid-layer top from Icebreaker made of Merino wool for a couple of seasons and love it; Icebreaker also make, for example, underwear, hats and glove liners made from this wool.

Helmets are becoming more and more common on the slopes (one of the editors of this book now always wears one, the other occasionally) and sales have been growing by 30 per cent a year for the last five years. They are becoming more aesthetically pleasing and warmer on cold days and cooler on hot ones due to temperature regulating materials and vents being improved. More and more are incorporating headphone technology so that you can use your phone or listen to music more easily. RED has a good range of helmets and its Tantrum Audex, for example, comes with bluetooth technology to link, for example, to a Motorola phone or an Ipod – and you can take the headphones out and use them separately.

Protective clothing is getting more popular too; Dainese has an extensive range to safeguard your back, knees and the like.

Watches that also measure altitude, number of runs completed, act as compasses and even monitor your heart rate are becoming more and more popular – Suunto is the brand to look for here.

It is essential to be properly prepared for free-riding. Never venture off-piste without companions and ensure you are all equipped with a transceiver, backpack, shovel, probe, first-aid kit and thermal body bag. For additional safety, consider an ABS pack, which incorporates two airbags that you can inflate if you are caught in an avalanche – the idea is that they (and you) stay on the surface and not be buried.

SNOWBOARD GEAR

It's official, white is the new black! After several years of black or muted earth coloured kit, this winter the majority of manufacturers have spotted the public's desire to have more colourful kit. Two of the biggest manufacturers are offering their top of the line boots (Burton's SL9 and Salomon's F LTD) in white rather than black.

This winter's boards are more colourful than ever too, with the return of bright and fluorescent colours; this harks back to the 1980s but also brings back an element of fun to snowboard design. Check the Ride range for the most adventurous graphics.

On the innovations front, Salomon has launched a new concept of binding called the Relay. It has a revolutionary soft heel hoop which allows the ankle to flex laterally, and is so comfortable it's a wonder that no one has come up with the idea before. It also has a cable that runs from the heel hoop to

Good gear guide

Arbor Push
Burton Vapor (base)
Volkl Selecta (detail of rear flute)
Ride DH (top and base) →

SNOW+ROCK TIP

ULTIMATE SNOWBOARD SET-UPS:

LIGHTWEIGHT TECHNICAL SET-UP

Burton SL9 Boot

Burton C60 Binding

Burton Vapor Board

FREESTYLE SET-UP

Vans Fargo Focus Boot

Ride Alpha Binding

Ride DH Board

WOMEN'S SET-UP

Salomon f22 boot

Salomon Relay Elite Binding

Arbor Push snowboard

↑ Burton SL9, in white

the toe area giving greater leverage for much less effort. The result is a binding that is both responsive and superbly comfortable.

Ride also has a new chassis on the Alpha, Beta, Delta and Sigma models that is super lightweight and very minimalist. Not only do they look fantastic, but they perform superbly and are very comfortable too. Flow has also designed a new chassis making it lighter and less bulky, and have incorporated new ratchets for ease of use and more tweakability. This will certainly make the conventional binding purists take another look.

On the board front, everyone is using shorter boards than over the last four or five years. Ski slopes are getting busier and it is getting increasingly difficult to open up and go full speed down the piste, so there is very little point in having a super aggressive, stiff speed machine. Instead, we are buying shorter, more freestyle orientated boards, and what they lack in outright speed, they make up with sheer fun and usability. Riders are learning new tricks and using the entire mountain as a terrain-park. And more people are buying a second board that is more free-ride or powder specific for the big powder days; boards such as the Volkl Selecta are particularly popular for this application and it's surprisingly good fun on-piste too.

WHY BUY IN THE UK

Prices within the UK are competitive with Europe and the range of choice available in the UK is far better. Shops in the mountains often tend to stock mainly local brands (eg French brands in France, Austrian or German in Austria). What's more, if you do find the product cheaper elsewhere in Europe Snow+Rock offers a price pledge on all products to give you the confidence to buy in the UK. It also offers a number of other exclusive guarantees to give you peace of mind to purchase in England, such as a comfort guarantee on all ski boots and a ski suitability and breakage guarantee.

Family holidays

Lessons from 17 years skiing with Kevin – sorry, with Alex

by **Chris Gill**

Another year has gone by, and another stage has been reached in the gradual progress of the Gill household through the gratifying process of child-rearing. Elder child Alex has now reached what is laughably called adult-hood – ie the age of 18. This could be taken to mean that he is now of an age when he can devote himself to selflessly looking after his mum and dad – you know, carrying the skis, fetching the lift passes, getting the breakfast baguettes, bagging a table for lunch – while amusing us constantly with his good-natured banter. As it turned out, he is of an age when he can arrange for six of his school mates to take a flat in the same resort so that he doesn't need to spend any of his waking hours in our company. So it goes. It could have been worse, I suppose: he could have arranged for six of his mates to inhabit our apartment. His absence did mean that I was able to ski comfortably at my own pace, rather than struggle to ski at his. But it did feel like an era had ended without warning. So: let's see what lessons that closed era taught me, year by year.

AGE 1: NORWEGIAN WOODS MK 1
Just to show how liberated we were, Val and I left Alex at home with his nanny while we had a week at Geilo in Norway. Two mistakes in one: Norway was wet and tedious, and we missed the little angel almost as much as we missed decent, affordable wine.

AGE 2: CHRISTMAS IN MONTCHAVIN

A pretty, rustic village free of cars, snowy nursery slopes, a ski-in/ski-out chalet right next to them and Ski Esprit's ever-capable nannies on hand to take charge while we had a Christmas lunch of egg and chips over in La Plagne. Perfect.

AGE 3: SHOME MISHTAKE?

This must have been a really bad trip, because I have obliterated it from my memory.

AGE 4: THE VDI DISASTER

The holiday from hell. Our bags failed to arrive (they went to Peking instead of Geneva) so we had to borrow stuff for ourselves and stretch our credit limits buying new clothes for Alex. But I digress. We didn't want to use the ESF for Alex's first ski lessons, but we had no choice – the small scale alternative was stricken by illness (a hazard with small-scale alternatives to anything, I guess). The result was disastrous. The ESF was understaffed, too; Alex's lesson was terminated early and British kids who didn't understand what was going on were lying in the snow sobbing when we turned up. We organised a parent rota to 'teach' the kids for the week. Judging by reports from readers, the culture of the ESF in many resorts still leaves a lot to be desired.

AGE 5: REST AND RECUPERATION

The scars caused by the ESF hadn't healed by the time we came to discuss our plans for the next season, so we allowed the lad a year off to build his strength up.

AGE 6: PROGRESS IN COURCHEVEL
The Jardin Alpin gondola is really intended to get people up to their swanky hotels in the woods above 1850, but we made good use of it as a beginner lift, getting off at the mid-station and snowploughing down the winding trail to the main resort. The main lesson, though, was that novice skiers don't really want to based in Le Praz, with no suitable local runs except a neglected nursery slope.

AGE 7: SURVIVAL IN NEW ENGLAND
American ski schools are widely recognised to be excellent, particularly for English-speakers. They did the business in Killington, getting Alex skiing down the mountain from virtually the first day. Watch out for frostbite, though, in chilly areas like this.

AGE 8: MIXED MESSAGES IN CHAMONIX
Chamonix was a risky choice for a family holiday; it worked pretty well, but one factor it underlined is the undesirability of nursery slopes that are on the floor of a steep valley (and therefore shady) and completely detached from other runs. Given his achievements in Killington, Alex should have been off that slope within minutes – not easily achieved when moving on involves bus-rides.

AGE 9: HINTERSTODER
One of my main regrets about our handling of the kids' development as skiers is that I didn't insist on more ski school lessons. I should have built on the basis of this quick trip, in the course of which Alex had a great day or two in a small group with a young instructor who rightly sensed that a bit of excitement was called for.

Family holidays

63

AGE 10: NORWEGIAN WOODS MK 2

The need to take a look at Norway's premier downhill resort, Hemsedal, was the trigger for this trip. It would have been a perfectly satisfactory week if only Hemsedal had had a liquor store. Alex's taste for speed was developing faster than his taste for control, which accounts for his demolition of sister Laura in a collision that could have produced serious injury.

AGE 11: VERBIER

Mid-life crisis time: this trip was in celebration of a Big Birthday of mine, and to add to the age concern it happened also to be the first time I had real trouble keeping up with Alex. Not because he was a better skier, of course, but because he still had no sense of danger. I should have sent him to ski school again, but somehow I've never had the moral fibre to make it happen.

AGE 12: LES ARCS

Our first self-catering trip, and our first trip with another family since the kids were babies. Having an apartment on the ground floor with patio doors opening on to the piste was fabulous, especially on a spring holiday when the kids wanted to be out on the snow as late as possible. Woodland runs above Peisey-Vallandry were a great hit with all the kids, mainly on account of the little piste-side off-piste adventures that the woods offered.

AGE 13: TIGNES

A great week on good snow, at a time when many lower resorts were barely functioning. Surprisingly, the wife-and-daughter half-day-skiing faction quite enjoyed themselves too, which goes to show that even a high-altitude ski-station can be a good place to relax in.

AGE 14: LES MENUIRES

The tourist office here kindly lent us an instructor for half a day, spent on the splendid slopes of La Masse, which again demonstrated to Alex that instructors are not necessarily something to be avoided.

AGE 15: SCHOOL TRIP TO SWITZERLAND

In my day at school, Fountains Abbey and the caves of Derbyshire were as far from the satanic mills of Yorkshire as school trips could take you. (I know, I know: 'Derbyshire? You were lucky ...') But it's clear to me (from video evidence) that school skiing trips are an absolutely excellent thing – like family skiing trips but with mates instead of sisters to ski with, and fun young teachers in place of dreary old parents. Alex's skiing came on by leaps and bounds, and he even won the ski school slalom race at the end of the week. Proud? Yes – and envious.

AGE 16: APATHY RULES

So impressed was Alex by his school trip that he displayed no interest in going back to a family trip the year after – and since his mother and sister can never raise much enthusiasm for cold holidays we didn't do a trip this year.

AGE 17: LES ARCS

Well, here we are: 16 years on from that misconceived trip to Norway without him, and 13 years on from that disastrous first lesson in Val-d'Isère, Alex spent our pre-Easter 'family' week in Les Arcs bombing around the slopes with his mates, I'm sure doing so at speeds I would rather not know about.

Earlier in the season he did another excellent school trip; but this time he came second in the end-of-week race. Maybe it's time for some more lessons, Alex?

↑ Age 11: Verbier

Family holidays

65

Buying property

Fancy a chalet or apartment on the slopes?

by **Dave Watts**

Buying your own place in a ski resort has been many people's ambition for years. And now more and more of us are doing just that. As well as the Alps, lots of Brits are now buying places in North America and in eastern Europe too – especially Bulgaria. So where should you look, what can you expect to pay, and what are the pitfalls to beware of?

Most people see the idea of a place in the snow as a mixture of pleasure and investment. They hope to use their place themselves for a few weeks a year and let it out for the rest of the winter (and perhaps for part of the summer too). Prices vary dramatically depending on where you buy and the size of the property. While you can expect to pay well over £1 million for a decent chalet in top resorts such as Val d'Isère and Megève, you can find decent sized apartments in France and Switzerland for £200,000 to £300,000 or less. And in Bulgaria, even £70,000 goes a long way.

So what should you look for when buying a home in the snow? First, you need to decide whether you want somewhere just for the skiing or which is in a resort that is lively and attractive in the summer as well. Many French resorts developed after the 1950s can be deadly dull in summer, whereas somewhere like Morzine or Chamonix is as busy or busier in summer as in winter. Second, if you want the place primarily for skiing and snowboarding you will want reliable snow. And with global warming likely to continue, that means going for somewhere with access to high, snow-sure slopes. Third, if you intend to use it yourself frequently, you will probably want somewhere within a couple of hours of an easily accessible airport. Fourth, make sure you understand the legal and taxation aspects of what you are considering purchasing – buying and running costs, all types of taxes and any resale restrictions. It is highly advisable to get professional advice on these. Fifth, make sure you understand any sale and leaseback type of arrangement or 'guaranteed return' from renting it out that you are offered – these can vary enormously and are particularly common in France where you can save VAT on the purchase price under certain circumstances. Sixth, if you are intending to rent the property out yourself don't overestimate the income you will get from it.

You also need to decide whether you want to buy a new or a resale property. Building restrictions in many areas of the Alps has severely curtailed the number of new properties being built. But, as Simon Malster of Investors in Property points out, 'New builds, especially in France, now tend to be of much higher quality and with much more spacious rooms than was the case in the past.' More and more old buildings are now being converted into high-quality apartments, particularly in villages near the major resorts.

PURE INTERNATIONAL

Grimentz is a little-known, unspoiled Swiss resort with some high snow-sure slopes and good-value property for sale ↓

WHERE TO BUY

Most British buyers still head for France. One reason for this is that second-home ownership by foreigners is banned in many parts of Austria and Switzerland – though more regions are gradually opening their doors. One of the most successful new French developments in the last few years has been Arc 1950, a brand new ski-in/ski-out, traffic-free village in the Les Arcs ski area, designed and built by Canadian company Intrawest. That has now been sold out and Intrawest has started selling properties in its second major new Alpine village – see the Flaine chapter for more on this.

The big resorts such as Méribel, Courchevel 1850 and Val d'Isère have seen prices soar and new building is being severely restricted. But there are some refurbished apartment buildings coming on the market. Bertie Sanderson, Director of Marketing for Erna Low Property, says: 'Properties in Courchevel 1850 are extremely difficult to come by, so I'm delighted that we have completely refurbished apartments in the Chalets du Forum, right in the centre of Courchevel 1850 – there are 55, from one to five bedrooms.' At over £500,000 for a two-bed, 67m² apartment, these are far from cheap. 'But 1850 is a Mecca for wealthy skiers,' says Sanderson. Erna Low also has refurbished apartments on the slopes in Méribel-Mottaret – a two-bed, 45m² apartment will cost around £285,000. Erna Low is also selling some good-looking new-build properties by developer ImmoConcepts. These include spacious five-bedroom, 160m² chalets in the old village of Tignes-Les-Brevières; the second phase of this development is now coming on the market – apartments starting at around £260,000 for 53m² – and they will share underground parking, a 24-hour reception, pool and sauna.

To get anything much cheaper in France you have to look at less mainstream resorts such as Chamrousse, near Grenoble where Jean-Claude Killy won the Olympic men's downhill in 1968. It's a functional family resort with almost 80km/49 miles of pistes – one-bed apartments start at £110,000 and four-bed chalets at £220,000. Zigi Davenport of Alpine Apartments Agency is just starting to sell newly built four-bed, four-bath chalets in St-François-Longchamps, a purpose-built resort linked to the Valmorel ski area, which is being smartened up. These will be selling for £260,000 for 100m² and the development will have a pool and fitness facilities.

SWITZERLAND OFFERS GOOD VALUE FOR MONEY

Simon Malster of Investors in Property has long held the view that Switzerland offers much better value for money than France. But, as in France, new building is banned or severely restricted in some places such as Crans-Montana and Saas-Fee. So developers are again turning to refurbishing existing buildings. Malster has apartments in a refurbished building from the 1970s in Saas-Fee and he expects prices to be around £290,000 for a two-bed, 65m² apartment.

Malster says there are rumours that Verbier may also introduce a building ban. But he prefers the other villages, which link in to Verbier's skiing: 'Best of all is Les Collons,' he says, 'because all the other villages face north and look down to the Rhône valley, but Les Collons is much higher (1800m/5,905ft) and is east- and south-facing with some lovely uncrowded ski pistes and wonderful views of the mountains, including the Matterhorn.' He has two chalet developments available here, one hi-tech modern chalet with huge windows and 270° panoramic views, and the other more traditional.

Ski...

...into the heart of Tuscany

- Abetone is Tuscany's leading ski resort • At 1500 metres ski the slopes and valleys of Val di Luce • Florence, Siena, Lucca and Pisa airport within 90 mins • Strong capital growth potential • Fractional ownership opportunities • Great savings when you buy off-plan *now* • Underground parking available • Use of spa and hotel facilities • Completion dates from November 2007

1 & 2 bedroom apartments from £105,000

0207 590 1624
property@ernalow.co.uk

Erna Low PROPERTY   savills

ernalowproperty.co.uk

A HOME IN THE SNOW IN TUSCANY?

Most people associate Tuscany with the summer: warm sunshine, rolling hills and vineyards, chianti, lovely old buildings and charming old cities and villages. It has all that. But it has some good skiing too. The main resort is Abetone in the Appennines, less than a couple of hours from Pisa and Florence.

The ski area covers 50km/31 miles of linked pistes between 1200m/3,940ft and 1900m/6,230ft, served by 20 lifts, which include a gondola and a couple of fast chairs. The runs are mainly easy cruising on blues and reds – good for families – and are prettily wooded on the lower part of the mountain, with open bowls above that offer some good off-piste. And from the highest point at Alpe tre Potenze, on a clear day you can see all the way to the Mediterranean and the islands beyond. The resort is surprisingly snow-sure for somewhere so far south and the season lasts well into April (which is when we visited in 2006) – due to a good snow record, extensive snowmaking and lots of north-facing slopes. There's a terrain-park with half-pipe and 3m/10ft jumps for snowboarders and skiers.

Part of the ski area and 10 to 15 minutes by car from Abetone is Val di Luce, currently just an alternative lift base and with a ski school office and a few apartments. But it will shortly be transformed by a new development of slope-side apartments and a hotel with properties on sale (some outright and some in fractional ownership) through Erna Low Property. Prices start at around £110,000 for a 48m² studio, and a two-bedroom apartment of 70m² costs around £190,000. The hotel will have a covered pool in the central square and spa facilities with sauna, steam and treatments available. And it is all set at 1500m/4,920ft at the foot of the slopes with two chair-lifts heading up the best open bowl in the ski area (see right) and another linking in to the slopes above Abetone.

So if you fancy a home in Tuscany with skiing all winter and the Tuscan sun and sights in summer, this development is well worth a look.

Traditional chalets will sell for from around £375,000 for three or four bedrooms and modern ones from around £700,000 for four or five bedrooms. Malster also likes the unspoiled and little-known resort of Grimentz (see our Resort Directory), which has high, snow-sure slopes, where you can have a chalet built to order for around £350,000, and two-bed apartments sell for around £230,000.

Other agents are now also starting to get keen on selling in Switzerland. Alpine Apartments Agency has some five-bed chalets in the charming village of Morgins (part of the Portes du Soleil), right on the slopes, for £600,000. And Pure International has refurbished apartments in Val d'Illiez near Champéry (again the Portes du Soleil ski area) with an outdoor thermal spa – huge 130M^2, two-bed apartments cost £320,000. It also has some lovely looking chalets in Grimentz, a selection of developments in Villars (very close to Geneva airport) and apartments in Veysonnaz and Crans-Montana.

Pure International also has two developments in the Hochkönig region of Austria (see our chapter on the ski area) including one overlooking an excellent golf course, which I can vouch for myself, after playing it in June. Prices start at around £260,000 for a two-bed, 87m^2 apartment. Investors in Property also has Austrian properties at Stadl and Turracher (which has its own small ski area – see Resort Directory), around 30 minutes' drive from Bad Kleinkirchheim (see chapter on page 132). Prices start at around £160,000 for a detached two- or three-bed chalet with use of pool and clubhouse.

GOING FURTHER AFIELD

Pure International sells a lot of properties in Canada. Kate Bermon told me: 'The Tremblant region is very popular: it has a lovely car-free village, lots of activities in the summer as well as skiing or boarding in the winter. And it's only a five-hour flight from the UK.' The many properties on offer include one-bed apartments from £130,000, and log cabins in a wooded setting by the lake for under £220,000 for four bedrooms. Erna Low also sells a lot of property in Tremblant village and is UK representative for the resort developer Intrawest. Pure International also has properties near Canmore in Alberta – the gateway to Banff National Park and its ski resorts.

If rock-bottom prices are your priority, look at Bulgaria. There is a huge building boom going on right now at Bansko (see chapter on page 711) but some people are worried that the infrastructure may not be able to cope with the rapid expansion. Nevertheless, you can pick up two-bed apartments of 60-70m^2 for around £40,000 to £70,000, says Amar Sodhi of Bulgarian specialists Avatar International.

THERE'S SNOW
PLACE LIKE HOME

If you dream of owning a home on the slopes no other company provides the variety of property, choice of first class destinations or level of expertise offered by PURE International. With a wide range of properties from stylish studios to exquisite family log cabins, PURE International offers dream homes in exceptional ski destinations in North America and Europe.

When the snow disappears during the hot summer months PURE properties offer plenty of four season fun including golf, sailing and hiking to keep even the most discerning traveller occupied.

CANADA SPAIN **SWITZERLAND**
ITALY **AUSTRIA** PORTUGAL
JAMAICA **USA** MEXICO

EXCEPTIONAL HOMES. UNIQUE ENVIRONMENTS

www.pureintl.com   contact@pureintl.com   +44 (0)20 7331 4500

PURE
INTERNATIONAL

Corporate ski trips

A great way to motivate your staff and clients

Most companies choose to get groups of staff or clients together out of the office occasionally for a whole variety of reasons. Team building, rewarding performance, bonding with clients, problem solving, communicating key messages and planning future strategy are just a few. Getting together in another boring UK hotel can seem a bit tedious – but getting together in a splendid ski resort environment is most certainly not. That's why more and more firms are doing just that.

The mountain environment is one that has lots of advantages for corporate events. The perceived status of ski resorts is high – whoever you invite will be in no doubt that they are being given a treat (as will their friends and business colleagues). And the clear fresh air, the sun and the snowy, dramatic mountain scenery have a huge and immediate impact on people arriving from the European lowlands and their dreary winters. There is a great sense of fun and liberation, and people are happy to cast inhibitions aside and let their hair down. And a winter sports break need not appeal just to skiers. Helena Kania went on a team building weekend to Morzine organised by her company Cable & Wireless and told us, 'I didn't set foot on skis or board but just loved the fresh air, sunshine, views, walks and meeting up with the others in mountain restaurants. And we all got on much better when we got back to work after sharing a great experience.'

HOW LONG FOR AND WHAT'S THE COST?

The answer is that it depends on your goals. Corporate trips of a few days are the norm – Thursday to Sunday, say. But you can have two full, action-packed days in the Alps by leaving on Friday after work and returning late on Sunday night – arriving back at work on Monday morning refreshed, invigorated and remotivated. Some companies take over a cluster of chalets for a week or two and have different groups moving in and out, staying for a variety of durations. Others hire helicopters for airport transfers and just go for one night. The cost can be a lot less than you'd think and, indeed, less than some of the alternatives, because UK hotel and restaurant costs are relatively high.

HOW BIG A GROUP?

In principle, your group can be any size you like. Melissa Long of The Corporate Ski Company says that the groups they deal with vary from 15 to several hundred people but that generally the average size is between 30 and 50. With really small groups, be aware that the social success is going to depend on how the individuals mesh.

Larger groups can work well but need to be expertly organised. When we were in Whistler a couple of years back, the whole of the 550-room Fairmont Chateau Whistler had been taken over by a medical conference. And in Squaw Valley this year, the whole of the new Village at Squaw had been taken over by Google for the week.

Someone with plenty of experience of handling large groups is Amin Momen of Momentum Travel. For the last few years he has organised the Swiss International City Ski Championships in Courmayeur, involving around 200 racers, plus lots of hangers-on.

↑ Some of the 2006 competitors after the end of the race

SWISS INTERNATIONAL CITY SKI CHAMPIONSHIPS

The City Ski Championships have been organised by weekend skiing specialist Momentum Ski and held annually in Courmayeur in Italy's Aosta valley since 2000. Among its attractions is the array of former skiing stars who turn up to set the pace. Former Olympic gold medallist Tommy Moe of the USA and Britain's downhill stars of the 1980s and 90s Konrad Bartelski and Graham Bell are regulars. They will be joined in 2007 by Austrian Olympic gold medal winner Patrick Ortleib. Around 200 skiers from 40 City firms take part in the event. In 2006, the fastest genuine amateur man was Eric Armellino of Lloyds of London and the fastest amateur woman was Michelle Muir of Accenture, with ex-pro racer Einar Johansen of Deutsche Bank, as usual, taking the former FIS racer title. There are team events too, as well as prizes for the over 40s and 50s sections, best wipeout and slowest time.

The Saturday GS race is the main event but only part of the attraction of this weekend. Three other races are held on the Friday: a team parallel slalom (a relay race with four in each team), the Volvo Radar Trap (speed skiing) and, new for 2007, the Crew Clothing boarder-cross. On the Friday evening, there's a welcome drinks party, dinner at various restaurants, late-night drinks in the Bar Roma; on the Saturday, there's a race-side buffet on the piste, champagne reception in the evening, followed by a gala presentation dinner and then ... clubbing till dawn. On Sunday the hard core either take advantage of Courmayeur's off-piste terrain on the Toula Glacier or heli-ski; others just enjoy Momentum's complimentary Bloody Marys at Christiania's on the slopes.

The 2007 event, from 15 to 18 March, promises to be even better than ever. Konrad Bartelski will again be running the Snow+Rock pre-race ski clinics, which are really popular with the competitors, and Graham Bell and Matt Chilton from the BBC will be doing the commentary (the Ski Sunday crew may even enter a team themselves). For more details contact Momentum on 020 7371 9111 or City Championships on 01787 249 604 or see www.cityskichampionships.com. The City Ski Championships are part of the City Championships Calendar.

Last season he organised a trip for Google Europe with over 700 involved – and they are threatening to involve 1,500 people in the 2007 trip. 'Such a large group is quite a challenge,' says Amin, 'but it helps enormously that we have such good local contacts in the resort. If strings need to be pulled to solve a problem, we know exactly which strings.'

WHERE TO GO AND WHAT KIND OF ACCOMMODATION?
How easy it is to settle on a resort for a corporate trip depends hugely on the nature of your project. If it's a group spread around the world that you want to get together, you could consider North American resorts as well as the Alps. But if they are UK or European based, the Alps would be best. Because corporate trips tend to be short, you'll want to keep the travel time to the minimum so that it doesn't dominate the proceedings. Transfer times from airports to resorts generally range from one to four hours, and you'll probably want to operate at the lower end of that range if you can. On the other hand, you may want your choice of resort to carry a message to your 'delegates'. Choosing Courchevel or St Moritz is effectively saying, 'No expense spared – nothing but the best for you.'

Whatever you do, choose a resort with a good snow record and/or extensive snowmaking. You don't want to invite people on a skiing break to find that there's no snow. Avoid early season for the same reason. A March trip to a high resort will mean good snow and it should mean strong sunshine, too. Don't get hung up on size – with only a couple of days to spend on the slopes, almost any resort has plenty of terrain, especially with good local guides to help you make the most of it. It's likely that not everyone in the group will want to

Corporate ski trips

go skiing or boarding, so you may want to choose a resort that has good walks available and maybe lots of other activities that can be organised, such as snow-shoeing, dog-sledding, snowmobiling, skating, curling, tobogganing, ballooning, flights in planes or helicopters or luxuriating in a spa enjoying treatments and massages.

As for accommodation, if it's a dozen people travelling out together for a relaxed couple of days, a swanky chalet might be good: see the 'Luxury Chalets' chapter on page 49 to get an idea of what's available.

If you are getting a large group together and need good conference facilities, you're playing a different ball game. Finding the right resort and accommodation, meeting rooms and support services can be a real headache, and it's in dealing with this sort of challenge that the services of a tour operator or event management company will really pay off. If you put them in charge of the whole event, you can make them responsible for staying within budget, including on-the-spot costs, as well as the basic accommodation and travel costs.

Melissa Long of The Corporate Ski Company says: 'Although we operate throughout the Alps, around 60 per cent of our groups go to Switzerland because of the excellent flight access and wider choice of 4- and 5-star hotels which tend to be more accommodating for short-stay and weekend corporate groups. Some of our more popular resorts are St Moritz, Zermatt, Grindelwald and Flims.'

ORGANISING THE DAYS AND EVENINGS

This is another area where the services of a tour operator or event management company will really pay off. You'll need to make sure everyone is equipped with suitable clothing, equipment and lift passes. You'll also want to organise tuition or guiding specially for your group. Make sure you have enough instructors/guides so that you can form groups of equal ability. You'll also want to ensure that activities for non-skiers are carefully choreographed, so that people do what they want to do and have their time filled (or have time off to relax if that's what they want). Lunch in a mountain restaurant can be an opportunity to get your group together, and if you choose one near the top of a lift that pedestrians can use, everyone will be able to get there easily. Another possibility, in good weather, is a swanky picnic, with plenty of champagne buried in the snow.

You might want to think about a race for delegates, though bear in mind that this won't appeal to the complete beginners in the group. Other forms of competition, such as on-snow treasure hunts, could be used to include non-skiers too. You might want to make these team events (eg relay races) to build relationships.

Then there are the evenings to consider. They are a time when all the group can be brought together, so it's important to think about how you're going to use those opportunities to best effect. You can create social events that reinforce your message – perhaps taking over a whole bar or a mountain restaurant, for example. In the right resort, dinner in a mountain restaurant could be followed by toboggan runs or torchlit descents on skis.

Corporate ski trips

Weekend breaks

Three days on the slopes can feel as good as a week

A weekend away with just one day off work can give you three great days on the slopes, leaving you with the feeling of having been away for ages and returning to work feeling really refreshed. And it does not need to cost you an arm and a leg, Dave Watts enthuses.

Short-break ski trips have become much more popular in the last few years, partly because of the growth of budget airlines. I was very sceptical of them before I tried them myself several years ago. But now I'm convinced they are a great idea. A quick fix of the white stuff really does seem almost as good as a week. I have had successful short breaks all over the place. My first was in the classic weekend destination of Chamonix, which has local areas suitable for all types of weather and snow conditions. Next came Zell am See in Austria, with skiing on the glacier at Kaprun. Then a weekend in Val-d'Isère at the time of the Premier Neige race – great fun. Other good pre-Christmas weekends have been in Courchevel and Saas-Fee. A January weekend in Courmayeur, a February one in Aosta (skiing Cervinia, Monterosa and Pila on successive days), March ones in Engelberg and Verbier, and April stays in Hochkönig in Austria and Abetone in Tuscany have all been great.

And I've met many other weekend converts, including people who rent apartments for the season and go out every other weekend and others who book up 12 or so weekend flights well in advance

Weekend breaks

and decide where to go when they know where the best snow is.

The key to making the most of your time is to catch late flights each way (or a very early flight out, allowing you to be on the slopes by lunch time) – so it helps if you live near a suitable airport. With the growth of budget airlines, there's a big choice of regional and destination airports to use as well as the big ones favoured by longer-established airlines. I've had excellently timed Ryanair flights to and from Salzburg and Pisa from Stansted as well as EasyJet to Geneva from Luton, for example. At the other extreme of the price range, of course, you could fly in your own private jet, with timings and departure and arrival airports suited to your needs – see what Jeffersons offer on the previous page.

We don't recommend flying to Munich if you are travelling out on a Friday or back on a Sunday – the queues on the motorway can be horrendous, as the whole of Munich seems to go weekend skiing, and the airport is on the far side of the city from the Alps. Similarly, allow plenty of time if you are driving back to Lyon airport on a Sunday evening – we encountered very heavy traffic after leaving Courchevel in what we had thought was good time.

Booking a rental car or transfer in advance is usually cheaper than arranging one after you arrive. Taxis can be ridiculously expensive compared with the cost of renting a car. For example, you would expect to pay over £200 each way between Geneva airport and Courchevel by taxi if you book locally – but renting a small car for the weekend would be much less than the one-way taxi price. In our experience, train and bus times between airports and resorts are more suitable for week-long visitors than for weekenders looking for maximum time on the slopes. Airport transfer companies such as

those listed in the reference section at the back of this book are worth trying; but you might waste valuable time waiting around if you go for a shared transfer.

Using a weekend specialist, such as one of those advertising in this chapter, makes sense if you don't want the hassle of making your own arrangements. They know the best resorts to go to, can arrange transfers or car hire and have special deals with hotels that do them good room rates or that might not otherwise take weekend bookings. Some arrange special weekend courses (eg with off-piste guides or even heli-skiing) and can arrange groups of similar standard for you to ski with. And local tour operator reps and contacts can save you valuable time arranging lift passes (beware of big weekend queues on Saturday and Sunday mornings) and equipment hire, and advise on local restaurants and other facilities.

CHOOSING A RESORT

As for choosing a resort, there are various considerations. Many people think they should go for a resort within a short drive of their arrival airport. But by definition, resorts close to major airports are close to large numbers of people poised to hit the slopes on fine weekends, which can mean queues for the lifts, crowds on the slopes and competition for hotel beds. These days, most resorts are within striking distance of a major airport and an hour's extra transfer time is not really that much if it gets you to quieter slopes.

Resorts close to Geneva include Chamonix, St-Gervais, Megève and Les Contamines (all in the Mont Blanc area and sharing an area lift pass), Flaine and La Clusaz in France, and Villars and Les Diablerets in Switzerland. All these are within an hour or so of

Geneva by car. Verbier and Crans-Montana in Switzerland are a bit further, as are the Three Valleys and other Tarentaise resorts – Val-d'Isère can be reached in under three hours now – and Morzine and the Portes du Soleil resorts in France. EasyJet's Nice flights put Isola 2000 within a 90km/56 mile drive.

Flying to Zürich opens up lots of other possibilities. Flims, Davos and Klosters are the nearest big resorts, and the less well-known resorts of Engelberg and Andermatt are within easy reach. St Anton and Lech in Austria are within striking distance, as are the resorts of the Montafon valley. Ryanair's Salzburg flights make most of the eastern Austrian resorts a short drive away.

In Italy, Courmayeur is a popular weekend destination and is easily accessible from Geneva through the Mont Blanc tunnel. Resorts such as Champoluc, Sauze d'Oulx and Sestriere are easily accessible from Milan or Turin. Ryanair's Verona flights put you very near the Sella Ronda resorts and Cortina d'Ampezzo, and Bergamo is convenient for Trentino resorts such as Madonna di Campiglio.

Unless you are booking at short notice when you know the snow is good, we'd be tempted to avoid low resorts such as Megève and Villars – unless you have transport to get you to more snow-sure slopes. And because you don't want your whole weekend ruined by a white-out, we'd also be tempted to avoid very high resorts where the skiing is entirely above the tree line – this rules out places such as Tignes and Val-Thorens in France, Obergurl in Austria and Cervinia in Italy. Another consideration is that hotels in big, popular winter resorts such as St Anton, Verbier and Val-d'Isère now often refuse to take weekend bookings except in very low season (eg early Jan or late March) because they can get more profitable week-long bookings. But more summer-oriented resorts, which generally have accommodation spare in winter, are worth considering – such as Chamonix, Morzine, Engelberg, Villars and Mürren.

WHAT ABOUT PRICE?

The cost can vary enormously. The flight and transfer are expensive fixed costs and obviously make a weekend proportionately more expensive than a full week. In general, through a good specialist tour operator you can expect to pay from around £350 a head for flights, car hire and a double room in a 3-star hotel or B&B for three nights, assuming two people sharing. With lift passes and meals you could be looking at around £500. For a 4-star hotel add another £100 or so.

MIDWEEK BREAKS

If you can get away midweek, there are many advantages. Flights (especially on budget airlines) should be cheaper, and possibly accommodation, too. And resorts that get busy at weekends, such as Verbier and Courmayeur, can be very quiet midweek in low season.

SNOWPIX.COM / IAN STRATFORD

← Chamonix is a great weekend destination – close to Geneva airport and with lots of accommodation

All-inclusive holidays

Come home on-budget

by **Chris Gill**

For anyone who wants to keep control of their holiday spending, there's nothing to beat an all-inclusive holiday. Perhaps surprisingly, no one sells winter sports packages that include absolutely everything. But there are a couple of companies that come close.

Club Med is the big name in this game, with huge hotels (called 'villages') in around 20 resorts in the Alps. The great majority are in France (it's a French company), but Club Med has taken over a handful of old hotels in Swiss resorts and also has places elsewhere.

Holidays are available with or without flights and transfers. They all include insurance. But the key feature of the package is that it includes all meals and drinks (including, within reason, bar drinks at most 'villages'). This is a French operation, so lunch is a serious meal. Usually, it's taken back at the village; most are in high resorts, where this is not difficult, but returning to base for lunch doesn't appeal to everyone. In a very few resorts Club Med has taken over a mountain restaurant or two, which is a better arrangement.

Generally, Club Med prices include your lift pass and tuition. Some do only half-day tuition, but most do a full day. Skiing or boarding equipment costs extra, but is usually available on site.

Most villages have childcare facilities, and for many Club Med regulars these are at the heart of the formula – though how well they will work for English-speaking kids must be open to doubt.

Equity Ski's pricing is a lot simpler, as well as different. They don't include lunch, and they include drinks with dinner only in the case of catered chalet holidays. But all their holiday prices include your equipment hire, as well as lift pass, insurance and either tuition or guiding around the slopes (it depends on where you are staying).

The Equity programme falls roughly into two halves. They offer a moderate number of Austrian and French resorts, in which they generally run their own catered chalets or hotels, and sometimes offer other hotels too. Then, in a larger number of Italian resorts, they offer two or three standard hotels that may be shared with other companies' clients, in the conventional way.

Equity's 30 or so resorts are a mix of established big names – La Plagne, Mayrhofen, Sestriere – and smaller, less well-known places such as St Michael and Le Corbier (part of Les Sybelles). It includes one or two interesting 'back-door' resorts attached to major ski areas – Claviere for the Milky Way, Folgarida for Madonna di Campiglio.

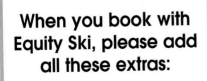

Flying to the snow

Competition means good deals for consumers

by **Chris Gill**

Most Brits going to the Alps go by plane; that's been the case since skiing became a mass-market activity in the 1960s. But most of us have traditionally travelled on one-week packages, using charter flights. What has changed in the last decade is that a growing number of us travel independently by air, often going for non-standard periods and paying bargain fares.

This change in our travelling habits has been brought about by budget airlines operating scheduled services, on which anyone can buy a seat, choosing flights to suit their own plans. The key player was EasyJet, which started cheap scheduled flights to the Alps in the mid-1990s. EasyJet and other major budget airlines have added more routes as well as more flights, while more minor airlines have entered the market. The budget flight business is clearly here to stay.

AIRLINES FOR THE ALPS

Budget airlines operate from most UK airports other than pricey Heathrow. Our map shows the arrival airports dotted around the Alps. There isn't so much scope here as in other parts of the Continent for budget airlines to use budget airports, but there are one or two unfamiliar names on the map. You can work out from the map which arrival airports are likely to work for your chosen resort. We're concentrating on the Alps, but budget airlines can also get you to the Pyrenees, the Massif Central and the Sierra Nevada.

EasyJet still has by far the biggest range of flights to the key Alpine destination airport of Geneva – seven provincial departure airports around the UK. The airline serves roughly nine Alpine airports from the London area. For those living south of London, the fact that it operates several routes from Gatwick will be important.

Ryanair has a lot of flights from Stansted (and some from Luton) to a number of useful airports, including places such as Friedrichshafen, which you may not have heard of but which is handy for St Anton and eastern Switzerland.

Flybe serves Geneva, Chambéry, Berne and Salzburg from Birmingham and Southampton.

Bmibaby has flights from Cardiff, Manchester, Birmingham and Nottingham to Geneva and some other relevant airports.

Jet2.com is based at Manchester and Leeds/Bradford, offering flights to Geneva and Chambéry.

Helvetic is a Swiss budget airline, based in Zürich. It now uses Luton, offering two daily flight to Zürich.

Thomsonfly goes to Grenoble and Salzburg from several provincial airports.

Don't overlook foreign national airlines – Air France, Alitalia, Austrian, Lufthansa – which fly between Heathrow (and sometimes major regional airports such as Birmingham and Manchester) and major home airports. They are increasingly competitive. **Swiss** International Air Lines operates several flights a day from Birmingham and Manchester to Zürich, from Heathrow and London City to Zürich and Geneva. And **British Airways** goes to lots of useful airports from a variety of UK airports.

TRAVEL TIPS
How low can you go?
Budget airline fares vary according to demand, and in general the cheapest are for midweek flights, early or late in the day, booked months in advance (or at the last minute). As a flight fills up, the fares go up; if it looks like the flight might not sell out, the fares go down again. You can pay less than £30 return if you time it right. We made trips last winter for which the cost of carrying skis and boots exceeded the basic fares we paid.

Flexibility Although the budget airlines won't normally give you a refund if you decide not to travel, most will now allow you to change the flight time or route, or the name of the passenger – but at a cost of perhaps £15 each way for each change. Check when you book, because the rules change.

Baggage Airline policies on baggage vary, and they are liable to change – so it's important to check. EasyJet allows hold baggage of 20kg per person. Ryanair has a mean baggage allowance of 15kg. Excess baggage is generally charged at £5/kg to £6/kg (for one flight) – the cost can mount up. Both these airlines now charge £15 per flight to carry skis. Major national airlines treat skis as part of your general baggage. Swiss carries one pair of skis or a snowboard free.

DON'T FORGET CHARTER FLIGHTS
We've been concentrating here on scheduled services, which allow a wide choice of travel arrangements. Charter flights, where a tour operator (or group of operators) takes over a plane for package holiday purposes, are sometimes sold on a seat-only basis – and you can find out about these, as well as scheduled flight options, by spending hours on the internet. Charter flights can allow you to use airports not served by scheduled services – eg Bolzano, for resorts in the Dolomites.

Flying to the snow

83

ONLINE BOOKING
Most budget airlines expect you to make your booking online. The web addresses of the airlines we list are given in the reference section at the back of the book, and will also be found as links on our own website at www.wtss.co.uk.

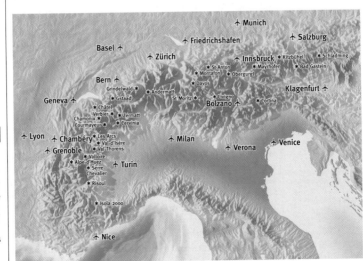

Drive to the Alps

And ski where you please

by **Chris Allan**

More and more people from Britain are doing what the French, the Germans and the Dutch have done for years, and driving to their Alpine resorts. It has various advantages, even for those going on a pretty standard week in the Alps. For many people, it's just less hassle than checking in at dawn for a flight from Gatwick, and less tedious than sitting around waiting for a delayed charter plane that's stuck in Majorca. For families (especially those going self-catering), it simplifies the job of moving half the contents of your house to the Alps. If there are four or five people in your party, the cost can be lower than travelling by air.

If you fancy something a bit more adventurous, taking a car opens up the exciting possibility of touring around several resorts in one trip, and even making up your plans as you go.

Cross-Channel ferries are faster and more pleasant than ever, with the possibility of a seriously good lunch on P&O's short crossings as an alternative to the quicker shuttle-trains through the tunnel. And the motorway networks in north-eastern France and on the approaches to the Alps have improved immensely in the last decade. You can now get to most resorts easily in a day, if you're based in south-east England, in some cases using motorways virtually all the way.

For us, the freedom factor is the key. If the snow's bad in your resort, if the lift queues are horrendous, or if the resort you've plumped for turns out to be a let-down, you don't have to grin and bear it – if you have a car, you can try somewhere else (provided of course that you haven't already invested in a weekly lift pass).

Another plus-point is that you can extend the standard six-day holiday by two days by taking only one extra day off work – crossing the Channel early on a Friday morning and returning nine days later on the Sunday evening. On the outward journey, we often spend a day in a different resort before moving on to our final destination late on the Saturday. After a full day on the slopes on the final Saturday, driving for a few hours before stopping for the night means you won't find Sunday's journey too demanding, and you may even have time for a traditional French Sunday lunch.

AS YOU LIKE IT

If you fancy visiting several resorts, you can use one as a base and make day trips to others when it suits you. This way, you can still take advantage of package holiday prices.

The key to turning this kind of holiday into a success is to go for a base that offers easy road access to other resorts. Our suggestions for France are in a separate chapter. A good choice in Austria is the Tirol: the resorts east of Innsbruck offer many options. Söll is a convenient base for exploring resorts such as Alpbach and Kitzbühel. Further east in Salzburgerland there are lots of possibilities – and the Ski Amadé lift pass described in our Austrian introduction means you can exploit them conveniently and economically. Western Austria is not ideal for this sort of holiday – many resorts are tucked away at the head of long valleys – but from St Anton you could make day trips to Ischgl and Serfaus, as well as nearby Lech and Zürs.

SAVE 20%
WHEN YOU SUBSCRIBE!

Subscribe to Daily Mail Ski & Snowboard magazine by Direct Debit and you'll save a massive 20%!* Published monthly from October to March, it has everything you need for an action-packed season:

- Essential reviews of resorts and tour operators
- Impartial tests of the latest skis, snowboards and accessories
- Expert tips and advice on helping you improve your technique
- **PLUS** exclusive holiday offers, health and fitness tips and all the latest news from the slopes

Don't miss out, subscribe today and have all the info you need delivered hot off the press and straight to your door. You'll pay a discounted rate of just £35.20 for 12 issues, which will last you two years!

WIN! A £2500 HOLIDAY and £2200 OF MUST-HAVE KIT

DAILY MAIL

SKi
& SNOWBOARD
www.skiandsnowboardmag.com

FREE! Bollé goggles
Amazing subscription offer

Bargain holidays
Are they a rip off?

Winter Olympics 2006
How everyone will benefit

Instant success
Amazing technique tips

Hawaii Five-Snow
Ultimate boarding adventure

Yodelaaeeeeooh!
Switzerland calling

Live your **DREAM**
28 brilliant ideas for amazing experiences... whatever your age

PRODUCTS ON TEST
30 ON-PISTE SKIS
10 BEGINNER SNOWBOARDS
9 ROCK HARD HELMETS

TOP RESORTS ✳ FINLAY MICKEL ✳ GLOBAL WARMING ✳ HOLIDAY OFFERS

Visit **www.subscription.co.uk/dmski/skfq**
or call **01858 438831** and quote **SKFQ**

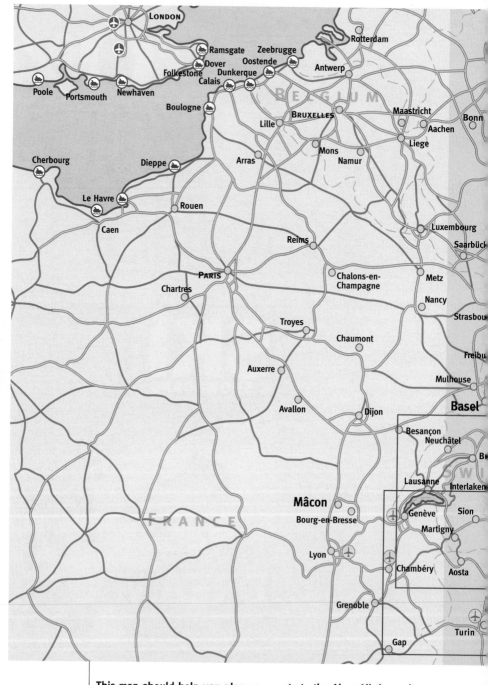

This map should help you plan your route to the Alps. All the main routes from the Channel and all the routes up into the mountains funnel through (or close to) three 'gateways', picked out on the map in larger type – Mâcon, Basel and Ulm. Decide which gateway suits your destination, and pick a route to it. Occasionally, using different Channel ports will lead you to use different gateways.

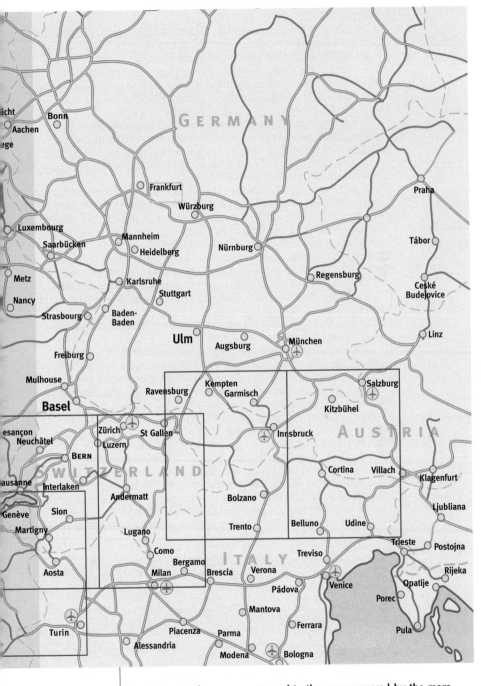

The boxes on the map correspond to the areas covered by the more detailed maps at the start of the main country sections of the book:
Austria page 120
France page 236
Italy page 422
Switzerland page 486

AROUND THE ALPS IN SEVEN DAYS

If you want to see as much of the Alps as possible, consider making a Grand Tour by car, moving every day or two to a different resort and enjoying the complete freedom of going where you want, when you want. Out of high season there's no need to book accommodation before you go, so you can decide at the last minute which part of the Alps and which countries to visit – going where the snow is best, unless you have other special requirements.

A touring holiday doesn't mean you'll be spending more time on the road than on the piste – provided you plan your route carefully. An hour's drive after the lifts have shut is all it need take. It does eat into your après-ski time, of course; you have to be prepared to trade beers in the bar for fruit juice in the car.

Italy is far more suitable for tourers than day-trippers, provided you're prepared to put up with some slow drives on winding passes. For example, you could start in Livigno, drive to Bormio and then to the Dolomites, visiting Madonna di Campiglio and Selva, and finish your Italian expedition in Cortina. A tour of resorts off the Valle d'Aosta in the west of the Italian Alps doesn't involve passes, but some long drives up to places like Cervinia and Champoluc.

Eastern Switzerland also offers a very attractive touring holiday. You could start in Davos/Klosters, take in Lenzerheide and Arosa and end up in Flims. With a little extra driving, you could even include St Moritz. Or tack Disentis, Sedrun and snowy Andermatt on to the end, leaving a short drive to Zürich airport.

There's no need to confine yourself to one country. You could imitate the famous Haute-Route by starting in Argentière in France and ending up in Switzerland's Saas-Fee, taking in Verbier and Zermatt along the way – even diverting to Crans-Montana if time permits and the conditions (for once) look promising. The Valle d'Aosta tour mentioned above could start and finish with a day or two in Megève, or the Portes du Soleil.

The major thing that you have to watch out for with a touring holiday is the cost of accommodation. Checking into a resort hotel as an independent traveller for a night or two doesn't come cheap, and can be a bit of a rip-off. You can save money by staying down the valley – and you don't necessarily have to drive up to the slopes in the morning: some valley towns are linked by lifts. For example, you can take a funicular from Bourg-St-Maurice up to Les Arcs; a gondola links Brides-les-Bains to Méribel.

TYRES / CHAINS

For several seasons we have used winter tyres made by a specialist Dutch company, Vredestein. The editorial Audi Allroad is shown here wearing Wintrac 'V'-rated tyres, good for 149mph. We've found these (like the company's Snowtracs) excellent both on-snow and off. We leave them on year-round – they are no noisier than standard tyres.

Chains are the normal way of dealing with deep snow; but many modern cars with wide wheels (like the Audi) can't take chains. The solution is clever Swiss gadgets called Spikes Spiders; a reader reports that they gave him 'excellent grip'. You can hire or buy from the UK agents.

www.vredestein.com
t 01933 677770

www.spikesspider.com
t 01706 819365

Drive to the French Alps

To make the most of them

by **Chris Gill**

If you've read the preceding chapter, you'll have gathered that we are keen on driving to the Alps in general. But we're particularly keen on driving to the French Alps. The drive is a relatively short one, whereas many of the transfers to major French resorts from Geneva airport are relatively long. And the route from the Channel is through France rather than Germany, which for Francophiles like us means it's a pleasant prospect rather than a vaguely off-putting one.

TRAVEL TIME

The French Alps are the number-one destination for British car-borne skiers. The journey time is surprisingly short, at least if you are starting from southern England. From Calais, for example, you can comfortably cover the 900km/560 miles to Chamonix in about nine hours plus stops – with the exception of the final few miles, the whole journey is on motorways. And except on peak weekends the traffic is relatively light, if you steer clear of Paris.

With some southern exceptions, all the resorts of the French Alps are within a day's driving range, provided you cross the Channel early in the day (or overnight). Weekend traffic jams used to make the journey from Albertville to the Tarentaise resorts (from the Trois Vallées to Val-d'Isère) a nightmare for drivers and coach passengers alike; thanks to road improvements for the 1992 Olympics these are nowhere near as serious as in the past, but the volume of traffic has built up over the last decade, and on peak-season Saturdays you can again encounter serious queues around Moûtiers, where there are traffic lights placed well away from the town, to minimise pollution.

DAY-TRIP BASES

As we explained in the previous chapter, a car opens up different kinds of holiday for the adventurous. Day-tripping, for example.

In the southern French Alps, Serre-Chevalier and Montgenèvre are ideal bases for day-tripping. They are within easy reach of one another, and Montgenèvre is at one end of the Milky Way lift network, which includes Sauze d'Oulx and Sestriere in Italy – you can drive on to these resorts, or reach them by lift and piste. On the French side of the border, a few miles south, Puy-St-Vincent is an underrated resort that is well worth a visit for a day – as is Risoul, a little further south. The major resorts of Alpe-d'Huez and Les Deux-Alpes are also within range, as is the cult off-piste resort of La Grave.

Getting to them involves crossing a high pass, but it's a major route and is kept open pretty reliably.

The Chamonix valley is an ideal destination for day-trippers. The Mont-Blanc lift pass covers Chamonix, Les Contamines, Megève and others. Flaine and its satellites are fairly accessible – and so are Verbier in Switzerland, if the intervening passes are open, and Courmayeur in Italy, via the Mont Blanc tunnel. You could stay in a valley town such as Cluses, to escape resort prices.

MOVING ON

A look at the map over the page shows that a different approach will pay dividends in the Tarentaise region of France. Practically all the resorts here – from Valmorel to Val-d'Isère – are found at the end of long winding roads up from the main valley. You could visit them all from a base such as Aime, but it would be hard work. If instead you stayed in a different resort each night, moving on from one to the next in the early evening, you could have the trip of a lifetime.

GETTING THERE

There are three 'gateways' to the different regions of the French Alps. For the northern Alps – Chamonix valley, Portes du Soleil, Flaine and neighbours – you want to head for Geneva. If coming from Calais or another short-crossing port, you no longer have to tangle with the busy A6 from Paris via Beaune to Mâcon and Lyon. The relatively new A39 autoroute south from Dijon means you can head for Bourg-en-Bresse, well east of Mâcon.

For the central Alps – the mega-resorts of the Tarentaise, from Valmorel to Val-d'Isère, and the Maurienne valley – you want to head for Chambéry. For the southern Alps – Alpe-d'Huez, Les Deux-Alpes, Serre-Chevalier – you want to head for Grenoble. And for either of these gateways you first of all head for Mâcon and turn left at Lyon.

If you are taking a short Channel crossing, there are plenty of characterful towns for an overnight stop between the Channel and Dijon – Arras, St-Quentin, Laon, Troyes, Reims.

From the more westerly Channel ports of Le Havre or Caen your route to Geneva Mâcon sounds dead simple: the A13 to Paris then the A6 south. But you have to get through or around Paris in the process. The most direct way around the city is the notorious périphérique – a hectic, multi-lane, urban motorway close to the centre, with exits every few hundred yards and traffic that is either worryingly fast-moving or jammed solid. If the périphérique is jammed it takes ages. The more reliable alternative is to take a series of motorways and dual carriageways through the south-west fringes of Greater Paris. It's a great help to have a competent navigator.

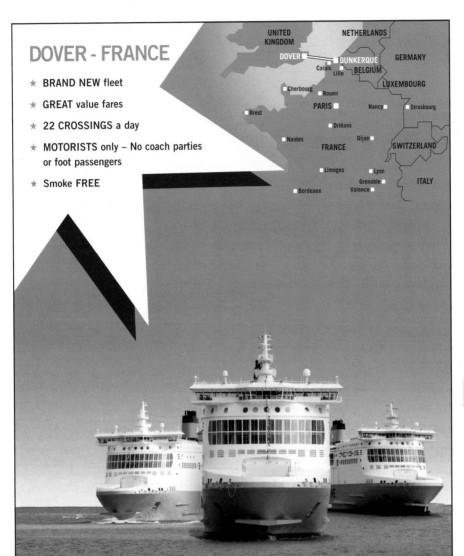

Drive to the French Alps

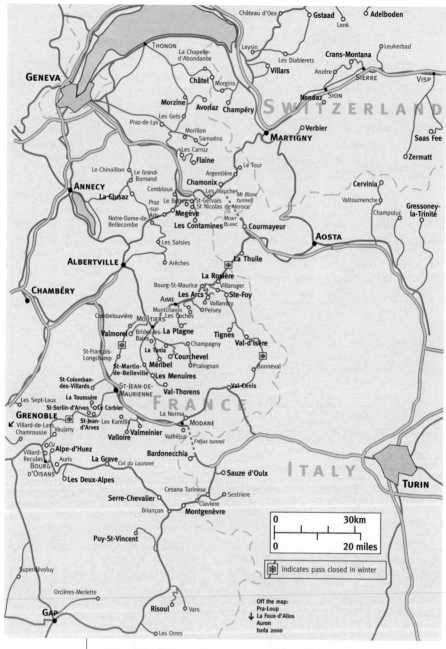

Château d'Oex   Gstaad   Adelboden
Lenk
Leysin   Crans-Montana   Leukerbad
THONON   Les Diablerets
La Chapelle-   Anzère   SIERRE
d'Abondance   Villars
Châtel   Morgins   VISP
GENEVA
Morzine   SWITZERLAND
Avoriaz   Champéry   Nendaz   SION
Les Gets
Praz-de-Lys   Verbier   Saas Fee
Morillon   MARTIGNY
Samoëns
Les Carroz   Zermatt
Flaine
Le Chinaillon   Le Grand-   Argentière   Le Tour
Bornand   Cervinia
ANNECY   Chamonix
La Clusaz   Combloux   Les Houches   Mt Blanc   Valtournenche
Praz-   Le Bettex   St-Gervais   tunnel   Champoluc   Gressoney-
-sur-   St Nicolas de Veroce   la-Trinité
Notre-Dame-de-   Ardy   Megève   MONT
Bellecombe   Les Contamines   BLANC   Courmayeur
Les Saisies   AOSTA
ALBERTVILLE   Arêches   La Thuile
La Rosière
CHAMBÉRY   Bourg-St-Maurice   Villaroger
AIME   Les Arcs   Ste-Foy
Montchavin   Vallandry
Combelouvière   MOÛTIERS   Les Coches   Peisey
Valmorel   Brides-les-   La Plagne
St-François-   Bains   Champagny   Tignes
Longchamp   La Tania   Val-d'Isère
St-Martin-   Méribel   Pralognan
St-Colomban-   de-Belleville   Les Menuires   Bonneval
des-Villards   ST-JEAN-DE-
Les Sept-Laux   La Toussuire   MAURIENNE   Val-Thorens   Val-Cenis
St-Sorlin-d'Arves   Le Corbier
GRENOBLE   St-Jean-   La Norma   FRANCE
Villard-de-Lans   d'Arves   Les Karellis   MODANE
Chamrousse   Vaujany   Valloire   Valmeinier
Oz   Alpe-d'Huez   Valfréjus   Fréjus tunnel
Villard-   Auris   La Grave   Bardonecchia
Reculas   BOURG-   Col du Lautaret
D'OISANS   Les Deux-Alpes   ITALY
Cesana Torinese   Sauze d'Oulx
Serre-Chevalier   Sestriere   TURIN
Briançon   Claviere
Montgenèvre
Puy-St-Vincent

0 _____ 30km
0 _____ 20 miles

✸ indicates pass closed in winter

Superdévoluy

Orcières-Merlette   Off the map:
Pra-Loup
GAP   Risoul   Vars   ↓ La Foux-d'Allos
Auron
Les Orres   Isola 2000

Pick the right gateway – Geneva, Chambéry or Grenoble – and you can
hardly go wrong. The approach to Serre-Chevalier and Montgenèvre
involves the 2060m/6,760ft Col du Lautaret; but the road is a major one
and is kept clear of snow or reopened quickly after a fall. Crossing the
French-Swiss border between Chamonix and Verbier involves two
closure-prone passes – the Montets and the Forclaz. When necessary,
one-way traffic runs beside the tracks through the rail tunnel beneath
the passes.

Travelling by rail

Let the train take the strain

by **Dave Watts**

Taking the train to the Alps can be a great way to get more time on the slopes without taking more time off work. You can leave on Friday night, arriving in your resort on Saturday morning, and return on the following Saturday night, arriving back home on the Sunday – eight days' skiing for five days out of the office. Even if you opt for a different service that doesn't deliver the eight-day week, travelling by train is one of the most restful (and environmentally friendly) ways to get to the Alps.

The most popular train destination, with several different direct and indirect services, is the Tarentaise valley in France – resorts such as Les Arcs, Val-d'Isère, Tignes, La Plagne, Courchevel, Méribel, Les Menuires and Val-Thorens. But you can travel by train to many other resorts. And many traditional resorts, especially in Switzerland, are on the rail network and therefore reachable without resorting to buses. How many times you'll have to change trains is another matter.

DIRECT TRAIN SERVICES TO THE FRENCH ALPS

Eurostar has a direct service to the Alps – you board the train at London Waterloo or Ashford in Kent and disembark at Moûtiers, Bourg-St-Maurice or Aime (between Moûtiers and Bourg-St-Maurice) in the Tarentaise valley, without changing trains en route. The special winter services will run from 23 December through to Easter weekend on 6/7 April (with the last trains returning the following weekend). Standard return tickets cost from £149 (£199 for Leisure

Select, which includes a bigger seat pitch, meals, and drinks with meals). Seats can also be booked as part of a package holiday. There's an overnight service (but not the first weekend) that allows you two extra days' skiing or boarding – it leaves on Friday night, arriving early on Saturday morning, and returns late Saturday evening, arriving back on Sunday morning. The service uses standard Eurostar carriages with no special sleeping arrangements – you just doze (or not) in your seat. The daytime service gives you no more than the standard six days on the slopes: both outward and return services leave on Saturday morning, arriving late afternoon.

INDIRECT TRAIN SERVICES TO THE FRENCH ALPS
All the other train services to the Alps involve a change somewhere along the line, but they can still be fairly convenient and also allow for extra time on the slopes. Unlike Eurostar, many of the other services are equipped with sleeping facilities.

The old Snowtrain from Calais no longer exists, but there is still an overnight sleeper service with the traditional bar/disco carriage. You now take the Eurostar to Paris from London Waterloo or Ashford on Friday afternoon and change trains at Paris Gare du Nord for an overnight service to Moûtiers, Aime and Bourg-St-Maurice. The return journey leaves the Alps on Saturday evening, arriving in Paris early on Sunday morning. This service runs from 19 January until 6 April and costs from £219 return including couchettes.

During the week daytime services operate from London Waterloo or Ashford to Paris Gare du Nord. You then need to cross the city to the Gare de Lyon – the change of station is not difficult, though, with a direct metro, regular buses and plenty of taxis at your disposal – for a TGV to Chambéry. This connects with a local TER train to the Tarentaise. Fares start from £99 return Standard Class and £179 return Leisure Select. Indirect services to many Alpine destinations via Brussels or Lille also run and involve only a change of platform.

Note that, unlike on most budget airline services, there is no extra charge for taking skis or a snowboard on a train service.

For more details of French rail services contact Rail Europe on 08701 244 646 for overnight ski trains or 08705 848 848 for Eurostar trains. Or visit www.raileurope.co.uk or www.eurostar.com.

PUTTING YOUR CAR ON A TRAIN
Sadly French Railways no longer runs suitable motorail services that you can put your car on overnight and wake up in the Alps. But Deutsche Bahn does. Its services from Hamburg and Dusseldorf to Salzburg and Innsbruck (both for a wide range of Austrian resorts), Lindau-Reutin (for western Austrian and eastern Swiss resorts), Villach (for Carinthian resorts) and Bolzano (for Dolomite resorts) seem likely to be of most interest for UK-based drivers. For more details call 08702 435363 or visit www.dbautozug.de.

Choosing your resort

Get it right first time

Most people get to go skiing or boarding only once or twice a year – and then only for a week at a time. So choosing the right resort is crucially important. Here is some advice on how to use our information to best effect, for the benefit of readers with relatively narrow experience of different resorts. Chamonix, Châtel and Courchevel are all French resorts, but they are as similar as chalk and Camembert. Start to consider resorts in other countries – Alpbach in Austria, say, or Zermatt in Switzerland – and the differences become even more pronounced.

Each resort chapter is organised in the same way, to help you choose the right resort. This short introduction takes you through the structure and what you will find under each heading we use.

GETTING A FEEL FOR THE PLACE

Our Costs ratings, ranging from ①②③④⑤⑥ to ①②③④⑤⑥, reflect the total cost of a week's holiday from Britain, including a typical package of flights plus half-board accommodation, a lift pass and meals and drinks on the spot. Three coins means on the low side of average, four means on the high side. Then, in the Ratings section, we rate each resort from 12 points of view – the more stars the better.

For major resorts, the next things to look at are our lists of the main good and bad points about the resort and its slopes, picked out with ✚ and ▬. These lists are followed by a summary in **bold type**, in which we've aimed to weigh up the pros and cons, coming off the fence and giving our view of who might like the resort.

You'll know by now whether this is, for example, a high, hideous, convenient, purpose-built resort with superb, snow-sure, challenging slopes but absolutely no nightlife; or a pretty, traditional village with gentle wooded slopes, ideal for beginners if only it had some snow.

THE RESORT

Resorts vary enormously in character and charm. At the extremes of the range are the handful of really hideous modern apartment-block resorts thrown up in France in the 1960s and the captivating old traffic-free mountain villages of which Switzerland has an unfair number. But it isn't simply a question of old versus new. Some purpose-built places can have a much friendlier feel than some long-established resorts with big blocky buildings. Some places can be remarkably strung out, whereas others are surprisingly compact; our

village plans are drawn to a standard scale, to help you gauge this. The landscape can have an important impact – whether the resort is at the bottom of a shady valley or on a sunny shelf with panoramic views. Some places are working towns as well as ski resorts. Some are full of bars, discos and shops; others are peaceful backwaters. Traffic may choke the streets; or the village may be traffic-free.

THE MOUNTAINS
The slopes Some mountains and lift networks are vast and complex, while others are much smaller and lacking variation.
Terrain-parks We summarise here the specially prepared fun-parks and other terrain features most resorts now arrange for freestylers.
Snow reliability This is a crucial factor for many people, and one that varies enormously. Ignore this at your peril.
For experts, intermediates, beginners Most (though not all) resorts have something to offer beginners, but relatively few will keep an expert happy for a week's holiday. As for intermediates, whether a resort will suit you really depends on your standard and inclinations.
For cross-country We don't pretend that this is a guide for avid cross-country skiers. But we do try to help.
Queues Monster queues are largely a thing of the past, but it still pays to avoid the resorts with the worst queues, especially in high season.
Mountain restaurants If you like a decent lunch, beware: some resorts offer miserable restaurants and food (eg many resorts in America).
Schools and guides This is an area where we rely heavily on readers' reports of their own or their friends' experiences.
Facilities for children Again, to be of real help we need first-hand reports from people whose children have actually used the facilities.

STAYING THERE
How to go The basic choice is between catered chalets, hotels and self-catering accommodation. Some resorts have few hotels or few chalets. Note that we now have chapters on smart apartments (page 45) as well as luxury chalets (page 49).
Eating out The range of restaurants varies widely. Even some big resorts, such as Les Arcs, may have little choice because most of the visitors stay in their apartments. Most American resorts offer lots of choice.
Après-ski Tastes and styles vary enormously. Most resorts have pleasant places in which to have an immediate post-skiing beer or hot chocolate. Some then go dead. Others have noisy bars and discos until the early hours.
Off the slopes This is largely aimed at assessing how suitable a resort is for someone who doesn't intend to use the slopes, such as a non-skiing spouse.
Staying up the mountain/down the valley If there are interesting options for staying in isolation on the slopes above the resort village or in valley towns below it, we pick them out.

Resort ratings at a glance

AUSTRIA

	ALPBACH	BAD GASTEIN	BAD KLEIN-KIRCHHEIM	ELLMAU	HINTERTUX	HOCHKÖNIG	ISCHGL	KITZBÜHEL
Page	127	129	132	135	138	143	150	156
Fast lifts	**	**	**	**	***	**	*****	***
Snow	**	***	***	**	*****	***	****	**
Extent	*	****	**	****	**	***	****	***
Expert	*	***	**	*	***	**	***	***
Intermediate	**	****	***	****	***	****	****	****
Beginner	****	**	**	****	**	***	**	**
Convenience	**	**	***	***	**	**	***	**
Queues	***	***	****	****	***	****	****	**
Restaurants‡	***	****	***	**	**	***	****	****
Scenery	***	***	***	***	***	***	***	***
Resort charm	*****	***	***	***	***	***	****	****
Off-slope	***	****	***	***	*	***	***	*****

	LECH	MAYRHOFEN	NAUDERS	OBERGURGL	OBERTAUERN	SAALBACH-HINTERGLEMM	SCHLADMING	SÖLDEN
Page	163	172	180	182	187	189	195	199
Fast lifts	****	***	***	****	*****	****	****	*****
Snow	****	***	****	*****	****	***	****	*****
Extent	****	***	**	**	**	***	***	***
Expert	****	*	***	**	***	**	**	***
Intermediate	****	***	****	***	****	****	****	****
Beginner	****	**	**	****	****	***	***	**
Convenience	***	*	**	****	****	****	***	**
Queues	****	*	****	*****	****	***	****	***
Restaurants‡	***	***	***	**	****	****	****	***
Scenery	***	***	***	***	***	***	***	***
Resort charm	****	***	****	****	**	****	***	**
Off-slope	***	****	***	**	**	**	****	**

	SÖLL	ST ANTON	ST JOHANN IN TIROL	STUBAI VALLEY	WESTENDORF	WILD-SCHÖNAU	ZELL AM SEE
Page	202	208	219	221	223	225	229
Fast lifts	**	***	**	***	**	**	***
Snow	**	****	**	*****	**	**	**
Extent	****	****	*	***	*	*	**
Expert	*	*****	*	***	**	*	**
Intermediate	****	***	***	***	***	**	***
Beginner	***	*	****	**	***	***	***
Convenience	**	***	***	**	***	***	**
Queues	***	**	****	***	****	***	**
Restaurants‡	**	***	****	**	***	**	***
Scenery	***	***	***	****	***	***	***
Resort charm	***	****	***	****	****	***	***
Off-slope	**	**	****	***	**	**	****

Note: Andorra is dealt with on the last page of the chapter

‡ Refers to mountain restaurants only

FRANCE

	ALPE-D'HUEZ	LES ARCS	AVORIAZ	CHAMONIX	CHATEL	LA CLUSAZ	LES CONTAMINES	COURCHEVEL
Page	241	250	260	264	274	279	281	283
Fast lifts	**	**	***	***	**	**	**	****
Snow	****	****	***	****	**	**	****	****
Extent	****	***	*****	***	*****	***	***	*****
Expert	****	*****	***	*****	***	***	***	****
Intermediate	****	****	****	**	****	****	****	*****
Beginner	*****	****	****	*	***	****	**	****
Convenience	****	****	*****	*	**	***	**	****
Queues	****	***	***	**	***	***	***	****
Restaurants‡	****	***	****	**	***	****	****	****
Scenery	****	***	***	*****	****	***	****	***
Resort charm	*	*	**	****	***	****	****	**
Off-slope	****	*	*	*****	**	***	**	***

	LES DEUX-ALPES	FLAINE	LES GETS	LA GRAVE	MEGEVE	LES MENUIRES	MERIBEL	MONTGENEVRE
Page	294	300	307	309	311	317	319	330
Fast lifts	**	**	**	***	*	***	****	*
Snow	****	****	**	***	**	****	***	****
Extent	***	****	***	*	*****	*****	*****	****
Expert	****	****	***	*****	**	****	****	**
Intermediate	**	*****	****	*	****	*****	*****	****
Beginner	***	*****	****	*	***	***	****	*****
Convenience	***	*****	***	***	**	*****	***	****
Queues	**	***	***	****	****	****	****	****
Restaurants‡	**	**	***	**	****	***	***	**
Scenery	****	****	***	****	*****	***	***	***
Resort charm	**	*	***	***	****	*	***	***
Off-slope	**	*	***	*	****	*	***	*

	MORZINE	LA PLAGNE	PUY-ST-VINCENT	RISOUL	LA ROSIERE	SAMOENS	SERRE-CHEVALIER	STE-FOY
Page	334	343	355	357	360	362	364	371
Fast lifts	**	**	**	*	**	**	**	*
Snow	**	****	***	***	***	***	***	***
Extent	*****	****	**	***	***	****	****	*
Expert	***	***	***	**	**	****	***	****
Intermediate	****	*****	***	****	***	*****	****	***
Beginner	***	****	***	****	*****	**	****	**
Convenience	**	*****	*****	****	***	*	***	***
Queues	***	***	***	****	***	****	***	*****
Restaurants‡	***	****	***	***	*	**	***	**
Scenery	***	****	****	***	***	****	***	***
Resort charm	***	*	**	**	***	****	***	***
Off-slope	***	*	*	*	*	***	**	*

FRANCE   ITALY

	ST-MARTIN-DE-BELLEVILLE	LES SYBELLES	LA TANIA	TIGNES	VAL-D'ISERE	VALMOREL	VAL-THORENS	
Page	374	377	382	388	398	409	411	
Fast lifts	***	*	****	***	****	*	****	
Snow	***	***	***	*****	*****	***	*****	
Extent	*****	*****	*****	*****	*****	***	*****	
Expert	****	**	****	*****	*****	**	****	
Intermediate	*****	***	*****	*****	*****	****	*****	
Beginner	**	****	**	**	***	*****	****	
Convenience	***	***	****	****	***	*****	*****	
Queues	****	****	****	****	****	***	***	
Restaurants‡	****	**	****	***	***	**	****	
Scenery	***	***	***	***	***	***	***	
Resort charm	****	*/****	***	**	***	****	**	
Off-slope	*	**	*	*	**	**	**	

	BORMIO	CERVINIA	CORTINA D'AMPEZZO	COURMAYEUR	LIVIGNO	MADONNA DI CAMPIGLIO	MONTEROSA SKI	PASSO TONALE
Page	426	428	434	439	444	448	450	454
Fast lifts	***	****	**	***	***	****	***	****
Snow	***	*****	***	****	****	***	****	****
Extent	**	***	***	**	**	***	***	**
Expert	*	*	**	***	**	**	****	*
Intermediate	***	****	***	****	***	****	****	***
Beginner	**	*****	*****	**	****	****	**	****
Convenience	***	***	*	*	**	***	***	***
Queues	***	***	****	***	****	****	****	****
Restaurants‡	****	***	****	****	***	***	**	**
Scenery	***	****	*****	****	***	****	****	***
Resort charm	****	**	****	****	***	***	***	*
Off-slope	****	*	*****	***	**	***	*	*

	SAUZE D'OULX	SELLA RONDA	SELVA	SESTRIERE	LA THUILE
Page	456	461	468	474	476
Fast lifts	**	***	***	**	**
Snow	**	****	****	****	****
Extent	****	*****	*****	****	***
Expert	**	**	**	***	**
Intermediate	****	*****	*****	****	****
Beginner	**	****	***	***	****
Convenience	**	***	***	***	***
Queues	***	***	***	***	****
Restaurants‡	***	****	****	**	*
Scenery	***	*****	*****	***	***
Resort charm	**	***	***	*	***
Off-slope	*	***	***	*	**

Resort ratings at a glance

99

‡ Refers to mountain restaurants only

SWITZERLAND   USA

Resort ratings at a glance

100

	ADELBODEN	ANDERMATT	AROSA	CHAMPERY	CRANS-MONTANA	DAVOS	FLIMS	GRINDEL-WALD
Page	492	494	496	499	501	503	509	511
Fast lifts	***	**	***	**	***	***	****	***
Snow	***	****	***	**	**	****	***	**
Extent	***	*	**	*****	***	*****	****	***
Expert	**	****	**	***	**	****	***	**
Intermediate	***	**	***	****	****	*****	*****	****
Beginner	****	*	****	**	***	**	****	***
Convenience	***	***	**	*	**	**	***	**
Queues	***	**	****	****	***	**	****	**
Restaurants‡	***	*	***	***	***	***	***	***
Scenery	****	***	***	****	****	****	***	*****
Resort charm	****	****	**	****	**	**	***	****
Off-slope	****	**	****	***	****	*****	***	****

	KLOSTERS	MÜRREN	SAAS-FEE	ST MORITZ	VERBIER	VILLARS	WENGEN	ZERMATT
Page	515	517	521	526	532	543	545	550
Fast lifts	***	***	****	****	**	***	***	*****
Snow	****	***	*****	****	***	**	**	****
Extent	*****	*	**	*****	*****	***	***	****
Expert	****	***	***	****	*****	**	**	*****
Intermediate	*****	***	****	****	***	***	****	****
Beginner	***	**	*****	**	**	****	***	*
Convenience	**	***	***	*	**	***	***	*
Queues	**	***	***	**	***	***	***	***
Restaurants‡	***	**	***	****	***	***	****	*****
Scenery	****	*****	****	****	****	***	*****	*****
Resort charm	****	*****	*****	*	***	****	*****	*****
Off-slope	****	***	****	*****	***	****	****	****

	CALIFORNIA				COLORADO			
	HEAVENLY	MAMMOTH	SQUAW VALLEY		ASPEN	BEAVER CREEK	BRECKEN-RIDGE	COPPER MOUNTAIN
Page	568	573	578		583	590	592	597
Fast lifts	***	****	***		***	*****	****	**
Snow	****	****	****		*****	*****	*****	*****
Extent	***	***	***		****	**	**	**
Expert	***	****	****		*****	****	****	****
Intermediate	****	****	**		*****	****	****	****
Beginner	****	****	****		*****	*****	****	****
Convenience	*	**	****		**	****	***	****
Queues	****	****	****		****	*****	****	****
Restaurants‡	*	*	*		***	**	**	*
Scenery	****	***	***		***	***	***	***
Resort charm	*	**	***		****	**	***	**
Off-slope	**	*	*		****	***	***	*

	KEYSTONE	SNOWMASS	STEAMBOAT	TELLURIDE	VAIL	WINTER PARK		
Page	599	601	603	606	608	615		
Fast lifts	****	***	**	*****	****	***		
Snow	*****	*****	****	****	*****	*****		
Extent	**	****	***	**	****	***		
Expert	***	*****	***	****	****	****		
Intermediate	****	*****	****	***	*****	****		
Beginner	****	*****	*****	*****	***	*****		
Convenience	**	****	***	****	***	***		
Queues	****	****	****	*****	**	****		
Restaurants‡	***	***	***	*	**	***		
Scenery	***	****	***	****	***	***		
Resort charm	**	**	**	****	***	**		
Off-slope	**	***	**	**	***	*		

	UTAH ALTA	THE CANYONS	DEER VALLEY	PARK CITY	SNOWBIRD			
Page	621	623	625	627	632			
Fast lifts	***	***	****	***	***			
Snow	*****	****	****	****	*****			
Extent	***	***	**	***	***			
Expert	*****	****	***	****	*****			
Intermediate	***	****	****	****	***			
Beginner	***	**	****	****	**			
Convenience	****	****	****	**	*****			
Queues	***	****	****	****	**			
Restaurants‡	**	***	****	**	*			
Scenery	***	***	***	***	***			
Resort charm	**	**	***	***	*			
Off-slope	*	**	**	***	*			

	REST OF THE WEST BIG SKY	JACKSON HOLE		NEW ENGLAND KILLINGTON	STOWE			
Page	636	640		647	651			
Fast lifts	***	**		**	**			
Snow	*****	****		***	***			
Extent	****	***		**	*			
Expert	****	*****		***	***			
Intermediate	****	**		***	****			
Beginner	*****	***		****	****			
Convenience	****	***		*	*			
Queues	*****	***		****	****			
Restaurants‡	*	*		*	**			
Scenery	***	***		***	***			
Resort charm	*	***		*	****			
Off-slope	**	***		*	*			

‡ Refers to mountain restaurants only

Resort ratings at a glance

101

Resort ratings at a glance

	WESTERN CANADA BANFF	BIG WHITE	FERNIE	KICKING HORSE	LAKE LOUISE	PANORAMA	SUN PEAKS	WHISTLER
Page	658	665	667	672	674	679	681	684
Fast lifts	****	***	**	**	***	***	***	****
Snow	****	*****	*****	****	***	***	****	****
Extent	****	***	***	***	****	**	***	****
Expert	****	***	*****	****	****	****	***	*****
Intermediate	****	****	**	***	****	***	****	*****
Beginner	***	****	****	***	***	****	****	***
Convenience	*	****	****	****	*	****	****	****
Queues	****	*****	****	*****	****	*****	*****	***
Restaurants‡	***	*	*	**	**	*	*	**
Scenery	****	***	***	***	*****	***	***	***
Resort charm	***	**	**	**	***	**	***	***
Off-slope	*****	**	**	*	****	*	**	**

	EASTERN CANADA TREMBLANT							
Page	696							
Fast lifts	****							
Snow	****							
Extent	*							
Expert	**							
Intermediate	***							
Beginner	****							
Convenience	****							
Queues	***							
Restaurants‡	**							
Scenery	***							
Resort charm	****							
Off-slope	***							

	ANDORRA ARINSAL	PAS DE LA CASA	SOLDEU	SPAIN BAQUEIRA	NORWAY HEMSEDAL	SWEDEN ÅRE	BULGARIA BANSKO	NEW ZEALAND QUEENSTOWN
Page	111	113	115	699	705	708	711	723
Fast lifts	**	***	***	**	**	**	****	**
Snow	****	****	****	***	****	***	***	**
Extent	*	***	***	**	*	**	*	*
Expert	*	*	*	***	**	**	**	***
Intermediate	**	***	***	****	****	****	****	***
Beginner	***	****	****	**	***	****	**	***
Convenience	***	****	***	***	**	***	**	*
Queues	***	***	***	****	****	****	****	***
Restaurants‡	*	**	**	**	*	***	***	*
Scenery	***	***	***	***	**	***	***	****
Resort charm	*	*	*	**	**	***	**	**
Off-slope	*	*	*	*	*	***	*	*****

‡ Refers to mountain restaurants only

Resort shortlists

To help you spot resorts that will suit you

To streamline the job of spotting the ideal resort for your own holiday, here are lists of the best ten or so resorts for 20 different categories. Some lists embrace European and North American resorts, but most we've confined to Europe, because the US has too many qualifying resorts (eg for beginners) or because the US does things differently, making comparisons invalid (eg for off-piste).

SOMETHING FOR EVERYONE
Resorts with everything from reassuring nursery slopes to real challenges for experts
Alpe-d'Huez, France p241
Les Arcs, France p250
Aspen, Colorado p583
Courchevel, France p283
Flaine, France p300
Mammoth, California p573
Vail, Colorado p608
Val-d'Isère, France p398
Whistler, Canada p684
Winter Park, Colorado p615

RELIABLE SNOW IN THE ALPS
Alpine resorts with good snow records or lots of snowmaking, and high or north-facing slopes
Chamonix, France p264
Cervinia, Italy p428
Courchevel, France p283
Hintertux, Austria p138
Lech/Zürs, Austria p163
Obergurgl, Austria p182
Saas-Fee, Switzerland p521
Val-d'Isère/Tignes, France pp398/388
Val-Thorens, France p411
Zermatt, Switzerland p550

INTERNATIONAL OVERSIGHTS
Resorts that deserve as much attention as the ones we go back to every year, but don't seem to get it
Alta, Utah p621
Andermatt, Switzerland p494
Bad Gastein, Austria p129
Big Sky, Montana p636
Les Contamines, France p281
Copper Mountain, Colorado p597
Flims-Laax, Switzerland p509
Monterosa Ski, Italy p450
Risoul, France p357
Telluride, Colorado p606

OFF-PISTE WONDERS
Alpine resorts where, with the right guidance and equipment, you can have the time of your life
Alpe-d'Huez, France p241
Andermatt, Switzerland p494
Chamonix, France p264
Davos/Klosters, Switzerland p503
La Grave, France p309
Lech/Zürs, Austria p163
Monterosa Ski, Italy p450
St Anton, Austria p208
Val-d'Isère/Tignes, France pp398/388
Verbier, Switzerland p532

103

MADE
to
MEASURE

01243 533 333
sales@mtmhols.co.uk
www.mtmhols.co.uk

ATOL 1006 ABTA V6471

SNOWPIX.COM / IAN STRATFORD

Chamonix rates highly for scenery and off-piste, as production manager Ian likes to point out (not to mention the great nightlife, tough skiing... that's enough Ian – Ed) →

POWDER PARADISES
Resorts with the snow, the terrain and (ideally) the lack of crowds that make for powder perfection
Alta/Snowbird, Utah pp621/632
Andermatt, Switzerland p494
Big Sky, Montana p636
Big White, Canada p665
Brighton/Solitude, Utah p634
Fernie, Canada p667
Grand Targhee, Wyoming p640
La Grave, France p309
Jackson Hole, Wyoming p640
Kicking Horse, Canada p672
Kirkwood, California p580
Monterosa Ski, Italy p450
Snowbasin, Utah p634
Ste-Foy, France p371

BLACK RUNS
Resorts with steep, mogully, lift-served slopes within the safety of the piste network
Alta/Snowbird, Utah pp621/632
Andermatt, Switzerland p494
Argentière/Chamonix, France p273
Aspen, Colorado p583
Beaver Creek, Colorado p590
Courchevel, France p283
Jackson Hole, Wyoming p640
Whistler, Canada p684
Winter Park, Colorado p615
Zermatt, Switzerland p550

CHOPAHOLICS
Resorts where you can quit the conventional lift network and have a day riding helicopters or cats
Aspen, Colorado p583
Crested Butte, Colorado p619
Fernie, Canada p667
Grand Targhee, Wyoming p640
Lech/Zürs, Austria p163
Monterosa Ski, Italy p450
Panorama, Canada p679
Verbier, Switzerland p532
Whistler, Canada p684
Zermatt, Switzerland p550

WEATHERPROOF SLOPES
Alpine resorts with snow-sure slopes if the sun shines, and trees in case it doesn't
Les Arcs, France p250
Courchevel, France p283
Courmayeur, Italy p439
Flims, Switzerland p509
Schladming, Austria p195
Selva, Italy p468
Serre-Chevalier, France p364
Sestriere, Italy p474
La Thuile, Italy p476

HIGH-MILEAGE PISTE-BASHING
Extensive intermediate slopes with big lift networks
Alpe-d'Huez, France p241
Davos/Klosters, Switzerland p503
Flims/Laax, Switzerland p509
Milky Way: Sauze d'Oulx (Italy), Montgenèvre (France) pp456/330
Paradiski, France p341
Portes du Soleil, France/Switz p353
Sella Ronda, Italy p461
Selva, Italy p468
Les Sybelles, France p377
Three Valleys, France p386
Val-d'Isère/Tignes, France pp398/388
Whistler, Canada p684

MOTORWAY CRUISING
Long, gentle, super-smooth pistes to bolster the frail confidence of those not long off the nursery slope
Les Arcs, France p250
Breckenridge, Colorado p592
Cervinia, Italy p428
Cortina, Italy p434
Courchevel, France p283
Megève, France p311
La Plagne, France p343
Snowmass, Colorado p601
La Thuile, Italy p476
Vail, Colorado p608

RESORTS FOR BEGINNERS
European resorts with gentle, snow-sure nursery slopes and easy, longer runs to progress to
Alpe-d'Huez, France p241
Les Arcs, France p250
Bansko, Bulgaria p711
Cervinia, Italy p428
Courchevel, France p283
Flaine, France p300
Montgenèvre, France p330
La Plagne, France p343
Saas-Fee, Switzerland p521
Soldeu, Andorra p115

MODERN CONVENIENCE
Alpine resorts where there's plenty of slope-side accommodation to make life easy
Les Arcs, France p250
Avoriaz, France p260
Courchevel, France p283
Flaine, France p300
Les Menuires, France p317
Obertauern, Austria p187
La Plagne, France p343
Puy-St-Vincent, France p355
La Tania, France p382
Tignes, France p388
Valmorel, France p409
Val-Thorens, France p411

BACK-DOOR RESORTS
Cute little Alpine villages linked to big, bold ski areas, giving you the best of two different worlds
Les Brévières (Tignes), France p388
Champagny (La Plagne), France p343
Leogang (Saalbach), Austria p189
Montchavin (La Plagne), France p343
Peisey (Les Arcs), France p250
Le Pré (Les Arcs), France p250
Samoëns (Flaine), France p362
St-Martin (Three Valleys), France p386
Stuben (St Anton), Austria p218
Vaujany (Alpe-d'Huez), France p249

SNOW-SURE BUT SIMPATICO
Alpine resorts with high-rise slopes, but low-rise, traditional-style buildings
Andermatt, Switzerland p494
Arabba, Italy p463
Argentière, France p273
Les Contamines, France p281
Ischgl, Austria p150
Lech/Zürs, Austria p163
Monterosa Ski, Italy p450
Obergurgl, Austria p182
Saas-Fee, Switzerland p521
Zermatt, Switzerland p550

SPECIALLY FOR FAMILIES
Alpine resorts where you can easily find accommodation surrounded by snow, not by traffic and fumes
Les Arcs, France p250
Avoriaz, France p260
Flaine, France p300
Lech, Austria p163
Montchavin (La Plagne), France p343
Mürren, Switzerland p517
Puy-St-Vincent, France p355
Risoul, France p357
Saas-Fee, Switzerland p521
Les Sybelles, France p377
Valmorel, France p409
Wengen, Switzerland p545

SPECIAL MOUNTAIN RESTAURANTS
Alpine resorts where the mountain restaurants can really add an extra dimension to your holiday
Alpe-d'Huez, France p241
La Clusaz, France p279
Courmayeur, Italy p439
Kitzbühel, Austria p156
Megève, France p311
St Johann in Tirol, Austria p219
St Moritz, Switzerland p526
Selva, Italy p468
Söll, Austria p202
Zermatt, Switzerland p550

DRAMATIC SCENERY
Resorts where the mountains are not just high and snowy, but spectacularly scenic too
Chamonix, France p264
Cortina, Italy p434
Courmayeur, Italy p439
Heavenly, California p568
Jungfrau resorts (Grindelwald, Mürren, Wengen), Switzerland pp511/517/545
Lake Louise, Canada p674
Megève, France p311
Saas-Fee, Switzerland p521
St Moritz, Switzerland p526
Selva, Italy p468
Zermatt, Switzerland p550

VILLAGE CHARM
Resorts with traditional character that enriches your holiday – from mountain villages to mining towns
Alpbach, Austria p127
Champéry, Switzerland p499
Courmayeur, Italy p439
Crested Butte, Colorado p619
Lech, Austria p163
Mürren, Switzerland p517
Saas-Fee, Switzerland p521
Telluride, Colorado p606
Wengen, Switzerland p545
Zermatt, Switzerland p550

LIVELY NIGHTLIFE
European resorts where you'll have no difficulty finding somewhere to boogy, and someone to do it with
Chamonix, France p264
Ischgl, Austria p150
Kitzbühel, Austria p156
Pas de la Casa, Andorra p113
Saalbach, Austria p189
St Anton, Austria p208
Sauze d'Oulx, Italy p456
Sölden, Austria p199
Val-d'Isère, France p398
Verbier, Switzerland p532

OTHER AMUSEMENTS
Alpine resorts where those not interested in skiing or boarding can still find plenty to do
Bad Gastein, Austria p129
Chamonix, France p264
Cortina, Italy p434
Davos, Switzerland p503
Gstaad, Switzerland p561
Innsbruck, Austria p146
Kitzbühel, Austria p156
Megève, France p311
St Moritz, Switzerland p526
Zell am See, Austria p229

Our resort chapters

How to get the best out of them

FINDING A RESORT

The bulk of the book consists of the chapters listed on the facing page, devoted to individual major resorts, plus minor resorts that share the same lift system. Sometimes we devote a chapter to an area not dominated by one resort, in which case we use the area name (eg Les Sybelles, Monterosa). Chapters are grouped by country: first, the five major European countries; then the US and Canada (where resorts are grouped by states or regions); then minor European countries; then Japan, and lastly the southern hemisphere. Within each group, resorts are ordered alphabetically – except that each section ends with Short Turns: a handful of short chapters covering minor resorts.

Short cuts to the resorts that might suit you are provided (on the pages preceding this one) by a table of comparative **star ratings** and a series of **shortlists** of resorts with particular merits.

At the back of the book is an **index** to the resort chapters, combined with a **directory** giving basic information on hundreds of other minor resorts. If the resort you are looking up is covered in a chapter devoted to a bigger resort, the page reference will take you to the start of that chapter, not to the exact page on which the minor resort is described.

There's further guidance on using our information in the chapter on 'Choosing your resort', on page 95 – designed to be helpful particularly to people with little or no experience of resorts, who may not appreciate how big the differences between one resort and another can be (ie like chalk and cheese).

READING A CHAPTER

The **cost** of visiting each resort is rated on a scale of one to six – ①②③④⑤⑥ to ①②③④⑤⑥ – reflecting the typical cost of a one-week trip based on a half-board package from the UK, plus a lift pass and an allowance for lunch in mountain restaurants. We assume two people sharing a room – even in the US, where package prices are often based on four people sharing.

Star ratings summarise our view of the resort in 12 respects, including how well it suits different standards of skier/boarder. The more stars, the better.

We give phone numbers and internet addresses of the **tourist office** (in North America, the ski lift company) and phone numbers for recommended **hotels**. We give a cost rating for hotels: the higher the price, the more coins shown.

The UK tour operators offering **package holidays** in each resort are listed in the directory at the back of the book, not in the main chapters.

Our **mountain maps** show the resorts' own classification of runs – so those for the US and Canada show green, blue and black runs, and no red ones. On some maps we show black diamonds to indicate expert terrain without defined runs. We do not distinguish single-diamond terrain from the steeper double-diamond.

We include on the map any lifts definitely planned for construction for the coming season.

We use the following symbols to identify **fast lifts**:

 fast chair-lift

 gondola

 'chondola' – chair/gondola

 cable-car

 railway/funicular

THE WORLD'S BEST WINTER SPORTS RESORTS

To find a minor resort, or if you are not sure which country you should be looking under, consult the index/directory at the back of the book, which lists all resorts alphabetically.

Our resort chapters

107

come to Andorra
come to Vallnord

Andorra

Andorra is now the fourth most popular winter sports destination on the British market, attracting some 80,000 package holidaymakers – not far behind Italy and well ahead of Switzerland or North America. With all these people basically travelling to two ski areas, it's difficult to get away from fellow Brits. It's also difficult to escape from traffic and construction sites – Andorra has lots of both.

Andorra used to be seen primarily as a cheap and cheerful holiday destination, aimed mainly at younger singles and couples looking for a good time in the duty-free bars and clubs as well as learning to ski or snowboard. But things have changed. In recent years, some more upmarket hotels have been built (though they often resemble Spanish summer package hotels, with their self-service buffet meals). And lots of money has been pumped in to developing powerful lift systems and piste-grooming fleets that many well-known Alpine resorts would be proud of; this makes the slopes much more attractive to intermediates as well as beginners. Reporters tell us the cost of drinks as well as packages has edged up, and even Arinsal now seems to attract more families than youths. Andorra no longer competes with eastern Europe for the budget market; it costs more, and delivers much more.

One thing remains unchanged, happily: the ski schools have always been excellent, with lots of native English-speaking instructors, and standards in this key part of the Andorran recipe are holding up.

Andorra has a relatively reliable snow record. Its situation close to both the Atlantic and the Mediterranean oceans, together with the high altitude of its resorts, means it usually gets substantial natural snowfalls. It has also invested heavily in snowmaking. This combination means you can book Andorra months in advance with some confidence. And an early reservation is necessary: late bookers can have difficulty finding an Andorra package.

Both package holiday prices and prices for drinks and extras such as instruction and equipment rental are generally lower than in the Alps. Beer is reportedly no cheaper than in the UK, but large, unmeasured servings of spirits mean that nightlife can be very lively. Some reporters have found duty-free luxury goods prices not the super-bargains they had expected.

The sight of cranes is still common, as hotels and apartments are built to keep up with demand. It is no longer true to say that the resorts resemble giant construction sites, but they all have construction sites within them (or on the edge of them, as they expand in sprawling fashion along the roadside).

STAYING DOWN THE VALLEY
Several valley towns can be used as bases, either to use the slopes of one resort or to explore several resorts in the course of a week.

One obviously strong candidate here is **Encamp**, which has a powerful 18-seat gondola giving a quick way into the whole of the Grandvalira ski area shared by Soldeu and Pas de la Casa. Encamp seemed to us the least attractive of the valley towns (not least because of its situation on the traffic-choked main road), but we can't claim to have examined it closely and a couple of reporters

LIFT PASSES

Ski Andorra
The Ski Andorra pass covers all Andorran areas and allows skiing at any single one of them each day. For five non-consecutive days in high season: €162; for five consecutive days in low season €152.

Phone numbers
From abroad use the prefix +376.

TOURIST OFFICES

Ski Andorra
t 805200
skiandorra@ski
andorra.ad
www.skiandorra.ad

Arcalis
t 739600
ito.reserves@
andorra.ad
www.vallnord.com

have recommended it. It is certainly cheap.

La Massana is a more appealing town, and since the 2004/05 season it has been linked to the Pal-Arinsal ski area by gondola. It is also 6km/4 miles closer to Arcalis, which is attractive to intermediates and experts. **Ordino** is slightly nearer still to Arcalis, and pleasantly rustic, but has no direct access to slopes.

The capital of **Andorra la Vella** is not far down the valley from Encamp but is a more attractive base for someone wanting a more rounded holiday (though still choked by traffic and 'appalling' resultant fumes). The duty-free shopping could fill a page, but probably the most interesting feature is the Caldea spa – 'probably the best off-slope activity in Andorra', according to a reporter. The interior is laid out in a 'Hanging Gardens of Babylon' style, and the facilities are very impressive – indoor and outdoor pools, with fountains and waterfalls, saunas, hot-tubs, Turkish baths, sunbeds, hydrotherapy, massage ... even a grapefruit bath! There are plenty of high-quality, if relatively expensive, hotels. Andorra la Vella is not a big place, and most hotels are within easy walking distance of the centre. There is plenty of choice when it comes to dining out and plenty of bars and nightclubs that stay open until 4am. The clientele is mainly Andorran and Spanish.

OUTINGS TO ARCALIS

Arcalis is the most remote area of slopes in Andorra, tucked away at the head of a long valley, and most British visitors to Andorra (or at least to Soldeu) never hear about it. But it makes a very worthwhile day trip, particularly from Arinsal and Pal; the trip is short, and the lifts are covered by the Vallnord lift pass. The variety of the terrain at Arcalis is greater than in most of the main resorts, the slopes are usually deserted except at weekends (when locals pour in) and the snow is usually the best you will find. It provides excellent intermediate and beginner terrain, but of all Andorra's resorts it has the most to offer experts, including lots of off-piste between the marked runs. 'A real jewel – the boarder in our group (who has visited a few Alpine resorts) was in heaven,' says a 2006 reporter.

There is no accommodation at the mountain, just a day lodge and a lot of car parking, but buildings are now springing up along the Vall d'Ordino leading up to it. Buses are not frequent.

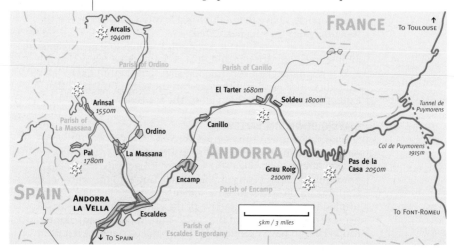

Arinsal

Not the prettiest village or the most impressive slopes in Andorra, but a cheap, lively base and popular with novices

COSTS

① ② ③ ④ ⑤ ⑥

RATINGS

The slopes

Fast lifts	**
Snow	****
Extent	*
Expert	*
Intermediate	**
Beginner	***
Convenience	***
Queues	***
Mountain restaurants	*

The rest

Scenery	***
Resort charm	*
Off-slope	*

NEWS

For 2005/06, a new six-pack was opened to serve the blue runs at Arinsal; and a quad chair replaced the Tossa drag-lift.

An 80m/260ft moving carpet was installed in the beginners' area at Arinsal, and snowmaking was increased in Pal.

REPORTS WANTED

Recently we have had few reports on this resort. If you go there, please do send us a report.

The best reports earn a copy of the next edition, and can lead to free lift passes in future.

See page 12.

➕ Lively bars

➕ Ski school geared to British needs

➕ Cable-car link with Pal and shared lift pass with Arcalis great assets for intermediates

➕ Pretty, tree-lined slopes in Pal

➖ Very confined and bleak local slopes

➖ Runs to village need good snow to be open, and don't lead to centre

➖ Long, linear and rather dour village, with no focus

➖ Obtrusive construction sites

Arinsal is the most British-dominated resort in Andorra, largely because British tour operators are able to offer packages here at tempting prices. The resort attracts mainly first-time skiers and riders; reports suggest that Arinsal, like the rest of Andorra, is managing to attract more families and fewer binge drinkers.

THE RESORT

Arinsal is a long, narrow village of grey, stone-clad buildings, near the head of a steep-sided valley north of Andorra la Vella. Development in recent years has been rapid.

The gondola from the village centre is the main way to and from the slopes and staying close to it is convenient; the alternative chair-lift, 1km/0.5 miles out of town, is largely irrelevant – though you can stay next to it and ski to the door in good conditions. Or you can drive to the top of the gondola. There is some accommodation at Pal, but it is a bus-ride from the lift base. There is also attractive accommodation in the lower town of La Massana (see Andorra introduction); it is 6km/4 miles closer to Arcalis and now has a gondola link to Pal's slopes.

Reporters have commented on the friendliness of the locals – 'We were made to feel very welcome.'

THE MOUNTAINS

The area above Arinsal is an open, east-facing bowl. Pal, in contrast, has the most densely wooded slopes in Andorra, calling to mind American resorts. Most face east; those down to the link with Arinsal face north.

Slopes Arinsal's slopes consist essentially of a single, long, narrow, bowl above the upper gondola station at Comallempla, served by a network of chairs and drags, including a new quad and six-pack. Almost at the top is the cable-car link to and from Pal. Pal's slopes are widely spread around the mountain, with four main lift bases, all reachable by road. The main

one, La Caubella, at the opposite extreme from the Arinsal link, is the arrival point of the gondola from La Massana. The lift pass now covers Arcalis too – see Andorra introduction.

Terrain-parks Arinsal's big freestyle area claims to be the most radical in southern Europe. It has its own lift and includes a huge half-pipe, big jump, terrain-park with spines, fun-boxes, rails and quarter-pipes, boarder-cross and a chill-out area. But a 'frustrated' snowboarder found the park closed for much of his January 2006 visit.

Snow reliability With most runs above 1950m/6,400ft, north-easterly orientation and an impressive 371 snow-guns, snow is relatively assured. Grooming is 'excellent'.

Experts These aren't great mountains for experts, but there are short, sharp black slopes at Arinsal – one now deliberately ungroomed – and quite long and challenging reds (and one black) as well as a mogul area at Pal. There are also off-piste free-ride areas marked on the map in both Arinsal and Pal – the latter offering some great tree-skiing – and because most visitors are beginners and intermediates, they do not get tracked-out so quickly.

Intermediates Arinsal offers a reasonable range of difficulty, but any confident intermediate is going to want to explore the much more interesting, varied and extensive Pal slopes.

Beginners Around half the guests here are beginners. Arinsal and Pal both have gentle nursery slopes set apart from the main runs; they can get very crowded at peak times. A new moving carpet has improved access to the slope at Arinsal. There are long easy runs to progress to, as well.

KEY FACTS

Resort	1470m
	4,820ft
Slopes	1550-2560m
	5,090-8,400ft
Lifts	28
Pistes	63km
	39 miles
Green	10%
Blue	39%
Red	39%
Black	12%
Snowmaking	19km
	12 miles

OUR WEBSITE

Go to our website at wtss.co.uk for resort news, links to resort sites, a build-your-own resort shortlist system and reader forums.

Phone numbers
From abroad use the prefix +376.

TOURIST OFFICES

Arinsal
t 737000
palarinsal@vallnord.
com
www.vallnord.com
Pal
t 737000

Snowboarding It's a good place to learn. But over half the lifts are drags, and some of them are vicious. And there are some tedious flat sections in Pal too. We're told crash helmets are compulsory in the terrain-park.
Cross-country There isn't any.
Queues Arinsal's gondola builds queues to return to the village at peak times. The cable-car link can close if the wind is high.
Mountain restaurants Mainly self-service, crowded, with snack food ('basic', says a 2006 visitor). The restaurant at Comallempla is said to run a barbie if the weather permits.
Schools and guides Over half the instructors are native English-speakers. The reports we have are all positive – 'one of the best; modern teaching methods, proper initial assessment before grouping'; 'first class'. But groups can be large – up to 15, quotes a 2006 reporter. Private lessons are said to be good value.
Facilities for children There are now two ski kindergartens for four- to eight-year-olds in Pal and nurseries for younger children at Pal and Arinsal.

STAYING THERE

How to go There is a wide choice of hotel and self-catering packages.
Hotels Rooms in the hotel Arinsal (835640) are not large, but it is well run, ideally placed and has a pleasant bar. The Princesa Parc (736500) is a big, glossy 4-star place close to the gondola, with a swanky spa. The Xalet Verdu (737140) is a smooth little 3-star. The St Gotthard (836005) is big but popular, except for its position a long way down the hill from the gondola. The Micolau (835052) is a characterful stone house, close to the centre, with simple rooms and a jolly, beamed restaurant. If there is snow to the valley, you can ski to the Crest (835866) at the old chair-lift station.
Self-catering There is a reasonable choice of places. Aparthotel Sant Andreu is simple but comfortable, with a relaxed bar-restaurant on site.
Eating out The Surf disco-pub does grills. Cisco's is a Tex-Mex place in a lovely wood and stone building. The Rocky Mountain is popular for steaks. El Rusc and Micolau do good food.
Après-ski Arinsal has plenty of lively bars and discos, such as Quo Vadis, El Cau, Surf, Rocky Mountain and El Cisco's (a major snowboarder hangout). El Derby is heaving on karaoke night. If, like us, you prefer something quieter, head for the bar of the hotel Arinsal.
Off the slopes There are lots of activities, but a 2006 reporter felt that family entertainment was limited in the evenings. Andorra la Vella is half an hour away by infrequent bus or inexpensive taxi.

Pas de la Casa

Andorra's liveliest resort – great if you like that kind of thing; we prefer to ski the extensive Grandvalira from a quieter base

COSTS

① ② ③ ④ ⑤ ⑥

RATINGS

The slopes

Fast lifts	***
Snow	****
Extent	***
Expert	*
Intermediate	***
Beginner	****
Convenience	****
Queues	***
Mountain restaurants	**

The rest

Scenery	***
Resort charm	*
Off-slope	*

NEWS

For 2005/06 a new six-pack, Estany, was installed on the north-west facing slopes on the French side of the border. This is the first step in realisation of a long-planned link with the small French area of Porté-Puymorens.

Also last season, a fast quad replaced two beginner drag-lifts at Grau Roig.

OUR WEBSITE

Go to our website at wtss.co.uk for resort news, links to resort sites, a build-your-own resort shortlist system and reader forums.

➕ The joint lift pass with Soldeu means the ski area now rivals many major resorts in the Alps for size

➕ Andorra's liveliest nightlife

➕ Attractive accommodation at Grau Roig

➖ Pas is an eyesore and the centre suffers from traffic (and fumes)

➖ Weekend crowds from France

➖ Very few woodland slopes – unpleasant in bad weather

The tour op brochures (and the few readers' reports we get) all say that Pas is Andorra's wildest party resort, and we don't doubt it. Having driven through it and skied down to it, we are quite happy to stay over the hill in Soldeu – or, for doorstep access to the Grandvalira slopes, at secluded Grau Roig.

THE RESORT

Sited right on the border between Andorra and France, Pas de la Casa owes its development as much to duty-free sales to the French as to skiing. It is a sizeable collection of dreary concrete-box-style apartment blocks and hotels, a product of the late 1960s and early 1970s. One reporter draws attention to 'loads of restaurants with plastic-covered faded images of burgers and chips'. Quite. Most accommodation is conveniently placed near the lift base and slopes. The town centre boasts plenty of cheap shops and bars, as well as a sports centre. Reporters complain that the heavy traffic generates fumes, although attempts have been made to keep some areas traffic-free in the evenings, according to a 2006 reporter. The resort attracts a lot of French and Spanish families, as well as Brits.

You can now drive to central Andorra via a toll tunnel which avoids the Port d'Envalira pass; you exit near Grau Roig (pronounced 'Rosh'). This is a mini-resort in an attractively wooded setting that acts as the access point for day visitors arriving by road, but it also makes a good base.

THE MOUNTAINS

The Grandvalira ski area offers an extensive 193km/120 miles of pistes – comparable to big-name Alpine resorts such as Kitzbühel and Les Deux Alpes. With the exception of a couple of attractively wooded slopes in the central valley, the slopes above Pas are all open, and vulnerable to bad weather. Soldeu is more sheltered.

Slopes The home slopes, facing north-east, descend from a high, north–south ridge; lifts go up to it at four points. Runs on the far side of the ridge converge on Grau Roig, where there is some wooded terrain at the head of the valley. And a single lift goes on further west to the bowl of Llac del Cubill and the rest of the Grandvalira ski area. On the far side of this bowl is the arrival station of the 6km/4 mile gondola up from Encamp. In the opposite direction out of Pas, a new six-pack has begun an expansion over the French border – see news.

Terrain-parks There is a 'freestyle circuit' at Grau Roig; a terrain-park and boarder-cross course at Pas (best suited to beginners and intermediates).

Snow reliability The combination of height and lots of snowmaking means

SKI ANDORRA / NUTS

Most of the slopes are open, with some woods around Grau Roig →

KEY FACTS

Resort	2100m
	6,890ft

GrandValira (Soldeu/El Tarter/Pas/Grau Roig)	
Slopes	1710-2560m
	5,610-8,400ft
Lifts	64
Pistes	193km
	120 miles
Green	16%
Blue	33%
Red	31%
Black	20%
Snowmaking	68km
	42 miles

REPORTS WANTED

Recently we have had few reports on this resort. If you go there, please do send us a report.

Phone numbers
From abroad use the prefix +376.

Central reservations phone number
For all resort accommodation call 801060.

TOURIST OFFICE

t 871900
info@grandvalira.com
www.grandvalira.com

good snow reliability and a season that often reaches late April. But on both our most recent visits the snow has been better in Soldeu.

Experts There are few challenges on-piste – the black runs are rarely of serious steepness, and moguls are sparse. But there seem to be plenty of off-piste slopes inviting exploration – a reader recommends the bowls above Grau Roig, in particular.

Intermediates The local slopes cater for confident intermediates best, with plenty of top-to-bottom reds on the main ridge; they do rather lack variety – and can be tricky for more timid intermediates, for whom Soldeu makes a better base.

Beginners There are beginner slopes in both Pas and Grau Roig – those in Grau Roig were improved for last season. The Pas area is a short but inconvenient bus-ride out of town. Progression to longer runs is easier in Grau Roig.

Snowboarding Boarding is popular with the young crowd the resort attracts. Drags are usually avoidable.

Cross-country There are loops totalling 12km/7 miles below Grau Roig.

Queues Queues are rarely serious during the week. But at weekends and French school holidays some can develop, especially at Grau Roig – confirmed by a 2006 visitor. But the new quad should keep beginners moving at Piolet.

Mountain restaurants There are routine places at the ridge above Pas and the top of the gondola from Encamp – 'the worst I've found' says a 2006 reporter. In contrast, the Rifugi dels Llacs dels Pessons at the head of the Grau Roig bowl is a cosy, beamed table-service restaurant with excellent food – booking recommended.

Schools and guides The ski school has a high reputation – good English.

Facilities for children There are ski kindergartens at Pas and Grau Roig, and a non-ski one at the latter.

STAYING THERE

How to go There are lots of apartments and hotels and a few chalets.

Hotels Himalaia-Pas (735 515) has a pool and is 'comfortable and recommendable', says a reporter. The Grau Roig hotel (755 556) is in a league of its own for comfort and seclusion. Beware of hotels catering to the 18-30 crowd.

Eating out It's not a resort for gourmets – though one reporter had 'good charcuterie and paella at the restaurant next to the Burger King' and another 'quail and foie gras' at Husky. A 2006 reader was impressed by the 'friendly and welcoming' attitude of restaurant staff in most places and the good value menu options.

Après-ski Après-ski is very lively. The Marseilles, Milwaukee and Underground bars are popular. The Billboard is 'by far the best club'.

Off the slopes Off-slope activity is limited to shopping, visiting the leisure centre or taking a trip to Andorra la Vella for more of the same.

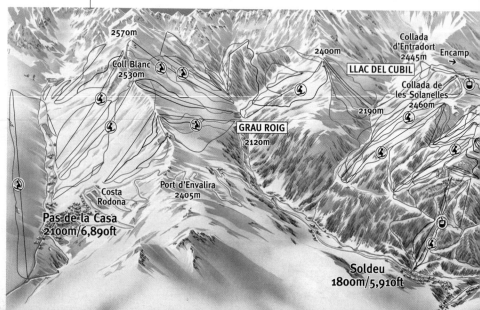

Soldeu

For most visitors to Andorra, the best all-round bet – a reasonably pleasant village, centrally placed in the most impressive ski area

NEWS

For 2006/07 a six-pack is due to replace the oldest chair-lift in Soldeu, the Espiolets 2, which runs parallel to the main gondola.

For 2005/06 two moving carpets were added to the beginner areas at Riba Escorxada above El Tarter, and at El Forn above Canillo.

A new mountain restaurant, Pi de Magdia, opened at Riba Escorxada, offering gourmet or self-service choices.

+ Joint lift pass with Pas de la Casa means the ski area now rivals many major resorts in the Alps for size

+ Not as rowdy a resort as it once was

+ Excellent beginner and early intermediate terrain

+ Ski school has excellent British-run section for English-speaking visitors

– Slopes can get very crowded

– Very little to interest experts

– Village is on the main road through Andorra and suffers heavy traffic

– Some hotels are way out of town

– Not much to do off the slopes

If we were planning a holiday in Andorra, it would be in Soldeu (or the isolated hotel at Grau Roig, up the road – covered in the Pas de la Casa chapter). Despite the traffic, it is the least unattractive village, and its local slopes are the most interestingly varied (though crowded). It shares with neighbouring Pas de la Casa 193km/120 miles of pistes – an area now known as Grandvalira, whose lift system includes four modern gondolas, nine six-packs and six fast quads.

THE RESORT

The village is an ever-growing ribbon of modern buildings – not pretty, but mainly with traditional stone cladding – on a steep hillside, lining the busy road that runs through Andorra from France to Spain. Most are hotels, apartments or bars, with the occasional shop; for serious shopping – or any other off-slope diversions – you have to head down to Canillo (see end of this chapter) or Andorra la Vella.

The steep hillside leads down to the river, and the slopes are on the opposite side. A gondola and new six-pack take you to the heart of the slopes at Espiolets, and a wide bridge across the river forms the end of the

piste home, with elevators to take you up to the gondola.

El Tarter, a few miles by road and 200m/66oft vertical down the valley, and Canillo, another 200m/66oft lower, offer alternative lifts into the slopes. Between all three resorts, hotels and apartments are being built along the main road and sold under the Soldeu banner – so check carefully where your proposed accommodation is. If you are staying a bus-ride from Soldeu, you can leave skis, boards and boots (for a fee) at the bottom or top (cheaper, says a reporter) of the gondola. The new Grandvalira bus service (included in the area pass) runs hourly along the valley towards Andorra la Vella – you can hop on or off at different sectors.

Like most black runs in this area, the smoothly groomed piste on the left (down to El Tartar) doesn't deserve its classification →

THE MOUNTAINS

The Grandvalira ski area offers an extensive 193km/120 miles of pistes – which compares with big-name Alpine resorts such as Kitzbühel and Les Deux-Alpes. Soldeu's main local slopes are on open mountainsides above the woods, though there are runs in the woods back to all of the lift bases.

THE SLOPES
Pleasantly varied but crowded

The gondola rises over wooded, north-facing slopes to **Espiolets**, a broad shelf that is virtually a mini-resort – the ski school is based here, and there are extensive nursery slopes. From Espiolets, a gentle run to the east takes you to an area of long, easy runs served by a six-pack. Beyond that is an extensive area of more varied slopes, served by a quad and another six-pack, that links with the Pas de la Casa area. Going west from Espiolets takes you to the open bowl of **Riba Escorxada** and the arrival point of the gondola up from El Tarter. From here, another six-pack serves sunny slopes on Tosa dels Espiolets and a fourth goes to the high-point of Tossal de la Llosada and the link with **El Forn** above Canillo.

TERRAIN-PARKS
A good one

The terrain-park situated just above Riba Escorxada is fast gaining a reputation throughout Europe. There is

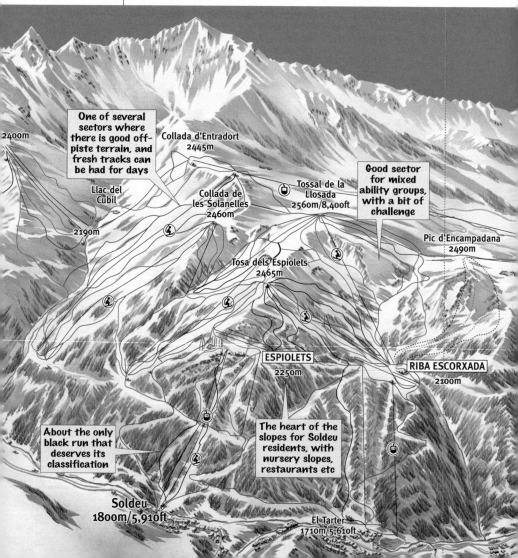

One of several sectors where there is good off-piste terrain, and fresh tracks can be had for days

2400m

Collada d'Entradort
2445m

Good sector for mixed ability groups, with a bit of challenge

Llac del Cubil

Collada de les Solanelles
2460m

Tossal de la Llosada
2560m/8,400ft

2190m

Pic d'Encampadana
2490m

Tosa dels Espiolets
2465m

ESPIOLETS
2250m

RIBA ESCORXADA
2100m

About the only black run that deserves its classification

The heart of the slopes for Soldeu residents, with nursery slopes, restaurants etc

Soldeu
1800m/5,910ft

El Tarter
1710m/5,610ft

fun for all levels in this little freestyle oasis. For beginners there is a 5m/16ft jump and a couple of fun-boxes to slide on. There is a reasonably well kept half-pipe, followed by a triple line of kickers that range between 8m and 16m (26ft and 52ft). This then goes into a nice big hip. There is a great selection of rails including a double rainbow S-box and two wall rides. A drag lift services the park.

SNOW RELIABILITY
Much better than people expect

Despite its name (Soldeu means Sun God) the slopes enjoy reliable snow. Most slopes are north-facing, with a good natural snow record and snowmaking on over a third of the pistes. The excellent grooming helps maintain good snow too.

FOR EXPERTS
Hope for good off-piste

It's a limited area for experts, at least on-piste. The Avet black run down to Soldeu deserves its grading, but most of the others would be no more than reds (or even blues) in many resorts. The blacks on Tosa dels Espiolets, for example, are indistinguishable from the neighbouring (and more direct) red and blue. But there is plenty of off-piste potential – notably in the bowl above Riba Escorxada, in the Espiolets and and Solanelles areas (we had a great time there in fresh powder on our last visit), and above El Forn. And the off-

Pic d'Encampadana
2490m

Pic de la Portella
2465m

Refreshingly quiet slopes, and the black could easily be a red

Encamp
1300m/4,270ft

RIBA ESCORXADA
2100m

If you're lucky you may find a snow-cat giving rides up to the top of these off-piste routes

EL FORN
2000m

Encamp is a cheap base and the gondola ride, though long, isn't quite as long as it looks here

Canillo
1500m/4,920ft

LIFT PASSES

GrandValira

Prices in €

Age	1-day	6-day
under 12	27	138
12 to 64	34	180
over 65	16	96

Free under 6, over 70

Beginner pass in each sector for beginners' area €21 per day

Notes

Covers all lifts in Soldeu, El Tarter, Canillo, Grau Roig and Pas de la Casa. Pedestrian and local day and half-day passes available.

Alternative passes

The Ski Andorra pass covers all Andorran areas and allows skiing at any single one of them each day. For five non-consecutive days in high season: €162; for five consecutive days in low season: €152.

boarding

Soldeu has become the home of snowboarding in the Pyrenees. More and more riders are coming here due to the board-friendly atmosphere and infrastructure of the resort. This is a perfect place for beginners to learn on the nice wide slopes that aren't too steep. Most of the runs including the nursery slopes are serviced by chair-lifts and not drags – ideal for less confident snowboarders. For the more advanced, Soldeu offers some good off piste, steeper areas and the best snow-park in the Pyrenees. Loaded snowboard shop in Soldeu is a real hub in the area, and the friendly staff will give you plenty of pointers.

piste remains untouched for days because most visitors are beginners and early intermediates. When conditions permit at weekends, a snowcat takes people up to Pic d'Encampadana, from where four off-piste routes (dotted on our map) descend to Riba Escorxada.

FOR INTERMEDIATES
Explore Grandvalira

There is plenty to amuse all but the very keenest intermediates. The area east of Espiolets is splendid for building confidence, while those who already have it will be able to explore the whole mountain. Riba Escorxada is a fine section for mixed ability groups. The Canillo/El Forn sector has an easy, little-used blue run along the ridge with excellent views all the way to Pal and Arinsal and an easy black in the valley. Many of the blues and reds have short steeper sections, preceded by a 'slow' sign and netting in the middle of the piste to slow you down.

FOR BEGINNERS
One of the best

This is an excellent place to start. The Espiolets nursery area is huge, and served by moving carpet lifts. There's a smaller area at Riba Escorxada, above El Tarter (which one reader reckons is better) with a new moving carpet and newly-improved slopes. They are relatively snow-sure, and there are numerous easy pistes to move on to (though the crowds can be off-putting). And the ski school is top-notch.

FOR CROSS-COUNTRY
Er, what cross-country?

There is no cross-country in Soldeu. There is some not far away at Grau Roig (see Pas de la Casa chapter), but Andorra's serious cross-country resort is La Rabassa, in the south-west corner of the country – 15km/9 miles of loops at an altitude of 2000m/6,560ft.

QUEUES
Crowds more of a problem

Most of Grandvalira's key lifts are high-speed chairs or gondolas, though there are a lot of slow lifts too. But the system seems to be able to cope. Great efforts are made to fill the bubbles on the gondola out of Soldeu; despite this, in the past it has generated queues, but these should be eased this season when the old double chair parallel to the gondola is upgraded to a six-pack. Allow time for the queue-prone Cubil chair back from Grau Roig. More of a problem than queues is crowds on the blue slopes (including lots of ski school classes snaking along) – the reds and blacks are much quieter. The final bend on the Esquirol run to El Tarter was named 'carnage corner' by one reporter, who recommends a return to the resort by lift for the inexperienced. El Tarter is very busy with local skiers at the weekend.

MOUNTAIN RESTAURANTS
Not a highlight

The mountain restaurants are crowded and the food generally dull (a notable exception is Rifugi dels Llacs dels Pessons – see Pas de la Casa). There is a choice of places at Espiolets, including table-service at Gall de Bosc, which was recommended by a reporter. The Pi de Migdia opened at Riba Escorxada this season and has table- and self-service options – reports please! The Roc de les Bruixes at El Forn claims to be 'gastronomic' but we lack reports on it. Reporters favour descending to El Tarter, particularly to the snack bar in the Hotel del Clos.

SCHOOLS AND GUIDES
One of the best for Brits

The scale of the teaching operation here is very impressive. The ski school is effectively run as two units. One deals with English-speaking clients, is led by an Englishman and has mostly

SCHOOLS

Soldeu
t 890591

El Tarter
t 890641

Canillo
t 890691

Classes
15hr: €101

Private lessons
€33 for 1hr

CHILDREN

Nurseries at Grau Roig and Soldeu
Ages 1 to 3 (Grau Roig), 2 to 3 (Soldeu); 2hr €16

Snow gardens run by ski schools
Ages 3 to 6; 2hr €19.50

Ski schools
For ages 5-11: 15hr: €96

GETTING THERE

Air Toulouse 196km/121 miles (3½hr).

Rail L'Hospitalet-Près-L'Andorre (25km/16 miles); buses and taxis to Soldeu.

ACTIVITIES

Indoor Thermal spas, bowling (at Pas), leisure centre (pools, hot-tub, gym)

Outdoor Helicopter rides, snowmobiling, dog-sledding, snow-shoeing, paragliding, paintballing, archery

Phone numbers
From abroad use the prefix +376.

Central reservations phone number
Call 890501.

TOURIST OFFICE

t 890500
info@grandvalira.com
www.grandvalira.com

native-English-speaking instructors. Some 40 per cent of the pupils are beginners, and the school has devised a special 'team-teaching' scheme to cope with this number of beginners. The school maintains its excellent reputation for teaching and friendliness. 'One of the reasons for returning to Soldeu', 'instructor was brilliant', 'everyone was very impressed, small classes of eight, English is first language, and good tuition' are typical comments.

FACILITIES FOR CHILDREN
With altitude
Children are looked after at the mid-mountain stations. There are nurseries at Espiolets, Riba Escorxada and El Forn for children from 12 months to three years old and Snow Gardens for three- to six-year-olds. The Mickey Snow Club (El Tarter) has Disney-themed play areas on the slopes.

STAYING THERE

HOW TO GO
Be careful where you stay
A wide range of UK tour operators offer packages here, mainly in hotels but with some apartments and chalets. Location is important – many places are a bus-ride from town.
Hotels The best hotels are far removed from the standards of a decade ago. The first five-star in the resort, Sport Hotel Hermitage, will open for 2006/07. ((((4) **Sport Hotel Village** (870500) By far the best in town, with style and space in the public areas – comfortable chairs and sofas, high ceilings, beams and picture windows. Built over the gondola station by the family that sold the land to the lift company. ((((3) **Sport** (870500) Comfortable, good lounge areas, lively bar and a popular basement disco-bar. But dull buffet-style food. ((((3) **Piolets** (871787) Pleasant enough, with a pool. Central. ((((3) **Himalaia** (878515) Refurbished, central.
Self-catering Most reporters are hotel-based but apartments are available.

EATING OUT
Some gourmand delights
We enjoyed excellent, satisfying meals at three rustic restaurants. Borda del Rector (Andorran-run, and with authentic Andorran cuisine), nearer to El Tarter than Soldeu, was our

favourite. The other two were both British-run: Snails and Quails, 3km/2 miles up the road in Bordes d'Envalira, and Fat Albert's in downtown Soldeu. L'Esquirol (Indian) and Pussycat have had good reports.

APRES-SKI
Lively
Après-ski is lively 'but not loutish' – mainly bars and rep-organised events (such as pub crawls with maybe 100 participants). The bar at Fat Albert's has videos shot on the mountain and often a live band. The Pussycat is a good late-night place, with changing party themes. The Piccadilly, under the Sport hotel, is popular. The Aspen and the nearby Avalanche attract a younger crowd. We liked the Villager. Expect noise from late-night revellers.

OFF THE SLOPES
Head downhill
There is little to amuse non-skiers in Soldeu itself. Down in Canillo is the smart Palau de Gel, and in Andorra la Vella the impressive Caldea spa, and some very serious shopping opportunities. Some of the bigger hotels have excellent sports facilities.

El Tarter 1710m/5,610ft

El Tarter has grown over recent years and is rather sprawling, with no real centre. Reporters recommend the hotels del Clos (851500) ('good food but up a steep hill') and del Tarter (802080). We have had good reviews of the big four-star Euro Esqui (736666) half-way to Soldeu ('very friendly staff, spacious rooms', with efficient minibus shuttle to El Tarter lifts). The local ski school is generally well-received, although one reporter says his children 'followed the instructor around without any feedback or instruction on technique'. Readers also complain that the resort is 'dull at night'. The Mosquit pizzeria has been recommended.

Canillo 1500m/4,920ft

If you like the idea of deserted local slopes and don't mind riding a gondola down at the end of the day, consider Canillo, which looks an acceptably pleasant spot as you drive through it. It has the impressive Palau de Gel – an Olympic ice rink plus pool, gym and other amenities.

Austria

Austria's holiday recipe is quite distinctive. It doesn't suit everybody, but for many holidaymakers, nothing else will do; in particular, France won't do. Austria is the land of cute little villages clustered around onion-domed churches – there are no monstrous, purpose-built, apartment-block resorts of the kind that are so common in France. It's the land of friendly wooded mountains, reassuring to beginners and timid intermediates in a way that bleak snowfields and craggy peaks will never be. It's the land of friendly, welcoming people who don't find it demeaning to speak their guests' language (if it's English, at least). And it's the land of jolly, alcohol-fuelled après-ski action – in many resorts, starting in mid-afternoon with dancing in mountain restaurants and going on as long as you have the legs for it. For many visitors to Austrian resorts the partying is as important as the skiing or riding. Of course, there are exceptions to all these norms.

In general, Austria isn't the first place you'll want to consider if reliably good snow is your top priority. (We should note here that there are some wonderful exceptions to this rule – Austria has some of the world's best glacier areas.) Most resorts are relatively low, and conditions are more likely to be problematic here than in higher resorts. But Austrian resorts have made great strides in their attempts to catch up with their rivals – most have radically increased their snowmaking capacity in the last decade. In midwinter, especially, lack of snow generally coincides with low night-time temperatures, even at low altitudes, and snowmaking comes into its own. And recent seasons have been bumper natural snow years for much of Austria.

It's the après-ski that strikes most first-time visitors as being Austria's unique selling point. The few French resorts that have lively après-ski are dominated by British or Scandinavian holidaymakers (and resort workers); the French themselves are noticeable by their absence, and you could be in London or Stockholm rather than in France.

But Austrian après-ski remains very Austrian – or perhaps German. Huge quantities of beer and schnapps are drunk, German is the predominant language and German drinking songs are common. So is loud Europop music. People pack into mountain restaurants at the end of the day – well, some time before the end of the day, actually – and girate in their ski boots on the dance floor, on the tables, on the bar, wherever there's room. There are open-air ice bars, umbrella bars and countless transparent 'igloo' bars in which to shelter from bad weather. In many resorts the bands don't stop playing until darkness falls, when the happy punters slide off in the general direction of the village to find another watering hole. After dinner the drinking and dancing starts again – for those who take time out for dinner, that is. Of course, not all Austrian resorts conform to this image. But lots of big-name ones with the best and most extensive slopes do. St Anton, Saalbach-Hinterglemm, Ischgl, Sölden and Zell am See, for example, fit this bill.

One thing that all Austrian resorts have in common is reliably comfortable accommodation – whether it's in 4-star hotels with pools, saunas and spas ('wellness centres'), or in great-value, family-run guest houses, of which Austria has thousands. Catered chalets

← All cute little villages with onion-domed churches, eh? Not quite: Austria has some of the best glacier areas in the Alps; Rettenbach, above Sölden, is linked to a second glacier, Tiefenbach

↑ Outdoor après-ski goes on at the Mooserwirt in St Anton no matter what the weather

WENDY KING

and self-catering apartments are in general much less widely available (though there are one or two resorts, such as St Anton and Kitzbühel, where catered chalets are more easily come by).

One thing to beware is Austria's strange aversion to credit cards. Reporter after reporter complains that many establishments do not accept cards – even quite upmarket hotels, as well as many ski lift companies. So check if they are accepted well in advance, and have access to plenty of cash. They usually do take 'EC' cards (a hangover from the days of the Eurocheque) and we hear that some debit cards are (or will be) part of the EC scheme.

Most Austrian resorts are real, friendly villages on valley floors, with skiing and boarding on the wooded slopes above them. They have expanded enormously since the war, but practically all the development has been in traditional chalet style, and the villages generally look good even without the snow that is the saving grace of many French and even some Swiss resorts. Unlike Courchevel and Verbier, many Tirolean resorts are as busy in July as in February.

Outside the big-name resorts, the skiing is often quite limited. There are many Austrian resorts that a keen skier could explore fully in half a day. Those who start their skiing careers in such resorts may not be worried by this; those who have tried the bigger areas of France and developed a taste for them may find the list of acceptable Austrian resorts quite a short one.

Unfortunately, several of the resorts on that shortlist bring you up against another problem – low altitude, and therefore the possibility of poor snow conditions. Kitzbühel is at 760m/2,490ft and Söll even lower. The top heights are relatively low, too – typically 1800m to 2000m (5,910ft to 6,560ft); as we note above, snowmaking is becoming more widespread, but it works only when the conditions are right. Many of these low resorts need only a shallow depth of snow to cover their pastures, but fluctuating temperatures bring the danger of slush alternating with ice. The resorts of the Arlberg region, at the western end of the Tirol – St Anton, Lech and Zürs – stand apart from these concerns, with excellent snow records and extensive skiing. And you can be fairly confident of good snow at Obergurgl, Obertauern and Ischgl, and of course on glaciers such as those at Hintertux, Stubai valley, Kaprun and Sölden. But for many other resorts our advice to those who care about snow is to book late, when you know what the snow conditions are like.

There are some extensive areas of slopes that are little known in the UK and well worth considering. Bad Gastein, Schladming, Ischgl, Sölden, the Montafon and Lech spring to mind.

Nightlife is not limited to drinking and dancing. There are lots of floodlit toboggan runs, and UK tour operator reps organise Tirolean, bowling, fondue, karaoke and other evenings. And not all resorts are raucous. Lech and Zürs, for example, are full of rich, cool, 'beautiful' people enjoying the comfort of 4-star sophisticated hotels. And resorts such as Niederau in the Wildschönau, Westendorf and Alpbach are pretty, quiet, family resorts.

Austrian resorts are now easier to get to independently using cheap flights. The standard arrival airports are Munich and Salzburg, and for western resorts Zürich. Don't overlook less well-known airports such as Klagenfurt in Carinthia and Friedrichshafen, just over the German border and handy for resorts in western Austria. But don't expect the car hire companies at these airports to be helpful in the matter of snow chains; you may have to buy your own.

GETTING AROUND THE AUSTRIAN ALPS

Austria presents few problems for the car-borne visitor, because practically all the resorts are valley villages which involve neither steep approach roads nor high altitude.

The dominant feature of Austria for the ski driver is the thoroughfare of the Inn valley, which runs through the Tirol from Landeck via Innsbruck to Kufstein. The motorway along it extends, with one or two breaks, westwards to the Arlberg pass and on to Switzerland. This artery is relatively reliable except in exceptionally bad conditions – the altitude is low, and the road is a vital transport link which is kept open in virtually any conditions.

The Arlberg – which divides Tirol from Vorarlberg, but which is also the watershed between Austria and Switzerland – is one of the

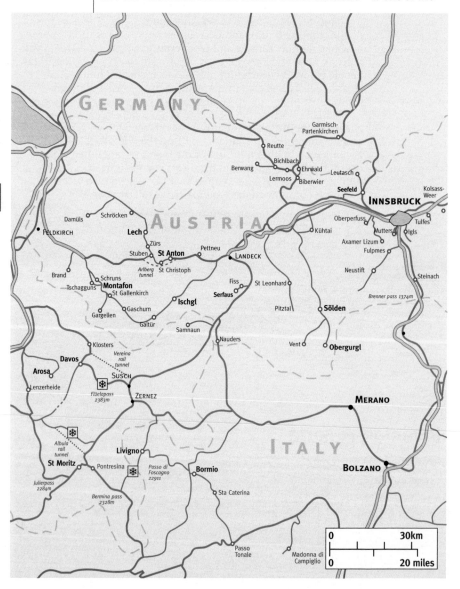

few areas where driving plans are likely to be seriously affected by snow. The east–west Arlberg pass itself has a long tunnel underneath it; this isn't cheap, and you may want to take the high road when it's clear, through Stuben, St Christoph and St Anton. The Flexen pass road to Zürs and Lech (which may be closed by avalanche risk even when the Arlberg pass is open) branches off just to the west of the Arlberg summit.

At the eastern end of the Tirol, the Gerlos pass road from Zell am Ziller over into Salzburg province can be closed. Resorts in Carinthia, such as Bad Kleinkirchheim, are usually reached by motorway, thanks to the Tauern and Katschberg tunnels. The alternative is to drive over the Radstädter Tauern pass through Obertauern, or use the car-carrying rail service from Böckstein to Mallnitz.

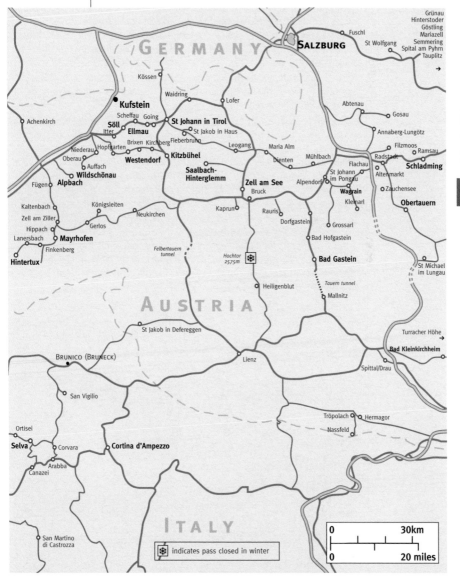

There are more extensive lift passes in the Alps than Salzburgerland's Ski Amadé, but they are very few. What's more, with a car you really could aim to get around most of the resorts it covers – they are clustered close together, no high passes are involved in getting from one resort to another, and many areas are geared to people arriving by car, with out-of-town lifts and serious car parks. (They are also conveniently close to Salzburg airport – last time we went we got an early cheap flight and were on the slopes in Flachau before lunch time; come departure day we skied till the end of the day, enjoyed some après-ski, had a leisurely drive to the airport and still had time to kill before our flight home.)

Some of the major components of the consortium are covered in their own chapters in the Austria section. In the Schladming chapter we also cover the smaller linked resorts of Haus in Ennstal and Pichl, as well as Schladming's elevated outpost of Rohrmoos. Also close to Schladming is Ramsau in Dachstein, which has slopes at village level but also a lift up to the lip of the Dachstein glacier. In the Bad Gastein chapter we cover not only the resorts in the Gastein valley, but also the next-door valley of Grossarl, which is linked over the hill to Dorfgastein.

We also have a chapter on the major area of Hochkönig's Winterreich. Though largely unknown on the British market, it has an extensive network of runs linking Mühlbach, Dienten and Maria Alm.

One of our half-page Short Turn chapters (grouped at the end of each country section) covers Wagrain, which is one of the main resorts in the biggest sub-region, the Salzburger Sportwelt. As well as the large three-valley system linking Wagrain to Flachau and Alpendorf/St Johann im Pongau, this area embraces a similarly extensive lift network linking Zauchensee, Flachauwinkl and Kleinarl, plus more modest lift systems at Filzmoos, Radstadt-Altenmarkt, Eben and Goldegg.

Considering the extent of the lift networks it covers (and the generally impressive efficiency of the lifts) the Ski Amadé pass is not expensive – 176 euros in high season. This is less than you'll pay for anything vaguely similar in France or Italy. Prices on the spot are not bad either – readers report prices in the mountain restaurants (which are very numerous) lower than in areas with a bigger international reputation.

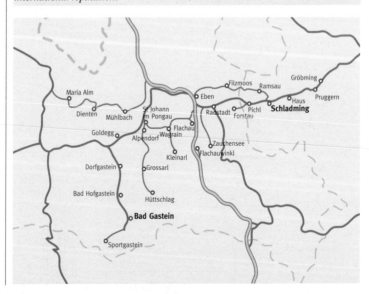

Alpbach

Small and beautiful: it's the pretty village and surroundings rather than the extent of the slopes that have attracted generations of Brits

COSTS

① ② ③ ④ ⑤ ⑥

RATINGS

The slopes

Fast lifts	**
Snow	**
Extent	*
Expert	*
Intermediate	**
Beginner	****
Convenience	**
Queues	***
Mountain restaurants	***

The rest

Scenery	***
Charm	*****
Off-slope	***

NEWS

For 2006/07 a fixed quad is to replace the Galtenberglift drag from Inneralpbach. It will end at Böglalm and should ease queues at the bottom. An eight-seat gondola replaced the two successive Pöglbahn double chairs in 2005/06, meaning the journey from Gmahkopf now takes seven minutes instead of 30.

The Galtenberg hotel was refurbished for 2005/06 and is now a 4-star with a spa and wellness centre.

Snowmaking was further increased in 2005/06.

For 2006/07 a lake between Alpbach and Reith is planned, to provide water for snowmaking.

REPORTS WANTED

Recently we have had few reports on this resort. If you go there, please do send us a report.

➕ Charming traditional village with a relaxed atmosphere – great for young children

➕ Handy, central nursery slopes

➕ Several other worthwhile resorts within day-trip distance

➕ Good, varied, intermediate terrain, not without challenges, but ...

➖ Slopes limited in extent and variety

➖ Main slopes are a shuttle-bus-ride away from the centre

➖ Few long easy runs for beginners to progress to

➖ Lower slopes can suffer from poor snow – though a north-facing aspect and increased snowmaking help

Alpbach is an old British favourite – there is even a British ski club, the Alpbach Visitors. It is exceptionally pretty and friendly, and inspires great loyalty in the visitors who take to it – a regular reporter who has been going for over 20 years claims only junior status.

THE RESORT

Alpbach is near the head of a valley, looking south across it towards the Wiedersbergerhorn, where most of the slopes are to be found. It's an exceptionally pretty, captivating place; traditional chalets crowd around the pretty church (the graves are lit by candles at night), and the nursery slopes are only a few steps away.

Alpbach is small, but it's not necessarily convenient. The main village is the place to stay for atmosphere and après-ski, but involves using a free shuttle-bus to and from Achenwirt, a mile away, where a gondola goes up to Hornboden. The backwater hamlet of Inneralpbach is much more convenient for the slopes, with its own gondola (new for last season) and chair-lift (new for 2006/07) into the slopes.

The Inn valley is a few miles north, and trips east to Kitzbühel or west to Innsbruck are possible. The Hintertux and Stubaier glaciers are within reach.

THE MOUNTAIN

Alpbach's slopes, on two flanks of the Wiedersbergerhorn, are small and simple. Piste grooming is excellent.
Slopes Chair-lifts and drags serve the open, north-facing slopes above the tree line, with black runs following the lift lines and reds (and a single blue) taking less direct routes. The runs are mostly of 200m to 400m (650ft to 1,300ft) vertical, but you can get 500m/1,650ft down the second stage of the Achenwirt gondola, and

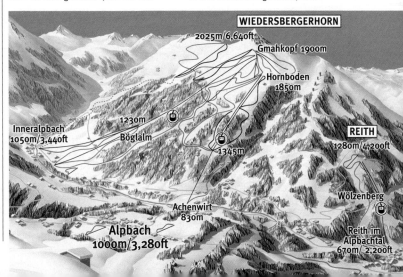

↑ The nursery slopes are in the village centre near the church

DAVID MAXWELL-LEES

KEY FACTS

Resort	1000m
	3,280ft
Slopes	670-2025m
	2,200-6,640ft
Lifts	20
Pistes	45km
	28 miles
Blue	15%
Red	70%
Black	15%
Snowmaking	31km
	19 miles

OUR WEBSITE

Go to our website at wtss.co.uk for resort news, links to resort sites, a build-your-own-shortlist system and reader forums.

rent
SPORT 2000
QUALITY RENTAL SYSTEM

www.sport2000rent.com

online booking

Phone numbers
From elsewhere in Austria add the prefix 05336.
From abroad use the prefix +43 5336.

TOURIST OFFICE

t 6000
info@alpbach.at
www.alpbach.at

1000m/3,300ft when snow is good down to valley level. Behind Gmahkopf is a short blue west-facing slope and a new red run built for the 2004/05 season. The tiny area at Reith (about 3km/2 miles down the valley from Achenwirt) is on the lift pass and, says a 2006 reporter 'well worth a morning's visit if Alpbach is busy and conditions are good – it was well-groomed and deserted on my visit.' It is accessed by an eight-seat gondola.

Terrain-parks There's a half-pipe at the top of the Achenwirt gondola which, during a 2006 visitor's stay, 'was poorly maintained and not re-shaped'.

Snow reliability Alpbach cannot claim great snow reliability, but at least most of the Wiedersbergerhorn faces north and two-thirds of the pistes are covered by snowmaking.

Experts Alpbach isn't ideal, but the reds and the three blacks (often groomed) are not without challenge, and runs of 1000m/3,300ft vertical are not to be sniffed at. There are a few off-piste routes to the valley, short tours are offered, and the schools apparently take the top classes off-piste. A 2006 reporter 'skied with a guide for three hours in untracked deep powder'.

Intermediates There is fine intermediate terrain; the problem is that it's limited. This resort is for practising technique on familiar slopes, not high mileage.

Beginners Beginners love the sunny nursery slopes beside the village. But the main slopes are not ideal for confidence-building: most are classified red (there are only a couple of blues).

Snowboarding There's some good free-riding terrain.

Cross-country 22km/14 miles of pretty cross-country trails rise up beyond Inneralpbach.

Queues According to 2005/06 visitors, the new gondola at Inneralpbach has helped relieve the main problem we have complained about in the past – queues for the Achenwirt gondola.

Mountain restaurants There are several mountain restaurants – each worth a visit. A 2005 reporter recommends 'the spit-roast chicken you order in advance at the Böglalm above Inneralpbach'.

Schools and guides Alpbach and Alpbach Aktiv are the two main ski schools. We have had excellent reports on both and the head of the Alpbach school is disabled and qualified to teach skiing to people with disabilities.

Facilities for children Reporters find the village very child-friendly, with good ski kindergartens; babysitters can be arranged by the tourist office.

STAYING THERE

How to go Hotels and pensions dominate in UK packages.

Hotels Of the smart 4-star places, the Alpbacherhof (5237) ('superb food and excellent service'), Alphof (5371) ('excellent, with friendly and welcoming staff') and ancient Böglerhof (5227) get most votes. The Berghof (5275) was recommended by a 2006 visitor as 'an excellent 3-star, wholesome half-board meals and only 20m from the nursery slopes'. And the simpler Haus Thomas (5944) ('very clean ... you feel like part of the family'), Haus Angelika (5339), and Haus Theresia (5386) have also been recommended by visitors. Pension Edelweiss (5268) is close to the nursery slopes and offers B&B and 'clean, spacious, good value apartments'.

Self-catering There is quite a bit to choose from now, easily bookable through the tourist office website.

Eating out The popular Post and Alphof both provide 'excellent food' according to a reporter, who also favoured the 'superb' Jakober and its non-smoking room. Wiedersbergerhorn in Inneralpbach has been recommended, as has the Rossmoos Inn for its lively Tirolean evenings, 'superb' food and toboggan run back to resort.

Après-ski At peak times this is typically Tirolean, with lots of noisy tea-time beer swilling in the bars of central hotels such as the Jakober and the Post. A 2005 reporter preferred the Farmer's Pub to the Waschkuchl bar. The ski schools put on a weekly 'ski show' on Wednesday evenings.

Off the slopes There are pretty walks and trips to Innsbruck and Salzburg. There are also an indoor swimming pool and an outdoor ice rink.

Bad Gastein

If you fancy 'taking the cure', there are few better resorts; even if you don't, you're likely to be impressed by the slopes (if not the towns)

COSTS

①②③④⑤⑥

RATINGS

The slopes

Fast lifts	**
Snow	***
Extent	****
Expert	***
Intermediate	****
Beginner	**
Convenience	**
Queues	***
Mountain restaurants	****

The rest

Scenery	***
Resort charm	***
Off-slope	****

NEWS

For 2005/06 more snowmaking was installed at Sportgastein. Following on from Bad Hofgastein's spa revamp, Bad Gastein's Felsentherme was renovated for 2004/05 and has a new Adventure Area that includes two pools and seven different saunas/steam rooms.

Sportgastein has the highest slopes and often the best snow in the valley ↓

+ Extensive, varied slopes

+ Excellent, testing long runs for confident intermediates

+ More reliable snow than in most low-altitude Austrian resorts

+ Lots of good, atmospheric, traditional mountain restaurants

+ Excellent thermal spas, but ...

− Main resorts are spa towns, without the usual Austrian resort ambience

− Bad Gastein itself has a steep, confined setting, with narrow streets

− Valley slopes are split into five areas and having a car is an advantage

− Timid intermediates and beginners are better off elsewhere

The Gastein valley is beginning to attract more Brits, to judge by our readers' reports. Rightly so – the slopes form one of Austria's bigger and more varied areas, and snow is more reliable than average. Steeply tiered Bad Gastein itself is a difficult place to like; we much prefer rustic Dorfgastein or spacious Bad Hofgastein – described at the end of this chapter. The valley needs a top-notch public transport system; the current one is criticised by some reporters.

THE RESORT

Bad Gastein sits near the head of the Gastein valley. It is an old spa that has now spread widely, but still has a compact core. A bizarre combination of buildings is laid out in a cramped horseshoe, set in what is virtually a gorge. The central area is steep and no pleasure at all to explore. Up the hill is a modern suburb with more of a ski-resort feel and access to the gondola up to the major sector, Stubnerkogel, which links with Bad Hofgastein's slopes. Across town, the double chair up Graukogel is a taxi-ride from the centre. Various ski-bus routes connect the villages and lift stations (including Sportgastein at the head of the valley and Dorfgastein down it). There are trains, too. The ski-bus service is not super-efficient, and a car is a big asset here. It also allows exploitation of the Ski Alliance Amadé lift pass, which covers over 30 resorts in the region.

THE MOUNTAIN

Most of the runs are on the open slopes above the tree line, though there are some woodland runs.
Slopes Stubnerkogel has runs in all directions from the peak, giving about 500m/1,640ft vertical on the open slopes above the tree line and rather more below it. There is night skiing once a week on the nursery slope. The much smaller Graukogel is unjustly neglected; its wooded runs are a great asset in bad weather, and quiet at other times. The high slopes of Sportgastein, in contrast, are more exposed both to wind and sun. We cover the slopes above Bad Hofgastein and Dorfgastein later in the chapter.
Terrain-parks There isn't one.
Snow reliability The area is higher than many Austrian rivals, and there is snowmaking on crucial sections.
Experts The few black runs are not severe, but many reds are long and

satisfying. Graukogel has some of the most testing slopes and is a great place to go in a blizzard. The other sectors have plenty of opportunities to go off-piste. Sportgastein is also worth the trip in good weather.

Intermediates Good for the confident, who will find long, leg-sapping runs in all the sectors in the valley. The timid are better off sticking to Schlossalm (see Bad Hofgastein, below).

Beginners Nursery slopes are scattered and none is ideal. The main slope at Bad Gastein is simply too steep. And progression is tricky – the genuinely easy blue runs are often boring paths.

Snowboarding The valley hosts snowboard events, but doesn't seem to cater particularly well for holiday boarders. There's still a fairly high proportion of drag-lifts.

Cross-country There are 90km/56 miles of trails, but they are all low down.

Queues A 2006 reporter found early-January crowds of Russians and waits of up to 30 minutes in Angertal and 5 to 10 minutes elsewhere. But a March reporter found no queues.

Mountain restaurants Atmospheric, traditional huts abound. The 'very inviting and totally refurbished' Jungerstube, Bergstadl, cosy Stubneralm, 'atmospheric' Hartlgut (from which you take a train or taxi back) and 'less frequented' Heitzingalm have been recommended.

Schools and guides A 2006 reporter had a lesson with the new Schnee Sports Schule Angertal with 'a first-class Croatian instructor'.

Facilities for children There are facilities for all-day care and there's a 'Fun Center' for kids at the top of the Stubnerkogel gondola which was a 'great success' with a 2006 reporter's small grandchildren. There's also a snow adventure park at Angertal.

STAYING THERE

How to go British tour operators sell mainly hotel-based packages.

Hotels There are lots of smart 4- and 3-star hotels with spa facilities. The Wildbad (37610) was rated 'excellent' by a 2005 reporter. The Grüner Baum (25160) is a lovely retreat, but wildly inconvenient (though they do have a hotel bus) except for langlauf.

Eating out There is a fair range of restaurants. The central Wirtshaus Jägerhäusl does excellent food in a warm, traditional atmosphere

(especially upstairs). The Vier Jahreszeiten, a short drive away in Böckstein, offers big portions, 'very good value and friendly service', according to a recent visitor.

Après-ski A 2006 reporter found the Hirschenhutte in the Angertal a 'good place to après'. The town feels generally subdued, but there are numerous popular bars and several discos – plus a casino. Highlights from a reporter include the 'boisterous' Bergfex, the 'cosy, friendly, wood-panelled' Hexenhäusl, the 'vibrant, Wild-West-style' Silver Bullet, the 'friendlier' Eden and the Weinfassl for 'dancing and drinking games'. Places for a quiet late drink include the smart Bellini bar and the Ritz cocktail bar.

Off the slopes The spa facilities are excellent and extensive. And interesting excursions are possible.

Bad Hofgastein

860m/2,820ft

Bad Hofgastein is a sizeable, quiet spa village set where the valley is wide.

THE RESORT

Although sprawling, the village has a pleasant pedestrianised centre. The slopes are reached by a funicular to Kitzsteinalm starting a long walk or short shuttle-bus-ride away; or you can take a longer bus-ride to Angertal.

THE MOUNTAINS

Schlossalm is a broad, open bowl, with runs through patchy woods both to Bad Hofgastein and Angertal.

The slopes Schlossalm is the valley's gentlest area, with sunny open slopes graded blue and red. But the top lifts lead to some challenging terrain, and the Kleine Scharte cable-car serves a serious 750m/2,460ft vertical, with a splendid long red run from Hohe Scharte to Kitzsteinalm or the valley floor.

Terrain-parks There isn't one.

Snow reliability Snowmaking is now fairly extensive, but snow-cover down to the bottom is unreliable, especially on the sunny Angertal slopes.

Experts There are no real challenges on the local pistes but there is ample opportunity to go off-piste.

Intermediates All intermediates will enjoy the Schlossalm slopes – and the more confident can go further afield.

Beginners You have to catch a bus to the limited nursery area at Angertal.

Snowboarding Pleasantly varied

Phone numbers
Bad Gastein
From elsewhere in Austria add the prefix 06434.
From abroad use the prefix +43 6434.
Bad Hofgastein
From elsewhere in Austria add the prefix 06432.
From abroad use the prefix +43 6432.
Dorfgastein
From elsewhere in Austria add the prefix 06433.
From abroad use the prefix +43 6433.

TOURIST OFFICE

For all resorts in the Gastein valley contact the Bad Hofgastein office.
t 3393
info@gastein.com
www.gastein.com

terrain, but no special facilities. Drag-lifts are dotted around every sector.

Cross-country Bad Hofgastein makes a fine base for cross-country when its lengthy valley-floor trails have snow.

Queues A 2006 visitor found that it could take 'the best part of an hour to get to the top' at Schlossalm using the queue-prone funicular (avoidable by bussing to Angertal) and cable-car (avoidable by taking chair-lifts).

Mountain restaurants Well up to the high local standards are Kleine Scharte, Hamburger Skihütte and Aeroplanstadl (its toilets 'in the form of a pristine mock cavern' are 'worth a visit'). Après-ski starts early at Aeroplanstadl.

Schools and guides One 2006 reporter booked a three-hour private lesson with the Bad Hofgastein school for an 'advanced beginner'. The instructor 'skied ahead most of the time, did not show a very high degree of interest and, overall, benefit was limited.'

Facilities for children See Bad Gastein.

STAYING THERE

How to go Mostly hotels.

Hotels Reporters have found the 4-star St Georg (61000), the central Salzburgerhof (62300) the Germania (6232) excellent value. In the village centre the Osterreichischer Hof (6216) is 'well-run' and has its own 'good' spa facilities. The 3-star Rauscher (64120) is handy for the shuttle-bus and

provides 'clean, spacious rooms and good food'.

Self-catering Accommodation can be organised through the tourist office.

Eating out There is a good range of restaurants. Piccola Italia is 'well worth a visit'. The Wintergarten is an intimate restaurant, the Maier one of the better informal places.

Après-ski Quiet by Austrian standards. At close of play the central Piccolo ice bar is popular; there are several good places for cakes, among them Café Weitmoser, a historic little castle. Later on, the Glocknerkeller and the Gasteiner Discostadl are among the bars playing disco music.

Off the slopes The Alpen Therme Gastein spa is 'huge', with several pools, and a 'river' as well as saunas, steam baths and restaurants. Other amenities include ice skating.

Dorfgastein 830m/2,720ft

Dorfgastein is a rustic village further down the valley. It has its own extensive slopes, accessed by a two-stage gondola or by chair-lifts starting 500m/1,640ft outside the village, linked with the slopes of Grossarl in the next valley. Runs are varied and long, with a good mix of open and wooded terrain amid lovely scenery. The low nursery slopes can be icy. There are a few shops and après-ski places.

Bad Kleinkirchheim

*Large resort with marvellous spa facilities and a ski area best
suited to intermediates (despite it being Franz Klammer's favourite)*

COSTS

① ② ③ ④ ⑤ ⑥

RATINGS

The slopes

Fast lifts	**
Snow	***
Extent	**
Expert	**
Intermediate	***
Beginner	**
Convenience	***
Queues	****
Mountain restaurants	***

The rest

Scenery	***
Resort charm	***
Off-slope	***

KEY FACTS

Resort	1090m
	3,580ft
Slopes	1100-2055m
	3,610-6,740ft
Lifts	26
Pistes	103km
	64 miles
Blue	17%
Red	75%
Black	8%
Snowmaking	97%

+ Mainly intermediate slopes
+ Virtually all the slopes have snowmaking
+ Superb spa facilities
+ Plenty to do off the slopes

− Spread-out town
− Still a lot of T-bars
− No terrain-park or half-pipe

BKK, as the locals call it, is downhill race hero Franz Klammer's favourite ski area – he learned to ski here, there's a World Cup downhill run bearing his name, and he is the proud owner of a mountain restaurant here. Not surprisingly, therefore, the resort has some serious skiing: 75 per cent of its slopes are graded red. But, surprisingly, there are few real challenges for experts. So the resort suits confident intermediates best. It's a traditional spa town but, unlike many of those, has mainly chalet-style buildings.

THE RESORT

Franz Klammer, 1976 Olympic downhill gold medallist and winner of a record 25 World Cup Downhills, was born in Mooswald, near Bad Kleinkirchheim. His mother runs a gasthaus with his brother and sister-in-law in Fresach, about 20km/12 miles from BKK. He learned to ski at BKK, and it remains his favourite resort.

BKK is tucked away on the edge of the Nock Mountain National Park in the province of Carinthia, in the far south-east of Austria, near the Italian and Slovenian borders. The nearest

airports are Klagenfurt (around 50 minutes away) and Ljubljana (90 minutes). Salzburg is less than two hours.

The old spa town has mainly chalet-style buildings with sloping roofs rather than the more austere blocks of some spa resorts. But it is very spread out along the valley, and the most convenient place to stay is near one of the main lifts out. A ski-bus links all the main lift stations, and some buses also go to St Oswald, a smaller village at the far end of the shared ski area. The spa facilities are excellent, with outdoor thermal pools (with

AISERBURG
055m/6,740ft

1905m

MAIBRUNN
1760m/5775ft

Priedröf
1965m/6,445ft

NOCKALM

Wieser Nock
1974m/6,480ft

Brunnach
1900m/6,235ft

1280m

St Oswald

1370m

1025m

Bad Kleinkirchheim
1090m/3,580ft

Feldkirchen ↓

NEWS

For 2005/06 two fast quads, the Wiesernock and the Scharten, replace two drags linking the Nockalm and St Oswald areas.

A new red and a black were built alongside the new quads. And in St Oswald a new red with a vertical of 580m/1,900ft was created.

The Thermal Romerbad spa is being renovated and extended in time for the 2006/07 season. It will have about a dozen new saunas, a salt bath and a new 50m/165ft outdoor pool with thermal water.

temperatures of between 28° and 34°C), different types of sauna (including a tepidarium: a sauna with a lower temperature so you can sit there longer), steam, solarium, hot-tub, massage and therapy rooms. There are also water slides, waterfalls and massage jets in the pools. 'We found the spas superb. They are a great way to unwind after skiing and mean there's plenty to do if the snow is limited, as it was for us,' says a recent reporter. The Thermal Romerbad is being renovated this year – see News.

THE MOUNTAIN

BKK's shady home slopes are linked to the sunnier ones above the neighbouring village of St Oswald. Throughout, they are mainly wooded and of intermediate standard (75 per cent are graded red).

The piste map doesn't mark most of the mountain restaurants but it does mark 'Rotes Sofa' and 'Hits am Lift' – for what these are see overleaf.

There is a speed course on the Kaiserburg run open to anyone, and it is free of charge.

The lift pass covers all the resorts in Carinthia – useful for visiting other resorts if you have a car.

Slopes BKK's main home slopes are reached by a two-stage gondola or a high-speed quad chair-lift from different parts of the village. The second stage of the gondola continues up to the area's high point, Kaiserburg (2055m/6,740ft), at one end of the ski area, where a couple of T-bars serve the highest slopes. The chair takes you to the other end of the same mountain face at Maibrunn at 1760m/5,775ft.

Pistes go down from both peaks to the gondola mid-station and a chair takes you back to above Maibrunn.

From the same end as the high-speed quad, successive double chair-lifts and a drag take you up the other side of the valley to the Priedröf and Nockalm slopes, which link in with St Oswald's slopes further along the valley. This area can also be accessed by a gondola midway between BKK and St Oswald, which can be reached by ski-bus. At St Oswald a gondola goes up to Brunnach at the far end of the shared ski area.

Two high-speed quads link the Nockalm and St Oswald slopes. Despite the new quads, there are few chairs in BKK, with the majority of the lifts being drags.

Terrain-parks There isn't one.

Snow reliability Being east of the Tauern Pass, BKK can have completely different weather from the rest of Austria. So snow reliability can be better or worse, depending on the season. In general BKK's main home slopes are north-facing and keep their snow best. The Nockalm-St Oswald slopes are more south-facing. Snowmaking was extended last season, and they claim that virtually all the pistes (97 per cent) are now covered.

Experts BKK has little to keep experts interested for a week. The best and most challenging black is the Franz Klammer World Cup run, which goes from Strohsack to the gondola base. There are two short black runs below Kaiserburg and another under the new Wiesernock quad. Off-piste tours that involve some hiking can be arranged (eg to the Mallnock and Klomnock mountains from the top of the gondola from St Oswald and on Falkert mountain, which can be accessed by taxi from BKK and then a T-bar followed by a hike).

Intermediates Virtually all the slopes in both BKK and St Oswald are ideal for good intermediates. Some 75 per cent of the slopes are graded red and many are long (up to 1000m/3,280ft vertical), wide and flattering. One of the most beautiful runs is the FIS K70 downhill run, graded red, which goes from top to bottom of the mountain away from all the lifts and through the trees in the lower section – on the left-hand side of our piste map. It is almost 5km/3 miles long (and rarely groomed, says a local). There are two other long top-to-bottom red runs in this area too, as well as the Franz Klammer black. The Nockalm and St Oswald sectors also have long red runs (and T-bars to allow you to stay on the top runs), and the two new quads make it easier to get between these sectors.

Beginners There are nursery slopes and drag-lifts for beginners at both BKK and St Oswald – the St Oswald ones are at the top of the Nockalm gondola and much warmer and sunnier in mid-winter, when the low BKK ones are in the shade. One reporter told us, 'I had to take my kids off the BKK nursery slope because they were freezing. But they loved the sunny slope at St Oswald.' Once off the nursery slopes, there is an easy blue run at the top of Nockalm and a long blue all the way from the top to the bottom of the gondola here.

Snowboarding Although the main lifts are all gondolas or chairs, there are a lot of T-bars around, which less experienced boarders may not like. And there's no terrain-park or half-pipe.

Cross-country BKK takes cross-country seriously, with 54km/34 miles of tracks, some as high as 1900m/6,230ft at the top of the Nockalm.

Queues We have no reports of lift queues being much of a problem.

Mountain restaurants There are 22 mountain restaurants and huts. The newest is the panoramic Nock In at the top of Brunnach above St Oswald, which was built for 2004/05. Franz Klammer's table-service Skibar is at the mid-station of the gondola from BKK. You might even meet the great man himself having lunch or a beer here (especially in January); he is

always happy to have a chat and sign autographs.

Schools and guides There are four schools to choose from, three based in BKK and one in St Oswald.

Facilities for children There's a non-skiing kindergarten for children from age two upwards at the foot of the gondola from BKK. New last season was First Steps, where children from two and a half upwards can learn to ski while playing.

STAYING THERE

How to go Several UK tour operators feature BKK.

Hotels Of the three 5-star hotels, the Pulverer (744) and Thermenhotel Ronacher (282) are both near the high-speed chair and nursery slope and have excellent spa facilities. The other is the St Oswald (591). There are 17 4-stars, several 3-stars and lots of gasthofs too. BKK boasts 26 hotels with swimming pools and 50 solariums.

Self-catering There are lots of self-catering apartments to rent.

Eating out Being a large village with a lot of summer visitors means there are plenty of places for eating out, including a lot of hotel restaurants open to the public. The Loy Stub'n in the Hotel Pulverer comes highly recommended by a recent reporter: 'a high quality, not too typically Austrian meal, in very pleasant surroundings with excellent service'.

Après-ski A lot of the après-ski takes place in the hotels, but there are a few interesting bars to try. Near the BKK gondola base are several popular places: the Almstube, Viktoria Pub, Club MC 99 and the Take Five Dancing Club.

Off the slopes There are superb spa facilities, which are great for non-slope users and for skiers and boarders looking to soothe their aching limbs. You can buy lift tickets that include the use of the thermal swimming pools. There are also some good walks, including the Spa Boulevard route at the top of the gondola from St Oswald, a tennis centre, squash courts, an outdoor ice rink, curling, snowtubing, horse-riding, horse-drawn sleigh rides and a 4km/2 mile floodlit toboggan run. Those with cars can also visit Villach (36km/22 miles away) for a shopping spree or carry on across the border into Italy.

Ellmau

Our favourite base on the extensive Ski Welt circuit – combines charm with convenience – just hope the snow holds up

COSTS

① ② ③ ④ ⑤ ⑥

RATINGS

The slopes

Fast lifts	**
Snow	**
Extent	****
Expert	*
Intermediate	****
Beginner	****
Convenience	***
Queues	****
Mountain restaurants	**

The rest

Scenery	***
Resort charm	***
Off-slope	***

KEY FACTS

Resort	800m
	2,620ft

Entire Ski Welt	
Slopes	620-1890m
	2,030-6,200ft
Lifts	93
Pistes	250km
	155 miles
Blue	43%
Red	48%
Black	9%
Snowmaking	180km
	112 miles

- Extensive slopes, Austria's largest linked ski and snowboard area
- Pretty, friendly slopes
- Excellent nursery slopes
- Cheap by Austrian standards
- Quiet, charming family resort – more appealing than neighbouring Söll
- Massive recent investment in snowmaking has paid off, but ...

- Ski Welt is at low altitude, and snow quality can suffer
- Main lift a bus-ride from village – though reachable via a drag-lift
- Upper-mountain runs are mostly short, and offer little for experts or adventurous intermediates
- Limited range of nightlife
- Ski Welt slopes can get crowded at weekends and in high season

If you like the sound of the large, undemanding Ski Welt circuit, Ellmau has a lot to recommend it as your base – quieter than Söll, but with more amenities than other neighbours such as Scheffau (covered in the Söll chapter). And Austria's largest snowmaking system makes the area less risky than it was.

THE RESORT

Ellmau sits at the north-eastern corner of the Ski Welt. Although sizeable, it remains quiet, with traditional chalet-style buildings, welcoming bars and shops, and a pretty church. It has a compact centre, but accommodation is scattered – so the buses around the resort are important (and now better organised say reporters). There is accommodation out by the funicular to the main slopes but we prefer to stay near the heart of the village. A guest card entitles you to various discounts, including entry to the leisure centre.

THE MOUNTAIN

The Ski Welt is the largest mountain circuit in Austria. It links Going, Scheffau, Söll, Itter, Hopfgarten and Brixen. The piste map covering this huge area is, not surprisingly, difficult to comprehend. A recent reporter highly recommends the 'new plastic 3D map – a big improvement on the huge paper version'. Most runs are easy, and short – which means that getting around the area can take time, despite increasing numbers of fast lifts. Westendorf is covered by the Ski Welt pass, though its local slopes are not

NEWS

For 2006/07 a six-pack with heated seats will replace the Tanzboden drag-lift below Hartkaiser and Brandstadl.

In 2005/06 the Kummereralm, a six-seater chair, replaced the T-bar (Weissachlift) up to Eiberg. This area was also extended by two red runs, and the new Kummereralm restaurant was built. The Bergkaiser panoramic restaurant was built at the top of the Hartkaiser. Ellmau's first terrain-park opened near the Kaiser-express, and it will be extended for 2006/07.

Snowmaking was increased again last season; it now covers 70 per cent of the pistes in the Ski Welt region.

A 3D MountMap piste map of the Ski Welt area was on sale for 5 euros – the first ski region in Austria to have one.

ON YOUR OWN?

You can team up with other skiers/boarders by turning up at 10am or 1pm at one of seven designated points in the Ski Welt; there are stickers to identify participants, and even a website forum for making prior arrangements.

linked (you need to take a bus from Brixen); Westendorf now has a link to the Kirchberg-Kitzbühel slopes – see the Westendorf chapter. These, along with Waidring, Fieberbrunn and St Johann are possible day trips and covered by the Kitzbüheler Alpenskipass.

Slopes The funicular railway on the edge of the village takes you up to Hartkaiser, from where a fine long red leads down to Blaiken (Scheffau's lift base station). A choice of gondolas take you up to Brandstadl. Immediately beyond Brandstadl, the slopes become rather bitty; an array of short runs and lifts link Brandstadl to Zinsberg. From Zinsberg, long, south-facing pistes lead down to Brixen. Then it's a short bus-ride to Westendorf's pleasant separate area, from which you can now reach the slopes of Kirchberg and Kitzbühel, via a slope and another short bus-ride. Part-way down to Brixen you can head towards Söll, and if you go up Hohe Salve you get access to a long, west-facing run to Hopfgarten.

Ellmau and Going share a pleasant little area of slopes on Astberg, slightly apart from the rest of the area, and well suited to the unadventurous and families. One piste leads to the funicular for access to the rest of Ski Welt. The main Astberg chair is rather inconveniently positioned, midway between Ellmau and Going.

We had a complaint from a 2006 reporter about inconsistent piste grading with some runs marked blue on the map but red on the mountain.

Terrain-parks For the first time last season Ellmau had its own park with kickers and rails near the Kaiserexpress.

Snow reliability With a low average height, and important links that get a lot of sun, the snowmaking that the Ski Welt has installed is essential and the Ellmau-Going sector now claims almost all its slopes are covered. This can, of course, only be used when it is cold enough and it cannot prevent slush and icy patches. The north-facing Eiberg area above Scheffau holds its snow well. Grooming is reported to be 'excellent' and a visitor last year found the snowmaking 'ace'. Several reporters also experienced great fresh powder all week in various visits.

Experts There are steep plunges off the Hohe Salve summit, a ski route from Brandstadl down to Scheffau and a little mogul field between Brandstadl and Neualm, but the area isn't really suitable unless you go off-piste.

Intermediates With good snow, the Ski Welt is a paradise for those who love easy cruising. There are lots of blue runs and many of the reds deserve a blue grading ('pale blue' says a recent reporter). It is a big area and you get a feeling of travelling around. The main challenge is when the snow isn't perfect – ice and slush can make even gentle lower slopes seem tricky. For timid intermediates the easy slopes of Astberg are handy.

Beginners Ellmau has an array of good nursery slopes covered by snowmaking. The main ones are at the Going end, but there are some by the road to the funicular. The Astberg chair opens up a more snow-sure plateau at altitude. The Brandstadl area has a section of short easy runs.

Snowboarding Ellmau is a good place to learn as its local slopes are easy.

Cross-country There are long, quite challenging trails (the Ski Welt area has a total of 170km/105 miles), but trails at altitude are lacking.

Queues Continued lift upgrades have greatly improved this once queue-prone area. With the exception of peak times, reporters comment on quiet and crowd-free slopes with 'few queues'.

Mountain restaurants The smaller places are fairly consistent in providing good-value food in pleasant surroundings. The Rübezahl above Ellmau is our favourite in the whole Ski Welt, but can be 'smoky and busy' according to a recent reporter. The Aualm, just below Brandstadl, is favoured, especially for its cakes and glühwein, but a recent visitor felt 'disappointed' with the new layout and change of staff. The Jagerhütte (below Hartkaiser) is good for 'home-made strudel' and 'excellent for a drinks stop', says a 2005 reporter, before enjoying the 'quiet and pleasant' home-run. The Hartkaiser 'has vastly improved in food quality, ambiance, and even has escalators to the loos', says a 2006 visitor. The Bergkaiser has 'quick service and good food'. The Hausleiten Stub'n is also worth a visit. The hut at Neualm, halfway down to Scheffau, has been recommended. The larger self-service restaurants are functional (the Jochstube at Eiberg is a pleasant exception) and suffer queues.

Schools and guides The three schools have good reputations – except that classes can be very large. Top is highly rated for children's lessons – and a 2005 reporter said, 'All our children

Across the valley from the ski slopes the Wilder Kaiser is a dramatic backdrop →

SNOWPIX.COM / CHRIS GILL

had a great time in different classes with Top, who made sure they were in English-only speaking groups. It was a very busy week but only our youngest was in the maximum class size of 12.' As well as the main schools there are mountaineering schools that organise tours in the Wilder Kaiser and the Kitzbühel mountains.

Facilities for children Ellmau is an attractive resort for families, described by a regular visitor as 'so child-friendly'. Top ski school is praised (see Schools). Kindergarten facilities seem to be satisfactory and include fun ideas such as a mini train to the lifts. Kinderland has its own fun-park and play areas. But we have had no recent reports.

STAYING THERE

How to go Ellmau is essentially a hotel and pension resort, though there are apartments that can be booked locally. **Hotels** The Bär (2395) is an elegant, relaxed Relais & Châteaux chalet, but twice the price of any other hotel. 'Very friendly and welcoming, wonderful food, reasonably priced house wine and a very good wellness centre,' wrote a 2005 reporter. 'Luxury without pretensions,' said another. The Hochfilzer (2501) is central, well equipped (with outdoor hot-tub) and popular with reporters (as is the simpler Pension Claudia, which it owns – use of hotel facilities allowed). Kaiserblick (2230), with good spa facilities and right by the piste, is recommended by a regular visitor who went with six families including 12 children. A 2006 reporter rates the Kaiserhof (2022) as 'very comfortable, friendly and had amazing food'. **Self-catering** There is a wide variety. The Landhof apartments continue to impress – 'spacious, immaculately

clean, well equipped' – with pool, sauna and steam room. A regular reporter rates the supermarket on the way out of town towards Going as 'excellent'.
Eating out The jolly Gasthof Lobewein is a splendid central chalet, with cheerful service in countless rooms and excellent food. The Cantina Bar has 'surprisingly good Mexican food', says a 2006 visitor.
Après-ski Cafes Kaiserstüberl and Bettina are good for coffee and cakes. Memory (which has internet facilities) is the early-evening riotous party pub. Pub 66 and Ötzi have regular events such as karaoke and 'erotic dancers'. The Ellermauer Alm at the Going end is 'superb fun'. Tour op reps organise events like bowling, sleigh rides, Tirolean folklore and tubing. There's an Instructors' Ball and ski displays with 'a party atmosphere' each week, and the toboggan run from the Astberg lift is recommended.
Off the slopes The KaiserBad leisure centre is good. There are many excursions available, including Salzburg and Vitipeno. Valley walks are spoiled by the busy main road. Heading up to Hartkaiser to relax on the terrace 'was a highlight for our non-skiers', writes a reporter.

Going 775m/2,540ft

Going is a tiny, attractively rustic village, ideal for families looking for a quiet time. It is well placed for the limited but quiet slopes of the Astberg and for the vast area of nursery slopes between here and Ellmau. Prices are low, but it's not an ideal base for covering the whole of the Ski Welt on the cheap unless you have a car for quick access to Scheffau and Söll. The Lanzenhof (2428) is a cosy central pension doing excellent traditional food in its woody dining rooms.

Ellmau

Hintertux/Tux valley

Small, unspoiled, traditional villages, high snow-sure glacier slopes and lots of other places down the valley covered by the lift pass

COSTS

① ② ③ ④ ⑤ ⑥

RATINGS

The slopes

Fast lifts	★★★
Snow	★★★★★
Extent	★★
Expert	★★★
Intermediate	★★★
Beginner	★★
Convenience	★★
Queues	★★★
Mountain restaurants	★★

The rest

Scenery	★★★
Resort charm	★★★
Off-slope	★

NEWS

The mid-mountain restaurant at Sommeralm was rebuilt for 2005/06.

Snowmaking was installed on the crucial link from Rastkogel to Eggalm and on other pistes in both areas. More snowmaking is planned for 2006/07 between Tuxer Joch and Sommerbergalm in the glacier area.

A short rope tow now gives access to the top station of the jumbo cable-car that forms the link between Rastkogel and Mayrhofen's slopes – so skiers no longer face a climb to the cable-car if they don't want to ski the often bumpy red run down.

➕ Hintertux has one of the best glaciers in the world, open summer as well as winter, with some great runs for intermediates and experts on guaranteed good snow

➕ Massive investment in new lifts has linked Lanersbach to Mayrhofen

➕ Some excellent off-piste opportunities

➕ A choice of quiet, unspoiled, traditional villages to stay in

➖ Lanersbach and Hintertux are a bus-ride apart

➖ Not for those who want a huge choice of shops and throbbing nightlife on their doorstep

➖ Not ideal for beginners or timid intermediates, with few easy runs to valley level

➖ Glacier can be cold and bleak in midwinter, and there are lots of T-bars and slow chairs

The Tux valley has always had its attractions, chief among them the Hintertux glacier, which arguably has the most challenging and interesting runs of any lift-served Alpine glacier. For guaranteed good snow, Hintertux is simply one of the best places to go. But the valley acquired much broader appeal in 2001 when the quieter, friendlier, non-glacial slopes above Lanersbach and its nearby twin, Vorderlanersbach were linked by fast new lifts with those above Mayrhofen and Finkenberg, down in the Zillertal. Together, they form a fair-sized circuit. With the glacier only 15 to 20 minutes away by bus, these quiet, unspoiled, traditional villages are attractive bases – for many people, more attractive than either Hintertux or Mayrhofen (covered in its own chapter).

The Tux valley, an extension of Mayrhofen's Zillertal, has a variety of small villages, linked by regular free ski-buses. A cheap (50c) night-bus also runs until 2am. Vorderlanersbach is the first village you come to, and Lanersbach is just beyond it. Both are small, traditional places with rustic buildings, narrow roads and paths, their quiet centres bypassed by the main road.

Both have gondola links into the local slopes; the Vorderlanersbach sector links with the Penken-Horberg slopes above Mayrhofen – see separate chapter. Hintertux is 15 minutes by bus beyond Lanersbach, at the head of the valley, a few minutes from the glacier lifts. There is also accommodation in Juns and Madseit.

There are some good rustic restaurants and bars and a few places along the valley with discos or live music. But nightlife tends to be quieter than in many bigger Austrian resorts.

The Tux valley and Mayrhofen lifts now form what is called the Ski and Glacier World Zillertal 3000. Lift passes for four days or more also cover the countless resorts in the rest of the Ziller valley.

Hintertux 1500m/4,920ft

THE RESORT
Tiny Hintertux is set at the end of the Tux valley. It is little more than a small collection of hotels and guest houses; there is another, smaller group of hotels near the lifts, which lie a 15-minute walk away from the village, across a car park that fills with day-visitors' cars and coaches, especially when snow is poor in lower resorts.

THE MOUNTAINS
Hintertux's slopes are fairly extensive and, for a glacier, surprisingly challenging. The glacier is one of the best in the world, with varied terrain that attracts national ski teams for summer training.
Slopes A series of three speedy gondolas takes you up from the base to the top of the glacier (vertical rise 1750m/5,740ft) in under 20 minutes. The first stage is an eight-seater up to Sommerbergalm, while the second and third stages (linked by a short slope at Tuxer Ferner Haus) have 24-person cabins. On the two lower stages there is a parallel smaller gondola which is pressed into service to meet demand

KEY FACTS

Resort	1500m
	4,920ft

Ski and Glacier World Zillertal 3000

Slopes	630-3250m
	2,070-10,660ft
Lifts	62
Pistes	225km
	140 miles
Blue	26%
Red	60%
Black	14%
Snowmaking	93km
	58 miles

Hintertux only

Slopes	1500-3250m
	4,920-10,660ft
Lifts	21
Pistes	86km
	53 miles

For Ziller valley

Slopes	630-3250m
	2,070-10,660ft
Lifts	177
Pistes	620km
	385 miles

LIFT PASSES

Zillertaler Superskipass

Prices in €

Age	1-day	6-day
under 15	17	84
15 to 18	27	134
over 19	35	168

Free under 6
Senior no deals
Beginner no deals

Notes

1-, 2- or 3-day passes cover Hintertux glacier, Eggalm, Rastkogel and Penken areas; 4-day and over passes include all Ziller valley lifts, ski-bus and railway. Part-day and pedestrian passes available.

OUR WEBSITE

Go to our website at wtss.co.uk for resort news, links to resort sites, a build-your-own resort shortlist system and reader forums.

at peak times. From Sommerbergalm, a fast quad chair serves the slopes below Tuxer Joch; from the top of this sector, an excellent secluded off-piste run goes down to the base station. Between the top of the glacier and Tuxer Ferner Haus there are further chairs and drag-lifts to play on and links across to another 1000m/3,300ft-vertical chain of lifts below Grosser Kaserer on the west. Behind Gefrorene Wand is the area's one sunny piste, served by a triple chair. Descent to the valley involves a short ascent to Sommerbergalm on the way, now achieved by a six-seater chair-lift.

Terrain-parks Europe's highest World Cup half-pipe is on the glacier (a popular hang-out throughout the summer), and there is a terrain-park.

Snow reliability Snow does not come more reliable than this. Even off the glacier, the other slopes are high and face north, making for very reliable snow-cover. The runs from Tuxer Ferner Haus down to Sommerbergalm have snowmaking as well and more is planned for 2006/07 between Tuxer Joch and Sommerbergalm.

Experts There is more to amuse experts here than on any other glacier, with a couple of serious black runs at

glacier level and steep slopes and ungroomed ski routes beneath. A lot of the off-piste is little used and one reporter said, 'We found untracked snow not far from the lifts two weeks after the last snowfall.'

Intermediates The area particularly suits good or aggressive intermediates. The long runs down from Gefrorene Wand and Kaserer are fun. And there is a pleasant, tree-lined ski route to the valley from Sommerbergalm and another from Tuxer Joch. Moderate intermediates will love the glacier.

Beginners There is a nursery slope at valley level, but the glacier isn't the ideal place to progress to.

Snowboarding There are some great off-piste opportunities, but boarders complain about the number of T-bars.

Cross-country See the Lanersbach information later in the chapter.

Queues There used to be huge queues at Hintertux when snow was poor elsewhere. Improved lifts have largely solved this problem. But the main runs can get crowded, and then it is best to head over to the quieter Kaserer lifts and runs.

Mountain restaurants The mountain restaurants tend to get very crowded and the big self-service places lack

Hintertux

SCHOOLS

Hintertux/Madseit
t 87755

Happy Skiing
t 87240

Luggis
t 86808

Tux 3000
t 87747

Classes
(Hintertux prices)
6 days (2hr am and
pm) €129

Private lessons
€48 for 1hr; each
additional person €15

CHILDREN

Guest kindergarten
(in Tux Tourist
Association building,
Lanersbach)
t 872240
Ages 1 to 3

Ski school
All the ski schools run
children's classes.
Hintertux school takes
children from 10am to
3pm (6 days including
lunch €186).

GETTING THERE

Air Salzburg
200km/124 miles
(3½hr); Munich
176km/109 miles
(3hr); Innsbruck
88km/55 miles
(1½hr).

Rail Local line to
Mayrhofen; regular
buses from station.

charm – 'rather soulless except for
Tuxerjochhaus,' as one visitor said. The
90-year-old Spannagelhaus is another
exception ('fun atmosphere,' says a
2006 reporter), and there are great
views from Gletscherhütte, at the top.
The rebuilt restaurant at
Sommerbergalm opened for 2005/06
and a reporter described it as
'excellent, with a great choice of food'.
Schools and guides There are now four
schools, which serve all the resorts in
Tux, but we lack reports on them. The
newest, Tux 3000, has special guiding,
touring and race-training programmes.
Facilities for children Most of the ski
schools run classes for children aged 4
to 14 and lunch is provided.

STAYING THERE

How to go Most hotels are large and
comfortable and have spa facilities, but
there are also more modest pensions.
Hotels Close to the lifts are the 4-star
Vierjahreszeiten (8525) and
Neuhintertux (8580), in which a 2005
reporter enjoyed the 'large and modern
spa' and 'unusually good and plentiful'
fare. Another relished the 'comfort and
hospitality' of the 4-star Alpenhof
(8550). We have enjoyed staying in the
3-star Hintertuxerhof (85300); good
food, sauna and steam room. Pensions
Kössler (87490) and Willeiter (87492)
are in the heart of the village.
Self-catering There are plenty of
apartments.
Eating out Restaurants are mainly
hotel-based. The Vierjahreszeiten is
pleasant and informal.
Après-ski There can be a lively après-
ski scene both at mid-mountain
(Sommerbergalm) and at the base; the
'very lively' Hohenhaus Tenne has
several different bars, the Rindererhof
has a popular tea dance, and there are
a couple of local bars. The cheap (50
cents) night-bus gets you to and from
the other villages until 2am, but
Hintertux is not the place for keen
clubbers.
Off the slopes The spa facilities are
excellent, including a thermal indoor
pool, but there are many more options
in Mayrhofen.

Lanersbach 1300m/4,270ft

Lanersbach and neighbouring
Vorderlanersbach have long been
attractive bases for anyone planning to
explore the multiple resorts of the
Zillertal and the higher Tuxertal. With

the construction of direct links,
via Rastkogel, with Mayrhofen's
slopes their attractions are now
greatly reinforced.

THE RESORT
Lanersbach is an attractive, spacious,
traditional village largely unspoiled by
the busy road up to Hintertux that
passes the main lift. Happily, the quiet
centre near the pretty church is
bypassed by the road, yet is within
walking distance of the gondola up to
Eggalm. The village is small and
delightfully uncommercialised, but it
has all you need in a resort. And prices
are relatively low. Vorderlanersbach is
even smaller, with a gondola up to the
Rastkogel area.

THE MOUNTAINS
Slopes The slopes of Eggalm, accessed
by the gondola from Lanersbach, offer
a small network of pleasantly varied,
intermediate pistes, usually delightfully
quiet. You can descend on red or blue
runs back to the village or to
Vorderlanersbach, where a gondola
goes up to the higher, open Rastkogel
slopes; here, two fast chair-lifts – one
a covered eight-seater – serve some
very enjoyable long red and blue runs
and link with Mayrhofen's slopes. The
linking run is classified red but can get
very mogulled and many people opt to
ride the 150-person cable-car down; a
short rope-tow now cuts out the need
to hike up to the top station. The run
back from Rastkogel to Eggalm is
marked red but is really quite easy and
is now served by snowmaking. The
alternative is to ride the gondola down
to Vorderlanersbach (there are no
pistes to the village) and catch the bus
to Lanersbach.
Terrain-parks The Mayrhofen and
Hintertux pipes and parks are easily
accessed.
Snow reliability Snow conditions are
usually good, at least in early season;
by Austrian standards; these are high
slopes and snowmaking was increased
on both the Eggalm and the Rastkogel
areas for 2005/06. But Rastkogel is
basically south-facing, so snow quality
can suffer.
Experts There are no pistes to
challenge experts, but there is a fine
off-piste route starting a short walk
from the top of the Eggalm slopes and
finishing at the village.
Intermediates The slopes suit
intermediates best – especially now

↑ This excellent glacier not only has the best snow for miles around most of the winter but offers lots of summer fun too

TVB TUX

ACTIVITIES

Indoor Bowling, tennis, squash, saunas, fitness rooms and pools in hotels open to public

Outdoor Ice rink, curling, winter hiking trails, paragliding, tobogganing, sleigh rides, cave excursion, snow-shoe tours

Phone numbers
From elsewhere in Austria add the prefix 05287.
From abroad use the prefix +43 5287.

TOURIST OFFICE

Tux
t 8506
info@tux.at
www.tux.at

that they are linked in to Mayrhofen's Penken slopes.

Beginners Both areas have nursery slopes (as do Madseit and Juns) but there are few ideal progression slopes – most of the easy runs are on the higher lifts of the Rastkogel sector.

Snowboarding The area isn't great for novices – there are drag-lifts dotted around, some in key places.

Cross-country There are 14km/9 miles of cross-country trails, alongside the Tux creek, between Madseit and Vorderlanersbach, and a 6km/4-mile skating track in Juns/Madseit.

Queues We have no reports of any problems. Indeed, Egglam can be delightfully quiet.

Mountain restaurants There's no shortage but most, though fairly rustic, are self-service with simple food; the small Lattenalm on Egglam is a table-service exception with a terrace that has splendid views of the Tux glacier.

Schools and guides There are four schools in the valley, but we lack recent reports on them.

Facilities for children The non-ski nursery takes children aged from one to three, and most of the schools take children from four years upwards. There's a new terrain-park, including a snow-tyre carousel and a bob-run, on the glacier.

STAYING THERE

How to go Lanersbach and Vorderlanersbach are essentially hotel-based resorts.

Hotels The Lanersbacherof (87256) is a good 4-star with pool, sauna, steam and hot-tub close to the lifts ('Very friendly, with good gourmet menu and great wine cellar,' says a 2005/06 season visitor), but it is also on the main road. The cheaper 3-star Pinzger (87541) and Alpengruss (87293) are similarly situated. In Vorderlanersbach the 3-star Kirchlerhof (8560) is 'really friendly, with comfortable rooms and excellent food', says a regular visitor.

Self-catering Quite a lot of apartments are available.

Eating out Restaurants are mainly hotel-based, busy, and geared to serving dinner early.

Après-ski Nightlife is generally quiet by Austrian standards, which suits us. We enjoyed the jolly Hühnerstall in Lanersbach (an old wooden building with traditional Austrian music). There is a disco or two.

Off the slopes Off-slope facilities are fairly good considering the size of the resorts. Some hotels have pools, hot-tubs and fitness rooms open to non-residents. There is a tennis centre in Vorderlanersbach which also has squash and bowling. Innsbruck and Salzburg are possible excursions.

Hochkönig

An unusual combination: small unspoiled villages and a large uncrowded ski area virtually unknown on the British market

COSTS

① ② ③ ④ ⑤ ⑥

RATINGS

The slopes
Fast lifts	**
Snow	***
Extent	***
Expert	**
Intermediate	****
Beginner	***
Convenience	**
Queues	****
Mountain restaurants	***

The rest
Scenery	***
Resort charm	***
Off-slope	***

NEWS

Two drag-lifts on Aberg were replaced by a six-pack for 2005/06. And a new 4-star hotel, Alpine Wellness Hotel Haller (7723), is due to open in Maria Alm for 2006/07.

KEY FACTS

Resorts	800-1070m
	2,620-3,510ft
Slopes	800-2000m
	2,620-6,560ft
Lifts	37
Pistes	150km
	93 miles
Blue	35%
Red	55%
Black	10%
Snowmaking	90km
	56 miles

- ➕ Traditional quiet villages
- ➕ Plenty of uncrowded beginner and intermediate terrain
- ➕ Friendly locals

- ➖ Little for experts except ski routes and off-piste
- ➖ Buses needed in parts and there are some slow chairs and T-bars

The picturesque Salzburgerland villages of Maria Alm, Hintermoos, Hinterthal, Dienten and Mühlbach combine to provide a sizeable ski area, best suited to intermediates and beginners. The lift system is not completely linked, so you'll have to drive or catch the ski buses to explore it all. The area is largely unknown on the British market and no big tour operators go there.

THE RESORT

Maria Alm, though small, is one of the two largest villages; it's a pretty place with a splendid old church boasting the highest spire in Salzburgerland. The peaks of the Selbhorn and Schonfeldspitze provide a dramatic backcloth. Hinterthal, the next real village up the valley, is even smaller – little more than a few 4-star hotels and chalets (some owned by the rich and famous) and a couple of ski shops and bars; it has some of the best mountain views in the region. Further up the road and over a pass is Dienten, a tiny, picturesque village with a handful of traditional hotels and guest houses. Mühlbach, at the eastern end of the ski area, is a similar size to Maria Alm and, unlike the other villages which are set off the main road, sprawls along it for quite a distance. The spectacular Hochkönig (which means 'High King') massif, from which the region gets its name, overlooks the village and can be seen from many of the slopes but is not part of the ski area.

THE MOUNTAIN

There are 150km/93 miles of pistes, on a par with well-known names such as Kitzbühel and Mayrhofen.

Slopes The main slopes spread along several small mountains running east along the valley from Maria Alm to Mühlbach. Many of the runs are north-facing and have splendid views over to the high peaks opposite. Just to the west of Maria Alm is the tiny little area of Hinterreit, where the British ski team trains. Maria Alm has its own small Natrun ski area, served by what was the world's first chondola (a mix of chairs and gondolas). An ungroomed ski route leads off the back to the main local Aberg-Langeck mountain and an eight-seat gondola; but most people catch the bus round to Aberg (you have to catch it back, too). You also need a bus from Aberg to the rest of the main ski area, starting at Hinterthal – but you can get back from Hinterthal to Aberg along a gentle track with some flat/uphill sections. From Hinterthal you can go via Dienten

Maria Alm is a pretty village and its church has the highest spire in Salzburgerland ➔

Phone numbers
From elsewhere in Austria add the prefix 06584 (Maria Alm and Hinterthal), 06461 (Dienten), 06467 (Mühlbach). From abroad use the prefix +43 and omit the initial '0'.

TOURIST OFFICES

region@hochkoenig.at
www.hochkoenig.at
Maria Alm
t 7816
Dienten
t 263
Mühlbach
t 7235

to Mühlbach (where the gondola back up is a bus-ride from the village centre). The piste map is poor – it would benefit from more detail and we understand it may be redesigned.
Terrain-parks Of the five terrain-parks, the biggest and best is on Aberg.
Snow reliability Although low altitude, the region is in a snow pocket, so tends to have good conditions for its height (and there was no shortage of snow on our April 2006 visit). Some 60% of the pistes have snowmaking.
Experts There are several ungroomed ski routes, the best of which is in a huge off-piste bowl behind the Aberg ridge. It is not well marked and having a guide is useful; a local says 'there are lots of ways in and it's better than Vail's back bowls'. With a guide you can explore other excellent off-piste too, such as in the trees off Aberg and on Schneeberg. There's one genuinely steep black piste on Aberg.
Intermediates The area between Hinterthal and Mühlbach is best for adventurous intermediates, with mainly challenging red runs. And you really get a feeling of travelling around between different valleys here. There are a few easy cruising blue runs in the centre of this area, served by fast chairs, and on Aberg.
Beginners All the villages have good nursery slopes, and the runs at the foot of the Aberg and by Hinterthal village are good progression runs.
Cross-country There are over 40km/25 miles of prepared tracks.
Queues Not usually a problem.
Mountain restaurants There are 37, including some nice little huts. We liked Griessbachhütte (an isolated hut with very simple food and good views

on Aberg's ski route); we also had good table-service Bauerngröstl at Tiergartenalm below Sunnhütte. A local also recommends the Tischlerhütte (Aberg), the Alm Bar (Hinterthal – good spare ribs) and Almhäust (just above Dienten – sun deck and umbrella bar).
Schools and guides All four main villages have schools, and many instructors speak good English.
Facilities for children The kindergartens at all the main base areas take children from the age of two. The ski schools take them from four.

STAYING THERE

How to go No big tour ops come here.
Hotels There are plenty of good hotels with spa and pool facilities. The Haus Salzburg (23497) in Hinterthal is a chalet-hotel run by an English couple (Carl is a ski instructor who also guides his guests once a week on the Hinterthal-Mühlbach 'safari').
Eating out The Ubergossene Alm just outside Dienten and the restaurant in the hotel Thalerhof in Maria Alm have good menus. Haus Salzburg (see Hotels) serves international rather than traditional Austrian food.
Après-ski Maria Alm is by far the most animated village. The Dengl Alm gets packed and has zither music, dancing and jolly bar staff in lederhosen. Almer Tenne has live music and a disco. Orgler Keller and Chili's are good for a quieter time. The Alm Bar in Hinterthal can be lively and opens till late, as does the Haus Salzburg bar. Saustall is a decent 'pub' in Mühlbach.
Off the slopes Maria Alm has curling, tobogganing, bowling, sleigh rides, swimming and nice walks.

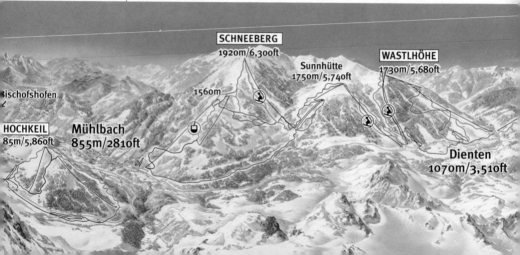

Your winter is here.

The Winterkingdom of Hochkönig — Part of Austria's largest ski paradise Ski amadé

Ski amadé is made up of five of Austria's leading ski regions, working in close harmony to bring you arguably the biggest and best ski experience in Austria! One lift pass provides access to over 860 km of skiing, served by 270 modern lifts. Ski amadé is the only region offering so much choice, for every level of ability – and we even guarantee the snow!

As you would expect from a top-class resort a network of ski services, rental and ski schools caters for every need. You will find all information about news & events, snow reports, live cams and much more on the website **www.hochkoenig.at** See you next winter!

Magical experience in Hochkönigs Winterreich
Maria Alm · Dienten · Mühlbach

LIVE DABEI
Ski **amade**
www.skiamade.com

HOCHKÖNIGs
WINTERREICH

ASTLHÖHE
om/5,68oft

ABERG-LANGECK
2000m/6,56oft

Gabühel
1635m/5,36oft

Hintermoos

HINTERREIT

Saalfelden

Dienten
1070m/3,51oft

HOCHMAIS

NATRUN
1100m

Maria Alm
800m/2,62oft

Hinterthal

www.gfb.at©2006

Innsbruck

Stay in a small, historic, cultured city and visit a different ski area every day, including one of Austria's best glacier areas

COSTS

① ② ③ ④ ⑤ ⑥

KEY FACTS

Resort	575m
	1,890ft
Slopes	800-3210m
	2,620-10,530ft
Lifts	75
Pistes	270km
	168 miles
Blue	32%
Red	49%
Black	19%
Snowmaking	53km
	33 miles

NEWS

Last season, the Mutters ski area re-opened after several years of closure – with three new lifts (an eight-seat gondola, a fast quad chair and a drag). A new fast quad also opened on the Patscherkofel slopes above Igls. In Oberperfuss, snowmaking was installed on the blue run from Stiglreith at mid-mountain down to the valley, and the whole of the Schlick 2000 area now has snowmaking.

For 2006/07, more snowmaking is planned in Oberperfuss from Stiglreith to Rangger Köpfl.

146

Innsbruck is not a ski resort in the usual sense. It is an historic university city of 138,000 inhabitants, with a vibrant cultural life, and is a major tourist destination in summer. The city has twice hosted the Olympic Winter Games, and is surrounded by little resorts that share a lift pass and are accessible by efficient bus services. Among them is a glacier that is one of best in the world – the Stubaier Gletscher (see the separate chapter on the Stubai valley). In 2005 the lift pass coverage was expanded by the addition of little Oberperfuss and the more distant Kühtai – at 2020m/6,630ft, one of Austria's highest resorts. Meanwhile, lower down, the slopes above Mutters finally reopened last season with three new lifts – an eight-seat gondola, a fast quad and a drag.

The Inn valley is a broad, flat-bottomed trench here, but Innsbruck manages to fill it from side to side. It is a sizeable city and, as you would expect from its Olympic background, it has an excellent range of winter sports facilities, as well as a captivating car-free medieval core. It has smart, modern, shopping areas, trendy bars and restaurants, museums (including, of course, one devoted to the Olympics), concert halls, theatres, a zoo and other attractions that you might seek out on a summer holiday, but normally wouldn't expect to find when going skiing.

Winter diversions off the slopes include 117km/73 miles of cross-country trails, some at valley level but others appreciably above it; curling and skating at the Olympic centre; several toboggan runs totalling 95km/59 miles, the longest (above Birgitz) an impressive 11km/7 miles and 1060m/3,480ft vertical; and rides on a four-man bob at Igls.

Not the least of the attractions of staying in such a place is that you don't pay ski resort prices for anything.

There are hotels, inns and B&Bs of every standard and style, with 3-star and 4-star hotels forming the nucleus. Among the more distinctive hotels are the grand 5-star Europa Tyrol (59310), the ancient 4-star Goldener Adler (571111) and the 3-star Weisses Kreuz (59479) in the central pedestrian zone, and the 4-star art nouveau Best Western Neue Post (59476).

As well as traditional Austrian restaurants there are several Italians, plus a smattering of more exotic alternatives from Mexican to Japanese.

There is an impressive 1400m/4,600ft vertical of slopes on the south-facing slopes of **Nordpark-Seegrube**. The focus of the slopes here is at Seegrube and is reached by cable-car (rebuilt for 2006/07) rising 1050m/3,450ft from Hungerburg on the outskirts of the city. Although there are red runs to the valley, the snow is not reliable. You go up here expecting to ski the red runs of 370m/1,210ft vertical below Seegrube, served by a chair-lift. A further stage of the cable-car rises 350m/1,150ft vertical to access the Karinne ski route, which is said to be very steep. If you ski it with a guide you can collect a T-shirt and certificate to prove it.

GLUNGEZER 2305m

2245m

Tulfes 920m

Hall in Tirol

↑ Innsbruck's old buildings look even more impressive because of the stunning mountain backdrop
INNSBRUCK TOURISMUS

OUR WEBSITE

Go to our website at wtss.co.uk for resort news, links to resort sites, a build-your-own resort shortlist system and reader forums.

facing slopes. A chair-lift from the bottom serves red and blue runs of 600m/1,970ft vertical. This leads to a drag up to the tree line serving a red run of 500m/1,640ft vertical. And this in turn leads to a drag and a chair-lift serving open red runs from the top at 2305m/7,560ft – almost 1400m/4,600ft above the village.

A major road runs southwards from Innsbruck over the Brenner pass to Italy – opening up the possibility of excursions to resorts in the Dolomites.

But for visitors, if not for residents, skiing usually means heading for the opposite side of the Inn trench.

The standard Innsbruck lift pass covers the lifts in all the resorts dealt with here, plus the slopes of Schlick 2000 above Fulpmes (see the Stubai valley chapter later in the book) and Glungezer above Tulfes.

Free ski-bus services run to and from all the lift-pass-covered areas, but only at the beginning and end of the day. A car makes life more convenient, especially if you are staying outside downtown Innsbruck.

There are terrain-parks at Seegrube, Axamer Lizum, the Stubaier Gletscher, Kühtai and Oberperfuss.

The runs on Glungezer are on north-

IGLS 900m/2,950ft
Igls seems almost a suburb of Innsbruck – the city trams run out to the village – but it is a small resort in its own right. Its famous downhill race course is an excellent piste.
The village of Igls is small and quiet, with not much in the way of diversions apart from the beautiful walks, an artificial ice rink, the Olympic bob run and the tea shops. You can stay in Igls, and a few UK operators sell packages there. Most hotels are small and in the centre of the village, a bit of a walk from the cable-car station. An exception is the family-run 4-star Sporthotel (377241), which occupies the prime site between the tram and the cable-car stations: 'Excellent facilities, good food and nice bar,' says a reporter.

Innsbruck

147

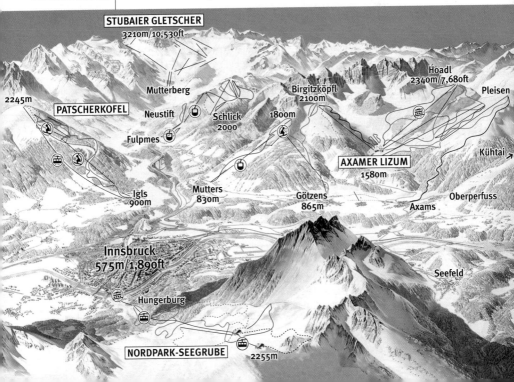

STUBAIER GLETSCHER
3210m/10,530ft

Hoadl
2340m/7,680ft

Pleisen

2245m

Mutterberg

Birgitzköpfl
2100m

PATSCHERKOFEL

Neustift

Schlick
2000

1800m

Kühtai

Fulpmes

AXAMER LIZUM
1580m

Oberperfuss

Igls
900m

Mutters
830m

Götzens
865m

Axams

Innsbruck
575m/1,890ft

Seefeld

Hungerburg

NORDPARK-SEEGRUBE
2255m

↑ The Stubai is one of the best glacier areas in the world – open summer and winter

TOURISM ASSOCIATION NEUSTIFT

LIFT PASSES

Innsbruck Gletscher Skipass

Prices in €

Age	1-day	6-day
under 15	12	96
15 to 18	19	128
19 to 59	24	160
over 60	19	128

Free under 7 (one-day pass only)

Beginner no deals

Alternative passes
Super-Skipass also covers days in the Arlberg (St Anton) and Kitzbühel. Day passes for individual areas available.

Phone numbers
Calling long-distance
Add the prefix given below for each resort. When calling from abroad use the country code 43 and omit the initial '0'.

Innsbruck, Igls, Mutters
0512

Axamer Lizum
05234

Oberperfuss
05232

Kühtai
05239

The skiing on Patscherkofel is very limited and revolves around the excellent, varied, long red run that formed the men's downhill course in 1976, when Franz Klammer took ski racing (and the Olympic gold medal) by storm. There is a blue-run variation on this run, but few other pistes. A cable-car rises 1050m/3,450ft from the village (and you can take it down if the lower runs are poor or shut). At the top, a chair rises a further 275m/900ft to the summit offering wonderful views over Innsbruck and ski routes back down. Two fast quads and a couple of drags serve the other slopes. There is a short beginner lift at village level, and another a short bus-ride up the hill. We have received mixed reports on the grooming of the trails.

Après-ski is quiet. The resort suits families but others might prefer to stay in Innsbruck.

STUBAIER GLETSCHER
The Stubaier Gletscher is one of the best glacier ski and snowboard areas in the world; it is open in summer as well as in winter. It is covered in more detail in the Stubai valley chapter later in the book.
The glacier is accessed by two alternative two-stage gondolas from the huge car park at Mutterberg. A third gondola takes you right to the top of the slopes.

On the glacier a variety of chair- and drag-lifts (including three six-person chairs) allow fabulous high altitude cruising on blue and red runs, which normally have excellent snow on slopes between 3200m and 2300m (10,500ft and 7,550ft). A lovely 10km/ 6 mile ungroomed ski route through a deserted bowl takes you down to the valley – or, if you start at the top, a descent of about 14km/9 miles and 1450m/4,760ft vertical is possible.

AXAMER LIZUM 1580m/5,180ft
The mountain outpost of the Inn-side village of Axams is a simple ski station and nothing more, but it does have some good slopes and reliable snow conditions – and, as a reporter says, 'You feel as if you are in a wilderness.'
Axamer Lizum could scarcely offer a sharper contrast to Igls. It offers much more varied slopes and a network of lifts, with the base station at a much higher altitude. The slopes here hosted all the Olympic Alpine events in 1976 except the men's downhill, and this is the standard local venue for weekends – hence the huge car park, which is the most prominent feature of the 'resort'.

The main slopes on Hoadl and Pleisen are blues and reds, almost entirely above the trees but otherwise nicely varied, and there is scope to 'play in gullies and bumps, as well as true off-piste', says a reporter. The vertical of the main east-facing slopes above the main lift station is 'only' 700m/2,300ft, but for good skiers at least there is the possibility (given good snow conditions) of a 1300m/ 4,260ft descent at the end of the day from Pleisen to the outskirts of Axams – an easy 6.5km/4 mile black. On the opposite side of the valley, a chair-lift serves a fairly easy black slope. Beyond it are the slopes of Mutters, which re-opened last season with three new lifts after being closed since 2001; there are plans to link the Axamer and Mutters slopes but there was no timescale for this when we went to press. Snowmaking now covers 70 per cent of the slopes and there is a new large restaurant with panoramic views on Hoadl. There are two good nursery lifts, and two ski schools.

You can stay up here – there is a 4-star hotel, the Lizumerhof (68244) at the lift base – 'nice rooms and decent modern Austrian cuisine' – and there are a couple of 3-stars, too. But there's

TOURIST OFFICES

Innsbruck
t 59850
office@innsbruck.info
www.innsbruck.info

Tulfes
t 78324
info@tulfes.at
www.tulfes.at

Igls
t 377101
igls@innsbruck.info
www.tiscover.com/igls

Fulpmes
t 62235
info@stubai.at
www.tiscover.com/
fulpmes

Neustift
t 2228
info@stubai.at
www.stubai.at

Axamer Lizum
t 68178
axams@innsbruck.info
www.tiscover.com/
axams

Mutters
t 548410
mutters@innsbruck.
info
www.tiscover.com/
mutters

Oberperfuss
t 81489
oberperfuss@
innsbruck.info

Kühtai
t 5222
kuehtai@
innsbruck.info

TVB INNSBRUCK

Three new lifts meant
that Mutters' local
slopes opened again
last season after
being closed since
2001 ↓

little in the way of après-ski apart from a couple of bars – the Alm bar is the most atmospheric – and you have to eat in your hotel or go to Axams.

There is also accommodation not far away at lower altitude in Axams – including six 3-star hotels – and in other nearby villages such as Götzens (one 4-star hotel, two 3-star gasthofs) and Birgitz (two 3-star hotels).

MUTTERS 830m/2,720ft
Almost as close to Innsbruck as Igls, Mutters is a charming rustic village at the foot of long slopes of 900m/2,950ft vertical. Its slopes were re-opened last season, served by three new lifts after being closed since 2001.
The gentle slopes suit beginners and families best. A new eight-seat gondola from the village serves a long blue run and an equally long toboggan run. Above that a new high-speed quad takes you to the summit at 1800m/5,900ft and serves a red run. There's also a T-bar which, along with the top chair, links to a long red run down to Götzens further along the valley.

There are plans to link the slopes with those of Axamer Lizum. But there was no definite timescale for this when we went to press.

The half-dozen hotels in the Mutters include 3-stars and 4-stars. There is a lively après-ski scene and great off-slope facilities including tennis courts, saunas, skating and curling.

OBERPERFUSS 815m/2,675ft
No, we hadn't heard of it, either – until the lifts on its local hill, Rangger Köpfl, were brought into the fold of the Innsbruck area lift pass.
The hill is a very limited one, with five lifts in a largely linear arrangement serving 17km/11 miles of easy-intermediate slopes – but an

impressive vertical of 1200m/3,940ft. For 2005/06 snowmaking was installed on the blue run from Stiglreith at 1400m/4,590ft at mid-mountain down to the valley and for 2006/07 there will be more snowmaking from Stiglreith to Rangger Köpfl. The village is small but self-sufficient, with most things you need (eg pharmacy, bakery) including a big 3-star hotel, the Krone (81465). It is prettily rustic, and targets the family market with the aid of a moving carpet lift on the nursery slopes. There is night skiing and tobogganing on Tuesdays and Fridays.

KÜHTAI 2020m/6,630ft
A collection of comfortable hotels spread along a high road pass 25km/16 miles west of Innsbruck – higher than equally snow-sure Obergurgl or Obertauern, but cheaper than either.
Glaciers apart, Kühtai's altitude means it must be one of Austria's most snow-sure resorts. That is its main attraction, given the limited nature of the village.

Six drags and three fast quad chairs serve red cruisers of 400m/1,310ft to 500m/1,640ft vertical on either side of the road, plus some token blue and black runs (which may be easier than the reds because they get less traffic). There is a good nursery slope, but no easy blues to graduate to. There's also a terrain-park with kickers and rails. The resort attracts families during school holidays (notably carnival) and crowds of day trippers on fine weekends – especially if lower resorts are short of snow – but is otherwise crowd-and queue-free. There are three mountain restaurants and two ski schools.

The village is quiet in the evening, but for its size has 'a reasonable selection of bars and restaurants', says a report – practically all in hotels. The 4-star hotels include the Jagdschloss (5201) – a much-developed old hunting lodge. A 2006 visitor recommends the 4-star Mooshaus (5207) – 'convenient for the slopes, excellent service and copious and delicious food'. The 3-star hotel Elisabeth (5240) has also been recommended – 'Very friendly, excellent food.'

Reporters say that English is not spoken everywhere – and there is little resort information in English, either on paper or on the resort web site.

There are several free postbuses from Innsbruck morning and afternoon, but the journey takes over an hour.

Ischgl

A unique combination: a typically cute Austrian village and high, snow-sure slopes typical of French purpose-built resorts

NEWS

For 2006/07 a new piste is planned for Samnaun – at the far left of our piste map. More snowmaking is planned for several runs at Samnaun, on the Palinkopf runs at Ischgl and at Galtür.

For 2005/06 a new table-service restaurant opened at the Pardorama complex at the top of the Pardatschgrat gondola. A new après-ski bar, the Mungaloch, was opened on Alp Trida. A new base station and shopping complex was built at the main access lift, the Silvrettabahn.

There are plans to expand the ski area to the right of our piste map with a new lift and runs in the next couple of years. There are also plans to link Kappl – a 15-minute bus-ride from Ischgl – with the Rendl area of St Anton. But no date for either of these has been announced.

- ＋ Charming old Tirolean village, expanded in sympathetic fashion
- ＋ High slopes with reliable snow
- ＋ Lots of good intermediate runs
- ＋ Superb modern lift system
- ＋ Three other nearby resorts to try
- ＋ Very lively après-ski

- ─ Not ideal for beginners or timid intermediates, for various reasons
- ─ Few seriously steep runs
- ─ Very little wooded terrain to give shelter in bad weather
- ─ Eurotrash-style après-ski – eg table dancing in plush 4-star hotels – and a lot of heavy drinking

For years we've been saying that Ischgl is unjustly neglected in Britain, mainly because of a shortage of package holidays to the resort, but that's now changing, with three major operators going there. Most reporters enthusiastically endorse our view that this is one of Austria's best. The lift system is particularly impressive: 62 per cent are fast lifts, putting the resort at the top of our fast lift league table. Unless cost is an obstacle or you insist on the woodland runs that are the Tirolean norm, put it on your Austrian shortlist.

Samnaun, over the Swiss border, is tour-op-free (as well as duty-free). But it's a charming, relaxed village, and for a party booking independently and including novices it makes a better base than Ischgl. Kappl, See and Galtür in the same valley as Ischgl are also worth considering for a quiet (and cheaper) time.

THE RESORT

Ischgl is a quite compact village tucked away on the Swiss border in the long, narrow Paznaun valley, south of St Anton; the ski area is shared with Swiss Samnaun. The wooded flanks of the valley rise steeply from the village, which gets almost no sun in early season.

The narrow main street plus a couple of side streets are traffic-free – the village is bypassed by the valley road up to Galtür – and at the west end of the pedestrian zone is the main access lift, the 24-person Silvrettabahn, up to the main mid-mountain focus of Idalp. Two other gondolas – one to Idalp, the other to Pardatschgrat, higher up – start close together on the eastern fringe of the village. An underground

moving walkway runs to these lifts from the heart of the village.

The buildings are practically all in traditional chalet style, and the place has a neat, prosperous air. There's a selection of lively bars and an excellent sports centre; shops are mainly confined to winter sports.

The underground walkway makes choice of location less important than it was, but the best spot, overall, is on or near the main street. Beware of accommodation across the bypass road, a long way from the lifts.

There are frequent ski-buses down the valley to Kappl and See and up it to Galtür, described at the end of this chapter. A car makes trips to St Anton viable. It's a very long taxi-ride from Samnaun, should you get stuck there.

THE MOUNTAINS

Ischgl is a fair-sized, relatively high, snow-sure area. Practically all the slopes are above the tree line, the main exception being the steep lower slopes above the village and a couple of short runs low in the Fimbatal.

You can leave skis and boots at Idalp and take the gondola down at the end of the day if you don't want to ski the steep valley runs with the homeward-bound crowds.

miles   0.5   1.0

N ↑

Pardatschgrat

Idalp

Idalp

km   1.0   2.0

THE SLOPES
Cross-border cruising

The sunny **Idalp** plateau, reached by two of the village gondolas, is the hub of the slopes. It can be very crowded, especially at ski school meeting time, lunchtime (lock up your skis!) and the end of the day. Pardatschgrat, reached by the third gondola, is about 300m/ 1,000ft higher. From here it's an easy run down to Idalp, where lifts radiate to a wide variety of mainly north-west- and west-facing runs. The main red runs from Idalp to Ischgl itself provoke regular complaints; neither is easy, conditions can be tricky, and beer-lubricated crowds don't help. The wide, quiet piste down the pretty Velilltal is much more pleasant. Quite a few people ride the gondolas down.

A short piste brings you from Idalp to the lifts serving the **Höllenkar** bowl, leading up to the area's south-western extremity and high point at **Palinkopf**. Runs from here lead down to the **Fimbatal**. On the Swiss side, the hub of activity is **Alp Trida**, surrounded by south- and east-facing runs with great views. From here a scenic red run goes down to Compatsch, where a short walk takes you to buses to Ravaisch – for the cable-car back – and Samnaun-Dorf. From Palinkopf there is a beautiful long run down an unspoiled valley to Samnaun-Dorf. It is not difficult, but it is excessively sunny in

parts and prone to closure because of avalanche risk. There is a long flat stretch at the end.

TERRAIN-PARKS
One of Europe's best

For freestylers the main park above Idalp, served by the Idjochbahn, is worth coming for alone. It is 750m/ 2,460ft long and well shaped and maintained. There is a box and four good rails dotted around, and several good intermediate and entry-level kickers and corner jumps. The main weakness is that there are no fluid lines allowing you to hit several obstacles in a row. The pipe is well maintained, although could be steeper. There is a smaller pipe in the separate kids' snowboard area. And there's another small park on the Swiss side.

SNOW RELIABILITY
Very good

All the slopes, except the runs back to the resort, are above 2000m/6,560ft and many of those on the Ischgl side are north-west-facing. So snow conditions are generally reliable and a 2006 reporter said, 'We've visited four years in a row and had excellent powder on three of them.' We also had non-stop fresh powder on our April 2006 four-day visit. There is snowmaking on various runs including several above Idalp, the two main

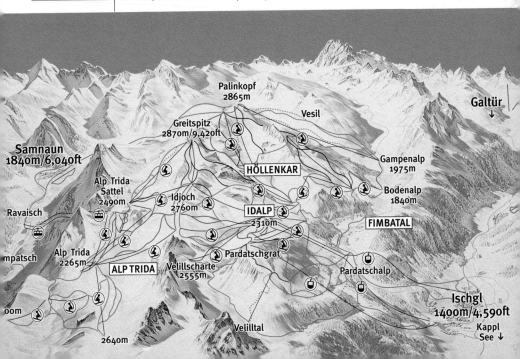

LIFT PASSES

VIP Skipass

Prices in €

Age	1-day	6-day
under 16	23	106
16 to 59	39	177
over 60	35	151

Free under 7

Beginner no deals

Notes
Covers all lifts in Ischgl and Samnaun and local buses. Half-day pass available. Passes for two days and over available only to those staying in Ischgl or Mathon on presenting a guest card. The lift pass office began taking credit cards last season.

Alternative passes
Regional pass covers Ischgl, Samnaun, Galtür, Kappl and See.

boarding

Ischgl has long been a popular spot for snowboarders, with its long, wide, well groomed slopes served by snowboard-friendly gondolas and high-speed chair-lifts. Although the off-piste terrain is less steep than in some other resorts, its above-the-tree-line, easily accessible nature and good snow record makes for great riding for most ability levels. Ischgl is home to one of Austria's best terrain-parks and Silvretta Sports and Intersport Mathoy are recommended snowboard shops.

descents to Ischgl, most of the Palinkopf runs and some key slopes on the Samnaun side. Piste grooming is reportedly 'very reliable'.

FOR EXPERTS
Not much on-piste challenge
Ischgl can't compare with nearby St Anton for exciting slopes, and some of the runs marked black on the piste map would be red elsewhere. But there is plenty of beautiful off-piste to be found with a guide and it doesn't get tracked out quickly. The best areas to head for are Greitspitz and Palinkopf – and the wooded lower slopes of the Fimbatal are delightful in a storm. There are also several ski routes. Ski route 39 is recommended to leave you 'suitably exhausted' after the testing 1000m/3,280ft descent. The best steep piste is 4, from Pardatschgrat towards Ischgl. The variant 4a, into Velilltal, is a ski route. Black 14a, from Greitspitz, is steeper than most. The bottom part of the red to the Pardatschgratbahn should really be a black – they need winch-cats to groom it and it's often icy.

FOR INTERMEDIATES
Something for everyone
Most of the slopes are wide, forgiving and ideal for intermediates.

At the tough end of the spectrum our favourite runs are those from Palinkopf down to Gampenalp – almost 900m/2,950ft vertical and at the edge of the ski area with great views of virgin slopes. There are also interesting and challenging black runs down the Höllspitz chair, and on Greitspitz. The reds from Pardatschgrat and Velillscharte down the beautiful Velilltal and the red from Greitspitz into Switzerland are great for quiet, high-speed cruising.

For easier motorway cruising, there is lots of choice, including those down to and around Alp Trida on the Swiss side – but on our April 2006 visit these were crowded. Timid intermediates should avoid the steep runs back to town – take the gondolas instead.

FOR BEGINNERS
Up the mountain
Beginners must go up the mountain to Idalp, where there are good, sunny, snow-sure nursery slopes served by drags and a fast chair. The blue runs on the east side of the bowl offer pleasant progression for fast learners. Over at Alp Trida there are further easy expanses – you can return by lift.

FOR CROSS-COUNTRY
Plenty in the valley
There are 48km/30 miles of track in the valley between Ischgl, Galtür and Wirl. This tends to be shady, especially in early season, and is away from the main slopes, which makes meeting downhillers for lunch inconvenient.

QUEUES
OK once you're up the mountain
Ischgl tops our fast lift league table – 62 per cent of its lifts are fast ones. But there can still be queues in the village. A reporter had a 30-minute wait at the Pardatschgratbahn, and we found big queues for the Silvrettabahn in April 2006 but they moved quickly. More of a problem was crowds on the runs, especially the easier runs on the Swiss side, where lots of people were skiing too fast and too close to others.

MOUNTAIN RESTAURANTS
Some good places
Mountain restaurants tend to be very crowded but quite good quality, with over half now offering table-service. The newest is the multi-story, glass sided Pardorama complex at the top of the Pardatschgrat where we had fabulous spicy prawns and Ox fillet steak on our 2006 visit. The Paznauner Thaya, above Bodenalp, is an attractive, rustic chalet with 'great spit-roasted chickens'. There is often a band playing on the terrace, or throbbing disco music. Down in Fimbatal is the Bodenalpe, a quieter, rustic table-service restaurant.

At Idalp there is a busy, big self-service cafeteria, and a good table-

↑ Almost all Ischgl's slopes are high above the tree line and served by high-speed chair-lifts
ISCHGL TOURISMUS

SCHOOLS

Ischgl
t 5257/5404

Classes
5 days (2hr am and pm) €156

Private lessons
€102 for 90 min; each additional person €14

CHILDREN

Kindergarten
(run by ski school at Idalp)
t 5257/5404
For non-skiing children (no small infants); 10am to 4pm

Ski kindergarten
(run by ski school at Idalp)
t 5257/5404
Ages 3 to 5; €43 per 4hr day; lunch available

Ski school
Takes children from the age of 5 (5 full days €145)

---

service alternative. The Schwarze Wand pizzeria at the top of Höllenkar is recommended by reporters, as is the Höllboden below it ('good desserts'). From Gampenalp you can be towed 5km/3 miles by snowmobile to the remote Heidelberger hütte – the way back involves 'a lot of poling, some climbs and a few gentle schusses'.

The restaurants on the Swiss side at Alp Trida are pleasant, quieter and generally recommended by reporters. At the Alp Bella, a 2006 reporter says: 'Choose the half chicken, a speciality.' Also highly rated are the Skihaus Alp Trida – 'best goulash soup ever' – and the Panorama Sattel (top of the Samnaun cable-car) – 'excellent food', 'splendid views'. Above the big Alp Trida self-service is the upmarket Marmotte (reservations needed) and the new Munggaloch bar.

SCHOOLS AND GUIDES
Best for late risers

The school meets up at Idalp and starts very late (10.30). In the past we've had rave reviews, but recent reporters said class sizes were large at around 12 people and their instructor spoke limited English. The school also organises off-piste tours.

FACILITIES FOR CHILDREN
High-altitude options

The childcare facilities are all up at Idalp – there's an enclosed learning zone and adventure garden with cartoon characters. But we have no reports of the service they provide.

STAYING THERE

HOW TO GO
Increasing choice of packages

Several British tour operators now feature Ischgl.

Hotels There is a good selection from luxurious and expensive to basic B&Bs.
(((((5) **Trofana Royal** (600) One of Austria's most luxurious hotels, with prices to match. A celebrity chef runs the kitchen. Sumptuous spa facilities.
(((((5) **Madlein** (5226) Convenient, 'hip', modern hotel. Pool, sauna, steam room. Nightclub and disco.
(((((5) **Elisabeth** (5411) Right by the Pardatschgrat gondola with lively après-ski. Pool, sauna and steam room.
(((((5) **Solaria** (5205) Near the Madlein and just as luxurious, with a 'friendly family atmosphere' and 'helpful staff'.
(((((5) **Brigitte** (5646) Highly recommended by a reporter. 'Central, but quiet', 'fantastic food'. Pool.
((((4) **Piz Tasna** (5277) Up hill behind church: 'Quiet location, friendly, lovely views over village, excellent food.'
((((4) **Goldener Adler** (5217) Recommended by two recent reporters. Convenient, modern hotel, with 'outstanding food'. Sauna and whirlpool.
((((4) **Sonne** (5302) Highly rated by reporters. In the centre of the village. Lively stube. Sauna, hot-tub, solarium.
(((3) **Olympia** (5432) 'Well-appointed, family-run' with 'good-sized rooms'. Bar and restaurant. Steam and solarium.
(((3) **Jägerhof** (5206) 'Jewel of a hotel,' said a reporter. Friendly, good food, large rooms. Sauna and steam.

Don't be fooled: you don't get this much sun in the village in early season
ISCHGL TOURISMUS

GETTING THERE

Air Innsbruck 100km/62 miles (1½hr); Zürich 300km/186 miles (3hr); Munich 300km/186 miles (3hr).

Rail Landeck (30km/19 miles); frequent buses from station.

ACTIVITIES

Indoor Silvretta Centre (bowling, billiards, swimming pool, sauna, solarium, massage), museums
Outdoor Skating, sleigh rides, hiking tours, 7km/4 miles floodlit toboggan run

www.sport2000rent.com
SPORT 2000 rent a sport
QUALITY RENTAL SYSTEM
Ski Boards Boots and more...

((⦿3 **Christine** (5346) Probably the best B&B in town. 'Huge rooms, nice views, good position near the lifts.'
((2 **Dorfschmeide** (5769) Small, central B&B with 'friendly service and a great location', says a 2006 reporter. Other recommendations include the Albona (5500), the Sylvia (5690), the Ida (50005), The Hotel (20150) – 'excellent food' – and the Post (5232) – 'luxurious and excellent gourmet food'.
Self-catering Some attractive apartments are available. The Golfais are conveniently placed by the Pardatschgrat gondola and have been recommended. A 2006 reporter was pleased with his apartment for four in the hotel Solaria (with use of its spa).

EATING OUT
Plenty of choice
Most of our reporters eat in their hotels. For a lighter meal such as pizza try the Nona, the Schatzi or the Trofana Alm, which is as much a bar as a restaurant, and for fondue or ribs the Kitzloch, with its galleries over the dance floor. The Allegra and Salz & Pfeffer 'pasta and pizza' have been recommended. The Grillalm and Salnerhof are popular, 'traditional Austrian fare, huge portions'. A reporter pronounces the Nudelhimmel (above the Höllboden bar) his favourite – local dishes at reasonable prices. The Nevada is also recommended, 'friendly staff, but little English is spoken'.

APRES-SKI
Very lively
Ischgl is one of the liveliest resorts in the Alps, from early afternoon on. Lots of people are still in ski boots late in the evening. At close of play head for Trofana Alm near the Silvrettabahn or the Schatzi bar of the hotel Elisabeth by the Pardatschgratbahn – with

indoor and outdoor bars and scantily clad dancing girls. The 'tremendously lively' Niki's Stadl across the road is a great place to sing along to live Austrian hits. The Kitzloch 'rocks', with dancing on the tables in ski boots. The bar at the hotel Sonne gets crowded and has live music. The Kuhstahl under the Sporthotel Silvretta and Fire & Ice ('expensive drinks') over the road are both lively all evening. The Höllboden bar is recommended for live music. Guxa ('a cigars and cocktails type of place') and Allegra liven up after dinner, and the Golden Eagle is 'good for live bands'. The huge Trofana Arena also has live bands (and a lap dancing club). The Coyote Ugly at the hotel Madlein – 'a lap dancing bar that just manages to avoid seediness' – has been recommended. There's a branch of the famous Pacha nightclubs, also in Ibiza and London – a bit 'tacky', says a visitor). The Living Room (hotel Grillalm) is allegedly 'more hands-on' than table dancing. And the club under the hotel Post has an ancient Roman theme.

OFF THE SLOPES
No sun but a nice pool
The village gets little sun in the middle of winter, and the resort is best suited to those keen to hit the slopes. But there's no shortage of off-slope activities. There are 24km/15 miles of well-marked and maintained walks (many at altitude), a 7km/4 mile floodlit toboggan run and a splendid sports centre. And you can browse upmarket shops, which sell Versace and Bogner. It's easy to get around the valley by bus and the Smuggler's Pass for pedestrians enables them to explore specially selected lifts for a day, walk and lunch with skiing friends.

Samnaun 1840m/6,040ft

Small, quiet duty-free Samnaun is in a corner of Switzerland more easily reached from Austria. A recent reporter saw no other Brits there all week.
There are four small components, roughly 1km/0.5 mile apart: Samnaun-Dorf, prettily set at the head of the valley is the main focus, with some swanky hotels and duty-free shops; Ravaisch, where the cable-car goes up; tiny Plan; and the hamlets of Laret and Compatsch, at the end of the main run down from the slopes (where there are several choices of lunchtime eateries). We've stayed happily on the edge of

Dorf in the Waldpark B&B (8618310), and have eaten well at La Pasta in the hotel Montana (8619000). Reporters recommend the Hotel Post (8619200) ('good food but pricey') and the Stammerspitze Cafe there. There's a smart AlpenQuell spa-pool-fitness centre.

The Schmuggler Alm is a popular après-ski spot and 'does the best pizza in the world', says a 2006 reporter.

Kappl 1260m/4,135ft

Kappl, a 15-minute bus-ride down the valley from Ischgl, is worth a visit – and if you want a quieter time, staying here is worth considering. Both the village, with a couple of dozen hotels and guest-houses on a shelf 100m/330ft above the valley floor, and the mountain are family-oriented. The Sunny Mountain area at the top of the access gondola has a big kindergarten, kids' restaurant and outside play area with a roundabout and tubing. There's a long floodlit toboggan run from here back to the village and valley floor.

The ski area is included on the area pass and has 40km/25 miles of sunny, largely south-facing pistes going up to 2640m/8,660ft. The slopes – served by an access gondola from the road and fast quads above it – offer plenty of variety, with several tough reds, including the 8km/5 mile Lattenabfarht down a deserted valley from the top to the valley floor with the option of a chair part-way down to take you back up. Most of the slopes are open, but there are some woodland runs for bad-weather days and all except the highest slopes are covered by snowmaking. And they are delightfully quiet compared with Ischgl. We had a great half-day here last April.

See 1050m/3,440ft

See, a 10-minute bus-ride further down the valley from Kappl, is also covered by the valley lift-pass and has 30km/19 miles of predominantly easy, largely north-facing slopes. It had great powder when we were there in April 2006 – excellent for making your first turns off-piste. There's a good nursery slope at the top of the access gondola and easy runs to progress to. Ski route 10 on the piste map turned out to be a proper groomed piste and is a beautiful run away from all lifts, round the back of the mountain and with spectacular views – a pleasant ski to

start with and then a road you cruise along admiring the views. It is worth a visit from Ischgl for those wanting easy, uncrowded runs and not minding the limited extent. Staying at See in one of the largely 3-star hotels and guest houses strung along the road is worth considering for families and those wanting a quiet time and to pay much lower prices than in Ischgl; but the village is not especially attractive and is spoiled by the road.

Galtür 1585m/5,200ft

Galtür hit the headlines when it was struck by a devastating avalanche in 1999, but the village centre has since been rebuilt and fortified and is now home to the Alpinarium, featuring an exhibition centre (signs only in German), climbing wall, internet and archive room, all built within avalanche-protection structures.

It is a charming, peaceful, traditional village clustered around a pretty little church, amid impressive mountain scenery at the head of the valley (and so unspoiled by through traffic). Sunnier, cheaper and much quieter than Ischgl, it is a good base for a quiet family holiday and mixed-ability groups – and the free buses to Ischgl are regular and quick. There are good 3- and 4-star hotels – the Almhof (8253), Flüchthorn (8202), Alpenrose (8201) and Ballunspitze (8214) have been recommended.

Galtür's own slopes (rising to 2295m/7,530ft), above a lift base at Wirl, a short bus-ride from the village, are not very challenging and can be bleak in poor weather; but the black runs are ideal for intermediates and there are fine nursery slopes. The area on the far right of the piste map, served by a slow double chair and a T-bar has some good off-piste in a bowl and among well-spaced trees. There is a small terrain-park at the top of the Soppalift drag. The school has a high reputation and offers small classes. Kinderland has its own tow, carousel and magic carpet. Galtür has 45km/28 miles of cross-country loops, some quite testing. The cosy, wooden Wieberhimml mountain hut has waitresses in traditional costume.

Off-slope facilities are limited, but there's a sports centre with pool, tennis and squash. Night skiing and sledding are available every Wednesday evening on floodlit slopes.

Phone numbers
Calling long-distance
Add the prefix given below for each resort. When calling from abroad use the country code 43 and omit the initial '0'.

Ischgl
05444

Galtür
05443

Kappl
05445

Samnaun
(Switzerland)
From elsewhere in Switzerland add the prefix 081.
From abroad use the prefix +41 81.

TOURIST OFFICES

Ischgl
t 5266
info@ischgl.com
www.ischgl.com

Galtür
t 8521
info@galtuer.com
www.galtuer.com

Kappl
t 6243
info@kappl.at
www.kappl.at

Samnaun
(Switzerland)
t 868 5858
info@samnaun.ch
www.samnaun.ch

Kitzbühel

The extensive slopes are mostly pretty tame; the medieval town at the base, though, is something special – cute and lively

RATINGS

The slopes

Fast lifts	★★★
Snow	★★
Extent	★★★
Expert	★★★
Intermediate	★★★★
Beginner	★★
Convenience	★★
Queues	★★
Mountain restaurants	★★★★

The rest

Scenery	★★★
Resort charm	★★★★
Off-slope	★★★★★

NEWS

For 2006/07 the triple chair at Ehrenbachhöhe and the Hanglalm T-bar in the Resterhöhe area will both be replaced by six-packs. More snowmaking is also planned for the Resterhöhe area.

The refurbished casino re-opened in summer 2006 with a new restaurant, and a new ice rink should be ready this season.

For 2005/06 the ski area of Westendorf was extended to meet the Kitzbühel area at Aschau, with an eight-seat Ki-West gondola from there up to the Gampen sector of Westendorf. And a new gondola was built to give access to Resterhöhe from Hollersbach near Mittersill, in the valley to the south. A 3-D piste map was also launched, costing 5 euros.

Sadly, the lift-served off-piste Bichlalm area has now closed.

➕ Large, attractive, varied slopes offering a sensation of travel

➕ Beautiful medieval town centre

➕ Vibrant nightlife

➕ Plenty of off-slope amenities, both for the sporty and not-so-sporty

➕ A surprisingly large amount of cheap and cheerful accommodation

➕ Jolly mountain restaurants

➕ New gondola has improved access to the high Resterhöhe slopes, for the best snow in the area, but ...

➖ Snow in other, lower sectors is often poor, especially on runs to the valley (though there's now quite a bit of snowmaking)

➖ Surprisingly little challenging terrain – though plenty of off-piste

➖ Disappointing nursery area

➖ Some crowded pistes

Kitzbühel is one of the big names of the ski world, largely thanks to its Hahnenkamm downhill race course – the most spectacular on the World Cup circuit. And there is a lot to like about the resort – particularly the beautiful, traffic-free centre, complete with cobbled streets and lovely medieval buildings, including expensive, elegant hotels. The big drawback is the ski area's low altitude, which means the snow quality on the lower slopes is unreliable. The last three seasons have been bumper snow years and on our last visit we encountered superb powder right down to the village, but that came after countless visits (over a 20-year period) blighted by ice and slush. Our advice is to book late, when you know the conditions are good.

Despite the glamorous reputation, this is no Gstaad: there is a huge amount of inexpensive accommodation which attracts low-budget visitors, many of whom are young and out to party in the resort's famous après-ski haunts.

THE RESORT

Set at a junction of broad, pretty valleys, Kitzbühel is a large, animated town, with separate areas of local slopes on each side. The beautiful walled medieval centre – with quaint church, cobbled streets and attractively painted buildings – is traffic-free and a compelling place to stay. Many visitors love the sophisticated, towny ambience and swanky shops and cafes. But the resort spreads widely, and busy roads surround the old town, reducing the charm factor somewhat. Visitors used to peaceful little Austrian villages are likely to be disappointed by its urban nature.

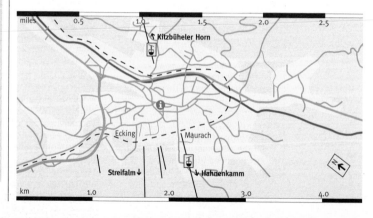

KEY FACTS

Resort	760m
	2,490ft
Slopes	800-2000m
	2,620-6,560ft
Lifts	56
Pistes	145km
	90 miles
Blue	37%
Red	43%
Black	20%
Snowmaking	65km
	40 miles

LIFT PASSES

Kitzbühel

Prices in €

Age	1-day	6-day
under 16	18	85
16 to 18	30	136
over 19	36	170

Free under 7

Senior no deals

Beginner seven free lifts (three in Kitzbühel)

Notes
Covers all lifts in Kitzbühel, Kirchberg, Jochberg, Pass Thurn, Mittersill/Hollersbach. 50% reduction on pool entry with passes for 2 days or more. Single ascent and hourly tickets, family reductions.

Alternative passes
Kitzbüheler Alpen-skipass covers five large ski areas – Kitzbühel, Schneewinkel (St Johann), Ski Welt, Alpbach and Wildschönau. Salzburg Super Ski Card covers 21 ski areas in the Salzburg province.

Kitzbühel's mix of open slopes higher up and patchy forest lower down is very attractive ➔

boarding

Kitzbühel has never been known as a snowboarders' hub. However they have recently tried to attract a more freestyle-orientated clientele, by building a decent terrain-park complete with half-pipe and coupled with a boarder-cross course. There are some good off-piste runs and fun natural obstacles on the Hahnenkamm and around Pengelstein. All major lifts are gondolas and chair-lifts – the area suits beginners and intermediates well.

The size of Kitz makes choice of location important. Many visitors prefer to be close to the Hahnenkamm gondola, south-west of the centre. Beginners should bear in mind that the Hahnenkamm nursery slopes are often lacking in snow, and then novices are taken up the Horn. Reporters continue to say the buses around town get overcrowded and some suggest taking taxis if you don't want to walk. A car is useful for visiting lots of other resorts covered by the Kitzbüheler Alpenskipass – though one of those, Westendorf, is now linked by the Ki-West gondola from near Aschau.

THE MOUNTAINS

Kitzbühel's extensive slopes – shared with Kirchberg and other, smaller villages – offer a very attractive mixture of entirely open runs higher up and patchy forest lower down. Most face north-east or north-west.

THE SLOPES
Big but bitty
The slopes are divided into four areas.

The **Hahnenkamm-Pengelstein** sector is by far the largest. After the Hahnenkamm gondola from the edge of the town, followed by a tedious walk along a flat piste, you descend into the bowl of Ehrenbachgraben, where several chair-lifts fan out. One goes up to Ehrenbachhöhe, the arrival point of lifts from Kirchberg. Another takes you to the gentle peak of Steinbergkogel, the high point of the sector. Beyond is the slightly lower peak of Pengelstein, whence several long west-facing runs go down to Aschau to meet the new extension of the Westendorf area (or ski-buses back towards Kirchberg) and Skirast, where there is a gondola back up.

Pengelstein is also the start of the 30-person cross-valley gondola to Wurzhöhe above Jochberg that was opened a couple of seasons ago. Further lifts then take you to the **Resterhöhe** sector above Pass Thurn.

This impressive peak-to-peak link has great views and is much quicker than using the old routes down to the valley and a bus-ride back. Resterhöhe is well worth the excursion, for better snow and fewer crowds, even though the gondola connection has brought more people over, says a 2006 visitor. Runs are short, but several new fast chairs have made the area more appealing.

The **Kitzbüheler Horn** is accessed by a gondola starting close to the railway station, some way from the centre. The second stage leads to the sunny Trattalm bowl, but the alternative cable-car takes you up to the summit of the Horn, from where a fine, solitary piste leads down into the Raintal on the east side. There's a blue piste and two ski routes back towards town.

There's floodlit skiing on Thursday and Friday on **Gaisberg**, a small area of slopes at Kirchberg, on the other side of the road from the main ski area.

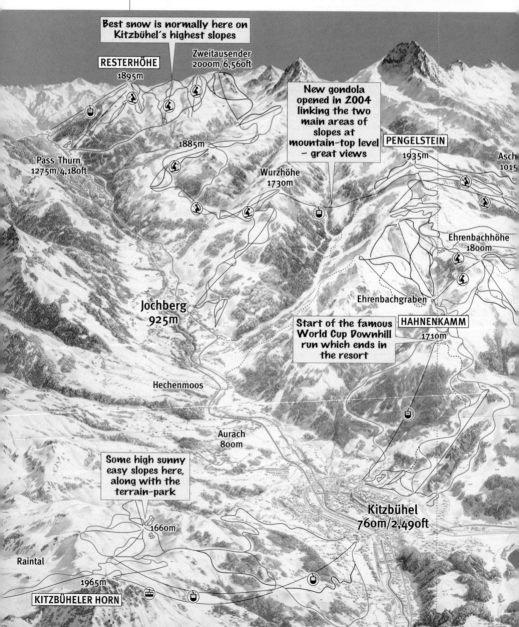

Best snow is normally here on
Kitzbühel's highest slopes

RESTERHÖHE
1895m

Zweitausender
2000m/6,56oft

New gondola
opened in 2004
linking the two
main areas of
slopes at
mountain-top level
– great views

PENGELSTEIN
1935m

Asch
1015

1885m

Pass Thurn
1275m/4,18oft

Wurzhöhe
1730m

Ehrenbachhöhe
1800m

Jochberg
925m

Ehrenbachgraben

HAHNENKAMM
1710m

Start of the famous
World Cup Downhill
run which ends in
the resort

Hechenmoos

Aurach
800m

Some high sunny
easy slopes here,
along with the
terrain-park

Kitzbühel
760m/2,49oft

1660m

Raintal

1965m

KITZBÜHELER HORN

THE HAHNENKAMM DOWNHILL

Kitzbühel's Hahnenkamm Downhill race, held in mid-January each year, is the toughest as well as one of the most famous on the World Cup circuit. On the race weekend the town is packed and there is a real carnival atmosphere, with bands, people in traditional costumes and huge (and loud) cowbells everywhere. The race itself starts with a steep icy section before you hit the famous Mausfalle and Steilhang, where even Franz Klammer used to get worried. The course (now thankfully served by snow-guns) starts near the top of the Hahnenkamm gondola and drops 860m/2,820ft to finish amid the noise and celebrations right on the edge of town. Ordinary mortals can now try most of the course after the race weekend, whenever the snow is good enough – it's an unpisted red ski route mostly. We found it steep and tricky in parts, even when going slowly – it must be terrifying at race speeds of 80mph or more. The course is normally closed from the start of the season until after the race.

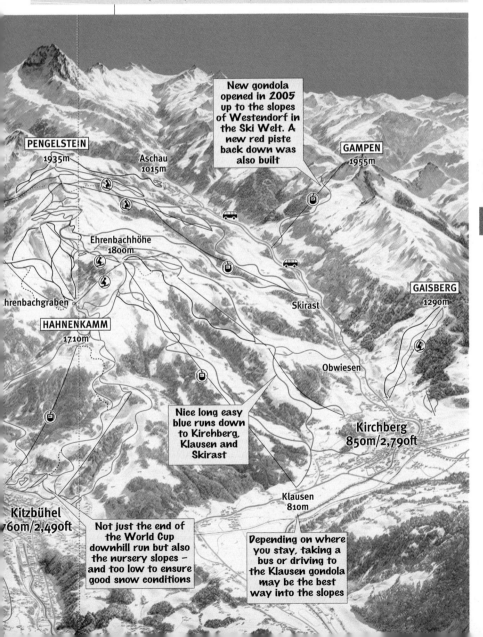

New gondola opened in 2005 up to the slopes of Westendorf in the Ski Welt. A new red piste back down was also built

PENGELSTEIN
1935m

Aschau
1015m

GAMPEN
1955m

Ehrenbachhöhe
1800m

hrenbachgraben

Skirast

GAISBERG
1290m

HAHNENKAMM
1710m

Obwiesen

Nice long easy blue runs down to Kirchberg, Klausen and Skirast

Kirchberg
850m/2,790ft

Klausen
810m

Kitzbühel
/60m/2,490ft

Not just the end of the World Cup downhill run but also the nursery slopes – and too low to ensure good snow conditions

Depending on where you stay, taking a bus or driving to the Klausen gondola may be the best way into the slopes

Sadly, the separate Bichlalm area, which offered lift- and snowcat-served off-piste is now closed.

TERRAIN-PARKS
Take the Hornbahn
The park is on the Kitzbüheler Horn and has an intermediate table-top jump, a quarter-pipe and several small rails and boxes. The half-pipe can be OK but isn't that well maintained. The park in Westendorf (now linked by gondola from near Aschau) is far bigger and better, and is littered with obstacles for all levels – worth the early start for park aficionados.

SNOW RELIABILITY
More snowmaking now
Even in an exceptionally good snow years such as the last three, some reporters complained of worn patches, ice and slush on the lower slopes. In a normal year, the lower slopes can be very tricky or bare at times (though the snow at the top is often OK). The problem is that Kitzbühel's slopes have one of the lowest average heights in the Alps. To make matters worse, the Horn is also sunny. The expansion of snowmaking in recent years has improved matters when it's cold enough to make snow – major runs right down to Kitzbühel, Kirchberg, Klausen and Jochberg are covered. But many slopes still remain unprotected. If snow is poor, head for Resterhöhe, which, as well as having the best natural snow, is to get more snowmaking for this season.

FOR EXPERTS
Plan to go off-piste
Steep slopes – pistes and off-piste terrain – are mostly concentrated around the bowl of Ehrenbachgraben. The most direct of these are challenging mogul fields. Nearby is the Streif red, the basis for the famous Hahnenkamm Downhill race (see the feature panel). When conditions allow, there is plenty of gentler off-piste potential elsewhere – some of it safely close to pistes, some requiring a guide.

FOR INTERMEDIATES
Lots of alternatives
The Hahnenkamm area is prime terrain. Good intermediates will want to do the World Cup downhill run, of course (see the feature panel). And the long blues of around 1000m/3,300ft vertical to Klausen from Ehrenbachhöhe and to

Skirast from Steinbergkogel or Pengelstein are also satisfying. The east-facing Raintal run on the Horn is excellent for good intermediates.

The runs above Jochberg are particularly good for mixed abilities and the short, high runs at Resterhöhe are ideal if you are more timid. There are also easy reds down to both Pass Thurn and Jochberg. Much of the Horn is good cruising.

FOR BEGINNERS
Not ideal
The Hahnenkamm nursery slopes are no more than adequate, and prone to poor snow conditions. The Horn has a high, sunny, nursery-like section, and quick learners will soon be cruising home from there on the long Hagstein piste. There are some easy runs to progress to if the snow is OK. But there are many more conveniently arranged places to start.

FOR CROSS-COUNTRY
Plentiful but low
There are nearly 40km/25 miles of trails scattered around, but all are at valley level and prone to lack of snow.

QUEUES
Still some problems
Since the old Hahnenkamm cable-car was replaced by a gondola, morning queues to get out of the town have been almost forgotten. However, once up the mountain there are bottlenecks at slow old chairs and drags, including the Steinbergkogel lift from Ehrenbachgraben. The Maierl chairs out of Kirchberg can also be tiresome. But we have had reports of queue-free weeks and maximum queues of ten minutes at half-term. Both the Horn and the Hahnenkamm can have crowded pistes – though reports suggest the recent gondola link with Jochberg has spread the traffic across sectors.

MOUNTAIN RESTAURANTS
A highlight
There are many attractive restaurants – 'One of the reasons we keep going back,' says one of our Kitz regulars. And, unlike in most resorts, they are well marked on the piste map. On the Horn, Hornköpfl-Hütte's good food and sunny terraces still get praised despite a slight climb to reach it. Alpenhaus 'does excellent self-service meals for great prices' but can get crowded; the Gipfelhaus is quieter with 'super views

GETTING THERE

Air Salzburg 80km/50 miles (1½hr); Munich 160km/99 miles (2hr); Innsbruck 95km/59 miles (1½hr).

Rail Mainline station in resort. Postbus every 15min from station.

SCHOOLS

Rote Teufel (Red Devil)
t 62500

Jochberg
t 5342

Wagstätt
t 20152

Reith
t 65496

Aurach
t 65804

Classes
(Rote Teufel prices) 6 days (2hr am and pm) €150

Private lessons
€150 for 2hr; each additional person €20

CHILDREN

There is no non-ski nursery, but babysitters and nannies can be hired.

Ski school
Most schools cater for small children, offering lunchtime supervision as well as lessons – generally from the age of 3 or 4 (6 days approx €160).

and a sheltered terrace'. Gasthof Hagstein is an attractive farmhouse. At Jochberg-Pass Thurn the Jägerwurzhütte and Trattenbachalm are recommended; Hanglalm has 'the best Kaiserschmarrn', and Panoraamaalm great views. In the Hahnenkamm sector we loved the rustic Seidlalm, right by the lower part of the downhill course, ('wonderful garlic soup' says a 2006 reporter) and had a jolly meal at Berghaus Tyrol below Ehrenbachhöhe. The Hockeckhütte has 'excellent food and an Austrian atmosphere'. Melkalm 'is worth the effort of finding'. The Hochbrunn has 'very friendly' staff and 'good strudel', the Steinbergkogel 'wonderful food'. The Kasereckhütte on the ski route to Jochberg is 'brilliant'. The expensive Hochkitzbühel at the top of the gondola has good food, but service has been criticised.

SCHOOLS AND GUIDES
Good recent reviews
A 2006 visitor found Rudi Sailer's 200-strong Red Devils 'a giant confidence booster' and he 'learnt more this week than ever before' and a 2005 reporter said 'enjoyable from start to finish. We progressed very quickly with our excellent instructor.' The other schools emphasise their small scale and personal nature. The Total school is the best established of these and includes video analysis. Lots of British instructors, reportedly.

FACILITIES FOR CHILDREN
Not an ideal choice
There is no non-ski nursery, but provided your children can take classes, you can deposit them at any of the schools. The Total school has supervision until 5pm.

STAYING THERE

HOW TO GO
Mainly hotels and pensions
Kitz is essentially a hotel resort.
Chalets A few tour operators run chalet-hotels here. Reporters have praised the 'ski to door' convenience of First Choice's chalet Karlberger.
Hotels There is an enormous choice, especially of 4-star and 3-star hotels.
(((((5) **Golfhotel Rasmushof** (65252) Right on the slopes by the finish area of the Hahnenkamm race, close to centre of town. 'Excellent service from friendly staff. Book a room overlooking the slopes (a golf course in summer).'
(((((5) **Tennerhof** (63181) Luxurious former farmhouse, with renowned restaurant. Beautiful panelled rooms.
((((4) **Schloss Lebenberg** (6901) Modernised 'castle' with smart pool; inconvenient location but free shuttle-bus. Free nursery for kids age 3-plus.
((((4) **Weisses Rössl** (625410) Smartly traditional, exclusive 5-star aparthotel.
((((4) **Goldener Greif** (64311) Historic inn, elegantly renovated; vaulted lobby-sitting area, panelled bar, casino.
((((4) **Jägerwirt** (6981) Modern chalet with 'helpful staff and wonderful food'. Not ideally placed.
((((4) **Schwarzer Adler** (6911) Traditional hotel, near centre, highly praised by a reporter: 'Great food and lovely leisure centre in basement.'
((((4) **Schweizerhof** (62735) Comfortable chalet right by Hahnenkamm gondola.
(((3) **Edelweiss** (75252) Recommended in 2005 for 'excellent food and accommodation'.
(((3) **Strasshofer** (62285) A favourite with a regular reporter – 'Central, family-run, friendly, good food, good

Kitzbühel

161

ACTIVITIES

Indoor Aquarena Centre (pools, slides, sauna, solarium, mud baths, aerated baths, underwater massage) – discounted entry with lift pass; indoor tennis hall, fitness centre, beauty centre, bridge, indoor riding school, bowling, museums, casino, cinema

Outdoor Ice rink (curling and skating), sleigh rides, snow-shoeing, ballooning, paragliding, wildlife park, 40km/25 miles of cleared walking paths (free guided tours)

Phone numbers
Kitzbühel
From elsewhere in Austria add the prefix 05356.
From abroad use the prefix +43 5356.
Kirchberg
From elsewhere in Austria add the prefix 05357.
From abroad use the prefix +43 5357.

TOURIST OFFICES

Kitzbühel
t 777
info@kitzbuehel.com
www.kitzbuehel.com
Kirchberg
t 2309
info@kirchberg.at
www.kirchberg.at

with children, quiet rooms at back.'
② **Mühlbergerhof** (62835) Small, friendly pension in good position.
Self-catering Many of the best (and best-positioned) are attached to hotels.

EATING OUT
Something for everyone
There is a wide range of restaurants to suit all pockets, including pizzerias and fast-food outlets (even McDonald's). The Neuwirt in the Schwarzer Adler hotel is regarded as the best in town and wins awards in food guides and the Schwedenkapelle is also highly rated. Good, cheaper places include the traditional Huberbräu-Stüberl ('good Austrian food'), Chizzo, Eggerwirt and, a little out of town with great views, Hagstein, which serves big pans of communal food for groups. Goldene Gams has a wide-ranging menu and both traditional and modern dining rooms. On Fridays and Saturdays you can dine at the top of the Hahnenkamm gondola. For something different take a taxi to Rosi's Sonnbergstubn. Choose the speciality lamb or duck and expect to be serenaded by Rosi herself, who sings to her guests after dinner.

APRES-SKI
A main attraction
Nightlife is a great selling point of Kitz. There's something for all tastes, from throbbing bars full of teenagers to quiet little places, nice cafes and smart spots for fur-coat flaunting.
Immediately after the slopes close, the town is jolly without being much livelier than many other Tirolean resorts. The Streifalm bar at the foot of the slopes is popular, with 'white pine and slate, open fire, widescreen TV and Europop music', as is the Sportcafe Hölzl. Cafes Praxmair, Kortschak, Langer and Rupprechter are among the most atmospheric tea-time places for cakes and pastries. Stamperl is a very lively bar. Later the American-style Highways bar and s'Lichtl (with thousands of lights hanging from the ceiling) get packed. Seppi's Pub is recommended for sport on TV, pizzas and the eccentric owner. The Python (formerly Olympia) and Take Five are the main discos. The Londoner Pub is a famous drinking place, well summarised by one visitor: 'Very crowded, very noisy and great fun, but the bar staff were mostly rude and arrogant.' La Fonda has been

recommended for the 'younger generation'. The Casino reopened last summer after a major refurbishment and with a new restaurant.

OFF THE SLOPES
Plenty to do
The lift pass gives a reduction for the pools in the impressive Aquarena leisure centre. There's a museum, and concerts are organised. The railway makes excursions easy (eg Salzburg).

Kirchberg 850m/2,790ft

THE RESORT
Kirchberg is a large, spread-out, lively village. There are three ways into the slopes, all a bus-ride from the village.

THE MOUNTAIN
Slopes The Maierl chair-lifts and the gondola from Klausen take you to Ehrenbachhöhe, at the heart of the Kitzbühel slopes. The gondola from Skirast meets chairs to Pengelstein which link to the gondola to Wurzhöhe. The separate small Gaisberg ski area is on the other side of the valley.
Snow reliability Kirchberg suffers from the same unreliable snow as Kitzbühel.
Experts Few challenging slopes.
Intermediates The main slopes back are easy cruises when snow is good.
Beginners There's a beginner lift and area at the foot of the Gaisberg slopes.
Snowboarding Kitzbühel has the edge, with the terrain-park on the Horn.
Cross-country There are plenty of trails – but they can suffer from lack of snow.
Queues There are some bottlenecks.
Mountain restaurants There are some good local huts.
Schools and guides We lack recent reports on the three schools.
Facilities for children There are non-ski and ski kindergartens.

STAYING THERE
How to go There's a wide choice of chalet-style hotels and pensions.
Hotels The 4-star Klausen (2128), close to the main gondola, and the Sporthotel Tyrol (2787), a bit out of the centre, have been recommended.
Self-catering There is some available.
Eating out Mostly in hotels, but there's a pizzeria and a steak house too.
Après-ski There's a toboggan run on Gaisberg. Nightlife is very lively.
Off the slopes Some hotels have swimming pools, saunas and so on.

Lech

If you can afford it, simply one of the best: a captivating blend of reliable snow, village charm and deeply comfortable hotels

COSTS

① ② ③ ④ ⑤ ⑥

RATINGS

The slopes
Fast lifts	****
Snow	****
Extent	****
Expert	****
Intermediate	****
Beginner	****
Convenience	***
Queues	****
Mountain restaurants	***

The rest
Scenery	***
Resort charm	****
Off-slope	***

NEWS

For 2006/07 the Trittalp and Seekopf lifts in Zürs will be equipped with covers and heated seats.

For 2005/06 a heated six-pack with covers replaced the Hexenboden triple chairs at the north end of Zürs.

The mountain guides office now also operates a ski school, Omeshorn Alpincenter, offering some competition for the main school.

+ Picturesque Alpine village

+ Sunny and usually uncrowded slopes with excellent snow record and extensive snowmaking

+ Fair-sized, largely intermediate piste network with some recently updated lifts, plus good, extensive off-piste

+ Easy access by bus to the slopes of St Anton and other Arlberg resorts

+ Some very smart hotels, including many offering ski-in ski-out convenience, notably at Oberlech

+ More and more heated chair-lifts

+ Lively après-ski scene, but ...

− Very much hotel-dominated, with few non-hotel bars or restaurants

− Surprising shortage, for a smart resort, of seductive shopping

− Local traffic intrudes on main street of Lech (and really spoils Zürs)

− Very few challenging pistes

− Nearly all slopes are above the tree line, and unpleasant in bad weather

− Blue runs back to the village are rather steep for nervous novices

− Generally expensive

− Less than ideal ski-bus service

− Still a few slow, old lifts

Lech and its higher, linked neighbour Zürs are the most fashionable resorts in Austria, each able to point to a string of rich and celebrated regular visitors, and pulling in Merc-borne Germans on an unmatched scale. But, like all such 'exclusive' resorts, they aren't actually exclusive in any real sense. A holiday here is unlikely to be cheap, but it doesn't have to cost a lot more than in countless other international resorts in the Alps. We don't feel out of place here, and neither would you. We often see Lech described as 'a very chic resort' – but it has none of the flash shops of St Moritz or Cortina, for example.

The real point about these resorts is that they offer a rare and attractive combination of impressive snowfall, traditional Alpine atmosphere and excellent hotels offering a truly personal service from their family owners.

THE RESORT

Lech is an old farming village set in a high valley that spent long periods of winter cut off from the outside world until the Flexen Pass road through Zürs was constructed at the end of the 19th century. (Even now, the road can be closed for days on end after an exceptional snowfall; a road tunnel is planned, but is not imminent.)

The village is attractive, with its upmarket chalet hotels built in traditional chalet style, its gurgling river plus bridges, its adequately impressive scenery and the high incidence of snow on the streets. But its appeal is dimmed by traffic on the main street that forms its spine (a regular complaint by reporters): although the pavements have been widened and parking is controlled, it can still get very busy, especially at weekends.

Britain is the resort's third most important market, but Brits are outnumbered 10:1 by Germans and 3:1 by Austrians.

The heart of the village is a short stretch of the main street beside the river; most of the main hotels are clustered here. Right on this street is the base station of the Rüfikopf cable-car, departure point for exploration of the Zürs slopes. A short walk away, across the river, are the Schlegelkopf chair-lifts, leading up into Lech's main area of slopes. Chalets, apartments and pensions are dotted around the valley, and the village spreads along

↑ The curving main street, beside the river to the right of the church, is rarely as traffic-free as this

LECH TOURIST OFFICE

LIFT PASSES

Arlberg Ski Pass

Prices in €

Age	1-day	6-day
under 16	23	113
16 to 19	36	163
20 to 64	39	189
over 65	36	163

Free no one, but season pass only €10 if under 8 or over 75

Senior senior min. age for women is 60

Beginner points ticket

Notes

Covers all St Anton, St Christoph, Lech, Zürs and Stuben lifts, and linking bus between Rauz and Zürs. Single ascent, half-day and afternoon 'taster' tickets available. Pass also covers Sonnenkopf (10 lifts) at Klösterle, 7km/4 miles west of Stuben (bus link from Stuben).

the main street for 2km/1.5 miles. Some of the cheaper accommodation is quite a walk from the lifts.

Not far from the centre is the cable-car up to Oberlech: a small, traffic-free collection of 4-star hotels set on the mountainside, with an underground tunnel system linking the hotels and lift station – used routinely to move baggage, and by guests in bad weather. The cable-car works until 1am, allowing access to the mother resort's much livelier nightlife.

Zug is a hamlet 3km/2 miles from Lech, with a lift into the Lech-Oberlech area. The limited accommodation here is mostly bed and breakfast, with one pricey 4-star hotel.

Lech is linked by lifts and runs to higher Zürs, described at the end of this chapter. There is a free ski-bus service between the two resorts. A consistent source of complaints in the past, this may be showing signs of improvement: this year, the only complaints are of excessive intervals between buses, rather than inadequate capacity. Buses also run to St Anton, St Christoph and Stuben, all covered by the Arlberg lift pass. For a small fee the post bus offers a direct and less crowded alternative.

The Sonnenkopf area at Klösterle, reached by ski-bus from Stuben, is also covered – 'Worth a trip,' say reporters, not least in bad weather for its combination of gondola rides and woodland runs.

THE MOUNTAINS

Practically all the slopes are treeless, the main exception being the lower runs just above the village. Practically all the slopes are quite sunny – very few are north-facing.

The toughest runs are classed as unpatrolled 'ski routes' or 'high-alpine touring runs', which are not protected against avalanche and should be skied only with a guide. We don't have much of a problem with the latter category – in other resorts, these off-piste runs would simply not appear on the piste map at all. But the ski route concept is bad news, reducing the resort's responsibility for runs that are a key part of the area, and that should be patrolled pistes. The only ways down to Zug, for example, are ski routes; the only way to complete the Lech-Zürs-Lech circuit (the Madloch-Lech run) is a ski route; and most of the identified runs from Kriegerhorn are ski routes. To add to the confusion, these routes may be closed if avalanche conditions are dangerous; some of them are groomed after a heavy snowfall; and in practice most people ski them (often into a piste-like state) without a guide or instructor. The St Anton chapter has more on this ludicrous state of affairs.

The piste map, which attempts to cover the whole of the Arlberg region in one view, was redesigned recently, but is still unclear or misleading in places – particularly around Oberlech.

KEY FACTS

Resort	1450m
	4,760ft

Arlberg region

Slopes	1305-2650m
	4,280-8,690ft
Lifts	86
Pistes	276km
	172 miles
Blue	38%
Red	51%
Black	11%
Snowmaking	58%

For Lech-Zürs only

Slopes	1450-2450m
	4,760-8,040ft
Lifts	33
Pistes	117km
	73 miles
Blue	39%
Red	48%
Black	13%

boarding

Lech's upper-crust image has not stood in the way of its snowboarding development. The jewel in the Arlberg crown has some of the best backcountry riding in Austria, and record snowfalls mean it is a popular destination for free-riders. Impeccable piste grooming makes for nice learning conditions, and most runs are serviced by modern chair-lifts and few drag-lifts; however, be careful on the west-facing slopes at Zürs, which have many flat/uphill sections.

THE SLOPES
One-way traffic

The main slopes centre on **Oberlech**, 250m/820ft above Lech (just below the tree line), and can be reached from the village by chair-lifts as well as the cable-car. The wide, open pistes above Oberlech are perfect for intermediates and there is also lots of off-piste. Zuger Hochlicht, the high point of this sector, gives stunning views.

The **Rüfikopf** cable-car takes Lech residents to the west-facing slopes of Zürs. This mountainside, with its high point at **Trittkopf**, is a mix of quite challenging intermediate slopes and flat/uphill bits. On the other side of Zürs the east-facing mountainside is of a more uniform gradient. Chairs go up to **Seekopf** with intermediate runs back down. There's a chair from Zürsersee

up to **Muggengrat** (the highest point of the Zürs area). This has a good blue run back under it and accesses a long, scenic, lift-free and quiet red (beware the steep top section) with lots of nearby off-piste options back down towards Zürs – but it is a fair walk back to Zürs at the end. Another chair from Zürsersee – slow and vulnerable to closure by wind – goes up to Madloch-Joch and the long, scenic ski route back to the fringes of Lech, completing a clockwise circuit. You can peel off part-way down and head for Zug and the slow chair-lift up to the Kriegerhorn above Oberlech, instead.

TERRAIN-PARKS
In Lech only

Just above the Schlegelkopf and visible from town lies what has become one of the best snow-parks in Austria. There are three kicker lines, separated into easy, public and pro categories, which will suit new kids on the block as well as seasoned pros. The kickers are outstanding, with well-shaped mellow transitions that are great for learning on. There are all types of rails and boxes, including flat, kinked and rainbow rails and boxes that culminate in a wall ride.

SNOW RELIABILITY
One of Austria's best

Lech and Zürs both get a lot of snow. Lech gets an average of almost 8m/26ft of snow between December and March, almost twice as much as St Anton and three times as much as Kitzbühel; but Zürs gets 50% more than Lech. The altitude is high by Austrian resort standards and there is excellent snowmaking, helping to counter the sunny exposure of Lech and much of Zürs.

This combination, together with excellent grooming, means that the Lech-Zürs area normally has good coverage from early December until late April.

FOR EXPERTS
Off-piste is main attraction

There is only one black piste on the map, and there is no denying that for the competent skier who prefers to stick to patrolled runs the area is very limited. There are the two types of off-piste route referred to earlier, which most people are happy to undertake without guidance. But experts will get a lot more out of the area if they do have a guide, as there is plenty of excellent off-piste other than the marked ski routes, much of it accessed by long traverses. Especially in fresh snow, it can be wonderful.

Many of the best runs start from the top of the fast Steinmähder chair, which finishes just below Zuger Hochlicht. Some routes involve a short climb to access bowls of untracked powder. From the Kriegerhorn there are shorter off-piste runs down towards Lech and a very scenic long ski route down to Zug (followed by a slow chair and a rope tow to pull you along a flat area). Most runs, however, are south- or west-facing and can suffer from sun. At the end of the season, when the snow is deep and settled, the off-piste off the shoulder of the Wöstertäli from the top of the Rüfikopf cable-car down to Lech can be superb. There are also good runs from the top of the Trittkopf

Zuger Hochlicht
238om

Kriegerhorn
2175m

There is no proper piste down to Zug, only ski-routes and entirely off-piste runs – an insane arrangement

Zug
1510m

1950m

244om

SONNENKOPF

1840m

MUGGENGRAT

2450m/
8.04oft

Glattingrat
2300m

If you like to get away from the lift system, this long red is a must

Klösterle
1075m

cable-car in the Zürs sector, including a tricky one down to Stuben.

Experts will also enjoy cruising some of the steeper red runs and will want to visit St Anton during the week, where there are more challenging pistes as well as more off-piste.

Heli-lifts are available to a couple of remote spots, at least on weekdays.

FOR INTERMEDIATES
Flattering variety for all

The pistes in the Oberlech area are nearly all immaculately groomed blue runs, the upper ones above the trees, the lower ones in wide swathes cut through them. It is ideal territory for leisurely cruisers not wanting surprises. And even early intermediates will be able to take on the circuit to Zürs and back, the only significant red involved being the beautiful long ski route back to Lech from the top of the Madloch chair in Zürs. It shouldn't be difficult but, because it's a ski route, it is groomed only occasionally, and several readers have found it unpleasantly mogulled. 'They should make it a proper pisted run,' complained one. We couldn't agree more.

It's worth noting that the final blue-run descents to Lech (as opposed to Oberlech) are uncomfortably steep for nervous novices.

SCHOOLS

Lech
t 2355

Oberlech
t 2007

Zürs
t 2611

Omeshorn Alpincenter Lech
0664 788 7723

Classes
(Lech prices)
6 days (2hr am and 2hr pm) €169

Private lessons
€205 for 1 day; each additional person €16

CHILDREN

All mini-clubs run 9am to 4pm, Sun to Fri

Miniclub Lech
t 21610
Ages from 3 – must be toilet trained

Little Zürs
t 224515
Ages from 3 – must be toilet trained

Kinderland Oberlech
t 2007
Ages from 2½

Babysitting list
Held by tourist office.

Ski school
From 4½ to 14:
6 days €157

More adventurous intermediates should take the fast Steinmähder chair to just below Zuger Hochlicht and from there take the scenic red run all the way to Zug (the latter part on a ski route rather than a piste). And if you feel ready to have a stab at some off-piste for the first time, Lech is an excellent place to try it.

Zürs has many more interesting red runs, on both sides of the village. We like the north-west-facing reds from Trittkopf and the usually quiet east-facing Muggengrat Täli, which starts in a steep bowl – you can take the plunge, or skirt it on a catwalk.

FOR BEGINNERS
Easy slopes in all areas
The main nursery slopes are in Oberlech, but there is also a nice dedicated area in Lech. There are good, easy runs to progress to, both above and below Oberlech.

FOR CROSS-COUNTRY
Picturesque valley trail
A 15km/10 mile trail starts from the centre of Lech and leads through the beautiful but shady valley, along the Lech river to Zug and back. A reporter recommends the Älpele for lunch en route. In Zürs there is a 4km/2.5 mile track to the Flexen Pass and back.

QUEUES
A few complaints
The resort proudly boasts that it limits numbers on the slopes to 14,000 for a more enjoyable experience. Most reporters also stress how much quieter Lech's slopes are than St Anton's. There have been significant lift improvements in recent years: feedback is generally positive, but there are still one or two bottlenecks – the Schlegelkopf fast quad out of Lech gets very busy first thing and the crucial ('slow and cold')Madloch double chair at the top of the Zürs area generates peak-time queues on the Lech-Zürs-Lech circuit. Some readers mention the Rüfikopf cable-car to Zürs as generating queues. The new six-pack in Zürs has improved access to Hexenboden. Reporters have also praised the care taken by attendants to help children on to lifts.

MOUNTAIN RESTAURANTS
On the up
Proper mountain restaurants are not a highlight – the hotel owners of

Oberlech and Zürs no doubt see to that – but they have improved in recent years, persuading us last year to up the rating from ** to ***.

Rud-Alpe on the lower slopes above Lech is a rustic place, built using the timbers of an old hut. 'Excellent decor, food and service,' says one reporter; 'best lunch on the mountain,' enthuses another. The 'lively' Kriegeralpe, higher up, has been extended so it can open in winter as well as in summer. Rustic and charming, it is 'always full', writes a disappointed visitor. One reader commented that it has a 'limited menu, but is good for drinks'. The Cia (just above Lech) is also worth a try.

The Schröfli Alm, just above the base of the Seekopf lift, is a pleasant chalet. The self-service Seekopf restaurant does 'quality food at decent prices' and has a good sun terrace – recommended by two reporters this year. The cosy Palmenalpe above Zug, which is being refurbished for 2006/07, offers 'stunning views' and 'huge pizzas', but it too is very crowded.

Not surprisingly, lunch in Oberlech is a popular choice. There are several big sunny terraces set prettily around the piste. Quite often you'll find a live band playing outside one. Reader recommendations include the 'rustic' Ilga Stube, the lovely old Alter Goldener Berg, the Mohnenfluh and the Petersboden hotel's round tent. But the Burgwald is 'the best', insists one reporter this year.

Zug is another popular low-altitude option. The Rote Wand does 'a fine lunch' and the Alpenblick is also recommended. The Klösterle is said to occupy a 'beautiful old chalet'.

SCHOOLS AND GUIDES
Excellent in parts
The ski schools of Lech, Oberlech and Zürs all have good reputations and the instructors speak good English. Group lessons are divided into no fewer than 10 ability levels. One past visitor enjoyed 'the best lessons I have ever had'. Another reader experienced 'flexible, small classes' and 'friendly instructors'. Last season the mountain guides office started a new school, Omeshorn Alpincenter – reports welcome. In peak periods, you should book instructors and guides well in advance, as many are booked every year by regular visitors.

GETTING THERE

Air Zürich 200km/
124 miles (2½hr);
Innsbruck 120km/
75 miles (1½hr).
Friedrichshafen
130km/81 miles
(1½hr).

Rail Langen (17km/
10 miles); regular
buses from station,
buses connect with
international trains.

FACILITIES FOR CHILDREN
Oberlech's fine, but expensive

Oberlech makes an excellent choice for
families who can afford it, particularly
as it's so convenient for the slopes.
Reporters have praised the family-
friendly approach, and attention paid
to children using the lifts: 'Mountain
staff were really polite and helpful.'
The Sonnenburg and the Goldener
Berg have in-house kindergartens.
Children of visitors staying in Oberlech
have free access to the kindergarten
there, Kinderland. Reporters tell us the
Oberlech school is great for children,
with small classes, good English
spoken and lunch offered.

STAYING THERE

HOW TO GO
Surprising variety

The accommodation ranges from luxury
hotels to simple but spotless B&Bs.
Hotels There are three 5-stars, over 30
4-stars and countless modest places.

LECH

(((((5) **Arlberg** (2134-0) Patronised by
royalty and celebrities. Elegantly rustic
chalet, centrally set. Pool. 'Good food
and service – probably the best in

Lech,' says a 2006 report.
(((((5) **Post** (2206-0) Lovely old Relais
& Chateaux place on main street with
pool, sauna. 'Absolutely first class.'
((((4) **Angela** (2407) Perfect for keen
skiers: in a piste-side location up the
hill from the Schlegelkopf chair-lift.
((((4) **Brunnenhof** (2349) Highly
recommended by a 2006 reporter.
'Food and service were excellent.'
((((4) **Haldenhof** (2444-0) Friendly and
well run, with antiques and fine
paintings. 'Totally brilliant – probably
the best food I have had anywhere in
the world,' enthuses a reporter.
((((4) **Krone** (2551) One of the oldest
buildings, in a prime spot by the river.
'Food and service faultless,' says one
reader. But small rooms and some
noise, according to a 2006 visitor.
'Superb' wellness centre with pool .
((((4) **Monzabon** (2104) 'Characterful,
with friendly staff,' says a reporter. Pool
and an indoor ice rink.
((((4) **Tannbergerhof** (2202-0)
Splendidly atmospheric inn on main
street, with outdoor bar and popular
disco (tea time as well as later). Pool.
(((3) **Pension Angerhof** (2418) Beautiful
ancient pension, with wood panels and
quaint little windows.

Lech

ACTIVITIES

Indoor Tennis, hotel swimming pools and saunas, squash, museum, ice rink

Outdoor Cleared walking paths, ice rink, toboggan run (from Oberlech), horse-drawn sleigh rides

OBERLECH

(((4) **Burg Vital** (2291-930) 'Excellent – no criticism,' said a reporter.

(((4) **Burg** (2291-0) Sister hotel of Burg Vital – same facilities and with famous outdoor umbrella bar.

(((4) **Montana** (2460) Welcoming chalet run by the family of racer Patrick Ortlieb. 'Good food, wine,' says a 2006 reporter. Pool, smart wellness centre.

(((4) **Sonnenburg** (2147) Family-run chalet with a relaxed, traditional atmosphere. Good children's facilities. Pool, impressive wellness centre.

Other recommendations include the 4-star Schmelzhof (37500), with a children's nursery, **Gästehaus Lavendel** (2657) ('fantastic; huge breakfasts') and **Pension Sabine** (2718) in Oberlech – 'comfortable and charming with spa facilities.' Praised again in 2006.

Self-catering There is lots available to independent bookers.

Chalets There are a couple run by British tour operators, including Total's chalet-hotel with pool and sauna.

EATING OUT
Mainly hotel-based

There are over 50 restaurants in Lech, but nearly all of them are in hotels.

Angela
★★★★
Lech am Arlberg

4* on the ski slopes of Lech entice you with outstanding quality service and excellent cuisine.

Hotel Angela
Family Walch Fernandez
A-6764 Lech am Arlberg
Tel +43.5583.2407 Fax +43.5583.2407.15
angela.hotel@lech.at, www.hotel-angela.at

Reporter recommendations include the Krone, Ambrosius (above a shopping arcade), and the Post, which serves modern Austrian food. The Madlochblick has a typically Austrian restaurant, very cosy with good solid food, and Rudi's Stamperl is 'top-notch and reasonably priced'. Hûs Nr 8 is one of the best non-hotel restaurants and does 'good fondue' (a contradiction in terms, some would say). Schneggarei does good pizza. Bistro S'Casarole is a small casual place with a short menu of excellent grills. The Fux does 'excellent modern/Asian food, utterly un-Austrian' and the Lecher Stube (hotel Gotthard) is 'very good value' – recommended by a 2006 visitor. The Olympia is suggested for cakes and coffee stops.

In Oberlech, hotel Montana is a 2006 reporter's favourite. There is said to be good fondue at Alter Goldener Berg.

In Zug, the Rote Wand is excellent for fondues, kaiserschmarren and a good night out, but is said to be 'frighteningly expensive'. Reporters recommend the 'simple and charming' Alphorn, and the Gasthof Älpele 3km/ 2 miles from the road, up the valley on the cross-country route, reached by covered wagons attached to snowcats.

APRES-SKI
Good but expensive

At Oberlech, the umbrella bar of the Burg hotel is popular immediately after the slopes close, as is the champagne bar in hotel Montana.

Down in Lech the outdoor bars of hotels Krone (in a lovely setting by the river) and Tannbergerhof (where there's an afternoon disco) are popular. Later on, discos in the hotels Kristberg, Arlberg, Almhof-Schneider and Krone liven up too. The latter's Side Step specialises in 60s and 70s music. The Ilga is a good place for a drink, as is S'Pfefferkörndl. Schneggarei's music (rap to funky house) makes a change from Austrian drinking songs early and late. The smart, modern Fux bar and restaurant has live music, pop art in the toilets and a huge wine list. Archiv is good for cocktails and attracts a younger crowd.

Zug makes a good night out: you can take a sleigh-ride for a fondue at the Rote Wand, Klösterle or Auerhahn, then a visit to the Rote Wand disco.

After 7.30pm the free resort bus becomes a pay-for bus called James, which runs until 4am.

Phone numbers
From elsewhere in Austria add the prefix 05583.
From abroad use the prefix +43 5583.

TOURIST OFFICES

Lech
t 2161
info@lech-zuers.at
www.lech-zuers.at

Zürs
t 2245
info@lech-zuers.at
www.lech-zuers.at

OFF THE SLOPES
At ease

Many visitors to Lech don't indulge in sports and the main street often presents a parade of fur-clad strollers. The range of shopping is surprisingly limited, with Strolz's plush emporium (including a champagne bar) right in the centre the main attraction.

It's easy for pedestrians to get to Oberlech or Zug to meet friends for lunch. The village outdoor bars make ideal posing positions. There are various sporting activities and 29km/18 miles of walking paths ('well-marked and popular') – the one along the river to Zug is 'outstandingly' beautiful, and recommended by several readers.

There is a floodlit sledging run from Oberlech to town: 'Loved by kids and not to be missed,' says a reporter.

Zürs 1720m/5,640ft

Ten minutes' drive towards St Anton from Lech, Zürs is almost on the Flexen Pass, with good snow virtually guaranteed. Austria's first recognisable ski lift was built here in 1937. But, apart from the excellent hotels, we find Zürs a difficult place to like. It has nothing resembling a centre, few shops – and the traffic to/from Lech doesn't so much intrude as ruin the place.

The village is a fraction the size of Lech, but matches its bigger neighbour with three 5-star hotels. We stayed at the 5-star Zürserhof (25130) and found it excellent – great service, food and spa facilities. There are eight 4-stars. Of these, the Alpenhotel Valluga (24260) is a warmly welcoming, traditional chalet in a prime position close to the Zürserseebahn. A couple of reporters liked the Hirlanda (2262) for its convenient location and 'excellent food and service.'

If you want to eat out, it will probably be in another hotel. The Kaminstüble (hotel Schweizerhaus) has been recommended for 'fabulous food and service' and Toni's Einkehr (hotel Flexen) is reported to be 'good value'. Nightlife is quiet. Vernissage, at the Select Alpenrose (22710), is said to be the best nightspot. There's a disco in the Edelweiss hotel (26620) and a piano bar in the Alpenhof (21910).

Many of the local Zürs instructors are booked for the entire season by regular clients, and more than 80 per cent of them are booked privately.

Lech

Mayrhofen

Traditional British favourite, much improved by terrain expansion a few years ago, with relatively reliable snow and access to a glacier

COSTS

① ② ③ ④ ⑤ ⑥

RATINGS

The slopes

Fast lifts	★★★
Snow	★★★
Extent	★★★
Experts	★
Intermediates	★★★
Beginners	★★
Convenience	★
Queues	★
Mountain restaurants	★★★

The rest

Scenery	★★★
Resort charm	★★★
Off-slope	★★★★

NEWS

A new 160-person cable-car (Austria's largest) is due to open in December 2006, going from Mayrhofen to Ahorn and starting closer to Mayrhofen than the cable-car it replaces (though it still won't be close to most accommodation). The Gerent T-bar in the Horberg area was replaced by a fast six-pack last season.

Snowmaking was increased in the Finkenberg area for 2005/06.

➕ Good terrain for confident intermediates

➕ Snow more reliable than usual in the Tirol, plus the snow guarantee of the Hintertux glacier nearby

➕ Several nearby areas on the same lift pass, and reached by free bus

➕ Lively après-ski – though it's easily avoided if you prefer peace

➕ Excellent children's amenities

➕ Wide range of off-slope facilities

➖ Often long queues for gondola to Penken – which is inconveniently sited for many visitors

➖ Slopes can be crowded

➖ Many short runs, though linked Lanersbach slopes are longer

➖ Few steep pistes – though they do include Austria's steepest

➖ No runs back to the village from Penken – the main area of slopes

➖ Smaller Ahorn area – the best bet for novices – is completely separate

Mayrhofen has long been a British favourite. Many visitors like it for its lively nightlife, but it's also an excellent family resort, with highly regarded ski schools and kindergartens and a fun pool with special children's area. The liveliest of the nightlife is confined to a few places, easily avoided by families. And there are quieter alternative bases, including Finkenberg (covered in this chapter) and Lanersbach (covered in the Hintertux chapter).

Mayrhofen's main Penken-Horberg slopes are entirely above the tree line, with no pistes down to valley level. The upside is better-than-average snow, for the Tirol; the downside, shorter-than-average runs (typically around 350m/1,150ft vertical). The linked Lanersbach sector opens up some welcome longer runs.

THE RESORT

Mayrhofen is a fairly large resort sitting in the flat-bottomed Zillertal. Most shops, bars and restaurants are on the one main, long, largely pedestrianised street, with hotels and pensions spread over a wider area. As the village has grown, architecture has been kept traditional.

Despite its reputation for lively après-ski, Mayrhofen is not dominated by lager louts. They exist, but tend to gather in a few easily avoided bars. The central hotels are mainly slightly upmarket, and overall the resort feels pleasantly civilised (though we have had a few complaints about traffic).

The main lift to Penken is set towards one end of the main street, and the new cable-car to the much smaller Ahorn sector will start 200m/65oft further along the road. The free bus service can be crowded and it finishes early (5pm), so location is important. The original centre, around the market, tourist office and bus/railway stations, is now on the edge of things. The most convenient

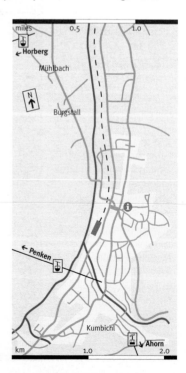

| Resort | 630m |
| | 2,070ft |

Ski and Glacier World Zillertal 3000

Slopes	630-3250m
	2,070-10,660ft
Lifts	62
Pistes	225km
	140 miles
Blue	26%
Red	60%
Black	14%
Snowmaking	93km
	58 miles

Mayrhofen-Lanersbach only (ie excluding Hintertux glacier)

Slopes	630-2500m
	2,070-8,200ft
Lifts	49
Pistes	157km
	98 miles

For Ziller valley

Slopes	630-3250m
	2,070-10,660ft
Lifts	177
Pistes	620km
	385 miles

area is on the main street, close to the Penken gondola station.

Free buses linking the Zillertal resorts mean you can easily have an enjoyably varied week visiting different areas on the Ziller valley lift pass, including the extensive Arena slopes linking Zell am Ziller to Königsleiten and Gerlos – and the excellent glacier up at Hintertux. But if you plan to spend a lot of time on the glacier, consider staying in Lanersbach (see Hintertux chapter).

The buses get packed at peak times, so it's worth planning your outings carefully ('Get the 8am bus and you'll be in Hintertux just as the lifts open,' recommends a reporter).

THE MOUNTAINS

Practically all Mayrhofen's slopes are above the tree line, and many are challenging reds. When you buy a lift pass, make sure it covers the Hintertux glacier, unless you are absolutely confident that you won't want to try it.

THE SLOPES
Rather inconvenient
The larger of Mayrhofen's two areas of slopes is **Penken-Horberg**, accessed by the main jumbo gondola from one end of town. It is also accessible via

gondolas at Hippach and Finkenberg, both a bus-ride away. You cannot get back to Mayrhofen on snow – you can catch the main gondola down or, if snow cover is good, you can descend to either Finkenberg or Hippach on unpisted ski routes (though these are often closed). The buses back from Finkenberg run only at hourly intervals.

A big cable-car links the Penken area with the **Rastkogel** slopes above Vorderlanersbach, which is in turn linked to **Eggalm** above Lanersbach – see the Hintertux chapter. These links are a great asset, and the run to Eggalm has been made more reliable by snowmaking being installed over the past two seasons. Getting back from Rastkogel on skis means braving a red run that can be heavily mogulled, but a rope-tow up to the top station of the cable-car means you no longer face a climb to avoid that run.

The smaller, gentler **Ahorn** area is good for beginners and is due to be served by a new 160-person cable-car for 2006/07, starting closer to town than the old one.

TERRAIN-PARKS
Comprehensive
One of the finest parks in the Alps (sponsored by Burton Snowboards) is built beneath the Sun-Jet chair-lift on

Mayrhofen

173

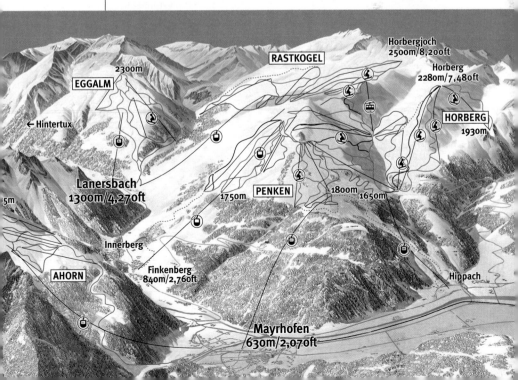

LIFT PASSES

Zillertaler Superskipass

Prices in €

Age	1-day	6-day
under 15	17	84
15 to 18	27	134
over 19	33	168

Free under 6
Senior no deals
Beginner no deals

Notes
1-, 2- or 3-day passes cover Mayrhofen areas only; 4-day and over passes include all Ziller valley lifts, ski-bus and railway. Part-day and pedestrian passes available for local areas.

SCHOOLS

Die Roten Profis (Manfred Gager)
t 63800

Total (Max Rahm)
t 63939

Mount Everest (Peter Habeler)
t 62829

Mayrhofen 3000 (Michael Thanner)
t 64015

Classes
(Roten Profis prices)
6 days (2½hr am or pm) €105

Private lessons
1 day: €118 for 1 person

boarding

Mayrhofen has long been popular with snowboarders from around the globe. And there is a large British contingent who make this town their winter home because of the extensive off-piste available. This said, however, beginners may have a hard time getting around as the terrain tends to be relatively steep, the nursery slopes are somewhat inconvenient to get to and the area still has quite a few drag-lifts. Intermediates and upwards will, however, relish the abundance of good red runs, and easily accessible off-piste. The terrain-park is one of the best in Europe.

Penken – but it can get crowded. There's an easy beginner line, an intermediate line and a pro line of tabletops ranging between 3 and 19 metres in length as well as a big hip jump. Every year there are more and more combinations of kinked, curved and flat boxes and rails for all levels. The half-pipe isn't on par with the rest of the park; but there is a 360m/1,180ft long super-pipe in Hintertux.

SNOW RELIABILITY
Good by Austrian standards
Although the lifts go no higher than 2500m/8,200ft, the area is better than most Tirolean resorts for snow-cover because the slopes are mostly above 1500m/4,920ft. Snowmaking covers nearly all the main slopes in the Penken-Horberg area, and is starting to appear on Rastkogel. And Hintertux has one of the best glaciers in the Alps.

FOR EXPERTS
Commit Harakiri
Austria's steepest piste, called Harakiri, opened three seasons ago under the Knorren chair, with a claimed gradient of 78 per cent or 38°. It is certainly steep for a European piste and when we tried it, the run was mogul-free, but rock hard except near the edges – not surprisingly, it was delightfully deserted. A 2006 reporter described it as 'one hell of a ride'. It does offer a worthwhile challenge for the brave but is quite short. The black run under the Schneekar chair on Horberg is a good, fast cruise when groomed, but there are few other steepish pistes. The long unpisted trail to Hippach is quite challenging but rarely has good snow because of its low altitude. There is, however, some decent off-piste to be found, such as from the top of the Horbergjoch at the top of Rastkogel – we had a great time there in fresh powder – and under the cable-car linking to Lanersbach. You can also try the other resorts covered by the valley lift pass.

FOR INTERMEDIATES
On the tough side
Most of Mayrhofen's slopes are on the steep side of the usual intermediate range – great for confident or competent intermediates. And the Lanersbach expansion a few years ago made the area much more interesting for avid piste-bashers, with some good long runs on Rastkogel and delightfully quiet runs on Eggalm. But many of the runs in the main Penken area are quite short. And (except on Ahorn) there are few really gentle blue runs, making the area less than ideal for nervous intermediates or near-beginners. The overcrowding on many runs can add to the intimidation factor.

If you're willing to travel, each of the main mountains covered by the Ziller valley pass is large and varied enough for an interesting day out.

FOR BEGINNERS
Overrated: big drawbacks
Despite its reputation for teaching, Mayrhofen is not ideal for beginners. The Ahorn nursery slopes are excellent – high, extensive and sunny – but intermediate mates will want to be on Penken. The Penken nursery area is less satisfactory and there are very few easy blues to progress to.

FOR CROSS-COUNTRY
Go to Lanersbach
There is a fine 20km/12 mile trail along the valley to Zell am Ziller, plus small loops close to the village. But snow down here is not reliable. Higher Vorderlanersbach has a much more snow-sure trail.

QUEUES
Still a real problem
The Penken jumbo-gondola is very oversubscribed at peak times. Reports of queues of 45 or 60 minutes at the morning peak are still common. An alternative is to take the bus to the Horberg gondola at Hippach. There are queues to get down at the end of the

day, too. The slopes can also get very crowded, causing queues for some lifts – a nuisance with so many short runs.

MOUNTAIN RESTAURANTS
Plenty of them
Most of Penken's many mountain restaurants are attractive and serve good-value food, but they can get crowded in peak season. The Schneekar restaurant at the top of the Horberg section has been highly recommended ('excellent lunch' and 'table-service, traditional food, open fire, wooden beams, leather sofa, sometimes with a jazz pianist' say two reporters). The Almstüberl at the mid-station of the Finkenberg gondola 'was usually quiet when others were packed'. Vronis Skialm remains a firm favourite with reporters ('fabulous steaks'). Schiestl's Sunnalm and Kressbrunnalm have also been recommended.

SCHOOLS AND GUIDES
Excellent reputation
Mayrhofen's popularity is founded on its schools, and a high proportion of guests take lessons. We have received many positive reports over the years, but a few negative ones too – including, strangely, reports of a shortage of English-speaking instructors. More reports would be welcome.

FACILITIES FOR CHILDREN
Good but inconvenient
Mayrhofen majors on childcare and the facilities are excellent. But there is a lot to be said for resorts where children don't have to be bussed around and ferried up and down the mountain.

HOW TO GO
Plenty of mainstream packages
There is a wide choice of hotel holidays available from UK tour operators, but few catered chalets.
Hotels Most of the hotels packaged by UK tour operators are centrally located, a walk from the Penken gondola.
(((((5) **Elisabeth** (6767) The resort's only 5-star – 'Superb, with excellent food and service,' says a 2005 guest. Casino.
((((4) **Manni's** (633010) Well-placed, smartly done out; pool.
((((4) **Kramerwirt** (6700) Lovely hotel, oozing character, 'friendly and helpful staff, good rooms, interesting food'.
(((3) **Strass** (6705) Right by the Penken gondola. Lively bars, disco, fitness centre, pool; but very big and with a down-market feel ('Brits in football shirts') and rooms that lack style.
(((3) **Neuhaus** (6703) 'First-class facilities,' says a reporter; good food but rooms above the bar are not ideal.
(((3) **Rose** (62229) Well placed, near centre. Good food.
(((3) **Neue Post** (62131) Convenient family-run 4-star on the main street – 'good food and nice big rooms'.
(((3) **Waldheim** (62211) Smallish, cosy 3-star gasthof, near the gondola.

EATING OUT
Wide choice
Manni's is good for pizzas ('but expensive, especially for wine'). Wirthaus zum Griena is a 'wonderful old wooden building with traditional cuisine'. We had good lamb and pepper steak at Tiroler Stuben. Tour op reps use the Mount Everest in the Andrea hotel. A 2005 visitor enjoyed lunch at Mo's.

GETTING THERE

Air Salzburg 175km/109 miles (3hr); Munich 190km/118 miles (2½hr); Innsbruck 75km/47 miles (1hr).
Rail Local line through to resort; regular buses from station.

ACTIVITIES

Indoor Bowling, adventure pool, two hotel pools open to the public, massage, sauna, squash, fitness centre, indoor tennis centre, indoor riding-school, chess, pool and billiards

Outdoor Ice rink, curling, horse sleigh rides, 45km/28 miles of cleared paths, snow-shoeing, snowmobiling, hang-gliding, paragliding, ballooning, panoramic flights, tobogganing, tubing

OUR WEBSITE

Go to our website at wtss.co.uk for resort news, links to resort sites, a build-your-own resort shortlist system and reader forums.

Phone numbers
From elsewhere in Austria add the prefix 05285.
From abroad use the prefix +43 5285.

TOURIST OFFICES

Mayrhofen
t 6760
info@mayrhofen.at
www.mayrhofen.at

Finkenberg
t 62673
info@finkenberg.at
www.finkenberg.at

APRES-SKI
Lively but not rowdy

Après-ski is a great selling point. At close of play, the umbrella bar, at the top of the Penken gondola, the Ice Bar at the hotel Strass and Nicki's Schirmbar, in the Brücke hotel, get packed out. Some of the other bars in the Strass are rocking places later on, including the Speak Easy, with live music; but the Sport's Arena disco is said to be 'for the kids'. Recent visitors have preferred the Apropos ('great music') and Brücke's Schlüssel Alm ('still the best all-round late-night venue'). Mo's American theme bar and Scotland Yard remain popular with Brits, but you might judge the latter to be 'dated, dirty and smoky'. The Neue Post bar and the Passage are good for a quiet drink. The hotel Elisabeth has a small casino (though one reporter said it was 'usually deserted').

OFF THE SLOPES
Good for all

Innsbruck is easily reached by train. There are also good walks and sports amenities, including the swimming pool complex – with saunas, solariums and lots of other fun features. Pedestrians have no trouble getting up the mountain to meet friends for lunch.

Finkenberg 840m/2,760ft

Finkenberg is a much smaller, quieter village than Mayrhofen.

THE RESORT

Finkenberg is no more than a collection of traditional-style hotels, bars, cafes and private homes. There is a pretty central area around the church, but most of the buildings (and hotels) are spread along the busy, steep, winding main road up to Lanersbach. Beware slippery pavements. Some hotels are within

walking distance of the gondola, and many of the more distant ones run their own minibuses; there is also an inefficient village minibus service.

THE MOUNTAIN

Finkenberg shares Mayrhofen's main Penken slopes.

Slopes A two-stage gondola gives direct access to the Penken slopes – and in good conditions you can ski back to the village on a ski route (though it is often closed).

Snow reliability The local slopes are not as well-endowed with snowmaking as those on Mayrhofen's side, but more was added for last season.

Experts Not much challenge, except off-piste and the Harakiri piste.

Intermediates The whole area opens up from the top of the gondola.

Beginners There's a village nursery slope, but it's a sunless spot, and good conditions are far from certain.

Snowboarding No special facilities.

Cross-country Cross-country skiers have to get a bus up to Lanersbach.

Queues We've had reports of 20-minute queues at peak times for the gondola to and from the Penken.

Mountain restaurants See the recommendations given for Mayrhofen.

Schools and guides The Finkenberg School has a good reputation.

Facilities for children There's a non-ski nursery, and the ski nursery takes children from age four.

STAYING THERE

Hotels The Sporthotel Stock (6775), owned by the family of former downhill champion Leonard Stock, enjoys pole position near the gondola station, and has great spa facilities. The Eberl (62667) is recommended by a 2005 reporter – 'attentive staff, excellent food' – but avoid the annexe rooms, and the Kristall (62840) was completely renovated for 2005/06 and is 150m/500ft from the gondola, it has a 'superb wellness spa'. All these are 4-stars.

Eating out Mainly in hotels, notably the Eberl.

Après-ski The main après-ski spots are the Laterndl Pub at the foot of the gondola ('jumping as the lifts close') and Finkennest ('welcoming, cosy, weird decor', but 'more civilised than the Laterndl').

Off the slopes Curling, ice-skating, swimming and good local walks.

Montafon

Extensive slopes with separate areas covered by a single lift pass – and some attractive places to stay, well off the beaten package path

NEWS

For 2005/06 in Silvretta Nova, the Vermiel six-pack replaced three drag-lifts from the central valley. The Nova six-seater (also from the central valley, new in 2004/05) was fitted with heated seats.

Work has begun on extending the NovaPark terrain-park (which the lift company aims to make 'one of the largest and best terrain-parks in the Alps'). On Hochjoch, a 3.5km/2 mile piste extension means you can now ski from the top down to Silbertal in the valley.

For 2006/07 more snowmaking is planned for the whole Montafon area, particularly Silvretta Nova, Schruns, Golm and Gargellen.

ALPENSZENE MONTAFON

Schruns is a towny little place with shops catering for locals and summer tourists as well as skiers ↓

The 40km/25 mile-long Montafon valley contains no fewer than 11 resorts and five main lift systems. Packages from the UK are few (accommodation to suit tour operators is not easy to find), but for the independent traveller the valley is well worth a look – especially the Silvretta Nova area (linking Gaschurn and St Gallenkirch) and high, tiny, isolated Gargellen.

The Montafon is neglected by the UK travel trade. Its location in Vorarlberg, west of the Arlberg pass, makes it a bit remote from the standard Austrian charter airport of Salzburg – and the valley is said to lack the large hotels that big operators apparently need.

But it is not undiscovered by independent travellers from the UK and we have had several positive reports on the area in the last few years.

The valley runs south-east from the medieval city of Bludenz – parallel with the nearby Swiss border. The first sizeable community you come to is Vandans, linked to its Golm ski area by gondola. Next are Schruns, at the foot of Hochjoch, and Tschagguns, across the valley at the foot of Grabs. Further on are St Gallenkirch and Gaschurn, at opposite ends of the biggest area, Silvretta Nova. Up a side valley to the south of St Gallenkirch is Gargellen, close to the Swiss border – a tiny village, but not unknown in Britain.

The valley road goes on up to Partenen. You can take a cable-car from Partenen to Trominier, and then a minibus (covered by the area lift pass) on up to Bielerhöhe and the Silvrettasee dam, at the foot of glaciers and Piz Buin (of sunscreen fame) – the highest peak in the

Vorarlberg. Bielerhöhe is a great launch pad for ski-tours, and there are high, snow-sure cross-country trails totalling 22km/13 miles on and around the frozen lake. From here you can ski down to Galtür, near Ischgl. Some of the ski schools organise trips, with the return to Bielerhöhe by snow-cat; you end the day with a long run back down to Partenen.

There are more ordinary cross-country trails along the valley, and an 11km/7 mile woodland trail at Kristberg, above Silbertal – up a side valley to the east of Schruns. Trails total over 100km/62 miles.

The shared valley lift pass covers the post-bus service ('comprehensive, and not too crowded') and the Bludenz-Schruns trains, as well as the 62 lifts – so exploration of the valley does not require a car.

The top heights hereabouts are no match for the nearby Arlberg resorts; but there is plenty of skiing above the mid-mountain lift stations at around 1500m/4,920ft, and most of the slopes are not excessively sunny, so snow reliability (aided by snowmaking on quite a big scale) is reasonable. Practically all the pistes are accurately classified blue or red, but there are plentiful off-piste opportunities (including quite a few 'ski routes'). There are terrain-parks in most sectors, the newest being NovaPark at Silvretta Nova, which also features a half-pipe and is being expanded.

There are 10 ski schools in the valley, operating in each of the different ski areas. And eight ski kindergartens take kids from age three.

Tobogganing is popular, and there are several runs on the different mountains – the Silvretta Nova's 6km/4 mile floodlit run down to St Gallenkirch being the most impressive.

For those with a car, there is accommodation in various smaller villages in addition to those dealt with

KEY FACTS

Resorts	655-1425m	
	2,150-4,680ft	
Slopes	680-2395m	
	2,230-7,860ft	
Lifts		62
Pistes		222km
		138 miles
Blue		50%
Red		36%
Black		14%
Snowmaking		97km
		60 miles

TOURIST OFFICE

Montafon
t 722530
info@montafon.at
www.montafon.at

The tourist office is in
Schruns, so from
elsewhere in Austria
add the prefix 05556,
from abroad use the
prefix +43 5556.

below. For example, a reader
highly recommends the hotel Adler
in St Anton im Montafon ('excellent
food, large pool'), at the entrance to
the valley.

GARGELLEN 1425m/4,680ft

**Gargellen is a real backwater – a
tiny, friendly village tucked up a
side valley, with a small but varied
piste network on Schafberg that is
blissfully quiet.**
The eight-person gondola from the
village up to the Schafberg slopes
seems rather out of place in this tiny
collection of hotels and guest houses,
huddled in a steep-sided, narrow
valley. The runs it takes you to are
gentle, with not much to choose
between the blues and reds; but there
is lots of off-piste terrain including five
ski routes. A special feature is the day-
tour around the Madrisa – a small-
scale off-piste adventure taking you
over to Klosters in Switzerland. It
involves a 300m/1,000ft climb (which
can take 40 minutes, observes a recent
reporter), but is otherwise easy.

The altitude of the village (the
highest in the Montafon) and north-
east facing slopes make for reasonable
snow reliability. And there is
snowmaking on one of the several
pistes to the valley, which include a
couple of excellent, scenic away-from-
the-lifts runs at the extremities of the
area. With care you can ski to the door
of some hotels, including the highly
rated hotel Madrisa (6331) – 'Fantastic

food, superb staff, excellent facilities.
The hotel made the holiday,' enthuses
a 2006 visitor. Behind the hotel is a
rather steep nursery slope. There are
four pleasant mountain restaurants:
the Schafberghüsliat the top of the
gondola and two rustic huts at the tree
line – the Obwaldhütte ('very
traditional, good value') and the Kessl
Hütte. The Obwaldhütte holds a weekly
après-ski party after the lifts close,
followed by a torchlit descent. (Slide
shows and bridge are more typical
evening entertainments.) The Barga
pizzeria at the foot of the Vergalden
drag can also be reached by walkers.

SCHRUNS 700m/2,300ft

**Schruns is the most rounded resort in
the valley – a towny little place, with
the shops in its car-free centre catering
for locals and for summer tourists.**
A cable-car and gondola go up from
points outside the village into the
Hochjoch slopes. Above the trees is a
fair-sized area of easy blue runs, with
the occasional red alternative, served
by slow chairs and drags and the fast
eight-seat Seebliga chair. There are
restaurants at strategic points – the
Wormser Hütte is a climbing refuge
with 'stunning' views, while the Kapell
restaurant has a good table-service
section. Parents can leave their kids
under supervision at the huge NTC
Dreamland children's facility at the top
of the cable-car, by the skier services
building. The blue run from Kreuzjoch
back to Schruns is exceptional: about
12km/7.5 miles long and over
1600m/5,250ft vertical. Snow-guns
cover the lower half of this, plus the
Seebliga area.

Easily accessible across the valley
are the limited slopes of Grabs, above
the formless village of Tschagguns, and
the more extensive area of Golm,
where a gondola goes from Vandans
up to a handful of chairs and drags
serving easy slopes above the trees,
and offering a vertical descent of over
1400m/4,590ft. A six-pack goes to the
top of the area, linked via a ski tunnel
to a quad on the Aussergolm slopes
on the back of the hill. This serves the
Diabolo black run, reputedly the
steepest in the Montafon. Snow-guns
cover two major upper slopes, and the
run to the valley.

MONTAFON TOURISMUS

← The Golm area is just one of five main ski
areas in the valley

Piz Buin 3310m · Bielerhöhe · 2275m/7.46oft · 2100m · 2150m · SCHAFBERG · Grüneck 2085m · 2010m · 1720m · 1850m · Gargellen 1425m/4,68oft · Hochegga 1600m · 1520m · GOLM · rtenen · 1480m · SILVRETTA NOVA · 1000m · St Gallenkirch 900m/2,95oft · Kreuzjoch 2395m/7,86oft · GRABS · Tschagguns · Vandan 655m/2510 · Gaschurn 1000m/3,28oft · Gortipohl · 2300m · Schruns 700m/2,300ft · 1850m · HOCHJOCH · 1335m · Silbertal 890m · Kristberg

Phone numbers

Gargellen
From elsewhere in Austria add the prefix 05557.
From abroad use the prefix +43 5557.

Schruns
From elsewhere in Austria add the prefix 05556.
From abroad use the prefix +43 5556.

Gaschurn
From elsewhere in Austria add the prefix 05558.
From abroad use the prefix +43 5558.

TOURIST OFFICES

Gargellen
t 6303
tourismus@gargellen.at
www.gargellen.at

Schruns
t 721660
info@schruns-tschagguns.at
www.schruns.at

Gaschurn
t 82010
info@gaschurn-partenen.com
www.gaschurn-partenen.com

As you are reminded frequently, Ernest Hemingway ensconced himself in Schruns in 1925/26, and his favourite drinking table in the hotel Taube (72384) can be admired. The Löwen (7141) and the Alpenhof Messmer (72664) are elegant, well-equipped 4-stars with big pools, the former a hub of the 'quite lively' après-ski scene.

GASCHURN / ST GALLENKIRCH
1000m/3,28oft / 900m/2,95oft
Silvretta Nova is the biggest lift and piste network in the valley. As a result, German cars fill to overflowing the huge car parks at the valley lift stations. Gaschurn is an attractive place to stay.

The two main resorts here are quite different. Whereas St Gallenkirch is strung along the main road and spoiled by traffic, Gaschurn is a pleasant village, bypassed by the valley traffic, with the wood-shingled Posthotel Rössle (8333) in the centre.

The lift network covers two parallel ridges running north-south, with most of the runs on their east- and west-facing flanks. The slopes are accessed from three points along the valley. A gondola from Gaschurn (prone to serious peak-season queues) takes you up to the east ridge, while another gondola from St Gallenkirch goes up to Valisera on the west ridge. A chair-lift

to Garfrescha gives access to the central valley from Gortipohl – on the road between the two resorts. The lifts out of the central valley are queue prone. There is snowmaking on one-third of the area, with cover to two valley stations; more is planned for this season.

This is generally the most challenging area in the valley, with as many red as blue runs, and some nominal blacks. Most of the slopes are above the tree line, typically offering a modest 300m/98oft vertical. The Rinderhütte six-pack serves more red pistes from the top of the area. There is lots of off-piste potential, including steep (and quite dangerous) slopes down into the central valley. The map shows four 'ski routes'.

There are lots of mountain restaurants, many impressive in different ways. At the top of the east ridge, the state-of-the-art Nova Stoba has seats for over 1,500 people in various rooms catering for different markets, including splendid panelled rooms with table service. The big terrace bar gets seriously boisterous in the afternoons. At the top of the other ridge is the splendidly woody Valisera Hüsli. A 2005 reporter recommends the strudel and glühwein at Zur Brez'n and, snow permitting, searching out the unmapped Lammhütta on run 1a down to Gaschurn: 'Basic but lovely.'

Nauders/Reschenpass

A rustic village remotely set high up on the border with Italy (and close to Switzerland) – a good base for an international tour by car

COSTS

① ② ③ ④ ⑤ ⑥

RATINGS

The slopes

Fast lifts	★★★
Snow	★★★★
Extent	★★
Expert	★★★
Intermediate	★★★★
Beginner	★★
Convenience	★★
Queues	★★★★
Mountain restaurants	★★★

The rest

Scenery	★★★
Charm	★★★★
Off-slope	★★★

NEWS

For 2005/06 a six-pack replaced the Geissloch drag-lift at Piengtal. Two red runs were added from the top: the former itinerary was reclassified.

And there's a new drag-lift at village level, serving the beginner slopes next to the gondola station.

At Schöneben, the home run was widened and improved.

➕ High-altitude slopes, by Tirolean standards – so relatively snow-sure

➕ Attractively traditional village

➕ Grand views from the top lift

➕ Day trips to various places, including St Moritz in Switzerland, are a possibility, but ...

➖ That's just as well – the local slopes are rather limited in extent

➖ Main Nauders lifts are a bus-ride from the village, with Schöneben and Haider Alm further away still

Nauders is in the Tirol, but only just – it's 3km/2 miles from the Swiss border, and its lifts run up to the Italian one. And the Skiparadies Reschenpass area of which Nauders is the main element also includes two other small resorts just over the pass in Italy – Schöneben and Haider Alm. Swiss outings to Bad Scuol or even St Moritz are possible – or to Samnaun, which connects with Ischgl, back in Austria. All in all, it makes an interesting departure from the Tirolean norm.

THE RESORT

Nauders is a rustic, not overly commercialised village just short of the crest of the Reschenpass to Italy – but happily bypassed by the main road. It's a quiet family resort, with chalet-style guest-houses dotted along narrow lanes (some of them one-way).

The bit of Italy just over the pass is part of the Süd Tirol, where place names in German dominate.

THE MOUNTAINS

Nauders' home slopes at Bergkastel start about 2km/1 mile outside the village, reached by a free shuttle-bus. The opportunity to visit other resorts covered by the Reschenpass lift pass effectively doubles the terrain. An outing to Switzerland is tempting: there aren't many resorts within day-trip range of St Moritz, but this is one.

Slopes The main lift to **Bergkastel** is a powerful gondola up to the mid-mountain meeting area (2200m/ 7,220ft), just above the tree line. Beyond here there are three main options: take an eight-seat chair another 400m/1,310ft up the wide slopes of Bergkastelspitz; move across to a new six-pack on the next hill; or continue to another six-pack chair on Tscheyeck, surmounted by a drag to the area high-point at 2850m/9,350ft.

There are a couple of runs back to the valley – the Talabfahrt red is a beautiful, wide swathe through trees.

Schöneben is the name of a mountainside above the little village of Reschen and of the company operating lifts on it. From the valley station about 1km/0.5 miles outside Reschen a gondola goes up to a mid-mountain lift hub, just above the tree line. There are wide, gentle slopes above and below this point, served by a six-pack chair, a couple of more challenging runs served by two chairs beyond it, and an easy, undulating, highly enjoyable red run back to the valley, widened and improved for 2005/06.

The third area, **Haider Alm**, is named in the same fashion: Haider Alm is the tree-line focus of the lifts above the village of St Valentin. This is the most limited of the areas. But any mountain with 1200m/3,940ft vertical has to be worth a visit.

Terrain-parks There's a half-pipe in Nauders, a small park at Haider Alm and a carving course at Schöneben.

Snow reliability The slopes are quite good for snow. The pistes of Schöneben and Haider Alm are almost entirely covered by artificial back-up, as are a good proportion of those at Nauders, most of which get a lot of afternoon sun. We've found the grooming to be immaculate.

Experts The Reschenpass area is not ideal for experts looking for a challenge, but there are satisfying runs. Die Schwarze, on Tscheyeck, just about deserves its black classification, and is designated a bumps run. The blacks at Schöneben used to be red, and

Nauders

KEY FACTS

Resort	1400m
	4,590ft
Slopes	1400-2850m
	4,590-9,350ft
Lifts	26
Pistes	111km
	69 miles
Blue	37%
Red	43%
Black	20%
Snowmaking	90km
	56 miles

OUR WEBSITE

Go to our website at wtss.co.uk for resort news, links to resort sites, a build-your-own resort shortlist system and reader forums.

Phone numbers
From elsewhere in Austria add the prefix 05473.
From abroad use the prefix +43 5473.

TOURIST OFFICE

t 87220
office@nauders.info
www.nauders.info
www.reschenpass.net

properly so. There is a lot of off-piste terrain accessible from the Tscheyeck chair (including ways down to Nauders itself), and there are red-classified ski routes from the drag above it.

Intermediates Basically, all the slopes here make excellent intermediate terrain. They don't add up to a huge amount, but with three areas to play in there is no lack of variety. The long descents to the valley at Nauders and Schöneben are very satisfying.

Beginners Nauders is not an ideal place for complete beginners because the village nursery slopes are some way out. A new lift for 2005/06 has improved the area beside the gondola, but most beginner lessons take place at mid-mountain.

Snowboarding Facilities include the half-pipe on the Nauders slopes.

Cross-country There are four cross-country trails – amounting to 40km/25 miles of track in all – of differing levels of difficulty around Nauders itself. There are further accessible trails down in the (rather shady) Inn valley, over the Swiss border, and over in Italy.

Queues The place seems to attract weekend crowds, but we would be surprised if lift queues were much of a problem at other times.

Mountain restaurants At Nauders there are four; Lärchenalm is the first choice – a cosy chalet with efficient table-service. At Schöneben there are three restaurants at mid-mountain, including a pleasant, woody self-service. At the far edge of the area is an extremely rustic Schihütte.

Schools and guides There are two ski schools at Nauders; among their offerings are off-piste courses.

Facilities for children There's a learning area behind the children's restaurant at Bergkastel (classes from age three years), and a separate snow-garden. Nauderix Guest Kindergarten takes children from the age of two.

STAYING THERE

How to go You're on your own here: we know of no packages.

Hotels Most of the hotels are comfortable 4-stars. The Central (872210), Nauderer Hof (87704), Maultasch (86101) and Tirolerhof (86111) are well-equipped possibilities in the village. Nearer the lifts are the Neue Burg (87700), and the Erika (872170). For a friendly welcome in a simpler place, you won't beat the Pension Reiterhof (87263).

Eating out Many of the eateries are hotel-based. The hotel Almhof is a popular choice, with an attractive, lively pizzeria; the Aladin is another pizza and pasta joint. The Stadlwirt is recommended for more traditional food. The Gasthof Goldener Löwe is a traditional old inn.

Après-ski There are several options. The cramped, dark Traktor bar maybe has the edge on the similar Yeti. The hotel Almhof has an external round bar that is less noisy – though maybe not when the dancing girls are on display.

Off the slopes There is quite a bit to do, including long toboggan runs from Bergkastel and Kleiner Mutzkopf (a separate hill), curling lanes, tennis, ice skating, squash, bowling, and public swimming pools in hotels. There are 50km/31 miles of marked walks shown on a special map.

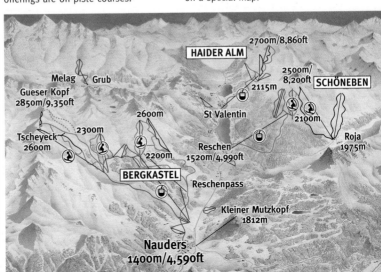

Obergurgl

A rare combination of extreme altitude and traditional Alpine atmosphere keeps the regulars going back, despite the drawbacks

COSTS
① ② ③ ④ ⑤ ⑥

RATINGS

The slopes

Fast lifts	★★★★
Snow	★★★★★
Extent	★★
Expert	★★
Intermediate	★★★
Beginner	★★★★
Convenience	★★★★
Queues	★★★★★
Mountain restaurants	★★

The rest

Scenery	★★★
Resort charm	★★★★
Off-slope	★★

NEWS

For 2005/06 snowmaking was extended to cover two runs below the Schermerspitze chair-lift.

And a golf-themed bar/restaurant has opened at the hotel Riml, complete with putting green and simulators.

➕ Glaciers apart, one of the Alps' most reliable resorts for snow – especially good for a late-season holiday

➕ Excellent area for beginners, timid intermediates and families

➕ Large areas of easy off-piste terrain

➕ Mainly queue- and crowd-free

➕ Traditional-style village with very little traffic

➕ Jolly tea-time après-ski

➖ Limited area of slopes, with no tough pistes and no terrain-park or half-pipe

➖ Exposed setting, with very few sheltered slopes for bad weather

➖ Few off-slope leisure amenities except in hotels

➖ Village is spread out and disjointed

➖ For a small Austrian resort, hotels are rather expensive

➖ Unremarkable mountain restaurants

A loyal band of visitors go back every year to Obergurgl or higher Hochgurgl, booking a year in advance in recognition of the limited supply of beds. They love the high, snow-sure, easy intermediate slopes, the end-of-the-valley seclusion and the civilised atmosphere in the reassuringly expensive hotels.

We're unconvinced. If we're going to a bleak, high, snow-sure resort where there is not much to do but ski or board, we'd rather go somewhere with more skiing or boarding to do. But, of course, most such places aren't in Austria – important to some – and their hotels might be less reassuringly expensive.

THE RESORT

Obergurgl is based on a traditional old village, set in a remote spot, the dead end of a long road up past Sölden. It is the highest parish in Austria and is usually under a blanket of snow from November until May. The surrounding slopes are bleak.

Obergurgl has no through traffic and few day visitors. The village centre is mainly traffic-free, and entirely so at night. Village atmosphere is relaxed during the day, jolly immediately after the slopes close, but rather subdued later at night; there are some nightspots, but most people stay in

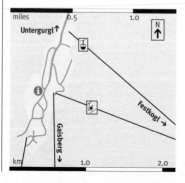

their hotels. The resort is popular with British families and well-heeled groups looking for a relaxing winter break.

Despite its small size, this is a village of widely separated parts; moving between them means long walks, a shuttle-bus ('excellent, prompt service,' says a recent visitor), or taxis charging a flat rate of 5 euros. At the northern entrance to the resort is a cluster of hotels near the main Festkogl gondola, which takes you to all the local slopes. The road then passes another group of hotels set on a little hill to the east, around the ice rink (beware steep, sometimes treacherous walks here). The village proper starts with an attractive little square with church, fountain, and the original village hotel (the Edelweiss und Gurgl). Just above are the Rosskar and Gaisberg chair-lifts to the local slopes. There is an underground car park in the centre of the village.

Hochgurgl, a gondola-ride away, is little more than a handful of hotels at the foot of its own slopes. It looks like it might be a convenience resort dedicated to skiing from the door, but in practice it isn't: from nearly all the hotels you have to negotiate roads and/or stairs to get to or from the

boarding

Obergurgl is a traditional ski destination, attracting an affluent and (dare we say it?) 'older' clientele. The resort is actually pretty good for snowboarding. Beginners will be pleased to find that most of the slopes can be reached without having to ride drag-lifts. And there's some good off-piste potential for more advanced riders. But the lack of any terrain features is a major drawback for most.

snow. Hochgurgl is even quieter than Obergurgl at night.

In the valley at 1795m/5,900ft is Untergurgl – linked by gondola to Hochgurgl and by regular ski-buses to Obergurgl. For a budget base, it is worth considering. For a day out, it's a short bus or car trip to Sölden (see separate chapter), and a long car trip to Kühtai (a worthwhile high area near Innsbruck). Much closer is the tiny touring launch-pad of Vent.

THE MOUNTAINS

The gondola between Obergurgl and Hochgurgl means that the two can be thought of as forming a single area (though the gondola closes absurdly early at 4pm). Even so, the slopes are quite limited. Most of the slopes are very exposed – there are few woodland runs to head to in poor conditions. Wind and white-outs can shut the lifts and, especially in early season, severe cold can curtail enthusiasm.

The lift pass is quite expensive for the relatively small area, but we're told the low-cost upgrade to cover a day in Sölden, sold last season, is likely to be repeated. Piste grooming is very good. Some reporters have complained of poor signposting.

THE SLOPES
Limited cruising

Obergurgl is the smaller of the two linked areas. It is in two sections. The gondola and the Rosskar fast quad chair from the village go to the higher Festkogl section. This is served by two drags and a chair up to 3035m/9,960ft. From here you can head down to the gondola base or over to the second section, Gaisberg, with its high point at Hohe Mut, reached by a long, slow single chair. Two chairs (one fast) now serve the lower, lightly wooded part of this area. Gaisberg is also reached via a double chair from the village.

There are two runs called 'varientenabfahrt', one of them the only run from Hohe Mut. The term is not explained; when we visited these were pretty wild itineraries – ungroomed, largely unmarked, possibly unpatrolled; take care. There are 8km/ 5 miles of night skiing ('excellent').

The slopes of **Hochgurgl** consist of high, gentle bowls, with fast lifts – chairs and a gondola – serving the main slopes above the village, but drags serving the more testing outlying slopes. From the top stations there are spectacular views to the Dolomites. A single run leads down through the woods from Hochgurgl to Untergurgl.

Obergurgl

183

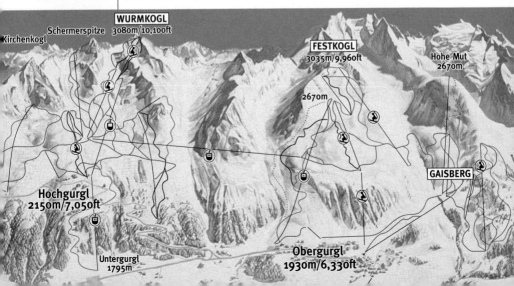

WURMKOGL
Schermerspitze 3080m/10,100ft
Kirchenkogl

FESTKOGL
3035m/9,960ft

Hohe Mut
2670m

2670m

2670m

GAISBERG

Hochgurgl
2150m/7,050ft

Untergurgl
1795m

Obergurgl
1930m/6,330ft

include a day on Sölden's slopes will be available again this season.

Hochgurgl has the bigger area of easy runs, and these make good cruising. For more challenging intermediate runs, head to the Vorderer Wurmkogllift, on the right as you look at the mountain. Less confident intermediates may find the woodland piste down from Hochgurgl to the bus stop at Untergurgl tricky.

The Obergurgl area has more red than blue runs but most offer no great challenge to a confident intermediate. There is some easy cruising around mid-mountain on the Festkogl. The blue run from the top of the Festkogl gondola down to the village, via the Gaisberg sector, is one of the longest cruises in the area. And there's another long enjoyable run down the length of the gondola, with a scenic off-piste variant in the adjoining valley.

In the Gaisberg area, there are very easy runs in front of the Nederhütte and back towards the village.

FOR BEGINNERS
Fine for first-timers or improvers
The inconveniently situated Mahdstuhl nursery slope above Obergurgl is adequate for complete beginners. And the gentle Gaisberg run – under the chair out of the village – is ideal to move on to as soon as a modicum of control has been achieved. The easy slopes served by the Bruggenboden chair are also suitable.

The Hochgurgl nursery slopes are an awkward walk from the hotels, but otherwise satisfactory. And there are good blue slopes to move on to.

The quality of the snow and piste preparation make learning here easier than in most lower Austrian resorts.

CROSS-COUNTRY
Limited but snow-sure
Three small loops, one each at Obergurgl, Untergurgl and Hochgurgl, give just 12km/7 miles of trail. All are relatively snow-sure and pleasantly situated. Lessons are available.

QUEUES
Few problems
Major lift queues are rare. An early season visitor this year reports 'no queues at all'. There can be high-season queues for the village lifts at the start of ski school, but these tend to clear quickly, except in severe weather when other lifts are closed.

↑ Most of the terrain is exposed and high above the tree line – snow-sure but very vulnerable to being closed by bad weather; this is the Wurmkogl area, above Hochgurgl

SNOWPIX.COM / CHRIS GILL

TERRAIN-PARKS
Sorry, no
We understand that there are still no plans to revive the terrain-park, half-pipe and quarter-pipe that were scrapped a few years ago.

SNOW RELIABILITY
Excellent
Obergurgl has high slopes and is arguably the most snow-sure of Europe's non-glacier resorts – even without its snowmaking, which has been increased again this year. It has a long season by Austrian standards.

FOR EXPERTS
Not generally recommendable
There are few challenges on-piste – most of the blacks could easily be red, and where they deserve the grading it's only for short stretches (for example, at the very top of Wurmkogl). But the Hohe Mut ski route can have big moguls, and there is a lot of easy off-piste to be found with a guide – and the top school groups often go off-piste when conditions are right. This is a well-known area for ski touring, and we have reports of very challenging expeditions on the glaciers at the head of the valley.

FOR INTERMEDIATES
Good but limited
There is some perfect intermediate terrain here, made even better by the normally flattering snow conditions. The problem is, there's not much of it. Keen piste-bashers will quickly tire of travelling the same runs and be itching to catch the bus to Sölden, down the valley – we are told the arrangement to upgrade a week's lift pass to

CHILDREN

Alpina, Austria and Hochfirst hotels
Kindergartens in these hotels

Bobo's ski-kindergarten
From age 3

Ski schools
Take children over the age of 5 (6 full days) €180)

SCHOOLS

Obergurgl
t 6305
Hochgurgl
t 6265

Classes
(Obergurgl prices)
6 days (2hr am and pm) €180
Private lessons
€118 for 2hr

MOUNTAIN RESTAURANTS
Unremarkable choice

Perhaps because the villages are so easily accessible for lunch, mountain huts are neither numerous nor very special. The jolly Nederhütte at Gaisberg is one of the best, with 'tasty and huge portions'. Carnivores will relish the ribs, but the menu is probably unique in Austria in offering several identified vegetarian dishes. David's Skihütte is 'very friendly', cheerful and good value. The small hut at Hohe Mut serves 'good, tasty, local dishes' and has fabulous glacial views from its terrace.

At Hochgurgl, Wurmkoglhütte is a big, pleasantly woody and spacious 'reasonably priced' self-service, but it gets too busy according to a 2006 visitor. The tiny hut above it at Wurmkoglgipfel does limited food.

SCHOOLS AND GUIDES
Further good news

We continue to receive positive reports of the Obergurgl school, with good English spoken, a maximum of nine per group and excellent lessons and organisation. One reporter found the instructors 'patient and supportive, and chose routes that built confidence'. Another reader this year rated her class 'a very positive and pleasant experience'. Demand for private instruction appears to be increasing and it is advisable to book ahead during peak periods.

FACILITIES FOR CHILDREN
Check out your hotel

Children's ski classes start at five years and children from age three can join Bobo's ski-kindergarten. There's lunchtime supervision for ski school and kindergarten children alike. Many hotels offer childcare of one sort or another, and the Alpina has been particularly recommended.

HOW TO GO
Plenty of good hotels

Most tour operators feature hotels and pensions. Demand exceeds supply, and for once it is true that you should book early to avoid disappointment.
Hotels Accommodation is of high quality: most hotels are 4-stars, and none is less than a 3-star. Couples have been surprised to be asked to share tables even at 4-star hotels.

A cheaper option is to stay down the valley in Untergurgl, where the 4-star Jadghof (6431) is recommended. Some hotels don't accept credit cards. ((((4) **Edelweiss und Gurgl** (6223) The focal hotel – biggest, oldest, one of the most appealing; on the central square, near the main lifts. Pool and outdoor whirlpool.
((((4) **Alpina de Luxe** (6000) Big, smart, excellent children's facilities. Pool.
((((4) **Bergwelt** (6274) Recommended as 'very smart'. Beauty and spa facilities, including outdoor pool.
((((4) **Hochfirst** (63250) 'Superb' spa facilities, comfortable, four or five minutes from gondola. Ski-bus stop right outside. Casino.
((((4) **Crystal** (6454) Near the Festkogl lift. If you don't mind the ocean-liner appearance, it's one of the best.
((((4) **Gamper** (6545) 'Excellent,' says a reporter – 'Good food, friendly staff.' Far end of town, past the square.
((((4) **Gotthard-Zeit** (6292) 'Elegant', spacious, comfortable, good food. Spa facilities. Small pool. Sun terrace. Recommended too for skiing convenience, but a 'steep walk back from the village' if you are on foot.
((((4) **Jenewein** (6203) 'Convenient with attractive spa facilities,' says a reporter.
(((3) **Wiesental** (6263) 'Excellent,' said a recent visitor. Comfortable, well situated, good value. Sun terrace popular for lunch and après-ski.
(((3) **Granat-Schlössl** (6363) Amusing pseudo-castle, surprisingly affordable.
((2) **Alpenblume** (6278) Good B&B hotel, well-placed for Festkogl lift.
((2) **Gurgl** (6533) B&B near Festkogl lift; friendly, pizzeria, same owners as Edelweiss und Gurgl.
((2) **Schönblick** (6251) B&B with downhill walk to main lifts, 'very clean, big rooms, hearty breakfast, friendly'.
Hochgurgl has equally good hotels.
(((((5) **Hochgurgl** (6265) The only 5-star in the area. Luxurious, with pool.
((((4) **Angerer Alm** (6241) 'Staff were

Obergurgl

185

↑ As you can (we hope) see, Obergurgl stretches quite a way – and the high bit is quite a bit higher than the low bit
OBERGURGL TOURIST OFFICE

GETTING THERE

Air Innsbruck 90km/56 miles (2hr); Salzburg 288km/179 miles (3hr); Munich 240km/149 miles (4hr).

Rail Train to Ötz; regular buses from station, transfer 1½hr.

ACTIVITIES

Indoor Pools, saunas, whirlpools, steam baths and massage in hotels; bowling, indoor golf, billiards, library

Outdoor Natural ice rink, snow-shoe outings, winter hiking paths

Phone numbers
From elsewhere in Austria add the prefix 05256.
From abroad use the prefix +43 5256.

TOURIST OFFICE

t 6466
info@obergurgl.com
www.obergurgl.com

really friendly and nothing was too much trouble,' said a reporter. Pool. (((3 **Sporthotel Ideal** (6290) Well situated for access to the slopes. Pool. (((3 **Laurin** (6227) Well-equipped, traditional rooms, excellent food. **Self-catering** The Lohmann is modern and well placed for the slopes, less so for the village centre below. The 3-star Pirchhütt has apartments close to the Festkogl gondola, and the Wiesental hotel has more central ones.

EATING OUT
Wide choice, limited range

Hotel à la carte dining rooms dominate. Remember, credit cards are not widely accepted. A reporter recommends the independent and rustic Krumpn's Stadl (where staff dress in traditional clothing). The Hexenkuchl in the Jenewein receives favourable reports, serving 'good quality Austrian food'. The Romantika at the hotel Madeleine and the Belmonte are popular pizzerias. Hotels Alpina, Hochfirst ('food excellent, good wine selection') and Gotthard-Zeit have been recommended. The Angerer Alm does 'good meals in relaxing surroundings'. The two restaurants in the Edelweiss und Gurgl are reportedly 'superb', and food at the Josl 'excellent'. Up the mountain, Nederhütte (which has a fondue evening with live music, which 'rocks', says a reporter) and David's Skihütte ('a real hut atmosphere') are both open on some evenings and popular snowmobile destinations. The 5-star hotel Hochgurgl is recommended for a 'delicious' treat.

APRES-SKI
Lively early, quiet later

Obergurgl is more animated in the evening than you might expect. The Nederhütte mountain restaurant is the place for lively table-dancing and should not be missed, enthuses a 2006 reporter ('fantastic'). You ski home afterwards though (or ride down on a snowmobile, says a reporter). All the bars at the base of the Rosskar and Gaisberg lifts are popular at close of play – the Umbrella Bar outside the Edelweiss hotel is particularly busy in good weather and the Pic-Nic is said to be lively. The Hexenkuchl at the Jenewein is also popular and a recent reporter enjoyed the 'excellent' and 'popular sun terrace' at the Wiesental.

Later on, the crowded Krumpn's Stadl barn is the liveliest place in town with live music on alternate nights. The Josl Keller is popular with all ages and gets busy. The Jenewein and Edelweiss und Gurgl hotels have atmospheric bars. The Lodge is a 'smart' new bar at the Hotel Bellvue. The Austria-keller disco is 'good fun' and attracts an extraordinary age range – 6 to 60. There's a casino at the Hochfirst.

Hochgurgl is very quiet at night except for Toni's Almhütte bar in the Olymp Sporthotel – one of three places with live music. There's also the African Bar disco.

OFF THE SLOPES
Very limited

There isn't much to do during the day, with few shops and limited public facilities. Innsbruck is over two hours away by post-bus. Sölden (20 minutes away) has a leisure centre and shopping facilities. Pedestrians can walk to restaurants in the Gaisberg area to meet friends for lunch and there are 15km/9 miles of hiking paths. The health suite at the Hochfirst is said to be open to non-residents. One reporter enjoyed the ski school display – held on Tuesdays at the top of the Festkogl lift ('great atmosphere for all the family').

Obertauern

High, snow-sure, French-style purpose-built resort on a small scale but with acceptable architecture and Austrian après-ski

COSTS

① ② ③ ④ ⑤ ⑥

RATINGS

The slopes

Fast lifts	*****
Snow	****
Extent	**
Expert	***
Intermediate	****
Beginner	****
Convenience	****
Queues	****
Mountain restaurants	****

The rest

Scenery	***
Resort charm	**
Off-slope	**

NEWS

For 2005/06 the new Monte Flu quad replaced the Flubachalm drag-lift on the lower slopes on the left hand side of our piste map.

REPORTS WANTED

Recently we have had few reports on this resort. If you go there, please do send us a report.

The best reports earn a copy of the next edition, and can lead to free lift passes in future. See page 12.

- ➕ Excellent snow record
- ➕ Efficient modern lifts
- ➕ Slopes for all abilities
- ➕ Good mountain restaurants
- ➕ Lively but not intrusive après-ski
- ➕ Compact resort core, but...

- ➖ Village lacks traditional charm and spreads along the pass a long way
- ➖ Peaks are not high, so slopes are of limited vertical and extent is too small for keen piste-bashers
- ➖ Lifts and snow can suffer from exposure to high winds

If you like the après-ski jollity of Austria but have a hankering for the good snow of high French resorts, Obertauern could be just what you're looking for. The terrain is a bit limited by French standards, and the village can't compete with the chocolate-box charm of some lower traditional villages. But if you've grown up on slush and ice in lower Austrian resorts, moving up in the world by 1000m/3,300ft or so will be something of a revelation.

THE RESORT

In the land of picture-postcard resorts grown out of rustic villages, Obertauern is different – a mainly modern development at the top of the Tauern pass road. Built in (high-rise) chalet style, it's not unattractive – but it lacks a central focus of shops and bars. Although the core is compact, accommodation is spread widely along the road.

THE MOUNTAIN

The slopes and lifts form a circuit around the village and the Tauern pass road that can be travelled either way in a couple of hours. Visitors used to big areas will soon start to feel they have seen it all. Runs are short and vertical is limited – most major lifts are in the 200m to 400m (660ft to 1,310ft) range. Reporters complain that there are a lot of flat areas at the bottom of pistes that can make getting to the next lift hard work. And a 2006 reporter who visited during a week when it snowed every day said, 'The resort has the worst signage of any I have skied and the lack of piste edge marking was a safety hazard in poor visibility.' While pistes are numbered on the mountain, they are not on the map.

Slopes Most pistes are on the (normally) sunny slopes to the north of the road and village: a wide, many-faceted basin of mostly gentle runs, some combining steepish pitches with long schusses. The slopes on the other side of the road – on Gamsleitenspitze,

to the south-west – are generally quieter and have some of Obertauern's most difficult runs. There is floodlit skiing from the Edelweisbahn twice a week.

Terrain-parks There is a terrain-park on the northern fringe of the area – the left-hand side of our piste map.

Snow reliability The resort has exceptional snow reliability because of its altitude. But lifts can be closed by wind (which may blow snow away too).

Experts There are genuinely steep black pistes from the top Gamsleiten chair, but it is prone to closure. And a 2006 reporter said, 'The icy racing piste beneath the Schaidbergbahn is also a challenge.' Reporters recommend joining an off-piste guided group to explore the area.

Intermediates Most of Obertauern's circuit is of intermediate difficulty. Stay low for easier pistes, or try the tougher runs higher up; you can't complete the whole circuit without venturing on to reds. In the Hochalm area, the Seekareck and Panorama chairs take

KEY FACTS

Resort	1740m
	5,710ft
Slopes	1630-2315m
	5,350-7,600ft
Lifts	26
Pistes	95km
	59 miles
Blue	59%
Red	37%
Black	4%
Snowmaking	85km
	53 miles

OUR WEBSITE

Go to our website at wtss.co.uk for resort news, links to resort sites, a build-your-own resort shortlist system and reader forums.

Phone numbers
From elsewhere in Austria add the prefix 06456.
From abroad use the prefix +43 6456.

TOURIST OFFICE

t 7252
info@obertauern.com
www.obertauern.com

you to challenging runs. The chair to Hundskogel leads to a red and a black. And over at the Plattenkar quad there are splendid black/red runs.

Beginners Obertauern has very good nursery slopes, but they are spread around and beginners must choose accommodation carefully to avoid long walks – there are no ski-buses. The Schaidberg chair leads to a drag-lift serving a high-altitude beginners' slope and there is an easy run back home.

Snowboarding Drag-lifts are optional and Blue Tomato is a specialist school.

Cross-country There are 17km/11 miles of trails in the heart of the resort.

Queues When nearby resorts have poor snow, non-residents arrive by the bus-load. However, the modern lift system is impressively efficient. The Sonnenlift double chair and the Grünwaldkopfbahn quad from the bottom end of the resort generate queues at ski school start time.

Mountain restaurants Mountain restaurants are plentiful and good, but crowded. A 2005 visitor recommends the Edelweisshütte, Treff 2000 and the Hochalm for 'lots of fun' in addition to food. A 2006 reporter recommends the 'modest' Flubachalm with 'traditional Austrian dishes', the self-service Dikt'nalm with 'beautiful new loos' and the 'jolly atmosphere' of the tiny Achenrainhutte.

Schools and guides There are six schools. Frau Holle school has a 'caring attitude' and 'excellent English'. A recent visitor found Willi Grillitsch school 'very efficient' and another was

pleased with an Australian snowboard instructor and liked 'the minibus to take boarders back to base at the end of the lessons'.

Facilities for children Most of the schools take children.

STAYING THERE

How to go Two major British tour operators offer packages here.

Hotels Practically all accommodation is in hotels (mostly 3-star and 4-star) and guest houses. The following have been recommended: Steiner (7306) – 'last word in luxury and great food'; Frau Holle (7662) – 'comfortable rooms and great breakfast'; Kohlmayr (7272) – 'excellent ambiance'; Enzian (72070) – 'very good facilities'; Schütz (72040) – pool and spa; Edelweiss (7245) – Beatles memorabilia from the filming of 'Help'; Gamsleiten (72860) – 'definitely upmarket'; Alpina (7336).

Eating out The choices are mostly hotels and the busy après-ski bars at the foot of the lifts. The lively old Lürzer Alm does 'terrific food'.

Après-ski It's lively and varied. The Latsch'n Alm, with terrace and dancing, is good at tea time. Monkey's Heaven and the People bar have dancing. The Lürzer Alm disco 'lives up to its wild, young crowd reputation' says a 2006 visitor. The Taverne has various bars, a pizzeria, and a disco. The Römerbar is worth a look.

Off the slopes There's an excellent, large sports centre – no pool, though. Salzburg is an easy trip.

Saalbach-Hinterglemm

A compelling blend of lively, traditional-style villages and extensive, varied, prettily wooded slopes; pity they are mostly so sunny

COSTS

① ② ③ ④ ⑤ ⑥

RATINGS

The slopes
Fast lifts	****
Snow	***
Extent	***
Expert	**
Intermediate	****
Beginner	***
Convenience	****
Queues	***
Mountain restaurants	****

The rest
Scenery	***
Resort charm	****
Off-slope	**

KEY FACTS

Resort	1000m
	3,280ft
Slopes	930-2095m
	3,050ft-6,870ft
Lifts	55
Pistes	200km
	124 miles
Blue	45%
Red	48%
Black	7%
Snowmaking	on all main slopes

+ Large, well-linked, intermediate circuit, good for mixed groups

+ Impressive lift system

+ Saalbach is a big but pleasant, affluent village, lively at night

+ Village main streets largely traffic-free

+ Lifts and pistes are conveniently close to centres of both villages

+ Atmospheric mountain restaurants

+ Large snowmaking installation

+ Sunny slopes, but ...

− Most slopes are low as well as sunny, and the snow suffers

− Limited steep terrain

− Nursery slopes in Saalbach are not ideal – sunny, and crowded in parts

− Saalbach spreads along the valley – some lodgings are far from central

− Hinterglemm sprawls along a long street with no clearly defined centre

− Saalbach can get rowdy at night

Saalbach-Hinterglemm is one of Austria's major resorts, with a claimed 200km/ 124 miles of pistes. Compared with other big names nearby, it emerges well: it has more challenging intermediate terrain and better mountain restaurants than the Ski Welt (Söll, Ellmau etc), more impressive lifts and snowmaking than Kitzbühel, and has the edge on both in terms of village altitude and ski convenience.

But look further afield for your comparisons, and you become more aware of what a weakness it is to have most slopes facing south, especially when those slopes are mainly below the 1900m/6,230ft mark. There is a limit to what snowmaking can achieve, especially in February and March.

THE RESORT

Saalbach and Hinterglemm are separate villages, their centres 4km/ 2.5 miles apart, which have expanded along the floor of their dead-end valley. They haven't quite merged, but they have adopted a single shared

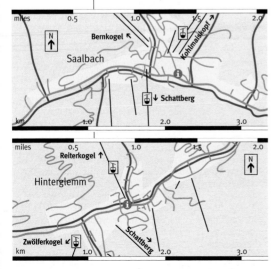

marketing identity. This doesn't mean they offer a single kind of holiday.

Saalbach is an attractive, typically Austrian village, with traditional-style (although mostly modern) buildings huddled together around a classic onion-domed church. But it is more convenient than most Austrian villages, with lifts into three sectors of the slopes starting close to the traffic-free village centre; the result is close to an ideal blend of Austrian charm with French convenience.

Saalbach has a justified reputation as a party town – but those doing the partying seem to be a strangely mixed bunch. Big-spending BMW and Mercedes drivers, staying in the smart, expensive hotels that line the main street, share the bars with teenagers (including British school kids) spending more on alcohol than on their cheap and cheerful pensions out along the road to Hinterglemm. It can get very rowdy, with drunken revellers still in their ski boots long after dark.

Hinterglemm also has lifts and runs close to the centre, and offers quick access to some of the most interesting slopes. It is a more diffuse collection

↑ This clever shot of the point where Saalbach meets Leogang exaggerates somewhat the drama of the Leoganger Steinberge group beyond

SAALBACH-HINTERGLEMM TOURIST OFFICE

NEWS

For 2006/07 an eight-seat gondola is planned to replace the double chair linking Schattberg Ost and Schattberg West.

A six-pack with heated seats and covers is expected to replace the two drag-lifts on the slopes of Wildenkarkogel.

At Leogang, the Riederfeld red run to the valley is due to be improved.

For 2005/06 two six-packs with heated seats and covers replaced two T-bars to Kohlmaiskopf and Bründlkopf.

And an eight-seat gondola replaced the double chair to Hochalm at Lengau. The Hochalm six-seat chair above it was equipped with heated seats.

of hotels and holiday homes, where prices are lower and less cash is flashed. The main street, lined with bars and hotels, has been relieved of through traffic, though it is not quite traffic-free. It is lively without being rowdy, and for many people is the more attractive option.

In both villages, the amount of walking depends heavily on where you stay. There is an excellent valley bus service, but it isn't perfect: it finishes early, gets very busy at peak times and doesn't get you back to hotels in central Hinterglemm, or to hotels set away from the main road. Taxis are plentiful and not expensive.

Several resorts in Salzburg province are reachable by road – including Bad Hofgastein, Kaprun and Zell am See, the last a short bus-ride away.

THE MOUNTAINS

The slopes form a 'circus' almost entirely composed of intermediate, lightly wooded slopes.

THE SLOPES
User-friendly circuit
Travelling anticlockwise, you can make a complete circuit of the valley on skis, crossing from one side to the other at Vorderglemm and Lengau. You have to tackle a red run from Schattberg West, but otherwise can stick to blues. Going clockwise, you have to truncate the circuit because there is no lift on the south side at Vorderglemm – and there is more red-run skiing to do (and a black if you want to do the full circuit).

On the south-facing side, five

sectors can be identified, each served by a lift from the valley – from west to east, **Hochalm, Reiterkogel, Bernkogel, Kohlmaiskopf** and **Wildenkarkogel**. The links across these south-facing slopes work well: when traversing the whole hillside you need to descend to the valley floor only once – at Saalbach, where the main street separates Bernkogel from Kohlmaiskopf. The Wildenkarkogel sector connects via Seidl-Alm to the slopes of **Leogang**; a small, high, open area leads to a long, north-facing slope down to the base of an eight-seat gondola near Hütten, 3km/2 miles from Leogang village.

The north-facing slopes are different in character: two widely separated and steeper mountains, one split into twin peaks. An eight-seat gondola rises from Saalbach to **Schattberg Ost**, where the high, open, sunny slopes behind the peak are served by a fast quad. The slightly higher peak of **Schattberg West** is reached by gondola from Hinterglemm. A new gondola is planned for 2006/07 to replace the double chair between Schattberg Ost and Schattberg West.

The second north-facing hill is **Zwölferkogel**, served by a two-stage eight-seat gondola from Hinterglemm. A six-pack and drag-lift serve open slopes on the sunny side of the peak, and a second gondola from the valley provides a link from the south-facing Hochalm slopes.

The Hinterglemm nursery slopes are well used, and floodlit every evening.

TERRAIN-PARKS
Excellent
There's a terrain-park with half-pipe on the north-facing slopes just above Hinterglemm (floodlit and 'loved' by a recent reporter's teenagers), and another below Kl. Asitz on the way to Leogang. Below Seidl-Alm there's a boarder-cross course. Several dedicated 'carving' and 'mogul' zones are dotted around the area.

SNOW RELIABILITY
A tale of two sides
The south-facing slopes are in the majority, and can suffer when the sun comes out. Most are above 1400m/ 4,590ft; on the other hand, most are below 1900m/6,235ft. The north-facing slopes keep their snow better but can get icy. The long north-facing run down to Leogang often has the best snow in the area. Piste maintenance is good,

LIFT PASSES

Skicircus Saalbach Hinterglemm Leogang

Prices in €

Age	1-day	6-day
under 16	18	86
16 to 18	29	138
over 19	36	173

Free under 6

Senior no deals

Beginner points card

Notes
Covers Saalbach, Hinterglemm and Leogang, and the ski-bus; also Reiterkogel toboggan run at night. Part-day passes available. Supplement for swimming pool.

Alternative passes
Salzburg Super Ski Card covers all lifts and pistes in Salzburgerland including Zell am See, Kaprun, Schladming and Bad Gastein.

boarding

Saalbach is great for boarding. Slopes are extensive, lifts are mainly chairs and gondolas (though there are some connecting drags), and there are pistes to appeal to beginners, intermediates and experts alike – with few flats to negotiate. For experienced boarders, there's plenty of off-piste terrain between the lifts.

and snowmaking – improved substantially in recent years – now covers many top-to-bottom runs; but the low altitude is a problem that won't go away.

FOR EXPERTS
Little steep stuff

There are a few challenging slopes on the north-facing side. The long (4km/2.5 mile) Nordabfahrt run beneath the Schattberg Ost gondola is a genuine black – a fine fast bash first thing in the morning if it has been groomed. The Zwölferkogel Nordabfahrt at Hinterglemm is less consistent, but its classification is justified by a few short, steeper pitches. The World Cup downhill run from Zwölferkogel is interesting, as is the 5km/3 mile Schattberg West-Hinterglemm red (and its scenic 'ski route' variant). Off-piste guides are

available, but snow conditions and forest tend to limit the potential.

FOR INTERMEDIATES
Paradise for most

This area is ideal for both the mileage-hungry piste-basher and the more leisurely cruiser, although one nervous third-weeker found the slopes too challenging and gave up after two days, warns a recent visitor. For those looking for more of a challenge, the most direct routes down from Hochalm, Reiterkogel, Kohlmaiskopf and Hochwartalm are good fun. Only the delightful blue from Bernkogel into Saalbach – 'the ultimate cruiser', to quote one visitor – gets really crowded at times.

The north-facing area has some more challenging runs, with excellent relentless reds from both Schattberg West and Zwölferkogel, and a section

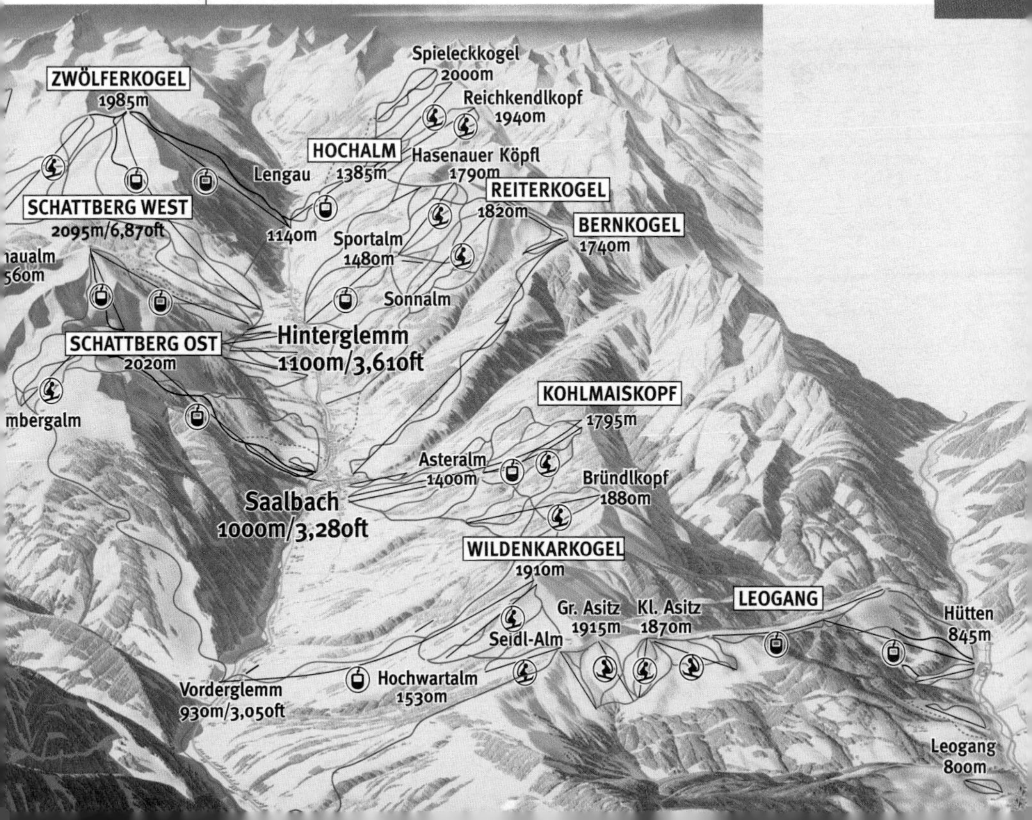

Saalbach-Hinterglemm

of relatively high, open slopes around Zwölferkogel – good for mixed-ability groups wishing to ski together, a happy reporter points out. None of the black runs is beyond an adventurous intermediate. The long, pretty cruise to Vorderglemm gets you right away from lifts – but one 2006 visitor suggests the lower section should be classified red, having witnessed 'a fair amount of distress at the end of the day'. Our favourite intermediate run is the long, off-the-main-circuit cruise on north-facing snow down to Leogang.

FOR BEGINNERS
Best for improvers
Saalbach's two nursery slopes are right next to the village centre. But they are south-facing and the upper one gets a lot of through-traffic. The lower one is very small but the lift is free.

Alternatives are trips to the short, easy runs at Bernkogel and Schattberg.

Hinterglemm's spacious nursery area is separate from the main slopes and 'very good', says a recent reporter. It is north-facing, so lacks sun in midwinter but is more reliable for snow later on.

There are lots of easy blue runs to move on to, especially on the south-facing side of the valley, which 'more than satisfied' a 2006 reporter's group.

FOR CROSS-COUNTRY
Go to Zell am See
Some 10km/6 miles of trails run beside the road along the valley floor from Saalbach to Vorderglemm, between Hinterglemm and the valley end at Lindlingalm, and there is a high trail on the Reiterkogel. In mid-winter the valley trails get very little sun, and are not very exciting. The area beyond nearby Zell am See offers more scope.

QUEUES
Only a problem in high season
Queues are a problem only in high season, when the lifts from Saalbach up the south-facing slopes can cause waits of up to 15 minutes at peak times, at the end as well as the start of the day. A mid-February visitor found 30-minute queues for the Schönleiten gondola up from Vorderglemm 'all day except first thing in the morning'. High-season queues can also arise for the chair to Hasenauer Köpfl. The fast six-packs now serving the upper slopes at Kohlmaiskopf and Bründlkopf have improved access there. The gondola

between Hinterglemm and Schattberg has reduced queues at the end of the day and the one planned for 2006/07 should greatly improve the link from Schattberg Ost to Schattberg West.

MOUNTAIN RESTAURANTS
Excellent quality and quantity
The area is liberally scattered with around 40 attractive huts, most serving good food. Many have pleasant rustic interiors and a lively ambience.

On the south-facing slopes, the Panoramaalm on Kohlmaiskopf and the Walleggalm on Hochalm serve particularly good food. The 'cosy' Thurneralm close to Bründlkopf serves 'delicious BBQ ribs and the best glüwein', says a 2006 visitor. Across in the Hinterglemm direction, reporters recommend the 'enterprising' Rosswaldhütte, not least for its 'excellent rösti'. The Bärnalm near the top of the Bernkogel chair does 'good food, good value'; the Westernstadl lower down has a 'cowboy-themed interior'. The Grabenhütte, tucked away from the main piste, is recommended by a reporter this year ('fantastic home-made sausages') – the return route follows a 'bumpy' un-pisted track. The Wildenkar Hütte has a big terrace and possibly the loudest mountain-top music we've heard, with resident DJ from mid-morning. The rustic Alte Schmiede at the top of the Leogang gondola is recommended for its 'good food' including 'the best pizza in the area', although you may have to wait for it.

The Simalalm at the base of the Limbergalm quad chair is 'great for the sun and the views'. On the north-facing slopes, the Bergstadl – halfway down the red run from Schattberg West – has stunning views and good food. Ellmaualm, at the bottom of the Zehner lift has been praised, the toilets being an 'outstanding' feature.

↑ Zwölferkogel, on the left, has everything from easy, sunny slopes to a proper shady black going down to a new gondola connecting with Hochalm, on the right

SAALBACH-HINTERGLEMM TOURIST OFFICE

CHILDREN
Several hotels have nurseries

Ski schools
Some take children in miniclubs from about age 3 and can provide lunchtime care. From about age 4½, children can join ski school (€142 for 6 days – Fürstauer prices)

GETTING THERE
Air Salzburg 90km/ 56 miles (2hr); Munich 218km/135 miles (3½hr).

Rail Zell am See 19km/12 miles (40min); hourly buses.

SCHOOLS AND GUIDES
Plenty of choice
We're all in favour of competition, but nine schools seems rather too much of this particular good thing. We get conflicting reports. With Fürstauer one visitor's children made excellent progress – but a beginner had some complaints. Last season a visitor using Aamadall Snow Academy had 'a very good instructor who took us from snowplough to parallel', but a previous reporter did not like the 'wide ranging standard in the class'. A Hinterglemm boarder had 'worthwhile' lessons with Hinterglemmer.

FACILITIES FOR CHILDREN
Hinterglemm tries harder
Saalbach doesn't go out of its way to sell itself to families, although it does have a ski kindergarten. Hinterglemm has some good hotel-based nursery facilities – the one at the Theresia is reportedly excellent.

STAYING THERE

HOW TO GO
Cheerful doesn't mean cheap
Chalets We are aware of a few 'club hotels' but Saalbach isn't really a chalet resort.
Hotels There are a large number of hotels in both villages, mainly 3-star and above. Be aware that some central hotels are affected by disco noise and front rooms by all-night street noise.
SAALBACH
((((④ **Alpenhotel** (6666) Luxurious, with open-fire lounge, disco, small pool.
((((④ **Berger's Sporthotel** (6577) Liveliest of the top hotels, with a daily tea dance, and disco. Small pool.

((((④ **Kendler** (62250) Position second to none, right next to the Bernkogel chair. Classy, expensive, good food.
((((④ **Saalbacher Hof** (71110) Retains a friendly feel despite its large size; 'excellent wellness centre'.
((((④ **Gartenhotel Eva** (7144) 'Small, good quality with sophisticated, simple, low calorie food,' said a reporter.
(((③ **Haider** (6228) Best-positioned of the 3-stars, right next to the main lifts.
(((③ **Kristiana** (6253) Near enough to lifts but away from night-time noise. 'Excellent food.' Sauna, steam bath.
HINTERGLEMM
((((④ **Theresia** (74140) Hinterglemm's top hotel, and one of the best for families. Out towards Saalbach, but nursery slopes nearby. Pool.
((((④ **Egger** (63220) 'I'll stay here next time, on the slopes,' says a reader.
(((③ **Wolf** (63460) Small but well-equipped 4-star in excellent position. 'Superb food and gala dinners.' Pool.
(((③ **Sonnblick** (6408) Convenient 3-star in a 'quiet location' with 'friendly service' and 'the comfiest holiday beds I have slept in', says a guest. 'Buffet breakfast excellent and tasty choice at dinner,' says a recent visitor.
((② **Haus Ameshofer** (8119) Beside piste at Reiterkogel lift. 'Great value ski-in, ski-out B&B,' says a reporter.
Self-catering There's a big choice of apartments for independent travellers.

EATING OUT
Wide choice of hotel restaurants
This is essentially a half-board resort, with few non-hotel restaurants. Peter's restaurant, at the top of Saalbach's main street, is atmospheric and serves excellent meat dishes cooked on hot stones. One reader enjoyed the

Phone numbers
Saalbach
From elsewhere in Austria add the prefix 06541.
From abroad use the prefix +43 6541.
Leogang
From elsewhere in Austria add the prefix 06583.
From abroad use the prefix +43 6583.

excellent food, with 'an emphasis on the meatier, richer dishes', at the Hotel Neuhaus. The Wallner Pizzeria on the main street is good value. The Auwirt hotel on the outskirts of Saalbach has a good à la carte restaurant. A reader recommends the 'reindeer steaks and marvellous atmosphere' at the Berger Hochalm, '3km up the toboggan track'.

APRES-SKI
It rocks from early on
Après-ski is very lively from mid-afternoon until the early hours and can get positively wild. Most places are packed by 4pm. In Saalbach the Bäckstättstall is recommended for tea-dancing. The rustic Hinterhagalm has live bands and rock music; when it closes around 6pm, the crowds slide down to Bauer's Ski-alm and try to get into the (already heaving) old cow shed. The tiny Zum Turm (next door to the church) is a medieval jail that also offers 'unusual bar games'.

Castello's 'at the bottom of the main street' is the place to be, according to one visitor. The Neuhaus Taverne has live music and attracts a mature clientele. Bobby's Pub is cheap, often full of British school kids, has bowling and serves Guinness. King's Disco livens up after midnight. Arena disco has go-go dancers and is very popular, as is Berger's Sporthotel.

In Hinterglemm there are a number of ice bars, popular at close of play, including the central Gute Stube of hotel Dorfschmiede, with loud music blasting out and people spilling into the street. A wider age group enjoys the live music later on at the smart, friendly Tanzhimmel – an open, glass-fronted bar with a dance floor. The Hexenhäusl gets packed. One recent reporter rates the rustic goat-themed Goasstall 'the best and loudest bar in the area'. Bla Bla is small and smart, with reasonable prices. The Almbar has good music and some dancing.

Tour operator reps organise tobogganing, sleigh rides and bowling.

OFF THE SLOPES
Surprisingly little to do
Saalbach is not very entertaining if you're not into winter sports. There are few shops other than supermarkets and ski shops – even those failed to impress a 2006 reporter. There are paths beside the cross-country trails and the Saalbach toboggan run. There are excursions to Salzburg.

Leogang 800m/2,620ft
A much less expensive alternative to Saalbach-Hinterglemm.

THE RESORT
Leogang is quiet, attractive and rather scattered. It's best to stay in the hamlet of Hütten, near the gondola into the main ski area.

THE MOUNTAIN
The village is linked to the eastern end of the Saalbach-Hinterglemm circuit.
Slopes A gondola from Hütten takes you into the ski area. The local slopes tend to be delightfully quiet.
Snow reliability The local slopes have some of the best snow in the region, being north- and east-facing, with snowmaking on the ski home run.
Experts Not much challenge locally.
Intermediates Great long red run cruise home from the top of the gondola. Plus the circuit to explore.
Beginners Good nursery slopes by the village, and short runs to progress to.
Snowboarding The whole area is great for boarding and there's a terrain-park.
Cross-country The best in the area. There are 20km/12 miles of trails, plus a panoramic high-altitude trail.
Queues No local problems.
Mountain restaurants A couple of good local huts. A recent visitor recommends the Forsthofalm – 'the nicest I have ever been in'.
Schools and guides Leogang Altenberger school has a high reputation – 'excellent service and lessons; highly recommended'.
Facilities for children There is a non-ski nursery, and children can start school at four years old.

STAYING THERE
Hotels The luxury Krallerhof (8246) has its own nursery lift, which can be used to get across to the main lift station. The 4-star Salzburgerhof (73100) is well placed, a two-minute walk from the gondola; sauna and steam.
Self-catering There are quiet apartments available.
Eating out Restaurants are hotel-based. The upscale Krallerhof has excellent food and the much cheaper Gasthof Hüttwirt has a high reputation.
Après-ski The rustic old chalet Kraller Alm is very much the focal tea-time and evening rendezvous.
Off the slopes Excursions to Salzburg are possible.

Schladming

Old valley town with pleasant main square and extensive intermediate slopes on four linked mountains

COSTS

① ② ③ ④ ⑤ ⑥

RATINGS

The slopes
Fast lifts   ****
Snow   ****
Extent   ***
Expert   **
Intermediate ****
Beginner   ***
Convenience ***
Queues   ****
Mountain
restaurants ****

The rest
Scenery   ***
Resort charm ***
Off-slope   ****

NEWS

For 2005/06 the old Gleiming gondola on Reiteralm was replaced by a new eight-seater one. And a new piste was built at the base of the Kaibling six-pack on Hauser Kaibling, which connects with the red Prenner piste that goes back to the valley.

For 2006/07 a new gondola with a mid-station is due to replace the bottom Planai West chair and go to Lärchkogel in the heart of the Planai slopes.

KEY FACTS

Resort	745m
	2,440ft

Schladming Ramsau/Dachstein area	
Slopes	745-2015m
	2,440-6,610ft
Lifts	90
Pistes	167km
	104 miles
Blue	29%
Red	61%
Black	10%
Snowmaking	100%

➕ Extensive slopes in four sectors

➕ Excellent slopes for intermediates

➕ Very sheltered slopes, among trees

➕ Lots of good mountain restaurants

➕ Appealing town with friendly people and a life independent of tourism

➕ Extensive snowmaking, good grooming and shady slopes mean good piste conditions, but ...

➖ The mainly north-facing runs can be cold in early season

➖ Slopes lack variety

➖ Very little to entertain experts

➖ Nursery slopes are inconvenient if you stay near the village centre

➖ Runs to valley level are not easy

➖ Not much lively nightlife

Since its four previously separate mountains were linked by lifts and pistes, Schladming has been able to compete with major resorts that are better known internationally. A keen intermediate who wants to make the most of the links and the reassuringly consistent slopes can get a real sense of travelling around on the snow. But if you like the spice of variety and the thrill of a serious challenge, you might find it all rather tame.

The resort does not offer one of Austria's wildest après-ski scenes, but most of our reporters don't mind that and enjoy its established, valley-town ambience.

THE RESORT

The old town of Schladming has a long skiing tradition and has hosted World Cup races for many years.

The town has a pleasant, traffic-free main square, prettily lit at night, around which you'll find most of the shops, restaurants and bars (and some appealing hotels). The busy main road bypasses the town and is separated from it by a river. Much of the accommodation is close to the centre and can be noisy into the early hours because of nearby bars. The modern sports centre and tennis halls are five minutes' walk from the centre.

Schladming sits at the foot of Planai, one of four mountains that are now linked to form a fair-sized network. A gondola starting a few

minutes' walk from the centre goes most of the way up this home mountain. To the east is the small, attractively rustic village of Haus, where a cable-car and gondola go up to the highest of the four linked mountains, Hauser Kaibling. From the western suburbs of Schladming there will be a new gondola up Planai for 2006/07 and there are chair-lifts towards the next mountain to the west, Hochwurzen. The lifts pass through Rohrmoos, a quiet, scattered village set on an elevated slope that forms a giant nursery area. Rohrmoos makes an excellent base for beginners who aren't looking for lively nightlife.

There are timetabled buses between the villages and lift bases, but they are not as frequent as reporters wished.

Reporters have been impressed with

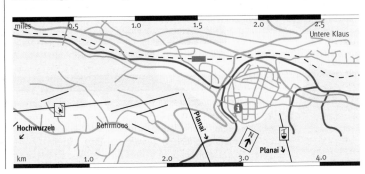

THE SLOPES
Four linked sectors – and more

Each of the linked sectors is quite a serious mountain with a variety of lifts and runs to play on. **Planai** and **Hauser Kaibling** are linked at altitude via the high, wooded bowl between them. But the links with **Hochwurzen** (where you can try night skiing, boarding or tobogganing, though it is not included on the lift pass) and with the fourth linked mountain, **Reiteralm**, are at valley level. Getting around the whole area can take time – and involves some uninteresting linking runs. The link between Planai and Hochwurzen involves riding the new gondola to/from the mid-station, whichever way you are travelling.

Some people who want to spend time on Reiteralm prefer to get the bus, or a taxi, to one of the lift bases at Pichl or Gleiming. You also have to do this (with a change of bus on the way) to reach unlinked areas such as **Fageralm**, which has mainly gentle intermediate and beginner runs, slow lifts and is usually uncrowded.

Several lower runs run across roads that aren't well signposted and a 2006 reporter says, 'Parents take note: there is a real danger of being hit by a car.'

There are handy ski lockers to rent at the Planai base station.

TERRAIN-PARKS
Three to try

There are two terrain-parks and half-pipes on the main linked area.

SNOW RELIABILITY
Excellent in cold weather

The northerly orientation of the slopes and good maintenance help keep the slopes in better shape than in some neighbouring resorts, and the serious snowmaking operation makes it a particularly good choice for early holidays; coverage is comprehensive, and the system is put to good use (to the point that one reporter found it 'a constant irritation'). The steep bottom part of the World Cup downhill run back to town can get extremely icy.

↑ Nearly all Schladming's slopes are sheltered and tree lined

LIFT PASSES

Ski Alliance Amadé Ski Pass

Prices in €

Age	1-day	6-day
under 17	17	84
17 to 19	30	152
over 20	33	171

Free under 6
Senior no deals
Beginner no deals
Notes
Day pass price is for Schladming Ramsau Dachstein only; part-day tickets also available. Passes for two days or more cover the 865km/ 538 miles of pistes and 270 lifts in five regions: Dachstein Tauern; Gastein; Salzburger Sportwelt; Grossarl; Hochkönig Winterreich.

Alternative pass
Salzburg Super Ski Card: all lifts in Salzburgerland including Zell am See, Kaprun and Saalbach-Hinterglemm.

the free photo e-mail service at the top of the Planai and Reiteralm gondolas. Another neat free souvenir is offered by the Skiline terminals at the Planai base. At the end of the day you can obtain a printout showing lifts used, height gained and distance covered.

THE MOUNTAINS

Most pistes are on the wooded north-facing slopes above the main valley, with some going into the side valleys higher up; there are a few open slopes above the trees. All four mountains have similar terrain, with mainly red runs of much the same pitch.

Piste maps, and discrepancies between different versions (runs red on one, blue on the other; marked on one, not on the other) continue to provoke criticism.

Apart from the main slopes we describe here, there are several other separate mountains nearby and shown on the main piste map – Fageralm, Galsterbergalm, Ramsau, the Dachstein glacier and Stoderzinken. The Ski Alliance Amadé lift pass also covers many other resorts. Trips to Bad Gastein are feasible by rail (with at least one change). Drivers can also visit Wagrain/Flachau, Kleinarl and Hochkönig. Tour operators organise day trips. Having a car is useful for getting the most out of the lift pass.

boarding

Schladming is popular with boarders. Most lifts on the spread-out mountains are gondolas or chairs, with some short drags around. The area is ideal for beginners and intermediates, except when the lower slopes are icy, though there are few exciting challenges for expert boarders bar the off-piste tree runs. The Blue Tomato snowboard shop runs the specialist snowboard school.

www.sport2000rent.com

online booking

FOR EXPERTS
Strictly intermediate stuff
Schladming's status as a World Cup downhill venue doesn't make it macho. The steep black finish to the Men's Downhill course and the moderate mogul runs at the top of Planai and Hauser Kaibling are the only really challenging slopes. Hauser Kaibling's off-piste is good, but limited.

FOR INTERMEDIATES
Red runs rule
The area is ideal for intermediate cruising. The majority of runs are red but it's often difficult to distinguish them from many of the blues.

The open sections at the top of Planai and Hauser Kaibling have some more challenging slopes. And the two World Cup pistes, and the red that runs parallel to the Haus downhill course to the village, are ideal for fast intermediates in good snow conditions but can get very icy and tricky. If they are bad, many prefer to ride the gondola down.

Hauser Kaibling has a lovely meandering blue running from top to bottom for the less confident intermediates, and Reiteralm has some gentle blues with good snow. Runs are well groomed, so intermediates will find the slopes generally flattering.

FOR BEGINNERS
Good slopes but poorly sited
The ski schools generally take beginners to the extensive but low-altitude Rohrmoos nursery area – fine if you are based there, a discouraging bus-ride away if you are not. Another

novice area near the top of Planai is more convenient for residents of central Schladming and has better snow, but the runs are less gentle.

FOR CROSS-COUNTRY
Extensive network of trails
Given sufficient snow-cover, there are 400km/250 miles of trails in the region, and the World Championships have been held at nearby Ramsau. There are local loops along the main valley floor and between Planai and Hochwurzen.

QUEUES
Avoid peaks at Planai
The Planai gondola can have morning queues at peak-season and weekends, but generally reporters have found few problems. A reporter recommends going to quiet Fageralm on exceptionally busy days.

MOUNTAIN RESTAURANTS
A real highlight
There are plenty of attractive rustic restaurants in all sectors, and they receive more praise from reporters than for virtually any other resort in Austria ('too many – we couldn't decide which to try', 'the best I have ever been to'). The 'spacious', attractive Schladminger Hütte, at the top of the Planai gondola is recommended as is nearby Onkel Willi's Hütte (live music, indoor nooks and crannies. large terrace). The terrace of the Weitmoosalm is very pleasant in the sun, as is the one at the Schaf-Alm ('excellent service, incredible food'). The Holzhackerstub'n on the lower part of the World Cup run

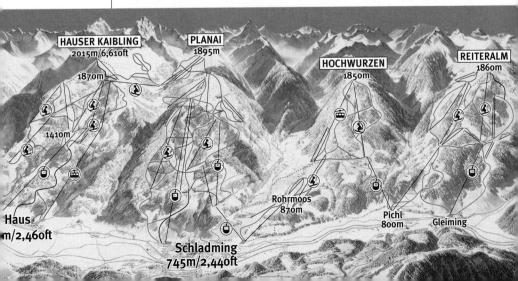

HAUSER KAIBLING
2015m/6,610ft
1870m
1410m

PLANAI
1895m

HOCHWURZEN
1850m

REITERALM
1860m

Rohrmoos
870m

Pichl
800m   Gleiming

Haus
m/2,460ft

Schladming
745m/2,440ft

CHILDREN

The ski schools take children from age 4 (€190 for 5 days including lunch – Tritscher price).

GETTING THERE

Air Salzburg 90km/ 56 miles (1½hr).

Rail Main line station in resort.

ACTIVITIES

Indoor Swimming pool, fitness club, tennis, sauna

Outdoor Ice skating, curling, tobogganing, sleigh rides, 30km/ 19 miles of cleared paths

Phone numbers
Schladming
From elsewhere in Austria add the prefix 03687.
From abroad use the prefix +43 3687.
Haus
From elsewhere in Austria add the prefix 03686.
From abroad use the prefix +43 3686.

TOURIST OFFICES

Schladming
t 22777
urlaub@schladming.at
www.schladming.at
www.skiamade.com
Haus
t 22340
info@haus.at
www.haus.at

---

has 'high quality freshly made food'. On Reiteralm 'you absolutely must visit' the Gasslhöh-Hütte to try the 'mega huge' spare ribs with jacket potato and garlic sauce. On Hauser Kaibling it's worth looking out for the sign to the tiny Kulmhoferhütte to experience real mountain hut atmosphere, complete with fur-lined walls. Higher up, the hut off the Almlift feels wonderfully isolated, with great views and soup. Mitterhausalm is good. The Knapplhof at Hauser Kaibling is full of ski-racing mementos.

SCHOOLS AND GUIDES
Generally okay reports
We have generally had good reports in the past, but a recent visitor found the Tritscher school 'badly organised'.

FACILITIES FOR CHILDREN
Rohrmoos is the place
The extensive gentle slopes of Rohrmoos are ideal for building up youngsters' confidence.

STAYING THERE

HOW TO GO
Packages mean hotels
Packaged accommodation is in hotels and pensions, but there are plenty of apartments for independent travellers.
Hotels Most of the accommodation is in modestly priced pensions but there are also a few more upmarket hotels.
((((4) **Sporthotel Royer** (200) Big, smart and comfortable, a few minutes' walk from the main Planai lift. Pool, sauna.
(((3) **Posthotel** (22571) Characterful old inn with great position on the main square (formerly called the Alte Post). 'Good food, helpful staff, good spa.' But some small rooms.
(((3) **Stadttor** (24525) Similarly priced, although less charming and well placed. 'Friendly, helpful staff and excellent food,' says a 2006 reporter.
(((3) **Kirchenwirt** (22435) Just off the main square. 'Traditional atmosphere, wonderful food,' 'great value for money'.
(((3) **Neue Post** (22105) Large rooms, friendly, good food, central.
(((3) **Zum Kaiserweg** (22038) Family run. Very near the new Planai West gondola. 'Good value, excellent food.'
(((3) **Rohrmooser Schlössl (61237)** Just downhill from the new Planai West gondola. 'Really friendly', with 'excellent food and views'.
Self-catering Haus Girik (22663) is close to the Planai gondola.

EATING OUT
Some good places
Recommendations include the Kirchenwirt hotel ('fine home cooking'), Giovanni's (for pizza), Gasthof Brunner ('good value'), Talbachschenke ('good grills and atmosphere') and Neue Post hotel ('good but expensive').

APRES-SKI
Explore the side streets
Some of the mountain restaurants are lively at the end of the afternoon, but down in the town there's a real lack of animation. Charly's Treff (with umbrella bar) opposite the Planai gondola is the main exception (and has great photos of local hero Arnold Schwarzenegger). The little Siglu has 'a good atmosphere' but quickly gets 'overcrowded and smoky'. The Schladminger Hütte at the top of the gondola has live music at après-ski time on Wednesdays and the gondola stays open to bring you down.
Later on, recent reporters have complained that the town is quiet ('lack of a buzz in the evening') even though many of the central bars stay open until dawn. We liked the brewpub, Schwalbenbräu. The Beisl is a smart bar but a 2005 visitor found it 'lifeless'. In contrast, the Neiderl is 'small but friendly'. Szenario is 'quite cosy, with very eclectic music choices'. Hanglbar has occasional karaoke and 'generally a good atmosphere'. Maria's Mexican is 'relaxing' with chilled music and margaritas. The Porta is a 'smart place with the best music and ambience'. The Sonderbar, a disco with three bars, is reportedly 'lacking in class'.

OFF THE SLOPES
Good for all but walkers
Non-skiers are fairly well catered for. There's a floodlit 7km/4 mile toboggan run at Hochwurzen, a pool and an ice rink. Some mountain restaurants are easily reached on foot. The town shops and museum are worth a look. Train trips to Salzburg are easy. Buses run to the old walled town of Radstadt.

Haus 750m/2,460ft

Haus is a real village with a life of its own and its own ski schools and kindergartens. The user-friendly nursery slopes are between the village and the gondola. There's a railway station, so excursions are easy, but off-slope activities and nightlife are very limited. Hotel prices are generally lower here.

FRANK HEUER

Sölden

A traditional valley town dominated by traffic and throbbing après-ski/nightlife – but with excellent slopes reaching glacial heights

➕ Excellent snow reliability, with access to two glaciers

➕ Fairly extensive network of slopes suited to adventurous intermediates

➕ Impressive lift system

➕ Very lively après-ski/nightlife, but ...

➖ It can get rowdy at times

➖ Busy road through sprawling village

➖ Some central hotels are distant from the two main access lifts

➖ Inconvenient beginners' slopes

➖ English not widely spoken

A couple of big UK tour operators now have Sölden in their brochures, but still very few Brits go there (and you might find the lack of English-speakers in the resort a drawback). Nevertheless, Sölden deserves a close look from keen intermediates keen on Austrian après-ski. It has recently invested massively in new lifts to link its extensive glaciers to the lower slopes, and there are some seriously long runs. Nightlife is not for the faint-hearted, or prudish.

THE RESORT

Despite its traditional Tirolean-style buildings and wooded valley setting, Sölden is no beauty: it is a large, traffic-filled place that sprawls along both sides of a river and busy main road. The resort attracts a young, lively crowd – mostly Dutch and German – bent on partying.

Gondolas from opposite ends of town go up to Sölden's home slopes – the peak of Gaislachkogl and the lift junction of Giggijoch. A free, 'very efficient' shuttle-bus serves both lift stations. Isolated high above the town is the satellite resort of Hochsölden – a handful of 4-star hotels, the attractions of which we fail to see.

THE MOUNTAIN

Practically all the slopes you spend your days on are above the trees, though there are red runs through trees to the village. Two recent reporters noted that they skied all the runs in three days. It seems that last season's low-cost pass upgrade to cover a day in nearby Obergurgl is going to be repeated for 2006/07.

Slopes The two similar-sized home sectors are linked by chair-lifts (one a new six-pack) out of the Rettenbachtal that separates them. Fast lifts from the Giggijoch sector lead to the Rettenbach glacier, and on to the Tiefenbach. Our attempts to get to the glaciers have always been thwarted by the weather;

SNOWPIX.COM / CHRIS GILL

We confess that we don't understand the appeal of fighting your way through this crowd beside Sölden's main street to get a beer, and then standing around in the gathering gloom drinking it ➔

KEY FACTS

Resort	1380m
	4,530ft
Slopes	1370-3250m
	4,490-10,660ft
Lifts	34
Pistes	150km
	93 miles
Blue	35%
Red	45%
Black	20%
Snowmaking	40 km
	25 miles

AUSTRIA

200

a 2006 reporter liked the extent and variety of the glacier slopes, but not the 'long trek' to get there.

Terrain-parks Two in winter above Giggijoch: one has a half-pipe, kickers and rails; the other a boarder-cross run with waves and jumps.

Snow reliability The slopes are high and mainly north-east- or south-east-facing; there is some snowmaking; and there are two extensive glaciers. So snow is usually good. Grooming is generally good.

Experts None of the black pistes dotted around Sölden's map is serious, and some are silly; but there are quite a few non-trivial reds. And there are extensive off-piste possibilities with a guide. At the top of the valley is one of the Alps' premier touring areas.

Intermediates Most of Sölden's main slopes are genuine red runs ideal for keen intermediates, and there are some serious verticals to be racked up – almost 1700m/5,500ft from Gaislachkogl to the village. There are several easy blacks. The long, quiet red down to Gaislachalm is relatively easy, and ideal for high-speed cruising. Giggijoch offers gentler gradients, but the blues here gets extremely crowded. Less confident intermediates should beware the tricky red runs to town from Giggijoch and Rettenbachtal; the latter is marked black on the ground.

Beginners The beginners' slopes are situated inconveniently – just above the village at Innerwald – and are prone to poor snow. Near-beginners can use the blues at Giggijoch. Stay away from Hochsölden.

Snowboarding Sölden is not ideal for beginners but there's great free-riding for experienced boarders. And all drag-lifts can be avoided.

Cross-country There are a couple of uninspiring loops by the river, plus small areas at Zwieselstein and Vent.

Queues Recent reporters found big queues at the Einzeiger and Seekogl chairs on the way to and from the glacier – taking the Rettenbachtal ski route home allows you to avoid Seekogl. The new six-pack up from the Rettenbachtal has improved the link from Giggijoch to Gaislachkogl.

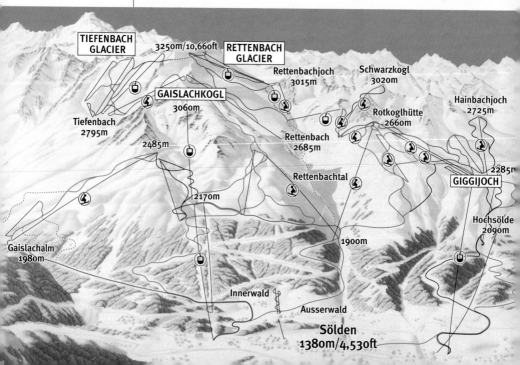

OUR WEBSITE

Go to our website at wtss.co.uk for resort news, links to resort sites, a build-your-own resort shortlist system and reader forums.

Phone numbers
From elsewhere in Austria add the prefix 05254.
From abroad use the prefix +43 5254.

TOURIST OFFICE

t 5100
info@soelden.com
www.soelden.com

Mountain restaurants The self-service places around Giggijoch can get very crowded. To escape the crowds try the cluster of places around Gaislachalm, or the big, modern Schwarzkogl on run 24. Gampealm, towards the end of piste 11, is a fine panoramic spot. A couple of recent visitors enjoyed the rustic Eugens Obstlerhütte.
Schools and guides The three schools all restrict class sizes to seven or eight. A reporter last year had a 'good' private lesson with the main school.
Facilities for children The ski kindergarten takes children from the age of three. There are special family lift pass deals.

STAYING THERE

How to go There are few UK packages.
Hotels The warmly welcoming Central (22600) is not only central (midway between the two gondolas) but also the biggest and best in town – the only 5-star; beautiful pool. We were very happy in the Stefan, right next to the Giggijoch gondola; good food. The Regina (2301) is recommended by a reporter. Several reporters have enjoyed Gasthof Grauer Bar (2564). The Grüner-Hof B&B (2477) above town on run 7 is highly praised and has a 'suite of saunas and steam rooms'. Self-catering apartments at the Posthäusl (3138) are good.
Eating out We repeatedly end up in the Tavola in the hotel Rosengarten, because it doesn't take reservations, and haven't been disappointed. Reader recommendations include Cafe Hubertus, Nudeltopf and Corso for pizza; and s'Pfandl at Ausserwald for Tirolean food.
Après-ski Sölden's après-ski is justly famous. It starts up the mountain, notably at Giggijoch, and progresses via packed bars in the main car park and main street to countless places with live bands and throbbing discos (a recent reporter recommends the PartyHaus and Lawine), routinely accompanied by table dancing and/or striptease. Zum Kuckuck is a new bar at the Giggijochbahn. There are nightly toboggan evenings, with drinking and dancing, before a 6km/4 mile floodlit run back to town from Gaislachalm.
Off the slopes There's a sports centre, a swimming pool and an ice rink. Trips to Innsbruck are possible. Aqua Dome is a thermal spa centre at Längenfeld.

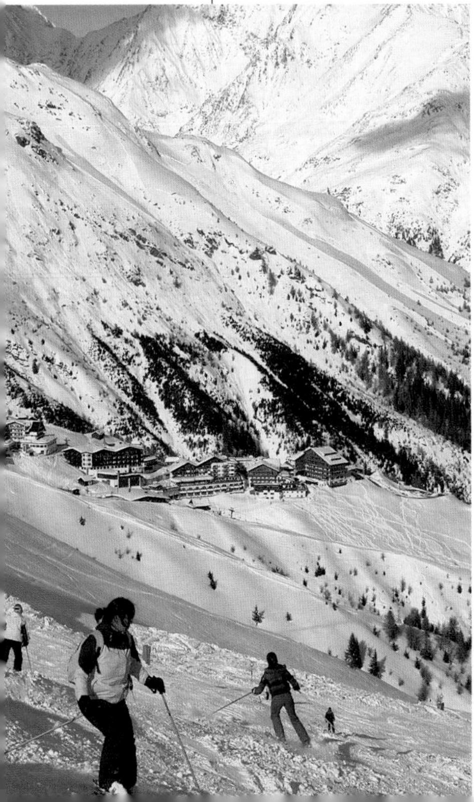

SNOWPIX.COM / CHRIS GILL
One way to escape the rowdy nightlife of downtown Sölden is to stay in isolation up in Hochsölden ↓

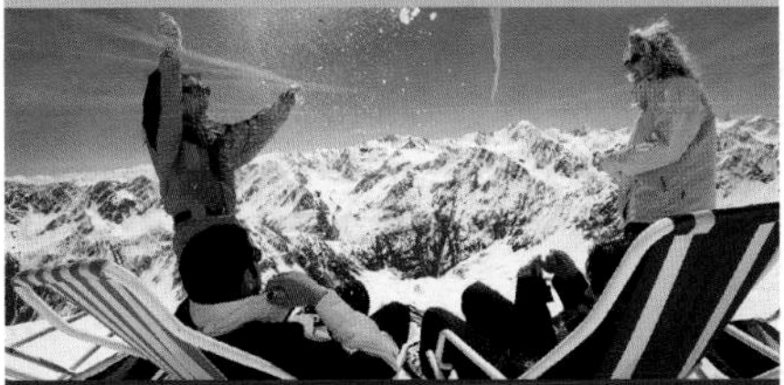

Söll

The ski area is big, but the attractive village is surprisingly small and intimate. Shame it is not set right by the lifts

RATINGS

The slopes

Fast lifts	**
Snow	**
Extent	****
Expert	*
Intermediate	****
Beginner	***
Convenience	**
Queues	***
Mountain restaurants	**

The rest

Scenery	***
Resort charm	***
Off-slope	**

NEWS

For 2006/07 the Tanzboden drag-lift below Hartkaiser and Brandstadl is due to be replaced by a six-pack with heated seats.

In 2005/06 another six-pack, the Kummereralm, replaced the Weissachlift T-bar up to Eiberg. This area was also extended with two new red runs, and a new Kummereralm restaurant was built. The Bergkaiser panoramic restaurant was also built at the top of the Hartkaiser.

KEY FACTS

Resort	700m
	2,300ft

Entire Ski Welt	
Slopes	620-1830m
	2,030-6,000ft
Lifts	93
Pistes	250km
	155 miles
Blue	43%
Red	48%
Black	9%
Snowmaking	180km
	112 miles

➕ Part of Ski Welt, Austria's largest linked ski and snowboard area

➕ Local slopes are the highest in the Ski Welt and north-facing, so they keep their snow relatively well

➕ Plenty of cheap and cheerful pensions for those on a budget

➕ Pretty village with lively après-ski

➕ Massive recent investment in snowmaking has paid off, but ...

➖ Ski Welt is at low altitude, and snow quality can suffer

➖ Long walk or inadequate bus service between the village and the lifts

➖ Little to amuse experts or to challenge good intermediates

➖ Ski Welt slopes can get crowded at weekends and in high season – especially above Söll

➖ Mostly short runs in local sector

Söll has long been popular with British beginners and intermediates, attracting a mixture of singles looking for a fun week and families looking for a quiet time.

When the snow is good, as it has been for much of the last three seasons, Söll can be a great place for a holiday – cruising the attractive and undemanding pistes of Austria's largest linked area. Its main real drawback has always been the lack of altitude and the consequent danger of poor natural snow. But this problem has been tackled by a massive investment in snowmaking, and over 70 per cent of the Ski Welt's 250km/155 miles of piste are now covered by snow-guns – the biggest snowmaking operation in Austria. This ensures the main pistes and links stay open, though it can't prevent slush and ice developing.

Many visitors are surprised by the small size of the village and the long distance between it and the slopes.

THE RESORT

Söll is a small, pretty, friendly village; you can explore it in a few minutes. New buildings are traditional in design and there's a huge church near the centre which, according to a reporter, is well worth a visit at dusk as the graveyard is lit with candles. The pretty scenery adds to Söll's charm, and it benefits from being off the main road. There aren't many shops.

The slopes are a bus- or taxi-ride or a 15-minute walk from the centre, the other side of a busy road with a pedestrian tunnel underneath. You can leave your equipment at the bottom of the gondola for a small charge.

There is some accommodation out near the lifts, but most is in or around the village centre and the ski-bus service is heavily criticised by reporters ('crowded', 'totally inadequate', 'we wasted 40 minutes queuing' were 2006 comments). Being on the edge of the village nearest the lifts is best for those who are prepared to walk to the slopes. The other side of town has the advantage that you can board the bus there before it gets too crowded. Some guest houses are literally miles from the centre and lifts, and the ski-bus does not serve every nook and cranny of this sprawling community.

THE MOUNTAINS

The Ski Welt linked circuit includes Hopfgarten, Itter, Söll, Scheffau, Ellmau, Going and Brixen. It is the largest linked area in Austria, and will easily keep an early or average intermediate amused for a week. But that doesn't make it a Trois Vallées. It is basically a typically small, low, pastoral Austrian hill multiplied several times. One section is much like another, and most slopes best suit early to average intermediates. Runs are mostly short and scenery attractive rather than stunning – although the views from Hohe Salve are impressive.

Westendorf is separate (see separate chapter) but covered by the area pass. The Kitzbüheler Alpenskipass also covers many other

↑ The snow on the low-altitude Ski Welt slopes isn't always this good; but the last three seasons have been bumper snow years

DAVID MAXWELL-LEES

GETTING THERE

Air Salzburg 94km/58 miles (2hr); Innsbruck 73km/45 miles (1½hr).

Rail Wörgl (13km/8 miles) or Kufstein (15km/9 miles); bus to resort.

ACTIVITIES

Indoor Swimming, sauna, solarium, massage, bowling, squash

Outdoor Natural ice rink (skating, curling), sleigh rides, 3km/ 2 miles of floodlit ski and toboggan runs, walks, paragliding

STAYING THERE

HOW TO GO
Mostly cheap, cheerful gasthofs
The major mainstream tour operators offer packages here.
Hotels There is a wide choice of simple gasthofs, pensions and B&Bs, and an adequate amount of better-quality hotel accommodation – mainly 3-star.
《《③ **Greil** (5289) Attractive 4-star, but out of the centre far from the lifts.
《《③ **Postwirt** (5221) Attractive, central, traditional 4-star with built-in stube.
《《③ **Bergland** (5454) Small 3-star, well placed between the village and lifts.
《《③ **Alpen Panorama** (5309) 3-star far from lifts but with own bus stop; wonderful views; pleasant rooms; good cakes.
《《③ **Tulpe** (5223) Next to the lifts.
《② **Feldwebel** (5224) Central 3-star.
《② **Hexenalm** (5544) Next to the lifts.
《② **Gasthof Tenne** (5282) B&B gasthof between centre and main road.
Chalets There are few catered chalets but a couple of big 'club hotels' run by British tour operators.
Self-catering The central Aparthotel Schindlhaus has nice accommodation, though the best apartments in town are attached to the Bergland hotel.

EATING OUT
A fair choice
Some of the best restaurants are in hotels. The Greil and Postwirt are good, but the Schindlhaus is said to be the best. Giovanni does excellent pizzas, while other places worth a visit include the Dorfstub'n and the Venezia.

APRES-SKI
Still some very loud bars
Söll is not as raucous as it used to be, but it's still very lively and a lot of places have live music. The Salvenstadl (Cow Shed) bar was recommended as 'the best with live music' by a recent reporter. The Whisky Mühle is a large disco that can get a little rowdy, especially after other bars close. Buffalo's is popular and the Hotel Austria bar 'was packed whenever a football match was on TV'. There's a floodlit piste and separate toboggan run – both from top to bottom of the gondola.

OFF THE SLOPES
Not bad for a small village
You could spend a happy day in the wonderfully equipped Panoramabad: taking a sauna, swimming, lounging about. The large baroque church would be the pride of many tourist towns. There are numerous coach excursions, including trips to Salzburg, Innsbruck and even Vipiteno over in Italy.

Scheffau 745m/2,440ft

This is one of the most attractive of the Ski Welt villages.

THE RESORT
Scheffau is a rustic little place complete with pretty white church. It is spacious yet not sprawling and has a definite centre, a kilometre off the busy main road, which increases its charm at the cost of convenience – you can ski to the Ski Welt lifts at Blaiken

sauna. The Zum Wilden Kaiser (8118) – 'sauna and good fish dishes' – Blaiken (8126) and Waldhof (8122) are good value gasthofs near the gondolas. And the central Gasthof Weberbauer (8115) is said to be 'good value' and 'efficient'.

Eating out There aren't many village restaurants. Donatello is a 'good pizza place', says a 2005 visitor

Après-ski 'Non-existent,' says one happy reporter – but another last year said the Red Bull had 'full-on hardcore music in a tent'. The usual reporganised events such as bowling and tobogganing are available.

Off the slopes Walking apart, there is little to do. Tour operators organise trips to Innsbruck and Salzburg.

Hopfgarten 620m/2,030ft

Hopfgarten is an unspoiled, friendly, traditional resort off the main road.

THE RESORT
The village is a good size: small enough to be intimate, large enough to have plenty of off-slope amenities. Most hotels are within five minutes' walk of the lift to Rigi.

THE MOUNTAIN
Hopfgarten is at the western extremity of the Ski Welt.

Slopes Hopfgarten offers queue-free access to Rigi and Hohe Salve – the high point of the main Ski Welt circuit.

Terrain-parks None locally but it's a short bus-ride to Westendorf, where there is a park.

Snow reliability The resort's great weakness is the poor snow quality on the south-west-facing home slope.

Experts Experts should venture off-piste for excitement.

Intermediates When snow is good, the runs down to Hopfgarten and the nearby villages of Brixen and Itter are some of the best in the Ski Welt.

Beginners There is a beginners' slope in the village, but it is sunny as well as low; lack of snow-cover means paying for a lift pass to higher slopes.

Snowboarding The Ski Welt is best suited to free-riding the extensive intermediate slopes.

Cross-country Hopfgarten is one of the best cross-country bases in the area. There are fine trails to Kelchsau (11km/7 miles) and Niederau (15km/ 9 miles), and the Itter-Bocking loop (15km/9 miles) starts nearby.

(where there are several hotels) but you need a bus to get back.

THE MOUNTAIN
Scheffau is well placed for the Ski Welt's best (and most central and snow-sure) section of pistes.

Slopes Two gondolas (including an eight-seater) give rapid access directly to Brandstadl.

Snow reliability Eiberg is the place to go when snow is poor.

Experts The pistes above Blaiken are some of the longest and steepest in the Ski Welt.

Intermediates This is as good a base as any in the area.

Beginners The nursery slope is in the village, making Scheffau a poor choice for mixed-ability parties; but a reporter rates the easy blues at Brandstadl as 'excellent for beginner snowboarders'.

Cross-country See Söll and Ellmau.

Queues The second gondola has cut weekend queues at Blaiken.

Mountain restaurants See Söll, Ellmau.

Schools and guides The school is well regarded, but groups can be large. A reporter's private snowboarding lesson was 'the best I've ever had'.

Facilities for children Both the ski kindergarten and non-ski nursery have good reputations. The children's ski area and school 'Kinder-Kaiserland' is also reported to be 'very good'. And excellent progress was made by a four-year-old at Ski Esprit's nursery.

STAYING THERE
How to go Major operators offer packages here.

Hotels The best hotels – both with pool, sauna and steam room – are the 4-star Kaiser (8000) and 3-star Alpin (8556) – 'excellent food, lots of choice, spacious rooms'. Pool ('a bit cold') and

Phone numbers
Calling long-distance
Add the prefix given
below for each resort.
When calling from
abroad use the
country code 43 and
omit the initial 0.

Söll
05333
Scheffau
05358
Hopfgarten
05335
Itter
05335
Brixen
05334
Ski Welt TO
05358

TOURIST OFFICES
Söll
t 5216
info@soell.com
www.soell.at
Scheffau
t 7373
scheffau@skiwelt.at
www.scheffau.com
Hopfgarten
t 2322
hopfgarten@hohe-
salve.com
www.hopfgarten.at
Itter
t 2670
itter@hohe-salve.com
www.tiscover.at/itter
Brixen
t 8433
brixen@skiwelt.at
www.brixenimthale.at
Ski Welt
t 505
info@skiwelt.at
www.skiwelt.at

Westendorf's trails are close.
Queues We've had no reports of
morning queues to leave the village
since an eight-seater gondola replaced
the old chair-lift two seasons ago.
Mountain restaurants See Söll.
Schools and guides Partly because
Hopfgarten seems to attract large
numbers of Australians, English is
widely spoken in the two schools.
Facilities for children Hopfgarten is a
family resort, with a nursery and ski
kindergarten.

STAYING THERE
How to go Cheap and cheerful
gasthofs, pensions and little private
B&Bs are the norm here.
Hotels The comfortable hotels
Hopfgarten (3920) and Sporthotel
Fuchs (2420) are both well placed for
the main lift.
Eating out Most of the restaurants are
hotel-based, but there are exceptions,
including a Chinese and a pizzeria.
Après-ski Après-ski is generally quiet,
though a lively holiday can usually be
ensured if you go with Aussie-
dominated Contiki Travel.
Off the slopes Off-slope amenities
include swimming, riding, bowling,
skating, tobogganing and paragliding.
The railway makes trips to Salzburg,
Innsbruck and Kitzbühel possible.

Itter 700m/2,300ft

Itter is a tiny village halfway around
the mountain between Söll and
Hopfgarten, with nursery slopes close
to hand and a gondola just outside the
village into the Ski Welt, via Hochsöll.
There's a hotel and half a dozen
gasthofs and B&Bs. The school has a
rental shop, and when conditions are
good this is a good beginners' resort.

Brixen 800m/2,620ft

It may not be pretty, but Brixen has a
queue-free, high-capacity gondola up
to the main Ski Welt slopes.

THE RESORT
Brixen im Thale is a very scattered
roadside village at the south-east edge
of the Ski Welt, close to Westendorf.
The main hotels are near the railway
station, a bus-ride from the lifts.

THE MOUNTAIN
Brixen is on the south side of the main
Ski Welt circuit, and a short bus-ride

from separate Westendorf.
Slopes The gondola takes you to
Hochbrixen, where lifts diverge for
Hohe Salve and Söll, or Astberg and
Ellmau. There's a small area of north-
facing runs, including nursery slopes,
on the other side of the village. Last
year a regular visitor reported a nasty
incident involving a liftie who was
inside his hut and therefore failed to
stop a chair-lift when her 10-year-old
son slipped and fell under it, and who
then threw her son at the seat of the
chair. We hope this was a one-off.
Terrain-parks None locally but there's a
good park nearby at Westendorf.
Snow reliability A chain of snow-guns
on the main south-facing piste helps to
preserve the snow as long as possible
and the area continues to benefit from
major investment in snowmaking.
Experts The black run alongside the
Brixen gondola is one of the few
challenging pistes in the area.
Intermediates When snow is good,
Brixen has some of the best slopes in
the Ski Welt – including some
challenging ones.
Beginners The nursery slopes are
secluded and shady, but meeting up
with friends for lunch is a hassle – the
area is a bus-ride from the village.
Snowboarding See Söll.
Cross-country In addition to valley-
floor trails, a 3km/2 mile loop up the
mountain at Hochbrixen provides fine
views and fairly reliable snow.
Queues Lift upgrades have improved
the once queue-prone area.
Mountain restaurants The Filzalm
above Brixen has been recommended.
Schools and guides The ski school
runs the usual group classes, and mini-
groups for five to seven people.
Facilities for children There is an all-
day ski kindergarten.

STAYING THERE
How to go There are plenty of hotels
and pensions.
Hotels Alpenhof (88320) and Sporthotel
(8191) are both 4-stars with pools.
Eating out Mainly hotel-based, but the
restaurant opposite the gondola has
been recommended.
Après-ski Après-ski is quiet, but livelier
Westendorf is a short taxi-ride away.
Off the slopes Activities include tennis,
hotel-based spa facilities and days out
to Salzburg, Innsbruck and Kitzbühel.

St Anton

If what you seek is dumps, bumps, boozing and bopping, there's nowhere quite like it – with a neat Tirolean town as a bonus

COSTS

① ② ③ ④ ⑤ ⑥

RATINGS

The slopes

Fast lifts	★★★
Snow	★★★★
Extent	★★★★
Expert	★★★★★
Intermediate	★★★
Beginner	★
Convenience	★★★
Queues	★★
Mountain restaurants	★★★

The rest

Scenery	★★★
Resort charm	★★★★
Off-slope	★★

NEWS

For 2006/07 St Anton's 70th anniversary as a resort will be celebrated with the opening of a jumbo gondola to replace the first stage of the queue-prone cable-car to Galzig. The modern 'ferris-wheel' design will allow direct access at ground level. Each cabin will carry 24 people, giving three times the carrying capacity of the existing lift.

For 2005/06 a fast six-pack with covers replaced the Valfagehr triple chair at Alpe Rauz.

At Rendl, part of the valley run was improved and access to the gondola made easier with a new escalator to replace the steep staircase.

208

+ Varied terrain for experts and adventurous intermediates – and a lot of it, once you include Lech-Zürs, a bus-ride away

+ Heavy snowfalls, backed up by a fair amount of snowmaking

+ Very lively après-ski, from mid-afternoon onward

+ Despite expansion, the resort retains some traditional charm – and the animated village centre is mainly car-free

+ Improved lift system has cut queues from the base areas, but ...

− Still some queues up the mountain

− Slopes far from ideal for beginners or timid intermediates

− Pistes can get very crowded – some of them dangerously so

− Most of the tough stuff is off-piste – including many popular runs

− Main slopes get a lot of sun, quickly affecting the snow conditions

− Resort spreads widely, with long treks from some lodgings to key lifts and bars

− Can get rowdy, with noisy drunks in the central streets in the early hours

St Anton is undeniably a big-league resort. For competent skiers and riders with an appetite for non-stop action and the stamina to keep up with it, we'd rate it even higher: it is one of the great resorts, with an après-ski scene that can be as taxing as the splendid bowls below the Valluga. The combination draws ski bums from around the world, as well as lots of regular holiday visitors.

But it won't suit everyone, as our list of − points makes clear. If you are thinking of trying an Austrian change from Val-d'Isère, or of taking a step up from Kitzbühel, take full account of this list.

Those going back to St Anton after a long interval may be amazed to find that the railway has disappeared – moved from the centre to the fringe of the village for the 2001 Alpine World Ski Championships. Those new to the resort may simply wonder why it has a featureless gap between the town and the lifts.

Yet again we have to report zero progress in improving the dangerously busy piste down the Steissbachtal and on down to the village. What's needed, as we have been saying for four years, is a new piste to the village from Galzig.

THE RESORT

St Anton is at the foot of the road up to the Arlberg pass, at the eastern end of a lift network that spreads across to St Christoph and over the pass to Stuben. These two tiny villages are described at the end of the chapter.

The resort is a long, sprawling mixture of traditional and modern buildings crammed into a narrow valley. It used to be sandwiched between the busy bypass road and the mainline railway; but the railway was moved in 2000, and where there were tracks there is now a little area of parkland.

Although it is crowded and commercialised, St Anton is full of character, its traffic-free main street

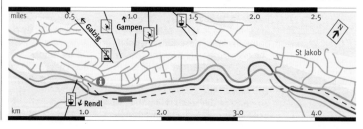

Fang chair-lift, which gives access to the Nasserein gondola, was built.

On the other side of the main road a gondola goes up to the Rendl area. This is linked one-way by rope tows and a moving carpet from the end of St Anton's main street – but the return still involves a bus-ride or short walk.

St Anton spreads up the hill to the west of the centre, towards the Arlberg pass – first to Oberdorf, then Gastig, 10 minutes' walk from the centre. Further up the hill are the suburbs of Dengert and Moos – a long way out, but quite close to the slopes.

Regular buses go to Stuben, Zürs and Lech (the latter two described in the Lech chapter) and the much less well-known but worthwhile Sonnenkopf area above Klösterle. The ski-buses are free but involve a couple of changes. These buses can get crowded early and late in the day and have provoked several complaints by recent reporters. For a small fee, the post-bus offers a direct, less-crowded alternative. Minibus-style taxis can be economic if widely shared.

Serfaus, Nauders, Ischgl and Sölden are also feasible outings by car.

THE MOUNTAINS

The main slopes are essentially open: only the lower Gampen runs and the run from Rendl to the valley offer much shelter from bad weather.

St Anton vies with Val-d'Isère for the title of 'resort with most underclassified slopes'. There are plenty of blue pistes that would be red in many other resorts, and plenty of reds that would be black – although, paradoxically, none of the blacks is seriously steep.

Many of the most popular steep runs marked on the piste map are classified as 'ski routes'. These have widely spaced markers but they are essentially ungroomed and, more importantly, are not patrolled and are protected from avalanches only 'in the immediate vicinity of the markers'.

Clearly you should not ski such runs alone, and the piste map recommends them only for people with 'alpine experience or with a ski instructor'. In theory this puts these routes out of bounds for many holidaymakers – absurd, when these runs lie at the heart of the resort's appeal. On Rendl there is a lift serving no pistes but only a single ski route, which more or less

↑ The run down to Rauz is long, lift-free and satisfying

AMANDA MCCORMICK

KEY FACTS

Resort	1305m
	4,280ft

Arlberg region	
Slopes	1305-2650m
	4,280-8,690ft
Lifts	86
Pistes	276km
	171 miles
Blue	38%
Red	51%
Black	11%
Snowmaking	58%

St Anton, St Christoph and Stuben	
Slopes	1305-2650m
	4,280-8,690ft
Lifts	40
Pistes	120km
	75 miles

lined by traditional-style buildings. It is an attractively bustling place, day and night. Its shops offer little in the way of entertainment, but meet everyday needs well – self-catering reporters have observed that it has a 'wonderful Spar', for example.

The main hub of the resort is around the base stations of the lifts to Galzig – a fancy jumbo gondola, replacing the inadequate cable-car this year – and Gampen (a fast quad chair). The main street is only a short walk from these lifts, and for most purposes a location on or close to this main street is ideal.

The resort spreads down the valley, thinning out before broadening again to form the suburb of Nasserein. This backwater now has an eight-person gondola up to Gampen, and makes an appealing base for a quiet time. The nightlife action is a short bus-ride or 15-minute walk away ('quite a hike'). Staying in the suburbs of St Anton, between the centre and Nasserein, is also a more attractive idea since the follows the line of the lift. Why is it not a patrolled piste?

The Arlberg piste map also shows (at Stuben and Lech) lots of 'high-alpine touring runs', which are not marked on the ground at all and not protected against avalanche. Read the Lech chapter for more on these.

The Arlberg lift companies seem determined to present all their widely spread terrain in a single view. The map was redesigned recently, and is considerably improved – but smaller, separate maps would be better.

Reporters regularly complain of poor and limited piste grooming; many blue runs are steep enough to develop moguls when snow is soft. The local cable TV, showing the state of the pistes and queues, can be very useful.

THE SLOPES
Large linked area
St Anton's slopes fall into three main sectors, two of them linked.

The major sector is that beneath the local high-spot, the **Valluga**, accessed by a jumbo gondola to Galzig, then a cable-car. The tiny top stage of the cable-car to the Valluga itself is mainly for sightseeing – you can take skis or a board up only if you have a guide to lead you down the tricky off-piste run to Zürs. The slightly lower station of Valluga Grat gives access to St Anton's famous high, sunny bowls, and to the long, beautiful red/blue run to Rauz, at the western end of St Anton's own slopes. From here there's a new six-pack, the Valfegehrbahn, to return, or you can go on to explore the

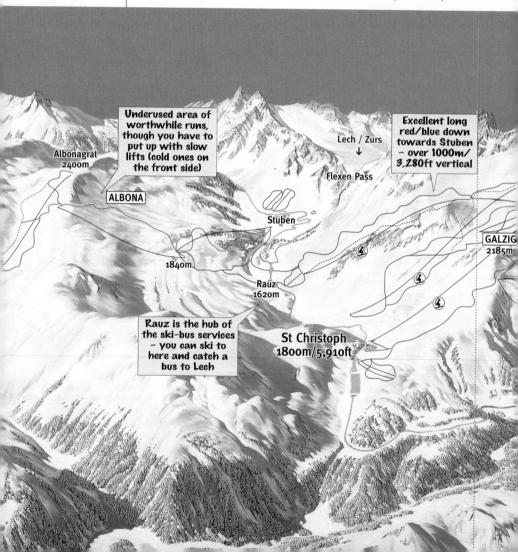

Albonagrat
2400m

Underused area of worthwhile runs, though you have to put up with slow lifts (cold ones on the front side)

ALBONA

1840m

Lech / Zürs
↓

Flexen Pass

Stuben

Rauz
1620m

Excellent long red/blue down towards Stuben – over 1000m/ 3,280ft vertical

GALZIG
2185m

Rauz is the hub of the ski-bus services – you can ski to here and catch a bus to Lech

St Christoph
1800m/5,910ft

THE VALLUGA RUNS

The off-piste runs in the huge bowl beneath the summit of the Valluga, reached by either the Schindlergrat chair or the Valluga I cable-car, are justifiably world-famous. In good snow, this whole area is an off-piste delight for experts.

Except immediately after a fresh snowfall, you can see tracks going all over the mountain. There are two main ski routes marked on the piste map – both long, steep descents that quickly get mogulled. The Schindlerkar is the first you come to and it divides into two – the Schindlerkar gully being the steeper option. For the second, wider and somewhat easier Mattun run, you traverse further at the top. Both these feed down into the Steissbachtal where there are lifts back up to Galzig and Gampen.

There are of course more adventurous ways down than the identified ski routes. The Schweinströge starts off in the same direction as the red run to Rauz, but you traverse the shoulder of the Schindler Spitze and descend a narrow gully. Perhaps the ultimate challenge is to ski off the back of the Valluga – a great adventure, according to readers who have done it. More info in our off-piste feature panel.

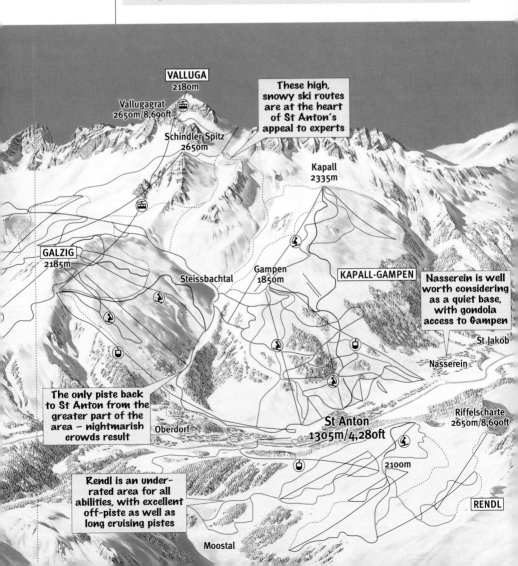

LIFT PASSES

Arlberg Ski Pass

Prices in €

Age	1-day	6-day
under 16	23	113
16 to 19	36	163
20 to 64	39	189
over 65	36	163

Free no one, but season pass only €10 if under 8 or over 75

Senior senior min. age for women is 60

Beginner points ticket

Notes Covers all St Anton, St Christoph, Lech, Zürs and Stuben lifts, and linking bus between Rauz and Zürs. Single ascent, half-day and afternoon 'taster' tickets available. Pass also covers Sonnenkopf (10 lifts) at Klösterle, 7km/4 miles west of Stuben (free bus link from Stuben).

rather neglected slopes of Stuben.

These high runs can also be accessed by riding the Schindlergrat triple chair, though some involve a half-hour hike – even so, this can be quicker than waiting for the cable-car, as an energetic reporter proved last season.

Other runs from **Galzig** go south-west to St Christoph and east into the Steissbachtal.

Beyond this valley, with lift and piste links in both directions, is the **Kapall-Gampen** sector, reachable by chair-lift from central St Anton or gondola from Nasserein. From Gampen at mid-mountain, pistes lead back to St Anton and Nasserein. Or you can ride a six-pack on up to Kapall to ski the treeless upper mountain.

A handful of lifts (including a fast six-pack to Gampberg) serve the west-facing runs at the top of **Rendl**, with a single north-facing piste returning to the gondola bottom station.

The slopes above **Stuben**, described at the end of the chapter, should not be overlooked.

TERRAIN-PARKS
Head for Rendl
The 200m/660ft-long park on Rendl, just below the top of the gondola, doesn't touch the park over in neighbouring Lech maintenance-wise, but it will easily keep beginners and intermediates entertained. Due to its narrow nature the park has only a single kicker line, in the form of 3-, 6- and 12-metre tabletops and a corner jump. Around the jumps are various rails. There's a large A-framebox, a small rainbow, an A-frame rail and a flat slidebox.

SNOW RELIABILITY
Generally very good cover
If the weather is coming from the west or north-west (as it often is), the Arlberg gets it first, and as a result St Anton and its neighbours get heavy falls of snow. They often have much

better conditions than other resorts of a similar height, and we've had great fresh powder here as late as mid-April. But many of the slopes face south or south-east, causing icy or heavy conditions at times. It's vital to time descents of the steeper runs off the Valluga to get decent conditions, or you can find yourself in trouble.

The lower runs are now well equipped with snowmaking, which generally ensures the home runs remain open. As an April visitor said, 'Pistes were kept open while surrounded by green fields.'

FOR EXPERTS
One of the world's great areas
St Anton vies with Chamonix, Val-d'Isère and a handful of other resorts for the affections of experts. There are countless opportunities for going off-piste, and guidance is very desirable. Read the feature panels on the Valluga runs (on the previous page) and off-piste routes (facing page).

Lower down, there are challenging runs in many directions from both Galzig and Kapall-Gampen. These lower runs can be doubly tricky if the snow has been hit by the sun. Ski route 34 from Kapall has been re-directed away from the main runs to follow a steeper and 'much more interesting' descent into the Mattun valley.

Don't overlook the Rendl area, which has plenty of open space served by the top lifts, and several quite challenging itineraries. This is a great area for a mixed group, especially.

One of our reporters particularly liked the quieter Sonnenkopf area, down-valley from Stuben, for its excellent off-piste route to Langen. See also the Stuben section.

Each of the main sectors has its toughest piste classified as black; a couple deserve their classification, but most don't – the Fang race course from Gampen used to be red, in fact. The distinction between reds and blacks is in general a fine one.

boarding

Many consider St Anton as the Mecca of Austrian free-riding. Countless steep gullies and backcountry powder fields with challenging terrain form a big draw for advanced riders. The Arlberg Snowboard academy has a great reputation for showing all levels where best to apply their respective skills – whether you are a beginner on the wide-open pistes, or a more advanced rider wanting guidance through the trees or steep and deep off-piste. Rendl is an excellent mountain for free-riders and freestylers alike.

The Arlberg region is an off-piste skier's dream – renowned for its consistently high snowfall record, incredible deep powder and enormous diversity of terrain. We invited Piste to Powder Mountain Guides to give us an introduction to the possibilities. Remember you should never explore far off-piste without a guide.

Mountain Guides
St. Anton – Austria

Piste to Powder
Mountain Guides

All day guiding 9am to 5pm. Choose from four skill levels. All safety equipment provided.

t 01661 824318
00 43 664 174 6282
info@pistetopowder.com
www.pistetopowder.com

Runs from Rendl

After initial practice close to the pistes, the natural progression is to go beyond the furthest lift to access the wide rolling bowls of powder of Rossfall.

More serious routes from Rendl take you well away from all lifts. The North Face, accessed from the Gampberg six-seat chair, offers challenging terrain to the intermediate/confident off-piste skier. The Riffel chair-lifts access the imposing Hinter Rendl – a gigantic high-mountain bowl offering a huge descent down to St Anton, often in deep powder. A variant involves a climb to Rendl Scharte and a demanding descent with sections of 35° down the remote Malfontal to the village of Pettneu and a taxi back to St Anton.

Runs from Albona, above Stuben

Stuben's outstanding terrain, reached from the Albonagrat chair, is suited to the more experienced off-piste skier, as the descents are long. The open tree lines of the Langen forest, where the powder is regularly knee to waist deep, form some of the world's finest tree skiing. A 30-minute climb from Albonagrat, with skis on shoulder, opens up further outstanding terrain from Maroikopfe – either west, down undulating open slopes to Langen, or east, down steep 40° slopes to Ferwalltal, where this glorious run ends with a glass of wine at an old hunting lodge.

Runs from the Valluga

The legendary runs from the summit cable-car of the Valluga must be on the tick list of all keen and experienced off-piste skiers – the North Face, Bridge Couloir or East Couloir. Your pulse will race as you trace a steep ski line between cliff bands in the breathtaking scenery of the Pazieltal, leading down to Zürs. Here, at the top of the Madloch chair-lift and after a short hidden climb, you will be roped down into the steep Valhalla Couloir, accessing 1200m/3,940ft vertical of open slopes ending in the hamlet of Zug, close to Lech.

St Anton

213

FOR INTERMEDIATES
Some real challenges
St Anton is well suited to good, adventurous intermediates. As well as lots of testing pistes, they will be able to try the Mattun ski route and the easier of the Schindlerkar routes from Valluga Grat (see feature panel). The run from Schindler Spitze to Rauz is very long (over 1000m/3,300ft vertical), varied and ideal for good (and fit) intermediates. Alternatively, turn off from this part-way down and take the Steissbachtal to the lifts back to Galzig. The Kapall-Gampen section is also interesting, with sporty bumps among trees on the lower half. Good

PISTE TO POWDER

Far from the piste, the Albonagrat down to Langen is a classic
↓

intermediates may enjoy the men's downhill run from the top to town.

Timid intermediates will find St Anton less to their taste. There are few easy cruising pistes; many blues get bumpy, especially just after a snowfall. The most obvious cruisers are the short blues on Galzig and the Steissbachtal (aka 'Happy Valley'). These are reasonably gentle but get uncomfortably crowded (see 'Queues'). When the Steissbachtal is closed, the only piste home from Galzig is a steepish black run. The blue from Kapall to Gampen is wide and cruisy.

In the under-rated Rendl area a variety of trails suitable for good and

moderate intermediates criss-cross, including the long and genuinely blue Salzböden, which can be combined to great effect with the relatively cruisy red Riffel run above it. There is a long tree-lined run (over 1000m/3,300ft vertical from the top) back to the valley gondola station. This is the best run in the area when visibility is poor, but it has some quite awkward, steep and narrow sections and gets very busy at the end of the day – early intermediates beware.

FOR BEGINNERS
Far from ideal
The best bet for beginners is to start at Nasserein, where the nursery slope is less steep than the one close to the main lifts. There are further slopes up at Gampen, and a short, gentle blue run at Rendl, served by an easy drag-lift. But there are no easy, uncrowded runs for beginners to progress to. A mixed party including novices would be better off staying in Lech or Zürs; more advanced skiers who want to explore St Anton can get on the bus.

FOR CROSS-COUNTRY
Limited interest
St Anton is not a great cross-country resort, but trails total around 35km/ 22 miles and snow conditions are usually good. There are a couple of uninspiring trails near town, another at St Jakob 3km/2 miles away, and a pretty trail through trees along the Ferwalltal to the foot of the Albona area. There is also a tiny loop at St Christoph.

QUEUES
Improvements continue, but ...
Queues are not the problem they once were, thanks to continuing lift upgrades – now including replacement of the cable-car to Galzig by a jumbo gondola for 2006/07. This should slash waiting times in the village. But there are still problems up the mountain, notably the Valluga cable-car from Galzig. In peak season, especially when powder beckons, queues here can run into hours.

Also at mid-mountain, queues for the Schindlergrat chair appear to have been eased by the fast Arlenmähder chair allowing access to the run to Rauz without going to the top. The new Valfegehr six-seat chair at Rauz has improved the return from Stuben to St Anton, although one reporter

experienced two breakdowns during a February visit. The Zammermoos chair out of the Steissbachtal still generates queues; but at least it has a (little used) singles line.

At Rendl, the gondola gets busy when poor weather closes the other lifts, but one reporter was surprised to find it very 'orderly and polite'. One 2006 visitor witnessed lift attendants filling chairs during busy periods.

Perhaps more of a worry than the lift queues are the crowded pistes. Clearly the worst (at least when the top Valluga runs are open) is the Steissbachtal and the home run below it, which can be uncomfortably crowded even in January and a nightmare on a peak weekend. So acute is this problem at times that several reporters have recommended heading over to Rauz or St Christoph and getting a bus back to town rather than tangling with the Steissbachtal. There was talk of improvements last year, but nothing has appeared – and the real solution to this long-standing problem is an alternative blue run from Galzig to the village, to relieve the pressure. When heavy snow closes the top runs on the Valluga, the crowds shift to Rendl, where the home run again gets unpleasantly busy.

MOUNTAIN RESTAURANTS
Plenty of choice
It may not be a proper mountain restaurant, but we often seem to end up lunching in St Christoph at the atmospheric Hospiz Alm, famed for its slide down to the toilets as well as its table-service food. Most reporters love it ('couldn't have chosen anywhere more cheering'; 'it pleased even the fussiest eater in our group') – but a couple of visitors complain of 'appalling' service this year. The Arlberg Taja is a 'jolly and welcoming' nearby alternative.

But next time we are resolved to stay high and try the newish Verwall Stube at Galzig – a serious table-service place with great views, said to be 'in a class of its own'. Other Galzig recommendations include the Ulmer Hütte near the top of the Arlenmähder chair, the big, smart self-service restaurant at Galzig itself for 'superb views and tasty food'. Lower down, the Sennhütte offers 'excellent choices'. The Rodelalm on Gampen is a 'real hut with good food at low prices and a lovely fire'; 'great knuckles of pork'.

CHILDREN

Kindergarten
t 3451
From age 30mnth;
must be toilet trained

Ski schools
Both Austrian schools
take children aged
from 5 (6 days
including lunch €288
at Arlberg school)

Just above the village, the Mooserwirt serves typical Austrian food at what seems a high price, but 'the portions are absolutely massive'; the Heustadl is popular with 'good choices and efficient service'; the Krazy Kanguruh does burgers, pizzas and snacks, and Taps Bar next door does 'good goulash soup'. Over on Rendl, the self-service Rendl restaurant has great views but gets very busy. Better to head down the valley run to the 'rustic and welcoming' Bifang-Alm, for regional specialities and excellent service.

SCHOOLS AND GUIDES
Mixed reports
The St Anton school and the Arlberg school are now under the same ownership but continue to operate separately. The Arlberg school generates conflicting reports: one reporter commented, 'Not enough attention was paid to putting equal standards together and groups were big.' Another complained of old-fashioned technique: 'They need to turn the clock forward.' But some reporters are very happy: 'Children and parents were delighted.' And one 2006 group made 'rapid progress'. Another

reader joined a top-level guided group and was impressed with the 'superb value' and 'non-stop high mileage covered'.

We have skied with excellent guides from Piste to Powder, a specialist off-piste outfit run by British guide Graham Austick, and have had good reports from readers ('A good balance of guiding to instruction and a professional attitude to safety') – although reader reports suggest some guides are better than others. Another reporter highly recommends Snoworks: 'instructional-skiing holidays' which complement guiding with instruction. We have reports of tour ops being stopped from supplying their own ski host to show guests around the pistes unless they hire an instructor too.

FACILITIES FOR CHILDREN
Nasserein 'ideal'
The youth centre attached to the Arlberg school is excellent, and the special slopes both for toddlers (at the bottom) and bigger children (at Gampen) are well done. At Nasserein there is a moving carpet lift on the baby slope, and a reporter rates this an 'absolutely ideal' place to stay with young kids.

St Anton

215

GETTING THERE

Air Innsbruck 100km/62 miles (1½hr); Zürich 200km/124 miles (3hr); Friedrichshafen 140km/87 miles (1½hr).

Rail Mainline station in resort.

STAYING THERE

HOW TO GO
Austria's main chalet resort

There's a wide range of places to stay, from quality hotels to cheap and cheerful pensions and apartments.

Chalets Plenty of catered chalets are offered by UK operators. Flexiski's Amalien Haus has a great position on the main street, and is getting a makeover for this season. Nasserein makes a convenient chalet base.

Hotels There is one 5-star hotel and lots of 4- and 3-stars and B&Bs.

(((((5) **Raffl's St Antoner Hof** (2910) Best in town, but its position on the bypass is less than ideal. Pool.

((((4) **Schwarzer Adler** (22440) Centuries-old inn on main street. Widely varying bedrooms. 'Good service', 'lovely pool'.

((((4) **Alte Post** (2553) Atmospheric place on main street with lively après-ski bar.

((((4) **Post** (2213) Comfortable if uninspiring 4-star at the centre of affairs, close to both lifts and nightlife.

((((4) **Sporthotel** (3111) Central position, varied bedrooms, good food. Pool.

(((3) **Grischuna** (2304) Welcoming and family-run in peaceful position up the hill west of town; close to the slopes.

(((3) **Goldenes Kreuz** (22110) A comfortable B&B hotel halfway to Nasserein, ideal for cruising home.

(((3) **Nassereinhof** (3366) Close to the Nasserein gondola. Family-run with sauna and steam room. Recommended for 'good home-cooked food'. Other recommendations include: Haus Pirker (2310), the 'friendly' Rendlhof (3100) in Nasserein, Haus Matt Rudi (3291) and the Bachseite (3866) ('large rooms and a most welcoming host').

Self-catering There are plenty of apartments available but package deals are few and far between. Reporters like the Bachmann apartments ('really excellent', 'spacious and comfortable') and the H Strolz ('well equipped') – both in Nasserein.

EATING OUT
Mostly informal

Places such as the Trödlerstube and Reselhof serve big portions of traditional Austrian food. The village museum's restaurant does 'excellent' upmarket food and wine in elegant panelled rooms. Quite different in style is Ben.venuto ('excellent food', 'impeccable service'), in the Arlberg-well.com building: stark decor and eclectic menu. Scotty's, Pomodoro (pizza) and the Train (fondue) are popular with reporters. The Sporthotel Steakhouse is said to be 'excellent' and the Dolce Vita does 'good meals with friendly service'. A reporter this year enjoyed the 'very good set menus' at the Grossmauer Chinese.

ACTIVITIES

Indoor Swimming pool (also hotel pools open to the public, with sauna and massage), fitness centre, tennis, squash, bowling, museum, cinema in Vallugasaal

Outdoor Swimming pool, cleared walking paths, natural ice rink (skating, curling), sleigh rides, snow-shoeing, tobogganing, paragliding

The cosy Sonnbichl is recommended for its 'superb home-cooked food'. In Nasserein, the Tenne is noted for game dishes and Robi's Rodel-Stall at the end of the toboggan run has a cosy log fire.

APRES-SKI
Throbbing till late

St Anton's bars rock from mid-afternoon until the early hours. Après-ski starts in a collection of bars on the slopes above the village. The Krazy Kanguruh is probably the most famous but is 'dull' according to this year's visitors. The Mooserwirt has an 'infectious happy buzz' and is now the 'in' place, filling up with revellers as soon as the lunch trade finishes – reputedly dispensing more beer than any other bar in Austria. The Heustadl is 'the best place to boogie Tirolean style, and shouldn't be missed'. All this is followed by a slide down the piste in the dark. The bars in town are in full swing by 4pm, too. Most are lively, with loud music; sophisticates looking for a quieter time are less well provided for. The Hazienda and, for late-night dancing, the Stanton and Piccadilly ('good live music') are

popular choices. Reporters have recommended Scotty's (in Mark Warner's chalet-hotel Rosanna, with happy hour), Bar Cuba ('a good party'), Jacksy's ('a relaxed pub'), Pub 37, Bobo's, Alibi and Funky Chicken. The St Antoner Hof is suggested for pre-dinner 'canapés and champagne'. In Nasserein, the Fang House and 'jolly' Sonnegg are recommended.

OFF THE SLOPES
Some improvement

St Anton is a resort for keen skiers and riders. But the fitness, swimming and skating facilities of Arlberg-well.com are impressive and highly recommended by reporters. The village is lively during the day, but has few diverting shops. Getting by bus to the other Arlberg resorts is easy, as is visiting Innsbruck by train. Some of the better mountain huts are accessible by lift or bus. A reporter suggests using the winter walking trails to visit Pettneu.

STAYING DOWN THE VALLEY
Nice and quiet

Beyond Nasserein is St Jakob. It can be reached on snow, but is dependent on the free shuttle-bus in the morning.

St Anton

217

Phone numbers
St Anton
From elsewhere in
Austria add the prefix
05446.
From abroad use the
prefix +43 5446.
Stuben
From elsewhere in
Austria add the prefix
05582.
From abroad use the
prefix +43 5582.

TOURIST OFFICES

St Anton
t 22690
info@stantonam
arlberg.com
www.stantonamarlberg.
com
St Christoph
www.tiscover.com/
st.christoph
Stuben
t 399
info@stuben.at
www.stuben.com

Stuben 1405m/4,610ft

Stuben (in Vorarlberg) is linked by lifts and pistes over the Arlberg pass to St Anton (in Tirol). There are infrequent buses from the village to Lech/Zürs, and more frequent ones from Rauz, the roadside lift station for St Anton.

Dating back to the 13th century, Stuben is a small, unspoiled village, with an old church, a few unobtrusive hotels, a school, two or three bars, a couple of banks and a few little shops. Heavy snowfalls add to the charm.

The Albona above Stuben makes a refreshingly quiet change from the busy slopes of St Anton. It has north-facing slopes that hold powder well and some wonderful, deserted off-piste descents including beautiful long runs down to Langen and to St Anton. A regular visitor recommends the small Rasthaus Ferwall for lunch at the end of a the latter. Staying within the lift network, the Berghaus is repeatedly recommended, not least for 'excellent rösti'. But a reporter who visited Stuben on a Monday lunchtime was surprised to find most places closed. The slow village chair can be a cold ride but blankets are available. A

quicker and warmer way to get to St Anton in the morning, if you have a car, is to drive up the road to Rauz. Stuben has sunny nursery slopes separate from the main slopes, but lack of easy runs to progress to makes it unsuitable for beginners. A covered moving carpet has improved the link between Stuben and St Anton, at Rauz, omitting the need to ride the awkward drag-lift.

Evenings are quiet, but several places have a pleasant atmosphere. The charming old Post (7610) is a very comfortable 4-star with a fine restaurant.

St Christoph 1800m/5,910ft

A small collection of pricey hotels, restaurants and bars just down from the summit of the Arlberg pass. There are decent beginner slopes served by drag-lifts and a fast quad chair-lift to the heart of St Anton's slopes, but the blue back down is not an easy run to progress to. It's quiet at night. The best hotel of all is the huge 5-star Arlberg-Hospiz (2611), with luxurious health and spa facilities – recommended by a reporter for expensive but fine gourmet dining.

St Johann in Tirol

A traditional Tirolean resort appealing to those who want to spend as much time on jolly restaurant terraces as on the slopes

- Traditional traffic-free town centre
- Lots of good mountain restaurants
- Plenty of off-slope activities
- Relatively good snow record
- Easy to visit other resorts on the lift pass; just as well, because ...

- Local slopes very limited, with little to interest experts or keen, mileage-hungry intermediates
- Can be crowded on peak weekends, or when nearby resorts with less reliable snow are suffering

This friendly resort is an attractive place for beginners and leisurely part-timers who like to spend as much time having drinks and lunch as they do actually cruising the slopes. Keener and more proficient skiers and boarders will soon get bored unless they are prepared to visit surrounding resorts – nearby ones covered by the local pass, others by the Kitzbüheler Alpenskipass.

THE RESORT

St Johann is a sizeable valley town where life doesn't revolve entirely around skiing. Reporters emphasise the friendliness of the locals. The attractive traffic-free centre, where most of the hotels are found, is wedged between a railway track, main roads and rivers. The main access lift from the village is a gondola to the top; it's about a ten-minute walk from the centre, including a level crossing and walking beside a busy road. But there is the alternative of staying in hotels near the lift base. There is also accommodation in the hamlet of Eichenhof to the east.

The local pass covers several other resorts to the north and east; Fieberbrunn and Waidring's Steinplatte are particularly worth a visit. There's a reasonable bus service between the resorts. The Kitzbüheler Alpenskipass covers the whole region, and Kitzbühel itself is only 10 minutes by car or train.

THE MOUNTAINS

St Johann's local slopes are on the north-facing side of the Kitzbüheler Horn – the 'back' side of Kitzbühel's 'second' and smaller mountain.

Slopes From the top of the gondola a choice of north-facing pistes lead back through the trees towards town – mainly reds on the upper mountain, blues lower down. A sunnier sector of west-facing pistes lead down to another gondola at Oberndorf.

Terrain-parks There is a half-pipe at the Eichenhof lift and a jumps area above the Hochfeld chairs.

Snow reliability St Johann gets more snow than neighbouring Kitzbühel and the Ski Welt, and this, together with its largely north-facing slopes, means that it often has better conditions. It also has substantial snowmaking.

Experts There is nothing here to challenge an expert. The long black run on the piste map is really a moderate red. Off-piste is limited.

219

Kitzbüheler Horn 2000m
Harschbichl 1700m/5,580ft
Bergstation Penzing 1465m
Jodlalm 1500m
Oberndorf
Eichenhof
St Johann in Tirol 650m/2,130ft
Hochfeld

↑ Solid, ancient
buildings form the
centre of the town

TVB ST JOHANN IN TIROL

KEY FACTS

Resort	650m
	2,130ft
Slopes	670-1700m
	2,200-5,580ft
Lifts	17
Pistes	60km
	37 miles
Blue	41%
Red	47%
Black	12%
Snowmaking	28km
	17 miles

Phone numbers
From elsewhere in
Austria add the prefix
05352.
From abroad use the
prefix +43 5352.

TOURIST OFFICE

t 63335
info@stjohanntirol.at
www.stjohanntirol.at

AUSTRIA

220

Intermediates The slopes are varied.
But keen piste-bashers will ski them all
in a day and are likely to want to go
on to explore nearby resorts. Decent
intermediates have a fairly direct-
running piste between Harschbichl and
town, plus the black mentioned above.
There are some easier red runs on the
top part of the mountain, but the best
(3a and 4b) are served by slow lifts.
The less adventurous can take gentle
pistes from the gondola mid-station.
Beginners Most beginners rate St
Johann highly, but one dissenting voice
last year said the nursery slopes at
Eichenhof are a bit steep, while those
who start from Hochfeld have to ride a
tricky chair once off the nursery slope.
Snowboarding It's drag-lifts or nothing
on the nursery slopes.
Cross-country Given good snow, St
Johann is one of the best cross-country
resorts in Austria. The wide variety of
trails totals 75km/47 miles.
Queues Rare except at peak times – but
slow lifts is a common complaint.
Mountain restaurants With 14
restaurants spread over its small area,
St Johann must have the highest hut
density in Europe. All those tried by
one reporter had 'excellent food –
especially the Hochfeld'.
Harschbichlhütte is also recommended
for 'excellent gulaschsuppe'. Our
favourite is the Angerer Alm, just
above the gondola mid-station, with
good local food and an amazing wine
cellar. Bassgeigeralm is a rustic
restaurant on the Oberndorf side and
the Grander Schupf at Eichenhof is
recommended this year.
Schools and guides The instructors of
the St Johann school continue to
impress reporters, but in the past we
have heard of large classes and
'dreadful management and
organisation'. No such problems with
the newish Wilder Kaiser school,
though, rated 'very highly' by reporters.

Facilities for children There are no
longer any nursery facilities in the
resort. Bobo's, at the ski school, offers
a mini-club for the under 5s.

STAYING THERE

How to go British tour operators
concentrate on hotels, but there are
numerous apartments available.
Hotels All hotels are 3- or 4-star. There
are dozens of B&B pensions.
The 4-star Sporthotel Austria (62507)
is near the lift, with pool, sauna and
steam. The Post (62230) is a 13th-
century inn on the main street – 'By far
the nicest,' says a regular. Recent
visitors recommend the Park (62226),
'very well run, very friendly, food
enjoyable and plentiful'. The Fischer
(62332) has a new children's play area,
is central, with 'friendly and helpful
staff' and 'excellent' food.
Self-catering There are plenty of
apartments to rent.
Eating out A recent reporter found
'plenty of good places to eat', including
the Rustica (Italian) and the Lange
Mauer (Chinese). Villa Masianco is said
to be 'lovely' and 'very good value'. The
Huber-Bräu brewery serves good food
but closes early. For a special meal,
locals recommend the Ambiente.
Après-ski Ice bars and tea dancing greet
you as you come off the slopes – Max
Pub at the bottom of the main piste has
'free-flowing alcohol and blaring europop'. In town there are lots of bars that
reporters have enjoyed, including
Bunny's Pub with its 'good, alternative
music' and 'youthful crowd'. Tour op
reps organise outings and the resort
itself puts on an event most evenings.
Off the slopes There's a public pool
with sauna, steam-room, solarium and
spa facilities, indoor tennis, ice rink,
curling, tobogganing and 40km/25
miles of cleared walks. Easy outings by
rail to Salzburg or Innsbruck.

Stubai valley

A choice of pretty little villages with their own wooded slopes, and one of the best glaciers in the world at the head of the valley

COSTS

①②③④⑤⑥

RATINGS

The slopes
Fast lifts	✲✲✲
Snow	✲✲✲✲✲
Extent	✲✲✲
Expert	✲✲✲
Intermediate	✲✲✲
Beginner	✲✲
Convenience	✲✲
Queues	✲✲✲
Mountain restaurants	✲✲

The rest
Scenery	✲✲✲✲
Resort charm	✲✲✲✲
Off-slope	✲✲✲

NEWS

For 2006/07 work to improve the glacier's Mutterberg base station is expected to begin. And a terrain-park and boarder-cross course are planned for the Schaufelschuss slope.

At Fulpmes (Schlick 2000), a blue run is expected to open between the gondola mid-station and the valley. Previously the only way back was to use a ski route or take the gondola down. Snowmaking will be added to cover the new run.

➕ High, snow-sure glacier slopes plus lower bad-weather options

➕ Quiet, pretty Tirolean villages

➖ Beginners are better off sticking to the lower slopes

➖ Not much to challenge experts

Think Austrian glaciers, and the Stubaier Gletscher is likely to feature near the top of your list. It is the country's largest glacier ski area, and among the world's best. For a winter holiday you need non-glacial slopes as well, for the bad-weather days – and the Stubai valley has plenty in the Schlick 2000 area above Fulpmes, Elfer above the village of Neustift and Serles above Mieders.

The Stubai valley lies a short drive south of Innsbruck. It is a long valley (about 30km/19 miles) with countless hamlets dotted along it – and a handful of bigger villages; three have their own wooded slopes and lift systems, and are described in this chapter. Together the valley offers a sizeable 130km/81 miles of mostly intermediate terrain, all covered by the Stubai-Superski lift pass (which also covers the shuttle-bus). All the villages have impressive toboggan runs.

The **Stubaier Gletscher** offers an extensive area of runs between 3200m/10,500ft and 2300m/7,550ft accessed by two alternative two-stage gondolas from the huge car park at Mutterberg to the two mid-mountain stations of Eisgrat and Gamsgarten. A third gondola from Eisgrat takes you right to the top of the slopes.

The glacier area is broken up by rocky peaks giving more sense of variety than is normal on a glacier. Chairs (including three six-packs) and drag-lifts serve fabulous cruising runs, blue and red, all of which normally have excellent snow, naturally. There is also a lovely 10km/6 mile ungroomed ski-route (Wilde Grub'n) down to the valley – a run of 1450m/4,760ft vertical from the top of the glacier. And there is good off-piste to be explored with a guide.

There aren't the challenges here that there are on the Hintertux glacier. But there are some good long runs, including two blacks – one is a pretty steep mogul field – and a couple of ski routes. For intermediates it is splendid territory, with lots of fabulous cruising. Novices are better off learning lower down, but there is a short beginner slope at Gamsgarten.

The area is popular with

snowboarders. There are lots of natural hits and kickers across the mountain, and a new terrain-park is planned for 2006/07 with rollers, boxes and a boarder-cross course.

There's also a cross-country loop.

Queues are no longer a serious problem. On a busy weekend there can be short delays at the gondola mid-station and at the Eisjoch six-pack.

The mountain huts vary in character. The cute little cabin at Jochdohle – Austria's highest restaurant – gives great views, and the Dresdnerhütte is said to be charming and uncrowded. Zur Goldenen Gams has table-service.

There is a ski school at the glacier. Club Micky Maus is a comprehensive childcare facility at Gamsgarten. Children ski for free when both parents join ski school.

Après-ski starts up the mountain in the lively snow bar at Gamsgarten.

NEUSTIFT 1000m/3,280ft
The major village closest to the glacier, 20km/12 miles away and served by regular buses. It's an attractive, traditional Tirolean village, with limited local slopes at Elfer.

The slopes at Elfer consist of a narrow chain of runs and lifts from Elferhütte at 2080m/6,820ft down to the village. Apart from one short blue run at altitude, the pistes are all red and there's not much to entice experts, but it is a quiet place for intermediates to practise. This area is north-east-facing; there is a sunny nursery slope at village level, on the other side.

There are lots of 3- and 4-star hotels. The 3-star Tirolerhof (3278) is excellent – comfortable and relaxed; good food. It has a hire shop, and the owner is a qualified instructor and guide. The central 4-star Sonnhof

KEY FACTS

Resort	935-1000m
	3,070-3,280ft
Slopes	935-3210m
	3,070-10,530ft
Lifts	33
Pistes	130km
	81 miles
Blue	47%
Red	41%
Black	12%
Snowmaking	some

OUR WEBSITE

Go to our website at wtss.co.uk for resort news, links to resort sites, a build-your-own resort shortlist system and reader forums.

Phone numbers
From elsewhere in Austria add the prefix 05226.
From abroad use the prefix +43 5226.

TOURIST OFFICE

t 2228
info@stubai.at
www.stubai.at

(2224) is also recommended. For families, the 4-star Gasteigerhof in Gasteig (2746) is suggested; it has a pool and children's fun area.

Nightlife is focused on the Dorf, Bierfassl, Hully Gully and the Romansstuben. Most restaurants are hotel-based. Past recommendations include Bellafonte's pizzas and the atmospheric Hoferwirt.

Neustift has quite a lot to offer off the slopes: a good leisure centre and numerous activities.

FULPMES 935m/3,070ft

Fulpmes (with its satellite village of Telfes) sits at the foot of Schlick 2000, the most extensive of the lower ski areas. The pretty village is said to be the sunniest in the Stubaital. It attracts few British visitors.

The ski area at Schlick 2000 sits in a sheltered bowl beneath the Sennjoch. A two-stage gondola takes you to Kreuzjoch (2135m/7,000ft), from where a series of chair- and drag-lifts serve a few short, mainly north-east-facing blue and red runs and a ski route. The runs suit intermediates best, with some 'genuinely testing' sections. A long blue winds its way down the valley from the Sennjoch at 2225m/7,300ft and is due to be extended to the valley bottom for 2006/07. The main beginner area is beside the gondola

mid-station at Froneben. There's also a new children's area, Ronny's Kinderland, with moving carpets and fun features. Schlick 2000 is a good area for snowboarders, with a free-ride zone on the Sennjoch and a terrain-park lower down, at Schlickeralm. There are two schools, but spoken English is reported to be poor.

There's a good choice of 3- and 4-star hotels, most with pools and spa facilities. The 4-star Stubaierhof (62226) is central, with a pool and children's play room. Eating out is generally hotel-based.

The nearest leisure centre is in Neustift, but Fulpmes has tobogganing, sleigh rides and ice skating.

MIEDERS 980m/3,220ft

Mieders is near the entrance to the Stubai valley, 15 minutes' drive from Innsbruck. It's an unspoiled village with its own tiny area of slopes.

The slopes of Serles are limited to a couple of blues and a short red, but there are several ski routes and 40km/25 miles of marked cross-country tracks above 1600m/5,250ft. A newish eight-person gondola takes you to Kopponeck at 1680m/5,510ft, where a couple of drag-lifts serve the upper runs. There are a couple of mountain restaurants. The village has a small selection of hotels and guest houses.

STUBAIER GLETSCHER
3210m/10,530ft

1720m

ELFER 2080m

Sennjoch 2225m

SCHLICK 2000

Neustift 1000m/3,28oft

Schlickalm

SERLES 1680m

Fulpmes 935m

Froneben

Telfes

Mieders 980m

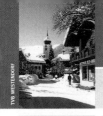

Westendorf

This cute little village now offers access to a vast amount of terrain and should start attracting a lot more keen intermediates

223

COSTS

① ② ③ ④ ⑤ ⑥

RATINGS

The slopes
Fast lifts	**
Snow	**
Extent	*
Expert	**
Intermediate	***
Beginner	***
Convenience	***
Queues	****
Mountain restaurants	***

The rest
Scenery	***
Resort charm	****
Off-slope	**

NEWS

For 2005/06 the long-awaited link with the Kirchberg-Kitzbühel slopes opened: a new 4km/2.5 mile red piste (with snowmaking) down to near Aschau from the Gampen area, with a new eight-seat Ki-West gondola back. Shuttle-buses take you from the bottom of the gondola to the Pengelstein gondola at Skirast. All the Kirchberg-Kitzbühel and Ski Welt lifts are covered by the Kitzbüheler Alpenskipass (see 'Alternative passes' in the Söll chapter).

OUR WEBSITE

Go to our website at wtss.co.uk for resort news, links to resort sites, a build-your-own resort shortlist system and reader forums.

TVB WESTENDORF

Most of Westendorf's local pistes are of genuine red gradient
→

- ➕ Charming traditional village
- ➕ Access to the extensive Ski Welt circuit (via nearby Brixen), and to Kitzbühel's slopes (from last season)
- ➕ Good local beginners' slopes
- ➕ Jolly if rather limited après-ski scene

- ➖ Local slopes are limited in extent, and mainly of genuine red gradient
- ➖ Short bus rides to reach both Ski Welt circuit and Kitzbühel's slopes
- ➖ Slopes are at low altitude, and snow quality can suffer

Westendorf is worth considering as a base for keen intermediates. As well as its own small area of serious red runs, it now has easy access to the extensive area of slopes shared by Kitzbühel and Kirchberg as well as to the main Ski Welt slopes. And its own slopes are worth a day trip for confident intermediates based in Ski Welt resorts such as Söll and Ellmau or in Kitzbühel or Kirchberg.

THE RESORT

Westendorf is a small village with a charming main street and attractive onion-domed church (it was once declared 'Europe's most beautiful village' in a floral competition). The centre is close to the nursery slopes but a five-minute walk from the main gondola outside the village.

THE MOUNTAIN

The local slopes are small, but you can get into the Ski Welt circuit easily via a bus to Brixen and then a gondola – and into the Kitzbühel-Kirchberg slopes by taking the new red piste to Aschau and then a bus.

Slopes A two-stage gondola takes you to Talkaser, from where one main north-west-facing red run goes back to the resort (with blue options on the lower half). Short west- and east-facing

pistes at the top run below the peaks of Choralpe, Fleiding and Gampen. A couple of red runs from Fleiding go down past the lifts to hamlets served by buses; a recent reporter particularly enjoyed these. The piste grooming was excellent said a 2005 visitor. There's weekly floodlit skiing.

Terrain-parks There's a good terrain-park with jumps, boxes, rails and a half-pipe, with something for all levels.

Snow reliability Westendorf's snow reliability is a bit better than some other Ski Welt resorts and nearly all of its pistes now have snowmaking.

Experts The slopes are among the most testing in the Ski Welt area, and we guess it's possible to have a lot of fun off-piste with a guide.

Intermediates Nearly all the local terrain is genuinely red in gradient, though we see they have regraded some former reds to blues. The main Ski Welt area has lots of easier inter-

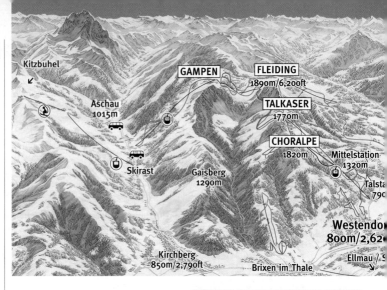

Kitzbühel

GAMPEN FLEIDING
1890m/6,200ft

Aschau
1015m TALKASER
1770m

Skirast CHORALPE
1820m Mittelstation
1320m

Gaisberg
1290m Talst
79(

Westendo
800m/2,62

Kirchberg
850m/2,790ft Ellmau / S

Brixen im Thale

KEY FACTS

Resort	800m
	2,620ft

Westendorf only	
Slopes	800-1890m
	2,620-6,200ft
Lifts	13
Pistes	45km
	28 miles
Blue	49%
Red	40%
Black	11%
Snowmaking	40km
	25 miles

For Ski Welt	
Slopes	620-1890m
	2,030-6,200ft
Lifts	93
Pistes	250km
	155 miles
Blue	43%
Red	48%
Black	9%
Snowmaking	180km
	112 miles

SPORT 2000 **rent**
QUALITY RENTAL SYSTEM

www.sport2000rent.com

online booking

Phone numbers
From elsewhere in Austria add the prefix 05334 (05358 for Ski Welt Tourist Office). From abroad use the prefix +43 5334 (+43 5358 for Ski Welt Tourist Office)

TOURIST OFFICES

Westendorf
t 6230
info@westendorf.com
www.westendorf.com

Ski Welt
t 505
info@skiwelt.at
www.skiwelt.at

mediate runs but getting there involves a bus. Now that the link with Kitzbühel-Kirchberg has been built, it is a lot easier to access their good mix of intermediate runs.

Beginners Extensive village nursery slopes are Westendorf's pride and joy. There are a couple of genuine blues to progress to, but the reds are real reds (as are some of the regraded blues).

Snowboarding There are some tedious catwalks at altitude.

Cross-country There are 25km/15 miles of local cross-country trails along the valley but snow-cover is erratic.

Queues Given good conditions, queues are rare, and far less of a problem than in the main Ski Welt area. If poor weather closes the upper lifts, queues can become long.

Mountain restaurants Alpenrosenhütte is woody and warm, with good food; reporters enjoyed the quiet, pleasant Brechhornhaus; the Choralp (top of gondola) gets busy but is 'reasonably priced'; the Gassnerwirt is good but you have to bus back to town.

Schools and guides The three ski schools have quite good reputations, though classes can be large. One reporter tells of her teenager's 'excellent' private lesson with the Top school: 'He's been skiing since he was three, but this was a revelation.' Others praise the Westendorf school: 'teachers very good, good value, great prize-giving in town hall' and 'excellent instructor, good English'.

Facilities for children Westendorf sells itself as a family resort. The nursery and the ski kindergarten open all day.

STAYING THERE

How to go A couple of mainstream operators offer packages here.

Hotels There are central 4-star hotels – the Jakobwirt (6245) and the 'excellent' Schermer (6268) – and a dozen 3-star ones. The 3-star Post (6202) is good value, central and 'traditional and charming but the half-board dinner was bland with rushed service'. Among more modest guest houses, Haus Wetti (6348) is popular, and away from the church bells. Pension Ingeborg (6577) has been highly recommended and is next to the gondola station.

Self-catering The Schermerhof apartments are of good quality.

Eating out Most of the best restaurants are in hotels – the Schermer, Jakobwirt and Mesnerwirt are good. The Wastlhof and Klingler have also been recommended. Get a taxi to Berggasthof Stimlach for a good evening out.

Après-ski Nightlife is quite lively, but it's a small place with limited options. The Liftstüberl, at the bottom of the gondola, is packed at the end of the day. The Moskito Bar has live music and theme nights but is said by one reporter to be 'a bit of a dive'. The Village Pub, next to the hotel Post, is very popular with 'good Irish craic' and sells draught Guinness. A 2005 reporter enjoyed the 'good atmosphere and live music' of In's Moment, run by a Scot.

Off the slopes There are excursions by rail or bus to Innsbruck and Salzburg. Walks and sleigh rides are very pretty. In February, the Jump and Freeze night is recommended viewing – 'all good fun' in a party atmosphere.

Wildschönau

Wildschönau is the dramatic-sounding name for a valley with a group of family-friendly resorts each with small areas of slopes above

225

COSTS

① ② ③ ④ ⑤ ⑥

RATINGS

The slopes
Fast lifts	**
Snow	**
Extent	*
Expert	*
Intermediate	**
Beginner	***
Convenience	***
Queues	***
Mountain restaurants	**

The rest
Scenery	***
Resort charm	***
Off-slope	**

NEWS

For 2005/06 a second six-pack replaced the two top drag-lifts on Schatzberg above Auffach. For 2006/07 new blue and red pistes will be created near here too. And a new beginners' lift will be installed at Niederau.

A night bus service between Auffach and Niederau now runs Thursday to Sunday from 8pm to 3am.

- ➕ Traditional, family-friendly villages
- ➕ Good nursery slopes at Niederau and Oberau
- ➕ Jolly après-ski scene

- ➖ Three separate ski areas, linked by ski-buses
- ➖ Each area has limited slopes
- ➖ Natural snow reliability not the best (but extensive snowmaking)

Niederau, Oberau and Auffach are contrasting villages with contrasting small areas of slopes on a shared lift pass. The area best suits families and those looking for a friendly, relaxing holiday rather than hitting the slopes non-stop.

THE RESORT

Niederau has long been a favourite resort with British beginner and early intermediate skiers. It is the main resort in the Wildschönau and is quite spread out, with a cluster of restaurants and shops around the gondola station forming the nearest thing to a focal point. But few hotels are more than five minutes' walk from a main lift.

Auffach, 7km/4 miles away, is a smaller, quieter, attractive old village and has the area's highest and most extensive slopes.

On a low col between the two is **Oberau** – almost as big as Niederau and the valley's administrative and cultural centre.

The villages are unspoiled, with traditional chalet-style buildings. Roads are quiet, except on Saturdays, and the valley setting is lovely.

THE MOUNTAINS

Niederau's slopes are spread over a wooded mountainside that rises no higher than 1600m/5,250ft. The slopes at Auffach continue above the tree line to 1905m/6,250ft.

Slopes The main lift from Niederau is an eight-person gondola to Markbachjoch. A few minutes' walk away is the alternative chair-lift, and above it is a steep drag to the high point of Lanerköpfl. Beginner runs at the bottom of the mountain are served by several short drag-lifts. The whole area is very small, and we skied most of the area in less than two hours on our 2004 visit. There's a sizeable 'Race 'n' Boarder Arena'; races are run here, but you can also take race-training lessons.

A reliable free bus goes to Auffach. Its sunny, east-facing area, consisting almost entirely of red runs, goes up to

The small area of mainly tree-lined slopes best suits people looking for a leisurely time rather than avid piste-bashers ➔

KEY FACTS	
Resort	830m
	2,720ft
Slopes	830-1905m
	2,720-6,250ft
Lifts	25
Pistes	70km
	43 miles
Blue	21%
Red	62%
Black	17%
Snowmaking	27km
	17 miles

Schatzberg, with a vertical of 1000m/3,280ft. The main lift up is a two-stage gondola and two six-packs (one new for 2005/06) serve the top runs. Again the area is very small.

The Kitzbüheler Alpen ski pass covers resorts in the Schneewinkel, Kitzbühel ski region, Ski Welt and Alpbachtal as well.

Terrain-parks There's a 90m/300ft half-pipe and a terrain-park with a quarter-pipe, jumps, snake, wave and fun-box served by a drag-lift on Schatzberg.

Snow reliability The low altitude means that natural snow reliability is relatively poor. But almost 40 per cent of the pistes have snowmaking, including the main runs down at both Niederau and Auffach from top to bottom. And Auffach has most of its runs above mid-mountain, making for more reliable snow there than at Niederau. Grooming is good.

Experts The several black pistes are short and not severe. We skied the main black piste from the bottom of the drag-lift below Lanerköpfl to Niederau when it was well groomed and thought it great for fast carving, but of almost blue gradient for much of its length. A couple of Niederau's black pistes have now been converted to ungroomed and unpatrolled ski routes, which were bumpy and had patchy snow when we skied them. There are off-piste routes to be found, too – such as the Gern route, which is marked on the piste map, from the top

of Schatzberg down a deserted valley to the road a little way from Auffach.

Intermediates Niederau's red runs generally merit their status but there's no blue run from top to bottom. The main black piste mentioned above is enjoyable, but the blue to reach it is just a path. Auffach has more intermediate terrain, with several short reds at the top, and the long main piste from the top to the village is attractive. But all this does not add up to very much – keen intermediate piste-bashers will be able to ski it all in a day. The slopes are best suited to confident but leisurely intermediates who are happy to take it easy and have a relaxing holiday.

Beginners There are excellent nursery slopes at the top and bottom of Niederau's main slopes, but the low ones don't get much sun in midwinter. Auffach has nursery slopes near the gondola mid-station. Oberau has its own nursery slopes, with a short black run above them. A problem is the lack of really easy longer runs to progress to.

Cross-country There are 50km/30 miles of trails along the valley, which are good when snow is abundant.

Queues One recent reporter said, 'Very little queueing.' Another complained of queues for the Niederau gondola. We saw long queues for the beginner drag-lifts (which may be eased by the new beginner lift planned for 2006/07).

Mountain restaurants These are scarce but good, causing lunchtime queues as

Joel 1970m

SCHATZBERG 1905m/6,250ft

Schönanger

MARKBACHJOCH 1500m

LANERKÖPFL 1600m/5,250ft

Thierbach 1175m

Auffach 875m/2,870ft

Roggenboden

Mühltal 780m

← Hopfgarten

Niederau 830m/2,720ft

Oberau 935m/3,070ft

wildschönau
exciting   relaxing

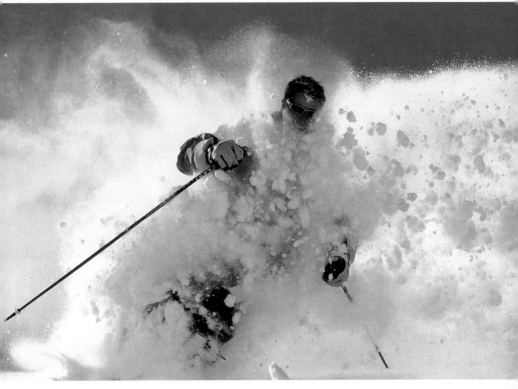

Wildschönau - Tyrol
Niederau - Oberau - Auffach - Thierbach

The 70km of piste give skiers everything they are looking for, steep slopes and gentle family runs. The Wildschönau offers its guests a lift capacity that sets it aside from other resorts. With two gondolas, three chair lifts and 20 drag lifts there is no time lost by queuing and there are no overcrowded lifts.

The gentle Wildschönau hills are particularly suitable for families but there are also plenty of opportunities for experienced skiers, e.g. the FIS runs for the giant slalom and Super G and some magnificent deep-snow slopes. There is also a measured section where skiers can test their top speed. Carvers and snowboarders are welcome on all pistes and the Schatzberg mountain offers an enormous fun park with a half pipe, high jump, fun-box, snake, quarter pipe and wave ride both for fun and competition.

WILDSCHÖNAUER
BERGBAHNEN

Lift Company, A-6313 Wildschönau
Phone +43 5339 5353-0, Fax 5353-44
buero@schatzbergbahn.at **www.schatzbergbahn.at**

For more information contact:
Tourist Office
A-6311 Wildschönau
Phone +43 5339 8255-0, Fax 8255-50
E-Mail: info@wildschoenau.com
www.wildschoenau.com

WILDSCHÖNAU
aufregend entspannend Tirol

↑ Cross-country is popular here, with 50km/30 miles of trails along the valley

TVB WILDSCHÖNAU

ski schools take a break. Many people lunch in the villages.

Schools and guides The ski schools have good reputations both for English and for teaching beginners, and a recent reporter raved about his beginner lessons. But classes can be large.

Facilities for children The kindergarten and nursery take kids from age two.

STAYING THERE

How to go There are a number of attractive hotels and guest houses in the three main villages – many with pools. Several major operators run packages to Niederau and Oberau.

Hotels In Niederau the 4-star Sonnschein (8353) and the Austria (8188) are central recommendations. The Vicky, run by Thomson, has 'friendly staff, excellent food, brilliant crèche', says a recent reporter. The 3-star Kellerwirt (8116) in Oberau dates from 1200 and was highly recommended by a 2006 reporter ('comfort, character, excellent food').

Eating out The restaurants at the hotels Alpenland and Wastl-Hof in Niederau have been recommended.

Après-ski Niederau has a nice balance of après-ski, neither too noisy for families nor too quiet for the young and lively. Bobo's Heustadl bar is popular at tea time. The Almbar and

the Cave bar – 'where it all happens, live bands twice a week' – are popular later on. The Drift-Inn at hotel Vicky has also been recommended. Cafe Treff is an internet cafe.

The other villages are quieter, once the tea-time jollity is over for the night.

Off the slopes There are excellent sleigh rides, horse-riding trips and organised walks as well as the Slow Train Wildschönau – on wheels not rails – which offers varied excursions. Several hotel pools are open to the public, and there's an outdoor ice rink. There's a long toboggan run at Auffach, from the mid-station of the gondola down to the bottom – a distance of 4km/2.5 miles. And on Wednesday and Thursday evenings tobogganing is organised next to the night skiing above Oberau. Shopping excursions to Innsbruck are possible.

OUR WEBSITE

Go to our website at wtss.co.uk for resort news, links to resort sites, a build-your-own resort shortlist system and reader forums.

Phone numbers
From elsewhere in Austria add the prefix 05339.
From abroad use the prefix +43 5339.

TOURIST OFFICE

t 8255
info@wildschoenau.com
www.wildschoenau.com

Zell am See

A real one-off, this: a charming lakeside town, with varied local slopes and a very worthwhile glacier option nearby at Kaprun

COSTS

① ② ③ ④ ⑤ ⑥

RATINGS

The slopes

Fast lifts	***
Snow	**
Extent	**
Expert	**
Intermediate	***
Beginner	***
Convenience	**
Queues	**
Mountain restaurants	***

The rest

Scenery	***
Resort charm	***
Off-slope	****

NEWS

For 2005/06 a six-pack with covers and heated seats replaced a T-bar at Sonnenalm. And a 2km/1 mile long red run was opened beneath it.

A 4-star hotel, the Mavida Balance, opened in Schüttdorf.

Snowmaking was increased, and now covers 90 per cent of the skiable area.

For 2006/07 a six-pack with covers is planned to replace the Almbahn double chair at Maiskogel above Kaprun, extending to the top of the mountain. A new red piste is also planned at the top.

- ➕ Pretty, tree-lined slopes with great views down to the lake
- ➕ Lively, but not rowdy, nightlife
- ➕ Charming old town centre with beautiful lakeside setting
- ➕ Lots to do off the slopes
- ➕ Huge range of cross-country trails
- ➕ Kaprun glacier nearby
- ➕ Varied terrain including a couple of genuine black runs

- ➖ Sunny, low slopes often have poor conditions despite snowmaking, which makes the area more limited
- ➖ Trek to lifts from much of the accommodation, and sometimes crowded buses
- ➖ Less suitable for beginners than most small Austrian resorts
- ➖ The Kaprun glacier gets lengthy queues when it is most needed

Zell am See is not a rustic village like most of its Austrian rivals, but a lakeside summer resort town with a charming old centre. For a small area, Zell's slopes have a lot of variety and some slightly challenging terrain, but not enough to keep a keen intermediate or expert happy for long. Zell is close to Kaprun and its Kitzsteinhorn glacier; but if snow is in short supply, Zell visitors have no special claim – you have to queue for access along with visitors coming from Saalbach, Kitzbühel and other low resorts.

THE RESORT

Zell am See is a long-established, year-round resort town set between a large lake and a mountain. Its charming, traffic-free medieval centre is on a flat promontory, and the resort has grown up around this attractive core.

A gondola at the edge of town (served by ski-buses) goes up the southern arm of the horseshoe-shaped mountain. You can also stay 2km/1 mile west of Zell in the Schmittental, in the centre of the horseshoe, where there are two cable-car stations. A more radical alternative is to stay 3km/2 miles south of Zell in Schüttdorf, where there is another gondola and large car park. But it is a characterless dormitory with little else going for it. Cross-country skiers and families wishing to use the Areitalm nursery stand to gain most from staying in Schüttdorf – and perhaps those with a car planning multiple outings to Kaprun.

Kaprun's snow-sure glacier slopes are only a few minutes by crowded buses ('best to get on at the bus station', says a reporter – getting on in Schüttdorf can be a problem).

Saalbach is easily reached by bus and Bad Hofgastein by train. At a push, Wagrain, Schladming and Obertauern are car trips.

THE MOUNTAINS

Zell's horseshoe-shaped mountain has the easiest runs along the open ridges, with steeper pistes descending through woods to the Schmittental.

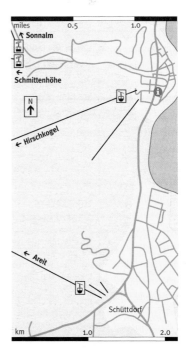

KEY FACTS

Resort	755m
	2,480ft

Zell and Kaprun	
Slopes	755-3030m
	2,480-9,940ft
Lifts	57
Pistes	132km
	82 miles
Blue	43%
Red	38%
Black	19%
Snowmaking	
	290 guns

Zell only	
Slopes	755-2000m
	2,480-6,560ft
Lifts	29
Pistes	77km
	48 miles

Kaprun only	
Slopes	785-3030m
	2,580-9,940ft
Lifts	28
Pistes	55km
	34 miles

THE SLOPES
Varied but limited

The lifts from Zell and Schüttdorf go up along the southern arm of the horseshoe mountain to the high-point at Schmittenhöhe, meeting a cable-car up from the Schmittental. The several lifts on the back of the hill and on the sunny slopes of the northern arm of the horseshoe (including a new six-pack) are accessed via Schmittenhöhe or by riding another cable-car from Schmittental to Sonnalm.

Black runs descend from various points to Schmittental; intermediate runs go down the southern arm to Zell and Schüttdorf.

TERRAIN-PARKS
Man-made and 'natural'

There's a half-pipe on Schmittenhöhe and a newly improved terrain-park on the Kaprun glacier.

SNOW RELIABILITY
Good snowmaking, but lots of sun

Zell am See's slopes can be badly affected by the sun. Ninety per cent are now covered by snow-guns, including the sunny home run to Schüttdorf. But holidays can still be marred by slush, ice and bare patches low down. The Kaprun glacier is snow-sure, but oversubscribed when snow is short in the region. Good grooming and quiet pistes have pleased reporters.

FOR EXPERTS
Several blacks, but still limited

Zell has more black runs than most resorts this size, but they barely deserve the classification, and don't hold out much of a challenge to experts. The blacks are usually immaculately groomed and little used – great if you like that kind of thing, especially first thing in the morning when they are completely deserted. Off-piste opportunities are limited.

FOR INTERMEDIATES
Bits and pieces for most grades

Good intermediates have a choice of fine, long runs, but this is not a place for high mileage. All blacks are usually within a confident intermediate's capability, and the red home run from Areitalm to Schüttdorf is almost equally as testing – great when conditions are good, but a struggle for many at the end of a warm day. The wide Sonnkogel runs are relatively quiet – great for carving. The timid can cruise the southern ridge blues.

Kaprun's high, snow-sure glacier runs are also ideal for intermediates not looking for too great a challenge.

FOR BEGINNERS
Two low nursery areas

There are small nursery slopes at Schmittental and at Schüttdorf, both covered by snow-guns. There are short, easy runs at Schmittenhöhe, Areitalm and Breiteckalm; some are used by complete beginners when snow conditions are poor lower down, but it means buying a lift pass.

FOR CROSS-COUNTRY
Excellent if snow allows

The valley floor has extensive areas – 30km/19 miles – including a superb area on the Kaprun golf course. At altitude there are short loops, above Zell and on the Kitzsteinhorn.

QUEUES
A few bottlenecks

Zell am See doesn't have many problems once you are on the mountain, but reporters regularly experience lengthy waits for the main cable-cars and gondolas. A 2006 visitor endured a 25-minute wait for the gondola out of Schüttdorf. There may be long queues for the Zell and Schmittental lifts too – the Sonnalm cable-car is said to be quieter than the

LIFT PASSES

Europa Sportregion Kaprun–Zell am See

Prices in €

Age	1-day	6-day
under 16	18	86
16 to 18	28	137
over 19	36	172

Free under 6

Senior no deals

Beginner points card

Notes

Covers Zell and Kaprun, and buses between them. One-day price is for Schmittenhöhe (Zell) only.

Alternative passes

Kitzsteinhorn-only and Maiskogel-only day passes. Salzburg Super Ski Card covers huge area round Salzburg province from Abtenau to Zell and is available for three days or more.

boarding

Zell is well suited to boarders and most lifts are chairs, gondolas or cable-cars. You'll also find plenty of life in the evenings. The Kaprun glacier has powder in its wide, open bowl. But it also has a high proportion of drag-lifts – a day of this and the 'small walk' to enter the terrain-park exhausted some reporters who said that a chair-lift would be most welcome. Snowboard Academy is a specialist school.

others. When snow is poor there are few daytime queues at Zell – many people are away queueing at Kaprun. The queue for the bus back from Kaprun was said by a recent reporter to be 'chaotic – a heaving mass, all scrambling and fighting to get on'.

MOUNTAIN RESTAURANTS
Plenty of little refuges

There are plenty of cosy, atmospheric huts dotted around the Zell slopes, helpfully named on the piste map. Among the best are Glocknerhaus, Kettingalm, Areitalm ('gets busy'), Breiteckalm and Blaickner's Sonnalm ('the best strudel'). Pinzgauer Hütte, in the woods behind Schmittenhöhe, is regularly recommended by reporters ('superb'); snowmobiles will tow you back to the lifts ('great fun'). The Schmiedhofalm has 'great views' and serves regional specialities ('best Tirolean pancake we've had'). The Berghotel at Schmittenhöhe is good, but expensive. Its bar with loud music

is lively in the afternoons (see Après-ski). The Panorama-Pfiff gets crowded, but 'has wonderful views and quite good food'. The Ebenbergalm just above the village has 'excellent home cooked food'.

SCHOOLS AND GUIDES
A wide choice

There is a choice of schools in both Zell am See and Kaprun. We get few reports, but a 2005 visitor had 'excellent' lessons with a 'delightful board instructor' at the main Zell school. Groups are said to be quite large. There are specialist cross-country centres at Schüttdorf and at Kaprun.

FACILITIES FOR CHILDREN
Schüttdorf's the place

We have no recent reports on the childcare provisions, but staying in Schüttdorf has the advantage of direct gondola access to the Areitalm snow-kindergarten. There's a children's adventure park on the mountain.

SCHOOLS

Zell am See
t 56020

Sport Alpin
t 0664 453 1417

Snowboard Academy
t 0664 253 0381

Classes
(Zell prices)
5 days (2hr am and pm) €140

Private lessons
€50 for 1 hr; €10 for each additional person

GUIDES

Ski Safari
t 0664 336 1487

CHILDREN

Kinderskiwelt Areit
t 56020
Ages from 2; with ski lessons for children over 3

Babysitter list
At the tourist office

Ski schools
Take children from age 4 (5 days including lunch €195)

GETTING THERE

Air Salzburg 80km/ 50 miles (2hr); Munich 230km/ 143 miles (3hr).

Rail Station in resort.

STAYING THERE

HOW TO GO
Choose charm or convenience
Lots of hotels, pensions and apartments.
Hotels A broad range of hotels (more 4- than 3-stars) and guest houses.
(((4) **Salzburgerhof** (7650) Best in town – the only 5-star. It is nearer the lake than the gondola, but has courtesy bus and pool.
(((4) **Tirolerhof** (7720) Excellent 4-star in the old town. 'Greatly improved' pool, hot-tub and steam room. 'Very comfortable, very friendly and efficient staff', 'good bar' say reporters.
(((4) **Eichenhof** (47201) On outskirts of town, but popular and with a minibus service, great food and lake views.
(((4) **Alpin** (7690) Modern 4-star chalet next to the Zell gondola.
(((4) **Zum Hirschen** (7740) Comfortable 4-star, easy walk to gondola. Sauna, steam room, splash pool, popular bar.
(((4) **Schwebebahn** (72461) Attractive 4-star in secluded setting in the Schmittental, by the cable-cars.
(((4) **Romantikhotel Zell am See** (72520) 4-star close to lake and centre. 'Very good, really wild decor, friendly.'
(((4) **Lebzelter** (7760) A family hotel in the pedestrian area – 'friendly and welcoming, excellent food and good sports bar,' say this year's reporters.
((2) **Margarete** (72724) B&B in the Schmittental, by the cable-cars.
Self-catering Lots of options. Lederer is mid-range and close to the Ebenberg lift (linking to the gondola). More comfortable and central are the 3-star Diana (72436) and Seilergasse.

STAYING UP THE MOUNTAIN
Several options
As well as the Berghotel (72489) at Schmittenhöhe cable-car, the Breiteckalm (73419), Sonnalm (73262) and Pinzgauer Hütte (53472) restaurants have rooms.

EATING OUT
Plenty of choice
Zell has more non-hotel places than is usual in a small Austrian resort. The Ampere is quiet and sophisticated; Giuseppe's is a popular Italian with excellent food; and Kupferkessel and Traubenstüberl both do wholesome regional dishes. There are Chinese restaurants in Zell and Schüttdorf. Car drivers can try the excellent Erlhof at Thumersbach.

APRES-SKI
Plenty for all tastes
Après-ski is lively and varied, with tea dances and high-calorie cafes, plus bars and discos aplenty. 'Even as a 55-year-old I had a great time pubbing,' says a reporter. When it's sunny, Schnapps Hans ice bar outside the Berghotel, up at Schmittenhöhe, really buzzes, with 'great music, a crazy DJ and dancing on tables and on the bar. All ages loved it'. The Diele disco bar rocks – endorsed by a 2006 reporter as 'the place to be' for music and videos. The Resi (formerly Crazy Daisy) on the main road has two crowded bars and still seems popular. Villa Crazy Daisy has three lively bars in a new location. Classic has a live band and 60s and 70s music. The 'excellent' Viva disco allows no under 18s. Or try the smart Hirschenkeller, the cave-like Lebzelter Keller and the Sportstüberl, with nostalgic ski photos on the walls.

OFF THE SLOPES
Lots of choices
There is plenty to do in this year-round resort. The train trip to Salzburg is a must, Kitzbühel is also well worth a visit and Innsbruck is within reach.
You can often walk across the frozen lake to Thumersbach, plus there are good sports facilities, a motor museum, sleigh rides and alpine flights. There are marked paths at Schmittenhöhe.

Indoor Swimming, sauna, solarium, massage, fitness centre, spa, tennis, squash, bowling, rifle range, museums, cinema, library

Outdoor Ice rink, curling, walking, ice sailing, ice surfing, tobogganing, horse-riding, plane flights, sleigh rides, paragliding

Phone numbers
Zell am See
From elsewhere in Austria add the prefix 06542.
From abroad use the prefix +43 6542.
Kaprun
From elsewhere in Austria add the prefix 06547.
From abroad use the prefix +43 6547.

TOURIST OFFICE

Zell am See/Kaprun
t 7700
welcome@europa
sportregion.info
www.europasport
region.info

Kaprun 785m/2,580ft

Apart from providing Zell's snow guarantee, Kaprun is worth considering as a destination in its own right.

THE RESORT

Kaprun is a spacious, charming and quite lively village. The main road to the glacier bypasses it, leaving the centre pleasantly quiet.

THE MOUNTAIN

There is a small area of easy intermediate slopes on the outskirts of the village at **Maiskogel**, served by five lifts, including a cable-car and fast quad. A new six-pack with covers is due to replace an old double chair for 2006/07. There is also a separate nursery area. But most people will want to spend most of their time on the slopes of the nearby **Kitzsteinhorn** glacier or on Zell am See's slopes. Buses to and from both are often crowded at peak times – it's worth timing your trips carefully. The lift pass covers only one ascent of the Kitzsteinhorn access gondola per day.

Slopes A 15-person, two-stage gondola has replaced the Kitzsteinhorn funicular, which suffered a tragic fire in autumn 2000. The first-stage runs parallel with an older eight-seat gondola, ending in the same mid-mountain area. The second stage, up to the Alpincenter and main slopes, runs parallel to a fast quad chair. The main slopes are in a big bowl above the Alpincenter, served by a cable-car, lots of T-bars and three chairs. The area above the top of the Alpincenter is open in summer and is particularly good for an early pre-Christmas or late post-Easter break.

Snow reliability Snow is nearly always good because of the glacier. And there's snowmaking too.

Queues Queues have always been a problem here. Some reports tell of 15-minute waits for the access gondola (down as well as up) and up to 10 minutes for the upper lifts. See Zell am See for comments on the buses home.

Mountain restaurants There are three decent mountain restaurants – the Gletschermühle (recommended in 2006 for 'awesome views, rock music and selection of weekly specials') and Krefelderhütte near the Alpincenter, and the Häusalm near the gondola mid-station. All these get busy. Bella Vista at the top of the mountain has

good views and is 'reasonably priced', says a recent reporter.

Experts There's little to challenge experts except for some good off-piste; the one slightly tough piste starts at the very top.

Intermediates Pistes are mainly gentle blues and reds and make for great easy cruising on usually good snow. From Alpincenter there is an entertaining red run down to the gondola mid-station. This is our favourite run on the mountain, though it does get crowded. There's also a good unpisted ski route.

Beginners There are two nursery slopes in the village and some gentle blues on the glacier to progress to.

Snowboarding There's a newly improved terrain-park on the glacier and some excellent natural half-pipes.

Cross-country Trails on the Kaprun golf course are good, but at altitude there is just one short loop – at the top of the glacier.

Schools and guides There are several ski schools.

Facilities for children All of the schools offer children's classes and there's a kindergarten in the village.

STAYING THERE

How to go There are some catered chalets and chalet-hotels.

Hotels The Orgler (82050), 'spacious' Mitteregger (8207) and Tauernhof (8235) are among the best hotels.

Après-ski Nightlife is quiet, but the Baum bar is lively. The new Kitsch & Bitter is recommended for 'great live music and cocktails'.

Eating out Good restaurants include the Dorfstadl, Hilberger's Beisl and Schlemmerstube.

Off the slopes Off-slope activities are good, and include a fine sports centre with outdoor rapids. A 2006 reporter enjoyed the 'rustic' bowling at the Sportsbar.

Rauris 950m/3,120ft

Rauris is a small village in a quiet dead-end valley south-east of Zell, about 25km/16 miles by road. There are a couple of 4-star hotels, but most are 3-stars. Across the valley from the village are nursery drag-lifts and a six-seat gondola accessing 30km/19 miles of intermediate slopes with a vertical of 1250m/4,100ft; in total 10 lifts, including a new eight-seat gondola serving blue slopes at the top.

Fieberbrunn

Novices could do worse than try Fieberbrunn, with its good nursery slopes, pretty, easy pistes and jolly Tirolean atmosphere. An expansion of the slopes this season will add new off-piste terrain, but the pistes remain limited.

KEY FACTS

Resort	800m
	2,620ft
Slopes	835-2020m
	2,740-6,630ft
Lifts	10
Pistes	35km
	22 miles
Blue	35%
Red	60%
Black	5%
Snowmaking	43%

best for rent

www.sport2000rent.com

TOURIST OFFICE

t 05354 56304
fieberbrunn@
pillerseetal.at
www.pillerseetal.at

THE RESORT

Fieberbrunn sprawls along the valley road for 2km/1 mile, but has classic Tirolean charm: wooden chalets, pretty church, cosy bars and coffee shops. Most accommodation is in hotels and pensions. Much of the village is set back from the road and railway, so that peace is interrupted only by church bells. Light sleepers can stay in hotels out near the main lift station, served by regular but sometimes crowded buses from the village.

THE MOUNTAINS

Two gondolas diverge from a station a little way from the village, with lifts above them ultimately meeting on the upper slopes of Lärchfilzkogel (1645m/5,400ft). One sector consists mainly of blue runs, the other mainly

of easy reds, all mostly below the tree line. Across a valley behind this peak are separate lifts going up to the high point of 2020m/6,630ft on Hochhörndl, with further open red slopes. A big new gondola is being put in here for 2006/07, extending the slopes down to a new valley station and so opening up a new off-piste area. The resort is boarder-friendly, hosting major competitions in its Lords of the Boards terrain-park at the base of the area, with half-pipe.

There are broad nursery slopes at the base. Graduation to long, gentle runs beneath the gondolas is easy.

Fieberbrunn has better snowfall than is usual at this altitude, and it has snowmakers on the home slopes.

Weekday queues are rare outside the morning ski-school rush. Sunny weekends are busy. There is a handful of good mountain restaurants.

Seefeld

Seefeld is a smart, all-round winter holiday resort in a pretty setting, with superb cross-country trails and off-slope activities, and a couple of small, separate areas of downhill slopes. Innsbruck is not far away.

KEY FACTS

Resort	1200m
	3,940ft
Slopes	1200-2100m
	3,940-6,890ft
Lifts	25
Pistes	45km
	28 miles
Blue	70%
Red	30%
Black	0%
Snowmaking	15km
	9 miles

TOURIST OFFICE

t 05212 2313
info@seefeld.at
www.seefeld.at

THE RESORT

A classic post-war Tirolean tourist development, Seefeld is well designed in traditional Tirolean style, with a large, pedestrian-only centre. Lots of people come here for the curling, skating and swimming rather than the skiing. The upmarket nature of the resort is reflected in the hotels – there are three 5-stars and some 30 4-stars. The village is on a main railway line.

THE MOUNTAINS

The slopes are in two main sectors – Gschwandtkopf and Rosshütte. Both are on the outskirts, served by a regular free shuttle-bus. The nursery slopes on Geigenbühel, close to the centre of the village are broad and gentle, with snowmaking. Gschwandtkopf is a rounded hill of 300m/980ft vertical

and intermediate runs on two main slopes. Rosshütte is more extensive, and has a terrain-park and half-pipe. The top of Rosshütte can be reached by a funicular – 'very efficient' says a reader – and then a cable-car. A new panorama restaurant at the top is planned for 2006/07. There is a cable-car across to the separate peak of Härmelekopf, also reachable from the valley by two six-seat chairs. Both sectors have long runs of 800m/2,620ft vertical to the base station.

Rosshütte has some seriously steep off-piste challenges for experts and will offer intermediates an interesting day out from Innsbruck – but the terrain is too limited for a week's stay.

Seefeld's 262km/163 miles of excellent cross-country trails are some of the best in the Alps – and Winter Olympics events and the Nordic World Ski Championships have been held here.

TVB SERFAUS

Serfaus

A compelling combination: the charm of a nearly car-free Austrian village with extensive high slopes (175km/109 miles claimed) and fairly reliable snow; virtually unknown in the UK – a lack of English speakers may be a drawback.

KEY FACTS

Resort	1430m
	4,690ft
Slopes	1200-2750m
	3,940-9,020ft
Lifts	53
Pistes	175km
	109 miles
Blue	20%
Red	70%
Black	10%
Snowmaking	85km
	53 miles

TOURIST OFFICE

t 05476 6239
info@serfaus.com
www.serfaus.com

THE RESORT

Serfaus is attractive and friendly, with chalet-style buildings set on a sunny shelf. It is largely traffic-free, with an underground railway running through the village to the lifts at the far end, via two stops en route. Comfortable, chalet-style hotels abound.

Most visitors are well-heeled Germans, many of them family groups. There are several après-ski bars, but evenings are quiet. There is a very long toboggan run to the village.

THE MOUNTAINS

A gondola goes up to the huge mid-mountain focus of Komperdell (1980m/6,500ft), with vast kids' facilities. There's a broad area of intermediate slopes above here, with some good long runs down to the village. A chain of lifts and runs extends west over two more ridges, ending an extraordinary 11km/7 miles from the village. It's all good intermediate stuff; the blacks dotted around, with a couple of exceptions, are more like tough reds. But there are ski routes, and plenty of off-piste.

Another village gondola leads to the slopes of Fiss (1435m/4,710ft), where there are wide sunny slopes served by a long gondola to Schönjoch and shorter shady runs beyond. You can take a 10km/6 mile red run to Fiss – of blue gradient, with good views.

Most of the slopes are above the tree line, and with good snowmaking the area is fairly snow-sure, despite the sun. Queues are not a problem.

The mid-station nursery slopes are good, and there is ample opportunity for progression to longer runs. Cross-country is big here.

Short turns

235

Wagrain

Wagrain is a towny little resort at the centre of a lift system that is typical of many in Salzburgerland – spreading widely across several low, partly wooded ridges. Flachau and Alpendorf/St Johann are at its extremities.

SNOWPIX.COM / CHRIS GILL

KEY FACTS

Resort	850m
	2,790ft
Slopes	850-2190m
	2,790-7,190ft
Lifts	64
Pistes	200km
	124 miles
Blue	20%
Red	75%
Black	5%

TOURIST OFFICE

t 06413 8448
info@wagrain.info
www.wagrain.info
www.sportwelt-
amade.com

THE RESORT

Wagrain is an unremarkable valley village where life does not revolve entirely around skiing. The lift stations are on the fringes of the village and served by ski-buses – one up at the elevated suburb of Kirchboden, along with the nursery slopes and the excellent Wasserwelt pool complex.

THE MOUNTAINS

It's an impressive lift system, with a lot of fast chairs and gondolas. From Wagrain, a gondola to Grafenberg leads to an area of short lifts and runs and so to Hirschkogel above Alpendorf, a satellite of St Johann im Pongau. To the east, from Kirchboden, another gondola goes to Griessenkareck, at the top of the slopes down to Flachau. It's a big area – 15km/9 miles from end to end – with some good, long, although easy runs. The slopes are practically all graded red, with a few blues dotted around. The reds are generally not very testing, but they are genuine reds, and none of the home runs is really easy. The few stretches of black are for purely decorative purposes. Despite the altitude, most of the upper slopes are fairly open. Some get too much sun for comfort, and snow reliability is not a strong point. There are lots of attractive mountain restaurants.

The Salzburger Sportwelt lift pass area includes another similar lift system (tantalisingly close but connected only by buses) to the south, linking Zauchensee, Flachauwinkl and Kleinarl – much more easily accessed from Wagrain or Flachau than St Johann. There are also smaller areas at Filzmoos and Radstadt/Altenmarkt.

France

Over one-third of British skiers and snowboarders choose France for their holidays each year, almost double the number who go to Austria, the next most popular country. It's not difficult to see what attracts us to France. The country has the biggest lift and piste networks in the world; for those who like to cover as many miles in a day as possible, these are unrivalled. Most of these big areas are also at high altitude, ensuring high-quality snow for a long season. And French mountains offer a mixture of some of the toughest, wildest slopes in the Alps and some of the longest, gentlest and most convenient beginner runs.

French resort villages can't be quite so uniformly recommended; but, equally, they don't all conform to the standard image of soulless, purpose-built service stations, thrown up without concern for appearance during the boom of the 1960s and 1970s. Many resorts are based on more traditional villages, or offer these as an option. Another advantage of smaller villages and less well-known resorts is that they tend to be cheaper. Some of the big-name resorts can now be very expensive – none more so than Courchevel 1850, where you can pay quite silly prices for hotel rooms, food and drink.

Towards the front of the book there is a special chapter on driving to the French Alps – still very popular, especially with people going self-catering, despite the growth of the budget airlines. The French Alps are easy to get to by car, and luxurious apartments are becoming more and more common as property developers see the market opportunities.

237

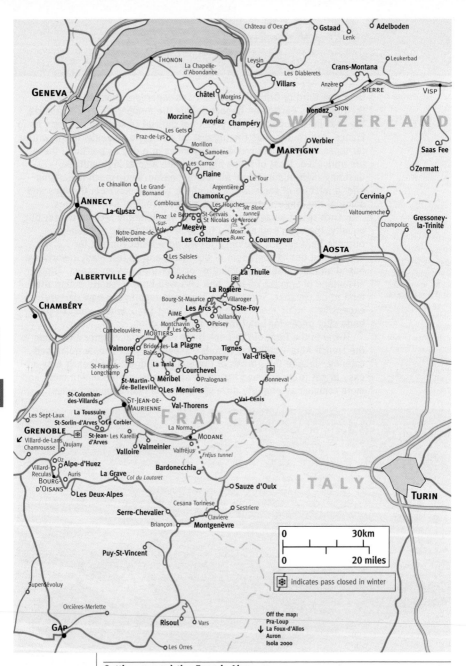

Château d'Oex · ○ Gstaad · ○ Adelboden
Lenk
THONON · Leysin · ○ Leukerbad
La Chapelle-d'Abondance · Les Diablerets · Crans-Montana
GENEVA · Villars · Anzère ○ · SIERRE · VISP
Châtel · Morgins
Morzine · Avoriaz · Champéry · Nendaz · SION
Les Gets · SWITZERLAND
Praz-de-Lys ○ · Morillon · ○ Verbier
Samoëns · MARTIGNY · Saas Fee
Les Carroz · ○ Zermatt
Flaine · Le Tour
Le Chinaillon · Le Grand-Bornand · Argentière · Cervinia
ANNECY · Combloux · Chamonix · Les Houches · Mt Blanc · Valtournenche · Gressoney-la-Trinité
La Clusaz · Praz- · Le Bettex · St-Gervais · tunnel · Champoluc
sur- · St Nicolas de Véroce
Notre-Dame-de- · Arly · Megève · MONT
Bellecombe · Les Contamines · BLANC · Courmayeur
Les Saisies · AOSTA
ALBERTVILLE · Arèches · La Thuile
La Rosière
CHAMBÉRY · Bourg-St-Maurice · Villaroger
Les Arcs · Ste-Foy
AIME · Vallandry
Montchavin · Peisey
Combelouvière · MOUTIERS · Les Coches
Valmorel · Brides-les- · La Plagne · Tignes
Bains · Champagny · Val-d'Isère
St-François- · La Tania
Longchamp · Courchevel
St-Martin- · Méribel · Pralognan · Bonneval
St-Colomban- · de-Belleville · Les Menuires
des-Villards · ST-JEAN-DE- · Val-Thorens · Val-Cenis
Les Sept-Laux · La Toussuire · MAURIENNE
St-Sorlin-d'Arves · Le Corbier · FRANCE
GRENOBLE · St-Jean- · Les Karellis · La Norma
Villard-de-Lans · d'Arves · MODANE
Chamrousse · Vaujany · Valloire · Valmeinier · Valfréjus
Villard- · Oz · Alpe-d'Huez · Fréjus tunnel · ITALY
Reculas · Auris · La Grave · Bardonecchia
BOURG- · Col du Lautaret · TURIN
D'OISANS · Les Deux-Alpes · Sauze d'Oulx
Cesana Torinese · Sestriere
Serre-Chevalier · Claviere
Briançon · Montgenèvre

Puy-St-Vincent

0 · 30km
0 · 20 miles

✳ indicates pass closed in winter

Superdévoluy

Orcières-Merlette

Off the map:
Pra-Loup
↓ La Foux-d'Allos
Auron
Isola 2000

GAP · Risoul · Vars

Les Orres

Getting around the French Alps

Pick the right gateway – Geneva, Chambéry or Grenoble – and you can hardly go wrong. The approach to Serre-Chevalier and Montgenèvre involves the 2060m/6,760ft Col du Lauteret; but the road is a major one and kept clear of snow or re-opened quickly after a fall. Crossing the French-Swiss border between Chamonix and Verbier involves two closure-prone passes – the Montets and the Forclaz. When necessary, one-way traffic runs beside the tracks through the rail tunnel beneath the passes.

ANY STYLE OF RESORT YOU LIKE

The main drawback to France, hinted at above, is the monstrous architecture of some of the purpose-built resorts. But not all French resorts are hideous. Certainly, France has its fair share of Alpine eyesores, chief among them central Les Menuires, central La Plagne, Flaine, Tignes, Isola 2000 and Les Arcs. But all these places have learned from past mistakes, and newer developments there are being built in a much more attractive, traditional chalet style. The later generation of purpose-built resorts, such as Valmorel, La Rosière and La Tania, have been built in much more sympathetic style than their predecessors. The big advantages of the high, purpose-built resorts are the splendid quality and extent of the slopes they serve, the reliability and quality of the snow, and the amazing slope-side convenience of most of the accommodation.

If you prefer, there are genuinely old mountain villages to stay in, linked directly to the big lift networks. These are not usually as convenient for the slopes, but they give you a feel of being in France rather than in a winter-holiday factory. Examples include Montchavin or Champagny for La Plagne, Vaujany for Alpe-d'Huez, St-Martin-de-Belleville, Les Allues or Brides-les-Bains for the Trois Vallées, and Les Carroz, Morillon or Samoëns for Flaine. There are also old villages with their own slopes that have developed as resorts while retaining some or all of their rustic ambience – such as Serre-Chevalier and La Clusaz.

Megève deserves a special mention – an exceptionally charming little town combining rustic style with sophistication; shame about the traffic. It has now been overtaken for the award for being the most chic and expensive resort by Courchevel 1850, largely because of the latter's popularity not just with the Paris jet set but also with rich Russians.

And France has Alpine centres with a long mountaineering and skiing history. Chief among these is Chamonix, which sits in the shadow of Mont Blanc, Europe's highest peak, and is the centre of the most radical off-piste terrain in the Alps. Chamonix is a big, bustling town, where winter sports go on alongside tourism in general. By contrast, simple La Grave is at the foot of mountains that are almost as impressive – the highest within France.

IMPROVING APARTMENTS

One of the most welcome developments on the French resort scene in recent years has been the availability of genuinely comfortable and stylish apartments, in contrast to the cramped and, frankly, primitive places that have dominated the market since the 1960s – see the luxury apartments chapter.

PLAT DU JOUR

France has advantages over most rival destinations in the gastronomic stakes. While many of its mountain restaurants serve fast food, most also do at least a plat du jour that is in a different league from what you'll find in Austria or the US. It is generally possible to find somewhere to get a half-decent lunch and to have it served at your table, rather than queuing repeatedly for every element of your meal. In the evening, most resorts have restaurants serving good, traditional French food as well as regional specialities. And the wine is decent and affordable.

Many French resorts (though not all) have suffered from a lack of nightlife, but things have changed in recent years. In resorts dominated by apartments with few international visitors, there may still be very little going on after dinner, but places such as Méribel are now distinctly lively in the evening.

France is unusual among European countries in using four grades of piste (instead of the usual three). The very easiest runs are classified green; except in Val-d'Isère, they are reliably gentle. It's novices who care most about choosing just the right sort of terrain to build confidence, so this is a genuinely helpful system, which ought to be used internationally.

AVOID THE CROWDS

French school holidays mean crowded slopes, so they are worth avoiding if possible. The country is divided into three zones, with three fortnight holidays staggered over a four-week period from early February to early March – with two zones overlapping in late February – so expect that period to be particularly busy.

Alpe-d'Huez

Impressive and sunny slopes above a hotchpotch of a purpose-built village, but with attractive alternative bases that we prefer to stay in

COSTS

① ② ③ ④ ⑤ ⑥

RATINGS

The slopes

Fast lifts	**
Snow	****
Extent	****
Expert	****
Intermediate	****
Beginner	*****
Convenience	****
Queues	****
Mountain restaurants	****

The rest

Scenery	****
Resort charm	*
Off-slope	****

NEWS

For 2006/07 access from Alpe-d'Huez to Auris-en-Oisans should be improved by a new high-speed quad due to replace the slow two-person Louvets chair-lift.

In 2005/06 a six-pack replaced the three drag-lifts at Les Bergers. Also the Romains lift was removed and a second tow added to the Rif Nel to improve access to the beginner slopes there.

A moving carpet was installed at the beginner area at Oz-en-Oisans last season. And a new 3-star hotel with 33 rooms and a swimming pool is due to open there in December 2006.

Alpe-d'Huez's lower slopes are gentle and, if they didn't get too crowded, would be ideal for beginners →

➕ Extensive, high, sunny slopes, split interestingly into various sectors

➕ Huge snowmaking installation

➕ Vast, gentle, sunny nursery slopes

➕ Efficient lift system, mostly

➕ Some good, surprisingly rustic mountain restaurants

➕ Livelier than most purpose-built resorts

➕ Pleasant alternative bases in outlying villages and satellites

➖ In late season the many south-facing runs can be icy early and slushy later

➖ Some main intermediate runs get badly overcrowded in high season

➖ Many of the tough runs are very high, and inaccessible in bad weather

➖ Practically no woodland runs to retreat to in bad weather

➖ Sprawling resort with a hotchpotch of architectural styles, no central focus and very little charm

There are few places to rival Alpe-d'Huez for extent and variety of terrain – in good conditions it's one of our favourites. But, in late season at least, despite ever-expanding snowmaking, the 'island in the sun' suffers from the very thing it advertises: strong sun means that ice can spoil mornings on the main slopes, however alluring the prospect of slushy moguls in the afternoons.

The village has few fans, but if you don't like the sound of it you always have the alternative of staying in rustic Vaujany (with its mighty cable-car), Villard-Reculas, or in the modern ski stations of Oz-en-Oisans or Auris. The whole area is increasingly being referred to as the Massif des Grandes Rousses.

THE RESORT

Alpe-d'Huez is a large village spread across an open mountainside high above the Romanche valley east of Grenoble, and it has grown in a seemingly unplanned way. Its buildings come in all shapes, sizes and designs (including a futuristic church which hosts weekly organ concerts). Many buildings look scruffy and in need of renovation, although some wood cladding and general smartening-up can now be seen. A couple of recent reporters remarked how friendly and welcoming the locals were, compared with other French resorts.

It is a large, amorphous resort; the nearest thing to a central focus is the main Avenue des Jeux in the middle, where you'll find the swimming pool, ice skating and some of the shops, bars and restaurants. The rest of the resort spreads out in a triangle, with lift stations at two of the apexes.

The bus service around the resort is free with the lift pass, and there's a bucket-lift (with a piste beneath it)

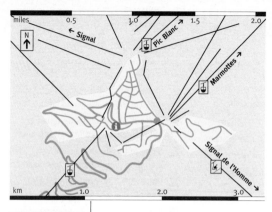

KEY FACTS

Resort	1860m
	6,100ft
Slopes	1120-3320m
	3,670-10,890ft
Lifts	84
Pistes	245km
	152 miles
Green	31%
Blue	26%
Red	28%
Black	14%
Snowmaking	
	770 guns

running through the resort to the main lifts at the top. This is handy but slow, and some people don't like the need to jump on and off it as it moves. It doesn't operate in the evenings.

A short distance from the main body of the resort (and linked by chair-lift) are two satellite 'hamlets'. Les Bergers, at the eastern entrance to the resort, is convenient for the slopes (with its own nursery area). It is fairly self-contained, with a couple of bar/restaurants and several shops near the slopes, but it's a trek from most of the other resort facilities. A chalet suburb is expanding this quarter uphill – convenient for skiing but even more remote from the village centre. L'Eclose, to the south of the main village, is less convenient but a 2006 reporter said 'it now has some lively bars and good restaurants and is a pleasant 15-minute walk over a snowfield into town'. There is also accommodation down the hill in the old village of Huez, linked by lift. Another 2006 reporter enjoyed staying down there in the small L'Ancolie hotel at 'almost half the cost we were quoted by hotels in town'.

Outings by road are feasible to other resorts covered on a week's lift pass, including Serre-Chevalier and Les Deux-Alpes. A helicopter also does day trips to Les Deux-Alpes for a surprisingly modest fee and a bus goes twice a week (Wed and Thurs) but you need to book.

THE MOUNTAINS

Alpe-d'Huez is a big-league resort, ranking alongside giants like Val-d'Isère or La Plagne for the extent and variety of its slopes. Practically all the slopes are above the tree line, and there may be precious little to do when a storm socks in; the runs around Oz are your best bet (if you can get to them).

Reporters find the piste grading unreliable, making it a rather unnerving place for timid intermediates. For example, the Hirondelles run (now graded blue rather than green), is still singled out by reporters as being tricky, with a tendency to develop big bumps. You may find some reds rather tame, then find others 'steeply mogulled halfway down'.

THE SLOPES
Several well-linked areas
The slopes divide into four sectors, with good connections between them, though a recent reporter complained of having to pole or walk between lifts.

The biggest sector is directly above the village, on the slopes of **Pic Blanc**. The huge Grandes Rousses gondola, otherwise known as the DMC (a reference to its clever technology), goes up in two stages from the top of the village. Above it, a cable-car goes up to 3320m/10,890ft on Pic Blanc itself – the top of the Sarenne glacier. There is an alternative way to the glacier now that a third stage has been added to the Marmottes gondola, which also serves a lower area of challenging runs at Clocher de Macle. The longest piste in the Alps – the 16km/10 mile Sarenne – starts from Pic Blanc (see the feature panel).

The Sarenne gorge separates the main resort area from **Signal de l'Homme**. It is crossed by a down-and-up fast chair-lift from the Bergers part of the village. From the top you can take excellent north-facing slopes towards the gorge, or head south to Auris or west to tiny Chatelard.

LIFT PASSES

Visalp

Prices in €

Age	1-day	6-day
under 16	24	133
16 to 59	36	187
over 60	24	133
Free under 5, over 72		

Beginner day pass
€11.80

Notes
Covers all lifts in
Alpe-d'Huez, Auris,
Oz, Vaujany and
Villard-Reculas. Half-
day passes available.
Discounts for families
and regular visitors.
Two-day plus pass
covers sports centre,
ice rink, swimming
pools, concerts, two
museums and shuttle
service. Six-day or
more pass allows one
day's skiing at one of
Serre-Chevalier, Puy-
St-Vincent and the
Milky Way in Italy,
and two days in Les
Deux-Alpes.

Alternative passes
Passes for Auris only,
Oz-Vaujany only,
Villard-Reculas only.

On the other side of town from
Signal de l'Homme is the small **Signal**
sector, reached by drag-lifts next to the
main gondola or by a couple of chairs
lower down. Runs go down the other
side of the hill to the old village of
Villard-Reculas. One blue run back to
Alpe-d'Huez is floodlit twice a week.

The generally quieter **Vaujany-Oz**
sector consists largely of north-west-
facing slopes, accessible from Alpe-
d'Huez via good red runs from either
the mid-station or the top of the DMC
gondola. At the heart of this sector is
Alpette, the mid-station of the cable-
car from Vaujany. From here a
disastrously sunny red goes down to
Oz, a much more reliable blue goes
north to the Vaujany home slopes
around Montfrais, and a shady black
plunges down to Enversin, just below
Vaujany, offering an on-piste descent
of 2200m/7,220ft from Pic Blanc – not
the biggest vertical in the Alps, but not
far short. The links back to Alpe-d'Huez
are by the top cable-car from Alpette,
or a gondola from Oz.

TERRAIN-PARKS
A choice
There's a good boarder-cross course
and new advanced park by the Babars
drag, and a 1.5km/1 mile terrain-park
with half-pipe, jumps and rollers near
the main lift base. There's another
terrain-park near Auris and a
'beginners' park above Vaujany.

SNOW RELIABILITY
Affected by the sun
Alpe-d'Huez is unique among major
purpose-built resorts in the Alps in
having mainly south- or south-west-
facing slopes. The strong southern sun
means that late-season conditions may
alternate between slush and ice on
most of the area, with some of the
lower runs being closed altogether.
There are shady slopes above Vaujany
and at Signal de l'Homme. The Pic
Blanc glacier is small.

In more wintry circumstances the
runs are relatively snow-sure, the
natural stuff being backed up by
extensive snowmaking on the main
runs above Alpe-d'Huez, Vaujany and
Oz. But reports suggest that neither
the grooming nor the snowmaking is
as enthusiastic as we would wish.

FOR EXPERTS
Plenty of blacks and off-piste
This is an excellent resort for experts,
with long and challenging black runs
(and reds that ought to be black) as
well as serious off-piste (see feature
box). The slope beneath the Pic Blanc
cable-car, usually an impressive mogul-
field, is reached by a 300m/1,000ft
tunnel from the back side of the
mountain. Despite improvements to
the tunnel exit, the start of the actual
slope is often awkward. The slope is of
ordinary black steepness, but can be
very hard in the mornings because it
gets a lot of sun.

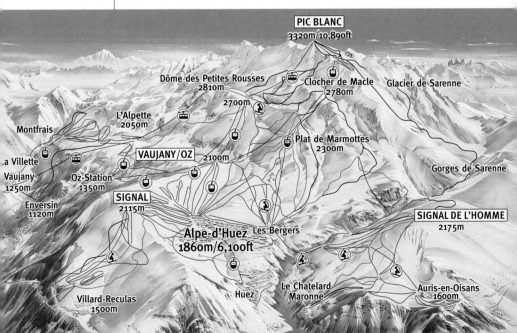

The long Sarenne run on the back of the Pic Blanc is described in a special feature panel. We've never found the black Fare piste to Enversin open, but reporters rate it as one of the best – 'a demanding but highly enjoyable descent through the trees'. Some of the upper red pistes are tough enough to give experts a challenge. These include the Canyon and Balme runs accessed by the Lièvre Blanc chair-lift from the gondola mid-station – runs which are unprepared and south-facing, and steep enough to be classified black in many resorts. Above this, the Marmottes II gondola serves steep black runs from Clocher de Macle, including the beautiful, long, lonely Combe Charbonniere.

FOR INTERMEDIATES
Fine selection of runs

Good intermediates have a fine selection of runs all over the area. In good snow conditions the variety of runs is difficult to beat. Every section has some challenging red runs to test the adventurous intermediate. The most challenging are the Canyon and Balme runs, mentioned previously. There are lovely long runs down to Oz and to Vaujany, with space for some serious carving. The Villard-Reculas and Signal de l'Homme sectors also have long challenging reds. The Chamois red from the top of the gondola down to the mid-station is quite narrow, and miserable when busy and icy and/or heavily mogulled. Fearless intermediates should enjoy the super-long Sarenne black run.

For less ambitious intermediates, there are usually blue alternatives, except on the upper part of the mountain. The main Couloir blue from the top of the big gondola is a lovely run, well served by snowmaking, but it does get scarily crowded at times.

There are some great cruising runs

above Vaujany; but the red runs between Vaujany and Alpe-d'Huez can be too much for early intermediates. Unless you are prepared to travel via Oz on gondolas, you are effectively confined to one sector or the other.

Early intermediates will also enjoy the gentle slopes leading back to Alpe-d'Huez from the main mountain, and the Signal sector.

FOR BEGINNERS
Good facilities

The large network of green runs immediately above the village is as good a nursery area as you will find anywhere. The drag-lifts at Les Bergers were replaced by a new six-seat chair for 2005/06, making that part much easier for novices. Sadly, these slopes get very crowded and carry a lot of fast through-traffic. A large area embracing half a dozen runs has been declared a low-speed zone, but the restriction is not policed and so achieves very little. All in all, with a special lift pass covering 11 lifts, Alpe-d'Huez makes a good choice.

FOR CROSS-COUNTRY
High-level and convenient

There are 50km/31 miles of trails, with three loops of varying degrees of difficulty, all at around 2000m/6,560ft and consequently relatively snow-sure.

QUEUES
Generally few problems

Even in French holiday periods, the modern lift system ensures there are few long hold-ups. The village bucket-lift is said to generate lengthy queues first thing. Queues can build up for the gondolas out of the village, but the DMC shifts its queue quickly and the bottom section can be avoided by taking alternative lifts to the quieter second stage.

The small Pic Blanc cable-car is no longer the bottleneck it was, thanks to the Marmottes III gondola, which now offers an alternative way to the glacier.

Although they may not cause queues, there are lots of old drag-lifts scattered around.

Over much of the area a greater problem than lift queues is that the main pistes can be unbearably crowded. We and many reporters rate the Chamois and Couloir runs from the top of the DMC among the most crowded we've seen. The red to Oz, beneath the Poutran gondola, is also singled out by reporters as being too busy for comfort – 'Carnage all the way,' said one.

MOUNTAIN RESTAURANTS
Some excellent rustic huts
Mountain restaurants are generally good – even self-service places are welcoming, and there are many more rustic places with table-service than is usual in high French resorts. One of our favourites is the cosy little Chalet du Lac Besson – endorsed by both 2005 ('fabulous place') and 2006 ('tender lamb with garlicky gratin') reporters – on the cross-country loops north of the DMC gondola mid-station; the route to it, now with piste status (the Boulevard des Lacs), is still not easy to follow.

The pretty Forêt de Maronne hotel at Chatelard, below Signal de l'Homme, is 'a delightfully quiet sun-trap', enthuses a reporter, and has a good choice of traditional French and International cuisine: 'The chicken satay kept us raving about the place all week.' The Bergerie at Villard-Reculas has good views and is 'highly recommended'.

The Combe Haute, at the foot of the Chalvet chair in the gorge towards the end of the Sarenne run, is welcoming but gets very busy. The Signal is quieter and has 'postcard views'. The terrace of the Perce-Neige, just below the Oz-Poutran gondola mid-station, attracts crowds. The Plage des Neiges at the top of the nursery slopes is one of the best places available to beginners. Chantebise 2100, at the DMC mid-station, offers 'slick and cheerful table service and is reassuringly expensive'. The Cabane du Poutat, halfway down from Plat de Marmottes, is recommended for good food but we've had a report of a '30 minute delay to be served'. The Marmottes itself has had mixed reviews – 'good value main courses' but 'a tiny microwaved cheeseburger in a soggy, stale bun'.

The restaurants in the Oz and Vaujany sectors tend to be cheaper, but no less satisfactory. At Montfrais, the Airelles is a rustic hut, built into the rock, with a roaring log fire, atmospheric music and excellent, good-value food ('The best plat du jour I have ever eaten,' says a 2005 reporter). The Auberge de l'Alpette also gets enthusiastic reviews emphasising that it is 'really good value', as does the Chardon Bleu for 'excellent French country cooking'. The P'Oz is also worth a visit.

SCHOOLS AND GUIDES
Contrasting reports
Recent reports on the ESF branches here are mixed: 'The kids progressed very well,' said one, but two others sound worrying alarms. 'Appalling,' said a reporter whose daughter was found 'sobbing after being shouted at', while another child 'was curled in a ball crying, totally ignored'. 'Don't even

SCHOOLS
ESF
t 0476 809423
International
t 0476 804277

Classes (ESF prices) 6 days (3hr am and 2½hr pm) €177
Private lessons €36 for 1hr, for 1 or 2 people.

GUIDES
Mountain guide office
t 0476 804255

OFF-PISTE FOR ALL STANDARDS
There are vast amounts of off-piste terrain in Alpe-d'Huez, from fairly tame to seriously adventurous. Here we pick out just a few of the many runs to be explored – always with guidance, of course.

There are lots of off-piste variants on both sides of the Sarenne run that are good for making your first turns off-piste. The Combe du Loup, a beautiful south-facing bowl with views over the Meije, has a black-run gradient at the top, and you end up on long, gentle slopes leading back to the Sarenne gorge. La Chapelle Saint Giraud, which starts at Signal de l'Homme, is another excellent itinerary for off-piste novices. Its vertical drop of 630m/2,070ft includes a series of small confidence-boosting bowls, interspersed with gentle rolling terrain.

For more experienced and adventurous off-piste skiers, the Grand Sablat is a classic which runs through a magnificently wild setting on the eastern face of the Massif des Grandes Rousses. This descent of 2000m/6,560ft vertical includes glacial terrain and some steep couloirs. You can either ski down to the village of Clavans, where you can take a pre-booked helicopter or taxi back, or traverse above Clavans back to the Sarenne Gorge. In the Signal sector, there are various classic routes down towards the village of Huez or to Villard-Reculas.

The north-facing Vaujany sector is particularly interesting for experienced off-piste enthusiasts. Route finding can be very tricky, and huge cliffs and rock bands mean this is not a place to get lost. From the top of Pic Blanc, a 40-minute hike takes you to Col de la Pyramide at 3250m/10,660ft, the starting point for the classic itinerary La Pyramide with a vertical of over 2000m/6,560ft. Once at the bottom of the long and wide Pyramide snowfield, you can link into the Vaujany pistes.

THE LONGEST PISTE IN THE ALPS – AND IT'S BLACK?

It's no surprise that most ski runs that are seriously steep are also seriously short. The really long runs in the Alps tend to be classified blue, or red at the most. The Parsenn runs above Klosters, for example – typically 12km to 15km (7 to 9 miles) long – are manageable in your first week on skis. Even Chamonix's famous Vallée Blanche off-piste run doesn't include steepness in its attractions.

So you could be forgiven for being sceptical about the 'black' Sarenne run from the Pic Blanc: even with an impressive vertical of 2000m/6,560ft, a run 16km/10 miles in length means an average gradient of only 11% – typical of a blue run. Macho-hype on the part of the lift company, presumably?

Not quite. The Sarenne is a run of two halves. The bottom half is virtually flat (boarders beware) but the top half is a genuine black if you take the direct route – a demanding and highly satisfying run (with stunning views) that any keen, competent skier will enjoy. The steep mogul-field near the top can be avoided by taking a newly created easier option (or by using the new Marmottes III gondola); and the whole run can now be tackled by an adventurous intermediate. The run gets a lot of sun, so pick your time with care – there's nothing worse than a sunny run with no sun.

CHILDREN

Les Crapouilloux
t 0476 113923
From age 2; 9.30-5.30

Les Intrépides
t 0476 112161
Ages 6mnth to 3yr;
8am-6.30

Les Eterlous (ESF)
t 0476 806785
Ages 2½ to 5

Tonton Mayonnaise
(International school
Ages 2½ to 3½;
10am-12 noon

Club des Marmottes
(International school)
Ages from 4

Club Med nursery
From age 4, with or
without lessons

Ski schools
Take children from 4
to 16 (ESF 6 days
€166)

GETTING THERE

Air Lyon 150km/
93 miles (3hr);
Geneva 220km/137
miles (4hr); Grenoble,
99km/62 miles
(1½hr).

Rail Grenoble (63km/
39 miles); daily buses
from station.

think about going to the ESF,' said another. Groups can be big: one reporter counted an astonishing 25 in one class. We continue to get favourable reports of Masterclass, an independent school run by British instructor Stuart Adamson – 'I would go back to Alpe-d'Huez just to ski with them,' says one. Class sizes are limited to eight. Advance booking for high season is necessary. The Bureau des Guides also has a good reputation.

FACILITIES FOR CHILDREN
Positive reports
Les Crapouilloux day-care centre is 'very well organised' and has been recommended, as has tour operator Crystal's childcare operation. The children's garden and nursery at Vaujany have been recommended.

STAYING THERE

HOW TO GO
Something of everything
Chalets UK tour operators run quite a few chalet-hotels, and some are offering smaller chalets in the new development above Les Bergers.
Hotels There are more hotels than is usual in a high French resort, and there's a clear downmarket bias, with more 1-stars than 2- or 3-stars, and only two 4-stars.
(((4 **Royal Ours Blanc** (0476 803550) Central. Luxurious, with good food. Superb fitness centre. Free (but often oversubscribed) minibus to the lifts.
(((3 **Au Chamois d'Or** (0476 803132) Good facilities, modern rooms, one of the best restaurants in town and well placed for main gondola.
(((3 **Cimes** (0476 803431) South-facing rooms, excellent food; close to cross-

resort lift and pistes.
(((3 **Grandes Rousses** (0476 803311) A recent visitor says, 'Great atmosphere, charming Madame, goodish food and a good guitarist.' Close to the lifts.
((2 **Mariandre** (0476 806603) Comfortable hotel with good food, recommended by readers. Some small rooms. Next to the bucket-lift.
((2 **Gentianes** (0476 803576) Close to the Sarenne gondola in Les Bergers; a range of rooms, the best comfortable.
Self-catering There is an enormous choice available. The Pierre et Vacances apartments near the Marmottes gondola in Les Bergers offer good facilities, but as usual in France they are too small if fully occupied. The Maison de l'Alpe close to the DMC has been recommended for its ideal location and good facilities.

EATING OUT
Good value
Alpe-d'Huez has dozens of restaurants, some of high quality; many offer good value by resort standards. The Crémaillère is recommended by a frequent visitor. Au P'tit Creux has 'excellent food and ambience' but is said to be 'getting expensive'. The 'outstanding' Génépi is a friendly old place with good cuisine. The Pomme de Pin is repeatedly approved. Of the pizzerias, L'Origan 'served fabulous pizza and pasta'; Pinocchio 'gets very busy early', says a reporter, who also liked the 'enormous helpings' at Smithy's Tavern (Tex-Mex). The Edelweiss is recommended for its 'excellent value set menus and grills'. The Nabab (Moroccan) was recommended by a 2006 reporter for 'tender slow-cooked lamb in a room decorated like a Turkish harem'.

peak retreats

Beat the crowds
Traditional resorts

0870 770 0408

www.peakretreats.co.uk

ABTA W5537

The off-slope
facilities, including
this open-air pool,
are good →

NUTS.FR/JP NOISILLIER/
OT ALPE-D'HUEZ

APRES-SKI
Getting better all the time

There's a wide range of bars, some of which get fairly lively later on. Of the British-run bars, the Roadhouse in Crystal's hotel Vallée Blanche and the Underground in Neilson's hotel Chamois are established favourites – but a recent reporter thought the Underground 'smoke-filled and claustrophobic'. The Crowded House in Crystal's Hermitage hotel was recommended as a 'quiet' alternative with a pool table – but a 2006 reporter found it 'dirty, shabby, frequented by a very young crowd'. The small but 'lively' Sphere bar is popular after the lifts close. O'Sharkey's (with 'comfortable leather sofas') and the Pacific (sister bar to the one in Val d'Isère) are also popular. Smithy's can get pretty rowdy late on. The live bands at the Yeti make for 'some great nights' but a 2006 reporter said it had 'all the atmosphere of a youth club.'

The Etalon and Free Ride cafes ('relaxed, cheery atmosphere with great sports videos') are also recommended. And the Dutch-run Melting Pot does good tapas and is great for a relaxed drink, as is the Zoo. The Sporting is 'a great bar with class bands but the highest prices in town'; this and the Igloo club liven up in peak season.

OFF THE SLOPES
Good by purpose-built standards

There is a wide range of facilities, including an indoor pool, an open-air pool (boxer-style cozzies not allowed), Olympic-size ice rink and splendid sports centre – all of this covered by the lift pass. There's also an ice-driving school and a toboggan run. Visits to the Ice Cave are highly recommended by reporters. Shops are numerous but limited in range. The helicopter excursion to Les Deux-Alpes is amusing. There are well-marked walkers' trails and there's a pedestrian lift pass. A special route map is also available. The better mountain restaurants are widely spread – some too remote for pedestrians.

247

Selected chalet in Alpe-d'Huez

ADVERTISEMENT

ACTIVITIES

Indoor Sports centre (tennis, gym, squash, aerobics, swimming, shooting range, climbing wall), cinemas, concerts, theatre, library, museum

Outdoor Ice rink, curling, cleared walking paths, tobogganing, snow-shoeing, microlight flights, sightseeing flights, ice cave, off-road vehicle tours, hang-gliding, paragliding, ice driving school, snowmobiles, quad-bikes

Phone numbers From abroad use the prefix +33 and omit the initial '0' of the phone number.

TOURIST OFFICE

Alpe-d'Huez
t 0476 114444
info@alpedhuez.com
www.alpedhuez.com

Villard-Reculas

1500m/4,920ft

Villard-Reculas is a secluded village just over the hill (Signal) from Alpe-d'Huez, complete with an old church, set on a small shelf wedged between an expanse of open snowfields above and tree-filled hillsides below. Following the installation of a fast quad chair up to Signal a few years back, the village is becoming more popular. Its visitor beds are mainly in self-catering apartments and chalets, booked either through the tourist office or La Source – an English-run agency that also runs a comfortable catered chalet in a carefully converted stone barn. There is one 2-star hotel, the Beaux Monts (0476 803032). There is a store 'almost like a trading post' and a couple of bars and restaurants.

The local slopes have something for everyone – including a nursery slope at village level – and there is a branch of the Ecole du Ski Français.

But a recent reporter warns 'the place is dull at night' and 'beginners will be stuck here because the runs that link to the rest of the wonderful skiing are very undergraded'. Two near-beginners in his party were 'very put off'.

Oz-en-Oisans

1350m/4,430ft

The purpose-built ski station above the old village of the same name is now a 'thriving small resort', says a reporter who has an apartment there. It has been built in an attractive style, with much use of wood and stone, and has a ski school, sports shops, nursery slopes, bars, restaurants, supermarket, skating rink and large underground car park. But another reporter complains that there is still no nightlife. There is a hotel, the Hors Piste (0476 794240). Two gondolas whisk you out of the resort – one goes to Alpette above Vaujany and the other goes in two stages to the mid-station of the DMC above Alpe-d'Huez. The main run home is liberally endowed with snow-guns, but it needs to be. One clear advantage of staying here is that the slopes above Oz are about the best in the area when heavy snow is falling – and those based elsewhere may not be able to reach them.

SMART APARTMENTS – SEE FEATURE

The Chalet des Neiges apartments are in chalet-style buildings with pool, sauna and restaurant.

Auris 1600m/5,250ft

Auris is a series of wood-clad, chalet-style apartment blocks with a few shops, bars and restaurants pleasantly set close to the thickest woodland in the area. It's a fine, compact family resort, with a ski school, nursery and a ski kindergarten. Beneath it is the original old village, complete with attractive, traditional buildings, a church and all but one of the resort's hotels. Staying here with a car you can drive up to the lift base or make excursions to other resorts.

Unsurprisingly, evenings are quiet, with a handful of bar-restaurants to

choose from. The Beau Site (0476 800639), which looks like an apartment block, is the only hotel in the upper village. A couple of miles down the hill, the traditional Auberge de la Forêt (0476 800601) gives you a feel of 'real' rural France.

Access to the slopes of Alpe-d'Huez is no problem (but returning to Auris may prove difficult for novices – the top section of Signal de L'Homme is a bit steep). There are plenty of local slopes to explore, for which there is a special lift pass. Most runs are intermediate, though Auris is also the best of the local hamlets for beginners.

Vaujany 1250m/4,100ft

Vaujany is a quiet, small (though growing) village perched on the hillside opposite its own sector of the domain. Hydroelectric riches have financed huge continuing investment. There's a giant 160-person cable-car that whisks you into the heart of the Alpe-d'Huez lift system and a two-stage gondola that takes you to the local slopes.

The village has two sections, built at different levels up the steep mountainside facing the ski area. The top section, high above, is a pleasant mix of the original rustic village and traditional-style additions. It's linked to the lower village by an impressive glass-domed escalator, and is the hub of the resort in the evenings. It has a pedestrianised main street with the village's only supermarket (small), several restaurants, a play area, the tourist office and some apartments.

The lower section, called Le Village, has been built in traditional style around the cable car and gondola stations. It's a large pedestrianised complex of spacious, mid-range apartments, with a good ski shop, pizzeria, bakery, bar, cafe and cavernous underground car-park. On the same level, at the entrance to the resort, is a small church, some very old rustic buildings, the Igloo Gourmand cafe-bar and a couple of hotels (one is the Ski Peak-run Rissiou, which has been recommended by a reporter). Ski Peak also runs comfortable, tastefully decorated catered chalets in Vaujany and La Villette (see below); a minibus service for guests is available. An elevator takes you down from here to the superb sports centre with a pool.

There's also a mini-funicular which brings skiers, who have skied down the long red run from the heart of the ski area down to beneath the village, back up to the cable car, gondola and village. Other than this run, there are no slopes back to the village. You can, however, ski back to the mid-station of the gondola on a blue run. Beginner children are taken to a gentle roped-off area here at the gondola mid-station and adult beginners to the nursery slope at the cable-car mid-station. There's a good self-service restaurant with sunny terrace right by the children's learning area. The ski school (adult's and children's) and nursery have all been praised by reporters. Near the mid-station of the gondola is the tiny, rustic hamlet of La Villette (with a tiny but excellent bar-restaurant).

Phone numbers
From abroad use the prefix +33 and omit the initial '0' of the phone number.

TOURIST OFFICES

Villard-Reculas
t 0476 804569
info@villard-reculas.com
www.villard-reculas.com

Oz-en-Oisans
t 0476 807801
info@oz-en-oisans.com
www.oz-en-oisans.com

Auris
t 0476 800910
info@auris.en.oisans.com
www.auris-en-oisans.com

Vaujany
t 0476 807237
info@vaujany.com
www.vaujany.com

Alpe-d'Huez

249

Les Arcs

Three typical purpose-built resorts plus a cute, upmarket alternative – with access to an exceptional variety and extent of slopes

COSTS

① ② ③ ④ ⑤ ⑥

RATINGS

The slopes
Fast lifts	**
Snow	****
Extent	***
Expert	*****
Intermediate	****
Beginner	****
Convenience	****
Queues	***
Mountain restaurants	***

The rest
Scenery	***
Resort charm	*
Off-slope	*

NEWS

2006/07 will bring a long-overdue major improvement to the main lifts above Arc 2000: a fast six-seat covered chair moving 3,000 people an hour will replace the queue-prone Plagnettes chair to Col de la Chal. That chair will start higher than at present, and so will take over the role of the Bosses drag-lift, which will be removed. Eighty new snow-guns are planned.

In Arc 1950 another apartment building will open, with the final one completed for 2007/08. Spa facilities, open to all, are also predicted. Development at the hotel Golf in Arc 1800 will also include a spa complex.

250

+ A wide variety of pistes and easily accessed off-piste terrain

+ Exceptional amounts of genuinely black piste skiing above Arc 2000

+ Cable-car link to La Plagne opens up a vast amount of terrain

+ Some excellent woodland runs

+ Mainly traffic-free villages with easy slope access from most lodgings

+ Option of staying in quiet, more traditional, lower villages

+ Very easy rail access from UK

+ Arc 1950 offers a rare blend of convenience and ambience, but ...

– Other village centres lack charm, and aren't always so convenient

– Few off-slope diversions

– Still a lot of slow old chair-lifts

– Very quiet in the evenings, and limited choice of bars/restaurants

– No green runs for novices to progress to – normally a feature of French resorts

– But lots of flat linking runs to annoy snowboarders

– Accommodation in high villages is nearly all in apartments

We've always liked Les Arcs' slopes: they offer impressive variety, including some of the longest descents in the Alps, and plenty of steep stuff. And the link with La Plagne puts these resorts in the same league as the Three Valleys. Keen mixed-ability groups should have Les Arcs on their shortlists.

The main villages have always put us off – fairly functional, but drab. But the new Arc 1950 mini-village is something else: a resort that's even more conveniently arranged than the others, and a lot more pleasant to inhabit.

THE RESORT

Les Arcs is made up of four modern resort units, linked by road, high above the railway terminus town of Bourg-St-Maurice. The four villages are all purpose-built and apartment-dominated, and offer doorstep access to the snow with no traffic hazards, but the original three lack Alpine charm, off-slope activities and much evening animation. There's a special feature panel on the fourth – the much more attractive Arc 1950 – a couple of pages on.

Reporters repeatedly comment on the friendliness of the locals.

Arc 1600 was the first Arc. For rail travellers it is the obvious choice, with a funicular railway up from Bourg-St-Maurice. 1600 is set in the trees and has a friendly, small-scale atmosphere; and it enjoys good views along the valley and towards Mont Blanc. The central area is particularly good for families: uncrowded, compact, and set on even ground. But it is very quiet in the evening. Above the village, chair-lifts fan out over the lower slopes, leading to links to the other Arcs.

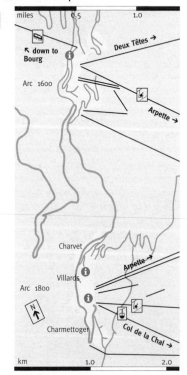

Arc 1600

Deux Têtes →

← down to Bourg

Arpette →

Charvet

Arpette →

Villards

Arc 1800

Charmettoger

Col de la Chal →

KEY FACTS

Resort	1600-2120m
	5,250-6,960ft
Slopes	1200-3225m
	3,940-10,580ft
Lifts	56
Pistes	200km
	124 miles
Green	1%
Blue	51%
Red	30%
Black	18%
Snowmaking	12km
	7 miles

Paradiski area	
Slopes	1200-3250m
	3,940-10,660ft
Lifts	141
Pistes	425km
	264 miles
Green	5%
Blue	56%
Red	27%
Black	12%

Much the largest of the villages is Arc 1800. It has three sections, though the boundaries are indistinct. Charvet and Villards are small shopping centres, mostly open-air but still managing to seem claustrophobic. Both are dominated by huge apartment blocks. More easy on the eye is Charmettoger, with smaller, wood-clad buildings nestling among trees. There are also apartments up the hillside in Le Chantel. The lifts depart from Villards – chair-lifts to mid-mountain, and the big Transarc gondola to Col de la Chal above Arc 2000.

Arc 2000 is just a few hotels, apartment blocks and the Club Med, huddled together in a bleak spot, with little to commend it but immediate access to the highest, toughest skiing. Although some more upmarket apartments have been built over the last few years, there is only a handful of restaurants and shops.

Just below Arc 2000 and linked to it by a short gondola, the new mini-village of Arc 1950 is now almost complete and already impressive – see feature panel later in this chapter.

There are lifts all around Arc 1950 and 2000, including the Varet gondola up towards the Aiguille Rouge.

At the southern end of the area, linked by pistes but reachable by road only by first descending to the main valley, is Peisey-Vallandry. The long-awaited cable-car link with La Plagne opened here for 2003/04. At the northern end of the ski area is the rustic hamlet of Le Pré. These outlying bases are described at the end of the chapter.

THE MOUNTAINS

Les Arcs' terrain is notably varied; it has plenty of runs for experts and intermediates and a good mixture of high, snow-sure slopes and low-level woodland runs ideal for bad weather.

The cable-car from Plan-Peisey gives access to La Plagne, covered by the Paradiski passes. Any doubts about the value of this link have now disappeared; even from Arc 1950 you can be at the cable-car in 20 minutes, ready for a long day at La Plagne.

Day trips by car to Val-d'Isère/ Tignes or the Three Valleys are possible – both covered for a day with the six-day Paradiski passes.

THE SLOPES
Well planned and varied
Arc 1600 and Arc 1800 share a west-facing mountainside laced with runs down to one or other village. At the southern end is an area of woodland runs down to Peisey-Vallandry.

From various points on the ridge above 1600 and 1800 you can head down into the wide Arc 2000 bowl. Across this bowl, lifts take you to the highest runs of the area, from the Aiguille Rouge and the Grand Col. As well as a variety of steep north-west-facing runs back to Arc 2000, the Aiguille Rouge is the start of a lovely long run (over 2000m/6,560ft vertical and 7km/4 miles long) right down to the hamlet of Le Pré near Villaroger. Arc 2000 has runs descending below village level, to the lift base and car park at Pré-St-Esprit, about 300m/985ft lower.

SNOWPIX.COM / CHRIS GILL

The Chalets de l'Arc restaurant is just far enough above Arc 2000 to count as a mountain restaurant, and is the only notable one on the slopes of Les Arcs. In the distance, the slopes of La Rosière, and then the Mont Blanc massif →

On the lower half of the Aiguille Rouge is a speed-skiing run, which is sometimes open to the public; the fee includes helmet, goggles and skis.

TERRAIN-PARKS
State of the art

Above Arc 1600 and below Arpette, and served by the Clair Blanc chair-lift, lies Apocalypse Parc – a facility so extensive that it deserves its own website, www.apocalypse-parc.com. For years, this has been one of the most advanced parks in the Alps – on a par with Avoriaz. Three kicker lines, green, red and black, account for all levels of jumping, coupled with a nice rail and box line, equally varied and fun for all. Along the far side of the park lies a 500m/1,640ft long boarder-cross course. Not surprisingly, the park is popular, and the lift gets huge queues at peak times. In addition to the main park there is a well-shaped

and big half-pipe located at Arc 2000 that is floodlit and stays open until late, plus a second boarder-cross course. There was also a small rails park above Peisey-Vallandry last season – not marked on the piste map, but recommended by a reader.

SNOW RELIABILITY
Good – plenty of high runs

A high percentage of the runs are above 2000m/6,56oft and when necessary you can stay high by using lifts that start around that altitude. Most of the slopes face roughly west, which is not ideal. Those from the Col de la Chal and the long runs down to Le Pré are north-facing, and the blacks on the Aiguille Rouge face near enough north to keep their snow well, even in spring. The limited snowmaking is being gradually extended. Reporters are still finding that grooming can be 'economical'.

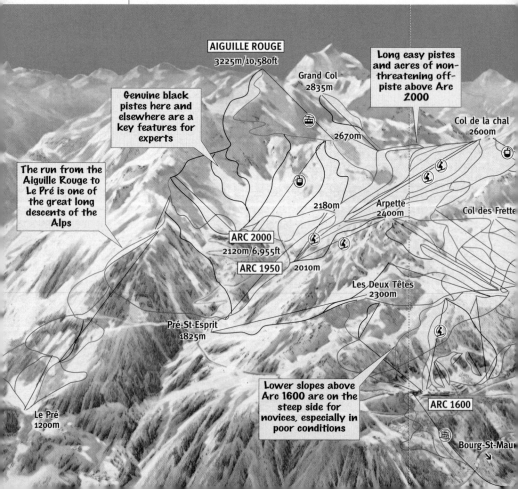

FOR EXPERTS
Challenges on- and off-piste

Les Arcs has a lot to offer experts – at least when the high lifts are open (the Aiguille Rouge cable-car, in particular, is often shut in bad weather).

There are a number of truly black pistes above Arc 2000, and a couple in other areas. After a narrow shelf near the top (which can be awkward), the Aiguille Rouge-Le Pré run is superb, with remarkably varying terrain throughout its vertical drop of over 2000m/6,560ft. There is also a great deal of off-piste potential. There are steep pitches on the front face of the Aiguille Rouge and secluded runs on the back side, towards Villaroger. A short climb to the Grand Col from the chair-lift of the same name gives access to several routes, including a quite serious couloir and an easier option. From Col de la Chal there is an easy route down to Pont Bodin near Nancroix. The wooded slopes above 1600 are another attractive possibility and there are open slopes beside the pistes all over the place.

FOR INTERMEDIATES
Plenty for all abilities

One strength of the area is that most main routes have easy and more difficult alternatives, making it good for mixed-ability groups. There are plenty of challenges, yet less confident intermediates are able to move around without getting too many nasty surprises. An exception is the solitary Comborcière black from Les Deux Têtes down to Pré-St-Esprit. This long mogul-field justifies its rating and can be great fun for strong intermediates. The Malgovert red, from the same point towards Arc 1600, can be equally tricky – it is narrow and often mogulled.

The woodland runs at either end of the domain, above Peisey-Vallandry

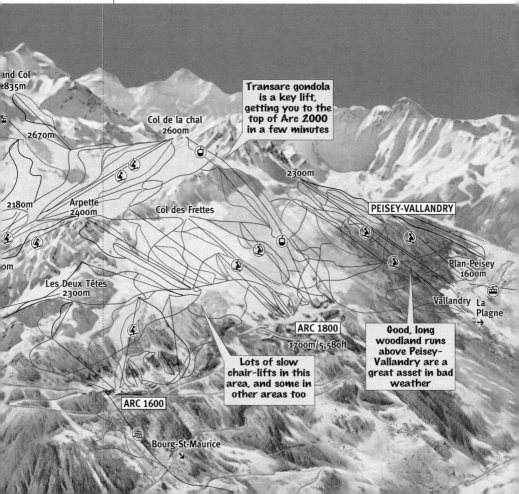

and Col
2835m

2670m

Col de la chal
2600m

Transarc gondola is a key lift, getting you to the top of Arc 2000 in a few minutes

2300m

2180m

Arpette
2400m

Col des Frettes

PEISEY-VALLANDRY

Plan-Peisey
1600m

om

Les Deux Têtes
2300m

Vallandry La Plagne
→

ARC 1800
1700m/5,580ft

Good, long woodland runs above Peisey-Vallandry are a great asset in bad weather

Lots of slow chair-lifts in this area, and some in other areas too

ARC 1600

Bourg-St-Maurice
↘

ski freshtracks.co.uk
holiday adventures
for all standards
+44 (0)20 8410 2022
abta 2811 atol 5064
SKI CLUB FRESHTRACKS

boarding

Les Arcs has always been a hotspot for snowboarders. Regis Rolland, founder of A-Snowboards (recently renamed APO), has for years been exploiting the potential of some of the most varied board-friendly terrain in Europe and has played a huge part in popularising the sport here. Les Arcs is home to incredible backcountry, mainly located in the back bowls of Arcs 2000. Gullies, trees, natural jibs and hits, steep terrain – this place has it all. The good mix of terrain also means that there are plenty of wide-open rolling slopes for beginners, especially in Vallandry or just above Arc 1800. Be careful of the long traverses on near-flat-cat-tracks and some of the blues at Arc 2000. Most of the area is serviced by fast chair-lifts and gondolas, which is an added bonus. For freestyle junkies, there is a great terrain-park; but don't stay in Peisey-Vallandry if you plan to use it – the trip to get there 'takes hours'.

LIFT PASSES

Grand Domaine Les Arcs

Prices in €

Age	1-day	6-day
under 14	29	140
14 to 59	39	186
over 60	33	158

Free under 6, over 72
Beginner six free lifts

Notes
Covers Les Arcs lifts. Half-day pass and one-day Paradiski extension available.

Paradiski Découverte

Prices in €

Age	6-day
under 14	154
14 to 59	205
over 60	174

Free under 6, over 72
Beginner no deals

Notes
Covers lifts in all La Plagne areas and one-day Paradiski extension. Also covers a day in each of the Three Valleys, Val-d'Isère-Tignes, Les Saisies, Pralognan.

Paradiski

Prices in €

Age	1-day	6-day
under 14	34	172
14 to 59	46	229
over 60	39	195

Free under 6, over 72
Beginner no deals

Notes
Covers all lifts in Les Arcs area and La Plagne area. Six-day pass covers a day in each of the Three Valleys, Val-d'Isère-Tignes, Les Saisies, Pralognan. Family reductions.

and Le Pré, and the bumpy Cachette red down to 1600, are also good for better intermediates. We especially like the Peisey-Vallandry area: its well groomed, tree-lined runs have a very friendly feel and are remarkably uncrowded much of the time, allowing great fast cruising. Good intermediates can enjoy the Aiguille Rouge-Le Pré run (which now has only red and blue variants on the lower half – no black).

The lower half of the mountainside above 1600/1800 is good for mixed-ability groups, with a choice of routes through the trees. The red runs down from Arpette and Col des Frettes towards 1800 are quite steep but usually well groomed.

Cautious intermediates have plenty of blue cruising terrain. Many of the runs around 2000 are rather bland and prone to overcrowding. Edelweiss is a newish blue down to Arc 1950 from Col des Frettes. The blues above 1800 are attractive but also crowded. A favourite blue of ours is Renard, high above Vallandry, usually with excellent snow.

And, of course, you have the whole of La Plagne's slopes to explore if you get bored locally.

FOR BEGINNERS
1800 or Peisey-Vallandry best

There are 'ski tranquille' nursery-slope zones above each of the three main Arcs, and at mid-mountain above Peisey-Vallandry; though we and readers haven't found them always tranquil. The slopes at Arc 1600 are rather steep, while those at 2000 are crowded with through-traffic at times. The sunny, spacious slopes at 1800 and Peisey-Vallandry are better – but, perversely, 1800's free lifts are very limited and P-V has none, so you need a lift pass. In all sectors there are long, easy blue runs to move on to.

FOR CROSS-COUNTRY
Very boring locally

Short trails, mostly on roads, is all you can expect, but the pretty Nancroix valley's 40km/25 miles of pleasant trails are easily accessible by free bus.

QUEUES
Slow chairs more of a problem

Reporters have few complaints about queues, except in one or two places, though during half-term one visitor found the worst queues she had ever experienced and 'manic' pistes above 1800. A boarder complains of 'huge' peak-season queues at the Apocalypse terrain-park lift. In sunny weather, Arc 2000 attracts the crowds. The gondola to the shoulder of the Aiguille Rouge forms non-trivial queues but the main problem has been the chair to Col de la Chal; happily, a more powerful chair is going in for next season – see News. There are often 'shocking queues' for the Aiguille Rouge cable-car – 45 minutes, complained one high-season reporter.

A bigger issue than queues is the time taken riding slow old chair-lifts, some of them very long – Comborcière, Mont Blanc and Plan Bois come in for particular criticism. At peak periods crowded pistes can be a problem, too. The cable-car link to La Plagne seems to cope with demand.

MOUNTAIN RESTAURANTS
Not much choice high-up

The proper mountain restaurants are mainly unremarkable. An exception is the Chalets de l'Arc, just above Arc 2000 – built in traditional wood and stone, and providing 'very good service and food' (including notably good home-baked bread). Below Arc 2000, the 500-year-old Belliou la Fumée at Pré-St-Esprit is set beside a car park;

OUR WEBSITE

Go to our website at wtss.co.uk for resort news, links to resort sites, a build-your-own resort shortlist system and reader forums.

SCHOOLS

ESF Arc 1600
t 0479 074309

ESF Arc 1800
t 0479 074031

ESF Arc 2000
t 0479 074752

Arc Aventures (ESI)
t 0479 074128

Darentasia
t 0479 041681

New Generation
t 0479 010318
www.skinewgen.com

Initial-Snow
t 0612 457291

Club des Sports
t 0479 078205

Spirit 1950
t 0479 042572

Classes (ESF prices)
6 days (2½hr am or pm) €134

Private lessons
€37 for 1hr, for 1 or 2 people

SNOWPIX.COM / CHRIS GILL

The wooded slopes above Peisey-Vallandry, seen here from the far side of the cable-car link with La Plagne, are a great asset in bad weather, provided you can get to them →

---

but it is charmingly rustic, and judged the best in the resort by two 2006 reporters. At even lower altitude, the Ferme ('simple but excellent value') and Aiguille Rouge ('nice omelettes') down at Le Pré are both friendly, with good food.

A 2006 reporter recommends the 'great selection of food' at Arpette, above 1800. The restaurant at Col de la Chal has fabulous views but is otherwise ordinary. The little Blanche Murée, slightly out of the way below the Transarc mid-station, is good for a simple table-service lunch in the sun. Above Vallandry, the Poudreuse has a 'fair choice of meals', although 'drinks at the bar are expensive – beware'. The Solliet above Le Pré has good views across the valley to La Rosière.

There are lots of options in the main villages, of course, some accessible on skis. Readers' recommendations include the Aiguille Grive on the fringes of 1800, the Chalet de l'Arcelle and Chez Fernand at 1600 1950 and Chalet de Luigi at 1950.

SCHOOL AND GUIDES
Several, including a Brit school

The ESF here is renowned for being the first in Europe to teach ski évolutif, where you start by learning parallel turns on short skis, gradually moving on to longer skis. Progress can be spectacular. Past reports on the ESF have been mainly critical, and this year are mixed; grumbles include a tendency to guide instead of teach, and a children's class numbering 22. The International school (aka Arc Aventures) has impressed reporters. New Generation, well established in Courchevel and Méribel, started up in Vallandry three seasons ago; a 2006 reader had 'the most instructive lesson ever' with them. Another Vallandry reporter recommends Snow-Escape's private lessons. The Spirit school in 1950 has received good reports this year for both adult and children's classes, with 'small classes, very good instructors with good English'. Another 2006 visitor recommends the off-piste discovery days.

Les Arcs

255

CHILDREN

Arc 1600:
Garderie La Cachette
t 0479 077050
8.30 to 6pm; ages
4mnth to 11yr

**Arc 1800: Les
Pommes de Pins**
t 0479 042431
8.30 to 12 noon; 1.30
to 5pm; ages 3 to 6

Arc 2000:
t 0479 076425
8.30 to 12 noon; 1.30
to 5pm; ages 3 to 6

Club Med
(at Arc 2000) has full
childcare facilities –
this is one of their
'family villages'.

Ski school
The ESF branches in
all three stations take
children from 3:
6 days (2hr am or
pm) €134

Excellent chalets
Childcare service
On-line booking
On-line chalet videos

01243 780 405
or go to
www.skibeat.co.uk

FACILITIES FOR CHILDREN
Good reports

Spirit 1950 reportedly provides good
care and facilities for smaller children,
returning them well-fed and rested. We
have received good reports in the past
on the Pommes de Pin facilities in Arc
1800. Comments on children's ski
classes have been favourable, too:
'Classes were crowded but teaching/
childcare was good.' There is a
children's area at 1800, complete with
moving carpet lifts, a sledging track
and a climbing wall. There are also a
couple of discovery pistes, at 1800 and
1600, for children to find out about
flora and fauna of the Alps.

STAYING THERE

HOW TO GO
New chalets and apartments

Most resort beds are in apartments.
There is a long-established Club Med
presence in Arc 2000 and a new,
smarter 'village' opened last season at
Peisey-Vallandry.

Chalets There are now several catered
chalets in the Peisey-Vallandry area
(see the end of the chapter), and Le
Pré has a couple, but there are hardly
any in the high Les Arcs 'villages'.

Hotels The choice of hotels in Les Arcs
is gradually widening.

(((⁴ **Mercure**(1800) (0479 076500)
Locally judged to be worth four stars
rather than its actual three.

((⁽³⁾ **Golf** (1800) (0479 414343) An
expensive but good 3-star, with 'great
ambience around its Jazz Bar', a sauna,
gym, kindergarten, covered parking.
Spa facilities are planned for 2006/07.

(((³ **Cachette** (1600) (0479 077050)
Renovated in the mid-1990s. 'Very
nice' but it can be 'dominated by kids',
say reporters – not surprising as 1600's
childcare facilities are here.

(⁽²⁾ **Aiguille Rouge** (2000) (0479
075707) Daily free ski guiding.

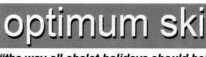

GETTING THERE

Air Geneva 156km/97 miles (3½hr); Lyon 200km/124 miles (3½hr); Chambéry 127km/79 miles (2½hr).

Rail Bourg-St-Maurice; frequent buses and direct funicular to resort.

Phone numbers
From abroad use the prefix +33 and omit the initial '0' of the phone number.

SMART APARTMENTS – SEE FEATURE

The various apartment developments at Arc 1950 (see panel below) vary in style and space, but the general level of comfort is exceptionally high by French standards. In Arc 2000 the Chalet des Neiges and Chalet Altitude offer 'luxury' apartments, with pool etc. The Alpages de Chantel above Arc 1800 is typical of MGM apartments – attractive and comfortable, with pools, saunas and gyms. It is very convenient for skiing, but a bit isolated.

The Ruitor apartments, set among trees between Charmettoger and Villards (in Arc 1800), are reported to be 'excellent in all respects'. L'Aiguille Grive apartments are reportedly spacious and convenient.

EATING OUT
Good choice in Arc 1800

In Arc 1600 and 2000 there are very few restaurants. In 2000 Chez Eux gets the thumbs-up for 'excellent' Savoyard meals: 'All eight of us were complimentary – a rare event!' 1800 has a choice of about 15 restaurants; an ad-based (so not comprehensive) guide is given away locally. The Petit Zinc restaurant in the Golf hotel has haute cuisine and high prices; it has a Friday evening seafood buffet. Chalet Bouvier has been highly recommended by a reporter who knows his food. The Chalet de Milou has gourmet cuisine, 'including excellent fish'. The Gargantus is a decent, informal place. Readers have been satisfied by 'enormous portions' at Equipage and 'good food and great service' at the Triangle. Casa Mia is an excellent all-rounder with exceptionally friendly service ('Good food but expensive wine,' says one recent visitor). The Mountain Café does much more than the Tex-Mex it advertises, and copes well with big family parties. Chez les Filles is worth a visit for 'exceptional views' and 'good food'. A drive half-way down the mountain, the woody, welcoming Bois de Lune at Montvenix has perhaps the best food in the area. At 1950, Hemingway's Café does an 'excellent value three-course dinner'. Chalet de Luigi specialises in Italian ham, Chez Anne in Savoyard specialities. East does Indian etc.

APRES-SKI
Arc 1800 is the place to be

1800 is the liveliest centre. The JO bar is open until the early hours and has a friendly atmosphere with live music. The friendly Red Hot Saloon has bar games and 'surprisingly good' live music. A reporter enjoyed the cocktails, atmosphere and live music at the Jungle Café. The Fairway disco keeps rocking until 4am and the Apokalypse 'isn't terrible'. Reporters also like the Jazz Bar in the Hotel Golf – 'good ambience, great Mexican Bloody Mary'. And the Gabotte in Place Miravaldi is favoured for its 'cosy upstairs bar'. The Arpette mountain restaurant is also recommended this year – especially the 'fun, up-beat torchlit descent'.

ARC 1950: WHERE NORTH AMERICA MEETS EUROPE

The first phase of the brand-new resort of Arc 1950, a little way down the hill from Arc 2000, opened in December 2003; by December 2005 it was almost complete – a fully functioning mini-resort with powerful attractions. It is high and relatively snow-sure; absolutely traffic-free (cars have to be parked in the multi-storey pay-garage that runs under the whole place); very conveniently laid out, offering ski in/ski out lodgings; comfortable, with apartments of a standard much higher than the French norm; and it is built in a traditional, easy-on-the-eye style. The credit goes to Canadian company Intrawest, developer of Whistler and other stylish resort villages in North America. This is its first venture into Europe. Others will follow (see Flaine chapter).

All the accommodation at present is in apartments, furnished to a high standard. The living rooms we have seen are spacious, at least by French standards, but some incorporate tiny kitchens – and the bedrooms are mostly compact. The outdoor hot-tubs and pools, saunas and steam rooms are added attractions – as are the 'animations' planned every evening, such as fireworks and live music.

Last season we were impressed by how established the place feels already – and by how much more pleasant it is than most other purpose-built resorts in France. You can eat out in a different place each night, there is a reasonable choice of après-ski bars, and the key facilities are in place – a tiny but well stocked supermarket, a bakery, a gift shop, a crêperie, ski and board equipment shops. There is a free gondola up to Arc 2000, perched higher up the steep hillside, but we didn't feel the need to use it.

A further apartment-hotel building will open for 2006/07 and the final development for 2007/08.

ACTIVITIES

Indoor Squash (1800), saunas, solaria, multi-gym (1800), cinemas, games rooms, concert halls, bowling (1800)

Outdoor Natural skating rinks (1800/2000), tobogganing, organised snow-shoe outings, dog-sledding, 10km/6 miles cleared paths, hang-gliding, horse-riding, sleigh rides, ice grotto, 'snowtubbing' (2000)

UK Representative
Erna Low Consultants
9 Reece Mews
London SW7 3HE
t 0870 750 6820
info@ernalow.co.uk
www.ernalow.co.uk

SNOWPIX.COM / CHRIS GILL

Arc 1950 is a lot more attractive than your average purpose-built French resort, and is as conveniently laid out as the best of them ↓

In 1600 the Bar des Montagnes opposite (and belonging to) the hotel Cachette has games machines, pool and live bands, and can be quite lively even in low season, and a reporter has recommended the Beguin. Another recommends the Aubreuvoir for 'good live bands most nights'.

In 2000 the Red Rock is 'good for youngsters but too crowded for grown-ups'; a reporter's verdict is that the Tavern (also at 2000) is 'best all round'. The Whistler's Dream, in the Chalet des Neiges, could be worth a try. There is bowling at 1800 and skating at 1800 and 2000. At 1950, Chalet de Luigi at 1950 has a bar and a

nightclub, Hemingway's a bar, and the Belles Pintes is an Irish-style pub.

The cinemas at 2000, 1800 and 1600 have English films weekly.

OFF THE SLOPES
Very poor
Les Arcs is not the place for an off-the-slopes holiday. There is very little to do, though several of the newer apartment blocks have pools. You can visit the Beaufort dairy and go shopping in Bourg-St-Maurice and there are a few walks – nice ones up the Nancroix valley. There's also an ice grotto at the top of the Transarc, which pedestrians can reach.

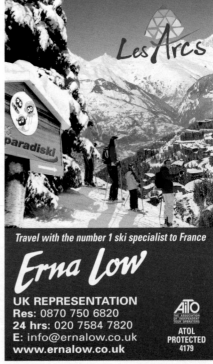

Peisey-Vallandry
1600m/5,250ft

Plan-Peisey and Vallandry are recently developed lift-base resorts above the old village of Peisey, which has a bucket-lift up to Plan-Peisey. They market themselves as Peisey-Vallandry, and the cluster of villages hereabouts is known collectively as Peisey-Nancroix. Clear as mud, eh?

Both Vallandry and Plan-Peisey are still small and quiet, but are fast developing. Quite a few UK tour operators now offer chalets here. And there is a swanky Club Med.

The cable-car to La Plagne leaves from Plan-Peisey, which has one hotel, a few shops, bars and restaurants but no real focus other than the lift station. A fast six-seat chair takes you into the slopes. The hotel Vanoise (0479 079219) has been recommended by readers for its position, food and staff ('very welcoming, very French') with few British guests. Reporters recommend the Cordée ('excellent, frequented by locals'), Armoise ('superb food, exceptional value menus') and Solan ('brasserie, cosy inside, large terrace'). The Flying Squirrel is British-run, has a popular happy hour, live music, 'gourmet-burgers', weekly quiz night and live sport on TV.

Vallandry is a few hundred metres away and linked by shuttle-bus. A fast quad takes you into the slopes. More development has gone on here recently, with lots of new chalets and a small pedestrian-only square at the foot of the slopes with a small supermarket and a ski shop.

SMART APARTMENTS – SEE FEATURE
Among the modern developments are some notable self-catering properties. L'Orée des Cimes is a comfortable CGH development with a stylish pool and great views.

There are several 'great, locally owned' restaurants. Recommendations from reporters include the Calèche for excellent duck, the Dahu, the Bergerie de Raphael, the Refuge and L'Ourson. There is a crêperie by the Vanoise Express ('good for galettes'). Jimmy's bar is popular, especially with the Dutch, but 'noisy'. Mont Blanc Bar is a Brit hang-out and Marlu more French. The Forêt is a Beatles-themed bar-restaurant, next to a slope-side Ski Olympic chalet-hotel.

2006 readers enjoyed staying in the characterful old village of Peisey which dates back 1,000 years and has a fine baroque church. The other, mostly old, buildings include a few shops and a couple of bars and restaurants – a reader enjoyed 'wonderful fondue' at the Ormelune. There are several catered chalets down here run by UK tour operators.

Nancroix is a roadside hamlet notable mainly for the excellent Ancolie restaurant.

Le Pré 1200m/3,940ft

Le Pré is a charming, quiet, rustic little hamlet with three successive chair-lifts (the first two quite slow) going up to a point above Arc 2000. It has a couple of small bar-restaurants and a couple of British-run chalets, including a rustic one that owners Martin and Deirdre Rowe renovated and run themselves under the Optimum brand. We can personally vouch for their good food, free-flowing wine, jolly bar and basic but adequate bedrooms. But Le Pré is not at all suitable for beginners.

Les Granges 1200m/3,940ft

A reader writes to recommend this hamlet at the mid-station of the funicular up from Bourg, reached from 1600 by two red runs and a winding blue following a minor road. There is a good (but low and sunny) free nursery slope. Splendid isolation – no bars, no restaurants, trains stop at 7.30pm, and taxis from Arc 1600 or Bourg are not cheap unless shared.

Bourg-St-Maurice
850m/2,790ft

Bourg-St-Maurice is a real French town, with cheaper hotels and restaurants and easy access to other resorts for day trips. The funicular starts next to the TGV station and goes straight to Arc 1600 in seven minutes – but beware, the last one down is at 7.30pm. Hostellerie du Petit-St-Bernard (0479 070432) has been reported to be a reasonable 2-star hotel – 'looks run-down, but friendly with super food'. Another reporter enjoyed the cheap and cheerful Savoyard (0479 070403), despite the noise: 'Take earplugs to sell to other guests.' A 2006 reporter recommends a traditional Savoyard restaurant, the Tsablo: 'excellent' and 'good value'.

Les Arcs

259

Avoriaz 1800

The 'ski to and from the door' purpose-built resort option on the French side of the big Portes du Soleil circuit

COSTS

① ② ③ ④ ⑤ ⑥

RATINGS

The slopes
Fast lifts	✱✱✱
Snow	✱✱✱
Extent	✱✱✱✱✱
Expert	✱✱✱
Intermediate	✱✱✱✱
Beginner	✱✱✱✱
Convenience	✱✱✱✱✱
Queues	✱✱✱
Mountain restaurants	✱✱✱✱

The rest
Scenery	✱✱✱
Resort charm	✱✱
Off-slope	✱

NEWS

Great news for 2006/07: the old Chaux Fleurie chair (a key link from Avoriaz to Châtel and a long-standing bottleneck) is due to be replaced by a six-pack.

A new terrain-park, the Biotop, was built for 2005/06, with wooden rails to be 'totally integrated to the environment of the forest'.

KEY FACTS

Resort	1800m
	5,900ft

Portes du Soleil	
Slopes	950-2300m
	3,120-7,550ft
Lifts	209
Pistes	650km
	404 miles
Green	14%
Blue	39%
Red	37%
Black	10%
Snowmaking	
	577 guns

Avoriaz only	
Slopes	1100-2275m
	3,610-7,460ft
Lifts	38
Pistes	150km
	93 miles

➕ Good position on the main Portes du Soleil circuit, giving access to very extensive, quite varied runs

➕ Generally has the best snow in the Portes du Soleil

➕ Accommodation right on the slopes

➕ Good children's facilities

➕ Snowy paths entirely free of cars are an attractive formula, but ...

➖ Non-traditional architecture, which some find ugly

➖ Much of Portes du Soleil is low for a major French area, with the risk of poor snow or bare slopes low down

➖ Can get very crowded at weekends

➖ Little to do off the slopes

➖ Few hotels or chalets – mostly no-frills, cramped apartments

If Avoriaz sounds like the kind of thing you like, you'll probably like it. Unlike many purpose-built resorts it is truly car-free, with cars kept completely separate from its reliably snow-covered paths and pistes. The snow is thanks to the altitude, which the resort has made a half-hearted attempt to emphasise by re-branding itself Avoriaz 1800. As for us – we're more at home lower down, in the cosy chalets of Châtel 1200 or Morzine 1000 (see separate chapters).

THE RESORT

Avoriaz 1800 is a purpose-built, traffic-free resort perched above a dramatic, sheer rock face. From the edge of town horse-drawn sleighs or snowcats transport people and luggage from car parks to the accommodation – or you can borrow a sledge for a small deposit and transport your own. The problem of horse mess has been cut since horses now wear 'nappies' and staff on snowmobiles scoop up what escapes! Cars are left in paid-for outdoor or underground parking – choose the latter to avoid a chaotic departure if it snows. You can book space.

As our scale plan suggests, it's a compact place, with everything close to hand (turn forward to Chamonix, for a striking comparison). But the village is set on quite a slope; elevators inside the buildings (and chair-lifts outside, during the day) mean moving around is no problem except when paths are icy, but if you plan to go out much in the evening, it's worth staying near the central focus. Wherever you stay, you should be able to ski from the door.

The village is all angular, dark, wood-clad, high-rise buildings, mostly apartments. But the snow-covered paths and pistes give the place quite a friendly Alpine feel.

The evenings are not especially lively, but reporters have enjoyed 'a good ambience, both day and night',

and a 'brilliant parade in half-term week, with a fire-eating display'. Family-friendly events are laid on all season. A floodlit cliff behind the resort adds to its nocturnal charm.

You can also stay in the lower hamlets of Ardent and Les Prodains.

Avoriaz is on the main lift circuit of the Portes du Soleil – for an overview, look at our separate chapter. It has links to Châtel in one direction and Champéry (Switzerland) in the other – both covered in separate chapters. It is above the valley resort of Morzine, to which it is linked by gondola (but not by piste). The slopes of Morzine and Les Gets, on the far side of Morzine, are part of the Portes du Soleil but not on the core circuit; both are covered in their own chapters. Car trips to Flaine and Chamonix are possible.

LIFT PASSES

Portes du Soleil

Prices in €

Age	1-day	6-day
under 16	25	120
16 to 59	37	179
over 60	30	143

Free under 5

Beginner 1 day
€19.30 (Avoriaz only)

Notes
Covers all lifts in all resorts, plus shuttle-buses. Half-day pass also available.

Alternative passes
Avoriaz-only pass; snowboarder passes for limited areas.

REPORTS WANTED

Recently we have had few reports on this resort. If you go there, please do send us a report.

The best reports earn a copy of the next edition, and can lead to free lift passes in future.
See page 12.

THE MOUNTAINS

The slopes closest to Avoriaz are bleak and treeless, but snow-sure. The main Portes du Soleil circuit is easily done by intermediates of all abilities. Going clockwise avoids two snags in Morgins – the excessively sunny lower slopes of Bec de Corbeau and the uphill walk to the next lift. The booklet-style piste map gives a reasonably clear picture of each resort along the way. The circuit breaks down at Châtel, where you need the frequent shuttle-bus.

THE SLOPES
360° choice

The village has lifts and pistes fanning out in all directions.

Facing the village are the slopes of **Arare-Hauts Forts** and, when snow conditions allow, there are long, steep runs down to Les Prodains.

The lifts off to the left go to the **Chavanette** sector on the Swiss border – a broad, undulating bowl. Beyond the border is the infamous Swiss Wall – a long, impressive mogul slope with a tricky start, but not the terror it is cracked up to be unless it's icy (it gets a lot of sun). It's no disgrace to ride the chair down – lots of people do. At the bottom of the Wall is the open terrain of Planachaux, above Champéry, with links to the even bigger open area around Les Crosets and Champoussin.

Taking a lift up through the village of Avoriaz to the ridge behind it is the way to the prettily wooded **Lindarets-Brocheaux** valley, from where lifts and runs in the excellent Linga sector lead to Châtel. A couple of reports suggest piste marking could be improved.

TERRAIN-PARKS
Still leading the way

There are now three parks near Avoriaz. The main park is Arare, next to the Bleue du Lac piste; it has its own drag-lift and is a pro-park and often used for high profile contests. Four big kickers with red and black take-offs, big rails and a wall ride are the order of the day. Beginners and intermediates should head to the La Chapelle park, accessible via the Tour or Prolays chair-lifts. This is littered with jumps of all sizes and a good rail line. Many of the pros still come here as it is such good fun. The third park is the Biotop – strictly a rail park situated in the trees and part of La Chapelle. Nicely constructed wooden rails line this new addition – great for progressing on. Just above the town centre next to the Prodains lift is a good super-pipe. Avoriaz does a brilliant job of keeping the parks maintained, and as a result a lot of riders make this their winter home.

SNOW RELIABILITY
High resort, low slopes

Although Avoriaz itself is high, its slopes don't go much higher – and some parts of the Portes du Soleil circuit are much lower. Considering their altitude, the north-facing slopes below Hauts Forts hold snow well. In general, the snow in Avoriaz is usually much better than over the border on the south-facing Swiss slopes. But when snow was sparse on our January 2005 visit we found the smooth, grassy, lower slopes of Les Gets much better than the rocky ones around Avoriaz, which need more snow cover.

Reporters generally say that grooming is good.

FOR EXPERTS
Several challenging runs

Tough terrain is scattered about. The challenging runs down from Hauts Forts to Prodains (including a World Cup downhill) are excellent. There is a tough red and several long, truly black

Champéry-Les Crosets ↓   ↓ Champéry

Pointe de Mossettes
2275m

CHAVANETTE 2215m

ARARE-
HAUTS FORTS

âtel

l du
achaux
20m

Avoriaz 1800

DARETS-BROCHEAUX

Les Lindarets
1495m

Ardent
1200m

Les Prodains
1145m

Morzine
1000m/3,28oft

SCHOOLS

ESF
t 0450 740565

International (L'Ecole de Glisse)
t 0450 740218

Alpine (AASS)
t 0450 747691

Classes
(ESF prices)
6 days (2½hr am and pm) €148

Private lessons
€33 for 1hr, for 1 or 2 people

CHILDREN

Les P'tits Loups
t 0450 740038
9am to 6pm; ages 3mnth to 5yr; 6 days €185

Annie Famose Children's Village
t 0450 740446
9am to 5.30 (skiing 9.30 to 12 noon and 1.30 to 4pm); ages 3 to 16; 6 days with meal €220

Club Med
This is a 'family village', with comprehensive childcare facilities

Ski schools
Take children from 4 to 12 (6 days €133)

runs, one of which cuts through trees – useful in poor weather. Two chair-lifts serve the lower runs, which snow-guns help to keep open. The Swiss Wall at Chavanette will naturally be on your agenda, and Châtel is well worth a trip. The black runs off the Swiss side of Mossettes and Pointe de l'Au are worth trying, and one reporter had a 'very good day' here exploring off-piste with a guide. Four 'snow-cross' runs – ungroomed but avalanche controlled and patrolled – have been introduced in the Hauts Forts, Lindarets, Chavanette and Mossettes areas. They are marked on the piste map, closed when dangerous and an excellent idea.

FOR INTERMEDIATES
Virtually the whole area
Although some sections lack variety, the Portes du Soleil is excellent for all grades of intermediates when snow is in good supply. Timid types not worried about pretty surroundings need not leave the Avoriaz sector; reporters recommend the 'wonderfully quiet' and 'scenic' blues to Prodains. Arare and Chavanette are gentle, spacious and above the tree-line bowls. The Lindarets area is also easy, with pretty runs through the trees, but several reporters complain about long flat sections where poling is required. Champoussin has a lot of easy runs, reached without too much difficulty via

Les Crosets and Pointe de l'Au. Better intermediates have virtually the whole area at their disposal. The runs down to Pré-la-Joux and L'Essert on the way to Châtel, and those either side of Morgins, are particularly attractive – as are the long runs down to Grand-Paradis near Champéry when snow conditions allow. Brave intermediates may want to take on the Wall, but Pointe de Mossettes offers an easier route to Switzerland.

FOR BEGINNERS
Convenient and good for snow
The nursery slopes seem small in relation to the size of the resort, but are adequate because so many visitors are intermediates. The slopes are sunny, yet good for snow, and link well to longer, easy runs. The main problem can be the crowded pistes. One recent reporter complains crowds and collisions on the Plateau area made progress 'painfully slow' for novices taking classes there.

FOR CROSS-COUNTRY
Varied, with some blacks
There are 45km/28 miles of trails, a third classified as black, mainly between Avoriaz and Super-Morzine, with other fine trails down to Lindarets and around Montriond. The only drawback is that several trails are not loops, but 'out and back' routes.

QUEUES
Main problems now gone
Most of the bad queues have been eliminated by new high-speed lifts. When the old chair from Lindarets towards Châtel is replaced for 2006/07 (see News), the main long-standing problem will be queues for the cable-car at Prodains. Recent visitors report few other problems. At weekends crowds on the pistes (especially around the village) can be bad, with care needed to avoid collisions.

boarding

Avoriaz was one of the pioneers of snowboarding in France, and the first terrain-park to be built in the country was here in 1993. They now have three parks and a half-pipe, as well as special non-groomed snow-cross areas full of natural obstacles (see 'For experts'). Check www.snowparkavoriaz.com for details. Terrain-park lift passes are available at 30 euros for two days. It is well worth hiring a guide here to exploit the vast quantity of good off-piste riding too. There are also plenty of wide, easy slopes and now very few drag-lifts left, making this a great resort for beginners and intermediates as well. Chalet Snowboard, the first chalet company to target snowboarders, has a couple of chalets at Les Prodains.

↑ Avoriaz was one of the pioneers of snowboarding in France and is a very popular snowboard destination

OT AVORIAZ / V. CANET-PORET

GETTING THERE

Air Geneva 80km/ 50 miles (2hr); Lyon 200km/124 miles (3½hr).

Rail Cluses (42km/ 26 miles) or Thonon (45km/28 miles); bus and cable-car to resort.

ACTIVITIES

Indoor Health centre 'Altiform' (sauna, gym, hot-tub), squash, ice rink, Turkish baths, cinema, bowling **Outdoor** Ice rink, snake slides, mountain biking on snow, dog-sledding, hot air ballooning, ice diving, walking paths, horse-drawn carriage tours, helicopter flights

Phone numbers
From abroad use the prefix +33 and omit the initial '0' of the phone number.

TOURIST OFFICE

t 0450 740211
info@avoriaz.com
www.avoriaz.com

MOUNTAIN RESTAURANTS
Good choice over the hill
The rustic chalets in the hamlet of Les Lindarets form one of the great concentrations of mountain restaurants in the Alps. The jolly Crémaillière has wonderful chanterelle mushrooms and great atmosphere, but on a good day it's difficult to beat the Terrasse. Near the top of the gondola from Morzine, the rustic Grenouille du Marais has good food, views and atmosphere. The 'friendly' table-service Abricotine does 'excellent galettes' and is 'good value'. The Refuge des Brocheaux at Les Brocheaux offers 'efficient service and a good menu'. Pas de Chavanette, at the top of the Swiss Wall, has been recommended. Check out the chapters on the other Portes du Soleil resorts too.

SCHOOLS AND GUIDES
Try AASS
The ESF has a good reputation; classes can be large, but we had reports in 2005 of 'great instruction' and very successful private snowboard lessons. The Avoriaz Alpine Ski School has British instructors and has been highly recommended, especially for 'quite excellent children's lessons'. A 2006 reporter tried both ESF and AASS for private lessons; he thought the AASS's higher price wasn't justified and criticised its 'haphazard admin system'. However, his son rated the advanced snowboard lessons as 'excellent'.

FACILITIES FOR CHILDREN
'Annie Famose delivers'
The Village des Enfants, run by ex-downhill champ Annie Famose, is a key part of the family appeal of Avoriaz. Its facilities are excellent – a chalet full of activities and special slopes complete with Disney characters. There's a snowboard village too.

STAYING THERE

HOW TO GO
Self-catering dominates
Alternatives to apartments are few.
Chalets There are several available – comfortable and attractive but mainly designed for small family groups.
Hotels There is one good hotel and a Club Med 'village'.
◖◖◖ **Dromonts** (0450 740811) The original core of the resort, taken over and renovated by a celebrity French chef and in the *Hip Hotels* guidebook.
Self-catering Past reporters have said that some apartments needed refurbishing, and others are typically 'basic and cramped'. But the Falaise apart-hotel, Douchka, Sepia and Datcha ('very basic') residences have all been recommended.

EATING OUT
Good; booking essential
There are more than 30 restaurants (though a reporter last year criticised the 'limited variety'). The hotel Dromonts has a gastronomic restaurant with an excellent set-price six-course meal and a simpler Table du Marché restaurant. The Bistro and Cabane have been recommended for 'good food and value', as have the Fontaines Blanches and Douchka for Savoyard food, Intrêts for 'pizza and pasta' and 'table-barbecues and Savoyard fare', Au Briska for a cosy night out and Falaise for 'good pizza'. You can buy in advance meal vouchers for dinner in a range of five restaurants, when you book Pierre & Vacances apartments. 'Restricted menu but excellent value,' says a reporter.

APRES-SKI
Lively, but not much choice
A few bars have a good atmosphere, particularly in happy hour. The Yeti is busy at 4pm. The Tavaillon attracts Brits and has Sky TV, and the Fantastique is worth a visit. For late-night dancing the Choucas and the Place have bands. Going down to Morzine is possible.

OFF THE SLOPES
Not much at the resort
Those not interested in the slopes are better off in Morzine – though Avoriaz does have the Altiform Fitness Centre, with saunas and hot-tubs. Pedestrians are not allowed to ride the chair-lifts, which is a shame.

Avoriaz 1800

263

Chamonix

Traditional old mountain town with great atmosphere and towering mountains above offering stunning views and off-piste for experts

COSTS

①②③④⑤⑥

RATINGS

The slopes

Fast lifts	★★★
Snow	★★★★
Extent	★★★
Expert	★★★★★
Intermediate	★★
Beginner	★
Convenience	★
Queues	★★
Mountain restaurants	★★

The rest

Scenery	★★★★★
Resort charm	★★★★
Off-slope	★★★★★

NEWS

For 2005/06 a fast six-pack replaced the old quad to L'Index at La Flégère. For 2006/07, the slow Col Cornu quad from Les Vioz at Le Brévent which serves three red runs is due to be replaced by a fast six-pack.

A new lift pass, the Mont Blanc Unlimited, will be introduced for 2006/07 and is a step up from the Cham'Ski pass. It will cover all the Chamonix areas including Les Houches and unlimited use of the top Grands Montets cable car plus a day in Courmayeur.

➕ A lot of very tough terrain, especially off-piste

➕ Amazing cable-car, for the famous Vallée Blanche (or just the views)

➕ Stunning views of peaks and glaciers

➕ Lots of different resorts and areas covered on Mont Blanc lift pass

➕ Town steeped in Alpine traditions, with lots to do off the slopes

➕ Easy access by road, rail and air – excellent weekend destination

➖ Several separate mountains: mixed ability groups are likely to have to split up, and the bus service gets mixed reviews

➖ Pistes in each area are quite limited

➖ The few runs to the valley are often closed – and tricky when open

➖ Bad weather can shut the best runs

➖ Still some old lifts and queues

➖ Few nice mountain restaurants

➖ Crowds and lots of road traffic

Chamonix could not be more different from the archetypal high-altitude, purpose-built French resort. Unless you are based next to one mountain and stick to it, you have to drive or take a bus each day. There are all sorts of terrain, but it offers more to interest the expert than anyone else, and to make the most of the area you need a mountain guide rather than a piste map. Chamonix is neither convenient nor conventional.

But it is special. The Chamonix valley cuts deeply through Europe's highest mountains and glaciers. The views are stunning and the runs are everything really tough runs should be – not only steep, but high and long. If you like your snow and scenery on the wild side, give Chamonix a try. But be warned: there are those who try it and never go home – including lots of Brits.

THE RESORT

Chamonix is a long-established tourist town that over the years has spread for miles along its valley in the shadow of Mont Blanc – the scale map below is one of the biggest in these pages.

On either side of the centre, just within walking distance, are lifts to two of the dozen slope areas in the valley – the famous cable-car to the Aiguille du Midi, and a gondola to Le Brévent. Also on the fringe of the centre is the nursery slope of Les Planards. All the other lift bases involve bus-rides – the nearest being the cable-car to La Flégère at the village of Les Praz.

Chamonix is a bustling town with scores of hotels and restaurants, visitors all year round and a lively Saturday market. The car-free centre of town is full of atmosphere, with cobbled streets and squares, beautiful old buildings, a fast-running river, pavement cafes crowded with shoppers and tourists sipping drinks and staring at the glaciers above. Not everything is rosy: unsightly modern buildings have been built on to the periphery (especially near the Aiguille du Midi cable-car station), some of the lovely old buildings have been allowed to fall into disrepair, and at times traffic clogs the streets around the car-free centre.

← to Les Houches

Les Pélerins

Les Bossons

↓ Mont Blanc tunnel

↓ Aiguille du Midi

Les Praz

to Argentière →

km   1.0   2.0   3.0   4.0   5.0

That's it folks: the famous Vallée Blanche, with Mont Blanc on the right

OT CHAMONIX-MONT BLANC / PASCAL TOURNAIRE

KEY FACTS

Resort	1035m
	3,400ft
Slopes	1035-3840m
	3,400-12,600ft
Lifts	47
Pistes	147km
	91 miles
Green	20%
Blue	34%
Red	33%
Black	13%
Snowmaking	96 guns

Chamonix's shops deal in everything from high-tech equipment to tacky souvenirs. But reporters often comment on the number and excellence of the former, and Chamonix remains essentially a town for mountain people rather than for poseurs. A 2006 reporter particular praises Snell Sports: 'One of the best shops in the Alps for serious skiers.'

Strung out for 20km/12 miles along the Chamonix valley are several separate lift systems, some with attached villages, from Les Houches at one end to Le Tour at the other. Regular buses link the lift stations and villages but can get very crowded and aren't always reliable – that to Les Houches is reportedly especially poor. There is an evening service, but it is said to finish too early. Like many reporters, we rate a car as essential. A car also means you can get easily to other resorts covered by the Mont Blanc pass, such as Megève and Les Contamines, and Courmayeur in Italy.

The obvious place to stay for the full Chamonix experience is in downtown Chamonix. If you plan to ski mainly Argentière, Le Tour or Les Houches, staying nearby clearly makes sense.

Once you get over the fact that the place is hopelessly disconnected, you come to appreciate the upside – that Chamonix has a good variety of slopes, and that each of the different areas is worth exploring. Practically all the slopes are above the tree line.

THE SLOPES
Very fragmented

The areas within the Chamonix valley – there are 11 in total – are either small, low, beginners' areas or are much higher up, above the wooded slopes that plunge to the valley floor, reached by cable-car or gondola.

The modern six-seat gondola for **Le Brévent** departs a short, steep walk from the centre of town, and the cable-car above takes you to the summit. The black run back to the valley was improved for 2004/05 – not before time. At **La Flégère**, like Le Brévent, the runs are mainly between 1900m and 2450m (6,230ft and 8,040ft), sunny and with stunning views of Mont Blanc. The two new fast chair-lifts (see News) and the cable-car linking La Flégère and Le Brévent now makes this side of the valley more user-friendly – though reporters have found the cable-car often closed by high winds.

A cable-car or chair-lift take you up to **Les Grands Montets** above Argentière. Much of the best terrain is still accessed by a further cable-car, of relatively low capacity. This costs extra – five euros a trip – with the Cham'Ski pass, but unlimited use is included with the new Mont Blanc Unlimited pass. But it still attracts big queues. The Herse chair takes you a lot of the way up but doesn't access some of the best off-piste or the lovely Point de Vue black. The area can be very cold in early season when it gets little sun.

Le Tour has an area of mainly easy pistes. It is also the starting point for good off-piste runs, some of which end up over the border in Switzerland.

Sheltered pistes descend to Vallorcine from where you can return using a relatively new gondola.

Les Houches is now covered as a separate Short Turns entry – see the end of the French section of the book.

There is a valley piste map and an informative little Cham'Ski handbook, which includes all the local area piste maps, with brief descriptions of each run and assessments of suitability for different abilities. But for navigation purposes the individual piste maps available at each area are best.

Most of our reporters have been more impressed than they expected with the piste grooming, but not with the signposting of the runs ('virtually non-existent', 'horrendous').

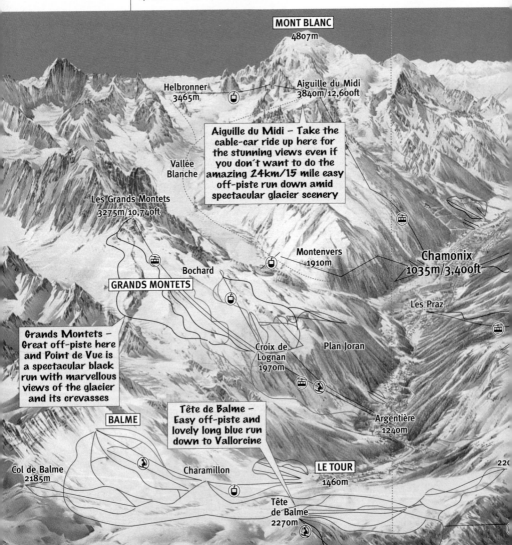

MONT BLANC
4807m

Helbronner
3465m

Aiguille du Midi
3840m/12,600ft

Vallée
Blanche

Aiguille du Midi – Take the cable-car ride up here for the stunning views even if you don't want to do the amazing 24km/15 mile easy off-piste run down amid spectacular glacier scenery

Les Grands Montets
3275m/10,740ft

Montenvers
1910m

Chamonix
1035m/3,400ft

Bochard

GRANDS MONTETS

Les Praz

Grands Montets – Great off-piste here and Point de Vue is a spectacular black run with marvellous views of the glacier and its crevasses

Croix de
Lognan
1970m

Plan Joran

Argentière
1240m

BALME

Tête de Balme – Easy off-piste and lovely long blue run down to Vallorcine

Col de Balme
2185m

Charamillon

LE TOUR
1460m

Tête
de Balme
2270m

220

TERRAIN-PARKS
It's natural
For years talk of a terrain-park here was sacrilege because of the excellent natural hits and off-piste terrain. However, due to popular demand, and several winters of poor snow conditions, one has been built at Les Bossons as an extra attraction. It in no way stands up to the bigger parks elsewhere, but usually has an average jump or two. Its forte is the good line of small to medium rails and boxes and its own drag-lift.

SNOW RELIABILITY
Good high up; poor low down
The top runs on the north-facing Grands Montets slopes above

Argentière are almost guaranteed to have good snow, and the season normally lasts well into May. The risk of finding the top lift shut because of bad weather is more of a worry. There's snowmaking on the busy Bochard piste and the run to the valley, which can now be kept open late in the season. Le Tour has a snowy location and a good late-season record. The largely south-facing slopes of Brévent and Flégère suffer in warm weather, and the steep runs to the resort are often closed. Don't be tempted to try these unless you know they are in good condition – they can be lethal. Some of the low beginners' areas have snowmaking.

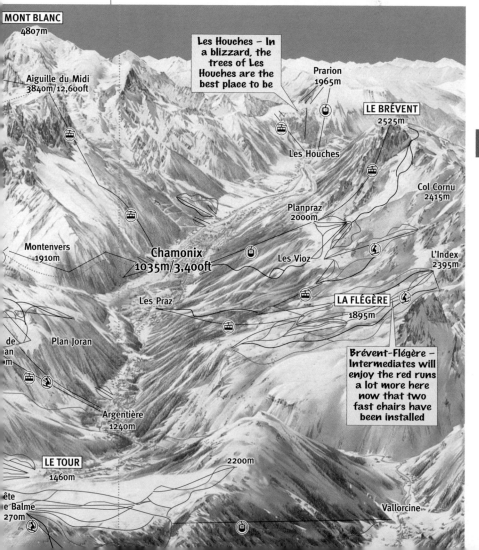

MONT BLANC
4807m

Aiguille du Midi
3840m/12,600ft

Les Houches – In a blizzard, the trees of Les Houches are the best place to be

Prarion
1965m

LE BRÉVENT
2525m

Les Houches

Col Cornu
2415m

Planpraz
2000m

Montenvers
1910m

Chamonix
1035m/3,400ft

Les Vioz

L'Index
2395m

Les Praz

LA FLÉGÈRE
1895m

Plan Joran

Brévent-Flégère – Intermediates will enjoy the red runs a lot more here now that two fast chairs have been installed

de
an
m

Argentière
1240m

LE TOUR
1460m

2200m

ête
e Balme
270m

Vallorcine

FOR EXPERTS
One of the great resorts

Chamonix is justifiably renowned for its extensive steep terrain, and for impressively deep snow. To get the best out of the area without putting your life at risk you really need to have a local guide. There is also lots of excellent terrain for ski-touring on skins. See the feature panel, facing.

The Grands Montets cable-car offers stunning views from the observation platform above the top station – if you've got the legs and lungs to climb the 121 steep metal steps. (But beware: it's 200 more steps down from the cable-car before you hit the snow.) The ungroomed black pistes from here – Point de Vue and Pylones – are long and exhilarating. The former sails right by some dramatic sections of glacier, with marvellous views of the crevasses.

The Bochard gondola serves a challenging red and a moderate black. Alternatively, head directly down the Combe de la Pendant bowl for 1000m/ 3,28oft vertical of wild, unpisted mountainside. The continuation down the valley side to Le Lavancher is equally challenging; it suffers frequently from lack of snow.

At Le Brévent there's more to test experts than the piste map suggests – there are a number of variations on the runs down from the summit. Some are very steep and prone to ice. The runs in the sunny Col de la Charlanon are uncrowded and include one red piste and lots of excellent off-piste if the snow is good.

At La Flégère there are further excellent challenging slopes – in the Combe Lachenal, crossed by the linking cable-car, for example – and a pretty tough run back to the village when snow-cover permits. Le Tour boasts little tough terrain on-piste but there are good off-piste routes from the high points to the village, towards Vallorcine or into Switzerland.

FOR INTERMEDIATES
It's worth trying it all

For less confident intermediates, the Col de Balme area above Le Tour is good for cruising and usually free from crowds. There are excellent shady runs on the north side of Tête de Balme, served by a quad. When conditions permit, you can head right down to Vallorcine and ride the gondola back up.

THE VALLEE BLANCHE

This is a trip you do for the stunning scenery. The views of the ice, the crevasses and seracs – and the spectacular rock spires beyond – are simply mind-blowing. The run, although exceptionally long, is not steep – mostly effortless gliding down gentle slopes with only the occasional steeper, choppy section to deal with. In the right conditions, it is well within the capability of a confident intermediate (but rather too flat for snowboarders). If snow is sparse, the run can turn tricky – there can be patches of sheet ice, exposed stones and rocks, and narrow snow bridges over gaping crevasses. And if fresh snow is abundant, different challenges may arise. Go in a guided group – dangerous crevasses lurk to swallow those not in the know. The trip is popular – on a busy day 2,500 people do it; book in advance at the Maison de la Montagne or other ski school offices. To miss the worst of the crowds go very early on a weekday, or in the afternoon if you are a good skier and can get down quickly.

The amazing Aiguille du Midi cable-car takes you to 3840m/12,600ft. Across the bridge from the arrival station on the Piton Nord is the Piton Central; the view of Mont Blanc from the 3842 cafeteria (claimed to be the Europe's highest restaurant) – a stair-climb higher – should not be missed, and it gives you the opportunity to adjust to the dizzying altitude. A tunnel delivers you to the infamous ridge-walk down to the start of the run. Be prepared for extreme cold up here. There is (usually) a fixed guide-rope for you to hang on to, and many parties rope up to their guides. You may still feel envious of those nonchalantly strolling down in crampons; you may wish you'd stayed in bed.

After that, the run seems a doddle. There are variants on the classic route, of varying difficulty and danger. Lack of snow often rules out the full 24km/15 mile run down to Chamonix; a stairway and slow gondola link the glacier to the station at Montenvers, for the half-hour mountain railway-ride down to the town.

Chamonix is renowned as an extreme sports Mecca, with arguably some of the best off-piste skiing in the world. And while thrill seekers and off-piste specialists are spoilt for choice, there is plenty for those looking for their first powder experience too.

Les Houches and Le Tour, at opposite ends of the Chamonix Valley, are ideal for a first taste off the beaten track. The forested slopes of Les Houches are easy to navigate on bad-weather days, with gentle blue runs bringing you back to the valley. Le Tour's open slopes are perfect for a foray into deep snow in between the pistes, with firmer ground just a few reassuring metres away.

Snowboarders flock to La Flégère after a snowfall, its array of boulders and drop-offs turning it into a massive terrain-park. The open bowl of Combe Lachenal is easily accessed from the top of the Index lift, and the south-facing slopes of this ski area provide excellent spring skiing.

From the top of Les Grands Montets (3275m/10,740ft) skiing is mostly off-piste and on glacial terrain. The vast north-facing slope of La Face is fairly steep but with plenty of room for tracks. The steep, extensive area reached via the Point de Vue piste offers stupendous views, plus snow conditions that are often among the best in the valley. The Grands Montets also gives access to the steep Pas de Chèvre run. Skiing under the colossal granite spire of Le Dru, with views of Mont Blanc and the Vallée Blanche in the distance, is an unforgettable experience. The Couloir du Dru and the Rectiligne are also on this face, reserved for the adventurous – with some slopes of 40/45°.

These are just some of the off-piste options in the Chamonix valley, but the possibilities are endless. Together with ski-touring itineraries like the Haute Route (Chamonix to Zermatt), and heli-skiing on the Italian side of Mont Blanc and in neighbouring Switzerland, the wealth of off-piste on offer could keep you skiing for a lifetime. We haven't mentioned here the Vallée Blanche, because it is covered in a separate feature panel in this chapter.

More adventurous intermediates will also want to try the other three main areas, though they may find the Grands Montets tough going (and crowded). The bulk of the terrain at Le Brévent and La Flégère provides a sensible mix of blue and red runs; at Le Brévent the slopes have been redesigned to achieve this. And the two new fast chair-lifts (see News) make these linked areas much more enjoyable to spend a day on.

If the snow and weather are good, join a guided group and do the Vallée Blanche (see feature panel opposite).

A day trip to Courmayeur makes an interesting change of scene, especially when the weather is bad (it can be sunny there when Chamonix's high lifts are closed by blizzards or high winds).

FOR BEGINNERS
Best to learn elsewhere
If there is snow low down, the nursery lifts at La Vormaine, Les Chosalets, Les Planards and Le Savoy are fine for first-timers, who will not be bothered by speed-merchants there. But the separation of beginners' slopes from the rest inhibits the transition to real runs, and makes lunchtime meetings of mixed groups difficult. The slopes on the south side of the valley – Les Planards, in particular – can be dark and cold in mid-winter, as the editorial

daughter can testify. Le Savoy is sunny, but devoid of restaurants. Better to learn elsewhere, and come to Chamonix when you can appreciate the tough terrain.

FOR CROSS-COUNTRY
A decent network of trails
Most of the 42km/26 miles of prepared trails lie along the valley between Chamonix and Argentière. There are green, blue, red and black loops. All these trails are fairly low; they're cold and shady in midwinter, and they fade fast in the spring sun.

QUEUES
Morning and afternoon problems
The main lifts from the valley at Chamonix and Argentière produce queues at peak times – and getting down when the home runs are closed can be as bad as getting up the mountain in the morning. A 2006 reporter experienced queues of over an hour to get up the Flégère cable-car (there's a booking system to get down at the end of the day here).

There are still long queues for the top cable-car on Les Grands Montets – often all day long. When they reach 30 minutes a booking system operates, so you can go skiing until it's your turn to ride – often an hour or more later. The replacement of the slow Herse chair by

CHILDREN

Panda Club
t 0450 558612
Ages 3 to 12; 8.30-
5pm; includes ski
lessons

Babysitter list
Available from the
tourist office

Ski schools
Take children aged 3
to 12 (6 days from
€190 – ESF price)

SCHOOLS

ESF
t 0450 532257
Evolution 2
t 0450 559022
White Sensations
t 0450 911425
(UK 0870 241 5809)

Classes
6 half days: €168
Private lessons
€37 for 1hr, for 1 or
2 people

GUIDES

**Compagnie des
Guides**
t 0450 530088
Chamonix Experience
t 0450 540936

a six-pack has relieved the pressure there and on the Bochard gondola – a 2005 visitor confirms this. And the new gondola at Vallorcine seems to be queue-free 'even on Saturdays'. Crowded pistes are reported to be more of a problem in places – most notably at Lognan.

In poor weather Les Houches gets crowded and the queues for the Bellevue cable-car can then be bad.

MOUNTAIN RESTAURANTS
Surprisingly dull

The Bergerie de Planpraz on Le Brévent is the most attractive option – built in wood and stone, with self- and table-service. Food and service are 'excellent'; but it gets very busy. The little Panoramic at the top enjoys amazing views over to Mont Blanc and the food is fine. Altitude 2000 provides table-service at rip-off prices and one reporter rates the attitude of the waiters as 'absolutely terrible'. There's a self-service place at La Flégère with a large terrace and excellent views.

On the Grands Montets the Plan Joran serves good food and does table- (try the 'trilogie cuisine – three small dishes served on one plate' says a 2006 reporter) and self-service, but gets busy, according to a reporter. There's also an indoor picnic area. The restaurant at

Lognan has been smartly renovated. The rustic Chalet-Refuge de Lognan, off the Variante Hôtel run to the valley, and overlooking the Argentière glacier, has marvellous food and is very popular (book a table) – 'well worth the bit of poling to get back to Lognan', says a 2006 reporter. The Crèmerie du Glacier, just off the Pierre à Ric red down to Argentière, has 'fast and friendly service, generous portions and a cosy atmosphere', says a 2006 visitor.

At the top of the Le Tour gondola, the Chalet de Charamillon is an adequate self-service and there's a picnic area. The Refuge du Col de Balme – a short hike from the lifts – is charming, but we've had mixed reports of the service.

SCHOOLS AND GUIDES
The place to try something new

The schools here are particularly strong in specialist fields – off-piste, glacier and couloir skiing, ski-touring, snowboarding and cross-country. English-speaking instructors and mountain guides are plentiful, and specialist Chamonix tour operators can arrange them in advance for guests. At the Maison de la Montagne is the main ESF office and the HQ of the Compagnie des Guides, which has taken visitors to the mountains for 150 years. Both now offer ready-made

boarding

The undisputed king of free-ride resorts, Chamonix is a haven for advanced snowboarders who relish the steep and wild terrain. This means, however, that in peak season it gets crowded and fresh snow gets tracked out very quickly. The rough and rugged nature of the slopes means it is not best suited for beginners but to more experienced adventurous riders, willing to try true all-mountain riding. If you do the Vallée Blanche, be warned: the usual route is flat in places. Check out former British champ Neil McNab's excellent extreme backcountry camps at www.mcnabsnowboarding.com. Most areas are equipped mainly with cable-cars, gondolas and chairs. However, there are quite a few difficult drags at Le Tour that cause inexperienced boarders problems – though you can avoid these if you are ready to contend with cat tracks to take you to other lifts, according to a reporter.

GETTING THERE

Air Geneva 86km/ 53 miles (1½hr); Lyon 226km/140 miles (3hr).

Rail Station in resort, on the St Gervais-Le Fayet/Vallorcine line.

Direct TGV link from Paris on Friday evenings and at weekends.

week-long 'tours' taking clients to a different mountain or resort each day. We have a good report of the ESF Ski Fun Tour, where they ski a different Mont Blanc region resort each day, transport included: 'Fantastic – we cannot speak highly enough of the guides.' Competition is provided by a number of smaller, independent guiding and teaching outfits. Evolution 2 'never disappoints', writes a reporter. Chamonix Experience offers a full range of options, from classic itineraries and Italian heli-skiing to hidden off-piste routes and avalanche courses.

FACILITIES FOR CHILDREN
Better than they were

The Panda Club is used by quite a few British visitors and reports have been enthusiastic. The Argentière base can be inconvenient for meeting up with children for the afternoons. The Club Med nursery seems to go down well too. UK tour operator Esprit Ski has chalets here, with a nursery in the Sapinière chalet-hotel near the Savoy nursery slope.

Beware the tendency to keep children on the valley nursery slopes for the convenience of the school.

STAYING THERE

HOW TO GO
Any way you like

There is all sorts of accommodation, and lots of it. The tourist office has a 'useful central booking system'. Call 0450 532333 or email reservation@ chamonix.com.

Chalets Many are run by small operators that cater for this specialist market. Quality tends to be high and value for money good by comparison with resorts that have wider appeal.

Hotels A wide choice, many modestly priced, and the vast majority with fewer than 30 rooms. Bookings for a day or two are no problem – the peak season is summer.

(((((4) **Albert 1er** (0450 530509) Smart, 100-year-old chalet-style hotel with 'truly excellent' and 'reasonably priced' food (Michelin stars) but expensive rooms (especially in the farmhouse annexe). Indoor-outdoor pool.

(((((4) **Auberge du Bois Prin** (0450 533351) A small modern chalet with a big reputation; great views; bit of a hike into town; closer to Le Brévent.

(((((4) **Mont-Blanc** (0450 530564) Central, luxurious.

Chamonix

271

FRANCE

272

ACTIVITIES

Indoor Sports
complex (swimming
pool, sauna, steam
room, tennis, squash,
ice rink, fitness room,
climbing wall), Alpine
museum, library,
cinemas, bowling

Outdoor Ice rink,
snow-shoeing,
walking paths,
tobogganing, dog-
sledding, ice-climbing,
paintballing

((((④ **Jeu de Paume** (Lavancher) (0450
540376) Alpine satellite of a chic
Parisian hotel: a beautifully furnished
modern chalet halfway to Argentière:
'Tasteful, friendly staff ... lovely';
endorsed in 2006 as 'welcoming,
relaxed and unpretentious'.
(((④ **Grand Hotel des Alpes** (0450
553780) Newly renovated, elegant
central hotel with pool, sauna, hot-tub.
Friendly, largely Italian staff.
(((③ **Alpina** (0450 534777) Much the
biggest in town: modernist-functional
place just north of centre.
(((③ **Croix-Blanche** (0450 530011)
Central, dates from 1793, 'rooms
furnished in simple regional style'.
(((③ **Gourmets & Italy** (0450 530138)
Spot-on central mid-price B&B hotel.
(((③ **Labrador** (Les Praz) (0450 559009)
Scandinavian-style chalet close to the
Flégère lift. Good restaurant.
(((③ **Prieuré** (0450 532072) Mega-
chalet on northern ring-road – handy
for drivers, quite close to centre.
(((③ **Vallée Blanche** (0450 530450)
Smart, low-priced 3-star B&B hotel,
handy for centre and Aiguille du Midi.
((② **Richemond** (0450 530885)
Traditional, comfortable, with good
public areas. 'Excellent, very good
value, superb food,' says one reporter.
'Rather faded,' writes another.
((② **Arve** (0450 530231) Central, by the
river; small rooms. 'Good value and
superb service from owners.'
(① **Faucigny** (0450 530117) Cottage-
style; in centre.
     Also recommended by reporters are
the 'boutique hotel with rooms varying
from a suite to bunks' Clubhouse
(0450 909656), the 'friendly' Morgane
(0450 535715) with a pool, the
'spacious, clean and modern rooms' of
Gustavia (0450 530031), the 'modern
and Savoyard-style smart' Hermitage
(0450 531387), and the 'reasonable
and so convenient for Le Brévent'
Savoyard (0450 530077).

SMART APARTMENTS – SEE FEATURE

Many properties in UK package
brochures are in convenient but
cramped blocks in Chamonix Sud. The
Balcons du Savoy and Ginabelle are a
cut above the rest: more spacious,
great views, pool, gym, steam etc.

EATING OUT
Plenty of quality places

The top hotels all have excellent
restaurants and there are many other
good places to eat. The Sarpé is a
lovely 'mountain' restaurant and the
Impossible is rustic but smart and
features good regional dishes. We
always enjoy the Atmosphere, by the
river, despite its two-sitting system
('excellent', 'cosy, trendy, friendly
efficient service' say recent reporters).
The National, next door, is also
reported to be 'very good'. The Panier
des Quatre Saisons is another favourite
('good food at reasonable prices') –
much better than its shopping-gallery
setting would suggest.
     Reader recommendations include
Maison Carrier in the Albert 1er hotel
('Bustling, rustic with great value
traditional food'), the Calèche ('good
food, atmosphere and service') and the
Petit Moulin ('tiny, excellent, especially
for veggies'). The Monchu is good for
Savoyard specialities, as is the
'outstanding' Chaudron – a 2005
reporter's favourite ('excellent service').
The Bergerie is traditional and
'fantastic', according to another visitor
and the popular Casa Valerio does
'fabulous pasta' and 'excellent pizza'.
The Spiga d'Oro is a recommended
Italian, over a 'lovely' deli.
     There are a number of ethnic
restaurants – Mexican, Spanish,
Japanese, Chinese, Indian etc and lots
of brasseries and cafes.

↑ The Bochard gondola on the Grands Montets accesses a vast amount of off-piste

ED CHESTER

Phone numbers
From abroad use the prefix +33 and omit the initial '0' of the phone number.

TOURIST OFFICES

Chamonix
t 0450 530024
info@chamonix.com
www.chamonix.com

Argentière
t 0450 540214
info@argentiere.com

APRES-SKI
Lots of bars and music
Many of the bars around the pedestrianised centre of Chamonix get crowded for a couple of hours at sundown – none more so than the Choucas video bar. During the evening, The Pub ('friendly staff and good British/Irish beer') and the Bar'd Up are busy. The Chambre Neuf at the Gustavia hotel remains so until late: 'Live music and dancing on the bar,' says a 2006 reporter. The Micro Brasserie is 'very good', with live bands and DJs. No Escape replaced Wild Wallabies for last winter and is a 'funky, upmarket restaurant and lounge bar'; it joins Privilege, as a place aimed 'at a more discerning clientele who like their après-ski at a slightly less frantic pace'.

The Brit-run 'small but cosy' Dérapage has happy hours early and mid-evening; L'Expedition is 'small and friendly'. There's a lively variety of nightclubs and discos. The Choucas (again), and Garage are popular. The Cantina sometimes has live music and is open late. Bar Terrasse has live music every night and serves 'a good snack menu till 10pm'.

A fire in February 2006 on the rue du Moulin unfortunately destroyed some of Chamonix's most famous bars. Cybar, Bar du Moulin, the Queen Vic and Dick's Tea bar all suffered fire and water damage. When we went to press, the tourist office says the buildings will be rebuilt but is uncertain if it will be for 2006/07. In the meantime, the Queen Vic is looking to lease an alternative building, and a new bar, the Soul Food cafe, opened on the rue du Moulin towards the end of last season 'with bags of atmosphere'.

OFF THE SLOPES
An excellent choice
There's more off-slope activity here than in many resorts. Excursion possibilities include Annecy, Geneva, Martigny, Courmayeur and Turin. The Alpine Museum is 'very interesting', the library has a good selection of English language books and there's a good sports centre and swimming pool.

Argentière 1240m/4,070ft

The old village is in a lovely setting towards the head of the valley – the Glacier d'Argentière pokes down towards it and the Aiguille du Midi and Mont Blanc still dominate the scene down the valley. There's a fair bit of modern development but it still has a rustic appeal.

A number of the hotels are simple, inexpensive and handy for the village centre – but it's a fair hike (uphill on the way back) or a bus-ride to and from the slopes. The 3-star Grands-Montets (0450 540666), on the other hand is handy for the slopes but a hike to the village. It's a large chalet-style building and 'offers all the comfort and service of a 4-star' says an impressed 2006 visitor; 'luxurious rooms and a superb pool' says another. The family-run Montana (0450 541499) provides 'lovely rooms, excellent food', the Couronne (0450 540002) is basic but 'good value', the Dahu (0450 540155) 'excellent value'.

Restaurants and bars are informal and inexpensive; the 'wonderful setting and mouth-watering menu' at Jeu de Paume at Lavancher (see Chamonix hotels) proves the exception. A 2005 reporter recommends Luigi's ('excellent duck') and a 2006 reporter says the Stone, with its 'authentic pizzas and a few pasta dishes, is giving Luigi's a run for its money'. The Dahu is recommended for its 'lovely terrace' and is 'busy with locals and residents both early and later'. The Office is always packed with Brits and Scandinavians and has live bands and 'terrific cooked breakfasts', but one 2006 reporter found the food somewhat mediocre and the service rather inept'. The Savoy bar is another traditional favourite – 'lively, friendly, well priced'. The 'friendly' Rencard plays reggae music and serves food. The Rusticana is 'laid back' and does 'excellent steaks': 'Seems to be the new in-place,' says a 2006 visitor.

Châtel

A distinctively French base in an ideal position for exploring the huge Portes du Soleil circuit which spans the French-Swiss border

274

- ➕ Very extensive, pretty, intermediate terrain – the Portes du Soleil
- ➕ Wide range of cheap and cheerful, good-value accommodation
- ➕ Pleasant, lively, French-dominated old village, still quite rustic in parts
- ➕ Local slopes are among the best in the Portes du Soleil and relatively queue-free
- ➕ Easily reached – one of the shortest drives from the Channel, and close to Geneva

- ➖ Traffic congestion can be a problem at weekends and in peak season
- ➖ Both the resort and the slopes are low for a French resort, with the resulting risk of poor snow – though snowmaking is now extensive
- ➖ Some main lifts are a bus-ride from the village centre
- ➖ Best nursery slopes are reached by bus or gondola

Châtel offers an attractive blend of qualities much like that of Morzine – another established valley village in the Portes du Soleil. Morzine is a bit more polished, Châtel (with a claimed 40 working farms) more rustic. But its key advantage is that it is part of the main Portes du Soleil (PdS) circuit. There is a gap in the circuit at Châtel, filled by buses; but this is more of an irritant to those passing through than for Châtel residents, for most of whom the excellent local bus services are part of the daily routine. At weekends it's worth trying the slopes of nearby Chapelle d'Abondance, which are pleasantly uncrowded.

THE RESORT

Châtel lies near the head of the wooded Dranse valley, at the north-eastern limit of the French-Swiss Portes du Soleil ski circuit.

It is a much expanded but still attractive old village. Modern unpretentious chalet-style hotels and apartments rub shoulders with old farms where cattle still live in winter.

Although there is a definite centre, the village sprawls along the road in from lake Geneva and the diverging roads out – up the hillside towards Morgins and along the valley towards the Linga and Pré-la-Joux lifts.

Lots of visitors take cars and the centre can get clogged with traffic – especially at weekends. Street parking is difficult but there is underground (paid-for) parking and day car parks at Linga and Pré-la-Joux (where the parking can still get very full in peak season despite the provision of new spaces). Other main French Portes du Soleil resorts are easy to reach by piste, but not by road.

The free resort bus service is approved by most reporters. A central location gives you the advantage of getting on the ski-bus to the outlying lifts before it gets very crowded, and

simplifies après-ski outings – the night bus finishes at 9.30pm. But there is accommodation near the Linga lift if first tracks are the priority.

A few kilometres down the valley is the rustic village of La Chapelle-d'Abondance (see end of chapter).

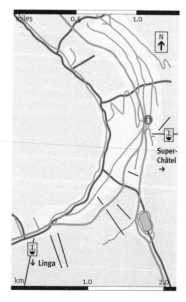

The mountains in the distance are the Dents du Midi in Switzerland, beyond Champéry →

SNOWPIX.COM / CHRIS GILL

THE MOUNTAINS

Châtel sits between two sectors of the main Portes du Soleil circuit, each offering a mix of open and wooded slopes, and linked by an 'excellent, practically continuous though sometimes crowded' free bus service. The circuit is easily done by intermediates of all abilities and there are sectors within it that you are likely to want to spend time exploring without doing the whole circuit more than once or twice during a week. The booklet-style piste map gives a fairly clear picture of each sector.

THE SLOPES
Two sectors to choose between
Directly above the village is **Super-Châtel** – an area of easy, open and lightly wooded slopes, accessed by a gondola or two-stage chair. From here you can embark on a clockwise Portes du Soleil circuit by heading south to the Swiss resort of Morgins, travelling via Champoussin and Champéry to cross back into France above Avoriaz. Or you can head north for the slopes straddling a different bit of the Swiss border, above **Torgon**. You can also access these slopes by chair-lifts from Petit Châtel, down the valley.

An anticlockwise circuit starts outside the village with a lift into the

Linga sector – a gondola from Villapeyron or a choice of fast chairs from Pré-la-Joux. The fastest way to Avoriaz is via Pré-la-Joux. There is night-skiing on the Stade de Slalom run on Linga every Thursday.

TERRAIN-PARKS
Head for Super-Châtel
There's a terrain-park, with 15 features of varying difficulty, at Super-Châtel, plus a 120m/390ft long half-pipe and an 800m/half-mile long boarder-cross course. Music blasts out to help motivate you for the tricks. La Chapelle-d'Abondance also has a 360m/1,180ft long park with half-pipe. A special park-only pass is now available (18.70 euros a day).

SNOW RELIABILITY
The main drawback
The main drawback of the Portes du Soleil is that it is low, so snow quality can suffer when it's warm. Châtel is at only 1200m/3,940ft and some runs home can be tricky or shut. But a lot of snowmaking has been installed at Super-Châtel and on runs down to resort level. Linga and Pré-la-Joux are mainly north-facing and generally have the best local snow. The pistes to Morgins and Lindarets, in contrast, get full sun. Grooming could be better, according to a 2005 visitor.

Châtel

275

SCHOOLS

ESF
t 0450 732264

International
t 0450 733192

Stages Henri Gonon
t 0450 732304

Francis Sports
t 0450 813251

Snow Ride (Ecole de Glisse)
t 0608 337651

Bureau des Moniteurs Virages
t 0680 028763

Classes
(ESF prices)
6 half-days (2¹/₂hr am or pm) €111

Private lessons
€33 for 1hr, for 1 or 2 people

FOR EXPERTS
Some challenges

The best steep runs – on- and off-piste – are in the Linga and Pré-la-Joux area. Beneath the Linga gondola and chair, there's a pleasant mix of open and wooded ground, which follows the fall line directly. And there's a mogul field between Cornebois and Plaine Dranse, which has been described as 'steeper and narrower than the infamous Swiss Wall in Avoriaz'. An area under the Cornebois chair, known to the locals as Happy Valley, is also popular. There's also a great off-piste route from Tête du Linga down the valley of La Leiche – hire a guide. Two pistes from the Rochassons ridge are steep and kept well groomed. There are some genuine blacks and good off-piste opportunities on the way to Torgon from Super-Châtel, including a long run down to Barbossine, which is quite narrow and tricky at the top.

FOR INTERMEDIATES
Some of the best runs in the area

When conditions are right the Portes du Soleil is an intermediate's paradise. Good intermediates need not go far from Châtel to find amusement; Linga and Plaine Dranse have some of the best red runs on the circuit. The moderately skilled can do the PdS circuit without problem, and will particularly enjoy runs around Les Lindarets and Morgins. Even timid types can do the circuit, provided they take one or two short-cuts and ride chairs down trickier bits. But some blues are said to be difficult: the 'narrow, steep and icy' route to

Morgins provoked a complaint from one reporter last year, who witnessed skiers 'in tears' on its top section. The chair from Les Lindarets to Pointe de Mossettes leads to a red run into Switzerland, which is a lot easier than the 'Swiss Wall' from Chavanette and speeds up a journey round the circuit.

Expeditions to the Hauts-Forts runs above Avoriaz are worthwhile. Timid intermediates should note: the runs back to Plaine Dranse are real reds.

Don't overlook the Torgon sector, which has some excellent slopes including some challenging ones.

FOR BEGINNERS
Three possible options

There are good beginners' areas at Pré-la-Joux (a bus-ride away) and at Super-Châtel (a gondola-ride). And there are nursery slopes at village level if there is snow there. Reporters have praised the Super-Châtel slopes and lifts, which 'allow the beginner to progress' and 'safely practise' on gentle gradients away from the main runs. Getting up to them is a bit of an effort, though. The home run to the village of Super-Châtel is not recommended – it is narrow, busy and steep at the end, which, coupled with often poor and icy conditions, makes it very tricky for beginners and timid intermediates. The Pré-la-Joux slopes are said to have 'less variety of slopes and quite a steep drag-lift'.

FOR CROSS-COUNTRY
Pretty, if low, trails

There are 14 pretty trails along the river and through the woods on the

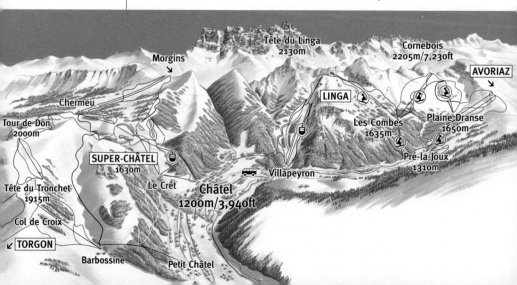

CHILDREN

Mouflets Garderie
t 0450 813819
Ages 3mnth to 6yr;
8am to 7pm; half-day
€24

Le Village des Marmottons
t 0450 733379
Ages 3 to 6; 6 days
€334 (with lunch)

Ski schools
ESF, International and
Francis Sports take
children from age 4 or
5 (ESF 6 half-days
€120)

GETTING THERE

Air Geneva 75km/
47 miles (1½hr).
Rail Thonon les Bains
(40km/25 miles).

ACTIVITIES

Indoor Bowling,
cinemas, library,
painting and drawing
lessons
Outdoor Ice rink,
walks, salto
trampoline, bob-sled
run, paragliding, farm
visits, cheese factory
visits, ice-diving,
snow-shoe excursions
(60km/37 miles of
trails shared with
Morgins – special
route map available)

OUR WEBSITE

Go to our website at
wtss.co.uk for resort
news, links to resort
sites, a build-your-
own resort shortlist
system and reader
forums.

---

lower slopes of Linga, but snow-cover can be a problem. The tourist office produces good maps with suggested routes and trail times.

QUEUES
Bottlenecks have been eased
Queues have been eased throughout the Portes du Soleil circuit in recent years by the introduction of several fast chair-lifts. And two more giving access to the Linga sector of the Châtel slopes are due to be in place for the 2006/07 season – see News. But you can still face queues to get down from Super-Châtel if the slope back is shut by poor snow. And queues for the gondola out of the village form when school parties gather: 'It is common to share your lift with a buzz of hyperactivity,' writes a visitor. Reporters have also found lengthy queues at the Tour de Don and Chermeu drag-lifts at certain times of day, causing difficulties for skiers rushing back to Super-Châtel to pick up children from ski school.

MOUNTAIN RESTAURANTS
Some quite good local huts
Atmospheric chalets can be found, notably in a cluster at Plaine Dranse – the Bois Prin, Tan ô Marmottes, Vieux Chalet ('fabulous meal, low ceilinged, laden with teddies, run by a mad woman'), Chaux des Rosées and Chez Denis have been recommended. In the Linga area the Ferme des Pistes, 'a cosy alpine barn, complete with stable-door', is said to do 'simply the best tarte aux pommes'. The Perdrix Blanche at Pré-la-Joux scarcely counts as a mountain restaurant, but is an attractive (if expensive and crowded) spot for lunch. At Super-Châtel the Portes du Soleil at the foot of the Coqs drags is much better than the big place at the top of the gondola. The Escale Blanche is worth a visit. Don't forget to check out chapters on other Portes du Soleil resorts – particularly Avoriaz.

SCHOOLS AND GUIDES
Plenty of choice
There are six ski and snowboard schools in Châtel. The International school has been recommended by a reporter, but another was 'very disappointed' with her private lesson. The ESF came in for praise, with comments such as 'very helpful and customer-focused instructors', and 'skiing progressed by leaps and

---

bounds', reinforced recently by a regular reporter.

FACILITIES FOR CHILDREN
Good reports
The Marmottons nursery has good facilities, including toboggans, painting, music and videos, and children are reportedly happy there. Francis Sports ski school has its own nursery area with a drag lift and chalet at Linga: 'Very organised, convenient and reasonably priced.' The ESF had a rave report from a regular visitor: 'I continue to be very impressed.' His eight-year-old grandson has always received 'sympathetic instruction from English-speaking instructors' and has made excellent progress.

STAYING THERE

HOW TO GO
A wide choice, including chalets
Although this is emphatically a French resort, packages from Britain are no problem to track down. A 2006 reporter praised the personal service he received from a Ski Addiction weekend visit: 'Met me at train station, waited at hotel then took me to hire shop, guided me round slopes, nothing was too much trouble.'
Chalets A fair number of UK operators have places here, including some Châtel specialists.
Hotels Practically all the hotels are 2-stars, mostly friendly chalets, wooden or at least partly wood-clad. None of the 3-stars is particularly well placed.
((③ **Macchi** (0450 732412) Modern chalet, most central of the 3-stars.
((③ **Fleur de Neige** (0450 732010) Welcoming chalet on edge of centre; Grive Gourmande restaurant is one of the best in town.
((③ **Lion d'Or** (0450 813440) In centre, 'basic rooms, good atmosphere'.
(② **Belalp** (0450 732439) Simple chalet with small rooms, but 'very good food'. The Carnotzet restaurant does good braserade.
(② **Choucas** (0450 732257) Recently refurbished. 'Friendly owner.' Approved of again by a 2006 reporter.
① **Kandahar** (0450 733060) One for peace-lovers: a Logis by the river, a walkable distance from the centre.
① **Rhododendrons** (0450 732404) 'Great service, friendly, comfortable, clean.'
Self-catering Many of the better places are available through agencies

popular with the British and has a DJ or live music every night (the caramel vodka is recommended). The Avalanche is a very popular English-style pub with a 'good atmosphere and live music' and has internet facilities. The Godille – close to the Super-Châtel gondola and crowded when everyone descends at close of play – has a more French feel. The 'small and cosy' Isba is the locals' choice, and shows extreme sports videos. The bar in hotel Soldanelles has been recommended. The bowling alley, the Vieille Grange du Père Crincheux, also has a good bar.

OFF THE SLOPES
Less than ideal
Those with a car easily visit places like Geneva, Thonon and Evian. There are some pleasant walks, you can visit the cheese factory or the two cinemas, or join in daily events organised by the tourist office.

The Portes du Soleil as a whole is less than ideal for non-skiers who like to meet their more active friends for lunch: they are likely to be at some distant resort at lunchtime and very few lifts are accessible to pedestrians.

La Chapelle-d'Abondance
1010m/3,310ft
This unspoiled, rustic farming community, complete with old church and friendly locals, is 5km/3 miles along a beautiful valley from Châtel. 'A car and a bit of French are virtually essential,' says a reporter. It's had its own quiet little north-facing area of easy wooded runs for some years, but has more recently been put on the Portes du Soleil map by an outlying gondola that links it to the slopes between Torgon in Switzerland and Super-Châtel.

Nightlife is virtually non-existent – just a few quiet bars, a cinema and torchlit descents.

The hotel Cornettes (0450 735024) is an amazing 2-star, run by the Trincaz family since 1894, with 2-star rooms but 4-star facilities, including an indoor pool, sauna, steam room and hot-tubs. It has an atmospheric bar and an excellent restaurant doing extremely good-value menus (but 'disappointing' desserts, comments one reporter). Look out for showcases with puppets and dolls and eccentric touches, such as ancient doors that unexpectedly open automatically.

↑ It's an unpretentious old village, with a very French feel to it, that sprawls along the main road
WENDY-JANE KING

FRANCE

*ski*addiction

- Chalet & Hotels
- Short breaks
- Short transfer
- Self drive option
- Off piste courses
- Heli-skiing specialist

www.skiaddiction.co.uk
sales@skiaddiction.co.uk

Tel: 01580 819349

Est Since 1989

Phone numbers
From abroad use the prefix +33 and omit the initial '0' of the phone number.

TOURIST OFFICES

Châtel
t 0450 732244
touristoffice@
chatel.com
www.chatel.com

**La Chapelle-
d'Abondance**
t 0450 735141
ot.lachapelle@
valdabondance.com
www.valdabondance.
com

specialising in Châtel or in self-drive holidays. The Gelinotte (out of town but near the Linga lifts and children's village) and the Erines (five minutes from the centre) look good. The Avenières is right by the Linga gondola. Châtel's supermarkets are reported to be small and over-crowded. There is a large supermarket out in the direction of Chapelle d'Abondance.

EATING OUT
Fair selection
There is an adequate number and range of restaurants. Our favourite for a serious dinner is the Table d'Antoine, the restaurant of the hotel Chalet d'Alizée – excellent food, charming patronne. The Fleur de Neige hotel has a pricey gastronomic restaurant (La Grive Gourmande). The woody Vieux Four carries its rustic ornamentation a bit far for our taste, but it does ambitious dishes alongside Savoyard specialities and is approved by readers. The Pierrier and the Fiacre are more modest, everyday restaurants doing a range of grills as well as Savoyard specialities. The Moroccan chef at the Hotel Soldanelles cooks a 'veritable feast'. The Refuge du Milles Pâtes does 'bargain' set menus. Out of town, the Ripaille, almost opposite the Linga gondola, is popular with the locals and highly rated by reporters, especially for its fish and the 'fantastic local Gamay wines'. The hotel Cornettes in La Chapelle-d'Abondance is worth a trip – see later section.

APRES-SKI
All down to bars
Châtel is getting livelier, especially at the weekends. The Tunnel bar is very

La Clusaz

Attractive, scenic, distinctively French all-rounder; we like it a lot –
but we'd like it a lot more if it were 500m higher

COSTS

① ② ③ ④ ⑤ ⑥

RATINGS

The slopes
Fast lifts	**
Snow	**
Extent	***
Expert	***
Intermediate	****
Beginner	****
Convenience	***
Queues	***
Mountain restaurants	****

The rest
Scenery	***
Resort charm	****
Off-slope	***

NEWS

For 2006/07 the Patinoire gondola is to be upgraded.

There are longer-term plans to add two new chairs on L'Etale and build a new hotel 'Au Coeur du Village'.

REPORTS WANTED

Recently we have had few reports on this resort. If you go there, please do send us a report.

The best reports earn a copy of the next edition, and can lead to free lift passes in future.

See page 12.

+ Traditional village in scenic setting

+ Extensive, interesting slopes – something for everyone

+ Very French atmosphere

+ Very short transfer from Geneva, and easy to reach by car from UK

+ Good, rustic mountain restaurants

+ Good cross-country trails

− Snow conditions unreliable because of low altitude (by French standards)

− Lots of slow old chair-lifts

− Crowded at weekends

Few other major French resorts are based around what is still, essentially, a genuine mountain village that exudes rustic charm and Gallic atmosphere. Combine that with more than 200km/125 miles of largely intermediate slopes, above and below the tree line, and there's a good basis for an enjoyable, relaxed week. Snowmaking is continually increased, but of course it makes no difference if the temperatures are too high.

THE RESORT

The village is built beside a fast-flowing stream at the junction of a number of narrow wooded valleys. As it has developed into an international resort it has had to grow in a rather rambling and sprawling way, with roads running in a confusing mixture of directions. But, unlike so many French resorts, La Clusaz has retained the charm of a genuine and friendly mountain village, and the new buildings have been built in chalet style and blend in well, for the most part. Les Etages is a much smaller centre of accommodation south of the main town.

As one of the most accessible resorts from Geneva and Annecy, La Clusaz is good for short transfers, but it does get crowded, and there can be weekend traffic jams.

THE MOUNTAINS

Like the village, the slopes are rather spread out. There are five main areas, each connecting with at least one other.

Slopes Several points in La Clusaz have lifts giving access to the predominantly west- and north-west facing slopes of L'Aiguille. From here you can reach the slightly higher and shadier slopes of the La Balme area and a gondola returns you to Côte 2000 on L'Aiguille. La Balme is a splendid, varied area with good lifts.

Going the other way from L'Aiguille leads you to L'Etale and then the Transval cable-car, which shuttles people between the two areas. From the bottom of L'Etale, you can head back along another path to the village and the gondola up to the Beauregard sector, which, as the name implies, has splendid views and catches a lot of sunshine. From the top of Beauregard you can link via an easy piste and a two-way chair-lift with Manigod. From here you can move on to L'Etale.

Terrain-parks The park – on the Aiguille – has quarter- and half-pipes, tables, rails and boarder-cross runs.

Snow reliability Most runs are west- or north-west facing and tend to keep their snow fairly well, even though most of the area is below 2000m/6,500ft. The best snow is on the north-west-facing slopes at La Balme. In late season, the home runs can be dependent on snowmaking – but the runs linking La Balme and l'Etale to the village do not have any, so you may have to use lifts to descend.

Experts The piste map doesn't seem to have a lot to offer experts, but most sectors present off-piste variants, and there are more serious adventures to undertake. The best terrain is at La Balme – the black Vraille run, which leads to the speed-skiing slope, is seriously steep. On the opposite side of the sector, the entirely off-piste Combe de Bellachat can be reached.

The Noire run down the face of Beauregard can be tricky in poor snow

KEY FACTS

Resort	1100m
	3,610ft
Slopes	1100-2470m
	3,610-8,100ft
Lifts	56
Pistes	132km
	82 miles
Green	32%
Blue	32%
Red	27%
Black	9%
Snowmaking	
	74 acres

Phone numbers
From abroad use the prefix +33 and omit the initial '0' of the phone number.

TOURIST OFFICE

La Clusaz
t 0450 326500
infos@laclusaz.com
www.laclusaz.com

OUR WEBSITE

Go to our website at wtss.co.uk for resort news, links to resort sites, a build-your-own resort shortlist system and reader forums.

and is often closed. The Tétras on L'Etale is steep only at the top; the Mur Edgar bumps run on L'Aiguille is steep but short. L'Aiguille has a good off-piste run down the neglected Combe de Borderan and the long Lapiaz black piste runs down the Combe de Fernuy from Côte 2000.

Intermediates Early intermediates will delight in the gentle slopes at the top of Beauregard and over on La Croix-Fry at Manigod. L'Etale and L'Aiguille have more challenging but wide blue runs. More adventurous intermediates will prefer the steeper slopes of La Balme.

Beginners There are nursery slopes at village level, and better ones up on Beauregard and at Crêt du Merle. The Beauregard area has lovely gentle blue runs to progress to; those from Crêt are steeper, but there is a green.

Snowboarding Most of the drag-lifts are avoidable. There are some good nursery slopes, served by chair-lifts, and cruising runs to progress to. La Balme is great for good free-riders.

Cross-country The region has much better cross-country facilities than many resorts, with around 70km/43 miles of loops of varying difficulty.

Queues These aren't a problem, except on peak weekends or if the lower slopes are shut because of snow shortage.

Mountain restaurants A highlight: there are lots of them and most are rustic and charming, serving good, reasonably priced food. Readers repeatedly recommend the Télémark above the chair-lift to L'Etale. The 'very

attractive' Chez Arthur at Crêt du Merle has table-service tucked away behind the crowded self-service. The Relais de L'Aiguille at Crêt du Loup is also popular. The Bercail is 'good but very crowded'.

Schools and guides We've had mixed reports of the ESF ('large classes', 'poor instruction', 'very satisfied'). Reports suggest the smaller Sno Academie is more reliable.

Facilities for children We've had mixed reports about the kindergarten too.

STAYING THERE

How to go La Clusaz is offered mostly by smaller operators.

Hotels Small, friendly 2- and 3-star family hotels are the mainstay of the area; luxury is not an option here. The Carlina (0450 024348) is said by a reporter to be the best. A 2006 reporter recommends the Alp'Hotel (0450 024006) for 'excellent' food and 'very friendly' staff.

Self-catering There's quite a good choice, but some are out of town.

Eating out There's a wide choice of restaurants, some a short drive away, including the Vieux Chalet (one of our favourites). The St Joseph at the Alp'Hotel is regarded as the best in the village. The Cordée and the Outa are great value for money.

Après-ski The 'olde worlde' Caves du Paccaly has live music. Pub le Salto has Sky TV and draught Guinness.

Off the slopes There's an excellent aquatic centre and good walks.

Les Contamines

A charming, unspoiled French village with its own area of reliably snowy slopes and easy road access to nearby big-name resorts

COSTS

① ② ③ ④ ⑤ ⑥

RATINGS

The slopes

Fast lifts	**
Snow	****
Extent	***
Expert	***
Intermediate	****
Beginner	**
Convenience	**
Queues	***
Mountain restaurants	****

The rest

Scenery	****
Resort charm	****
Off-slope	**

NEWS

Snowmaking was increased for last season and more is planned for 2006/07.

For 2004/05 a fast quad, the Montjoie, replaced the drag-lift at Etape: it serves the lower Signal runs.

➕ Traditional, unspoiled French village
➕ Fair-sized intermediate area
➕ Good snow record for its height
➕ Lift pass covers nearby resorts

➖ Not ideal for beginners
➖ Quiet nightlife
➖ Lifts a bus-ride from main village
➖ Can be some lengthy queues

Only a few miles from the fur coats of Megève and the ice-axes of Chamonix, Les Contamines is a charming contrast to both, with pretty wooden chalets, impressive old churches, a weekly market in the village square and prices more typical of rural France than of international resorts. Its position at the shoulder of Mont Blanc gives it an enviable snow record. What more could you want?

THE RESORT

The core of the village is compact, but the resort as a whole spreads widely, with chalets scattered over a 3km/2 mile stretch of the valley, and the main access lift is 1km/half a mile from the centre. There's expanding development by the lift at Le Lay but you can stay in the charming village centre, a shuttle-bus-ride away. Bizarrely, the local pass appears not to cover the buses. The Mont Blanc pass does cover them, plus the lifts of Chamonix and Megève (among other resorts). A car is useful.

THE MOUNTAINS

Most of the slopes are above the tree line and there are some magnificent views, though the runs down from Signal are bordered by trees (as is the run from La Ruelle down to Belleville).
Slopes From Le Lay a two-stage gondola climbs up to the slopes at Signal. Another gondola leads to the

Etape mid-station from a car park a little further up the valley, with a fast quad above it. Above these, a sizeable network of open, largely north-east-facing pistes fans out, with lifts approaching 2500m/ 8,200ft in two places. You can drop over the ridge at Col du Joly to south-west-facing runs down to La Ruelle, with a single red run going on down to Belleville. From Belleville, a 16-person gondola runs back up to La Ruelle, followed by a fast chair to Col du Joly.
Terrain-parks There's a terrain-park with jumps, rails, big air and boarder-cross, accessed by the fast Tierces chair-lift. A second area, on the Loyers piste, features more jumps, rails and a 120m/390ft super-pipe – floodlit twice weekly.
Snow reliability Many of the shady runs on the Contamines side are above 1700m/5,580ft, and the resort has a justifiable reputation for good snow late into the season, said to be the result of proximity to Mont Blanc.

281

OUR WEBSITE

Go to our website at wtss.co.uk for resort news, links to resort sites, a build-your-own resort shortlist system and reader forums.

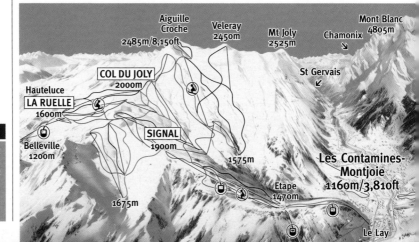

KEY FACTS

| Resort | 1160m |
| | 3,810ft |

Les Contamines-Montjoie/Hauteluce

Slopes	1160-2485m
	3,810-8,150ft
Lifts	24
Pistes	120km
	75 miles
Green	19%
Blue	21%
Red	36%
Black	24%
Snowmaking	
	125 guns

Phone numbers
From abroad use the prefix +33 and omit the initial '0' of the phone number.

TOURIST OFFICE

t 0450 470158
info@lescontamines.com
www.lescontamines.com

AGENCE NUTS / OT LES CONTAMINES

It's a pretty village and its position right by Mont Blanc gives it an enviable snow record →

There's snowmaking on the home runs from Signal down to the valley.

Experts The steep western section has black runs, which are enjoyable but not terribly challenging. But there is substantial and varied off-piste terrain within the lift system and outside it – including a 'seriously steep and challenging' descent to Megève.

Intermediates Virtually all the runs are ideal for good intermediates, with a mix of blues and reds that one recent reporter described as 'very similar – more like purple'. Some of the best go from the gondola's top station to its mid-station and others are served by the Roselette and Bûche Croisée lifts. Given good snow, the south-facing runs down to La Ruelle are a delight. And the black runs are enjoyable for good intermediates. Timid intermediates might find sections of many blue runs too steep for comfort.

Beginners In good snow, the village nursery area is adequate for beginners. There are other areas at the mid-station and the top of the gondola. The piste map shows no long greens to progress to but reporters tell of a 'very gentle green run from Col du Joly back to Le Signal' that is not on the map. Beginners will want to take the gondola down to the village at the end of the day, as the only run down is a red one that can be icy.

Snowboarding There are quite a few drag-lifts, including four marked on the piste map as difficult, so inexperienced boarders beware. But there is excellent off-piste boarding on offer.

Cross-country There are trails of varying difficulty totalling 26km/16 miles. One loop is floodlit twice a week.

Queues There can be 15- to 20-minute peak-period queues for the gondolas, especially if people are bussed in from other resorts with less snow. The main bottleneck at Etape, where the lower gondolas meet, has been relieved by the fast quad parallel to the second stage. A 2006 visitor said that in a two-week stay the longest time she spent in a queue was five minutes.

Mountain restaurants There are quite a few lovely rustic huts – not all of which are marked on the piste map. The Ferme de la Ruelle is a jolly barn, and the Grange just above it does a 'great-value plat du jour'. Roselette and Bûche Croisée (also known as R'mize à Louis) are two cosy chalets that have been recommended again by 2006 reporters, and the 'reasonably priced' Chez Gaston has great views.

Schools and guides We have mixed reports on the ESF – one expert was pleased with his 'fluent English-speaking' instructor, but his brother was lost by the school and 'got a snooty remark' when he rejoined them. Excursions are offered, including trips to the Vallée Blanche. There's an alternative International school, and mountain guides. One 2006 visitor enjoyed the 'challenging off-piste' found for him by Miage Aventure.

Facilities for children The kindergarten, next to the central nursery slopes, takes children from age one. Children can join ski school from age three.

STAYING THERE

How to go There are some catered chalets and a dozen modest hotels.

Hotels The 3-star Chemenaz (0450 470244) at Le Lay is praised: 'Comfortable, best food in the village.'

Eating out Recommendations include the Husky, Auberge du Barattet and the Op Traken ('lovely fondues') – and the Savoisien and the Auberge du Chalézan for Savoie specialities.

Après-ski Après-ski is quiet, but there are several bars. The Saxo near the gondola has been recommended; the Ty Breiz has live music and is 'the only lively bar', say reporters. There are weekly events such as music and free vin chaud by the village fountain (on Saturdays) and torchlit descents.

Off the slopes There are good walks, a toboggan run, snowmobiling, dog-sledding, snow-shoeing and a natural ice rink, but St-Gervais, Megève and Chamonix have more to offer.

Courchevel

A resort of many parts – mostly modern, mostly not pretty; 1850 is famously pricey – more so since the Russians started coming

COSTS

① ② ③ ④ ⑤ ⑥

RATINGS

The slopes

Fast lifts	****
Snow	****
Extent	*****
Expert	****
Intermediate	*****
Beginner	****
Convenience	****
Queues	****
Mountain restaurants	****

The rest

Scenery	***
Resort charm	**
Off-slope	***

NEWS

For 2006/07 a new 4-star hotel (Cheval Blanc) with spa is planned for 1850 and the Aiglon hotel is to be renovated and upgraded. A new 2-star – the Chanrossa – is planned for 1550.

For 2005/06 a six-pack chair, the Chapelets, replaced the Signal and Bel Air drags in 1650. The line of the old Signal drag is now a skiable off-piste run. An impressive kids' zone, Les Indiens, has been created, with various diversions.

The Grangettes gondola up from 1550 was upgraded.

- ➕ Extensive, varied local terrain to suit everyone from beginners to experts – plus the rest of the Three Valleys
- ➕ Lots of slope-side accommodation
- ➕ Impressive lift system, piste maintenance and snowmaking
- ➕ Wooded setting is pretty, and useful in bad weather
- ➕ Choice of four very different villages – only 1850 is notably expensive
- ➕ Some great restaurants, and good après-ski by French standards

- ➖ Some pistes get unpleasantly crowded (but they can be avoided)
- ➖ Rather soulless villages, with intrusive traffic in places
- ➖ 1850 has some of the priciest hotels, bars and mountain restaurants in the Alps, and it's getting worse
- ➖ Losing a little of its French feel as more and more British visitors – and now Russians – discover its attractions
- ➖ Little to do away from the slopes, especially during the day

Courchevel 1850 – the highest of the four components of this big resort – has long been the favourite Alpine hangout of the Paris jet set, and they have now been joined by wealthy Russians. Its top hotels and restaurants have always been among the most expensive in the Alps, and the influx of Russians has pushed up prices even further, while pushing service standards down.

But don't be put off: a holiday here doesn't have to cost a fortune (especially in the lower villages), the atmosphere is not generally exclusive, and Courchevel's list of ➕ points is enough to attract more and more Brits. Even so, it remains much more French than Méribel, over the hill, as well as having better snow.

The slopes are excellent: Courchevel is the most extensive and varied sector of the whole Three Valleys. Many visitors never leave this sector, which has everything from long gentle greens to steep couloirs.

Le Praz is an overgrown but still pleasant village, 1550 is quieter and good for families, 1650 has more of a village atmosphere than it seems from the road through, and the posh bits of 1850 are stylishly woody. But overall the resort is no beauty. Well, nothing's perfect.

283

OT COURCHEVEL

There are some wooded slopes above 1850, but more below, including some excellent black pistes →

KEY FACTS

| Resort | 1260-1850m |
| | 4,130-6,070ft |

Three Valleys	
Slopes	1260-3230m
	4,130-10,600ft
Lifts	183
Pistes	600km
	373 miles
Green	14%
Blue	40%
Red	36%
Black	10%
Snowmaking	
	1920 guns

| Courchevel/ | |
La Tania only	
Slopes	1260-2740m
	4,130-8,990ft
Lifts	63
Pistes	150km
	93 miles
Green	22%
Blue	37%
Red	33%
Black	8%
Snowmaking	
	563 guns

LIFT PASSES

Three Valleys

Prices in €

Age	1-day	6-day
under 13	32	158
13 to 59	42	210
over 60	36	168
Free under 5, over 72		

Beginner mini-pass
for eight lifts €13.50
a day

Notes
Covers Courchevel, La
Tania, Méribel, Val-
Thorens, Les Menuires
and St-Martin.
Family reductions;
pedestrian and half-
day passes. Six-day
pass valid for a day
in Espace Killy
(Tignes-Val-d'Isère),
Paradiski (La Plagne-
Les Arcs), Pralognan
and Les Saisies.

Alternative pass
Courchevel/La Tania
only, with one-day
Three Valleys
extension available.

THE RESORT

Courchevel is made up of four varied villages, generally known by numbers very loosely related to their altitudes. A road winds up from Le Praz (1300) past 1550, through 1650 to 1850. On the slopes, things work a bit differently: runs go down from 1850 to 1550 and 1300, but the slopes of 1650 form a distinct sector.

1850 is the largest village, and the focal point of the area, with most of the smart nightlife and shops. Two gondolas go over its lower slopes towards the links with Méribel and the rest of the Three Valleys. Although the approach is dreary and the centre not much better, parts are conspicuously upmarket, with some very smooth hotels on the slopes just above the village centre, and among the trees of the Jardin Alpin (a suburb served by its own gondola). There's a spreading area of smart private chalets.

You can pay through the nose to eat, drink and stay, but more affordable places are not impossible to find. Pressure on the restaurants is highest when big-spending Russians are in town – in early January and the second week in March – but we are no longer getting reports from readers unable to get a table.

1650 by contrast is 'calm and uncrowded, a world away from 1850', as a reader puts it. The main road up to 1850 cuts through but there's also an attractive old village centre, lively bars and quietly situated chalets. Its local slopes (whose main access is a gondola) are also relatively peaceful.

1550 is a quiet dormitory, a gondola or chair ride below 1850. It has the advantage of having essentially the same position as 1850, with cheaper accommodation and restaurants. But it's a long trip to 1850 by road if you want to go there in the evening.

Le Praz (or 1300) is an old village set amid woodland. It remains a pleasant spot despite expansion triggered by the 1992 Olympics – the Olympic ski jump is a prominent legacy. Ancient gondolas go up to 1850 and towards Col de la Loze, for Méribel. It is 'excellent' for pre-skiing children. But novices face rides down from as well as up to ski school.

Efficient free buses run between and within the villages. Champagny is an easy road outing, for access to the extensive slopes of La Plagne.

THE MOUNTAINS

Although there are plenty of trees around the villages, most of the slopes are essentially open, with the notable exception of the runs down to 1550 and to Le Praz, and the valley between 1850 and 1650. These are great areas for experts when the weather closes in. Many reporters recommend buying only a Courchevel pass and then one-day extensions for the Three Valleys as necessary.

THE SLOPES
Huge variety to suit everyone
A network of lifts and pistes spreads out from 1850, which is very much the focal point of the area. The main axis is the **Verdons** gondola, leading to a second gondola to La Vizelle and a nearly parallel cable-car up to La Saulire. These high points of the **Saulire-Creux** sector give access to a wide range of terrain above Courchevel (including a number of couloirs), to Méribel and all points to Val-Thorens. To the left of the Verdons gondola is the Jardin Alpin gondola, which leads to runs back to 1850, and serves the higher hotels until 8pm. It also gives access via the valley of Prameruel to the Chanrossa slopes above 1650.

To the right looking up from 1850

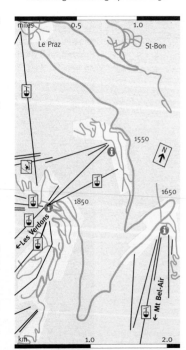

SCHOOLS

ESF in 1850
t 0479 080772

ESF in 1650
t 0479 082608

ESF in 1550
t 0479 082107

ESF Centre Pralong
t 0479 011581

Ski Academy
t 0479 081199

Supreme
t 0479 082787
(UK: 01479 810800)

New Generation
t 0479 010318
www.skinewgen.com

Magic in Motion
t 0479 010181

Oxygène
t 0479 551745

Classes
(ESF 1850 prices)
6 days (2½hr am and pm): €264

Private lessons
€70 for 1½hr

GUIDES

Bureau des guides
t 0479 010366

the Chenus gondola goes towards the **Loze-Praz** sector, a second link with Méribel. Runs go back to 1850, and through the woods to La Tania (see separate chapter) and Le Praz.

There are various ways up from 1650 to the minor high-points of Bel Air and Signal, and on into the **Chanrossa** sector. From here you can link across via the valley of Prameruel to Saulire-Creux, or ride long drag-lifts to the far end of the sector, where there is another link to Saulire-Creux via the col of Chanrossa.

TERRAIN-PARKS
Something for everyone
There are four designated freestyle areas in Courchevel – the canyon-style mounds and kids' fun area at Verdons, the humps and bumps course at Biollay, the boarder-cross at Pralong and the main terrain-park at Plantrey. Plantrey is accessible via the Ecureuil chair lift, and the Epicea poma lift services the park itself. It is a picturesque 600m/1,970ft long park that has a pro and intermediate kicker line, various handrails and boxes. There is also an 80m/26oft average-sized half-pipe that is well maintained.

SNOW RELIABILITY
Very good
The combination of Courchevel's orientation (its slopes are north- or north-east facing), its height, an

abundance of snowmaking and excellent piste maintenance usually guarantees good snow down to at least the 1850 and 1650 villages. A reporter comments: 'On a week when snow was relatively scarce in the Alps, we were pleasantly surprised by the quality and quantity of the snow.' On countless visits we have found that the snow is usually much better than in neighbouring Méribel, where the slopes get more sun. The runs to Le Praz are still prone to closure in warm weather. Daily maps are available, showing which runs have been groomed overnight (normal in America but very rare in Europe).

FOR EXPERTS
Some black gems
There is plenty to interest experts, even without the rest of the Three Valleys.

The most obvious expert runs are the couloirs you can see on the right near the top of the Saulire cable-car. The three main ways down were once designated black pistes (some of the steepest in Europe), but now only the Grand Couloir remains a piste – it's the widest and easiest of the three, but you have to pick your way along the narrow, bumpy, precipitous access ridge to reach it.

There is a lot of steep terrain, on- and off-piste, on the shady slopes of La Vizelle, both towards Verdons and towards the link with 1650. Some of

boarding

Despite being an upmarket resort, Courchevel has always been a popular resort with snowboarders. The resort has never been afraid to draw in sideways sliders, so much so that there are four separate areas designated to snowboarding. There are miles of well-groomed pistes, and the lifts are in general very modern and quick with few drag-lifts. As it is very expensive, Courchevel best suits intermediates and advanced riders who can fully take advantage of this resort's resources. The big snowboard hangout in 1850 is 'Prends ta luge et tire toi', a combined shop/bar/internet cafe..

the reds on La Vizelle verge on black and the black M piste is surprisingly little used. If you love moguls, try the black Suisses and Chanrossa runs – and the off-piste moguls under the Chanrossa chair. For a change of scene and a test of stamina, a couple of long (700m/2,300ft vertical), genuinely steep blacks cut through the trees to Le Praz.

In good snow conditions you can ski all the way down (around 2000m/6,560ft vertical) from La Saulire to Bozel, way below Le Praz, over meadows and through trees on the final section, and catch a bus back.

There is plenty of off-piste terrain to try with a guide – see the feature panel later in the chapter.

FOR INTERMEDIATES
Paradise for all levels

The Three Valleys is the greatest intermediate playground in the world, but all grades of intermediates will love Courchevel's local slopes too.

Early intermediates will enjoy the gentle Pyramides and Grandes Bosses blues above 1650, and the Biollay and Pralong blues above 1850. Those of average ability can handle most red runs without difficulty. Our favourite is the long, sweeping Combe de la Saulire from top to bottom of the cable-car first thing in the morning, when it's well groomed and free of crowds; but it's a different story at the end of the day – cut up snow and very crowded. Creux, behind La Vizelle, is

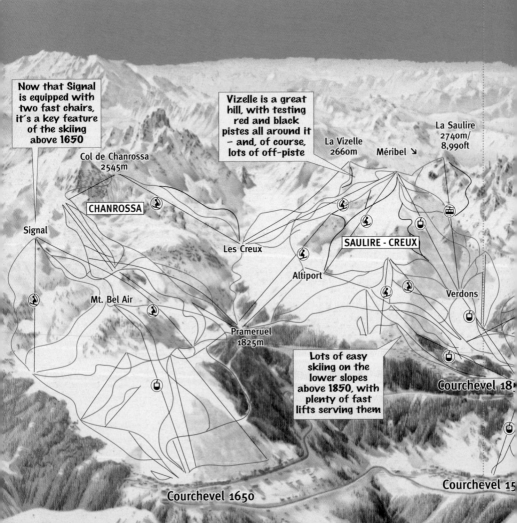

Now that Signal is equipped with two fast chairs, it's a key feature of the skiing above 1650

Vizelle is a great hill, with testing red and black pistes all around it – and, of course, lots of off-piste

Col de Chanrossa 2545m

La Vizelle 2660m

Méribel ⟍

La Saulire 2740m/ 8,990ft

CHANROSSA

Signal

Les Creux

SAULIRE - CREUX

Altiport

Verdons

Mt. Bel Air

Prameruel 1825m

Lots of easy skiing on the lower slopes above 1850, with plenty of fast lifts serving them

Courchevel 18•

Courchevel 15

Courchevel 1650

OT COURCHEVEL
The heart of
Courchevel's highly
varied slopes – Vizelle
and Saulire ➜

another splendid, long red that gets
bumpy and unpleasantly crowded later
on. Marmottes from the top of Vizelle
is quieter and more challenging.

The Loze-Praz sector has excellent
blues and reds down towards 1850
and 1550 and through the trees
towards La Tania – long, rolling cruises.
Over at 1650, the Chapelets and
Rochers reds right at the edge of the
whole Three Valleys ski area are great
fun for fast cruising, although the new
six-pack serving them means they are
now more heavily used.

FOR BEGINNERS
Great graduation runs
There are excellent nursery slopes
above both 1650 and 1850. At the
former, lessons are likely to begin on
the short drags close to the village,
but quick learners will soon be able to
go up the gondola. The best nursery
area at 1850 is at Pralong, above the
village, near the airstrip. A reporter
points out that getting to it from the
village isn't easy, unless you go by
road. A blue path links this area with
chairs to 1650, so adventurous novices
can soon move further afield. The
Bellecôte green run down into 1850 is

an excellent, long, gentle slope – but it
is used by skiers returning to the
village and does get unpleasantly
crowded. It is served by the Jardin
Alpin gondola, and a drag that is one
of eight free beginner lifts. 1550 and Le
Praz have small nursery areas, but
most people go up to 1850 for its
more reliable snow.

FOR CROSS-COUNTRY
Long wooded trails
Courchevel has a total of 66km/
41 miles of trails, the most in the Three
Valleys. Le Praz is the most suitable
village, with trails through the woods
towards 1550, 1850 and Méribel. Given
enough snow, there are also loops
around the village.

QUEUES
Not a problem
Even at New Year and in mid-February,
when 1850 in particular positively teems
with people, queues are minimal,
thanks to the excellence of the lift
system. However, there can be a build-
up at 1850 for the gondolas and chairs,
notably in 'bad weather conditions and
just after ski school meeting-up time'.
The Biollay chair is very popular with

ONE OF THE BEST PLACES IN THE WORLD FOR OFF-PISTE SKIING

Courchevel's image is of up-market luxury and pampered piste skiing. But it is one of the world's best resorts for off-piste too. Manu Gaidet is a Courchevel mountain guide and a ski instructor with the Courchevel ESF. He is also one of the world's top free-riders and won the Freeride World Championship three years running. We asked him to pick out a few of the best runs.

These suggested routes are limited to the Courchevel valley. In addition, there is great off-piste in the rest of the Three Valleys. And directly from the resort you can heli-ski in Italy and Switzerland (it is banned in France). But never venture off-piste without a qualified ski instructor or mountain guide and safety equipment.

For a first experience off-piste, the Tour du Rocher de l'Ombre is great. Access is easy from the left of the Combe de la Saulire piste and you are never far from the piste. It is very quiet, the slope is very broad and easy and you get a real sense of adventure as you plan your way between the rocks. And the view of the Croix des Verdons is impressive. Keep to the left for the best snow.

The Courchevel **ESF** is the largest ski school in Europe with over 700 instructors. They can help you find the best off-piste and explore it safely. For phone numbers see the schools list. The websites of the three different branches (1550, 1650, 1850) can be accessed through www.courchevel.com

Les Avals is one of my favourite routes. The easiest way to get to it is to take the Roc Merlet piste from the top of the Chanrossa chair-lift. Leave the piste on the right as soon as you can, then climb up and cross the ridge. Once you've arrived at a group of rocks (in the form of towers) descend the south side. This run is not technically difficult and is particularly beautiful in spring conditions. Another possibility from the Chanrossa chair is to traverse towards the Aiguille du Fruit. Almost anywhere along this very wide slope, you can choose your spot to start skiing down to rejoin the end of the Chanrossa black piste at the bottom. A technically more difficult run, for experienced off-piste skiers only, is Plan Mugnier. This starts with a 20-minute walk from the top of the Chanrossa chair but you are normally rewarded by very good snow because the slope you ski down faces north. Le Curé is in the Saulire area: this narrow gully starts under a towering rock and offers a steady 35° slope; it is only for expert skiers who don't mind climbing to the Doigt du Curé starting point.

Courchevel

289

CHILDREN

Kindergarten (1850)
t 0479 080847
Ages from 18mnth;
9am-5pm

Les Pitchounets (1650)
t 0479 083369
Ages from 18mnth;
9am-5pm

Babysitting list
Contact tourist office.

Ski schools
Most offer lessons
from the age of 3 or 4
(ESF 1850 prices
€239 for 6 days).

the ski school (which gets priority) and can be worth avoiding. Queues for the huge Saulire cable-car are rare. Many lifts have American-style singles lines, which seem to be working better now than when they were first introduced.

MOUNTAIN RESTAURANTS
Good but can be very expensive
Mountain restaurants are plentiful and pleasant, but it is sensible to check the prices; for table-service restaurants reservations may be needed.

If we're paying the bill, our favourite (supported by many readers) is the Bel Air, at the top of the gondola above 1650 – good simple food ('omelettes to die for'), friendly and efficient table-service, and a splendid tiered terrace; booking essential. The Casserole, at the bottom of the Signal chair, was found to be 'very expensive but portions are big, and the salads are very good'.

Cap Horn, near the airstrip, has now taken over as leading lunchtime rip-off, according to a local who says it has a 'scarily' expensive wine list, specifically catering for the rich Russians toting wads of dollars. A reporter talks of food which was 'cold and dry' and says the place is 'like Cannes in the

Alps'. Chalet de Pierres, on the Verdons piste is not far behind, pricewise. But it is a comfortable, smooth place built in traditional style and reporters agree it does good food: 'great unfussy mountain food and very nice staff' is a typical comment. It has a wonderful array of desserts and is easily accessible for pedestrians.

The Bergerie on the Bellecôte piste still has 'a lot of atmosphere but the prices are now quite steep'. A 2006 reader found that the food at the Arc en Ciel (top of the Verdons gondola) 'lived up to our fond memories of it'. The Soucoupe has good food and views, but we hear the table-service section upstairs is imposing two fixed lunchtime sittings, which rules it out for us. The Panoramic at the top of Saulire has a good table-service section.

SCHOOLS AND GUIDES
Size is everything
Courchevel's branches of the ESF add up to the largest ski school in Europe, with over 700 instructors. We lack recent reports – no doubt partly because there is a wide choice of attractive alternatives.

STAYING THERE

HOW TO GO
Value chalets and apartments

Huge numbers of British tour operators go to Courchevel.

Chalets There are plenty of chalets available. In 1850 several operators offer notably comfortable chalets, and a few genuinely luxurious ones.

Flexiski has the cosily traditional Anemone and the more modern Chinchilla, being revamped for next season in contemporary style. Kaluma and Descent both have swanky 10-bed places with all the trimmings. Among the features of Scott Dunn's flagship Aurea is a 7.5m/25ft pool in the basement. Supertravel's portfolio now includes the lovely Montana.

Although not quite in that league, Total has several properties, including a couple of neat modern places up in the Jardin Alpin.

Mark Warner and Ski Olympic have chalet-hotels; the latter's central Les Avals is said to be 'just brilliant'.

In 1650 Le Ski has 16 comfortable chalets, including three brand-new for 2006/07. A 2005 reporter found 'the food excellent and the chalet staff friendly, helpful and unassuming'. Small Scottish operator Finlays has six chalets in 1550, and a couple up in 1850. Family-specialist Esprit Ski has several chalets and chalet-apartments down in Le Praz.

Hotels There are nearly 50 hotels in Courchevel, mostly at 1850 – including more 4-stars than anywhere else in France except Paris – 14 at the last count with 9 in the top '4-star luxe' category. And we hear that two more superhotels are about to be unveiled – the revamped Aiglon and newly built Cheval Blanc.

COURCHEVEL 1850

(((((5) **Les Airelles** (0479 003838) 'Super flash and over the top. The most expensive hotel in the Alps.'

(((((5) **St Joseph** (0479 081616) Like a plush country house 'with 14 fab rooms and two stunning apartments'.

(((((5) **Mélézin** (0479 080133) Superbly stylish and luxurious – and in an ideal position beside the Bellecôte slope.

(((((5) **Carlina** (0479 080030) Luxury piste-side pad, next to Mélézin.

(((((5) **Byblos** (0479 009800) Spacious public rooms, good pool, sauna, steam complex.

(((((4) **Bellecôte** (0479 081019) Our favourite among the more swanky places – it offers some Alpine

---

Ski Academy is an independent group of French instructors – 'one brilliant, another OK', 'excellent and attentive', said two past reporters. Magic in Motion has been rated 'good, but not outstanding'. Supreme in 1850 (British owned and mainly staffed by British instructors) has had mixed reviews – the criticisms, interestingly, involving a French not British teacher.

New Generation is another British-run school. We joined a group lesson with them last year and were very impressed by their US-style of teaching: they ask the students to set their goals for the lesson on the gondola ride up and then try to help them achieve them. We nearly all opted for skiing chopped-up, off-piste snow with style, and all felt we had improved a lot by the end of the morning. We continue to receive rave reviews about this outfit from reporters, for adults and children alike: 'Head and shoulders above any other ski school I've come across in the Alps,' says a 2006 reporter, summing up previous reports neatly.

The Bureau des Guides runs all-day off-piste excursions.

FACILITIES FOR CHILDREN
Lots of chalet-based options

In the past reporters have found the ski kindergarten at 1850 over-stretched, with 19 children in a class of five to seven-year-olds. But one reader said her three-year-old daughter was happy and 'skiing on reins quite well by the end of the week'. Magic in Motion has a wide range of ski/board programmes for kids. The ESF at 1850 offers VIC (Very Important Children) lessons for English-speaking children between 6 and 12 years with a maximum of six children per group. Several tour operators run their own nurseries using British nannies and there are now rentananny agencies.

Courchevel

291

ACTIVITIES

Indoor Ice rink, climbing wall, gymnasium, bowling, exhibitions, concerts, cinemas, language and computer courses, cookery courses, library
In hotels: health and fitness centres (swimming pools, saunas, steam-room, hot-tub, water therapy, weight-training, massage)

Outdoor Hang-gliding, paragliding, flying lessons, snow-shoe excursions, ice-climbing, snowmobile rides, ice karting, ballooning, horse-drawn sleigh rides, cleared paths, tobogganing, flight excursions

OUR WEBSITE

Go to our website at wtss.co.uk for resort news, links to resort sites, a build-your-own resort shortlist system and reader forums.

FRANCE

292

---

atmosphere as well as sheer luxury. ((((④ **Chabichou** (0479 080055) Distinctive white building, right on the slopes; family-run, friendly and rustic with very good food plus the option of a restaurant with 2 Michelin stars.
((((④ **Les Grandes Alpes** (0479 000000) 4-star on piste by main lifts. Readers enthuse: 'Personal service. Luxurious rooms.' 'Brilliant food.'
(((③ **Rond Point** (0479 080433) Family atmosphere, central position.
(((③ **Croisette** (0479 080900) Next to main lifts above the Jump bar. 'Simple and clean, staff very helpful.'
(((③ **Courcheneige** (0479 080259) On Bellecôte piste. 'A real find: lovely staff, good food.' Quiet.
(((③ **New Solarium** (0479 080201) Newly renovated, near first stop on Jardin Alpin gondola, 'sensible prices and very friendly service'.
(((③ **Sivolière** (0479 080833) Newly renovated, set among pines.

COURCHEVEL 1650
(((③ **Golf** (0479 009292) Rather impersonal 3-star, in a superb position on the snow next to the gondola.
(((③ **Seizana** (0479 014646) Stylish and central (over road from the gondola).

COURCHEVEL 1550
(((③ **Ancolies** (0479 082766) 'A real find,' said a US visitor impressed by the friendly staff and excellent food.

LE PRAZ
(((③ **Peupliers** (1300) (0479 084147) Smartly renovated and expanded, good restaurant – but prices now 'approach 1850 levels', we hear.

SMART APARTMENTS – SEE FEATURE
Leaving aside the swanky private chalets you can rent through local agents, the best bets are the Chalets les Montagnettes at the top end of 1650 – a choice of apartments and semi-detached chalets – and the Chalets du Forum in the heart of 1850.

EATING OUT
Pick your price
There are a lot of good, very expensive restaurants in Courchevel. A non-comprehensive pocket guide is distributed locally.

In 1850, among the best, and priciest, are the Chabichou (a 2006 visitor recommends the three course set menu lunch – 'absolutely fantastic'), and the Bateau Ivre – both with two Michelin stars. Other reporters praise the Chapelle ('fabulous and filling meal of lamb cooked on an open fire'). A 2006 reader had a 'great

meal' at the Anerie 'in a cosy and rustic setting'. A reporter liked the pizzas but not the soup at the Via Ferrata and was concerned to watch the staff smoking in the kitchen. Also mentioned by readers are the Cloche ('good atmosphere'), the Tremplin ('exemplary lamb', expensive but 'worth every penny') and the Cendrée ('a wonderful Italian', 'good value'). The Saulire (aka Chez Jaques) is a reliable spot that we have enjoyed, endorsed by a 2006 reporter for 'excellent service and food – a bargain by local standards'. Another recommends the Mangeoire's 'good simple food at acceptable prices, considering there is live music every night'. We've had mixed reports about the Locomotive, with railway-theme decor and a varied menu: 'Lots of character, good music, food and wine,' said one 2005 reporter; 'Very average food and service, overpriced,' said a 2006 visitor. The hotel Tovets is reported to have 'reasonable prices and delicious food'. A local recommends the Grand Café (underneath the hotel St Joseph) for good Asian cuisine. A 2005 visitor enjoyed the large helpings at the Tex Mex Kalico.

In 1550, the Oeil du Boeuf is good for grills. The Cortona does good-value pizza.

In 1650 the smart hotel Seizena has quickly built a good reputation for 'inventive, reasonably priced' food; and the cosy Eterlou's 'good traditional' food and 'wide range of pizzas' have led to many recommendations from readers. Montagne and the Petit Savoyard ('divine fillet steak and pâté de foie gras dish') also do good French and Savoyard food, pizza and pasta.

In Le Praz, Bistrot du Praz is expensive but excellent – 'a foodie's treat'. The Ya-ca is small and 'very French'. We've had excellent meals at the hotel Peupliers (good pepper steak) but we hear that prices are on the rise.

APRES-SKI
1850 has most variety
If you want lots of nightlife, it's got to be 1850. There are some exclusive nightclubs, such as the Caves, with top Paris cabaret acts and sky-high prices. The popular Kalico ('open until 4am') has DJs and cocktails. The Bergerie has themed evenings – food, music,

Phone numbers
From abroad use the
prefix +33 and omit
the initial '0' of the
phone number.

entertainment – but prices are high.

The 'buzzing' Jump at the foot of the main slope seems to be the place to be as the lifts close – to the point where some judge it 'very unpleasant'. The 'reasonably priced yet stylish Equipe' has free WiFi internet. Others have liked the 'cool and trendy zinc-look S'no Limit' and the new Milk Pub, set underground with live music, 'sensible-ish prices and a young crowd'. One reader comments that there is 'no real large meeting place for après-ski'. The Saulire (aka Chez Jacques) and the cheap and cheerful Potinière are also popular. Piggys is described as 'fur coats, pampered dogs and sky-high prices' and as 'the world's only medieval themed French/Irish wine bar/pub/disco featuring a drawing room and library'. Irresistible. Mangeoire has 'an excellent Piano bar (with high Piggys-style prices) and is extremely lively from about 11pm'.

Cinemas in 1850 and 1650 show English-speaking films.

One reader's 20-something kids found 'plenty to do' in 1650. The 'lively, friendly' Bubble is the hub; with satellite TV, internet access, cheap bar prices, a happy hour, some strong local beers and frequent live music, it has a largely British clientele. One reader's favourite last year was the Signal bar. Rocky's Bar (in chalet-hotel Avals) is popular and 'good for watching sport', with all that that entails. Remonte Pente is a tiny French bar. The New Space Bar has pool, games and live music or DJs and the local disco (now called the Taverne) stays open till 4am.

In 1550 the Chanrossa bar is British-dominated, with occasional live music, the Taverne also has English owners. In Le Praz the Escorch'vel bar is 'a good, lively place'.

OFF THE SLOPES
1850 isn't bad
There are a fair number of shops in 1850, plus markets at most levels. There's an ice-driving circuit and an ice-climbing structure. Snow-shoeing among the trees is growing in popularity. A pedestrian lift pass for the gondolas and buses in Courchevel and Méribel makes it easy for non-slope users to meet up the mountain for lunch. And you can take joyrides from the altiport. A non-skier's guide to Courchevel, Méribel and La Tania is distributed by the tourist office.

Courchevel

293

Les Deux-Alpes

Sprawling resort with a long, narrow ski area that will disappoint many intermediates; popular for summer skiing and boarding

COSTS

① ② ③ ④ ⑤ ⑥

RATINGS

The slopes

Fast lifts	**
Snow	****
Extent	***
Expert	****
Intermediate	**
Beginner	***
Convenience	***
Queues	**
Mountain restaurants	**

The rest

Scenery	****
Resort charm	**
Off-slope	**

NEWS

For last season, two old chair-lifts from the central slope area to just below Tête Moute were replaced by the fast Bellecombes six-pack. And the bottleneck Grand Nord piste was widened – though we are sceptical of how much this will have helped alleviate overcrowding.

On the Pied Moutet side, another fixed-grip quad chair was installed to improve access from the north end of town.

➕ High, snow-sure slopes, including an extensive glacier area

➕ Varied high-mountain terrain, from motorways to steep off-piste slopes

➕ Excellent, sunny nursery slopes

➕ Stunning views of the Ecrins peaks

➕ Lively resort with varied nightlife

➕ Wide choice of affordable hotels

➖ Piste network modest by mega-resort standards – we're sceptical about the claimed 220km/137 miles – and badly congested in places

➖ The home runs are either steep and icy or dangerously overcrowded – so people queue for a lift down instead

➖ Virtually no woodland runs

➖ Spread-out, traffic-choked resort

➖ Few appealing mountain restaurants

We have a love–hate relationship with Les Deux-Alpes. We quite like the buzz of the village – arriving here is a bit like driving into Las Vegas from the Nevada desert – and we understand the appeal of its vibrant nightlife. We love the high-Alpine feel of its main mountain, and the good snow to be found on the north-facing pistes at mid-mountain. But we're very unimpressed by the extent of those pistes, and we hate the congestion that results when most of the town's 35,000 visitors are crammed on to them. Crowding apart, keen intermediates spoiled by high-mileage French mega-resorts (and not up to the excellent off-piste) will simply find the usable area of slopes rather small.

THE RESORT

Les Deux-Alpes is a narrow village sitting on a high, remote col. Access is from the Grenoble-Briançon road to the north. The village is a long, sprawling collection of hotels, apartments, bars and shops, most lining the busy main street and the parallel street that completes the one-way traffic system. The resort has a lively ambience.

The village has grown haphazardly over the years, and there is a wide range of building styles, from old chalets through 1960s blocks to more sympathetic recent developments. It looks better as you leave than as you arrive, because all the balconies face the southern end of the resort.

Lifts are spread fairly evenly along the village and there is no clear centre, but a couple of focal points are evident. Alpe de Venosc, at the south end of town, has many of the nightspots and hotels, the most character, the fewest cars, the best shops and the Diable gondola up to the tough terrain around Tête Moute. More generally useful is the Jandri Express from the middle of the resort, where there is a popular outdoor ice rink and some good restaurants and bars. The village straggles north from here, becoming less convenient the further you go.

The free shuttle-bus service saves on some very long walks from one end of town to the other.

The six-day pass covers a day in several nearby resorts including Alpe-d'Huez and Serre-Chevalier. Helicopter trips to Alpe-d'Huez are good value at £40 return – a 'must', says a reporter. More economical is the shuttle-bus service on Wednesdays and Thursdays.

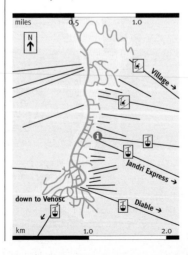

KEY FACTS

Resort	1650m
	5,410ft
Slopes	1300-3570m
	4,270-11,710ft
Lifts	51
Pistes	220km
	137 miles
Green	20%
Blue	40%
Red	21%
Black	19%
Snowmaking	
	191 guns

THE MOUNTAINS

For a big resort, Les Deux-Alpes has a disappointingly small piste area, despite recent improvements. Although extremely long and tall (it rises almost 2000m/6,560ft), the main sector is also very narrow, with just a few runs on the upper part of the mountain, served by a few long, efficient lifts. The piste-grading is rather inconsistent and some runs are graded differently on the map and on the mountain. A 2006 reporter confirms our view: 'A real lack of mileage; we skied pretty much everything in a day.' The piste map is inadequate, especially for the central area around Toura and Crêtes.

THE SLOPES
Long, narrow and fragmented
The western **Pied Moutet** side of Les Deux-Alpes is relatively little used. It is served by lifts from various parts of town but reaches only 2100m/6,890ft. As well as the short runs back to town, which get the morning sun, there's an attractive north-facing red run down through the trees to the small village of Bons. The only other tree-lined run in Les Deux-Alpes goes down to another low village, Mont-de-Lans.

On the eastern side of the resort, the broad, steep slope immediately

above it offers a series of relatively short, challenging runs, down to the nursery slopes ranged at the bottom. With the exception of a long winding green run, which gets very crowded, these runs are now all classified as black, and rightly so: they are usually mogulled (some are never groomed), and often icy when not softened by the afternoon sun. As a result, many visitors ride down in the gondolas.

The ridge of **Les Crêtes** above the village has lifts and gentle runs along it, and behind it lies the deep, steep Combe de Thuit. Lifts span the combe to the main mid-mountain station at 2600m/8,530ft, now known as **Toura**, at the foot of the slopes on La Toura. The middle section of the mountain, above and below this point, is made up primarily of blue cruising runs and is very narrow. At one point, there is essentially just a single run down the mountain – the Grand Nord, which is a real bottleneck late in the day. The only alternative is to take the (partly flat) blue Gours run to the bottom of the combe, where a chair-lift takes you up to Les Crêtes. This pleasant run passes the base of the Fée chair, serving an isolated, under-used black run, and a slightly easier parallel red.

The top **Glacier du Mont de Lans** section, served by drag-lifts and the

Les Deux-Alpes

295

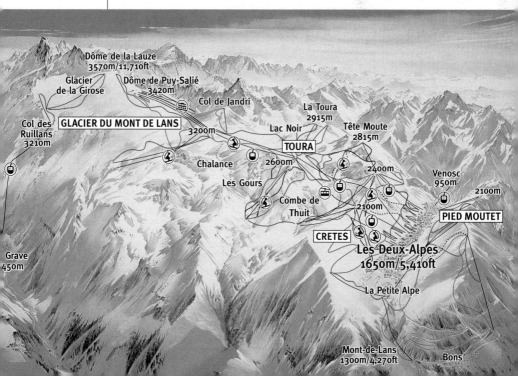

FRANCE

↑ The resort's huge
summer terrain-park
on the glacier makes
it popular year-round

OT LES DEUX-ALPES /
STEPHANE CERVOS

LIFT PASSES

Super ski pass

Prices in €

Age	1-day	6-day
under 13	28	120
13 to 59	35	165
over 60	28	124

Free under 5, over 72

Beginner four free
drag-lifts

Notes
Covers all lifts in Les
Deux-Alpes and entry
to swimming pool
and ice rink. Half-day
and pedestrian
passes available. Also
family rates. Six-day
pass includes access
to La Grave and one
day's skiing in Alpe-
d'Huez, Serre-
Chevalier, Puy-St-
Vincent and the Milky
Way.

Alternative passes
Ski Sympa covers 21
lifts.

warmer underground funicular, has
some fine, very easy runs, which afford
great views and are ideal for beginners
and the less adventurous. You can go
from the top here all the way down to
Mont-de-Lans – a descent of 2270m/
7,450ft vertical that is the world's
biggest on-piste vertical, as far as we
know. A walk (or snowcat tow) in the
opposite direction takes you over to
the slopes of La Grave – a splendid
area for advanced skiers with a guide
(now covered by the Deux-Alpes pass).

TERRAIN-PARKS
A real highlight
The heavyweight terrain-park is located
on the Toura run in the winter then
shifts up to the glacier in the summer
and gets even bigger. Easily one of the
top parks in Europe, there is
something for everyone here (including
beginners). All sizes of kickers, hips,
rails and boxes will keep all levels
challenged throughout the day. The
highlights of this 800m/2,620ft long
park are the impeccable super-pipe
and the big gap jump. Additionally
there are DJs playing music, a BBQ
area and a snowskate park.

SNOW RELIABILITY
Excellent on higher slopes
The snow on the higher slopes is
normally very good, even in a poor
winter. Above 2200m/7,220ft most of
the runs are north-facing, and the top
glacier section guarantees good snow.
More of a concern is bad weather
shutting the lifts, or extremely low
temperatures at the top. But the runs
just above the village face west, so
they get a lot of afternoon sun and can
be slushy or icy. There's snowmaking
on some of the lower slopes – but a
January visitor skiing on rocky pistes
saw it used 'not once'.

FOR EXPERTS
Off-piste is the main attraction
With good snow and weather
conditions, the area offers wonderful
off-piste sport – see the feature panel
on the facing page. There are serious
routes that end well outside the lift
network, with verticals of over
2000m/6,560ft. Reporters consistently
recommend the renowned descent to
St-Christophe (hire a guide, who will
arrange transport back); one who
visited in January 2006 said, 'Though
the resort's slopes were hard-packed,
this run offered superb powder.'
  A weekly Free Respect event
promotes off-piste safety, with free
advice and free-ride competitions.
  The Super Diable chair-lift, from the
top of the Diable gondola, serves the
steepest black run around. The brave
can also try off-piste variations here.
  If the conditions are right, an outing
to the slopes of La Grave is a must.

FOR INTERMEDIATES
Limited cruising
Les Deux-Alpes can disappoint keen
intermediates. A lot of the runs are
either rather tough – some of the blues

boarding

*Les Deux-Alpes has become a snowboard Mecca over the last few years. Its cheap
and cheerful atmosphere has attracted snowboarders from all over the world – the
limited pisted slopes aren't as off-putting to boarders. The resort is open all year
round, the terrain-park being the summer's main attraction and home to various
camps. The kick-off to the French winter season begins here with a huge 'Mondial
du Snowboard' event – on 27–29 October in 2006. In town there are good
trampoline facilities and a huge airbag to get a feeling of what air-time is all
about. Although the focus is on the terrain-park, the free-riding terrain is not to be
underestimated, with plenty of steep challenging terrain (including that in the
nearby resort of La Grave). Beginners will find the narrow, flat crowded areas
mid-mountain and the routes down to the village intimidating. Most of the lifts
on the higher slopes are chairs, and there's a specialist Primitive snowboard school.*

OFF-PISTE CHALLENGES FOR EVERYONE FROM NOVICE TO EXPERT

The off-piste routes in Les Deux-Alpes are numerous and varied in difficulty, the easiest permitting skiers even of an intermediate level to enjoy their first 'free-ride experience'. We've asked Jeremy Edwards of the European Ski and Snowboard School to share some of his favourites.

For something slightly technical, both sides off the Bellecombes red piste – 2800m-2300m (9,190ft-7,550ft) – offer a wide range of varying terrain; it's important to take care here – there are several small cliff faces. For those keen to tackle couloirs – steep, narrow slopes between rocks – this descent offers small ones that are ideal for your first attempts; they can be avoided, though.

Traversing across the top of the black Grand Couloir piste leads to the North Rachas area, with off-piste faces that offer cold snow conditions all winter. The first large valley leads to three couloirs – one fairly broad and easy, the other two much narrower and steeper, and certainly not for the timid. Traversing further leads to a much wider descent that avoids the three couloirs.

The **European Ski and Snowboard School** does classes and guiding in small groups. Its instructors are of several nationalities, but all speak excellent English.
t 00 33 476 797455
europeanskischool@worldonline.fr
www.europeanskischool.co.uk

For tree skiing it's best to head for the Vallée Blanche area, reached via the lifts on Pied Moutet. The north-east face, towards the chair-lift at Bons, offers great routes over generally deserted wooded terrain with excellent cold snow conditions.

Strong skiers will enjoy the famous Chalance run, which starts just below the glacier and descends 1000m/3,280ft vertical to the Gours run; there are several variations, mixing wide open slopes and rocky pitches. These faces are at times subject to quite a high avalanche risk because of wind slab.

Traversing above the north face of the Chalance leads to the couloir Pylone Electrique – a steep, narrow 200m/660ft-long couloir with the reward below it of an excellent wide powder field of moderate gradient. A rest on the Thuit chair-lift is a must after this adrenalin-charged descent.

These routes and many more play a large part in the off-piste free-ride courses offered by the European Ski and Snowboard School.

Les Deux-Alpes

British orientated ski and snowboard school

Summer and winter

Quality instruction all in English

British instructors

Ski group courses

Adults or children Maximum 8 per group in 3-hour sessions over 5/6 days at all levels. Video analysis, progress reports, medals. Certificates for children.

Natural born skiers Whole mountain philosophy. Maximum 4 per group in 2-hour sessions over 5 days. Higher levels. Lift queue priority.

Free ride for experienced skiers. Discover Les Deux Alpes off-piste. 3 or 6 days, half or full days.

Private tuition on a 2-hourly basis, all levels. Ski, Snowboard, Telemark, Snowblades.

La Grave Guided trips to this off-piste Mecca.

Race camps Summer and winter.

Snowboard courses First go, Improving, Snow park, Free ride. Maximum 4 per group in 2-hour sessions over 3 or 6 days. Lift queue priority.

SCHOOLS

ESF
t 0476 792121

International St-Christophe
t 0476 790421

European
t 0476 797455

Primitive Snowboard (Salomon)
t 0607 907135

Ski Privilege
t 0476 792344

Easiski
t 0476 795884

Damien Albert
t 0476 795038

Classes
(ESF prices)
6 half days (2¼hr am or pm) €127.50

Private lessons
€32 for 1hr

GUIDES

Bureau des guides
t 0476 113629

CHILDREN

Crèche – 2 Alpes 1800
t 0476 790262
Ages 6mnth to 2yr; 8.30-5.30

Bonhomme de Neige
t 0476 790677
Ages 2 to 6; 8.30-5.15 (also activity centre for ages 6 to 17)

Jardins des Neiges
t 0476 792121
Ages 4 to 6; 9.15-12 noon, 2.30-5pm; 6 mornings €107.50

Ski schools
Classes for ages 6 to 12 (6 mornings €107.50 with ESF)

could be reds – or boringly bland. The runs higher up generally have good snow, and there is some great fast cruising, especially on the mainly north-facing pistes served by the chair-lifts off to the sides. You can often pick gentle or steeper terrain in these bowls as you wish, but avid piste-bashers will explore all there is to offer in a couple of days. Many visitors take the opportunity of excursions to Alpe-d'Huez and Serre-Chevalier.

Less confident intermediates will love the quality of the snow and the gentleness of most of the runs on the upper mountain. Their problem might lie in finding the pistes too crowded.

FOR BEGINNERS
Good slopes
The nursery slopes beside the village are spacious and gentle. The run along the ridge above them is excellent, too. The glacier also has a fine array of very easy slopes. But there is a lot of lift-riding to do between all this.

FOR CROSS-COUNTRY
Needs very low-altitude snow
There are small, widely dispersed areas. La Petite Alpe, near the entrance to the village, has a couple of snow-sure but very short trails. Given good snow, Venosc, reached by a gondola down, has the only worthwhile picturesque ones. Total trail distance is 25km/16 miles. You can ski the Mont de Lans glacier with a qualified guide.

QUEUES
Can be a problem
Les Deux-Alpes has some impressive lifts, but the village is large, and queues at the morning peak can be 'diabolically' long for the Jandri Express and Diable gondolas. The eight-seat chair from the mid-station to the glacier has reduced the bottleneck for the second stage. Problems can also

occur when people are bussed in because snow is in short supply elsewhere. The top lifts are prone to closure if it's windy, putting pressure on the lower lifts. We have repeated reports of queues for the gondolas back to the village when people decline to tackle the tricky blacks or the crowded green run back down.

MOUNTAIN RESTAURANTS
Still limited
There are mountain restaurants at all the major lift junctions, but they are generally pretty poor. The Diable au Coeur, opened at the top of the Diable gondola a couple of seasons ago but the Chalet de la Toura, in the middle of the domain at about 2600m/8,530ft, is still said to be 'probably the best restaurant on the mountain'. The Panoramic has been recommended again this year for its 'mouth-watering cuisine' – but 'it gets very crowded and there's no queuing system'.

SCHOOLS AND GUIDES
We are all Europeans now
A 2006 reporter 'highly recommends' Easiski who were 'very helpful and friendly'. We have a positive recent report on the tuition and organisation of the European school, composed of instructors of various nationalities, all (we are assured) speaking good English. Class sizes are small – as few as four pupils if you go for their advanced classes.

FACILITIES FOR CHILDREN
Fine for babies
Babies from six months to two years old can safely be entrusted to the village nursery. The kindergarten takes kids from two to six years, and there are chalet-based alternatives run by UK tour operators. There are also four free T-bars for children at the village level.

GETTING THERE

Air Lyon 160km/ 99 miles (3½hr); Grenoble 120km/ 75 miles (2½hr); Chambéry 126km/ 78 miles (3hr); Geneva 230km/ 143 miles (4½hr).

Rail Grenoble (70km/43 miles); four daily buses from station.

ACTIVITIES

Indoor Swimming pool, hot-tub, sauna, sports centres (Club Forme, Tanking Center), cinemas, games rooms, bowling, museum, library

Outdoor Ice rink, donkey rides, snowmobiles, helicopter flights, paragliding, quad bikes, snow-shoeing, Kanata (Inuit) village visit

Phone numbers
From abroad use the prefix +33 and omit the initial '0' of the phone number.

TOURIST OFFICE

t 0476 792200
les2alp@les2alpes.com
www.les2alpes.com

STAYING THERE

HOW TO GO
Wide range of packages
Les Deux-Alpes has something for most tastes, including that rarity in high-altitude French resorts, reasonably priced hotels.

Chalets Several UK tour operators run catered chalets but some use apartments. Mark Warner now runs what was the smartest hotel in town (the Bérangère) as a chalet-hotel (on-piste, at the less convenient north end of resort, pool, sauna, steam).

Hotels There are over 30 hotels, of which the majority are 2-star or below. There's a Club Med 'village' here, too.

⑫ **Mariande** (0476 805060) Highly recommended, especially for its 'excellent' five-course dinners. At Venosc end of resort.

⑫ **Chalet Mounier** (0476 805690) Smartly modernised. Good reputation for its food, and well placed for the Diable bubble and nightlife. Swimming pool and fitness room.

⑫ **Souleil'Or** (0476 792469) Looks like a lift station, but pleasant and comfortable, and well placed for the Jandri Express gondola. The rooms and food are reportedly 'fantastic'.

⑫ **Les Lutins** (0476 792152) Central. Reportedly the 'best value' and 'best location in the resort'.

⑫ **Brunerie** (0476 792223) 'Basic and cheerful', large 2-star with plenty of parking and quite well positioned.

SMART APARTMENTS – SEE FEATURE
Many of the apartments are stuck out at the north end of the resort – well worth avoiding. Cortina has 15 brand-new spacious apartments at the south end, with sauna, steam room and hot-tubs. Alpina Lodge is central and right by the slopes.

EATING OUT
Plenty of choice
The hotel Bérangère has an excellent restaurant and the Chalet Mounier has a high reputation. The Petite Marmite has good food and atmosphere at reasonable prices. Bel'Auberge does classic French and is 'quite superb'. The Patate, the Cloche (formerly the Dahu) and Crêpes à Gogo are also recommended. Visitors on a budget can get a relatively cheap meal at Bleuets bar, the Vetrata or the Spaghetteria. One regular visitor says that Smokey Joe's Tex-Mex is the best value for money in the resort.

APRES-SKI
Unsophisticated fun
Les Deux-Alpes is one of the liveliest of the French resorts, with plenty of bars, several of which stay open until the early hours. Smithy's is a 'massive party venue'. The Windsor bar is another noisy British enclave. Corrigans and Smokey Joe's are recommended. The Baron is said to be the haunt of inebriated teenagers. Bar Brésilien is apparently quieter than in previous years. The Avalanche is reportedly 'still the best club', and the Opéra is recommended by locals, but a recent visitor found it to be too far out of the resort. There are quieter places, too – the 'cosy, friendly' Bleuets is recommended.

The resort has contrived a couple of ways of dining at altitude – you can snowmobile to the glacier and back, eating on the way, or at full moon you can ski or board back to town after dinner (accompanied by ski patrollers).

OFF THE SLOPES
Not recommended
Les Deux-Alpes is not a particularly good choice for people not hitting the slopes. The pretty valley village of Venosc is worth a visit by gondola, and you can take a scenic helicopter flight to Alpe-d'Huez. There are lots of scenic walks and a good pool. Several mountain restaurants are accessible to pedestrians. Snowcat tours across the glacier provide wonderful views.

STAYING DOWN THE VALLEY
Worth considering
Close to the foot of the final ascent to Les Deux-Alpes are two near-ideal little hotels for anyone thinking of travelling around to Alpe-d'Huez, La Grave and Serre-Chevalier, both Logis de France – the cheerful Cassini (0476 800410) at Le Freney and the even more appealing Panoramique (0476 800625) at Mizoën – approved of by a reporter this year for 'hearty food, informative Dutch hosts' and (not least) the 'wondrous' panorama.

A 2006 reporter stayed down in Venosc – linked by a gondola that 'stops at 7pm'. There are several small villages close together here: 'Ours was Bourg d'Arud, very small and quiet, no shops. We found only one restaurant and one bar, and both were closed a lot of the time. It was a 400m uphill walk to the gondola – leave skis and boots in lockers near the slopes.'

Flaine

Uncompromisingly modern, high-altitude resort sharing a big, broad area of varied slopes with more rustic alternatives

300

COSTS

① ② ③ ④ ⑤ ⑥

RATINGS

The slopes

Fast lifts	**
Snow	****
Extent	****
Expert	****
Intermediate	*****
Beginner	*****
Convenience	*****
Queues	***
Mountain restaurants	**

The rest

Scenery	****
Resort charm	*
Off-slope	*

NEWS

A new red run, Aventurine, opened for 2005/06, connecting the blue Tourmaline and Olivine pistes. It is intended to redirect some of the crowds returning to Flaine at the end of the day.

Also, the red Faust run was further developed and snowmaking was extended to reach to the bottom of the 14km/9 mile long blue Cascades run down to Sixt.

There are plans to expand Flaine by up to 4,500 beds over the next decade. Canadian developer Intrawest has sold the first units in the Flaine Montsoleil development – read the feature panel later in the chapter for more information.

+ Big, varied area, with plenty of terrain to suit everyone

+ Reliable snow in the main bowl

+ Compact, convenient, mainly car-free village, right on the slopes

+ Excellent facilities for children

+ You can stay in traditional villages on the lower fringes of the area

+ Scenic setting, and glorious views

+ Very close to Geneva but ...

− Weekends can be busy as a result

− Austere 1960s Bauhaus buildings of Flaine itself are not easy to like

− In bad weather main Flaine bowl offers little to do, and links to outer sectors of the area may be closed

− Lots of slow old chair-lifts

− No proper hotels in Flaine itself

− Nightlife not a highlight

− Little to do off the slopes (in Flaine)

Flaine is best known as a convenient resort catering particularly well for families, but it has a much broader appeal than that. The Grand Massif may not be quite in the same league as the Three Valleys and the new Paradiski area, but in extent its slopes are almost a match for Val-d'Isère/Tignes.

Flaine's family orientation is underlined by the domination of self-catering accommodation. Its few hotels have now all been taken over by tour operators such as Club Med and Crystal. But you open up more accommodation options by considering the outlying villages – Les Carroz, Samoëns and Morillon (the last two now covered in the separate Samoëns chapter). Not only are they more attractive, rounded places to stay in, but also they offer some sheltered forest slopes for bad-weather days.

THE RESORT

The concrete Bauhaus-style blocks that form the core of Flaine were conceived in the sixties as 'an example of the application of the principle of shadow and light'. They look particularly shocking from the approach road – a mass of blocks nestling at the bottom of the impressive snowy bowl. From the slopes they are less obtrusive, blending into the rocky grey hillside. For us, the outdoor sculptures by Picasso, Vasarely and Dubuffet do little to improve Flaine's austere ambience.

The more recent development of Hameau-de-Flaine is built in a much more attractive chalet style – but is inconveniently situated 1km/0.5 miles from the slopes and main village.

In Flaine proper, everything is close by: supermarket, sports rental shops, ski schools, main lifts out etc. The resort itself is also easy to get to – only 70km/43 miles from Geneva, and about 90 minutes from the airport.

There are two parts to the main resort. The 'club' hotels – and some apartments – are set in the lower part, Forum. The focus of this area is a snow-covered square with buildings on three sides, the open fourth side blending with the slopes. Flaine Forêt, up the hillside and linked by lift, has its own bars and shops, and most of the apartment accommodation.

There are children all over the place; they are catered for with play areas, and the resort is supposed to be traffic-free. In fact, roads penetrate the village and you don't have to go far to encounter traffic; but the central Forum itself, leading to the pistes, is pretty safe.

The bus service to/from Hameau is 'excellent' but runs only to Forêt, not Forum. A car gives you the option of visiting the Portes du Soleil, Chamonix, Megève or Courmayeur (via the Mont Blanc tunnel).

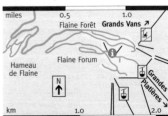

KEY FACTS

Resort	1600m
	5,250ft

Grand Massif (Flaine, Les Carroz, Morillon, Samoëns, Sixt)	
Slopes	700-2480m
	2,300-8,140ft
Lifts	78
Pistes	265km
	165 miles
Green	11%
Blue	42%
Red	36%
Black	11%
Snowmaking	
	218 guns

For Flaine only	
Slopes	1600-2480m
	5,250-8,140ft
Lifts	28
Pistes	120km
	75 miles
Green	13%
Blue	37%
Red	42%
Black	8%

THE MOUNTAINS

The Grand Massif is an impressive area, with plenty of scope for any level of skier or boarder, provided you can get to all of it – the greater part of the domain lies outside the main Flaine bowl and the links can be closed by excessive wind or snow.

THE SLOPES
A big white playground

The day begins for most people at the **Grandes Platières** jumbo gondola, which speeds you in a single stage up the north face of the Flaine bowl to the high-point of the Grand Massif, and a magnificent view of Mont Blanc.

Most of the runs are reds (though there are some blues curling away to skier's right, and one direct black). There are essentially four or five main ways down the barren, treeless, rolling terrain back to Flaine, or to chairs in the middle of the wilderness.

On the far right, the Cascades blue run leads away from the lift system behind the Tête Pelouse down to the outskirts of Sixt, dropping over 1700m/ 5,580ft vertical in its exceptional 14km/ 9 mile length. The gentle/flat top half is hard work, so we're not greatly concerned that the run isn't reliably

open – but readers seem more impressed than we are. At the end you can get buses (often crowded) to the lifts at Samoëns – the timetable is on the piste map. Or explore the slopes of Sixt – very quiet, with a non-trivial 700m/2,300ft vertical. End up at Salvagny in the middle of the slopes to get a less crowded bus.

On the other side of the Tête Pelouse, a broad catwalk leads to the experts-only **Gers** bowl. At the bottom, a flat trail links with the lower (and more interesting) half of the Cascades run or there's a drag back to the ridge.

Back at Platières, an alternative is to head left down the long red Méphisto to the **Aujon** area – again mostly red runs but with some blues further down. The lower slopes here are used as slalom courses. This sector is also reachable by gondola or drag-lifts from below the resort.

The eight-seat Grands Vans chair, reached from Forum by means of a slow bucket-lift (aka télébenne), gives access to the extensive slopes of Samoëns, Morillon and Les Carroz. You come first to the wide Vernant bowl, equipped with three fast chair-lifts. Beyond here the lie of the land is complicated. In good snow there is a choice of blues and reds winding down

LES GRANDES PLATIERES
2480m/8,140ft

Tête Pelouse   Tête des Lindars

Tête de Véret
2315m   AUJON
                                         2035m

GERS   Les Grands
1715m   Vans   Flaine
         2205m   1600m/5,250ft

Tête des Saix   Vernant
2120m

Sixt   Les Molliets

                 1900m

Samoëns Village
720m/2,360ft   LES CARROZ
                         1500m   1140m/3,740ft

                SAMOENS
                1600m

Vercland   Morillon
                  1100m
         MORILLON
         700m ↓

LIFT PASSES

Grand Massif

Prices in €

Age	1-day	6-day
under 12	25	127
12 to 15	27	140
16 to 59	35	173
over 60	27	140

Free under 5, over 75
Beginner 4 free lifts
Notes
Covers all the lifts in Flaine, Les Carroz, Morillon, Samoëns and Sixt.
Alternative passes
Flaine area only.

to **Les Carroz** or **Morillon**, the latter with a halfway point at 1100m/3,610ft. While there is a choice of blue, red and black runs on the top section above **Samoëns 1600**, the runs below here to Vercland are challenging.

Piste grooming is repeatedly commended but signing could still be improved. The piste map is rubbish – hopelessly ambitious in trying to cover such a big and complex area in a single view. In the middle of the area are several distinct bowls that are simply not detectable on the map.

TERRAIN-PARKS
Cater for kids to experts
There's a big terrain-park (called the JamPark Pro – standing for Jib and Air Maniacs) in the Aujon area of Flaine. Watch out for the 'downright dangerous' Aujon drag-lift, though, which is still as much of a challenge as the park. There's an intermediates' park under the Charionde 2 chair on the Samoëns side, with green, red and black options and a variety of rails. And there's a kids' park, JamPark Kids, with a boarder-cross run under the Esserts quad on the Morillon side.

SNOW RELIABILITY
Usually keeps its whiteness
The main part of Flaine's slopes lie on the wide north- and north-west-facing flank of the Grandes Platières. Its direction, along with a decent height, means that it keeps the snow it receives. There is snowmaking on the greater part of the Aujon sector and on the nursery slopes. The runs towards Samoëns 1600 and Morillon 1100 are north-facing too, and some lower parts have snowmaking, but below here can be tricky or closed. The Les Carroz runs are west-facing and can suffer from strong afternoon sun, but a couple of runs have snowmaking.

FOR EXPERTS
Great fun with guidance
Flaine's family-friendly reputation tends to obscure the fact that it has some seriously challenging terrain. But much

of it is off-piste and, although some of it looks like it can safely be explored without guidance, this impression is mistaken. The Flaine bowl is riddled with rock crevasses and potholes, and should be treated with the same caution that you would use on a glacier. We are told that these hazards cause deaths most years.

All the black pistes on the map deserve their grading. The Diamant Noir, down the line of the main gondola, is a challenging 850m/2,790ft descent, tricky because of moguls, narrowness and other people, rather than great steepness; the first pitch is the steepest, with spectators applauding from the chair-lift.

To skier's left of the Diamant Noir are several short but steep off-piste routes through the crags.

The Lindars Nord chair serves a shorter slope that often has the best snow in the area, and some seriously steep gradients. Mind the chair doesn't whack you as you exit.

The Gers drag-lift, outside the main bowl, serves great expert terrain. The Styx piste is a proper black, but nearby off-piste slopes reach 45°. The main Gers bowl is a great north-facing horseshoe of about 550m/1,800ft vertical, powder or moguls top to bottom, all off-piste, ranging from steep to very steep. There are more adventurous ways in from the Grands Vans and Tête de Véret lifts.

There are further serious pistes on the top lifts above Samoëns 1600.

There are some scenic off-piste routes from which you can be retrieved by helicopter – such as the Combe des Foges, next to Gers.

FOR INTERMEDIATES
Something for everyone
Flaine is ideal for confident intermediates, with a great variety of pistes (and usually the bonus of good snow conditions, at least above Flaine itself). As a reporter puts it, 'There may not be many challenging runs, but there are very few dull ones.' The diabolically named reds that dominate

boarding

Flaine suits boarders quite well – there's lots of varied terrain and plenty of off-piste with interesting nooks and crannies, including woods outside the main bowl. The key lifts are now chairs or gondolas (but beware the absurdly vicious Aujon drag-lift, which serves the terrain-park). There are two other terrain-park options, including one for kids. Black Side is the local specialist shop, in the central Forum.

Following its spectacularly successful development of Arc 1950, just below Arc 2000, Canadian developer Intrawest is moving on to Flaine. If you are on the lookout for Alpine property, or simply wanting to be aware of high-quality apartment accommodation that you might use a couple of years down the line, you'll want to know what they are up to. The Intrawest combination of comfortable accommodation and obsessively thorough and coherent design produces exceptional results, whether you look at Whistler, Squaw Valley, Mammoth Lakes or Arc 1950. And it produces results quickly: it was difficult to believe, walking around Arc 1950 in the winter of 2006, that the first apartments were occupied less than three years before, in the summer of 2003.

Close to the high point of the access road to Flaine, Intrawest now plans to build Flaine Montsoleil, a development of 500 apartments plus associated shops and restaurants, and a water leisure centre. Montsoleil will be linked by lift and piste to Flaine itself, and will be a short taxi-ride from the larger resort should you feel the need for a wider choice of après-ski activity.

The development is being planned to make the most of the panoramic, sunny site. The first development, Les Terrasses d'Eos, will be built at the resort's southern entrance. The architecture is described as 'contemporary and welcoming', using mainly wood and stone finishes – and from the drawings we have seen it does seem more modern in style than the apartments in Arc 1950. The apartments will have large windows and balconies to make the most of the sunlight and the surrounding landscape.

Facilities will include an outdoor heated swimming pool, an indoor jacuzzi next to it, a sauna/hammam fitness room and underground parking.

Part of the Intrawest formula for success is to sell its developments off-plan. Although nothing exists yet, the first 91 apartments in Flaine Montsoleil were put on sale in late June 2006, and 75 were sold in a day. So the signs are that the momentum Intrawest has established in Arc 1950 is going to be maintained. The whole development is scheduled for completion in 2012.

Flaine

SCHOOLS

ESF
t 0450 908100

International
t 0450 908441

**Moniteurs
indépendants**
t 0607 195609

François Simond
t 0450 908097

Classes (ESF prices)
6 days (3hr per day)
€120

Private lessons
€35 for 1hr, for 1 or
2 people

CHILDREN

Les P'tits Loups
t 0450 908782
Ages 6mnth to 3yr

**Rabbit Club and
Fantaski**
t 0450 908100
Ages 3 to 12; 9am-
5pm; 6 days with
lunch €215

La Souris Verte
t 0450 908441
Ages from 3

**MMV Hotels Flaine
and Aujon**
t 0492 126212
Ages 18mnth to 14yr

**Cap'Vacances les
Lindars**
t 0471 508081

Club Med Flaine
t 0450 908166
For babies aged from
4mnth

Ski school
For ages 5 to 12:
€100 for 6 days, 3hr
per day (ESF prices)

the Flaine bowl are not really as hellish as their names imply – they tend to gain their status from short steep sections rather than overall difficulty. The relatively direct Faust is great carving territory, at least in January when it isn't cluttered. There are gentler cruises from the top of the mountain – Cristal, taking you to the Perdrix chair, or Serpentine, all the way home. The blues at Aujon are excellent for confidence building, but the drag serving them is just the opposite.

The connections with the slopes outside the main bowl are classified blue but several blue-run reporters have found them tricky because of narrowness, crowds or poor snow. Once the connection has been made, however, all intermediates will enjoy the long tree-lined runs down to Les Carroz, as long as the snow is good. The Morillon slopes are also excellent intermediate terrain – the long green Marvel run to Morillon 1100 is an easy cruise with excellent signs along the way explaining (in English as well as French) the local wildlife.

Crowds on the lower slopes returning to Flaine have been a source of complaint, but the problem should be relieved to some degree by the new red Aventurine piste, allowing better skiers to go left well above the village.

FOR BEGINNERS
Fairly good
There are excellent nursery slopes right by the village, served by free lifts which make a pass unnecessary until you are ready to go higher up the mountain. The area is roped off, but it is still used as a short cut back to the village by other skiers. There are no long green runs to progress to in the Flaine bowl but there are some gentle blues over on skier's right, beneath Tête Pelouse. If you have a really nervous intermediate to deal with, it's worth driving or bussing down the access road to the green at Vernant.

CROSS-COUNTRY
Very fragmented
The Grand Massif claims 64km/40 miles of cross-country tracks but only about 17km/10 miles of that is around Flaine itself. The majority is on the valley floor and dependent on low snow. There are extensive tracks between Morillon and Les Carroz, with some tough uphill sections.

QUEUES
A few problems
Recent investment in new lifts has eliminated many trouble spots, and several reporters have had queue-free weeks, even in high season. But there can be problems when the resorts are full and at weekends (the area is very close to Geneva). Towards the end of the day expect delays at the Vernant chair to get back to the Flaine bowl (an alternative is to descend to one of the lift-bases along the access road, and catch a bus) and at Les Molliets – 'horrendous' at times, partly thanks to frequent failure of the machinery or its power supply.

Queues elsewhere can build up at weekends and when the lifts out of the Flaine bowl are shut due to high winds or when the weather is warm and the lower resorts have poor snow. (When this happens, the queues to go down can be worse than those to go up.)

MOUNTAIN RESTAURANTS
Back to base, or quit the bowl
In the Flaine bowl, there are few restaurants above the resort's upper outskirts, but a 2006 reporter commends the 'friendly and reasonable-value' self-service at Grandes Platières. The rustic Blanchot, at the bottom of the Serpentine run, has 'friendly staff' and 'excellent food', but it can get crowded. At Forum level, across the piste from the gondola, is the welcoming Michet ('definitely worth a visit'), with very good Savoyard food and table service, and the 'rustic' Eloge. Up the slope a bit, the Cascade is self-service but with a good terrace and 'very pleasant' proprietors. Epicéa has a rustic atmosphere, a terrace and has had rave reviews, but service may be stretched. Up at Forêt level, the Bissac has a good atmosphere, traditional decor and excellent food.

Outside the Flaine bowl, we love the remote Chalet du Lac de Gers (book in advance and ring for a snowcat to tow you up from the Cascades run) – simple food but splendid isolation and views of the frozen lake. We also had an excellent plat du jour at the cosy and rustic Igloo above Morillon, but service gets overstretched. This year, the 'hearty portions' at the self-service Telemark in that sector have been recommended. The 'outstanding food' at the rustic Chalet les Molliets near the bottom of the Molliets chair receives praise again this year.

↑ Forum is quite some way below Forêt (there's a lift between the two parts of the resort)

OT FLAINE / PHOTOZOOM

SCHOOLS AND GUIDES
Getting better
We've had few reports recently on the ESF. A 2006 reporter found private lessons with the International school a 'hit or miss' affair, and was not at all impressed with one instructor's 'disappearance' before the end of his children's lesson. The small Super Ski has 'small classes, good instruction'.

FACILITIES FOR CHILDREN
Parents' paradise?
Flaine prides itself on being a family resort, and the number of English-speaking children around is a bonus. There are some free children's lift passes available in low season weeks.

Crystal's 'well organised and popular' hotel Le Totem has good childcare facilities for residents only.

STAYING THERE

HOW TO GO
Plenty of apartments
Accommodation is overwhelmingly in self-catering apartments.
Chalets There are few catered chalet options, but they include a couple of Scandinavian-style huts in Hameau.

GETTING THERE
Air Geneva 90km/ 56 miles (1½hr).

Rail Cluses (30km/ 19 miles); regular bus service.

The 'excellent food, friendly staff, good rooms' and childcare facilities of Crystal's Totem club-hotel continue to impress reporters.
Hotels All the hotels are now run by tour operators. B&B is available at the Cascade restaurant.
Self-catering The best apartments are out at Hameau – ' fabulous' says one reporter this year. In Flaine Forêt, the Forêt and Grand Massif apartment buildings are attractively woody.

EATING OUT
Enough choice for a week
A 2006 reporter enjoyed the 'lovely local specialities' in the 'rather cramped' pizzeria Chez Pierrot. The Perdrix Noire in Forêt is good but not cheap. Chez Daniel offers a good range of Savoyard specialities, and is good with kids. The 'lively' Brasserie les Cîmes is recommended for 'very good local food, good prices, very friendly service'. A couple of places close to the village and described under 'Mountain restaurants' are open in the evening – the Michet and the Bissac. The Ancolie in Hameau is said to be worth the trip for its 'great food' and 'beautiful wooden chalet interior'.

Hôtel Le Bois de la Char

Your stay right on the pistes

Les Carroz-d'Arâches
40 minutes from Geneva Airport
10 minutes from highway A40

Tel: 00 33 (0) 4 50 90 06 18
E-mail: contact@hotel-boisdelachar.com
Website: www.hotel-boisdelachar.com

Photo credit: PHOTOTEM – Claude Monvoisin

ACTIVITIES

Indoor Swimming pool, sauna, solarium, gymnasium, massage, bowling, cinema, billiards, climbing wall, cultural centre with art gallery and library

Outdoor Ice rink, snowshoe excursions, dog-sledding, paragliding, helicopter rides, snow scooters, quad bikes, ice-driving

OUR WEBSITE

Go to our website at wtss.co.uk for resort news, links to resort sites, a build-your-own resort shortlist system and reader forums.

Phone numbers
From abroad use the prefix +33 and omit the initial '0' of the phone number.

TOURIST OFFICES

Flaine
t 0450 908001
welcome@flaine.com
www.flaine.com

Les Carroz
t 0450 900004
info@lescarroz.com
www.lescarroz.com

APRES-SKI
Signs of life
You can eat and drink into the early hours here if you move around a bit – but you don't have much choice of venue. The White pub has a big screen TV, rock music and punters trying to get pints in before the end of happy hour. The Flying Dutchman is 'very lively 5-7pm, very friendly, tends to wind down around 11'. The bar at the bowling alley has a 'family atmosphere earlier on, turns into a pub after 11' and is 'the only place still serving food until 3am'. The Cubain is Flaine's only nightclub, but the drinks are 'very expensive' and the 'music not up to much'. The 'very French' Diamant Noir pool hall is open late and sometimes has 'good live music'.

OFF THE SLOPES
Curse of the purpose-built
Flaine is not recommended for people who don't want to hit the slopes. But there is a great ice-driving circuit where you can take a spin (literally) in your car or theirs. Snowmobiling and dog-sledding are popular, and there's a cinema, gymnasium and swimming pool. Save your souvenir shopping in the few shops in Forum for the one evening a week when there is a free hands-on display of large wooden games, enjoyed by visitors of all ages.

Les Carroz 1140m/3,740ft

This is a sprawling, sunny, traditional, family resort where life revolves around the village square with its pavement cafes, restaurants and

interesting little shops. It is a sizeable place – much bigger than Flaine, in fact – that has a lived-in feel of a real French village, with more animation than Flaine, at least in the afternoon – 'a delight' says a recent visitor. But a thorough report last year confirmed that the après-ski scene doesn't amount to much: the Marlow pub is popular at close of play but soon becomes quiet; Pointe Noire, next-door, is cheaper and more animated; Carpe Diem is devoid of customers until the other places close.

Last year we had a rave review of the Brit-run hotel Belles Pistes (0450 900017) – 'ideal: staff A1, food good, close to lifts'. A 2006 reporter backs up his recommendation of the 'well-managed, perfectly situated, excellent value' Bois de la Char (0450 900618), noting 'an improvement in the restaurant'. The hotel Arbaron (0450 900267) has been commended for food, views and airport transfers.

SMART APARTMENTS – SEE FEATURE
Les Fermes du Soleil is an MGM development of five chalet-style buildings, with comfortable apartments and a good pool, jacuzzi and sauna.

The recently upgraded gondola starts a steep 300m/1,000ft walk up from the centre – the nursery drag is a help or you can catch the free ski-bus. It serves some excellent slopes in the woods above the village, as well as launching you off into the Grand Massif, so this is a great place to be on a bad-weather day.

The ski school's torchlit descent is 'not to be missed' – ending with vin chaud and live jazz in the square.

Les Gets

Friendly village with a very French feel to it and two local areas of slopes. But not a good base for the main Portes du Soleil circuit

COSTS

①②③④⑤⑥

RATINGS

The slopes

Fast lifts	**
Snow	**
Extent	***
Expert	***
Intermediate	****
Beginner	****
Convenience	***
Queues	***
Mountain restaurants	***

The rest

Scenery	***
Resort charm	***
Off-slope	***

Extent rating
This relates only to the Les Gets/Morzine slopes, not the whole Portes du Soleil.

Piste map
The whole local area is covered by the map in the Morzine chapter.

NEWS

For 2006/07 a new bus service is planned to link Les Gets, Morzine, St Jean-d'Aulps and Avoriaz. And a new mountain restaurant called Grande Ourse is due to open at the top of the terrain-park on Mont Chéry. Pedestrians are to be given priority on Rue du Centre in town.

For 2005/06 the terrain park and boarder-cross were relaid together and new features added. Two new pistes were built on the Grand Cry children's play area on Chavannes. More snowmaking was installed and several pistes were widened.

➕ Good-sized, varied local piste area shared with slightly lower Morzine – plus excellent, neglected Mont Chéry

➕ Attractive chalet-style village, with through-traffic kept on fringes

➕ Relatively short drive from the UK

➕ Few queues locally

➕ Part of the vast Portes du Soleil ski pass region, but ...

➖ To get to Avoriaz and the main Portes du Soleil circuit is a real slog, unless you drive to Ardent

➖ Modest altitude means there is always a risk of poor snow, though increased snowmaking has helped

➖ Few challenging pistes

➖ Too many slow, old chairs

➖ Weekend crowds

The area that Les Gets shares with Morzine offers the most extensive slopes in the Portes du Soleil, and in some respects Les Gets is the better base for them. But if the main Portes du Soleil circuit is a priority, stay closer to it.

THE RESORT

Les Gets is an attractive, sunny, much-expanded village of traditional chalet-style buildings, on the low pass leading from the A40 autoroute at Cluses to Morzine. The main road bypasses the village centre, which is partly car-free with more pedestrianisation planned for this season and has plenty of attractive food and other shops and restaurants lining the main street. There's also a popular outdoor ice rink, which adds to the charm. It's good for families.

Although the village has a scattered appearance, most facilities are close to the main lift station – and the free 'petit train' road-train shuttle is a cute way of travelling around. The village is fairly quiet in the evenings but gets busier and livelier at weekends.

THE MOUNTAINS

Les Gets is not an ideal base for the Portes du Soleil, but its local slopes are extensive. The local pass saves a fair bit on a Portes du Soleil pass, and makes a lot of sense for many visitors.
Slopes The main local slopes – accessed by a gondola and fast chair-lift from the nursery slopes beside the village – are shared with Morzine, and are mainly described in that chapter. On the opposite side of Les Gets is Mont Chéry, accessed by a gondola and parallel chair. The slopes include some of the most challenging in the area, and are usually very quiet. Both sectors offer wooded and open slopes.

Snow reliability The nursery slopes benefit from a slightly higher elevation than Morzine, but otherwise our general reservations about the lack of altitude apply. A lot more snow-guns have improved runs to the resort. The front slopes of Mont Chéry face south-east – bad news at this altitude; but grooming is good, and the other two flanks are shadier. On our January 2005 visit, when snow was sparse, we found the Les Gets pistes much better than in the higher Three Valleys resorts and Avoriaz (largely because the grassy slopes need less snow cover) and better than in neighbouring Morzine.
Terrain-parks There's a park on the upper slopes of Mont Chéry with kickers, hip jumps, a gap jump, quarter-pipes and a boarder-cross.
Experts Black runs on the flank and back of Mont Chéry chair are quite steep and often bumped. In good snow there is plenty to do off-piste, including some excellent wooded areas.
Intermediates High-mileage piste-bashers might prefer direct access to the main Portes du Soleil circuit, but the local slopes have a lot to offer – including excellent reds on Mont Chéry.
Beginners The village nursery slopes are convenient, and there are better, more snow-sure ones up at Chavannes, with plenty of easy runs to progress to.
Snowboarding The local slopes are good for beginners and intermediates.
Cross-country There are 18km/11 miles of good, varied loops on Mont Chéry and Les Chavannes.
Queues See the Morzine chapter for general observations. Mont Chéry is

307

KEY FACTS

Resort	1170m
	3,840ft

Portes du Soleil	
Slopes	950-2300m
	3,120-7,550ft
Lifts	209
Pistes	650km
	404 miles
Green	14%
Blue	39%
Red	37%
Black	10%
Snowmaking	
	577 guns

Morzine-Les Gets only	
Slopes	1000-2010m
	3,280-6,590ft
Lifts	48
Pistes	110km
	68 miles

OUR WEBSITE

Go to our website at wtss.co.uk for resort news, links to resort sites, a build-your-own-shortlist system and reader forums.

Phone numbers
From abroad use the prefix +33 and omit the initial '0' of the phone number.

TOURIST OFFICE

t 0450 758080
lesgets@lesgets.com
www.lesgets.com

OT LES GETS / PIERRE WITT

Les Gets has grown into quite a large village but remains attractive and has a very French 'feel' to it, unlike many more 'international' resorts
→

crowd-free. But there are still a lot of slow, old chairs.

Mountain restaurants See Morzine.

Schools and guides Our latest reports of the ESF are mixed. A 2005 reporter says Ecole International's private lessons 'brought me on'. The 'good but pricey' British Alpine Ski & Snowboard School has a branch here.

Facilities for children There are comprehensive resort facilities. Family-specialist tour operator Esprit Ski is moving in here from 2006/07 and Ski Famille and Ski Hillwood are also family specialists. The British-run Snowkidz nursery takes babies as well as infant skiers, and is reported to be 'superb – absolutely faultless'.

STAYING THERE

How to go Several tour operators have catered chalets; we've had good reports of Total's operation.

Hotels We stayed at the Ferme de Montagne (0450 753679) in 2005 and loved it (see the luxury chalets chapter – but it's as much a small hotel as a chalet). It is a beautifully renovated

farmhouse with eight luxury bedrooms, gourmet food, ski guiding, sauna, outdoor hot-tub, brilliant massage therapist (try the hot stones); on the edge of town at La Turche. The Crychar (0450 758050), 100m/330ft from central Les Gets at the foot of the slopes, is one of the best 3-star hotels ('first rate, ideal location, great restaurant' said a 2006 reporter). The 2-star Alpen Sports (0450 758055) is a friendly, family-run hotel ('Excellent food and good value for money,' says a reporter; 'Soundproofing and room size not good,' says another). We've had good reports of the Nagano (0450 797146), the Marmotte (0450 758033) – 'great maître d'; large, warm pool' – and the Alpages (0450 758088) – 'friendly, good heated outdoor pool' – all 3-star.

Self-catering The central Sabaudia apartments have a pool and hot-tub.

Eating out The Ferme de Montagne (see Hotels) has wonderful food, beautifully presented in a splendid renovated wooden dining room. The Tyrol and the Schuss are good for pizza, the rustic Vieux Chêne for Savoyard specialities. The Flambeau, Tanière and Tourbillon have been recommended.

Après-ski Après-ski is quiet, especially on weekdays. The Irish Pub, Canadian Bar above it, Boomerang, Copeaux and the Bush (Scottish owned and with Sky Sports) are recommended by reporters. The Igloo is a popular disco.

Off the slopes There's a well-equipped fitness centre with a pool, and an artificial ice rink. The Mechanical Music Museum is strongly recommended by a reporter (barrel organs and music boxes, for example, with guided tours in English). There's a cinema; husky rides and snow-shoeing are possible. There is a good selection of shops and visits to Geneva, Lausanne and Montreux are feasible.

La Grave

A world apart: an unspoiled mountain village beneath high, untamed off-piste slopes, some of them extreme and very hazardous

➕ Legendary off-piste mountain

➕ Usually crowd-free

➕ Usually good snow conditions

➕ Link to Les Deux-Alpes

➕ Easy access by car to other nearby resorts

➖ Rather dour village

➖ Poor weather means lift closures – on average, two days per week

➖ Suitable for experts only, despite some easy slopes at altitude

➖ Nothing to do off the slopes

La Grave enjoys legendary status among experts. It's a quiet old village with around 500 visitor beds and just one serious lift – a small stop-start gondola serving a high, wild and almost entirely off-piste mountainside. The result: an exciting, usually crowd-free area. Strictly, you ought to have a guide, but in good weather many people go it alone.

THE RESORT

La Grave is a small, unspoiled mountaineering village set on a steep hillside facing the impressive glaciers of majestic La Meije. It's rather drab, and the busy road through to Briançon doesn't help. But it has a rustic feel, some welcoming hotels, friendly inhabitants and prices that are low by resort standards. The single serious lift starts just below the centre. Storms close the slopes on average two days a week – so a car is useful for access to nearby resorts.

THE MOUNTAIN

A slow two-stage 'pulse' gondola (with an extra station at a pylon halfway up the lower stage) ascends into the slopes and finishes at 3200m/10,500ft. Above that, a short walk and a drag-lift give access to a second drag serving twin blue runs on a glacier slope of about 350m/1,150ft vertical – from here you can ski to Les Deux-Alpes. But the reason that people come here is to explore the legendary slopes back towards La Grave. These slopes offer no defined, patrolled, avalanche-protected pistes – but there are two marked itinéraires (with several variations now indicated on the 'piste' map) of 1400m/4,590ft vertical down to the pylon lift station at 1800m/5,910ft, or all the way down to the valley – a vertical of 2150m/7,050ft.

Slopes The Chancel route is mostly of red-run gradient; the Vallons de la Meije is more challenging but not too steep. People do take these routes

KEY FACTS

Resort	1450m
	4,760ft
Slopes	1450-3550m
	4,760-11,650ft
Lifts	4
Pistes	5km
	3 miles
Green/Blue	100%

The figures above relate only to pistes; practically all the skiing – at least 90% – is off-piste

Snowmaking	none

OUR WEBSITE

Go to our website at wtss.co.uk for resort news, links to resort sites, a build-your-own resort shortlist system and reader forums.

Phone numbers From abroad use the prefix +33 and omit the initial '0' of the phone number.

TOURIST OFFICE

t 0476 799005
ot@lagrave-lameije.com
www.lagrave-lameije.com

without a guide or avalanche protection equipment, but we couldn't possibly recommend it.

There are many more demanding runs away from the itinéraires, including couloirs that range from the straightforward to the seriously hazardous, and long descents from the glacier to the valley road below the village, with return by taxi, bus, or strategically parked car. The dangers are considerable (people die here every year), and good guidance is essential. You can also descend southwards to St-Christophe, returning by bus and the lifts of Les Deux-Alpes.

Terrain-parks There aren't any.

Snow reliability The chances of powder snow on the high, north-facing slopes are good, but if conditions are tricky there are no pistes to fall back on apart from the three short blue runs at the top of the gondola.

Experts La Grave's uncrowded off-piste slopes have earned it cult status among hard-core skiers. Only experts should contemplate a stay here – and then only if prepared to deal with bad weather by sitting tight or struggling over the Col du Lautaret to the woods of Serre-Chevalier.

Intermediates The itinéraires get tracked into a piste-like state, and adventurous intermediates could tackle the Chancel. But the three blue runs at the top of the gondola won't keep

anyone occupied for long. The valley stations of Villar d'Arène and Lautaret, around 3km/2 miles and 8km/5 miles to the east respectively, and Chazelet, 3km/2 miles to the north-west, offer very limited slopes with a handful of intermediate and beginner runs.

Beginners Novices tricked into coming here can go up the valley to the beginner slopes at Le Chazelet, which has two cannons for snowmaking.

Snowboarding There are no special facilities for boarders, but advanced free-riders will be in their element on the open off-piste powder.

Cross-country There is a total of 20km/12 miles of loops in the area.

Queues Normally, there are short queues only at weekends. If snow conditions back to the valley are poor, queues can build up for the gondola down from the mid and lower stations.

Mountain restaurants Surprisingly, there are three decent mountain restaurants; the best is the refuge on the Chancel itinéraire. A 2005 reporter enjoyed the food at the Haut-Dessus, at the top, 'particularly the pizzas'.

Schools and guides There are a dozen or so guides in the village, offering a wide range of services through their bureau. See also Hotels below.

Facilities for children Babysitting can be arranged through the tourist office.

STAYING THERE

How to go There are a few simple hotels.

Hotels The Edelweiss (0476 799093) is a friendly 2-star with 'comfortable rooms and a phenomenal wine list' as well as a cosy bar and restaurant. The long-established Skiers Lodge operation – all-inclusive week-long packages, including guiding – has moved into the old hotel des Alpes in the centre of the village (reservations 0450 533119). A 2005 visitor had an 'excellent' week, advising that 'you need to get really fit beforehand'.

Self-catering Bookable through the tourist office.

Eating out Most people eat in their hotels, though there are alternatives.

Après-ski The standard tea-time après-ski gathering place is the central Glaciers bar, known to habitués as chez Marcel. The Vieux Guide gets crowded later. The Vallons and Bois des Fées are two other possibilities.

Off the slopes Anyone not using the slopes will find La Grave much too small and quiet.

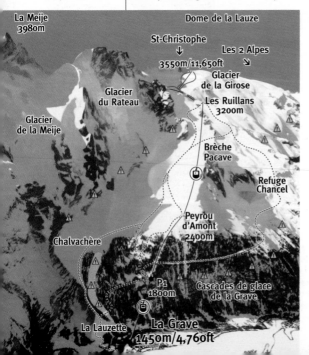

Megève

One of the traditional old winter holiday towns; best for those who enjoy relaxed cruising among splendid scenery

COSTS

① ② ③ ④ ⑤ ⑥

RATINGS

The slopes

Fast lifts	*
Snow	**
Extent	*****
Expert	**
Intermediate	****
Beginner	***
Convenience	**
Queues	****
Mountain restaurants	****

The rest

Scenery	*****
Resort charm	****
Off-slope	****

NEWS

For 2005/06 the Alpette double chair on Rochebrune was replaced by a fast six-pack. More snowmaking is planned for the Rochebrune/Alpette area for this season.

We are told that there are medium-term plans to link Praz-sur-Arly to Megève.

➕ Extensive easy slopes

➕ Scenic setting, with splendid views

➕ Charming old village centre, with very swanky shopping

➕ Some lovely luxury hotels

➕ Both gourmet and simple mountain lunches in attractive surroundings

➕ Excellent cross-country trails

➕ Great for weekends

➕ Great when it snows – woodland runs with no one on them

➕ Plenty to do off the slopes

➖ With most of the slopes below 2000m/6,560ft there's a risk of poor snow – although the grassy terrain does not need a thick covering, and snowmaking has improved a lot

➖ Lots of slow, old lifts remain – a real irritant to mileage-hungry skiers

➖ Three separate mountains, two linked by lift but not by piste, and the third not linked at all

➖ Not many challenging pistes – though there is good off-piste

➖ Very muted après-ski scene

Megève is the essence of rustic chic. It has a medieval heart but it was, in a way, the original purpose-built French ski resort – developed in the 1920s as an alternative to St Moritz. And, although Courchevel took over as France's swank resort ages ago, Megève's smart hotels and chalets still attract 'beautiful people' with fur coats and fat wallets. Happily, you don't need either to enjoy it. And it is enjoyable – the list of plus points above is as long as they come.

The risk of poor snow still makes us wary of low resorts like this. But it is true that a few inches of snow is enough to give skiable cover on the grassy slopes, and when a storm socks in this is a great place to be, as we have confirmed more than once in recent years.

The resort's managers can't do much about the altitude. What they could do, though, is drag the lift system into this century. Only one in seven of the area's lifts is fast, putting Megève close to the bottom of our fast lifts league table. For such an affluent resort, the lack of investment is disgraceful.

THE RESORT

Megève is in a lovely sunny setting and has a beautifully preserved, traditional, partly medieval centre, which is pedestrianised and comes complete with open-air ice rink, horse-drawn sleighs, cobbled streets and a fine church. Lots of smart clothing, jewellery, antique, gift and food shops add to the chic atmosphere.

The main Albertville-Chamonix road bypasses the centre, and there are expensive underground car parks. But the resort's clientele arrives mainly by car and the resulting traffic jams and fumes are a major problem. It's worst at weekends, but can be serious every afternoon in high season.

The clientele are mainly well-heeled French couples and families, who come here as much for an all-round winter holiday as for the slopes themselves.

What they don't come for is après-ski action. The tea-time atmosphere is muted, and later on the nightlife is smart rather than lively.

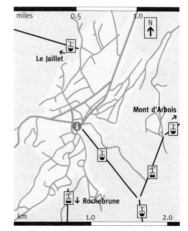

KEY FACTS

Megève only	
Resort	1100m
	3,610ft
Slopes	850-2355m
	2,790-7,730ft
Lifts	89
Pistes	325km
	202 miles
Green	17%
Blue	30%
Red	40%
Black	13%
Snowmaking	
	445 guns

A gondola within walking distance of central Megève gives direct access to one of the three mountains, Rochebrune. This sector can also be reached directly by a cable-car from the southern edge of town. The main lifts for the bigger Mont d'Arbois sector start from an elevated suburb of the resort – though there is also a cable-car link from Rochebrune. The third sector, Le Jaillet, starts some way out on the north-west fringes of the town.

Staying close to one of the main lifts makes a lot of sense. Some accommodation is a long walk from the lifts, and the half-hearted free bus services are a source of complaints, although a first-time visitor this year armed with a timetable from the tourist office found it reliable. There are several alternative bases (which offer some good-value lodging) on the fringes of the area. St-Gervais and Le Bettex above it have gondola access (St-Gervais is described at the end of this chapter). But beware slow access lifts from otherwise attractive spots such as St-Nicolas and Combloux. The most recently linked village, La Giettaz, is out on a limb but offers interesting local terrain.

The standard weekly lift pass covers Les Contamines, and the Mont Blanc pass also covers Chamonix and Courmayeur, reached through the Mont Blanc road tunnel. A car is handy for visiting these resorts.

THE MOUNTAINS

The three different mountains provide predominantly easy intermediate cruising, much of it prettily set in the woods and with some spectacular views. The wooded slopes make it a great resort to head for in poor weather. Some reporters complain that the piste grading is inconsistent. Signposting is poor, not helped by an imprecise piste map.

THE SLOPES
Pretty but low
The biggest, highest and most varied sector is **Mont d'Arbois**, accessible not only from the town but also by a gondola from La Princesse, way out to the north-east of town, with extensive free car parking. It offers some wooded slopes but is mainly open.

The slopes above the resort are sunny, but there are north-east-facing slopes to Le Bettex and on down to St-Gervais. A two-stage gondola returns you to the top. You can work your way over to Mont Joux and up to the small Mont Joly area – Megève's highest slopes. And from there you can descend to the backwater village of St-Nicolas-de-Véroce (there's a splendid red run along the ridge with spectacular views of Mont Blanc); tediously slow chair-lifts bring you back to Mont Joux.

From the Mont d'Arbois lift base,

You can see why we give Megève five stars for scenery. This view of Mont Blanc was taken from the Mont Joux area →

LIFT PASSES

Evasion Mont Blanc

Prices in €

Age	1-day	6-day
under 15	26	127
15 to 59	33	159
over 60	30	143

Free under 5, over 80

Beginner no deals

Notes
Covers lifts at Les Contamines as well as Megève.

Alternative passes
Day and half-day passes for Megève only; weekly Mont Blanc passes (all resorts in the Mont Blanc area plus Courmayeur in Italy); Jaillet-Combloux-Giettaz pass (Le Jaillet, Christomet, la Giettaz and Combloux); pedestrian pass for Megève.

the Rocharbois cable-car goes across the valley to **Rochebrune**. Alpette is the starting point for Megève's historic downhill course, now revived as an off-piste route, and narrow enough to be quite tricky. A network of gentle, wooded, north-east-facing slopes, served by drags and mainly slow chair-lifts, lead across to the high-point of Côte 2000, which often has the best snow in Megève.

The third area is **Le Jaillet**, accessed by gondola from just outside the north-west edge of town, or from Combloux, linked by a series of long, gentle tree-lined runs. In the other direction is the high-point of Le Christomet, which is now linked to the slopes of **Le Torraz**, above La Giettaz, a tiny resort half-way to La Clusaz. As part of the development, a very welcome fast chair-lift was installed on Le Christomet. The slopes of La Torraz are worth visiting, not least for the spectacular views from the summit, but the link is a bit of a mess – and can involve miles of skating and poling, depending on snow conditions, plus an awkward bit of narrow steep stuff.

TERRAIN-PARKS
Music to motivate
There is a 320m/1,050ft slope on Mont Joux with a half-pipe, quarter-pipe, pyramid and a section of challenging moguls. A sound system at the bottom helps to motivate the faint-hearted. And there's a small park, Snowtap – on the upper slopes at Combloux.

SNOW RELIABILITY
The area's main weakness
The problem is that the slopes are low, with very few runs above 2000m/6,560ft, and partly sunny – the Megève side of Mont d'Arbois gets the afternoon sun. So in a poor snow year, or in a warm spell, snow on the lower slopes can suffer badly.

Fortunately, the grassy slopes don't need much depth of snow. And the resort has an extensive snowmaking network (some runs are now entirely covered, including the long red Olympique run at Rochebrune) but that can't work in warm weather. There is also a high standard of piste grooming.

FOR EXPERTS
Off-piste is the main attraction
One of Megève's great advantages for expert skiers is that there is not much competition for the powder – you can

often make first tracks on challenging slopes many days after a fresh dump.

The Mont Joly and Mont Joux sections offer the steepest slopes. The top chair here serves a genuinely black run, and the slightly lower Epaule chair has some steep runs back down and also accesses some good off-piste, as well as pistes, down to St-Nicolas.

The steep area beneath the second stage of the Princesse gondola can be a play area of powder runs among the trees. Cote 2000 has a small section of steep runs, including good off-piste.

The terrain under the Christomet chair could be a good spot to practise off-piste technique, given decent snow.

FOR INTERMEDIATES
Superb if the snow is good
Good intermediates will enjoy the whole area – there is so much choice it's difficult to single out any particular sectors. Keen skiers are likely to want to focus on the fast lifts, and happily several of these serve excellent terrain – the Princesse and Bettex gondolas on Mont d'Arbois, the Fontaine and Alpette chairs on Rochebrune and the Christomet chair in the Le Jaillet sector. But don't confine yourself to those – there are lots of other interesting areas, including the shady north-east-facing slopes on the back of Mont d'Arbois and Mont Joux and the front of Rochebrune, and the genuinely red/black slopes of La Giettaz.

It's a great area for the less confident. A number of comfortable

Megève

313

SCHOOLS

ESF
t 0450 210097

International
t 0450 587888

Freeride
t 0450 930352

Summits
t 0450 933521

Classes (ESF prices)
5 mornings (2½hr)
€133

Private lessons
€37 for 1hr, for 1 or
2 people

GUIDES

Compagnie des Guides
t 0450 215511

boarding

Boarding doesn't really fit with Megève's traditional, rather staid, upmarket image. But free-riders will find lots of untracked off-piste powder for days after new snowfalls. It's a good place to try boarding for the first time, with plenty of fairly wide, quiet, gentle runs and a lot of chair-lifts and gondolas; though there are a fair number of drag-lifts, they are generally avoidable. There are no specialist snowboard schools, but all the ski schools offer boarding lessons. There's a terrain-park on Mont Joux and a smaller one above Combloux.

runs lead down to Le Bettex and La Princesse from Mont d'Arbois, while nearby Mont Joux accesses long, problem-free runs to St-Nicolas. Alpette and Cote 2000 are also suitable.

Even the timid can get a great deal of mileage in. All main access lifts have easy routes down to them (there is now a blue down the Princesse gondola). There are some particularly good, long, gentle cruises between Mont Joux and Megève via Mont d'Arbois. But in all sectors you'll find long, easy blue runs.

FOR BEGINNERS
Good choice of nursery areas

There are beginner slopes at valley level, and more snow-sure ones at altitude on each of the main mountains. There are also plenty of very easy longer green runs to progress to – one reporter favoured those at Combloux.

FOR CROSS-COUNTRY
An excellent area

There are 43km/27 miles of varied trails spread throughout the area. Some are at altitude (1300m–1550m/ 4,270ft–5,090ft), making lunchtime meetings with Alpine skiers simple.

QUEUES
Few weekday problems

Megève is relatively queue-free during the week, except at peak holiday time. But school holidays and sunny Sunday crowds can mean some delays. The Lanchettes drag between Cote 2000 and the rest of the Rochebrune slopes gets busy ('ridiculously long waits', writes a 2005 visitor) – as does the cable-car linking the two mountains. Crowded pistes at Mont Joux and Mont d'Arbois can also be a problem. But out of peak season, slow lifts and breakdowns (eg of the gondola from St Gervais) provoke more complaints than queues or crowds. And on a snowy day (especially in January), the slopes can be delightfully quiet as the pampered clientele stay in bed.

MOUNTAIN RESTAURANTS
Something for all budgets

Megève has some chic, expensive, gourmet mountain huts but plenty of cheaper options too. Booking ahead is advisable for table-service places.

The Mont d'Arbois area is very well endowed with restaurants. There are two suave places popular with poseurs with small dogs and fur coats – the Club House and the Idéal 1850. The Mont d'Arbois self-service has a varied menu. Chalet des Princesses (formerly Chez Tartine) is 'beautifully located' half-way down the Princesse gondola. The Ravière, tucked away in the woods near La Croix chair, is a tiny rustic hut that does a set meal and where booking is essential. The Igloo, 'quiet but expensive', with wonderful views of Mont Blanc, has both self- and table-service sections. At the base of the Mont Joux lift, Chez Marie du Rosay is recommended.

Prices are lower on the back side of the hill. The hut at the bottom of the Mont Rosset chair offers 'great food' and 'friendly staff', say recent reporters. Above St-Nicolas are several little chalets offering great charm and good food and views at modest prices.

Our favourite on Rochebrune is Alpette, atop the ridge – excellent all-round views outside, a good atmosphere inside, friendly people, good food. At the foot of the Cote 2000 slopes is the popular Auberge de la Cote 2000, a former farm ('We went in for a drink and staggered out three hours and five courses later,' writes a reporter); Radaz, up the slope a little, enjoys better views but can get busy. A reporter enjoyed his Christmas Day lunch at the Super Megève. And Chalet Forestier is a 'cosy' retreat.

On Le Jaillet the Auberge du Christomet is highly rated for its 'plats du jour' and 'touches of real originality' about the food. It is also accessible to walkers, and gets booked out. We hear the Face au Mont Blanc at the top of the gondola does a great

This is the one of Megève's many good mountain huts: the Auberge du Christomet on the back of Le Jaillet →

SNOWPIX.COM / CHRIS GILL

CHILDREN

Meg'Accueil
t 0450 587784
Ages 18mnth to 12yr
Club des Piou-Piou
t 0450 589765
Ages 3 and 4
La Princesse
t 0450 930086
Ages from 2½

Ski schools
The schools run classes for ages from 3 or 4 (ESF prices: 5 mornings €97 for ages 3 and 4, €117 for ages 5 to 12).

GETTING THERE

Air Geneva 70km/ 43 miles (1hr); Lyon 180km/112 miles (2½hr).

Rail Sallanches (12km/7 miles); regular buses from station.

fixed-price buffet. A 2006 visitor found the Auberge de Bonjournal on the link to La Giettaz was 'well placed, well priced and excellent'.

SCHOOLS AND GUIDES
Several good options
The International school has traditionally been more popular with readers than the ESF, but we have several reports of successful private lessons with the ESF. Both main schools offer expeditions to the Vallée Blanche and heli-skiing (in Italy), as well as normal teaching. Individual guides are available. We had a great morning powder skiing in the trees with Alex Périnet (06 8542 8339).

FACILITIES FOR CHILDREN
Language problems
The kindergartens offer a wide range of activities. But lack of English-speaking staff could be a drawback. The slopes are family-friendly and the schools rated by reporters (see above). There's a snow garden at Le Bettex.

STAYING THERE

HOW TO GO
Few packages
Relatively few British tour operators go to Megève, but there is an impressive range of accommodation.
Chalets A few UK tour operators offer catered chalets. For a cheap and very cheerful base, you won't do better than Stanford's Sylvana – a creaky, unpretentious old hotel, reachable on skis, run along chalet lines.
Hotels Megève offers a range of exceptionally stylish and welcoming

hotels, and there are simpler places, too.
((((4) **Mont Blanc** (0450 212002) Megève's traditional leading hotel – elegant, fashionable, central.
(((4) **Chalet du Mont d'Arbois** (0450 212503) Prettily decorated Relais & Châteaux hotel in a secluded position near the Mont d'Arbois gondola.
((((4) **Fer à Cheval** (0450 213039) Rustic-chic at its best, with a warmly welcoming wood-and-stone interior and excellent food. Close to the centre. 'A memorable stay,' writes a reporter.
(((3) **The Prairie** (0450 214855) Central, 'reasonably priced' B&B. Close to the Chamois lift.
(((3) **Coin du Feu** (0450 210494) 'Very well managed' chalet midway between Rochebrune and Chamois lifts.
(((3) **Grange d'Arly** (0450 587788) Quite close to the centre and the bus station. A beautifully furnished chalet: 'excellent' said a 2006 reporter.
(((3) **Ferme Hôtel Duvillard** (0450 211462) Smartly restored farmhouse, perfectly positioned for the slopes, at the foot of the Mont d'Arbois gondola.
((2) **Sévigné** (0450 212309) Ten minutes from the centre, but 'really delightful – very quaint, excellent food'.
Self-catering There are some very comfortable and well-positioned apartments – not cheap. Prices are lower in Combloux.

EATING OUT
Very French
Lots of upmarket restaurants – many recommended in the gastro guides. The multi-starred Ferme de Mon Père and the restaurants in all the best hotels are excellent but very pricey.

The fashionable Cintra, also expensive, is 'great for fresh seafood'.

The Brasserie Centrale 'serves almost anything you ask for', says an impressed reporter. The Flocons de Sel is recommended for its 'excellent service'. The Prieuré is 'highly recommended – lots of atmosphere, excellent food, good value', as is the Bistrot ('great salads and pizzas'). The Delicium is also popular.

Some reporters wish there was more variety, while others say that you get this and lower prices too in the centres outside Megève. This is true 'especially in Combloux', says a 2006 reporter.

APRES-SKI
Strolling and jazz
Megève is a pleasant place to stroll around after the lifts close, but exciting it isn't. If there are atmospheric bars for a post-piste beer, they have eluded us. And those looking for loud disco-bars later on will also be disappointed. Our favourite place was the Club de Jazz (aka the 5 Rues) – a very popular, if rather expensive, jazz club-cum-cocktail bar, that gets some big-name musicians and opens from tea-time to late. But a change of management did not impress a 2005 reporter: 'It's cold, impersonal, and the pure jazz seems to have given way to more rock and roll.' The Cocoon is popular with Brits, and the Wake-Up attracts seasonaires. The casino is more slot machines than blackjack tables.

OFF THE SLOPES
Lots to do
There is a 'fantastic' sports centre with pool, an outdoor ice rink, three cinemas and a weekly market. Trips to Annecy and Chamonix are possible. Walks are excellent, with 50km/30 miles of marked paths classified for difficulty on a special map. Meeting friends on the slopes for lunch is easy.

STAYING UP THE MOUNTAIN
Several possibilities
As well as mid-mountain Le Bettex, there are hotels on Mont d'Arbois.

St-Gervais 850m/2,790ft
St-Gervais is a handsome 19th-century spa town set in a narrow river gorge, on the far side of Mont d'Arbois, with access to the slopes via a 20-person gondola from just outside the town. It's an urban but pleasant place, with interesting food shops and cosy bars, thermal baths and an Olympic skating rink. Prices are noticeably lower than in Megève. Buses are reported to be regular and convenient. Two hotels convenient for the gondola are the Liberty Mont Blanc (0450 934521), a pleasantly traditional 2-star, and the 'quite charming' 3-star Carlina (0450 934110) with a small pool and sauna. The Val d'Este (0450 936591) and its restaurant have been recommended.

On the opposite side of St-Gervais is a rack-and-pinion railway, which in 1904 was intended to go to the top of Mont Blanc but actually takes you to the slopes of Les Houches.

Les Menuires

The bargain base for the Three Valleys – with an increasing amount of stylish accommodation as well as the original dreary blocks

NEWS

For 2006/07 the second stage of the new gondola up to Roc des 3 Marches should be opened. Last winter the first stage of the eight-seat lift replaced the Combes chair out of Les Menuires. A 4-star hotel, the Kaya, is planned for Reberty.

A new leisure centre opened for 2005/06, with pools, saunas, steam room, hot-tubs and gym.

- ➕ The cheapest base for the 3V
- ➕ Great local slopes on La Masse, and quick links with Val-Thorens
- ➕ Extensive snowmaking
- ➕ Lots of slope-side accommodation
- ➕ New, outlying parts of the resort are much more attractive than the core
- ➕ Good specialist food shops, although they are found in ...

- ➖ Gloomy indoor shopping malls
- ➖ Resort core is dominated by big, dreary apartment blocks
- ➖ Main intermediate and beginner slopes get a lot of sun
- ➖ No woodland slopes
- ➖ Some of the lower slopes get dangerously crowded as well as over-exposed to the sun

Les Menuires is developing in the right way, adding traditional-style satellites where you can ignore the brutal architecture at the core of the resort. And the Belleville valley has a lot of terrain, including the excellent, challenging slopes on La Masse, rarely used by visitors from the other valleys.

THE RESORT

The original buildings that surround the main lift base, La Croisette, are among the worst examples of the thoughtless building of the 1960s/70s. The main centre has a particularly dire indoor shopping gallery. But the resort is trying hard to lose its reputation as one of the ugliest in the Alps. In outposts such as Reberty and Hameau des Marmottes, the latest additions are in stone-and-wood chalet style – and the accommodation is good, too. These outposts have their own shops and bars – Les Bruyères is now a more-or-less self-contained resort.

THE MOUNTAINS

Les Menuires is set at about the tree line, with almost entirely open slopes.
Slopes The major part of the network spreads across the broad, west-facing mountainside between Les Menuires and St-Martin, with links to the Méribel valley at four points (mostly red runs, with one tricky blue) as well as a link up the valley to Val-Thorens. The new gondola and a fast chair go up from La Croisette. Lifts to La Masse, a more challenging mountain, start below the village – a gondola and a chair-lift.
Terrain-parks There's a new terrain-park with slides, tables, pyramids and snow-cross above Reberty.
Snow reliability La Masse's height and orientation ensure good snow for a long season. The west-facing slopes have lots of snowmaking but the snow lower down is often icy or slushy.
Experts The upper slopes of La Masse are virtually all of stiff red/soft black steepness. Dame Blanche is a particularly fine black, on the front of the hill – we'd love to catch it when

317

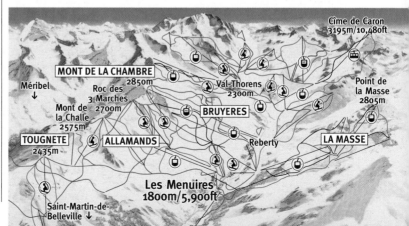

Cime de Caron
3195m/10,480ft

MONT DE LA CHAMBRE
2850m

Méribel ↓

Roc des
3 Marches
2700m

Mont de
la Challe
2575m

TOUGNETE
2435m

ALLAMANDS

Mont de
la Challe

Val-Thorens
2300m

BRUYERES

Reberty

Point de
la Masse
2805m

LA MASSE

Les Menuires
1800m/5,900ft

Saint-Martin-de-
Belleville ↓

recommends the 'good, reasonably priced' food at the Ours Blanc hotel.
Schools and guides The ESF has the monopoly here. We have had good reports this year: 'Particularly friendly and helpful.'
Facilities for children This is very much a family resort. Family Ski Company has its own nursery in Reberty – and sends a minder with kids going to ski-school, to make up for ESF 'brutality'.

STAYING THERE

How to go Some big UK tour operators offer holidays here, and some chalet operators have a presence in Reberty. There is a Club Med above Reberty.
Chalets The cluster known as Reberty Village has been virtually taken over by UK chalet operators – particularly Family Ski and Ski Olympic.
Hotels None of the hotels is above 3-star grading, although a new 4-star is planned for Reberty. Ours Blanc (0479 006166) is the best – a chalet-style 3-star on the slopes above Reberty 1850. The Bruyères (0479 007510) is set on the lower fringe of Les Bruyères.

SMART APARTMENTS – SEE FEATURE
In contrast to the blocks of the main resort, there are lots of more recent apartment developments in chalet style on the slopes south of the resort centre. Just above it at La Sapinière is the excellent new Residence Montalys and the Chalets les Montagnettes. Further up in Reberty 2000 is Les Alpages, an MGM development with 12m pool; and further up still the Chalets du Soleil, with pool. Down the slope in Balcons des Bruyères is Les Chalets de l'Adonis, with 10m pool.
Eating out Though some restaurants lack atmosphere, most serve good food. Alternatives to Savoyard include Italian and Tex-Mex. The Trattoria, with its 'good menu' and 'rustic French' ambience, has been recommended. Set menus at the Refuge are 'reasonably priced' with 'particularly good' tartiflette. The Marmite de Géant has 'excellent food and pleasant atmosphere' and 'is good value'. Chalet-boy night off is no problem in Reberty: the Ferme, on the spot, is 'always good'.
Après-ski There is no shortage of bars in La Croisette, but many are within the dreadful shopping gallery. The Taverne bar in Les Bruyères is 'lively and welcoming'. There are discos.
Off the slopes This is a resort for keen skiers and boarders.

FRANCE

318

KEY FACTS

Resort	1800m
	5,910ft

Three Valleys	
Slopes	1260-3230m
	4,130-10,600ft
Lifts	182
Pistes	630km
	391 miles
Green	14%
Blue	40%
Red	36%
Black	10%
Snowmaking	
	1823 guns

Les Menuires / St-Martin only	
Slopes	1450-2850m
	4,760-9,350ft
Lifts	37
Pistes	160km
	99 miles
Green	10%
Blue	40%
Red	38%
Black	12%
Snowmaking	
	365 guns

OUR WEBSITE

Go to our website at wtss.co.uk for resort news, links to resort sites, a build-your-own resort shortlist system and reader forums.

Phone numbers
From abroad use the prefix +33 and omit the initial '0' of the phone number.

TOURIST OFFICE

t 0479 007300
lesmenuires@
lesmenuires.com
www.lesmenuires.com

groomed, or after fresh snow. There is also a huge amount of off-piste, including Vallon du Lou – a broad, sweeping route towards Val-Thorens that used to be marked as an itinerary.
Intermediates With good snow, you may be content with the local slopes, which are virtually all blue and red. In poor snow you can head up to Val-Thorens on blue runs. Don't miss La Masse – the blacks are not super-steep – but beware the steep Masse drag-lift.
Beginners There are wide and gentle slopes and a special lift pass for beginners, but the snow quality on the nursery slopes is a worry. The blue slopes you progress to can get extremely crowded.
Snowboarding The number of drags is low and dwindling further year by year; but there are some flattish sections of piste in places. There are huge amounts of terrain to suit free-riders.
Cross-country There are 28km/17 miles of prepared trails along the valley floor between St-Martin and Val-Thorens.
Queues The fast lifts up from La Croisette seem to have largely solved the problem of queues there, but have perhaps contributed to the worsening problem of acute overcrowding on the slopes down to the resort centre.
Mountain restaurants There are few remarkable places in this sector of the 3V. However, 2006 visitors were 'very impressed' with the new Grand Lac, at the base of the Granges chair ('superb toilets'). Just above Les Menuires is very pleasant but quite pricey Etoile. At higher altitude there are 'huge meals' and 'excellent value' at the Alpage, on the 4 Vents piste and 'reasonably priced' self-service food at the top of Roc des 3 Marches with 'great views'. Many people head down to the villages for lunch; you retain some sense of being on the mountain at the 'good value' Ferme, beside the piste at Reberty and a regular reporter

Méribel

The enduring British favourite: a comfortable, upmarket chalet-style resort in the centre of the wonderful Three Valleys

COSTS

① ② ③ ④ ⑤ ⑥

RATINGS

The slopes
Fast lifts	****
Snow	***
Extent	*****
Expert	****
Intermediate	*****
Beginner	****
Convenience	***
Queues	****
Mountain restaurants	***

The rest
Scenery	***
Resort charm	***
Off-slope	***

NEWS

For 2006/07 a six-pack will replace the Chatelet chair serving the Plattières snowpark. A new three-part restaurant is planned for the base of the Mont Vallon gondola.

For 2005/06, an escalator was installed to ease access to the pistes from the main village square. A new restaurant, the Darbollées, opened just below Rond Point. On the slopes, a new mogul area was created between the Lagopède red and Bartavelle black runs, a protected beginners' area was designated below the Plattières 2 gondola and an avalanche training zone was created near the bottom of the Plan des Mains chair.

➕ In the centre of the biggest linked lift network in the world – ideal for intermediates, great for experts, too

➕ Pleasant chalet-style architecture

➕ Impressive lift system

➕ Excellent piste maintenance and snowmaking; nevertheless ...

➖ Not the best snow in the 3V, especially on the afternoon-sun side

➖ Pistes can get very crowded

➖ Sprawling main village, with lots of accommodation far from the slopes

➖ Expensive

➖ Full of Brits (holds the record for number of UK operators, at 67)

➖ Méribel-Mottaret and Méribel-Village satellites are rather lifeless

For keen piste-bashers who like to rack up the miles but dislike tacky purpose-built resorts, Méribel is difficult to beat. The Three Valleys can keep anyone amused for a fortnight – and Méribel-Mottaret, in particular, has quick access to every part. Unlike other purpose-built resorts, Méribel has always insisted on chalet-style architecture. What more could you ask? Well, our ➖ points are mostly non-trivial, and other Three Valleys resorts have the edge in some respects. For better snow opt for Courchevel or Val-Thorens. For less crowded runs, Courchevel 1650. For a smaller village, St-Martin or La Tania. For lower prices, Les Menuires. For a lower concentration of Brits, anywhere. But the other resorts have their drawbacks too. Regular visitors love Méribel.

THE RESORT

Méribel occupies the central valley of the Three Valleys system and consists of two main resort villages.

The original resort is built on a single steepish west-facing hillside with the home piste running down beside it to the main lift stations at the valley bottom. All the buildings are wood-clad, low-rise and chalet-style, making it one of the most tastefully designed of French purpose-built resorts. A road winds up from the village centre to Rond Point des Pistes, and goes on through woods to the outpost of the Altiport (a snow-covered airstrip).

The resort was founded by a Brit, Peter Lindsay, in 1938, and has retained a strong British presence ever since – 'More like Kensington than France,' commented a reporter. It spreads widely, and although some accommodation is right on the piste, much depends on use of buses (or tour operator minibuses). There are collections of shops and restaurants at a couple of points on the road through the resort – Altitude 1600 and Plateau de Morel. The lodgings at Altiport enjoy splendid isolation in the woods, and are 'normally Brit-free'.

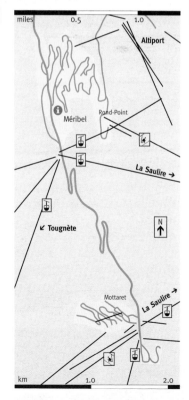

The newer satellite of Méribel-Mottaret is centrally placed in the Three Valleys ski area, offering swift access to Courchevel, Val-Thorens and Les Menuires. Development started beside the piste on the east-facing slope, but the resort has spread up the opposite hillside and further up the valley. Both sides are served by lifts for pedestrians – but the gondola up the east-facing slope stops at 7.30pm and it's a long, tiring walk up.

Mottaret looks modern, despite wood cladding on its apartment blocks. Even so, it's more attractive than many other resorts built for slope-side convenience. It has far fewer shops and bars and much less après-ski than Méribel, and some visitors have found it 'lacking in atmosphere'.

The hamlet of Méribel-Village, on the road from Méribel to La Tania and Courchevel, has a chair-lift up to Altiport with a blue run back and has developed into a pleasant mini-resort. There are some luxury chalets and apartments here but little else apart from a fitness centre, bar, pizzeria and a couple of restaurants.

There are some alternative bases lower down the mountain (and price scale) – see the end of this chapter.

Local buses are free but readers continue to complain that they are inadequate. Many UK tour operators run their own minibus services to and from the lifts. A car is mainly of use for outings to other resorts. Lift passes for six days or more give you a day in Val-d'Isère-Tignes and Paradiski.

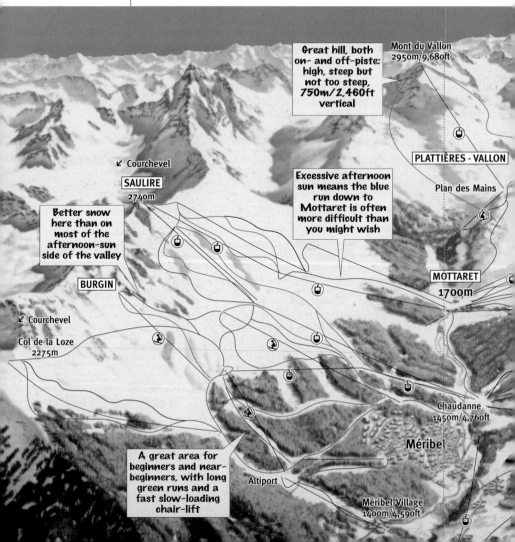

Great hill, both on- and off-piste: high, steep but not too steep, 750m/2,460ft vertical

Mont du Vallon
2950m/9,680ft

PLATTIÈRES - VALLON

Plan des Mains

Excessive afternoon sun means the blue run down to Mottaret is often more difficult than you might wish

⬐ Courchevel

SAULIRE
2740m

Better snow here than on most of the afternoon-sun side of the valley

BURGIN

⬐ Courchevel

Col de la Loze
2275m

MOTTARET
1700m

Chaudanne
1450m/4,760ft

Méribel

A great area for beginners and near-beginners, with long green runs and a fast slow-loading chair-lift

Altiport

Méribel-Village
1400m/4,590ft

THE MOUNTAINS

Most of the slopes are above the tree line, but there are some sheltered runs for bad-weather days. Piste classification is not always reliable – a problem compounded by exposure of many slopes to a lot of sun. Daily maps are available showing which runs were groomed overnight.

THE SLOPES
Highly efficient lift system
The Méribel valley runs roughly north-south, and in late season you soon get into the habit of skiing one side in the morning and the other after lunch.

On the morning-sun side, a gondola rises from Méribel to **Tougnète**, from where you can get down to Les

Menuires or St-Martin-de-Belleville. You can also head for **Mottaret** from here. From there, a fast chair then a drag take you to another entry point for the Les Menuires runs in the next valley.

On the afternoon-sun side, gondolas leave both Méribel and Mottaret for **Saulire**. From here you can head back down towards either village or over the ridge towards Courchevel 1850.

South of Mottaret are some of the best slopes in the **Plattières-Vallon** sector. The Plattières gondola ends at another entry point to Les Menuires. To the east of this is the big stand-up gondola to the top of Mont du Vallon (wonderful views from the top). A fast quad from near this area goes south up to Mont de la Chambre, giving direct access to Val-Thorens.

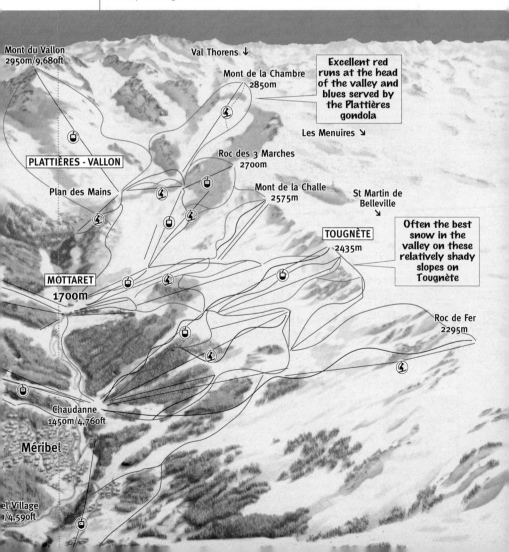

Mont du Vallon
2950m/9,68oft

Val Thorens ↓

Mont de la Chambre
2850m

Excellent red runs at the head of the valley and blues served by the Plattières gondola

Les Menuires ↘

PLATTIÈRES - VALLON

Roc des 3 Marches
2700m

Plan des Mains

Mont de la Challe
2575m

St Martin de Belleville ↘

TOUGNÈTE
2435m

Often the best snow in the valley on these relatively shady slopes on Tougnète

MOTTARET
1700m

Roc de Fer
2295m

Chaudanne
1450m/4,76oft

Méribel

el-Village
1/4,59oft

The morning sun hits
the original part of
Mottaret, but not the
piste from Saulire in
the foreground – still
rock-hard after a
baking the previous
afternoon ↗

SNOWPIX.COM / CHRIS GILL

FRANCE

322

KEY FACTS

Resort	1400-1700m	
	4,590-5,580ft	
Three Valleys		
Slopes	1260-3230m	
	4,130-10,600ft	
Lifts		183
Pistes		600km
		373 miles
Green		16%
Blue		38%
Red		36%
Black		10%
Snowmaking		
		1920 guns
Méribel only		
Slopes	1400-2950m	
	4,590-9,680ft	
Lifts		53
Pistes		150km
		93 miles
Green		11%
Blue		46%
Red		31%
Black		12%
Snowmaking		
		650 guns

TERRAIN-PARKS
There's a choice
There are two parks in the area. The
main 'Moon' park (www.moonpark.net)
is accessible by the Arpasson drag-lift
just above the Tougnète gondola mid-
station. There are two half-pipes, one
much larger than the other. A triple
kicker line for all levels with smooth
take offs. The rails here are quite
advanced, as is the big spine jump. At
times the park suffers from a lack of
maintenance, in which case you can
head up the valley to the Plattières
snow-park above Mottaret; this has a
smaller set of obstacles but is worth a
visit, especially for intermediates.

SNOW RELIABILITY
Not the best in the Three Valleys
Méribel's slopes aren't the highest in
the Three Valleys, and they mainly face
east or west; the latter get the full
force of the afternoon sun. So snow
conditions are often better elsewhere.
And grooming seems to be rather
better in neighbouring Courchevel.
   The lower runs have substantial
snowmaking and lack of snow is rarely
a problem, but ice or slush at the end
of the day can be. The north-west-
facing slopes above Altiport generally
have decent snow.
   At the southern end of the valley,
towards Les Menuires and Val-Thorens,
a lot of runs are north-facing and keep
their snow well, as do the runs on
Mont du Vallon.

FOR EXPERTS
Exciting choices
The size of the Three Valleys means
experts are well catered for. In the
Méribel valley, head for Mont du
Vallon – voted 'the best skiing in the

whole of the Three Valleys' by one
reporter's group. The long, steep
Combe du Vallon run here is classified
red; it's a wonderful, long fast cruise
when groomed, but presents plenty of
challenge when mogulled. And there's
a beautiful off-piste run in the next
valley to the main pistes, leading back
to the bottom of the gondola.
   A good mogul run is down the side
of the double Roc de Tougne drag-lift
which leads up to Mont de la Challe.
And there is a steep black run down
the Tougnète gondola back to Méribel,
unrelenting most of the way.
   At the north end of the valley the
Face run was built for the women's
downhill in the 1992 Olympics. Served
by a fast quad, it's a splendid cruise
when freshly groomed, and you can
terrify yourself just by imagining what
it must be like to go straight down.
   Nothing on the Saulire side is as
steep or as demanding as on the other
side of the valley. The Mauduit red run
is quite challenging, though – it used
to be black.
   Throughout the area there are good
off-piste opportunities – see feature
panel later in this chapter.

FOR INTERMEDIATES
Paradise found
Méribel and the rest of the Three
Valleys is a paradise for intermediates;
there are few other resorts where a
keen piste-basher can cover so many
miles so easily. Virtually every slope in
the region has a good intermediate run
down it, and to describe them would
take a book in itself. For less
adventurous intermediates, the run
from the second station of the
Plattières gondola above Mottaret back
to the first station is ideal, and used a

LIFT PASSES

Three Valleys

Prices in €

Age	1-day	6-day
under 13	32	158
13 to 59	42	210
over 60	36	168

Free under 5, over 72

Beginner seven free lifts in Méribel-Mottaret area

Notes
Covers Courchevel, La Tania, Méribel, Val-Thorens, Les Menuires and St-Martin. Family reductions; pedestrian and half-day passes. Six-day pass valid for a day in Espace Killy (Tignes-Val-d'Isère), Paradiski (La Plagne-Les Arcs), Pralognan and Les Saisies.

Alternative passes
Méribel pass covers Méribel and Méribel-Mottaret only. One-day Three Valleys extension available.

lot by the ski school. It is a gentle, north-facing, cruising run and is generally in good condition. But below that the run can get tricky and bumpy later in the day; 'Carnage when the beginner classes went up,' said one reporter. 'People spreadeagled everywhere, with the bloodwagons overwhelmed,' said another. The run into Mottaret on the other side of the valley also gets dangerously icy and crowded. The lift company needs to solve both these problems, which spoil an otherwise ideal intermediate area.

Even early intermediates should find the runs over into the other valleys well within their capabilities, opening up further vast amounts of intermediate runs. Go to Courchevel or Val-Thorens for the better snow.

Virtually all the pistes on both sides of the Méribel valley will suit more advanced intermediates. Most of the reds are on the difficult side.

FOR BEGINNERS
Strengths and weaknesses
Méribel has an excellent slope for beginners, but it's out of the resort at Altiport, which is a bit of a nuisance. There is a small nursery slope at Rond-Point, at the top of the village, mainly used by the children's ski school.

The Altiport area is accessible from the village by the Morel chair-lift, or by free bus. Once you have found your feet, a free drag-lift takes you half-way

up a long, gentle, wide, tree-lined green run – ideal except that it can get crowded and have good skiers speeding through. Next, a longer drag takes you to the top of this run, then a chair a bit higher, then another chair higher still, on to an excellent blue usually blessed with good snow.

FOR CROSS-COUNTRY
Scenic routes
There are about 33km/21 miles in total. The main area is in the pine forest near Altiport, a pleasant introduction to those who want to try cross-country for the first time. There's also a loop around Lake Tuéda, in the nature reserve at Mottaret, and for the more experienced an itinéraire from Altiport to Courchevel.

QUEUES
3V traffic a persistent problem
Huge lift investment over the years has paid off in making the area virtually queue-free most of the time, despite the huge numbers of people. Generally, if you do find a queue, there is an alternative quieter route you can take. The real problems result from the tidal flows of people between the three valleys, in the morning (when the tide coincides with the start of ski school) and in the late afternoon. Reporters this year were concerned that the lift staff were not filling up the gondolas at busy times – 'very frustrating'. The

Méribel

323

boarding

Méribel is a favourite for British snowboarders. The terrain is good and varied, with a lot more tree runs than in neighbouring Val-Thorens. There are some very good steep runs that stay relatively untracked on the Campagnol and Combe Vallon. There is a real wealth of red runs here for intermediates, and beginners have a good selection of mellow runs between Méribel proper and satellite Mottaret. Beware some of the flat sections on the main routes to and from Val-Thorens – the Ours down to Mottaret is very hard work. Specialist shops include Board Brains (in Méribel) and Quiksilver Gotcha Surf (in Mottaret).

SCHOOLS

ESF Méribel
t 0479 086031

ESF Méribel-Mottaret
t 0479 004949

Magic in Motion
t 0479 085336

New Generation
t 0479 010318
www.skinewgen.com

Snow Systems
t 0479 004022

Classes
(ESF prices)
6 half-days (2½hr per day): €160

Private lessons
From €93 (for an afternoon)

GUIDES

Mountain guide office
t 0479 003038

queue for the Tougnète gondola at Méribel towards Les Menuires was eased by the installation of a fast chair in 2004; but you can still find big queues for the Plattières gondola at Mottaret towards Les Menuires ('nightmarish' says a 2006 visitor), the Côte Brune chair to Mont de la Chambre and the Plan des Mains chair (used by everyone returning from Val-Thorens to avoid the ridiculously flat 'blue' Ours run that goes directly down the valley).

MOUNTAIN RESTAURANTS
Less than wonderful
There are lots of places on the piste map, but few that are worth singling out – and not enough to meet the demand, so many get very crowded (you might want to take lunch early or late). A 2006 reader's favourite was the 'small and cosy' Arpasson at the mid-station of the Tougnète gondola for 'a variety of good-value choices'. The Chardonnet, at the mid-station of the Mottaret-Saulire gondola, has table-service and excellent food, but is expensive. The large terrace at the Rhododendrons, at the top of the Altiport drag, is also expensive but remains a popular spot. Some 2006 visitors found the 'ever popular' Rond Point, just below the mid-point of the Rhodos gondola 'expensive' and preferred the 'good pasta and service' as well as the views from the new Darbollées, a bit lower down. The 'delightfully quaint' Crêtes, below the top of the Tougnète gondola, continues to provide 'good food and service'. Lower down, at the bottom of the Roc de Tougne drags, the Togniat has 'very good self-service food'. The pricey Altiport hotel scarcely counts as a mountain restaurant, but has a great outdoor buffet in good weather and the 'best tarts in town'. Two self-service places notable for their views are the Pierres Plates, at the top of

Saulire, and the Sittelle (‘good choice of cooked and cold buffet lunches’) above the first section of the Plattières gondola.

SCHOOLS AND GUIDES
No shortage of instructors
The ESF is by far the biggest school, with over 300 instructors. It has a special international section with instructors speaking good English. Recent reports have been mixed. A 2005 reporter said, 'A couple in our chalet had two private lessons with an ESF instructor who was late both times and smelt strongly of alcohol (at 11.30am!).' The ESF offers useful alternatives to standard classes, such as off-piste groups, heli-skiing on the Italian border and Three Valleys tours.

Some 2006 beginners praise Snow Systems for their 'superb service' and 'absolutely fantastic' lessons. Magic in Motion, the second largest school, also offers heli-skiing, couloir and extreme sessions as well as normal lessons. But recent reports have been variable; one 2006 visitor found their smaller groups a 'refreshing change' from ESF; but another felt the instructors 'didn't have much enthusiasm' and didn't like the way they spoke to some of the children. New Generation, a British school which operates in Courchevel and Méribel, continues to receive excellent reports. One reader said, 'I cannot recommend them highly enough, they were patient and kept groups small.' A 2005 reporter 'progressed quickly in a group of only three; the instructor explained and demonstrated techniques clearly'.

FACILITIES FOR CHILDREN
Tour operators rule
We guess readers needing childcare use the facilities of chalet operators who run their own nurseries – we rarely get reports on resort facilities.

Méribel has a lot of very good off-piste to discover, as well as the pistes that the Three Valleys is famous for. We asked Pierre-François Papet, head of Méribel's Snow Systems ski school, to pick out some of the best off-piste runs for skiers with at least some off-piste experience. Don't tackle them without guidance.

Some of the best snow is to be found on the north-facing run accessed from the 3 Vallées 2 chair-lift at Val-Thorens. Ducking the rope at the top takes you into varied terrain mixing couloirs and gentle slopes, with exposures from north-east to north-west. Eventually you join the red Lac de la Chambre piste.

The run from near Roc de Fer to Le Raffort, a mid-station on the gondola from Brides-les-Bains, is an adventure with exceptional views. You ride the Olympic chair-lift, go along the ridge, then ski down a gentle bowl to finish among the trees.

The wide, west-facing slope above Altiport is enjoyable when the snow is fresh – varied terrain, from average to steep, some open some wooded, reached from the Tétras black run.

There are lots of runs suitable for more accomplished off-piste skiers. One is a descent known as The Cairn from the Mouflon piste at the top of the Plattières gondola; it starts in a fairly steep couloir and becomes wider, with a consistent pitch, until you reach the Sittelle piste.

The Roc de Tougne drag-lift accesses some challenging runs. To the right of the Lagopède red piste is an area we call the Spot – a rather technical and steep descent to the Sittelle piste. Alternatively, a 15-minute hike brings you to the Couloir du Serail, leading to the Mouflon red piste – one of my favourites because of the vertical, the constant pitch and the quality of snow.

The Col du Fruit is a local classic, far away from the lifts and resorts. You ride the Creux Noirs chair-lift in Courchevel, then walk along the ridge for 15 minutes before descending through the national park to Lac de Tueda and the cross-country tracks ... 800m/2,620ft of flat ground from the Mottaret lifts.

Mont Vallon offers a big choice of routes and exposures – quite steep at the top but with easier slopes from the middle. The challenging northern couloir starts at the top of the Campagnol run.

Snow Systems is a ski school that operates from both Méribel and Mottaret. As well as group and private on- and off-piste lessons, they run children's lessons, snowboard lessons and instructor training.

t 0479 004022
www.snow-systems.com

Méribel

325

FRANCE

326

Phone numbers
From abroad use the prefix +33 and omit the initial '0' of the phone number.

CHILDREN

Les Saturnins
t 0479 086690
Ages 18mnth to 3yr;
6 days €208
Kids Etcetera
t 0479 007139
From 3mth to 6yr
Les Piou Piou
t 0479 086031 (Mér)
t 0479 004949 (Mot)
Ages 3 to 5; 9am-5pm; 6 days €208
Childminder list
Available from the tourist office.

Ski school
The ESF runs classes for ages 5 to 13: 6 half-days (2½hr) from €98.40.

STAYING THERE

HOW TO GO
Huge choice but few bargains
Package holidays are easy to find, both with big UK tour operators and smaller Méribel specialists.
Chalets Méribel has more chalets dedicated to the British market than any other resort, and over 50 operators offering them – many, as you may have noticed, advertising their properties in these pages. What really distinguishes Méribel is the range of recently built luxury chalets. Some are perfectly positioned for the slopes, but many rely on minibuses to compensate for their inconvenient locations.
  Méribel specialists include Meriski, whose portfolio includes some of our favourites; Purple Ski, with impressive places in every part of the resort, including the lovely Iamato in Village; and Bonne Neige (see Staying down the valley). At the top of the market, VIP has several sumptuous looking places, mostly with saunas and hot-tubs; sister company Snowline has some not far behind. Descent International has four of the best chalets. The Lodge in the Belvédère area moves into the Supertravel programme this year, straight into the number one slot.
  Of the few chalet-hotels, Mark Warner's Tarentaise (with a sauna and hot-tub) has a great position, right on the piste at Mottaret.
Hotels Méribel has some excellent hotels, but they're not cheap.
《《《④ **Grand Coeur** (0479 086003) Our favourite almost-affordable hotel in Méribel. Just above the village centre. Welcoming, mature building with plush lounge. Magnificent food. Huge hot-tub, sauna, etc.
《《《④ **Altiport** (0479 005232) Modern and luxurious hotel, isolated at the foot of the Altiport lifts. Convenient for

Courchevel, not for Val-Thorens.
《《《④ **Mont-Vallon** (0479 004400) The best hotel at Mottaret; good food, and excellently situated for the Three Valleys' pistes. Pool, sauna, squash, fitness room, etc.
《《③ **Arolles** (0479 004040) Right on the slopes at Mottaret. 'Friendly, unpretentious, good food, highly recommended.' Pool and sauna.
《《③ **Adray Télébar** (0479 086026) Welcoming piste-side chalet with pretty, rustic rooms, good food and popular sun terrace.
《《③ **Parc Alpin** (0479 082963) Newly renovated luxury chalet at 1600 with pool, sauna and wi-fi internet.
《② **Roc** (0479 086416) A good-value B&B hotel, in the centre, with a bar-restaurant and crêperie below.
SMART APARTMENTS – SEE FEATURE
Les Fermes de Méribel (in Méribel-Village) is a classic tasteful MGM development of six large chalets with the usual impressive pool.

EATING OUT
Fair choice
There is a reasonable selection of restaurants, from ambitious French cuisine to pizza and pasta. For the best food in town, in plush surroundings, there are top hotels – Grand Coeur ('so pleased, we ate there several times'), Allodis and Kouisena ('traditional food at justifiably high prices'). Other recommendations from readers include: Chez Kiki – 'the best steaks'; the Taverne – 'relaxed atmosphere' but 'can be expensive'; the Tremplin – 'good pizzas'; Enfants Terribles – 'wonderful roast beef carvery'; Refuge – 'lovely crêpes'; Grange – 'excellent food and service'; Oasis – 'good meals at a reasonable price'; Cactus Café – 'quick service and good value'; the 'tiny' Bibi Phoque – 'good value for money' food including crêpes; Cava – for 'service, food and value'.

www.skichaletsmeribel.co.uk

Méribel

327

GETTING THERE

Air Geneva 135km/
84 miles (3½hr); Lyon
185km/115 miles
(3½hr); Chambéry
95km/59 miles
(1½hr).

Rail Moûtiers
(18km/11 miles);
regular buses to
Méribel.

Other alternatives include the Galette, the Fromagerie and Cro-Magnon up the hill in Morel – all popular for raclette and fondue. The Blanchot, just below Altiport, offers the choice of two dining areas, one dedicated to dishes of the region. Scott's does good American-style food.

At Les Allues, the Tsaretta will pay for a taxi to ferry you to the creations of the Australian chef. The Chaumière offers 'good value inclusive menus in pleasant, rustic surroundings'. The Chemina is another recommendation as is the Martagon at Le Raffort between Méribel and Les Allues.

APRES-SKI
Méribel rocks – loudly

Méribel's après-ski revolves around British-run places. Dick's Tea Bar is well established but is remote from the slopes. At close of play it's the piste-side Rond Point that's packed – happy hour starts around 4pm – and has live music and 'almost infamous toffee vodka'. The terrace of Jack's, near the main lift stations, remains popular.

The ring of bars around the main square do good business at tea time. The Taverne (sister to Dick's Tea Bar)

gets packed. Just across the square is the Pub, with videos, pool and sometimes a band. There are a couple of alternatives to the loud pubs complained about in the past. The Poste 'serves the best vin chaud' and is a 'more French option than the bars closer to the slopes'. The Barometer has a good atmosphere and lots of leather seating.

There is late dancing at Scott's (next to the Pub) and, of course, there's Dick's Tea Bar. One reader was put off by the queues at the Pub, another liked its 'busy atmosphere'.

In Mottaret the bars at the foot of the pistes get packed at tea time – Rastro ('as good as ever' and 'good value', comment regular visitors) and Down Town are the most popular, though reporters say that Zig-Zag has lower prices. Later on the Rastro disco gets going.

Both villages have a cinema.

OFF THE SLOPES
Flight of fancy

Méribel is not really a resort for people who want to languish in the village, but it is not unattractive and has some good facilities. There's a good public

ACTIVITIES

Indoor Parc Olympique (ice rink, swimming pool, climbing wall, karting on ice), fitness centres in hotels, bowling, library, two cinemas, museum, heritage tours

Outdoor Flying lessons and excursions, snow-mobiles, snow-shoe excursions, cleared paths, ice climbing, ice karting, paragliding, dog-sledding, hot air ballooning, paintball

TOURIST OFFICE

t 0479 086001
info@meribel.net
www.meribel.net

swimming pool and an Olympic ice rink (hockey matches sometimes). You can also take joyrides in the little planes that operate from the altiport.

The pedestrian's lift pass covers all the gondolas, cable-cars and buses in the Méribel and Courchevel valleys, and makes it very easy for pedestrians to meet friends for lunch. There are pleasant, marked walks in the Altiport area and a signposted trail through some of the hamlets down to Les Allues (return from there or Le Raffort in the Olympic gondola).

A non-skier's guide to Courchevel, Méribel and La Tania is distributed free by the tourist office.

STAYING DOWN THE VALLEY
Quieter, cheaper choices
For the 1992 Olympics the competitors were accommodated in **Brides-les-Bains** (600m/1,970ft), an old spa town way down in the valley, and a gondola was built linking it to Méribel. It offers a quieter, cheaper alternative to the higher resorts and has some simple hotels, adequate shops and 'plenty of good-value restaurants and friendly bars used by locals', says a reporter. Ski Weekends runs a chalet-hotel here.

There is a casino, but evenings are distinctly quiet. The long gondola ride to and from Méribel (about 25 minutes) is tedious, can be cold, stops 'ridiculously early' at 5pm and arrives at a point that's a bit of a trek from the main lifts up the mountain. But in good conditions you can ski off-piste to one or other of the mid-stations at the end of the day (or in exceptional conditions down to Brides itself). Given a car, Brides makes a good base for visiting other resorts.

Some UK tour operators have places in the old village of **Les Allues**, close to a mid-station on the gondola from Brides-les-Bains. The pick of the chalets is probably Bonne Neige's Les Allodis, a carefully converted barn ('Absolutely brilliant, the best chalet holiday ever, excellent food,' said a 2004 reporter) plus one other chalet, St Joseph – there's a hot-tub and a sauna in each. Ski Blanc have six good-looking chalets too, including one with a hot-tub. Next door to one of them is an independent British-run playgroup. There are a couple of bars – and a good-value, well-renovated hotel, the Croix Jean-Claude (0479 086105); rooms are small, though.

Méribel

329

OT MERIBEL / J-M GOUEDARD

Chalets, chalets, chalets wherever you look; not all are as dinky as these ones, mind you →

Montgenèvre

The snowiest part of the Milky Way circuit reaching across to Sauze d'Oulx in Italy – now with through-traffic buried in a tunnel

COSTS

① ② ③ ④ ⑤ ⑥

RATINGS

The slopes

Fast lifts	*
Snow	****
Extent	****
Expert	**
Intermediate	****
Beginner	*****
Convenience	****
Queues	****
Mountain restaurants	**

The rest

Scenery	***
Resort charm	***
Off-slope	*

NEWS

A tunnel designed to take through-traffic out of Montgenèvre was completed last season.

In 2005 a new centre opened in the village with an auditorium, 200-seat cinema and day-care centre for children from the age of three months to six years old.

330

➕ Good snow record, and local slopes largely north-facing – often the best snow in the Milky Way area

➕ Plenty of intermediate cruising and good, convenient nursery slopes

➕ Few queues on weekdays, unless people are being bussed in from other resorts with poor snow

➕ A lot of accommodation close to the slopes, and some right on them

➕ Great potential for car drivers to explore other nearby resorts

➖ Poor base for exploring the Italian Milky Way resorts unless you have use of a car

➖ Lots of slow lifts and mainly short runs in local area

➖ Little to challenge experts on-piste

Montgenèvre is set on a minor pass between France and Italy, at one end of the big cross-border Milky Way network. On snow, it's a time-consuming trek from here to Sestriere and Sauze d'Oulx at the far end (you may have to ride some slow lifts down as well as up). But you can get to these worthwhile resorts much more quickly by car, which also facilitates day trips in the opposite direction to other excellent French resorts such as Serre-Chevalier. Thanks to the pass setting, the local slopes shared with Claviere (in Italy, but very close) often have the best snow in the region.

The village is pleasant, and must be much more so now that main road traffic has been consigned to a 400m/1,310ft tunnel, with the result that the village is no longer separated from the main north-facing slopes. (The tunnel seems to have opened during last season, so not all visitors got the benefit of it.)

THE RESORT

Montgenèvre is a narrow roadside village set on a high pass only a mile from the Italian border – this is an area where the euro has really simplified things. Cheap and cheerful cafes, bars and restaurants line the road running along the bottom of the nursery slopes, now happily free of through-traffic, giving an animated atmosphere sometimes missing from French resorts. And tucked away off the main road is a quite pleasant old village, complete with quaint church and friendly natives. The place gets a lot of weather – sometimes wind but also snow, which adds to the charm factor when the sun comes out.

The slopes are convenient, despite the road; most of the accommodation is less than five minutes from a lift. Some of the newer accommodation is uphill, away from the slopes – but there is a free shuttle-bus. The main lifts are gondolas from opposite ends of the village. On the village side of

the col are the south-facing slopes of Le Chalvet. The more extensive north-facing slopes of Les Gondrans are across the main road, with nursery slopes at the bottom. Both sectors have piste links with Claviere, gateway to the other Italian resorts of the Milky Way – Sansicario, Sestriere and Sauze d'Oulx.

The best way to get to other resorts is by car. Serre-Chevalier and Puy-St-Vincent, with lift pass sharing arrangements, are easily reached, and well worth an outing each. Different lift pass options cater for most needs.

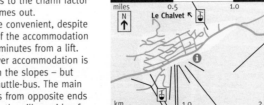

KEY FACTS

Resort	1850m
	6,070ft

Montgenèvre-Monts de la Lune (Claviere)

Slopes	1850-2630m
	6,070-8,630ft
Lifts	38
Pistes	100km
	62 miles
Green	11%
Blue	27%
Red	42%
Black	20%
Snowmaking	
	26 hectares

For the whole Milky Way area

Slopes	1390-2825m
	4,560-9,270ft
Lifts	88
Pistes	400km
	249 miles
Blue	24%
Red	56%
Black	20%
Snowmaking	120km
	75 miles

THE MOUNTAINS

Montgenèvre's local slopes are best suited to leisurely intermediates, with lots of easy cruising on blues and greens, both above and in the woods.

Run gradings on the local area and Milky Way piste maps have differed in the past, which can be confusing – however, none of the blacks is much more than a tough red.

THE SLOPES
Nicely varied

The major north-facing sector now named **Les Gondrans** offers easy intermediate slopes above the mid-mountain gondola station, with more of a mix of runs lower down. It has a high-altitude link via Collet Vert into the slopes above Claviere (**L'Aigle**). This whole area around the border is attractively broken up by rocky outcrops and woods and the scenery is quite spectacular.

The runs of the sunny sector across the road – **Le Chalvet** – are mainly on open slopes above its mid-mountain gondola station. When conditions permit, a 'charming' long blue run from this sector goes down to Claviere, for access to Italy. But on some maps this run is marked as an itinéraire, which would normally mean that it is not patrolled. Check the situation before you start if skiing alone.

TERRAIN-PARKS
High and remote

There's a terrain-park with a half-pipe and boarder-cross near the Prarial chair

and a free-ride zone higher up on the Gondrans sector, next to the Observatoire chair.

SNOW RELIABILITY
Excellent locally

Montgenèvre has a generally excellent snow record, receiving dumps from westerly storms funnelling up the valley. The high north-facing slopes naturally keep their snow better than the south-facing area, but both have snowmaking on the main home pistes.

FOR EXPERTS
Limited, except for off-piste

There are very few challenging pistes locally. Many of the runs are overclassified. There is, however, ample off-piste terrain. The remote north-east-facing bowl beyond the Col de l'Alpet on the Chalvet side is superb in good snow and has black and red pistes, too. The open section between La Montanina and Sagnalonga on the Italian side is another good powder area. Those with a car should visit Sestriere for the most challenging runs. Heli-skiing can be arranged on the Italian side.

FOR INTERMEDIATES
Plenty of cruising terrain

The overclassified blacks are just right for adventurous intermediates, though none holds the interest for very long. The pleasantly narrow tree-lined runs to Claviere from Pian del Sole, the steepest of the routes down in the Chalvet sector and the runs off the back of Col de l'Alpet are all fine in

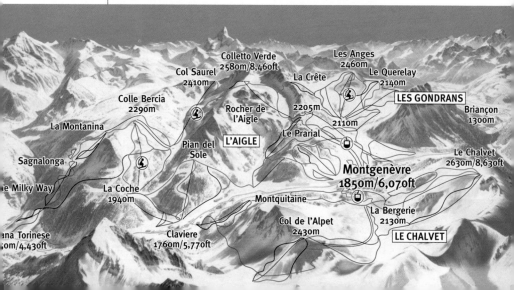

The shady main slopes run down to the sunny village →

LIFT PASSES

Montgenèvre-Monts de la Lune

Prices in €

Age	1-day	6-day
under 12	22	109
12 to 59	27	135
over 60	22	109

Free under 6, over 75
Beginner no deals

Notes
Covers Montgenèvre and Claviere lifts. 6-day and over Galaxie pass allows free day at Alpe-d'Huez, Deux-Alpes, Puy-St-Vincent and Serre-Chevalier.

Alternative passes
Montgenèvre only and Voie Lactée (Milky Way) area passes available.

SCHOOLS

ESF
t 0492 219046
A-Peak
t 0492 218330

Classes (ESF prices)
6 half days (2½hr)
€95
Private lessons
€32 for 1hr

CHILDREN

Village kindergarten
t 0492 215250
Ages 3mnth to 6yr
ESF kindergarten
t 0492 219046
Ages 3 to 5

Ski school
For ages 5 to 12
(6 half days €91)

small doses.

Average intermediates will enjoy the red runs, though most are short. On the major sector, both the runs from Collet Vert – one into Italy and one back into France – can be great fun.

Getting to Cesana via the lovely sweeping run starting at the top of the Serra Granet double-drag, and heading home from Pian del Sole, is easier than the gradings suggest, and can be tackled by less adventurous intermediates, who also have a wealth of cruising terrain high up at the top of the Les Anges sector. The runs down to the village are flattering cruises.

Further afield, the run down to Claviere from the top of the Gimont drags, on the Italian side, is a beautifully gentle cruise.

FOR BEGINNERS
Good for novices and improvers
There is a fine selection of convenient nursery slopes with reliable snow at the foot of the north-facing area. Progression to longer runs could not be easier, with a very easy blue starting at Les Anges, leading on to a green and finishing at the roadside 600m/1,970ft below.

FOR CROSS-COUNTRY
Having a car widens horizons
Montgenèvre is the best of the Milky Way resorts for cross-country enthusiasts, but it's useful to have a car. The two local trails, totalling 17km/11miles, offer quite a bit of variety, but a further 60km/37 miles of track starts in Les Alberts, 8km/5 miles away in the Clarée valley.

QUEUES
No problems most of the time
The slopes are wonderfully uncrowded during weekdays, provided surrounding resorts have snow. Some lifts become crowded at weekends and when nearby Bardonecchia is lacking snow. And queues for the two gondolas out of the village can occur first thing. Links with Italy have improved but some walking can be involved and many of the lifts are still old and slow. Reporters praise the lift attendants.

MOUNTAIN RESTAURANTS
Head for Italy
The few mountain restaurants in the Montgenèvre sector are of the large self-service canteen variety, but 2006 reporters enjoyed the 'very friendly'

Bergerie, in the Chalvet sector, for its 'wholesome, good food' and 'marvellous views'. In the Claviere sector there is a choice of atmospheric little mountain huts, such as the 'cosy' and 'friendly' Montanina Restaurant at the top of the chair lift from Sagnalonga. Alternatively there are plenty of places to eat back in the village.

SCHOOLS AND GUIDES
Encouraging reports
A 2006 reporter found the ESF 'well organised, with English speaking instructors friendly and helpful'. They found that some 'prompting' was needed to get children in the right groups, but praised the friendliness and the 'secure area with indoor and outdoor facilities' for younger children.

FACILITIES FOR CHILDREN
Hugely improved
With the intrusive main road traffic removed, Montgenèvre would now seem a fine family resort. Reports on the school's children's classes have been complimentary of both class size and spoken English.

GETTING THERE

Air Turin 98km/ 61 miles (2hr); Grenoble 145km/ 90 miles (3hr); Lyon 253km/157 miles (4½hr).

Rail Briançon (12km/ 7 miles) or Oulx (15km/9 miles); buses available from both five times a day.

ACTIVITIES

Indoor Cinema

Outdoor Natural ice rink, snow-shoeing, snowmobiling, walking, heritage tours, horse-riding

Phone numbers From abroad use the prefix +33 and omit the initial '0' of the phone number.

TOURIST OFFICE

Montgenèvre
t 0492 215252
info@montgenevre.
com
www.montgenevre.com
Claviere
t 0122 878856
claviere@
montagnedoc.it
www.claviere.it

boarding

There's plenty to attract boarders to Montgenèvre. There are good local beginner slopes and long runs on varied terrain for intermediates. The only real drawback is that many of the lifts in the area are drags, and you will have to use them to get around – getting over to Sestriere and back involves lots (and some flat sections to skate along as well). There are some excellent off-piste areas for more advanced boarders. Snow Box is the local specialist shop.

STAYING THERE

HOW TO GO
Limited choice
UK tour operators concentrate on cheap and cheerful catered chalets, though some apartments are also available and a few operators also package hotels.
Hotels There is a handful of simple places offering good value.
② **Valérie** (0492 219002) Central rustic old 3-star. 'Quiet and nicely French.'
② **Napoléon** (0492 219204) 3-star on the roadside.
① **Alpet** (0492 219006) Basic 2-star near the centre.
① **Chalet des Sports** (0492 219017) Among the cheapest rooms in the Alps.
Self-catering Résidences La Ferme d'Augustin are simple, ski-to-the-door apartments on the fringes of the main north-facing slopes, five minutes' walk (across the piste) from town.

EATING OUT
Cheap and cheerful
There are a dozen places to choose from. The 'pick of the bunch' is reportedly the Estable – 'a great find, full of locals'. We also have good reports of the Refuge ('excellent and extensive menu') and the Jamy – 'very good value set menu'. The 'magnificent calzone pizzas' at the 'no-frills' Italian-run Captain's Table are said to be 'perfect for hungry people on a budget'. A trip to Claviere is worthwhile – reporters have testified to the excellence of the restaurants.

APRES-SKI
Mainly bars, but fun
The range is limited. The Graal is a friendly, unsophisticated place; the Ca del Sol bar is a cosy place with open fire. The Chaberton, with pool tables, is also recommended, although a 2006 visitor found it 'pretty quiet'. The 'infamous' Blue Night disco is popular, it 'supplies half-decent music and not too over-priced drinks till very, very late', attracting a very mixed crowd to

its 'friendly and permissive atmosphere'. The Refuge, the Crepouse and the Jamy are the focal cafe-bars at tea time.

OFF THE SLOPES
Very limited
There is a weekly market and you can walk the cross-country routes, but the main diversion is a bus-trip to the beautiful old town of Briançon.

STAYING UP THE MOUNTAIN
Easily arranged, recommended
The Sporthotel Sagnalonga, halfway down the piste to Cesana (on the Italian side of the border) and reached by chair-lift or snowmobile, is recommended by two reporters – 'good-value self-service meals', but 'it's in need of redecoration'. Even at half-term you get the immaculately groomed local slopes to yourself until skiers based elsewhere arrive, mid-morning. It's quiet in the evenings, but livens up considerably when Italian weekenders arrive to party. It's in the First Choice package programme.

Claviere 1760m/5,770ft

Claviere is a small, traditional village, barely a mile to the east of Montgenèvre and just over the border in Italy. It's no great beauty, and the main road to Montgenèvre and Briançon that divides it in two has an obvious impact, but visitors seem to like its quiet, relaxed ambience, and are ready to go again.

The slopes of Montgenèvre are as easily reached as those on the Italian side of the border. Unbelievably, there is no shared pass sold here; you have to buy day extensions for the French slopes, or buy a shared pass up the road in Montgenèvre.

Claviere's nursery slope is small and steep but usually uncrowded and snow-reliable. We have had mixed reports of its ski school – from 'lovely instructors, brilliant with the kids' to 'only average' and 'big classes'.

Morzine

A large, lively, year-round resort with its own attractive slopes and linked by lift to the main Portes du Soleil circuit

COSTS

① ② ③ ④ ⑤ ⑥

RATINGS

The slopes
Fast lifts	**
Snow	**
Extent	*****
Expert	***
Intermediate	****
Beginner	***
Convenience	**
Queues	***
Mountain restaurants	***

The rest
Scenery	***
Resort charm	***
Off-slope	***

NEWS

For 2005/06 the Nabor double chair used by beginners at Le Pléney was replaced by a quad. A new mountain restaurant at the bottom of the Pointe de Nyon serving Savoyard specialities was built. And 200 new underground parking places were built in the village centre.

For 2006/07 a new quad chair is planned to replace two drag-lifts on the Nyon plateau. And a new spa centre, Massages du Monde, is also planned.

➕ Part of the vast Portes du Soleil

➕ Larger local piste area than other Portes du Soleil resorts

➕ Good nightlife by French standards

➕ Quite attractive old town

➕ One of the easiest drives from the Channel (a car is very useful here)

➕ Few queues locally

➕ Lots of tree-lined runs

➖ Just off the main Portes du Soleil circuit

➖ Bus-ride or long walk to lifts from much of the accommodation

➖ Low altitude means there is an enduring risk of poor snow, despite increased snowmaking

➖ Few tough pistes for experts

➖ Weekend crowds

Morzine is a long-established year-round resort, popular for its easy road access, traditional atmosphere and gentle wooded slopes, where children do not get lost and bad weather rarely causes problems. For keen piste-bashers wanting to travel the Portes du Soleil circuit regularly, the main drawback is having to take a bus and cable-car or several lifts to get to the main circuit.

Such problems can be avoided by taking a car or using a tour operator who will drive you around. The little-used Ardent gondola, a short drive from Morzine, is a particularly neat option, giving the alternative of a shorter circuit that misses out Avoriaz, where the worst crowds tend to be found.

THE RESORT

Morzine is a traditional mountain town sprawling along both sides of a river gorge. In winter, under a blanket of snow, its chalet-style buildings look charming, and in spring the village quickly takes on a spruce appearance. Morzine is a family resort, and village

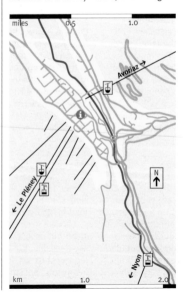

ambience tends to be fairly subdued – but there is plenty of après-ski action.

The centre is close to the river, around the tourist office. Restaurants and bars line the street up to the lifts to Le Pléney, where a busy one-way street runs along the foot of the slopes. Accommodation is widely scattered, and a good multi-route bus service (including two electric buses, introduced a few of seasons ago) links all parts of the town to outlying lifts, including those for Avoriaz.

As the extensive network of bus routes and a growing number of hotel mini-buses imply, Morzine is a town where getting from A to B can be tricky. The best plan is to stay in the centre of town or near one of the gondolas. Our view is that the resort suits car drivers is widely shared. But the roads are busy and the one-way system takes some getting used to.

THE MOUNTAINS

The local slopes suit intermediates well, with excellent areas for beginners and near-beginners too. Reporters have praised the system of Discovery Routes around the Portes du Soleil – choose an animal that suits your ability and follow the signs displaying it.

KEY FACTS

Resort	1000m
	3,280ft

Portes du Soleil	
Slopes	950-2300m
	3,120-7,550ft
Lifts	209
Pistes	650km
	404 miles
Green	14%
Blue	39%
Red	37%
Black	10%
Snowmaking	
	577 guns

Morzine-Les Gets only	
Slopes	1000-2010m
	3,280-6,590ft
Lifts	48
Pistes	110km
	68 miles
Green	12%
Blue	35%
Red	44%
Black	9%

LIFT PASSES

Portes du Soleil

Prices in €

Age	1-day	6-day
under 16	25	120
16 to 59	37	179
over 60	30	143

Free under 5

Beginner no deals

Notes
Covers all lifts in all resorts, plus shuttle-buses. Half-day pass also available.

Alternative passes
Morzine-Les Gets pass pass available(free for over 75s).

THE SLOPES
No need to go far afield
Morzine is not an ideal base for the Portes du Soleil main circuit but it has an extensive local area shared with Les Gets (covered in a separate chapter).

A gondola rises from the edge of central Morzine to **Le Pléney**. (The parallel cable-car is for the hotel and ski school kids only, unless the gondola breaks down.) Numerous routes return to the valley, including a run down to Les Fys – a quiet junction of chairs which access **Nyon** and, in the opposite direction, the ridge separating Morzine from the Les Gets slopes. The Nyon sector has two peaks – Pointe de Nyon and Chamossière – accessible from Nyon and Le Grand Pré respectively. Nyon can also be accessed by cable-car, situated a bus-ride from Morzine. Beyond Chamossière are two more ridges – Le Ranfolly and La Rosta. In the valley between these two, no fewer than five chair-lifts have their base stations clustered together.

Beyond Les Gets, **Mont Chéry** is notably quiet, and well worth a visit.

Across town from the Le Pléney sector – a handy 'petit train' shuttle service runs between the two – is a gondola leading (via another couple of lifts and runs) to Avoriaz and the main Portes du Soleil circuit. You take the gondola down at the end of the day to get back to Morzine (there's no piste back). Alternatives are a bus-ride or short drive to either Les Prodains, from where you can get a (queue-prone) cable-car to Avoriaz or a chair-lift into the **Hauts Forts** slopes above it, or to Ardent, where a gondola accesses Les Lindarets for lifts towards Châtel, Avoriaz or Champéry. The tree-lined slopes at Les Lindarets are good in poor visibility and the area at the top of the gondola is a good place for mixed ability groups to meet up. Car trips to Flaine and Chamonix are feasible. The piste map, signposting and grooming are all good.

TERRAIN-PARKS
Mont Chéry, or head for Avoriaz
Nothing locally, except a boarder-cross, aimed at children, in the Zone Enfant at the top of Les Chavannes. So head

Morzine

335

boarding

Morzine is very popular with boarding seasonaires because of the extensive slopes, the splendid terrain-parks in Avoriaz and the lower prices here. Chalet Snowboard, one of the first chalet companies to target snowboarders, has chalets here and former British champ Becci Malthouse runs the British Alpine Ski & Snowboard School. Specialist boarding shops include The Park and Misty Fly. The slopes in Morzine are great for all abilities of rider, with very few drag-lifts and flat areas. Plenty of tree-lined runs make for scenic and interesting snowboarding and the more adventurous should hire a guide to go to explore off-piste.

up to one of the three terrain-parks in Avoriaz (see Avoriaz chapter) or to Mont Chéry (see Les Gets chapter).

SNOW RELIABILITY
Poor

Morzine has a very low average height, and it can rain here when it is snowing higher up. A recent reporter had 'three days of heavy rain up to 1800m on our January visit'. But on our 2005 visit, when snow was sparse throughout the Alps, we found the skiing good because little coverage is needed on the rock-free grassy pastures that you ski on. There is some snowmaking,

most noticeably on runs linking Nyon and Le Pléney, and on the home runs.

FOR EXPERTS
A few possibilities

The runs down from Pointe de Nyon and Chamossière are quite challenging, as are the black runs down the back of Mont Chéry and the excellent Hauts Forts blacks at Avoriaz. There is plenty of off-piste scope; the open slopes of Chamossière offer some of the best local possibilities, and Mont Chéry at Les Gets is also worth exploring. For further off-piste ideas, see the feature panel later in this chapter.

Chamossière 2000m

Le Ranfolly 1850m

La Ros

POINTE DE NYON
2010m/6,590ft

Our favourite local hut, Chez Nannon, close to good challenging runs

Nyon 1420m

Le Grand Pré

Les Chavannes 1485m

La Turch

LE PLÉNEY
1510m

Les Gets
1170m/3,840ft

← Avoriaz

Lovely easy blue run away from all the lifts

Morzine
1000m/3,280ft

The gondola is a link to Avoriaz from the centre of town. But you have to catch it down too – there's no piste back

FOR INTERMEDIATES

Something for everyone

Good intermediates will enjoy the challenging red and black down from Chamossière. Mont Chéry, on the other side of Les Gets, has some fine steepish runs which are usually very quiet, as everyone heads from Les Gets towards Morzine.

Those looking for something less steep have a great choice. Le Pléney has a compact network of pistes that are ideal for groups with mixed abilities: there are blue and red alternatives down to every lift.

One of the easiest cruises on Le

Pléney is a great away-from-it-all, snow-gun-covered blue from the top to the valley lift station. Heading from Le Ranfolly to Le Grand Pré on the blue is also a nice cruise. And the slopes down to Les Gets from Le Pléney are easy when conditions are right (they face south).

The fast chairs on Le Ranfolly and La Rosta now make these sectors more attractive, serving easy blacks and cruising reds.

And, of course, there is the whole of the extensive Portes du Soleil circuit to explore by going up the opposite side of the valley.

La Rosta

Pointe de la Turche

Underused, quiet sector with some of the steepest runs in the area and great red run cruising

If you're driving, park here and take the fast chair into the slopes

MONT CHÉRY
1850m

Chavannes
1485m

La Turche

Les Perrières

Col de l'Encrenaz
1435m

Les Gets
1170m/3,840ft

SCHOOLS

ESF
t 0450 791313

International
t 0450 790516

BASS
t 0871 7801500 (UK)

Classes
(ESF prices)
6 half days (2½hr am or pm) €115

Private lessons
€34 for 1hr for 1 to 3 people

GUIDES

Mountain Office
t 0450 747223

FOR BEGINNERS
Good for novices and improvers

The wide village nursery slopes are convenient, and benefit from snow-guns, though crowds are reported to be a problem. Some of the best progression runs are over at Nyon, and the slopes between Avoriaz and Morzine are also recommended. Adventurous novices also have the option of easy pistes around Le Pléney. Near-beginners can get over to Les Gets via Le Pléney, and return via Le Ranfolly.

FOR CROSS-COUNTRY
Good variety

There are 95km/60 miles of varied cross-country trails, not all at valley level. The best section is in the pretty Vallée de la Manche beside the Nyon mountain up to the Lac de Mines d'Or, where there is a good restaurant. The Pléney-Chavannes loop is pleasant and relatively snow-reliable.

QUEUES
Few problems when snow is good

Queues are not usually a problem in the local area. But we have had complaints of overcrowding,

particularly in the Ranfolly-Rosta area and of waits for the old Rosta chair. The Nyon cable-car and Belvédère chair-lift (Le Pléney) are weekend bottlenecks. Long waits at the Morzine to Pléney gondola can be avoided by using the adjacent chairs, suggests a reporter. The cable-car from Les Prodains is queue-prone at peak periods (but again, there are chair-lift alternatives).

MOUNTAIN RESTAURANTS
Some excellent huts

We have had several very enjoyable Savoyard lunches at the rustic Chez Nannon near the top of the Troncs chair between Nyon and Chamossière. A 2006 reporter raves about the new Pointe du Nyon restaurant ('we swapped our boots for slippers, the food was good quality and the pizzas were named after footballers!'). The nice little Atray des Neiges at the foot of the d'Atray chair is also good. The tiny Lhottys hut has had mixed reviews ('amazing fresh seafood', 'mediocre spaghetti Bolognese', 'inadequate toilets'). The Vaffieu at the top of the Folliets chair has had several recommendations ('nice fondue', 'liked

↑ It's a big, sprawling resort; the far side is the link to Avoriaz

OT MORZINE / F REINHART

The **ESF** Morzine has 155 instructors offering group and private lessons at every level. For off-piste guiding, instructors can be hired for groups of up to six people, by the day and half day.

t 0450 791313
f 0450 791770
info@esf-morzine.com
www.esf-morzine.com

the food, service, location and atmosphere'), as has the Nabor at Pléney ('really good food, friendly'). The Mouflon at the top of Rosta has 'good food but bad toilets'. The Tanière in Les Gets, at the bottom of the Chavannes chair, is recommended for its 'varied food and lower prices'. The self-service on Mont Chéry is 'one of the better examples of the breed'. Also on Mont Chéry, two 2006 visitors recommend the Chanterelle on the back of the mountain ('lasagne to die for') and the rustic Ancrenaz Bar. A 2005 reporter found many small huts overcrowded even midweek in January.

SCHOOLS AND GUIDES
Good reports
The British Alpine Ski & Snowboard School (BASS) is pricey but gets good reports: 'absolutely first class; personalised, friendly service'; '£100 for a 2-hour private lesson with Becci Malthouse a bargain!'; 'my five-year old was skiing down the blues by the end of the week'. The beginners in a 2005 reporter's group had private lessons with 'great instructors' from the ESF (which is half the price). Another visitor and his grown-up daughter had a private lesson with 'an excellent instructor' at International: 'It was money very well spent.'

Morzine

339

OFF-PISTE RUNS IN THE PORTES DU SOLEIL AREA

The Portes du Soleil offers a lot of great lift-served off-piste terrain. We asked the ESF Morzine to give us a run-down on some of the highlights on the French side. Like all serious off-piste runs, these should not be done without guidance.

Morzine – Nyon/Chamossière area
From the Chamossière chair-lift (2000m/6,560ft), heading north brings you to two runs – one on the same north-west slope as the pistes, the other via a col down the north-east slope to the the Nyon cable-car (1020m/3,350ft) in the Vallée de La Manche – a wild area, with a great view of Mont Blanc at first.

Avoriaz area – two suggestions
From the the Fornet chair-lift (2220m/7,280ft) on the Swiss border, you head west to descend a beautiful, unspoiled bowl leading down to the village of L'Erigné (1185m/3,890ft). In powder snow you descend the west-facing slopes of the bowl; when there is spring snow, you traverse right to descend the south-facing slopes. Medium-pitch slopes, for skiers and snowboarders.

From the top of the Machon chair-lift (2275m/7,460ft) you traverse west, beneath the peaks of Les Hauts Forts, across Les Crozats de la Chaux – a steep, north-facing slope. You then turn north to descend through the forest to the cable-car station at Les Prodains (1150m/3,770ft). Testing terrain, for very good skiers – the traverse is dangerous following a snowfall.

Châtel area
From the top of the Linga chair-lift (2040m/6,690ft), you head north-west to cross the ridge on your right at a recognisable col and then head down the La Lèche slope to the drag-lift of the same name (1550m/5,090ft). It's a north-facing slope with powder snow. This run starts in a white wilderness, taking you through trees back to civilisation. Steep slopes – for good skiers only.

FACILITIES FOR CHILDREN
Various possibilities

The facilities of the Outa nursery are quite impressive, but we've received reports of poor English and low staff ratios. There is a big children's area, the Zone Enfant, in the Chavannes area. An ESF childcare centre, Club des Piou-Piou looks after children between the ages of 3 and 12 after skiing ('Our younger children were quite happy, the older ones a little bored,' says a 2006 visitor). The Dérêches Farm offers days learning about animals, snow-shoeing and tobogganing. A 2006 reporter recommends both Jack Frosts and Powderbabies nanny services – 'they come to your chalet with toys etc'. Tour operators Esprit Ski and Ski Famille have good facilities.

STAYING THERE

HOW TO GO
Good-value hotels and chalets

The tour operator market concentrates on hotels and chalets.

Chalets There's a wide choice, but position varies enormously and you need to check this carefully before booking. Snowline has six central places (most with hot-tub and/or sauna). Reporters recommend the independently run Farmhouse (0450 790826): 'excellent service, good ski guide'; 'gourmet dinner with fine wines and invaluable mini-bus service to the lifts'. A 2006 snowboarder reporter recommends Ride&Slide's chalets and service.

Hotels The handful of 3-star hotels includes some quite smart ones; and there are dozens of 2-stars and 1-stars.
(((4) **Airelles** (0450 747121) Central 3-star close to Pléney lifts and Prodains and Nyon bus routes. Good pool.
(((4) **Champs Fleuris** (0450 791444) Comfy 3-star next to Pléney lifts. Pool.
(((4) **Dahu** (0450 759292) 3-star linked to centre by footbridge over river; good restaurant; pool. Private shuttle to lifts.
((3) **Tremplin** (0450 791231) Next to lifts; 'friendly, good food, small rooms'.
((3) **Viking** (0450 791169) is now run by Crystal. On the slopes at top of gondola. Evening entertainment. Pool and childcare.
((3) **Bergerie** (0450 791369) Rustic chalet, in centre. Friendly staff. Pool.
((2) **Côtes** (0450 790996) Simple 2-star on the edge of town. Pool.
((2) **Equipe** (0450 791143) One of the best 2-stars; next to the Pléney lift.

Self-catering The Télémark apartments, close to the Super-Morzine gondola, and the Udrezants, by the Prodains cable-car, have been recommended.

EATING OUT
A reasonable choice

The best restaurant in town is probably in hotel Samoyede, which offers traditional and modern cuisine – we enjoyed lobster ravioli, truffle risotto and scallops. The hotel Airelles has a fine restaurant and the hotel Dahu also has good food. The Chamade looks the part (elegant table settings) but reports are mixed. The Grange does 'excellent food, but at a price'. Locals rate the Chalet Philibert highly. The unpretentious Etale was popular with 2006 visitors ('excellent friendly service and a good plat du jour at lunchtime', 'our favourite'). Café Chaud is popular for fondue and the Pique Feu does Savoyard food at 'reasonable prices'. The Tyrolien has 'tartiflette to die for' and 'well presented steaks and fondues'. Clin d'Oeil has been praised.

APRES-SKI
One of the livelier French resorts

On Tuesday evenings there's a 'ski retrospective' on the slopes at Le Pléney, and on Thursdays there's a torchlight descent and floodlit skiing.

Nightlife is good by French resort standards. Bar Robinson is basic but always busy as the slopes empty. The Dixie has sport on TV, MTV, a cellar bar and some live music. Between the slopes and the centre, and all in the same building are: the Cavern, which is popular with resort staff; the Coyote for arcade games and DJ; the Boudha Café, with Asian decor. At the nearby Crepu dancing on the tables in ski boots to deafening music seems compulsory. L'Opéra (which advertised 'nuits torrides' of striptease and lap dancing last time we heard) and Laury's are late-night haunts.

OFF THE SLOPES
Quite good; excursions possible

There is an excellent ice rink, with ice hockey matches and skating galas. There are two cinemas. Some hotels have pools open to non-residents. 'Morzine is a shopper's paradise,' says a recent visitor. Buses run to Thonon for more shopping, and car owners can drive to Geneva, Annecy or Montreux. There are lots of pretty walks and a cheese factory you can visit.

Paradiski

The new mega-area: a single cable-car gives residents of Les Arcs more space and residents of La Plagne more challenges

KEY FACTS

Paradiski area	
Slopes	1200-3250m
	3,940-10,660ft
Lifts	141
Pistes	425km
	264 miles
Green	5%
Blue	56%
Red	27%
Black	12%

December 2003 saw the opening of the world's largest cable-car – a double-decker holding 200 people – which swoops low across a wooded valley to link the French resorts of Les Arcs and La Plagne. The result is that the two resorts can claim a joint ski area, called Paradiski, that is one of the biggest in the world. With 425km/264 miles of pistes and 141 lifts, it beats most of the established mega-areas; only the Three Valleys and the Portes du Soleil are significantly bigger. Add in a lot of off-piste terrain and you could argue the new area is bigger than either.

The new cable-car, called the Vanoise Express, spans the 2km/1 mile-wide valley between Plan-Peisey (in the Les Arcs area) and a point 300m/980ft above Montchavin (in La Plagne).

The linking of these two major resorts is good news for the great British piste-basher who likes to cover as much ground as possible. For those who like a bit of a challenge, getting from your home base to both far-flung outposts of the Paradiski area – Villaroger in Les Arcs and Champagny-en-Vanoise in La Plagne – would make quite a full day.

The new link is also good for experts. Those based in either resort can more easily tackle the north face of La Plagne's Bellecôte, finishing the run in Nancroix. Those based in La Plagne who are finding the piste skiing a bit tame can easily get across to Les Arcs' Aiguille Rouge.

If you want to make the most of the new link it makes sense to stay near one of the cable-car stations. But once you start to study the piste maps you realise that it's easily accessible from many other bases.

On the Les Arcs side, **Plan-Peisey** and nearby **Vallandry** are in pole position. They are basically small, low-rise, modern developments, but built in a much more sympathetic style than the original Les Arcs resorts. They are quiet places to stay, but are expanding rapidly and a few UK operators have chalets there. You can also stay in the unspoiled old village of **Peisey**, 300m/980ft below and linked by bucket-lift to Plan-Peisey.

It's easy to get to the cable-car station at Plan-Peisey from the main resort parts of Les Arcs. One lift and a blue run is all it takes to get there from **Arc 1800**, which is the most attractive of the main resort units. From quieter **Arc 1600**, along the mountainside from 1800, it takes two lifts. **Arc 2000** and the stylish new **Arc 1950** development seem further away, over the ridge that separates them from 1600 and 1800; but all it takes is one fast chair to the ridge and one long blue run down the other side. Beyond and below the bowl of Arc 2000, **Le Pré** and **Villaroger** are not ideal starting points.

On the La Plagne side, the obvious place to stay is **Montchavin**, which is below the Vanoise Express station. Montchavin is a well-restored

LIFT PASSES

Paradiski
Covers lifts in whole
Paradiski area.
6-day pass €229
(over 60 €195; under
14 €172). Also covers
a day in the Three
Valleys, Val-d'Isère-
Tignes, Les Saisies
and Pralognan-en-
Vanoise.

Paradiski Découverte
Covers lifts in Les
Arcs area or La
Plagne area plus one
day Paradiski
extension.
6-day pass €205
(over 60 €174; under
14 €154). Pass also
covers a day in the
Three Valleys, Val-
d'Isère-Tignes, Les
Saisies, Pralognan.

OUR WEBSITE

Go to our website at
wtss.co.uk for resort
news, links to resort
sites, a build-your-
own-shortlist system
and reader forums.

UK Representative
Erna Low Consultants
9 Reece Mews
London SW7 3HE
t 0870 750 6820
info@ernalow.co.uk
www.ernalow.co.uk

traditional old village with modern
additions built in traditional style. **Les
Coches**, across the mountain from the
station, is most easily reached with the
help of a lift. It is entirely modern, but
built in a traditional style. From either,
one lift brings you to the cable-car.

The other parts of La Plagne are
some way from the cable-car. But one
long lift is all it takes to get from
monolithic **Plagne-Bellecôte** up to
L'Arpette, from which point it's a single
long blue descent. The most attractive
of the resort villages, **Belle-Plagne**, is
only a short run above Plagne-
Bellecôte. From the villages further
across the bowl – **Plagne-Villages**,
Plagne-Soleil, dreary **Plagne-Centre**,
futuristic **Aime-la-Plagne** – you have to
ride a lift to get to Plagne-Bellecôte.
From **Plagne 1800**, below the bowl,
add another lift. From the villages
beyond the bowl – rustic, sunny
Champagny-en-Vanoise and expanding
Montalbert – it's going to be pretty
hard work.

RIDING THE VANOISE EXPRESS

The cable-car ride from one resort to
the other takes less than four minutes.

The system is designed to be able
to operate in high winds, so the risk of
getting stranded miles from home is
low. It can shift 2,000 people an hour,
and end of the day crowds don't seem
to be a problem.

The lift company offers a six-day
pass covering the whole Paradiski
region, which is perhaps most likely to
appeal to people based in the villages
at either end of the lift, who might
divide their time between the two ski
areas as the mood takes them – one
day here, the next there.

But it also offers a pass (Paradiski
Découverte) which includes just one
day's use of the Vanoise Express and
the lifts in the other resort.

Alternatively, you can also buy one-
day extensions to a Les Arcs or La
Plagne six-day lift pass. These cost
less at weekends (18 instead of 25
euros) because demand is less then.

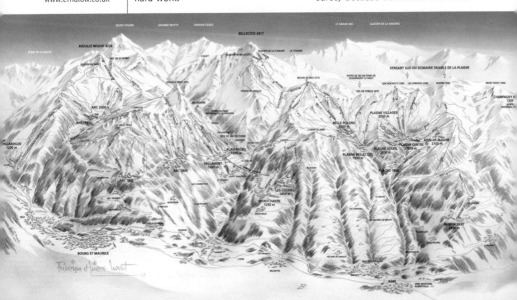

La Plagne

Villages from the rustic to the futuristic spread over a vast area of intermediate terrain – mainly high and snow-sure

343

COSTS

① ② ③ ④ ⑤ ⑥

RATINGS

The slopes
Fast lifts	**
Snow	****
Extent	****
Expert	***
Intermediate	*****
Beginner	****
Convenience	*****
Queues	***
Mountain restaurants	****

The rest
Scenery	****
Resort charm	*
Off-slope	*

NEWS

For 2006/07, a six-pack will replace the Charmettes and the Bouclet drag-lifts from La Roche to Aime-la-Plagne. A new blue run will also be created to the chair, as an alternative to the Emile Allais black. In Les Coches, the Orgere drag and the Plan Bois chair up to the mid-mountain nursery area will be replaced by a six-pack. Snowmaking will again be further extended.

For 2005/06 the Arpette chair (from Plagne-Bellecôte towards Montchavin and the Vanoise Express) was upgraded to an eight-seater.

■ Extensive intermediate slopes, plus plentiful, excellent off-piste terrain

■ Cable-car link with Les Arcs adds even more terrain

■ Good nursery slopes

■ High and fairly snow-sure – and with some wonderful views

■ Purpose-built resort units are convenient for the slopes

■ Attractive, traditional-style villages lower down share the slopes

■ Wooded runs of lower resorts are useful in poor weather

■ Pistes in the main bowl don't offer much challenge – or much vertical

■ Pistes get very crowded in places

■ Still lots of slow old chair-lifts

■ Lower villages can suffer from poor snow – sunny Champagny especially

■ Unattractive architecture in some of the higher resort units

■ Hardly any green runs for nervous beginners to go on to – though some blues are very easy

■ Nightlife very limited

With 225km/140 miles of its own slopes and 85 per cent of these being blue or red, the La Plagne area is an intermediate's paradise. And with much-needed lift improvements over the last few years, plus the link with Les Arcs, the resort is going up in our estimation. It has a reputation for plug-ugly, soulless, purpose-built villages and some of them justify that view. But there are 10 different villages to choose from – and as well as delightful old mountain villages at the foot of the slopes, there are some quite attractive purpose-built centres, too.

Experts prepared to hire a guide can have a splendid time off-piste, with some long descents which are often deserted and untracked compared with the classic off-piste runs of more macho resorts like Val-d'Isère.

THE RESORT

La Plagne consists of no fewer than 10 separate 'villages'; six are purpose-built at altitude in the main bowl, on or above the tree line and linked by road, lifts and pistes; the other four are scattered around outside the bowl. Each is self-contained, with its own shops, bars, restaurants, schools and lift pass offices.

Even the core resorts vary a lot in character. The first to be built, in the 1960s, was Plagne-Centre – still the

focal point for shops and après-ski. Typical of its time, it has ugly blocks and dreary indoor 'malls' that house a reasonable selection of shops, bars and restaurants. Recent developments are more pleasing to the eye.

Lifts radiate from Centre to all sides of the bowl, the major one being the big twin-cable gondola to Grande Rochette. A cable-car goes to the even more obtrusive 'village' of Aime-la-Plagne – a group of monolithic blocks. Below these two, and a bit of a backwater ('a dormitory', says one

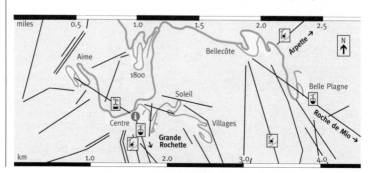

KEY FACTS

Resort	1800-2100m	
	5,900-6,890ft	

La Plagne only

Slopes	1250-3250m	
	4,100-10,660ft	
Lifts		105
Pistes		225km
		140 miles
Green		8%
Blue		59%
Red		25%
Black		8%
Snowmaking		
		277 guns

For Paradiski area

Slopes	1200-3250m	
	3,940-10,660ft	
Lifts		141
Pistes		425km
		264 miles
Green		5%
Blue		56%
Red		27%
Black		12%

SNOWPIX.COM / CHRIS GILL

Acres and acres of gently undulating terrain, seen here from Belle-Plagne ↓

reader), is Plagne 1800, where the buildings are small-scale and chalet-style – indeed many are offered as catered chalets on the UK market. Access to the main bowl from here is by lifts to Aime-la-Plagne, and reporters comment that a drag-lift, the Lovatière, links with no other lifts.

A little way above Plagne-Centre is the newest development, Plagne-Soleil, with attractive modern chalets. This area is officially attached to Plagne-Villages, which is a rather strung-out but attractive collection of small-scale apartments and chalets in traditional style, handy for the slopes and with lift link to Plagne-Centre.

The two other core resort units are a bus-ride away, on the other side of a low hill. The large apartment buildings of Plagne-Bellecôte form a wall at the foot of the slopes leading down to it. Some way above it is Belle-Plagne – as its name suggests, easy on the eye, with a neo-Savoyard look, and entirely underground parking. Although Belle-Plagne is highly convenient for skiing, reporters complain of exhaustion when moving between the different levels in the evening, despite public lifts.

Lifts from Plagne-Bellecôte provide links to two of the lower resorts in the valleys outside the bowl – the old village of Montchavin and its more recently developed neighbour Les Coches, at the northern extremity of the area. Beyond Grande Rochette, at the southern extremity, is rustic Champagny. Beyond Aime-la-Plagne, at the western extremity, is little Montalbert. For a description of these villages, see the end of this chapter.

A free bus system between the core villages within the bowl runs until after midnight. But you may have to change in Plagne-Centre. Lifts from Belle-Plagne to Plagne-Bellecôte, Aime-la-Plagne to Plagne-Centre, and Plagne-Centre to Plagne-Villages all run until 1am.

A cable-car from above Montchavin gives access to the slopes of Les Arcs via Peisey-Vallandry. How appealing this will seem may depend on where in the wide La Plagne area you are based, but most readers who try it enjoy their day at Les Arcs. Trips by car to Val-d'Isère-Tignes or the Three Valleys are possible – and each is covered for a day with a six-day Paradiski or Paradiski Découverte pass.

THE MOUNTAINS

The majority of the slopes in the main bowl are above the tree line, though there are trees scattered around most of the resort centres. The slopes outside the bowl are open at the top but descend into woodland. The gondola up to the exposed glacier slopes on Bellecôte, to the west of the main bowl, is prone to closure by high winds or poor weather.

THE SLOPES
Multi-centred; can be confusing

La Plagne boasts 225km/140 miles of pistes over a wide area that can be broken down into seven distinct but interlinked sectors. From Plagne-Centre you can take a lift up to **Le Biolley**, from where you can head back to Centre, to Aime-la-Plagne or down gentle runs to **Montalbert**, from where you ride several successive lifts back up. But the main lift out of Plagne-Centre leads up to **La Grande Rochette**. From here there are good sweeping runs back down and an easier one over to Plagne-Bellecôte, or you can drop over the back into the mainly south-facing **Champagny** sector, for excellent long runs and great views

Plagne-Centre
A GRANDE ROCHETTE
2500m
s Verdons
2500m
Col de Forcle
2270m
Belle-Plagne
Plagne-Bellecôte ↓
Les Borseliers
ROCHE DE MIO
2700m
Col de la Chiaupe
2550m
Bellecôte
3417m
Champagny-le-Haut
Le Planay
Champagny-en-Vanoise
1250m

over to Courchevel.

From Plagne-Bellecôte and Belle-Plagne, you can head up to **Roche de Mio**, and have the choice of a gondola, or two successive fast chairs (the first of which also accesses Champagny). From Roche de Mio, runs spread out in all directions – towards La Plagne, Champagny or **Montchavin/Les Coches**. This sector can also be reached by taking a chair (upgraded to an eight-seater for last season) from Plagne-Bellecôte to L'Arpette.

From Roche de Mio you can also take a gondola down then up to the **Bellecôte glacier**. The top chair is normally shut in winter – but if open, it offers excellent snow and stunning views. You can descend 2000m/6,560ft vertical to Montchavin, with a not-difficult off-piste stretch in the middle.

Several reporters have complained that some runs are more difficult than their grading suggests, while others are easier. Some also complain that the signing can be confusing. There are a lot of slow old lifts still around. The piste map marks half a dozen drag-lifts as 'difficult', and reporters say some are very much so.

TERRAIN-PARKS
Lots of choices
There are four terrain-parks in the area. Belle-Plagne, Montchavin/Les Coches and Champagny all have decent parks; however, the new Snowpark above Plagne-Centre, serviced by the

Colorado chair-lift, is in a league of its own when up to scratch. With 25,000 square metres and over 20 obstacles, this is a freestyle wonderland. There are ride-on rails and boxes for first-timers as well as huge kinked monsters, rainbows and a wall-ride to challenge the best of them. Kicker-wise, from the smallest to the biggest of jumps, it's all here.

SNOW RELIABILITY
Generally good except low down
Most of La Plagne's runs are snow-sure, being at altitudes between 2000m and 2700m (6,560ft and 8,860ft) on the largely north-facing open slopes above the purpose-built centres. The lift company is nearing the end of a five-year plan to increase snowmaking on the links to all the villages. The north-facing runs to Montchavin/Les Coches and Montalbert, plus a few runs around Plagne-Centre and most of those into Plagne-Bellecôte and Belle Plagne, have guns at the moment. But even here cover can be patchy if the weather is warm. The two sunny runs to Champagny are often closed.

FOR EXPERTS
A few good blacks and off-piste
There are two great black runs from Bellecôte to the chair-lift up to the gondola mid-station at Col de la Chiaupe – both beautiful long runs with a vertical of some 1000m/3,280ft

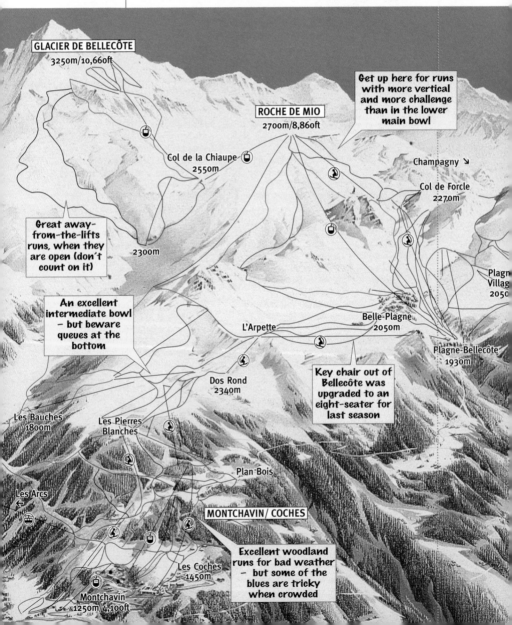

GLACIER DE BELLECÔTE
3250m/10,66oft

ROCHE DE MIO
2700m/8,86oft

Get up here for runs with more vertical and more challenge than in the lower main bowl

Col de la Chiaupe
2550m

Champagny ↘

Col de Forcle
227,0m

Great away-from-the-lifts runs, when they are open (don't count on it)

2300m

An excellent intermediate bowl – but beware queues at the bottom

L'Arpette

Belle-Plagne
2050m

Plagne Village 2050

Plagne-Bellecôte
1930m

Key chair out of Bellecôte was upgraded to an eight-seater for last season

Dos Rond
2340m

Les Bauches
1800m

Les Pierres Blanches

Plan Bois

Les Arcs

MONTCHAVIN/ COCHES

Excellent woodland runs for bad weather – but some of the blues are tricky when crowded

Les Coches
1450m

Montchavin
1250m/4,10oft

boarding

With such a huge amount of terrain, there is something for everyone in La Plagne. Expert free-riders, however, are advised to hire a guide as there is so much hidden terrain to be had off the mainly motorway-style pistes. When light gets flat hit the lower tree runs, as the open nature of the higher slopes will be a nightmare. Although this is a great place for beginners, with huge wide-open rolling pistes, be careful as there is also a lot of flat land, especially above Belle-Plagne, the tunnel in the middle of the Inversens run and the blue run linking Montchavin with Les Bauches. Make sure to get enough speed, or to avoid such areas, or you'll be doing a lot of walking. Although most drag-lifts have been replaced there are still several unavoidable ones – the more difficult ones are marked on the resort piste map.

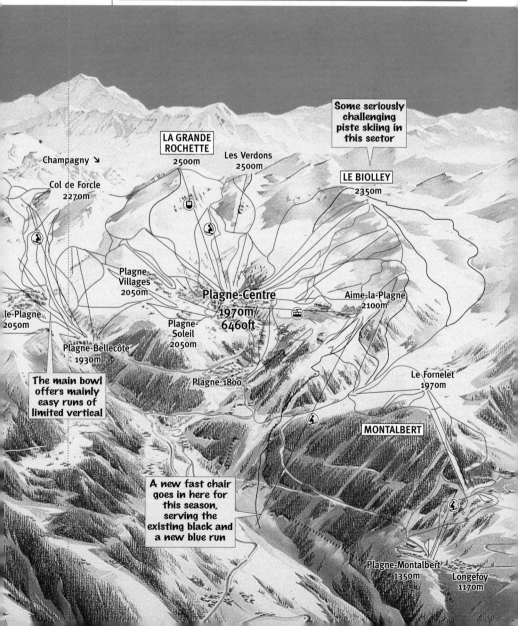

Some seriously challenging piste skiing in this sector

LA GRANDE ROCHETTE 2500m

Les Verdons 2500m

Champagny ↘

Col de Forcle 2270m

LE BIOLLEY 2350m

Plagne-Villages 2050m

Plagne-Centre 1970m/ 6460ft

Aime-la-Plagne 2100m

le-Plagne 2050m

Plagne-Soleil 2050m

Plagne-Bellecôte 1930m

Plagne 1800

Le Fornelet 1970m

The main bowl offers mainly easy runs of limited vertical

MONTALBERT

A new fast chair goes in here for this season, serving the existing black and a new blue run

Plagne-Montalbert 1350m

Longefoy 1170m

FRANCE

348

that take you away from the lift system. But these are often closed because of too much or too little snow.

The long Emile Allais black run down from above Aime-la-Plagne is little-used, north-facing and very enjoyable in good snow. The drag-lifts back up are to be replaced by a new six-seat chair for 2006/07. The Coqs and Morbleu runs, also in the Aime-la-Plagne sector, are seriously steep.

But experts will get the best out of La Plagne if they hire a guide and explore the vast off-piste potential – which takes longer to get tracked out than in more 'macho' resorts.

FOR INTERMEDIATES
Great variety

Virtually the whole of La Plagne's area is a paradise for intermediates, with blue and red runs wherever you look.

For early intermediates there are plenty of gentle blue motorway pistes in the main La Plagne bowl, and a long, interesting run from Roche de Mio back to Belle Plagne, Les Inversens (involving a tunnel). The blue runs either side of L'Arpette, on the Montchavin side of the main bowl, are glorious cruises. In poor weather the best place to be is in the trees on the gentle runs leading down to Montalbert. The easiest way over to Champagny is from the Roche de Mio-Col de Forcle area rather than from Grande Rochette.

Better intermediates have lots of delightful long red runs to try. There are challenging red mogul pitches down from the glacier. Roche de Mio to Les Bauches is a drop of 900m/ 2,950ft – the first half, Le Clapet, is a fabulous varied run with lots of off-

piste diversions possible; the second half, Les Crozats, was changed from black to red for 2003/04 – not surprisingly, it can be tricky for timid intermediates. A blue run carries on to Montchavin, but much of this is flattish, and hard work.

The Champagny sector has a couple of tough reds – Kamikaze and Hara-Kiri – leading from Grande Rochette. And the long blue cruise Bozelet has one surprisingly steep section. The long, sweeping Mont de la Guerre red, with 1250m/4,100ft vertical from Les Verdons to Champagny, is also a great run in good snow (a rare event).

FOR BEGINNERS
Excellent facilities for the novice

La Plagne is a good place to learn, with generally good snow and above-average facilities for beginners, especially children. Each of the main centres has nursery slopes on its doorstep. There's a free drag-lift in each resort as well. There are no long green runs to progress to, but no shortage of easy blues. The Plan Bois area above Les Coches has good gentle slopes. But the blue runs back into Plagne 1800 and Montchavin are difficult for novices.

CROSS-COUNTRY
Open and wooded trails

There are 85km/53 miles of prepared cross-country trails scattered around. The most beautiful of these are the 30km/19 miles of winding track set out in the sunny valley around Champagny-le-Haut. The north-facing areas have more wooded trails that link the various centres. It's best to have a car if you want to make the most of it all.

SCHOOLS

ESF
Schools in all centres.
t 0479 090668 (Belle Plagne)

Oxygène (Plagne-Centre)
t 0479 090399

EL Pro (Belle-Plagne)
t 0479 091162

Reflex (Plagne 1800)
t 0613 808056

Evolution 2 (Montchavin)
t 0479 078185

Classes (ESF prices)
6 half-days €175

Private lessons
€86 for 2hr for 1-2 people

QUEUES
Main problems being sorted

La Plagne used to have some big bottlenecks. Recent lift upgrades have eased some of the worst problems, but even so one March visitor grew weary of the many five-minute queues when getting around the area. The upgrading of the Arpette chair from Plagne-Bellecôte towards Montchavin has reduced the queues for that. But reporters still complain of queues for the Roche de Mio gondola, despite its renovation, and there are still several lifts that can generate queues that you can't avoid, once you've descended to them – at Les Bauches for example, and in the Champagny sector – especially at the Verdons Sud lift, warns one reader. The gondola to the glacier is queue-prone when snow is poor lower down.

Crowds on the pistes are now as much of a problem as lift queues, particularly above Plagne-Bellecôte and Belle-Plagne in the afternoon, and at Roche de Mio – 'very crowded, quite dangerous' comments a recent reporter, while another advises retreating to the quieter slopes of Montalbert, Les Coches or Montchavin.

MOUNTAIN RESTAURANTS
An enormous choice

Mountain restaurants are numerous, varied and crowded only in peak periods, as many people eat in one of the resorts – particularly Champagny or Montchavin/Les Coches.

The sunny, panoramic Champagny slopes are particularly well served. Our favourite places are the recently built Chalet des Verdons Sud, with excellent food and service on a big terrace or in the warmly woody interior, and La Rossa, at the top of the Champagny gondola – friendly staff, good, basic cooking. Readers also recommend the 'terrific' Roc des Blanchets, at the top of the Borseliers chair-lift. All three have self-service snack bars as well as table-service restaurants.

Two great rustic restaurants in which to hole up in poor weather for a long lunch of Savoyard dishes are Chez Pat du Sauget, above Montchavin, and Au Bon Vieux Temps, just below Aime-la-Plagne.

Chalet des Colosses above Plagne-Bellecôte and Chalets des Inversens at Roche de Mio ('fabulous views, good food') have been highly recommended. The little Breton cafe at the bottom of

La Plagne

349

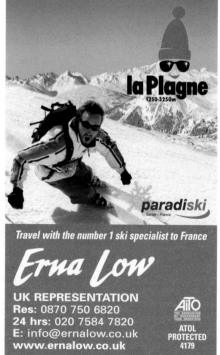

The **most** choice combined with all the **local** knowledge

www.laplagnechalets.co.uk

CHILDREN

Nursery (Belle-Plagne)
t 0479 090668
Ages 18mnth to 3yr

Les P'tits Bonnets
(Plagne-Centre)
t 0479 090083
Ages from 10wk

Marie Christine
(Centre)
t 0479 091181
Ages 2 to 6

ESF nurseries and snow nurseries (ages from 2 or 3):
Aime 0479 090475
Village and Soleil
0479 090440
Belle 0479 090668
Centre 0479 090040
Bellecôte 0479 090133
1800 0479 090964

Ski schools
Children's classes are available up to 12 or 16 depending on the village: ESF Belle-Plagne 6 half-days €153 (€185 during French February school holidays).

GETTING THERE

Air Geneva 149km/93 miles (3½hr); Lyon 196km/122 miles (3½hr); Chambéry 92km/57 miles (2½hr).

Rail Aime (18km/11 miles) and Bourg-St-Maurice (35km/22 miles) (Eurostar service available); frequent buses from stations.

---

the Quillis lift has been recommended as has the 'very French' Chalet du Friolin at Les Bauches. The Forperet, an old farm above Montalbert, is popular ('superb views, good value') and does good tartiflette.

Other reader recommendations include the Bergerie, with 'fantastic fireplace', above Plagne-Villages, Crystal des Neiges, Carroley, Plan Bois, Arpette, Dou du Praz, and the 'friendly' Plein Soleil.

SCHOOLS AND GUIDES
Better alternatives to ESF
Each centre has its own ESF school. High-season classes can be much too large (up to 20) and good spoken English cannot be relied upon. One youngster 'was left in floods of tears, with her confidence completely destroyed'. But reports about private lessons are generally positive, the school in Les Coches has come in for praise, and one 2006 visitor had an excellent experience with an ESF guide.

However, the consensus seems to be that the alternatives to the ESF are preferable. The Oxygène school in Plagne-Centre has impressed most reporters: 'Worked very hard with us, and was very patient.' 'Superb with our children, very friendly, made everything into a game.' But one commented, 'Nothing special but no problems either.' We have had glowing reports on the El Pro school in Belle-Plagne ('good English, asked us what we wanted to do, strong focus on technique and safety'). We have also had good reports on Evolution 2 (based in Montchavin): 'One of the most positive and best value experiences I've had in a while.' Reflex is the newest school (based in 1800), and a reporter said of a private lesson, 'The best for several years; humorous, pitched at the right level to test and enjoy.' Antenne Handicap offers private lessons for skiers with any kind of disability.

FACILITIES FOR CHILDREN
Good choice
Children are well catered for with facilities in each of the villages. The nursery at Belle-Plagne is 'excellent, with good English spoken'. Be wary, however, of ESF classes (see 'Schools and Guides'). A Club Med at Aime-la-Plagne is one of their 'family' villages. Several UK chalet operators run childcare services.

STAYING THERE

HOW TO GO
Plenty of packages
The resort is very apartment-dominated, but there are alternatives. There are two Club Meds.
Chalets There's a large number available – the majority are fairly simple, small, and located in 1800. But new chalets in the lower villages are proving very popular now that La Plagne is linked with Les Arcs.
Hotels There are very few, all of 2-star or 3-star grading.
(2) **Araucaria** (0479 092020) Very modern new 3-star at Plagne-Centre.
(2) **Balcons** (0479 557655) 3-star at Belle-Plagne. Pool.
(2) **Carlina** (0479 097846) New, very promising-looking 3-star slope-side on the fringe of Belle-Plagne.
(2) **Terra Nova** (0479 557900) Big, 120-room 3-star in Plagne-Centre.
Self-catering There is a huge amount of apartment accommodation; much of it is very ordinary, but there is more good accommodation being built.

SMART APARTMENTS – SEE FEATURE

The Chalets les Montagnettes in Belle-Plagne are spacious with good views. and the MGM Les Hauts Bois apartments in Aime-la-Plagne are highly recommended by a reader – 'friendly, not a bad size'. A new 4-star residence, the Pelvoux, opened in Plagne-Centre last year.

EATING OUT
A surprising amount of choice
Throughout the resort there is a good range of casual restaurants including pizzerias and traditional Savoyard places serving raclette and fondue.
Reader recommendations in Plagne-Centre include the Métairie ('the most enjoyable we've encountered in the Alps'), the Vega ('pricey but friendly with excellent food'), the Maison ('easy going relaxed place serving good pizzas, until 1am'), and the Refuge ('great meal in charming, rustic atmosphere', 'very reasonable').
In Plagne-Villages, the Casa de l'Ours is good for pizzas and steaks, the Grizzli is 'superb' for Savoyard food – 'worth visiting for the chocolate cake alone'. In Plagne 1800, the Loup Garrou, the Petit Chaperon Rouge and the Mama Mia pizzeria have been praised as has the Loup Blanc – 'great food, good service'. At Aime-la-Plagne, Au Bon Vieux Temps (see Mountain

ACTIVITIES

Indoor Sauna and solarium in most centres, squash (1800), fitness centres (Belle-Plagne, 1800, Centre, Bellecôte), library (Centre), climbing wall, cinemas, bowling, craft courses

Outdoor Heated swimming pool (Bellecôte), bob-sleigh (La Roche), marked walks, tobogganing, paragliding, snowmobiles, ice-climbing, ice rink, snow quad-bikes, paintball, snow-shoeing, dog-sledding

Phone numbers
From abroad use the prefix +33 and omit the initial '0' of the phone number.

restaurants) is open in the evening and the Soupe au Schuss, now called the Cave, buried deep in the main block, has 'exceptional' food.

In Plagne-Bellecôte, the Ferme and Chalet des Colosses have been recommended. In Belle-Plagne, so have Pappagone pizzeria, the Chalet Maître Kanter ('good value'), the Cloche ('good duck breast in bilberry sauce') and the Face Nord ('very friendly, lovely rabbit'). The Matafan has 'a homely feel and great pierre chaude'.

APRES-SKI
Bars, bars, bars

Though fairly quiet during low season, La Plagne has a wide range of après-ski, catering particularly for the younger crowd. Plagne-Centre has night skiing on the slalom slope.

In Belle-Plagne, the Tête Inn and the Cheyenne are the main bars. The Maître Kanter has been recommended. The King Café, now called No Bl'm Café, with a massive TV and occasional live music, is the liveliest bar in Plagne-Centre. Plagne 1800 is fairly

quiet at night – though the Mine (complete with old train and mining artefacts) is an exception: 'Get there early for a seat; quiz night and rock bands recommended.' Another reader recommends upstairs at the Loup Garrou. Plagne-Bellecôte is very limited at night, with only one real bar – Showtime, which is popular for karaoke. But there is bowling, and tubing. Aime-la-Plagne is also quiet.

The Luna (Plagne-Centre), the Jet 73 (Plagne-Bellecôte) and the Saloon (Belle-Plagne) are the main discos. There are cinemas at Aime, Bellecôte and Plagne-Centre.

OFF THE SLOPES
OK for the active

As well as the sports and fitness facilities, winter walks along marked trails are pleasant: 'There are enough walks to keep you busy for six days,' says one reporter. It's also easy to get up the mountain on the gondolas, which both have restaurants at the top. The Olympic bob-sleigh run is a popular evening activity (see feature box). Excursions are limited.

STAYING IN THE LOWER RESORTS
A good plan

Montchavin (1250m/4,100ft) is based on an old farming hamlet and has an attractive traffic-free centre. The cable-car link with Les Arcs starts from 300m/980ft above the village, and is reached by a fast chair. There are adequate shops, a kindergarten and a ski school. Reaching La Plagne involves a series of lifts; but the local slopes have quite a bit to offer –

La Plagne

351

Selected chalets in La Plagne

↑ The reassuringly padded bob-raft is much the cheapest way to experience the thrill of the bob-sleigh run – and quite exciting enough for most people

OT LA PLAGNE / J FAVRE

UK Representative
Erna Low Consultants
9 Reece Mews
London SW7 3HE
t 0870 750 6820
f 020 7589 9531
info@ernalow.co.uk
www.ernalow.co.uk

OUR WEBSITE

Go to our website at wtss.co.uk for resort news, links to resort sites, a build-your-own resort shortlist system and reader forums.

TOURIST OFFICES

La Plagne:
t 0479 097979
bienvenue@
la-plagne.com
www.la-plagne.com

Montchavin-Les Coches
t 0479 078282
info@
montchavin-
lescoches.com
www.montchavin-
lescoches.com

Montalbert
t 0479 097733
maison.montalbert@
la-plagne.com
www.montalbert.com

Champagny-en-Vanoise
t 0479 550655
info@champagny.com
www.champagny.com

pretty, sheltered runs, well endowed with snowmaking, with nursery slopes at village level and up at Plan Bois. Those who venture further can return from Roche de Mio or the Bellecôte glacier (off-piste) in one lovely long swoop. The more usual way home involves some of the trickiest blue runs we have encountered. Après-ski is quiet, but the village doesn't lack atmosphere and has a couple of nice bars, a nightclub, cinema and night skiing. The Bellecôte hotel (0479 078330) is convenient for the slopes.

Les Coches (1450m/4,760ft) is 2km/ 1 mile away and shares the same slopes. It is a sympathetically designed, quiet, modern mini-resort with a traffic-free centre. It has its own school and kindergarten. The Last One pub is good for après-ski, with a big screen TV and live bands. Poze (for pizza) and Taverne du Monchu are recommended for eating out. There's a shuttle to the cinema in Montchavin.

Montalbert (1350m/4,430ft) is a traditional but much expanded village

with quicker access into the main area – though it's a long way from here across to the Bellecôte glacier or the Les Arcs link. The local slopes are easy and wooded – a useful insurance against bad visibility. The Aigle Rouge (0479 555105) is a simple hotel.

SMART APARTMENTS – SEE FEATURE
The Chalets de Montalbert and Les Granges units are 'simply furnished but pleasantly spacious'.

Champagny-en-Vanoise (1250m/ 4,100ft) is a charming village in a pretty, wooded setting, with its modern expansion done sensitively. It is at the opposite end of the slopes from the link to Les Arcs but well placed for an outing by taxi or car to Courchevel. Given good snow, there are lovely runs home (though not recommended for near-beginners). There are several hotels, of which the two best are both Logis de France. The Glières (0479 550552) is a rustic old hotel with varied rooms, a friendly welcome and good food. The Ancolie (0479 550500) is smarter, with modern facilities (recommended by a 2004 reporter). The Alpina (0479 550459) is 'consistently good for both food and rooms', says a regular visitor, and is close to the lift.

SMART APARTMENTS – SEE FEATURE
Les Alpages de Champagny is an impressive-looking chalet-style development, new for 2006/07, with a pool and sauna.

The village is quiet in the evenings but the restaurant Poya is highly rated again this year for a 'delightful atmosphere, a wonderful view and excellent food at reasonable prices'.

TRY THE OLYMPIC BOB-SLEIGH RUN – YOU CAN NOW DO IT SOLO

If the thrills of a day on the slopes aren't enough, you can round it off by having a go on the bob-sleigh run that was built specially for the 1992 Winter Olympics. Note that it is open on certain afternoons and early evenings only. The floodlit 1.5km/1 mile run drops 125m/410ft and has 19 bends. You can go in a proper four-man 'taxi-bob' (100 euros in 2006), a padded driverless bob-raft (34 euros), or, the latest craze, a mono-bob, 95 euros.

We tried the mono-bob and hurtled down solo at 100kph/62mph (in excess of the advertised speed!) lying almost horizontally – a great thrill, though we have to admit that we did close our eyes on a couple of the sharper bends (the pressure in the turns can be as high as 3g). Whether it is worth £70 to scare yourself silly is your call. With the taxi-bob, you are one of three passengers wedged in a real four-man bob behind the driver. You reach a maximum advertised speed of 110kph/68mph. Most people find the bob raft's 80kph/50mph quite thrilling enough. Be sure your physical state is up to the ride. It's a good idea to book ahead – and there are minimum age limits. Additional insurance is available (holiday policies may not be valid).

Portes du Soleil

Low altitude, largely intermediate circuit of slopes straddling the French-Swiss border, with a variety of contrasting resorts to stay in

The Portes du Soleil vies with the Trois Vallées for the title 'World's Largest Ski Area', but its slopes are very different from those of Méribel, Courchevel, Val-Thorens and neighbours. The Portes du Soleil's slopes are spread out over a large area, and not all are linked – but most are part of an extensive circuit straddling the French-Swiss border. You can travel the circuit in either direction, with a short bus-ride needed at Châtel. There are smaller areas to explore slightly off the main circuit. The runs are great for keen intermediates who like to travel long distances and through different resorts. There are few of the tightly packed networks of runs that encourage you to stay put in one area – though there are exceptions in one or two places. The area also has some nice rustic mountain restaurants, serving good food in pleasant, sunny settings.

The lifts throughout the area have been improved in recent years, with several new high-speed chair-lifts eliminating some bad bottlenecks – though there are still plenty of drags and slow chairs. But the slopes are low by French standards, with top heights in the range 2000m to 2300m (6,560ft to 7,550ft), and good snow is far from assured (though snowmaking has been expanded in recent years). When the snow is good you can have a great time racing all over the circuit. But the slopes can get very crowded, especially at weekends and in the Avoriaz area.

Purpose-built **Avoriaz** has the most snow-sure slopes and is especially good for families, with a big snow-

The pretty village of Morgins in Switzerland, seen from a run down from the French side →

SNOWPIX.COM / CHRIS GILL

FRANCE

354

SNOWPIX.COM / CHRIS GILL

The Portes du Soleil is a good area for mountain restaurants – these are at Plaine Dranse in the Châtel sector ↓

garden right in the heart of the car-free village. And it is good for snowboarders and freestylers, with three terrain-parks and now snow-cross areas.

The other French resort on the main circuit is **Châtel**. Given good snow, it has some of the best runs in the area – though they are mostly quite short. It is an old and quite characterful village, but traffic is a nuisance at times. It has some good beginner areas – at resort level and up the mountain.

Morzine is close to Avoriaz. It is linked by lift but there's no piste all the way back to town. It's a summer as well as a winter resort – a pleasant, bustling little town with good shops and restaurants, busy traffic and long walks to the lifts from much of the accommodation – countered by increasing use of hotel minibuses. The local slopes are extensive, and linked to those of the slightly higher, quieter,

traditional village of Les Gets. But they are low, and good snow is certainly not assured. You can use Morzine as a base to ski the main Portes du Soleil circuit, but it's not ideal. Linked **Les Gets** is another attractive family resort, at slightly higher altitude; it is even further off the main circuit, and if skiing that circuit is a priority you are better off elsewhere – unless you have a car to drive to Ardent's gondola.

On the Swiss side, **Champéry** is a classic, charming Swiss village – but again just off the main circuit. You have to take a cable-car down from the main slopes as well as up to them – or, if there is enough snow, take a piste that ends out of town and then ride a bus.

Champoussin and **Les Crosets** are purpose-built mini-resorts set on the very extensive open slopes between Champéry and Morgins, with fairly direct links over to Avoriaz. **Morgins**, in contrast to Champéry, has excellent local slopes – but they are low and the linking runs from Châtel are very sunny and prone to poor conditions or even closure. Its more serious local runs on the Swiss side are enjoyable and prettily wooded, but they are also limited in extent.

On a spur off the main circuit are the slopes above **Torgon** in Switzerland (with splendid views over Lake Geneva). This area can be reached from above Châtel and is usually quiet even when the rest of the circuit is packed. Almost linked, too, is **La Chapelle d'Abondance** in France – down the valley from Châtel.

Puy-St-Vincent

Underrated small modern resort with limited but varied slopes – good for young families who haven't been spoilt by mega-resorts

COSTS

①②③④⑤⑥

RATINGS

The slopes
Fast lifts	**
Snow	***
Extent	**
Expert	***
Intermediate	***
Beginner	***
Convenience	*****
Queues	***
Mountain restaurants	***

The rest
Scenery	****
Resort charm	**
Off-slope	*

NEWS

There are new apartments at 'Station 1800', some with indoor pool.

For 2005/06 a new chair was installed from 1400 and a new long blue run, La Balme, was made, from the red Bois des Coqs slope down to 1400.

KEY FACTS

Resort	1400-1600m
	4,590-5,250ft
Slopes	1250-2700m
	4,100-8,860ft
Lifts	13
Pistes	60km
	37 miles
Green	18%
Blue	41%
Red	35%
Black	6%
Snowmaking	10km
	6 miles

Dog-sled rides are among the limited range of off-slope activities →

+ Mostly convenient, purpose-built resort that isn't too hideous

+ Good variety of slopes with challenges for all abilities

+ Friendly locals

+ Splendid scenery

+ Some great cross-country routes

– Slopes very limited in extent

– Upper village has only apartment-based accommodation

– Queues in French holidays

– Mainly slow old lifts

– Limited après-ski/restaurants

– Not a lot to do off the slopes

Puy-St-Vincent's ski area may be limited, but we found ourselves liking it more than we expected before we went. It offers a decent vertical and a lot of variety, including a bit of steep stuff. Provided you pick your spot with care, it makes an attractive choice for a family not hungry for piste miles.

THE RESORT

Puy-St-Vincent proper is an old mountain village. The modern resort of PSV is basically a two-part affair – the minor part, Station 1400, is just along the mountainside from PSV proper at 1400m/4,590ft; the major part, Station 1600, is a few hairpins further up (yes, at 1600m/5,250ft), consisting of long, low apartment blocks. Spreading up the hillside from here are newer developments in a more traditional style – gradually being identified as Station 1800. Some of the accommodation is slope-side, but not all – take care if this matters. We and our reporters have found PSV friendly ('even the lift operators').

THE MOUNTAINS

Within its small area, PSV packs in a lot of variety, with runs from green to black that justify their gradings.

Slopes There are gentle slopes between the two villages, but most of the runs are above 1600. A fast quad goes up to the tree line at around 2000m/6,560ft. Entertaining red runs go back down, and a green takes a less direct route. The main higher lift is a long chair to 2700m/8,860ft, serving excellent open slopes of red and genuine black steepness. Drags to either side serve further open runs here, and access splendid cruising runs that curl around the edges of the area into the woods – one linking to a newly created blue, La Balme, all the way down to 1400. 1400 now has a six-pack up into the main slopes. The six-day Galaxie pass covers a series of major resorts beyond Briançon. More to the point, it also covers a day's skiing above the valley hamlet of Pelvoux, 10 minutes' drive away. This area has quiet, very rewarding blue, red and black runs, and a vertical of over 1000m/3,280ft.

355

Phone numbers From abroad use the prefix +33 and omit the initial '0' of the phone number.

Terrain-parks There is a floodlit terrain-park with half-pipe at 1600.

Snow reliability The slopes face north-east and are reasonably reliable for snow. Snowmaking has increased and now covers one run down to 1400 and several above 1600.

Experts The black runs are short but genuinely black, and are 'totally ungroomed, with serious moguls'. There are off-piste routes to be tackled with guidance. There are itinéraires outside the piste network, including one to the valley.

Intermediates Size apart, it's a good area for those who like a challenge – but there aren't many very easy runs.

Beginners Beginners should be happy on either of the nursery slopes, and on the long green from 2000m/6,56oft.

Snowboarding Boarders are not allowed on the Rocher Noir drag-lift.

Cross-country There are 30km/19 miles of cross-country trails, including some splendid routes between 1400m and 1700m (4,59oft and 5,575ft), ranging from green to black difficulty.

Queues In a family resort like this,

there are bound to be some problems in French holiday times – but with fast chairs at the lower levels these should now be confined to the upper slopes.

Mountain restaurants There is a modern but pleasantly woody place at mid-mountain, but the sunny terraces of 1600 get most of the business.

Schools and guides You have a choice of French and International ski schools, and a British tour operator, Snowbizz, has its own school, which reporters have found 'excellent'; it provides free guiding in the afternoons, as well as 'good instruction' in small groups.

Facilities for children There are nurseries taking children from 18 months in 1400 and 1600, and both schools run ski kindergartens.

STAYING THERE

How to go A number of UK operators now offer accommodation here; most of it is in self-catering apartments.

Hotels There are three cheap hotels in 1400, but none in 1600.

SMART APARTMENTS – SEE FEATURE

The new Gentianes apartments at 1800 are 'good-sized, very reasonably priced', with use of indoor pool. Handy for slopes but not for shops.

Eating out The bar-restaurants serve 'a rather monotonous range of dishes'.

Après-ski Après-ski amounts to a few bar-restaurants in each village.

Off the slopes There are 30km/19 miles of paths. Paragliding, dog-sled rides, tobogganing and outdoor skating are available. The cinema shows English-speaking films. With a car you can visit the historic town of Vallouise.

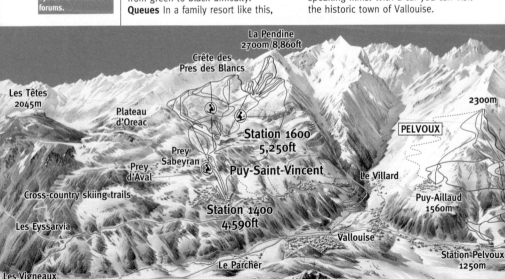

Risoul

Modern, villagey resort with a range of accommodation in an attractive setting – and a big area of slopes shared with Vars

COSTS

① ② ③ ④ ⑤ ⑥

RATINGS

The slopes
Fast lifts	*
Snow	***
Extent	***
Expert	**
Intermediate	****
Beginner	****
Convenience	****
Queues	****
Mountain restaurants	***

The rest
Scenery	***
Resort charm	**
Off-slope	*

NEWS

For 2005/06 the Peyrefolle drag-lift in the Risoul sector was replaced by a chair.

➕ One of the more attractive and convenient purpose-built resorts

➕ Scenic slopes linked with Vars add up to a fair-sized area

➕ High resort, reasonably snow-sure

➕ Good resort for beginners, early intermediates and families

➕ Plenty of good-value places to eat

➖ Still lots of long drag-lifts

➖ Not too much to challenge expert skiers and boarders

➖ Long airport transfers

➖ Little to do off the slopes

Slowly but surely the international market is waking up to the merits of the southern French Alps. Were they nearer Geneva, Risoul and its linked neighbour Vars would be as well known as Les Arcs and Flaine – the village of Risoul is more attractive than either. Brush up your school French before you go.

THE RESORT

Risoul, purpose-built in the late 1970s, is a quiet, apartment-based resort, popular with families. Set among the trees, with excellent views over the Ecrins national park, it is made up of wood-clad buildings – mostly bulky, but with some concessions to traditional style. It has a busy little main street that, surprisingly, is very far from traffic-free. But the village meets the mountain in classic French purpose-built style, with sunny restaurant terraces facing the slopes. Reporters have commented on the friendliness of the natives. The village does not offer many resort amenities. Airport transfers (usually from Turin) can take four hours.

THE MOUNTAINS

Together with neighbouring Vars, the area amounts to one of the biggest domains in the southern French Alps – marketed as the Forêt Blanche. **Slopes** The slopes, mainly north-facing, spread over several minor peaks and bowls, and connect with the sunnier slopes of neighbouring Vars via the Pointe de Razis and the lower Col des Saluces. The upper slopes are open, but those back to Risoul are prettily wooded, and good for bad-weather days. The link itself no longer involves drag-lifts, but overall there are still too many long and steep drag-lifts. Piste grooming seems to have improved – 'excellent' says a 2006 visitor, but the gradings and markings are unreliable.

357

There are lots of places for lunch at the foot of the slopes
→

KEY FACTS

Resort	1850m
	6,070ft

The entire Forêt Blanche ski area

Slopes	1660-2750m
	5,450-9,020ft
Lifts	57
Pistes	180km
	112 miles
Green	16%
Blue	38%
Red	36%
Black	10%
Snowmaking	
	104 guns

Terrain-parks There are two good terrain-parks – with half-pipes, boarder-cross, hand-rail and big air – one near the base, the other high up.

Snow reliability Risoul's slopes are all above 1850m/6,070ft and mostly north-facing, so despite its southerly position snow reliability is reasonably good. Snowmaking is fairly extensive and is being extended. Visitors recommend going over to the east-facing Vars slopes for the morning sun, and returning to Risoul in the afternoon.

Experts The pistes in general do not offer much to interest experts. However, Risoul's main top stations access a couple of steepish descents. And there are some good off-piste opportunities if you take a guide.

Intermediates The whole area is best suited to intermediates, with some good reds and blues in both sectors. Almost all Risoul's runs return to the village, making it difficult to get lost.

Beginners Risoul's local area boasts some good, convenient, nursery slopes with a free lift, and a lot of easy longer pistes to move on to.

Snowboarding There is a lot of good free-riding to be done throughout the area, although beginners might not like the large proportion of drag-lifts. There are weekly competitions.

Cross-country There are 45km/28 miles of cross-country trails in the whole domain. A trail through the Peyrol forest links the two resorts together.

Queues Outside French school holidays, the slopes are impressively quiet. There may be a wait to get back from Vars at the end of the day.

Mountain restaurants Most people return to the village terraces, but the mountain restaurants have increased in quantity and quality. A 2006 visitor

found the self-service Tetras just 'OK'. Snack Attack, near the Forêt Blanche apartments, pleased a recent visitor, and the Refuge de Valbel is recommended.

Schools and guides We had a good report on the ESF this year. 'The instructors were excellent for both adults and kids – patient, with good English. Classes no bigger than eight.' There is also an Internationale school.

Facilities for children Risoul is very much a family resort. It provides an all-day nursery for children over six months. Both ski schools operate ski kindergartens, slightly above the village, reached by a child-friendly lift (one parent reckons many other drags have a dangerous 'whiplash' effect).

STAYING THERE

How to go Most visitors stay in self-catering apartments, but there are a few hotels and more chalets are becoming available from UK operators. A 2006 reporter found Crystal's club hotel the Morgan 'basic but perfectly adequate', although it could be 'surprisingly' noisy.

Hotels The 'value for money' Chardon Bleu (0492 460727) is right on the slopes. You can also stay overnight at the Tetras mountain refuge (0492 460983) at 2000m/6,560ft.

Self-catering The Constellation Forêt Blanche apartments, although small, are said to be 'in an excellent position, well-equipped and pristine'; the Bételgeuse and Pégase are new.

Eating out There's plenty of choice for eating out, from pizza to good French food, and it's mostly good value – the Ecureuil ('very friendly, excellent food, good prices') is highly recommended this year, as is the 'excellent' Chalet.

Après-ski Après-ski in the centre is reportedly now 'very lively' and goes on through the night, with half a dozen 'extremely friendly' bars and three clubs to move between. The best bars are, apparently, the Place ('noisy and fun') and the 'trendy' Caribbean-themed Babao. For a quieter drink, try the Chalet or the Eterlou.

Off the slopes There is little to do; excursions to Briançon are possible.

Vars 1850m/6,070ft

THE RESORT

Vars includes several small, old villages on or near the road running southwards towards the 2110m/6,920ft Col de Vars. But for winter visitors it mainly consists of purpose-built Vars-les-Claux, higher up the road. The resort has convenience and reasonable prices in common with Risoul, but is bigger and has far more in the way of amenities. There are a lot of block-like apartments, but Vars-les-Claux is not a complete eyesore, thanks mainly to surrounding woods. There are two centres: the original, geographical one – where the main gondola starts – has most of the accommodation and shopping; Point Show is a collection of bars and shops, 10 minutes' walk away at another main lift station.

Vars-Ste-Marie makes a more attractive base now that fast chairs take you to the top of La Mayt.

THE MOUNTAINS

There are slopes on both sides of the village, linked by pistes and by chair-lift at the lower end of Les Claux. Lifts also run up from both sides of Ste-Marie, lower down the mountain.

Slopes The wooded, west-facing Peynier area is the smaller sector, and reaches only 2275m/7,460ft – though there are good long descents down to Les Claux and Ste-Marie. The main slopes are in an east-facing bowl with direct links to the Risoul slopes at the top and at the Col des Saluces. There's a speed-skiing course at the top (access via the ski school). Beneath it are easy runs, open at the top but descending into trees.

Terrain-parks There's a terrain-park above Les Claux.

Snow reliability The main slopes get the morning sun, and are centred at around 2000m/6,560ft, so snow reliability is not as good as in Risoul, but snowmaking is widespread.

Experts There is little of challenge for experts, though the Crête de Chabrières top section accesses some off-piste, an unpisted route and a tricky couloir at Col de Crevoux. The Olympic red run from the top of La Mayt down to Ste-Marie is a respectable 920m/3,020ft vertical.

Intermediates Most of the area is fine for intermediates, with a good mixture of comfortable reds and easy blues, particularly in the main bowl.

Beginners There is a nursery area close to central Vars, with lots of 'graduation' runs throughout the area. Quick learners will be able to get over to Risoul by the end of the week.

Snowboarding There is good free-riding to be done throughout the area, although beginners might find the number of drag-lifts a problem.

Cross-country There are 25km/16 miles of trails in Vars itself. Some start at the edge of town, but those above Ste-Marie are more extensive.

Queues Queues are rare outside the French holidays, and even then Vars is not overrun as some family resorts are.

Mountain restaurants There are several in both sectors, but a lot of people head back to the villages for lunch. The Cassette, at the bottom of the Mayt chair, 'delighted' a 2005 visitor and is approved by 2006 visitors.

Schools and guides Lack of English speaking has been a problem.

Facilities for children The ski school runs a nursery for children from two years old. There is a ski kindergarten.

STAYING THERE

How to go There are a few small hotels, but Les Claux is dominated by apartment accommodation.

Hotels The Caribou (0492 465043) is the smartest of the hotels and has a pool. The Ecureuil (0492 465072) is an attractive, modern chalet (no restaurant).

Eating out The range of restaurants is impressive, with good-value pizzerias, crêperies and fondue places. A 2005 reporter says the Taverne du Torrent is 'excellent with reasonable prices' and found the food at Chez Plumot to be 'truly haute cuisine'.

Après-ski Après-ski is animated at tea-time, less so after dinner – except at weekends when the discos warm up.

Off the slopes The amenities are rather disappointing, given the size of Vars: 35km/22 miles of walking paths, a cinema and an ice rink – and that's it.

Phone numbers
From abroad use the prefix +33 and omit the initial '0' of the phone number.

La Rosière

The sunniest slopes in the Tarentaise, but also about the snowiest;
the link to La Thuile in Italy adds a vital extra dimension

COSTS

① ② ③ ④ ⑤ ⑥

RATINGS

The slopes
Fast lifts	**
Snow	***
Extent	***
Expert	**
Intermediate	***
Beginner	*****
Convenience	***
Queues	***
Mountain restaurants	*

The rest
Scenery	***
Resort charm	***
Off-slope	*

NEWS

For 2006/07 there will be two new hotels and further new apartment developments at Les Eucherts.

For 2005/06 the Snowcross des Zittieux free-ride area (patrolled but not groomed) opened by the Sevolière lift.

+ Attractive purpose-built resort with glorious views towards Les Arcs
+ Fair-sized area of slopes shared with La Thuile in Italy
+ Sunny home slopes
+ Heli-skiing over the border in Italy
+ Good nursery slope
+ Gets big dumps of snow when storms sock in from the west, but ...

– Winds can close lift links with Italy
– Snow affected by sun in late season
– Lots of slow old lifts
– Few on-piste challenges for experts
– One run is much like another – though La Thuile is more varied
– Limited après-ski
– Few off-slope diversions

Like Montgenèvre, a long way to the south, La Rosière enjoys a position on the watershed with Italy that brings the twin attractions of big dumps of snow and access to cheap vino rosso. The former is crucial: given the sunny orientation of the slopes – very unusual in a modern French resort – average snowfalls wouldn't do the trick. The Chianti is less significant, because there are few attractive restaurants in which to consume it (see La Thuile chapter).

THE RESORT

La Rosière has been built in attractive, traditional chalet style beside the road that zigzags its way up from Bourg-St-Maurice towards the Petit-St-Bernard pass to Italy (closed to traffic in winter – the Italian side becomes a piste). It's a quiet place with a few shops and friendly locals; don't expect lively nightlife. The most convenient accommodation is in the main village near the lifts, or just below, in Le Gollet or Vieux Village. Growth continues, notably by the second main lift at Les Eucherts.

THE MOUNTAINS

La Rosière and La Thuile in Italy share a big area of slopes, now called Espace San Bernardo. La Rosière's sunny home slopes are south-facing with great views over the valley to Les Arcs and La Plagne. The link with Italy's slopes is prone to closure because of high winds or heavy snow.
Slopes Two fast chairs at either end of the village take you into the heart of the slopes, from where a series of drags and chairs, spread across the mountain, takes you up to Col de la Traversette. From there, you can get over the ridge and to the lifts, which link with Italy at Belvedere.
Terrain-parks There is a terrain-park served by the Poletta drag lift, just above the village centre. And there's a boarder-cross course by the Fort lift.
Snow reliability The slopes get a lot of snow from storms pushing up the valley, but in late season the sunny orientation takes its toll.
Experts Other than excellent heli-skiing from just over the Italian border (see La Thuile) and guided off-piste, there is little excitement for experts. The steepest terrain is on the lowest slopes, down the Marcassin run to Le Vaz and down the Ecudets run close to the village. There's also a new free-ride area above Ecudets, which has replaced two black runs, reached via the Sevolière or Roches Noires lifts.

360

La Thuile
Belvedere 2610m/8,56oft
Col du Petit
Saint Bernard
2190m
Le Roc Noir
2400m
COL DE LA TRAVERSETTE
2385m
Le Gollet
1175m
La Rosière
1850m/6,07oft
Les Eucherts
Le Vaz
1500m

KEY FACTS

Resort	1850m
	6,070ft

Espace San Bernardo	
Slopes	1175-2610m
	3,850-8,560ft
Lifts	35
Pistes	150km
	93 miles
Green	9%
Blue	36%
Red	40%
Black	15%
Snowmaking	
	Over 300 guns

For La Rosière only	
Slopes	1175-2385m
	3,850-7,820ft
Lifts	20
Pistes	47km
	29 miles

Phone numbers
From abroad use the
prefix +33 and omit
the initial '0' of the
phone number.

TOURIST OFFICE

t 0479 068051
info@larosiere.net
www.larosiere.net

Intermediates There's a fair amount to explore if you take into account La Thuile. The main part of La Rosière's area is a broad open mountainside offering straightforward red and blue pistes. More interesting is the Fontaine Froide red, dropping 750m vertical through woods to the Ecudets chair, far below the village. The red beyond Col de la Traversette has good snow and views, but is narrow at the top. You can avoid it by taking the chair.

Beginners There are good nursery slopes and short lifts near the village and near Les Eucherts.

Snowboarding The long drag-lift to Italy means the resort is best-suited to those content to stay on the French side. There are three 'Snowzones', including a terrain-park, boarder-cross course and free-ride area.

Cross-country There are 7km/4.5 miles of trails near the altiport.

Queues Queues are not usually a problem. Apart from peak times, getting out of the village is quicker now that the lift is a six-pack.

Mountain restaurants Most people have lunch in the village. Mountain recommendations include the self-service Plan du Repos for its 'friendly staff, huge pasta portions and lovely salads', the San Bernardo (on the border) and the Vieux Chalet (at the bottom of the Ecudets chair) for snacks ('very friendly service'); it is a popular poor-weather retreat.

Schools and guides There are three schools. Evolution 2 is praised for its 'small groups' and 'friendly instructors', who are especially good with children. And we have a similar report of the ESF this year, for both children's groups and private lessons with 'pleasant' instructors.

Facilities for children Club des Galopins has a snow garden, and British tour operators Esprit and Thomson run nurseries.

STAYING THERE

How to go A number of British tour operators now offer packages here.

Hotels There are a few 2-star hotels in the village, and more in the valley. Two interesting new places are slated to open for 2006/07: the 10-room luxury Chalet Matsuzaka and a bigger chalet at Les Eucherts doing half-board for groups.

Chalets There are now several companies operating chalets here.

SMART APARTMENTS – SEE FEATURE

The best places are newly built at Les Eucherts. The Cimes Blanches is a classic MGM development with attractive pool, jacuzzi, sauna. A wellness centre is due to be added for 2006/07. The Balcons units can accommodate larger groups.

Eating out A useful pocket guide to restaurants is distributed locally. The Génépi (formerly the Oustal) is recommended by a 2006 visitor for 'good quality food, service and a lovely atmosphere'. The Turia is a rustic, smarter establishment in the centre. The Marmottes is said to serve 'good salads'. The 'charming' Ancolie does 'good food, but with slow service'. The popular Relais du Petit St Bernard is now the MacKinley.

Après-ski Après-ski is limited to a couple of bars in the village.

Off the slopes There are scenic flights and walks, an indoor climbing wall and a cinema. The ski schools offer paragliding and organise various non-skiing expeditions on foot. You can visit the St Bernard dogs. Mountain restaurants are inaccessible on foot.

Staying up the mountain The Hotel San Bernardo (0165 841444), on the border and reachable only on skis, provided a memorable two-night stay for an adventurous reporter – 'simple, comfortable and peaceful', with a 'spectacular collection of grappas'.

La Rosière

361

Samoëns

Characterful but inconvenient base for the extensive and varied Grand Massif, shared with Flaine and Les Carroz

RATINGS

The slopes

Fast lifts	**
Snow	***
Extent	****
Expert	****
Intermediate	*****
Beginner	**
Convenience	*
Queues	****
Mountain restaurants	**

The rest

Scenery	****
Resort charm	****
Off-slope	***

NEWS

Two new ski schools appeared in Samoëns last winter – 360 International and Ski Session.

The Fermes de Samoëns opened for 2005/06: a new apartment development just outside the village. The Aero, a new hotel with some apartments, also opened last winter in Samoëns 1600.

Excellent nursery slopes at 1600 – but progression to longer runs isn't so easy ↘

- ➕ Lovely historic village, with traffic-free centre and weekly market
- ➕ Lift into big, varied area shared with Flaine and Les Carroz, with slopes to suit everyone
- ➕ Glorious views from top heights
- ➕ Very close to Geneva, but ...

- ➖ Weekends can be busy as a result
- ➖ Access lift is way outside the village – yet has no return piste
- ➖ Slow lifts above mid-mountain
- ➖ Not ideal for beginners
- ➖ Surprisingly intrusive traffic
- ➖ Nightlife not a highlight

The impressive Grand Massif area is chiefly associated in Britain with high, purpose-built, apartment-dominated Flaine; but the network can also be accessed from much more attractive traditional villages – Les Carroz, Morillon and Samoëns. And the cutest of these, if not the most convenient, is Samoëns.

THE RESORT

Samoëns is a 'Monument Historique' – once a thriving centre for stone-masons, with their work much in evidence. There is a small traffic-free centre of narrow streets lined by appealing food shops, and nearby a pretty square (sadly not traffic-free) with a stone fountain, an ancient linden tree, a fine church and other medieval buildings. Also nearby is a nominally car-free area of modern development. The village as a whole retains the feel of 'real' rural France. There is a good weekly market.

The long-awaited eight-seat gondola from village level was opened in 2003, supposedly transforming Samoëns into a proper ski resort. Well, not quite. The base station is a drive or a bus-ride from most accommodation – and yet there is no run back to it. For non-beginners with a car, the slow old gondola at Vercland (now queue-free) is still worth considering.

THE MOUNTAINS

Most of the skiing directly above Samoëns is on open slopes beneath Tête des Saix, from which point there are links to the next-door Morillon sector and the slightly more distant sectors of Les Carroz and Flaine (both covered in the Flaine chapter).

Slopes The two gondolas from the valley arrive at separate points on the 'hilly plateau' of Samoëns 1600. This mini-resort is also reachable by road. Tête des Saix is reached by parallel chair-lifts in two stages. These slow lifts are a real drawback: a couple of six-packs are urgently needed. From the Tête you can descend to Morillon or Les Carroz; one more (fast) chair is needed for access to the Flaine bowl.

Terrain-parks There is a terrain-park above 1600, and another at Morillon.

Snow reliability The slopes above Samoëns face due north, so above 1600 snow is fairly reliable. There is snowmaking around 1600.

362

peak retreats

Beat the crowds
Traditional resorts

0870 770 0408

www.peakretreats.co.uk

ABTA W5537

alpsaccommodation

Premier Chalets and Apartments
Samoëns, Grand Massif

Tel: 0033 (0)4 50 90 83 55

www.alpsaccommodation.com

How to go A few specialist UK operators now go to Samoëns. **Hotels** We and readers have enjoyed the Neige et Roc (0450 344072), a walk from the centre – 'friendly staff, excellent food, big spa area'. Avoid the annexe, though. The central Glaciers (0450 344006) is recommended. **Chalets** We have glowing reports of two owner-run chalets – Marie Stuart and Alps Accommodation's Moccand.

SMART APARTMENTS – SEE FEATURE

Self-catering accommodation is mostly modest, but above-average places include the Fermes de Samoëns (with pool). Peak Retreats has several chalets, and Alps Accommodation some spacious apartments.

Eating out The Table de Fifine is a short drive from the centre, but a fine spot – beautiful wooden interior, satisfying food. A 2006 reporter enjoyed 'great food' at the Bois de Lune and recommends the Louisiane for its 'great' wood-oven pizzas.

Après-ski There are several bars, including an Irish pub, Covey's, rated by an Irish reporter as 'authentic' – but also 'pricey', says a 2006 visitor. **Off the slopes** Samoëns offers quite a range of activities. We enjoyed a guided tour of the church one evening. Snowmobiling up at Samoëns 1600 is wilder than is usual in the Alps. There is an outdoor, covered ice rink, hosting regular hockey matches.

KEY FACTS

Resort 720-1600m
2,360-5,250ft

Grand Massif ski area (Samoëns and all linked resorts)

Slopes	700-2480m
	2,300-8,140ft
Lifts	78
Pistes	265km
	165 miles
Green	11%
Blue	40%
Red	38%
Black	11%
Snowmaking	25%

Massif ski area (excluding Flaine)

Slopes	700-2120m
	2,300-6,700ft
Lifts	54
Pistes	145km
	90 miles

PISTE MAP

Samoëns is covered on the Flaine map

Phone numbers

From abroad use the prefix +33 and omit the initial '0' of the phone number.

TOURIST OFFICES

Samoëns
t 0450 344028
infos@samoens.com
www.samoens.com

Morillon
t 0450 901576
info@ot-morillon.fr
www.ot-morillon.fr

Experts The upper pistes on Tête des Saix are among the most testing in the Grand Massif, and there is lots of good off-piste in the valleys and bowls between Samoëns and Flaine.

Intermediates If you can put up with the slow lifts mentioned above, Samoëns makes a perfectly satisfactory base for all but the most timid intermediates, who might be better off in Morillon. From Tête des Saix you have a wide choice of good long runs in various directions. In good snow the valley runs to Vercland are highly enjoyable – the black is very little steeper than the red, and used less.

Beginners Beginners must buy a pass (there is a special one at about 15 euros a day) and go up to 1600. There are snow-sure, gentle slopes for absolute beginners up there – excellent when not crowded at peak times – but no long green runs to progress to. Morillon is a better bet.

Snowboarding Beware drag-lifts on the nursery slopes.

Cross-country There are trails on the flat valley floor around Samoëns, and more challenging ones up the valley beyond Sixt and up at Col de Joux Plane (1700m/5,580ft).

Queues This year we have reports of queues building up at 1600 for access to Tête des Saix.

Mountain restaurants There are places to eat at Samoëns 1600, but the most captivating places are above Morillon and Les Carroz – see Flaine chapter.

Schools and guides A reader this year had a 'poor' lesson with the ESF and a 'much better one' from 360 International, one of two new schools – the other is Ski Session. Another 2006 visitor found the ESF's private boarding instruction 'very good' but noted large numbers in group classes.

Facilities for children There is a newly built kindergarten, and ski lessons are available.

Morillon 700m/2,300ft

Morillon is a couple of miles down the valley from Samoëns. Not quite in the Samoëns league but still a pretty, rustic village, Morillon makes a more convenient base, with an efficient gondola from the upper fringes of the village to the mini-resort of Morillon 1100 (Les Esserts) – also reachable by road. Up here there is a large and 'delightful' ski kindergarten plus good slopes for adult beginners – including a fabulous long green run (Marvel) through the forest, away from lifts. There are new apartments right on the piste up here – but it's 'dead as a dodo in the evenings'. Back in the village, the 'very friendly' hotel Morillon, a short walk from the gondola, is recommended again.

SMART APARTMENTS – SEE FEATURE

Les Marmottes is a spacious chalet with an impressive kitchen.

Flaine

363

Serre-Chevalier

Villages that are an odd mixture of ancient and modern sit beneath an extensive and varied area of slopes

COSTS

① ② ③ ④ ⑤ ⑥

RATINGS

The slopes

Fast lifts	**
Snow	***
Extent	****
Expert	***
Intermediate	****
Beginner	****
Convenience	***
Queues	***
Mountain restaurants	***

The rest

Scenery	***
Resort charm	***
Off-slope	**

NEWS

For 2005/06 three much-needed fast six-seat chairs were installed. They replace the Forêt and Rouge drags above L'Aravet, the Clôt Gauthier chair above Fréjus and the Grand Serre chair above Grand Alpe.

Also for 2005/06, the red Cucumelle run was remodelled, but the planned blue piste to Chantemerle did not materialise.

Snowmaking was installed around the Grand Serre chair.

MGM is building new apartments in Chantemerle and the Hotel le Rif Blanc in Le Monêtier is under new ownership and being refurbished. Both should be ready for December 2006.

For 2006/07 snowmaking is due to be expanded in Le Monêtier.

364

➕ Big, varied mountain, with something for everyone

➕ Interesting mixture of wooded runs and open bowls with lots of off-piste

➕ One of the few big French areas based on old villages with character

➕ Good-value and atmospheric old hotels, restaurants and chalets

➕ Lift pass covers days elsewhere

➕ Generally quiet slopes, but ...

➖ Serious crowds in central sectors in French holidays

➖ Despite recent improvements, still too many slow, old lifts on upper mountain – some vicious drags

➖ Busy road runs through the resort villages, with traffic jams at times

➖ A lot of indiscriminate new building

➖ Limited nightlife

➖ Few off-slope diversions

Serre-Chevalier is a big-league resort, but isn't well known internationally. We like it a lot: it's one of the few French resorts where you can find the ambience you might look for on a summer holiday – a sort of Provence in the snow, with lots of small, family-run hotels and restaurants housed in old stone buildings.

The slopes are likeable, too. They are split into different segments, so you get a real sensation of travel. What really sets the area apart from the French norm are the woodland runs, making Serre-Chevalier one of the best places to be when snow is falling or wind is blowing – though there are plenty of open runs, too.

It has been let down by an outdated lift system and a lack of up-market accommodation. Happily both these issues are being tackled: three six-packs were installed last season (but more are needed) and some plush new MGM apartments are due to open for the coming season. Who knows, it might become much more internationally famous soon – so get there quickly.

THE RESORT

The resort is made up of a string of 13 villages set on a valley floor running roughly north-west to south-east, below the north-east-facing slopes of the mountain range that gives the resort its name. From the north-west – coming over the Col du Lautaret from Grenoble – the three main villages are Le Monêtier (or Serre-Che 1500), Villeneuve (1400) and Chantemerle (1350), spread over a distance of 8km/5 miles. Finally, at the extreme south-eastern end of the mountain, is Briançon (1200) – not a village but a

town (the highest in France). Nine smaller villages can be identified, and some give their names to the communes: Villeneuve is in the commune of La Salle les Alpes, for example. Confusing.

Serre-Chevalier is not a smart resort, in any sense. Although each of its parts is based on a simple old village, there is a lot of modern development, which ranges from brash to brutal, and even the older parts are roughly rustic rather than chocolate-box pretty. (A ban on corrugated iron roofs would help.) Because the resort is so spread out, the impact of cars and buses is

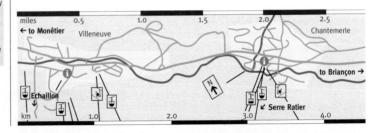

↑ The resort is made up of 13 villages spread along the valley floor beneath the mountain range that gives it its name
AGENCE ZOOM

difficult to escape, even if you're able to manage without them yourself. But when blanketed by snow the older villages and hamlets do have an unpretentious charm, and we find the place as a whole easy to like. Every year reporters stress how friendly and welcoming the people are, hardly the norm in France: 'I have never skied a friendlier place,' said one 2006 visitor.

There are few luxury hotels or notably swanky restaurants; on the other hand, there are more hotels in the modestly priced Logis de France 'club' here than in any other ski resort. This is a family resort, which fills up (even more than most others) with French children in the February high season. You have been warned.

The heart of the resort is **Villeneuve**, which has two gondolas and a fast quad chair going up to widely separated points at mid-mountain. The central area of new development near the lifts is brutal and charmless. But not far away is the peaceful hamlet of Le Bez, which has a third gondola, and across the valley is the old stone village of Villeneuve, its quiet main street lined by cosy bars, hotels and restaurants.

Not far down the valley, **Chantemerle** gives access to opposite ends of the mid-mountain plateau of Serre Ratier via a gondola and a cable-car, both with second stages above. Chantemerle has some tasteless modern buildings in the centre and along the main road. The old sector is a couple of minutes' walk from the lifts, with a lovely church and most of the small hotels, restaurants, bars and nightlife. However, a lot of accommodation is across the main road – 'Quite a long walk from the lifts,' says a weary visitor.

At the top of the valley, **Le Monêtier** has one main access lift – a fast quad chair to mid-mountain, reached from the village by bus or a 10-minute walk (downhill in the morning, uphill at the

end of the day and tricky when ice is around, though you can leave your boots at the lift base). Le Monêtier is the smallest, quietest and most unspoiled of the main villages, with a bit of a Provençal feel to its narrow streets and little squares, and new building which is mostly in sympathetic style. Sadly, the through-road to Grenoble, which skirts the other villages, bisects Le Monêtier; pedestrians stroll about bravely, hoping the cars will avoid them.

Briançon has a gondola from right in the town to mid-mountain and on almost to the top. The area around the lift station has a wide selection of modern shops, bars, restaurants, hotels, and a casino, but no character. In contrast, the 17th-century fortified upper quarter is a delight, with narrow cobbled streets and traditional restaurants, auberges and patisseries. Great views from the top, too.

Ski-buses, covered on the free guest card, circulate around each village and link all the villages and lift bases along the valley. But they finish quite early, to the annoyance of some reporters (the local navettes stop soon after the lifts close, and the valley buses at approximately 7pm), and at least one reporter found the service inadequate; taxis aren't cheap.

A six-day area pass (or rather your receipt) covers a day in each of Les Deux-Alpes, Alpe-d'Huez, Puy-St-Vincent and the Milky Way. All of these outings are possible by public transport, but are more attractive to those with a car. If driving through France, you are likely to approach over the high and beautifully dramatic Col du Lautaret, which required chains on our recent visit and is very occasionally closed because of avalanche danger.

Turin airport is closer than Lyon, with easier road access than there or Grenoble.

Serre-Chevalier

365

KEY FACTS

Resort	1350-1500m
	4,430-4,920ft
Slopes	1350-2735m
	4,430-8,970ft
Lifts	68
Pistes	250km
	155 miles
Green	21%
Blue	27%
Red	38%
Black	14%
Snowmaking	45km
	28 miles

LIFT PASSES

Grand Serre-Che

Prices in €

Age	1-day	6-day
under 12	25	124
12 to 64	35	170
over 65	25	124

Free under 6, over 75

Beginner Two free
lifts and limited pass
in each area:
Villeneuve €13.30;
Monêtier €9.50;
Chantemerle €13.30

Notes
Covers all lifts in
Briançon,
Chantemerle,
Villeneuve and Le
Monêtier. Passes of
six days or more give
one day in each of
Les Deux-Alpes, Alpe-
d'Huez, Puy-St-
Vincent and Voie
Lactée (Milky Way).
Reductions for
families.

Alternative passes
Passes covering
individual areas of
Serre-Chevalier.

THE MOUNTAINS

Trees cover almost two-thirds of the
mountain, providing some of France's
best bad-weather terrain (we had a
great day here despite the upper lifts
all being closed by high winds). The
Serre-Chevalier massif is not
particularly dramatic, but from the
peaks there are fine views of the Ecrins
massif, the highest within France (ie
not shared with Italy).

The trail map and signposting have
both been improved recently, but the
map remains infuriatingly unclear and
imprecise in places and a 2006
reporter found the signposting 'fairly
intermittent and not consistent across
the sectors'. More reports welcome.

Piste classification is unreliable –
many reds, in particular, could be
classified blue, but there are
occasional stiff blues, too.

THE SLOPES
Interestingly varied and pretty
Serre-Chevalier's 250km/155 miles of
pistes are spread across four main
sectors above the four main villages.
The sector above **Villeneuve** is the
most extensive, reaching back a good
way into the mountains and spreading
over four or five identifiable bowls. The
main mid-station is Fréjus. This sector
is reliably linked to the slightly smaller
Chantemerle sector well below the tree
line. The link from Chantemerle to
Briançon is over a high, exposed col
via a six-pack. The link between
Villeneuve and **Le Monêtier** is liable to
closure by high winds or avalanche
danger. Travelling from here towards
Villeneuve involves a red run, so timid
intermediates have to use the bus.

TERRAIN-PARKS
Fully featured
Legendary French ripper Guillaume
Chastagnol and the Serre Che Brigade
have been building the freestyle
infrastructure here for several years,
trying to improve the terrain-parks.
There's a park under the Aravet
gondola that leaves from Villeneuve,
with a very good half-pipe, big-air
jump and quarter-pipe. For the more
classic terrain-park, which has four
average-sized kickers and a few rails,
head to the bottom of the lifts in Le
Monêtier. There are two boarder-cross
courses: one above Chantemerle and
one above Villeneuve.

SNOW RELIABILITY
Good – especially upper slopes
Most slopes face north or north-east
and so hold snow well, especially high
up (there are lots of lifts starting above
2000m/6,560ft). The weather pattern is
different from that of the northern Alps
and even that of Les Deux-Alpes or
Alpe-d'Huez, only a few miles to the
west. Serre-Che can get good snow
when there is a shortage elsewhere,
and vice versa. There is snowmaking
on long runs down to each village.
Piste grooming is generally excellent.

FOR EXPERTS
Deep, not notably steep
There is plenty to amuse experts –
except those wanting extreme steeps.

The broad black runs down to
Villeneuve and Chantemerle are only
just black in steepness, but they are
fine runs with their gradient sustained
over an impressive vertical of around
800m/2,620ft. One or the other may be
closed for days on end for racing or
training. The rather neglected Tabuc
run, sweeping around the mountain
away from the lifts to Le Monêtier, has
a couple of genuinely steep pitches but
is mainly a cruise; it makes a fine end
to the day. For moguls, look higher up
the mountain to the steeper slopes
served by the two top lifts above Le
Monêtier and the three above
Villeneuve. The runs beside these lifts
– on and off-piste – form a great
playground in good snow. The more
roundabout Isolée black is a reader's
favourite – 'scenic and challenging'
after a rather scary ridge start.

There are huge amounts of off-piste
terrain throughout the area; on a
recent visit we had a great morning in
the trees above Villeneuve and
Chantemerle. There are plenty of more
serious off-piste expeditions, including:
Tête de Grand Pré to Villeneuve (a
climb from Cucumelle); off the back of
L'Eychauda to Puy-St-André (isolated,
beautiful, taxi-ride home); L'Yret to Le
Monêtier via Vallon de la Montagnolle;
Tabuc (steep at the start, very
beautiful). The experts' Mecca of La
Grave is nearby. And the Compagnie
des Guides runs heli-skiing trips to
nearby Italy, where the practice is legal.

FOR INTERMEDIATES
Ski wherever you like
Serre-Chevalier's slopes ideally suit
intermediates, who can buzz around
without worrying about nasty surprises

The term 'natural playground' could have quite easily been coined in Serre-Chevalier. The slopes are littered with natural obstacles that seem made for confident snowboarders to keep them happy. Try the Cucumelle slope and the areas around the Rocher Blanc lift at Prorel for such terrain. For beginners and intermediates the many drag-lifts can be a problem, as can the flat areas – one reporter's group stayed mostly in the Chantemerle sector, simply because they could cover a lot of ground using three major chair-lifts. Generation Snow in Chantemerle is a school that offers all sorts of courses from beginners' lessons to advanced freestyle courses.

on the way. On the trail map red runs far outnumber blues – but most reds are at the easy end of the scale and the grooming is usually good, so even nervous intermediates shouldn't have problems with them.

There's plenty for more adventurous intermediates, though. Many runs are wide enough for a fast pace. Cucumelle on the edge of the Villeneuve sector is a favourite – a beautiful long red, away from the lifts, with a challenging initial section. The red runs off the little-used Aiguillette chair in the Chantemerle sector (which we dubbed the 'Lost Chair' on our last visit because it was so quiet while other areas were packed) are worth seeking out – quiet, enjoyable fast cruises. Aya and Clos Galliard at Le Monêtier and the wonderful long run from the top to the bottom of the gondola at Briançon (with great views of the town) are other favourites.

If the reds are starting to seem a bit tame, there is plenty more to progress to. Unless ice towards the bottom is a problem, the (often well-groomed) blacks on the lower mountain should be first on the agenda, and the bumpier ones higher up can be tackled if snow is good.

FOR BEGINNERS
All three areas OK
All three main villages have nursery areas (at Chantemerle the area is small, and you generally go up to Serre Ratier or Grand Alpe – both rated as good by a beginner reporter) and there are some easy high runs to progress to. Villeneuve has excellent green runs above Fréjus. Both sectors have green paths down from mid mountain which are narrow, and not enjoyable when the runs become rutted and others are speeding along. Le Monêtier's easy runs are at resort level, next to excellent nursery slopes, and beginners have recommended it for 'better snow and fewer people'. But progression to long runs here isn't so easy, and the link to Villeneuve involves the red Cucumelle run.

FOR CROSS-COUNTRY
Excellent if the snow is good
There are 35km/22 miles of tracks along the valley floor, mainly following the gurgling river between Le Monêtier and Villeneuve and going on up towards the Col du Lautaret.

Serre-Chevalier

367

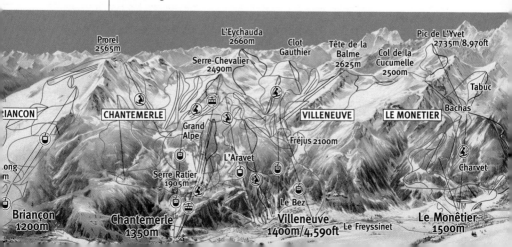

SCHOOLS

ESF In all centres
t 0492 241741

Génération Snow
(1350)
t 0492 242151

Evasion (1350)
t 0492 240241

Buissonnière (1400)
t 0492 247866

Eurekaski
t 0679 462484
t 01326 375710 (UK)

Axesse (1400)
t 0662 765354

Altitude (1400)
t 0608 025182

International (1500)
t 0683 025182

Classes (ESF prices)
6 half days €93

Private lessons
€34 for 1hr

GUIDES

Montagne Aventure
(1350)
t 0492 240551

Bureau des Guides
(1400)
t 0492 247590

Montagne à la carte
(1400)
t 0492 247320

Montagne et Ski
(1500)
t 0492 244681

CHILDREN

Les Schtroumpfs
t 0492 247095
Ages 6mnth upwards;
9am-5pm

Les Poussins
t 0492 244003
Ages 8mnth upwards;
9am-5pm

Les Eterlous
t 0492 244575
Ages 18mnth to 6yr
(6mnth to 6yr out of
school holidays);
9am-5pm

Ski school
Snow gardens for
ages 3 to 5; from age
7 children can join ski
school classes (ESF 6
half-days €89).

QUEUES
Investment at last

A range of big lifts means there are few problems getting out of the valley. But the many old, slow lifts at altitude still cause queues, as well as slowing down the whole process of exploration: 'frustrating' says a 2006 reporter. The new lifts that went in last season have helped but more are needed. Bottlenecks include the slow and unreliable Balme chair on the way to Le Monêtier, the Fréjus chair above the Pontillas gondola and the Crête drag-lift it links with – 'Avoid them,' warns one 2006 reporter. Another advises avoiding the Bois des Coqs drag-lift above Chantemerle: 'vicious take-off, some horrid turns, very steep in parts – evil'.

More than most resorts, Serre-Chevalier seems to fill up with French families in the February holidays, producing serious mid-mountain queues, especially in the central sectors, but for one 2006 visitor the queues 'were not as dreadful as we expected in the central sections'.

The lower slopes above Chantemerle, in particular, can get hideously crowded, particularly when snow conditions are poor and progress therefore slow – head for the Aiguillette chair in these circumstances (see 'For Intermediates').

MOUNTAIN RESTAURANTS
Some good places

Mountain restaurants are quite well distributed (and, usefully, marked clearly on the piste map).

The Villeneuve sector holds the aces. L'Echaillon, just below the top of the Casse du Boeuf quad, is a lofty chalet with open fire and a table-service section doing excellent food. Just above here, the Bivouac de la Casse is another attractive chalet with both self-service and 'first-class' table-service (inside and out). Pi Maï in the hamlet of Fréjus, a fine retreat on a bad day, set a little way below the Fréjus lift station, is 'highly acclaimed' with 'the best hot chocolate in the resort'. The Fermière, just above Pi Maï, is 'basic but good value', with lengthy queues for food at times. The Bercail D'Abord at the top of the Aravet lift is a 'good relaxed place'.

In the Chantemerle sector, the busy Soleil pleases reporters – 'good food, sun trap', 'excellent food for good prices'. The Relais de Ratier is said to be

'cheaper than elsewhere' and has been praised for 'excellent fresh-cooked food'. The Grand Alpe is spacious, and also 'a bit cheaper than some of the others'.

In the Briançon sector, the 'attractive' Pra Long chalet at the gondola mid-station has good views and food in both table- and self-service sections is 'excellent'. The little Chalet de Serre Blanc just down from the top of Prorel has great views and reasonable prices.

Above Le Monêtier the choice is between the self-service Bachas at mid-mountain, 'ideal for those who want to get back on the slopes as soon as possible', and the cosy, friendly Peyra Juana (popular with the locals) much lower down, which we and readers alike have enjoyed, although a 2005 visitor found it 'somewhat expensive'. Both get packed on bad-weather days.

SCHOOLS AND GUIDES
Nearly all good

We have received a number of reports on the Ecole de Ski Buissonnière over the years – most of them full of praise but with one distressing experience of early-intermediate boarders being put together with a couple of experts.

Eurekaski, British-run by BASI instructors, gets consistently good reports. Its 'exceptionally good teachers were the main reason for returning to the resort for the third successive year' for some 2006 visitors, and they are going back in 2007. Another reporter who took two private lessons 'learned more than I have previously in a week'. Classes with a maximum size of six range from beginner to free-ride masterclass. EurekaSki also offer special one-day Avalanche Awareness courses, including training on how to use transceivers and how to choose the safest routes off-piste, as well as some fun off-piste skiing.

We lack recent reports of group classes with the ESF. 'Children's classes seemed to have two instructors,' observed one February 2006 reporter. But another saw 'tiny kids in groups of 12 to 13 with one instructor'. Some 2005 visitors had private lessons and found 'friendly instructors who gave good advice'. The Internationale school 'gave the impression of being rather more professional than the ESF', and one reporter saw 'small groups of five to six children maximum'.

On our 2004 visit we had a great

GETTING THERE

Air Turin 108km/
67 miles (1½hr);
Grenoble 92km/
57 miles (2hr); Lyon
208km/129 miles
(3hr).

Rail Briançon (6km/
4 miles); regular
buses from station.

morning skiing off-piste with Bertrand
Collet of Axesse ski school and guiding
service (which specialises in off-piste
and advanced techniques).

FACILITIES FOR CHILDREN
Facilities at each village
The Ecole de Ski Buissonnière has
been praised in the past, and Les
Schtroumpfs in Villeneuve was in 2006:
'Brilliant, and the baby loved it.'

STAYING THERE

HOW TO GO
A good choice of packages
There's a wide choice of packages from
UK tour operators, offering all kinds of
accommodation.
Chalets Several operators offer chalets
in the different parts of the resort. A
2005 visitor found ' imaginative' food
and a 'friendly team' of staff at
Inghams' club hotel Lièvre Blanc. Chez
Bear is a wonderful conversion of an
18th-century farmhouse into a luxury
chalet for 10 – remotely set above
Briançon, but the owners will ferry you
around in their minibus.
Hotels One of the features of this
string of little villages is the range of

attractive family-run hotels – many of
them part of the Logis de France.
LE MONÊTIER
⟨⟨⟨③ **Auberge de Choucas** (0492
244273) Smart, wood-clad rooms, and
'excellent, seven-course dinners in
stone-vaulted restaurant – but
mediocre breakfast and erratic service'.
⟨② **Europe** (0492 244003) Simple well-
run Logis in heart of old village, with
pleasant bar and 'very good' food.
⟨② **Alliey** (0492 244002) 'Excellent
rooms with an indoor/outdoor spa.'
Michelin-star restaurant (see Eating out).
VILLENEUVE
⟨② **Christiania** (0492 247633) Civilised,
family-run hotel on main road,
crammed with ornaments.
⟨② **Vieille Ferme** (0492 247644) Stylish
conversion on the edge of the village.
⟨② **Cimotel** (0492 247822) Modern and
charmless, with good-sized rooms and
'excellent' food.
① **Chatelas** (0492 247474) Prettily
decorated simple chalet by river.
CHANTEMERLE
⟨② **Plein Sud** (0492 241701) Modern;
pool, sauna; 'superbly run by a Brit'.
⟨② **Boule de Neige** (0492 240016)
Comfortable, friendly, in the old centre.
① **Ricelle** (0492 240019) Charming, but
across the valley from the slopes in
Villard-Laté. Good food.

The new Hameau du Rocher Blanche,
which MGM is building by the slopes in
Chantemerle (pool, gym, jacuzzi, sauna,
steam), will be a cut above what was
on offer before. The hotel Alliey (see
above) in Le Monêtier has apartments
too. Snowgums are two apartments in
a hamlet a five-minute drive from
Chantemerle (ski-bus stop nearby).

EATING OUT
Unpretentious and traditional
In Le Monêtier, there are several good
hotel-based options. At the upper end,
the Alliey restaurant is now called
L'Antidote, has a Michelin star, serves
a 'unique' menu and is 'well worth a
meal there'; and the Auberge du
Choucas has a good reputation. Further
down the price bracket, the Europe has
reliable French cooking at reasonable
prices. The Boîte à Fromages is said to
do a 'magnificent' fondue. The Kawa
and the Belotte are both recommended
for their 'cosy atmosphere, good staff
and excellent value'.
 In Villeneuve the Swedish-run Vieille
Ferme is a 'great, stylish eating place'.
The Marotte, a tiny stone building with

classic French cuisine in the old part of Villeneuve, 'offers a wide choice of very good food at very reasonable prices'. The Refuge specialises in fondue and raclette. And there are good crêperies – try the Petit Duc, or the Manouille. Over in Le Bez, the Bidule is said to have 'first-class food and service, at good value' and is recommended by locals. L'Ours Blanc and Passé Simple ('terrific pizzeria') have been recommended.

In Chantemerle, the Couch'où is good value for fondue and raclette, and has a pizzeria upstairs. The candlelit Crystal is the smartest, most expensive place in Chantemerle; the rustic Ricelle offers 'amazing value'.

APRES-SKI
Quiet streets and few bars
Nightlife seems to revolve around bars, scattered through the various villages, and several reporters complain of it being too quiet (though that doesn't bother us personally).

In Le Monêtier the British-run Alpen has a happy hour, free nibbles and welcoming staff; the Que Tal warms up later on. In Villeneuve, Loco Loco in the old village was reportedly 'the place to go, with funky music and a French atmosphere'; but a 2005 visitor took a dim view, reporting 'tedious music and high prices'. The Frog has 'good local beer' and the Yeti is 'very lively and enjoyable' and for 'serious fun seekers'. In Chantemerle the Kitzbühel shows sporting events on TV and 'does good pizzas'. The other Chantemerle bars to look out for are the Taverne de la Biere, the Extreme bar and the new Triptyque ('popular and trendy'). After everything else has closed, a karaoke bar with 'an erratic door policy' may still let you in.

In Briançon, the Auberge Mont Prorel, right by the gondola base, had live music and was full of Brits and Danes rounding off their day when we paid a tea-time visit.

OFF THE SLOPES
Try the hot baths
Serre-Chevalier doesn't hold many attractions for non-slope-users, and it's certainly not for avid shoppers, but the old town of Briançon is well worth a visit. There is a leisure complex with pools, sauna, hot-tub and steam room. Briançon also has an ice hockey team – their games make 'a good night out', says one reporter. Visitors have enjoyed the various indoor-outdoor thermal bath in Le Monêtier, which makes a great place to watch the sun go down – you need to book. (There are ambitious plans to develop the bath into a swanky spa for 2007.) There is a public swimming pool and health spa near the hotel Sporting in Villeneuve. Each of the main villages has a cinema. Chantemerle and Villeneuve have outdoor ice rinks, and there is good walking on 'well-prepared trails'.

STAYING UP THE MOUNTAIN
Worth considering
Pi Maï (0492 248363) above Villeneuve (see Mountain restaurants) and the chalet-hotel Serre-Ratier (0492 205288) above Chantemerle have rooms.

OT STE-FOY / MARK JUNAK

Ste-Foy-Tarentaise

Tasteful development of new chalets and apartments at the foot of deserted slopes with excellent off-piste but very few pistes

COSTS

① ② ③ ④ ⑤ ⑥

RATINGS

The slopes
Fast lifts	*
Snow	***
Extent	*
Expert	****
Intermediate	***
Beginner	**
Convenience	***
Queues	*****
Mountain restaurants	**

The rest
Scenery	***
Resort charm	***
Off-slope	*

NEWS

A fast new six-pack to the east of the resort's bowl is scheduled for 2006/07, serving one new red and one new blue run, as well as making some off-piste routes more easily accessible. For the future, the resort is investigating installing more snowmaking, and construction in the satellite village of La Bataillettaz will continue.

For 2005/06 a new children's area opened near the ski school, and the nursery drag at the base of the slopes was upgraded to a moving carpet. Another new blue run was created at the top of the second lift (one was also created for 2004/05).

+ No crowds

+ Lots of off-piste and untracked powder

+ Cheap lift pass and good-value lodging

+ Other resorts you can visit nearby

– Small resort with limited après-ski

– Very small piste network and till now only slow chair-lifts

– It's best to have a car

The area has been developed only since 1990; but there has been a recent building boom and now there's quite a choice of apartments and chalets to rent. But the millions who flock to the nearby mega-resorts of Val-d'Isère, Tignes and Les Arcs still rarely give it a thought and those in the know – and that includes an increasing number of Brits – are well rewarded. It's an uncrowded gem with some wonderful off-piste slopes for experts and intermediates. Lots of instructors and guides from the big resorts come here on their days off and some bring their off-piste groups here to escape the crowds back home.

THE RESORT

Until a few seasons ago there was not much accommodation at the Ste-Foy ski station. Now more and more is being built, all in the traditional Savoyard style of wood and stone.

Ste-Foy Station (sometimes called Bonconseil) is set 4km/2.5 miles off the main road between Val-d'Isère and Bourg-St-Maurice: turn off at La Thuile, just after the village of Ste-Foy. A complex at the foot of the lifts houses the tourist and ticket office, a couple of cafe/bars, a pizzeria, a small supermarket and well-equipped ski-shops. Zigzags has been there for years and these days gets good reports. The newer competitors are both part of the

Skiset chain, the newest of these is near the alternative focus area that emerged last season on the other side of the main lift. It includes the children's area, the ski school, a newsagent, the Iceberg piano bar and the gourmet Bergerie restaurant.

If you don't have a car, it's most convenient to stay at the ski station, as the free buses to and from Ste-Foy village and other local hamlets aren't very frequent and don't run in the evenings. To make the most of nearby resorts, however, and some excellent but not local restaurants, it's a good idea to have a car. Parking can be rather challenging, but this was helped last season by a new car park with 104 free places in the centre of the resort.

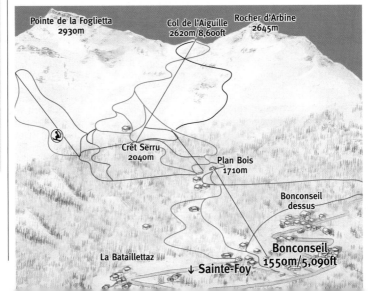

Pointe de la Foglietta 2930m

Col de l'Aiguille 2620m/8,600ft

Rocher d'Arbine 2645m

Crêt Serru 2040m

Plan Bois 1710m

Bonconseil dessus

Bonconseil 1550m/5,090ft

La Bataillettaz

↓ Sainte-Foy

THE MOUNTAIN

Up till now Ste-Foy's deserted slopes have been accessed by three slow quad chairs, rising one above the other to the Col de l'Aiguille. This season, a new six-pack, in the bowl to the east of the area, is set to open – see our piste map. Several major resorts – Val-d'Isère, Tignes, Les Arcs (via Villaroger), La Plagne and La Rosière – are all within easy reach by car. You are entitled to a day at each for around 22 euros a time on presentation of a Ste-Foy six-day pass – which at 105 euros last season was around half the price of Val-d'Isère. A day pass was a bargain 19 euros – compared to 40 in Val.

Slopes The top lift accesses almost 600m/1,970ft of vertical above the tree line and superb, long off-piste routes on the back of the mountain. The two lowest chairs serve a few pleasant runs through trees and back to the base station. The new six-pack will serve an above-the-tree line blue and red, and make some off-piste routes more accessible. Most reporters have been amazed by the amount of terrain the few lifts access: 'Looking at the map gives no indication of the variety of options available,' said one. But don't come here for miles of groomed pistes or modern lifts.

Terrain-parks There has not been an official park for the last couple of seasons, but last season a patrolled off piste area dedicated to freestyle was introduced, between two red pistes above the tree line.

Snow reliability The slopes face north or west. Snow reliability is good on the former but can suffer on the latter, especially as there is snowmaking only on the run down to the resort.

Experts Experts can pass happy times on and off the sides of Ste-Foy's black and red runs, exploring lots of easily accessible off-piste and trees in the huge bowl. Two black runs, Morion and Crystal Dark, are now designated free-ride areas, unpisted but avalanche controlled. If there's been fresh snow, Ste-Foy can't be beaten for snaring first tracks. The lack of crowds means you can still make fresh tracks days after a storm. There's more serious off-piste on offer too, for which you need a guide. There are wonderful runs from the top of the lifts down through deserted old villages, either to the road between Ste-Foy and Val-d'Isère or back to the base, and a splendid route which up till now started with a hike up to the Pointe de la Foglietta, and takes you through trees and over a stream down to the tiny village of Le Crot. The new six-pack should make this route more easily accessible (ie no hike!). The ESF runs group off-piste trips, with transport back to the station. There's also a Bureau des Guides which can arrange heli-skiing.

Intermediates Intermediates can enjoy 1000m/3,28oft vertical of uncrowded reds and the new lift should open up some higher cruising runs.The red from the Col de l'Aiguille is a superb test for confident intermediates, who would also be up to the off-piste routes, especially the Monal route back to base. Anyone who doesn't fancy trying off-piste will tire of the limited runs in a day or two and be champing at the bit to get to Val d'Isère or Les Arcs – although the new runs may help.

Beginners Not the best place, but there have been improvements at the base, including a children's area near the ski school, and a moving carpet lift on the small nursery slope. After that you can progress to a green run off the first chair and a couple of gentle blues off the second – and the slopes are pleasantly quiet.

Snowboarding Great free-riding terrain, with lots of trees and powder between the pistes to play in, plus a dedicated freestyle area for building kickers.

Cross-country No prepared trails, but ask the tourist office about marked itinerary routes such as Planay Dessus.

Queues Except in peak season and on fresh powder days, despite all the new building and slow lifts, reporters have still failed to find queues at Ste-Foy.

Mountain restaurants There are two rustic restaurants at the top of the first chair. Recent reporters rate the Brevettes more highly ('friendly and lively', 'good omelettes') than Chez Léon. Both are small, so it's best to book. The Maison à Colonnes, at the base of the first lift, gets consistently good write-ups. There's also an open-air snack-bar, the Chalet La Foglietta, at the top of the second lift.

Schools and guides We've had good reports of ski school, especially for children (from age four).

Facilities for children Children under seven ski free. There is a nursery, Les P'tits Trappeurs, which takes children from age three to 11. The UK tour operator Première Neige also runs a nursery (its own guests take priority).

STAYING THERE

How to go Various small tour operators can organise chalets and hotels here. Ste-Foy is about 20 minutes from the Eurostar terminal at Bourg-St-Maurice.

Hotels We continue to get glowing reports of Auberge sur la Montagne (0479 069583), just above the turn-off at La Thuile. Yellow Stone Chalet (0479 069606) at the ski station has been highly recommended (a 2006 visitor found it 'great value at the upper end of the market'). For a more French experience try the Ferme du Baptieu (0479 069752). Hotel Monal (0479 069007), in Ste-Foy village, is a basic 2-star, with a games room, bar and two restaurants.

Chalets and self-catering Gîte de Sainte Foy station and Première Neige both have several chalets and apartments (worthy of our 'smart apartments' label) here, with catered and self-catered options. Chalet Number One, in the village of La Masure, is run by former British snowboard champion Lloyd Rogers. 2006 reporters recommend 'great views and food' at Chalet Chevalier in the hamlet of Planay-Dessous. And one

of our assistant editors has one of the MGM chalets to rent (see www.ste-foy-chalet.co.uk). The tourist office runs a central reservation system.

Eating out In the village of Le Miroir, Chez Mérie is excellent (for lunch as well as dinner). So is the Auberge sur la Montagne. In Ste-Foy village, the Grange at the Monal does 'good food'. Chez Léon, up the mountain, opens by arrangement in the evenings. At the station the Maison à Colonnes is 'cosy and fun', and the Bec de l'Ane pizzeria does takeaway as well as eat-in. Chez Alison offers simple fare while the Bergerie is more upmarket and offers a delivery service (but a 2006 reporter was 'disappointed – the food was over fussy and badly cooked').

Après-ski Pretty quiet. Reporters enjoyed the new Iceberg piano bar. The Pitchouli is the place to go for a drink later on. It has table football and sometimes live music. The bar of the Monal can get busy, too.

Off the slopes There's not a lot to do off the slopes, but paragliding, dog-sledding and snow-shoeing are available. The pool and spa at the Balcons de Ste-Foy apartments are open to non-residents for a fee.

Phone numbers
From abroad use the prefix +33 and omit the initial '0' of the phone number.

TOURIST OFFICE

t 0479 069519
stefoy@wanadoo.fr
www.saintefoy.net

Ste-Foy-Tarentaise

373

www.Sainte-Foy.info

The website for:

* Beautiful chalets
* Sainte Foy Ski movies
* Webcams
* Restaurant
* Delicatessen shop
* Swimming pool
* Sauna, Spa & Fitness
* Conference center

www.sainte-foy.info
Tel: +33 (0) 479 06 97 18

Première Neige

Exclusively in Sainte Foy, France

Luxury selection of chalets & apartments on the slopes

Fantastic skiing, empty slopes no queues. Catered & self catered service with flexible dates. In resort Concierge Service. Crèche, Childcare & Transfers.

Tel: UK +44 (0)870 383 1000
email: snow@premiere-neige.com
www.premiere-neige.com

St-Martin-de-Belleville

*Explore the Three Valleys from a traditional old village – and so
avoid the Méribel crowds who descend on it for lunch*

COSTS

① ② ③ ④ ⑤ ⑥

RATINGS

The slopes
Fast lifts	★★★
Snow	★★★
Extent	★★★★★
Expert	★★★★
Intermediate	★★★★★
Beginner	★★
Convenience	★★★
Queues	★★★★
Mountain restaurants	★★★★

The rest
Scenery	★★★
Resort charm	★★★★
Off-slope	★

NEWS

For 2005/06, MGM
opened the Chalets
du Gypse, an
upmarket apartment
development and a
spa and beauty
centre open to all.

KEY FACTS

Resort	1400m
	4,590ft

Three Valleys	
Slopes	1260-3230m
	4,130-10,600ft
Lifts	182
Pistes	630km
	391 miles
Green	14%
Blue	40%
Red	36%
Black	10%
Snowmaking	
	1823 guns

Les Menuires / St-Martin only	
Slopes	1450-2850m
	4,760-9,350ft
Lifts	37
Pistes	160km
	99 miles
Green	10%
Blue	40%
Red	38%
Black	12%
Snowmaking	
	355 guns

➕ Attractively developed traditional
village with pretty church

➕ Easy access to the whole of the
extensive Three Valleys network

➕ Long, easy intermediate runs on
rolling local slopes

➕ Extensive snowmaking keeps local
runs open in poor conditions, but ...

➖ Snow at resort level suffers from
altitude, and sun in the afternoon

➖ No green runs for beginners to
progress to

➖ The climb up from the lower part of
the village can be taxing

➖ Limited après-ski

➖ Few off-slope diversions

**St-Martin is a lived-in, unspoiled village with an old church (prettily lit at night),
small square and buildings of wood and stone, a few miles down the valley
from Les Menuires. As a quiet, inexpensive, attractive base for exploration of the
Three Valleys as a whole, it's unbeatable.**

THE RESORT

In 1950 St-Martin didn't even have
running water or electricity. It remained
a backwater until the 1980s, when
chair-lifts were built linking it to the
slopes of Méribel and Les Menuires.
The old village, set on a steep slope,
has been developed, of course, but the
new buildings fit in well, and it
remains small – you can walk around it
in a few minutes. The main feature
remains the lovely old 16th-century
church – prettily floodlit at night. There
are some good local shops and few
'touristy' ones. A regular visitor was
pleased to report how 'unobtrusive'
the newish gondola station is.

THE MOUNTAINS

The whole of the Three Valleys can
easily be explored from here.
Slopes A gondola followed by a fast
quad take you to a ridge from which
you can access Méribel on one side
and Les Menuires on the other.
Terrain-parks There isn't a terrain-park
in the St-Martin sector, but you can
get to those above Les Menuires and
Méribel relatively easily.
Snow reliability The local slopes face
west and get the full force of the
afternoon sun, and the village is quite
low. There is now snowmaking from
top to bottom of the main run to the
village, and reporters agree that it is
impressively effective at keeping the
run open, but higher runs (eg Verdet)
are less secure. Many people ride the
gondola down if snow is poor. A 2006

visitor found piste marking 'erratic'
Another has said, 'In poor visibility it is
quite easy to go off-piste
unintentionally.'
Experts Locally there are large areas of
gentle and often deserted off-piste. A
reader recommends the descent from
Roc de Fer to the village of Béranger.
Head to La Masse for steep north-
facing slopes.
Intermediates The local slopes are
pleasant blues and reds, mainly of
interest to intermediates – including
one of our favourite runs in the Three
Valleys: the long, rolling, wide
Jerusalem red. The Verdet blue from
the top of the Méribel lifts is a

MONT DE LA CHAMBRE
2850m
Méribel
Roc des
3 Marches
↓ Mont de 2700m
la Challe
2575m
TOUGNETE
2435m
ALLAMANDS
Les Menuires
1800m/5,900ft
Saint-Martin-de-
Belleville ↓
Saint-Martin-de-Belleville
1400m/4,590ft

wonderful easy cruise with great views and is usually very quiet.

Beginners St-Martin is far from ideal – there's a small nursery slope but no long green runs to progress to.

Snowboarding There is some great local off-piste free-riding available.

Cross-country There are 28km/17 miles of trails in the Belleville valley.

Queues Queues are not usually much of a problem outside peak periods, but St-Martin's popularity as a lunch destination leads to 'often massive queues in the afternoon' for the St-Martin 2 chair.

Mountain restaurants There are three atmospheric old places on the run down to the village. Chardon Bleu ('good, not too expensive') and Corbeleys near the mid-mountain lift junction are good for lunch, and the Loy, lower down, is busy as the lifts close. 2006 readers were again 'most impressed' with the Grand Lac at the bottom of the Granges chair – 'friendly with good food'. St-Martin itself is a major lunch destination. For a real treat, La Bouitte in nearby St-Marcel is one of the best restaurants in the Three Valleys (see Eating out) – you ski to it off-piste, and the owners will ferry you to a lift afterwards.

Schools and guides A 2005 reporter had a private ESF lesson on off-piste skiing and said the instructor was 'good at analysing his faults but not so good at teaching him how to improve'. Friends of another visitor found the 'instructors spoke English and were helpful' and enjoyed their lessons.

Facilities for children The Piou Piou club and ESF take children from two-and-a-half years old from 9am to 5pm.

STAYING THERE

How to go For a small village there's a good variety of accommodation.

Hotels The Alp Hôtel (0479 089282), at the foot of the slope by the main lift and close to the nursery, 'continues to be good but lacks a little atmosphere' and reporters were again disappointed by the food. A 2006 visitor was 'made to feel very welcome' by the owners of the 'charming' Saint-Martin (0479 008800), right on the slope, and the Edelweiss (0479 089667) is in the village itself. All are 3-stars. La Bouitte (0479 089677) in St-Marcel (see Eating out) has four lovely rooms – spacious, woody and furnished with antiques.

Chalets Les Chalets de St Martin has operated here ever since the first lift was built – 'I'd recommend them,' says a 2005 visitor. The Alpine Club – which isn't really a club – operates the Ferme de Belleville, a nicely renovated 400-year-old farmhouse in the heart of the old village, with personal service from the proprietors, a British couple.

SMART APARTMENTS – SEE FEATURE

The stylish new CGH/MGM development Les Chalets du Gypse is well placed beside the piste, with a smart pool. Les Chalets de St Martin has a variety of self-catered chalets and apartments.

Eating out For such a small village there is a good variety of restaurants. Readers still enjoy the Montagnard's 'fabulous' Savoyard food, but it and the 'high quality' Voûte, recommended for its salads and pizzas, 'are continuing to move upmarket', says a 2006 visitor. The Lachenal is said to do 'good mid-priced food' and the

Phone numbers
From abroad use the
prefix +33 and omit
the initial '0' of the
phone number.

Grenier, in the hotel St-Martin is 'good
quality with excellent presentation',
'great for an expensive lunch'.

The Etoile des Neiges is a smart,
traditionally French restaurant, but a
2006 reporter is 'annoyed by the lack
of effort ... to keep up with rising
standards elsewhere'. By which he
probably means standards set locally
by La Bouitte, just up the road in the
next village, St-Marcel, and now
boasting a Michelin star. We have had
several superb meals here.

Après-ski The Pourquoi Pas? is cosy,
with a roaring log fire and comfortable
easy chairs and sofas, 'friendly staff'
and 'a large British clientele'. Brewski's

has basic wooden chairs, live bands,
karaoke evenings and the like –
'appealing to the younger boarding
crowd'. A 2006 reader found the
Eterlou a 'much better place to gather
at the end of the day', but not if you
are a non-smoker apparently. The
Dalhia, at the bottom of the gondola,
'makes a good rendezvous'.

Off the slopes If you don't use the
slopes, there are better places to base
yourself. However, a 2006 visitor found
the tourist office very helpful in
arranging dog-sledding and cross-
country skiing excursions. There are
also pleasant walks, a sports hall, and
musical events in the church.

Les Sybelles

Chalk-and-cheese resorts linked rather tenuously by slow lifts to form an area that's one of the biggest in the Alps, at least on paper

COSTS

① ② ③ ④ ⑤ ⑥

RATINGS

The slopes
Fast lifts	*
Snow	***
Extent	*****
Expert	**
Intermediate	***
Beginner	****
Convenience	***
Queues	****
Mountain restaurants	**

The rest
Scenery	***
Resort charm	
– Le Corbier	*
– La Toussuire	**
– St-Jean	****
– St-Sorlin	****
Off-slope	**

NEWS

For 2005/06 the journey to the top of Le Corbier's local ski area was speeded up by the installation of a six-pack from the centre of the resort.

For 2004/05 four much-needed six-packs were installed to improve links between resorts. Two go from St-Sorlin up to Les Perrons, two from La Toussuire via Grande Verdette to Tête de Bellard.

+ Extensive area of largely easy intermediate slopes and gentle, uncrowded off-piste

+ Inexpensive by French standards

+ Unusual mixture of stark, purpose-built resorts and old villages

– Lift network still painfully slow to get around, despite improvements

– Few pistes steep enough to interest adventurous intermediates

– Après-ski limited and quiet

– Mainly simple accommodation

– Few off-slope diversions

Les Sybelles is not a resort but a lift network linking a handful of little-known resorts in the Maurienne massif in the French Alps. When formed in 2003, Les Sybelles' 310km/193 miles of pistes put it straight into the big league, alongside such giants as Val-d'Isère-Tignes.

Our first visit to the newly launched Les Sybelles gave us a bit of a shock; we had forgotten just how slow progress can be on a mountain with 70 slow lifts and just one fast one. Matters have since improved – four more fast chairs for 2004/05, and one more last season. But Les Sybelles still languishes at the bottom of our fast-lift league table – and installation of fast lifts out of the big resorts without similar improvements at altitude seems sure to create queue problems in peak season for the drag-lifts that form the links. So we still say: more six-packs, please.

The resorts are sharply contrasting in character. La Toussuire and Le Corbier are most politely described as modern, functional and downmarket, while St-Sorlin-d'Arves and St-Jean-d'Arves are largely unspoiled, traditional villages that have recently expanded tastefully and attracted some major UK tour operators.

The links between the resorts are high – mostly between 2000m and 2600m (6,560ft and 8,530ft) – so they are relatively snow-sure. They are also easily negotiated by adventurous intermediates, consisting of easy reds and tough blues (one or two of which might be better classified red). But getting from one resort to another can be slow going, because of slow lifts.

Visitors to St-Jean and St-Sorlin warn that the long road up from the valley is seriously worrying – winding, narrow in places, with precipitous drops often without barriers, all compounded by a poor surface.

LE CORBIER 1550m/5,090ft
Le Corbier is centrally placed, with direct links to St-Jean-d'Arves in one direction and La Toussuire in the other, as well as a high link to St-Sorlin.

THE RESORT
Designed in the 1960s, Le Corbier is a no-compromise functional resort. Most of its accommodation is in eight inner-city-style tower blocks – one as high as

19 storeys – with subterranean shops beneath. To our eye, it looks like a mistake. But it does accommodate its 9,000 visitors efficiently in the minimum space, and in functional terms it is hard to criticise – it is compact, family-friendly and traffic-free with all ski-in/ski-out accommodation. The apartment blocks line the foot of the slopes, and in the other direction the resort's balcony setting gives good views of the valley. It sells itself firmly as a family resort and runs a French Family Championship with teams made up of mother, father and one child. And the resort assures us that all new building will be in traditional style.

THE MOUNTAIN
Le Corbier's local ski area has 90km/56 miles of gentle pistes. Although the altitudes are modest (top height 2265m/7,430ft, resort 1550m/5,090ft), there are hardly any trees.

Slopes The new Sybelles Express, a six-seat fast chair, rises over 700m/2,300ft vertical to Pte du Corbier from where pistes and lifts go along the

Slopes	1300-2620m
	4,270-8,600ft
Lifts	73
Pistes	310km
	193 miles
Green	17%
Blue	40%
Red	36%
Black	7%
Snowmaking	
	233 guns

ridge to the hub of Les Sybelles at Pte de L'Ouillon. Runs spread across a wide, north-east-facing mountainside return to the resort, and there are links at the extremities to La Toussuire and St-Jean-d'Arves.

Terrain-park There's a park on the lower slopes just above the resort.

Snow reliability The mix of reasonable altitude and lack of crowds cutting up the pistes means the snow tends to stay in fairly good condition. The slopes get the morning sun, but there is snowmaking on all the main pistes back to the resort. The low connection from La Toussuire is another problem spot, but there is also a higher link.

Experts The area lacks challenges – the one short black piste scarcely deserves a red grading. There are off-piste options in the valley between Le Corbier and La Toussuire.

Intermediates Le Corbier's gentle slopes are ideal cruising terrain, though the runs aren't very long and they rather lack variety.

Beginners There is an extensive nursery area with a moving carpet right in front of the resort, with gentle progression runs directly above.

Snowboarding The wide, open terrain is ideal for riders, as long as they don't want anything too challenging.

Cross-country There are narrow loops across the mountainside either side of the resort, one of which leads to La Toussuire and back. It's all a bit bleak.

Queues We have no reports of problems, but see introduction.

Mountain restaurants A past reporter says Le Charmun, at the foot of the Vadrouille area, 'was the restaurant of the week for us, with delicious crozets with wild mushrooms and lardons' and Chalet 2000 near the top was 'notable for its playful golden labrador as well as its welcome and food'.

Schools Our one past reporter judged the ESF 'disdainful, uncaring, very disorganised; bad tuition'.

Facilities for children The Nursery takes children from six months. A reporter praised the ski kindergarten (for age three up): 'Nice, well-equipped ski-park; good instructors.' Its location up on the pistes means a bit of a hike.

STAYING THERE

How to go There are several UK operators selling packages here.

Chalets Equity Ski runs its own chalet hotel, described by one reporter as 'clean, comfortable and very good

value' and approved by others, too.

Self-catering There's nothing larger than cramped two-bedroomed units on offer from central reservations.

Eating out Le Grillon, 3km/2 miles away in the Villarembert, makes a pleasant, rustic change from Le Corbier's tower blocks – and serves traditional French food.

Après ski Very quiet. The Equity Ski chalet-hotel bar is popular. The Roches Blanches restaurant in the centre includes a cosy bar area with an open fire. For dancing, the Président gets busy only at peak holiday periods.

Off the slopes There's a nice natural ice rink and a fitness centre. The outdoor pool is open, and you can go snowmobiling, among other things.

LA TOUSSUIRE 1700m/5,580ft

La Toussuire, along with Le Corbier, is one of the central resorts of the new network – the two have been linked at low altitude since 1986.

THE RESORT

La Toussuire has grown up over many years but is predominantly modern, with a car-free and snow-covered main street lined by dreary-looking buildings dating from the 1960s and 1970s. The resort has now spread widely from here, with wooden chalets as well as older hotels and small apartment blocks scattered across the mountainside.

THE MOUNTAIN

The local slopes amount to 45km/ 28 miles of pistes.

Slopes The resort sits in the pit of a wide bowl. Drags and chair-lifts (including two six-packs) rise just over 500m/1,640ft vertical to the high point of Tête de Ballard and the link to L'Ouillon. At one end of the bowl is the low-level link to Le Corbier and at the other the start of a long red run to the hamlet of Les Bottières of 900m/2,950ft vertical.

Terrain-park There's a boarder-cross course in the centre of the bowl.

Snow reliability With every run above 1800m/5,910ft snow-cover is fairly assured, but some of the slopes are rather exposed to the sun – particularly the low-level connection to Le Corbier.

Experts There are few challenges here, and not much space left between the pistes. The main interest is the ungroomed black Vallée Perdue run, which descends the valley separating

La Toussuire from Le Corbier, away from the lifts. But it gets a lot of sun, and snow conditions can suffer. The link lifts towards L'Ouillon open up off-piste routes down this valley.

Intermediates This is ideal terrain for cruisers who don't mind mainly short runs. The longer runs that go down to Les Bottières are some of the most appealing in the whole area.

Beginners There are nice, gentle nursery slopes immediately above the centre of the village, and good, easy progression slopes.

Snowboarding There are quite a few drag-lifts in the area.

Cross-country A narrow loop goes to Le Corbier, but it is in bleak surroundings close to the road. There are also loops on the lower slopes of Le Grand Truc.

Queues We have no reports of problems, but see introduction.

Mountain restaurants The Foehn at Le Marolay is recommended for its 'friendly service', the 'stunning views' and an interesting interior of old photos, carvings, etc. A 2006 reporter says the 'staff were even nice to our kids!' The Cigales, near the foot of the bowl, reportedly had 'good basic food and was friendly'. Another reader enjoyed the 'fantastic setting' and 'great vin chaud' of the refuge on the Bouyans blue run down to St-Colomban.

Schools A lack of English-speaking tuition can be a problem, as confirmed by a 2006 visitor with children. However, he also 'had a fantastic time in the ESF advanced adult class with a great bi-lingual teacher'.

Facilities for children The nursery accepts children from three to six. Language may be a problem.

STAYING THERE

How to go A few UK tour operators serve the resort.

Hotels There are several small 3-star and 2-star places. The 3-star Ruade (0479 830179) and Soldanelles (0479 567529) both have pools and saunas.

Self-catering The new Chalet Goélia residence, slightly outside the centre but linked to the slopes, is recommended. The Ecrins chalets are large 3-star apartments. Most others are cheap and not so cheerful.

Eating out The options are mostly inexpensive pizzerias and bar-restaurants.

Après-ski Fairly dire. There are a few bars, including the Tonneau. The Alpen Rock nightclub can get busy at peak French holiday time.

Off the slopes There's a reasonable amount to do, including snow-shoeing, snowmobiling, dog-sledding, skating on a ' very seedy' rink on the roof of a building in the main street, and hang-gliding.

Les Sybelles

379

↑ St-Sorlin has much the highest and most interesting slopes in the area on Les Perrons, the rocky ridge to the right. The gentler slopes of La Balme are to the left, and a small part of the village is visible in the lower centre

ST-SORLIN-D'ARVES 1500m/4,920ft

St-Sorlin is the major beneficiary of recent investment in fast chairs, gaining a slick link right to the top of the most interesting slopes in the area, on Les Perrons. This is now an excellent base for keen intermediates.

THE RESORT

St-Sorlin-d'Arves is a real, medium-sized village with a year-round life outside skiing. It's a picturesque collection of well-preserved traditional farmhouses, with a baroque church and long-established shops – fromagerie, boulangerie, crafts, etc – alongside more modern resort development. Its setting on a narrow shelf gives fine views but doesn't allow much room for expansion, so the village has grown in a ribbon-like fashion – not ideal for strolling around. Visitors have various complaints about the bus services.

THE MOUNTAIN

St-Sorlin's local slopes form the biggest single sector of the linked network, with 120km/75 miles of piste. Although very much an intermediate mountain, it does offer much more variety, including some steeper options, than the rest of the area.

Slopes There are two distinct sections. The lower, gentler left side on La Balme, reached by a choice of slow chairs from the village, is crammed with lots of short, easy runs. The higher, right side on Les Perrons, now reached by two successive fast six-packs, has long, sweeping, generally steeper pistes. The Vallons run off the back of Les Perrons (which forms the first part of the link to L'Ouillon and from there to the other resorts) and the runs from Petit Perron have added

a lot of interest to the local skiing.

Snow reliability Not bad. Les Perrons slopes are the highest in the area and the main runs back to the village are covered by snowmakers.

Experts There isn't much on-piste challenge, but Les Perrons has the best off-piste in the whole area; the slopes beneath the new Petit Perron chair look interesting.

Intermediates The long top-to-bottom reds on both sides of Les Perrons are the best pistes in the whole area. There is only one on the back and a couple on the front, but they have the whole mountain to themselves, giving a great away-from-it-all feel. La Balme has shorter, more leisurely runs.

Beginners The nursery slope is right by the village, and there are plenty of slopes to progress to on La Balme.

Snowboarding La Balme has a lot of drag-lifts.

Cross-country There's a narrow 16km/10 mile loop along a side valley past the foot of La Balme's Alpine area, with good views of the Aiguilles d'Arves.

Queues We have no reports of problems, but see introduction.

Mountain restaurants We enjoyed lunch and stunning views of the Aiguilles d'Arves on the sunny terrace of the rustic Bergerie at the top of the Plan Moulin chair at La Balme.

Schools A recent visitor reports 'exceptionally friendly and helpful instructors but big classes of up to 20'. A 2005 visitor was annoyed that the ESF shortened his child's pre-booked lessons with no cut in the price.

Facilities for children The Petits Diables nursery accepts children from three months. The ski kindergarten accepts kids from three-and-a-half years. Language is a likely problem.

Phone numbers
From abroad use the
prefix +33 and omit
the initial '0' of the
phone number.

TOURIST OFFICES

info@les-sybelles.com
www.les-sybelles.com
La Toussuire
t 0479 830606
info@la-toussuire.com
www.la-toussuire.com
Le Corbier
t 0479 830404
info@le-corbier.com
www.le-corbier.com
St-Sorlin-d'Arves
t 0479 597177
info@saintsorlin
darves.com
www.saintsorlindarves.
com
St-Jean-d'Arves
t 0479 597330
info@saintjeandarves.
com
www.saintjeandarves.
com
**St-Colomban-des-
Villards**
t 0479 562453
info@saint-colomban.
com
www.saint-colomban.
com
Les Bottières
t 0479 832709
info@bottieres-
jarrier.com
www.bottieres-
jarrier.com

STAYING THERE

How to go Some major UK tour
operators now offer holidays here –
see the index at the back of the book.
Hotels There are two small 2-star
places – both attractive chalets. The
Beausoleil (0479 597142) and Balme
(0479 597021) look the best bets.
Self-catering There are scores of small
properties (and the Grignotte bakery
sells 'the best bread ever encountered
in the Alps', says one reporter).
Eating out The choice is limited to
cheap and cheerful pizzerias and
raclette/fondue places. The Table de
Marie, Gargoulette ('friendly, decent
food, but frenetic and disorganised
service') and pizza and pasta above
the Avalanche bar have been
recommended. The Kalico, in the
Fermes de Saint Sorlin residence, is
said to have 'very good food' and 'a
good atmosphere'.
Après-ski St-Sorlin-d'Arves is even
quieter than the other major resorts. A
2004 reporter says, 'The Avalanche bar
was lively with a student-age clientele
and the Godille was more frequented
by locals but essentially dead. We did
not think the guide's warning that
there isn't much nightlife or many bars
would matter to us oldies, but in
practice it did.' You have been warned
– again.
Off the slopes There is not much to
do. Dog-sledding and snow-shoeing
are options, but it's fairly tame territory.

ST-JEAN-D'ARVES 1550m/5,090ft

Although small, St-Jean-d'Arves is quite
a scattered community. The original
old village, with the usual ancient
church, is set across the valley from
the slopes, which are at the mid-
mountain hamlet of La Chal. Here,
where a tasteful development of
chalet-style buildings is still expanding,
there are nursery slopes and the lift
link to and piste back from Le Corbier.

St-Jean/La Chal is not a good base
for anyone wanting to exploit the
larger area – a group that includes
most energetic beginners as well as
intermediates. The slow chair-lift
towards Le Corbier 'is enough to make
you cry every morning', says a 2006
reporter. The return slopes are
excessively sunny – bare and rocky
when we visited; snowmaking may
have improved matters, but a cure is
unlikely. Usually it will be better to
take the shuttle-bus to St-Sorlin to use
its fast lifts.

Off-slope diversions are few – dog-
sledding, cheese farm visits, snow-
shoeing. Plenty of open slopes for
sledging. Après-ski is basic, with a few
bars, an Irish pub and night-
tobogganing with music. The
Marmottes and the Fontaine du Roi
apartments are about the best self-
catering options in the whole area –
which is not saying much.

ST-COLOMBAN-DES-VILLARDS
1100m/3,610ft
St-Colomban-des-Villards is a tiny old
village in the next valley to La
Toussuire, only a few miles up from
the Maurienne valley.

In recent years it has developed a
chain of drags and chair-lifts on north-
and east-facing slopes to the south of
the village, with a high point at Mt
Cuinat, and is now linked to L'Ouillon,
at the hub of Les Sybelles. The run
down is reportedly 'interesting and
attractive', but the return lifts take an
hour. A battery of snowmakers keeps
the home slope open.

LES BOTTIERES 1300m/4,270ft
Down the mountain from La Toussuire,
this tiny hamlet offers little
infrastructure and extremely indirect
access to the main network – it takes
three lifts to get over to La Toussuire,
before setting off for L'Ouillon.

JM GOUÉDARD

La Tania

A very attractive budget base for the limitless slopes of Courchevel and Méribel – and not bad looking, for a purpose-built resort

382

+ Part of the Three Valleys – the world's biggest linked ski area

+ Quick access to the slopes of Courchevel and Méribel

+ Long, rolling, intermediate runs through woods back to the village

+ New green run above the village means it's now more attractive for beginners and timid intermediates

+ Greatly improved snowmaking

+ Attractive, small, traffic-free village

– Small development without much choice of après-ski – and no doctor or pharmacy

– Main nursery slope is part of the blue run to the village, and gets a lot of through-traffic

– Not the ideal launch-pad for expeditions to the far end of the Three Valleys

– Some accommodation is a long walk from the centre and the main lifts

La Tania does not try to compete with its more upmarket neighbours, Courchevel and Méribel. But it has carved out its own niche as a good-value, small, quiet, family-friendly base from which to hit the slopes of both neighbouring valleys. Trips to the furthest corners of the immense Three Valleys are certainly possible, but they obviously take more time than from better-placed starting points.

It is a second-generation purpose-built resort, and at 1350m/4,430ft about the lowest you'll find; its wood-clad buildings sit comfortably in a pretty woodland setting – quite a contrast to classic French ski stations like Les Menuires.

THE RESORT

La Tania is set just off the minor road linking Le Praz (Courchevel 1300) to Méribel. It has grown into a quiet, attractive, car-free collection of mainly ski-in, ski-out chalets and apartments set among the trees, most with good views. There are few shops other than food and sports shops and you can walk around it in a couple of minutes. But for such a small place there is a fair selection of bars and restaurants.

A gondola leads up into the slopes, and there are two wonderful sweeping intermediate runs down. The nursery slope is on your doorstep, and visitors say that La Tania is 'very child friendly'. The steepness of the longer runs above the village has, until now, been its key weakness. This was greatly improved for 2005/06 with the opening of the Plan Fontaine green run from Praz-Juget to the village, giving novices a long easy slope to progress to. But getting back from Courchevel still involves tackling a blue.

Free buses go to Courchevel; the hourly evening service is said to be erratic. For those with a car, Méribel is probably a bigger draw – and a lot nearer than Courchevel 1850.

THE MOUNTAINS

As well as good, though limited, local slopes, the Courchevel or the Méribel slopes are only two lifts away.
Slopes The gondola out of the village goes to Praz-Juget. From here a drag-lift takes you to Chenus and the slopes above Courchevel 1850 and a fast quad goes to the link with Méribel via Col de la Loze. An alternative way to the slopes above 1850 is to take two successive drag-lifts from the village to Loze. From all these points, varied, interesting intermediate runs take you back into the La Tania sector.
Terrain-parks There is no local terrain-park or half-pipe, but you can get to

Courchevel's four parks easily.

Snow reliability Good snow-cover down to Praz-Juget is usual all season. Snowmaking now covers the whole of the blue run back to the village; some reporters found this satisfactory, but others found the run became icy in the afternoon and preferred to ride the gondola down at times.

Experts There are no particularly testing runs directly above La Tania, but the Jean Blanc and Jockeys blacks from Loze to Le Praz are genuine challenges and there is good off-piste terrain beneath the Col de la Loze ridge and close by above Courchevel.

Intermediates There are two lovely, long, undulating intermediate runs back through the trees to La Tania – though there's little difference in gradient between the blue and the red,

and timid intermediates may want to use the new green. On the higher slopes you have a choice of three or four pistes. Both Lanches and Dou des Lanches (now reclassified from red to black) are excellent and challenging.

Beginners There is a good beginner area and lift right in the village and children are well catered for. But there's a lot of through traffic on the main slope. The new green run from Praz-Juget, due to be further improved for 2006/07, should make La Tania a lot more suitable for beginners.

Snowboarding It's easy to get around on gondolas and chairs, avoiding drags.

Cross-country There are trails at altitude with links through the woods to Méribel and Courchevel, which has an extensive 66km/41 miles of trails. To our non-specialist eye, this looks a good base.

La Tania

383

Col de Chanrossa 2545m
La Vizelle 2660m
Méribel
La Saulire 2740m/8,990ft
Méribel
CHANROSSA
Les Creux
SAULIRE - CREUX
Chenus 2245m
Col de la Loze 2275m
Mt. Bel Air
Altiport
Verdons
LOZE - PRAZ
Prameruel 1825m
Praz-Juget
Courchevel 1850
Courchevel 1650
Courchevel 1550
Le Praz 1260m/4,130ft
La Tania 1350m/4,430ft

KEY FACTS

Resort	1350m
	4,430ft

The Three Valleys

Slopes	1260-3230m
	4,130-10,600ft
Lifts	182
Pistes	630km
	391 miles
Green	14%
Blue	40%
Red	36%
Black	10%
Snowmaking	
	1823 guns

Courchevel/
La Tania only

Slopes	1260-2740m
	4,130-8,990ft
Lifts	63
Pistes	150km
	93 miles
Green	22%
Blue	37%
Red	33%
Black	8%
Snowmaking	
	563 guns

Queues A queue can build up for the village gondola but it is quick-moving, and one of the attractions of La Tania in general is the lack of crowds.

Mountain restaurants The 'excellent' Bouc Blanc, near the top of the gondola out of La Tania, has friendly table-service in a wood-clad dining room, good food and a big terrace. A 2006 visitor says 'lovely salads, always a good plat du jour and huge plates of chips for fussy kids'. Roc Tania, higher up at Col de la Loze, is tiny, but very pretty inside – good for a scenic coffee stop; one reader found the food good, another was disappointed with food and service.

Schools and guides Several 2005 reporters raved about the ESF: 'Unequivocally the lessons for myself and children were excellent.' One of the satisfied ESF clients went there because of 'appalling service' from Magic in Motion at the booking stage. We have no recent reports of the other schools. Supreme (a Brit-run school which has operated out of Courchevel 1850 for years, and branched out a couple of years back) and Snow Ball.

Facilities for children We have had excellent reports of the nursery run by UK tour operator Le Ski; they opened a second, larger one for 2005/06. The local Maison des Enfants kindergarten takes non-skiing children from the age of three; the Jardin des Neiges takes skiing children from the age of four. A list of babysitters is available from the tourist office.

STAYING THERE

How to go Over 30 British tour operators go here.

Hotels The Montana (0479 088008) is a slope-side 3-star next to the gondola with a sauna and fitness club. The Télémark (0479 088032), with bistro, opened a couple of years back. The Mountain Centre (0870 251006 in the UK or www.themountaincentre.com) has 'cheap backpacker-style accommodation and food'.

Chalets Several tour operators have selections of splendid newish ski-in, ski-out chalets with fine views, which reporters generally enjoy though we have had complaints of 'poor sound-

OT LA TANIA /
MARIE-AGNES SEJALON

The slopes are at the heart of the small village →

OUR WEBSITE

Go to our website at wtss.co.uk for resort news, links to resort sites, a build-your-own resort shortlist system and reader forums.

Phone numbers
From abroad use the prefix +33 and omit the initial '0' of the phone number.

TOURIST OFFICE
t 0479 084040
info@latania.com
www.latania.com

proofing' in some. The choice gets wider every year; Le Ski, for example, added two newly built slope-side chalets for 2005/06. We have had especially good reports of them and of Snowline.

Self-catering There are lots of apartments – and most are more spacious and better equipped than usual in France. The Saboia and the Christiania have been recommended. There is a deli and a bakery, as well as a small supermarket.

Eating out The Ferme de la Tania gets generally good reviews for its Savoyard fare – 'good service, good food'. The Farçon was back in favour this year: a reporter says, 'We had an excellent lunch, and it did not cost a fortune.' The Ski Lodge has 'damn good chilli burgers' and 'will do a deal for groups including all-you-can-eat-and-drink salad, chips and wine'. The Chanterelles is 'highly recommended' for crêpes and pizzas ('first-class meals at knockdown prices') and the Taïga does 'very good pizzas and is friendly

and quite cheap'. A 2004 reporter recommends the Marmottons for its tartiflette and a 2005 one the relatively new hotel Télémark as having 'a very good new restaurant'.

Après-ski The Ski Lodge has long been the focal après-ski place and has live bands. But it also now has some rivals. The hotel Télémark has 'civilised live music nightly' and the Taïga 'is quite smart, with cocktails and live music', according to 2005 reporters. The hotel Montana bar is also worth trying for a quiet drink and the 'nice locals' bar' – the Arbatte – is popular as the slopes close.

Off the slopes Unless you have a car, La Tania is not the best place for someone not intending to hit the slopes – too small and limited. However, snowmobile trips, snow-shoeing, paragliding and husky dog-sledding are possibilities, and the hotel Montana has a fitness club with a swimming pool. A non-skier's guide to Courchevel, Méribel and La Tania is distributed free by the tourist office.

La Tania

385

Selected chalets in La Tania

The Three Valleys

With the swankiest resort in the Alps at one end, and the highest at the other: the biggest lift-linked ski area in the world

CLEVER – book your sports gear in this resort!

www.sport2000rent.com

Despite competing claims, notably from the Portes du Soleil, in practical terms the Three Valleys cannot be beaten for sheer quantity of lift-served terrain. There is nowhere like it for a keen skier or boarder who wants to cover as much mileage as possible while rarely taking the same run repeatedly. It has a lot to offer everyone, from beginner to expert. And its resorts offer a wide range of alternatives – not only the widely known attractions of the big-name mega-resorts but also the increasingly appreciated low-key appeal of the smaller villages.

What's more, the area undersells itself. It should actually be known as the Four Valleys because several years ago it expanded south into the Maurienne. And the figures the individual resorts give us for their local ski areas add up to 630km/391 miles – but the Three Valleys claims only 600km/373 miles. So we'll forgive the fact that the lifts add up to a mere 182 when 200 are claimed. The central fact is that it's huge.

The runs of the Three Valleys and their resorts are dealt with in six chapters. The four major resorts are Courchevel, Méribel, Les Menuires and Val-Thorens, but we also give chapters to St-Martin-de-Belleville, a small village down the valley from Les Menuires, and La Tania, a modern development between Courchevel and Méribel.

None of the resorts is cheap. **Les Menuires** has some budget accommodation but its original

buildings are hard on the eye (new developments are now being built in a much more acceptable style). The slopes around the village get too much sun for comfort, but across the valley are some of the best (and quietest) challenging pistes in the Three Valleys on its north-facing La Masse. Down the valley from Les Menuires is **St-Martin-de-Belleville**, a charming traditional village which has been expanded in a sympathetic style. It has good-value accommodation and lift links into the slopes of Les Menuires and Méribel.

Up rather than down the Belleville valley from Les Menuires, at 2300m/ 7,550ft, **Val-Thorens** is the highest resort in the Alps, and at 3230m/ 10,600ft the top of its slopes is the high point of the Three Valleys. The snow in this area is almost always good, and it includes two glaciers where good snow is guaranteed. But the setting is bleak and the lifts are vulnerable to closure in bad weather. The purpose-built resort is very convenient. Visually it is not comparable to Les Menuires, thanks to

the smaller-scale design and more thorough use of wood cladding, but it still isn't to everyone's taste.

Méribel is a two-part resort. The higher component, **Méribel-Mottaret**, is the best placed of all the resorts for getting to any part of the Three Valleys system in the shortest possible time. It's now quite a spread-out place, with some of the accommodation a long way up the hillsides – great for access to the slopes, less so for access to nightlife. **Méribel** itself is 200m/660ft lower and has long been a British favourite, especially for chalet holidays. It is the most attractive of the main Three Valleys resorts, built in chalet style beside a long winding road up the hillside. Parts of the resort are very convenient for the slopes and the village centre; parts are very far from either. The growing hamlet of **Méribel-Village** has its own chair-lift into the system but is very isolated and quiet. You can also stay below Méribel in the valley town of **Brides-les-Bains**, or in hamlets along the route of the gondola that links it to Méribel.

Courchevel has four parts. 1850 is the most fashionable resort in France, and can be the most expensive resort in the Alps (though it doesn't have to cost a fortune to stay there). The less expensive parts – Le Praz (aka 1300), 1550 and 1650 – don't have the same choice of nightlife and restaurants. Many people rate the slopes around Courchevel the best in the Three Valleys, with runs to suit all standards.

La Tania was built for the 1992 Olympics, just off the small road linking Le Praz to Méribel. It has now grown into an attractive, car-free collection of chalets and chalet-style apartments set among the trees, and is popular with families. It has a good nursery slope and lovely long intermediate runs, with a green run back due to open for winter 2005/06.

Tignes

Stark apartment blocks and a bleak, treeless setting are the prices you pay for the high, snow-sure slopes and great, varied terrain

COSTS

① ② ③ ④ ⑤ ⑥

RATINGS

The slopes
Fast lifts	★★★
Snow	★★★★★
Extent	★★★★★
Expert	★★★★★
Intermediate	★★★★★
Beginner	★★
Convenience	★★★★
Queues	★★★★
Mountain restaurants	★★★

The rest
Scenery	★★★
Resort charm	★★
Off-slope	★

KEY FACTS

Resort	2100m
	6,890ft

Entire Espace Killy area	
Slopes	1550-3455m
	5,090-11,340ft
Lifts	90
Pistes	300km
	186 miles
Green	15%
Blue	46%
Red	27%
Black	12%
Snowmaking	26km
	16 miles

Tignes only	
Slopes	1550-3455m
	5,090-11,340ft
Lifts	48
Pistes	150km
	93 miles

388

- ➕ Good snow guaranteed for a long season – about the best Alpine bet
- ➕ One of the best areas in the world for lift-served off-piste runs
- ➕ Huge amount of terrain for all abilities, with swift access to the slopes of Val-d'Isère
- ➕ Lots of accommodation close to the slopes (though there is also quite a bit that involves some walking)
- ➕ Efforts to make the resort villages more welcoming are paying off

- ➖ Resort architecture not to everyone's taste (including ours)
- ➖ Bleak, treeless setting – and many slopes liable to closure during and after storms
- ➖ Still a few long, slow chair-lifts – though they are part way through an upgrading programme
- ➖ Near beginners looking for long green runs have to buy an area pass and go to the Val-d'Isère slopes
- ➖ Limited, but improving, après-ski

The appeal of Tignes is simple: good snow, spread over a wide area of varied terrain, shared with Val-d'Isère. Together the two resorts form the enormous Espace Killy – a Mecca for experts, and ideal for adventurous intermediates. The height of Tignes is crucial: a forecast of 'rain up to 2000m' means 'fresh snow down to village level in Tignes'.

We prefer to stay in Val, which is a more human place. But in many ways Tignes makes the better base: appreciably higher, more convenient, surrounded by intermediate terrain, with quick access to the Grande Motte glacier. And the case for Tignes gets stronger as results flow from the resort's campaign to reinvent itself in a more cuddly form. Cars have been largely pushed underground, new buildings are being designed in traditional styles and some old ones are getting a facelift. It all helps to combat the impression that you've landed on the Moon.

They have been improving their lifts as well, and in the last few seasons have, at last, got around to installing some fast chairs on the western side of the Tignes bowl, allowing more time to be spent on skis or board and less on slow lifts. But there are still a few key links that need upgrading.

These are some of the early Tignes apartment blocks. More recent developments have been much more tasteful, built in chalet style and using wood and stone. Shame they didn't think of that in the 1960s →

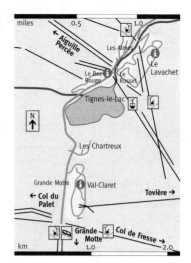

Tignes was created before the French discovered the benefits of making purpose-built resorts look acceptable. But things are improving. Traffic is now discouraged (and in places routed underground), and the villages are gradually acquiring a more traditional look and feel.

The original and main village – Tignes-le-Lac – is still the hub of the resort. Some of the smaller buildings in the central part, Le Rosset, are being successfully revamped in chalet style. But the place as a whole is dreary, and the blocks overlooking the lake from the quarter called Le Bec-Rouge will remain monstrous until the day they are demolished. It's at the point where these two sub-resorts meet – now a snowy pedestrian area, with valley traffic passing through a tunnel beneath – that the lifts are concentrated: a powerful gondola towards Tovière and Val-d'Isère and (new for 2006/07) a fast six-pack up the western slopes. Some attractive new buildings are being added both in the centre and on the fringes, in a suburb built on the lower slopes known as Les Almes. A nursery slope separates Le Rosset from the fourth component part, Le Lavachet, below which there are now good fast lifts up both sides of the valley. Like Le Rosset, Le Lavachet is an apartment development, but one that is much easier on the eye.

Val-Claret (2km/1 mile up the valley, beyond the lake) was also mainly developed after Le Rosset, and is a bit more stylish – though we don't side with those readers who claim to actually like the look of it. The main part of the village, Centre, is an uncompromisingly 1960s-style development on a shelf above the valley floor. Below this, high-speed chairs head up in three directions: to the western slopes, towards Val-d'Isère and to the Grande Motte. An underground funicular also accesses the Grande Motte.

Beside the road along the valley to the lifts is a ribbon of more recent development in traditional style, named Grande Motte (after the peak). The two levels of Val-Claret are linked by a couple of (unreliable) indoor elevators and stairs and by hazardous paths.

Below the main resort villages are

two smaller places. Tignes-les-Boisses, quietly set in the trees beside the road up, consists of a barracks and a couple of simple hotels. Tignes-les-Brévières is a renovated old village at the lowest point of the slopes – a favourite lunch spot, and a friendly place to stay.

Location isn't crucial, as a regular and very efficient free bus service connects all the villages until midnight – though in the daytime the route runs along the bottom of Val-Claret, leaving residents of Val-Claret Centre with some uphill hiking.

A six-day pass covers a day in some other resorts, including Paradiski (Les Arcs and La Plagne) and the Three Valleys, most easily reached with the aid of a car. Keep your pass and you'll get a loyalty discount off next year's. A 2006 reporter liked the system where you can buy a lift pass over the web and have it posted to you in advance – so avoiding queueing in resort.

The area's great weakness is that it can become unusable in bad weather. There are no woodland runs except immediately above Tignes-les-Boisses and Tignes-les-Brévières. Heavy snow produces widespread avalanche risk and wind closes the higher chairs.

Piste classification here is more reliable than in Val-d'Isère.

THE SLOPES
High, snow-sure and varied
Tignes' biggest asset is the **Grande Motte** – and the runs from, as well as on, the glacier. The underground

FRANCE

390

LIFT PASSES

L'Espace Killy

Prices in €

Age	1-day	6-day
under 13	30	144
13 to 59	40	192
over 60	61	163

Free under 5, over 75

Beginner five free lifts

Notes
Covers Tignes and
Val-d'Isère. Half-day
and pedestrian
passes available.
Discount on
presentation of lift
pass from any of
previous three
seasons. Six-day
passes and over are
valid for one day in
the Three Valleys,
Valmorel and
Paradiski (La Plagne-
Les Arcs), half-price
pass in Ste-Foy and
reduced price in La
Rosière.

Alternative passes
Tignes-only pass
available.

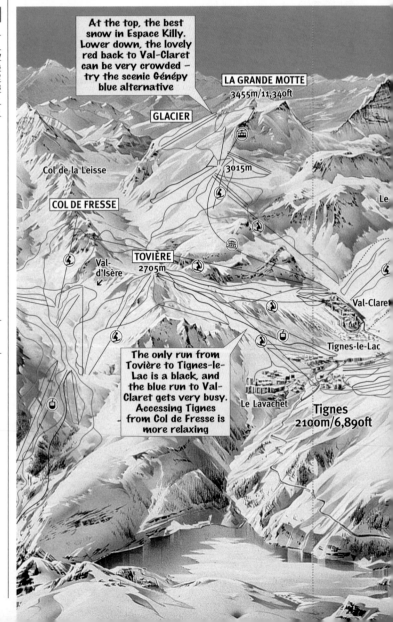

At the top, the best
snow in Espace Killy.
Lower down, the lovely
red back to Val-Claret
can be very crowded –
try the scenic Génépy
blue alternative

LA GRANDE MOTTE
3455m/11,340ft

GLACIER

Col de la Leisse

3015m

COL DE FRESSE

Le

TOVIÈRE
2705m

Val-
d'Isère

Val-Claret

Tignes-le-Lac

The only run from
Tovière to Tignes-le-
Lac is a black, and
the blue run to Val-
Claret gets very busy.
Accessing Tignes
from Col de Fresse is
more relaxing

Le Lavachet

Tignes
2100m/6,890ft

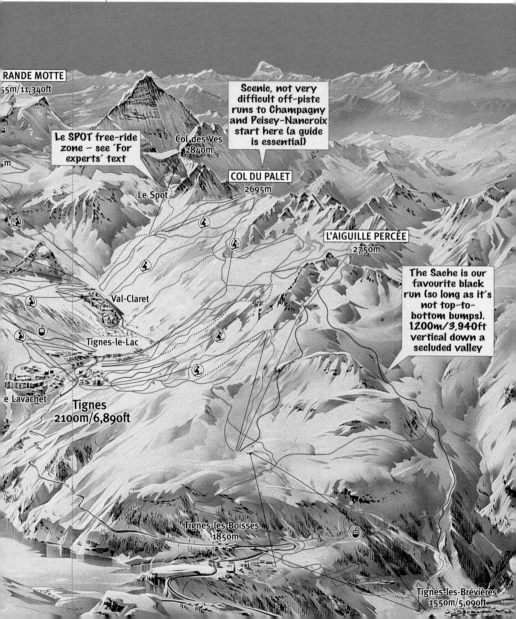

funicular from Val-Claret whizzes you up to over 3000m/9,840ft in seven minutes. There are blue, red and black runs to play on up here, as well as beautiful long runs back to the resort.

The main lifts towards Val-d'Isère are efficient: a high-capacity gondola from Le Lac to **Tovière**, and a fast chair with covers from Val-Claret to **Col de Fresse**. You can head back to Tignes from either: the return from Tovière to Tignes-le-Lac is via a steep black run but there are easier blue runs to Val-Claret.

Going up the opposite side of the valley takes you to a quieter area of predominantly east-facing slopes split into two main sectors, linked in both directions – **Col du Palet** and **l'Aiguille Percée**. This whole mountainside is at last being given the fast lifts it has needed for years – by 2006/07 there will be five of them.

The Col des Ves chair-lift, at the south end of the Col du Palet sector, now serves the new SPOT area – see 'News'. You can descend from l'Aiguille Percée to Tignes-les-Brévières on blue, red or black runs. There's an efficient gondola back.

TERRAIN-PARKS
New but not improved
Tignes was one of the first French resorts to build a terrain-park. This means that the local shaping crew are not short of experience and know how to build a good park. Whether they can be bothered to keep it maintained is another story. The park is in Val Claret and is long, has several small-to-medium-sized jumps, a hip and several medium-sized rails. On a good day the park is a lot of fun and the 120m/390ft long half-pipe is well shaped and a good size for those not comfortable with a super-pipe. It is right at the bottom of the mountain as well which means if you have the energy to hike, you can ride it for free. In the summer the park doubles in size and moves up to the Grande Motte for freestyle camps. There's also a boarder-cross as part of Le SPOT (see 'For experts').

SNOW RELIABILITY
Difficult to beat
Tignes has all-year-round runs (barring brief closures in spring or autumn) on its Grande Motte glacier. And the resort height of 2100m/6,890ft generally means good snow-cover right back to base for most of the long winter season – November to May. The west-facing runs down from Col de Fresse and Tovière to Val-Claret suffer from the afternoon sun, although they now have serious snowmaking. Some of the lower east-facing and south-east-facing slopes on the other side of the valley can suffer late in the season, too.

FOR EXPERTS
An excellent choice
Tignes has converted six of its black runs into 'Naturides', which means they are never groomed (a neat way of saving money!) but they are marked, patrolled and avalanche protected. Many of them are not especially steep (eg the Ves run – now renamed after local free-ride hero Guerlain Chicherit – was only recently promoted from red status). Perhaps the most serious challenge is the long black run from Tovière to Tignes-le-Lac, with steep, usually heavily mogulled sections (the top part, Pâquerettes, is now a 'Naturide' but the bottom part, Trolles, is a normal black). Parts of this run get a lot of afternoon sun. Our favourite black run (still a 'normal' black) is the Sache, from l'Aiguille Percée down a secluded valley to Tignes-les-Brévières,

Tignes is renowned for offering some of the best lift-served off-piste skiing in the world. There is a tremendous choice, with runs to suit all levels, from intermediate skiers to fearless free-riders and off-piste experts. Here's just a small selection.

For a first experience of off-piste, perhaps for a family, **Lognan** *is ideal. These slopes – down the mountainside between the pistes to Le Lac and the pistes to Val-Claret – are broad and not very difficult.*

One of our favourite routes is the **Tour de Pramecou**. *After a few minutes' walking at the bottom of the Grande Motte glacier, you pass around a big rock called Pramecou. There is then a multitude of possibilities, differing in difficulty – so routes can be found for skiers of different abilities.*

Petite Balme *is a run for good skiers only – access is easy but leads to quite challenging north-facing slopes in real high-mountain terrain, far from the pistes.*

To ski **Oreilles de Mickey** *(Mickey's Ears) you start from Tovière and walk north along the ridge to the peak of Lavachet, where you get a great view of Tignes. The descent involves three long couloirs, narrow and pretty steep, which bring you back to Le Lavachet.*

The best place to find fresh snow is the **Chardonnet** *couloirs – they face north, and never get the sun. The snow is always very good here. The route involves a 20-minute walk from the top of the Merle Blanc chair-lift.*

The **Vallons de la Sache** *is one of the most famous off-piste routes – a descent of 1200m/3,940ft vertical down a breathtaking valley in the heart of the National Park, overlooked by the magnificent Sache glacier. Starting from l'Aiguille Percée at 2750m/9,020ft you enter a different world, high up in the mountains, far away from the ski lifts. You arrive down in Les Brévières at 1550m/5,090ft, below the Tignes dam.*

One of the big adventures is to go away from the Tignes ski area and all signs of civilisation, starting from the Col du Palet. From there you can head for **Champagny** *(linked to La Plagne's area) or* **Peisey-Nancroix** *(linked to Les Arcs' area) – these are both very beautiful runs, and not too difficult. Your guide will arrange for a taxi back.*

Tignes

393

which can become very heavily mogulled (especially at the bottom).

But it is the off-piste possibilities that make Tignes such a draw for experts. Go with one of the off-piste groups that the schools organise and you'll have a great time. See the feature box for a few of the options.

The whole western side of the Tignes ski area has lots of off-piste possibilities. The terrain served by the slow, old Col des Ves double chair has been designated Le SPOT (Skiing the Powder of Tignes) area and has various ungroomed off-piste zones: Hardride for experts, Softride for the less experienced and Backcountry freestyle with jumps. It is explained at length on the back of the piste map. At Chalet Freeride here you can learn to use an avalanche transceiver, practise searching for avalanche victims, read the avalanche bulletins and study maps and photos of the terrain.

Schools and guides offer the bizarre French form of heli-skiing: mountaintop drops are forbidden, but from Tovière you can ski down towards the Lac du Chevril to be retrieved by chopper.

FOR INTERMEDIATES
One of the best

For the keen intermediate piste-basher the Espace Killy is one of the top three or four areas in France, or the world.

Tignes' local slopes are ideal intermediate terrain. The red and blue runs on the Grande Motte glacier nearly always have superb snow. The glacier run from the top of the cable-car has been regraded from blue to red but is wide and mostly easy on usually fabulous snow. The Leisse run down to the chair-lift is now classified black and can get very mogulled but has good snow. The long red run all the way back to town is a delightful long cruise – though often crowded. The roundabout blue alternative (Génépy) is much gentler and quieter.

From Tovière, the blue 'H' run to Val-Claret is an enjoyable cruise and generally well groomed. But again, it can get very crowded. There is lots to do on the other side of the valley and the runs down from l'Aiguille Percée to Tignes-les-Boisses and Tignes-les-Brévières are also scenic and fun. There are red and blue options as well

as the beautiful Sache black run – adventurous intermediates shouldn't miss it. The runs down from l'Aiguille Percée to Le Lac are gentle, wide blues.

FOR BEGINNERS
Good nursery slopes, but ...
The nursery slopes of Tignes-le-Lac and Le Lavachet (which meet at the top) are excellent – convenient, snow-sure, gentle, free of through-traffic and served by a slow chair and a drag. The ones at Val-Claret are less appealing: an unpleasantly steep slope within the village served by a drag, and a less convenient slope served by the fast Bollin chair. All of these lifts are free.

Although there are some fairly easy blues on the west side of Tignes, for long green runs you have to go over to the Val-d'Isère sector. You need an Espace Killy pass to use them, and to get back to Tignes you have a choice between the blue run from Col de Fresse (which has a tricky start) or riding the gondola down from Tovière. And in poor weather, the high Tignes valley is an intimidatingly bleak place – enough to make any wavering beginner retreat to a bar with a book.

FOR CROSS-COUNTRY
Interesting variety
The Espace Killy has 40km/25 miles of cross-country trails. There are tracks on the frozen Lac de Tignes, along the valley between Val-Claret and Tignes-le-Lac, at Les Boisses and Les Brévières and up on the Grande Motte.

QUEUES
Very few
The queues here depend on snow conditions. If snow low down is poor, the Grande Motte funicular generates queues; the fast chairs in parallel with it are often quicker, despite the longer

ride time. These lifts jointly shift a lot of people, with the result that the run down to Val-Claret can be unpleasantly crowded. The worst queues now are for the cable-car on the glacier – half-hour waits are common. And post-lunch queues at Les Brévières are not unknown.

Of course, if higher lifts are closed by heavy snow or high winds, the lifts on the lower slopes have big queues.

MOUNTAIN RESTAURANTS
A couple of good places
The restaurants at the top of the Chaudannes chair – the Alpage for self-service and Lo Soli for table-service – represented a huge improvement on the western side of the bowl when they were built a few seasons back. Their adjacent terraces share a superb view of the Grande Motte, and Lo Soli received a rave review from a 2006 reporter: 'Excellent food, ambience, service and hospitality; the gâteau d'agneau, Caesar salad and melt-in-the-mouth pot-au-feu deserve special praise.' On the side of the valley with the Val-d'Isère link the atmospheric chalet at the top of Tovière is 'fairly basic' but does 'very good portions'. A recent reporter found the 'service just OK, but food very good' at the modern but pleasantly woody Chalet du Bollin – just a few metres above Val-Claret. At the top of the Tichot chair from Val-Claret the Palet 'serves good food at good prices'.

The big Panoramic self-service restaurant at the top of the Grande Motte funicular has great views from its huge terrace, but its food gets poor reviews. There's an excellent table-service 'cuisine gourmande' restaurant here too, which one regular reporter describes as the 'top mountain eatery in Tignes; a veritable joy – excellent

↑ The top of Tovière can get much more crowded than this when the jumbo-gondola from Le Lac and the eight-person chair from the Val-d'Isère slopes are both full

OT TIGNES / C TATIN

CHILDREN

Les Marmottons
t 0479 065167
Ages 3 to 8.

Ski schools
Evolution 2 and 333 take children from age 5 and ESF takes children from age 4 (6 half-days €123).

GETTING THERE

Air Geneva 165km/103 miles (3½hr); Lyon 240km/ 149 miles (3½hr); Chambéry 130km/ 81 miles (2½hr)

Rail Bourg-St-Maurice (30km/19 miles); regular buses or taxi from station

rack of lamb, huge rib steak, tiramisu'.

There are lots of easily accessible (and often cheaper) places for lunch in the resorts. One ski-to-the-door favourite of ours in Le Lac is the ground-floor restaurant of the hotel Montana, on the left as you descend from l'Aiguille Percée. In Val-Claret the Fish Tank is described as 'very good value', the Carline self-service restaurant as having 'cheerful staff and hearty portions' and the Taverne des Neiges as having 'good food and service'. In Le Lac, the 'excellent' Arbina is popular (see 'Eating out'). In Les Brévières, a short walk round the corner into the village brings you to places much cheaper than the two by the piste. Sachette, for example, is crowded with artefacts from mountain life and offers 'lots of good cheese dishes' including 'superb tartiflette'. The Etoile des Neiges 'serves great, typical Savoyard food'.

SCHOOLS AND GUIDES
Plenty of choice
There are over half-a-dozen schools, including three specialist snowboard schools, plus various independent instructors. Reporters advise that pre-booking is 'essential' at busy times like Easter. A 2006 visitor was very impressed with the ESF – the nine-year old in their group was 'admirably looked after' and the instructor

showed 'great professionalism and understanding'. And a reporter on Evolution 2 said: 'Our beginner boarders got on well in the group lessons despite a class size of 10 and the instructor's poor English. We had a selection of private ski and boarding lessons, which were excellent.'

FACILITIES FOR CHILDREN
Mixed reports
We have had good reports on the Marmottons kindergartens – 'brilliant' says a father of a four-year-old this year – and the Spritelets ski classes arranged by Esprit Ski and Evolution 2: 'She loved her class and could snowplough by the end of the week.' But we have had a few poor reports on Evolution 2 in the past.

STAYING THERE

HOW TO GO
Improving range of options
All three main styles of accommodation are available through tour operators. And more luxury options are appearing.

Chalets The choice of catered chalets is increasing. Total Ski and Neilson both have several smart chalets, including some with pool, hot-tub and sauna. Child specialist Esprit Ski has a chalet hotel and several chalets here. Ski Olympic's Chalets Rosset and Madeleine have been

The kids' ski school classes don't get any smaller, do they? →

OT TIGNES / DANIEL ROUSSELOT

ACTIVITIES

Indoor 'Vitatignes' (sauna, Turkish baths, hot-tub, etc), Bains du Montana (pool, sauna, etc), Fitness Centre (spa treatments, weight training, fitness), Aquatonic Centre (spa and beauty treatments, fitness etc), multisports hall, yoga, squash, heritage centre, networked computer games, computer and video editing lessons

Outdoor Natural skating rink, hang-gliding, paragliding, helicopter rides, ice-diving, ice-driving, bungee trampolining, mini-quad bikes, ice-climbing, mountaineering, snow-shoeing, aircraft and microlight flights, ski-joring

recommended by reporters. Mark Warner has two chalet-hotels, one with an outdoor pool open from March. Snowstar's Chalet Chardon has a vast living room and was once owned by the late Robert Maxwell.

Hotels The few hotels are small and concentrated in Le Lac.

((3 **Campanules** (0479 063436) Smartly rustic chalet in upper Le Lac, with good restaurant. One reporter was impressed enough to suggest that it deserved a 4-star rating.

((3 **Village Montana** (0479 400144) Stylishly woody 3-star on the east-facing slopes above Le Lac (though a 2006 reporter says the rooms are starting to show their age), with 4-star suites section. Outdoor pool, sauna, steam, tub.

((3 **Lévanna** (0479 063294) Smart 3-star in central position in Le Lac – comfortable, with a 'generous hot-tub' but a 2006 reporter found 'friendly staff but a woeful lack of them'.

((3 **Diva** (0479 067000) Biggest in town (121 rooms). On lower level of Val-Claret, a short walk from lifts. 'Very comfy rooms, excellent meals.' Sauna.

(2 **Arbina** (0479 063478) Well-run place close to the lifts in Le Lac, with lunchtime terrace, crowded après-ski bar and one of the best restaurants.

(2 **Marais** (0479 064006) Prettily furnished, simple hotel in Les Boisses.

(1 **Génépy** (0479 065711) Simple Dutch-run chalet in Les Brévières.

SMART APARTMENTS – SEE FEATURE

There are lots of apartments available in all price ranges. A growing number of smart ones include L'Ecrin des Neiges apartments in lower Val-Claret and Residence Village Montana above Le Lac (both with pool, sauna and steam, though there's a charge for

their use). New for 2005/06 was the Ferme du Val-Claret, built by MGM at the foot of the Grande Motte funicular. In Les Brévières, the Chalets d'Ercule are a collection of good-looking individual chalets sleeping up to 16. More upmarket property is being built in Les Brévières and will be on sale though Erna Low – see the buying property chapter.

The Chalet Club in Val-Claret is a collection of simple studios, but has a free indoor pool, sauna and in-house restaurant and bar. The supermarket at Le Lac is reported to be 'comprehensive but very expensive'.

EATING OUT
Good places scattered about

The options in Le Lavachet are rather limited, though a 2005 reporter enjoyed Le Grenier with its 'excellent cold meats and tartiflette'. Finding anywhere with some atmosphere is difficult in Le Lac, though the food in some of the better hotels is good. The Campanules is 'a gastronomic delight', said a reporter. L'Escale Blanche was praised in 2006 for 'very good food and service'. The Arbina continues to provide 'outstanding food, very good value and first-class service'. Two recent visitors recommend the 'delicious food' at the 'quirky' Clin d'Oeil. Two others recommend Bagus Cafe's 'eclectic cuisine'. One 2006 visitor particularly highlights the Monday champagne nights at the Alpaka Lodge – 'a relaxed restaurant with duck breast the star attraction'.

In Val-Claret the Caveau is recommended for a special treat. You may have to wait at Petit Savoyard but the food and service are said to be worth it. The buffet at the Indochine

Phone numbers
From abroad use the prefix +33 and omit the initial '0' of the phone number.

has been strongly recommended by several reporters. Pizza 2000 has 'reasonable prices and helpful staff' but a reporter says La Pignatta 'slightly trumps it'. The Auberge des 3 Oursons was recommended for 'massive portions, friendly service'.

The Cordée in Les Boisses is said to offer unpretentious surroundings, great traditional French food, modest prices.

APRES-SKI
Hidden away
Recent reporters agree that there is plenty going on if you know where to find it. Val-Claret has some early-evening atmosphere, and happy hours are popular. Reporters differ on the merits of the Crowded House and Fish Tank (both popular with Brits), with the latter getting marginally more votes. Grizzly's is 'cosy and atmospheric, but you pay for the ambience'.

Le Lac is a natural focus for immediate après-ski drinks. The 'lively' Loop, with pool table, has a 'two for one' happy hour from 4 to 6pm. The bar of the hotel Arbina is our kind of spot – adequately cosy, friendly service. It's a great place to sit outside and people-watch. The Alpaka Cocktail

Bar is recommended as 'a real gem later on' and 'the cocktails slide down with too much ease'. Embuscade is said to be 'the only proper French bar in town'. The Red Lion in Les Almes has satellite TV (which attracts the football fans), pool and 'a good range of beers'. What was the most animated bar in Le Lavachet – Harri's – is now called Censored and still has a 'good atmosphere'. TC's bar is 'very friendly, with good music'.

Le Lac, Café de la Poste and Jack's are popular late haunts.

OFF THE SLOPES
Forget it
Despite the range of alternative activities, Tignes is a resort for those who want to use the slopes, where anyone who doesn't is liable to feel like a fish out of water. Some activities do get booked up quickly as well – a reporter said it was impossible to find a free dog-sledding slot in April. The ice skating on the lake includes a 500m/1,640ft circuit as well as a conventional rink. There's ice-driving at Les Brévières. A new sports centre, including a big pool, should be finished for 2006/07.

Tignes

397

Ski Olympic
Now in our 19th very successful season!

20 Outstanding Chalets
5 Fantastic Chalethotels
8 Top French Resorts

Our guests come back year after year because we offer excellent cuisine, complimentary wine, friendly and attentive staff, and free ski hosting.

Fly from Gatwick, Stansted, Manchester, and Birmingham, or travel via luxury overnight Snowcoach or Eurostar.

www.skiolympic.co.uk 01302 328820

AGENCE DES CIMES

your partner in Tignes

A small team in a local family agency with expert knowledge of the resort and the apartments on offer.

All-inclusive package:
accommodation + ski pass + ski rental

Easy booking at
www.agence-des-cimes.fr

Tel +33 479 06 43 29
Fax +33 479 06 57 51
Email: les.cimes@wanadoo.fr

Val-d'Isère

On- and off-piste playground with smart new lifts and reliable snow above a much-improved village with lively nightlife and lots of Brits

COSTS

① ② ③ ④ ⑤ ⑥

RATINGS

The slopes

Fast lifts	****
Snow	*****
Extent	*****
Expert	*****
Intermediate	*****
Beginner	***
Convenience	***
Queues	****
Mountain restaurants	***

The rest

Scenery	***
Resort charm	***
Off-slope	**

NEWS

For 2006/07 hands-free lift passes will, at last, be introduced throughout the Espace Killy.

For 2005/06 a new six-pack opened, going from the roadside at Le Laisinant up to above the top of the cable-car from Le Fornet. This means you no longer have to catch a bus if you ski one of the lovely runs down to Le Laisinant. It is also an alternative way of getting up the mountain in the morning.

Snowmaking has been installed on the Pissaillas glacier to make the summer skiing season last longer. And for 2006/07 snowmaking will be introduced on the Creux piste, down from Tovière towards Val-d'Isère.

➕ Huge area shared with Tignes, with lots of runs for all abilities

➕ Big recent investment in new lifts

➕ One of the great resorts for lift-served off-piste runs

➕ Once the snow has fallen, high altitude of slopes keeps it good

➕ Wide choice of schools, especially for off-piste lessons and guiding

➕ For a high Alpine resort, the town is attractive, very lively at night, and offers a good range of restaurants

➕ Wide range of package holidays – including swanky chalets

➕ Piste grooming and staff attitudes have improved noticeably

➖ Some green and blue runs are seriously undergraded and all runs back to the village are tricky (even the sole green if you're a novice)

➖ Not enough snowmaking and what there is could be used better

➖ You're quite likely to need the bus at the start and end of the day

➖ Most lifts and slopes are liable to close when the weather is bad

➖ Nursery slopes not ideal

➖ Main off-piste slopes get tracked out very quickly

➖ At times seems more British than French – especially in low season

➖ Increasingly pricey

Val-d'Isère is one of the world's best resorts for experts – attracted by the extent of lift-served off-piste – and for confident, mileage-hungry intermediates. But you don't have to be particularly adventurous to enjoy the resort.

The many drawbacks listed above are mainly not serious complaints, whereas most of the plus-points weigh heavily in the balance, The lift company has made a concerted effort in recent years to deal with key criticisms. Heavy investment in new lifts has eliminated bad bottlenecks, the piste grooming has been improved and they have even regraded some of their pistes, which should help timid intermediates to have more confidence in the piste map. But more regrading is needed, and the green run down to La Daille remains one of the most seriously undergraded we have come across. The village ambience has been improved recently too; and the resort has a huge selection of both chalet and hotel holidays on offer by UK tour operators – with some very luxurious options indeed. Overall, this is one of our favourite resorts in the world.

THE RESORT

Val-d'Isère spreads along a remote valley, which is a dead end in winter. The road in from Bourg-St-Maurice brings you dramatically through a rocky defile to the satellite mini-resort of La Daille – a convenient but hideous slope-side apartment complex and the base of lifts into the major Bellevarde sector of the slopes. The outskirts of Val proper are dreary, but as you approach the centre recent improvements become more evident: new wood- and stone-cladding, culminating in the tasteful pedestrian-only Val Village complex. Many first-time visitors find the resort much more pleasant than they expect a high

KEY FACTS

Resort	1850m
	6,070ft
Entire Espace Killy area	
Slopes	1550-3455m
	5,090-11,340ft
Lifts	90
Pistes	300km
	186 miles
Green	15%
Blue	46%
Red	27%
Black	12%
Snowmaking	26km
	16 miles

ARPAD PALFI

There are easy runs in Val-d'Isère but you have to know where to find them. This is Bellevarde ↓

French resort to be, and returning visitors generally find things improving.

Turn right at the centre and you drive under the nursery slopes and two of Val's big lifts up the mountains to a lot of new development beyond. Continue up the main valley instead, and you come to Le Laisinant, a peaceful little outpost with a new lift out of the valley for 2005/06, and then to Le Fornet and the fourth major lift station.

There is a lot of traffic around, but the resort is working to get cars under control and has made the centre more pedestrian-friendly.

The location of your accommodation isn't crucial. The main lift stations are linked by efficient free shuttle-buses; in peak periods you never have to wait more than a few minutes. But in the evening frequency plummets and dedicated après-skiers will want to be within walking distance of the centre. The developments up the side valley beyond the main lift station – Le

Châtelard and La Legettaz – are mainly attractive, and some offer ski-in/ski-out convenience. But you pay the price in the evening when the buses stop running. La Daille and Le Fornet have their (quite different) attractions for those less concerned about nightlife.

A car is of no great value around the resort, but simplifies outings to other resorts such as Ste-Foy and Les Arcs. A six-day lift pass gives a day in the Paradiski area (Les Arcs and La Plagne combined) and in the Three Valleys and 50 per cent off a pass in Ste-Foy, the locals' favourite outing.

THE MOUNTAINS

Although there are wooded slopes above the village on all sectors, in practice most of the runs here are on open slopes above the tree line and and a lot of lifts can close in bad weather. Piste grooming is better than it used to be, but we continue to get

Val-d'Isère

399

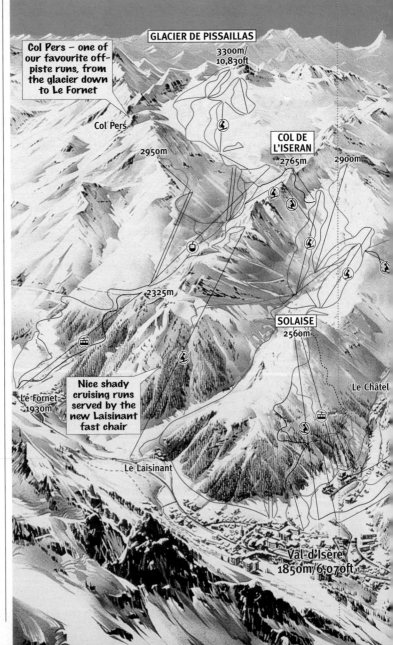

GLACIER DE PISSAILLAS

Col Pers – one of our favourite off-piste runs, from the glacier down to Le Fornet

3300m/10,830ft

Col Pers

2950m

COL DE L'ISERAN
2765m

2900m

2325m

SOLAISE
2560m

Le Châtel

Nice shady cruising runs served by the new Laisinant fast chair

Le Fornet
1930m

Le Laisinant

Val-d'Isère
1850m/6,070ft

LIFT PASSES

L'Espace Killy

Prices in €

Age	1-day	6-day
under 13	30	144
13 to 59	40	192
over 60	61	163

Free under 5, over 75

Beginner seven free lifts on nursery slopes

Notes
Covers Tignes and Val-d'Isère. Half-day and pedestrian passes available. Discount on presentation of lift pass from any of previous three seasons. Six-day passes and over are valid for one day in the Three Valleys, Valmorel and Paradiski (La Plagne-Les Arcs), half-price pass in Ste-Foy and reduced price in La Rosière.

Alternative passes
There is no separate pass for Val-d'Isère's lifts only.

complaints about the poor signing (particularly at piste junctions) and the piste grading: 'It's a joke,' reiterated a recent visitor. Many blue and some green runs are simply too steep, narrow and even bumpy; we are pleased to see that some pistes have been regraded, but more need to be.

If you plan a return visit, keep your lift pass – those with a week's pass bought in the last three years are entitled to a 'loyal customer' reduction.

The local radio carries weather reports in English as well as in French.

THE SLOPES
Vast and varied
Val-d'Isère's slopes divide into three main sectors, two reachable from the village. **Bellevarde** is the mountain that is home to Val-d'Isère's famous downhill course – the OK piste, which opens each season's World Cup Alpine circus in December (in 2006, on the weekend of 9/10 December for men and 16/17 December for women). You can reach Bellevarde quickly by underground funicular from La Daille or the powerful gondola from near the centre of town. From the top you can descend to the valley, play on a variety of drags and chairs at altitude or take a choice of lifts to the slopes of Tignes (see separate chapter).

Solaise is the other mountain accessible directly from the village. The Solaise Express fast quad chair-lift takes you a few metres higher than the parallel cable-car. Once up, a short drag takes you over a plateau and down to a variety of chairs that serve this very sunny area of predominantly gentle pistes. From near the top of this area you can catch the fast Leissières six-pack (which climbs over a steep ridge and then drops suddenly down the other side) over to the third main area, above and below the **Col de l'Iseran**. The area can also be reached

by the new chair-lift for 2005/06 from Le Laisinant or by cable-car from Le Fornet. The runs at Col de l'Iseran are predominantly easy, with access to the region's most beautiful off-piste terrain.

TERRAIN-PARKS
Beginners and experts welcome
Above the La Daille gondola and served by the Mont Blanc chair-lift lies a very good terrain-park (www.valdisere.com/winterpark). Maintenance can be a bit hit or miss, but on a good day this park has a bit of everything. There are four kicker lines, with jumps ranging from 3m/10ft in the blue line to 20m/70ft in the pro line. With more and more earth-work being done during the summer to pre-shape jumps, there are now up to five jumps in a row on some of the lines, so prepare your legs. New additions to the rail park make this one of the best in France, with flat downs, C rails, rainbows, a big box, a small box and much more. The boarder-cross is set up just outside the park and there are plans for a half-pipe. Or head over to the Tignes pipe.

SNOW RELIABILITY
Only early season issues
In years when lower resorts have suffered, Val-d'Isère has rarely been short of snow. Once a big dump of snow has fallen, the resort's height means you can almost always get back to the village. But even more important is that in each sector there are lots of lifts and runs above mid-mountain, between about 2300m and 2900m (7,550ft and 9,510ft). Many of the slopes face roughly north. And there is access to glaciers at Pissaillas or over in Tignes, although both take a while to get to. But snowmaking is not extensive enough (and not used well enough to judge by a December 2005 editorial visit) to ensure good skiing in early season before that first big dump.

FOR EXPERTS
One of the world's best

Val-d'Isère is one of the top resorts in the world for experts. The main attraction is the huge range of beautiful off-piste possibilities – see the feature panel.

There may be better resorts for really steep pistes – there are certainly lots in North America – but there is plenty on-piste to amuse the expert, despite the small number of blacks on the piste map. Many reds and blues are steep enough to get mogulled.

On Bellevarde the famous Face run is the main attraction – often mogulled from top to bottom, but not worryingly steep. Epaule is the sector's other black run – where the moguls are hit by long exposure to sun and can be slushy or rock-hard (it is prone to closure for these reasons too). There are several challenging ways down from Solaise to the village: all steep, though none fearsomely so (Piste X has now been regraded from a normal black run to a 'Naturide' – see Tignes chapter for what this means).

Wayne Watson of off-piste school Alpine Expérience puts a daily diary of off-piste snow conditions and runs on the web at www.alpineexperience.com.

FOR INTERMEDIATES
Quantity and quality

Val-d'Isère has just as much to offer intermediates as experts. There's enough here to keep you interested for several visits – though pistes can be crowded in high-season, and the less experienced should be aware that many runs are under-graded.

In the Solaise sector is a network of gentle blue runs, ideal for building confidence. And there are a couple of beautiful runs from here through the woods to Le Laisinant – ideal in bad weather, though prone to closure in times of avalanche danger.

Most of the runs in the Col de l'Iseran sector are even easier – ideal for early and hesitant intermediates. Those marked blue at the top of the glacier could really be classified green.

Bellevarde has a huge variety of runs ideally suited to intermediates of all levels. From Bellevarde itself there is a choice of green, blue and red runs of varying pitch. The World Cup Downhill OK piste is a wonderful rolling cruise when groomed. And the wide runs from Tovière normally give you the choice of groomed piste or moguls.

A snag for early intermediates is that runs back to the valley can be

Val-d'Isère

THE BEST LIFT-SERVED OFF-PISTE IN THE WORLD?

Few resorts can rival the extent of lift-served off-piste skiing in Val-d'Isère.

Some runs are ideal for adventurous intermediates looking to try off-piste for the first time. The Tour du Charvet goes through glorious scenery from the top of the Grand Pré chair-lift on the back of Bellevarde. For most of the way it is very gentle, with only a few steeper pitches. It ends up at the bottom of the Manchet chair up to the Solaise area. The Pays Désert is a very easy run from the top of the lift system on the Pissaillas glacier. The views are superb. You end up at the Pays Désert T-bar.

For more experienced off-piste skiers, Col Pers is one of our favourite runs. Again, it starts a traverse away from the Pissaillas glacier. You go over a pass into a big, wide, fairly gentle bowl with glorious views and endless ways down. If the snow is good, you can drop down into the Gorges de Malpasset and ski over the frozen Isère river back to the Fornet cable-car.

There are endless other off-piste options, such as Cugnai and Danaides on Solaise, Banane and the Couloir des Pisteurs on Bellevarde – and, of course, many more in Tignes.

boarding

Val-d'Isère's more upmarket profile attracts a different kind of holiday boarder to Tignes and is perhaps seen as Tignes' less hardcore cousin. But the terrain here is phenomenal and still draws a fair few boarders. The easier slopes are suitable for beginners, and there are now very few drag-lifts. There is a very good terrain-park, and specialist snowboard shops such as Misty Fly and Quiksilver Boardriders. Check your email and have a coffee at the snowboarder-run Powder Monkey cafe.

challenging. The easiest way is down to La Daille on a green run which would be classified blue or red in most resorts. It gets very crowded and mogulled by the end of the day. None of the runs from Bellevarde and Solaise back to Val itself is easy. Many early intermediates sensibly choose to ride the lifts down.

FOR BEGINNERS
OK if you know where to go
The nursery slope right by the centre of town is 95 per cent perfect; it's just a pity that the very top is unpleasantly steep. The lifts serving it are free.

Once off the nursery slopes, you have to know where to find easy runs; many of the greens should be blue, or even red. One local instructor admits: 'We have to have green runs on the map, even if we don't have so many green slopes – otherwise beginners wouldn't come to Val-d'Isère.'

A good place for your first real runs off the nursery slopes is the Madeleine green run on Solaise – served by a fast six-pack. The Col de l'Iseran runs are also gentle and wide, and not overcrowded. There is good progression terrain on Bellevarde, too. From all sectors, it's best to take a lift back down to the valley.

FOR CROSS-COUNTRY
Limited
There are a couple of loops in each of three areas – towards La Daille, on Solaise and out past Le Laisinant. More picturesque is the one going from Le Châtelard (on the road past the main cable-car station) to the Manchet chair. But keen cross-country enthusiasts should go elsewhere.

QUEUES
Few problems
Queues to get out of the resort have been kept in check by new lifts – most recently the big gondola to Bellevarde and the new six-pack from Le Laisinant. At Solaise the slow Lac chair up to the Tête Solaise can generate queues. Crowded pistes in high season is a more common complaint than queues these days.

MOUNTAIN RESTAURANTS
Acceptable – at long last
It's been a long, slow business, but Val has at last managed a three-star rating for mountain restaurants. They mainly consist of big self-service places with vast terraces at the top of major lifts. But there are exceptions, and they are gradually growing in number. The Fruitière at the top of La Daille

ARPAD PALFI

The Face 1992 Winter Olympic Downhill run from Bellevarde to the village is often mogulled from top to bottom ↓

gondola, a table-service place kitted out with stuff rescued from a dairy in the valley, is still popular. But the 'pleasantly woody' Edelweiss, above Le Fornet, is now a serious rival for the best food. We had delicious duck and fish there (reporters also send us rave reviews); you must reserve a table.

The 'friendly' but busy Trifollet with table service, about halfway down the OK run, 'serves one of the best tartiflettes in the Alps' and good plats du jour but a recent visitor complained that the waiters now try to rush you through to make the table available again. On the lower slopes at La Daille, and reachable on snow and by pedestrians, Tufs does good pizzas and a good-value buffet on the first floor.

If you are in a hurry, Marmottes, in the middle of the Bellevarde bowl, is an efficient self-service with a big sunny terrace. The small and friendly Bar de L'Ouillette, at the base of the Madeleine chair-lift, does good food at reasonable prices and the Datcha (with a small table service section) at the bottom of the Cugnai lift 'excellent salads, if expensive'. A 2006 reporter found the Tanière (popular with locals) better value, set between the two

chairs going up Face de Bellevarde.

Of course there are lots of places actually in the resort villages. When at Col de l'Iseran, one idea is to descend to the rustic Arolay ('excellent for both lunch and dinner, with a lovely terrace') at Le Fornet. The terrace of the Brussel's hotel in Val-d'Isère, right by the nursery slopes, has 'good food and excellent service' and the Grand Paradis, next door, is 'an enjoyable lunch venue, very well run and efficient'.

SCHOOLS AND GUIDES
A very wide choice
There is a huge choice of schools, guides and private instructors. But as they all get busy, at peak periods it's best to book in advance. Practically all the schools run off-piste groups at various levels of competence, as well as on-piste lessons. Outside the ESF, practically all the instructors and guides speak good English, and many are native English-speakers.

The Development Centre, based in the Precision Ski shop in the heart of the village, is a group of British instructors who offer intensive clinics for all levels of skier and have been highly praised. New Generation,

Val-d'Isère

another British-run school, also have a branch here. A 2006 reporter said, 'The morning we had with New Generation was one of the highlights of our holiday – lots of fun and we learned a lot too.'

Mountain Masters is a group of British and French instructors and guides, and a 2006 reporter said, 'They knew exactly how to take me over that seventh week plateau.' The Oxygène school gets mixed reviews.

Over recent years we've heard from lots of satisfied pupils of Snow Fun ('Good value and good instructors,' said a 2006 reporter) and Evolution 2. Reporters consistently praise Bernard Chesneau of Ski Mastery. Misty Fly is a specialist snowboard school.

Alpine Expérience and Top Ski specialise in guided off-piste groups – an excellent way to get off-piste safely without the cost of hiring a guide as an individual. We have had great mornings out with both. The weekly Henry's Avalanche Talks in Dick's Tea Bar are 'both entertaining and informative'. Heli-trips can be arranged from over the border in Italy – heli-drops are banned in France.

FACILITIES FOR CHILDREN
Good tour op possibilities
Many people prefer to use the facilities of UK tour operators such as Mark Warner, Ski Beat or Esprit. But there's a 'children's village' for three to eight year olds, with supervised indoor and outdoor activities on the village nursery slopes. A past reporter was 'very pleased' with the childcare there: 'The staff speak English, and are very organised, in particular about safety.'

HOW TO GO
Lots of choice
More British tour operators go to Val-d'Isère than anywhere else.

Chalets This is Planet Chalet, with properties at every level of the market. Many of the most impressive are in the side valley running south from the village – some in the elevated enclave of Les Carats. YSE is a Val-d'Isère specialist, with 25 varied chalets and the best and most entertaining 'no bullshit' brochure we've seen. Companies with properties at the top end of the market include VIP, Scott Dunn and Descent International. Le Ski has nine chalets including six splendid all-en-suite chalets grouped together just up from the main street (now with a big outdoor hot-tub) and two new luxurious ones for eight nearby for 2006/07. Total has a wide range, from cute old farmhouses to very smart apartments up in Les Carats. Ski Beat has five en-suite chalets. Finlays has half-a-dozen properties, with especially luxurious-looking ones in Le Fornet and Le Laisinant. There are several chalet hotels. Mark Warner has four, including the family-friendly Cygnaski, the nightlife hot spot Moris and the Val-d'Isère in the centre, which has its own outdoor swimming pool. Total has the modern Champs Avalin at La Daille. Esprit, the family specialist, has the Ducs de Savoie near the centre.

Hotels There are about 40 to choose from, mostly 2- and 3-star, but with an increasing number of plush ones.
((((4) **Barmes de L'Ours** (0479 413700) Recently built, and best in town. Good

CHILDREN

Le Village des Enfants
t 0479 400981
Ages 3 to 8; 9am-5.45 (Sun-Thu); 9am-2pm (Fri)

Le Petit Poucet
t 0479 061397
Ages from 3; 9am-5.30

Babysitter list
Contact tourist office.

Ski schools
Most offer classes. For example ESF runs classes for ages 5 to 17 (€195 to €330 for five days depending on age and ability). Snow Fun's Club Nounours takes children aged 3 to 6.

GETTING THERE

Air Geneva 180km/112 miles (4hr); Lyon 220km/137 miles (4hr); Chambéry 130km/81 miles (3hr)

Rail Bourg-St-Maurice (30km/19 miles); regular buses from station

ACTIVITIES

Indoor Swimming pool, sports hall (badminton, gym etc), weights room, cinema, fitness and health clubs, bridge, chess

Outdoor Ice rink, snow-shoeing, quad-bikes, snowmobiles, ice-climbing, dog-sledding, ice-driving, paragliding, scenic flights, farm visits, walking

position, close to slopes and centre. The fabulous rooms are in a different style on each floor. Three restaurants. Excellent indoor pool, and spa.

《《《④ **Christiania** (0479 060825) Big chalet. Chic but friendly. Pool, sauna.

《《《④ **Blizzard** (0479 060207) Comfortable. Convenient. Indoor-outdoor pool and sauna. Good food.

《《《④ **L'Aigle des Neiges** (0479 061888) Highly rated refurbished version of former Lattitudes. Cool and central.

《《③ **Savoyarde** (0479 060155) Rustic decor. Leisure centre. Good food (except for vegetarians). Small rooms.

《《③ **Brussel's** (0479 060539) Excellent location, right on nursery slope, with big terrace. Sauna, steam room, hot-tub.

《《③ **Grand Paradis** (0479 061173) Next to Brussels. Austrian owner. Good food.

《《③ **Kandahar** (0479 060239) Smart, newish building above Taverne d'Alsace on main street.

《《③ **Mercure** (0479 061293) Highly recommended by a reliable reporter: 'It doesn't look much from outside, but the food and wine list are excellent.'

《《③ **Sorbiers** (0479 062377) Modern but cosy B&B hotel, not far out. 'Clean, comfortable, good-sized rooms.'

《《③ **Samovar** (0479 061351) In La Daille. Traditional, with good food. 'Very friendly and helpful staff.'

《② **Auberge Saint-Hubert** (0479 060645) Centrally located, 'clean and good value for its 2-star rating'.

《② **Danival** (0479 060065) Piste-side location: 'Very reasonable if you're happy with no frills and B&B.'

SMART APARTMENTS – SEE FEATURE
Among the best are Chalets de Solaise (with outdoor pool) and Alpina Lodge

close to the centre, Chalets du Jardin Alpin at the foot of Solaise and Chalets du Laisinant (at Laisinant). Local agency Val-d'Isère Agence (0479 067350) has a large selection of places and a good brochure.

There are thousands of apartments available. UK operators offer lots, but they tend to get booked up early. The local supermarkets are well stocked.

EATING OUT
Plenty of good places
The 70-odd restaurants offer a wide variety of cuisines; there's a free *Guide des Tables* booklet covering 23, but many worthwhile places are missing.

The Grande Ourse, by the nursery slope, is one place to head for a top-of-the-range meal. Another is Les Clochetons, out in the Manchet valley (they run a free minibus to pick up and drop off clients) – we ate there in 2005 and enjoyed the foie gras and duck. The Table de l'Ours, in the Barmes de l'Ours hotel, has a Michelin star. The hotel Aigle des Neiges restaurants are rated highly by locals.

There are plenty of pleasant mid-priced places. The Perdrix Blanche went through a bad spell but has now improved again. Tufs, on the snow at La Daille, is open in the evenings (see 'Mountain restaurants'). The 'impressive' Austrian-influenced menu of the Schuss restaurant in the Grand Paradis hotel has been recommended. Bar Jacques is worth a visit for its no smoking policy and 'some of the best food in town'. Chez Nano (next to Dick's Tea Bar) and the Lodge are among the cheaper places. Family-run Chez Paolo is praised for its 'excellent

Val-d'Isère

407

pizzas and pastas', the Corniche for being 'traditional French, very enjoyable'; Casa Scara for 'good food, though the service was slow', and Grand Cocor for 'excellent food and choice'.

FRANCE

408

APRES-SKI
Very lively
Nightlife is surprisingly energetic, given that most people have spent a hard day on the slopes. There are lots of bars, many with happy hours followed by music and dancing later on.

The Folie Douce, at the top of the La Daille gondola, has become an Austrian-style tea-time rave, with music and dancing; you can ride the gondola down. At La Daille the bar at the Samovar hotel is 'a good spot for a beer after skiing'. In downtown Val, Bananas (cosy wooden chalet with nice terrace), Café Face ('warm and friendly'), the Moris pub (with live music) and the Saloon (underneath hotel Brussel's) fill up as the slopes close; the 'friendly' Boubou, Bar Jacques and the Perdrix Blanche are

popular with locals. Victor's bar is popular ('good cocktails') before it turns into a restaurant later on. The Pacific Bar has sport on big-screen TVs. Bar des Sports has some mountain atmosphere. The basement Taverne d'Alsace is quiet and relaxing.

Later on, the famous Dick's Tea Bar is the main disco and gets packed, but it receives mixed reports. The nearby Petit Danois is a good alternative and somewhat less frenetic than Dick's.

OFF THE SLOPES
A reasonable amount to do
Val is primarily a resort for those keen to get on to the slopes – though one non-skiing reporter was 'very satisfied' with the facilities. The swimming pool was quite recently renovated and the range of shops is better than in most high French resorts. Lunchtime meetings present problems: the easily accessible mountain restaurants are few, and your friends may prefer lunching miles away in places like Les Brévières.

Selected chalets in Val d'Isère ADVERTISEMENT

JEANNE CATTINI

Valmorel

The purpose-built resort the French got right: easy on the eye, as well as convenient; slopes extensive, but on the low side

RATINGS

The slopes

Fast lifts	*
Snow	***
Extent	***
Expert	**
Intermediate	****
Beginner	*****
Convenience	*****
Queues	***
Mountain restaurants	**

The rest

Scenery	***
Resort charm	****
Off-slope	**

NEWS

Links with the Longchamp ski area are greatly improved. For 2006/07 the outward Madeleine chair is to be upgraded; for 2005/06 the return Frêne drag lifts were replaced by a six-pack. A floodlit toboggan run was opened.

KEY FACTS

Resort	1400m
	4,590ft

For Grand Domaine

Slopes	1250-2550m
	4,100-8,370ft
Lifts	54
Pistes	152km
	94 miles
Green	33%
Blue	39%
Red	19%
Black	9%
Snowmaking	199 guns

For Domaine de Valmorel only

Slopes	1250-2405m
	4,100-7,890ft
Lifts	38
Pistes	95km
	59 miles

+ The most sympathetically designed French purpose-built resort

+ Largely slope-side accommodation

+ Extensive easy slopes linked to St-François-Longchamp give even the timid a chance to travel around

+ Beginners and children particularly well catered for

− Few challenging pistes

− Fairly low, so snow can suffer

− Most runs of limited vertical

− Little variety in accommodation

− Peak-season lift queues

− Still lots of slow lifts and drags

Built from scratch in the mid-1970s, Valmorel was intended to look and feel like a mountain village: a traffic-free main street with low-rise hamlets grouped around it. The end result is an attractive, friendly sort of place. The slopes are extensive by most standards and with good snow conditions there's enough here to keep everyone except real experts happy.

THE RESORT

Valmorel is the main resort in 'Le Grand Domaine' – a ski area shared with St-François and Longchamp, across the Madeleine pass. Bourg-Morel is the heart of the resort – a traffic-free street where you'll find most of the shops and restaurants. It's pleasant and usually lively, with a distinctly family feel. Scattered here and there on the hillside are the six 'hameaux' with most of the lodgings. Hameau-du-Mottet is convenient – it is at the top of the Télébourg (the cross-village lift) with good access to the main lifts and from the return runs. All the mega-ski areas of the Tarentaise are within driving distance.

THE MOUNTAINS

Variety is not lacking, and the extent is enough to provide interesting day-trips. There are still a lot drag-lifts and slow chairs.

Slopes The pistes are spread over a number of minor valleys and ridges either side of the Col de la Madeleine. The most heavily used route out of the village is the fast Altispace quad chair. From the top, a network of lifts and pistes takes you to the Col de la Madeleine and beyond that to Lauzière or the slopes of Longchamp and St-François. The Mottet and Gollet areas have their own runs back towards the village, or you can work your way round to the Beaudin and Madeleine sectors.

Terrain-parks There's a terrain-park, with a boarder-cross course, rails, quarter- and super-pipes, at the top of the Crève Coeur chair; a special park-only pass is available. There's also a boarder-cross at St-François.

Snow reliability With many runs below 2000m/6,560ft, good snow is not guaranteed. Mottet is north-facing and usually has the best snow. There's snowmaking on the nursery slopes and the main runs back to base.

Experts There are a few challenging pistes – the steepest are at Gollet and Mottet – but there is good off-piste that doesn't get skied out.

Intermediates The whole area – except for the steepest black runs – is ideal, though the main home run can be quite daunting at the end of the day. We have had mixed reports about piste grooming – one report says it is 'erratic, making some red runs tricky'.

Beginners There are dedicated learning areas ('Still the best we've seen, 10/10,' according to one reporter) right by the village for both adults and children.

Snowboarding There are decent intermediate runs – but new boarders will find some of the drag-lifts tricky.

Cross-country Trails adding up to 23km/14 miles can be reached by bus.

Queues The Altispace chair out of the resort is reportedly slow to start in the morning, and both village lifts can build big queues at peak times; depending on your location, you may be able to avoid these.

Mountain restaurants There are half a dozen or so. Banquise 2000, with a

Col du Mottet 2405m

Col du Gollet 1980m

MADELEINE

ST FRANCOIS LONGCHAMP

GOLLET MOTTET

2020m

2185m

Crey

Lauzière 2550m

Les Avanchers Valmorel 1400m

BEAUDIN

Longchamp 1650m

St François 1400m

Doucy Combelouvière

OUR WEBSITE

Go to our website at wtss.co.uk for resort news, links to resort sites, a build-your-own resort shortlist system and reader forums.

Phone numbers From abroad use the prefix +33 and omit the initial '0' of the phone number.

TOURIST OFFICE

t 0479 098555
info@valmorel.com
www.valmorel.com

great location at Col de la Madeleine, and Prariond ('beautiful building', 'wonderful views') have been recommended again this year. Also mentioned are the Altipiano for 'very good food and service' and the Alpage – 'very good location and good value'. Cagette is reported to have 'good food but a terrible queuing method'.

Schools and guides A 2005 reporter wrote, 'The charming teacher was excellent and spoke good English. She took us off-piste, on blacks and carving – gave us great variety.' A 2006 reporter said that his children's private lessons were 'very good', the instructor 'punctual and good'. Teaching for first-timers is a speciality of the resort.

Facilities for children Piou-Piou club is a comprehensive childcare facility run by the ski school, and children taking ski lessons can have lunch there, too. Advance booking is essential.

STAYING THERE

How to go Self-catering packages are the norm but there are some catered chalets, mainly aimed at families. One regular prefers staying in Combelouvière below Valmorel – 'sunnier and quieter'.
Hotels The Village Club du Soleil (0825 802805) is right on the slopes. The 'ideally located' 2-star Hotel du Bourg (0479 098666) is reportedly 'a bit faded but fit-for-purpose'.
Self-catering The Athamante et Valeriane apartments have been praised.
Eating out The Petit Prince ('excellent, friendly service'), the Marmite and Ski Roc win approval from 2006 reporters.
Après-ski Immediate après-ski centres on the lively outdoor cafes; after-dark activities centre on the main street.
Off the slopes It's not a great place to hang around but there are various activities. There's a fitness centre, cinema and a new toboggan run.

Val-Thorens

Europe's highest resort, with guaranteed good snow but also other attractions: stylish lodgings and good restaurants among them

COSTS

① ② ③ ④ ⑤ ⑥

RATINGS

The slopes
Fast lifts	★★★★
Snow	★★★★★
Extent	★★★★★
Expert	★★★★
Intermediate	★★★★★
Beginner	★★★★
Convenience	★★★★★
Queues	★★★
Mountain restaurants	★★★★

The rest
Scenery	★★★
Resort charm	★★
Off-slope	★★

NEWS

The 4-star Fitz Roy hotel, under new ownership, is due to be refurbished over the next two seasons and is hiring a top chef to compete with the Oxalys.

+ Extensive local slopes to suit all abilities, and good access to the rest of the vast Three Valleys

+ The highest resort in the Alps and one of the most snow-sure, with mainly north-facing slopes

+ Convenient, gentle nursery slopes

+ Not as much of an eyesore as most high, purpose-built resorts, with more and more smart lodgings

+ Compact village with direct slope access from most accommodation

− Can be bleak in bad weather – not a tree in sight

− Parts of the village are much less attractive to walk through in the evening than to ski past in the day

− Not much to do off the slopes

− Some very crowded pistes and dangerous intersections

− Still some queues – and really serious ones for the Cîme de Caron cable-car

For the enthusiast looking for the best snow available, it's difficult to beat Val-Thorens. That wonderful snow lies on some pretty wonderful slopes, and the village – always one of the better-designed high-altitude stations – gets more attractive as it continues to develop, and gain more smart accommodation.

But we still prefer a cosier base elsewhere in the Three Valleys. That way, if a storm socks in, we can play in the woods; if the sun is scorching, we have the option of setting off for Val-Thorens. The formula simply doesn't work the other way round. For a pre-Christmas or an April trip, though, it's the best base.

THE RESORT

Val-Thorens is built high above the tree line on a sunny, west-facing mountainside at the head of its valley, surrounded by peaks, slopes and lifts. The streets are supposedly traffic-free. Most visitors' cars are banished to car parks, except on Saturday. Workers' cars still generate a fair amount of traffic, though, and Saturdays can be mayhem. A reporter recommends booking parking in advance: 'It's cheaper and you are less likely to get a far distant parking spot.'

Many apartment blocks are designed with their 'fronts' facing the slopes, and their relatively dreary backs facing the streets. There are quite extensive shopping arcades, a fair choice of bars and restaurants, and a good sports centre.

It is a classic purpose-built resort, with lots of convenient slope-side accommodation. It's quite a complex little village; but since it's very compact – our scale plan is one of the smallest in these pages – it doesn't matter much where you stay and there is a free bus service which visitors praise. At its heart is the snowy Place de Caron, where pedestrians mix with skiers and boarders. Many of the shops and restaurants are clustered here, along with the best hotels, and the sports centre is nearby. The village is basically divided in two by a little slope (with a drag-lift) that leads down from here to the broad main nursery slope running the length of the village. The upper half of the village is centred on the Place de Péclet. A road runs across the hillside from here to the chalet-style Plein Sud area, where many of the most attractive new apartments have been built. The lower half of the village is more diffuse, with the Rue du Soleil winding down from the dreary bus station to the big Temples du Soleil apartments.

Seen from the slopes, the resort is not as ugly as many of its rivals. The buildings are mainly medium-rise and wood-clad; some are distinctly stylish.

miles 0.5 1.0

Mont de Péclet →

N ↑

ⓘ

ⓘ

Péclet →

Caron

Montée du Fond ↘

km 1.0 2.0

Snow as far as the eye can see. The resort is in the distance, left of centre. The col visible lower left is the top of the Bouchet chair in the fourth valley – at 3230m/10,600ft the high point of the whole Three Valleys →

KEY FACTS

Resort	2300m
	7,550ft

Three Valleys	
Slopes	1260-3230m
	4,130-10,600ft
Lifts	183
Pistes	600km
	373 miles
Green	14%
Blue	40%
Red	36%
Black	10%
Snowmaking	
	1920 guns

Val-Thorens only	
Slopes	1800-3230m
	5,900-10,600ft
Lifts	29
Pistes	170km
	106 miles
Green	12%
Blue	38%
Red	42%
Black	8%
Snowmaking	
	245 guns

THE MOUNTAINS

The main disadvantage of Val-Thorens is the lack of trees. Heavy snowfalls or high wind can shut practically all the lifts and slopes, and even if they don't close, poor visibility can be a problem.

THE SLOPES
High and snow-sure
The resort has a wide piste going right down the front of it, leading down to a number of different lifts. The big **Péclet** gondola, with 30-person cabins, rises 700m/2,300ft to the Péclet glacier, with a choice of red runs down. One links across to a wide area of intermediate runs served by lifts to cols either side of the **Pointe de Thorens**. You can take red or blue runs into the 'fourth valley', the Maurienne, from one of these – the **Col de Rosaël**, now served by the Grand Fond 30-person gondola.

Above **Orelle** in the Maurienne valley two successive chairs go up to 3230m/10,600ft on the virgin flanks of Pointe du Bouchet – the highest lift-served point in the Three Valleys, with stunning views. The former black run off the back of here is now off-piste because of crevasse and avalanche danger and the snow gets very windblown and icy – nice!

The 150-person cable-car to **Cîme de Caron** is one of the great lifts of the Alps, rising 900m/2,950ft in no time at all. It can be reached by skiing across from mid-mountain, or by coming up on the gondola, which starts below the village. From the top there is the choice of red and black pistes down the front, or a black into the Maurienne.

The relatively low **Boismint** sector is overlooked by many visitors, but is actually a very respectable hill, with a total vertical of 860m/2,820ft.

Chair-lifts heading north from the resort serve sunny slopes above the village and also lead to the Méribel valley. Les Menuires can also be reached via these lifts; the alternative Boulevard Cumin along the valley floor is nearly flat, and can be hard work, especially for kids – as the editorial offspring can confirm.

TERRAIN-PARKS
Adequate
There is a good terrain-park served by the Deux Lacs chair-lift that has over ten obstacles that include a quarter pipe, kicker line, hip and handrail line. There is a 110m/360ft long half-pipe that gets cut daily. The whole park is well maintained and often hosts local

boarding

Val-Thorens has always been popular with snowboarders as it is the highest and most snow-sure of the Three Valleys resorts, as well as having a younger and more affordable feel in comparison with Courchevel and Méribel. The terrain is rather bleak; however, there are great steep runs, gullies, and groomed pistes for all levels and forms of snowboarding. The lifts are now mainly chairs and gondolas, although one or two drag-lifts remain.

Three Valleys

Prices in €

Age	1-day	6-day
under 13	32	158
13 to 59	42	210
over 60	36	168

Free under 5, over 72
Beginner 5 free lifts
Notes
Covers Courchevel, La Tania, Méribel, Val-Thorens, Les Menuires and St-Martin. Family reductions; pedestrian and half-day passes. Six-day pass valid for a day in Espace Killy (Tignes-Val-d'Isère), Paradiski (La Plagne-Les Arcs), Pralognan and Les Saisies.
Alternative pass
Val-Thorens-Orelle only, with one-day Three Valleys extension available.

competitions. Beside the Peyron chair-lift in the Maurienne valley is a 1.5km/1 mile-long boarder-cross course, which will test the best of them. If neither of these are to your taste, neighbouring Les Menuires also has a good terrain-park next to the Boyes run.

SNOW RELIABILITY
Difficult to beat
Few resorts can rival Val-Thorens for reliably good snow-cover, thanks to its altitude and generally north-facing slopes. Snowmaking covers a lot of the key pistes, including the crowded south- and west-facing runs on the way back from the Méribel valley, and was extended last winter to include routes to and from the Orelle sector.

FOR EXPERTS
Lots to do off-piste
Val-Thorens' local pistes are primarily intermediate terrain. The fast Cascades chair serves a short but steep black run that quickly gets mogulled. The pistes down from the Cîme de Caron cable-car are challenging, but not seriously steep, and there's a sunny black run off the back into the fourth valley. The red Chamois, Falaise and

Variante runs from Col de Rosaël can get heavily mogulled and challenging (and a 2005 reporter found them 'full of out of control skiers and boarders who are not prepared for the conditions they find'). The sunny Marielle run, one of the routes from the Méribel valley, is one of the easiest blacks we've come across, but it can get crowded and be icy in the morning.

There is a huge amount of off-piste to explore with a guide – see the feature panel below.

FOR INTERMEDIATES
Unbeatable quality and quantity
The scope for intermediates throughout the Three Valleys is enormous. It will take a keen intermediate only 90 minutes or so to get to Courchevel 1650 at the far end, if not distracted by the endless runs on the way.

The local slopes in Val-Thorens are some of the best intermediate terrain in the region. Most of the pistes are easy reds and blues, made even more enjoyable by the excellent snow.

The snow on the red Col run is normally some of the best around. The blue Moraine below it is gentle and popular with the schools. The runs on

Val-Thorens

413

FABULOUS OFF-PISTE IN VAL-THORENS

Val-Thorens offers a huge choice of off-piste. And because of the high altitude, the snow stays powdery longer here than in lower parts of the Three Valleys.

For those with little off-piste experience, the Pierre Lory Pass run is ideal. It is a very large and gentle slope, and you access the pass by doing an easy traverse on the Chavière glacier from the top of the Col chair-lift. When you arrive at Pierre Lory Pass there are breathtaking views of the Aiguilles d'Arves in the Maurienne valley, and you will be just above the glacier du Bouchet, which you then ski down, rejoining the lift system at Plan Bouchet.

For those with more off-piste under their belt already, the Lac du Lou is a famous off-piste run of 1400m/4,590ft vertical. It is easily accessible from the top of the Cîme de Caron cable-car. The many ways into this long, wide valley allow plenty of variety and opportunities for making first tracks; because many of the slopes face north or north-west it is not unusual to find good powder most of the ski season, even in late April. The views are stunning and you'll notice the quietness and vastness of the whole valley.

La Combe sans Nom on the Maurienne side in the fourth valley, also accessible from the Cîme de Caron cable-car, usually offers superb skiing and snowboard conditions. There's a choice of south-, west- and, on the far side, some east-facing slopes, which makes for excellent spring skiing conditions.

For the more adventurous there are many options, including hiking up from the top of the Col chair-lift and skiing a long run over the Gébroulaz glacier down to Méribel-Mottaret.

But don't even think about doing any off-piste runs without a fully qualified guide or instructor. Route finding can be difficult, there can be avalanche danger, and hidden hazards such as cliffs and crevasses lurk.

the top half of the mountain are steeper than those back into the resort. The Grand Fond gondola serves a good variety of red runs. The recently improved Pluviomètre from the Trois Vallées chair is a glorious varied run, away from the lifts. Adventurous intermediates shouldn't miss the Cîme de Caron runs. The black run is not intimidating – it's very wide, usually has good snow, and is a wonderful fast cruise when freshly groomed.

FOR BEGINNERS
Good late-season choice

The slopes at the foot of the resort are very gentle and provide convenient, snow-sure nursery slopes, now with moving walkway lifts. There are no long green runs to progress to, but the blues immediately above the village are easy. The resort's height and bleakness make it cold in midwinter, and intimidating in bad weather.

FOR CROSS-COUNTRY
Try elsewhere

Val-Thorens is a poor base for cross-country, with only 4km/2.5 miles of local trails.

QUEUES
Persistent at the Cîme de Caron

Recent reports suggest that the longest queues are for the largest and most rewarding lifts, notably the Cîme de Caron cable-car, but also the gondolas. The queues move fairly quickly, but

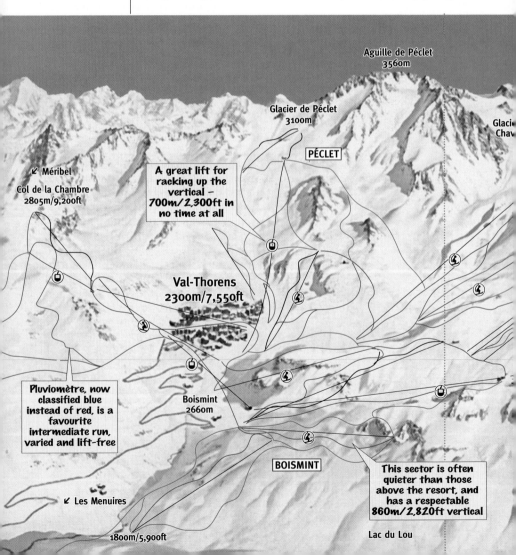

Aguille de Péclet
3560m

Glacier de Péclet
3100m

Glaci
Cha

PÉCLET

Méribel
Col de la Chambre
2805m/9,200ft

A great lift for racking up the vertical – 700m/2,300ft in no time at all

Val-Thorens
2300m/7,550ft

Pluviomètre, now classified blue instead of red, is a favourite intermediate run, varied and lift-free

Boismint
2660m

BOISMINT

This sector is often quieter than those above the resort, and has a respectable 860m/2,820ft vertical

Les Menuires

1800m/5,900ft

Lac du Lou

reporters warn that visits to the Cîme de Caron really need to be timed to miss the crowds (the view at the top is worth the wait, emphasise a couple of 2005 reporters – as if the runs were not). Get there very early if you can.

The Plein Sud six-pack chair-lift does a good job of getting the crowds out of the village towards Méribel and Courchevel, and delivers you to the Bouquetin gondola. Past reports of serious morning queues as people head out to tour the Three Valleys are no longer coming in. But in good weather the Rosaël chair back from the fourth valley is a serious bottleneck.

When snow is in short supply elsewhere, the pressure on the Val-Thorens lifts can increase markedly.

MOUNTAIN RESTAURANTS
Lots of choice

For a high, modern resort, the choice of restaurants is good. The Bar de la Marine, on the Dalles piste, does 'excellent and imaginative' food but it's pricey and service can get stretched; 2006 reports are mixed, as a result. The Moutière, near the top of the chair of the same name, is one of the more reasonably priced huts. The Plan Bouchet refuge in the Maurienne valley is very popular and welcoming, but bar service can be slow. You can stay the night there, too. The Chalet Plein Sud, below the chair of the same name, has excellent views but a 'rather limited menu'. The big Chalets du Thorens has been praised for 'fabulous

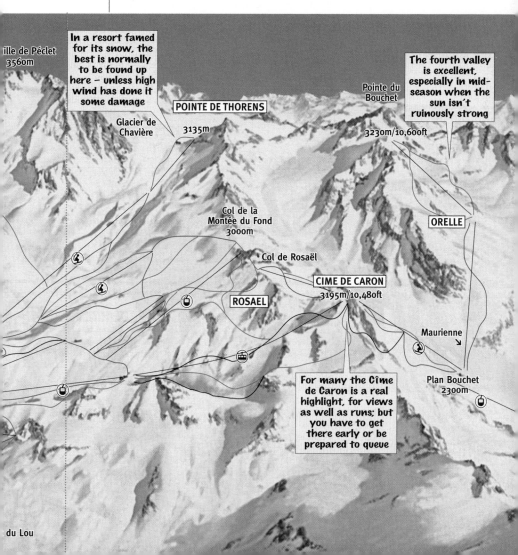

ille de Péclet
3560m

In a resort famed for its snow, the best is normally to be found up here – unless high wind has done it some damage

Glacier de Chavière

POINTE DE THORENS

3135m

Pointe du Bouchet

The fourth valley is excellent, especially in mid-season when the sun isn't ruinously strong

3230m/10,600ft

Col de la Montée du Fond
3000m

ORELLE

Col de Rosaël

CIME DE CARON
3195m/10,480ft

ROSAEL

Maurienne

For many the Cîme de Caron is a real highlight, for views as well as runs; but you have to get there early or be prepared to queue

Plan Bouchet
2300m

du Lou

GETTING THERE

Air Geneva 160km/ 99 miles (3½hr); Lyon 193km/120 miles (3½hr); Chambéry 112km/70 miles (2½hr).

Rail Moûtiers (37km/23 miles); regular buses from station.

SCHOOLS

ESF
t 0479 000286
Ski-Cool
t 0479 000492
Prosneige
t 0479 010700
International
t 0479 000196

Classes (ESF prices)
6 half-days (3hr am)
from €101
Private lessons
from €33 for 1hr

GUIDES

Mountain office
t 0689 292336

CHILDREN

Le Montana
t 0479 000286
Ages from 3mnth
Le Roc
t 0479 000286
Ages from 18 mnth.
Skiing tuition for 3 and over (Bambi club)

Ski school
All the schools offer classes for children aged 4 or 5 and over (ESF: 6 mornings from €92).

food, even if the service was poor', but another 2006 reporter found the 'confusing' self-service area and the music off-putting. The Genépi, on the run of the same name, has a 'lovely open fire' and 'very pleasant staff'. The Chalet de Caron was found to have 'one of the widest ranges of self-service meals' plus 'quick and efficient' service. The Chalet des 2 Lacs has 'the best food and is the best value', says a 2005 reporter. The Chalet des Deux Ours on the Blanchot run gets repeated recommendations – 'a dream; excellent quality food, large portions and reasonably priced'; 'fresh, tasty and imaginative food'.

SCHOOLS AND GUIDES
A mixed bag
The ESF, has a Trois Vallées group for those who want to cover a lot of ground while receiving lessons – available by the day or the week, and can include off-piste. The children of a 2005 visitor were taught in French despite 'being guaranteed that lessons would be in English'. Prosneige gets generally better reports; we have two enthusiastic reports this year from intermediates taking private lessons, and one of an absolute beginner who quit her ESF class after her first day, but who was rescued by Prosneige. Ski Cool class sizes are guaranteed not to exceed 10. They also have off-piste courses. There are several specialist guiding outfits.

FACILITIES FOR CHILDREN
Coolly efficient
Our most recent reporter on the ESF nursery found the facilities convenient and the service efficient. In spite of the fact that the staff were 'not particularly warm or friendly', by the end of the week all the children were 'comfortable' on skis. The Prosneige school takes children from age five.

STAYING THERE

HOW TO GO
Surprisingly high level of comfort
Accommodation is of a higher standard than in many purpose-built resorts – more comfortable as well as stylish.

Chalets These are catered apartments rather than real chalets, but many are quite comfortable.

Hotels There are plenty of hotels, and there's a Club Med, too.

((((5) **Fitz Roy** (0479 000478) The sole 4-star is a swanky but charming place with lovely rooms. New owners plan to refurbish and add a Michelin-starred chef. Pool. Well placed.

((((4) **Val Thorens** (0479 000433) Next door to Fitz Roy. 'Good service, good food and an excellent on the slopes location.' 'Comfortable and friendly.'

(((3) **Sherpa** (0479 000070) Highly recommended for atmosphere and food. Less-than-ideal position at the top of the resort.

(((3) **Val Chavière** (0479 000033) Friendly, convenient, 'good food and plenty of it'.

(((3) **Bel Horizon** (0479 000477) Friendly, family-run 3-star, popular with reporters – 'cuisine wonderful'.

SMART APARTMENTS – SEE FEATURE
Val-Thorens has quite a few above-average apartment developments, many in the Plein Sud area above the main village – Balcons de Val Thorens, Chalet Altitude, Chalet du Soleil, Chalet Val 2400 have all been recommended; some have a pool. On its own just above the village is the Chalet des Neiges, with pool. At the very bottom of the resort, the Residence Oxalys is exceptional, with its own wonderful restaurant (see 'Eating out') as well as a large lounge, pool and sauna. There are three Montagnettes developments in different locations. Reporters have also enjoyed staying in the Temples du Soleil, Orsière and Village Montana.

ACTIVITIES

Indoor Sports centre (spa, sauna, fitness room, hot-tub, tennis, squash, swimming pool, volleyball, table tennis, badminton, football), games rooms, music recitals

Outdoor Paragliding, sightseeing microlight flights, snowmobiles, snow-shoeing, ice-driving, walks, tobogganing

Phone numbers
From abroad use the prefix +33 and omit the initial '0' of the phone number.

TOURIST OFFICE

t 0479 000808
valtho@valthorens.com
www.valthorens.com

OT VAL-THORENS / BASILE / J C PIRONON

'Un station sans voiture et ski aux pieds,' it says here. C'est vrai ➔

EATING OUT
Surprisingly wide range
Val-Thorens has something for most tastes and pockets. The resort's excellent pocket guide contains a useful restaurant section.

Top of the range is the restaurant in the Residence Oxalys. This report is typical: 'Out of this world. In over half a century of French gastronomy I have never had a meal to compare with the inventiveness of this smart but friendly establishment. It is expensive but worth every penny.' We can't wait to try it ourselves.

The Fitz Roy and Val Thorens hotels do classic French food and were the best in town before Oxalys appeared. For something more regional, the best bets are the 'excellent' Vieux Chalet and the 'interesting' menu at the Galoubet. A 2006 reporter says that the 'efficient' Chaumière is a good, cheaper alternative. Other readers' recommendations include the 'steaks, veal escalope and mixed grill' at the Auberge des Balcons ('huge' but 'sometimes difficult to get a table'), Cabane ('very high quality cooking with real innovation and reasonably priced'), the Ferme de Rosalie ('good but limited menu'), the Montana ('good food and service'), El Gringo's ('great for Tex-Mex food' and 'very popular so get there early'), the Toit du Monde ('particularly good' and 'excellent value for money') and the Joyeuse Fondue. The Blanchot is an unusually stylish wine bar with a simple but varied carte and of course an excellent range of wines. Several pizzerias are recommended, including the 'cosy wood-clad' Scapin and the Grange ('good food and friendly staff').

APRES-SKI
Livelier than you'd imagine
Val-Thorens is more lively at night than most high-altitude ski-stations. The Red Fox up at Balcons is crowded at close of play, with karaoke. At the opposite extreme the Sherlock in the Temples du Soleil is 'always lively'. The Frog and Roastbeef at the top of the village is a cheerful British ghetto with a live band at tea time and half-price beer while it plays; real ale is sold, but a 2006 reporter says, 'It stank of vinegar. We did not linger.' It claims to be the highest pub in Europe. The Friends and the Viking pub are both lively bars on the same block. The Underground nightclub in Place de Péclet has an extended happy hour but 'descends into Europop' when its disco gets going. The Malaysia cellar bar is recommended for good live bands, and gets very crowded after 11pm. Quieter bars include the 'atmospheric without being overcrowded' O'Connells and the cosy Rhum Box Café (aka Mitch's).

OFF THE SLOPES
Forget it
There's a good sports centre, free weekly concerts in the church, a small cinema and twice-weekly street markets. You can get to some mountain restaurants by lift, and the 360° panorama from the top of the Cîme de Caron cable-car is not to be missed. But it is not a good bet for a holiday off the slopes.

The French Pyrenees

An underrated region with decent skiing and boarding at half the price of the Alps and villages that remain distinctly French

418

It took us a long time to get round to visiting the resorts of the French Pyrenees – mainly because we had the idea that they were second-rate compared with the Alps. Well, it is certainly true that they can't compete in terms of size of ski area with the mega-resorts of the Three Valleys and Paradiski. But don't dismiss them: they have considerable attractions, including price – hotels cost half as much as in the Alps, and meals and drinks are cheap.

The Pyrenees are serious mountains, with dramatic, picturesque scenery. They are also attractively French. Unlike the big plastic mega-resorts, many Pyrenean bases have a rustic, rural Gallic charm.

The biggest ski area – shared by **Barèges** and **La Mongie** – is called **Domaine Tourmalet**. Between them they have 100km/62 miles of runs (69 pistes) and 43 lifts. Most lifts are drags and slow chairs but they have three high-speed chairs. There is 20km/12 miles of cross-country.

The runs are best suited to intermediates, with good tree-lined runs above Barèges and open bowl skiing above La Mongie. The best bet for an expert is to try off-piste with a guide – one beautiful run away from all the lifts starts with a scramble through a hole in the rocks. There is a terrain-park, which was revamped last season. Rustic mountain huts are scattered around the slopes.

Barèges is a spa village set in a narrow, steep-sided valley, which gets little sun in midwinter; the lift base is at Tournaboup, 4km/2.5 miles up the valley and served by ski-bus. It's the second oldest ski resort in France and the pioneer of skiing in the Pyrenees. Accommodation is mainly in 2-star hotels such as the Igloo, Central and Europe, which reporters recommend for good food and a friendly welcome. One reporter stayed in nearby Luz in the Chimes hotel, describing the food as 'divine'. The rather drab buildings and one main street of Barèges grow on you, though there's little to do in the evenings other than visit the thermal spa and a restaurant. La Mongie, on the other hand, is a modern, purpose-built resort reminiscent of the Alps: 'Small friendly village, great restaurants but not cheap,' says a recent reporter.

Cauterets is another spa town but a complete contrast to Barèges. It is much bigger and set in a wide, sunny valley. It is a popular summer destination, and even in March we were able to sit at a pavement café with a drink after dinner. A new gondola takes you up to the slopes 850m/2,790ft above the town – you have to ride it down as well as up. There are only 35km/22 miles of slopes (mainly intermediate) set in a bowl that can be cold and windy.

But Cauterets' jewel is its cross-country, a long drive or bus-ride from town at Pont d'Espagne and served by a gondola. It is the start of the Pyrenees National Park and the old smugglers' route over the mountains between France and Spain. The 36km/22 miles of snow-sure cross-country tracks run up this beautiful deserted valley, beside a rushing stream and a stunning waterfall.

Font-Romeu has 54km/33 miles of pistes and 26 lifts, serving mainly easy and intermediate pistes, and is popular with families. The slopes get a lot of sun, but it has the biggest snowmaking set-up in the Pyrenees. When weekend crowds arrive both lifts and pistes can get crowded. It has 100km/62 miles of cross-country skiing. The village is a bus-ride from the slopes and hotels are mainly 2- and 3-star.

The other major Pyrenean resort is **St-Lary-Soulan**, a traditional village with houses built of stone, with a cable-car at the edge going up to the slopes, of which there are 100km/62 miles, mainly suiting intermediates. It has a terrain-park and half-pipe. There's a satellite called **St-Lary-Espiaube**, which is purpose-built and right at the heart of the slopes.

A recent reporter also visited other small resorts such as Formiguères, Eyne and Les Angles, and suggests staying down in a small valley town and visiting different resorts daily.

SNOWPIX.COM / CHRIS GILL

Les Houches

Varied, tree-lined area above a spread-out village at the entrance to the Chamonix valley. It has good intermediate cruising and is the best place in the valley to go when it's snowing hard – the trees make for good visibility.

KEY FACTS

Resort	1010m
	3,310ft
Slopes	950-1900m
	3,120-6,230ft
Lifts	18
Pistes	55km
	34 miles
Green	14%
Blue	27%
Red	50%
Black	9%
Snowmaking	67 guns

online booking
www.sport2000rent.com

TOURIST OFFICE

t 0450 555062
info@leshouches.com
www.leshouches.com

THE RESORT

Les Houches, 6km/4 miles from Chamonix, is covered by the new Mont Blanc Unlimited pass (see Chamonix). It's a pleasant village, sitting in the shade of the looming Mont Blanc massif. There is an old core with a pretty church, but modern developments in chalet style have spread along the road at the foot of the slopes, with the result that some of them are quite a walk from the lifts.

The village is quiet at night, but there are some pleasant bars and good restaurants including Vieilles Luges and the Terrain. Reporters enjoyed staying in the 3-star Bois (0450 545035), with its 'helpful staff and excellent restaurant'.

MGM has some good apartments with their own pool. Buses run to and from Chamonix all evening.

THE MOUNTAINS

The wooded area above Les Houches – popular when bad weather closes other areas – is served by a queue-prone cable-car and a gondola. There are open, gentle runs at the top of the main lifts (including nursery slopes), long, worthwhile blues and reds back towards the village and some particularly lovely woodland runs on the back of the mountain towards St-Gervais. It is the biggest single area of pistes in the Chamonix valley and has Chamonix's World Cup Downhill course.

In good weather the slopes are quiet and the views superb from the several attractive mountain restaurants, which are noticeably cheaper than others in the valley. Snow-cover on the lower slopes is not reliable, but there is a fair amount of snowmaking.

Short turns

419

ISOLA 2000 TOURIST OFFICE

Isola 2000

A flight to Nice and a short drive from there makes Isola easy to reach for a short break. It has slope-side accommodation and some snow-sure slopes. But the core of the resort village is dire: block-like and tatty.

KEY FACTS

Resort	2000m
	6,560ft
Slopes	1840-2610m
	6,040-8,560ft
Lifts	21
Pistes	120km
	75 miles
Green	15%
Blue	39%
Red	35%
Black	11%
Snowmaking	15km
	9 miles

TOURIST OFFICE

t 0493 231515
info@isola2000.com
www.isola2000.com

THE RESORT

Isola is a small, high, purpose-built resort close to the Côte d'Azur and easy to combine with a stay by the sea.

Built by a British property company at the end of the 1960s, the slope-side centre is a complex of block-like apartments, with shops, bars and restaurants in dark and tatty underground tunnels. Various owners have since worked hard to polish the image of the resort with new hamlets of more luxurious, wood-clad buildings. The Diva hotel (0493 231771) looks the best place to stay.

THE MOUNTAINS

The ski area spreads around the resort in a horseshoe shape. There are a couple of gondolas (one new for 2005/06) and a few fast chairs, but

there are still a lot of drag-lifts and slow chairs too.

Due to the great base height of Isola – the lowest of the slopes is at 1840m/6,040ft – most of the runs are above the tree line. Isola gets different weather from other major French resorts, so it can have masses of snow when the rest of the French Alps have none, and vice versa. Regular visitors say that they never find all the lifts open, but there is always snow – and plenty of sun.

Many of the runs suit confident intermediates best. They and experts will find the toughest runs in the St-Sauveur sector. There is more choice of blue runs in the Pélevos sector and excellent beginner slopes near the resort base. There are some surprisingly attractive restaurants on the slopes, including some just above the base, such as the Bergerie.

Val-Cenis

Val-Cenis is a marketing concept rather than a place. It comprises two quiet villages in the high and remote part of the Maurienne valley – Lanslebourg and Lanslevillard. A good place for half-term holidays, say readers.

KEY FACTS

Resort	1400m
	4,590ft
Slopes	1400-2800m
	4,590-9,190ft
Lifts	19
Pistes	80km
	50 miles
Green	21%
Blue	23%
Red	42%
Black	14%
Snowmaking	84 guns

TOURIST OFFICE

t 0479 052366
info@valcenis.com
www.valcenis.com

THE RESORT

Lanslevillard a pleasant spot directly at the foot of the slopes – off the road, randomly arranged and rustic, with a neat 'front de neige'. Lanslebourg is a long, linear place, spreading along the RN6 (a dead end in winter) with no real focus. It will become a more appealing base when the planned lift is built, up to the slopes above the village currently accessed only from the lower village of Termignon. There are modest hotels and a dozen restaurants in each village, and plenty of modern apartments. Lanslevillard has a leisure centre with rink and pool.

THE MOUNTAINS

There are lifts from base stations in and between the two villages – the main one a gondola starting near Lanslevillard. Above mid-mountain is a good range of open runs, served by chairs and drags. Below mid-mountain all the runs are prettily wooded. Most of the runs are north-facing, and there is snowmaking on the home runs, so snow reliability is quite good. There is ample off-piste and a few bump runs for experts. For intermediates there are top-to-bottom cruises of up to 1400m/ 4,590ft vertical. Lanslevillard has excellent nursery slopes; higher options include a very long and gentle green along the RN6 from the Col du Mont-Cenis.

There are extensive cross-country trails at Bessans, further up the valley. Queues are rare, even at half-term; the Lanslevillard gondola has been a problem, but an additional gondola opened for 2005/06.

The ESF school is consistently recommended: 'Friendly, good English.'

Valfréjus

Valfréjus is a small and unusual modern resort – purpose-built in the woods, with most of the skiing higher up above the tree line on slopes that were originally intended to extend over the border to Bardonecchia in Italy.

KEY FACTS

Resort	1550m
	5,090ft
Slopes	1550-2740m
	5,090-8,990ft
Lifts	13
Pistes	65km
	40 miles
Green	17%
Blue	48%
Red	22%
Black	13%
Snowmaking	16 guns

best for rent

TOURIST OFFICE

t 0479 053383
info@valfrejus.com
www.valfrejus.com

THE RESORT

The resort is a compact and quite pleasant affair, built on a narrow, shady shelf, with woods all around. There are several apartment blocks grouped around the main lift station, and chalets scattered here and there on the hillside. There are two hotels and 10 tourist residences in the resort. Restaurants in the village include a pizzeria and a crêperie. Après-ski is limited. Off the slopes, the limited activities include walking, skating and paragliding.

THE MOUNTAINS

A gondola goes up to the focus of the slopes at Plateau d'Arrondaz (2200m/ 7,220ft) and on to Punta Bagna (2735m/ 8,970ft). Beyond that point are sunny open slopes. There are runs of all grades through the trees to the village – and a glorious, long, away-from-the-lifts blue run (with off-piste variations along the way).

For experts there are a couple of genuine bumpy blacks, and good off-piste sport above the main plateau. Near-beginners might welcome more easy blues, but it would be a good place for confident intermediates to build their skills on good snow. There are nursery slopes at mid-mountain and village levels. The main open area is pretty snow-sure, but the lower runs are much less so. Queues are not a problem, but some of the chairs are very slow. The Punta Bagna, at the top of the gondola, is a 'basic' restaurant but has superb views, and the Bergerie at the mid-station has table-service.

Lessons are offered by the ESF and the International school, and there are three nurseries in the village.

BERNARD GRANGE / OT VALLOIRE

Valloire / Valmeinier

The old mountain village of Valloire shares with the mostly modern resort of Valmeinier the most extensive slopes in the Maurienne region, spreading widely over three mostly sunny sectors.

TOURIST OFFICE

t 0479 590396
info@valloire.net
www.valloire.net

THE RESORTS

Valloire still feels like a real mountain village, with a year-round population of 1,000, a 17th-century baroque church and plenty of crêperies, fromageries and reasonably priced restaurants. Events such as markets and ice carving competitions add to its lively air. It is free of through-traffic in winter, when the Col du Galibier pass is closed.

The hotel Aux Oursons (0479 590137) near the centre is comfortable and friendly, and has a small pool, hot-tub and sauna – and teddy bears everywhere (*ourson* means bear). The hotel de la Poste (0479 590347) is recommended. The Galibier (0479 590045) – 1km/0.5 mile from the centre but close to the Verneys chair-lift – and the central Valmonts apartments are both relatively new, with pool, sauna and steam room.

The Gastilleur restaurant in the Sétaz hotel on the main street is the gourmet choice, while Bistrot Chez Fred's reasonably priced brasserie food attracts such numbers that the place has been forced to expand into a heated tent on the terrace. The Grange is a rustic bar/crêperie, and the Asile des Fondues serves what you'd expect from the name in a beautiful old building with stone walls. Valloire is not the place to go if you want lively nightlife, though the Touring Bar attracts the teens and 20s.

The original old village of **Valmeinier** 1500 has expanded somewhat, with low-rise buildings that blend in well, and is closer to the link with Valloire. But the vast majority of visitors stay up the valley in the modern purpose-built satellite of Valmeinier 1800. Its low-rise chalet-style buildings line the bottom and side of the main slope and fit in well with their surroundings. It is a small, quiet, sunny place that mainly attracts French families on a budget looking for a hassle-free time and undemanding slopes. The Pierre & Vacances apartments are above average for the chain, right on the piste, with outdoor pool and sauna.

THE MOUNTAINS

Two gondolas from different parts of town access Valloire's two linked mountains. The Sétaz sector's shady slopes, the lower part tree-lined and the upper section open, generally have the best snow and the toughest slopes. The broad, open, west-facing slopes of Crey du Quart offer a choice of routes to link to the Valmeinier valley and to the lifts on to the west-facing slopes there. A gentle blue heads down from Grand Plateau to Valmeinier 1800, while a delightfully scenic and even gentler blue (with green alternative) leads to the Armera chair-lift. Snow on most of the slopes is affected by the sun, but there is a lot of snowmaking. The gondolas out of Valloire can have queues in the morning peak; other problems are rare.

Experts will find the area limited. The long Grandes Droze black run down to Valmeinier 1500 can present a challenge when the bumps build up, and the area from Crey du Quart down into the Valmeinier valley has some decent off-piste if the snow is good.

The vast majority of the slopes are ideal for intermediates of all standards. For easy cruising, head for the Crey du Quart sector which has gentle blues and almost-as-gentle reds everywhere. The red Praz Violette piste from the very tricky Combe drag-lift can be a wonderful cruise away from the crowds. There is further cruising in the Valmeinier sector. For more challenge, head over to Cretaz and try the highest runs, including the Cascade black, which often has excellent snow. Marmottes, down the gondola, is an excellent genuine red.

Both villages suit beginners well, with easy green runs to progress to; Valloire has nursery slopes both at village level and up the mountain.

Few of the mountain restaurants are memorable.

A 2005 reporter had 'superb' private lessons from an ESF instructor.

The six-day lift pass allows a cut-price day in the Trois Vallées (easily accessed from Orelle).

Italy

Italy's recent development as an international winter sports destination owed a lot to prices that were appreciably lower than those in other Alpine countries. It is still the cheapest of the four major Alpine countries, but it is not quite the bargain it was, so it now has to compete in terms of the quality of the holidays offered. And it is trying hard to do so – many resorts now have powerful, modern lifts and huge snowmaking systems. It has some enduring attractions, such as its good food and wine, jolly atmosphere and splendid scenery – especially in the Dolomites.

Italian resorts vary as widely in their characteristics as they do in location – and they are spread along the full length of the Italian border, from Sauze d'Oulx to the Dolomites. There are high, snow-sure ski stations and charming valley villages, and mountains that range from one-run wonders to some of the most extensive lift networks in the world.

A lot of Italian runs, particularly in the north-west, seem flatteringly easy. This is partly because grooming is immaculate, and partly because piste classification seems to overstate difficulty. Nowhere is this clearer than in the linked area of La Rosière in France and La Thuile – in Italy, despite the French-sounding name. Venturing from the Italian motorways to the French moguls is like moving from the shelter of the harbour to the open sea.

Many Italians based in the northern cities ski mainly at weekends, and it's very noticeable that many resorts become busy only at weekends. It's a great advantage for those of us who are there for the whole week. This pattern is especially noticeable at the chic resorts, such as Cortina, Courmayeur and Madonna, and resorts which have not yet found international fame such as the Monterosa region; it's much less pronounced in parts of the Dolomites favoured by German visitors who, like Brits, tend to go for a week.

In general, Italians don't take their skiing or boarding too seriously. A late start, long lunch and early finish are the norm – leaving the slopes delightfully quiet for the rest of us. Almost everywhere mountain restaurants are welcoming places, encouraging leisurely lunching. Pasta – even in the most modest establishment – is delicious. And eating and drinking on the mountain is still cheaper than in other Alpine resorts. But one drawback that many reporters remark upon is the primitive hole-in-the-ground toilets that are the norm in mountain restaurants (and sometimes in resorts too). Another is the ludicrous system in many self-service places where you have to queue to pay and then queue again to order your food or drink.

One thing that Italian resorts do have to contend with is erratic snowfall. While the snow in the northern Alps tends to come from the west, Italy's tends to come from storms arriving from the south. So it can have great conditions when other countries are suffering; or vice versa. Italian resorts have extensive snowmaking, and our observation is that they tend to use it more effectively than other Alpine countries. We have skied in Courmayeur and in the Dolomites when little natural snow had fallen, and in each case there was excellent cruising on man-made snow.

← Quiet early morning slopes and spectacular scenery are two of the attractions of Italian resorts. This is Cortina

Italy seems to be in the grip of a legislation fever at present, with mixed results. Italian bars and restaurants are now smoke-free, a huge improvement. And it is now compulsory for children (under 14, we understand) to wear helmets on the slopes. But many areas have also made off-piste illegal near their pistes – more on this in the editorial introduction to this edition.

DRIVING IN THE ITALIAN ALPS

There are four main geographical groupings of Italian resorts, widely separated. Getting to some of these resorts is a very long haul, and moving from one area to another can involve very long drives (though the extensive motorway network is a great help).

The handful of resorts to the west of Turin – Bardonecchia, Sauze d'Oulx, Sestriere and neighbours in the Milky Way region – are easily reached from France via the Fréjus tunnel from Modane, or via the good road over the pass that the resort of Montgenèvre sits on.

Further north, and somewhat nearer to Turin than Milan, are the resorts of the Aosta valley – Courmayeur, Cervinia, La Thuile and the Monterosa area are the best known. These (especially Courmayeur)

ITALY

424

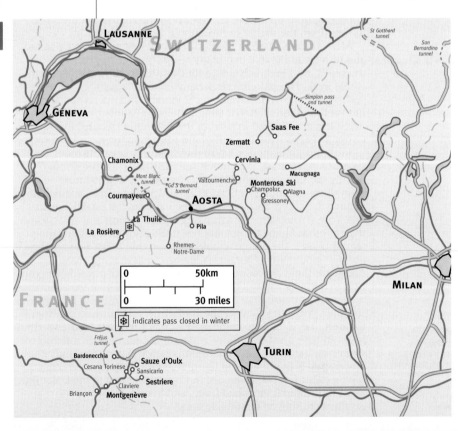

are the easiest of all Italian resorts to reach from Britain (via the Mont Blanc tunnel from Chamonix in France). The Aosta valley can also be reached from Switzerland via the Grand St Bernard tunnel. The approach is high and may require chains. The road down the Aosta valley is a major thoroughfare, but the roads up to some of the other resorts are quite long, winding and (in the case of Cervinia) high.

To the east is a string of scattered resorts, most close to the Swiss border, many in isolated and remote valleys involving long drives up from the nearest Italian cities, or high-altitude drives from Switzerland. The links between Switzerland and Italy are more clearly shown on our larger-scale Switzerland map at the beginning of that section than on the map of the Italian Alps included here. The major routes are the St Gotthard tunnel between Göschenen (near Andermatt) and Airolo – the main route between Basel and Milan – and the San Bernardino tunnel reached via Chur.

Finally, further east still are the resorts of the Dolomites. Getting there from Austria is easy, over the Brenner motorway pass from Innsbruck. But getting there from Britain is a very long drive indeed – allow at least a day and a half. We wouldn't lightly drive there and back for a week's skiing, though we routinely do as part of a longer tour including some Austrian resorts. It's also worth bearing in mind that once you arrive in the Dolomites, getting around the intricate network of valleys linked by narrow, winding roads can be a slow business – it's often quicker to get from village to village on skis. Impatient Italian driving can make it a bit stressful, too.

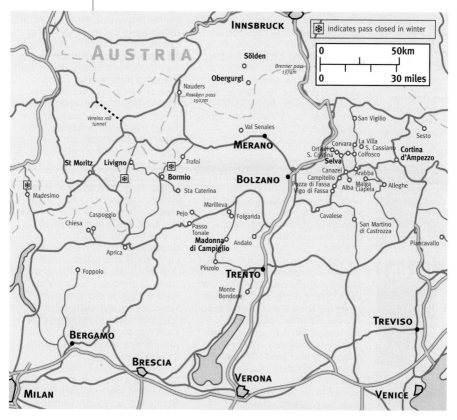

Bormio

One on its own, this: a tall, narrow mountain above a very unusual, historic town – a spa as well as a ski resort

COSTS

① ② ③ ④ ⑤ ⑥

RATINGS

The slopes

Fast lifts	***
Snow	***
Extent	**
Expert	*
Intermediate	***
Beginner	**
Convenience	***
Queues	***
Mountain restaurants	****

The rest

Scenery	***
Resort charm	****
Off-slope	****

NEWS

For 2005/06 the resort opened its first terrain-park, beside the Alpina run at Bormio 2000. Features include a 120m/390ft long super-pipe.

Over at Santa Caterina, expansion continues with the addition of a fast quad and a couple of red runs on the back of the mountain at Valle dell'Alpe.

426

➕ Good mix of high, open pistes and woodland runs adding up to some good long descents

➕ Worthwhile neighbouring resorts

➕ Attractive medieval town centre – quite unlike any other winter resort

➕ Good mountain restaurants

➖ Slopes all of medium steepness

➖ Rather confined main mountain, with second area some way distant

➖ Long airport transfers

➖ Crowds on Sundays

➖ Central hotels inconvenient

If you like ancient Italian towns and don't insist on a traditional Alpine resort atmosphere, you'll find the centre of Bormio very appealing – though you're unlikely to be staying right in the centre. Given the limited slopes of Bormio's own mountain, plan on taking the free bus out to the Valdidentro area and perhaps make longer outings – to Santa Caterina and maybe Livigno.

THE RESORT

Bormio, a spa since Roman times, has a splendid 17th-century town centre, with narrow cobbled streets and grand stone facades – very colourful during the evening promenade. It is in a remote spot, close to the Swiss border – though road improvements have cut the airport transfer to three hours.

The town centre is a 15-minute walk from the gondola station across the river to the south. There are reliable free shuttle-buses, but many people walk. Closer to the lifts is a suburban sprawl of hotels for skiers. Several major hotels are on Via Milano, leading out of town, which is neither convenient nor atmospheric.

THE MOUNTAINS

There's a nice mix of high, snow-sure pistes and lower wooded slopes. The main slopes are tall (vertical drop 1800m/5,900ft) and narrow. Most pistes face north-west.

Both the piste map and the piste marking need substantial improvement. The policy of opening certain lifts only at weekends and busy times (much the same thing) has provoked complaints.

The Valdidentro area, a short bus-ride out of Bormio, shouldn't be overlooked. The open and woodland runs are very pleasant and usually empty (and have great views). Day trips to Santa Caterina (20 minutes by bus) and Livigno (90 minutes) are covered by the Alta Valtellina lift pass. A six-day pass entitles you to a

discount rate on a one-day pass in St Moritz (three hours away).

Slopes The main access lift is an eight-seat gondola to the mid-mountain mini-resort of Bormio 2000, with a cable-car going on up to the top at over 3000m/9,840ft. An alternative gondola goes to Ciuk, and above this two fast chairs serve the top.

Terrain-parks The resort has opened its first terrain-park and super-pipe on the slopes at Bormio 2000. As well as the usual jumps and rails, there's also a separate beginner area.

Snow reliability Runs above Bormio 2000 are usually snow-sure, and there is snowmaking on the lower slopes, though this doesn't necessarily help in late March. The Valdidentro area is more reliable, and the high, shaded, north-facing slopes of Santa Caterina usually have good snow.

Experts There are a couple of short black runs in the main area, but the greatest interest lies in off-piste routes from Cima Bianca to both east and west of the piste area.

Intermediates The men's downhill course starts with a steep plunge, but otherwise is just a tough red, ideal for strong intermediates. Stella Alpina, down to 2000, is also fairly steep. Many runs are less tough – ideal for most intermediates. The longest is a superb top-to-bottom cruise. The outlying mountains are also suitable for early intermediates.

Beginners The nursery slopes at Bormio 2000 offer good snow, but there are no very easy longer pistes to move on to. Novices are better off at

Cresta Sobretta 2275m

Cima Bianca 3010m/9,880ft

Val di Sotto

Santa Caterina 1730m/5,675ft

BORMIO 2000   2200m   2500m

Ciuk 1620m

OGA-VALDIDENTRO

Bormio 1225m/4,020ft

Oga 1475m

Passo dello Stelvio Summer skiing

Le Motte 1430m   Isolaccia 1345m

KEY FACTS

Resort	1225m
	4,020ft

Bormio and Valdidentro	
Slopes	1225-3010m
	4,020-9,880ft
Lifts	26
Pistes	44km
	27 miles
Blue	28%
Red	65%
Black	7%
Snowmaking	30km
	19 miles

Bormio only	
Slopes	1225-3010m
	4,020-9,880ft
Lifts	16
Pistes	25km
	16 miles

OUR WEBSITE

Go to our website at wtss.co.uk for resort news, links to resort sites, a build-your-own-shortlist system and reader forums.

Phone numbers
From abroad use the prefix +39 (and do **not** omit the initial '0' of the phone number).

TOURIST OFFICE

t 0342 903300
infobormio@provincia.so.it
www.valtellinaonline.com

nearby Santa Caterina.
Snowboarding The new terrain-park is the main attraction. The slopes are too steep for novices, and there's little to attract experienced boarders either.
Cross-country There are some trails either side of Bormio, towards Piatta and beneath Le Motte and Valdidentro, but cross-country skiers are better off at snow-sure Santa Caterina.
Queues We have no recent reports, but the gondola that replaced the cable-car from the main car park to Bormio 2000 should have dealt with any problems low down. And there are now fast chairs up to Cima Bianca, relieving the pressure on the top cable-car. There should now be few problems outside carnival week.
Mountain restaurants The mountain restaurants are generally good. Even the efficient self-service at Cafe Bormio 2000 has a good choice of dishes. At the Rocca, above Ciuk, there is a welcoming chalet and a smart, modern place with table- or self-service. Cedrone, at Bormio 2000, has a good terrace and a play area for children. And Heaven 3000, at the top of Cima Bianca, opened a couple of years ago. Several reporters recommend the very welcoming Baita de Mario, at Ciuk, as a great place for a long lunch.
Schools and guides The only recent report we have is of the Nazionale school, which offered 'satisfactory lessons in English'.
Facilities for children The ski schools take children from the age of three, from 10am to 4pm. The Bormio 2000 school has a roped-off snow garden at mid-mountain with a moving carpet lift.

STAYING THERE

How to go There are plenty of apartments, but hotels dominate the package market.
Hotels Most of Bormio's 40-plus hotels are 2- and 3-star places. The 4-star Palace (0342 903131) is the most luxurious. The Posta (0342 904753) is in the centre of the old town – rooms vary widely. The Baita dei Pini (0342 904346) is the best placed of the top hotels – on the river, between the lifts and centre. The Ambassador (0342 904625) is close to the gondola.
Self-catering The modern Cristallo apartments have been recommended.
Eating out There's a wide choice. The Kuerc and Vecchia Combo are popular. There are excellent pizzerias, including the Jap. On the outskirts at San Antonio, the Rododendri and the 'atmospheric' Taula ('excellent modern food') are recommended.
Après-ski The après-ski starts on the mountain at the Rocca, and there are popular bars around the bottom lift stations. The Clem Pub, Cafe Mozart and the Aurora are popular. Shangri-La is a friendly bar. The Sunrise has taken over from the King's Club nightclub.
Off the slopes Diversions include thermal baths and the Roman baths, riding and walks in the Stelvio National Park. Excellent sports centre, ice rink and 'superb' swimming pool. St Moritz and Livigno are popular excursions.
Staying up the mountain The modern Girasole 2000 (0342 904652), at Bormio 2000, is simple but well run by an Anglo-Italian couple; lots of events for evening entertainment.

Cervinia

Mile after mile of high-altitude, easy, snow-sure cruising above a hotchpotch of a village; best for late-season trips

COSTS

① ② ③ ④ ⑤ ⑥

RATINGS

The slopes	
Fast lifts	****
Snow	*****
Extent	***
Expert	*
Intermediate	****
Beginner	*****
Convenience	***
Queues	***
Mountain restaurants	***

The rest	
Scenery	****
Resort charm	**
Off-slope	*

KEY FACTS

Resort	2050m
	6,730ft

Cervinia/ Valt'nenche	
Slopes	1525-3480m
	5,000-11,420ft
Lifts	24
Pistes	130km
	81 miles
Blue	30%
Red	59%
Black	11%
Snowmaking	37km
	23 miles

Cervinia/ Valt'nenche/ Zermatt combined	
Slopes	1525-3820m
	5,000-12,530ft
Lifts	57
Pistes	313km
	194 miles
Blue	22%
Red	60%
Black	18%
Snowmaking	98km
	61 miles

➕ Extensive mountain with miles of long, consistently gentle runs – ideal for early intermediates and anyone wary of steep slopes or bumps

➕ High, sunny and snow-sure slopes amid impressive scenery

➕ Excellent village nursery slope

➕ Link with Zermatt in Switzerland provides even more spectacular views and good lunches

➖ Very little to interest good or aggressive intermediates and above

➖ Little to do in bad weather – almost entirely treeless, and lifts prone to closure by wind

➖ Still a few slow old lifts

➖ Steep climb to main lifts, followed by lots of steps in station

➖ Rather dreary-looking village

➖ Few off-slope amenities

If there is a better resort than Cervinia for those who like gentle cruising in spring sunshine on mile after mile of easy, snow-sure, well-groomed slopes, we have yet to find it. And then there's the easiest of Zermatt's slopes just over the Swiss border, and linked by lift and piste.

But what about the rest of us? Well, to be frank, the rest of us are better off elsewhere. In particular, those who might be harbouring thoughts about bumps or powder over in Zermatt should probably think about staying there, not here. The link between the two resorts is unreliable, and the best of Zermatt's slopes take a while to reach – though the journey will be quicker for the coming season.

THE RESORT

Cervinia is at the head of a long valley leading off the Aosta valley on the Italian side of the Matterhorn. The old climbing village developed into a winter resort in a rather haphazard way, and it has no consistent style of architecture. It's an uncomfortable hotchpotch, neither pleasing to the eye nor as offensive as the worst of the French purpose-built resorts. The centre is pleasant, compact and traffic-free. But ugly surrounding apartment blocks and hotels make the whole place feel less friendly and welcoming than it could be.

A lot of people stay near the village centre, at the foot of the nursery slopes, which is obviously best for après-ski purposes. From 2006/07 it will also be much better for accessing the slopes because of a new six-pack replacing successive slow drag-lifts from here. This will now make a realistic alternative to an awkward uphill walk to the main lifts.

There are also modern developments above the main village, closer to the main lifts. Some hotels run their own shuttle-bus and the public bus from the Cieloalto complex,

for example, is reported to be 'efficient and well used'.

At weekends and public holidays, the resort can fill up with day trippers and weekenders from Milan and Turin. There are surprisingly few off-slope amenities, such as marked walks and spa facilities.

The slopes link to Valtournenche further down the valley (covered by the lift pass) and Zermatt in Switzerland (covered by a daily supplement, or a more expensive weekly pass).

Day trips by car are possible to Courmayeur, La Thuile and the Monterosa Ski resorts of Champoluc and Gressoney (all covered by the Aosta valley lift pass).

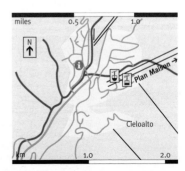

For 2006/07 five much needed new lifts are planned. Two chair-lifts will go from the bottom of the nursery slopes in the village, replacing four drag-lifts. A six-pack will go to Plan Torrette and meet an existing chair-lift, which will get you high enough to slide down to Plan Maison. A new quad, also from the bottom, will serve the nursery slopes. The Pancheron two-seat chair (right by the Matterhorn on the left of the ski area as you look at the piste map) has been dismantled, and there are plans to replace it but not until 2007/08.

In Valtournenche, a six-pack and two quads will replace three successive drag-lifts from Salette up to Colle Inf. Cime Bianche, hopefully making the journey much quicker. The old Roisette chair (the alternative way to get to the link with Cervinia) is due to be dismantled, so the new chairs will be the only way to Cervinia for 2006/07.

The cable-car from Cervinia to Plan Maison will be upgraded and its capacity increased. And snowmaking will be increased from the top of the Plan Torrette chair in Cervinia and from Colle Inf. Cime Bianche to Salette in Valtournenche.

SNOWPIX.COM / CHRIS GILL

See what we mean by the village being a hotchpotch? It doesn't look much better even when there's more snow than this. Good nursery slopes though ➔

The wide gentle slopes, generally good snow and lack of many drag-lifts (for 2006/07 onwards) make Cervinia pretty much ideal for beginner and early intermediate boarders. But there are some long, flat parts to beware of and there's not much to interest better boarders – just as there's not much to interest better skiers. Serious boarders will enjoy the terrain-park and there's an exclusive terrain-park pass that costs 21 euros a day; they could also try heli-boarding.

THE MOUNTAINS

Cervinia's main slopes are high, open, sunny and mostly west-facing. If the weather is bad, the top lifts often close because of high winds – and even the lower slopes may suffer poor visibility because of the lack of trees.

THE SLOPES
Very easy
Cervinia has the biggest, highest, most snow-sure area of easy, well groomed pistes we've come across, (and we're pleased to see they have reduced their claimed 200km of slopes to just 130km/81 miles – we never believed the former figure). The area has Italy's highest pistes and some of its longest (a claimed 13km/8 miles from Plateau Rosa to Valtournenche, interrupted only by a short drag-lift part-way – but see 'Snow reliability'). Nearly all the runs are accessible to average intermediates. The high number of red runs on the piste map is misleading: most of them would be classified blue elsewhere. There is now a handy quick-folding piste map that covers both Cervinia's and Zermatt's slopes fairly clearly. The slopes just above the village are floodlit some evenings.

The main lifts (a six-seat gondola and a parallel cable-car, which we've seen working only at peak times to help cut the queue) take you to the mid-mountain base of **Plan Maison**. The new six-pack from the village nursery slopes for 2006/07 followed by a slow chair will now make a viable alternative route to Plan Maison (though we fear there might be queues for the second chair at peak periods – reports welcome please). From Plan Maison a further gondola goes to Laghi Cime Bianche and then a giant cable-car goes up to **Plateau Rosa** and one link with Zermatt. The alternative link goes via three successive fast quads from Plan Maison up to a slightly lower point on the border. Between the fast quads and Laghi Cime Bianche, and going all the way back to the village, is a deep gorge that separates Cervinia's slopes into two main sections.

Plateau Rosa is the start of the splendid wide Ventina run. Part-way down you can branch off left down towards **Valtournenche**. The slopes here will be served by three new chair-lifts for 2006/07 (see News) above a modern gondola from Valtournenche.

There is also the very small, little-used **Cieloalto** area, served by a slow

Cervinia

old chair to the south of the cable-car at the bottom of the Ventina run. This has some of Cervinia's steeper pistes and the only trees in the area.

Several reporters complain of poor information and signing.

TERRAIN-PARKS
One of Italy's best

The 'Indian' terrain-park (www.indianpark.it) above Plan Maison is one of the best Italian parks. It is well maintained and includes a big pipe, boarder cross, three beginner jumps and big 10 and 18 metre advanced table-tops. Several rails and boxes are also now in place for different levels. For variety, try heading to Zermatt which has an equally impressive if not bigger freestyle area.

SNOW RELIABILITY
Superb

The mountain is one of the highest in Europe and, despite getting a lot of afternoon sun, can usually be relied on to have good snow conditions.

The village nursery slopes, the bottom half of the Ventina run, above Laghi Cime Bianche and the runs under the top chair-lifts down to Plan Maison have snowmaking, and more is planned for 2006/07 (see News).

But the run below the top of the gondola to lower-lying Valtournenche doesn't have snowmaking – and so is prone to bare patches and closure. We've often found it closed or hard and patchy in March, despite excellent snow elsewhere.

M. Cervino Matterhorn 4478m

Schwarzsee 2585m

Zermatt

Trockener Steg 2940m

Theodulpass 3290m

Crowds permitting, this is a great lift for racking up some vertical

PLATEAU ROSA 3480m/11,420ft

Colle Sup. Cime Bianche 2980m

Laghi Cime Bianche 2810m

Plan Maison 2555m

Plan Tourette

Slow old chairs keep this sector of pistes quiet

Cretaz

CIELOALTO

Cervinia 2050m/6,730ft

SCHOOLS

Cervino
t 0166 948744
Breuil
t 0166 940960
Matterhorn-Cervinia
t 0166 949523
Valtournenche
t 0166 92515

Classes
(Cervino prices)
6 days (2hr 45min per day) €155
Private lessons
€33 for 1hr for 1 person

FOR EXPERTS
Forget it

This is not a resort for experts. There is little readily accessible off-piste and high winds can blow the snow off what there is (though heli-drops with guides can be arranged). There are a few black runs scattered here and there, but most of them would be classified red elsewhere. Many reporters head over to Zermatt for more challenging slopes and will find it easier to reach them from 2006/07 – see 'The Zermatt connection' overleaf.

FOR INTERMEDIATES
Miles of long, flattering runs

Virtually the whole area can be covered comfortably by average intermediates. But, as a recent reporter

so aptly put it, 'Strong, aggressive intermediates will get bored quickly.' If you like wide, easy, motorway pistes, you'll love Cervinia: it has more long, flattering runs than any other resort. The easiest slopes are on the left as you look at the mountain. From top to bottom there are gentle blue runs and almost as gentle reds in the beautiful scenery beneath the Matterhorn.

The area on the right as you look at the mountain is best for adventurous intermediates. The Ventina red is a particularly good fast cruise. You can use the cable-car to do the top part repeatedly, or go all the way down to Cervinia (8km/5 miles and over 1400m/4,600ft vertical).

The runs down towards Valtournenche are great cruises and

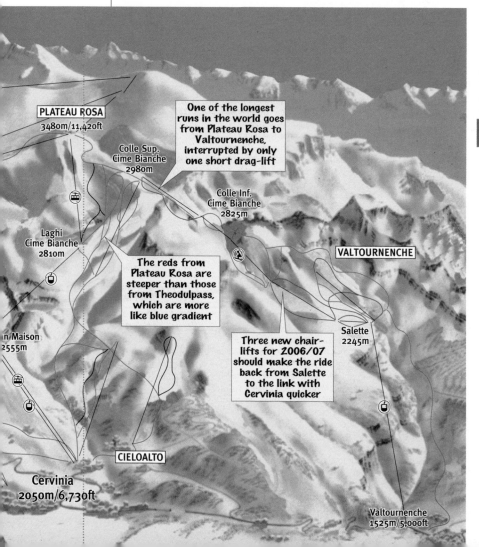

PLATEAU ROSA
3480m/11,420ft

Colle Sup.
Cime Bianche
2980m

One of the longest runs in the world goes from Plateau Rosa to Valtournenche, interrupted by only one short drag-lift

Colle Inf.
Cime Bianche
2825m

Laghi
Cime Bianche
2810m

The reds from Plateau Rosa are steeper than those from Theodulpass, which are more like blue gradient

VALTOURNENCHE

n Maison
2555m

Salette
2245m

Three new chair-lifts for 2006/07 should make the ride back from Salette to the link with Cervinia quicker

CIELOALTO

Cervinia
2050m/6,730ft

Valtournenche
1525m/5,000ft

THE ZERMATT CONNECTION

Getting to Zermatt's classic terrain on the Rothorn/Stockhorn sectors will be much quicker from 2006/07 because you'll be able to catch the new gondola from Furi to Rifelberg in the heart of the Gornergrat sector. Up till now, to reach that you had to descend to the village and then get a bus or taxi to lifts on the other side of town.

Make sure you leave plenty of time for your return journey. There can be long queues for the Klein Matterhorn cable-car (a reporter writes of an hour's wait) and for the alternative long, slow T-bars.

LIFT PASSES

Breuil-Cervinia

Prices in €

Age	1-day	6-day
under 8	8	44
8 to 12	24	131
13 to 64	32	174
over 65	24	131

Free no one

Beginner day pass for limited number of lifts €12

Notes
Covers all lifts on the Italian side of the border including Valtournenche. Half-day pass and individual section passes available. Also daily extension for Zermatt lifts.

Alternative passes
International pass covers all lifts on the Italian side plus Zermatt. Aosta Valley pass available.

OUR WEBSITE

Go to our website at wtss.co.uk for resort news, links to resort sites, a build-your-own resort shortlist system and reader forums.

many of the reds are more like blue gradient. The 13km/8 miles run all the way down is very satisfying, though the snow conditions on the lower part can be challenging.

FOR BEGINNERS
Pretty much ideal
Complete beginners will start on the good village nursery slope (which now has an excellent, long moving carpet), and should graduate quickly to the fine flat area around Plan Maison and its gentle blue runs. Fast learners will be going all the way from top to bottom of the mountain by the end of the week.

FOR CROSS-COUNTRY
Hardly any
There are a couple of short trails, but this is not a cross-country resort.

QUEUES
Few problems
Our 2006 reporters did not find queues a problem, at least on weekdays. But the main access lifts from Cervinia to Plan Maison can get crowded at the peak morning rush. Hopefully this will be less of an issue when the new six-pack is in place giving a speedy alternative way up from the village centre for 2006/07 – though it might create queues for the slow chair above it. Increased capacity for the cable-car out of town planned for 2006/07 should also help. There can be queues for many lower lifts when upper lifts are shut due to wind.

MOUNTAIN RESTAURANTS
OK if you know where to go
There are some good places if you know where to go. Toilet facilities have been a traditional cause of complaints from reporters, but several have now been improved. You can, of course, head over to Zermatt for lunch.

Our favourite restaurant, and readers', is the table-service section (there's self-service too) of Chalet Etoile, beneath the Rocce Nere chair-lift above Plan Maison: 'top quality cuisine in an authentic Italian style', 'fantastic pasta'. The more basic table-service section of Rifugio Teodulo at Theodulpass is also recommended – we had excellent pasta there. Booking is recommended at both. Several 2006 readers also recommend Bontadini at the top of the Fornet chair ('good value and superb view'). Other reporter tips include Tuktu at Plan Maison for

the 'best UK-style toilets in the area' (plus its 'good food and drink at reasonable prices') and the British-run Igloo, near the top of the Bardoney chair just off the Ventina piste, which serves huge burgers and again has 'a UK-style toilet'. Baita Cretaz, near the bottom of the Cretaz pistes, is good value ('the best Bombardinos').

The restaurants are cheaper and less crowded on the Valtournenche side. On the upper slopes there, the Motta does excellent food including goulaschsuppe that is 'out of this world' (and speciality hot white wine), and Lo Baracon dou Tene does a 'magnificent polenta con funghi'. A 2006 visitor commented that both were 'quite basic but had good atmosphere and were good value'.

SCHOOLS AND GUIDES
Generally positive reports
Cervinia has three main schools, Cervino, Breuil and Matterhorn-Cervinia. The Cervino school was praised by two 2006 reporters, one for the beginner group lessons; the other's children 'really enjoyed their lessons in a class of six English kids'. Another 2006 reporter said the instructors at the Breuil school were 'very good'.

FACILITIES FOR CHILDREN
No recent reports
The Cervino ski school runs a ski kindergarten. And there's a babysitting and kindergarten area at Plan Maison. Another kindergarten, Bianca Neve, opened a couple of seasons ago. But we lack recent reports on them. The slopes, with their long gentle runs, should suit families.

STAYING THERE

HOW TO GO
Plenty of hotel packages
Most of the big operators come here, offering a wide selection of hotels, though other types of accommodation are rather thin on the ground.
Hotels There are almost 50 hotels, mostly 2- or 3-stars, but there are a few 4-stars. Unless they run their own minibus to the slopes, choose your location with care.
((((4 **Hermitage** (0166 948998) Small, luxurious Relais et Château just out of the village on the road up to Cieloalto. Great views, pool, free bus to lifts. 'First class, good ambiance and service,' says a recent reporter.

Excelsior Planet (0166 949426)
Regularly recommended by reporters:
'Fantastic food and comfortable
facilities,' said one visitor this year.
Pool, spa facilities and minibus to lift.
In centre near Cretaz lifts.

Sporthotel Sertorelli (0166
949797) Excellent food, sauna and hot-
tub. Ten minutes from lifts.

Europa (0166 948660) Family run;
near Cretaz lifts. Pool. 'Exceptionally
friendly and helpful staff, very good
room.' Mixed views of the dinners.

Astoria (0166 949062) Right by
main lift station. Family run and
simple. 'Comfortable but that's all,'
says a reporter.

Marmore (0166 949057) Friendly,
family run, with 'quite good food'; on
main street – an easy walk to the lifts.

Al Piolet (0166 949161) The flood of
approval last year ('friendly' budget
place, recently refurbished 'to a high
standard', 'excellent – ski-in location',
'good meals') dried up this year.

Also recommended by recent
visitors are the Mignon (0166 949344)
– 'the best food we have ever eaten in
an Italian hotel'; the Gorret (0166
949044); and the Meynet (0166
948696) – 'super service'.

Self-catering There are many
apartments, but few are available via
UK tour ops. The Escargot ones in
Cieloalto are 'very spacious'.

EATING OUT
Plenty to choose from
Cervinia's 50 or so restaurants allow
plenty of choice. The Chamois and
Matterhorn are excellent, but quite
expensive. Casse Croute serves good
pizzas. The Copa Pan has a lively
atmosphere and is recommended by
several reporters. The Bricole and the
Nicchia have also been praised, and
the Maison de Saussure does 'very
good local specialities'. The Vieux
Grenier at the hotel Grivola does 'an
excellent pizza and is lively' and you'll
find 'good pizza and pasta' at Capanna
Alpina. The Pizzeria Bar Falcone and il
Rustico are recommended by a 2006
reporter for their 'reasonably priced
excellent local food and wine'. An
evening out at the Baita Cretaz
mountain hut makes a change.

APRES-SKI
Disappoints many Brits
Plenty of Brits come here looking for
action but find there isn't much to do
except tour the bars in and around the

main street. 'The best thing to do is
take a good book,' said a recent
reporter. The bar of the hotel Grivola,
next to the Vieux Grenier restaurant, is
attractively woody. The Copa Pan has
live music and is good value. The
Dragon Bar is popular with Brits and
Scandinavians and has satellite TV and
videos. The Ymeletrob, next door to
the Punta Maquignaz hotel, is 'cosy,
has live music and great canapés'.
Other recommendations include Lino's,
by the ice rink ('excellent pizzas and
cheap beer'), the Yeti and Hostellerie
des Guides (with mementos of the
owner's Himalayan trips). The discos
liven up at weekends.

OFF THE SLOPES
Little attraction
There is little to do for those who
don't plan to hit the slopes. The
pleasant town of Aosta is a four-hour
round trip. Village amenities include
hotel pools, a fitness centre and a
natural ice rink. The walks are
disappointing. The mountain
restaurants that are reachable by
gondola or cable-car are not special.

STAYING UP THE MOUNTAIN
To beat the queues
Up at Plan Maison, Lo Stambecco
(0166 949053) is a 50-room 3-star
hotel ideally placed for early nights
and early starts.

STAYING DOWN THE VALLEY
Great home run
Valtournenche, 9km/5.5 miles down
the road, is cheaper than Cervinia. The
village spreads along the steep,
winding road up to Cervinia, which is
often very busy.

A gondola leaves from the edge of
town and new lifts (see News) should
improve what was a very slow journey
after that. The exceptionally long run
back down is a nice way to end the
day – when it is in good condition (see
'Snow Reliability'). There's a fair
selection of simple hotels, of which the
3-star Bijou (0166 92109) is the best,
with a leisure centre and pool. Les
Rochers (0166 92119) has been
recommended by a 2006 visitor –
'Excellent food, and plenty of it, has a
shuttle bus and is very good value.'

On the road between the two
resorts, Les Neiges d'Antan (0166
948775 was strongly recommended to
us during a chair-lift ride in 2005. It
operates a shuttle-bus to the lifts.

Cortina d'Ampezzo

The scenery will take your breath away even if the slopes don't; take your posh frocks if you want to feel part of the evening scene

NEWS

For 2005/06 a six-pack, the Tofana Express, replaced the Col Taron and Piemerlo lifts at Socrepes.

And at Cristallo a fast quad, Padeon, replaced the old double chair up to Son Forca.

Also last season, a new mountain restaurant, the Son dei Prade, opened by the Olympia chair above Lacedèl.

434

- ➕ Magnificent Dolomite scenery – a quite exceptional setting
- ➕ Marvellous nursery slopes and good long cruising runs
- ➕ Access to the vast area covered by the Dolomiti Superski pass
- ➕ Attractive, although rather towny, resort, with lots of upmarket shops
- ➕ Good off-slope facilities
- ➕ No crowds or queues

- ➖ Several separate areas spread around all sides of the resort and linked by buses
- ➖ Erratic snow record
- ➖ Expensive by Italian standards
- ➖ Gets very crowded in town and in restaurants during Italian holidays
- ➖ Very little to entertain experts
- ➖ Mobile phones and fur coats may drive you nuts

Cortina is one on its own. Sure, it has a quantity of well-maintained, enjoyable intermediate slopes, and in one or two sectors it has efficient lifts. But you shouldn't even think about a holiday here if matters like these are top of your agenda – if skiing or riding from dawn to dusk is your priority.

If, on the other hand, you like lazy days centred around indulgent lunches on sunny terraces, gazing at scenery that is just jaw-droppingly wonderful, this is the place. Dramatic pink-tinged cliffs and peaks rising vertically from the top of the slopes ring the town, giving picture-postcard views wherever you look. Every time we go back, the memory has faded and our jaws drop again.

Cortina has a regular upmarket clientele from Rome and Milan, many of whom have second homes here and enjoy the strolling, shopping, people-watching and lunching as much as the slopes. A good proportion of visitors don't go near the slopes except to drive up to a 'mountain restaurant' for lunch.

As an occasional change from serious ski resorts, we love it.

THE RESORT

Although Cortina leapt to international prominence as host of the 1956 Winter Olympics, it is not a sporty place. Most people go not for any form of exertion but for the clear mountain air, the stunning views, the shopping, the cafes and the posing potential – 70% of all Italian visitors don't bother taking to the slopes. Cortina attracts the rich and famous from the big Italian cities. Fur coats and glitzy jewellery are the norm.

The resort itself is a widely spread town rather than a village, with exclusive chalets scattered around the outskirts. The centre is the traffic-free Corso Italia, full of chic designer clothes, jewellery and antique shops, art galleries and furriers – finding a ski shop can seem tricky. The cobbles and picturesque church bell tower add to the atmosphere. People quit the slopes early, and by 5pm hardly anyone is still in ski gear; the streets are packed

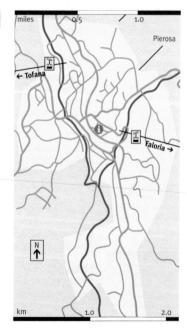

↑ Cortina is largely about mountain restaurants with fab views from their terraces; this one is Duca d'Aosta, down from Pomedes, and the view looks across the town to Faloria

SNOWPIX.COM / CHRIS GILL

with people parading up and down in their evening finery, shouting and gesticulating into their mobile phones. It's all pretty flat, so easy to get around in Gucci loafers.

Unlike most of the Dolomites, Cortina is pure Italy. The Veneto region has none of the Germanic traditions of the Südtirol. And everyone is 'friendly and welcoming,' say reporters.

Surrounding the centre is a busy one-way system, reportedly less traffic-clogged than it was last time we tackled it on a weekend. The lifts to the two main areas of slopes are a fair way from the centre, and at opposite sides of town. Other lifts are bus-rides away. There's a wide range of hotels, both in the centre and scattered on the outskirts. Staying centrally is best. The local bus service is good ('very efficient and punctual'), and free to ski-pass holders. A car can be useful, especially for getting to the outlying areas and to make the most of other areas on the Dolomiti Superski pass, but a recent visitor found parking 'inadequate'. San Cassiano is a short drive to the west, with links from there to Corvara and the other Sella Ronda resorts (see new Sella Ronda chapter).

KEY FACTS

Resort	1225m
	4,020ft
Slopes	1225-2930m
	4,020-9,610ft
Lifts	51
Pistes	140km
	87 miles
Blue	33%
Red	62%
Black	5%
Snowmaking	90%

THE MOUNTAINS

There is a good mixture of slopes above and below the tree line and new lifts are slowly replacing the old ones.

THE SLOPES
Inconveniently fragmented
All Cortina's smallish separate areas are a fair trek from the town centre. The largest is **Pomedes**, accessed by chair- and drag-lifts a bus-ride away. You can reach it by piste from **Tofana**, Cortina's highest area, accessed by cable-car from near the Olympic ice rink.

On the opposite side of the valley is the tiny **Mietres** area. Another two-stage cable-car from the east side of town leads to the **Faloria** area, from where you can head down to chairs that lead up into the limited but dramatic runs beneath **Cristallo**.

Other areas are reachable by road – in particular the road west over Passo Falzarego towards San Cassiano and the Sella Ronda area. (Taxis are an affordable means of access if shared.)

First is the small but spectacular Cinque Torri area. Its excellent north-facing cruising runs are accessed by a fast quad, followed by an ancient one-person chair; beyond that, a short rope

LIFT PASSES

Dolomiti Superski

Prices in €

Age	1-day	6-day
under 16	32	136
16 to 59	38	194
over 60	33	165

Free under 8
Beginner no deals

Notes
Covers 450 lifts and 1220km/758 miles of piste in the Dolomites, including all Cortina areas.

Alternative passes
Cortina d'Ampezzo covers all lifts in Cortina, San Vito di Cadore, Auronzo and Misurina.

tow leads to a sunny panoramic red run over the hill to Passo Giau.

Then comes the tiny Col Gallina area – north-facing, again – from where you can take a pleasant green to Cinque Torri. The cable-car from nearby Passo Falzarego up to Lagazuoi serves an excellent red run back down to the base station and accesses a longer red run down a beautiful 'hidden valley' to Armentarola on the fringe of the Alta Badia area. (For more on this run see the Sella Ronda chapter.)

Reporters consistently praise the excellent grooming and quiet slopes but complain about other things – too many to list – related to signs, piste classification and marking, and the piste map. But most reporters judge that Cortina's other charms more than make up for the grumbles.

One way to tour the area is to use special ski itineraries, maps for which are available at the tourist and ski pass offices. 'Skitour Olympia' takes you on the 1956 Olympic downhill, GS and slalom courses and the bob-sled run. 'Skitour Romantic Views' covers the Lagazuoi-Cinque Torri area.

TERRAIN-PARKS
Not a bad one
There is a terrain-park at Faloria that has some decent kickers and rails, and a half-pipe. It's not open to skiers.

SNOW RELIABILITY
Lots of artificial help
The snowfall record is erratic – it can be good here when it's poor on the north side of the Alps, and vice versa. But 90 per cent of the pistes are now covered by snowmaking, so cover is

good if it is cold enough to make snow. The run from Tofana to Pomedes involves a steep, narrow, south-facing section that often has poor snow conditions and is not infrequently closed.

FOR EXPERTS
Limited
The run down from Tofana mentioned above is deservedly graded black; it goes through a gap in the rocks, and gives wonderful views of Cortina way down in the valley below. There are short but genuinely black runs below Duc d'Aosta. Cortina's other major steep run goes from the top of the Cristallo area at Forcella Staunies . A chair-lift takes you to a south-facing couloir that is often shut due to avalanche danger or poor snow (tougher than it looks from below, warns a reporter).

Other than these two runs there are few challenges. There are some great long red runs though, and if it snows, you'll also have very little competition for first tracks. Heli-skiing is available.

FOR INTERMEDIATES
Fragmented and not extensive
To enjoy Cortina you must like cruising in beautiful scenery, and not mind doing runs repeatedly.

The runs at the top of Tofana are short but normally have the best snow. The highest are at over 2800m/9,190ft and mainly face north. But be warned: the only way back down is by the tricky black run described above or by cable-car. The reds in the linked Pomedes area offer good cruising and some challenges.

SCHOOLS

Cortina
t 0436 2911

Azzurra Cortina
t 0436 2694

Cristallo
t 0436 870073

Dolomiti
t 0436 862264

Classes
(Cortina prices)
6 days (2½hr per day)
€200

Private lessons
€44 for 1hr; each
additional person €14

GUIDES

Gruppa Guide Alpine
t 0436 868505

CHILDREN

Gulliver Park
at the Pocol ski area
t 0340 055 8399
9.30 to 4.30

Ski school
The schools offer all-
day classes for
children

boarding

Despite its upmarket chic, Cortina is a good resort for learning to board. The Socrepes nursery slopes are wide, gentle and served by a fast chair-lift. And progress on to other easy slopes is simple because you can get around in all areas using just chairs and cable-cars – though there are drags, they can be avoided. A specialist snowboard shop, Boarderline, organises instruction as well as equipment hire. There's little off-piste, but the best is to be found off the back of Cinque Torri, and the tiny Col Gallina area. There are some nice trees and natural undulations under the one-person chair at Cinque Torri. But a 2006 visitor 'did not see a boarder all week'.

Faloria has a string of fairly short north-facing runs – we loved the Vitelli red run, round the back away from the lifts. And the Cristallo area has a long, easy red run served by a fast quad.

It is well worth making the trip to Cinque Torri for wonderful, deserted fast cruising on usually excellent north-facing snow ('bliss,' says a 2006 reporter). And do not miss the wonderful 'hidden valley' red run from the Passo Falzarego cable-car.

FOR BEGINNERS
Wonderful nursery slopes
The Socrepes area has some of the biggest nursery slopes and best progression runs we have seen. Some of the blue forest paths can be icy and intimidating. But you'll find ideal gentle terrain on the main pistes.

FOR CROSS-COUNTRY
One of the best
Cortina has around 75km/47 miles of trails suitable for all standards, mainly in the Fiames area, where there is a cross-country centre and school. Trails include a 25km itinerary following an old railway from Fiames to Cortina, and there is a special beginner area equipped with snowmaking. Passo Tre Croci offers more challenging trails, covering 10km/6 miles. A Nordic area pass is now available.

QUEUES
No problem
Most Cortina holidaymakers rise late, lunch lengthily and leave the slopes early – if they get on to them at all. That means few lift queues and generally uncrowded pistes – a different world from the crowded Sella Ronda circuit. Queues can form for the cable-car to Lagazuoi, but most reporters are generally impressed. 'The lack of queues was one of the highlights of our holiday,' said one reporter. 'No queues even on a Saturday,' says another this year (many

Italian resorts are busiest at weekends). One visitor was delighted to find the slopes got emptier in the afternoons, as the Italians left the slopes, but that lifts stayed open as late as 5pm. There has been recent investment in new lifts too: a six-pack has replaced two lifts at Socrepes and an old double chair at Cristallo was upgraded to a fast quad.

MOUNTAIN RESTAURANTS
Good, but get in early
Lunch is a major event for many Cortina visitors. At weekends you often need to book or turn up very early to be sure of a table. Many restaurants can be reached by road or lift, and fur coats arrive as early as 10am to sunbathe, admire the views and idle the time away on their mobile phones. Skiers are often in a minority.

Although prices are high in the swishest establishments, we've found plenty of reasonably priced places, serving generally excellent food. A recent visitor says they are all 'brilliant – never found a bad one'. In the Socrepes area, the Rifugio Col Taron is highly recommended and the Rifugio Pomedes is endorsed by a 2006 visitor. The Piè de Tofana and El Faral are also good. El Soréi opened recently above Lacedèl. In the same area, the Son dei Prade at top of the Olympia lift is new this year.

At Cristallo the Rio Gere at the base of the quad chair is worth a visit, according to a 2006 reporter.

The restaurants at Cinque Torri – the Scoiattoli ('magnificent home-made pastas') and the Rifugio Averau ('marvellous pasta and great wine') – offer fantastic views. The Rifugio Fedare, over the back of Cinque Torri, is also recommended – 'great pasta with hare sauce'. Rifugio Lagazuoi, a short hike up from the top of the Passo Falzarego cable-car, also has great views.

Cortina d'Ampezzo

437

GETTING THERE

Air Venice 160km/
100 miles (2hr).
Treviso 132km/
82 miles (1³/₄hr).
Saturday and Sunday
transfers available for
hotel guests; advance
booking required.
35-minute heli-
transfers from Venice
also available.

Rail Calalzo (35km/
22 miles) or Dobbiaco
(32km/20 miles);
frequent buses from
station.

ACTIVITIES

Indoor Swimming
pool, saunas, health
spa, fitness centre,
ice stadium,
museums, art gallery,
cinema, indoor tennis
court, library

Outdoor Rides on
Olympic bob run,
snowrafting down
Olympic ski jump,
crazy sledging, snow-
shoe tours, sleigh
rides, 6km/4 miles of
walking paths,
tobogganing

OUR WEBSITE

Go to our website at
wtss.co.uk for resort
news, links to resort
sites, a build-your-
own resort shortlist
system and reader
forums.

Phone numbers
From abroad use the
prefix +39 (and do
not omit the initial '0'
of the phone
number).

TOURIST OFFICE

t 0436 866252
cortina@dolomiti.org
www.cortina.dolomiti.
org

SCHOOLS AND GUIDES
Mixed reports
Of the four ski schools, we've had
mixed reports of the Cortina school
over the years – though we lack recent
reports. The Gruppo Guide Alpine
offers off-piste and touring.

FACILITIES FOR CHILDREN
Better than average
By Italian standards childcare facilities
are outstanding, with all-day care
arrangements for children of practically
any age. However, given the small
number of British visitors, you can't
count on good spoken English. And
the fragmented area can make
travelling around with children difficult.
A recent reporter commented how well
the lift staff and instructors look after
children.

STAYING THERE

HOW TO GO
Now with more packages
Hotels dominate the market but there
are some catered chalets.
Hotels There's a big choice, from 5-star
luxury to 1-star and 2-star pensions.
(((((5) **Miramonti** (0436 4201)
Spectacularly grand hotel, 2km/1 mile
south of town. Pool.
(((((5) **Cristallo** (0436 881111) A hike
from the lifts and town centre, but
there's a shuttle bus. Has a wellness
centre.
((((4) **Poste** (0436 4271) Reliable 4-star,
at the heart of the town. Large rooms,
some with spa baths. 'We felt very well
looked after,' says a 2006 visitor.
((((4) **Ancora** (0436 3261) Elegant public
rooms. On the traffic-free Corso Italia.
((((4) **Victoria Parc**(0436 3246) Rustic,
family-run 4-star with small rooms but
good food, at the Faloria end of town.
Recommended by a 2006 reporter.
((((4) **Corona** (0436 3251) Family run
4-star, very friendly with good food and
lots of original art. Near Tofana lift.
((((4) **Park Faloria** (0436 2959) Near ski
jump, splendid pool, good food.
(((3) **Olimpia** (0436 3256) Comfortable
B&B hotel in centre, near Faloria lift.
(((3) **Menardi** (0436 2400) Welcoming
roadside inn, a long walk from centre
and lifts.
(((3) **Villa Resy** (0436 3303) Small and
welcoming, just outside centre, with
British owner.
(((3) **Des Alpes** (0436 862021) On the
edge of town. 'Excellent food and
service and friendly staff.'

(((2) **Montana** (0436 862126) 'Excellent
B&B. Amazing value and central
location,' says a reporter.
Self-catering There are some chalets
and apartments – usually out of town –
available for independent travellers.

EATING OUT
Huge choice
There's an enormous selection of
restaurants, both in town and a little
way out, doing mainly Italian food. The
very smart and expensive Toulà is in a
beautiful old barn, just on the edge of
town. Many of the best restaurants are
further out: the Michelin-starred Tivoli,
the Meloncino, the Leone e Anna, the
Rio Gere and the Baita Fraina.
Reasonably priced central restaurants
include the Cinque Torri, the Croda
(recommended by a 2006 reporter) and
the Passetto for pizza and pasta. The
Tavernetta and the Zanvor are the
latest additions to the dining scene.

APRES-SKI
Lively in high season
Cortina is a lively social whirl in high
season, with lots of well-heeled
Italians staying up very late.
   The Lovat is one of several high-
calorie tea-time spots. There are many
good wine bars: Enoteca has 700
wines and good cheese and meats;
Osteria has good wines and local ham;
and Villa Sandi and Dok-Dall'
Ava/L.P26 have been recommended. A
2006 reporter enjoyed drinks at the
Poste ('delicious Prosecco and
mandarin juice'). The liveliest bar is the
Clipper, with a bob-sleigh by the door.
Discos liven up after 11pm.

OFF THE SLOPES
A classic resort
Cortina attracts lots of people who
don't use the slopes. The town is
attractive and the shopping 'fabulous';
as well as high fashion 'you can get
anything and everything at the Co-
operative di Cortina'. Mountain
restaurants are accessible by road (a
car is handy). And there's plenty more
to do, such as swimming and skating.
There is an observatory at Col Drusciè
that has star-gazing tours. You can
have a run (with driver!) down the
Olympic bob-sleigh run and try
Adrenalin Park. There's horse jumping
and polo on the snow occasionally.
Excursions to Venice are easy. You can
visit World War 1 tunnels at Lagazuoi
or the memorial at Pocol.

Courmayeur

Stunning scenery and seductive, charming village, on the opposite side of the valley from its small area of slopes

NEWS

For 2006/07 a new eight-person gondola is due to open between Dolonne and Plan Checrouit. This will be another way into the slopes and make the piste back to Dolonne much more attractive to use during the day. The old Pra Neyron chair at the top of the gondola is due to be replaced by a six-pack.

The annual Swiss International Ski Championships, in association with Momentum Ski, are held here. This season's dates are 15 to 18 March 2007.

➕ Charming old village, with car-free centre and stylish shops and bars

➕ Stunning views of Mont Blanc massif

➕ Day trips to Chamonix (including doing the Vallée Blanche run) possible

➕ Heli-skiing available

➕ Comprehensive snowmaking

➕ Some good mountain restaurants

➖ Relatively small area, with mainly short runs; high-mileage piste-bashers should stay away

➖ Lack of nursery slopes and easy runs for beginners to progress to

➖ No tough pistes

➖ Slopes very crowded on Sundays

➖ Tiresome walk and cable-car journey between village and slopes

Courmayeur is a great place for a weekend away (or a day trip to escape bad weather in Chamonix), and we always look forward to a quick visit here. (That the village bars are among the most civilised in the skiing world is a factor, we admit.) Whether it makes sense for a week's holiday is another matter. Its pistes are best suited to competent intermediates, who are likely to have an appetite for mileage that Courmayeur will arouse but not satisfy. Off-piste, there is more to do; experts who hire a guide (and the odd helicopter) can have a fine time. And with a car you can explore several other worthwhile resorts nearby.

THE RESORT

Courmayeur is a traditional old Italian mountaineering village that, despite the nearby Mont Blanc tunnel road and modern hotels, has retained much of its old-world feel.

The village has a charming traffic-free centre of attractive shops, cobbled streets and well-preserved buildings. An Alpine museum and a statue of a long-dead mountain rescue hero add to the historical feel.

The centre has a great atmosphere, focused around the Via Roma. As the lifts close, people pile into the many bars, some of which are very civilised. Others wander in and out of the many small shops, which include a salami specialist and a good bookshop. At weekends people-watching is part of the evening scene, when the fur coats of the Milanese and Torinese take over.

The village is quite large, and its huge cable-car to Plan Checrouit is on the southern edge. There is no bus alternative to walking or driving to the lift, so having accommodation close to it is handy. Some hotels are a long walk away. Parking at the cable-car is very limited, but drivers can go to Entrèves, up the valley, where there is a large car park at the cable-car. For 2006/07 you will also be able to drive or catch a bus to a new gondola up

from Dolonne. You can leave skis, boards and boots in lockers up the mountain – highly recommended by several reporters.

Buses, infrequent but timetabled, go to La Palud, just beyond Entrèves, for the Punta Helbronner-Vallée Blanche cable-car. Taxis are easily arranged for evenings out.

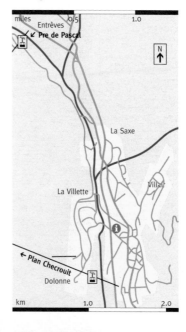

KEY FACTS

Resort	1225m
	4,020ft
Slopes	1210-2755m
	3,970-9,040ft
Lifts	16
Pistes	100km
	62 miles
Blue	26%
Red	57%
Black	17%
Snowmaking	20km
	12 miles

ITALY

440

LIFT PASSES

Courmayeur Mont Blanc

Prices in €

Age	1-day	6-day
6-7		46
8-11		139
12 to 64	37	186
over 65		139

Free under 6

Beginner two free nursery lifts

Notes
Covers all lifts in Val Veny and Checrouit, and the lifts on Mont Blanc up to Punta Helbronner. Single ascent on some lifts and half-day pass available. Passes for four days plus allow for at least one day in the Aosta valley, Flaine and Chamonix.

THE MOUNTAINS

The pistes suit intermediates, but are surprisingly limited for such a well-known, large resort. They are varied in character, if not gradient. Piste marking could be improved.

La Thuile and Pila are an easy drive or bus ride to the south, and Cervinia is reachable.

THE SLOPES
Small but interestingly varied
There are two distinct sections, both almost entirely intermediate. The east-facing **Checrouit** area, accessed by the Checrouit gondola, catches morning sun, and has open, above-the-tree-line pistes. The 25-person, infrequently running Youla cable-car goes to the top of Courmayeur's pistes. There is a further tiny cable-car to Cresta d'Arp. This serves only long off-piste runs but it is no longer compulsory to have a guide with you to go up it.

Most people follow the sun over to the north-west-facing slopes towards **Val Veny** in the afternoon. These are interesting, varied and tree lined, with great views of Mont Blanc and its

glaciers. Connections between the Checrouit and Val Veny areas are complex, with many alternative routes. The Val Veny slopes are also accessible by cable-car from Entrèves, a few miles outside Courmayeur.

A little way beyond Entrèves is La Palud, where a cable-car goes up in three stages to Punta Helbronner, at the shoulder of **Mont Blanc**. There are no pistes from the top, but you can do the famous Vallée Blanche run to Chamonix from here without the horrific ridge walk that forms the start on the Chamonix side. There are buses back from Chamonix through the Mont Blanc tunnel. Or you can tackle the tougher off-piste runs on the Italian side of Mont Blanc. None of these glacier runs should be done without a guide.

TERRAIN-PARKS
Just a boarder-cross
Like a lot of Italian resorts, Courmayeur has no terrain-park or half-pipe. However, there's now a 500m/1,640ft boarder-cross run – created a few years ago – near the top of the Plan de la Gabba high-speed chair.

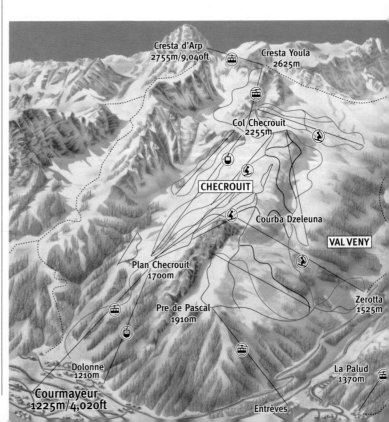

a deserted valley to Dolonne or Pré St Didier; or south through the Youla gorge to La Thuile.

On Mont Blanc, the Vallée Blanche is not a challenge (though there are more difficult variations), but the Toula glacier route on the Italian side from Punta Helbronner to Pavillon most certainly is, often to the point of being dangerous. There are also heli-drops available, including a wonderful 20km/12 mile run from the Ruitor glacier down into France – you ride the lifts back up from La Rosière and descend to La Thuile (a taxi-ride from Courmayeur). And you can do a day trip to Chamonix through the Mont Blanc tunnel.

FOR INTERMEDIATES
Ideal gradient but limited extent
The whole area is suitable for most intermediates, but it is small. The avid piste-basher will ski it in a day. It also lacks long, easy runs to suit the more timid.

The open Checrouit section is pretty much go-anywhere territory, but it is basically a red slope. The red run to the bottom of Dolonne run will be more accessible from 2006/07 now that you'll be able to catch the new gondola back. Timid skiers should head up the Pra Neyron chair (due to be replaced by a new six-pack this season) for access to the area's few blues. The Val Veny side of the mountain is basically steeper, with manageable blacks going close to the fall line and good reds and the occasional blue taking less direct routes. These runs link in with the pretty, wooded slopes heading down to Zerotta. The fast Zerotta chair dominates Val Veny, serving runs of varying difficulty over a decent vertical of 560m/1,800ft – including a long blue.

The Vallée Blanche, although off-piste, is easy enough for adventurous, fit intermediates to try. So is the local heli-skiing (from £90 a drop including a guide); you are picked up on the piste so there's no wasted time.

SNOW RELIABILITY
Good for most of the season
Courmayeur's slopes are not high – mostly between 1700m and 2250m (5,600ft and 7,400ft). Those above Val Veny face north or north-west, so keep their snow well, but the Plan Checrouit side is rather too sunny for comfort in late season. There is snowmaking on most main runs, so good coverage in early- and mid-season is virtually assured – we were there in a January snow drought and enjoyed decent skiing entirely on man-made snow.

FOR EXPERTS
Off-piste is the only challenge
Courmayeur has few challenging pistes. The black runs on the Val Veny side are not severe, and few moguls form elsewhere. But if you're lucky enough to find fresh powder – as we have been several times – you can have fantastic fun among the trees.

Classic off-piste runs go from Cresta d'Arp, at the top of the lift network, in three directions – a clockwise loop via Arp Vieille to Val Veny, with close-up views of the Miage glacier; east down

Courmayeur

441

boArding

Courmayeur's pistes suit intermediates, and most areas are easily accessible by novices as the main lifts are cable-cars, chairs and gondolas. But it's all a bit steep for absolute beginners. And beware of some flat sections in the Val Veny sector. The biggest draws for the more experienced are the off-piste routes. And there is a boarder-cross run.

↑ The Internazionale is the main red run from Col Checrouit to the Zerotta area; it can be much more crowded than this

SCHOOLS
Monte Bianco
t 0165 842477
Courmayeur
t 0165 848254

Classes
(Monte Bianco prices)
5 days (3hr per day)
€155
Private lessons
€33 to €42 for 1hr
for 1 person; each
additional person €10

GUIDES
Mountain guides
t 0165 842064

FOR BEGINNERS
Consistently too steep
Courmayeur is not well suited to beginners. There are several nursery slopes, none ideal. The area at Plan Checrouit gets crowded, and there are few easy runs for the near-beginner to progress to. The small area served by the short Tzaly drag, just above the Entrèves cable-car top station, is the most suitable beginner terrain, and it tends to have good snow.

FOR CROSS-COUNTRY
Beautiful trails
There are 35km/22 miles of trails scattered around Courmayeur. The best are the four covering 20km/12 miles at Val Ferret, served by bus. Dolonne has a couple of short trails.

QUEUES
Sunday crowds pour in
The Checrouit and Val Veny cable-cars suffer queues on Sundays and peak periods – a 2005 reporter experienced an 'absolutely awful' wait at 8am. There can be queues to go down as well as up. Queues may be alleviated for 2006/07 with the new gondola at Dolonne offering an additional way up and down. The infrequent Youla cable-car may require patience – mainly worth it for those heading off-piste. Overcrowded slopes on Sundays, particularly down to Zerotta, can also be a problem.

MOUNTAIN RESTAURANTS
Lots – some of them very good
The area is lavishly endowed with 27 establishments ranging from rustic little huts to larger self-service places. Most huts do table-service of delicious pizza, pasta and other dishes and it is best to reserve tables in advance. But there are also snack bars selling more basic fare and relying on views and sun to fill their terraces.

Several restaurants are excellent. Chiecco, next to the drag-lift with the same name at Plan Checrouit, serves some of the best food with friendly service – 'charming, knowledgeable, excellent wine list', 'wonderful pasta and amazing meat courses – expensive but worth it'. Maison Vieille, at the top of the chair of the same name, is a welcoming rustic place with superb home-made pastas (though a 2006 reporter was disappointed: 'previously had super meals there but service was haphazard this year; food was OK'). The pick of the Plan Checrouit places is Christiania (book a table downstairs) – 'best custard-filled bombolina ever'.

In Val Veny is another clutch of places worth trying. The jolly Grolla has good food and a sunny terrace with excellent views; the Fodze (just below Grolla) is a nice snack bar with some hot food; the Zerotta, at the foot of the eponymous chair, has a sunny terrace (though one 2006 reporter was disappointed with the food and preferred the nearby Petit Mont Blanc). One of the better snack bars is Courba Dzeleuna, just below the top of Dzeleuna chair, with incredible views and delicious home-made myrtle grappa (beware the alcohol-soaked berries left in the bottom of your glass). A 2005 visitor enjoyed an 'excellent lunch of charcuterie and cheese' there.

SCHOOLS AND GUIDES
Good reports
'We had the best instructor for ages – possibly ever,' said a reporter about the Monte Bianco ski school. There is a thriving guides' association ready to help you explore the area's off-piste; it has produced a helpful booklet showing the main possibilities.

FACILITIES FOR CHILDREN
Good care by Italian standards
Childcare facilities are well ahead of the Italian norm, but Courmayeur is far from an ideal resort for a young family.

MOMENTUM SKI

Weekend &
a la carte ski
holiday specialists

100% Tailor-Made

Premier hotels &
apartments

No. 1 specialists
in Courmayeur

020 7371 9111
www.momentumski.com

CHILDREN

'Fun park Dolonne
9am-4.30

Ski schools
Takes children from
age 5, 9am to 4.30,
(lesson am, play pm)
(5 days incl. lunch
€180)

GETTING THERE

Air Geneva 105km/
65 miles (2hr); Turin
150km/93 miles (2hr).

Rail Pré-St-Didier
(5km/3 miles); regular
buses from station.

ACTIVITIES

Indoor Swimming
pool and sauna at
Pré-St-Didier (5km/
3 miles), Alpine
museum, cinema,
library, art gallery,
sports centre with
climbing wall, ice rink,
curling, fitness centre,
indoor golf, squash,
tennis

Outdoor Walking
paths in Val Ferret,
paragliding, snow-
biking, dog-sledding

Phone numbers
From abroad use the
prefix +39 (and do
not omit the initial '0'
of the phone
number).

TOURIST OFFICE

t 0165 842060
info@aiat-monte-
bianco.com
www.aiat-monte-
bianco.com

STAYING THERE

HOW TO GO
Plenty of hotels
Courmayeur's long-standing popularity
ensures a wide range of packages
(including some excellent weekend
deals), mainly in hotels. Tour op
Momentum is a Courmayeur specialist
and can advise about and fix pretty
much whatever you want here. One or
two UK operators have catered chalets.
Hotels There are nearly 50 hotels,
spanning the star ratings.
((((4) **Grand Hotel Courmaison** (0165
831400) Luxury hotel 2km/1 mile from
town, with 'excellent food'. Pool.
((((4) **Gran Baita** (0165 844040) Luxury
place with antique furnishings,
panoramic views and 'superb food'.
Pool. Shuttle-bus to cable-car.
((((4) **Pavillon** (0165 846120)
Comfortable 4-star near cable-car, with
a pool. Friendly staff.
(((3) **Auberge de la Maison** (0165
869811) Small atmospheric 3-star in
Entrèves owned by the same family as
Maison de Filippo (see Eating Out).
(((3) **Walser** (0165 844824) Near main
road. 3-star. 'Good value hotel with
exemplary service.'
(((3) **Bouton d'Or** (0165 846729) Small,
friendly B&B near main square. 'Very
welcoming, owner ferries you to/from
lifts if you wish,' says a 2006 reporter.
(((3) **Berthod** (0165 842835) Friendly,
family-run hotel near centre.
(((3) **Grange** (0165 869733) Rustic,
stone-and-wood farmhouse in Entrèves.
(((3) **Triolet** (0165 846822) 'Excellent
location near lift. Comfy, well- furnished.'
((2) **Edelweiss** (0165 841590) Friendly,
cosy, good-value; close to the centre.
((2) **Lo Scoiattolo** (0165 846721) Good
rooms, good food, shame it's at the
opposite end of town to the cable-car.
SMART APARTMENTS – SEE FEATURE
The Grand Chalet is newly opened,
central and has spacious apartments
and jacuzzi, steam room and sauna.

EATING OUT
Jolly Italian evenings
There is a great choice, both in
downtown Courmayeur and within taxi
range; there's a handy promotional
booklet describing many of them (in
English as well as Italian). We've been
impressed by the traditional Italian
cuisine of both Pierre Alexis and
Cadran Solaire in Courmayeur. The
Terrazza ('best in town, wonderful local
food and great service' says a 2006

reporter) is a rising star. The Tunnel
pizzeria does a good job. The Mont-
Fréty ('good value', 'its antipasti is a
must'), the Padella ('great pizza,
raclette and fondue') and the Vieux
Pommier ('the place to go for fondue
and raclette') have been recommended
by reporters. Further afield, the touristy
but very jolly Maison de Filippo in
Entrèves is rightly famous for its fixed-
price, 36-dish feast. Also in Entrèves,
the Brenva has a separate steakhouse
serving huge steaks. At La Palud the
restaurant in the hotel Dente del
Gigante is recommended by a local.

APRES-SKI
Stylish bar-hopping
Courmayeur has a lively evening scene
– at weekends, at least – centred on
stylish bars with comfy sofas or
armchairs to collapse in, often serving
free canapés in the early evening. Our
favourites are the Roma ('Expensive,
but free nibbles,' says a 2006
reporter), the back room of the Caffè
della Posta and the Bar delle Guide.
The Cadran Solaire is where the big
money from Milan and Turin hangs
out. The Privé is excellent for cocktails.
The American Bar has good music and
a fine selection of wines. Poppy's is
recommended for drinks and pizza.
Maquis is the better of the two night
clubs in Entrèves.

OFF THE SLOPES
Lots on for non-slope users
If you're not interested in hitting the
snow you'll find the village pleasant –
parading up and down is a favourite
pastime for the many non-slope users
the resort attracts (especially at
weekends). You can go by cable-car up
to Punta Helbronner, by bus to Aosta,
or up the main cable-car to Plan
Checrouit to meet friends for lunch.
The huge sports centre is good (indoor
tennis and golf, climbing wall, skating,
curling, squash, gym, sauna, steam,
but no pool).

STAYING UP THE MOUNTAIN
Why would you want to?
Visiting Courmayeur and not staying in
the charming village seems perverse –
if you're that keen to get on the slopes
in the morning, this is probably the
wrong resort. But at Plan Checrouit,
the 1-star Christiania (0165 843572 –
see 'Mountain restaurants') has simple
rooms; the 3-star Baita (0165 846722)
is smarter; book way in advance.

Livigno

Lowish prices and highish altitude – a tempting combination, especially when you add in a quite pleasant Alpine ambience

RATINGS

The slopes

Fast lifts	***
Snow	****
Extent	**
Experts	**
Intermediates	***
Beginners	****
Convenience	**
Queues	****
Mountain restaurants	***

The rest

Scenery	***
Resort charm	***
Off-slope	**

NEWS

For 2005/06 a new restaurant and a couple of shops opened in the village.

KEY FACTS

Resort	1815m
	5,950ft
Slopes	1815-2800m
	5,950-9,190ft
Lifts	33
Pistes	110km
	68 miles
Blue	25%
Red	58%
Black	17%
Snowmaking	70km
	43 miles

- ✚ High altitude plus snowmaking means reliable snow
- ✚ Large choice of beginners' slopes
- ✚ Impressive modern lift system
- ✚ Cheap by the standards of high resorts, with the bonus of duty-free shopping (eg for new equipment)
- ✚ Cosmopolitan, friendly and quite smart village with some Alpine atmosphere
- ✚ Long, snow-sure cross-country trails

- ▬ No challenging pistes
- ▬ Long and gruelling transfers – 5hr from Bergamo, less from Innsbruck
- ▬ Slopes split into two quite widely separated areas
- ▬ Village is very long and straggling
- ▬ Few off-slope amenities
- ▬ Bleak setting, susceptible to wind
- ▬ Not many really comfortable hotels bookable through UK tour operators
- ▬ Nightlife can disappoint

Livigno offers the unusual combination of a fair-sized mountain, high altitude and fairly low prices. Despite its vaunted duty-free status, hotels, bars and restaurants are not much cheaper than in other Italian resorts, but shopping is – there are countless camera and clothes shops. As a relatively snow-sure alternative to the Pyrenees or to the smallest, cheapest resorts in Austria, Livigno seems attractive. But don't overlook the long list of drawbacks.

THE RESORT

Livigno is an amalgam of three villages in a wide, remote valley near the Swiss border – basically a string of hotels, bars, specialist shops and supermarkets lining a single long street. The buildings are small in scale and mainly traditional in style, giving the village a pleasant atmosphere. The original hamlet of San Antonio is the nearest thing Livigno has to a centre,

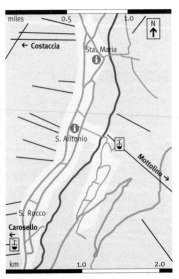

and the best all-round location. Here, the main street and those at right angles, linking it to the busy bypass road, are nominally traffic-free, but actually are not at all. The road that skirts the centre is constantly busy, and becomes intrusive in the hamlets of Santa Maria, 1km/0.5 miles to the north, and San Rocco, a bit further away to the south (and uphill).

Lifts along the length of the village access the western slopes of the valley. The main lift to the eastern slopes is directly across the flat valley floor from the centre.

The bus services, on three colour-coded routes, are free and fairly frequent, but can get overcrowded at peak times and stop early in the evening. A recent reporter found them confusing: 'there is no way to tell which way around they will go'. Taxis (including minibus taxis for groups) are an affordable alternative, but a 2006 reporter found them unreliable.

The lift pass covers Bormio and Santa Caterina, an easy drive or free bus-ride if the high pass is open, and a six-day pass entitles you to a discount on a day in St Moritz – a 'fantastic' day out, says a reader.

The airport transfer from Bergamo is long. The one from Innsbruck may be shorter, but reportedly causes travel sickness on a massive scale.

Livigno

Prices in €

Age	1-day	6-day
under 13	27	113
13 to 59	33	163
over 60	27	113

Free under 8

Beginner points card

Notes
Half-day passes and reduced Saturday passes available. Family reductions.

Alternative passes
Natur.card 6-day pass includes night-skiing and a day in St Moritz.

boarding

Livigno offers a refreshing sense of space. There really is something for everyone here, from big, wide, open and rolling motorways to natural gullies, hits, tree runs and powder. The back of Mottolino is a perfect example. As the resort stretches across such a long expanse, there is plenty of fun to be had between pistes as well as on them. Lower down there are some great tight tree runs sheltered from the wind. For three years Livigno was home to the Burton European Open, the biggest snowboard contest this side of the Atlantic, and this has left its mark on the terrain-park infrastructure, which continues to grow and is well maintained. Beginners be warned: practically all the smaller lower slopes are serviced by drags.

THE MOUNTAINS

The mainly open slopes, on either side of the valley, are more extensive than in many other budget destinations.

THE SLOPES
Improved links
There are three sectors, all of them suitable for moderate and leisurely intermediates.

A two-seat chair from the nursery slopes at the north end of the village take you up to **Costaccia**, where a long fast quad chair-lift goes along the ridge towards the **Carosello** sector. The blue linking run back from Carosello to the top of Costaccia is flat in places and may involve energetic poling if the snow conditions and the wind are against you. Carosello is more usually accessed by the optimistically named Carosello 3000 gondola at San Rocco, which goes up, in two stages, to 2750m/9,020ft. Most runs return

towards the village, but there are a couple on the back of the mountain, on the west-facing slopes of Val Federia, served by a six-pack.

The ridge of **Mottolino** is reached by an efficient gondola from Teola, a tiresome walk or a short bus-ride across the valley from San Antonio. From the top, you can descend to fast quads on either side of the ridge or, if you must, take a slow antique chair up the ridge to Monte della Neve. There is the alternative of a fast quad starting a little way up the Bormio road, and linking with a six-pack above.

There is a low-level link from the nursery drags at the bottom of Carosello to those below Costaccia, but a boarding reporter found it hard work and resorted to walking on the road.

Signposting is patchy and the piste map isn't helpful – runs are not named or numbered on it.

Night skiing is available on Thursdays.

Livigno

445

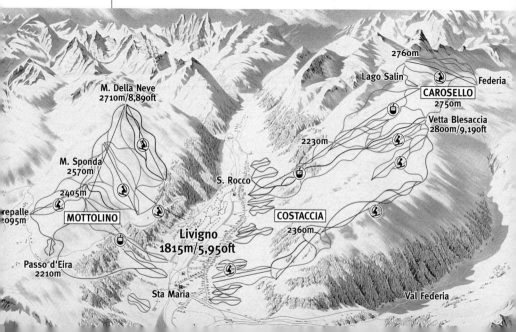

SCHOOLS

Livigno Inverno/Estate
t 0342 996276
Azzurra Livigno
t 0342 997683
Livigno Italy
t 0342 996739
Livigno Soc Coop
t 0342 970300
Madness Snowboard
t 0342 99779
Top Club Mottolino
t 0342 970822

Classes
(Livigno Inverno/
Estate prices)
6 days (2hr per day)
€85
Private lessons
€35 for 1hr; each
additional person €6

CHILDREN

Alì Babà
t 0342 978050
Ages 3 and over
Miniclub Top Club Mottolino
t 0342 970822
M'eating Point
t 0342 997822
Spazio Gioco Peribimbi
t 0342 970711
Ages 18mnth to 3yr;
8.30-1pm

GETTING THERE

Air Bergamo
200km/124 miles
(5hr).

Rail Tirano (48km/
30 miles), Zernez
(Switzerland, 28km/
17 miles); regular
buses from station,
weekends only.

TERRAIN-PARKS
Serious facilities
Just behind the Mottolino lies a large freestyle area divided into two sections. The main Mottolino park (www.livignopark.com) is a big park designed for advanced riders, used for the Burton European Open. It has a line of very big and intermediate kickers and a hip. This is bordered by a big super-pipe, often used for contests. There are advanced rails that are placed in and around the jumps as well. Beyond the half-pipe lies the smaller Snow-park Medio with nice lines of small to intermediate kickers, good entry-level rails of varying difficulty and a small boarder-cross.

SNOW RELIABILITY
Very good, despite no glacier
Livigno's slopes are high (you can spend most of your time around 2500m/8,200ft), and with snow-guns on the lower slopes of Mottolino and Costaccia, the season is long.

FOR EXPERTS
Not recommended
The piste map shows a few black runs, but these are not particularly steep. Even the all-black terrain served by the six-pack on Monte della Neve is really no more than stiff red in gradient. There is off-piste to be done.

FOR INTERMEDIATES
Flattering slopes
Good intermediates will be able to tackle all the blacks without worry. The woodland black run from Carosello past Tea da Borch is narrow in places and can get mogulled and icy at the end of the day. The red runs at Federia are now reportedly well groomed. Moderate intermediates have virtually the whole area at their disposal. The long run beneath the Mottolino gondola is one of the best – and there is also a long, under-used blue going less directly to the valley. Leisurely types have several long cruises available. The run beneath the fast chair at the top of Costaccia is a splendid slope for building confidence.

FOR BEGINNERS
Excellent but scattered slopes
A vast array of nursery slopes along the sunny lower flanks of Costaccia, and other slopes around the valley, make Livigno excellent for novices – although some of the slopes at the northern end are steep enough to cause difficulties. There are lots of longer runs to progress to.

CROSS-COUNTRY
Good snow, bleak setting
Long snow-sure trails (40km/25 miles in total) follow the valley floor, making Livigno a good choice, provided you don't mind the bleak scenery. There is a specialist school, and the resort organises major races.

QUEUES
Few problems these days
Despite reports of queues for the Costaccia chair at midday and short delays for the Carosello gondola in peak season, lift queues are not generally a problem. A bigger problem is that winds often close the upper lifts, causing crowds lower down.

MOUNTAIN RESTAURANTS
More than adequate
On Mottolino, the refuge at the top of the gondola is impressive, with smart self- and table-service sections, a solarium and a nursery, but 'immense' lunch-time queues. The rustic restaurants at Passo d'Eira and Trepalle are a good option for a quiet stop – the Trela is recommended for pizza. And there are some more charming places lower down. The welcoming Tea is at the base of the same sector. Costaccia's Berghütte is pleasantly rustic and sunny, with good food and a great atmosphere. The self-service place at the top of Carosello is acceptable and Tea da Borch, in the trees lower down, serves great food in a Tirolean-style atmosphere, though the run down can be tricky.

SCHOOLS AND GUIDES
Watch out for short classes
There are several schools. English is widely spoken, and reports are complimentary ('good instructors with excellent English'). Classes are short at only two hours, but are rated as great value for money. Private snowboard lessons were also praised in 2006. One complaint was that beginners spend too long on the nursery slopes.

FACILITIES FOR CHILDREN
Not bad for Italy
The schools run children's classes. The Livigno Inverno-Estate school's Alì-Babà nursery offers all-day care and the staff speak English.

↑ It's a long, long
village – seen here
from Carosello, with
the Mottolino lift base
across the valley
APT LIVIGNO

Phone numbers
From abroad use the
prefix +39 (and do
not omit the initial '0'
of the phone
number).

STAYING THERE

HOW TO GO
Lots of hotels, some apartments
Livigno has an enormous range of
hotels and a number of apartments.
There are some attractively priced
catered chalets from UK operators.
Hotels Most of the hotels are small 2-
and 3-star places, with a couple of 4-
stars out of the centre.
(((3) **Intermonti** (0342 972100) Modern
4-star with pool and other mod cons;
on the Mottolino side of the valley.
((2) **Bivio** (0342 996137) The only hotel
in central Livigno with a pool.
((2) **Steinbock** (0342 970520) Nice little
place, far from major lifts.
((2) **Loredana** (0342 996330) Modern
chalet on the Mottolino side. 'Pleasant
food, good rooms.'
((2) **Larice** (0342 996184) Stylish little 3-
star B&B well placed for Costaccia lifts.
((2) **Montanina** (0342 996060) Good
central 3-star.
((2) **Alpi** (0342 996408) In San Rocco,
not far from Carosello gondola.
'Absolutely the best; exquisite food.'
((2) **Camana Veglia** (0342 996310)
Charming old wooden chalet. Popular
restaurant, well placed in Santa Maria.
((2) **Silvestri** (0342 996255) 2-star in
the San Rocco area. 'Great staff,
comfortable rooms, filling meals.'
Self-catering All the big tour operators
that come here offer apartments.

EATING OUT
Improving, still value for money
Livigno has lots of traditional,
unpretentious restaurants, many hotel-
based. Hotel Concordia has some of
the best cooking in town and the
Helvetia also has 'good value and
good quality food.' The Baita and
Astoria are recommended for 'good
food and service'. Mario's wide-ranging

menu includes seafood, fondue and
steaks. Bait dal Ghet and Bivio are
popular with locals, and the Rusticana
does wholesome, cheap food. Pesce
d'Oro is good for seafood and Italian
cuisine. The Bellavista, Mirage, Grolla
and the Garden are also recommended.
Paprika is new place in the centre. A
2006 reporter ate three times at Echo,
– 'good and reasonably priced'.

APRES-SKI
Lively, but disappoints some
The scene in Livigno is quieter than
some people expect in a duty-free
resort. Pas de la Casa it is not – to the
relief of most reporters. Also, the best
places are scattered about, so the
village lacks evening buzz. At tea time
Tea del Vidal, at the bottom of
Mottolino, gets lively, as does the
Stalet bar at the base of the Carosello
gondola. The Caffè della Posta
umbrella bar, near the centre, is also
popular. Europe's highest brewery is in
production at Echo. Nightlife gets
going only after 10pm. Galli's pub, in
San Antonio, is 'a full-on party pub',
popular with Brits. The Kuhstall under
the Bivio hotel is an excellent cellar
bar with live music, as is the Helvetia,
over the road. The San Rocco end is
quietest, but Daphne's ('good fun') and
Marco's are popular. The stylish Art
Cafe is also recommended. Kokodi is
the main disco.

OFF THE SLOPES
Look lively, or go shopping
Livigno offers a small range of outdoor
alternatives to skiing and boarding –
horse-riding among them. And a 2006
visitor 'thoroughly enjoyed' the dog-
sledding. Walks are uninspiring and
there is no sports centre or public pool
(but the pool and spa in the hotel
Helvetia are accessible). The duty-free
shopping may make up for this. Trips
to Bormio and St Moritz are popular.

Livigno

447

Madonna di Campiglio

Chic, very Italian but rather spread-out resort with mainly easy intermediate local slopes amid stunning scenery

COSTS

① ② ③ ④ ⑤ ⑥

RATINGS

The slopes

Fast lifts	★★★★
Snow	★★★
Extent	★★★
Expert	★★
Intermediate	★★★★
Beginner	★★★★
Convenience	★★★
Queues	★★★★
Mountain restaurants	★★★

The rest

Scenery	★★★★
Resort charm	★★★
Off-slope	★★★

NEWS

There are plans to link Campiglio's Cinque Laghi slopes to those of Pinzolo, but they will not be in place for 2006/07.

For 2005/06 a high-speed quad replaced a drag-lift in the Pradalago sector.

ITALIA

448

italian ski specialists

it's
italiansafaris.com

+39 347 348 5757
info@italiansafaris.com

- ➕ Pleasant, friendly town in a pretty valley with splendid views at altitude
- ➕ Generally easy slopes, best for beginners and early intermediates

- ➖ Spread-out village and infrequent shuttle-bus service
- ➖ Quiet après-ski

Like Cortina, Campiglio is a pleasant Dolomite town with an affluent, almost exclusively Italian, clientele – though the scenery isn't in quite the same league. Folgarida and Marilleva (to which Campiglio's slopes are linked) and Pinzolo (which will be linked soon) are quite different and well worth exploring by adventurous intermediates and better. They are covered in our chapter on Trentino.

THE RESORT

Madonna is a long-established, traditional-style but largely modern town, set in a prettily wooded valley beneath the impressive Brenta Dolomites, with slopes in three linked sectors. The town spreads out along the approach roads but the centre is fairly compact: the cable-car to Cinque Laghi (to the west) and the gondola to Pradalago (to the north) bracket most of the central hotels, and are about a five-minute walk apart. Five minutes outside the centre is a gondola to Monte Spinale, leading to the Grostè sector; there is another gondola to Grostè starting a short bus-ride outside the town. Beyond this lift station are the main nursery slopes at Campo Carlo Magno. The town spreads south from the centre, past a frozen lake.

Madonna attracts an affluent Italian clientele; it has lots of smart shops. The village is busy all day, and promenading is an early evening ritual.

The free ski-bus is not frequent but some hotels run minibuses.

KEY FACTS

Resort	1520m
	4,990ft

Madonna, Folgarida,
and Marilleva
combined area

Slopes	1520-2505m
	4,990-8,220ft
Lifts	44
Pistes	120km
	75 miles
Blue	35%
Red	50%
Black	15%
Snowmaking	77km

BEWARE THE BEGINNER DRAGS

A couple of 2006
reporters point out
that the beginner
drag-lifts at Campo
Carlo Magno are
separately owned to
the main lifts and not
covered by the resort
pass. Rides cost
€1.50 each.

OUR WEBSITE

Go to our website at
wtss.co.uk for resort
news, links to resort
sites, a build-your-
own resort shortlist
system and reader
forums.

Phone numbers
From abroad use the
prefix +39 (and do
not omit the initial '0'
of the phone
number).

TOURIST OFFICE

t 0465 447501
info@campiglio.to
www.campiglio.to

THE MOUNTAINS

The Pradalago sector is linked by lift
and piste to Monte Vigo, and so to the
slopes of Folgarida and Marilleva – see
the Trentino chapter for more on these.
Slopes The terrain is mainly easy
intermediate, both above and below
the tree line. Reporters this year were
very impressed with the 'immaculate'
grooming and piste marking.
Terrain-parks The Ursus park, at
Grostè, includes boarder-cross, half-
and quarter-pipes and big air jumps.
Snow reliability Although many of the
runs are sunny, they are at a fair
altitude, and there has been hefty
investment in snowmaking. As a result,
snow reliability is reasonable.
Experts Experts should plan on
heading off-piste. The trees under the
Genziana chair are 'a good spot for
untracked snow'. But the 3-Tre race
course and Canalone on Cinque Laghi
and the Spinale Direttissima are steep.
For other steep runs head to Marilleva.
Intermediates Grostè and Pradalago
have long, easy runs, and early or
timid intermediates will love them.
Cinque Laghi, Madonna's racing
mountain, is a bit tougher, as are the
runs at Folgarida, Marilleva and
Pinzola, which adventurous
intermediates should explore (see
Trentino chapter).
Beginners The nursery slopes at
Campo Carlo Magno are excellent, but
do involve a bus-ride. The drag-lift
here is not covered by the main lift
pass and you have to buy a separate
day ticket when you get there.
Progression to longer runs is easy.
Snowboarding The resort is popular
with boarders and some major events
have been held here.
Cross-country There are 30km/19 miles
of pretty trails through the woods.
Queues Recent reporters have not
found queuing a worry, but there are

one or two bottlenecks. The Cinque
Laghi cable-car is tiny; it produces half-
hour queues which can be avoided by
using the two nearby slow chairs.
Mountain restaurants Reporters like
the table-service Cascina Zeledria (in
the trees off blue run 7 on Pradalago).
On our 2006 visit we lunched at
Viviani near the top of Pradalago and
enjoyed good local sausages. The
Malga Montagnoli in the lower part of
Grostè is a charming old (self-service)
refuge and Boch, higher up, has been
recommended, as has Cinque Laghi
('stunning views'). Restaurants are
well-marked on the piste map.
Schools and guides Language can be a
problem. A 2006 visitor found the
Nazionale school 'very good'; he was
the only Brit in his group but managed
OK as he spoke a little Italian.
Facilities for children Very limited.

STAYING THERE

How to go There is a wide choice of
hotels and some self-catering.
Hotels The 4-star Spinale (0465
441116) is convenient. The Savoia
Palace (0465 441004) is also 4-star –
'comfortable and friendly', but the
location can be noisy. The central
Arnica (0465 442227) does only
breakfast but does it very well ('super',
'very friendly owners'). The central
Milano (0465 441210), Bonapace (0465
441 019) and Crozzon (0465 442222),
all 3-stars, have been recommended by
readers, as has the 4-star Lorenzetti
(0465 441404). On our 2006 visit we
enjoyed our stay at the 4-star Zeledria
(0465 441010) at Campo Carlo Magno.
Eating out There are around 20
restaurants. 'All the ones we tried were
good,' says a reporter, and Belvedere,
the Antico Focolare, the Roi and Stube
Diana have all been recommended.
Another reporter enjoyed the 'artistic
dishes' at the pricey Alfiero, and
Locanda degli Artisti is 'worth the
expense for a special night out'. Some
of the mountain huts are also open.
Après-ski Après-ski is quiet. Franz-
Joseph Stube, Bar Suisse and Cantina
del Suisse are recommended. The
Alpes is perhaps the smartest club.
There's also a well-known disco – the
Zangola – which gets going very late.
Off the slopes Window-shopping,
skating on the lake and walking are
popular. There's also paragliding. A
reporter recommends taking the bus
out to Campo Carlo Magno for lunch.

Madonna di Campiglio

449

Monterosa Ski

Europe's best kept secret: three unspoiled villages beneath slopes with easy pistes and uncrowded off-piste for all standards

COSTS

① ② ③ ④ ⑤ ⑥

RATINGS

The slopes
Fast lifts	★★★
Snow	★★★★
Extent	★★★
Expert	★★★★
Intermediate	★★★★
Beginner	★★
Convenience	★★★
Queues	★★★★
Mountain restaurants	★★

The rest
Scenery	★★★★
Resort charm	★★★
Off-slope	★

NEWS

For 2005/06 a new eight-seat gondola above Champoluc replaced the two slow chairs from Crest up to Ostafa and a quad chair replaced the old triple from there to Colle Sarezza. This has speeded up access to the upper slopes considerably. In Alagna, the ancient cable-car to Punta Indren was closed for the 2005/06 season, but we are assured it will re-open for 2006/07, which is due to be its last season. There are plans to replace it with a cable-car from Passo dei Salati, which will be open for the 2007/08 season, it is hoped.

For 2006/07 more snowmaking is planned. And a beginner drag-lift at Gabiet, above Gressoney La Trinité, will be replaced by a triple chair.

➕ Fabulous intermediate and advanced off-piste, including heli-skiing

➕ Slopes usually very quiet weekdays

➕ Panoramic views

➕ Good snow reliability and grooming

➕ Quiet, unspoiled villages

➕ Three-valley lift/piste network gives a sensation of travel, but ...

➖ Virtually no choice of route when touring the three valleys on-piste

➖ Few challenging pistes – mainly easy cruising

➖ High winds can close links

➖ Few off-slope diversions

➖ Limited après-ski

Monterosa Ski's three resorts – Champoluc, Gressoney and Alagna – are popular with Italians weekenders, who drive up from Milan and Turin, but are hardly heard of on the international market. As a result, they retain a friendly, small-scale, unspoiled Italian ambience that we and a growing band of readers like a lot. Strangely, few UK tour operators feature the area. But that suits us, as it makes it more likely the area will retain its unique character.

The three-valley network of lifts and pistes is anything but small-scale: Alagna and Champoluc, at opposite ends, are no less than 17km/11 miles apart – slightly further apart than Courchevel and Val-Thorens. It's around a four-hour trip by road to get from Alagna to Champoluc if you miss the last lift. But a glance at the piste map reveals that the Italian network between the two extremes is skeletal compared with the full-bodied French one. Outside the piste network, however, is a lot of great off-piste terrain, some lift-served, which has long attracted experts.

It was only two seasons ago that Alagna became accessible by piste from the top of the Gressoney lifts. Expert skiers may be inclined to regret the fact that a splendid off-piste run was sacrificed; but that's progress. They have plenty more bowls to play in – and the Olen red piste is a cracker.

THE RESORT

There is one main village in each of the area's three long valleys. Champoluc in the western valley and Gressoney in the central one are both about an hour's drive up from the Aosta valley, to the south. Alagna is even more remote, and approached from the Italian lakes, to the east.

Champoluc is a pleasant but not notably pretty place, strung out along the valley road without much ski resort ambience – the centre, where there are a couple of good hotels, is more or less devoid of bars and inviting shops. The village gondola starts from a kind of micro-resort several minutes' walk up the road. You can store boots and skis/board there overnight. The valley road continues past several new hotels towards Frachey, where there is a chair-lift into the slopes.

Gressoney La Trinité is a quiet, neat little village, with cobbled streets, wooden buildings and an old church. It is about 800m/0.5 miles from the chair-lift into the local slopes, where there are a few convenient hotels. Links with the other valleys revolve around Stafal at the head of the valley, reached by bus (five euros for a pass). There is accommodation here, too. Gressoney St Jean, a bigger village, is 5km/3 miles down the valley and has its own separate slopes.

Alagna is a peaceful, rustic village with a solid church and some lovely old wooden farmhouses built in the distinctive Walser style. It bears no resemblance to a conventional ski resort. We visited on a sunny morning in March, and found the place deserted. The recently built gondola starts from an amazingly central station; it must be losing a fortune.

Trips to Cervinia, La Thuile, Courmayeur and Pila (all covered by the Aosta Valley pass) are possible by car.

KEY FACTS

Resort	1640m
	5,380ft
Slopes	1200-3260m
	3,940-10,700ft
Lifts	37
Pistes	180km
	112 miles
Blue	26%
Red	68%
Black	6%
Snowmaking	70km
	43 miles

OUR WEBSITE

Go to our website at wtss.co.uk for resort news, links to resort sites, a build-your-own resort shortlist system and reader forums.

THE MOUNTAINS

The slopes of Monterosa Ski are relatively extensive, and very scenic. The pistes are almost all intermediate (and well groomed), and the lifts are mainly chairs and gondolas, with few drag-lifts. The terrain is undulating and runs are long, but many lifts serve only one or two pistes.

The piste map is appalling – the worst in the northern hemisphere, and possibly the world. But the signposting on the pistes is clear. Reporters visiting at various times have found the top lifts making the connection between valleys closed by wind, severely limiting the available terrain.

Slopes Champoluc residents now reach Colle Sarezza on two successive gondolas and a quad chair. From the top a steep, narrow, bumpy run (which a lot of timid intermediates find very difficult) is the link with the long cruising runs below Colle Bettaforca. Taking the bus to the Frachey chair avoids the tricky top run.

At Stafal a cable-car followed by a fast chair bring you back towards Champoluc and two successive gondolas opposite take you to Passo dei Salati. From there, runs lead back down to Stafal and to Gressoney La Trinité and Orsia, both served by chair-lifts. Or you can head towards Alagna on the new pistes there.

From Alagna a modern gondola goes to Pianalunga at mid-mountain. From here, a cable-car (able to pause at a mid-station where a blue run

ends) now takes you to Passo dei Salati. The alternative from Pianalunga is a double chair leading to the tiny, ancient cable-car to Punta Indren (closed in 2005/06 but due to re-open for 2006/07). This serves a long ungroomed run ending in the middle of nowhere; an antique 'bucket' lift goes back up to the bottom of the cable-car. There are also lots of off-piste routes from Punta Indren, including routes to the Gressoney valley.

Gressoney St Jean and Antagnod, near Champoluc, have their own small areas of slopes. The St Jean slopes have only one lift but two recent reporters enjoyed half-days there. Antagnod is used by local instructors on bad-weather days and has some good off-piste terrain.

Terrain-parks Gressoney got a boarder-cross last season but there's no park. Big air jumps are sometimes constructed near the top of the gondola from Champoluc.

Snow reliability Generally good, thanks to altitude, extensive snowmaking and good grooming, though 2005/06 was a poor season for natural snow. A January 2006 visitor was impressed by the snowmaking – 'indistinguishable from the real thing' – but disappointed that the links out of the valley were closed because of lack of snow.

Experts The attraction is the off-piste, with great runs from the high points of the lift system in all three valleys and some excellent heli-drops. Among the adventures we've enjoyed here was a heli-drop on Monte Rosa, skiing down

↑ The Monterosa
massif makes a
spectacular backdrop.
The other side is
Switzerland: a
helicopter drops you
off and you ski down
(with a guide)
through amazing
glacier scenery to
Zermatt; you come
back off-piste after
taking lifts up

MONTEROSA TOURIST OFFICE

to Zermatt and returning off-piste from
the top of the Cervinia lifts. But the
closure of the Punta Indren cable-car
last season severely curtailed off-piste
opportunities there. A 2006 visitor
enjoyed the tree runs in Frachey.

Intermediates For those who like to
travel on easy, undemanding pistes,
the area is excellent, with long cruising
runs from the ridges down into the
valleys ('wonderful, carefree carving').
The new red Olen piste down towards
Alagna is a great blast. There isn't
much on-piste challenge for more
demanding intermediates, but those
willing to take a guide and explore
some of the gentler off-piste will have
a good time.

Beginners The high nursery slopes at
mid-mountain above Champoluc,
served by two moving carpets, are
better than the lower ones at
Gressoney. But neither area has ideal
gentle runs to progress to (moving on
to the Del Largo run above Frachey is
the best Champoluc option).

Snowboarding There's a new boarder-
cross at Gressoney and great off-piste
free-riding.

Cross-country There are long trails
around St Jean, and shorter ones up
the valley; Brusson, in the Champoluc

valley, has the best trails in the area.

Queues Few problems, say reporters.
Usually they occur only at weekends.
The worst bottleneck (when it is open)
is the tiny top cable-car on the Alagna
side, where waits of over an hour are
possible and where queues can form
even in mid-week. The double chair to
Belvedere, on the way back from
Frachey/Bettaforca to Champoluc, can
have long queues at the end of the
day. Pistes can get crowded at
weekends, too, but the off-piste is still
delightfully quiet.

Mountain restaurants The mountain
restaurants are generally simple, but
there are plenty of them. The following
have been enjoyed by reporters: the
'lively' Belvedere (one of the few
mountain restaurants in the region to
have a sit-down loo), the Ostafa
('excellent pasta', 'friendly staff') and
the Tana del Lupo above Champoluc;
the Mandria ('excellent and friendly')
and the 'small but charming' Chamois
at Punta Jolanda; the Bedemie and
Morgenrot above Orsia; the Del Ponte
above Gabiet; the Baita just below
Pianalunga; and the Sitten above
Stafal ('excellent specials and stunning
view'). Stadel Soussun above Frachey
is a bit out of the ordinary – 'charming,

Phone numbers
From abroad use the prefix +39 (and do **not** omit the initial '0' of the phone number).

with an excellent limited menu; booking essential'. A diversion to the right at the top of the run to Alagna brings you to the ancient Rifugio Guglielmina.

Schools and guides We have had mixed reports on the Italian ski schools but universally good reports about the Monterosa mountain guides ('Really excellent day,' said a recent reporter) and the ski school run by tour operator Ski 2 ('good, friendly instructors').

Facilities for children There is a special kids' ski school and snow-park at Antagnod near Champoluc and a mini-club at Gressoney St Jean.

STAYING THERE

How to go Surprisingly few tour operators feature the area. We've had good reports of Monterosa specialists Ski 2 ('great from pick-up to drop-off').

Hotels For a small place, Champoluc has a striking range of attractive hotels. Recent reporters liked the central Relais des Glaciers (0125 308721) – a welcoming 4-star with spa and shuttle to the gondola ('food excellent'). The central, creaky old Castor (0125 307117) is 'an absolute

gem' with 'good food and magnificent puddings'; it is managed by a British guy ('great fun') who married into the family that has owned it for generations. The Breithorn (0125 08734), just up the road, is the luxury option, with beautifully furnished public areas, beamed bedrooms and good spa facilities. 'It's a gem,' says one well-travelled reporter – 'superb service'. Food in the elegant dining room or more casual brasserie is excellent. A 2006 visitor recommends the Champoluc (0125 308088) for its 'charming owners, friendly staff, tasty and copious food and spacious rooms'. Out beyond the lift base are several interesting places. The California (0125 307977) is chiefly notable for the pop music themes applied to the rooms and the big saloon bar. The Rocher (0125 308711) is recommended by reporters as friendly and welcoming, with good food, spa and sauna.

At Gressoney La Trinité several reporters recommend the Jolanda Sport (0125 366140), with gym, saunas, pool; it's right by the lift. But one visitor was disappointed by the food – limited choice, especially for vegetarians. Another says of the nearby Residence (0125 366148), 'Friendliest hotel I've ever stayed at in the Alps.' The Dufour (0125 366139) and the Lysjoch (0125 366150) have also been mentioned. In Alagna, try the Monterosa (0163 923209) or Cristallo (0163 922822).

Eating out Both Gressoney and Champoluc have a few stand-alone restaurants (the Bistrot is recommended by a 2006 visitor); most are in hotels. The Walserchild in Gressoney got a good review from a recent reporter.

Après-ski Après-ski is quiet. In Champoluc, the bar of the hotel Castor is cosy and popular with resort workers; the Golosone is a small, atmospheric, authentic Italian wine bar; the Galion opposite the gondola is busy as the lifts close; the West Road pub in the hotel California has karaoke some nights. At weekends, the disco beneath the California gets going. Gressoney is even quieter; 'Schnee Blume bar is the best, but it has nothing to beat,' says a reporter, 'and the tour-op-organised wine tasting at Hirschstube was excellent.'

Off the slopes There is a natural ice rink at Champoluc; otherwise there's little to amuse those who don't head for the slopes.

Passo Tonale

Purpose-built village set on a high pass, with easy, snow-sure slopes and a new link to more challenging wooded terrain

COSTS

① ② ③ ④ ⑤ ⑥

RATINGS

The slopes

Fast lifts	****
Snow	****
Extent	**
Expert	*
Intermediate	***
Beginner	****
Convenience	***
Queues	****
Mountain restaurants	**

The rest

Scenery	***
Resort charm	*
Off-slope	*

TRENTINO

ITALIA

454

NEWS

For 2005/06 Passo Tonale's slopes were linked by a new piste to those of Pontedilegno in Lombardia . And for 2006/07 a new gondola will connect the two resorts. Pontedilegno's slopes were expanded last season by the addition of five new chair-lifts and 20km/12 miles of runs. This new connection makes the area much more attractive for exerienced intermediates and gives some welcome tree-lined runs to retreat to when it's snowing.

OUR WEBSITE

Go to our website at wtss.co.uk for resort news, links to resort sites, a build-your-own resort shortlist system and reader forums.

- ➕ Good value, basic accommodation
- ➕ Sunny, easy, snow-sure slopes
- ➕ Good for beginners and early or timid intermediates
- ➕ New link to Pontedilegno adds attractive, steeper, tree-lined runs

- ➖ Not much for experts or (except at Pontedilegno) adventurous intermediates
- ➖ Local slopes above the tree line and unpleasant in bad weather
- ➖ Purpose-built village lacks charm

Passo Tonale offers that rare combination of a fair-sized, uncrowded, snow-sure ski area and slope-side hotels at a bargain price. The resort lacks charm and pretty buildings but who cares? Reporters are unanimous that it's a great place for beginners. And now that it is linked to the slopes above Pontedilegno in Lombardia it is a more interesting destination for intermediates.

THE RESORT

Passo Tonale sits on a wide, treeless pass; it is in Trentino but right on the border with Lombardia. The village is a compact, functional affair, purpose-built for skiing and devoid of charm, with its hotels, shops, bars and restaurants spread along both sides of the busy through-road.

THE MOUNTAINS

The lift system is impressive, with seven fast chairs in the bigger of its two local areas of slopes. When we skied it in 2006 we rode only two slow lifts all morning – all the rest were high-speed chairs and a gondola.
Slopes Tonale's slopes are spread over two main sectors on opposite sides of the valley. The broad, south-facing area is much the larger, starts right in the village and is entirely novice and intermediate terrain served by a well-laid-out mix of chairs and drags. Runs are short because of the limited vertical. The north-facing Presena area is steeper, narrower and taller. First, there is an eight-seater gondola; above that a double chair-lift; and at the top, two drag-lifts on the Presena glacier going just over the 3000m mark (just short of 10,000ft). Both areas are entirely above the tree line and bad weather can mean white-outs and closures.

From last season, the Tonale slopes were linked to those of Pontedilegno in Lombardia by a blue/red run through the trees (mostly wide and easy but with a short, much steeper, section). Pontedilegno's slopes are generally

steeper and quieter than Passo Tonale's main area, served mainly by chair-lifts, five of them new for 2005/06. Last season, the only way back was by bus, but from 2006/07 there will be a gondola link.
Terrain-parks There's a park with jumps and a half-pipe served by the fast Valena chair at Passo Tonale.
Snow reliability Tonale is high, includes a glacier and has a lot of snowmaking, so is fairly snow-sure. But the main south-facing area gets a lot of sun, and there can be slush or ice in March and April. Pontedilegno's slopes are lower and more dependent on snowmaking. The new slopes there weren't open on our January 2006 visit because snowmaking hadn't been installed there then.
Experts This isn't a resort for experts. The black piste down the gondola on the Presena sector deserves its grading but is not a serious challenge. In the right conditions there are epic off-piste runs from the glacier, including the impressive 16km/10 mile Pisgana run towards Pontedilegno (a vertical of 1650m/5,410ft). Guidance needed.
Intermediates The south-facing slopes offer gentle terrain ideal for cruising; many of these runs are graded red but are really no more than gentle blue gradient. We particularly enjoyed the 4.5 km/3 mile Alpino piste down a deserted valley to the village. The runs at the top of the glacier are short and easy and we couldn't see much difference between the reds and the black marked here. Below that the run beneath the chair is no more than a cat-track but the black beneath the

Cima Presena 3015m/9,89oft

Corno Lacoscuro 3160m/10,36oft

PRESENA

Passo Paradiso 2585m

2120m

1905m/6,250ft

Vermiglio 1260m/4,140ft

Corno d'Aola 1920m/6,300ft

Valbione 1500m Temu

Tonale 1885m/6,18oft

Pontedilegno 1255m/4,120ft

Passo Contrabbandieri 2575m

2180m

2210m

Maga Valbiolo 2245m

2525m

2500m

www.sport2000rent.com

online booking

Phone numbers
From abroad use the prefix +39 (and do **not** omit the initial '0' of the phone number).

TOURIST OFFICE

t 0364 903838
tonale@valdisole.net
www.adamelloski.com

ADAMELLO SKI

The steepest piste in Tonale, under the gondola towards the Presena glacier ↓

gondola will be too much for timid intermediates, who should ride down. The runs at Pontedilegno are much more serious reds and deserve their grading and adventurous intermediates will enjoy the slopes here. You could use the regional pass and visit the Marilleva/Madonna area down the valley (free daily buses).

Beginners It's an excellent resort for novices. The sunny lifts on gentle slopes right by the village are ideal for beginners, and there are good longer progression runs higher up.

Snowboarding The gentle slopes and ability to get around mainly on chair-lifts means the area is good for beginner and intermediate boarders.

Cross-country There are 36km/22 miles with loops at Passo Tonale and in the valley and at altitude at Pontedilegno.

Queues We have no reports of queues.

Mountain restaurants The half-dozen mountain restaurants generally meet with readers' approval. We ate at Faita, with a terrace, small ground floor area and rustic dining room upstairs. Many people return to the resort for lunch.

Schools and guides We've heard of 'pure chaos' at ski school meeting times, with people milling around not knowing where to meet. But we also had two good 2006 reports on the Presena school ('instructor spoke excellent English, was very patient, encouraging and cheerful').

Facilities for children There's a kindergarten at hotel Miramonti for ages two to 12 and the ski school takes children from age four.

STAYING THERE

How to go Several tour operators feature Passo Tonale. You could consider staying in the much more traditional (and larger) village of Pontedilegno (and we suspect tour operators will move in soon).

Hotels There are around 30 hotels, most of them in the 3-star category. Reader recommendations include Adamello (0364 903886) – 'friendly, good service, clean'; Eden (0364 903946) – 'family-run, basic rooms, decent food, hot water inadequate'; Gardenia (0364 903769) – 'modern, clean, inexpensive, food basic'. To our eyes the 4-star Miramonti (0364 900501) looks to be the best (recently renovated with new pool and spa).

Self-catering There are 1400 beds in apartments, a few on the UK market.

Eating out Mainly hotel restaurants.

Après-ski Reader recommendations include the Magic Pub, El Bait and later on Heaven and the Miramonti disco.

Off the slopes If you are not intending to hit the slopes, forget Tonale. But there's snowmobiling, snow-shoeing, dog-sledding, ice skating and the hotel Miramonti pool is open to the public.

Passo Tonale

455

Sauze d'Oulx

'Suzy does it' still, up to a point – a lively village beneath an attractive area of slopes, but with persistent drawbacks

COSTS

① ② ③ ④ ⑤ ⑥

RATINGS

The slopes
Fast lifts	**
Snow	**
Extent	****
Expert	**
Intermediate	****
Beginner	**
Convenience	**
Queues	***
Mountain restaurants	***

The rest
Scenery	***
Resort charm	**
Off-slope	*

NEWS

For 2006/07 a new chair is expected to replace the old double accessing the slopes from the Jouvenceaux sector; we understand it will go directly to Sportinia, making life easier for novices.

For 2005/06 a quad replaced – at long last – the ancient double chair-lift between the village and Clotes.

There were various piste improvements: the lower section on the main run connecting Clotes to the village was widened and made easier for beginners.

Also last season, the Double Black terrain-park was expanded and a park-only pass introduced.

➕ Extensive and uncrowded slopes – great intermediate cruising

➕ Linked into Milky Way network

➕ Mix of open and tree-lined runs is good for all weather conditions

➕ Entertaining nightlife

➕ Some scope for off-piste adventures

➕ One of the cheapest major resorts there is – and more attractive than its reputation suggests

➖ Erratic snow record – and far from comprehensive snowmaking

➖ Still lots of ancient slow lifts

➖ Crowds at weekends

➖ Getting to the French end of the Milky Way takes forever

➖ Very few challenging pistes

➖ Mornings-only classes, and the best nursery slopes are at mid-mountain

➖ Steep walks around the village, and an inadequate shuttle-bus service

Sauze is cheap, cheerful and the closest decent-sized ski area to Turin, which helps to account for its enduring popularity with impecunious Brits flying into Turin and with the city's bourgeoisie looking for weekend homes. If you were a tabloid reader in the 1980s, you couldn't fail to notice that Sauze was dominated by British youth on the binge. But these days things are much more in balance, at weekends at least. It still has lively bars and shops festooned in English signs, but sober Brits like you and us need not stay away. When we visit, we always find ourselves liking it more than we expect to – as do many reporters.

But Sauze still has a problem: investment, lack of. With its acutely unreliable natural snow, it needs the kind of comprehensive snowmaking that the Sella Ronda resorts have. Until it gets it, booking a trip well in advance is going to be a gamble. And its programme of lift upgrading needs serious acceleration.

THE RESORT

Sauze d'Oulx sits on a sloping mountain shelf facing north-west across the Valle di Susa to the mountains bordering France.

Most of the resort is modern and undistinguished, made up of block-like hotels relieved by the occasional chalet, spreading down the steep hillside from the slopes. It rather gives the impression of falling behind the times, with none of the investment in smart, woody hotels and apartments that goes on in more dynamic resorts.

The village has an attractive old core, with narrow, twisting streets and houses roofed with huge stone slabs. There is a central car-free zone, but the rest of the village can be congested morning and evening. The roads have few pavements and can become icy.

Despite the decline in lager sales, the centre is still lively at night; the late bars are usually quite full, and the handful of discos do brisk business – at the weekend, at least. Noise can be a problem in the early hours.

Out of the bustle of the centre, there are secluded apartment blocks in quiet, wooded areas and a number of good restaurants also tucked away.

Most of the hotels are reasonably central, but the lifts are less so: the Clotes chair is at the top of the village, up a short but steep hill, and the Sportinia chair is an irritatingly long walk beyond that. Ski-buses (not covered by the lift pass) are infrequent, inadequate and absent around lunch-time. Getting to other resorts involves public buses with multiple changes in some cases. A car simplifies excursions, eg to French resorts such as Montgenèvre.

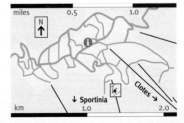

KEY FACTS

Resort	1510m
	4,950ft

Milky Way	
Slopes	1390-2825m
	4,560-9,270ft
Lifts	88
Pistes	400km
	249 miles
Blue	24%
Red	56%
Black	20%
Snowmaking	120km
	75 miles

Sauze d'Oulx-Sestriere-Sansicario	
Slopes	1390-2825m
	4,560-9,270ft
Lifts	51
Pistes	300km
	186 miles
Snowmaking	90km
	56 miles

The slopes of Sansicario aren't always quite this peaceful ↓

THE MOUNTAINS

Sauze's mountains provide excellent intermediate terrain. The piste grading fluctuates from year to year, but it doesn't matter much – many runs graded red or even black should really be graded blue; challenges are few.

THE SLOPES
Big and varied enough for most
Sauze's local slopes are spread across a broad wooded bowl above the resort, ranging from west- to north-facing. The main lifts are chairs, from the top of the village up to **Clotes** and from the western fringes to **Sportinia** – a sunny mid-mountain clearing in the woods, with a ring of restaurants and hotels and a small nursery area.

The high point of the system is **Monte Fraiteve**. From here you can travel west on splendid broad, long runs to **Sansicario** – and on to a two-stage gondola near **Cesana Torinese** that links with **Claviere** and then **Montgenèvre**, in France, the far end of the Milky Way (both are reached more quickly by car).

You normally get to **Sestriere** from the lower point of Col Basset, on the shoulder of M Fraiteve – but snow cover is unreliable and in our experience you normally have to use the gondola to descend the bottom half of the mountain. In bad weather, on the other hand, the gondola is prone to closure ('closed all week', says a 2006 visitor). There is an alternative red run from M Fraiteve itself, but snow is again not reliable on this sunny slope.

As in so many Italian resorts, piste marking, direction signing and piste map design are not taken seriously ('the map is an abysmal marketing vehicle for Coca-Cola').

TERRAIN-PARKS
Jump and grind
The Double Black terrain-park is in the Rio Nero bowl, just below Col Basset. There's no half-pipe, but a selection of jumps, spines and rails provide a choice for freestylers and a new beginner area was opened this year. Its location on the mountain means that it is probably easier to reach from Sestriere, via the gondola, than it is from Sauze. A park-only pass is now available (22 euros) which covers access from both resorts.

Sauze d'Oulx

LIFT PASSES

La Via Lattea

Prices in €

Age	1-day	6-day
under 12	15	81
over 12	31	163

Free under 10 (for pass of 4+ days)
Senior no deals
Beginner no deals
Notes
Covers lifts in Sauze d'Oulx, Sestriere, Sansicario, Cesana and Claviere. 4-hour pass available. 6-day pass allows one day in Montgenèvre.

SNOW RELIABILITY
Can be poor, affecting the links

The area is notorious for erratic snowfalls, suffering droughts with worrying frequency. Another problem is that many of the slopes get a lot of afternoon sun – the links with Sestriere are very vulnerable. Snowmaking has been increased throughout the area but coverage is still far from complete – around the Sportinia nursery slopes it is said to be 'woefully inadequate'. But reporters have been impressed by the efforts to keep runs open in poor conditions ('they worked miracles') and grooming is in general 'superb'.

FOR EXPERTS
Head off-piste

Very few of the pistes are challenging. The best slopes are at virtually opposite ends of Sauze's local area – a short, high, north-facing run from the shoulder of M Fraiteve, and the sunny slopes below M Moncrons. There are plenty of minor off-piste opportunities within the piste network, but the highlights are long, top-to-bottom descents of up to 1300m/ 4,270ft vertical from M Fraiteve, ending (snow permitting) at villages dotted along the valleys. The best known of these runs is the Rio Nero, down to the road near Oulx. When snow low down is poor, some of these runs can be cut short.

FOR INTERMEDIATES
Splendid cruising terrain

The whole area is ideal for confident intermediates who want to clock up the kilometres. For the less confident, the piste map doesn't help because it picks out only the very easiest runs in blue – there are many others that are manageable. The Belvedere and Moncrons sectors at the east of the area are served only by drags but offer some wonderful, uncrowded high cruising, some of it above the tree line.

The long runs down to Jouvenceaux are splendid, flattering intermediate terrain, as are those below Sportinia ('ideal for perfecting technique').

The slopes above Sansicario are also excellent – served by two fast quad chair-lifts – but the link via the shoulder of M Fraiteve can be problematic – a seriously steep double drag-lift on the way out, and the steepest pitch in the whole area on the way back. This should be dealt with by installation of a chair-lift.

At the higher levels, where the slopes are above the tree line, the terrain often allows a choice of route. Lower down are pretty runs through the woods, where the main complication can be route-finding. The mountainside is broken up by gullies, limiting the links between pistes that appear to be quite close together.

FOR BEGINNERS
There are better choices
There are signs that the resort is trying to improve life for novices but its village-level slopes are a bit on the steep side and the main nursery area is up the mountain, at Sportinia. Equally importantly, the mornings-only classes don't suit everyone. Once off the nursery slopes, the main problem is a psychological one – that most of the mountain is classified red, though the gradient is generally blue.

FOR CROSS-COUNTRY
Severely limited, even with snow
There is very little cross-country skiing, and it isn't reliable for snow.

QUEUES
Slow lifts the biggest problem
There can be irritating waits at Sportinia, especially when school classes set off, or just after lunch; otherwise the system has few bottlenecks. But there are few fast lifts – the dominance of ancient and terribly slow lifts was 'a major disappointment' for a 2006 visitor returning to the resort following a three-year gap. A quad has replaced the old double chair out of the village to Clotes – you no longer have to carry your skis on your lap; but the new chair is 'just as slow', and still gets queues. Breakdowns of elderly lifts may be a nuisance: the old one-person chair at Col Basset is an important link, and when it fails they may resort to 'dragging skiers behind snowmobiles', says a 2006 reporter. A February visitor reports that several lifts were opened only at weekends, when the Italian crowds arrive.

MOUNTAIN RESTAURANTS
Some pleasant possibilities
Restaurants are numerous and generally pleasant, though few are particularly special. If you like a civilised table-service lunch, head for the hotel Capricorno, at Clotes. It is not cheap, and midweek in low season it can be amazingly quiet. A reader this year liked the quiet Grangia for 'good value meals'. And Bar Clotes is 'a must' for hot chocolate stops and does 'great lasagne'. Reporters also recommend the Ciao Pais, further up the hill, 'a superb rustic restaurant, ideal when the weather closes in', writes one, but 'a bit pricey', according to another. The Clot Bourget has also pleased visitors and Bar Basset at Rio Nero is 'small and friendly with superb views'. There are several places at Sportinia; Capanna Kind is a 2006 reporter's favourite and does 'home-cooked food at very reasonable prices'. The Rocce Nere is praised again for 'good food and excellent service'. The Marmotta on M Triplex is one reader's tip for 'drinks and service with a smile'. The Soleil Boeuf above Sansicario is 'good value, with a nice sun terrace'.

SCHOOLS AND GUIDES
Lessons variable
One reporter found his daughter enthusiastic about her lesson (in a group of eight, in low season), and another writes of 'patient instructors with good English spoken', though past reports have been mixed.

FACILITIES FOR CHILDREN
Tour operator alternatives
Piccolo Dumbo takes children from 13 months old. You might also want to look at the nursery facilities offered by major UK tour operators in the chalets and chalet-hotels that they run here. All the schools take children from four years.

Sauze d'Oulx

boarding

Sauze has good snowboarding slopes – it's got local tree-lined slopes (with space in the trees, too), high, undulating, open terrain, and links to other resorts in the Milky Way. But although it has a fair number of chair-lifts, there are also lots of drags – a serious drawback for novice riders. There's a terrain-park just off the Col Basset chair, at Rio Nero (see 'Terrain-parks').

GETTING THERE

Air Turin 84km/
52 miles (1½hr).

Rail Oulx (5km/
3 miles); frequent
buses.

ACTIVITIES

Indoor Cinema, sauna,
solarium, massage

Outdoor Ice rink,
snowmobiling, ice-
climbing, snow-
shoeing

Phone numbers
From abroad use the
prefix +39 (and do
not omit the initial '0'
of the phone
number).

TOURIST OFFICES

Sauze d'Oulx
t 0122 858009
sauze@montagnedoc.
it
www.montagnedoc.it
www.vialattea.it

**Cesana Torinese
(Sansicario)**
t 0122 89202
cesana@montagne
doc.it

STAYING THERE

HOW TO GO
Packaged hotels dominate
All the major mainstream operators
offer hotel packages here, but there
are also a few chalets.
Hotels Simple 2-star and 3-star hotels
form the core of the holiday
accommodation, with a couple of
4-stars and some more basic places.
((((4) **Torre** (0122 859812) Cylindrical 4-
star landmark 200m/650ft below the
centre. Excellent rooms, 'good food',
'plenty of choice'; mini-buses to lifts.
(2) **Hermitage** (0122 850385) Neat
chalet-style hotel beside the home
piste from Clotes.
(2) **Gran Baita** (0122 850183)
Comfortable place in quiet, central
backstreet, with excellent food and
good rooms, some with sunset views.
(2) **Biancaneve** (0122 850160) Pleasant,
with smallish rooms. Near the centre.
(2) **Des Amis** (0122 858488) Down in
Jouvenceaux, but near bus stop; simple
hotel run by Anglo-Italian couple.
(2) **Stella Alpina** (0122 858731)
Between main lifts. Friendly Anglo-
Italian family doing 'excellent food'.
Endorsed by a 2006 reporter.
(2) **Villa Cary** (0122 850191)
Recommended by a recent reporter as
'cosy and welcoming' with good food.
(2) **Terrazza** (0122 850173) In a quiet
part of town, near the Clotes chair.
Self-catering Apartments and chalets
available, some through UK operators.

EATING OUT
Caters for all tastes and pockets
Typical Italian banquets of five or six
courses can be had in the upmarket
Godfather ('excellent food') and Cantun
restaurants. The Falco does a
particularly good three-course 'skiers'
menu'. In the old town, the Borgo and
the Griglia are popular pizzerias. The
Lampione does good-value Chinese,
Mexican and Indian food. The Pecore
Nere also gets good reviews.

APRES-SKI
Suzy does it with more dignity
Sauze's bars now impress reporters
young and old. Choice is wide, with
multiple happy hours.
   The Assietta terrace is popular for
catching the last rays of the sun at the
end of the day. The New Scotch bar in
the hotel Stella Alpina serves English
beer and is also popular ('high
standard of service'), as is the

Lampione, in the old town.
   After dinner, more places warm up.
One of the best is the smart,
atmospheric cocktail bar Moncrons,
which holds regular quiz nights. But a
2006 reporter's favourite is the Gran
Trun, a converted barn in the old part
of town, complete with resident
entertainer who 'loves you to request
all the old sing-a-long songs'.
Reporters also like the 'interesting'
Village Café with its many metal
artefacts; you can eat here too
('excellent pizzas'). The Cotton Club
provides good service, directors'
chairs, video screen and draught cider.
And a 2006 visitor also enjoyed Max's
and Scatto Matto. Miravallino is a 'very
Italian' cafe bar. Paddy McGinty's
offers 'a good variety of meals
including Mexican and steaks'. The
'very cosy' Derby is nice for a quiet
drink and a 'civilised chill-out' and the
Ghost Bar is the new place to go: it's
'lively, friendly and relaxed,' and
serves 'a wonderful array of burgers',
according to this year's reporters. Of
the discos, the Bandito is a walk away,
and popular with Italians. Schuss runs
theme nights and drink promotions.

OFF THE SLOPES
Go elsewhere
Shopping is limited, there are no
gondolas or cable-cars for pedestrians
and there are few off-slope activities.
Turin or Briançon are worth a visit.

STAYING UP THE MOUNTAIN
'You pays your money ... '
In most resorts, staying up the
mountain is one of the cheaper
options. Here, the reverse applies. The
4-star Capricorno (0122 850273), up at
Clotes, is the most attractive and
expensive hotel in Sauze. It's a
charming little chalet beside the piste,
with only eight bedrooms.
   Not quite in the same league are
the places up at Sportinia – though
reporters have enjoyed the isolation
and ski convenience.

Sansicario 1700m/5,580ft

Sansicario is ideally placed for
exploration of the whole Milky Way. It
is a modern, purpose-built, self-
contained but rather soulless little
resort, mainly consisting of apartments
around the small shopping precinct.
The 45-room Rio Envers (0122 811333)
is a comfortable, expensive hotel.

Sella Ronda

Endless intermediate slopes amid spectacular Dolomite scenery, with a choice of attractive valley villages, mainly German-speaking

COSTS

①②③④⑤⑥

RATINGS

The slopes
Fast lifts	***
Snow	****
Extent	*****
Expert	**
Intermediate	*****
Beginner	****
Convenience	***
Queues	***
Mountain restaurants	****

The rest
Scenery	*****
Resort charm	***
Off-slope	***

NEWS

In Alta Badia: for 2006/07 a gondola is planned to replace the Col Alto chair out of Corvara.

For 2005/06 three lifts were upgraded to fast quads: the Pralongià II drag at Corvara, the Pre dai Corf double chair above San Cassiano and the Pradüc lift joining La Villa to Pedraces.

And a new terrain-park was built on the Ciampai run at San Cassiano.

In Arabba: the Porto Vescovo cable-car was upgraded for 2005/06 as was the final stage of the Marmolada cable-car, serving the glacier.

The Carosello area has countless mountain restaurants giving great views from their terraces; this is Piz Sorega, directly above San Cassiano →

- ➕ Vast network of connected slopes – suits intermediates particularly well
- ➕ Stunning, unique Dolomite scenery
- ➕ Lots of mountain huts with good food
- ➕ Excellent value for money
- ➕ Extensive snowmaking – one of Europe's best systems, but ...

- ➖ They need it: natural snowfall is erratic in this southerly region
- ➖ Few challenges, and off-piste limited – possibly banned in places
- ➖ Most runs are of limited vertical
- ➖ Crowds on Sella Ronda circuit
- ➖ Still some old drag-lifts
- ➖ Après-ski not a highlight

The Sella Ronda is an amazing circular network of lifts and pistes taking you around the Gruppo Sella – a mighty limestone massif with villages scattered around it. Among the main attractions is the simply spectacular Dolomite scenery – like something Disney might have conjured up for a theme park. But the geology that provides the visual drama also dictates the nature of the slopes. Sheer limestone cliffs rise out of gentle pasture-land, which is where you spend your time. Individual runs are short; verticals of 500m/1,640ft are rare, while runs of under 300m/980ft are not. And there's scarcely a black run to be seen.

But the distances you can cover on skis are huge. In overall scale, the network rivals the famed Three Valleys in France. In addition to the main Sella Ronda circuit, major lift systems lead off it at three main points along the way – Selva, covered in the chapter after this – Corvara and Arabba. These three should obviously be on your shortlist as potential destinations. But there are other villages worth considering, notably Santa Cristina and Ortisei, next to Selva, and covered in that chapter; San Cassiano, which shares with Corvara the friendly Carosello area; and Canazei and Campitello, at the south-west corner of the circuit – in Trentino, and mainly covered in our separate chapter on that province.

This is one of the few areas where we unreservedly welcome continuous sunny weather; the snowmaking is fantastic, and we really don't want clouds and snow to interfere with our lunches gazing at the views. We say above that snowfall is erratic, but that is not to say it doesn't happen. In January 2006 we got uninterrupted sun, and lots of lovely pics as a result. In February a reporter got six days of blizzards, and two of low cloud with sunny spells. Bad luck, Jay!

461

KEY FACTS

Resort	1565m
	5,130ft

The linked lift network of Val Gardena, Alta Badia, Arabba, and the Canazei and Campitello slopes of Val di Fassa

Slopes	1235-2520m
	4,050-8,270ft
Lifts	186
Pistes	395km
	245 miles
Blue	38%
Red	53%
Black	9%
Snowmaking	276km
	172 miles

CHOOSING A BASE

It's important to pick the right resort. For good skiers, the best bases are Selva (covered in a separate chapter) and Arabba, an increasingly popular small village where classic Dolomite terrain gives way to longer, steeper slopes. Corvara is better for novices, with abundant gentle slopes both on and off the main circuit. Canazei has the most limited local slopes, but access to Arabba is speedy.

A vast network of slopes apparently requires a vast selection of piste maps – 12 in all, plus several variations. There are individual ones for each resort; some cover the main circuit, others do not. Reporters generally find them confusing: 'There are two maps numbered 6 for Arabba; the blue one covers the Sella Ronda, but the white does not.' To add to the confusion, the main resorts now promote additional tours, away from the main circuit. A World War 1 circuit is one.

The Dolomiti Superski pass covers not only the Sella Ronda resorts but dozens of others, amounting to an impressive 1220km/758 miles. We'd recommend anyone based in Corvara or San Cassiano to make a day trip to Cortina, ending the day with the famous 'hidden valley' run from Passo Falzarego – see feature panel.

Off-piste skiing in this area is limited but good – see feature panel.

THE SELLA RONDA CIRCUIT

The Sella Ronda is a unique circular tour around the Sella massif, easily managed in a day by even an early intermediate. The slopes you descend are almost all easy, and take you through Selva, Colfosco, Corvara, Arabba and Canazei (or at least the slopes above it). You can do the circuit in either direction by following very clear coloured signs. The clockwise route is slightly quicker and offers more interesting slopes. Reporters have found the anti-clockwise route tends to be less crowded though. Some resort piste maps incorporate a Sella Ronda map of the usual panoramic kind; map-literate people will want the proper topographical one with contour lines, from the tourist office (not lift stations).

The runs total around 23km/14 miles and the lifts around 14km/9 miles. The lifts take a total of about two hours (plus any queuing). We've done it in just three and a half hours excluding diversions and hut stops; five or six hours is a realistic time during busy periods, when there are crowds both on the pistes and on the lifts. If possible, choose low season or a Saturday, and set out early.

Not everyone likes it. 'It's a bit of a slog,' said one reporter. Others have found the circuit 'boring', and 'too busy and crowded'. And a 2006 visitor rated it 'over-hyped, over-sold and over-regimented'. Boarders beware: there are quite a few flat bits, which have deterred some visitors – a recent reporter's group exchanged their boards for skis after two days.

If you set out early, you can make more of the day by taking some diversions from the circuit. Among the most entertaining segments are the long runs down from Ciampinoi to Santa Cristina and Selva, from Dantercëpies to Selva, from the top of the Boe gondola back down to Corvara and from the top of the Arabba gondola. Take in all those in a day doing the circuit and you'll have had a good day.

Intermediates could take time out to explore the off-the-circuit Carosello area from Corvara. Groups of different abilities can do the circuit and arrange to meet along the way at some of the many welcoming rifugios.

LIFT PASSES

Dolomiti Superski

Prices in €

Age	1-day	6-day
under 16	32	136
16 to 59	38	194
over 60	33	165
Free under 8		
Beginner no deals		

Notes
Covers 450 lifts and
1220km/758 miles of
piste in Dolomites,
including all Sella
Ronda resorts.

ARABBA 1600m/5,250ft
**Arabba, diagonally opposite Selva on
the Sella Ronda circuit, is a small,
quiet village appealing particularly to
good skiers because of its relatively
steep, shady local slopes. Off the
circuit there is good skiing to be done
on the Marmolada glacier.**

THE RESORT
Arabba is a small, traditional-style
village; it is growing fast and we are
receiving more reports on it. Staying in
the older part involves an uphill walk
to reach the ski area, which provokes a
few complaints from reporters. A new
area of hotels and chalets has opened
higher up, better-placed for the lifts
and slopes. There's a small selection of
shops, bars and restaurants, but this is
not a place for lively nightlife.

THE MOUNTAIN
Arabba's local slopes cover 62km/38
miles and have some of the best
natural snow and steepest pistes in
the Dolomites. In various places
around Arabba, reporters reckon the
runs are at the steep end of their
classification, and in one or two cases
blues might be better classed as reds.
Runs from the high point of Porto
Vescovo are north-facing and longer
than most in the region. The
Marmolada glacier, beyond Arabba, is
open most of the winter and is
included on the main lift pass. It is a
trip to do as much for its spectacular
views as for skiing, though the red run
from top to bottom is a notable
1490m/4,900ft vertical.
Slopes The two-stage DMC gondola
and the newly upgraded cable-car
beside it rise almost 900m/2,950ft
vertical to the high point at Porto
Vescovo (2475m/8,120ft). From here a
choice of runs return to the village or
you can head off around the Sella
Ronda circuit, following a busy red run
to Pont de Vauz. From the mid-station
of the DMC, a series of chairs takes
you to Passo Padon and onwards to
the Marmolada glacier.
   On the opposite side of the village,
a fast quad gets you on the way to
Burz and Passo Campolongo. You can
then head directly down to Corvara
and the rest of the Sella Ronda or
divert right on to the quieter, gentle
Carosello slopes, shared by Corvara
and San Cassiano.
Terrain-park None in Arabba. There's a
half-pipe at Belvedere above Canazei.

Snow reliability Arabba offers some of
the most snow-sure slopes in the Sella
Ronda region. Good snow is far from
assured, but snowmaking is extensive
and the main runs are north-facing.
Experts Arabba has the best steep
slopes of all the Sella Ronda resorts.
The north-facing blacks and reds from
Porto Vescovo offer genuine challenges
and are great fun. Off-piste is limited –
see feature panel.
Intermediates The slopes suit
adventurous intermediates best. Most
are quite challenging and those on the
main circuit suffer from crowds.
Beginners It is not a good choice for
beginners. There is a small nursery
slope near the Burz chair, but access
to longer easy runs is tricky.
Snowboarding Porto Vescovo offers
some decent challenge. Most of the
lifts are now fast chairs or gondolas.
Cross-country There is one loop at
village level, between the ice-rink and
Alfauro.
Queues New lifts have vastly improved
access to and from the village.
Reporters note few problems, though
there can be queues at some key lifts
on the Sella Ronda circuit (one reader
had a 15-minute wait near Passo
Pordoi). The Burz quad now gives
faster access to Corvara and the new
cable-car to Porto Vescovo should
have removed any congestion there.
Despite upgrading of the three-stage
Marmolada cable-car, a 2006 visitor
had a 20-minute wait at the bottom
station.
Mountain restaurants Lots of choice,
from rustic huts to larger places. Most
are lively with good food. The Bec de
Roces and Col de Burz are both
suntraps (with 'amazing Bombardinos'
at the latter). Cherz above Passo di
Campolongo has great views of
Marmolada. The Luigi Gorze at the top
of the Porta Vescovo lifts has been
recommended for 'excellent food' and

Sella Ronda

'stunning panoramic views', as have the 'lively' Rifugio Plan Boe, and the Fodom ('first class, good value pizza') at the bottom of the Lezuo Belvedere chair below Passo Pordoi and Capanna Bill, near the Marmolada lifts, on the way back to Arabba ('good food, table-service').

Schools The local Arabba school offers group and private classes. Proguide guides off-piste – see feature panel.

Facilities for children The kindergarten at the ski school takes children from two years.

STAYING THERE

How to go Several UK tour operators offer packages. New accommodation has been built at the top end of town, closer to the lifts.

Chalets There are several chalets here, including a good selection from Neilson.

Hotels Of the dozen or so hotels, several get support from readers. The Portavescovo (0436 79139) has been described as 'excellent: wonderful food, nicely furnished rooms and a well-equipped fitness centre', but a 2006 reporter warns of a noisy disco every night and a chilly pool. The Malita (0436 79103) is 'comfortable with good food, at reasonable prices'. A 2006 group with members in both reports that the Evaldo (0436 791109) is better than either – 'great food', pool and sauna. It's away from the lifts, whereas the newish Mesdì (0436 79119) is close to the Burz lift with 'lovely rooms, health suite and wonderful 5-course dinners'. The B&B hotel Garni Royal (0436 79293) is 'a real gem' and offers 'incredible value for money' – large rooms, sauna, hot-tub and Turkish bath. The Al Forte

(0436 79329) is 'well appointed with good food, and built around the old fort, with fascinating public rooms'. The Sporthotel (0436 79321) sets 'high standards in all areas'.

Self-catering Self-catering accommodation is available.

Eating out Restaurant choice is limited, too. The central hotels all have busy restaurants. 7 Sass does 'wonderful enormous pizzas and little else'. Reporters love Miky's Grill in the Hotel Mesdì for great food and service ('the best steaks in the Alps'; 'the best restaurant in Arabba'). You can go up to Rifugio Plan Boè by snow-mobile for a 'special' 3-course dinner and dancing – 'the best meal we had'.

Après ski The après-ski is cheap but limited, which surprises some reporters – 'Still no bar with any life,' says one regular who lives in hope of an improvement. But the Stube bar is popular and said to attract tour op reps, instructors and young teenagers, and the 'friendly' Bar Peter gets a mention. The 'very smart' Treina is recommended as the liveliest bar by a couple of recent reporters. and cosy hotel bars are other options in the village. The atmospheric Rifugio Plan Boè up the mountain is good for a last drink on the pistes before heading back to the village – 'loud 70s, 80s and Europop music'. The Albergo Pordoi has 'the biggest selection of drinks in town'. It is possible to take a taxi to nearby Corvara (6km/4 miles away) for a more animated choice.

Off the slopes Off-slope diversions are few. There's a small selection of shops, cafes, and an ice-rink. Snowmobile excursions and sleigh rides are available. Helicopter rides to the Marmolada glacier are possible.

OFF-PISTE IN THE SELLA RONDA AREA

There are relatively few major off-piste routes in this area, because of the nature of the mountains – gentle pasture, surmounted by cliffs. But the routes that are available are spectacular.

The cable-car from Passo Pordoi gets you up on to the Sella massif. There are fairly direct descents from here back to the pass (the very sunny Forcella) or down the Val Lasties towards Canazei. But the classic run is the Val Mesdì, a long, shady couloir on the northern side of the Gruppo Sella down to Colfosco, reached by skiing and hiking across the massif.

Marmolada, the highest peak of the Dolomites, now reached by reasonably efficient lifts from Malga Ciapela, is the other obvious launching point. It offers a range of big descents on and off the glacier.

Proguide is a guiding outfit in Arabba offering guidance on these and other routes – go to www.proguide.it.

CORVARA 1570m/5,150ft

Gentle slopes at the heart of the Sella Ronda circuit. There are plenty of hotels, restaurants, bars and sports facilities, making Corvara one of the better bases in the area for families and novices.

THE RESORT

Corvara is the most animated village east of Selva and central to the Alta Badia region. The main shops and some hotels cluster around a small piazza, but the rest of the place sprawls along the valley floor – some accommodation is far from the lifts.

THE MOUNTAIN

Corvara is well-positioned with village lifts heading off to reasonably equidistant Selva, Arabba and San Cassiano. The local slopes are gentle and confidence-boosting.

Slopes A long gondola heads out of the village towards Boe and the clockwise Sella Ronda circuit. Two successive fast quads head in the opposite direction towards Colfosco and the anticlockwise route. The area around both lifts can get congested at peak times. A slow chair and a couple of drags take you towards the quieter Carosello slopes shared with San Cassiano. On the other side of town a new gondola is planned to replace the old chair to Col Alto for 2006/07 – this should improve access to San Cassiano and La Villa.

Terrain-park There is a new terrain-park on the Ciampai run towards San Cassiano.

Snow reliability Not reliable, but snow-guns cover most of the main runs.

Experts Very few of Corvara's slopes offer any real challenge and those that do are relatively short. There's hardly a black run to be seen – the one above Boé 'was red 28 years ago and is no harder now', a reporter points out. One reporter enjoyed the short black at Colfosco and there's the much longer World Cup run at La Villa. See the feature panel on off-piste runs.

Intermediates Intermediates are well-catered for around Corvara. The slopes are superb for cruising and confidence-boosting and there's a vast network of interconnected slopes to explore. The red underneath the Boè cable-car in Corvara is usually uncrowded and retains good snow. Or the adventurous can head for the steeper, wooded pistes above La Villa.

Beginners There's a small nursery area in the village and lots of easy runs to progress to.

Snowboarding Novices can make rapid progress on gentle slopes. A few awkward drag-lifts remain, but most can be avoided. There's a terrain-park on the way to San Cassiano.

Cross-country The Alta Badia area offers 30km/19miles of trails, including a valley loop on the way to Colfosco.

Queues New lifts have improved the area but we still receive complaints of queues to join the main circuit: the Boé gondola at peak times, the Borest chair between Corvara and Colfosco and the T-bar in Passo Campolongo are all mentioned. The length of the queue is often less of a problem than their character ('Lots of pushing and shoving'). The new gondola planned between the village and Col Alto should reduce any waiting times there.

Mountain restaurants Lots of choice. A 2006 reporter enjoyed 'brill lasagne and hunter's platter' at the Brancia, above Col Alto.

Schools There's a local branch of the Alta Badia school – reports welcome.

Facilities for children Kinderland by the ski school takes children from two years.

STAYING THERE

How to go There is a wide choice of accommodation, but some can be a walk from the lifts.

Hotels The hotel Posta Zirm (0471 836175) has a large spa facility, and is recommended by a recent reporter: 'Very good food, ski-in/ski-out, comfortable rooms.' Also recommended is the pensione Villa Tony (0471 836193): 'Very reasonably priced half-board, conveniently located on the main street.'

Eating out A reasonable choice. Most of the hotels have restaurants – the Stüa de Michil in the Perla has a Michelin star. See also San Cassiano.

Après ski The Posta Zirm in Corvara does a ski-boot tea dance but support may depend on tour ops organising group transport back to other villages. The hotel Tablè is recommended by reporters for its piano bar and good cakes. Other suggestions from a recent reporter are the smart bar in the Perla hotel and the 'self-consciously trendy' cocktail bar at the Marmolada.

Off the slopes There's a covered ice rink, indoor tennis courts and an outdoor artificial climbing wall.

TOURIST OFFICES

ALTA BADIA
www.altabadia.org
Corvara
t 0471 836176
corvara@altabadia.org
Colfosco
t 0471 836145
colfosco@altabadia.
org
San Cassiano
t 0471 849422
s.cassiano@altabadia.
org
La Villa
t 0471 847037
lavilla@altabadia.org

ARABBA
t 0436 780019
info@arabba.it
www.arabba.it

VAL DI FASSA
www.fassa.com
Canazei
t 0462 601113
infocanazei@fassa.
com
Campitello
t 0462 750500
infocampitello@fassa.
com

COLFOSCO 1645m/5,400ft
Colfosco is a smaller, quieter satellite of
Corvara, 2km/1 mile away. It has a fairly
compact centre with a sprawl of large
hotels along the road towards Passo
Gardena and Selva. It's connected to
Corvara by a horizontal chair-lift. In the
opposite direction, a gondola goes to
Passo Gardena. There are a couple of
short nursery slopes and the runs back
from Passo Gardena are lovely, long
cruises. Immediately above the village,
the Val Stella Alpina (aka Edelweisstal),
off the Sella Ronda circuit, offers gentle,
normally quiet pistes ideal for fast
cruising. The three pleasant restaurants
(see photo) can get very busy.

SAN CASSIANO 1530m/5,020ft
**A quiet village with easy slopes away
from the main Sella Ronda circuit, with
easy access to Passo Falzarego for the
famous 'hidden valley' run.**

THE RESORT
San Cassiano is a pleasant little
village, set in an attractive, tree-filled
valley. It is now bypassed by the road
to Cortina, and is working towards
becoming car-free. It's a quiet, civilised
resort, without much animation.

THE MOUNTAIN
The local slopes, the Carosello area
shared with Corvara, form a spur off
the main Sella Ronda circuit. Access to
the circuit takes time.
Slopes The newish gondola, a drive
from the centre, gets you off to a quick
start, rising 466m/1,530ft vertical to Piz
Sorega. From the top, fast chairs form
the link with La Villa, or you can head
for Pralongia and the long runs home.

THE 'HIDDEN VALLEY'

*If you like runs surrounded by spectacular scenery rather than the apparatus of
ski resorts, don't miss the easy red run from Lagazuoi, reached by cable-car from
Passo Falzarego. The pass is easily accessible from Cortina, but is better done
from San Cassiano because the run descends to a point near Armentarola, close
to San Cassiano. Shared taxis run an affordable shuttle service to the pass from
Armentarola. There's also a bus from San Cassiano, but a 2006 reporter says it is
'very crowded and slow'.*

*The run is one of the most beautiful we've come across, and usually delights
reporters. Views from the top of the cable-car are splendid, and the run offers
isolation amid sheer, pink-tinged Dolomite peaks and frozen waterfalls. Make
time to stop at the atmospheric Rifugio Scotoni near the end.*

*At the bottom, it's a long skate to a horse-drawn sled with ropes attached, which
tows you back to Armentarola (for a couple of euros). This is more of a challenge
than the run, and the risk of a pile-up if someone falls has concerned a couple of
reporters. At Armentarola there is a drag-lift up to a run back to San Cassiano.*

Terrain-park A new terrain-park was
opened for 2005/06 at Ciampai, near
La Brancia.
Snow reliability The Dolomites have an
erratic snowfall record, but problems
arise only when it is too warm to make
snow.
Experts Experts would be wise to stay
elsewhere. There are a few steeper
runs at La Villa, but not much else.
Intermediates Pretty much ideal if you
love easy cruising on flattering, well-
groomed runs.
Beginners There are nursery slopes is
a short bus-ride away at Armentarola,
and at the top of the gondola – not
ideal. But plenty of long, easy slopes
to progress to.
Snowboarding Endless carving on
quiet pistes, plus there's a new terrain-
park to try.
Cross-country There's a branch of the
DolomitiNordicski in Armentarola. It
offers tuition and equipment hire, as
well as a couple of trails.
Queues Few problems.
Mountain restaurants There are
countless options. Piz Sorega gets very
crowded – a reporter suggests going
down to the Pic Pre, which is 'badly
marked on the map and consequently
quiet'. The woody Saraghes is 'friendly
and popular' and the Pralongia is
'welcoming and cosy' with 'a wonderful
array of pastries and strudels'. And the
Punta Trieste has a collection of
wooden owls and is recommended for
'excellent spaghetti'.
Schools We have no reports of the
local school.
Facilities for children The school offers
the usual arrangements for children
and there are several kids' parks.

SNOWPIX.COM / CHRIS GILL

More restaurants: in their very limited area, the sunny slopes above Colfosco contain three: here are Stella Alpina (aka Edelweiss) and higher up Col Pradat, with Sassongher soaring 600m/1,970ft above the col; each is served by a gondola ↓

STAYING THERE

How to go There's a choice.

Hotels The 4-star Rosa Alpina (0471 849500) is a splendid place, coupling genuine comfort and great food with a relaxed atmosphere. Its three restaurants include the Michelin-starred St Hubertus; recognising that guests who like that kind of thing might like to try the other top-notch restaurants in the area, the adventurous owner lets rooms on a B&B basis, not half-board. You can stay up the mountain at the smart Las Vegas restaurant (0471 840138).

Eating out As well as the Rosa Alpina's St Hubertus there are two other Michelin-starred restaurants in the area; one, the Siriola in the hotel Ciasa Salares, is only a short drive away.

Après ski Après-ski starts up the mountain with loud music at Las Vegas. A 2006 reporter recommends staying late at the Utia on the home run and skiing down after dark ('the highlight of the week'). Nightlife is very limited: the Rosa Alpina has dancing and there's a bowling alley.

Off the slopes Walking in the pretty scenery is the main off-slope activity; swimming is the other.

LA VILLA 1435m/4,710ft

La Villa is similar to neighbouring San Cassiano in most ways – small, quiet, pretty, unspoiled. But the home pistes are challenging – genuine red and just about genuine black dropping 600m/1,970ft through woods to the village. Across the village, a fast chair serves a blue slope and a link to Pedraces.

PEDRACES 1325m/4,350ft

This small roadside village has a fast quad followed by a slow double chair to Santa Croce (2043m/6,700ft). There's a restaurant (and a church) at the top, and two restaurants at mid-mountain – a 2006 reporter enjoyed a 'cheap, sunny lunch' at the Lee hut as well as the 'pleasant' run from the top. There's a terrain-park (Dolomites Fun Park) at Piz la Villa and kids' snow-garden. Village amenities include a pool; and you can skate or watch horse-racing on the frozen lake.

CANAZEI AND CAMPITELLO

Canazei is a sizeable village at the south-west corner of the Sella Ronda circuit. Campitello next door is smaller and quieter. Both are covered in the chapter on Trentino.

Sella Ronda

Selva/Val Gardena

Pleasant village amid spectacular Dolomite scenery, with the vast Sella Ronda lift network on its doorstep

COSTS

① ② ③ ④ ⑤ ⑥

RATINGS

The slopes
Fast lifts	***
Snow	****
Extent	*****
Expert	**
Intermediate	*****
Beginner	***
Convenience	***
Queues	***
Mountain restaurants	****

The rest
Scenery	*****
Resort charm	***
Off-slope	***

NEWS

For 2006/07 fast quads are due to replace the Sotsaslonch drag above Plan de Gralba and the Sochers lift at Ciampinoi.

And at Alpe di Siusi, a six-pack is expected to replace the Paradiso double chair.

For 2005/06 a fast quad replaced the double chair from Monte Pana to Mont de Sëura above Santa Cristina. And a double chair was installed near Vallunga, just outside Selva, serving the lower runs at Dantercëpies.

A new red run was opened between Piz Sella and Mont Pana, which also provides an easier route to Ciampinoi, avoiding the tricky black run.

468

➕ Attractive village in an impressive wooded setting

➕ Excellent local slopes, with big verticals by Sella Ronda standards

➕ Mix of open and wooded slopes

➕ Excellent nursery slopes, but ...

➖ Progression to easy long runs involves bus-rides

➖ Bus services are far from ideal

➖ Busy road through the village

Selva (known to 'Ski Sunday' viewers as Val Gardena – the name of the valley) is one of the main bases to consider for a visit to the unique Sella Ronda region; the Sella Ronda as a whole is now covered in a separate chapter, immediately before this one – so here's a reminder of the characteristics of the area:

➕ Vast network of connected slopes – suits intermediates particularly well

➕ Stunning, unique Dolomite scenery

➕ Lots of mountain huts with good food

➕ Excellent value for money

➕ Extensive snowmaking – one of Europe's best systems, but ...

➖ They need it: natural snowfall is erratic in this southerly region

➖ Few challenges, and off-piste limited – possibly banned in places

➖ Most runs are of limited vertical

➖ Crowds on Sella Ronda circuit

➖ Still some old drag-lifts

➖ Après-ski not a highlight

Selva remains one of our favourites essentially because of the local slopes, including two race-courses through woods to the village that are among the most satisfying runs in the area – not least because they offer decent verticals. Beginners and near-beginners, though, are probably better off elsewhere – in Corvara or Colfosco.

THE RESORT

Selva is a long roadside village at the head of the Val Gardena, almost merging with the next village of Santa Cristina. It suffers from traffic but has traditional-style architecture and an attractive church. The valley is famed for wood carvings, which are on display (and sale) wherever you look.

The village enjoys a lovely setting under the impressive pink-tinged walls of Sassolungo and the Gruppo Sella –

a fortress-like massif about 6km/ 4 miles across that lies at the hub of the Sella Ronda circuit (see the separate chapter). Despite the World Cup fame of Val Gardena, Selva is neither upmarket nor brash. It's a good-value, civilised family resort – relaxed and family-friendly once you get away from the intrusive through-road into snowy fields.

For many years this area was part of Austria, and it retains a Tirolean charm. German is the main language, not

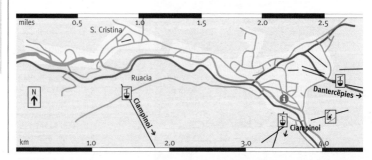

KEY FACTS

Resort	1565m
	5,130ft

The linked lift network of Val Gardena, Alta Badia, Arabba, and the Canazei and Campitello slopes of Val di Fassa

Slopes	1235-2520m
	4,050-8,270ft
Lifts	186
Pistes	395km
	245 miles
Blue	38%
Red	53%
Black	9%
Snowmaking	276km
	172 miles

Val Gardena-
Alpe di Siusi only

Slopes	1005-2520m
	3,300-8,270ft
Lifts	81
Pistes	175km
	109 miles
Blue	30%
Red	60%
Black	10%
Snowmaking	90km
	56 miles

Italian, and many visitors are German, too. Most places have two names: Selva is also known as Wolkenstein and the Gardena valley as Gröden. We do our bit to help with Italian unity by using the Italian place names. The local language, Ladin, also survives – giving a third name to some places.

Ortisei, the administrative centre of Val Gardena, is described at the end of the chapter; it is not so convenient for the Sella Ronda slopes.

From the village, gondolas rise in two directions. The Ciampinoi gondola goes south from near the centre of the village to start the anti-clockwise Sella Ronda route. The Dantercëpies gondola, for the clockwise Sella Ronda route, starts above the village at the top of the nursery slopes (but accessible via a central chair-lift and short run down). The most convenient position is near one of these gondolas. There are regular buses until early evening – three euros for a weekly card – but they generate regular complaints from reporters about infrequency, inadequate capacity (especially at the end of the day), poorly sited stops and lack of services to Corvara and Plan de Gralba. There is now a night bus between Selva and Ortisei. Many reporters use taxis, although they are expensive unless you share. All the four-star hotels run their own free transport.

The Dolomiti Superski pass covers not only Selva and the Sella Ronda resorts but dozens of others. It's an easy road trip to Cortina – worth it for the fabulous scenery alone.

469

THE MOUNTAIN

Selva's own slopes cover both sides of the valley, including the quieter Seceda area above Santa Cristina and Ortisei. Practically all are ideally suited to intermediates. Most of the lifts stay open until around 5pm in high season.

The local piste map covers Selva and Alpe di Siusi (accessed from Ortisei); there are several variations, which reporters find confusing. The maps show neither names nor numbers for the runs. Piste marking and signing also provoke complaints from reporters.

THE SLOPES
High mileage piste excursions
The **Ciampinoi** gondola accesses several shady pistes, including the famous World Cup Downhill run, leading back down to Selva and Santa Cristina. In the opposite direction, runs go on to **Plan de Gralba** – and so to the rest of the anticlockwise Sella Ronda circuit.

The **Dantercëpies** gondola serves excellent runs back to Selva and accesses the clockwise Sella Ronda

Dolomiti Superski

Prices in €

Age	1-day	6-day
under 16	32	136
16 to 59	38	194
over 60	33	165

Free under 8

Beginner no deals

Notes
Covers 450 lifts and 1220km/758 miles of piste in Dolomites, including all Sella Ronda resorts.

Alternative pass
Val Gardena-only pass.

boarding

Selva attracts few boarders. There's little to challenge experts and off-piste opportunities are limited, but the nursery slopes are good and there are lots of gentle runs to progress to. The main lifts out of the village are all gondolas or chairs. There's a terrain-park at Alpe di Siusi and a couple of half-pipes.

circuit via Corvara. A new double chair serves the quieter runs below it.

The sunny **Seceda** area is accessed by a gondola on the outskirts of Santa Cristina. This is also accessible by descending from Ciampinoi to ride an underground train across the valley. Runs descend to Santa Cristina or to Ortisei – a red run of about 7km/4 miles. And from Ortisei a cable-car on the other side of the valley takes you to and from **Alpe di Siusi** – a gentle elevated area of quiet, easy runs, cross-country tracks and walks. This area can also be accessed via the big gondola from the village of Siusi, to the west.

TERRAIN-PARKS
Head for the half-pipe
There are boarder-cross runs at Passo Sella by the Cavazes Grohmann chair and at Piz Sella by the Comici chair. And there's a new half-pipe and natural pipe at Plan de Gralba. Alpe di Siusi has a terrain-park and half-pipe by the Laurin chair, and a kids' park. Timed slalom runs are located in several areas – free to try.

SNOW RELIABILITY
Excellent when it's cold
The slopes are not high – there are few above 2200m/7,220ft and most are between 1500m and 2000m (4,920ft and 6,560ft). Natural snowfalls are erratic but Selva's slopes, like much of the area, are well covered by snowmaking. We have enjoyed excellent pistes here in times of severe natural snow shortage and our reporters are regularly impressed – 'a revelation', 'wonderful', 'stunning', 'unbelievable coverage and quality.' Problems arise only in poor snow years if it is too warm to make snow.

FOR EXPERTS
A few good runs
Experts may find the slopes too tame; there are few challenges, essentially no moguls (the blacks all get groomed) and a low likelihood of powder. There are few major off-piste routes, because of the nature of the terrain; see the feature

panel in the Sella Ronda chapter.

The Val Gardena World Cup piste, the Saslong, is one of several steepish runs between Ciampinoi and both Selva and Santa Cristina. Unlike many World Cup pistes it is kept in racing condition for Italian team practices, but it is open to the public much of the time. It's especially good in January, when it's not too crowded.

FOR INTERMEDIATES
Fast cruising on easy slopes
There are huge amounts of skiing to do, in several areas.

Competent intermediates will love the red and black descents from Dantercëpies and Ciampinoi to Selva.

The blue runs in the Plan de Gralba area are gentle; the red run to get there from Ciampinoi is a real obstacle – steep and crowded – but reporters find it worth the struggle. The high-altitude route back used to involve a tricky black run, but you now have the option of a new red run going to the Tramans chair and to Monte Pana. The quiet runs at Mont de Seura, above Monte Pana, are worth exploring.

The Alpe di Siusi above Ortisei is ideal for confidence-building – very gentle, quiet, amid superb scenery with no crowds. Runs are mostly short, the main exception being the red down to Saltria from Punta d'Oro offering 500m/1,640ft vertical.

The Seceda sector has good red and blue runs at altitude, and splendid runs to the valley – an easy blue/red back to Santa Cristina and the beautiful red Cucasattel, passing through a tight natural canyon to Ortisei.

FOR BEGINNERS
Great slopes, but ...
The village nursery slopes are excellent – spacious, convenient, and kept in good condition. There are lots of gentle, long runs to progress to, but Selva isn't the ideal base to access them. Plan de Gralba has easy blues, but you need to take a taxi to get there. Near-beginners would be better placed taking the bus to Ortisei and the cable-car to Alpe di Siusi.

OUR WEBSITE

Go to our website at wtss.co.uk for resort news, links to resort sites, a build-your-own resort shortlist system and reader forums.

FOR CROSS-COUNTRY
Beautiful trails
There are 98km/61 miles of trails, all enjoying wonderful scenery. The 12km/7 mile trail up the Vallunga-Langental valley is particularly attractive, with neck-craning views all around. Almost half the trails have the advantage of being at altitude, running between Monte Pana and across Alpe di Siusi.

QUEUES
Still a few problems
New lifts have vastly improved the area, and there are now fewer bottlenecks, especially away from the main Sella Ronda circuit. The trend continues for 2006/07 when two more lifts become fast quads (see News). However, the Dantercëpies gondola still generates complaints from reporters ('an absolute scrum till after 10') The old double chair from the town provides an alternative, but is 'very slow and takes ages'. Queues for the Ciampinoi gondola and the Piz

Seteur chair at Plan de Gralba are also mentioned by readers.

At Alpe di Siusi there has been a huge investment in lift upgrades. Almost all are now fast chairs and a six-pack is due to replace an old double for 2006/07.

MOUNTAIN RESTAURANTS
One of the area's highlights
There are lots of huts all over the area, and virtually all of them are lively, with helpful staff, good food, lots of character and modest prices. Reporters love them.

The Panorama is a small, cosy, rustic suntrap at the foot of the eponymous drag near the top of Dantercëpies. The 'attractive' restaurant at the bottom of the new Val double chair is worth a visit, according to a 2006 reporter. On the way down to Plan de Gralba from Ciampinoi, the Vallongia is tucked away on a corner of the piste. In the Plan de Gralba area the top station of the cable-car does excellent pizza; the Comici is atmospheric, with a big

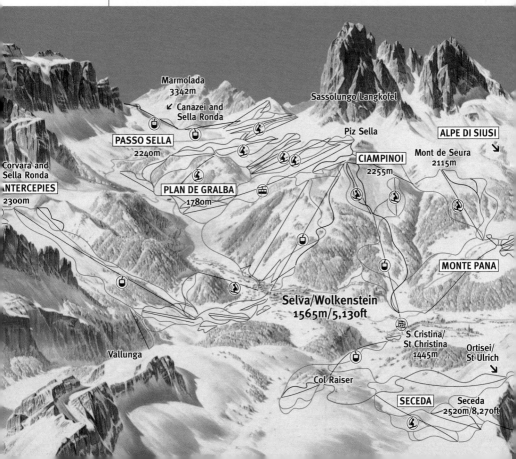

SCHOOLS

Factory Selva Gardena
t 0471 795156

2000
t 0471 773125

Classes
(Factory prices)
6 days €160

Private lessons
€34 for 1hr

CHILDREN

Kindergarten
0348 870 0661
From 4mnth to 7yr

Ski school
For age 4 to 12:
6 days €277, lunch
included (Factory
school price)

GETTING THERE

Air Verona 190km/
118 miles (3hr);
Bolzano 40km/
25 miles (45min);
Treviso 130km/81
miles (2½hr)

Rail Chiusa (27km/
17 miles); Bressanone
(35km/22 miles);
Bolzano 40km/
25 miles); frequent
buses from station

---

terrace. Piz Seteur has 'superb lasagne' and is also recommended late in the day (see Après-ski).

In the Seceda sector there are countless options. The cosy Sangon 'has bags of atmosphere', though another reporter pronounces Baita Gamsblut her favourite: 'Super rustic hut with a good menu and a warm, friendly atmosphere.' The Seceda does 'wonderful food, served by waitresses in miniskirts or leather shorts', which brightened one reporter's day. And a 2006 reporter reckons Daniel's Hütte is worth a mention ('very good').

On Alpe di Siusi the rustic Sanon refuge gets a good review, particularly since 'the barman came out to serenade us with his accordion'. The table-service restaurant at the bottom of the Monte Piz lift is also highly rated – 'good value', 'huge portions'. The Williams hut at the top of the Florian chair has 'superb views'.

SCHOOLS AND GUIDES
Positive reports

The Ski and Boarders Factory, run by 90s racing star Peter Runggaldier, gets favourable reports from readers: 'Good tuition, excellent English,' writes a 2006 reporter. Another praised the 'very beneficial' advanced level groups at the 2000 school. Private lessons with the Ski and Boarders Factory are said to be good value – but booking ahead is advised as it gets busy.

FACILITIES FOR CHILDREN
Good by Italian standards

There are comprehensive childcare arrangements, but German and Italian are the main languages here and English is not routinely spoken. That said, in the past we have had reports of very enjoyable lessons and of children longing to return. Casa Bambino at Santa Cristina provides daycare for toddlers.

STAYING THERE

HOW TO GO
A reasonable choice

Selva features in most major tour op brochures.

Chalets There is a fair choice of catered chalets, including some good ones with en suite bathrooms. Family specialist Esprit has chalets here, as does Total.

Hotels There are a dozen 4-stars in Selva, over 30 3-stars and numerous lesser hotels. Few of the best are well positioned.

⟨⟨③ **Gran Baita** (0471 795210) Large, luxurious sporthotel, with lots of mod cons including indoor pool. A few minutes' walk from centre and lifts. Highly recommended in 2006 ('they couldn't do enough for us').

⟨⟨③ **Granvara** (0471 795250) 'Just out of town but free hotel bus, great food and views and a spa. Recommended.'

⟨⟨③ **Aaritz** (0471 795011) Best-placed 4-star, opposite the Ciampinoi gondola, and with an open fire.

⟨⟨③ **Tyrol** (0471 774100) 'Friendly and fantastic value, handy for nursery slopes but bit of a way to Sella Ronda.'

⟨② **Rodella** (0471 794553) Just outside Selva but friendly pensione, with free taxi, spa and delicious meals.'

⟨② **Linder** (0471 795242) 'Friendly, family-run with good food.'

⟨② **Pralong** (0471 795370) An uphill walk from the centre, but 'one of the best hotels we've visited', says a reporter – endorsed again recently.

⟨② **Solaia** (0471 795104) 3-star chalet, superbly positioned for lifts and slopes.

⟨② **Pineta** (0471 795004) 'Good value for money,' says a 2006 reporter.

⟨② **Villa Seceda** (0471 795297) A 'friendly' B&B near the nursery slopes.

Self-catering There are plenty of apartments to choose from. We have had excellent reports of the Villa Gardena and Isabell apartments.

Passo Gardena (seen from Ciampinoi), with the excellent runs down the length of the Dantercëpies gondola descending into the woods →

SNOWPIX.COM / CHRIS GILL

ACTIVITIES

In Val Gardena:

Indoor Swimming pool, sauna, bowling, squash, ice rink, ice hockey, museum, concerts, cinema, billiards, tennis, climbing wall, fitness centre

Outdoor Sleigh rides, snow-shoeing, toboggan runs, paragliding, extensive cleared paths, climbing

Phone numbers
From abroad use the prefix +39 (and do **not** omit the initial '0' of the phone number).

TOURIST OFFICES

VAL GARDENA
t 0471 777777
info@valgardena.it
www.valgardena.it

Selva
t 0471 777900
selva@valgardena.it

Ortisei
t 0471 777600
ortisei@valgardena.it

EATING OUT
Plenty of good-value choices

The higher-quality restaurants are mainly hotel-based – reporters highly recommend Armin's Grill in the hotel of the same name, and the Sal Fëur in the Broi B&B. The Sun Valley Stübele does 'excellent pasta and pizza', says a 2006 visitor, as does Rino's. Another reader enjoyed 'wonderful goulash and dumplings' at Des Alpes. The Bellavista is also good for pasta, and Costabella is 'highly recommended' for Tirolean specialities.

APRES-SKI
Above average for a family resort

Nightlife is reasonably lively and informal, though the village is so scattered there is little on-street atmosphere. La Stua is an après-ski bar on the Sella Ronda route, with live music on some nights. For an early drink we are told that the Piz Seteur, above Plan de Gralba, is worth a little detour from the route – 'fun, loud and a bit raunchy' (you may find scantily clad girls dancing on the bar). For a civilised early drink try the good-value ski-school bar at the base of the Dantercëpies piste. Or the Costabella – cosy, serving good glühwein. Café Mozart on the main street is 'a great place for cakes'.

For thigh-slapping in Selva later on, the Laurinkeller has good atmosphere though it's 'quite expensive', while the popular Luislkeller is 'very German', 'lively' and 'packed', with loud music and barmaids in Tirolean garb. A 2006 reporter also enjoyed the new Goalies Irish bar with its hockey memorabilia – 'The music was particularly suited to 30 or 40 somethings.' The bar by the Ski Factory is said to be a 'jolly place' – and noted for its flaming cocktails.

The place to go after midnight is Dali, where a mixed British and Italian crowd dances till the small hours.

OFF THE SLOPES
Good variety

There's a sports centre, snow-shoeing, lovely walks, tobogganing and sleigh rides on Alpe di Siusi. One reporter enjoyed an organised bowling night ('great fun'). There is a bus to Ortisei, which is well worth a visit for its large hot-spring swimming pool, shops, restaurants and lovely old buildings.

Pedestrians can reach numerous good restaurants by gondola or cable-car. Car drivers have Bolzano and Innsbruck within reach and tour operators do trips to Cortina.

Ortisei 1235m/4,050ft

Ortisei is an attractive, prosperous market town with a life of its own apart from tourism. It's full of lovely buildings, pretty churches and pleasant shops. The local slopes aren't on the main Sella Ronda circuit. The lift to the Seceda slopes is easily reached from the centre by a 300m/980ft-long series of underground moving walkways and escalators; the Alpe di Siusi lifts are a similar distance out. The cable-car is now accessed via a long pedestrian footbridge, an improvement over the previous steep, icy uphill walk. The nursery area, school and kindergarten are at the foot of these slopes, but there's a fair range of family accommodation on the piste side of the road. The fine public indoor pool and ice rink are also here.

There are hotels and self-catering to suit all tastes and pockets and many good restaurants, mainly specialising in local dishes. A reporter recommends the Hotel Alpenheim (0471 796515): 'luxurious rooms', 'excellent food' but not central. Another says the Adler (0471 775000), which has a very impressive spa, is 'an excellent hotel'. Après-ski is quite jolly, and many bars keep going till late.

Sestriere

Altitude is the main attraction of this, Europe's first purpose-built resort; you could say it's the only attraction

COSTS

①②③④⑤⑥

RATINGS

The slopes
Fast lifts	**
Snow	****
Extent	****
Expert	***
Intermediate	****
Beginner	***
Convenience	***
Queues	***
Mountain restaurants	**

The rest
Scenery	***
Resort charm	*
Off-slope	*

NEWS

For 2006/07 the former Olympic village will be available for public use.

For 2005/06 an eight-seat gondola, with a mid-station, was opened up to Monte Fraiteve, for access to Sansicario.

And there's a new cable-car up from the town of Pragelato to Borgata.

- ➕ Local slopes suitable for most levels, with some tougher runs than in most neighbouring resorts
- ➕ Part of the extensive Milky Way area, now with improved links to Sansicario and Pragelato.
- ➕ Snowmaking covers all but one or two marginal slopes, but ...

- ➖ It needs to, given the very erratic local snowfall record
- ➖ The village is an eyesore, though smartened up or the 2006 Olympics
- ➖ For a purpose-built resort, not conveniently arranged
- ➖ Weekend and peak-period queues
- ➖ Little après-ski during the week

Sestriere was built for snow – high, with north-west-facing slopes – and it has very extensive snowmaking, too. So even if you are let down by the notoriously erratic snowfalls in this corner of Italy, you should be fairly safe here – certainly safer than in Sauze d'Oulx, over the hill. Whether this is a sensible basis for choosing to stay here is another question. When we go to Italy, we generally aim to go somewhere a bit more captivating.

THE RESORT

Sestriere was the Alps' first purpose-built resort, developed by Fiat's Giovanni Agnelli in the 1930s (and only now being sold, we hear). It sits on a broad, sunny and windy col, and neither the site nor the village, with its large apartment blocks, looks very hospitable – though the buildings have benefited from recent investment for the 2006 Winter Olympics. This is not the most convenient of purpose-built resorts, either – some of the walks are non-trivial. The satellite of Borgata, 200m/66oft lower, is less convenient for nightlife and shops. The valley town of Pragelato is a viable alternative base now that it has a cable-car link up to Borgata.

THE MOUNTAINS

The local skiing is on shady slopes, mainly open with some woodland, facing the village. Sestriere is at one extreme of the big Franco-Italian Milky Way area.

Slopes The local slopes, served by drags and chairs, are in two main sectors: Sises, directly in front of the village, and Motta, above Borgata; Motta is more varied and bigger, with almost twice the vertical. Across the valley, gondolas go up from Borgata for Sauze d'Oulx and from a car park west of the village for Sansicario and the rest of the Milky Way. For the return to Sestriere there are red runs

down both gondolas, but they are sunny and rarely open. Signposting and the piste map are poor. There's night skiing twice a week.

Terrain-parks Sestriere shares the Double Black terrain-park with Sauze d'Oulx at Col Basset, reached via the gondola. A special park pass is available for 22 euros.

Snow reliability With most of the local slopes facing north-west and ranging from 1840m to 2825m (6,040ft to 9,270ft), and an extensive snowmaking network, snow-cover is usually reliable, except on the runs down the gondolas mentioned above. The notoriously erratic snowfalls in the Milky Way often leave the rest of the area seriously short of snow.

Experts There is a fair amount to amuse experts – steep pistes served by the drags at the top of both sectors. There is a fair amount of off-piste, given snow. Don't count on it – or on moguls, which are erased religiously

Intermediates Both sectors also offer plenty for confident intermediates, who can explore practically all of the Milky Way areas, conditions permitting. The runs in the Motta sector offer more of a challenge.

Beginners The terrain is good for beginners, with several nursery areas and the gentlest of easy blue runs down to Borgata. But there is a lack of easy intermediate runs to progress to.

Snowboarding Sestriere has a reasonable number of chairs, but there are also lots of drag-lifts.

Not a pretty sight, though a reasonably pretty site →

SNOWPIX.COM / CHRIS GILL

KEY FACTS

Resort	2000m
	6,560ft
Milky Way	
Slopes	1390-2825m
	4,560-9,270ft
Lifts	88
Pistes	400km
	249 miles
Blue	24%
Red	56%
Black	20%
Snowmaking	120km
	75 miles
Sestriere-Sauze d'Oulx-Sansicario	
Slopes	1390-2825m
	4,560-9,270ft
Lifts	51
Pistes	300km
	186 miles
Snowmaking	90km
	56 miles

REPORTS WANTED

Recently we have had few reports on this resort. If you go there, please do send us a report.

OUR WEBSITE

Go to our website at wtss.co.uk for resort news, links to resort sites, a build-your-own-shortlist system and reader forums.

PISTE MAP

Sestriere is covered on the Sauze d'Oulx map a few pages back.

Phone numbers
From abroad use the prefix +39 (and do **not** omit the initial '0' of the phone number).

TOURIST OFFICE

t 0122 755444
sestriere@
montagnedoc.it
www.sestriere.it
www.montagnedoc.it
www.vialattea.it

Cross-country There are three loops covering a total of 8km/4 miles.

Queues The lifts are mainly modern, though there are still some inadequate old ones. But queues for the main lifts occur at the weekends and holidays. A recent reporter experienced a half-hour wait for the Cit Roc chair, which could be avoided by taking the Garnel chair instead. The lifts from Borgata to Sestriere should now be less of a bottleneck at the end of the day. Queues occur when poor weather closes the gondola link to Sauze, but the new lift to M. Fraiteve has improved the connection with Sansicario. Reporters here, as in Sauze, complain that some lifts may be kept closed during the week, to conserve either money or snow – when crowded pistes can also become a problem.

Mountain restaurants The Raggio di Sole in the Anfiteatro sector is a 'cosy log cabin'. Reporters also recommend the Tana della Volpe at the top of the Banchetta chair, the Alpette ('good portions, spectacular view') and the busy Gargote at Garnel ('excellent hot chocolates'). The Teit pizzeria at Borgata has 'good choices at reasonable prices', and the Capret is also worth a try. But on the whole the local restaurants are only fair. There are better ones further afield.

Schools and guides Lack of spoken English can be a problem. 'Well organised,' says a recent visitor.

Facilities for children There are no special facilities for children.

STAYING THERE

How to go Most accommodation is in apartments.

Hotels There are a dozen hotels, mostly 3-star or 4-star. You might want to stay near one of the gondolas. The Shackleton Mountain Resort (0122 750773) is new, and the former Olympic Village will offer accommodation from 2006/07. The Savoy Edelweiss (0122 77040) and the Du Col (0122 76990) are central, and just out of the village is the luxurious Principi di Piemonte (0122 7941). Grangesises offers an alternative base – it's 3km/1 mile from Sestriere and linked by bus.

Eating out There are plenty of options. Try Lu Periol for home-made ravioli and atmosphere. Tre Rubinetti is highly recommended for 'outstanding cooking' and an enormous wine list. The Antica Spelonca is 'cosy with an interesting menu'. Last Tango and the Baita are well regarded.

Après-ski Après-ski is quiet during the week, but the Prestige and Palace Due are two of the many little bars that liven up at weekends. The Pinky is one of the best of the bars that double as eateries, with low sofas in the classic Italian casual-chic style, an antipasto buffet and 'great choices of pizzas'.

Off the slopes There are some smart shops and there's a fitness centre, an ice rink, a sports centre and pool. Thanks to the new cable-car link from Borgata, it is now possible to visit the town of Pragelato.

Sestriere

475

La Thuile

An unusual combination of a revitalised mining town and a modern lift-base complex; extensive, easy slopes and a link with France

NEWS

For 2005/06 a quad chair with moving carpet loading replaced the old Belvedere double chair. It has a new location above the black run of the same name, between there and Fourclaz.

Snowmaking was also increased.

476

+ Fair-sized area with good lift system linked to La Rosière in France

+ Free of crowds and queues

+ Excellent beginner and easy intermediate slopes

+ Heli-skiing available, opening up some notably long descents

+ Some slope-side accommodation

– Most of the seriously tough pistes are low down, and most of the low, woodland runs are tough

– Mountain restaurants disappointing by Italian standards

– Winds can close lift links with France

– Not the place for lively après-ski

La Thuile deserves to be better known internationally. The slopes best suit beginners and intermediates looking for smooth cruises, but are not devoid of interest for experts, particularly if the snow conditions are good – and expeditions to La Rosière add interest. Those who try it seem to appreciate the quiet village as much as the quiet slopes.

THE RESORT

La Thuile is a resort of parts. At the foot of the lifts is the modern Planibel complex, with places to stay, a leisure centre, bars, shops and restaurants – like a French purpose-built resort, but with a distinctly Italian atmosphere. But many people find this rather soulless and prefer to stay in the old village across the river (served by a regular free bus service). Much of the old village has been restored and new buildings (and an underground car park) tastefully added. There are reasonable restaurants and bars.

The slopes link with La Rosière, over the border in France. Courmayeur is easily reached by car, and Cervinia is about an hour away.

THE MOUNTAINS

La Thuile has quite extensive slopes, with the great attraction that they are normally very uncrowded. Many runs are marked red, but deserve no more than a blue rating. The link with La Rosière adds adventure; the runs there are steeper, sunnier and bumpier – and the start of the route back is a fairly tricky red. By comparison, La Thuile is 'Heaven' for lifts and slope maintenance – endorsed by most reporters. Strong winds can close the high lifts, including the link.

Slopes The lifts out of the village take you to Les Suches, with shady black runs going back down directly to the village through the trees, and reds taking a more roundabout route. From here chairs take you to Chaz Dura for access to a variety of gentle bowls facing east. You can go off westwards from here to the Petit St Bernard road or across to the new quad up to Belvedere, the launch pad for excursions to La Rosière. Below Belvedere are the slopes of Gran Testa, served by a fast chairs and drags.

Terrain-parks None in La Thuile.

Snow reliability Most of La Thuile's slopes are north- or east-facing and above 2000m/6,560ft, so the snow generally keeps well. There's also a decent amount of snowmaking, and 'grooming is immaculate'.

Experts The steep pistes down through the trees from Les Suchest – the Diretta and Tre – are serious stuff. The

Chaz Dura
2580m

BELVEDERE
2610m/8,560ft

Col de
Fourclaz

COL DE LA
TRAVERSETTE
2385m
↙ La Rosière

Arnouvaz

Les
Suches
2200m

La Thuile
1440m/4,720ft

KEY FACTS

Resort	1440m
	4,720ft

Espace San Bernardo (La Rosière and La Thuile)	
Slopes	1175-2610m
	3,850-8,560ft
Lifts	35
Pistes	150km
	93 miles
Green	9%
Blue	36%
Red	40%
Black	15%
Snowmaking	
	Over 300 guns

OUR WEBSITE

Go to our website at wtss.co.uk for resort news, links to resort sites, a build-your-own-shortlist system and reader forums.

REPORTS WANTED

Recently we have had few reports on this resort. If you go there, please do send us a report.

Phone numbers
From abroad use the prefix +39 (and do **not** omit the initial '0' of the phone number).

TOURIST OFFICE

t 0165 883049
info@lathuile.it
www.lathuile.it

area above the Petit St Bernard road has some genuinely black terrain and plenty of off-piste – the fast quad means you can do quick circuits in this area. A 2006 reporter was still making fresh tracks three days after snowfall. The black Maisonettes, by the Arnouvaz chair, is reported to be quiet.

Heli-lifts are available. The Ruitor glacier offers a 20km/12 mile run to Ste-Foy, a short taxi-ride from La Rosière and the lifts back to La Thuile.

Intermediates La Thuile has some good intermediate runs. The bowls above Les Suches have many gentle blue and red runs, ideal for cruising. There are also long reds through the trees back to the resort. The red runs on the other side of the top ridge, down towards the Petit St Bernard road, offer more challenge. The road forms a roundabout red to the village, taking 11km/7 miles to drop 1100m; 'bleak' is one view, 'boring' probably nearer the mark; avoid at all costs in fresh snow.

Beginners There are nursery slopes at village level and up at Les Suches. There's a good gentle green run above there, and easy blues. Promenade is 'a very easy blue', but is served by drag-lifts. You ride the gondola back down.

Snowboarding These are great slopes for learning. You need ride only chair-lifts and the gondola, and most of the slopes are easy. For the more experienced there are great tree runs, good free-riding, and some good carving runs. But there are some frustratingly flat sections too.

Cross-country La Thuile has four loops of varying difficulty on the valley floor, adding up to 17km/11 miles of track.

Queues The lift system is excellent in general. Short queues may form at the gondola first thing, but not at the chair. Once up the hill, no problems: fast chairs dominate.

Mountain restaurants We haven't quite recovered from our last abortive

attempt to find a decent lunch here, but reports suggest an improvement. The Mélèze, near the top of the gondola, serves 'generous portions'. The Clotze, at the foot of the Chalets chair-lift, does 'tasty, reasonably priced food'. The Off Shore, above Arnouvaz, offers an 'excellent atmosphere'. A couple of places provide an incentive to tackle the long San Bernardo home run: the new Maison de Neige, is 'absolutely fabulous,' says a 2006 reporter – the 4-course menu is 'worth every penny'; and the Riondet serves 'good food at astonishing speeds'.

Schools and guides A recent reporter's parents received 'patient and effective tuition' and made excellent progress. They were 'delighted by the growth of confidence their instructors fostered'. Another reader had small classes early in the season ('really good').

Facilities for children There's an 'excellent' nursery, a Miniclub and snowgarden. Children over the age of five can join adult ski classes.

STAYING THERE

How to go The number of tour operators going there is increasing.

Hotels The choice is between the characterless 4-star Planibel, a few 3-stars and some simpler places. Reporters like the 'quiet, friendly, family-run' hotel du Glacier (0165 884137), a short walk above the lifts, and Chalet Eden (0165 885050), near the gondola ('excellent value').

Self-catering The Planibel apartments are spacious, by the lifts and great value. Some 'have been refurbished and are quite smart', but others are 'tired and urgently need refurbishing'.

Eating out Reader recommendations include the Bricole ('excellent house pasta'), the Créton ('the gorgonzola and walnut fagottini was outstanding'), the Lune for good value steaks and salads, and the Rascard ('tremendous jumbo prawns'). Early on, head for Chocolat and indulge in all things sweet – a cafe 'not to be missed'.

Après-ski Nightlife is 'not vibrant' and 'even quieter' than one reporter expected. The Bricole is the liveliest bar. The Fantasia disco at the Planibel warms up well after midnight.

Off the slopes There are few shops, but the Planibel complex has a good pool and there are several marked walks. Pedestrians can ride up the gondola for lunch.

Trentino

Not a resort, but a region with a few big resorts and a lot of smaller ones that deserve to be better known on the UK market

Trentino is a fabulously scenic region that is rather neglected by the British. It has a few large resorts – two of which are covered in their own chapters (Madonna di Campiglio and Passo Tonale) – resorts linked to the Sella Ronda (such as Canazei and Campitello, covered below) – and a lot of small ski areas that you may not have heard of. The following guide is not comprehensive; but it includes all the places that are likely to be of international interest, and more.

PASSO TONALE AND NEARBY

Passo Tonale is a good-value, high, snow-sure, purpose-built resort set on the border of Trentino and now linked to Pontedilegno in neighbouring Lombardia; its local slopes suit beginners and early intermediates best. Passo Tonale has its own chapter.

Just down the Val di Sole (which means Valley of Sun) is **Pejo** (1400m/4,590ft), a spa village with a narrow but tall slope area rising to 2340m/7,680ft, served by a gondola, three chair-lifts and a drag. Further down the valley are Marilleva and Folgarida, linked to Madonna di Campiglio (see below) – all these areas (and the resorts described in the 'Around Trento' section below) are covered by the Superskirama Adamello-Brenta ski pass. If you have a car, it is perfectly possible to explore all these areas in a week.

MADONNA DI CAMPIGLIO AND NEARBY

Madonna di Campiglio is a chic resort with mainly easy slopes that attracts an affluent, almost exclusively Italian clientele. It has its own chapter.

Its ski area is linked to those of the much smaller resorts of Marilleva and Folgarida. The slopes above **Marilleva** are excellent, steep, north-facing reds

(with a few blues higher up the mountain), much better for adventurous intermediates than Campiglio's main Pradalago slopes. And the snow is usually the best in the area because of the largely north-facing orientation. There's also a serious black run served by a two-stage chair from the resort to Doss della Pesa (2230m/7,320ft). There's also a gondola which links to a six-pack to Monte Vigo (2180m/7,150ft) and the links to Campiglio and Folgarida.

Marilleva itself is a modern resort consisting of several 1960s-style, ugly but functional, low-rise concrete buildings (most of them thankfully well screened by trees) built on a mid-mountain shelf at 1400m/4,590ft and reached by road or gondola from the lower part of the resort at 900m/2,950ft, on the valley floor.

The slopes down to **Folgarida** are gentler than those above Marilleva but in general somewhat more challenging than Campiglio's main slopes.

The main part of Folgarida itself is clustered around the gondola station at 1400m/4,590ft – and purpose-built in a much more traditional style than Marilleva. It feels much more upmarket, with smart hotels, a few shops and fur-clad patrons. There's another area of the resort at 1300m/4,270ft by another gondola station.

The lift companies are in the midst of a development that will link the Cinque Laghi slopes of Madonna di Campiglio with those above **Pinzolo** (780m/2,560ft), currently a 20-minute drive to the south. A gondola followed by a fast chair take you to the area's high point of Doss del Sabion (2100m/6,890ft), where there are great views of the Brenta massif. The area has mainly genuinely challenging red runs, an excellent groomed black (the Competition piste) and the snow keeps

in condition because most of the runs are northish facing. The Cioca and Patagonia reds are lovely steep cruises (though Cioca is steep enough to be a black in parts). Usefully, the average and maximum gradients of these and other runs are marked at the top of each (something we haven't seen before). The first two chair-lifts that are part of the link to Campiglio were there when we visited last season but we understand the link will not be complete for 2006/07. When it is, Madonna di Campiglio, with its outlying links to Pinzolo, Marilleva and Folgarida will be a much more attractive place for good intermediates to visit.

Pinzolo itself is not a conventional ski resort but the main town of the Val Rendena.

AROUND TRENTO

Trento is the main town of Trentino and its local hill – only a few minutes' drive away – is **Monte Bondone**. For a local hill it is excellent: half a dozen roadside chair-lifts serve partly wooded slopes here on Palon (2090m/6,860ft), with a longest run of 4km/2.5 miles dropping 800m/2,620ft and served by a fast quad chair. About 90 per cent of the small area is covered by snowmaking. There's a terrain-park. And great views to the Brenta

Dolomites around Madonna.

To the south-east of Trento, and closer to the town of Rovereto, are the small resorts of **Folgaria** (1165m/3,820ft – not to be confused with Folgarida near Madonna) and **Lavarone**. Lavarone has a handful of lifts, but Folgaria has more like 20, serving 60km/37 miles of runs with 100 per cent snowmaking.

To the north-west are the slopes on Paganella (2125m/6,970ft) shared by **Fai della Paganella** (1000m/3,280ft) and **Andalo** (1050m/3,440ft). Andalo is a sizeable resort and pleasant enough place with a small local town feel; a few small UK tour ops feature it. We visited for half a day in 2006 and enjoyed the small ski area very much. One new eight-seater gondola goes up from near the centre of Andalo and another leaves from a big car park nearby. Four of the other 15 lifts are high-speed chairs, with another planned for 2006/07. The runs are mainly genuinely challenging reds and can be long (a maximum vertical of almost 1100m/3,610ft); most are northish-facing and so keep their snow in good condition. We especially enjoyed the Dosa Larici and La Rocca reds down to Santel (the nearest lift base to Fai). There's a beginner area near the Andalo base but only a few short blue runs (all at the top) so we don't recommend it for novices or timid intermediates.

Trentino

479

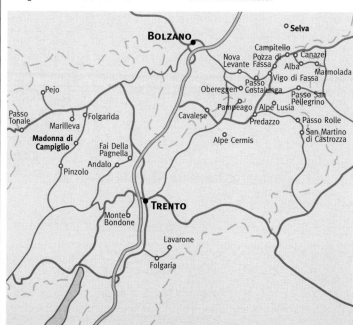

Trentino
Tread into Temptation

Trentino Marketing - ph: S. Angelani

Promise to enjoy yourself and we promise to entice you. Sun, snow, fast pistes, slow food - stray no further for your winter thrills. The Dolomites promise you the passion of Italy on seductive slopes. Trentino - for those who can resist everything except temptation.

www.trentino.to

TRENTINO

ITALIA

A single piste runs back to the village but it is often closed. The local Belvedere slopes are easy and the village nursery slope is good but inconvenient, and so unlikely to be used after day one.

Campitello (1445m/4,740ft) is a pleasant, unremarkable village, smaller and quieter than next-door Canazei, and still unspoiled. It's quiet during the day, having no slopes back to the village. A reporter recommends the 4-star hotel Soroghes (0462 750060). Another enjoyed a stay at the hotel Sella Ronda (0462 750525). Campitello has quite lively après-ski – the Da Giulio bar gets packed. There's an ice rink. A cable-car takes you up to the slopes. To get home you can take the cable-car down or take the piste to Canazei and catch a bus.

OTHER TRENTINO RESORTS

Still in the Val di Fassa, close to Canazei, **Alba** has its own slopes, linked to **Pozza di Fassa** further down the valley; over the road from Pozza another small area of slopes is linked to **Vigo di Fassa**. Not far from the valley town of Moena is the lift system of **Alpe Lusia**, but off to the east are more extensive slopes at **Passo San Pellegrino**, linked with **Falcade** – again, over the border in Veneto. Off to the east is another fair-sized lift network at **Passo Costalunga**, linked with **Nova Levante** (Welschnofen) in Alto Adige.

Continuing downstream, you are now in the Val di Fiemme. Near **Predazzo** there is a lift up to the slopes shared with **Pampeago** and with **Obereggen**, across the border in Alto Adige. Finally, the town of **Cavalese** has lifts up to the **Alpe Cermis** slopes.

To the south of the Val di Fassa/Val di Fiemme axis, a steep road over the high **Passo Rolle** – where there is a small network of drags and chairs serving easy slopes on either side of the road – leads down to the resort of **San Martino di Castrozza** (1470m/ 4,820ft). San Martino has a fabulous setting beneath a wall of Dolomite cliffs and peaks – the Pale di San Martino – soaring to over 3000m/ 9,840ft. The village is not notably cute – there are quite a few large, block-like buildings – but it is pleasant enough. The slopes, modest in extent and entirely intermediate in difficulty, are split into three sectors, only two of them linked (at altitude).

SELLA RONDA RESORTS

Canazei and Campitello in the **Val di Fassa** are in Trentino and the slopes above them are part of the famous Sella Ronda circuit; the **Marmolada** glacier is also in Trentino and is reachable on skis from Arabba on the Sella Ronda circuit. See the Sella Ronda chapter for a description of the skiing. Here we cover the main Trentino resorts linked to the Sella Ronda.

Canazei is a sizeable, bustling, pretty, roadside village of narrow streets, rustic old buildings, traditional-style hotels and nice little shops, set at 1465m/4,810ft beneath the Sella Ronda's most heavily wooded section of mountains. The grand 3-star hotel Dolomiti (0462 601106) in the centre is one of the original resort hotels; the charming, chalet-style Diana (0462 601477) is five minutes from the centre.

There are numerous restaurants and the après-ski is really animated. La Stua di Ladins serves local wines and the Husky and Roxy bars are worth a visit. Off-slope entertainment consists of beautiful walks and shopping. There's also a pool, sauna, Turkish baths and skating in neighbouring Alba.

A 12-person gondola is the only mountain access point, but it shifts the queues (which can be long) quickly.

Bardonecchia

A fairly extensive area, and a good base for touring other nearby French and Italian resorts. The local slopes, and the town itself, tend to be fairly quiet during the week, but lots of weekenders pour in from Turin.

KEY FACTS

Resort	1310m
	4,300ft
Slopes	1290m-2750m
	4,230-9,020ft
Lifts	26
Pistes	85km
	53 miles
Blue	41%
Red	49%
Black	10%
Snowmaking	30%

online booking
www.sport2000rent.com

TOURIST OFFICE

t 0122 99032
bardonecchia@
montagnedoc.it
www.montagnedoc.it

THE RESORT

Bardonecchia is a sizeable old railway town, with little Alpine charm but with a pleasant old quarter. It hosted the snowboard events of the 2006 Olympics. A regular visitor enthuses about the hotel des Geneys (0122 99001) – 'friendly; excellent food'. Après-ski is quiet, but not absent – there are some good-value bars and a couple of discos, at weekends at least. There is an 'excellent' ski-bus service.

THE MOUNTAINS

Two separate areas of slopes, either side of town, are each a free bus-ride away. The larger sector is a wide mountainside of north-facing runs, mostly in trees, above three valley lift stations – Campo Smith, Les Arnauds and Melezet. Most runs here are below

2200m/7,220ft. The other sector – Jafferau – is a tall, thin mountain of long, partly open, west-facing runs going appreciably higher (well above the trees). There are no groomed pistes to the bottom here. Despite an Olympics-inspired injection of new lifts, most are still slow (there are many drags). There are few queues during the week, though. The snow record isn't particularly good, but there is now extensive snowmaking on the larger sector, with mid-stations meaning you can stay above 1800m/5,910ft. There is little challenge for experts, but virtually the whole area is good for intermediates. Campo Smith and Melezet have nursery areas for beginners. For boarders there is a terrain-park and half-pipe but there are a lot of awkward drag-lifts to cope with. Mountain restaurants are generally pleasant and uncrowded.

Short turns

483

Macugnaga

Macugnaga consists of a pair of quiet, pretty villages dramatically set at the head of a remote valley, over the mountains from Zermatt and Saas-Fee. It's a place for a cheap holiday away from it all, with some skiing thrown in.

KEY FACTS

Resort	1325m
	4,350ft
Slopes	1325-2800m
	4,350-9,190ft
Lifts	12
Pistes	38km
	24 miles
Blue	30%
Red	65%
Black	5%
Snowmaking	some

TOURIST OFFICE

t 0324 65119
info@macugnaga.it
www.macugnaga.it

THE RESORT

The villages of Staffa and slightly higher Pecetto have a lot of traditional charm and enjoy a splendid setting close to the the towering east wall of Monte Rosa. Reporters remark on the friendly people and the good food. There is a 'lovely' wine shop, too. The bus service between the villages is reliable. There are a dozen small hotels; most manage 3-star status. The Girasole (0324 65052) is approved by a reporter this year – 'friendly, homely'.

THE MOUNTAINS

The slopes are in two separate sectors above the two villages.

Pecetto's lifts run up to Belvedere (1930m/6,330ft), at the foot of the Belvedere glacier. A chair-lift rises gently and very slowly from the village

to Burky, in the middle of the small, woody area of gentle runs.

Staffa has a couple of drags on an excellent nursery slope beside the village and a two-stage cable-car going over sunny slopes almost to the Swiss border. Drag-lifts up here serve short blue and slightly longer red and black runs, and there are good, varied red runs down the 1100m/3,610ft vertical of the top cable-car – the longest curling away to notch up 7.5km/5 miles. In the right conditions, off-piste possibilities from the cable-car are considerable, including a run north ending below Saas-Fee. Whether it's worth the long bus- or taxi-ride back ...

Reporters have approved of the piste grooming, the lack of queues, the 'very patient' and 'enthusiastic' ski instructors and the 'lovely, inexpensive' lunches in the several mountain restaurants.

SNOWPIX.COM / CHRIS GILL

Madesimo

Madesimo's mountain is great for Italian weekenders, who arrive in numbers. If you're planning a week, it's far from ideal. But we have a sneaking affection for the place – and we'd really like to do the run to Fraciscio.

KEY FACTS

Resort	1545m
	5,070ft
Slopes	1545-2880m
	5,070-9,450ft
Lifts	12
Pistes	60km
	37 miles
Blue	30%
Red	55%
Black	15%
Snowmaking	some

TOURIST OFFICE

t 0343 53015
aptmadesimo@
provincia.so.it
www.madesimo.com

SNOWPIX.COM / CHRIS GILL

The hotel Torre
should now have
been truncated ↓

THE RESORT

Madesimo sits in a remote, pretty side valley, a three-hour drive north from Bergamo that ends in a very dramatic hairpin-bend ascent. The village has some old farm buildings, but is mainly a piecemeal modern development. The delightful central church, narrow streets and little shops have until now been overlooked by an airport control tower (actually the hotel Torre), now truncated. A fair choice of hotels is available. Eating out is a highlight. Après-ski is fairly quiet.

THE MOUNTAINS

Madesimo's venerable cable-car was replaced by an eight-seat gondola for 2005/06, accessing the west-facing front and east-facing back of mountain. This should have solved any queue problems. From mid-mountain there are pleasant runs to the village, passing through pretty woodland, or you can cut across to the open slopes above Motta, now equipped with fast quads to deal with the weekend influx on the funicular from the valley town of Campodolcino. There is snowmaking on lower front runs, which get the afternoon sun. The top of the gondola serves the famous Canalone, a long, sweeping, easy black, but classed as off-piste. In theory there is also an off-piste route of 1600m/5,250ft vertical to Fraciscio, next to Campodolcino. The gondola also accesses the best intermediate runs, on the back of the mountain in the high Val di Lei. The nursery slopes are fine, but there are few really easy pistes to graduate to. There is a new terrain-park with half-pipe. The mountain restaurants are not particularly appealing.

Pila

Pila is little known outside Italy and offers a worthwhile surprise to those who visit. A fair-sized area of well-groomed, snow-sure slopes rises around a purpose-built resort, linked by gondola to the old Roman town of Aosta.

KEY FACTS

Resort	1800m
	5,910ft
Slopes	1550-2750m
	5,090-9,020ft
Lifts	14
Pistes	70km
	43 miles
Blue	12%
Red	73%
Black	15%
Snowmaking	15km
	9 miles

TOURIST OFFICE

t 0165 521055
info@pilaturismo.it
www.pilaturismo.it

THE RESORT

Pila is a car-free, purpose-built, ski-in/ski-out resort, with a mix of chalet-style buildings and large apartment blocks. Après-ski is quiet. Below the resort at 570m/1,870ft, 20 minutes away by gondola, 30 minutes by road, is Aosta, founded by the Romans. Aosta is a big, generally dreary town, but it has a pleasant traffic-free old centre, with cobbled streets and squares lined by shops and cafes (largely for locals). Aosta attracts large numbers of British school groups.

THE MOUNTAINS

Chair-lifts (some fast, but most slow) and a cable-car fan out from the village. There is an interesting mix of slopes. The tree line is notably high (about 2300m/7,550ft) and most runs are below it, making this an excellent bad-weather resort. Lifts go on up over open slopes to the top heights, where there are stunning views stretching from Mont Blanc in the west to the Matterhorn in the east. There are runs for all standards, but mostly they are reds, ranging from easy to stiff. The blacks don't amount to much, but there is extensive off-piste, a terrain-park and half-pipe. There are two short beginner lifts, but progression means using a very busy central run. Most of the slopes are north- or north-east facing and above 2000m/6,560ft and there's extensive snowmaking, so snow reliability is good (as is the grooming). There are few queues, except at weekends and for the gondola down to Aosta – 'huge from 3.30pm onwards'.

There are several good rustic mountain restaurants. La Châtelaine is a cosy retreat with a friendly owner.

Short turns

485

San Vigilio di Marebbe/Kronplatz

San Vigilio is the most charming and convenient of several resorts that share the Plan de Corones (aka Kronplatz) area of intermediate slopes in the Dolomites. It is little known in the UK but has a powerful lift system and great snowmaking.

KEY FACTS

Resort	1200m
	3,940ft
Slopes	1200-2275m
	3,940-7,460ft
Lifts	32
Pistes	103km
	64 miles
Blue	50%
Red	35%
Black	15%
Snowmaking	100%

best for rent

www.sport2000rent.com

TOURIST OFFICE

t 0474 555 447
info@kronplatz.com
www.kronplatz.com

THE RESORT

Brunico (Bruneck) is the main town (pop 120,000) of the area. Far more attractive is San Vigilio di Marebbe with a lift from the village (pop 1,200) and its own small linked area of slopes. It's a pretty little village with some good 3- and 4-star hotels and a couple of lively bars (including Bus Stop, complete with an air-conditioned bus for smokers).

THE MOUNTAINS

Out of the 32 lifts an astonishing 20 are gondolas and six are fast chairs. This heavy investment has been possible because of a 50 per cent subsidy on new lifts in the Sud Tirol because they count as public transport – amazing. The slopes have 100 per cent snowmaking, and it is used very well. On our 2006 visit we skied two long (1300m/4,270ft vertical), fabulously groomed black runs down towards Brunico in the morning, and both had a centimetre or two of fresh artificial 'powder' on top of corduroy – brilliant.

The area best suits early-to-average intermediates willing to take on challenges – though a keen piste-basher will ski all the runs in a day or two. The red runs are serious, and many blues are quite tough. There's an easy blue under the first stage of the gondola from San Vigilio and another reasonably easy one on San Vigilio's local slopes. These are linked by a cross-village gondola to the Plan de Corones area and will be linked for 2006/07 to Picolin in the next valley by a new red run and gondola. From there you'll be able to go by bus for a day on the Sella Ronda slopes, starting from La Villa. There are several attractive, rustic mountain restaurants.

Switzerland

Switzerland is home to some of our favourite resorts. We award ★★★★★ for resort charm and for spectacular scenery to only three resorts in this book – the essentially traffic-free Swiss villages of Wengen, Mürren and Zermatt. Many other Swiss resorts are not far behind. Many resorts have impressive slopes, too – including some of the biggest, highest and toughest runs in the Alps – as well as a lot of good intermediate terrain. For fast, queue-free lift networks, Swiss resorts are not known for setting the standards – too many historic cable-cars and mountain railways for that. But the real bottlenecks are steadily disappearing. And there are compensations – the world's best mountain restaurants, for one, and pretty reliable accommodation for another.

People always seem to associate Switzerland with high prices. In the recent past, we haven't found most Swiss resorts appreciably more expensive than most French ones – though some Swiss resorts, such as Zermatt, Verbier and St Moritz, do tend to be pricey. What is clear is that what you get for your money in Switzerland is generally first class.

Many Swiss resorts have a special relationship with the British, who invented downhill skiing in its modern form in Wengen and Mürren by persuading the locals to run their mountain railways in winter, and so act as ski lifts, and by organising the first downhill races. An indication of the continuing strength of the British presence in these resorts is that Wengen has an English church.

487

While France is the home of the purpose-built resort, Switzerland is the home of the mountain village that has transformed itself from traditional farming community (or health retreat) into year-round holiday resort. Many of Switzerland's most famous mountain resorts are as popular in the summer as in the winter, or more so. This creates places with a more lived-in feel to them and a much more stable local community. Many villages are still dominated by a handful of families lucky or shrewd enough to get involved in the early development of the area.

This has its downside as well as advantages. The ruling families are able to stifle competition and prevent newcomers from taking a slice of their action. Alternative ski schools, competing with the traditional nationally organised school and pushing up standards, are much less common than in other Alpine countries, for example. We are only now beginning to see this grip weakened, and only in some resorts.

Switzerland means high living as well as high prices, and the swanky grand hotels of St Moritz, Gstaad, Zermatt and Davos are beyond the dreams of most ordinary holidaymakers. (St Moritz now has an amazing five five-star hotels.) Even in more modest places, the quality of the service is generally high. The trains run like clockwork to the advertised timetable (and often they run to the top of the mountain, doubling as ski-lifts). The food is almost universally of good quality and much less stodgy than in neighbouring Austria. Even the standard rustic dish of rösti is haute cuisine compared to Austrian sausages. And in Switzerland you get what you pay for: the cheapest wine, for example, is not cheap, but it is reliable.

Perhaps surprisingly for such a traditional, rather staid skiing nation, Switzerland has gone out of its way to attract snowboarders. Davos may hit the headlines mainly when it hosts huge economic, conferences, but yards from the conference hall there are dudes getting big air on the Bolgen slope's training kickers. Little-known Flims claims Europe's best terrain-park.

GETTING AROUND THE SWISS ALPS
Access to practically all Swiss resorts is fairly straightforward when approaching from the north – just pick your motorway. But many of the high passes that are perfectly sensible ways to get around the country in summer are closed in winter, which can be inconvenient if you are moving around from one area to another.

There are very useful car-carrying trains in various places; they can cut out huge amounts of driving. One key link is between the Valais (Crans-Montana, Zermatt etc) and Andermatt via the Furka tunnel, and another is from Andermatt to the Grisons (Flims, Davos etc) via the Oberalp pass – closed to road traffic in winter but open to trains except after very heavy snowfalls. Another rail tunnel that's very handy is the Lötschberg, linking Kandersteg in the Bernese Oberland with Brig in the Valais.

St Moritz is more awkward to get to than other resorts. The main road route is over the Julier pass. This is normally kept open, but at 2285m/7,500ft it is naturally prone to heavy snowfalls that can shut it for a time. Fallbacks are car-carrying rail tunnels under the Albula pass and the Vereina tunnel from near Klosters – a relatively new option, having opened in 1999.

These car-carrying rail services are generally painless. Often you can just turn up and drive on. But carrying capacities are obviously

swissrent.com

Hire from swissrent a sport for complete freedom of choice with your winter sports equipment: skis, boards or boots, we have all the top brands and models, whatever your preference, whatever your style.

So be smart and hire from swissrent a sport. All over Switzerland at 50 outlets in 35 well-known winter sports resorts. Or wherever the action is.

For more information, prices or reservations visit our website at: www.swissrent.com

Your Ski Brand:

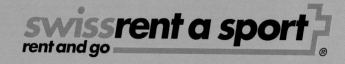

swissrent a sport
rent and go

Hire where the action is.

limited. Some services (eg Oberalp) carry only a handful of cars, and booking is vital. Others (eg Furka, Lötschberg, Vereina) are much bigger operations with much greater capacity – but that's a reflection of demand, and at peak times there may be long queues – particularly for the Furka tunnel from Andermatt, which Zürich residents use to get to the big Valais resorts. There is a car-carrying rail tunnel linking Switzerland with Italy – the Simplon. But most

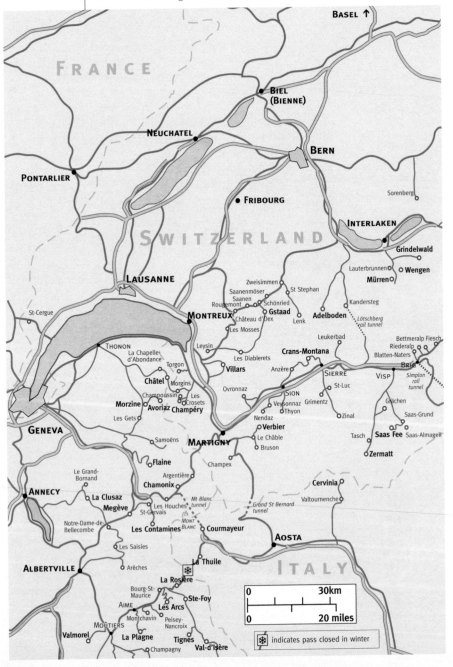

routes to Italy are kept open by means of road tunnels. See the Italy introduction for more information.

To use Swiss motorways (and it's difficult to avoid doing so if you're driving serious distances within the country) you have to buy a permit to stick on your windscreen (costing SF40 in 2006, and lasting from December 2005 to the end of January 2007). They are sold at the border, and are, for all practical purposes, compulsory.

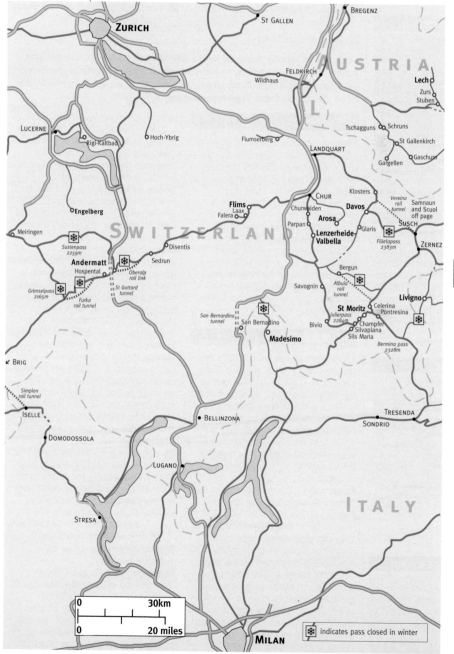

Adelboden

Chocolate-box village with plenty to do off the slopes – but also with an extensive ski area linked to Lenk

COSTS

① ② ③ ④ ⑤ ⑥

RATINGS

The slopes
Fast lifts	***
Snow	***
Extent	***
Expert	**
Intermediate	***
Beginner	****
Convenience	***
Queues	***
Mountain restaurants	***

The rest
Scenery	****
Resort charm	****
Off-slope	****

NEWS

For 2006/07 a six-pack is planned to replace a drag-lift at Bühlberg above Lenk. Snowmaking will be increased around the new lift.

For 2005/06 a quad replaced the main drag-lift from Boden on Höchsthorn.

492

KEY FACTS

Resort	1355m
	4,450ft
Slopes	1070-2355m
	3,510-7,730ft
Lifts	56
Pistes	170km
	106 miles
Blue	40%
Red	50%
Black	10%
Snowmaking	23km
	14 miles

OUR WEBSITE

Go to our website at wtss.co.uk for resort news, links to resort sites, a build-your-own resort shortlist system and reader forums.

+ Traditional, pretty mountain village in a splendid setting

+ Extensive slopes to suit all abilities, linked to Lenk

+ Good off-slope facilities

– Fragmented slopes – two sectors are a bus-ride away

– Few challenges on-piste – but plenty of off-piste opportunities

Adelboden is unjustly neglected by the international market: for intermediates looking for a relaxing holiday in pretty surroundings – and perhaps spending some time doing things off the slopes – it has a lot of appeal. Surprisingly, the resort literature includes English translations.

THE RESORT

Adelboden fits the traditional image of a Swiss mountain village: old chalets with overhanging roofs line the quiet main street (cars are discouraged), and 3000m/9,840ft peaks make an impressive backdrop. The village is compact, and there are efficient buses to the outlying areas (covered on the lift pass); the ideal location for most people is close to the main street. Adelboden is just to the west of the much better-known Jungfrau resorts (Wengen, Mürren etc). These resorts are within day-trip range, as is Gstaad to the west.

THE MOUNTAINS

Adelboden's slopes are split into five sectors – two of them unlinked and a bus-ride from the village. The rest of the sectors are linked, by piste if not by lift, and the ski area stretches across to the village of Lenk, with its own local slopes a bus-ride across the valley from the main body of slopes shared with Adelboden. The Swiss ski school runs American-style free mountain tours on Sundays.

Slopes Village lifts access three of the sectors. Schwandfeldspitz (aka Tschenten), just above the village, is reached by a cable-car/gondola hybrid. The main gondola to nearby Höchsthorn and then on to more remote Geils-Sillerenbühl starts down below the village at Oey (where there is a car park), but a connecting mini-gondola starts from close to the main street. This is much the biggest sector, with long, gentle runs (and some short, sharp ones) from 2200m down to 1350m (7,220ft down to 4,430ft) –

back to the village and over to Lenk.

Engstligenalp, a flat-bottomed high-altitude bowl, is reached by a cable-car 4km/2.5 miles south of the resort; Elsigenalp (another cable-car) is more remote, but more extensive.

Terrain-parks There's a good terrain-park at Hahnenmoos, with jumps, big-air and rail slides, but no longer a half-pipe. Sillerenbühl has a boarder-cross course and there's a natural playground at Engstligenalp.

Snow reliability Despite unimpressive top heights, snow reliability is not an acute concern: most slopes are above 1500m/4,920ft; Tschenten often has the best snow on its north-facing slopes. But this is not a place for a late holiday, or for skiing in a drought: the snowmaking is very limited.

Experts There are some genuine black pistes at Geils, and a less genuine one on Höchsthorn. Off-piste possibilities are good and remain untracked for much longer than in more macho resorts: the Laveygrat and Chummi chairs in the Geils bowl access routes down to both Adelboden and Lenk (though there are protected forest areas to avoid). Engstligenalp has off-piste potential too – and is a launching point for tours around the Wildstrubel.

Intermediates All five areas deserve exploration by intermediates. At Geils there is a lot of ground to be covered – and trips across to Lenk's gentle Betelberg area (covered by the lift pass) are possible.

Beginners There are good nursery slopes in the village and at the foot of nearby sectors. At Geils there are glorious long, easy runs to progress to.

Snowboarding Two specialist schools offer lessons. There's a free-ride zone at Engstligenalp. The many drag-lifts

are only gradually being replaced.

Cross-country There are extensive trails along the valley towards Engstligenalp with its high altitude, snow-sure circuit. There's also a short loop at Geils.

Queues The main gondola isn't entirely free of queues, and the Hahnenmoos gondola beyond it, up to the link with Lenk, is overdue for replacement – it has very limited capacity. The return from Lenk will be speeded up for 2006/07 by installation of a six-pack to replace another drag at Bühlberg. If snow low down is poor, the Engstligenalp cable-car produces queues. The main lift at Höchsthorn is now a quad chair.

Mountain restaurants There are numerous pleasant with terraces in the Geils sector – sadly not identified on the piste map. Aebi is particularly charming. The Standhütte is said to be 'small, simple, but good'.

Schools and guides Past reports on the Adelboden ski school have been mixed – 'caring, good English', but 'mix of abilities within group'.

Facilities for children The kindergarten takes children from three to five years. There's a snow-garden at Geils and another at Engstligenalp. Several hotels have childcare facilities and the resort runs a regular programme of children's events.

STAYING THERE

How to go The choice of how to go is wide. Several UK operators go there, and there are locally bookable chalets and apartments and some 30 pensions and hotels (mainly 3- and 4-star).

Hotels The 4-star Park Hotel Bellevue (673 8000) is expensive, but we have received good reports of its food and spa facilities. The central 3-star Adler Sporthotel (673 4141) is pretty and recommended. A wellness centre was added this year. The little Bären (673 2151) is a simple but captivating wooden chalet. The Huldi (673 8500) is 'very welcoming'.

Eating out Possibilities are varied, and include a couple of mountain restaurants. Guests on a half-board arrangement can 'dine around' at affiliated hotels twice a week.

Après-ski The après-ski is traditional, based on bars and tea rooms – a reader recommends Heuten and Schmidt. The Arte Bar offers a bit of artistic flair and, unusually, a wide range of spirits. A reader rates the main-street disco 'quite good'.

Off the slopes There is a fair bit to do – especially active things. There are indoor and outdoor curling and skating rinks, several toboggan runs, and hiking paths. There are hotel pools open to the public and an indoor public pool at Frutigen. Some mountain restaurants are easily reached on foot. Special lift passes are available for walkers.

Phone numbers
From elsewhere in Switzerland add the prefix 041.
From abroad use the prefix +41 41.

TOURIST OFFICE

t 673 8080
info@adelboden.ch
www.adelboden.ch

ADELBODEN TOURIST OFFICE

The setting is as attractive as the village ↓

Adelboden

493

Andermatt

A slow-paced, old-fashioned resort with some great steep, high terrain on- and off-piste (and the snowfall to go with it)

COSTS

① ② ③ ④ ⑤ ⑥

RATINGS

The slopes

Fast lifts	**
Snow	****
Extent	*
Expert	****
Intermediate	**
Beginner	*
Convenience	***
Queues	**
Mountain restaurants	*

The rest

Scenery	***
Resort charm	****
Off-slope	**

NEWS

There is now only one ski pass, called Gotthard Oberalp Arena (GOBA), which covers Sedrun, a short train-ride away over the Oberalp pass, as well as the Andermatt slopes.

KEY FACTS

Resort	1445m
	4,740ft
Slopes	1445-2965m
	4,740-9,730ft
Lifts	25
Pistes	130km
	81 miles
Blue	23%
Red	50%
Black	27%
Snowmaking	30km
	19 miles

REPORTS WANTED

There are some fine old chalets along the quiet main street →

+ Attractive, traditional village

+ Excellent snow record

+ Some excellent steep pistes, and great off-piste terrain – plus ski-touring opportunities

+ Easy access from Zürich

− Four separate areas of slopes are all fairly limited if you stay on-piste

− Unsuitable for beginners

− Limited off-slope diversions

− Little English spoken

− Cable-car queues at weekends

Little old Andermatt was rather left behind in the mega-resort boom of the 1960s and 1970s, but its attractions have not faded for those who like their mountains tall, steep and covered in deep powder. At first sight, it makes a tempting spot for a weekend break – but you'll be joined by the residents of Zürich, who arrive by the coachload and trainload. For a midweek break, it's superb.

THE RESORT

Andermatt is quite busy in summer and gets weekend winter business, but at other times seems deserted apart from soldiers from the local barracks. The town is quietly attractive, with wooden houses lining the dog-leg main street that runs between railway and cable-car stations, and some imposing churches. There are good road and rail links from Zürich, but in winter east-west links with the Grisons and the Valais rely on car-carrying trains. The town is big enough for reporters to appreciate the good minibus service to Gemsstock and Winterhorn.

THE MOUNTAINS

Andermatt's local skiing is split over three unlinked mountains, all limited in extent. The slopes are almost entirely above the trees. The lift pass covers Sedrun, 20 minutes away by train (included) to a tiny station just over the Oberalp pass – a good outing. The Sedrun skiing used to be an optional extra; since it is now standard, we have revised our 'Key facts'.

Slopes A two-stage cable-car from the edge of the village serves magnificent, varied slopes on the open, steep, north-facing and usually empty slopes of Gemsstock. Across town is the gentler, sunny Nätschen/ Gütsch area. And a bus- or train-ride along the valley is north-facing Winterhorn (above Hospental). There is also an isolated nursery slope further along at Realp. Piste marking is slack, which is bad news in a white-out.

Terrain-parks There are facilities (park and pipe) on Gemsstock. Sedrun has a half-pipe and park at Milez.

Snow reliability The area has a justified reputation for reliable snow. Piste grooming is generally good.

Experts It is most definitely a resort for experts. The north-facing bowl beneath the top Gemsstock cable-car is a glorious, long, steep slope (about 900m/2,950ft vertical), usually with excellent snow, down which there are countless off-piste routes, an itinerary and a piste. Outside the bowl, the Sonnenpiste is a fine open red run curling away from the lifts to the mid-station, with more off-piste opportunities. From Gurschen to the

village there is a black run, not steep but often tricky. Routes off the back of Gemsstock lead to the village, or to Hospental. Nätschen and Winterhorn both have black pistes and off-piste opportunities, including worthwhile itinerary routes.

Intermediates Intermediates needn't be put off Gemsstock: the Sonnenpiste can be tackled (and there are special groomed sections of the piste 'for carvers'), and there is a pleasant red run and some short blues at mid-mountain. Winterhorn's modest lift system offers pistes to suit all abilities down the 1000m/3,280ft vertical, while Nätschen's sunny mountain is well worth a visit. So is Sedrun, with a good choice of red runs starting from a railway halt in a snowy wilderness.

Beginners The lower half of Nätschen has a good, long, easy run. But this is not a good resort for beginners.

Snowboarding The cable-car accesses some great free-ride terrain.

Cross-country There are 40km/24 miles of loops along the valley.

Queues The Gemsstock cable-car can generate morning queues in the village and at mid-mountain when conditions are attractive, especially at weekends. Things take a while to get going after heavy snow.

Mountain restaurants They are present, but are still no more than adequate. The newish Gemsstockbar, at Gurschen, seems to be only a bar.

Schools and guides Bergschule Uri/ Mountain Reality, a guiding outfit run by local big wheel Alex Clapasson, is very pricey, and a recent reporter did not regret hiring a guide from the Swiss ski school instead.

Facilities for children There are slopes they can handle at Nätschen, and the Swiss school does classes. There's also a children's park at Sedrun.

STAYING THERE

How to go Andermatt's accommodation is in cosy 2- and 3-star hotels.

Hotels Gasthaus Sternen (887 1130) is an attractive central chalet with a cosy restaurant and bar. The lovely old 3-star Sonne (887 1226), between the centre and the lift, is welcoming and comfortable, with 'excellent service'. The neighbouring 2-star Bergidyll (887 1455) is a British favourite. Alpenhotel Schlüssel (888 7088) is 'good value', with spacious rooms.

Eating out A reporter praises the Sternen (see above) for 'generous portions, nicely cooked and very cosy surroundings'. The hotel Kronen's 'quite formal' Tre Passi restaurant has also been mentioned in dispatches.

Après-ski There are several cosy bars, which come alive on Saturdays – the Spycher and the Piccadilly in particular. The Curva at the hotel Monopol is 'very pleasant'. At weekends the Gotthard disco is said to be 'lively'.

Off the slopes There's a toboggan run at Nätschen. The fitness centre at the hotel Drei König is open to the public. There are maintained footpaths.

Andermatt

495

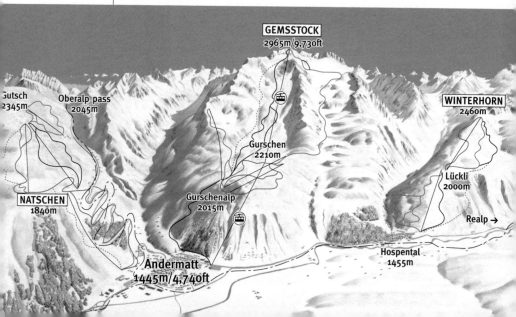

GEMSSTOCK
2965m/9,730ft

Gutsch
2345m

Oberalp pass
2045m

WINTERHORN
246om

Gurschen
2210m

Lückli
2000m

NATSCHEN
184om

Gurschenalp
2015m

Realp →

Andermatt
1445m/4,740ft

Hospental
1455m

Arosa

A classic all-round winter resort, where walking is as much part of the scene as skiing; choose your spot with care

COSTS

① ② ③ ④ ⑤ ⑥

RATINGS

The slopes

Fast lifts	***
Snow	***
Extent	**
Expert	**
Intermediate	***
Beginner	****
Convenience	**
Queues	****
Mountain restaurants	***

The rest

Scenery	***
Resort charm	**
Off-slope	****

NEWS

The FIS Snowboard World Championships will take place here from 13 to 20 January 2007.

For 2006/07 the resort plans to double the amount of snowmaking.

For 2005/06 two ski-routes on the Brüggerhorn became pistes – one red, one black. The terrain-park was improved.

And two new restaurants opened in the village.

A lift link with Lenzerheide-Valbella via Hörnli has been talked about for years, but now is shown as a forward plan on the piste maps of both resorts.

496

+ Classic winter sports resort ambience, with lots going on other than skiing and boarding

+ Some of the best cross-country loops in the Alps

+ Few queues

+ Choice of good nursery slopes at village or mid-mountain level

+ Relatively good snow reliability, and increasing amounts of snowmaking

+ Prettily wooded setting, complete with frozen lake, but ...

− Some very block-like buildings in main village around Obersee

− Spread-out village lacks a heart, and means some accommodation is inconveniently situated

− Slopes too limited for mileage-hungry intermediates

− Few challenging pistes for experts – though there is good off-piste

The classic image of a winter sports resort is perhaps an isolated, snow-covered Swiss village, surrounded by big, beautiful mountains, with skating on a frozen lake, horse-drawn sleighs jingling along snowy paths and people wrapped in fur coats strolling in the sun. Arosa offers exactly that. It's just a pity that many of its comfortable hotels date from that unfortunate era when wood and pitched roofs were out of fashion.

Its other serious weakness is the limited extent of slopes, coupled with a remote location that more or less rules out excursions to other resorts. Roll on the long-awaited link with Lenzerheide-Valbella, which would transform the appeal of Arosa to keen intermediates, in particular.

THE RESORT

High and remote, Arosa is in a sheltered basin at the head of a beautiful wooded valley, in sharp contrast to the open slopes above it. It's a long, winding drive or splendid rail journey from Chur (both take just under an hour).

The main resort development is around Obersee – a pretty spot, centred as you might guess on a frozen lake, but spoilt by the surrounding block-like buildings. Lifts go up from here into the Weisshorn sector of the slopes. The rest of Arosa is scattered, much of it spreading up the steep road separating Obersee from the older, prettier Inner-Arosa, where lifts from opposite extremities go up into both sectors of the slopes. Arosa is quiet; its relaxed ambience attracts an unpretentiously well-heeled clientele of families and older people. Very few of them are British.

Some accommodation is a long walk from the lifts, but there is an excellent free shuttle-bus and convenient parking.

THE MOUNTAINS

Arosa's slopes are situated in a wide, open bowl, facing north-east to south-east, with all the runs returning eventually to the village at the bottom. All the slopes are above the tree line, except those just above Obersee.

Slopes The slopes are spread widely over two main sectors. The major lift junction in the Weisshorn sector is Tschuggen (strangely un-named on the resort piste map), 500m/1,640ft away from the Mittelstation of the Weisshorn cable-car, and reachable from both Obersee and Inner-Arosa. From Mittelstation, you can take a chair to the lower peak of Brüggerhorn. The main access to the Hörnli sector is a slow gondola from below Inner-Arosa. Well-used walking paths wind across the mountainsides, and great care is needed where they cross the pistes. Piste marking is generally OK, although the blue run from the Brüggerhorn to Obersee is singled out by a 2006 reporter as being unclear at the top.

Terrain-parks There is a newly-improved park and a half-pipe.

KEY FACTS

Resort	1800m
	5,910ft
Slopes	1800-2655m
	5,910-8,710ft
Lifts	13
Pistes	60km
	37 miles
Blue	27%
Red	60%
Black	13%
Snowmaking	15km
	9 miles

Snow reliability The slopes are quite high, but the Weisshorn sector gets a lot of sun; the shadier Hörnli slopes hold their snow well. Grooming is good, and snowmaking on the home runs is often used. The resort plans to double its snowmaking to cover 30km/18 miles of pistes for 2006/07.

Experts Arosa isn't an obvious target for experts, but there is plenty of gentle off-piste terrain. The resort flirted briefly with exploitation of its ungroomed terrain, branding the Brüggerhorn 'Free Ride Mountain'. But that seems to have been abandoned, along with the associated ski-routes, two of which have become pistes – a red and a black, on Brüggerhorn.

Intermediates This is a good area for intermediates who aren't looking for high mileage or huge challenges. The runs from Hörnli are enjoyable cruises, the black including a short steeper pitch. The Weisshorn runs are generally steeper, with some rewarding reds. The long blue to Obersee from Brüggerhorn via Prätschli is a great way to end the day, with fab views of sunlit peaks from the shady piste.

Beginners The easy slopes up at Tschuggen are excellent and usually have good snow, but they get a lot of through traffic. Inner-Arosa has a quieter area for children ('nice and gentle,' says a 2006 reporter).

Snowboarding Bananas is the specialist school and Mountain Surf Club offers two-day free-ride camps.

Cross-country Arosa's modest 26km/16 miles of loops include some of the best and most varied in the Alps.

Queues Arosa does not suffer from serious queues – even in half-term. There can be waits for the Weisshorn cable-car, though our most recent reporters have had no problems.

Mountain restaurants There's a reasonable choice, several equipped with seriously indulgent sunbeds whereon you can lunch while sunbathing. Carmennahütte has scores. Tschuggenhütte has recently expanded and has choices for all the family. Alpenblick does 'very good food' and Hörnli is a 'welcoming hut in a dramatic position'.

Schools and guides Swiss and ABC are the main schools. Class sizes can be large. There's a lot of demand for private lessons.

Facilities for children Arosa's appeal as a family resort has led to Disney endorsement, with 12 hotels and the Swiss Ski school forming the Alpine Club Mickey Mouse. A 2006 reporter was 'very pleased' with his daughter's 'excellent, friendly instructors who spoke English'. Club Mickey also includes a kindergarten, kid's restaurants and games areas.

Arosa

497

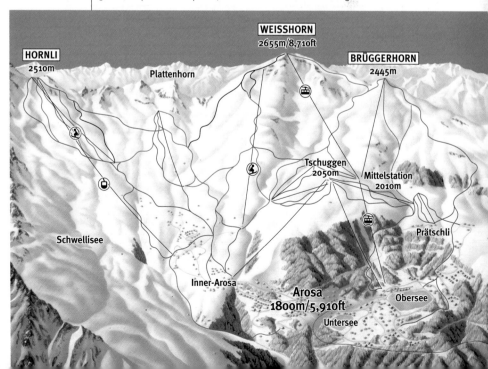

↑ Beyond the chalets of Inner-Arosa, a couple of the blocks that blight the lower part of the resort
AROSA TOURIST OFFICE

Phone numbers
From elsewhere in Switzerland add the prefix 081.
From abroad use the prefix +41 81.

TOURIST OFFICE
t 378 7020
arosa@arosa.ch
www.arosa.ch

STAYING THERE

How to go Arosa is a hotel resort, with a high proportion of 3- and 4-stars.
Hotels The sensitively modernised 4-star Waldhotel National (378 5555) with 'really special food' and direct access to the slopes is 'quite delightful'. The 4-star Sporthotel Valsana (378 6363) is recommended. The Tschuggen Grand (378 9999) is to add a wellness centre for 2006/07.
Eating out Most restaurants are hotel-based, some with a very high reputation. The Kachelofa-Stübli at the Waldhotel National is excellent. The Luna (for pasta) and Osteria Poltera (Swiss dishes) are new.

Après-ski Après-ski is quite lively. The Carmenna hotel by the ice rink has a popular piano bar. The Sitting Bull is busy and cheerful. Recommended bars include the Grischuna for grown-ups and Boomerang for kids (both with restaurants attached). The Blu club has a dance floor, games and snooker tables, and is said to be 'good fun'.
Off the slopes There's an indoor pool and plenty of outdoor alternatives. You can get a pedestrian's lift pass, and many mountain restaurants are reachable via 60km/37 miles of cleared, marked paths shown on a special map. Sleigh rides are popular, and there are indoor and outdoor ice rinks. Shopping is limited.

Selected chalet in Arosa

Champéry

Picture-postcard village which few UK tour operators feature these days, with access to the Portes du Soleil circuit

COSTS

① ② ③ ④ ⑤ ⑥

RATINGS

The slopes

Fast lifts	**
Snow	**
Extent	*****
Expert	***
Intermediate	****
Beginner	**
Convenience	*
Queues	****
Mountain restaurants	***

The rest

Scenery	****
Resort charm	****
Off-slope	***

NEWS

For 2005/06 the Palladium – the new Swiss national ice-sports centre – opened. It also includes an indoor swimming pool and tennis courts.

The MicroParc, a snow-park for beginners and youngsters, with rails and boxes, was opened beside the terrain-park at Les Crosets. The terrain-park was also improved with the addition of a new box, wall and rails.

+ Charmingly rustic mountain village
+ Cable-car or fast six-packs take you into the Portes du Soleil circuit
+ Quiet, relaxed – yet plenty to do off the slopes

– Local slopes suffer from the sun
– No runs back to the village – and sometimes none back to the valley
– Not good for beginners
– Not many tough slopes nearby

With good transport links and sports facilities, Champéry is great for intermediate skiers looking for a quiet time in a lovely place, especially if they have a car. Access to the Portes du Soleil circuit is not bad: Avoriaz is fairly easy to get to – and there may be fresh powder there when Champéry is suffering.

THE RESORT

Set beneath the dramatic Dents du Midi, Champéry is a village of old wooden chalets. Friendly and relaxed, it would be ideal for families if it wasn't separated from its slopes by a steep, fragmented mountainside.

Down a steepish hill, away from the main street, are the cable-car, sports centre and railway station.

THE MOUNTAINS

Once you get up to them, the local slopes are open, friendly and relaxing.
Slopes Champéry's sunny slopes are part of the big Portes du Soleil circuit, which links Avoriaz, Châtel (in France) Les Crosets, Champoussin and Morgins (see below). The village cable-car or fast six-seat chair-lift from Grand Paradis, a short free bus-ride from Champéry, go up to Croix de Culet, above the bowl of Planachaux. If snow is good there are a couple of pistes back to Grand Paradis, with an efficient

bus service back to the village, but no pistes back to Champéry.
Terrain-parks There is a good terrain-park at Les Crosets (which a reporter rates as the best in the area), half of which is natural. The 29 features include a quarter-pipe, gaps and kickers. A new beginners' park was added in 2006 (see 'News'). There's also a half-pipe that's floodlit twice a week.
Snow reliability The snow on the north-facing French side of the link with Avoriaz is usually better than on the sunnier Swiss side to the south. The local Champéry area would benefit from more snowmaking.
Experts Few local challenges and badly placed for most of the tough Portes du Soleil runs. The Swiss Wall, on the Champéry side of Chavanette, is intimidatingly long and bumpy, but not terrifyingly steep. There's scope for off-piste at Chavanette and on the broad slopes of Les Crosets and Champoussin.
Intermediates Confident intermediates have the whole Portes du Soleil at

↑ Champéry is a pretty village even when it's not covered by this much snow

KEY FACTS

| Resort | 1050m |
| | 3,440ft |

Portes du Soleil	
Slopes	950-2300m
	3,120-7,550ft
Lifts	209
Pistes	650km
	404 miles
Green	14%
Blue	39%
Red	37%
Black	10%
Snowmaking	
	577 guns

Swiss side only	
Slopes	1050-2275m
	3,440-7,460ft
Lifts	35
Pistes	100km
	62 miles

Phone numbers
From elsewhere in Switzerland add the prefix 024.
From abroad use the prefix +41 24.

TOURIST OFFICES

Champéry
t 479 2020
info@champery.ch
www.champery.ch
Les Crosets Champoussin
t 477 2077
info@valdilliez.ch
www.valdilliez.ch
Morgins
t 477 2361
touristoffice@morgins.ch
www.morgins.ch

their disposal. Locally, the runs home to Grand Paradis are good when the snow conditions allow. Les Crosets is a junction of several fine runs. There are slightly tougher pistes from Mossettes and Pointe de l'Au, Champoussin's leisurely cruising, and delightful tree-lined meanders to Morgins. A highlight is the quiet, beautiful, long blue from Col des Portes du Soleil to Morgins via the 'cute' restaurant at Tovassière.

Beginners The Planachaux runs, where lessons are held, are steepish and limited in extent.

Snowboarding Not ideal for beginners, and access to the Portes du Soleil circuit involves drag-lifts, many of which are quite steep. Good terrain-parks for experts though, and some good between-the-pistes powder areas.

Cross-country It's advertised as 10km/6 miles with 4km/2 miles floodlit every night, but it's very unreliable snow.

Queues Les Crosets is still a bottleneck at peak times. If snow is poor, end-of-the-day queues for the cable-car down are inescapable.

Mountain restaurants The local favourite is Chez Coquoz at Croix de Culet – lovingly prepared food, and a knockout wine list. Chez Gaby above Champoussin does 'marvellous rösti'. The tiny Lapisa on the way to Grand Paradis is delightfully rustic (they make cheese and smoke their own meats on site).

Schools and guides The few reports that we've had on the Swiss school are free of criticism ('professional but friendly'). The Freeride Company provides healthy competition.

Facilities for children The tourist office has a list of childminders. The Swiss ski school takes three to seven year olds.

STAYING THERE

How to go Limited packages available. Easy access for independent travellers.

Chalets We are not aware of any catered chalets.

Hotels Prices are low compared with smarter Swiss resorts. The Beau Séjour (479 5858) is friendly, family-run, with 'large rooms'. The National (479 1130) has 'friendly staff, lovely breakfast'. The Auberge du Grand Paradis (479 1167) is 'charmingly rustic but noisy'.

Self-catering Some apartments are available to independent travellers. Tour op Piste Artiste has a chalet.

Eating out A fair choice. Two excellent non-traditional places: Mitchell's bar has a good restaurant and the Café du Centre – 'modern Asian menu in a wonderfully restored building'. The Vieux Chalet (hotel Beau-Séjour) and the bistro in the hotel National have been recommended. Two of the best for local specialities are just outside the village: Cantines des Rives and Auberge du Grand Paradis.

Après-ski Mitchell's is popular at tea time – big sofas and a fireplace. Below the 'rather seedy' Pub, the Crevasse disco is one of the liveliest places. The Café du Centre has a micro brewery. Try the Bar des Guides in the hotel Suisse, or the Farinet's cellar nightclub.

Off the slopes Walks are pleasant and the railway allows excursions to Montreux, Lausanne and Sion. There's a big sports centre (see 'News').

Les Crosets 1660m/5,450ft

A good base for a quiet time and slopes on the doorstep. The Télécabine hotel (479 0300) is homely, with good food.

Champoussin 1580m/5,180ft

A good family choice – no through traffic, near the slopes, no noisy late-night revellers and the comfortable Royal Alpage Club hotel (pool, gym, disco, two restaurants – 476 8300).

Morgins 1350m/4,430ft

A fairly scattered, but attractive, quiet resort. The hotel Reine des Alpes (477 1143) is well thought of, and there are catered chalets. Of the ski schools, a reporter found the ESS 'very satisfactory'. The village kindergarten and nursery have been recommended. There's also a gentle nursery slope.

Crans-Montana

Sun-soaked slopes and stunning long-distance views above a big town base – not for those who love powder though

- ➕ Large, varied piste area
- ➕ Splendid setting and views
- ➕ Excellent, gentle nursery slopes
- ➕ Excellent cross-country trails
- ➕ Very sunny slopes, but ...

- ➖ Snow badly affected by sun
- ➖ Large town (rather than village), devoid of Alpine atmosphere
- ➖ Bus- or car-rides to lifts from much of the accommodation
- ➖ Few challenges except off-piste

When conditions are right – clear skies above fresh, deep snow – Crans-Montana takes some beating: the mountains you bounce down are charmingly scenic, the mountains you gaze at are mind-blowing, and you can forgive Crans-Montana its inconvenient, linear layout and towny feel. Sadly, conditions are more often wrong. Except in the depths of winter, the strong midday sun bakes the pistes.

THE RESORT

Set on a broad shelf facing south across the Rhône valley, Crans-Montana is really two towns, their centres a mile apart and their fringes merging. Strung along a busy road, the resort's many hotels, villas, apartments and smart shops are mainly dull blocks with little traditional Alpine character.

The resort is reached by road or by a fast funicular railway from Sierre. It depends heavily on summer conference business, so hotels tend to be formal, and visitors dignified. Crans is the more upmarket, with fancy shops. The main gondola stations are above the main road – there is a free shuttle-bus during the day but it can get crowded and it is 'not dependable' says a 2006 reporter.

There are other gondola bases and places to stay at Les Barzettes and at Aminona. Anzère is nearby, and you can get to Zermatt, Saas-Fee and Verbier by road or rail.

THE MOUNTAINS

Crans-Montana has slopes with few challenges and no nasty surprises, and there is a pleasant mix of open and wooded slopes. The views over the Rhône valley to the peaks bordering Italy are breathtaking.

The slopes The slopes are spread over a broad mountainside, with lifts from four valley bases. Gondolas from Crans and Montana meet at Cry d'Er – an open bowl descending into patchy forest. There is free night skiing here

501

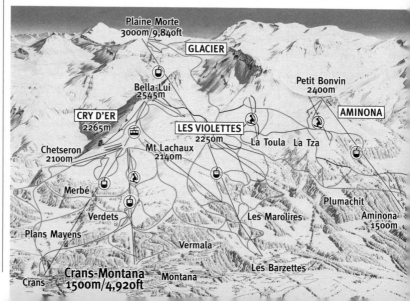

The resort has a stunning setting but the town itself doesn't look this attractive when there is less snow around (which is most of the time) ↗

CRANS-MONTANA TOURISME /
EMANUEL AMMON / AURA

KEY FACTS

Resort	1500m
	4,920ft
Slopes	1500-3000m
	4,920-9,840ft
Lifts	28
Pistes	140km
	87 miles
Blue	38%
Red	50%
Black	12%
Snowmaking	17km
	11 miles

OUR WEBSITE

Go to our website at wtss.co.uk for resort news, links to resort sites, a build-your-own resort shortlist system and reader forums.

Phone numbers
From elsewhere in Switzerland add the prefix 027.
From abroad use the prefix +41 27.

TOURIST OFFICE

t 485 0404
information@crans-montana.ch
www.crans-montana.ch

on Fridays The next sector, focused on Les Violettes, is accessed from Les Barzettes. A jumbo gondola goes up to the Plaine Morte glacier. The fourth sector is served by a gondola up from Aminona. Some of the runs down to the valley are narrow woodland paths, and signing is ridiculously slack.
Terrain-parks Aminona has a terrain-park, and there's a half-pipe in the more central Cry d'Er area.
Snow reliability The runs on the Plaine Morte glacier are limited and practically all the other slopes get a lot of direct sun. There is snowmaking on the main runs, but we have never found good snow on the runs down to the valley. A 2006 reporter tells of bare spots just 'two days after a 19 inch dump'.
For experts There are few steep pistes and the only decent moguls are on the short slopes at La Toula. There's plenty of off-piste, particularly beneath Chetseron and La Tza.
For intermediates Pistes are mostly wide, and many of the red runs don't justify the grading. They tend to be uniform in difficulty from top to bottom, with few surprises. Avid piste-bashers enjoy the length of many runs, plus the fast lifts and good links that allow a lot of mileage. The 11km/7 mile run from Plaine Morte to Les Barzettes starts with top-of-the-world views and powder, and finishes among pretty woods. The Piste Nationale downhill course is a good test of technique.
For beginners There are three excellent nursery areas, including the golf course fairways which are great learning slopes.
Snowboarding Despite the resort's staid image, boarding is very popular. There are a number of specialist shops and the Stoked snowboard school. The main lifts are chairs and gondolas, and the drag-lifts are usually avoidable.
For cross-country The 40km/25 miles of trails include a snow-sure glacier area.
Queues Investment in gondolas has

helped cut queues out of the village, and a 2006 visitor found the slopes were deserted before 10.30am.
Mountain restaurants There are 20 mountain restaurants, usefully marked on the piste map. Above Crans, Merbé is one of the most attractive (and expensive), Chetseron has good views and Chez Erwin 'gorgeous homemade cake'. Bella-Lui, Cabane des Violettes ('good food at fairly reasonable prices') and Petit Bonvin are worth a look.
Schools and guides The Swiss schools have attracted mainly favourable comments over the years.
Facilities for children These seem adequate, but we lack recent reports.

STAYING THERE

How to go There is a wide choice of hotels and apartments.
Hotels This conference resort has over 50 mainly large, comfortable, pricey hotels. Pas de l'Ours (485 9333) is our favourite – chic, attractive, wood and stone. Aïda Castel (485 4111) is also well-furnished in rustic style. Beau-Site (481 3312) is friendly and family-run.
Self-catering There are many apartments available.
Eating out A good variety of places, from French to Lebanese. The best is the Bistrot in the Pas de l'Ours hotel. The Chalet, Plaza, Rafael's, and Padrino have been recommended.
Après-ski One 2006 visitor was sadly disappointed with the lack of nightlife and atmosphere. Amadeus 2006 and Chez Nanette are tents on Cry d'Er, serving close-of-play vin chaud. The George & Dragon in Crans is one of the liveliest bars. Reporters recommend Bar 1900 and the Grange.
Off the slopes There are swimming pools (in hotels), two ice rinks, dog-sledding, snow-tubing, a cinema and a casino. There are also 60km/37 miles of walking. Sierre and Sion are close.

Davos

A glorious Alpine playground (for skaters and langlaufers as well as downhillers); but the resort is more like a city than a village

COSTS

①②③④⑤⑥

RATINGS

The slopes

Fast lifts	★★★
Snow	★★★★
Extent	★★★★★
Expert	★★★★
Intermediate	★★★★★
Beginner	★★
Convenience	★★
Queues	★★
Mountain restaurants	★★★

The rest

Scenery	★★★★
Resort charm	★★
Off-slope	★★★★★

NEWS

For 2006/07 Pischa, near Davos Dorf, will be designated a free-ride mountain. Two of the four drag-lifts will be removed; roughly half the runs will be ungroomed. The terrain-park, walking trail and children's area will remain.

There are plans to expand the slopes on Jakobshorn and to link it to Rinerhorn, making the latter much more easily accessible from the resort.

➕ Very extensive slopes

➕ Some superb, long, and mostly easy pistes away from the lifts, with trains to bring you back to base

➕ Lots of accessible off-piste terrain, with several marked itineraries

➕ Good cross-country trails

➕ Plenty to do off the slopes – from skating to shopping

➕ Some cute mountain restaurants

➖ Davos is a huge, city-like place, plagued by traffic, lacking Alpine atmosphere and après-ski animation

➖ Dreary block-style buildings spoil the views

➖ The slopes are spread over five separate areas

➖ Preponderance of T-bars is a problem for some visitors

➖ The only piste back to town from the main Parsenn area is a black run finishing on the outskirts

Davos was one of the original mega-resorts, with slopes on a scale that few resorts can better, even today. But it's a difficult resort to like. You can easily put up with slopes spread over separate mountains, some queue-prone lifts and lots of T-bars if that's the price of staying in a captivating Alpine village. But Davos is far from that.

Whether you forgive the flaws probably depends on how highly you value three key plus-points: the distinctive, super-long runs of the Parsenn area; being able to ski different runs each day; and the considerable off-piste potential. We value all three, and we always look forward to visiting, especially since the upgraded funicular to the Parsenn slopes removed what was the Alps' worst lift queue.

But you don't have to stay in Davos to enjoy its slopes: villagey Klosters offers a much more attractive alternative. It now gets a chapter of its own.

THE RESORT

Davos is set in a high, broad, flat-bottomed valley, with its lifts and slopes either side. Arguably it was the very first place in the Alps to develop its slopes. The railway up the Parsenn was one of the first built for skiers (in 1931), and the first drag-lift was built on the Bolgen nursery slopes in 1934. But Davos was already a health resort; many of its luxury hotels were built as sanatoriums.

Sadly, that's just what they look like. There are still several specialist clinics and it is for these, along with its conferences and sporting facilities, that Davos has become well known. The place has the grey, neat, rectilinear feel of a Swiss city rather than that of a mountain village.

It has two main centres, Dorf and Platz, about 2km/1 mile apart. Although transport is good, with buses around the town as well as the railway linking Dorf and Platz to Klosters and other villages, location is important. Easiest access to the slopes is from Dorf to the main Parsenn area, via the funicular railway; Platz is better placed for the Jakobshorn area, the big sports facilities, the smarter shopping and evening action.

Davos shares its slopes with the famously royal resort of Klosters, down the valley – an attractive village with good links into the Parsenn area and its own separate sector, the sunny

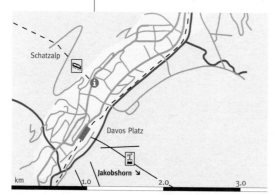

Schatzalp

Davos Platz

Jakobshorn ↘

km   1.0   2.0   3.0

Madrisa (see our new Klosters chapter for more detail).

Trips are possible by car or rail to St Moritz (the Vereina rail tunnel offers access to the Engadine area without having to negotiate the snowy Flüelapass) and Arosa, and by car to Flims-Laax and Lenzerheide.

Although the resort is reachable by train, the trip from Zürich airport involves two changes, and a reader strongly recommends the new DavosExpress coach transfer service.

THE MOUNTAINS

The slopes here have something for everyone, though experts and nervous intermediates need to choose their territory with care.

THE SLOPES
Vast and varied
You could hit a different mountain around Davos nearly every day for a week, but the out-of-town areas tend to be much quieter than the ones directly accessible from the resort. Lots of reporters remark on the immaculate grooming of the slopes.

The Parsennbahn funicular from Davos Dorf ends at mid-mountain, where a choice of fast six-pack or old funicular take you on up to the major lift junction of Weissfluhjoch, at one end of the **Parsenn**. The only run back to the valley is a black to the outskirts of Dorf. At the other end of the wide, open Parsenn bowl is Gotschnagrat, reached by cable-car from the centre of Klosters. There are excellent, exceptionally long intermediate runs

down to Klosters, and to other villages (see feature panel). From Davos Platz, a funicular goes up to Schatzalp, where there is a hotel, but the lifts above here are now closed.

Across the valley, **Jakobshorn** is reached by cable-car or chair-lift from Davos Platz; this is popular with snowboarders but good for skiers too. **Rinerhorn** and **Pischa** are reached by bus or (in the case of Rinerhorn) train. Pischa is due to become a designated free-ride area for 2006/07, with half the runs left ungroomed (and half the drag-lifts removed)

Beyond the main part of Klosters, a gondola goes up from Klosters Dorf to the sunny, scenic **Madrisa** area.

There are too many T-bars for the comfort of some reporters – Rinerhorn, Pischa and Madrisa have little else. It's time Davos invested in some chairs.

TERRAIN-PARK
Lots of choice
All four of the surrounding mountains now have functioning terrain-parks; the main one is the Sunrise park on Jakobshorn. It is open as early as November, weather permitting, and is by far the best in the area. It has a good variety of jumps, rails and a large number of boxes including a nice C-box. The park however is quite narrow and can feel cramped when crowded. Two pipes are the training grounds for a host of Swiss professionals, which shows the standard. The super-pipe at Bolgen, across the valley floor from Platz, is floodlit every evening. Training kickers are sometimes built at Bolgen, too.

boarding

Davos is a jack of all trades in terms of snowboard terrain. The mountain offers so much in terms of powder, tree runs, natural hits, cliffs and gullies for confident riders. The established boarder mountain is the Jakobshorn with its pipes, park and boarder-cross as well as night riding facilities and funky Jatzhütte. The terrain is vast and will keep any boarder entertained for a long time. Plans for 2007 include branding Pischa as a free-ride mountain, leaving a large chunk of the mountain ungroomed. One reporter says, 'There are no problems with crowds on this quiet mountain. The powder is amazing and there are endless kicker building spots with loads of windlips and cliff drops.' There are plenty of wide mellow slopes for beginners on Parsenn; however, watch out for the flats on the long runs down to the Schifer gondola. Top Secret is a specialist snowboard shop and school. There are several cheap hotels geared to snowboarders, notably the 180-bed Bolgenhof near the Jakobshorn, the Snowboardhotel Bolgenschanze and the Snowboarders Palace.

LIFT PASSES

Davos/Klosters

Prices in SF

Age	1-day	6-day
under 13	21	94
13-18	41	189
over 18	61	282

Free under 6

Senior No deals

Beginner Single and return tickets on main lifts in each area.

Notes
Covers all Davos and Klosters, the railway in the whole region and buses between the resorts.

Alternative passes
An array of passes is available for individual and combined areas (Parsenn/Gotschna, Jakobshorn, Pischa/Rinerhorn/ Madrisa).

SNOW RELIABILITY
Good, but not the best
Davos is high by Swiss standards. Its mountains go respectably high, too – though not to glacial heights. Not many of the slopes face directly south, but not many face directly north either. Snow reliability is generally good higher up but can be poor lower down. Snow-guns cover a couple of the upper runs on the Parsenn and several on the Jakobshorn, and the home runs from the Parsenn to Davos Dorf and Klosters. Piste grooming is excellent.

FOR EXPERTS
Plenty to do, on- and off-piste
A glance at the piste map may give the misleading impression that this is an intermediate's resort – there aren't many black runs. It's also true that the few that exist are not particularly testing – and since many are on the

steeper, lower, wooded slopes they are prone to closure. But they include some distinctive, satisfying descents. The Meierhofer Tälli run to Wolfgang is a favourite, and delighted a 2006 reporter ('quite steep and exciting') who found it closed on five previous visits. The run from Parsennhütte to Wolfgang is less challenging, and in the view of one reporter could be red.

What makes the area really interesting is that there are also half a dozen off-piste itineraries – runs that are marked but not prepared or patrolled. These are a key feature, adding up to a lot of expert terrain that can be tackled without expensive guidance (though not alone, of course). Some are on the open upper slopes, some in the woods lower down, some from the peaks right to the valley. Two of the steepest routes go from Gotschnagrat down beside the

Davos

505

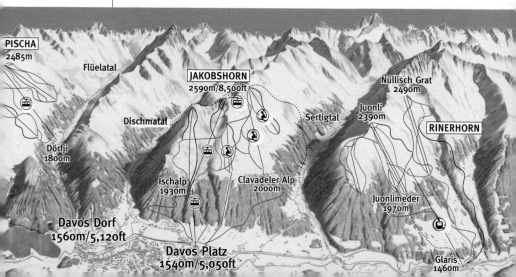

THE PARSENN'S SUPER-RUNS

The runs from Weissfluhjoch that head north, on the back of the mountain, make this area special for many visitors. The pistes that go down to Schifer and then to Küblis, Saas and Serneus, and the one that curls around the mountain to Klosters, are a fabulous way to end the day if you're based in Klosters, or one of the lower villages. If you are based in Davos, the return journey is by train (included in the lift pass) from one of the valley villages.

The runs are classified red but are not normally difficult (we have heard from reporters who did the run to Küblis on their second holiday, and one of your editors did the run to Klosters on his third day on skis, back in the days before the Schifer gondola was constructed). The latter parts can be challenging if they are not groomed, and you need to bear in mind that you are getting down to low altitudes by the end (Klosters is at 1190m/3,900ft, Küblis at 810m/2,560ft).

What marks these runs out is their sheer length (10-12km/6-7 miles) and the sensation of travel they offer – plus the welcoming huts in the woods towards the end (see 'Mountain restaurants'). You can descend the 1100m/ 3,610ft vertical to Schifer as often as you like and take the gondola back. Once past there, you're committed to finishing the descent.

---

infamous Gotschnawang slope – Drostobel and Chalbersäss.

Reporters also enjoyed heading away from the pistes above Serneus and Küblis and at Gotschnagrat ('tremendous variety').

There is also excellent 'proper' off-piste terrain, for which guidance is needed, and some short tours. Arosa can be reached with a bit of help from a train or taxi and from there you can travel on snow to Lenzerheide, but you'll need a train back. From Madrisa you can make tours to Gargellen in Austria. A reader also recommends the descent to St Antönien, north of Küblis, not least for 'spectacular views', returning by bus and train.

FOR INTERMEDIATES
A splendid variety of runs

For intermediates of any temperament, this is a great area. There are good cruising runs on all five mountains, so you would never get bored in a week. This variety of different slopes, taken together with the wonderful long runs to the Klosters valley, makes it a compelling area with a unique character.

The epic runs to Klosters and other places (described in the feature panel) pose few difficulties for a confident intermediate or even an ambitious near-beginner . And there are one or two other notable away-from-the-lifts runs to the valley. In particular, you

DAVOS TOURISMUS / SWISS-IMAGE

The sports facilities in Davos are excellent, and include several ice rinks ↓

SCHOOLS
Swiss Davos
t 416 2454
New Trend
t 413 2040
inandout snowsports
t 413 0888

Classes
(Swiss prices)
6 4hr days SF310
Private lessons
Half day SF200

CHILDREN
Pischa nursery
t 079 660 3168
Ages from 3; 10.30 to
4pm; SF15 per hour
Bobo Club
t 416 2454
Ages 4 to 10; 10am-
noon, 2pm-4pm; SF60
per day' SF15 per
hour.
Kinderhotel Muchetta
(at Wiesen)
t 404 1424
Ages from 6mnth
Babysitter list
At tourist office

Ski school
Takes ages 5 to 14 (5
days SF265)

can travel from the top of Madrisa back to Klosters Dorf via the beautiful Schlappin valley (it's an easy black – classified red until the mid-1990s).

The Jakobshorn has some genuine challenges. Rinerhorn is more of a cruise.

There will be ungroomed but marked routes on Pischa when it re-brands itself as free-ride territory for 2006/07. This is the gentlest of the Davos mountains, so it should be a good spot for first attempts at skiing deep snow in safety.

FOR BEGINNERS
Platz is the more convenient
The Bolgen nursery slope beneath the Jakobshorn is adequately spacious and gentle, and a bearable walk from the centre of Platz. But Dorf-based beginners face more of a trek out to Bünda – unless staying at the hotel of the same name.

There is no shortage of easy runs to progress to, spread around all the sectors. The Parsenn sector probably has the edge, with long, early intermediate runs in the main Parsenn bowl, as well as in the valleys down from Weissfluhjoch.

FOR CROSS-COUNTRY
Long, scenic valley trails
Davos has a total of 75km/47 miles of trails running in both directions along the main valley and reaching well up into Sertigtal, Dischmatal and Flüelatal. There is a cross-country ski centre and special ski school on the outskirts.

QUEUES
Worst one long gone
Some of the longest queues in the Alps were ended in 2002 with the upgrade of the first stage of the Parsenn funicular railway from Davos Dorf, tripling the lift's capacity. The existing lifts from the mid-station — a six-pack and second stage of the original railway — seem to be coping with the increased loading, although there can be problems during peak season. Queues can build up elsewhere for some cable-cars (including the one out of Klosters) at peak periods, although a recent visitor found more problems up the mountain at the Totalp chair and the Parsennhüttenbahn. Crowded pistes have raised some concern with readers – one 2006 visitor singled out those above Schifer in the Parsenn sector.

MOUNTAIN RESTAURANTS
Stay high or go low
The main high-altitude restaurants are dreary self-service affairs. The main exception is the highest of all: Bruhin's at Weissfluhgipfel – a great place for a hang-the-cost blow-out on a snowy day, with table-service of excellent rustic as well as gourmet dishes, and some knockout desserts. The table-service Gastro Alpin at Weissfluhjoch is also is said to be 'particularly good' and a 2006 reporter praised the 'friendly table-service' at the Skihütte Gruobenalp at Gotschnagrat.

There are other compelling places lower down in the Parsenn sector. A reader recommends 'big portions of chicken and noodles' at the Höhenweg bar at the Parsennbahn mid-station. The rustic 'schwendis' in the woods on the way down to the Klosters valley from the Parsenn still attract crowds. The Chesetta remains 'a particular favourite' with its 'super sun terrace' and 'very cosy interior'. Nearby, the Alte Conterser Schwendi is 'very friendly with good food'. These are fun places to end up as darkness falls – some sell wax torches to illuminate your final descent.

On Jakobshorn the Jatzhütte near the boarders' terrain-park is wild – with changing scenery such as mock palm trees, parrots and pirates. The Chalet Güggel on Jakobshorn is 'small and cosy – nice atmosphere but slow service'. On Pischa, the Mäderbeiz at Flüelameder is a friendly and spacious woody hut, cheering on a cold day. On the Rinerhorn, the Hubelhütte is the best bet.

SCHOOLS AND GUIDES
Decent choice
A reporter says that 'nearly all instructors spoke English and were skilled and friendly — both my kids had a terrific time'. There is an alternative ski school called New Trend (maximum of six in a class) and Top Secret is the competing snowboard school.

FACILITIES FOR CHILDREN
Not ideal
Davos is a rather spread-out place in which to handle a family. The kids' ski school operates a special Disney-themed slope at Bolgen. A reporter tells us the nursery is 'well organised, but even good instructors sometimes slip into German'.

Davos

507

GETTING THERE

Air Zürich 160km/ 99 miles (2hr by car, 3hr by rail or bus).

Rail Stations in Davos Dorf and Platz. 20 minutes from Davos to Klosters.

ACTIVITIES

Indoor Fitness centre, tennis, squash, swimming pools, sauna, solarium, massage, wellness centres, ice rink, cinema, casino, galleries, museums, libraries, badminton, golf-driving range, billiards, bridge

Outdoor Over 80km/ 50 miles of cleared paths (mostly at valley level), ice climbing, snow-shoe trekking, tobogganing, ice rink, curling, horse-riding, sleigh rides, paragliding

Phone numbers
From elsewhere in Switzerland add the prefix 081.
From abroad use the prefix +41 81.

TOURIST OFFICE

Davos
t 415 2121
info@davos.ch
www.davos.ch

STAYING THERE

HOW TO GO
Hotels dominate the packages
Although most beds are in apartments, hotels dominate the UK market.

Hotels A dozen 4-star places and about 30 3-stars form the core of the Davos hotel trade, though there are a couple of 5-stars and quite a few cheaper places, including B&Bs. You can book any hotel by calling 415 2121.

(((((5) **Flüela** (410 1717) The more atmospheric of the 5-star hotels, in central Dorf. Pool.

(((((4) **Waldhuus** (417 9333) Convenient for langlaufers. Quiet, modern, tasteful. Pool.

(((((4) **Sunstar Park** (413 1414) At far end of Davos Platz. Pool, sauna, games room. Recommended for 'excellent' food. New spa facilities.

(((((3) **Davoserhof** (414 9020) Our favourite. Small, old, beautifully furnished, with excellent food; well placed in Platz.

(((((3) **Parsenn** (416 3232) Right opposite the Parsenn railway in Dorf. An attractive chalet marred by the big McDonald's on the ground floor.

(((((3) **Berghotel Schatzalp** (415 5151) On the tree line 300m/1,000ft above Platz; reached by funicular (free to guests).

(((((3) **Panorama** (413 2373) In central Platz. Recommended by a 2006 reporter for 'excellent quality and good value' food. New piano bar.

((2) **Alte Post** (414 9020) Traditional and cosy; in central Platz. Popular with boarders.

((2) **Hubli's Landhaus** (417 1010) 5km/3 miles out at Laret, towards Klosters. Quiet country inn with sophisticated, expensive food, which a 2005 reporter describes as 'really special', and an 'attentive, friendly and helpful' owner.

(1) **Ochsen** (414 9020) Offers good-value dormitory accommodation.

EATING OUT
Wide choice, mostly in hotels
In a town this size, you need to know where to go – if you just walk around hoping to spot a suitable place to eat, you may starve. For a start, get the tourist office's Gastroführer booklet. The more ambitious restaurants are mostly in hotels. There is a choice of two good Chinese restaurants – the lavish Zauberberg in the Europe and the Goldener Drachen in the Bahnhof Terminus. Good-value places include the jolly Al Ponte (pizza and steak

both approved of), the Carretta (good for home-made pasta), the small and cosy Gentiana (with an upstairs stübli), and the Hotel Dischma's Röstizerria. An evening excursion out of town is popular. A recent reporter enjoyed a fondue evening at Höhenweg but warns that your ski pass isn't valid in the evening. Schatzalp (reached by a funicular), the Schneider and the Landhaus in Frauenkirch have also been recommended.

APRES-SKI
Lots on offer, but quiet clientele
There are plenty of bars, discos and nightclubs, and a large casino in the hotel Europe. But we're not sure how some of them make a living – Davos guests tend to want the quiet life. At tea time, mega-calories are consumed at the Weber, and the Schneider might be worth a look. The Scala has a popular outside terrace. The liveliest place in town is the rustic little Chämi bar (popular with locals); it has 'the best atmosphere later in the evening', according to a reporter. The smart Ex-Bar attracts a mixed age group. Nightclubs tend to be sophisticated, expensive and lacking atmosphere during the week. The most popular are the Cabanna and the Cava Grischa (both in the hotel Europe), the Rotliechtli, and Paulaner's. Bolgenschanze and Bolgen-Plaza are popular boarder hang-outs.

OFF THE SLOPES
Great, apart from the buildings
Provided you're not fussy about building style, Davos can be unreservedly recommended for those not planning to hit the slopes. The towny resort has shops and other diversions, and transport along the valley and up on to the slopes is good – though the best of the mountain restaurants are well out of range for pedestrians. The sports facilities are excellent; the natural ice rink is said to be Europe's biggest, and is supplemented by artificial rinks, both indoor and outdoor. Spectator events include speed skating as well as 'hugely popular' ice hockey – enjoyed by a reporter this year. And there are lots of walks up on the slopes as well as around the lake and along the valleys. There is a toboggan run on Rinerhorn, floodlit twice weekly, but the best in the area is the much longer run on Madrisa, at Klosters.

SWISS-IMAGE / MOUNTAIN
MARKETING AG

Flims

An unremarkable village, but one blessed with high, wide, sunny, varied slopes that deserve to be better known outside Switzerland

COSTS

① ② ③ ④ ⑤ ⑥

RATINGS

The slopes

Fast lifts	****
Snow	***
Extent	****
Expert	***
Intermediate	*****
Beginner	****
Convenience	***
Queues	****
Mountain restaurants	***

The rest

Scenery	***
Resort charm	***
Off-slope	***

Ski Boards Boots and more...

www.sport2000rent.com

rent a sport
QUALITY RENTAL SYSTEM

+ Extensive, varied slopes ideal for intermediates, shared with Laax

+ Impressive lift system with few queues most of the time

– Sunny orientation can cause icy or slushy pistes and bare lower runs

– Village very spread out, which can mean long walks or bus-rides

– Weekend crowds in high season

Flims gets the minor-resort treatment here only because hardly anyone from the UK goes there. It is by any measure a major resort – with 220km/137 miles of piste, one of the biggest in Switzerland. Flims itself in no great draw, but Laax and Falera are rustic alternatives linked in to the lift network.

THE RESORT

Flims is set on a sunny mountain terrace and has two parts. Dorf is the main village and lift base; it spreads along a busy road – but a bypass tunnel was being built when we visited in 2006. Waldhaus is a leafy suburb with the smart hotels (which run courtesy buses to the lifts). The slopes spread across to a busy lift station/hotel complex outside the village of Laax and a fast quad from Falera.

THE MOUNTAINS

Flims has extensive, varied slopes beneath high, exposed peaks, with a small glacier. There are some tree-lined runs. Trips are possible by car to Lenzerheide, Davos-Klosters and Arosa.
    The resort piste map shows 'free-

ride routes' without explaining whether they are avalanche-protected, and patrolled – scandalous.

Slopes There are powerful gondolas going into the heart of the slopes from both Flims Dorf and Laax (alongside a cable-car, of exceptional length). Above mid-mountain, there is a complex web of lifts and runs. A six-pack now serves the main Flims slopes below La Siala. The glacier offers limited vertical, but also accesses a superb black run away from the lifts to Alp Ruschein, of 1250m/4,100ft vertical. Some chairs (eg to Naraus) are designed for walkers – skis are taken off. Classification of runs often overstates difficulty.

Terrain-parks The 'very impressive' terrain-park at Crap Sogn Gion is claimed to be Europe's best, with drops, jumps, quarter-pipes, rails for all levels and a boarder-cross. The two

509

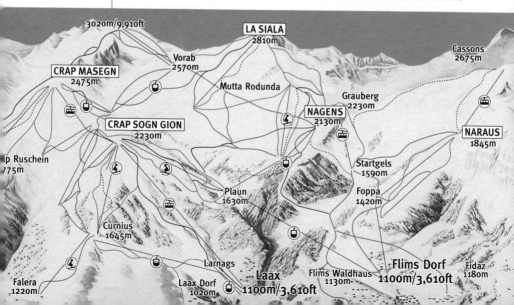

KEY FACTS

Resort	1100m
	3,610ft
Altitude	1100-3020m
	3,610-9,910ft
Lifts	27
Pistes	220km
	137 miles
Blue	29%
Red	33%
Black	28%
Snowmaking	13km
	8 miles

NEWS

For 2005/06 a six-pack replaced the drags between Nagens and La Siala. More snowmaking is planned for 2006/07. A tunnel is being built to remove through-traffic.

Phone numbers
From elsewhere in Switzerland add the prefix 081.
From abroad use the prefix +41 81.

TOURIST OFFICE

For Flims, Laax and Falera
t 920 9200
tourismus@alpenarena.ch
www.alpenarena.ch

half-pipes have walls up to 6.7m/22ft. The park has its own drag-lift. There's a half-pipe on the glacier.

Snow reliability Upper runs are fairly snow-sure, but those back to Flims can suffer from sun. The runs from Cassons and the black from the glacier are both prone to closure. Snowmaking is limited, and not shown on the piste map. 'Excellent' grooming.

Experts The few black pistes are not seriously steep except in patches, but the 'free-ride routes' add an extra dimension and there is abundant off-piste terrain too. In such a sunny area, timing your runs can be crucial to avoid rock-hard moguls.

Intermediates This is a superb area for all intermediates. Reporters are genuinely surprised by the extent and length of the slopes. The bowl below La Siala is huge and gentle. For the more adventurous and confident, there are plenty of reds and some blacks worth trying. The sheltered Grauberg valley is a favourite – long and fast. The long black Sattel run from the glacier is challenging only at the top. The men's World Cup Downhill piste from Crap Sogn Gion to Larnags is often beautifully groomed.

Beginners There's a nursery area in Dorf, and alternatives at Crap Sogn Gion and Nagens if snow is poor. The Foppa and Curnius areas have good easy runs to move on to.

Snowboarding This is a snowboard hot-spot. The park and pipe on Crap Sogn Gion have loud music from the adjacent bars. Regular high-profile competitions are held here. There's good free-riding to be had.

Cross-country There are 60km/37 miles of trails scattered around.

Queues Queues are generally rare, but the return chair at Alp Ruschein can generate long waits, and getting out of Flims and Laax at the weekend can be a slow process. A couple of slow chairs remain. High winds can close the exposed upper lifts.

Mountain restaurants All 17 are briefly described on the piste map. There are some stylish modern table-service places at altitude – Das Elephant and Capalari. Reporters love the Alpenrose (Startgels) by the Grauberg cable-car ('glorious views', 'excellent grills'). Tegia Curnius does 'good food at reasonable prices' but gets busy. Lower down are the smartly rustic Tegia Larnags and cosy Runcahöhe (popular with walkers as well).

Schools and guides Reporters have 'progressed very well' in group and private lessons, and in children's classes.

Facilities for children Children aged three and over can be looked after at one of the Kinderland centres. And there is a Snow Kids Village in the ski school. Nannies are available.

STAYING THERE

How to go Only a handful of UK tour operators feature Flims.

Hotels In Waldhaus a 2006 reporter enjoyed the Adula (928 2828) ('good spa facilities'). The award-winning Park Hotel (928 4848) has an ultra-modern wellness centre. And in Dorf the Vorab (911 1861) is close to the lifts and highly praised by a 2006 reporter for 'excellent food'.

Self-catering The tourist office has a long list of available apartments.

Eating out Most Flims restaurants are in hotels. Reporters recommend the Alpina, the Vorab and the Adula ('best gourmet restaurant in the area'); Little China (Park hotel) and Caverna (Bellevue) have also been suggested.

Après-ski Flims is pretty quiet. But the 'friendly' Iglu and the Stenna bar are packed at close of play. And a 2006 reporter recommends the Legna bar. Casa Veglia has live bands.

Off the slopes There's an enormous sports centre, with ice rink, and 60km/37 miles of marked walks. The shopping is limited. Chur is close.

Laax 1100m/3,610ft

The modern development at the base of the Crap Sogn Gion cable-car, Murschetg, now seems to be called Laax. Here, the high-tech Riders Palace (927 9700) is a trendy place to stay – with dorm as well as normal rooms. The village of Laax, now called Laax Dorf, is a quiet place a short drive/bus-ride away with a rustic centre and pleasant suburbs spreading around a lake. Here, the little Posta Veglia (921 4466) is the place to stay or eat – excellent food in a lovely old stube, and in a plainer restaurant behind. Endorsed by a 2006 visitor.

Falera 1220m/4,000ft

This tiny village is quiet and traffic-free and has good views over three valleys. Most accommodation is in apartments.

Grindelwald

Traditional summer-and-winter resort in a spectacular setting – better for scenery-gazing than bashing the pistes, thanks to slow lifts

COSTS

① ② ③ ④ ⑤ ⑥

RATINGS

The slopes
Fast lifts	***
Snow	**
Extent	***
Expert	**
Intermediate	****
Beginner	***
Convenience	**
Queues	**
Mountain restaurants	***

The rest
Scenery	*****
Resort charm	****
Off-slope	****

NEWS

For 2005/06 a section of the Oberjoch blue run at First became a slow-speed zone. Faster skiers and boarders are encouraged to use the adjacent red run.

The Hotel Eiger has a new wellness centre.

The are plans to replace the Honegg drag-lift (near Kleine Scheidegg) with a six-pack and to build a new terrain-park at the top – but not until 2007/08.

+ Dramatically set in magnificent scenery, directly beneath the towering north face of the Eiger

+ Lots of long, gentle runs, ideal for intermediates, with links to Wengen

+ Pleasant old village with long mountaineering history

+ Fair amount to do off the slopes, including splendid walks

– Main slopes accessed by a painfully slow, queue-prone (especially at weekends) gondola or by slow trains

– Few challenging pistes for experts

– Inconvenient for visiting Mürren

– Snow-cover unreliable

– Village gets very little midwinter sun

For stunning views from the town and the slopes, there are few places to rival Grindelwald. The village is nowhere near as special as Mürren or Wengen, just over the hill, but staying here does give you direct access to Grindelwald's own First slopes. But you can spend ages queueing for, waiting for or sitting in the gondola or trains up into the slopes shared with Wengen. (The gondola ride – the longest in Europe according to Grindelwald's literature – takes half an hour. The train to Kleine Scheidegg from Grindelwald takes about the same.) Grindelwald regulars accept all this as part of the scene.

THE RESORT

Grindelwald is set either side of a road along a narrow valley. Buildings are mainly traditional chalet-style. Towering mountains rise steeply from the valley floor, and the resort and main slopes get very little sun in January.

Grindelwald can feel very jolly at times, such as during the ice-carving festival in January, when huge ice sculptures are on display along the main street. The village is livelier at night than the other Jungfrau resorts of Wengen and Mürren. There's live music in several bars and hotels, but it isn't a place for bopping until dawn.

The main lifts into the slopes shared with Wengen are at Grund, right at the bottom of the sloping village. Near the opposite end of the village, a gondola goes to the separate First area. Trains run from the centre to Grund or direct to Kleine Scheidegg, and buses link the lift stations – but these get congested at times and reporters say they are too infrequent.

The most convenient place to stay for the slopes is at Grund. But this is out of the centre and rather charmless. There's a wide range of hotels in the heart of the village, handy enough for everything else, including the First area, at the foot of which are nursery slopes, ski school and kindergarten.

Trips to other resorts are not very easy, but you can drive to Adelboden. Getting to the tougher, higher slopes of Mürren is a lengthy business unless you go to Lauterbrunnen by car.

THE MOUNTAINS

The major area of slopes is shared with Wengen and offers a mix of wooded slopes and open slopes higher up. The smaller First area is mainly open, though there are wooded runs to the village.

THE SLOPES
Broad and mainly gentle
From Grund, near the western end of town, you can get to **Männlichen** by an appallingly slow two-stage gondola or to **Kleine Scheidegg** by an equally slow cog railway. The slopes of the separate south-facing **First** area are

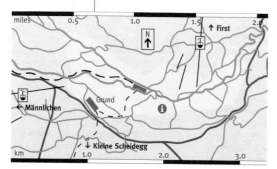

miles	0.5		1.0		1.5	↑ First	2.0

N ↑

← Männlichen

Grund

ⓘ

↓ Kleine Scheidegg

km	1.0		2.0		3.0

KEY FACTS

| Resort | 1035m |
| | 3,400ft |

Jungfrau region

Slopes	945-2970m
	3,100-9,740ft
Lifts	41
Pistes	213km
	132 miles
Blue	25%
Red	61%
Black	14%
Snowmaking	60km
	37 miles

First-Männlichen-Kleine-Scheidegg

Slopes	945-2485m
	3,100-8,150ft
Lifts	30
Pistes	160km
	99 miles

LIFT PASSES

Jungfrau Top Ski Region

Prices in SF

Age	1-day	6-day
under 16	28	144
16 to 19	45	230
20 to 61	56	288
over 62	50	259

Free under 6
Beginner points card

Notes
Covers Wengen, Mürren and Grindelwald, trains between them and Grindelwald ski-bus. Day pass price is for First-Kleine Scheidegg-Männlichen area only.

Alternative passes
Passes available for Grindelwald and Wengen only and for Mürren only. Non-skiers pass available.

reached by a long, slow gondola starting a bus-ride east of the centre.

From all over the slopes there are superb views, not only of the Eiger but also of the Wetterhorn and other peaks. Piste marking is poor; a reporter this year singles out the Männlichen slopes as particularly confusing ('marking is non-existent'). The piste map is clear, but huge.

TERRAIN-PARKS
First things first
First is the place to head for. There is a terrain-park with rails, boxes and jumps, a super-pipe and a boarder-cross course.

SNOW RELIABILITY
Poor
Grindelwald's low altitude and the lack of much snowmaking mean this is not a resort to book far in advance or for a late-season holiday. First is sunny, and so even less snow-sure than the main area. We have also had reports of 'patchy' piste grooming.

FOR EXPERTS
They are trying
The area is quite limited for experts, but there is some fine off-piste if the snow is good. Heli-trips with mountain guides are organised. The black run on First beneath the gondola back to town is quite tough, especially when the snow has suffered from the sun.

FOR INTERMEDIATES
Ideal intermediate terrain
In good snow, First makes a splendid intermediate playground, though the general lack of trees makes the area less friendly than the larger Kleine Scheidegg-Männlichen area. The runs

to the valley are great fun. Nearly all the runs from Kleine Scheidegg are long blues or gentle reds. On the Männlichen there's a choice of gentle runs down to the mid-station of the gondola – and in good snow, down to the bottom. For tougher pistes, head for the top of the Lauberhorn lift and the runs to Kleine Scheidegg, or to Wixi (following the start of the downhill course). The north-facing run from Eigergletscher to Salzegg often has the best snow late in the season.

FOR BEGINNERS
Depends where you go
The Bodmi nursery slope at the bottom of First is scenic but not particularly convenient according to a 2006 reporter, who says 'the chore of getting to and from it with small children was too much'. It can also suffer from the sun and its low altitude – a recent reporter said Grindelwald instructors used it despite it being icy, full of craters and spoiled by fast skiers and tobogganers racing through. A section of the Oberjoch blue run at First is now a designated slow speed zone for novices. Kleine Scheidegg has a better, higher beginner area and splendid long runs to progress to, served by the railway.

FOR CROSS-COUNTRY
Good but shady
There are 25km/16 miles of prepared tracks. Almost all of this is on the valley floor, so it's shady in mid-winter and may have poor snow later on.

QUEUES
Can be dreadful at peak times
We still receive mixed reports on queues. Waiting times for the gondola

SCHOOLS

Grindelwald Sports
t 854 1280

Buri Sport (snowboard)
t 853 3353

Snowsports Kleine Scheidegg
t 855 1545

Classes
(Sports prices)
5 full days SF270

Private lessons
SF320 for 1 day

CHILDREN

Kinderhort Sunshine
t 853 0440
Ages from 1mnth to 8yr; 9.30-4pm (SF68 per day)

Kinderhort Murmeli
t 077 414 91 08
9.30-4.30; ages 6mnth to 7yr

Snowli Kinderclub
t 854 1280
Ages from 3; 9.30-4pm; SF50 per day

Ski schools
Take children from age 4 (5 days SF270)

boarding

Intermediates will enjoy the area most – the beginners' slopes can be bare, while experts will hanker for Mürren's steep, off-piste slopes. First is the main boarders' mountain, not only because of the terrain-park and big pipe but also because of the open free-ride terrain accessed via the top lifts. There are quite a few drags.

and train at Grund can be very bad in high season, especially at weekends – partly because children up to 15 can ski free if a parent buys a pass on Saturday. Some reporters have told of half-hour waits for the gondola, which then takes a further half-hour to get to the top. You may find long waits for the gondola down from First when the lower runs are closed.

MOUNTAIN RESTAURANTS
Wide choice
See the Wengen chapter for options around Kleine Scheidegg and down towards Wengen. Brandegg, on the railway, is recommended for 'wonderful' apple fritters and its sunny terrace. Berghaus Bort does 'very good Alpler macaroni', and the popular Jägerstubli, off the Rennstrecke piste, serves 'the best raclette ever,' according to a 2006 visitor. The Berghaus Aspen, above Grund, is also recommended this year. There are splendid views from Männlichen, and the Berggasthaus at the top is recommended by a reader. The Spycher has a cosy indoor bar plus deckchairs and an ice-bar, which also serves sandwiches. At First, Café Genepi, at the bottom of the Oberjoch

chair, is 'a must' for Flammenkuchen (thin pizza) and a good place to begin your après-ski, says a 2006 visitor.

SCHOOLS AND GUIDES
Mixed views
Recent reports declare the main school, Grindelwald Sports, 'very good'; spoken English is normally excellent. But one reporter had a 'wasted' first day, because abilities were not assessed before the class. However, 'the teachers (three in three days!) were excellent'. The Privat school offers off-piste guiding.

FACILITIES FOR CHILDREN
Good reputation
See above, but a past reporter who put four children through the Grindelwald mill praised caring and effective instructors. 'Faultless' was the verdict from a 2006 parent, but he found the First area to be inconvenient and busy for families with small children. The First mountain restaurant runs a day nursery, which is a neat idea, and the Sunshine nursery is at the top of Männlichen.

Grindelwald

513

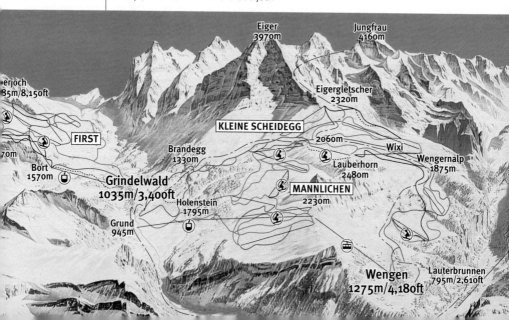

Eiger 3970m

Jungfrau 4160m

Eigergletscher 2320m

erjoch 35m/8,15oft

KLEINE SCHEIDEGG

2060m

FIRST

Brandegg 1330m

Wixi

Wengernalp 1875m

70m

Lauberhorn 2480m

Bort 1570m

Grindelwald 1035m/3,400ft

MANNLICHEN 2230m

Holenstein 1795m

Grund 945m

Wengen 1275m/4,18oft

Lauterbrunnen 795m/2,610ft

GETTING THERE

Air Zürich 195km/
121 miles (3hr); Bern
70km/43 miles
(1½hr).

Rail Station in resort.

ACTIVITIES

Indoor Sports centre
(swimming pool,
sauna, steam, fitness
room, games room),
indoor ice rink,
bowling, curling,
concerts, cinema

Outdoor 80km/
50 miles of cleared
paths, train rides to
Jungfraujoch, ice rink,
tobogganing, snow-
shoe excursions,
climbing, paragliding,
glacier tours, sleigh
rides

Phone numbers
From elsewhere in
Switzerland add the
prefix 033.
From abroad use the
prefix +41 33.

TOURIST OFFICE

t 854 1212
touristcenter@
grindelwald.ch
www.grindelwald.com

STAYING THERE

HOW TO GO
Limited range of packages

The hotels UK tour operators offer are
mainly at the upper end of the market.
Hotels There's a 5-star, a dozen 4-stars
and plenty of more modest places.
(((((5) **Grand Regina** (854 8600) Big
and imposing 5-star; right next to the
station. Nightly music in the bar. Pool.
(((4) **Belvedere** (854 5757) Family-run,
close to the station. 'Wonderful' pool.
Recommended by a 2006 visitor on his
fifth stay.
((((4) **Schweizerhof** (854 5858) 4-star
chalet at west end of the centre, close
to the station. Pool.
(((4) **Spinne** (854 8888) Central 4-star
which a reporter 'cannot praise enough:
friendly, superb food, good rooms'.
(((3) **Hirschen** (854 8484) Family-run 3-
star by nursery slopes. Good food.
(((3) **Derby** (854 5461) Popular, modern
3-star next to station, with 'first-class'
service, good food and great views.
(((3) **Eigerblick** (854 1020) A bit away
from the station but 'great service,
including free taxi'. Huge bedrooms.
(1) **Hotel Wetterhorn** (853 1218) Cosy,
simple chalet way beyond the village,
with great views of the glacier.
Self-catering The apartments of hotels
Hirschen and Eiger are recommended.

EATING OUT
Hotel based

There's a wide choice of good hotel
restaurants. Among the more traditional
places are: the Bistro-Bar Memory in the
Eiger; Schmitte in the Schweizerhof;
Challi-Stübli in the Kreuz; and the Alte
Post. The Fiescherblick's Swiss Bistro is
'brilliant but expensive'. The Kirchbühl
and Oberland are good for vegetarians.
Hotel Spinne has many options: Italian,
Mexican, Chinese and the candlelit
Rôtisserie for a special romantic meal.
Onkle Tom's Hutte is recommended for
pizza. The Latino does Italian home
cooking.

APRES-SKI
Getting livelier

Tipirama at Kleine Scheidegg is a fun
place immediately after skiing ('vibrant
and welcoming'), sometimes with DJs
and live bands. Pumuckl's offers a
similar experience on First. For
'unforgettable' speciality coffees try the
Rancher bar, says a 2006 reporter. The
Holzer bar is also suggested as a good
drinking spot on the way down to
Grund. In town, the terrace of the C&M
Café is good for coffee and cake. There
are a handful of bars that aim to keep
going late. The Espresso bar in the
Spinne hotel seems to be the liveliest
and the Hotel Eiger has a couple of
choices – the Memory Bar also offers
'reasonably priced food', especially on
burger night (Sundays). From there,
people head for the Mascelero club.

OFF THE SLOPES
Plenty to do, easy to get around

There are many cleared paths with
magnificent views, especially around
First – and there's a special (though
expensive) pedestrian bus/lift pass.
Many of the mountain huts are
accessible to pedestrians. A trip to
Jungfraujoch is spectacular (see below),
and excursions by train are easy to
Interlaken. Tobogganing has
undergone a renaissance, with runs up
to 15km/9 miles on First (the world's
longest – bear in mind it's a two-and-
a-half-hour uphill walk from the top of
the gondola) and 57km/35 miles of
runs in total. There's also a cinema,
and ice hockey and curling matches to
watch. There's an excellent sports
centre with pool. Helicopter flights
from Männlichen are recommended.

STAYING UP THE MOUNTAIN
Several possibilities

See the Wengen chapter for details of
rooms at Kleine Scheidegg. The
Berghaus Bort (854 4099), at the
gondola station in the middle of the
First area, is an attractive alternative.

THE JOURNEY TO THE TOP OF EUROPE

*From Kleine Scheidegg you can take a train through the Eiger to the highest
railway station in Europe – Jungfraujoch at 3450m/11,330ft. The journey is a bit
tedious – you're in a tunnel except when you stop to look out of two galleries
carved into the sheer north face of the Eiger – magnificent views over to
Männlichen, and then over the glacier. At the top is a big restaurant complex.
There's an 'ice palace' carved out of the glacier and a viewing tower with
fabulous views of the Aletsch glacier (a UNESCO World Heritage Site).
The cost is SF50.50 with a Jungfrau lift pass for three days or more.*

Klosters

*Ski the extensive slopes of Davos from a traditional village base –
now with through-traffic banished to a bypass*

➕ Splendid long intermediate runs back to the village from the Parsenn

➕ Lots of accessible off-piste terrain,

➕ Some cute mountain restaurants

➕ Pleasant traditional village, now bypassed by the valley traffic

➕ Very extensive slopes, shared with Davos, but ...

➖ The slopes are spread over five widely separated areas

➖ Preponderance of T-bars is a problem for some visitors

➖ Queue-prone cable-car into the main Parsenn area

In a word association game, 'Klosters' might trigger 'Prince of Wales'. The queue-prone cable-car to Gotschna and the Parsenn is named after him. Don't be put off: Klosters is not particularly exclusive, and it does have a lot going for it.

The village – potentially a really charming place – will have a lot more going for it since the bypass opened for last winter. We didn't get the chance to visit last season, but we look forward to finding the place transformed – not only with much less traffic but with a bit more animation in the streets, now that pedestrians don't go in fear of their lives.

THE RESORT

Klosters is a comfortable, quiet village with a much more appealing Alpine flavour than Davos. Klosters Platz is the main focus – a collection of upmarket, traditional-style hotels around the railway station, at the foot of the steep, wooded slopes of Gotschna. Traffic bound for Davos and the Vereina rail tunnel, an acute problem, was removed by the opening of a bypass in December 2005.

The village spreads along the valley road for quite a way before fading into the countryside; there's then a second concentration of building in the even quieter village of Klosters Dorf, base of the gondola to Madrisa.

THE MOUNTAINS

Most of the runs are on open slopes above steeper woodland.
Slopes A cable-car from the railway station in Platz takes you to the Gotschnagrat end of the Parsenn area shared with Davos, and a newly upgraded gondola from Dorf takes you up to the scenic Madrisa area. There's also a separate little slope at Selfranga, a suburb of Platz.
Terrain-parks The Madrisa area has a boarder-cross course, and there are more options on the other mountains. The Selfranga area has a new park, which is floodlit in the evenings.
Snow reliability It's usually good higher up but the home runs are quite low and not so reliable.
Experts The extensive off-piste possibilities are the main appeal. There are several marked itineraries.
Intermediates There are excellent cruising runs in all five ski areas.
Beginners There is a slope between Dorf and Platz, plus Selfranga; but the slopes of Madrisa are more appealing.
Snowboarding Local slopes are good, but more boarders stay in Davos.
Cross-country There are 35km/22 miles of trails and lots more up at Davos; a Nordic ski school offers lessons.
Queues Queues for the Gotschna cable-car can be a problem at weekends and peak holiday times. The

KEY FACTS

Resort	1190m
	3,900ft
Slopes	810-2845m
	2,660-9,330ft
Lifts	54
Pistes	310km
	193 miles
Green	19%
Blue	43%
Black	38%
Snowmaking	39km
	24 miles

Phone numbers
From elsewhere in Switzerland add the prefix 081.
From abroad use the prefix +41 81.

TOURIST OFFICE

t 410 2020
info@klosters.ch
www.klosters.ch

Madrisa gondola was upgraded for 2005/06, improving the journey time.
Mountain restaurants There are a number of atmospheric huts in the woods above the village – see Davos chapter. The restaurants on the Madrisa slopes are 'disappointing'.
Schools and guides There is a choice of three ski and snowboard schools. One reader recommends the Saas, with 'excellent English-speaking instructors'.
Facilities for children The ski schools offer classes for children from the age of four and the Madrisa Kids' Club takes children aged two to six.

STAYING THERE

How to go There is a wide choice of packages offered by UK tour operators.
Hotels There are some particularly attractive hotels. For most people, central Platz is the best location. Here, the Chesa Grischuna (422 2222) is a firm favourite, combining traditional atmosphere with modern comfort – and a lively après-ski bar. The Alpina (410 2424) is 'wonderful, with very helpful staff and excellent spa,' says a 2006 reporter. The 2-star Bündnerhof (422 1450), 400m/1,310ft from the train/lift station, provides 'extremely good value' half-board. Next door, the very cosy old Wynegg (422 1340) is a perennial favourite with British visitors. In Dorf, the Sunstar Albeina (423 2100) is not particularly convenient but is cheaper than the other 4-stars, has a good spa and is 'friendly, with good food' says a fourth-time visitor.
Self-catering Apartments are available through local agencies.

Eating out Good restaurants abound, but a reporter comments that there is a shortage of the cheap and cheerful variety. Top of the range is the Walserhof, with two Michelin stars. Al Berto's serves 'wonderful' pizza and the rösti at the Alpina is recommended. The Casanna at Platz serves 'excellent steaks' and the Chesa Grischuna is recommended for 'fabulous venison' and good wines at moderate prices.
Après-ski In the village, the Chesa Grischuna is a focus from tea-time onwards, with its live music, bowling and restaurant. A reporter enjoyed the music 'at a volume which allowed you to converse'. The hotel Vereina is recommended for its piano bar.

Gaudy's at the foot of the slopes is a popular stop after skiing 'if you're happy to drink in a tent', as is the lively bar at the 4-star Alpina and the warmly panelled Wynegg. The 'popular' Gotschna bar, near the base station, is 'friendly' and colourful inside. The Rossli bar is a 'nicely busy' place to watch sport on TV.

The Casa Antica is a small disco that livens up on Saturday night. The Kir Royal, under the hotel Silvretta Park, is bigger and more brash.
Off the slopes Klosters is an attractive base for walking and cross-country skiing, and tobogganing is popular – there is an exceptional 8.5km/5 mile run from Madrisa to Saas. A reporter this year recommends the return hike from Schifer ('a nice adventure'). There is a leisure centre with an ice rink, and some hotel pools are open. You can take the train to the interesting old town of Chur.

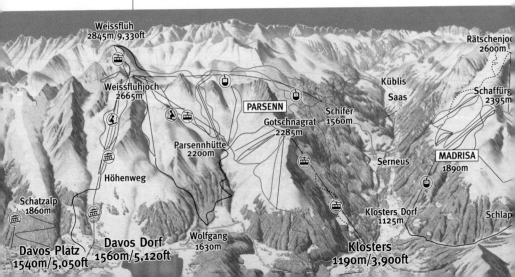

Mürren

*The dinky, car-free mountain village where the British invented
downhill ski racing; stupendous views from one epic run*

COSTS

①②③④⑤⑥

RATINGS

The slopes

Fast lifts	★★★
Snow	★★★
Extent	★
Expert	★★★
Intermediate	★★★
Beginner	★★
Convenience	★★★
Queues	★★★
Mountain restaurants	★★

The rest

Scenery	★★★★★
Charm	★★★★★
Off-slope	★★★

NEWS

For 2006/07 a fast
quad is due to
replace the Engetal
drag-lift up to Birg.
The return to this lift
from the runs at
Obere Hubel used to
involve a short walk,
but there's now a
short rope tow to
cover the distance.

And a cable-car will
replace the funicular
from Lauterbrunnen
in the valley to
Grütschalp.

miles   0.5
↑ down to Lauterbrunnen
Allmendhubel
Schilthorn
N ↑
↓ down to Stechelberg
km   0.5   1.

The views of the
Eiger, Mönch and
Jungfrau are quite
amazing →

➕ Tiny, charming, traditional village,
with 'traffic-free' snowy paths

➕ Stupendous scenery, best enjoyed
descending from the Schilthorn

➕ Good sports centre

➕ Good snow high up, even when the
rest of the region is suffering

➖ Extent of local pistes very limited,
no matter what your level of
expertise

➖ Lower slopes can be in poor
condition

➖ Quiet, limited nightlife

**Mürren is one of our favourite resorts. There may be other mountain villages
that are equally pretty, but none of them enjoys views like those from Mürren
across the deep valley to the rock faces and glaciers of the Eiger, Mönch and
Jungfrau: simply breathtaking. Then there's the Schilthorn run – 1300m/4,270ft
vertical with an unrivalled combination of varied terrain and glorious views.**

**But our visits are normally one-day affairs; holidaymakers, we concede, are
likely to want to explore the extensive intermediate slopes of Wengen and
Grindelwald, across the valley. And that takes time.**

**It was in Mürren that the British more or less invented modern skiing. Sir Arnold
Lunn organised the first ever slalom race here in 1922. Some 12 years earlier his
father, Sir Henry, had persuaded the locals to open the railway in winter so that
he could bring the first winter package tour here. Sir Arnold's son Peter has
been a regular visitor since he first skied here in November 1916.**

THE RESORT

Mürren is set on a shelf high above the
valley floor, across from Wengen, and
can be reached only by cable-car from
Stechelberg (via Gimmelwald) or from
Lauterbrunnen to a mountain railway at
Grütschalp. You can't fail to be struck
by Mürren's tranquillity and beauty.
Paths and narrow lanes weave
between little wooden chalets and a
handful of bigger hotel buildings – all
normally blanketed by snow.

A two-stage cable-car takes you up
to the high slopes of Birg and the
Schilthorn. Nearby lifts go to the main
lower slopes, and a funicular halfway
along the village accesses others.

Mürren's traffic-free status is being
somewhat eroded; there are now a few
delivery trucks. But the place still isn't
plagued by electric carts and taxis in
the way that most other traditional
'traffic-free' resorts now are, and
reporters are generally very impressed
with the place.

KEY FACTS

Resort	1650m
	5,410ft

Jungfrau region
Altitude	945-2970m
	3,100-9,740ft
Lifts	41
Pistes	213km
	132 miles
Blue	25%
Red	61%
Black	14%
Snowmaking	60km
	37 miles

Mürren-Schilthorn only
Slopes	1650-2970m
	5,410-9,740ft
Lifts	12
Pistes	53km
	33 miles

LIFT PASSES

Jungfrau Top Ski Region

Prices in SF
Age	1-day	6-day
under 16	28	144
16 to 19	45	230
20 to 61	56	288
over 62	50	259

Free under 6
Beginner points card
Notes
Covers Wengen, Mürren and Grindelwald, trains between them and Grindelwald ski-bus. Day pass price is for Mürren-Schilthorn area only.
Alternative passes
Passes available for Grindelwald and Wengen only and for Mürren only. Non-skiers pass available.

SCHOOLS

Swiss
t 855 1247

Classes
6 2hr days SF180
Private lessons
SF120 for 2hr for 1-4 persons

It's not the place to go for lively nightlife, shopping or showing off your latest gear to admiring hordes. It is the place to go if you want tranquillity and stunning views. The village is so small that location is not a concern. Nothing is more than a few minutes' walk.

THE MOUNTAIN

Mürren's slopes aren't extensive (53km/33 miles in total). But it has something for everyone, including a vertical of some 1300m/4,270ft. And those happy to take the time to cross the valley to Wengen-Grindelwald will find plenty of options.

THE SLOPES
Small but interesting
There are three connected areas around the village, reaching no higher than 2145m/7,040ft. The biggest is **Schiltgrat**, served by a fast quad chair behind the cable-car station. A funicular goes from the middle of the village to the nursery slope at **Allmendhubel** – from where a run and a fast chair take you to the slightly higher **Maulerhubel**. Runs go down from here to Winteregg, on the railway.

Much more interesting are the higher slopes reached by cable-car to **Birg**. Below Birg, the Engetal area has a new quad serving short, steep, shady slopes. Two chair-lifts below the Engetal serve some snow-sure intermediate slopes. The final stage of the cable-car takes you up to the Schilthorn and its revolving restaurant, made famous by the James Bond film *On Her Majesty's Secret Service*. In good snow you can ski down to Lauterbrunnen – almost 16km/10 miles and 2175m/7,135ft. The Inferno race (see separate box) takes place over this course, snow permitting. Below Winteregg, it's all boring paths.

TERRAIN-PARKS
Affirmative
We can scarcely believe it, but there is a terrain-park and half-pipe on the lower slopes of Schiltgrat.

SNOW RELIABILITY
Good on the upper slopes
The Jungfrau region does not have a good snow record – but Mürren always has the best snow in the area. When Wengen-Grindelwald (and Mürren's lower slopes) have problems, the Schilthorn and Engetal often have packed powder snow because of their height and orientation – north-east to east. The runs from below Engetal to Allmendhubel and parts of the lower slopes have snowmaking – and one reporter complains of it being left on at midday, forming 'lumps of wet icing sugar', while another tells of bare patches on the lower slopes being left that way. A more recent reporter tells of 'random piste grooming despite half of Mürren being closed because of the cable-car problems'.

FOR EXPERTS
One wonderful piste
The run from the top of the Schilthorn starts with a steep but not terrifying slope, in the past generally mogulled but now more often groomed. It flattens into a schuss to Engetal, below Birg. Then there's a wonderful, wide run with stunning views over the valley to the Eiger, Mönch and Jungfrau. Since the chair-lifts were built here you can play on these upper runs for as long as you like, before resuming your descent. Below the lifts you hit the Kanonenrohr (gun barrel). This is a very narrow shelf with solid rock on one side and a steep drop on the other – protected by nets. After an open slope and scrappy zig-zag path, you arrive at the 'hog's back' and can descend towards the village on either side of Allmendhubel.

From Schiltgrat a short, serious mogul run – the Kandahar – descends towards the village, but experts are more likely to be interested in the off-piste runs into the Blumental – both from here (the north-facing Blumenlucke run) and from Birg (the sunnier Tschingelchrachen) – or the more adventurous runs from the Schilthorn.

boarding

Like many Swiss resorts, Mürren has a traditional image, but it is trying to move with the times and offer a more snowboard-friendly attitude – and the major lifts are cable-cars and chair-lifts. The terrain above Mürren is suitable mainly for good free-riders – it's steep, with a lot of off-piste. Intermediates will find the area tough and limited; nearby Wengen is ideal, and much better for beginners.

CHILDREN

Snowgarden
Ages 18mnth to 5yr; 9.30-12noon; 1.30-4pm.

Ski school
Takes ages 5 and over (6 2hr days SF180).

FOR INTERMEDIATES
Limited, but Wengen nearby

Keen piste-bashers will want to make a few trips to the long cruising runs of Wengen-Grindelwald. The best easy cruising run in Mürren is the north-facing blue down to Winteregg. The reds on the other low slopes can get mogulled, and snow conditions can be poor. The area below the Engetal normally has good snow, and you can choose your gradient

Competent, confident intermediates should consider tackling the Schilthorn run if snow conditions are good.

FOR BEGINNERS
Not ideal, but adequate

The nursery slopes at Allmendhubel, at the top of the funicular, are on the steep side. And there are not many easy runs to graduate to – though the blue down the Winteregg chair is easy, and a couple of blues are served by the long Gimmeln drag and the less tiring Schiltgrat chair.

FOR CROSS-COUNTRY
Forget it

There's a 6km/4 mile loop along the valley, between Stechelberg and Lauterbrunnen. But snow is unreliable at valley height.

QUEUES
Generally not a problem

Mürren doesn't get as crowded as Wengen and Grindelwald, except on sunny Sundays. There can be queues for the cable-cars – usually when snow shortages bring in people from lower resorts. The top stage has only one cabin, so capacity is limited.

MOUNTAIN RESTAURANTS
Nothing outstanding

Piz Gloria revolves once an hour, displaying a fabulous 360° panorama of peaks and lakes. We don't like the ambience here, but one reporter tells of 'a very nice goulash soup' and says, 'It is incredible value for money just for the view (and cheaper than Méribel).' By the Engetal chair-lifts, the Schilthornhütte is small and rustic and 'does excellent special coffees'. Lower down, the rustic Suppenalp in the Blumental is quietly set and 'cosy with excellent food', but gets no sun in January. A recent reporter talks of 'friendly service' and 'fantastic goulash soup and macaroni with apple sauce'. As you might expect, Sonnenberg is sunnier and readers have enjoyed 'marvellous rösti' and speciality coffees. Gimmeln is a self-service place with a large terrace, famous for its

Mürren

519

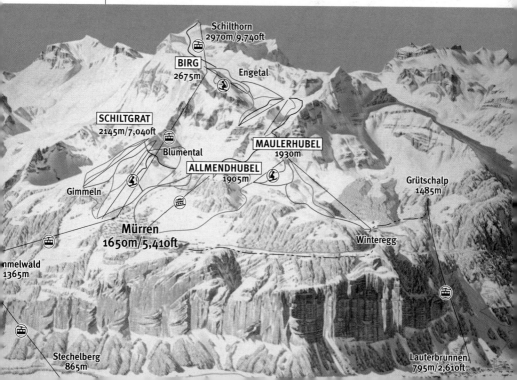

THE INFERNO RACE

Every January 1,800 amateurs compete in Mürren's spectacular Inferno race. Conditions permitting, and they usually don't, the race goes from the top of the Schilthorn right down to Lauterbrunnen – a vertical drop of 2175m/7,140ft and a distance of almost 16km/10 miles, incorporating a short climb at Maulerhubel. The racers start individually at 12 second intervals; the fastest finish the course in around 15 minutes, but anything under half an hour is very respectable.

The race was started by Sir Arnold Lunn in 1928, when he and his friends climbed up to spend the night in a mountain hut and then raced down in the morning. For many years the race was organised by the British-run Kandahar Club, and there is still a strong British presence among the competitors.

GETTING THERE

Air Zürich 195km/ 121 miles (3½hr); Bern 70km/43 miles (1½hr).

Rail Lauterbrunnen; transfer by mountain railway and tram.

ACTIVITIES

Indoor Alpine Sports Centre: swimming pool, sauna, solarium, steam bath, massage, fitness room, gymnasium, squash, library, museum

Outdoor Ice rink, curling, ice-climbing, tobogganing, 12km/ 7 miles cleared paths, snow-shoeing

OUR WEBSITE

Go to our website at wtss.co.uk for resort news, links to resort sites, a build-your-own resort shortlist system and reader forums.

Phone numbers
From elsewhere in Switzerland add the prefix 033.
From abroad use the prefix +41 33.

TOURIST OFFICE

t 856 8686
info@muerren.ch
www.wengen-muerren.ch

apple cake. Winteregg does something similar, as well as 'superb rösti' and 'the best burger east of the Rockies'. Both have little playgrounds for kids.

SCHOOLS AND GUIDES
Declining standards?
Sadly, we have received a poor review of the school this year. A regular visitor found his competent daughters of 10 and 13 placed in a groups of infants – and his complaint met with a rude response.'

FACILITIES FOR CHILDREN
Adequate
There is a nursery slope with a rope tow. The Kinderhort nursery takes children from 18 months old and the ski school takes them from five years.

STAYING THERE

HOW TO GO
Mainly hotels, packaged or not
A handful of operators offer packages to Mürren.
Hotels There are fewer than a dozen hotels, ranging widely in style.
((((4) **Anfi Palace** (856 9999) Victorian pile near station.
((((4) **Eiger** (856 5454) Plain-looking 'chalet' blocks next to railway station, widely recommended; good blend of efficiency and charm; good food; pool.
(((3) **Alpenruh** (856 8800) Attractively renovated chalet next to the cable-car. Due to receive a spa for 2006/07.
(((3) **Edelweiss** (856 5600) Block-like but friendly; good food and facilities – endorsed by a 2006 visitor.
(((3) **Jungfrau** (855 6464) Perfectly placed for families, in front of the baby slope and close to the funicular.
((2) **Alpenblick** (855 1327) Simple, small, modern chalet near station.
Self-catering There are plenty of chalets and apartments in the village for independent travellers to rent.

EATING OUT
Mainly in hotels
The main alternative to hotels is the rustic Stägerstübli – a bar as well as restaurant. The locals eat in the little diner at the back. The food at the Eiger hotel is good, and the Bellevue and Alpenruh get good reports.

APRES-SKI
Not devoid of life
The Eiger Bar (in the Eiger guest house, not the hotel) is the Brits' meeting place. The Iglu bar near the bottom of the Allmendhubel train makes a good stop at the end of the day. The tiny Stägerstübli is cosy, and the place to meet locals. The Anfi Palace's Balloon bar is an attempt at a trendy cocktail bar; it also has a weekend disco, the Inferno. The Bliemlichäller disco in the Blumental hotel caters for kids, the Tächi disco in the Eiger for a more mixed crowd.

OFF THE SLOPES
Tranquillity but not much else
There isn't a lot to amuse people who don't hit the slopes except the scenery and a very good sports centre with an outdoor ice rink. Excursions to Bern and Interlaken are easy and friends can readily return to the village for lunch. The only problem with meeting at the top of the cable-car is the expense.

STAYING DOWN THE VALLEY
A cheaper option
Lauterbrunnen is a good budget base, with a resort atmosphere and access to both Wengen and Mürren until late. We've happily stayed at the Schützen (855 2032) and Oberland (855 1241); the Silberhorn (856 2210) is highly recommended by a 2006 visitor for excellent food and value, and a lively bar. For more of a pub atmosphere, he recommends the bar in the Horner hotel.

Saas-Fee

Charming car-free village with spectacular scenery and snow-sure but rather less captivating slopes

RATINGS

The slopes
Fast lifts	★★★★
Snow	★★★★★
Extent	★★
Expert	★★★
Intermediate	★★★★
Beginner	★★★★★
Convenience	★★★
Queues	★★★
Mountain restaurants	★★★

The rest
Scenery	★★★★
Charm	★★★★★
Off-slope	★★★★

NEWS

For 2005/06 a new eight-seater gondola was built from mid-mountain to the top at Saas-Grund. The double Längfluh chair was replaced by a quad. And a big new restaurant opened at Morenia, at mid-mountain.

The resort has acquired four electric buses – a much cheaper alternative to the electric taxis.

For 2006/07 a new six-pack (only the resort's second chair-lift) is planned for the Morenia area.

There are plans to develop the slopes around Britanniahütte with a six-pack, but there are no dates for this.

The two top lifts on Saas-Fee's glacier provide snow-sure slopes in summer as well as winter →

➕ Spectacular setting amid high peaks and glaciers

➕ Traditional, 'traffic-free' village

➕ Most of the runs are at exceptionally high altitude, and snow-sure

➕ Good off-slope facilities – even a mountain for non-skiing activities

➖ Disappointingly small area of slopes, with mainly easy runs

➖ Still lots of T-bars

➖ Glacier limits off-piste exploration

➖ Much of the area is in shadow in midwinter – cold and dark

➖ Bad weather can shut the slopes

Saas-Fee is one of our favourite places – a sort of miniature Zermatt without the conspicuous consumption. And good snow is guaranteed, even late in the season: the altitude you spend most of your time at – between 2500m and 3500m (8,200ft and 11,480ft) – is unrivalled in the Alps.

But we tend to drop in here for a couple of days at a time, so the limited extent of the slopes never becomes a problem; for a week's holiday, it would. Top to bottom there is an impressive 1800m/5,900ft vertical – but there aren't many alternative ways down. Keen, mileage-hungry intermediates should look elsewhere, as should experts (except those prepared to go touring). For the rest, it's a question of priorities and expectations. Over to you.

THE RESORT

Like nearby Zermatt, Saas-Fee is a high-altitude mountain village centred on narrow streets lined by attractive old chalets and free of cars (there are car parks at the resort entrance) but not free of electric taxis and hotel etc vehicles. On most other counts, Saas-Fee and its more exalted neighbour are a long way apart in style.

There are some very smart hotels (plus many more modest ones) and plenty of good eating and drinking places. But there's little of the glamour and greed that, for some, spoil Zermatt – and even the electric taxis here are driven at a more considerate pace. Saas-Fee still feels like a village, with its cow sheds more obviously still containing cows. The village may be chilly in January, but when the spring sun is beating down, it is a beautiful place just to stroll around and relax in.

Depending on where you're staying and which way you want to go up the mountain, you may do more marching through the village than strolling, though. It's a long walk from one end to the other. Three major lifts start

KEY FACTS

Resort	1800m
	5,910ft
Slopes	1800-3500m
	5,910-11,480ft
Lifts	22
Pistes	100km
	62 miles
Blue	25%
Red	50%
Black	25%
Snowmaking	8km
	5 miles

from the southern end of the village, at the foot of the slopes, and lots of the hotels and apartments (particularly cheaper ones) are 1km/0.5 mile or more away. The biggest lift, though – the Alpin Express gondola – starts from a more central location. Your hotel may run a courtesy taxi, and there are now little public buses. You can store kit near the lifts, which helps.

The village centre has the school and guides' office, the church and a few more shops than elsewhere, but it doesn't add up to much. On a sunny day, though, the restaurant terraces by the nursery slopes at the south end of the village are a magnet, with stunning views up to the ring of 4000m/13,120ft peaks – you can see why the village is called 'The Pearl of the Alps'.

The slopes of Saas-Almagell and Saas-Grund are not far away ('highly recommended for a day or two' by a 2006 visitor), and you can buy a lift pass that covers all these resorts and buses between them. The Saas Grund slopes rise to 3100m/10,170ft. There is a footpath down to Saas-Almagell, which one reporter enjoyed skiing down. Day trips by car/train to Zermatt are also possible and a day there is now covered by the six-day lift pass.

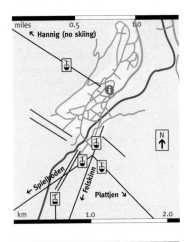

THE MOUNTAIN

The area is a strange mixture of powerful modern lifts (a two-stage 30-person gondola followed by an underground funicular which take you up 1700m/5,580ft vertical) and a lot of old-fashioned T-bars (there are only two chair-lifts). Blame the glaciers, which move too quickly for chair-lifts. Readers complain about the 'walks and climbs' involved in getting from one lift to another. Take it easy when climbing

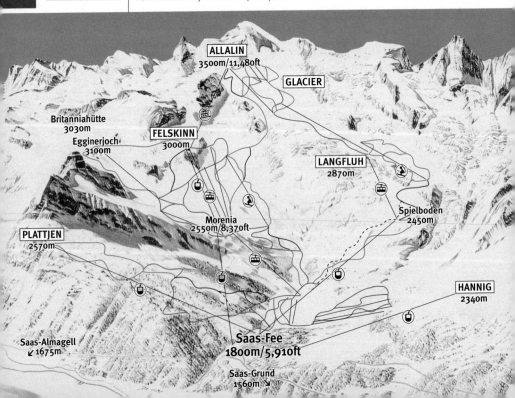

Ski Boards Boots and more...

boarding

Saas-Fee has backed snowboarding from its inception. The terrain suits intermediates and beginners best but while the main access lifts are gondolas, cable-cars and a funicular, nearly all the rest are T-bars. The high altitude means the resort is a favourite for early season and summer riding (the British team often chooses Saas-Fee as a training ground for this reason). Carvers should check out Längfluh and Morenia for well-groomed pistes to shred down. Half-pipe enthusiasts will love the perfect pipe next to the good terrain-park at Morenia. The Popcorn bar and shop is the favourite spot for après-snowboard beers.

LIFT PASSES

Saas-Fee

Prices in SF

Age	1-day	6-day
under 16	37	182
over 16	61	303

Free Under 6

Senior No deals

Beginner Pass for village nursery lifts only.

Notes
Covers lifts in Saas-Fee only. A six-day pass covers a day in Zermatt. Single and return tickets on most main lifts. Afternoon pass available. Family reductions available.

Alternative passes
Pass for whole valley available. Also separate passes for each of the other Saastal ski areas (Saas-Grund, Saas-Almagell, Saas-Balen).

OUR WEBSITE

Go to our website at wtss.co.uk for resort news, links to resort sites, a build-your-own resort shortlist system and reader forums.

out of the top lift station: the altitude of 3500m/ 11,480ft means some people feel faint because of the thin air.

The upper slopes are largely gentle, while the lower mountain, below the glacier, is steeper and rockier, needing good snow-cover. There is very little shelter here in bad weather: during and after heavy snowfalls you may find yourself limited to the nursery area.

Saas-Fee is one of the leading resorts for mountaineering and ski touring and the extended Haute Route from Chamonix via Zermatt ends here.

THE SLOPES
A glacier runs through it
There are two routes up to the main **Felskinn** area. The 30-person Alpin Express gondola, starting across the river from the main village, takes you to Felskinn via a mid-station at Morenia. The alternative is a short drag across the nursery slope at the south end of the village, and then the Felskinn cable-car. From Felskinn, the Metro Alpin underground funicular hurtles up to **Allalin**. From below here, two drag-lifts access the high point.

Also from the south end of the village, a gondola leaves for Spielboden. This is met by a cable-car which takes you up to **Längfluh**. Between Felskinn and Längfluh is an off-limits glacier area. A very long drag-lift from Längfluh takes you to a point where you can get down to the Felskinn area. These two sectors are served mainly by drag-lifts, and you can get down to the village from both.

Another gondola from the south end of the village goes up to Saas-Fee's smallest area, **Plattjen.**

TERRAIN-PARKS
Well developed
The 42 Crew (www.42crew.ch) are renowned for building great parks and maintaining them all year round. The big Morenia park has a plethora of kickers, rails and boxes and a truly

world-class half-pipe. However these will be intimidating for novices, who should head to the beginner and snow-skate park in Stafelwald near the nursery slopes, which has small jumps and rails. In summer a park is built on the glacier and you will often see pro riders honing their skills there.

SNOW RELIABILITY
Good at the highest altitudes
Most of Saas-Fee's slopes face north and many are above 2500m/8,200ft, making this one of the most reliable resorts for snow in the Alps. The glacier is open most of the year. There has been substantial recent investment in snow-guns but reporters say they aren't used enough. Piste grooming remains 'excellent'.

FOR EXPERTS
Not a lot to keep your interest
There is not much steep stuff, except on the bottom half of the mountain where the snow tends not to be as good (a short black run from Felskinn is the exception). The slopes around the top of Längfluh often provide good powder, and there are usually moguls above Spielboden. The blacks and the trees on Plattjen are worth exploring. The glacier puts limits on the local off-piste even with a guide – crevasse danger is extreme. But there are extensive touring possibilities.

FOR INTERMEDIATES
Great for gentle cruising
Saas-Fee is ideal for early intermediates and those not looking for much of a challenge. For long cruises, head for Allalin. The top of the mountain, down as far as Längfluh in one direction and as far as Morenia in the other, is ideal, with usually excellent snow. Gradients range from gentle blues to slightly steeper reds which can build up smallish bumps. For more of a challenge, head across to Längfluh.

The 1800m/5,900ft vertical descents

SCHOOLS

Swiss
t 957 2348

Eskimos Snowboard
t 957 4904

Classes
5 3hr days SF183

Private lessons
SF60 for 1hr

CHILDREN

Kindertagesstätte Murmeli (Marmots Club)
t 957 4057
Ages 1mnth to 6yr;
9am-5pm; SF70 per day

Nursery
t 958 7575
In Hotel Schweizerhof

Glückskäfer
t 79 225 8154
Evening babysitting service

Ski school
From age 4 (from SF34 per day). Full junior ski school from age 5 (5-day ski courses SF183)

from the top to the village are great tests of stamina – or, if you choose, an enjoyable long cruise with plenty of view stops. The lower runs have steepish, tricky sections and can have poor snow, especially if it isn't cold enough to make artificial snow – timid intermediates might prefer to take a lift down from mid-mountain.

Plattjen has a variety of runs, all of them fine for ambitious intermediates, and often under-used.

FOR BEGINNERS
A great place to start
We say 'great' – a reporter who took a beginner last year said 'perfect'. There's a good, large, out-of-the-way nursery area at the edge of the village, as snow-sure as any you will find. Those ready to progress can head for the gentle blues on Felskinn just above Morenia – it's best to return by the Alpin Express. There are also gentle blues at the top of the mountain, from where you can head down to Längfluh. Again, use the lifts to return to base.

A useful beginners' pass covers all the short lifts at the village edge, for those not ready to go higher.

FOR CROSS-COUNTRY
Good local trail and lots nearby
There is one short (6km/4mile) pleasant trail at the edge of the village. It snakes up through the woods, providing about 150m/490ft of climb and nice views. There's more (26km/16 miles) in the Saas valley.

WORLD'S HIGHEST REVOLVING LUNCH?

If you fancy 360° views during lunch, head up to the world's highest revolving restaurant at Allalin, where you can get a different vista with starters, mains and pud. It's only the bit of floor with the tables on it that revolves; the stairs stay put (along with the windows – watch your gloves). The other two revolving cafes in the Alps are also in Switzerland – at Mürren and Leysin – and we rate the views there better. But it's an amusing novelty that most visitors enjoy, and lunch is OK too. To reserve a table next to the windows phone 957 1771.

QUEUES
Persistent problems
Reporters still complain of an 'uncomfortable scrum' to get on the Alpin Express gondola first thing in the morning, and note that the whole journey to the top may take over an hour – but it is quite a long way. A recent reporter confirms that the Felskinn cable-car still regularly produces big queues, and another waited for 30 minutes during the afternoon up at Längfluh. The drag-lifts at the top of the mountain are persistent offenders.

MOUNTAIN RESTAURANTS
Fair choice, but it's no Zermatt
The restaurants at the main lift stations are functional; at least the table-service one at Allalin revolves – see separate box. The best places are slightly off the beaten track: the Berghaus Plattjen (just down from Plattjen) and the cosy Gletschergrotte, halfway down from Spielboden (watch for the arrow from the piste). If you're up for a trek – about 15 minutes each way – the Britanniahütte is special: a real climbing refuge, with atmosphere and views. The restaurant at the top of Plattjen has 'friendly service and the best rösti in the resort'. At Spielboden there are 'great views' of tricky slopes and a 'good selection of rösti'. At Längfluh the large terrace has spectacular views of huge crevasses, but the food is 'basic'. A 2006 reporter says the new 'giant' Morenia has 'excellent food and massive choice'. If you go to Saas-Grund a 2005 visitor says that the restaurant at the very top is good – 'more like an Alpine climbing hut than a ski eatery'.

SCHOOLS AND GUIDES
Mixed reactions
It's a choice between the Swiss school and Eskimos. Reports of the Swiss school are mixed. In the past we have heard positive things about the Eskimos school, with private snowboard lessons being 'rewarding'.

GETTING THERE

Air Sion 70km/
43 miles (1hr);
Geneva 234km/
145 miles (3½hr);
Zürich 246km/
153 miles (4hr);
Milan 250km/
155 miles (3hr).

Rail Brig (38km/
24 miles); regular
buses from station.

ACTIVITIES

Indoor Bielen leisure
centre (swimming,
hot-tub, steam bath,
whirlpool, solarium,
sauna, aerobics,
massage, tennis,
badminton, gym,
bodyforming,
aquafitness), cinema,
museums

Outdoor 30km/
19 miles of cleared
paths, horse carriage
rides, ice rink
(skating, curling,
snowbowling),
tobogganing, snow
tubing, ice-climbing,
snow-shoeing, dog-
sledding

Phone numbers
From elsewhere in
Switzerland add the
prefix 027.
From abroad use the
prefix +41 27.

TOURIST OFFICE

t 958 1858
to@saas-fee.ch
www.saas-fee.ch

FACILITIES FOR CHILDREN
Good reports
The school takes children from four
years old, and reports are generally
positive. Last year some children 'really
enjoyed' their lessons but this year a
reporter's daughter was 'so frustrated'
by being put in much too low a group
for her. Classes as big as 15 have been
spotted. For younger ones, several
hotels have an in-house kindergarten.

STAYING THERE

HOW TO GO
Check the location
Quite a few UK tour operators sell
holidays to Saas-Fee. But there are
surprisingly few chalet holidays.
Hotels There are over 50.
((((5) **Fletschhorn** (957 2131) Elegant
chalet in woods, with original art and
individual rooms, a trek from the
village and lifts, but fabulous food.
(((5) **Ferienart** (958 1900) Lovely
relaxed place, despite 5-star status.
Central, with excellent facilities
including swish spa. A 2005 reporter
found some rooms not up to scratch
and judged the food 'good but not
exceptional'.
(((4) **Schweizerhof** (958 7575) Stylish,
in quiet position above the centre.
'Fantastic food, friendly staff, excellent
kindergarten, wonderful service.' Pool
and new health facilities.
((3) **Beau-Site** (958 1560) 4-star in
central, but not convenient, position.
Good food. Pool. A 2006 reporter was
very impressed by the staff.
((3) **Christiania** (957 3166) 'Thoroughly
recommended' 3-star 'delivering much
more than our expectations', says a
2005 visitor.
((3) **Alphubel** (958 6363) At the wrong
end of town, praised by reporters for
its own 'brilliant nursery'.
((3) **Waldesruh** (958 6464) Strongly
recommended by a reporter: 'Best
situation for the Alpin Express.'
((3) **Astoria** (957 1133) 'Very handy for
the Alpin Express, excellent, friendly,'
says a reporter. Whirlpool and sauna.
((3) **Hohnegg** (957 2268) Small rustic
alternative to the Fletschhorn, in a
similarly remote spot.
((3) **Jägerhof** (957 1310) Adjacent to
nursery slopes. 'The service was simply
phenomenal,' says a 2005 visitor.
((2) **Belmont** (958 1640) The most
appealing of the hotels looking directly
on to the nursery slopes.
Self-catering Most apartments featured

by UK operators are at the north end
of the village, but they are generally
spacious and well equipped.

EATING OUT
Good variety – but book a table
Gastronomes will want to head for the
highly acclaimed and expensive but
excellent Fletschhorn – 'The best meal
I've ever had,' says a 2006 reporter.
Our favourite is the less formal
Bodmen, which has great food (from
rösti to fillet steak) and rustic
ambience. Both these are along paths
into the woods. The hotel Ferienart's
several restaurants include a Thai one
that we have enjoyed. Boccalino is
cheap and does pizzas. The rustic Alp-
Hitta has 'a lot of atmosphere' and
does 'reasonable' food. The hotel
Dom's restaurant does endless
varieties of rösti. The Ferme is
'excellent'. Arvu Stuba, Zur Mühle,
Gorge, Feeloch and the Sport-Hotel's
Tischgrille have all been recommended.

APRES-SKI
Excellent and varied
Late afternoon, Nesti's Ski-Bar, Zur
Mühle and the little snow-bars near the
lifts are all pretty lively, especially if
the sun's shining. The Black Bull, with
outdoor seating only, is reportedly still
the 'in place'. Later on, Nesti's and the
Alpenpub keep going till 1am. Popcorn
is 'relaxed' and as popular as ever. The
night club, Poison, advertises
'legendary parties' fuelled by shots and
shakers. The Metro Bar is 'like being in
a 19th-century mine shaft full of people
trying to share the few stools'. Why-
Not is the place for a Guinness. The
Happy bar's cheap drinks sessions are
popular. The Metropol, with American
diner, Crazy Night disco and other
bars, 'doesn't liven up till late'.

OFF THE SLOPES
A mountain for pedestrians
The whole of the Hannig mountain is
dedicated to walking, paragliding and
tobogganing, which a recent reporter
rates as 'terrific – all visitors should try
it'. Hannig offers 'great views' of the
glacial slopes. In the village, the
splendid Bielen leisure centre boasts a
25m/80ft pool, indoor tennis courts
and a lounging area with sunlamps.
There's also the interesting Saas
museum and the Bakery Museum,
where children can make bread. Don't
miss the largest ice cave in the world,
carved out of the glacier at Allalin.

St Moritz

Ignore the stuffy, monstrous five-star hotels: you don't need to be rolling in it to enjoy this panoramic high-altitude playground

NEWS

Last season marked 150 years since the first hotel, the Kulm, opened in St Moritz. The hotel itself received a revamp. A new residential and retail complex, The Murezzan, opened in the town centre.

Also for 2005/06 a special children's chair-lift opened on the nursery slopes at Provulèr, in Celerina.

There are plans to develop the Lagalb-Diavolezza slopes for 2008/09.

- ➕ Wonderful panoramic scenery
- ➕ Off-slope activities second to none
- ➕ Extensive, mainly intermediate slopes
- ➕ High, and fairly snow-sure
- ➕ Good après-ski, for all tastes
- ➕ Good mountain restaurants, some with magnificent views

- ➖ A sizeable town, with little traditional Alpine character and some hideous block buildings
- ➖ Several unlinked mountains, and inadequate valley bus service
- ➖ Runs on home mountain all fairly easy and most lacking variety
- ➖ Expensive

St Moritz is Switzerland's most famous 'exclusive' winter resort: glitzy, expensive, fashionable and, above all, the place to be seen – a place for an all-round winter holiday, with an unrivalled array of wacky diversions such as polo, golf and cricket on snow, and countless festivals. It has long been popular with upper-crust Brits, who stay in the top hotels in order to go sledging. Well, OK: in order to descend the world-famous Cresta Run. But like all such self-consciously smart resorts, it makes a perfectly good destination for anyone.

The town of St Moritz is undeniably an eyesore. But you may find, as we do, that you can ignore the scar, and appreciate the beauty of St Moritz's spectacular setting regardless. This is one of those areas where our progress on the mountain is regularly interrupted by the need to stand and gaze.

THE RESORT

St Moritz has two distinct parts. Dorf is the fashionable main part, on a steep hillside above the lake. It has two main streets – lined with boutiques selling Rolex watches, Cartier jewellery and Hermes scarves – a few side lanes and a small main square. A funicular takes you from Dorf to the slopes of Corviglia, also reached by cable-car from Dorf's other half, the spa resort of St Moritz Bad, down beside the lake. Everything in Bad is less prestigious. Many of the buildings are block-like, and spoil otherwise superb views. There are no lifts from St Moritz itself into the second major area of slopes, Corvatsch – a bus-ride away.

In winter the lake is used for eccentric activities including horse and greyhound racing, show jumping, polo, 'ice golf' and even cricket. It also makes a superb setting for walking and cross-country skiing, which is very big in the area; the Engadine Ski Marathon is held down the valley every March – over 12,000 racers take part.

The town's clientele is typified by the results of a Cresta Run race we saw on one of our visits. In the top 30 were three Lords, one Count, one Archduke and a Baronet. But the race

was won by a local Swiss guy.

For our money Bad is the better base, with the advantage that you can ski back to it from Corvatsch as well as Corviglia. Celerina, down the valley

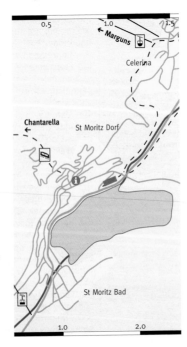

↑ You don't have to buy your lunch at the Fuorcla Surlej refuge to share the fantastic view of Plz Bernina

SNOWPIX.COM / CHRIS GILL

KEY FACTS

Resort	1770m
	5,810ft
Slopes	1730-3305m
	5,680-10,840ft
Lifts	56
Pistes	350km
	217 miles
Blue	20%
Red	70%
Black	10%
Snowmaking	70km
	43 miles

For Corviglia only	
Slopes	1730-3055m
	5,680-10,020ft
Lifts	23
Pistes	158km
	98 miles

with a lift towards Corviglia, is the obvious alternative, and an attractively rustic one (see end of this chapter). But there are other options – 'chocolate-box-pretty' Sils Maria, for example, has immediate access to the Corvatsch slopes via Furtschellas.

There are good rail links from Zürich, but it's quicker to drive to the resort. A car is handy, too: the valley bus service (needed for access to Corvatsch) is free with the lift pass but scandalously inadequate at peak times. And a car greatly speeds up visits to the outlying mountains. Trips are possible to Davos and other resorts.

THE MOUNTAINS

There are lots of long, wide, well-groomed runs with varied terrain – practically all on open slopes above the trees. The 350km/217 miles of pistes are in three separate areas, covered on three gigantic piste maps; our maps show only the two main areas close to St Moritz. Piste signing is unhelpful: pistes are numbered on the map, but not on the ground.

THE SLOPES
Big but broken up
From St Moritz Dorf a two-stage railway goes up to **Corviglia**, a lift junction at the eastern end of a sunny and rather monotonous area of slopes facing east and south over the main valley. The peak of Piz Nair, reached

from here by cable-car, separates these slopes from the less sunny and more varied ones in the wide bowl above **Marguns** – and gives fabulous views across the valley to Piz Bernina. From Corviglia you can (snow permitting) head down easy paths to Dorf and Bad; you'll probably pass through Salastrains – a major focus of activity just above Dorf, with nursery slopes, restaurants and two hotels. There is a red run from Marguns to Celerina.

From Surlej, a few miles from St Moritz, a two-stage cable-car takes you to the north-facing slopes of **Corvatsch**, which reach glacial heights. From the mid-station at Murtèl you have a choice of reds to Margun-Vegl and Alp Margun. From the latter you can work your way to **Furtschellas**, also reached by cable-car from Sils Maria. If you're lucky with the snow, you can end the day with the splendid Hahnensee run, from the northern limit of the Corvatsch lift system at Giand'Alva down to St Moritz Bad – a black-classified run that is of red difficulty for most of its 6km/ 4 mile length. The run often opens at about noon, when the snow is soft. It's a five-minute walk from the end of the run to the cable-car up to Corviglia.

The third area consists of two peaks on opposite sides of the road to the Bernina pass to Italy, about 20km/ 12 miles away – Diavolezza and Lagalb. The bus takes 50 minutes. You can now ski from Diavolezza to the base of Lagalb with the aid of a short rope

Piz Nair
3055m
Piz Grisch
Las Trais Fluors
Munt da S. Murezzan
266om
Glüna
CORVIGLIA
2485m
MARGUNS
2280m
Suvretta
Signal
Salastrains
Chantarella
2005m
St Moritz Dorf
1820m/5,97oft
Celerina
1730m/5,68oft
St Moritz Bad
1770m/5,81oft

SWITZERLAND

528

tow; plans have been announced to install two new chair-lifts in 2008 to form a properly united ski area.

Diavolezza (2980m/9,780ft) has excellent north-facing pistes of 900m/2,95oft vertical, down under its big 125-person cable-car, and a very popular and spectacular off-piste glacier route beneath Piz Bernina to Morteratsch. This requires a bit of energy and nerve. After a gentle climb, you skirt the glacier on a narrow ledge, with crevasses waiting to gobble you up on the right. At the end of the 30-minute slog, a welcoming ice bar greets you. After that, it's downhill over the glacier, with splendid views.

Lagalb (2960m/9,710ft) is a smaller area with quite challenging slopes – west-facing, 850m/2,790ft vertical – served by an 80-person cable-car.

It's worth noting that from mid-March the Lagalb cable-car runs until 5pm and the Diavolezza one until 5.30. We found a sunny run from 2900m/9,51oft a great way to end the day.

TERRAIN-PARKS
Improved

The terrain-park on Corviglia is only two years old and is a welcome addition for freestylers in the area. The park was actually designed with female pro skiers and snowboarders and advanced riders in mind and is home to some of the biggest contests for females. There are three lines, with the hardest comprising a big 12m/39ft table jump. There are straight, kinked and rainbow rails and boxes of all sizes, and the park always has a great relaxed atmosphere to learn in.

SNOW RELIABILITY
Improved by good snowmaking

This corner of the Alps has a rather dry climate, but the altitude means that any precipitation is likely to be snowy. The top runs at Corvatsch are glacial and require good snow depths to be safe – a 2006 reporter discovered them closed during her February visit. There is snowmaking in every sector and piste grooming is excellent.

FOR EXPERTS
Dispersed challenges

If you're looking for challenges, you're liable to find St Moritz disappointing on-piste. The few serious black runs are scattered about in different sectors and few are genuine blacks; those at

PIZ CORVATSCH
3450m
3305m/10,84oft
Culöz das las Furtschellas
2800m
Fuorcla Surlej
2760m
Murtèl
2700m
Val Fex
Giand'Alva
2645m
Margun-Vegl
2405m
Alp Margun
2270m
FURTSCHELLA
2310m
Hahnensee
2155m
Sils Maria
1795m
St. Moritz Bad
1770m/5,81oft
Surlej
1870m

LIFT PASSES

Upper Engadine

Prices in SF

Age	1-day	6-day
under 13	24	115
13 to 16	47	227
Over 17	70	339

Free under 6

Senior no deals

Beginner no deals

Notes
Covers all lifts in
Corviglia, Corvatsch,
Diavolezza-Lagalb and
Zuoz, and includes
the Engadine bus
services and certain
stretches of the
Rhätische Bahn
railway.

Alternative passes
Half-day and day
passes available for
individual areas
within Upper
Engadine.

boarding

Despite the high prices and glitzy image, the terrain in St Moritz is boarder-friendly and there's a special boarder's booklet with a lot of good information. The best free-ride terrain is on the Corvatsch side, but be warned – there are several drag-lifts in the area. Most of the area is serviced by chairs, gondolas, cable-cars and trains; beginners will enjoy the rolling blue runs and intermediates will relish the plethora of challenging red runs. A lot of money has been pumped into building a very good terrain-park on Corviglia. Specialist shop Playground in Paradise will help with all your equipment needs.

Lagalb and Diavolezza are the most challenging, and include one of the few sizeable mogul-fields – the Minor run down the Lagalb cable-car (though it's seriously steep only at the start). But there is good off-piste terrain, and it doesn't get tracked out. There is an excellent north-facing slope immediately above Marguns, for example. Experts often head for the tough off-piste runs on Piz Nair or the Corvatsch summit. More serious expeditions can be undertaken – such as the Roseg valley from Corvatsch.

FOR INTERMEDIATES
Good but flattering
St Moritz is great for intermediates. Most pistes on Corviglia are very well groomed, easyish reds that could well have been classified blue – ideal cruising terrain, or monotonous, depending on your requirements. The Marguns bowl is more interesting, including some easy blacks and the pleasant Val Schattain run away from the lifts. The Corvatsch-Furtschellas area is altogether more varied, interesting and challenging, as well as higher and wider. There are excellent red runs in both parts of the area, including descents to the two valley stations – particularly the Furtschellas one; do these in the morning, and return to St Moritz Bad via the lovely Hahnensee run – an easy black. Use the low-altitude way back to the Corvatsch sector from Furtschellas, to avoid a lot of tedious skating. The runs from the Corvatsch top station are genuinely red in parts, with fabulous views of Piz Bernina.

Diavolezza is mostly intermediate stuff, too. There is an easy open slope at the top, served by a fast quad, and a splendid long intermediate run back down under the lift. The link to Lagalb requires use of a black, but it is of red-run gradient. Lagalb has more challenging pistes – basically two good reds and a genuine black.

FOR BEGINNERS
Not ideal
Beginners start up at Salastrains or Corviglia, or slightly out of town at Suvretta. Celerina has good, broad nursery slopes at village level and a new child-friendly lift. Ironically, in a resort full of easy red runs, progression from the nursery slopes to longer runs is rather awkward – there are few blue runs without a difficult section.

FOR CROSS-COUNTRY
Excellent
The Engadine is one of the premier regions in the Alps for cross-country, with 180km/112 miles of trails, including floodlit loops, amid splendid scenery and with fairly reliable snow. A reporter recommends the lessons at the Langlauf Centre near the Hotel Kempinski. For cross-country the best bases are outside St Moritz – Sils or Silvaplana, suggests one reporter.

QUEUES
Not much of a problem
St Moritz has invested heavily in new lifts in recent years, especially on Corviglia and Marguns – fast chairs everywhere. The area as a whole has a lot of modest-sized cable-cars – both for getting up the mountain from the resort and for access to peaks from mid-mountain. Queues can result, but reporters have had good experiences lately. Happy reporters comment that many St Moritz visitors are late risers and don't ski after lunch, leaving the slopes quiet at the start and end of the day.

MOUNTAIN RESTAURANTS
Some special places
Mountain restaurants are plentiful, and include some of the most glamorous in Europe. Prices can be high, but standards can be disappointing. Last season we had the worst rösti in a skiing lifetime at the otherwise attractive Chamanna. The piste maps

GETTING THERE

Air Zürich 200km/ 124 miles (3hr); Upper Engadine airport 5km/3 miles.

Rail Mainline station in resort.

SCHOOLS

Swiss
t 830 0101
Suvretta
t 836 3600

Classes
(Swiss prices)
6 2hr days SF230
Private lessons
SF95 for 1hr

CHILDREN

Schweizerhof hotel
t 837 0707
Ages from 3; 9.30-6pm; Mon-Sat; SF35 per day

Ski school
Ages from 5; pick-up service and all-day care available

have helpful pictures and descriptions of all of the restaurants.

On Corviglia, the top lift station houses several restaurants run under the umbrella title of Mathis Food Affairs, including the famous Marmite. Much better for charm is the Paradiso, with panoramic views from the terrace; or the Lej de la Pêsch, behind Piz Nair. A 2006 reporter recommends the Salastrains and the Chasellas, a satellite of the Suvretta hotel.

On the Corvatsch side, a good place for a stormy day is the rustic Alpetta, near Alp Margun – 'nice food, lovely atmosphere and a great bar' (table-service inside). On the other hand Fuorcla Surlej, on the Fuorcla run from the glacier, is a good-weather option: a refuge serving basic food very slowly, but with a view from the ramshackle terrace that is among our top three. Hahnensee, on the lift-free run of the same name down to Bad is a splendid place to pause in the sun on the way home; it was closed last season, but should reopen for 2006/07.

SCHOOLS AND GUIDES
Internal competition
There are two main schools, the St Moritz and the Suvretta (see 'Hotels'). A 2006 reporter received 'excellent' instruction from the latter. The St Moritz Experience runs heli-trips and some hotels have their own instructors for private lessons.

FACILITIES FOR CHILDREN
Choose a hotel with a nursery
Children wanting lessons have a choice of schools, but others must be deposited at a hotel nursery. Club Med has its usual good facilities. Reports suggest that classes with the Swiss school can have mixed ability levels, with better kids getting bored.

STAYING THERE

HOW TO GO
Several packaged options
Packages are available, but many people make their own arrangements. There is a Club Med – its all-inclusive deal cuts the impact of high prices. The tourist office can provide a list of apartments.

Hotels Over half the hotels are 4-stars and 5-stars – the highest concentration of high-quality hotels in Switzerland. This year we are persuaded by a reader to list one of the resort's famous 5-stars; the others – the glossy Carlton, the staid but revamped Kulm, the Gothic Badrutt's Palace and the 'new' Kempinski Grand Hotel des Bains – leave us cold.

(((((5) **Suvretta House** (818 363636) The 5-star for skiers, in a secluded ski-in/ski-out location 2km/1 mile out of town, at the base of its own branch of the lift system, and with its own ski school. 'Splendid views, magnificent fitness centre and pool – difficult to fault, except that jackets and ties must be worn after 6pm.' Rules us out, then.

(((4) **Crystal** (836 2626) Big 4-star in Dorf, as close to the Corviglia lift as any. Recently renovated.

(((4) **Schweizerhof** (837 0707) 'Relaxed' 4-star in central Dorf, five minutes from the Corviglia lift, with 'excellent food and very helpful staff'.

(((4) **Albana** (836 6161) 4-star in Dorf, with walls adorned with big game trophies bagged by proprietor's family.

(((3) **Laudinella** (836 0000) Our Bad favourite: refreshing, innovative place – you can dine enjoyably in any of six different restaurants in the hotel.

(((3) **Monopol** (837 0404) Good value (for St Moritz) 4-star in centre of Dorf. Excellent breakfasts, hot-tub, sauna.

(((3) **Steinbock** (833 6035) 'Friendly, understated, comfortable,' In Dorf.

ACTIVITIES

Indoor Swimming pool, sauna, solarium, golf range, tennis, squash, museums, beauty/health centre, casino, library

Outdoor Ice skating, curling, cricket on snow, tobogganing, hang-gliding, golf on frozen lake, kitesailing, bobsleigh rides, Cresta run, 180km/ 112 miles cleared paths, sky diving, horse-riding, polo tournaments

Phone numbers
From elsewhere in Switzerland add the prefix 081.
From abroad use the prefix +41 81.

TOURIST OFFICES

St Moritz
t 837 3333
information@stmoritz.ch
www.stmoritz.ch

Celerina
t 830 0011
info@celerina.ch
www.celerina.ch

Pontresina
t 838 8300
info@pontresina.com
www.pontresina.com

(((3) **Nolda** (833 0575) One of the few chalet-style buildings, close to the cable-car in Bad.
((2 **Bellaval** (833 3245) A two-star between the station and the lake.

EATING OUT
Mostly chic and expensive
It's easy to spend £50 a head eating out in St Moritz – without wine – but you can eat more cheaply. We liked the excellent Italian food at the down-to-earth Cascade in Dorf and the (pricier) three restaurants in the Chesa Veglia, though one reporter considers it a rip-off. The two top restaurants, Jöhri's Talvo at Champfèr and Bumanns Chesa Pirani in La Punt, both approach the top restaurants in London or Paris for quality and price. We also liked the rustic Landhotel Meierei, by the lake.

Try an evening up at Muottas Muragl, between Celerina and Pontresina, for the spectacular views, splendid sunset and unpretentious dinner. The food at the Chesa Rosatsch hotel at Celerina attracts non-resident diners and is recommended. The Post Haus is a slick new restaurant in the Murezzan development.

APRES-SKI
Caters for all ages
There's a big variety of après-skiing age groups here. The fur coat count is high – people come to St Moritz to be seen. At tea time, head for Hanselmann's – 'fabulous tea and strudels' but 'the place is a bit dull'.

Bobby's Pub attracts a young crowd, as does the loud music of the Stübli, one of three bars in the Schweizerhof: the others are the Muli, with a country and western theme and live music, and the chic Piano Bar. The Enoteca is the place to sample 'wonderful wines', according to a 2006 visitor. The Cresta, at the Steffani, is popular with the British, while the Cava below it is louder, livelier and younger. The Diamond has a bar and a disco. Readers rate the piano bar at the

---

Albana Hotel 'cosy and welcoming'.
The two most popular discos are Vivai (expensive) at the Steffani, and King's at Badrutt's Palace (even more expensive; jackets and ties required). And if they don't part you from enough of your cash, try the casino.

OFF THE SLOPES
Excellent variety of pastimes
Even if you lack the bravado for the Cresta Run, there is lots to do. In mid-winter the snow-covered lake provides a playground for bizarre events but in March the lake starts to thaw. There's an annual 'gourmet festival', with chefs from all over the world. The Engadin museum is said to be 'very interesting'. And the shopping is simply 'incredible', enthuses another visitor.

There are well-marked walking trails around the area and a separate map is available.

Some hotels run special activities, such as a curling week. Other options are hang-gliding and indoor tennis. There's a public pool in Bad.

One reporter was bowled over by a train trip on the Bernina Express to Italy, with 'amazing bends and scenery; the high spot of our visit'.

STAYING UP THE MOUNTAIN
Excellent possibilities
Next door to each other at Salastrains are two chalet-style hotels, the 3-star Salastrains (833 3867), with 60 comfy beds, and the slightly simpler and much smaller Chesa Chantarella (833 3355). Great views, and no queues.

Celerina 1730m/5,680ft

At the bottom end of the Cresta Run, Celerina is unpretentious and villagey, if quiet, with good access to Corviglia. It is sizeable, with a lot of second homes, many owned by Italians (the upper part is known as Piccolo Milano). There are some appealing small hotels (reporters like Chesa Rosatsch 837 0101) and a couple of bigger 4-stars.

THE CRESTA RUN

No trip to St Moritz is really complete without a visit to the Cresta Run. It's the last bastion of Britishness (until recently, payment had to be made in sterling) and male chauvinism (women need an invitation from a club member).

Any adult male can pay around £200 for five rides (helmet and lunch at the Kulm hotel included). You lie on a toboggan (aptly called a 'skeleton') and hurtle head-first down a sheet ice gully from St Moritz to Celerina. Watch out for Shuttlecock corner – that's where the ambulances ply their trade.

Verbier

Big chalet-style resort that attracts powderhounds and affluent nightlife lovers from all over the world

COSTS

①②③④⑤⑥

RATINGS

The slopes
Fast lifts	**
Snow	***
Extent	*****
Expert	*****
Intermediate	***
Beginner	**
Convenience	**
Queues	***
Mountain restaurants	***

The rest
Scenery	****
Resort charm	***
Off-slope	***

KEY FACTS

Resort	1500m
	4,920ft

4 Valleys area
Slopes	1500-3330m
	4,920-10,930ft
Lifts	95
Pistes	410km
	255 miles
Blue	33%
Red	41%
Black	26%
Snowmaking	50km
	31 miles

Verbier, Bruson and Tzoumaz/Savoleyres sectors only (covered by Verbier pass)
Slopes	1500-3025m
	4,920-9,920ft
Lifts	38
Pistes	150km
	93 miles
Blue	33%
Red	33%
Black	34%
Snowmaking	20km
	12 miles

OUR WEBSITE

Go to our website at wtss.co.uk for resort news, links to resort sites, a build-your-own resort shortlist system and reader forums.

532

➕ Extensive, challenging slopes with a lot of off-piste and long bump runs

➕ Upper slopes offer a real high-mountain feel plus great views

➕ Pleasant, animated village in a sunny, panoramic setting

➕ Lively, varied nightlife

➕ Much improved lift system, piste grooming and on-mountain signposting, but ...

➖ Reporters still complain that it's difficult to find your way around

➖ Some overcrowded pistes and areas

➖ The 4 Valleys network is much less wonderful than it looks on paper

➖ Sunny lower slopes will always be a problem, even with snowmaking

➖ Some long walks/rides to lifts

➖ Lots of off-piste is tracked out quickly

We have been criticising Verbier ever since the first edition of this book back in 1994. At last we feel we're getting somewhere. Its lift system has been improved considerably and its queues have shrunk except for a couple of key, but optional, lifts. Its grooming, ski schools and snowmaking have got better and it has completely renewed its formerly atrocious on-mountain signposting and linked it to its piste map. But reporters still complain they can't find their way around – hopefully the new piste numbering system will help (see News).

For experts prepared to hire a guide to explore off-piste, Verbier is one of the cult resorts worldwide. And for vibrant nightlife it is difficult to beat. With its claimed 410km/255 miles of pistes, Verbier also seems at first sight to rank alongside the French mega-resorts that draw keen piste skiers, such as the Three Valleys and Paradiski. But it doesn't; Three Valleys and Paradiski devotees will be sorely disappointed by the 4 Valleys network, which is an inconveniently sprawling affair, with lots of traversing to get to the far end and back. And Verbier's local pistes are confined and crowded.

THE RESORT

Verbier is an amorphous sprawl of chalet-style buildings in an impressive setting on a wide, sunny balcony facing spectacular peaks. It's a fashionable, informal, very lively place that teems with cosmopolitan visitors. Most are younger than visitors to other big Swiss resorts.

Most of the shops and hotels (but not chalets) are set around the Place Centrale and along the sloping streets stretching both down the hill and up it to the main lift station at Médran 500m/ 1,640ft away. Much of the nightlife is here, too, though bars are rather scattered. These central areas get unpleasantly packed with cars at busy times, especially weekends. More chalets and apartments are built each year, with many newer properties inconveniently situated along the road to the lift base for the secondary Savoleyres area, about 1.5km/1 mile from Médran.

The Médran lift station is a walkable distance from the Place Centrale, so staying there has attractions, and there is accommodation close to the lift which is sufficiently distant from nightlife to avoid late-night noise. If nightlife is not a priority, staying somewhere near the upper (north-east) fringes of the village may mean that you can almost ski to your door – and there is a piste linking the upper nursery slopes to the

The top of Mont-Fort feels like the top of the world. Col des Gentianes down there is a fraction of the way down Tortin, 1300m/ 4,270ft vertical away →

NEWS

For 2006/07 a six-pack with covers is planned from La Combe (near Les Ruinettes) to Attelas. More snowmaking is planned for the La Chaux area and the terrain-park. And we are told that work is under way on numbering the pistes, which should make it much easier for people to find their way around the slopes; let's hope that happens for 2006/07 too.

For 2005/06 a major new lift – a 'chondola', a mix of eight-seat gondolas and six-seat chairs on the same lift – was installed between Les Ruinettes and La Chaux via the ridge at Côte de Brunet. It replaced the Combes 2, Chaux 1 and Fontanys chairs, and you can ride it both ways and get off at the Brunet ridge or at the terminus.

The slope from Col des Gentianes to La Chaux was remodelled so the run straight down can be groomed. And a new mountain restaurant called Chalet Carlsberg opened at La Combe.

Further afield, a new fast quad from Siviez to Cambatzeline, en route to Greppon Blanc, replaced the Novelli double chair for 2005/06. And the quad chair from Veysonnaz to above Thyon was replaced by an eight-seat gondola.

one in the middle of the village. But in practice most people just get used to using the free buses, which run efficiently on several routes until 7pm. Some areas have quite an infrequent service. We are told that from 7pm to 8.30 there is a special taxi service that will drop you at any of the usual bus stops for five francs per person.

Verbier is at one end of a long, strung-out series of interconnected slopes, optimistically branded the 4 Valleys ('bit of a cheek calling itself the 4 Valleys', says a 2006 reporter) and linking Verbier to Nendaz, Veysonnaz, Thyon and other resorts. These other resorts have their own pros and cons. All are appreciably cheaper places to stay than Verbier, and some are more sensible bases for those who plan to stick to pistes rather than venture off-piste – the Veysonnaz-Thyon sector, in particular, is much more intermediate-friendly than Verbier. As bases for exploration of the whole 4 Valleys, only Siviez is much of an advance on Verbier. They are much less lively in the evening. You can also stay down in the valley village of Le Châble, which has a gondola up to Verbier and on into the slopes. Across the valley, Bruson is more attractive as a place to visit for a day than to stay in. These alternatives are all described at the end of the chapter.

Chamonix and Champéry are within reach by car. But a car can be a bit of a nuisance in Verbier itself. Parking is tightly controlled; your chalet or hotel may not have enough space for all guests' cars, which means a hike from the free parking at the sports centre or paying for garage space.

THE MOUNTAINS

Essentially this is high-mountain terrain. There are wooded slopes directly above the village, but the runs here are either bumpy itinéraires or winding paths. There is more sheltered skiing in other sectors – particularly above Veysonnaz.

THE SLOPES
Very spread out

Savoleyres is the smaller area, reached by a gondola from the north-west end of the village. This area is underrated and generally under-used. It has open, sunny slopes on the front side, and long, pleasantly wooded, shadier runs on the back. You can take a catwalk across from Savoleyres to the foot of Verbier's main slopes. These are served by lifts from Médran, at the opposite end of the village.

Two gondolas rise to **Les Ruinettes** and then on to **Les Attelas**. From Les Attelas a small cable-car goes up to Mont Gelé, for steep off-piste runs only. Heading down instead, you can go back westwards to Les Ruinettes, south to La Chaux or north to Lac des Vaux. From Lac des Vaux chairs go back to Les Attelas and on to Chassoure, the top of a wide, steep and shady off-piste mogul field leading down to **Tortin**, with a gondola back.

For 2005/06 the link between Les Ruinettes and La Chaux was greatly improved by the new chondola (see News). The local La Chaux slopes are served by an additional slow chair-lift and are the departure point of a jumbo cable-car up to Col des Gentianes and the glacier area. A second, much smaller cable-car then goes up to the **Mont-Fort** glacier, the high point of the 4 Valleys. From the top a long, very steep black run leads down to very shallow reds served by drag-lifts. Below them there's another off-piste route down to Tortin; the whole north-facing run from the top to Tortin is almost 1300m/4,270ft vertical. A cable-car returns to Col des Gentianes.

Below Tortin is the gateway to the rest of the 4 Valleys, **Siviez**, where one

chair goes off into the long, thin **Nendaz** sector and a new fast quad installed for 2005/06 heads for the **Thyon-Veysonnaz** sector, via a couple of lifts and a lot of catwalks.

Allow plenty of time to get to and from these remote corners – the taxi-rides home are expensive.

The slopes of **Bruson** are described briefly at the end of this chapter.

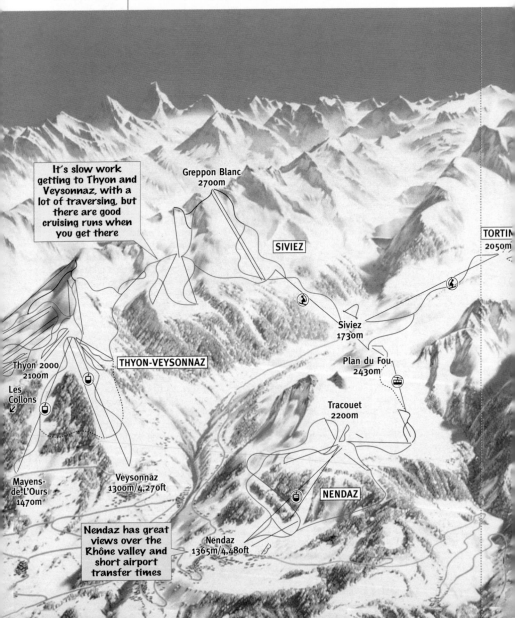

It's slow work getting to Thyon and Veysonnaz, with a lot of traversing, but there are good cruising runs when you get there

Greppon Blanc
2700m

SIVIEZ

TORTIN
2050m

Siviez
1730m

THYON-VEYSONNAZ

Plan du Fou
2430m

Thyon 2000
2100m

Les
Collons

Tracouet
2200m

Mayens-
de-L'Ours
1470m

Veysonnaz
1300m/4,270ft

NENDAZ

Nendaz has great views over the Rhône valley and short airport transfer times

Nendaz
1365m/4,480ft

TERRAIN-PARKS
Expert and beginner options

The 1936 Neipark, Verbier's main freestyle area, is at La Chaux (www.neipark.ch). The park has four separate lines that they term soft, medium, hard and rail. These are made up of kickers, gap jumps, step-ups, and hips. The rails are varied with boxes and rails of all types and a skate-style pyramid, which is the outstanding feature and gives the park its identity. There is a chill-out zone with deckchairs and DJs. A day terrain-park pass can be purchased, and freestyle coaching is available (check www.snowschool.ch for details). A second smaller park in Savoleyres is more geared to beginner freestylers.

SNOW RELIABILITY
Improved snowmaking

The slopes of the Mont-Fort glacier always have good snow. The runs to Tortin are normally snow-sure too. But nearly all of this is steep, and much of

MONT-FORT
3330m/10,930ft

The top and bottom dotted lines here are the Gentianes and Tortin itinéraires, skied by most good skiers but technically off-piste. Outrageous – they should be official black pistes

Col des Gentianes
2950m

The most crowded run in Verbier (if not the world) – from Attelas to Les Ruinettes

Mont Gelé
3025m

Chassoure
2740m

LES ATTELAS
2730m

La Chaux
2260m

TORTIN
2050m

LES RUINETTES
2200m

Lac des Vaux
2545m

Col des Mine
2320m

Our favourite run in Verbier: the Vallon d'Arbi itinéraire

Bruson

Le Châble

Vallon d'Arbi

The best (along with La Chaux) and quietest intermediate slopes

SAVOLEYRES

Verbier
1500m/4,920ft

Savoleyres
2355m

La Tzoumaz
1500m/4,920ft

skifreshtracks.co.uk

holiday adventures
for all standards

+44 (0)20 8410 2022
abta 2911 abtol 5064

LIFT PASSES

4 Valleys/Mon-Fort

Prices in SF

Age	1-day	6-day
under 16	47	223
16 to 19		271
20 to 64	67	319
over 65	50	239

Free under 6
Beginner no deals

Notes
Covers all lifts and ski-buses in Verbier, Mont-Fort, Bruson, La Tzoumaz, Nendaz, Veysonnaz and Thyon. Part-day passes available. Reductions for families.

Alternative passes
Verbier pass, La Tzoumaz/Savoleyres pass and Bruson-only pass available.

it is formally off-piste. Most of Verbier's main local slopes face south or west and are below 2500m/8,200ft – so they can be in poor condition at times. There is snowmaking on the main run down all the way from Attelas to Médran; and more is planned at La Chaux for 2006/07, as part of a long-term plan to have 60 per cent of the pistes covered. The north-facing slopes of Savoleyres generally hold their snow well.

FOR EXPERTS
The main attraction
Verbier has some superb tough slopes, many of them off-piste and needing a guide – see the separate feature panel on this. There are few conventional black pistes; most of the runs that might have this designation are now defined as itinéraires – which means they are 'marked, not maintained and not controlled'. But they do seem to be closed if unsafe or if snow cover is insufficient. We'd like to see them given official black piste status, so you know where you stand better. The blacks that do exist are mostly indistinguishable from nearby reds. The front face of Mont-Fort is an exception: a long mogul field, with a choice of gradient from seriously steep to intimidatingly steep. The World Cup run at Veysonnaz is a steepish, often icy red, ideal for really speeding down. The two itinéraires to Tortin are both excellent in their different ways. The one from Chassoure is just one wide, steep slope, normally a huge mogul field. The north-facing itinéraire from Gentianes is longer, less steep, but feels much more of an adventure (keep left for quieter and shallower slopes and better snow, right for steeper moguls where the crowds go). There is an entertaining itinéraire from Greppon Blanc, at the top of the Siviez sector, into the next valley.

FOR INTERMEDIATES
Hit Savoleyres – or Veysonnaz
Many mileage-hungry intermediates find Verbier disappointing. The intermediate slopes in the main area are concentrated between Les Attelas and the village, above and below Les Ruinettes, plus the little bowl at Lac des Vaux and the sunny slopes at La Chaux. This is all excellent and varied intermediate territory, but there isn't much of it – to put it in perspective, this whole area is no bigger than the tiny slopes of Alpbach – and it is used by the bulk of the visitors staying in one of Switzerland's largest resorts. So it is often very crowded, especially the otherwise wonderful sweeping red from Les Attelas to Les Ruinettes. Even early intermediates should taste the perfect snow on the glacier. The red run served by the T-bars is really of gentle blue steepness. And the red path from Col des Gentianes to La Chaux is not too difficult, but its high-mountain feel can be unnerving and it's no disgrace to ride the cable-car down instead.

There is excellent easy blue-run skiing at La Chaux (including a 'slow skiing' piste, though this was not heavily policed when we were there). Thankfully, getting back from La Chaux to Les Ruinettes is now a lot easier as you can ride the new 'chondola' instead of taking a tricky red run.

Intermediates should exploit the under-used Savoleyres area. This has good intermediate pistes, usually better snow and far fewer people (especially on Sundays). It is also a good hill for mixed abilities, with variations of many runs. From here, there is an easy way to Médran but there may be no easy way down to that link from the top of Savoleyres.

The Thyon-Veysonnaz and Nendaz sectors are worth exploring (those not willing to take on the itinéraires have to ride down to Tortin; and down from Plan du Fou to get to Nendaz).

boarding

Verbier has become synonymous with extreme snowboarding and is generally seen as a free-riders' resort, with powder, cliffs, natural hits and trees all easily accessible. For years the Bec des Rosses has been the home to the Verbier extreme contest, one of the most high-profile events of the sort on the calendar. There is a lot of steep and challenging terrain to be explored with a guide, but the pistes and itinéraires will provide most riders with plenty to think about. The main area is serviced by chair-lifts and gondolas with no drags and there is a good terrain-park at La Chaux, which improves every year. Beginners should stick to the lower blue runs and the Savoleyres area (but there are several drag-lifts there).

Verbier has some of the best, most extensive and most varied off-piste in the world, and major free-ride competitions are held there every year. Here, with the help of former British ski team members Chris and brother Andy David, who head up Altitude Extreme, we pick out just a few of the off-piste runs on offer.

The Col de Mines and Vallon d'Arbi itinéraires, accessible from Lac de Vaux, are relatively easy (and usually less crowded and skied out than the better-known Tortin and Gentianes itinéraires) – the former is a long, open slope back to Verbier and the latter a very beautiful run in a steep-sided valley down to La Tzoumaz. Fontainay, accessible from the chondola that was new last season, is an itinéraire that is great for learning how to deal with moguls, steeps or powder.

Stairway to Heaven is usually quiet and its snow is kept in good condition by the lack of crowds and its shady orientation. It starts a short ski, pole and climb from Col des Gentianes. Then you drop over the ridge into a deserted valley, and it's a long, relatively easy ski in powder down to Tortin, pretty much parallel to the popular Gentianes itinéraire.

The Mt Gelé cable-car, when it is open, offers some of the most amazing terrain accessible anywhere by lift, with long runs down to Siviez on steep but open slopes, before a long scenic traverse and schuss along the valley. Alternatively, go down the opposite side of the mountain through the steep rock face towards Lac de Vaux , not a route for the faint of heart but a must for adrenalin junkies if conditions are good. The many couloirs accessible from Attelas can also be fantastic. But don't even think of attempting them if they are closed by the ski patrol – they regularly slide and can be very dangerous.

Altitude Extreme advises that whenever skiing or boarding off-piste, safety equipment such as transceivers, helmets, back protection, shovels and probes should always be worn and carried. They also run clinics on how to use all this equipment – an essential prerequisite for anyone venturing off the beaten track in search of powder or new thrills.

Altitude Extreme is a partner of Altitude Snowsport School, the largest British-run school in Switzerland, based exclusively in Verbier. Altitude Extreme's experienced and professional coaches specialise in clinics to improve technique on more challenging terrain.

t 00 41 27 771 6006
www.altitude-verbier.com

Verbier

537

SWITZERLAND

538

FOR BEGINNERS
OK but not ideal

There are sunny nursery slopes close to the middle of the village and at Les Esserts, at the top of it. These are fine provided they have snow (they have a lot of snowmaking, which helps). For progression, there are easy blues at La Chaux (you can ride the new chondola back to Les Ruinettes) and the back side of Savoleyres (from where you can ride the gondola down).

FOR CROSS-COUNTRY
Surprisingly little on offer

Verbier is limited for cross-country. There's a 4km/2.5 mile circuit in Verbier, 6km/3.5 miles at Les Ruinettes-La Chaux and 30km/19 miles down at Le Châble/Val de Bagnes.

QUEUES
Not the problem they were

Verbier's queue problems have been greatly eased by recent investment in powerful new lifts. But the high-capacity gondola from Les Ruinettes to Attelas has increased the overcrowding on the pistes back down (and at the top where we have had to search hard to find space to put our skis on amidst a horde of others); the new chair planned to Attelas for 2006/07 may make the piste-overcrowding even worse. The mega-queues at Tortin for Chassoure are a thing of the past. But the cable-car from Tortin to Col des Gentianes can produce queues, and the Mont-Fort cable-car above it can still generate very long ones. Some queues at the main village lift station at Médran can arise if Sunday visitors fill one of the gondolas down at Le Châble, but the crowds shift quickly.

We have reports of queues for outdated double chairs and for inadequate drag-lifts in the outlying 4 Valleys resorts – notably the Greppon Blanc drags on the way to Veysonnaz.

MOUNTAIN RESTAURANTS
Disappointing in main area

There are not enough huts, which means queues and overcrowding in high season. Savoleyres is the best area. The Poste hotel by the Tzoumaz chair takes some beating for value and lack of crowds and the rustic Marmotte serves 'excellent rösti'. The Namasté is recommended by a 2005 reporter – 'the best restaurant on the mountain, reservations almost always essential'. Le Sonalon, on the fringe of the village, is 'excellent, with great views', but reached off-piste, as is the nearby La Marlenaz ('what a great find, hearty and well recommended').

In the main area, the rustic Chez Dany at Clambin, on the off-piste run on the southern fringe of the area, is about the best, and gets packed – booking needed. Carrefour, with a large terrace, is popular and well-situated at the top of the village. The restaurants at Les Ruinettes – table-service upstairs – have big terraces with splendid views. The Olympique at Les Attelas is a good table-service restaurant. Everyone loves the Cabane Mont Fort – a proper mountain refuge off the run to La Chaux from Col des Gentianes – get there early or book a table. We have no reports yet on the Chalet Carlsberg (new for 2005/06).

SCHOOLS AND GUIDES
Good reports

There's no shortage of schools to choose between. Adrenaline gets good reviews, particularly for its private lessons. A 2006 reporter praised his Swiss instructor with European Snowsport. Altitude was started by top British instructors in 2001 – though we lack reports on them. British instructor Warren Smith runs his Ski Academy here. Powder Extreme specialises in off-piste. We skied with both Warren Smith and Powder Extreme in 2005 and thought them both good.

FACILITIES FOR CHILDREN
Wide range of options

The Swiss school's facilities in the resort are good, and the resort attracts quite a lot of families. The playground up at La Chaux has also received favourable reports. The possibility of leaving very young babies at the Schtroumpfs nursery is valuable.

There are considerable reductions on the lift pass price for families on production of your passports.

GETTING THERE

Air Geneva
170km/106 miles
(2hr)

Rail Le Châble (7km/
4 miles); regular
buses to resort or
gondola

STAYING THERE

HOW TO GO
Plenty of options
Given the size of the place there are
surprisingly few apartments and
pensions available, though those on a
budget have inexpensive B&B options
in Le Châble. Hotels are expensive in
relation to their grading. Given a
sleeping bag you can bed down at the
sports centre for about £10 a night –
and that includes the use of the pool.
Chalets Verbier is the chalet-party
capital of Switzerland. Companies large
and small have properties here,
including Verbier specialists such as
Ski Verbier, who we have had good
reports of, and who have 14 chalets
and a hotel, including one with an
indoor pool and several with steam,
sauna and outdoor hot-tub. Flexiski has
the very comfortable chalet Bouvreuil.
Right at the top of the market, Descent
has two superb chalets.
Hotels There is one 5-star hotel, five 4-
star, 13 3-star and a few simpler places.
((((5) **Chalet d'Adrien** (771 6200) Relais
& Chateaux. A beautifully furnished
low-rise 25-room chalet, with top-notch
cooking. Next to the Savoleyres lift.

((((4) **Rosalp** (771 6323) Relais &
Chateaux. Comfortable rooms but the
great attraction is the food in Roland
Pierroz's Michelin-starred restaurant.
Sauna, steam, hot-tub. Good position
midway between centre and Médran.
((((4) **Montpelier** (771 6131) Very
comfortable 4-star, but out of town
(free courtesy bus). Pool.
((((4) **Vanessa** (775 2800) Central 4-star
with spacious apartments as well as
rooms; 'Great food,' says a reporter.
((((3) **Rotonde** (771 6525) Much cheaper,
well positioned 3-star between centre
and Médran; some budget rooms.
((((3) **Verbier Lodge** (771 6666) Novel
log-built 3-star with stylish modern
fittings, offering packages with tuition
or heli-skiing. On southern fringe,
beyond Médran – reachable on skis.
((((3) **Poste** (771 6681) Well placed 3-
star midway between centre and
Médran; pool. Some rooms small.
'Friendly staff and great food.'
((2) **Farinet** (771 6626) Central 3-star
hotel, British-owned, with a focal
après-ski bar on its elevated terrace.
Self-catering Few UK tour operators
offer apartments, but they can be
booked locally.

Verbier

539

the cheapest but excellent steaks').

For Swiss specialities, try the Relais des Neiges, the Robinson, the Caveau, Au Mignon, Au Vieux Verbier by the Médran lifts or Esserts by the nursery slopes. The ever-popular Fer à Cheval does reasonably priced pizza and other simple dishes. A 2006 reporter found 'top British gastropub food at reasonable prices' downstairs in the Pub Mont-Fort. Arguably the best-value Italian food in town is at Al Capone, out near the Savoleyres gondola, but a 2006 reporter preferred Borsalino. Harold's Snack internet cafe is a 'reasonable burger joint'.

You can be ferried by snowmobile up to Chez Dany or the Marmotte for a meal, followed by a torchlit descent.

EATING OUT
Plenty of choice

There is a very wide range of restaurants; a pocket guide is given away locally which would be much more useful if all its advertisers gave some clues about price.

The Michelin-starred Rosalp is clearly the best (and most expensive) in town, and among the best in Switzerland – splash out on the seven-course Menu Gastronomique if you can afford it. We have had two delicious meals there. The Pinte bistro in the hotel basement is a less expensive option – worth trying. The 5-star Chalet d'Adrien also has two tempting options, with a starred chef at work in the gastronomique Astrance. The Grange is also serious about its food.

King's is one of our favourites – innovative food in a stylish, clublike setting. We've also had excellent meals in the stylish Millénium. The Ecurie was recommended by a 2006 reporter ('not

APRES-SKI
Throbbing but expensive

It starts with a 4pm visit to either the tents of 1836, halfway down from Les Ruinettes, or the Offshore Café at Médran, for people-watching, milk shakes and cakes. The nearby Big Ben pub is 'great and lively on a sunny afternoon'. Au Mignon at the bottom of the golf course has become popular since it was given a large sun deck.

Then if you're young, loud and British, it's on to the Pub Mont-Fort – there's a widescreen TV for live sport. The Nelson and Fer à Cheval are popular with locals. The Farinet is particularly good in spring, its live band playing to the audience on a huge, sunny terrace.

After dinner the Pub Mont-Fort is again popular (the shots bar in the cellar is worth a visit). Crok No Name has good live bands or a DJ. Murphy's Irish bar in the Garbo hotel is popular,

with a good resident DJ. King's is a quiet candlelit cellar bar with 60s' decor – 'hip crowd, good music'. New Club is a sophisticated piano bar, with comfortable seating and a more discerning clientele. The Farm Club is seriously expensive – on Friday and Saturday packed with rich Swiss paying SF220 for bottles of spirits. You'll find us having a quiet nightcap in the basement Bar'Jo, across the road.

The Casbah, in the basement of the Farinet hotel, has a North African theme. Taratata is a friendly club that seems to be growing in popularity. The Icebox has 'a 70s party atmosphere'. Big Ben is 'lively, crowded and friendly'.

OFF THE SLOPES
No great attraction

Verbier has an excellent sports centre (with pool, saunas and hot-tubs), some nice walks and a big alpine museum, but otherwise not much to offer if you don't want to hit the slopes. Montreux is an enjoyable train excursion from Le Châble, and Martigny is worth a visit for the Roman remains and art gallery. The spa complex at Lavey-les-Bains has been highly recommended by a reporter. Various mountain restaurants are accessible to pedestrians. There's floodlit tubing etc on the nursery slope at Les Esserts on Saturday and Sunday.

Nendaz 1365m/4,480ft

Nendaz is a big resort with over 17,000 beds, but is little known in Britain. Although it appears to be centrally set in the 4 Valleys, getting to and from the other sectors is a slow business unless you drive/take a bus to Siviez ('To get into the Verbier skiing takes a decent skier about an hour,' said a 2006 reporter). In other respects it has attractions, relatively low prices among them. Airport transfers are quick, especially from Sion (20 minutes away).

THE RESORT
Nendaz itself is a large place with great views of the Rhône valley. Most of the resort is modern but built in traditional chalet style, and the original old village of Haute-Nendaz is still there, with its narrow streets, old houses and barns, and baroque chapel dating from 1499.

THE MOUNTAIN
Nendaz has its own area of slopes and a link to rest of the 4 Valleys via Siviez.
Slopes There's a 12-person gondola straight to the top of the local north-facing slopes at Tracouet. Here there are good, snow-sure nursery slopes plus blue and red intermediate runs.

Intermediates and better can head off down the back of Tracouet to a cable-car that takes you to Plan du Fou at 2430m/7,970ft. From there you can go down to Siviez and the links to Verbier one way and Veysonnaz and Thyon the other. To return to Nendaz you have to negotiate an itinéraire from Plan du Fou (or take the cable-car down) followed by a black run.
Terrain-parks There is a terrain-park.
Snow reliability Nendaz sits on a north-facing shelf so its local slopes don't get the sun that affects Verbier.
Experts Access to the tough stuff is a bit slower from here than from Verbier.
Intermediates The local slopes are quite varied, but not very extensive.
Beginners There are good nursery slopes at Tracouet.
Snowboarding The terrain is fine but there are quite a few drag-lifts.
Cross-country There are 15km/9 miles of cross-country tracks.
Queues There may be queues at Siviez at the end of the day.
Mountain restaurants The Tracouet has been praised for its sunny terrace and the Cabane de Balavaux under the Prarion chair for its 'excellent food'.
Schools and guides There are four ski schools plus mountain guides.
Facilities for children The schools have a nursery area at Tracouet and there's a resort kindergarten (Le P'tit Bec).

STAYING THERE
How to go A new UK chalet company, Ted Bentley, has launched a catered chalet operation there for 2006/07.
Hotels There are a four small hotels. The Mont-Fort (288 2616) has been newly renovated and modernised.
Self-catering There is no shortage of apartments and chalets to rent.
Eating out The Zinc restaurant of the

ACTIVITIES
Indoor Sports centre (swimming pools, ice rink, curling, squash, sauna, solarium, steam bath, hot-tub), cinema

Outdoor 25km/ 16 miles of cleared walking paths, paragliding, hang-gliding, snow-shoeing, tobogganing

Mont-Fort looks good and the Mont Rouge hotel restaurant, Vieux-Chalet and (out of town on the road to Siviez) the Vieux Nendaz have been recommended.

Après-ski There are plenty of bars and four discos; a 17-year-old reporter recommended the Cactus Saloon as one of the livelier spots.

Off the slopes Nendaz has 70km/43 miles of walks, an ice rink, fitness centre, climbing wall and squash courts.

Siviez 1730m/5,680ft

Siviez is a small huddle of buildings in an isolated spot, where the slopes of Verbier, Nendaz and Veysonnaz/Thyon meet. Among them is the 2-star hotel de Siviez (288 1623). It is an ideal base from which to explore the whole 4 Valleys lift network, and the new fast quad to Cambatzeline for 2005/06 has made this easier. Being set a little way down the valley from Tortin, at the foot of the steep itinerary runs from Chassoure and Mont-Fort, means it is also an excellent base for exploration of the tough skiing of Verbier – you can end the day with a descent of 1600m/5,250ft vertical from Mont-Fort; no noise in the evenings; perfect.

Veysonnaz 1300m/4,270ft

Veysonnaz is a small, quiet resort, sunny in the afternoon, at the foot of an excellent long red slope from the ridge above Thyon. It is an attractive old village complete with church. It has adequate bars, cafes and restaurants, a disco and a 'good' sports centre with swimming pool. Accommodation is mainly in apartments. Of the two hotels, the 'very comfortable' Chalet Royal (208 5644) is preferable to the 'tired-looking' Magrappé, which is the focus of noisy après-ski. Taking a car means you can drive to Siviez for quick access to the Verbier or Nendaz slopes – a slow business by lift and piste. The link up to Thyon has been improved by the new eight-seat gondola.

Thyon 2000 2100m/6,890ft

Thyon 2000 (why not Thyon 2100, we wonder?) is a functional, purpose-built collection of plain, medium-rise apartment blocks just above the tree line at the centre of the Thyon-Veysonnaz sector of the 4 Valleys. It has the basics – bakery, supermarket, newsagent, a couple of bar-restaurants. There's a terrain-park and a kindergarten as well as a ski school and indoor pool.

Les Collons 1800m/5,910ft

At the foot of a broad, east-facing slope down from Thyon 2000, this is a couple of strings of chalets along roads following the hillside, mostly apartments but also a couple of modest hotels including the 3-star Cambuse (281 1883). There's a much wider range of bars, restaurants and other diversions than up in Thyon.

Le Châble 820m/2,690ft

Le Châble is a busy roadside village in the valley, at the bottom of the hairpin road up to Verbier. It is linked to Verbier by a queue-free gondola that goes on (without changing cabins) to Les Ruinettes and Les Attelas, which means access to the slopes can be just as quick as from Verbier. Le Châble is on the rail network, and is also convenient for drivers who want to visit other resorts in the Valais or further afield. And it is handy for Bruson, just a short bus-ride up the mountainside facing Verbier. There are several modest hotels, of which the 2-star Giétroz (776 1184) is the pick.

Bruson 1000m/3,280ft

Bruson is a small village on a shelf just above Le Châble, and reached by a short free bus-ride. Its lifts are covered by the Verbier pass. From the village a slow chair goes up over gentle east-facing slopes dotted with chalets to Bruson les Forêts (1600m/5,250ft).

The open slopes above Bruson les Forêts are served by a quad chair up to the ridge, on the far side of which is a short drag-lift serving a tight little bowl. In addition to the intermediate pistes served by these lifts there are large areas of underused off-piste terrain, notably through woods on the front side accessed by the drag on the back. The off-piste down the back towards Orsières is good; you return by train. For years there have been plans to develop Bruson – building a lift from Le Châble to mid-mountain, extending the lift network and building a lift up from Orsières. A new Intrawest village is at the planning stages here. For now, it remains a great place to escape Verbier crowds.

Phone numbers
From elsewhere in Switzerland add the prefix 027.
From abroad use the prefix +41 27.

TOURIST OFFICES

Verbier
t 775 3888
info@verbier.ch
www.verbier.ch

Nendaz
t 289 5589
info@nendaz.ch
www.nendaz.ch

Siviez
www.siviez-nendaz.ch

Veysonnaz
t 207 1053
tourism@veysonnaz.ch
www.veysonnaz.ch

Thyon 2000 / Les Collons
t 281 2727
info@thyon-region.ch
www.thyon-region.ch

Le Châble and Bruson
t 776 1682
bagnestourisme@verbier.ch

Villars

Traditional year-round resort with local low-altitude slopes and a much needed but far-flung glacier

COSTS

① ② ③ ④ ⑤ ⑥

RATINGS

The slopes
Fast lifts	★★★
Snow	★★
Extent	★★★
Expert	★★
Intermediate	★★★
Beginner	★★★★
Convenience	★★★
Queues	★★★
Mountain restaurants	★★★

The rest
Scenery	★★★
Resort charm	★★★★
Off-slope	★★★★

NEWS

For 2006/07 a faster eight-person gondola is due to replace the old four-person one from the village to Roc d'Orsay

➕ Pleasant, relaxing year-round resort	➖ Unreliable snow-cover
➕ Fairly extensive intermediate slopes linked to Les Diablerets	➖ Overcrowded mountain restaurants
➕ Good nursery slopes	➖ Short runs on the upper slopes
➕ Quite close to Geneva airport	➖ Getting up the mountain may mean a slow, often crowded train journey or a bus-ride out to the gondola
➕ Good range of off-slope diversions	

With its mountain railway and gentle low-altitude slopes, Villars is the kind of place that has been overshadowed by modern mega-resorts. But for a relaxing and varied family holiday the attractions are clear – and the link with Les Diablerets and its high glacier, now known as Glacier 3000, adds to the appeal.

THE RESORT

Villars sits on a sunny shelf, looking across the Rhône valley to the Portes du Soleil. A busy high street lined with a variety of shops gives it the air of a pleasant small town; all around are chalet-style buildings, with just a few block-like hotels.

You can travel to the centre of Villars on a picturesque cog train which goes on up to the slopes. It leaves from Bex in the valley, which is served by direct trains from Geneva airport (as is Aigle, a bus-ride from Villars). A gondola at one end of town is the main lift; stay nearby if you can, since shuttle-buses get crowded at peak times. You can also stay in Gryon.

The Glacier-Alpes Vaudoises pass covers Villars, the linked slopes of Les Diablerets and Glacier 3000, plus Leysin and Les Mosses, both of which are easy jaunts by rail or road. Other resorts (eg Champéry and Verbier) are within driving distance.

543

Floriettaz
2120m/6,96oft

Gstaad Reusch ↓

Cabane
2525m

Sex Rouge
2970m/9,74oft

Iseneau
1760m

GLACIER 3000

Col du Pillon
1545m

MEILLERET
1950m

Croix des Chaux
2020m/6,63oft

Petit Chamossaire
2035m/6,68oft

Laouissalet

Les Diablerets
1200m/3,940ft

LES CHAUX
1750m

Chaux de Conches

Grand mossaire
...120m

Chaux Ronde
1985m

Alpe des Chaux

Roc d'Orsay
2000m

BRETAYE
1805m

Sodoleuvre

Les Fracherets
1515m

Col de Soud
1525m

La Rasse
1350m

Villars
1300m/4,27oft

Barboleuse
1200m/3,940ft

Gryon
1115m/3,66oft

The slopes suit novices
and intermediates ↗

SNOWPIX.COM / CHRIS GILL

KEY FACTS

Resort	1300m	
	4,270ft	
Villars, Gryon and Les Diablerets, but excluding Glacier 3000		
Slopes	1115-2120m	
	3,660-6,960ft	
Lifts	36	
Pistes	100km	
	62 miles	
Blue	40%	
Red	50%	
Black	10%	
Snowmaking	10km	
	6 miles	

Phone numbers
From elsewhere in
Switzerland add the
prefix 024.
From abroad use the
prefix +41 24.

TOURIST OFFICE

t 495 3232
information@villars.ch
www.villars.ch

THE MOUNTAINS

There's a good mix of open and
wooded slopes throughout the area.
Slopes The train goes up to the col of
Bretaye, which has intermediate slopes
on either side, with a maximum vertical
of 300m/980ft back to the col and
much longer runs back to the village.
To the east, open slopes (often spoilt
by sun) go to La Rasse and the link to
the Les Chaux sector. The gondola
from town takes you to Roc d'Orsay,
from where you can head for Bretaye
or back to Villars. From Bretaye you
can head for the slow two-way chair-lift
which is the connection to Les
Diablerets. The piste map and marking
are both poor. 'If you don't know the
resort, skiing in bad visibility would be
stressful,' said a reader last year.
Terrain-parks There are parks at Les
Chaux and Chaux Ronde, and a half-
pipe at Les Diablerets.
Snow reliability Low altitude and
sunny slopes mean snow reliability
isn't good. There is some snowmaking,
but the SF12 million investment
planned is badly needed. If local snow
is poor, head for Glacier 3000.
Experts The main interest for experts is
off-piste. Heli-skiing is available.
Intermediates The local slopes and Les
Diablerets offer a good variety and add
up to a fair amount of terrain. The
lengthy trip to Glacier 3000 for the
splendid red run down the Combe
d'Audon is worth it for the adventurous.
Beginners Beginners will enjoy the
village nursery slopes and riding the
train to Bretaye. There are gentle runs
here, too, but it's also very crowded.
Snowboarding There are quite a few
drag-lifts, including some on the link
with Les Diablerets.
Cross-country The trails up the valley
past La Rasse are long and pretty, and
there are more in the depression
beyond Bretaye (44km/27 miles in all).

Queues Queues appear for the lifts at
Bretaye mainly at weekends and peak
periods, and the buses and train can
get overcrowded.
Mountain restaurants They are often
oversubscribed, especially at Bretaye
and the Meilleret sector of Les
Diablerets. The Golf is expensive but
good, as is the Col-de-Soud ('best rösti
ever'); Lac des Chavonnes (open at
peak periods) is worth the walk.
Schools and guides The Villars ski
school – aka Ecole Moderne – and the
Swiss ski school get good reports. A
2006 visitor found the Swiss school
'brilliant. They taught us while keeping
the skiing fun. Even my picky seven-
year-old really took to the instructors.'
Riderschool is a snowboard specialist.
Facilities for children Both ski schools
run children's classes. There is also a
non-ski nursery for children up to six.

STAYING THERE

How to go Several tour operators offer
packages here. We have received
glowing reports on the Club Med. If
you fancy sleeping in a hi-tech tent out
in the wilds, go to www.whitepod.com.
Hotels The Golf (496 3838) is popular
('great, family tries hard'). The Eurotel
Victoria (495 3131) lacks style but is
near the gondola. The Bristol (496
3636) is not, but offers 'comfort, good
food and service'. All are 4-star.
Eating out Many restaurants are based
in hotels. Apart from these, the
Sporting is recommended for pizza and
the Vieux-Villars for local specialities.
Après-ski Charlie's, the Central, the
Sporting and the Mini-Pub are popular
bars. The Bowling bar can be a laugh;
and there's the El Gringo disco.
Off the slopes Paragliding and hang-
gliding are available, plus tennis,
skating, snow-shoeing, swimming,
'excellent' walks, and trips on the train
– to Lausanne for instance.

Wengen

A charming old village amid stunning scenery, where life revolves around the mountain railway; the slopes, somehow, are secondary

➕ Some of the most spectacular scenery in the Alps

➕ Tiny, traditional, nearly traffic-free Alpine village

➕ Lots of long, gentle runs, ideal for intermediates, leading down to Grindelwald

➕ Nursery slopes in heart of village

➕ Mountain railways suit non-skiers

➕ Calm, unhurried atmosphere

➖ Limited terrain for experts and adventurous intermediates

➖ Despite some snowmaking, snow conditions are unreliable on the sunny lower slopes

➖ Trains to slopes from here and from Grindelwald are slow – and there are quite a few drags and slow chairs

➖ Getting to Grindelwald's First area can take hours

➖ Subdued in the evening, with little variety of nightlife

Given the charm of the village, the friendliness of the locals and the drama of the scenery, it's easy to see why many people love Wengen – including large numbers of Brits who have been going for decades. But non-devotees should think carefully about the drawbacks before signing up.

Slow lifts is one of them. The mountain railway up to Kleine Scheidegg is the definitive slow lift; the trains are also crowded (don't expect a seat) and infrequent – you live by the timetable. These days, you do have a viable alternative: the Männlichen cable-car station, destroyed in the devastating avalanches of 1999, was rebuilt in the heart of the village – much more convenient, so much more popular, so prone to queues at peak times. But at least you don't need a timetable.

545

THE RESORT

Wengen is set on a shelf high above the Lauterbrunnen valley, opposite Mürren, and reached only by a cog railway, which carries on up the mountain as the main lift. Wengen was a farming community long before skiing arrived; it is still tiny, but it is dominated by sizeable hotels, mostly of Victorian origin. So it is not exactly pretty, but it is charming and relaxed, and almost traffic-free. The only traffic is electric hotel taxi-trucks, which gather at the station to pick up guests, and a few ordinary engine-driven taxis. (Why, we wonder?)

The short main street is the hub of the village. Lined with chalet-style shops and hotels, it also has the ice rink and village nursery slopes right next to it. The nursery slopes double

Grand scenery, and fairly grand hotels →

LIFT PASSES

Jungfrau Top Ski Region

Prices in SF

Age	1-day	6-day
under 16	28	144
16 to 19	45	230
20 to 61	56	288
over 62	50	259

Free under 6

Beginner points card

Notes
Covers Wengen, Mürren and Grindelwald, trains between them and Grindelwald ski-bus. Day pass price is for First-Kleine Scheidegg-Männlichen area only.

Alternative passes
Passes available for Grindelwald and Wengen only and for Mürren only. Non-skiers pass available.

as the venue for floodlit ski-jumping and parallel slalom races.

The views across the valley are stunning. They get even better higher up, when the famous trio of peaks comes fully into view – the Mönch (Monk) protecting the Jungfrau (Maiden) from the Eiger (Ogre).

The main way up the mountain is the regular, usually punctual trains from the southern end of the street to Kleine Scheidegg (about a half-hour journey), where the slopes of Wengen meet those of Grindelwald. The cable-car is a much quicker way to the Grindelwald slopes, and now starts conveniently close to the main street.

Wengen is small, so location isn't as crucial as in many other resorts. The main street is ideally placed for the station. There are hotels on the home piste, convenient for the slopes. Those who don't fancy a steepish morning climb should avoid places down the hill below the station.

You can get to Mürren by taking the train down to Lauterbrunnen, followed by a cable-car and connecting train to Winteregg (where you can get a chair-lift up and ski down to the village) or to Mürren itself and then walk though the village to the other lifts. Alternatively you can take an (infrequent) bus to Stechelberg followed by a cable-car up. The Jungfrau lift pass covers all of this. Outings further afield aren't really worth the effort.

THE MOUNTAINS

Although it is famous for the fearsome Lauberhorn Downhill course – the longest and one of the toughest on the World Cup circuit – Wengen's slopes are best suited to early intermediates. Most of the Downhill course is now open to the public. But the steepest section (the Hundschopf jump) can be avoided by an alternative red route. The majority of Wengen's runs are gentle blues and reds, ideal for cruising.

THE SLOPES
Picturesque playground
Most of the slopes are on the Grindelwald side of the mountain. From the railway station at Kleine Scheidegg you can head straight down to Grindelwald or work your way across the mountain with the help of a couple of lifts to the top of the Männlichen. This area is served by drag- and chair-lifts, and can be reached directly from Wengen by the cable-car. There are a few runs back down towards Wengen from the top of the Lauberhorn, but below Kleine Scheidegg there's really only one.

TERRAIN-PARKS
Not yet, but planned
The nearest parks are at First and Mürren, but these are a fair trek to get to. There are plans for a new park at the top of the Honegg lift (near Kleine Scheidegg), but not until 2007/08.

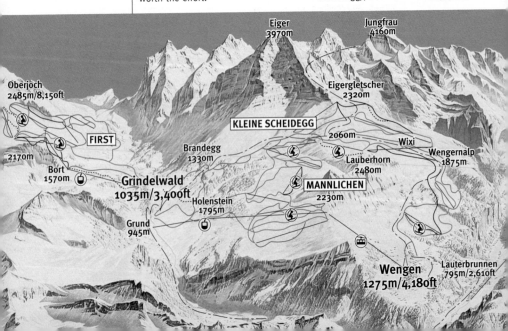

Resort	1275m
	4,180ft

Jungfrau region	
Slopes	945-2970m
	3,100-9,740ft
Lifts	41
Pistes	213km
	132 miles
Blue	25%
Red	61%
Black	14%
Snowmaking	60km
	37 miles

First-Männlichen-Kleine-Scheidegg only	
Slopes	945-2485m
	3,100-8,150ft
Lifts	30
Pistes	160km
	99 miles

SNOW RELIABILITY
How well do they use the guns?

Most slopes are below 2000m/6,560ft, and at Grindelwald they go down to less than 1000m/3,280ft. Very few slopes face north and the long blue run back to the village suffers from sun and lack of altitude. Failure to make use of snowmaking has been criticised in the past. But this year's reporters suggest a slight improvement in both snowmaking and piste preparation, with few complaints, although one visitor wrote of 'haphazard' grooming.

FOR EXPERTS
Few challenges

Wengen is quite limited for experts. The only genuine black runs in the area are parts of the Lauberhorn World Cup Downhill and a couple of pistes from Eigergletscher towards Wixi including Oh God (which used to be off-piste).

There are some decent off-piste runs such as White Hare from under the north face of the Eiger and more adventurous runs from the Jungfraujoch late in the season (see the Grindelwald chapter for more about going to the Jungfraujoch).

For more serious challenges it's well worth going to nearby Mürren, around an hour away. Heli-trips with mountain guides are organised if there are enough takers.

FOR INTERMEDIATES
Wonderful if the snow is good

Wengen and Grindelwald share superb intermediate slopes. Nearly all are long blue or gentle red runs – see Grindelwald chapter. The run back to Wengen is a relaxing end to the day, as long as it's not too crowded.

For tougher pistes, head for the top of the Lauberhorn lift and then the runs to Kleine Scheidegg, or to Wixi (following the start of the Downhill course). You could also try the north-facing run from Eigergletscher to Salzegg, which often has the best snow late in the season.

FOR BEGINNERS
Not ideal

There's a nursery slope in the centre of the village – it's convenient and gentle, but the snow is unreliable. There's a beginners' area at Wengernalp and another on the Grindelwald side of Kleine Scheidegg, but to get back to Wengen you either have to take the train or tackle the run down, which can be tricky, with several flat sections. There are plenty of good, long, gentle runs to progress to above Grindelwald.

FOR CROSS-COUNTRY
There is none

There's no cross-country in Wengen itself. There are 17.5km/11 miles of tracks down in the Lauterbrunnen valley, where the snow is unreliable.

QUEUES
Improving, but a long way to go

The Männlichen cable-car has helped cut the queues for the trains but both can still be crowded at peak periods. It is best to avoid travelling up at the same time as the ski school. Weekend invasions can increase the crowds on the Grindelwald side, especially on a Saturday, when children up to 15 can ski free if a parent buys a pass. There are plans to improve connections around Kleine Scheidegg with the upgrading of the Honegg drag to a six-pack for 2007/08. Queues up the mountain have been alleviated a lot in the last few years by the installation of fast chairs. The newish Innerwengen quad has made 'a big improvement' and this year's reporters experienced few problems. But there are still quite a few drags and slow chairs.

MOUNTAIN RESTAURANTS
Plenty of variety

A popular but pricey place for lunch is the Jungfrau hotel at Wengernalp, where the rösti is excellent and the views of the Jungfrau are superb. The highest restaurant is the popular Eigergletscher. If you get there early on a sunny day, you can grab a table on

Wengen

547

boarding

Wengen is not a bad place for gentle boarding – the nursery area is not ideal, but beginners have plenty of slopes to progress to, with lots of long blue and red runs served by the train and chair-lifts. Getting from Kleine Scheidegg to Männlichen means an unavoidable drag-lift though. And the slope back to Wengen is narrow and almost flat in places, so you may have to scoot. For the steepest slopes and best free-riding, experts will want to head for Mürren.

GETTING THERE

Air Zürich 195km/ 121 miles (3½hr); Bern 70km/43 miles (1½hr).

Rail Station in resort.

SCHOOLS

Swiss
t 855 2022

Privat
t 855 5005

Classes
(Swiss prices)
6 3hr days SF245

Private lessons
SF140 for 2hr

CHILDREN

Playhouse
t 855 1414
From 18mnth; 9pm-5pm; Sun-Fri

Sunshine
t 853 0440
Ages 1mnth upwards

Babysitters
List available from tourist office.

Ski school
The Swiss school takes ages 4 up (6 3hr days SF245)

---

the narrow outside balcony and enjoy magnificent views of the glacier, and 'lovely menu of the day – lamb, beans and potato', says a recent reporter. The station buffet at Kleine Scheidegg gets repeated rave reviews, so it's not surprising that it also gets packed – the take-away rösti and sausage are a popular option ('the best food we had on the mountain,' says a 2006 visitor). The Grindelwaldblick is a worthwhile trudge uphill from Kleine Scheidegg, with great food and views of the Eiger, and the Berggasthaus at the top of Männlichen is also recommended ('excellent soups and salads').

The Allmend, near the top of the Innerwengen chair and the train stop, is reportedly 'delightful', with 'friendly service' and wonderful views of the valley from the terrace. We've had conflicting reviews for Mary's Cafe situated at the end of the World Cup runs. One reporter says it is 'cosy and serves excellent food'; another found it had 'lost its character now it is owned by the Regina hotel'; a recent visitor found it 'very comfy, with open fires', but was disappointed by the food. For restaurants on the slopes towards Grindelwald, see that chapter.

In the village, the 'magnificent and relaxing' restaurant at the Hotel Caprice is recommended this year – they will even provide slippers so you don't have to wear your boots.

SCHOOLS AND GUIDES
Healthy competition

Reports on the Swiss school are generally good, and this year we've received a glowing report. A reporter's partner was 'full of praise for the consideration shown by the instructors' and 'beaming with delight and confidence' following her private lesson. The independent Privat school has also been recommended for private lessons. Guides are available for heli-trips and powder excursions.

FACILITIES FOR CHILDREN
Conveniently placed

It is an attractive and reassuring village for families. The nursery slope is in the centre and the Playhouse takes children from 18 months. A 2006 parent praised the children's classes – 'the best so far by a mile. My four year old really enjoyed all the different activities.'

The train gives easy access to higher slopes.

STAYING THERE

HOW TO GO
Wide range of hotels

Most accommodation is in hotels. There is only a handful of catered chalets (and no especially luxurious ones). Self-catering apartments are few, too.

Hotels There are about two dozen hotels, mostly 4-star and 3-star, with a handful of simpler places.

(((4 **Beausite Park** (856 5161) Reputedly the best in town. Good pool, steam and massage. But poorly situated at top of nursery slopes – a schlep up from the main street.

(((4 **Wengener Hof** (856 6969) No prizes for style or convenience, but recommended for peace, helpful staff and spacious, spotless rooms with good views.

(((4 **Sunstar** (856 5200) Family-friendly, modern hotel on main street right opposite the cable-car. Comfortable rooms which are gradually being refurbished; lounge has a log fire. Live music most evenings. Pool with views. Recommended by a couple of 2006 reporters ('superb', 'friendly', 'children's menu').

(((4 **Silberhorn** (856 5131) Comfortable, modern 4-star in central position opposite station, with a choice of restaurants, frequently praised by reporters.

(((4 **Caprice** (856 0606) Small, smartly furnished chalet-style hotel just above the railway. Sauna and steam room. 'Comfortable and friendly'; 'fabulous views, children's menu'. Kindergarten.

(((3 **Belvédère** (856 6868) Some way out, but we have good reports of buffet-style meals ('good for families'), spacious rooms and grand art nouveau public rooms. Endorsed by a 2006 reporter ('excellent value for money').

(((3 **Alpenrose** (855 3216) Long-standing British favourite; eight minutes' climb to the station, which rules it out for us. Small, simple rooms, but good views; 'first-class' food; friendly staff.

(((3 **Eiger** (856 0505) Very conveniently sited, right next to the station. Focal après-ski bar. Comfy modern rooms.

((2 **Falken** (856 5121) Further up the hill. Another British favourite, known affectionately as 'Fawlty Towers'.

Self-catering The hotel Bernerhof's decent Résidence apartments are well positioned just off the main street, and hotel facilities are available to guests.

ACTIVITIES

Indoor Swimming
pool (in Beausite Park
and Victoria
Lauberhorn hotels),
sauna, solarium,
whirlpool, massage
(in hotels), cinema
(with English films),
art gallery and
museum

Outdoor Ice rink,
curling, 50km/
31 miles of cleared
paths, tobogganing,
snow-shoeing, hang-
gliding, helicopter
flights

OUR WEBSITE

Go to our website at
wtss.co.uk for resort
news, links to resort
sites, a build-your-
own resort shortlist
system and reader
forums.

Phone numbers
From elsewhere in
Switzerland add the
prefix 033.
From abroad use the
prefix +41 33.

TOURIST OFFICE

t 855 1414
info@wengen.ch
www.wengen-
muerren.ch

EATING OUT
Lots of choice
Most restaurants are in hotels. They
offer good food and service. The Eiger
has a traditional restaurant and a
stube with Swiss and French cuisine.
The Bernerhof has good-value
traditional dishes. The little hotel
Hirschen has good steaks. There's no
shortage of fondues in the village and
several bars do casual food. Da Sina
does 'excellent steaks' and is
recommended by a couple of visitors
this year. Cafe Gruebi has been
recommended for 'the most wonderful
cakes'. The Jungfrau at Wengernalp has
an excellent restaurant – but you have
to get back on skis or on a toboggan.

APRES-SKI
It depends on what you want
People's reactions to the après-ski
scene in Wengen vary widely,
according to their expectations and
appetites.

If you're used to raving in Kitzbühel
or Les Deux-Alpes, you'll rate Wengen
dead, especially for young people. If
you've heard it's dead, you may be
pleasantly surprised to find that there
is a handful of bars that do good
business both early and late in the
evening. But it is only a handful of
small places. The bar at the Bumps
section of the home run is a popular
final run stop-off. A 2006 reporter
enjoyed the Start Bar on the
Lauberhorn – but it's a long ski down
afterwards. And the Pickle-Bar (Hotel
Eiger) and the tiny, 'always welcoming'
Eiger Bar are popular at the end of the
day. The traditional Tanne is a 'friendly
and relaxing' wine bar – but quite
pricey according to reporters – and the
funky Chili's, almost opposite, is lively.
Sina's, a little way out by Club Med,
usually has live music and karaoke.
The Caprice bar is also recommended,
as is the 'homely' Rock's. There are

discos and live music in some hotels.
The cinema often shows English-
language films.

OFF THE SLOPES
Good for a relaxing time
Wengen is a superb resort for those
who want a completely relaxing
holiday, with its unbeatable scenery
and pedestrian-friendly trains and
cable-car (there's a special, though
expensive, pass for pedestrians). It's
easy for mixed parties of skiers and
non-skiers to meet up for lunch on the
mountain, but rides on the lifts can be
time-consuming. There are some lovely
walks, ice skating and a curling club –
a popular activity with reporters.
Several hotels have health spas.
Excursions to Interlaken and Bern are
possible by train, as is the trip up to
the Jungfraujoch (see the Grindelwald
chapter). Helicopter flights from
Männlichen are recommended.

STAYING UP THE MOUNTAIN
Great views
You can stay at two points up the
mountain reached by the railway: the
expensive Jungfrau hotel (855 1622) at
Wengernalp – with fabulous views –
and at Kleine Scheidegg, where there
are rooms in the big Scheidegg Hotels
(855 1212) and dormitory space above
the Grindelwaldblick restaurant (855
1374) and the station buffet. The big
restaurant at Männlichen has rooms.

STAYING DOWN THE VALLEY
The budget option
Staying down in Lauterbrunnen will
halve your costs and give faster access
to Mürren, at the price of a much
longer journey time to Kleine
Scheidegg when you want to ski
Wengen or Grindelwald. The trains run
until 11.30pm and are included in your
lift pass. See Mürren chapter for hotel
recommendations.

THE BRITISH IN WENGEN

*There's a very strong British presence in Wengen. Many Brits have been returning
for years to the same rooms in the same hotels in the same week, and treat the
resort as a sort of second home. There is an English church with weekly services,
and a British-run ski club, the DHO (Downhill Only) – so named when the Brits
who colonised the resort persuaded the locals to keep the summer railway running
up the mountain in winter, so that they would no longer have to climb up in
order to ski down again. That greatly amused the locals, who until then had
regarded skiing in winter as a way to get around on snow rather than a pastime
to be done for fun. The DHO is still going strong and organises regular events
throughout the season.*

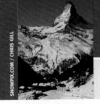

Zermatt

A magical combination of nearly everything you could want from a ski resort, both on and off the slopes

COSTS

① ② ③ ④ ⑤ ⑥

RATINGS

The slopes
Fast lifts	★★★★★
Snow	★★★★
Extent	★★★★
Expert	★★★★★
Intermediate	★★★★
Beginner	★
Convenience	★
Queues	★★★
Mountain restaurants	★★★★★

The rest
Scenery	★★★★★
Charm	★★★★★
Off-slope	★★★★

NEWS

At last, for 2006/07 a new eight-seater gondola will run from Furi up to Riffelberg, near where the fast chair departs. It will have a mid-station at Schweigmatten, just below Furi by the cross-country tracks. This will mean you no longer have to walk or ride through town to get from Klein Matterhorn to the other sectors of Zermatt's slopes. And you'll no longer have an uphill walk to Furi to get from the Gornergrat to the Klein Matterhorn sector.

For 2007/08, there are plans to build a chair-lift from Sunnegga to Findeln and Breitenboden (above Grunsee).

For 2005/06 the old Sunnegga-Blauherd gondola was replaced by a 'chondola' – a fast lift offering a choice of travelling in eight-seat cabins or on six-seat chairs.

- ✚ Wonderful, high and extensive slopes in three/four varied areas
- ✚ Spectacular high-mountain scenery, dominated by the Matterhorn
- ✚ Charming, if rather sprawling, old mountain village, largely traffic-free
- ✚ Reliable snow at altitude
- ✚ World's best mountain restaurants
- ✚ Extensive helicopter operation
- ✚ Nightlife to suit most tastes
- ✚ Smart shops
- ✚ Linked to Cervinia in Italy

- ▬ Main lifts may be a long walk, or a crowded bus- or taxi-ride from home
- ▬ Beginners should go elsewhere
- ▬ Europe's most expensive lift pass
- ▬ Some restaurants and hotels very expensive – so choose carefully
- ▬ Slow train up to Gornergrat annoys some people, but can be avoided
- ▬ Some lift queues at peak periods
- ▬ Annoying electric taxis detract from the car-free village ambience
- ▬ Walking can be treacherous on uncleared hard snow or ice

You must try Zermatt before you die. Few places can match its combination of excellent advanced and intermediate slopes, reliable snow, magnificent scenery, Alpine charm and mountain restaurants with superb food and stunning views.

Zermatt has its drawbacks – see the long list above (though one major grouse of the Klein Matterhorn sector not being properly connected to the other mountains will disappear for the 2006/07 season – see 'News'). For us, and for virtually all our reporters, these pale into insignificance compared to its attractions, which come close to matching perfectly our notion of the ideal winter resort. It's one of our favourites – and one of us regularly takes his holiday here.

THE RESORT

Zermatt started life as a traditional mountain village, developed as a mountaineering centre in the 19th century, then became a winter resort. Summer is as important as winter here.

The central part of the village is car-free. But the village doesn't have the relaxed, rustic feel of other car-free resorts, such as Wengen and Saas-Fee. Zermatt is big business, and it shows. The clientele is more overtly part of the jet set, and the electric taxis ferrying people around are more intrusive and aggressive. Most restaurants and hotels are owned by a handful of families. Many of the workers are brought in from outside the area – but that is probably one of the reasons for the increased friendliness and improved service in recent years.

The village sprawls along either side of a river, mountains rising steeply on each side. It is a mixture of chocolate-box chalets and modern buildings, most in traditional style. You arrive by rail or taxi from Täsch, where cars have to be left for a fee. They can be left for free at more distant Visp, from where you can also get a train. The main street runs away from the station, lined with luxury hotels, restaurants and shops.

The resort attracts an older age group than you get in rival resorts with comparable slopes, such as Val-d'Isère or St Anton and there's not as much of the youthful vitality you get there.

The cog railway to Gornergrat starts from near the main station. The Sunnegga underground funicular towards Rothorn is a few minutes' walk

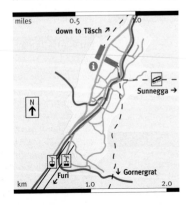

↑ Everywhere you go in Zermatt the views are fabulous. The pointed mountain top centre of this pic is the Klein Matterhorn, home to the highest cable-car station and piste in Europe

KEY FACTS

Resort	1620m
	5,310ft

Zermatt only

Slopes	1620-3820m
	5,310-12,530ft
Lifts	33
Pistes	183km
	114 miles
Blue	25%
Red	59%
Black	16%
Snowmaking	61km
	38 miles

Zermatt-Cervinia-Valtournenche combined

Slopes	1525-3820m
	5,000-12,530ft
Lifts	57
Pistes	313km
	194 miles
Blue	22%
Red	60%
Black	18%
Snowmaking	98km
	61 miles

away but the gondola to the Glacier and Schwarzsee areas (and the link to Cervinia) is at the opposite end of the long village. Walking from the station to the Glacier lifts can take 15 to 20 minutes. And be warned: walking anywhere (especially in ski boots) can be unpleasant because of treacherous icy paths and electric taxis and solar-powered buses darting around. The free buses get very crowded (especially at the end of the day bringing people back from the Glacier area). You can take an electric taxi instead (and keep costs down by sharing).

When the new gondola from Furi to Riffelberg opens, staying near the gondola to Furi will be convenient for the slopes. But being near the Gornergrat and Sunnegga railways, near the station end of the main street is more convenient for most shops, bars and restaurants (as well as the other two ways up to the slopes). Some accommodation is up the steep hill across the river in Winkelmatten – you can ski back to it from all areas and it has its own reliable bus service.

Getting up to the village from Täsch is no problem. There's a smart new station and underground car-park (SF11 a day) there and you can wheel luggage trolleys straight from the car-park onto and off the trains. You are met at the other end by electric and horse-drawn taxis and hotel shuttles.

THE MOUNTAINS

551

Practically all of the slopes are open, above the trees – the runs served by the Sunnegga funicular are the main exception.

A single piste map now covers both Cervinia's and Zermatt's slopes fairly clearly, ending past confusion over different names for the same point on the border. In Cervinia, they give you a handy quick-folding version. But the Zermatt version is bigger, cumbersome, and, strangely, fails to name the lifts despite them all having letters next to them; bizarre.

Some runs in all sectors and all the runs on Stockhorn are now 'ski runs' rather than normal pistes. On the resort piste map this classification is defined as 'protected' (from avalanches, we presume) 'and marked, but not prepared and not checked at the end of the day'. If it's correct that these runs are not checked, you should of course never descend them alone.

On our recent visits we have been impressed by service improvements: the lift staff are polite and helpful, there are useful announcements in several languages (including English) on the train and some cable-cars and there are free tissues at most lift stations (just as in America).

SWITZERLAND

552

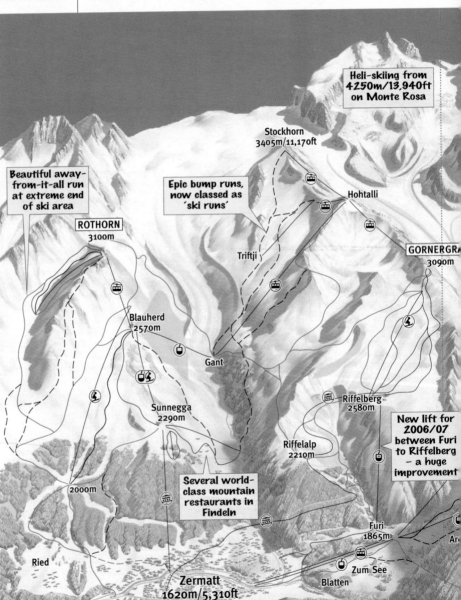

Heli-skiing from 4250m/13,940ft on Monte Rosa

Stockhorn
3405m/11,170ft

Hohtalli

Beautiful away-from-it-all run at extreme end of ski area

Epic bump runs, now classed as 'ski runs'

ROTHORN
3100m

Triftji

GORNERGR
3090m

Blauherd
2570m

Gant

Sunnegga
2290m

Riffelberg
2580m

New lift for 2006/07 between Furi to Riffelberg – a huge improvement

Riffelalp
2210m

2000m

Several world-class mountain restaurants in Findeln

Furi
1865m

Ar

Ried

Zum See

Zermatt
1620m/5,310ft

Blatten

Zmutt

boarding

Boarders in soft boots have one big advantage over skiers in Zermatt – they have much more comfortable walks to and from the lift stations! Even so, there aren't many snowboarders around. The slopes are best for experienced free-riders, because tough piste and off-piste action is what Zermatt is really about; plus there's the world-class terrain-park above Trockener Steg on the glacier. There is, however, an excellent little beginner area at Blauherd, complete with moving carpet lift, which we've seen many beginner snowboarders having lessons on. The main lifts are boarder-friendly: train, funicular, gondolas and cable-cars, and there aren't too many flat bits. But there are still a few T-bars. Stoked is a specialist school.

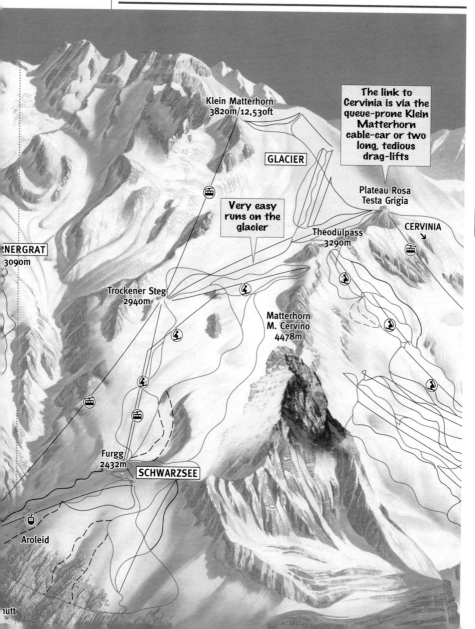

Klein Matterhorn
3820m/12,530ft

The link to
Cervinia is via the
queue-prone Klein
Matterhorn
cable-car or two
long, tedious
drag-lifts

GLACIER

Plateau Rosa
Testa Grigia

Very easy
runs on the
glacier

Theodulpass
3290m

CERVINIA

NERGRAT
3090m

Trockener Steg
2940m

Matterhorn
M. Cervino
4478m

Furgg
2432m

SCHWARZSEE

Aroleid

Zermatt

553

ıutt

LIFT PASSES

Zermatt

Prices in SF

Age	1-day	6-day
under 16	26	166
16 to 19	44	282
20 to 64	52	332
over 65	44	282

Free under 9

Beginner no deals

Notes
Covers all lifts on the Swiss side of the border. A 6-day pass covers a day in Saas-Fee. Half-day passes and single-ascent tickets on some lifts also available.

Alternative passes
International pass covers all lifts on the Swiss side plus Cervinia; Peak Pass available for pedestrians.

THE SLOPES
Beautiful and varied

Zermatt's piste map divides the slopes into several sectors and markets some of them as 'paradises' – which we think bizarre. So we are dropping the paradises and dividing the slopes into four main sectors.

The **Rothorn** sector (incorporating the lift company's Sunnegga sector) is reached by an underground funicular starting by the river, not far from the centre (the tunnel you walk through to reach it was badly in need of renovation on our 2006 visit). A new 'chondola' (chair/gondola hybrid) now goes on up from the top to Blauherd, where a cable-car goes up to Rothorn itself.

From the top of this area you can make your way – via south-facing slopes served by snowmaking – to Gant in the valley between Sunnegga and the second main area, **Gornergrat**. A 125-person cable-car links Gant to Hohtälli, on the ridge above Gornergrat. A gondola makes the link back from Gant to Sunnegga. Gornergrat can be reached directly from Zermatt by cog railway trains which leave every 24 minutes and take 30 or 40 minutes to get to the top – arrive at the station early to get a seat on the right-hand side and enjoy the fabulous views. It can be a long journey if you have to stand.

From Gornergrat there's a piste to Schweigmatten, just below Furi, where the new gondola (see News) will take you up to Furi or back up to Riffelberg on the Gornergrat sector. From Furi, a cable-car up to Trockener Steg and then the spectacular Klein Matterhorn cable-car take you to the top of the third and highest sector – now known as the **Glacier** area. The Glacier area gives access to Cervinia – make sure you have an appropriate pass.

From Furgg, towards the bottom of the Glacier area, a stop-start gondola goes up to the top of the small but worthwhile **Schwarzsee** area (also reached by gondola from Furi).

There are pistes back to the village from all four areas – though some of them can be closed or tricky due to poor snow conditions. They can be hazardous at the end of the day due to crowds and speeding skiers – particularly the black from Furgg.

TERRAIN-PARKS
One of Switzerland's best

Gravity Park on the Glacier area is one of Switzerland's best winter and summer parks. There are usually two pipes, one of which is a super-pipe, that sit next to an array of kickers, rails, a quarter-pipe and wall-ride. The park is set up nicely so that you can choose either a kicker or rail line, and practise several hits in a row. A mini rail area at the top of the park is a perfect initiation to sliding on metal.

SNOW RELIABILITY
Good high up, poor lower down

Zermatt has rocky terrain and a relatively dry climate. But it also has some of the highest slopes in Europe, and quite a lot of snowmaking.

Three of the four sectors go up to over 3000m/9,840ft, and the Glacier area has summer skiing. There are loads of runs above 2500m/8,200ft, many of which are north-facing, so guaranteeing decent snow except in freak years.

Snowmaking machines serve some of the pistes on all four areas, from about 3000m/9,840ft to under 2000m/6,560ft. Coverage was increased for 2005/06, including on a key south-facing run from Rothorn to Gant. Piste grooming is excellent.

FOR EXPERTS
Good – with superb heli-trips

If you love long mogul pitches the 'ski runs' (see second page of this chapter) at Triftji, below Stockhorn, are the stuff of dreams. From the top of the Stockhorn cable-car there's a run down to the T-bar that serves a wide, long face that can be one vast mogul field – steep, but not extremely so. Being north-facing and lying between 3400m and 2700m (11,150ft and 8,860ft), the snow keeps in good condition long after a new snowfall. But be warned: this whole area does not open until February. There's another great 'ski run' down from Hohtälli to Gant.

There are two wonderful 'ski runs' from Rothorn, with spectacular views of both the village and the Matterhorn. But they need good snow-cover to be really enjoyable. At Schwarzsee there are several steep north-facing gullies through the woods.

There are marvellous off-piste possibilities from the top lifts in each sector, but they aren't immediately obvious to those without local knowledge. They are also dangerous because of rocky and glacial terrain. You can join daily ski-touring groups, but there aren't straightforward off-piste groups as there are in resorts such as Val-d'Isère and Méribel; you have to hire a guide privately for a full day, so to make it economic you need to form your own group. The Ski Club of Great Britain usually hires a guide for off-piste skiing once a week – a recent reporter had 'an awesome day of powder' with them.

Zermatt is the Alps' biggest heli-trip centre; the helipad resembles a bus station at times, with choppers taking off every few minutes. There are only two or three main drop-off points, so you are likely to encounter other groups on the mountain. The classic run is from over 4000m/13,100ft on Monte Rosa and descends over 2000m/6,560ft vertical through wonderful glacier scenery to Furi; for most of its length it is not steep but getting off the end of the glacier can be tricky and involves walking along narrow rocky paths above long drops or side-stepping down steep slopes, depending on the amount of snow around that season.

FOR INTERMEDIATES
Mile after mile of beautiful runs

Zermatt is ideal for adventurous intermediates. Many of the blue and red runs tend to be at the difficult end of their grading. There are very beautiful reds down lift-free valleys from both Gornergrat (Kelle) and Hohtälli (White Hare) to Gant – we love these first thing in the morning, before anyone else is on them. A variant to Riffelalp (Balmbrunnen) ends up on a narrow wooded path with a sheer cliff and magnificent views to the right.

On Rothorn, the 5km/3 mile Kumme run, from Rothorn itself to the bottom of the Patrullarve chair, also gets away from the lift system and has an interesting mix of straight-running and mogul pitches. The reds and black served by the Hörnli drag at Schwarzsee are excellent. In the Glacier sector the reds served by the fast quad chair from Furgg are long, testing and gloriously set at the foot of the Matterhorn. The Furggsattel chair from Trockener Steg serves more pistes with stunning views, notably the 1100m/3,610ft-vertical Matterhorn piste – a red that is of no more than blue gradient for much of its considerable

is at Blauherd – but even this can get very busy. And there are no long easy runs to progress to except above Trockener Steg, which can be bitterly cold and windy.

FOR EVERYONE
Spectacular cable-car and ice cave
The Klein Matterhorn cable-car is an experience not to miss if the weather is good. There are stupendous views from the left side down to the glacier and its crevasses, as the car swings steeply into its hole blasted out of the mountain at the top. When you arrive, you walk through a long tunnel, to emerge on top of the world for the highest piste in Europe – walk slowly, the air is thin here and some people have altitude problems. The ice grotto cut into the glacier here is well worth a visit, with 'incredible ice carvings'.

FOR CROSS-COUNTRY
Fairly limited
There's a 4km/2.5 mile loop at Furi, 3km/2 miles of trails near the bottom of the gondola to the Glacier area and another 12 to 15km/7 to 9 miles down at Täsch (don't count on good snow). There are also 'ski walking trails', best tackled as part of an organised group.

QUEUES
Main problems being solved
Zermatt has improved its lift system hugely in recent years, eliminating major bottlenecks. But a few problems remain. Both the lifts out of Gant are prone to queues at times; we waited over 30 minutes for the cable-car in mid-morning last March. The high-speed quad from Furgg can get busy now that the Schwarzsee gondola is dumping people nearby. The Klein Matterhorn cable-car has queues much of the time. You may find there's only standing room on the Gornergrat train, which can be tiring and uncomfortable: 'Better to wait for the next one,' says a reporter. One thing we love about Zermatt is getting the 8am train with the lifties and restaurant staff. It arrives at the top just as they are dropping the rope to open the pistes, and you have the slopes to yourself for an hour or two. We have a complaint about people going in or out of the lower-level funicular entrance at Sunnegga getting mixed up in the queue of people waiting to get on the new chondola at peak periods.
The village buses, not surprisingly,

length (it must be graded red because of a short much steeper pitch near the end, which has a lot of less confident intermediates struggling).

For such less adventurous intermediates, the best runs are the blues from Blauherd on Rothorn and above Riffelberg on Gornergrat, and the runs between Klein Matterhorn and Trockener Steg. Of these, the Riffelberg area often has the best combination of good snow and easy cruising, and is popular with the school. Blauherd gets afternoon sun, but the snowmaking means that the problem is more often a foot or more of heavy snow near the bottom than bare patches.

In the Glacier sector most of the runs, though marked red on the piste map, are very flat and represent the easiest slopes Zermatt has to offer, as well as the best snow. The problem here is the possibility of bad weather because of the height – high winds, extreme cold and poor visibility can make life very unpleasant (and if you are skiing into a head-wind downhill progress can be very slow).

Even an early intermediate can make the trip to Cervinia, crossing at Theodulpass rather than taking the more challenging Ventina run from Testa Grigia/Plateau Rosa.

Beware the run from Furgg to Furi at the end of the day, when it can be chopped up, mogulled in places and very crowded (the only reason it is graded black that we can see, because it isn't very steep). A much more relaxed way is the beautifully scenic Weiss Perle run from Schwarzsee (the Stafelalp variant is even more scenic but has a short uphill section). Or you can ride the gondola from Schwarzsee.

FOR BEGINNERS
Learn elsewhere
Zermatt is to be avoided by beginners. The best snow-sure nursery slope area

SCHOOLS
Swiss
t 966 2466

Stoked
t 967 7020

Summit
t 967 0001

European Snowsport
t 967 6787

Classes (Swiss prices)
5 days (10am to 3.30 with lunch break)
SF295

Private lessons
SF160 for 2hr for 1 or 2 people

CHILDREN

Kinderparadies
t 967 7252
Ages from 3mnth

Hotel Nicoletta
t 966 0777
Ages 2 to 8

Kinderclub Pumuckel (Hotel Ginabelle)
t 966 5000
Ages from 30mnth

Kinderhort (Stoked)
t 967 7020
Ages from 3; 9am-3.30

Private babysitters
Tourist office has list.

Ski school
Both schools take children from age 6; 5 full days incl. lunch SF340 (Swiss prices). Snowli Village for ages 4 to 5: SF385 for 5 days.

cannot handle demand at the end of the day at the foot of the slopes from the Glacier area ('The chaos resulted in a fight over a taxi,' says a reporter).

SCHOOLS AND GUIDES
Competition paying off
The main Swiss school has a history of critical reports from readers but has allegedly improved recently.

There's a 'brilliant' separate Stoked snowboard school, of which we generally have good reports. This has combined with The SkiSchool and is made up of talented young instructors, some of whom are British and all of whom speak good English. One reader says they had 'a complete beginner confident on reds after three lessons', but another in 2005 was disappointed by the initial 'lack of instruction' in the group classes. Group sizes are said to be small. There are now two other schools staffed mainly by Brits – Summit and European Snowsport – though we lack reports on either.

FACILITIES FOR CHILDREN
Good hotel nurseries
The Nicoletta and Ginabelle hotels have nurseries. The Kinderparadies, 200m/66oft from the station, takes children from three months – 'the Swiss kids in the resort go there so it must be good', says a 2006 reporter. Stoked/The SkiSchool runs Snowflakes, for children aged at least four years old, at Trockener Steg and a kindergarten for kids from three years at Schwarzsee. There's a snow-garden at Riffelberg.

STAYING THERE

HOW TO GO
A wide choice, packaged or not
Chalets Several operators have places here; many of the most comfortable are in apartment blocks. Reporters have praised Total Ski's operation here. VIP has two luxury chalets here for the first time in 2006/07.
Hotels There are over 100 hotels, mostly comfortable and traditional-

---

THE WORLD'S BEST MOUNTAIN RESTAURANTS

Even reporters who don't normally stop long for lunch usually succumb to temptation here. The choice of restaurants is enormous, the food usually excellent (but it helps not to be vegetarian), the small hut-based places very atmospheric (some with spectacular views), the table-service friendly (if over-worked). It is impossible to list here all those worth a visit – so don't limit yourself to those we mention. It is best to book; check prices are within your budget when you do!

Down at Findeln below Sunnegga are several attractive, busy, pricey, rustic restaurants. After two visits last winter our current favourite – and that of many reporters – is Chez Vrony (we had wonderful carpaccio, calves liver, service and views from the first floor terrace; not cheap but well worth it). We've also enjoyed excellent lamb at Findlerhof (aka Franz & Heidy's). Reporters also praise Paradies ('good views, great rösti'), Adler ('prompt food and friendly service') and Enzian ('less busy than others').

The simple hut at Tuftern has great views from the terrace, sells good Heida wine from the highest vineyard in Europe and does a basic menu of home-made soup, cheese and cold sausage and 'wonderful apple spice cake'; you can also watch deer feeding here at the end of the afternoon. Othmar's Skihutte, below the Patrullarve chair, has a 'good and large selection of fish and seafood'.

The restaurants at Fluhalp (which often has live music on the terrace) and Grünsee have beautiful, isolated situations, and the large terraces at Sunnegga and Rothorn have great views. All these are part of the Matterhorn Group and do decent food.

The Kulmhotel, at 3100m/10,170ft at Gornergrat, has both self-service and table-service restaurants, with amazing views of lift-free mountains and glaciers. Readers also rate the Riffelberg at Gornergrat ('great quality for a very reasonable price') and Moos on the home run from Riffelberg.

At Furi, the Restaurant Furri (excellent rösti and scrumptious tarts) has a large sun terraces and cosy interior. The hotel at Schwarzsee is right at the foot of the Matterhorn, with staggering views and endless variations of rösti. Down the hill from here Stafelalp is simple, but it is charmingly situated. Up above Trockener Steg, Gandegghütte has stunning views of the glacier. On the way back to the village below Furi, Zum See is a charming old hut with a reputation of being Zermatt's best – we've eaten well there in the past but two 2006 reporters were disappointed with both the food and slow service; it is certainly usually packed with people still eating lunch at 4.30pm. Blatten is 'excellent' too.

Wherever you go, don't miss the local alcoholic coffee – in its many varieties.

GETTING THERE

Air Geneva
244km/152 miles
(4hr by rail); Zürich
248km/154 miles
(5hr by rail); Sion
80km/50 miles
(1½hr).

Rail Station in resort.

ACTIVITIES

Indoor Sauna, tennis,
squash, hotel
swimming pools
(some open to
public), salt water
pool, fitness centre,
indoor golf, climbing
wall, casino, billiards,
bowling, gallery,
library, concerts,
Alpine museum,
cinema

Outdoor Ice rinks,
curling, sleigh rides,
30km/19 miles
cleared paths, snow-
shoeing, helicopter
flights, paragliding,
climbing, bungee
trampolining, ice-
climbing

style 3-stars and 4-stars, but taking in the whole range.

《《《⑤ **Mont Cervin** (966 8888) Biggest in town. Elegantly traditional. Good pool and new wellness centre.

《《《⑤ **Zermatterhof** (966 6600) Traditional 'grand hotel' style with piano bar and pool.

《《《⑤ **Riffelalp Resort** (966 0555) Up the mountain, recent smart extension, pool, spa, own evening trains. A 2006 reporter says, 'Impeccable service, fabulous breakfasts, stunning location.'

《《《④ **Alex** (966 7070) Close to station. Reporters love it ('wonderful', 'amazing hospitality'). Pool. Dancing.

《《《④ **Ambassador** (966 2611) Peaceful position near Gornergrat station. Large pool; sauna. Mixed reports on the food.

《《《④ **Monte Rosa** (966 0333) Well-modernised original Zermatt hotel, near southern end of village – full of climbing pictures and mementos.

《《《④ **Ginabelle** (966 5000) Smart pair of chalets not far from Sunnegga lift; has own ski nursery as well as day care.

《《《④ **Nicoletta** (966 0777) Modern chalet quite close to centre, with nursery.

《《《④ **Sonne** (966 2066) Traditionally decorated, in quiet setting; 'superb Roman Bath complex'.

《《《④ **Beau-Site Parkhotel** (966 6868) Highly recommended by a recent reporter. 'Faultless service with nouvelle meals of four to five courses.'

《《③ **Julen** (966 7600) Charming, modern-rustic chalet over the river, with Matterhorn views from some rooms.

《《③ **Butterfly** (966 4166) 'Small, friendly, as well furnished as the Alex, but much better food,' says a reporter.

《《③ **Atlanta** (966 3535) No frills, but 'friendly service'; close to centre, with Matterhorn views from some rooms.

《② **Alpina** (967 1050) Modest but very friendly, and close to centre.

《② **Bahnhof** (967 2406) Right by Gornergrat station. Cheapest place to stay in town (SF95 a night for twin room with shower, SF30 a night for a dormitory bed; with communal kitchen). Other recommendations include the Dufour (966 2400) – 'only a 2-star but deserves much more, wonderful roomy bedrooms with the best view in the world'; Mirabeau (966 2660) – 'sophisticated and friendly', new wellness centre; Derby (966 3999) – 'good value'; Biner (966 5666) – 'organic food'; Mischabel (967 1131) – 'cheap for Zermatt'; Metropol (966 3566) – 'excellent, good dining'; Christiania (966 8000) – 'good value';

Perren (966 5200) – 'excellent'; and the Alpen Resort (966 3000) – 'first-class facility, a winner'.

Self-catering There is a lot of apartment accommodation, but not much finds its way to the UK package market. We have enjoyed staying in the hotel Ambassador apartments, with free use of all its facilities such as a pool and a sauna, and Apartment Scott available through Ski Solutions. The Vanessa complex was recommended by a reporter. The tourist office web site has apartments.

EATING OUT
Huge choice at all price levels

There are over 100 restaurants to choose from: top-quality haute cuisine, through traditional Swiss food, Chinese, Japanese and Thai to egg and chips. There is even a McDonald's.

In 2006 we enjoyed a couple of dinners at the Pipe (tiny with interesting dishes with Asian/West Indian influence). Mood's (see Après-ski) does 'outstanding' fish. The Schäferstube (Hotel Julen) is the place for a gourmet meal according to a reporter, who enjoyed 'heavenly lamb' there. The Mazot is highly rated and highly priced. At the other end of the scale, Du Pont has good-value pasta and rösti; Grampi's, Broken, Roma and Postli do good pizzas. The Schwyzer Stübli has local specialities and live Swiss music and dancing.

Rua Thai in the basement of the hotel Abana Real has been recommended for 'excellent Thai in attractive surroundings'. Fuji in the same building is a good Japanese.

Chez Heini serves excellent lamb and the owner sings after dinner. Giuseppe's doesn't look much, but has the best Italian food in town. The Zur Alten Muhle does 'excellent steaks and venison'. Da Mario, Casa Rustica, the Swiss Chalet, the Derby, the Avenstube ('good trout'), the Old Spaghetti Factory (in the hotel Post complex), the Stockhorn Grill ('excellent local lamb'), Tony's Grotta ('expensive but excellent Italian'), the Walliserkanne ('fine pizza'), and the Walliserhof ('good value set menu') have all been recommended by readers.

APRES-SKI
Lively and varied

There's a good mix of sophisticated and informal fun, though it helps if you have deep pockets. On the way back

↑ The Matterhorn,
with the Gornergrat
train leaving
Riffelberg station on
its way down to
Zermatt

SNOWPIX.COM / CHRIS GILL

OUR WEBSITE

Go to our website at
wtss.co.uk for resort
news, links to resort
sites, a build-your-
own resort shortlist
system and reader
forums.

Phone numbers
From elsewhere in
Switzerland add the
prefix 027.
From abroad use the
prefix +41 27.

TOURIST OFFICE

t 966 8100
zermatt@wallis.ch
www.zermatt.ch

to a lively disco (Broken) and live music (Pink) and a selection of restaurants.

At Grampi's 'watch out for the Elton John impersonator – very entertaining', says a 2006 reporter. Z'Alt Hischi (in an old house, serves huge measures of spirits) and the Little Bar (crowded if there are ten people in) are good for a quiet drink. The Hexen Bar is cosy too. The hotel Alex draws a mature clientele for eating, drinking and dancing. The Hotel Pollux has 'lively music in its bar' and 'a general party ambience'.

OFF THE SLOPES
Considerable attractions
Zermatt is an attractive place to spend time. As well as pricey jewellery and clothes shops, there are interesting places selling food, wine, books and art. It is easy (but expensive) for pedestrians to get around on the lifts (purchase the Peaks Pass) and meet others for lunch, and there are some nice walks – a special map is available. The Ice Grotto at Klein Matterhorn and the Alpine museum in town are worth seeing (both regularly recommended by reporters). You can take a helicopter trip around the Matterhorn. There is a cinema, and a reader tells us the free village guided tour is 'well worth doing'. For an icy experience, visit (or stay at) the Igloo up on Gornergrat.

STAYING UP THE MOUNTAIN
Comfortable seclusion
There are several hotels at altitude, of which the pick is the Riffelalp Resort at the first stop on the Gornergrat railway (see 'Hotels', above) – but the evening train service is a bit limited. At the top of the railway, at 3100m/10,170ft, is the Kulmhotel Gornergrat (966 6400) – an austere building but recently renovated.

STAYING DOWN THE VALLEY
Attractive for drivers
In Täsch, where visitors must leave their cars, there are six 3-star hotels costing less than half the price of the equivalent in Zermatt. The Täscherhof (966 6262) – 'fine, comfortable and with a reasonably priced restaurant' – and the Walliserhof (966 3966) – 'a very good option' – were recommended by 2006 reporters. Täsch is very quiet at night; it's just a 13-minute ride from Zermatt, with trains every 20 minutes for most of the day; the last train down is 11.20pm. Taxis can operate up to the edge of Zermatt.

from the Glacier or Schwarzsee sectors there are lots of restaurants below Furi for a last drink and sunbathe. Hennu Stall blasts out loud music in a very un-Zermatt-like fashion but attracts huge crowds. We preferred the delicious red wine and fruit tarts at Zum See. On the way back from Rothorn, Othmar's Hütte has great views and organises dinners followed by tobogganing down, and the Olympia Stübli often has live music. Near the church at Winkelmatten, the Sonnenblick is 'a great place to watch the sun set'.

Promenading the main street checking out expensive shoes and watches is a popular early-evening activity. The Papperla Pub is one of the few popular early places (it's crowded after dinner, too, and has a nightclub downstairs). Elsie's bar is wood-panelled, atmospheric and gets packed with an older crowd both early and late. The North Wall is frequented by seasonal workers.

The Vernissage is our favourite bar in town for a quiet evening drink. It is an unusual and stylish modern place, with the projection room for the cinema built into the upstairs bar and displays of art elsewhere. Mood's was designed by the same guy and has a good cocktail bar downstairs, wood-panelled restaurant above and a comfortable bar done out in nautical fashion at the top.

Later on, the hotel Post complex has something for everyone, from a quiet, comfortable bar (Papa Caesar's)

SNOWPIX.COM / CHRIS GILL

Les Diablerets

An unspoiled, traditional and sunny but spread-out village that for many makes a more sensible base than Villars, to which it is linked: from here you have a choice of two sectors of slopes, and fast access to the local glacier.

KEY FACTS

Resort	1150m
	3,770ft
Slopes	1115-3000m
	3,660-9,840ft
Lifts	46
Pistes	125km
	78 miles
Blue	39%
Red	60%
Black	1%
Snowmaking	some

TOURIST OFFICE

t 0492 3358
info@diablerets.ch
www.diablerets.ch

THE RESORT

Les Diablerets tends to be rather overshadowed by its better-known neighbours, Gstaad and Villars – but is in many ways a more attractive base than either. The chalets of the village spread widely across its broad valley, but it does have something of a central focus around the simple old Auberge de la Poste. It is quiet but not lifeless in the evening. There's a 7km/4 mile evening toboggan run down from the Mazots restaurant (head torches supplied). There are also ice rinks for skating and curling.

THE MOUNTAINS

Two fast quads in sequence take you to the top of the wooded Meilleret sector, and the link to Villars. A gondola in the centre of town takes you in the opposite direction to sunny Isenau, with higher open slopes at the top. From Isenau there's a red run down to Col du Pillon and the cable-car to and from the Diablerets glacier – or Glacier 3000. You can also reach the glacier cable-cars by bus from town. On Glacier 3000, you'll find short blue runs at over 3000m/9,840ft, stunning views and a terrain-park – 'It's one of the best I've seen,' says a reader. The ideal way down is the long red Combe d'Audon – a wonderful run away from all the lifts, descending over 1000m/ 3,300ft to Oldenalp. The slopes of the lower, local sectors are unremarkable, but pleasant intermediate stuff. The link with Villars, involving a slow two-way chair, is well worthwhile for red-run skiers. Snow reliability away from the glacier is not great – especially on sunny Isenau. There are cross-country loops along the valley.

Engelberg

Engelberg is an easy 2.5 hour train ride from Zürich airport (even less by car), which makes it great for short breaks. It has one of the biggest verticals in the Alps, awesome off-piste and some good intermediate slopes.

ENGELBERG TOURIST OFFICE

KEY FACTS

Resort	1050m
	3,440ft
Slopes	1050-3020m
	3,440-9,910ft
Lifts	24
Pistes	82km
	51 miles
Blue	30%
Red	67%
Black	3%
Snowmaking	some

TOURIST OFFICE

t 041 639 7777
welcome@engelberg.ch
www.engelberg.ch

THE RESORT

Engelberg was popular with Brits in the early 20th century but its grand Victorian hotels have a faded look and have been joined by chalet-style buildings and concrete blocks. It is more of a town than a village. The 12th-century monastery and its cheese-making shop are worth a visit. It's a bus-ride or long walk to the lifts from most hotels. The Europe (041 639 7575) is central, the Terrace (041 639 6666) is served by a funicular and run on club-hotel lines. The Yucatan is the main après-ski bar.

THE MOUNTAINS

The main slopes rise almost 2000m/ 6,560ft above the town by three successive lifts: a gondola and two cable-cars, the top one rising above glacial crevasses and rotating 360° on the way. Weekend queues can be long.

Pistes are limited and fragmented by the glaciers and rugged terrain, and they suit strong intermediates best: most runs are steep reds and there are few easy cruises. Beware of the seriously steep and usually mogulled black between Titlis and Stand. There's a good isolated beginner area near the mid-station of the gondola.

There is superb off-piste for experts who hire a guide. The classic Laub run is 1000m/3,280ft vertical down an immensely wide face with a consistent pitch and magnificent views of town. But we enjoyed even more the 2000m/ 6,560ft vertical Galtiberg run, which starts over glaciers and ends among mountain streams and trees: we saw only three other people on it. There's plenty more off-piste, too. The Ritz (at the bottom of the Laub) and Jochpass mountain restaurants are rustic.

Gstaad

Despite its exclusive reputation, Gstaad is an attractive, traditional village where anyone could have a relaxing holiday. But the slopes are very fragmented, and not snow-sure – most are below 2100m/6,890ft.

KEY FACTS

Resort	1050m
	3,440ft
Slopes	950-3000m
	3,120-9,840ft
Lifts	62
Pistes	250km
	155 miles
Blue	48%
Red	36%
Black	16%
Snowmaking	some

online booking
www.sport2000rent.com

TOURIST OFFICE
t 033 748 8181
gst@gstaad.ch
www.gstaad.ch

THE RESORT

Gstaad is a year-round resort in a spacious, sunny setting amid friendly, wooded mountains, its traffic-free main street lined by chalet-style hotels, smart shops and cafes. Most of the accommodation is in private chalets and apartments, the rest in 3-star hotels and above – including the landmark 5-star Palace. Restaurants are mainly hotel-based, and expensive. In season après-ski is lively. Off-slope activities are good – the tennis centre and pool complex are impressive.

THE MOUNTAINS

There are four main areas of slopes, covered by a single, confusing map. Most slopes are below the tree line.

Three sectors are accessed via lifts scattered around the fringes of Gstaad and served by a shuttle-bus. The largest sector is above Saanenmöser and Schönried, reached by train. Movement around this sector will be improved this year by a new chair-lift linking the slopes above Zweisimmen and St Stephan at altitude.

Snow-cover can be unreliable except on the Glacier des Diablerets – covered by the pass, but 15km/9 miles away.

Few runs challenge experts. Black runs rarely exceed red or even blue difficulty. There is off-piste potential – some steep. Given good snow, this is a superb area for intermediates, with long, easy descents in the major area to the villages scattered around its edges. The nursery slopes at Wispile are adequate, and there are plenty of runs to progress to. Time lost on buses or trains is more of a problem than queues. Mountain restaurants are plentiful, and most are attractive.

Short turns

561

Lenzerheide

Lenzerheide is the senior partner with Valbella in an extensive area of intermediate slopes in a pretty setting around a lake, all at a decent altitude – worth considering, although the villages are not chocolate-box pretty.

KEY FACTS

Resort	1470m
	4,820ft
Slopes	1230-2865m
	4,040-9400ft
Lifts	28
Pistes	155km
	96 miles
Blue	35%
Red	45%
Black	20%
Snowmaking	25%

best for rent
www.sport2000rent.com

TOURIST OFFICE
t 081 385 1120
info@lenzerheide.ch
www.lenzerheide.ch

THE RESORTS

Lenzerheide is a sprawling village – a pleasant enough place once you get away from the minor through-road that is at its centre. The road runs past a prettily wooded lake to Valbella, a more amorphous collection of holiday accommodation on the sunny slopes north of the lake, and over a low pass to the smaller village of Parpan. There are plenty of comfortable hotels, and a wonderful luxury rustic retreat in the Guarda Val. An influx of weekend visitors enlivens the après-ski scene.

THE MOUNTAINS

The slopes are on the two sides of the valley, facing due east and west. Links across the valley are by bus, but within each sector there are links across the mountainside – so a circuit is possible.

All around the circuit there are separate lifts serving the wooded lower slopes and the open upper slopes – with lots of appealing restaurants dotted around at the mid-stations, and at some of the tops. The east-facing, morning-sun slopes are mainly fairly gentle, with top heights around the 2300m/7,550ft mark. The west-facing slopes have more character, both in skiing and visual terms, including a run on the back of the dramatic peak of the Rothorn (2865m/9,400ft). Piste classification overstates difficulty, and there are few challenges. But there is considerable off-piste potential.

The lift system is a mix – there are a couple of six-packs, but there are also quite a few old chairs and drags. Queues may appear at weekends. Snow reliability is reasonable, at least on the east-facing slopes; there's snowmaking, and good grooming.

USA

Most people who give it a try find America is pretty seductive, despite the relatively small size of its ski areas. Key factors for us are the relatively deserted pistes, the quality of accommodation and the excellent, varied resort restaurants. Nearly everyone is also struck by the high standards of service and courtesy, and the immaculate piste grooming. Depending on the resort, you may also be struck by the cute Wild West ambience and the superb quality of the snow. Of course, US skiing does have some distinct disadvantages, too. Read on.

We have organised our American chapters in regional sections – California, Colorado, Utah, Rest of the West and New England.

Most American resorts receive serious amounts of snow – average snowfall is typically in the region of 6m to 12m (20ft to 40ft) in a season. And most have serious snowmaking facilities too. What's more, they use them well – they lay down a base of snow early in the season, rather than patching up shortages later.

There are wide differences in quantity and quality of snowfall, both between individual resorts and between regions – we discuss some of these in our regional introductions.

Piste grooming is taken very seriously – most American resorts set standards that the best Alpine resorts are only now attempting to match. Every morning you can expect to step out on to perfect 'corduroy' pistes. But this doesn't mean that there aren't moguls – far from it. It's just that you get moguls where the resort says you can expect moguls, not everywhere. Some resorts even go so far as to groom half the width of some runs, leaving the other half mogulled.

The slopes of most American resorts are blissfully free of crowds – a key advantage that becomes more important every year as the pistes of Europe become ever more congested. If you want to ride those new shaped skis through turns at the speeds they were designed for, take them to the States. And, because the slopes are mostly below the tree line, they offer good visibility in bad weather.

Most American resorts offer free guided tours of the area. Lift queues are short, partly because they are highly disciplined: spare seats on chair-lifts are religiously filled, with the aid of cheerful, conscientious attendants. Piste maps and tissues are freely available at the bottom of most lifts. Mountain 'hosts' are on hand to advise you about the best possible routes to take. School standards are uniformly high. And facilities for children are impressive, too.

Many Europeans have the idea that American resorts don't have off-piste terrain, but this seriously misrepresents the position. It's true that resorts practically always have a boundary, and that venturing beyond it into the 'backcountry' may be discouraged or forbidden. But within the boundary there is often very challenging terrain that is very much like off-piste terrain in an Alpine resort, but with the important advantage that it is patrolled and avalanche-controlled – so you don't need to hire a guide. We rate this as one of the great attractions of American resorts.

There are drawbacks to the US, of course. One is that many resorts have slopes that are very modest in extent compared with major Alpine areas. But many US resorts (in Colorado and California, in

← Lots of American have slopes with nicely spaced trees – and what's more, with gradients ranging from the gentle to the seriously steep; this is Heavenly, where a few years back we had a fabulous day in the trees on the Nevada side

563

particular) are very close to each other – so if you are prepared to travel a bit, you won't get bored. Roads are good, and car hire is cheap; but you should budget for buying snow-chains – we've yet to find a US rental company that will provide them. The roads you're likely to be driving on are major ones, well engineered with gentle gradients, but if a storm socks in you still will need chains – and be prepared to use them. Hiring a 4WD should help, but doesn't guarantee that you won't need chains.

A more serious problem is that the day is ridiculously short. The lifts often shut at 3pm or 3.30. That may explain another drawback – the dearth of decent mountain restaurants. The norm is monster self-service refuelling stations – designed to minimise time off the slopes. Small restaurants with table-service and decent food are rare.

It's also true that in many resorts the mountains are slightly monotonous, with countless similar trails cut through the forest. You don't usually get the spectacular mountain scenery and the distinctive high-mountain runs of the Alps.

The classification of pistes (or trails, to use the local term) is different from that in Europe. Red runs don't exist. The colours used are combined with shapes. Green circles correspond fairly closely to greens in Europe (that is, in France, where they are mainly found). American blue squares largely correspond to blues in Europe, but

SNOWPIX.COM / CHRIS GILL

You get moguls where you expect them and not where you don't; Heavenly, again ↘

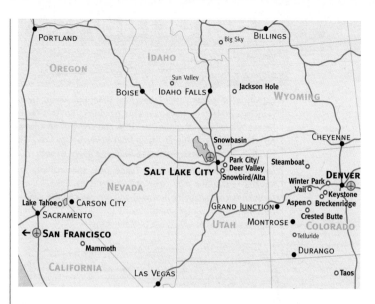

also include tougher intermediate runs that would be red in the Alps; these are sometimes labelled as double-squares, although in some resorts a hybrid blue-black grading is used instead. Black diamond runs correspond to steeper European reds and easier European blacks. But then there are multiple diamonds. Double-diamond runs are seriously steep – often steeper than the steepest pistes in the Alps. A few resorts have wildly steep triple-diamonds.

It comes as a surprise to many first-timers that many chair-lifts in the States do not have safety bars; even on chairs that have them, you will find Americans curiously reluctant to use them, and if you manage to deploy the bar you will find your companions very eager to raise it as soon as the top station is in view. They worry more about getting trapped on the chair than about falling off it. Weird.

US resort towns vary widely in style and convenience. There are old restored mining towns such as Telluride, Crested Butte and Aspen, genuine cowboy towns such as Jackson Hole, purpose-built monstrosities such as Snowbird, and even skyscraping gambling dens such as Heavenly. There is an increasing number of neat, car-free modern base villages. Two important things the resorts have in common are good-value, spacious accommodation and restaurants that are good, reasonably priced and varied in cuisine. Young people should be aware that the rigorously enforced legal age for drinking alcohol is 21; if you are 22 but look younger, carry evidence of age.

In the end, your reaction to skiing and snowboarding in America may depend mainly on your reaction to America. If repeated cheerful exhortations to have a nice day wind you up – or if you like to ride chair-lifts in silence – perhaps you'd better stick to the Alps.

Crossing the pond is never going to be cheap, but the basic cost is lower than you might think: you can get room-plus-hire-car February packages to California for under £600; with the £ at over $1.80, eating out is not expensive; and it's not difficult to find rooms with kitchenettes where you do your own catering. But lift passes, tuition and childcare are very expensive – they can be double what you would pay in the Alps. You can often save, especially on lift passes, by buying in advance through tour operators.

California? It means surfing, beaches, wine, Hollywood, Disneyland and San Francisco cable-cars. Nevada means gambling. But this region also has the highest mountains in continental USA and some of America's biggest winter resorts, usually reliable for snow from November to May. What's more, winter holidays here are less expensive than you might expect.

Most visitors head for the Lake Tahoe area. Spectacularly set high in the Sierra Nevada 322km/200 miles east of San Francisco, Lake Tahoe is ringed by skiable mountains containing 14 downhill and 7 cross-country centres – the highest concentration of winter sports resorts in the USA. Then, a long way south (more often reached from LA), there is Mammoth.

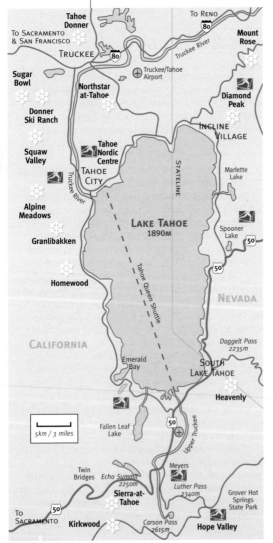

566

MAJOR RESORTS

Mammoth has the real drawback that it is rather isolated – it's a long drive from Tahoe, or from Los Angeles. But it is an impressive mountain that is worth considering – it's much higher than the Tahoe resorts, for one thing – and well placed if you fancy a visit to Disneyland as part of the trip. It gets its own chapter, a few pages on.

In the Tahoe area, two resorts stand out from the herd, at least in terms of size. Both now get their own chapters.

Heavenly is the biggest in the area, and has at the foot of its slopes much the biggest development – the bizarre town of South Lake Tahoe, which straddles the state line and owes its development to gambling on the Nevada side. It makes an obvious base, if you like the sound of it.

Squaw Valley, the biggest north-shore resort, comes a close second to Heavenly in terms of area, but has only recently developed a base village.

These resorts may have the extent and variety of slopes to keep you amused for a week, but the real appeal of a holiday in this area is that you can easily visit several resorts, spending a day or two at each. You could visit them all from a single base using a car, and most using buses and boats. A two-centre holiday with some time at the north end of the lake and some time at the south would be excellent.

We give Short Turns entries at the end of the California/Nevada section to the four second-division resorts – **Alpine Meadows, Kirkwood, Northstar** and **Sierra-at-Tahoe**. All are appreciably smaller than Heavenly and Squaw, but all offer a worthwhile 2,000 to 2,500 acres of terrain.

SUGAR BOWL

Resort	2100m
	6,890ft
Slopes	2100-2555m
	6,890-8,390ft
Lifts	8
Pistes	1,500 acres
Green	17%
Blue	45%
Black	38%
Snowmaking	
	500 acres

DIAMOND PEAK

Resort	2040m
	6,700ft
Slopes	2040-2600m
	6,700-9,700ft
Lifts	6
Pistes	655 acres
Green	18%
Blue	46%
Black	36%
Snowmaking	75%

MOUNT ROSE

Resort	2520m
	8,260ft
Slopes	2410-2955m
	7,900-9,700ft
Lifts	6
Pistes	1,200 acres
Green	20%
Blue	30%
Black	50%
Snowmaking	20%

HOMEWOOD

Resort	1900m
	6,230ft
Slopes	1900-2400m
	6,230-7,880ft
Lifts	7
Pistes	1,260 acres
Green	15%
Blue	50%
Black	35%

MINOR RESORTS

Most of the smaller resorts around Tahoe are not 'destination' resorts of the kind that you find in Colorado or the Alps. A few have no nearby accommodation at all; but there are lots of B&Bs and motels scattered around the lake, and a couple of quite pleasant small towns.

The obvious alternative to staying in South Lake Tahoe or Squaw Valley is the small tourist town of Tahoe City, on the lake's north-west shore – especially handy for Squaw Valley and Alpine Meadows. It has a range of touristy shops and some good restaurants and bars. One regular Tahoe reporter suggests Incline Village at the north-east corner of the lake (handy for Diamond Peak and Mount Rose) for its 'country charm and ambience, and friendly people'.

All the resorts covered below are worth a day visit, offering quiet slopes of 450-550m (1,480-1,800ft) vertical and areas from 650 to 1,500 acres. We made quick visits to three last winter, and have reader reports on the fourth.

The one we're most keen to go back to, without question, is **Sugar Bowl**. This was the first Sierra Nevada area to be developed, next to the railway from the Bay area to Truckee (and so away from the lake); but with five fast quads, there is nothing antique about it now. Sugar Bowl claims a huge average snowfall of 500in a year. We were impressed by the varied terrain, including lots of genuine black and double-diamond runs from the higher lifts as well as good cruising; the single-black Silver Belt is rated by an experienced American reader as his favourite run in the US. There is lodging at the base in The Inn, and a small development of condos is under way at the Mt Judah base, near the smart day lodge.

In sharp contrast to Sugar Bowl is **Homewood**, where all the slopes are served by slow chair-lifts, and the views are as much of an attraction as the slopes. Reporters tell us it has the best lake views of all the Tahoe resorts, and there are a couple of mountain restaurants from which to enjoy them. The resort is set right on the western shore of the lake, so access is quick and easy. The notably quiet slopes include plenty of short black pitches as well as cruisers.

Mount Rose has much the highest base elevation in the Tahoe area – a good 600m/1,970ft above the lake – and with an annual snowfall average of 400in you can generally depend on great snow. The last couple of years have seen big changes here: a second six-pack, and relocation of the quad it replaced to open up the Chutes – a shady bowl mainly of serious double-diamond gradient. This bowl separates the front face of the mountain, with a row of blue and easy black runs to the base, from a wider, gentler, lightly wooded area known variously as East Bowl or Slide Bowl. Both have a lot to offer, especially for someone staying in Heavenly who may be finding the groomed stuff monotonous and the ungroomed stuff too challenging.

Diamond Peak is the smallest of these resorts, with the least to offer – a narrow area consisting basically of a long ridge served by one fast chair; there are great lake views from the run along the ridge and from the terrace of Snowflake Lodge – a little hut selling snacks – at the end of it. There are black runs off the ridge, but nothing seriously steep.

SOME GENERALITIES

The mountains get a lot of snow: these resorts often have the deepest snowfall in North America. Rockies powder connoisseurs are inclined to brand the snow as wet 'Sierra Cement'. The snow can be heavy – our 2006 visit was spoiled by rain. But most people find the snow just fine, particularly in comparison with what you would expect in the Alps. On our previous trip we had two of the best days of the season, skiing powder in the trees of Heavenly and Mammoth.

Most of the resorts mainly attract weekend visitors from the cities of California's coastal area. Peak weekends apart, the slopes are uncrowded, and queues are rare.

In the past our main reservation has been the character of the resorts themselves; they don't have the traditional mountain-town ambience that we look for in the States.

But things are changing. At Heavenly a gondola goes up from a new car-free plaza in South Lake Tahoe. Squaw Valley now has an attractive base 'village'. Northstar is building a new, much bigger base village. And a new pedestrian village opened a couple of years back in Mammoth – linked to the slopes by gondola.

Heavenly

It's unique: fabulous lake and 'desert' views from interestingly varied slopes above a tacky lakeside casino town

HEAVENLY SKI RESORT / SCOTT MARKEWITZ

COSTS

①②③④⑤⑥

RATINGS

The slopes

Fast lifts	★★★
Snow	★★★★
Extent	★★★
Expert	★★★
Intermediate	★★★★
Beginner	★★★★
Convenience	★
Queues	★★★★
Mountain restaurants	★

The rest

Scenery	★★★★
Resort charm	★
Off-slope	★★

NEWS

For 2005/06 Nightlife, a night-time terrain-park, was built just above California Lodge. It opens from 5pm to 9pm on Thursday to Saturday.

There are plans for the North Bowl and Olympic chairs on the Nevada side to be replaced by a fast quad, but it is unlikely to take place until 2007/08.

568

➕ Spectacular setting, with amazing views of Lake Tahoe and Nevada

➕ Fair-sized mountain that offers a sensation of travelling around

➕ Large areas of widely spaced trees, largely on intermediate slopes – fabulous in fresh powder

➕ Some serious challenges for experts

➕ Numerous other worthwhile resorts within an hour's drive

➕ A unique nightlife scene

➕ Good snow record plus impressive snowmaking facilities

➖ South Lake Tahoe, where you stay, is a bizarre and messy place spreading along a busy highway

➖ No trail back to South Lake Tahoe

➖ Gondola very vulnerable to closure by high winds

➖ If tree-skiing is not good, or if you are not up to it, you are mainly confined to easy groomed blues

➖ If natural snow is in short supply, most of the challenging terrain is likely to be closed

➖ Very little traditional après-ski

A resort called Heavenly invites an obvious question: just how close to heaven does it take you? Physically, close enough: with a top height of 3070m/10,070ft and vertical of 1075m/3,530ft, it's the highest and biggest of the resorts set around Lake Tahoe. Metaphorically, it's not quite so close. In particular, anyone who (like us) is drawn to Heavenly partly by its exceptionally scenic setting is likely to be dismayed by the appearance and atmosphere of South Lake Tahoe.

The official line is that the place has been transformed into something like a European ski resort by the gondola between downtown and the mountain, and by the opening of a pedestrian 'village' around its base. We don't buy that. It's great to have a gondola from downtown and the 'village' is quite smart (though quiet and small). But the general feel of South Lake Tahoe isn't much affected.

THE RESORT

Heavenly is on California's border with Nevada, at the south end of Lake Tahoe. Other resorts around the lake are easily visited from a base here.

Heavenly's base-town – South Lake Tahoe – is primarily a summer resort. In this respect it is unusual, but not unique. What really sets it apart is that its economy is driven by gambling. The Stateline area at its centre is dominated by a handful of monstrous hotel-casinos located just inches on the Nevada side of the line. These brash but comfortable hotels offer good-value accommodation (subsidised by the gambling), swanky restaurants and big-name entertainers, as well as roulette wheels, craps and card games – and endless slot machines into which gambling-starved Californians feed bucketloads of quarters. It's bizarre to walk through the the gambling areas in ski gear, with skis over your shoulder.

The casinos are a conspicuous part of the amazing lake views from the

lower slopes (though not from above mid-mountain). They look like a classic American downtown area, which you'd expect to be full of shops and bars. But they are actually just a cluster of high-rise blocks bisected by the seriously busy US Highway 50. The rest of the town spreads for miles along this pedestrian-hostile road – dozens of low-rise hotels and motels (some quite smart, but many rather shabby), stores, wedding chapels and so on. The general effect is less dire than it might be, thanks to the camouflage of the tall trees that blanket the area.

The new 'village', built a few years ago on the California side of the stateline right next to the base of the gondola, is an improvement, providing a downtown après-ski focus (essentially one bar) and pedestrianised area that the resort has lacked. But this could have been done much better (eg the new ice rink has a huge chiller/generator right next to it). Despite this, it is now the obvious place to stay.

KEY FACTS

Resort	1900m
	6,230ft
Slopes	1995-3070m
	6,540-10,070ft
Lifts	30
Pistes	4,800 acres
Green	20%
Blue	45%
Black	35%
Snowmaking	70 %

Some of the casino-hotels are within five minutes' walk of the 'village' and gondola, making these an attractive choice even for those not keen on the gambling and entertainment, but others are enough of a hike away to justify using the shuttle buses. And much of the cheaper accommodation is literally miles away. If that's where you're staying, you may prefer to access the mountain from the original lift base, the refurbished California Lodge, up a heavily wooded slope 2km/1 mile out of South Lake Tahoe. That way, you'll be able to ski down at the end of the day instead of riding a lift down to the town base.

Like the town, the slopes spread across the border into Nevada – and there are two other lift bases, which can easily be reached by road, around the mountain in Nevada. There are 'adequate' free shuttle-bus services to the three out-of-town bases. A car is still handy to explore the other resorts around Lake Tahoe and to get to many of the best restaurants.

There's a useful TV programme at 7.30am *Another Heavenly Morning* which covers weather and snow conditions. You can visit Squaw Valley by coach and return by boat across the lake.

THE MOUNTAIN

Practically all of Heavenly's slopes are cut through forest, but in many areas the forest is not dense and there is excellent tree skiing. As always in America, this 'off-piste' terrain is avalanche controlled. But it's 'patrolled' only by hollering; since collision with a tree may render you unconscious, don't ski the trees alone.

THE SLOPES
Interestingly complex
The gondola between downtown and the mountain is a great improvement. But it can be closed far too often if it's windy (as several reporters have found). Heavenly's mountain is complicated, and getting from A to B requires more careful navigation than is usual on American mountains (eg it's not obvious from the piste map that it's much better to take the Comet rather than the Dipper chair back from Nevada to the California side). Quite a few of the links between different sectors involve flat tracks.

There is a fairly clear division between the California side of the mountain (directly above South Lake Tahoe) and the Nevada side (above

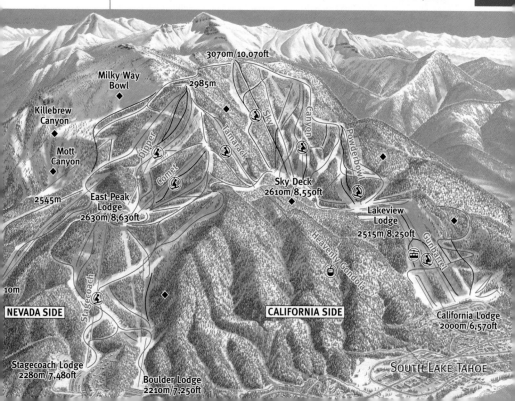

CALIFORNIA

570

LIFT PASSES

Heavenly

Prices in US$

Age	1-day	6-day
under 13	36	216
13 to 18	63	348
19 to 64	70	420
over 65	56	336
Free under 5		

Beginner combined lesson/lift pass/ equipment deals

Notes
Prices are what you pay at a ticket window in the resort. Reduced prices available to international visitors who pre-book through a UK tour operator. It is not necessary to buy a complete holiday package to obtain these prices.

Stagecoach Lodge and Boulder Lodge). Near the Nevada border you can see beautiful views over Lake Tahoe in one direction and the arid Nevada 'desert' in the other.

On the California side there are four fast chairs on the upper mountain. The steep lower slopes are served by the Tram (cable-car) and Gunbarrel fast chair.

On the Nevada side, above East Peak Lodge, is an excellent intermediate area, served by two fast quad chairs, with a downhill extension served (only at weekends, warn reporters) by the Galaxy chair. From the fast Dipper chair back up, you can access the open terrain of Milky Way Bowl, leading to the seriously steep gladed runs of Mott and Killebrew canyons, served by the Mott Canyon chair. Below East Peak Lodge are runs down to Nevada's two bases, only the Stagecoach having a fast chair back up – it takes an eternity from Boulder Lodge.

TERRAIN-PARKS
Four to choose between
Heavenly is home to four terrain parks. Low Roller Terrain Park, between Groove and Patsy's chair-lifts below the top of the lifts up from California Lodge has beginner features such as small jumps and boxes for novice park riders. An 2.5m/8ft high mini-pipe is on the cards for next year as well. High Roller California park, near the top of the Canyon chair, services expert riders; there are big kicker lines, and all sorts of jibs including an awesome pyramid jib-box feature and three-level box. Below this, off Ridge Run, is a beast of a super-pipe with 7m/22ft walls. High Roller Stateline, found to the side of the Tamarack chair, was set up as a boarder-cross course last season. High Roller Nightlife, served by the World Cup lift at the California base, is open Thursday to Saturday, 5pm-9pm.

SNOW RELIABILITY
No worries
Heavenly was one of the first resorts to invest heavily in snowmaking. The system now covers around 70% of the trails and ensures that most sections are open most of the time. In recent years California has recorded some of the deepest snow-cover of any North American resort, and Heavenly is now able to claim a five-year average of an impressive 360 inches.

FOR EXPERTS
Some specific challenges
The black runs under the California base lifts – including The Face and Gunbarrel (often used for mogul competitions) – are seriously steep and challenging and lots of people were struggling on the top-to-bottom icy bumps on our 2006 visit. Ellie's, at the top of the mountain, may offer continuous moguls too, but was groomed and a great fast cruise when we were there. There's some really steep stuff on the Nevada side. Milky Way Bowl provides a gentle single-diamond introduction to the emphatically double-diamond terrain beyond it. The extremely steep, densely wooded Mott and Killebrew canyons have roped gateways; be warned, these are genuine double-black-diamond tree runs. The Mott Canyon chair is slow, but you may welcome the rest it affords.

Elsewhere, especially on the California side from the Sky chair, there are excellent ungroomed slopes with widely spaced trees – tremendous fun when conditions are right. Some wooded slopes are identified on the trail map, but you are not confined to those. The trail map gives a good indication of the density of trees, and the grading of nearby trails gives a good idea of steepness.

↑ This is close to the bottom of the gondola. Highway 50, motels and casino-hotels certainly make a different resort ambience from any other ski resort we know

SNOWPIX.COM / CHRIS GILL

FOR INTERMEDIATES
Lots to do
Heavenly is excellent for intermediates. The California side offers a progression from the relaxed cruising of the long Ridge Run, starting right at the top of the mountain, to more challenging blues dropping off the ridge towards Sky Deck. Confident intermediates will want to spend some time on the Nevada side, where there is more variety of terrain, some longer runs down to the lift bases and more carving space. There are some great top-to-bottom cruises down to Stagecoach Lodge (served by a fast chair) and Boulder Lodge (served by very slow chairs). And adventurous intermediates will enjoy exploring the tree runs from the fast Sky chair on the California side (see 'For experts').

FOR BEGINNERS
An excellent place to learn
There's an excellent beginner area at the top of the gondola and others at the California base lodge and Boulder Lodge in Nevada. On the California side there are gentle green runs served by lifts at the top of the cable-car.

FOR CROSS-COUNTRY
A separate world
You can try Adventure Peak at the top of the gondola. But the serious stuff is elsewhere around the lake – notably at the Spooner Lake Cross Country Area: over 80km/50 miles of prepared trails. Organised moonlit tours are popular.

QUEUES
Gondola a problem
The gondola has morning queues ('sometimes 20 minutes' says a 2006 reporter) when it can be worth taking the shuttle to the much quieter Stagecoach Lodge base. There are also queues to ride the gondola down at the end of the day. Ignore the signs telling you to set off ridiculously early to catch the gondola; it keeps going and our advice is to ski till whenever you like, then have a beer at the bar near the top of the gondola until the queue disappears. Sadly the gondola seems to close because of wind too often, when you have to catch a bus to another base to get up the mountain. We also have a 2006 report of 20-minute queues for the Sky and Canyon chairs on the California side.

MOUNTAIN RESTAURANTS
Even refuelling is problematic
We have long considered the on-mountain catering grossly inadequate, especially in bad weather. We used to like the table-service Lake View Lodge at the top of the tram from California Lodge but even that served mediocre food on our 2006 visit. East Peak Lodge was recently renovated and the menu widened. The other options consist of outdoor decks serving BBQs and pizzas (hugely unenjoyable in a blizzard, as we can testify) and grossly overcrowded cafeterias.

Heavenly

571

boarding

Heavenly's varied natural terrain makes a perfect natural playground for advanced free-riders. Intermediates will have fun too, as there are plenty of gentle powder runs, served mainly by chair-lifts. And there are good areas for beginners. Heavenly has four terrain-parks and is home to the South Shore Soldiers spring freestyle camps (www.southshoresoldiers.com). The Block is pro rider Marc Frank Montoya's snowboarders' hotel in South Lake Tahoe. Each room is designed by a snowboard-associated brand and is the place to stay in the area (www.blockattahoe.com).

The tremendous views over the lake are a relief from the bumps on the way down to California Lodge (the bumps are much bigger and steeper higher up this run!) →

SCHOOLS AND GUIDES
Mixed reports
A recent reporter joined the school for two days and was delighted to find only two in her class. However, another skier, looking for advanced tuition, found the attitude of the organisers 'terrible, really patronising'.

FACILITIES FOR CHILDREN
Comprehensive
We lack recent feedback but a past reporter praised the day care and ski school facilities.

STAYING THERE

HOW TO GO
Hotel or motel?
Accommodation in the South Lake Tahoe area is abundant and ranges from the huge casinos to small motels. **Chalets** UK tour operators run some good catered chalets.
Hotels Of the main casino hotels, Harrah's (775 558 6611) and Harveys (775 558 2411) are the closest to the gondola. Rooms booked on the spot are expensive; packages are cheaper. The Block (530 544 2936) is a snowboarders' hotel – see 'Boarding'.
(((4 **Embassy Suites** (530 544 5400) Luxury suites in a modern, traditional-style building close to the gondola.
(((4 **Marriott's Timber Lodge** (530 542 6600) Part of the new 'village'.
(((3 **Forest Suites** (530 541 6655) Right by the gondola, pools, hot-tubs, 'enormous rooms, very luxurious'.
(2 **Holiday Lodge** (530 544 4101) Opposite the gondola. 'Comfortable, breakfast included, pool, hot-tub.'
(2 **Station House Inn** (530 542 1101) Recommended again in 2006: 'full cooked breakfast at no extra charge'.
(2 **Tahoe Chalet Inn** (530 544 3311) Clean, friendly, near casinos. Back rooms (away from highway) preferable.
(2 **Timber Cove Lodge** (530 541 6722) Bland but well run, with lake views from some rooms.
Self-catering Plenty of choice. We've had a rave report about The Ridge Tahoe condos near Stagecoach Lodge.

EATING OUT
Good value
The casino hotels' all-you-can-eat buffets offer fantastic value. They have some more ambitious 'gourmet' restaurants too – some high enough to give superb views (try Harrah's 18th floor and Harvey's 19th). The sprawling

resort area offers a huge variety. Reporters' suggestions include Applebee's ('the best value meals'), Hunan Garden ('best Chinese buffet ever'), Cecile's ('excellent and reasonable'), Fresh Ketch at Tahoe Keys Marina ('wonderful fresh fish and harbour views') and Zephyr Cove Resort ('excellent, reasonable, marvellous sunset views'. For breakfast, join the locals at the Driftwood Cafe.

APRES-SKI
Getting better
Things have looked up in the last few years for 4pm drinking: there's now an Austrian-style igloo bar near the top of the gondola and Fire and Ice at the foot of it (with an outdoor seating area with fires and heaters). Both get busy and form an après-ski focus. McP's, over the main highway from the gondola, is a locals' hangout. Later on, the casinos on the Nevada side of the stateline aren't simply opportunities to throw money away: top-name entertainers are also to be found in them. And you can dance and dine your way across the lake aboard a paddle steamer.

OFF THE SLOPES
Luck be a lady
If you enjoy gambling you're in the right place. If you want to get away from the bright lights, try a boat trip on Lake Tahoe, snowmobiling a short drive from South Lake Tahoe, or a hot-air balloon ride. Pedestrians can use the cable-car or the gondola to share the lake views and at Adventure Peak, at the top of the gondola, you can go tubing, snow-biking, tobogganing and snow-shoeing.

GETTING THERE
Air San Francisco 274km/170 miles (3½hr); Reno 89km/55 miles (1¼hr); South Lake Tahoe, 15min.

ACTIVITIES
Indoor Casinos, spas, art galleries, multiplex cinema, museums

Outdoor Lake cruises, snowmobiling, snow-shoeing, snowtubing, sleigh rides, dog-sledding, hot springs, fishing, hot-air ballooning, ice skating, factory outlet shops

OUR WEBSITE
Go to our website at wtss.co.uk for resort news, links to resort sites, a build-your-own resort shortlist system and reader forums.

Phone numbers Different area codes are used on the two sides of the stateline. For this chapter, therefore, the area code is included with each number.

From distant parts of the US, add the prefix 1. From abroad, add the prefix +1.

TOURIST OFFICE
t 775 586 7000
info@vailresorts.com
www.skiheavenly.com

INTRAWEST MOUNTAIN RESORTS

Mammoth Mountain

A big, sprawling mountain above a car-oriented, sprawling but pleasantly woody resort, a six-hour drive from Los Angeles

COSTS

① ② ③ ④ ⑤ ⑥

RATINGS

The slopes

Fast lifts	****
Snow	****
Extent	***
Expert	****
Intermediate	****
Beginner	****
Convenience	**
Queues	****
Mountain restaurants	*

The rest

Scenery	***
Resort charm	**
Off-slope	*

NEWS

For 2006/07 a local history and geology centre, Top of the Sierra, will open at the Panorama Lookout Station.

For 2005/06 dining facilities at the Main Lodge were revamped: a new food court, Broadway Marketplace, and slope-side bar opened there.

The resort wants to redevelop the Eagle base area. Plans include another moving carpet and lift for the nursery slope and a new plaza, including a hotel, shops and an ice rink. Work is expected to begin in 2007 with completion in 2008/09.

MAMMOTH MOUNTAIN SKI AREA

The upper slopes are high, seriously steep and often very deeply snow-covered →

- ➕ One of North America's bigger ski hills, with something for everyone
- ➕ Good mix of open Alpine-style bowls and classic American wooded slopes
- ➕ Impressive good snowfall record
- ➕ Uncrowded slopes most of the time
- ➕ Mightily impressive terrain parks
- ➕ Good views, including more Alpine drama than usual in the US

- ➖ Mammoth Lakes is a rather straggling place with no focus, where life revolves around cars
- ➖ Most accommodation is miles from the slopes – though development is taking place at the lift bases
- ➖ Weekend crowds in high season
- ➖ Trail map and signing still poor
- ➖ Wind can be a problem

Mammoth may not be mammoth in Alpine terms – from end to end, it measures less than one-third of the size of Val-d'Isère/Tignes, in area it's more like one-sixth – but it is big enough to amuse many people for a week. It can be a superb mountain for anyone who is happy in deep snow, but is equally suited to families and mixed-ability groups looking for groomed runs. The main thing it has lacked is a real village at the base.

You have to applaud the efforts of Intrawest, owner of Whistler and now of various key plots of land here, to put this right by building a new pedestrian 'village' (which we are encouraged to call The Village) on the edge of sprawling Mammoth Lakes, connected by a gondola to one of the main lift bases. If your lodgings are at The Village, no doubt its restaurants and boutiques will attract your custom. But we'd be surprised if it ever has much impact on the resort as a whole. You can't ski down to The Village, so most visitors based elsewhere (ie the majority) will ignore it. Mammoth will remain what it has always been: a resort that expects you to arrive by car, and get around by car.

573

THE RESORT

The mountain is set above Mammoth Lakes, a small year-round resort town that spreads over a wide area of woodland. The place is entirely geared to driving, with no discernible centre – hotels, restaurants and little shopping centres are scattered along the four-lane highway called Main Street and Old Mammoth Road, which crosses it. The buildings are generally timber-clad in traditional style – even McDonald's has been tastefully designed – and are set among trees, so although it may be short on village ambience, the place has a pleasant enough appearance – particularly when under snow.

The town meets the mountain at two lift bases, both a mile or two from most of the hotels and condos.

The major base is Canyon Lodge, with a big day lodge and four chairlifts; there are hotels, condos and individual homes in the area below the lodge. Not far from here, Intrawest has

KEY FACTS

Resort	2425m
	7,950ft

Mammoth only	
Slopes	2425-3370m
	7,950-11,050ft
Lifts	28
Pistes	3,500 acres
Green	25%
Blue	40%
Black	35%
Snowmaking	
	477 acres

June Mountain only	
Slopes	2300-3075m
	7,550-10,090ft
Lifts	7
Pistes	500 acres
Green	35%
Blue	45%
Black	20%
Snowmaking	none

built phase one of its pedestrian development, The Village, which is linked to Canyon Lodge by a gondola.

The minor base, with a single six-pack, is Eagle Lodge (previously Little Eagle – also known as Juniper Springs, which strictly is the name of the condos built at the base) – which, if plans go ahead, will be redeveloped for the 2007/08 season.

A road runs along the north fringe of the mountain past an anonymous chair-lift base to two other major base areas: The Mill Cafe, with two fast chairs, and Main Lodge, a mini-resort with three fast access lifts and a big day lodge. You can stay here, in the Mammoth Mountain Inn; but who wants to be based four miles from the resort's 50 restaurants? Not us.

Shuttle-buses run on several colour-coded routes serving the lift bases (though they are reported to be erratic in the mornings). Night buses run via The Village until midnight. A car is useful.

The Mammoth lift pass also covers June, a small mountain half an hour's drive north, chiefly attractive for its astonishingly people-free slopes. See feature box, later in this chapter.

The drive up from Los Angeles takes six hours (more in poor conditions); but it is not without interest. You pass through the Santa Monica mountains close to Beverly Hills, then the San Gabriel mountains and Mojave Desert (with the world's biggest jet-plane parking lot) before reaching the Sierra Nevada range.

There are plans to extend Mammoth Lakes' small airport to take jet flights, but progress seems slow.

THE MOUNTAIN

The 28 lifts access an impressive area, suitable for all abilities. The highest runs are open, the lower ones more sheltered by trees.

Finding your way around is not easy at first. Many of the chair-lifts now have names (the traditional practice was to give them numbers), but the trails are still ill-defined: the map shows trails by means of isolated symbols, not continuous lines, and signposting of runs on the mountain is sporadic. On the lower part of the mountain this is mainly an inconvenience. But higher up there are real dangers in poor visibility. The map uses six classifications, including green/blue and blue/black – somewhat pointless, when you often end up on the wrong trail anyway.

THE SLOPES
Interesting variety
From **Main Lodge** the two-stage Panorama gondola goes via McCoy Station right to the top. The views are great, with Nevada to the north-east and the jagged Minarets to the west. There are countless ways down the front of the mountain, which ranges from steep to very steep – or vertical if the wind has created a cornice, as it often does. Or you can go off the back, down to **Outpost 14**, whence chairs 14 or 13 bring you back to lower points on the ridge. The third option is to follow the ridge, which eventually brings you down to the Main Lodge area. This route brings you past an easy area served by a double chair, and a very easy area served by the Discovery fast quad.

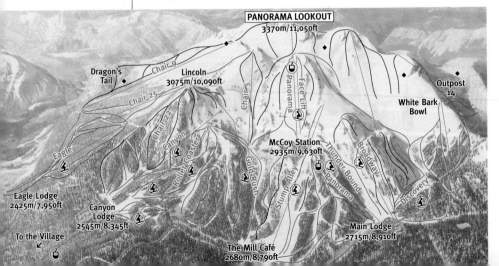

PANORAMA LOOKOUT
3370m/11,050ft

Dragon's Tail
Chair 9
Lincoln
3075m/10,090ft
Chair 25
Chair 22
Canyon
Roller Coaster
Chair 5
Face Lift
Panorama
Outpost 14
White Bark Bowl
McCoy Station
2935m/9,630ft
Broadway
Thunder Bound
Panorama
Eagle
Gold Rush
Stump Alley
Discovery
Eagle Lodge
2425m/7,950ft
Canyon Lodge
2545m/8,345ft
Main Lodge
2715m/8,910ft
To the Village
The Mill Café
2680m/8,790ft

Mammoth Mountain

Mammoth has always encouraged snowboarding since its early days. A huge amount has been spent on the terrain-parks, and this tends to overshadow just how good the mountain's natural terrain really is. Almost entirely serviced by fast chairs and gondolas, this is a snowboarder's heaven. There are bowls, chutes, tree runs and cliffs dotted around the mountain, and you will be hard-pressed not to find something to your liking. Take the Panorama gondola and drop into the back bowls for plenty of powder runs. There are heaps of not-so-steep and wide runs for beginners on the lower parts of the resort. The terrain-parks are about the best you will find. Wave Rave snowboard shop has a huge selection of gear.

Prices in US$

Age	1-day	6-day
under 13	35	159
13 to 18	53	240
19 to 64	70	319
over 65	35	159

Free under 7, over 80

Beginner pass covering Chair 7, Eagle Express and Discovery only

Notes
Covers all lifts at Mammoth and June Mountains. Afternoon pass available.

Alternative pass
Pass covering June Mountain only.

McCoy Station can also be reached using the Stump Alley fast chair from **The Mill Cafe**, on the road up from town. The fast Gold Rush quad from here takes you into the more heavily wooded eastern half of the area. This has long, gentle runs served by lifts up from **Canyon Lodge** and **Eagle Lodge** and seriously steep stuff as well as some intermediate terrain on the subsidiary peak known as Lincoln, served by lifts 25 and 22.

TERRAIN-PARKS
Among the best
There are three parks. Main park, situated above Main Lodge, is massive. Everything here is up to pro standard. Giant kickers, huge rails and the famous super-duper pipe (183m/600ft long, with 7m/22ft walls) loom over the car park. For intermediate to advanced riders, South park by the Roller Coaster fast chair is a real playground. Two tree-lined itineraries force you to choose between rails or kickers. These flowing lines allow you to hit 6 to 7 obstacles in a row – perfect. There's also a boarder-cross here. The Family Fun Park by Canyon Lodge has a fun mini-pipe, various micro-scale rails, boxes and mini-jumps, coupled with a great atmosphere to learn in. All the parks are groomed daily and often have original features you won't find anywhere else. The parks can get very crowded on the weekends.

SNOW RELIABILITY
A long season
Mammoth has an impressive snow record – an annual average of 385 inches, which puts it ahead of major Colorado resorts and about on a par with Jackson Hole. Mammoth is appreciably higher than other Californian resorts, and it has an ever-expanding array of snow-guns, so it enjoys a long season – staying open as late as 4 July in many years. The mountain faces roughly north; the relatively low and slightly sunny slopes down to Eagle Lodge are affected by warm weather before others. Strong winds are not uncommon on the upper mountain; some lifts are kept going in surprisingly breezy conditions – one reporter was blown over at the top. The snow quality can be affected by these winds, too. This is not always a bad thing – the 'wind-compacted powder' can be 'just like spring snow'.

FOR EXPERTS
Some very challenging terrain
The steep bowls that run the width of the mountain top provide wonderful opportunities for experts. There are one or two single-diamond slopes, but most are emphatically double-diamond affairs requiring a lot of bottle.
There is lots of challenging terrain lower down, too; Chair 5, Chair 22 and Broadway are often open in bad weather when the top is firmly shut,

JUNE MOUNTAIN: THE WORLD'S QUIETEST SLOPES?

June Mountain, a scenic half-hour drive from Mammoth, is in the same ownership and covered by the lift pass. It makes a pleasant haven if Mammoth is busy. When Mammoth isn't busy, June is quite simply deserted; on a March weekday we skied run after run without seeing another person.

A double chair goes up from the car park at 2290m/7,510ft over black slopes (often short of snow) to a lodge, June Meadows Chalet. A quad chair serves a gentle blue-run hill, and a double chair goes over very gentle green runs to a quad serving short but genuinely black slopes on June Mountain itself (3100m/ 10,175ft). There are three terrain-parks, two jib-parks and a super-pipe.

and their more sheltered slopes may in any case have the best snow. (The top of Chair 22 is higher than the very top of Heavenly, remember.) There are plenty of good slopes over the back towards Outpost 14, too. Many of the steeper trails are short by Alpine standards (typically under 400m/1,300ft vertical), but despite this we've enjoyed some great powder days here.

FOR INTERMEDIATES
Lots of great cruising

Although there are exceptions, most of the lower mountain, below the tree-line, is intermediate cruising territory. What's more, Mammoth's piste maintenance is generally good, and many slopes that might become mogulled are kept easily skiable. 'Very flattering,' says one visitor.

As you might hope, the six-point trail difficulty scale – which we haven't tried to replicate on our own small trail map – is a good guide to what you'll find on the mountain.

Some of the mountain's longest runs above Eagle, blue-blacks served by chairs 9 and 25, are ideal for good intermediates. There are also some excellent, fairly steep, woodland trails down to The Mill Cafe.

Most of the long runs above Eagle Lodge, and some of the shorter ones above Canyon Lodge, are easy cruises. There is a variety of terrain, including lots of gentle stuff, at the western extremity of the slopes, both on the front side and on the back side.

FOR BEGINNERS
Excellent

Chair 7 and Chair 17 (named the Schoolyard Express) at Canyon Lodge and Discovery Chair at Main Lodge serve quiet, gentle green runs – so as soon as you're off the nursery slopes you get an encouraging taste of real skiing. Excellent instruction, top-notch grooming and snow quality usually make progress speedy ('My eight-year-old son was skiing blue-diamond runs by the end of the week').

FOR CROSS-COUNTRY
Very popular

Two specialist centres, Tamarack and Sierra Meadows (ungroomed), provide lessons and tours. There are 30km/19 miles of trails at Tamarack, and lots of scenic ungroomed tracks, including some through the pretty Lakes Basin area: 70km/43 miles of trails in all.

QUEUES
Normally quiet slopes

During the week the lifts and slopes are usually very quiet, with few queues: 'empty', 'deserted', say reporters. And an April 2006 visitor reports only 5-10 minutes at most for the busiest areas. But even the efficient lift system can struggle when 15,000 visitors arrive from LA on fine peak-season weekends. That's the time to try the wonderfully uncrowded June Mountain, half an hour away.

MOUNTAIN RESTAURANTS
Not a lot of choice

The only real mountain restaurants are at mid-mountain McCoy Station. This offers 'a good choice' of roasts, Italian, Asian and other dishes – but does get 'very busy'. The Parallax table-service restaurant next door does satisfying food with a calm atmosphere and a splendid view from its picture windows. The other on-mountain possibility in good weather is the primitive outdoor BBQ at Outpost 14, on the back of the hill.

Most people eat at the lift bases. Talons at Eagle Lodge has its fans. The Mill Cafe is 'pleasant' but the 'choice of food was limited', according to one visitor. The Mountainside Grill at the revamped Mammoth Mountain Inn is also recommended. And Canyon Lodge offers Mexican, Italian, Asian and more. The Broadway Marketplace is the new venue in the Main Lodge for breakfast and lunch.

SCHOOLS AND GUIDES
Excellent reports

Reporters are favourably impressed by the school, which apparently contains growing numbers of Scottish instructors. A 2006 visitor writes of 'very sympathetic' instructors and small classes. You can encounter the general American problem that you usually get a different instructor every day. There are some special 'camps' for experts, and for women.

FACILITIES FOR CHILDREN
Family favourite

Mammoth is keen to attract families. The Woollywood school, based in the Panorama gondola station, works closely with the Small World childcare centre. We've had glowing reports; one reporter rated the facilities as 'second to none'. Canyon Kids (at Canyon Lodge) was recommended in 2006.

GETTING THERE

Air Los Angeles 494km/307 miles (5hr); Reno 270km/168 miles (3hr).

ACTIVITIES

Indoor Fitness centres, museum, art galleries, cinema, concerts

Outdoor Snow-shoeing, dog-sledding, snowmobiling

OUR WEBSITE

Go to our website at wtss.co.uk for resort news, links to resort sites, a build-your-own resort shortlist system and reader forums.

Phone numbers
From distant parts of the US, add the prefix 1 760.
From abroad, add the prefix +1 760.

TOURIST OFFICE

t 934 0745
info@mammoth-mtn.com
www.mammoth
mountain.com

STAYING THERE

HOW TO GO
Good value packages
A good choice of hotels (none very luxurious or expensive) and condos. The condos tend to be out of town, near the lifts or on the road to them.
((((4) **Mammoth Mountain Inn** (934 2581) Way out of town at Main Lodge. Recently refurbished. 'Spacious and comfortable, perfect for access to the slopes but rather isolated'.
(((3) **Quality Inn** (934 5114) Good main street hotel with a big hot-tub.
(((3) **Alpenhof Lodge** (934 6330) Comfortable and friendly, in central location. Shuttle-bus stop and plenty of restaurants nearby.
(((3) **Austria Hof Lodge** (934 2764) Ski-out location near Canyon Lodge, recommended by a reporter, despite modest-sized rooms.
(((3) **Sierra Nevada Rodeway Inn** (934 2515) Central, good value, 'great spa'.
(((3) **Holiday Inn** (924 1234) Central location, large, comfortable rooms and 'great restaurant'. Pool.
Self-catering The Juniper Springs Lodge is near lifts and town. Close to the Canyon Lodge base-station, the 1849 Condominiums are spacious and well equipped. The Mammoth Ski and Racquet Club, a 10-minute walk from the same lifts, is very comfortable. There is an 'excellent' supermarket in the Minaret Mall, with good discounts.

EATING OUT
Outstanding choice
Reporters continue to be impressed by the 50+ restaurants, varying widely in style, cost and location. Start with a copy of the local menu guide. One reporting couple had a great time

dining in a different restaurant every day for a fortnight. Meshing their findings with other reports, we offer the following guidance: Slocums Grill – very good meal in wood-panelled room; Angel's – popular, good-value diner; Ocean Harvest – great atmosphere and wonderful fish; Nevados – best in town, excellent modern cooking; Chart House – excellent seafood, varied meat dishes; Alpenrose – intimate chalet-style place, good food; Matsu – small, simple, with delicious Asian food; Berger's – 'excellent giant burgers'; Old Mammoth Grill – traditional diner, 'good bar'.

Also recommended are Shogun for Japanese and Gomez's for Mexican food. A recent visitor says that the meal he had at the Lakefront up at Twin Lakes was 'the best ever in a ski resort'. We've had excellent dinners at Skadi and Whiskey Creek, too. Sand Dollar Sushi and Sake (for Japanese), Lulu and the Side Door cafe are the latest additions in The Village.

APRES-SKI
Lively at weekends
The liveliest immediate après-ski spot is the Yodler, at Main Lodge – a chalet transported from Switzerland, so they say. A new bar, Tusks, has also opened at Main Lodge – apparently great for viewing the high jinks in the terrain-parks. Later on, things revolve around a handful of bars, which come to life at weekends. The Clocktower Cellar is reported to be 'best in town – lively, friendly, good music, great choice of beers'. Whiskey Creek is the liveliest (and stays open latest); it has live bands at weekends. Slocums is popular with locals and 'ideal for an after-dinner drink'. Grumpy's is a sports bar. One reporter enjoyed the venues in The Village. He says you shouldn't miss Hawaiian-style Lakanuki's with its 'bikini tree' or Dublin's Irish Pub (with Fever disco).

OFF THE SLOPES
Mainly sightseeing
There are various things to be done outdoors, including skating. But a 2006 reporter didn't find much of interest at any of the bases. You can go sightseeing by car (preferably 4WD). The town of Bishop, 40 minutes' drive south, makes an amusing day out. Factory-outlet shopping is recommended for bargains. Mono Lake is reported to be 'well worth a visit'.

Squaw Valley

Now the most compelling base in the Tahoe area – great terrain for novices and experts, above an attractive new 'village'

COSTS

① ② ③ ④ ⑤ ⑥

RATINGS

The slopes

Fast lifts	★★★
Snow	★★★★
Extent	★★★
Expert	★★★★
Intermediate	★★
Beginner	★★★★
Convenience	★★★★
Queues	★★★★
Mountain restaurants	★

The rest

Scenery	★★★
Resort charm	★★★
Off-slope	★

NEWS

For 2006/07 two children's areas are planned: one at Papoose and an educational fort at mid-mountain. More snowmaking is expected and some new terrain may open.

For 2005/06 the Papoose Lodge and Learning Centre opened in the beginner area at Far East. And the terrain-parks received improvements.

KEY FACTS

Resort	1890m
	6,200ft
Slopes	1890-2755m
	6,200-9,050ft
Lifts	34
Pistes	4,000 acres
Green	25%
Blue	45%
Black	30%
Snowmaking	
	400 acres

➕ Lots of challenging runs and 'off-piste' terrain of varying difficulty

➕ Impressive snow record

➕ Superb beginner slopes

➕ Convenient, pleasant, modern 'village' at the base

➖ Not for mile-hungry intermediates

➖ Lifts prone to closure by wind

➖ Adventurous skiers need guidance to really exploit the area

➖ Limited range of village amenities

➖ A bit pricey

With the construction by Intrawest of a neat little pedestrian resort at the base, Squaw is at last a proper destination. It can't rival Heavenly for nightlife or for quantity of groomed runs, but it's now our favourite base in the Tahoe area.

THE RESORT

'The Village at Squaw Valley' has been built at the base of the main lifts by Intrawest, of Whistler/Arc 1950 fame. For a built-from-scratch development it is very successful, although still very small and limited in what it offers. In classic Intrawest style, it consists of neat, linked, apartment buildings carefully arranged around traffic-free streets and squares, with a handful of restaurants and shops strategically placed. It meets the main slopes at one end, close to the cable-car.

The self-contained, luxurious conference-oriented Resort at Squaw Creek is linked into one end of the lift network by its own chair-lift.

Squaw is the major resort at the north end of Lake Tahoe, about an hour's drive from South Lake Tahoe and Heavenly. There are daily shuttle-buses, and you can go by boat.

THE MOUNTAINS

Squaw offers 4,000 acres of terrain (a lot, by US standards) on six linked peaks. The peaks and high bowls of the area are treeless, but much of the terrain is lightly wooded – a very attractive mixture.

Squaw has no trails marked on its mountain map, and few signs or other aids to route-finding on the ground. In some sectors, adventurous but not truly expert skiers could find themselves in real difficulty.

Slopes There are several distinct sectors. Two impressively powerful lifts leave the village – a jumbo gondola (as in Verbier and Val-Thorens) and a big cable-car (called, strangely, the Cable Car). They rise 600m/1,970ft to the twin stations of Gold Coast and High Camp (linked by a pulse gondola). Above them is a gentle area of beginner slopes, and beyond that

SQUAW PEAK 2710m/8,900ft

EMIGRANT 2650m/8,700ft

GRANITE C 2755m/9,0

KT-22 2500m/8,200ft

Headwall

Gold Coast

High Camp 2500m/8,200ft

Shirley Lake

SNOW KING 2300m/7,550ft

KT-22 Express

Squaw One

Gold Coast

High Camp

Far East Express

Arrows mark the general direction and classification of runs, which are shown only as coloured lifts on the resort map

Squaw Valley
1890m/6,200ft

the three highest peaks of the area. Each has lifts of modest vertical – much the biggest is on Squaw Peak's Headwall six-pack: 535m/1,750ft.

From High Camp you can descend into a steep-sided valley from which the Silverado chair is the return. This is an area where guidance is essential.

Two peaks are accessed directly from the village. The fast quad to KT-22 gives a quick access to countless steep routes. Snow King is an excellent intermediate hill, unjustly neglected because of its slow lift access.

Squaw's cable-car runs in the evenings to serve the floodlit slopes and the dining facilities at High Camp.

Terrain-parks There are three impressive terrain-parks – Belmont is for kids and novices; Central or Riviera Park is great for intermediates and even good fun for advanced riders; Mainline is the big pro park, home of the Squaw super-pipe and all sorts of boxes and rails.

Snow reliability An impressive 450 inches on average, plus snowmaking.

Experts The possibilities for experts on KT-22, Squaw Peak and Granite Chief – plus the Silverado valley – are huge, with lots of steep chutes and big mogul fields; many extreme skiing and boarding movies are made here. But at first it is very difficult to identify routes that are safe and (if not absolutely expert) within your competence – go with an instructor.

Intermediates Blue-run skiers have a choice of some lovely cruises in the Emigrant and Snow King sectors (especially the one to the Resort at Squaw Creek), and a three-mile top-to-bottom run. There is lots of steep blue and easy black terrain in which to develop deep-snow or mogul skills – particularly around the Siberia, Solitude and Granite Chief lifts.

Beginners The Papoose nursery area has a gentle slope served by a double chair-lift – a special beginner lift pass is available. There's a superb choice of easy runs to progress to at altitude.

Snowboarding This is one of the most snowboarder friendly resorts in California. The higher areas are full of steep and deep gullies, cliff drops, kicker building spots and tree runs. The Silverado and Granite Chief lifts are especially good for free-riding. And the three terrain-parks are great.

Cross-country There are 18km/11 miles of groomed trails at Squaw Creek.

Queues Fast lifts now serve each sector, but there are still several old chairs, notably around Emigrant.

Mountain restaurants The mid-mountain facilities are not inspiring, except in terms of views.

Schools and guides Ski Your Pro runs adult group lessons hourly. There are specialist workshops including women-only and teenage camps.

Facilities for children Squaw Kids takes children from three years. Two kids' areas are planned for 2006/07.

STAYING THERE

How to go Accommodation choice has widened with the new village.

Hotels The Plumpjack Inn (800-323 7666) is our favourite – comfortable, stylish, convenient (next to The Village and the cable-car). The Resort at Squaw Creek (800-403 0206) offers luxury rooms and leisure facilities.

Self-catering The Village has well-appointed ski-in/ski-out condos.

Eating out The Plumpjack Inn has an excellent restaurant; the Balboa Cafe, run by the same people, also has an impressive menu. The alternatives in The Village are more routine – the Auld Dubliner Irish pub, a pizza/pasta joint, a sushi place, the High Sierra Grill for steaks etc. The Olympic House, just outside The Village, does excellent genuine tapas. Dining up the mountain is possible at Alexander's.

Après-ski The Olympic House has several venues, all quiet when we visited. The Zenbu is said to come to life later on, and has the requisite lasers. In The Village, the places listed above mostly function as bars, too.

Off the slopes High Camp has an ice-rink and other activities. The Trilogy Spa offers a range of body-pampering treatments. Or you can take a paddle steamer cruise across Lake Tahoe.

Squaw Valley

579

Alpine Meadows

Squaw Valley's next-door neighbour has similar, lightly wooded terrain, with runs of all classifications and an impressive snow record, but a modest total vertical of 550m/1,800ft. There's nothing but a day lodge at the base.

SNOWPIX.COM / CHRIS GILL

KEY FACTS

Resort	2085m
	6,840ft
Slopes	2085-2635m
	6,840-8,640ft
Lifts	14
Pistes	2,400 acres
Green	25%
Blue	40%
Black	35%
Snowmaking	runs
served by 12 of 14
lifts

TOURIST OFFICE

t 530 583 4232
info@skialpine.com
www.skialpine.com

THE RESORT?

There is no resort in the European sense of the word. The base day-lodge has 'uninspiring' self-service and table-service restaurants. Lots of lodgings close-by in lakeside Tahoe City.

THE MOUNTAIN

The slopes are lightly wooded, with broad open runs between glades. The base sits in a broad bowl, and outside that are two back bowls. The base is surrounded by excellent beginner slopes with a variety of slow lifts. The major mountain access lift is a six-pack going close to the top of Ward Peak; the runs back are blue, but this lift also accesses a wide range of high black runs (single- and double-diamond), some of them involving long traverses. Lower down the bowl is

generally blue terrain, served mainly by a fast quad. There is also a double chair on the upper slopes, accessing double-diamond runs in the front bowl and single diamonds in one of the back bowls. The lower slopes back here are served by a new fast quad. Separated from Ward Peak by a low saddle is Scott Peak; a double chair goes up over the steep black slopes on the front, and on the back pleasant blue runs are served by a triple. The resort boundary is open – expeditions require guidance. There's a terrain-park with a super-pipe just above the base. With a top-notch average snowfall of 460 inches, Alpine Meadows is known for its long season and excellent spring snow. A regular visitor warns of '10-minute lift lines on weekends'. There is a little Mid-Mountain Chalet on the hill – self-service, but pleasantly woody and welcoming.

Kirkwood

Kirkwood is renowned for its powder, and has a lot to offer experts and confident intermediates. It makes a great outing from South Lake Tahoe, but the small base village is also an increasingly attractive place to stay.

KIRKWOOD MOUNTAIN RESORT

KEY FACTS

Resort	2375m
	7,800ft
Slopes	2375-2985m
	7,800-9,800ft
Lifts	12
Pistes	2,300 acres
Green	15%
Blue	50%
Black	35%
Snowmaking	4 runs

TOURIST OFFICE

t 209 258 6000
info@kirkwood.com
www.kirkwood.com

THE RESORT

Kirkwood is reached from South Lake Tahoe over two high passes; heavy snowfall often closes the road. There is a cheap shuttle-bus, arriving at 9.30.

A small 'village' with ski-in, ski-out apartment accommodation is taking shape at the base. There are several bars and restaurants, a recreation centre with outdoor pool, spa and sun deck, and an ice rink on the edge of the village plaza. Après-ski is limited.

THE MOUNTAIN

The resort sits at the centre of a semi-circle of slopes, lightly wooded at the top, more densely at the bottom. The lift system consists almost entirely of slow chair-lifts. One goes up to the top of the main bowl above the base, as does a fast quad. These two long lifts

also give access to bowls to left and right of the main one. All three bowls have black slopes at the top, and easier runs lower down, served by their own shorter chairs. Beyond the left-hand bowl is a lightly wooded mountainside of blue/black gradient served by two more chairs, with various fairly adventurous ways back to the front mountain. Beginners have an excellent area to themselves at Timber Creek, with its own base lodge and now a fast quad chair serving the blue runs above the nursery slopes.

Kirkwood is an excellent resort for experts and adventurous intermediates, and fine for beginners, but limited for intermediates who are not happy to tackle black runs. Deep snow is part of the attraction: Kirkwood claims an annual average snowfall of over 500 inches, and readers report 'top class snow – far better than Heavenly'.

Northstar-at-Tahoe

Northstar is a classic US-style mountain, with runs cut through dense forest – and lacking variety, to some extent. The resort is reinventing itself, with a new base village under way and an upscale hotel on the drawing board.

KEY FACTS

Resort	1930m
	6,330ft
Slopes	1930-2625m
	6,330-8,610ft
Lifts	17
Pistes	2,420 acres
Green	25%
Blue	50%
Black	25%
Snowmaking	50 %

TOURIST OFFICE

t 530 562 1010
verticalplus@northstar
attahoe.com
www.skinorthstar.com

THE RESORT

Northstar is in the middle of building what amounts to a new village at the base. Phase one, with around 100 condos and quite a few new shops centred on a pedestrian plaza with an ice rink, opened last season. New restaurants are now opening. Phase two is due to open for 2006/07. Phase three, a walk away, is not imminent. But a Ritz-Carlton luxury hotel in a new exclusive suburb called The Highlands is planned for completion in 2009.

THE MOUNTAIN

The whole area is very sheltered and good for bad-weather days. It enjoys long views in various directions. The lift system is very slick – ★★★★★.

A gondola and a fast quad – new for 2005/06 – go up to a lodge at Big Springs, only 160m/520ft above the village. From this point three fast chairs (one a six-pack, new for 2006/07) radiate to serve a broad bowl with some short steep pitches at the top, with easier blue runs lower down and around the ridges – these giving excellent runs to the village of almost 700m/2,300ft vertical. From the ridge you can access the Backside, a steeper bowl with a central fast quad chair rising 575m/1,890ft and serving a row of easy black runs; and – another four black runs with a modest vertical of 390m/1,280ft on Lookout Mountain. The two runs close to the liftline are seriously steep. Snowfall is a respectable 350 inches on average, and 50 per cent snowmaking. There are no less than six terrain-parks, to suit all abilities; as well as a super-pipe there is a standard pipe. You can eat at two or three places on the hill.

Sierra-at-Tahoe

Sierra makes a natural day trip target for those staying in South Lake Tahoe to ski Heavenly; it isn't as compelling as Kirkwood, but is easier to get to – a 25-minute drive, off the main Highway 50.

KEY FACTS

Resort	2210m
	7,250ft
Slopes	2025-2700m
	6,640-8,850ft
Lifts	10
Pistes	2,000 acres
Green	25%
Blue	50%
Black	25%

TOURIST OFFICE

t 530 659 7453
sierra@
boothcreek.com
www.sierratahoe.com

THE RESORT

There is nothing at the base but a day lodge with several eateries and bars and a car park. Free shuttle buses operate from South Lake Tahoe. The trees provide shelter, so in principle it's a good place to be in bad weather. But bear in mind that the road from South Lake Tahoe passes over the 2250m/7,380ft Echo Summit, which may require snow chains

THE MOUNTAINS

Sierra is a Colorado-style resort, with runs cut on densely wooded slopes; it has a vertical of 675m/2,210ft, 2,000 acres and nine lifts including three fast quads. Sierra claims an impressive average of 420 inches of snow a year.

The slopes are spread over two flanks of Huckleberry Mountain, above the base lodge, and West Bowl, off to one side. Both sectors include a fast quad chair among their lifts. The front of Huckleberry and West Bowl both offer good intermediate cruising plus some genuine single-diamond blacks. The Backside of Huckleberry has easier blue and green slopes, with blue and green routes back to the base. There are five gates in the area boundary accessing backcountry terrain, and half-day tours guided by ski patrollers for $25. The Playground at the base has tubing as well as a nursery slope with a fast quad. There are six terrain-parks, including a super-pipe with 5m/17ft walls, and a standard pipe. In addition to the day lodge at the base, there's a restaurant at the top of the hill (appropriately called Grandview) and a BBQ at the bottom of West Bowl – a rare opportunity in these parts to slump in a deck-chair.

Colorado

Colorado was the first US state to market its resorts internationally and is still the most popular American destination for UK visitors. And justifiably so: it has the most alluring combination of attractive resorts, slopes to suit all abilities and excellent, reliable snow – dry enough to justify its 'champagne powder' label. It also has direct scheduled and charter flights to Denver – a real advantage.

Colorado has amazingly dry snow. Even when the snow melts and refreezes, the moisture seems to be magically whisked away, leaving it in soft powdery condition. Even in times of snow shortage, the artificial snow is of a quality you'll rarely find in Europe. And like most north American rivals, Colorado resorts generally have excellent, steep, ungroomed terrain that has enormous appeal to the adventurous because you don't need guidance to ski it safely.

The resorts vary enormously. If you want cute restored buildings from the mining boom days of the late 1800s, try the dinky old towns of Telluride or Crested Butte or the much bigger Aspen. Others major on convenience –

such as Aspen's modern satellite, Snowmass. Some resorts deliberately pitch themselves up-market, with lots of glitzy, pricey hotels – such as Vail and Beaver Creek – while others are much more down to earth – such as Winter Park and Copper Mountain.

There is a cluster of resorts west of Denver which can be combined in a holiday tour by car. You could visit these while staying in cheaper accommodation in a valley town such as Frisco. As well as the resorts we cover in detail, you could think about quick visits to some others – notably high, steep Arapahoe Basin, up the valley from Keystone; and snow-sure Loveland, visible from the main I70 highway from Denver.

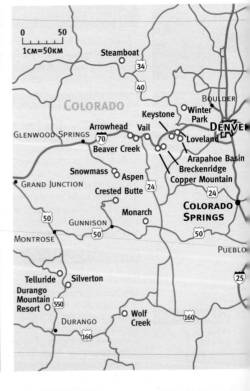

ASPEN / DOUG CHILD

Aspen

Don't be put off by the ritzy image – with a fun, historic town and quiet, extensive slopes, this is America's best resort

① ② ③ ④ ⑤ ⑥

RATINGS

The slopes	
Fast lifts	★★★
Snow	★★★★★
Extent	★★★★
Expert	★★★★★
Intermediate	★★★★★
Beginner	★★★★★
Convenience	★★
Queues	★★★★
Mountain restaurants	★★★

The rest	
Scenery	★★★
Resort charm	★★★★
Off-slope	★★★★

Our extent rating relates to the whole Aspen-Snowmass area. Aspen alone would rate ★★

NEWS

For 2006/07 an additional 20-30 acres of terrain is planned for the Deep Temerity sector at Aspen Highlands. This follows the opening of a triple chair and new advanced/expert terrain there last season.

Work to upgrade Aspen Mountain's Silver Queen gondola cabins should be complete for 2006/07.

The Hyatt Grand Aspen hotel opened near the gondola last season.

➕ Notably uncrowded slopes, even by American standards

➕ Attractive, characterful old mining town, with lots of smart shops

➕ Lively, varied nightlife

➕ Great range of restaurants

➕ Excellent Snowmass just up the road

➖ Slopes split over three separate mountains (four if you count Snowmass, as you should), though there's efficient, free transport

➖ Some accommodation in Aspen town is a bus-ride from the lifts

➖ Expensive

Aspen is our favourite American resort. We love the town and we love the extensive and varied skiing. We admit that this affection for the skiing depends heavily on the presence of Snowmass, a little way down the valley, which is covered in a separate chapter, and Aspen Highlands – so to get to most of the slopes you have to ride a bus. That doesn't put us off, and doesn't seem to worry readers who report on the place – so it shouldn't deter you, either.

You can forget the filmstar image. Yes, many rich and famous guests jet in to the local airport, and for connoisseurs of cosmetic surgery the bars of Aspen's top hotels can be fascinating places. But most celebs keep a low profile; and, like all other 'glamorous' ski resorts, Aspen is actually filled by ordinary holidaymakers.

THE RESORT

In 1892 Aspen was a booming silver-mining town, with 12,000 inhabitants, six newspapers and an opera house. But Aspen's fortunes took a nose-dive when the silver price plummeted in 1893, and by the 1930s the population had shrunk to 700 or so, and handsome Victorian buildings had fallen into disrepair. Development of the skiing started on a small scale in the late 1930s. The first lift was opened shortly after the Second World War, and Aspen hasn't looked back.

Now, the historic centre – with a typical American grid of streets – has been beautifully renovated to form the core of the most fashionable ski town in the Rockies. There's a huge variety of bars, restaurants, shops and art galleries – some amazingly upmarket. Spreading out from this centre, you'll find a mixture of developments, ranging from the homes of the super-rich through surprisingly modest hotels and motels to the mobile homes for the workers. Though the town is busy with traffic, it moves slowly and pedestrians effectively have priority in much of the central area.

Aspen is very unusual in being a cute town with a major lift close to the centre: the Silver Queen gondola

straight to the top of Aspen Mountain is only yards from some of the top hotels, and the streets running away from the lift base are lined by the restaurants and shops that make Aspen what it is. Downtown Aspen is quite compact by American resort standards, but it spreads far enough to make the free ski-bus a necessity for many visitors staying less centrally.

The other mountains are out of town, served by efficient buses from a station near the gondola base – 'fantastic and super-frequent' says a 2006 reporter. A couple of miles out of town, Aspen Highlands now has some limited accommodation; 12 miles away, Snowmass is a proper resort, and now gets its own chapter.

Sundeck
3415m/11,210ft

The fast Ajax
chair serves a
good high area
of blues and
easy blacks

Ajax

Copper Bowl

308om/10,110ft

Face of Bell

Ruthie's

Good cruising
served by this
unusual chair –
a fast double

Bell is an excellent
hill for those not
up to the double-
diamond runs
that dominate
other black areas

Spar Gulch

Silver Queen

Grand Junction

ASPEN MOUNTAIN

Long top-to-
bottom cruises
down Spar Gulch
and Copper Bowl

Aspen
2425m/7,95oft

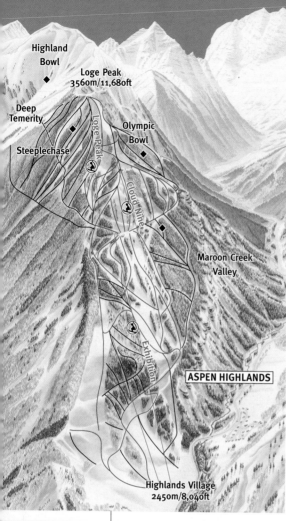

Highland
Bowl

Loge Peak
3560m/11,680ft

Deep
Temerity

Olympic
Bowl

Steeplechase

Loge Peak

Cloud Nine

Maroon Creek
Valley

Exhibition

ASPEN HIGHLANDS

Highlands Village
2450m/8,040ft

West Summit
3015m/9,900ft

SPEN HIGHLANDS

Cliffhouse
2965m/9,720ft

West Buttermilk

BUTTERMILK

West
Buttermilk
2655m/
8,710ft

Summit

ack
ɔm/
oft

Main
Buttermilk
2400m/788oft

THE MOUNTAINS

Aspen has lots for every ability; you just have to pick the right mountain. All of them have regular, free guided tours, given by excellent amateur ambassadors. The ratio of acres to visitor beds is high, and the slopes are usually blissfully uncrowded. Most of the slopes are in the trees. Lift passes are discounted heavily for purchase in advance or through tour operators – check out your options well in advance of travelling.

THE SLOPES
Widely dispersed

Each of the three local mountains is worth a visit – though novices should note that Aspen Mountain has no green runs. Much the most extensive mountain in the area is at Snowmass – see separate chapter.

Once you are up the gondola, a series of chairs serves the ridges of **Aspen Mountain**. In general, there are long cruising blue runs along the valley floors and short, steep blacks down from the ridges.

Buttermilk is the least challenging mountain, served by a fast quad from the fairly primitive main base lodge. The runs fan out from the top in three directions – back to the base, or down to the slow Tiehack chair, or down to the fast quad at West Buttermilk.

Aspen Highlands consists essentially of a single ridge served by three fast quad chairs, with easy and intermediate slopes along the ridge itself and steep black runs on the flanks – very steep ones at the top. And beyond the lift network is Highland Bowl, where gates give access to a splendid open bowl of entirely double-black gradient. There are free snowcat rides from the top of the lifts to the first access gate of Highland Bowl, but if these are not operating, it's a 20-minute hike. All the other gates require further hiking. The Deep Temerity triple chair accesses new advanced and expert terrain below Highland Bowl and Steeplechase. The views from the upper part of Highlands are the best that Aspen has to offer – the famous Maroon Bells that appear on countless postcards. There is a base lodge with underground parking and a Ritz-Carlton aparthotel.

Signposting could be better where runs merge: 'You're not sure which run you are on,' writes one reporter; but

KEY FACTS

Resort	2425m
	7,950ft

Aspen Mountain	
Slopes	2425-3415m
	7,950-11,210ft
Lifts	8
Pistes	673 acres
Green	0%
Blue	48%
Black	52%
Snowmaking	
	210 acres

Aspen Highlands	
Slopes	2450-3560m
	8,040-11,680ft
Lifts	5
Pistes	970 acres
Green	18%
Blue	30%
Black	52%
Snowmaking	
	110 acres

Buttermilk	
Slopes	2400-3015m
	7,870-9,900ft
Lifts	9
Pistes	435 acres
Green	35%
Blue	39%
Black	26%
Snowmaking	
	108 acres

Total with Snowmass	
Slopes	2400-3815m
	7,870-12,510ft
Lifts	44
Pistes	5,206 acres
Green	10%
Blue	45%
Black	45%
Snowmaking	
	613 acres

another reader liked the novel idea of attaching piste maps to chair-lifts. The Ski TV channel is recommended viewing for slope information.

TERRAIN-PARKS
Some of the world's best
Aspen has a terrain-park of a kind on each of its hills. Advanced riders should head to Buttermilk's Crazy T'rain Park, since 2002 home of the Winter X Games. The park stretches over 3km/2 miles and is said to be the longest in the world. Different sections include a log rail area, big kicker sections, hip jump, box and rail-park and a super-pipe. Aspen Mountain and Aspen Highlands have what they term 'natural' parks. Kickers, natural hits, a road gap and rails are dotted around the mountain, as opposed to being in designated areas, and are marked on the piste maps so you can ride the mountain from top to bottom and do some freestyle along the way.

SNOW RELIABILITY
Rarely a problem
Aspen's mountains get an annual average of 300 inches of snow – not in the front rank, but not far behind. In addition, all areas have substantial snowmaking. Immaculate grooming adds to the quality of the pistes.

FOR EXPERTS
Buttermilk is the only soft stuff
There's plenty to choose from – all the mountains except Buttermilk offer lots of challenges.

Aspen Mountain has a formidable array of double-black-diamond runs. From the top of the gondola, Walsh's, Hyrup's and Kristi are on a lightly wooded slope and link up with Gentleman's Ridge and Jackpot to form the longest black run on the mountain. A series of steep glades drops down from Gentleman's Ridge. The central Bell ridge has less extreme single-diamonds on both its flanks, including some delightful lightly wooded areas. On the opposite side of Spar Gulch is another row of double-blacks, collectively called the Dumps, because waste was dumped here in the silver-mining days.

At Highlands there are challenging runs from top to bottom of the mountain. Consider joining a guided group as an introduction to the best of them. Highland Bowl, beyond the top lift, is superb in the right conditions: a big open bowl with pitches from a serious 38° to a terrifying 48° – facts you can check in the very informative Highlands Extreme Skiing Guide leaflet. Within the lift system, the Steeplechase area consists of a number of parallel natural avalanche chutes, and their elevation means the snow stays light and dry. The Deep Temerity lift has opened up more than 200 acres of double black terrain. The Olympic Bowl area on the opposite flank of the mountain has great views of the Maroon Bells and some serious moguls. Thunderbowl chair from the base serves a nice varied area that's often underused.

LIFT PASSES

Four Mountain Pass

Prices in US$

Age	1-day	6-day
under 13	49	270
13 to 17	66	378
18 to 64	78	444
over 65	71	402

Free under 7

Senior over 70: $199 for unlimited period

Beginner included in price of lessons

Notes

Covers Aspen Mountain, Aspen Highlands, Buttermilk and Snowmass, and shuttle-bus between the areas. Substantial savings on lift passes for four days or more if you purchase them more than seven days in advance or through certain tour operators – and if you plan a two-week trip, there's a 'buy 8 get 6 days free' offer if you book before 1 December.

OUR WEBSITE

Go to our website at wtss.co.uk for resort news, links to resort sites, a build-your-own resort shortlist system and reader forums.

ASPEN SKIING COMPANY / PAUL MORRISON

← Sundeck restaurant on Aspen Mountain gives great views across to Highlands; to European eyes, the two ought to have been linked by now

boarding

There is a huge amount of terrain to explore, which will satisfy all levels of boarder – especially when you include Snowmass (see separate chapter). For more mellow carving runs and gentle free-riding head to Buttermilk, the least testing of the mountains – but also home to the most serious terrain-park. Until April 2001 snowboarding was banned on Aspen Mountain, but now you can enjoy all of its excellent terrain; here and on Highlands there are countless good runs and tree lines. The hills are drag-lift-free, with few flat sections.

FOR INTERMEDIATES
Grooming to die for

Most intermediate runs on Highlands are concentrated above the mid-mountain Merry-Go-Round restaurant, many served by the Cloud Nine fast quad chair. But there are good slopes higher up and lower down – don't miss the vast, neglected expanses of Golden Horn, on the eastern limit of the area.

Aspen Mountain has its fair share of intermediate slopes, but they tend to be tougher than on the other mountains. Copper Bowl and Spar Gulch, running between the ridges, are great cruises early in the morning but can get crowded later. Upper Aspen Mountain, at the top of the gondola, has a dense network of well-groomed blues. The unusual Ruthie's chair – a fast double, apparently installed to rekindle the romance that quads have destroyed – serves more cruising runs and the popular Snow Bowl, a wide, open area with moguls on the left but groomed on the right and centre.

The Main Buttermilk runs offer good, easy slopes to practise on. And good intermediates should be able to handle the relatively easy black runs – when groomed, these are a real blast on carving skis. It's also a great place for early experiments off-piste.

FOR BEGINNERS
Can be a great place to learn

Buttermilk is a great mountain for beginners. West Buttermilk has beautifully groomed, gentle, often deserted runs, which got a new quad recently. The easiest slopes of all, though, are at the base of the Main Buttermilk sector – on Panda Hill.

Despite its macho image, Highlands boasts the highest concentration of green runs in Aspen, served by the fast Exhibition chair.

FOR CROSS-COUNTRY
Backcountry bonanza

There are 60km/37 miles of groomed trails between Aspen and Snowmass in the Roaring Fork valley – the most extensive maintained cross-country system in the US. And the Ashcroft Ski Touring Centre maintains around 35km/21 miles of trails around Ashcroft, a mining ghost-town. The Pine Creek Cookhouse (970 925 1044) – excellent food and accessible by ski, snow-shoe or horse-drawn sleigh only – recently reopened following a devastating fire. Aspen is at one end of the famous Tenth Mountain Division Trail, heading 370km/230 miles north-east almost to Vail, with 12 huts for overnight stops.

GET THE BEST OF THE SNOW, ON- AND OFF-PISTE

Aspen offers special experiences for small numbers of skiers or riders.

Fresh Tracks *The first eight skiers to sign up each day get to ride the gondola up Aspen Mountain at 8am the next morning, and to get first tracks on perfect corduroy or fresh powder. Free! But take your time over the descent: if you get back to the base before the normal lift opening time, you'll have to wait, like everyone else.*

Off-piste Tours *On Wednesdays backcountry guides lead expert skiers and riders around the famous expert terrain of Highlands – a similar deal is available in Snowmass. 10am–3pm, $119.*

Powder Tours *Spend the day finding untracked snow in 1,500 acres of backcountry beyond Aspen Mountain, with a 10-passenger heated snowcat as your personal lift. You're likely to squeeze in about 10 runs in all. You break for lunch at an old mountain cabin. Full day, $295.*

SCHOOLS

Aspen
t 923 1227

Classes
Full day (5hr) $122,
incl.tax

Private lessons
$365 for a half day
(3hr) for up to 5
people.

CHILDREN

Buttermilk:
Powder Pandas
t 920 0935
Ages 3 to 6 (5 to 7
for snowboarding);
shuttle-bus from
Aspen.

Snowmass:
Big Burn Bears
t 923 0570
From age 3½

Snow Cubs
t 923 0563
Ages 8wk to 3½yr

Grizzlies
t 923 0580
Ages 5 and 6
(snowboarding for 5
to 7).

All-day non-skiing
nurseries
Several

Ski school
Takes ages 7 to 12,
US$360 for 5 days
(5¼hr per day, lunch
included).

ACTIVITIES

Indoor The Aspen
Club and Spa (racquet
ball, swimming,
weights, aerobics,
sauna, steam room,
hot-tubs, ice skating);
Aspen Recreation
Centre (swimming
complex and ice rink),
cinemas, theatre,
naturalists' evenings

Outdoor Ice skating,
snow-shoe tours,
snowmobiles

QUEUES
Few problems
There are rarely major queues on any
of the mountains. At Aspen Mountain,
the gondola can have delays at peak
times; although this lift is being
upgraded, it seems the changes are
directed at improving comfort and
views, not capacity. There are
alternatives to the top, but the Shadow
Mountain chair is said to be 'old and
slow', with an uphill walk to reach it.
Aspen Highlands is almost always
queue-free, even at peak times. The
two lifts out of Main Buttermilk
sometimes get congested.

MOUNTAIN RESTAURANTS
Good by American standards
On Aspen Mountain the Sundeck has
'one of the best self-service restaurants
you'll find', with great views across to
Highland Bowl. And there's a table-
service area, Benedict's, offering
'wonderful food.' A 2006 reporter
reckons Bonnie's is also worth a visit.
At Highlands the Cloud Nine Alpine
bistro is the nearest thing you will find
in the States to a cosy Alpine hut, with
great views and excellent food –
thanks to an Austrian chef.
On Buttermilk the mountaintop
Cliffhouse is known for its 'Mongolian
Barbecue' stir-fry bar and great views.

SCHOOLS AND GUIDES
Simply the best?
There's a wide variety of specialised
instruction – mountain exploration
groups, off-piste tours, adrenaline
sessions, women's groups, and so on.
Past reporters have praised the small
group lessons ('the best class ever';
'wonderful instruction') and a 2006
visitor enjoyed 'good value' beginner
classes. But another 2006 reader was
unimpressed: 'not enough mileage
covered and I didn't get my video
analysis as promised'. The Wizard Ski
Deck is an indoor ski and snowboard
simulator used in combination with
some classes or private lessons.

FACILITIES FOR CHILDREN
Choice of nurseries
We have no recent reports, but past
reports on the childcare arrangements
have always been first class. Young
children are bussed to and from
Buttermilk's very impressive Fort Frog.
The Kids' Trail Map is a great idea. But
Snowmass has clear advantages for
families with young children.

STAYING THERE

HOW TO GO
Accommodation for all pockets
There's a mixture of hotels, inns,
B&Bs, lodges and condos.
Chalets Several UK tour operators have
chalets here – some very luxurious.
Hotels There are places for all budgets.
Most smaller hotels provide an après-
ski cheese and wine buffet, which can
be quite a spread. A new hotel, the
Hyatt Grand Aspen (803 9400), has
opened near the gondola.
((((5 **St Regis Aspen** (920 3300)
Opulent city-type hotel, near gondola.
With a fancy spa facility.
((((5 **Little Nell** (920 4600) Stylish,
modern hotel right by the gondola,
with popular bar. Fireplaces in every
room, outdoor pool, hot-tub, sauna.
((((5 **Jerome** (920 1000) Step back a
century: Victorian authenticity
combined with modern-day luxury.
Several blocks from the gondola.
(((4 **Lenado** (925 6246) Smart modern
B&B place with open-fire lounge,
individually designed rooms.
((3 **Hotel Aspen** (925 3441) Best
'moderate' place in town, 10 minutes
from lifts; comfortable, pool, hot-tubs.
((3 **Boomerang Lodge** (925 3416)
Lloyd-Wright-inspired architecture,
seven blocks from the centre,
comfortable, pool, hot-tub.
((3 **The Mountain Chalet** (925 7797)
Cosy lodge five minutes from gondola.
Pool, sauna and fitness room.
(2 **Tyrolean Lodge** (925 4595) On the
main street; 'great, with great deals';
but no hot-tub.
Self-catering The standards here are
high, even in US terms. Many of the
smarter developments have their own
free shuttle-buses. The Gant is luxurious
and close to the gondola. Chateau
Roaring Fork and Eau Claire, four
blocks from the gondola, are spacious
and well furnished.

EATING OUT
Dining dilemma
As you'd expect, there are excellent
upmarket places, but also plenty of
cheaper options – and an easy way to
economise in many smarter places is
to choose from the bar menu.
Piñons serves innovative American
food. Syzygy is a suave upstairs place
with live jazz from 10pm. Pacifica
Seafood Brasserie is top-notch. The
basement Steak Pit is a long-
established and reliable favourite. The

Elevation features 'original Andy Warhol artworks on the wall' and 'superb modern food'. The Hostaria, Campo de Fiori and Manrico are good Italians. Cache Cache does good-value Provençal. Ute City Bar & Grill is good for local game, the Cantina serves Mexican and Jimmy's does 'excellent' steaks. A 2006 reporter rates Little Annies ('good meals, huge portions').

Cheaper recommendations include: Bentley's (main courses $8 upwards), Boogie's (a 50s-style diner, great for families), Main Street Bakery & Café, Mezzaluna, Hickory House ('very good ribs') and New York Pizzas ('excellent'). Old favourite the Red Onion is judged by one 2006 visitor to be 'over-rated'.

APRES-SKI
Lots of options
As the lifts shut, a few bars at the bases get busy – notably Iguana's at Highlands, the Ajax Tavern in Aspen. The Bar at the Little Nell is a great place for gazing at face-lifts.

Many of the restaurants are also bars – Jimmy's (spectacular stock of tequila), Mezzaluna, Red Onion, and Ute City, for example. The J-bar of the Jerome hotel still has a traditional feel.

Shooters Saloon is a splendid country-and-western dive with pool and line-dancing. For pool in more suave circumstances, there's Aspen Billiards adjoining the fashionable Cigar Bar, with its comfortable sofas (and smoking permitted!). The Popcorn Wagon is the place for munchies after the bars close. You can get a week's membership of the famous members-only Caribou club.

OFF THE SLOPES
Silver service
Aspen has lots to offer, especially if your credit card is in good shape. There are literally dozens of art galleries, as well as the predictable clothes and jewellery shops. Just wandering around town is pleasant, and there are plenty of shops selling affordable stuff – the 'super cool' Explore Bookshop, for one. Glenwood Springs is 'well worth a visit'. The best mountain restaurants are awkward for pedestrians to get to. Many hotels have excellent spa facilities. The Aspen Recreation Center at the base of Highlands has a huge swimming complex and an indoor ice rink. Hot-air ballooning is also recommended.

Aspen

589

JACK AFFLECK

Beaver Creek

The exclusive modern resort lacks charm, and prices are high – but the quiet, varied slopes make a great day trip from Vail

COSTS

① ② ③ ④ ⑤ ⑥

RATINGS

The slopes
Fast lifts	*****
Snow	*****
Extent	**
Expert	****
Intermediate	****
Beginner	*****
Convenience	****
Queues	*****
Mountain restaurants	**

The rest
Scenery	***
Resort charm	**
Off-slope	***

NEWS

For 2006/07 a new area, Stone Creek Chutes, is expected to open to the east of Rose Bowl. It will offer 180 acres of expert glades.

For 2005/06 the resort's 10th fast quad replaced the Larkspur triple chair, serving Larkspur Bowl.

➕ Blissfully quiet slopes, in sharp contrast to nearby Vail

➕ Mountain has it all, from superb novice runs to daunting mogul-fields

➕ Fast chair-lifts all over the place

➕ Compact, traffic-free village centre

➖ Rather urban feel to the village core – far from the Wild West atmosphere Europeans might look for

➖ Very expensive

➖ Disappointing mountain restaurants – the best ones are members-only

Beaver Creek gets rather overshadowed by big sister Vail, but is in many ways more rewarding; we wouldn't dream of making a trip to Vail without spending a day or two in Beaver. So why not do it the other way round? The prices in this exclusive resort are one obstacle; but the key one is that we'd rather stay in a village that feels a bit more like a holiday resort, less like a small city.

THE RESORT

Beaver Creek, 10 miles to the west of Vail, was developed in the 1980s. It is unashamedly exclusive, with a choice of top-quality hotels and condos right by the slopes. It centres on a smart but rather severe pedestrian area with escalators to the slopes, exclusive shops, exquisite bronze statues and an open-air ice rink. The choice of bars and restaurants is limited; Vail is a 25-minute bus-ride away.

The lift system spreads across the mountains through Bachelor Gulch, with its Ritz-Carlton hotel, to Arrowhead, a slope-side hamlet with luxury condos, less pricey than Beaver Creek. At valley level below Bachelor Gulch is Beaver Creek Landing, where a

fast chair now leads in to the slopes. This forms the natural access point for Vail visitors, or those staying in the valley town of Avon. Alternatively there's a regular free shuttle to the village from the free valley car parks.

Resorts within day-trip range by car include Vail, Breckenridge and Keystone (owned by Vail Resorts and covered by multi-day lift passes), Arapahoe Basin and Copper Mountain.

THE MOUNTAINS

All the slopes are below the tree-line, though there are some more open areas. Free mountain tours are held four days a week.

Slopes The slopes immediately above Beaver Creek divide into two sectors,

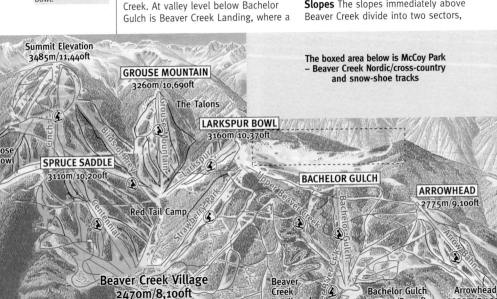

The boxed area below is McCoy Park – Beaver Creek Nordic/cross-country and snow-shoe tracks

Summit Elevation 3485m/11,440ft

GROUSE MOUNTAIN 3260m/10,690ft

The Talons

LARKSPUR BOWL 3160m/10,370ft

Rose Bowl

SPRUCE SADDLE 3110m/10,200ft

BACHELOR GULCH

ARROWHEAD 2775m/9,100ft

Red Tail Camp

Beaver Creek Village 2470m/8,100ft

Beaver Creek Landing ↓

Bachelor Gulch 2470m/8,100ft

Arrowhead 2255m/7,400ft

KEY FACTS

Resort	2470m
	8,100ft
Slopes	2255-3485m
	7,400-11,440ft
Lifts	16
Pistes	1805 acres
Green	34%
Blue	39%
Black	27%
Snowmaking	
	605 acres

OUR WEBSITE

Go to our website at wtss.co.uk for resort news, links to resort sites, a build-your-own resort shortlist system and reader forums.

LIFT PASSES

See Vail chapter.

Central reservations phone number
1 800 427 8308
(toll free from within the US).

Phone numbers
From distant parts of the US, add the prefix 1 970.
From abroad, add the prefix +1 970.

TOURIST OFFICE

t 845 9090
bcinfo@vailresorts.com
beavercreek.snow.com

each accessed by a fast quad chair – one centred on Spruce Saddle, with lifts above it reaching 3485m/11,430ft, the other Bachelor Gulch Mountain (which links to Arrowhead). Between these two sectors are Grouse Mountain and Larkspur Bowl.

Terrain-parks Park 101 is a small beginners' park, Zoom Room has intermediate-level features and Moonshine has big jumps and rails, best suited to advanced riders. There's a 120m/390ft long super-pipe and a new beginner area is planned for the nursery slopes. Park-ology is a park and pipe programme designed to offer tuition mainly to kids.

Snow reliability An impressive annual snow record (average 310 inches) plus extensive snowmaking means you can relax. Grouse Mountain can suffer from thin cover (some call it Gravel Mountain). Grooming is excellent ('never before seen eight bashers working on one slope during the day').

Experts There is quite a bit of intimidatingly steep double-diamond terrain. In the Birds of Prey and Grouse Mountain areas most runs are long, steep and moguled from top to bottom (but watch the grooming map – when one of these is groomed it makes a great fast cruise, especially the Birds of Prey downhill race-course). There are great steep glades on Grouse, and more opening for this season in the new Stone Creek Chutes. The Larkspur Bowl area has three short, steep mogul runs.

Intermediates There are marvellous long, quiet, cruising blues almost everywhere you look, including top-to-bottom runs with a vertical of 1000m/3,280ft. The Larkspur and Strawberry Park chairs serve further cruising runs – and lead to yet more ideal terrain, served by the Bachelor Gulch and Arrowhead fast chairs.

Beginners There are excellent nursery slopes at resort level and at altitude (there's a family zone at the top of the Cinch chair) – 'Snow stayed light and powdery here all week,' says a recent visitor. And there are plenty of easy longer runs to progress to, including runs from top to bottom.

Snowboarding Good riders will love the excellent gladed runs and perfect carving slopes. The resort is great for beginners, too, with special teaching methods and equipment that claim to help you learn quicker.

Cross-country There's a splendid,

mountain-top network of tracks at McCoy Park (over 32km/20 miles), reached via the Strawberry Park lift.

Queues The slopes are delightfully deserted and virtually queue-free, even at peak times – although a 2006 reporter says the Cinch Express can get busy mid-morning.

Mountain restaurants There's not much choice. The 'pleasant' and 'good-value' Spruce Saddle at mid-mountain is the main place – a food court in a spectacular log and glass building. Red Tail Camp is basic but does decent barbecues.

Schools and guides We've had good reports. Last year one 'timid intermediate' was transformed by her group lesson into a 'daredevil'.

Facilities for children Small World Play School looks after non-skiing kids from two months to six years from 8.30 to 4.30. We've had good reports on the children's school and there are splendid adventure trails and play areas.

STAYING THERE

How to go There's a reasonable choice of packages.

Hotels There are lots of upmarket places, including the Ritz-Carlton, Inn at Beaver Creek and Park Hyatt.

Self-catering There's a wide choice of condos available.

Eating out SaddleRidge is luxurious and packed with photos and Wild West artefacts. Toscanini, the Golden Eagle Inn, Dusty Boot and Beaver Creek Chophouse are all recommended. You can take a sleigh ride to one of several beautiful log cabins on the slopes – Beano's, Allie's or Zach's. .

Après-ski Try the Coyote Cafe, Whiskey Elk and McCoys (live bands).

Off the slopes There are smart boutiques and galleries, an impressive ice rink, hot-air balloon rides and some great shows and concerts.

Beaver Creek

591

Breckenridge

A sprawling resort with a cute 'Wild West' core, beneath a wide but flawed mountain; increasing amounts of slope-side accommodation

COSTS

① ② ③ ④ ⑤ ⑥

RATINGS

The slopes

Fast lifts	****
Snow	*****
Extent	**
Expert	****
Intermediate	****
Beginner	****
Convenience	***
Queues	****
Mountain restaurants	**

The rest

Scenery	***
Resort charm	***
Off-slope	***

NEWS

A new eight-seat gondola is expected to open for 2006/07, going from the Transportation Centre on the outskirts of town via the base of Peak 7 to the base of Peak 8. In due course Peak 7 will get a base village, and the Peak 8 base will be redeveloped.

For 2005/06 North America's highest lift, Imperial Express, opened on Peak 8, reaching a height of 3915m/12,840ft. It accesses 400 acres of expert terrain, previously reached by a 45-minute hike.

And the Skyway Skiway – a run and bridge connecting Peak 8 to the town – opened a year earlier than planned.

592

➕ Local mountains have something for all abilities – good for mixed groups

➕ Shared lift pass with nearby Keystone and Arapahoe Basin and not-so-nearby Vail and Beaver Creek

➕ Efficient lifts mean few queues

➕ Lively bars, restaurants and nightlife by US standards

➕ Some slope-side accommodation

➕ Restored Victorian mining town, with mainly sympathetic new buildings

➕ One of the nearest major resorts to Denver, so relatively short transfer

➖ Limited intermediate terrain, and few long runs

➖ Best advanced slopes can be closed by wind

➖ At 2925m/9,600ft the village is one of the highest you will encounter. At this extreme altitude there is a real risk of sickness for visitors coming straight from lower altitudes

➖ The 19th-century style gets a bit overblown in places, and there are some out-of-place modern buildings

➖ Main Street is just that – always busy with traffic

Breckenridge is very popular with first-time visitors to Colorado, and it's not a bad introduction to the place. Some of its drawbacks are non-trivial, though. The top slopes are exceptionally high (accessed by America's highest lift), and high winds have limited our exploration more than once. Like many readers, we have been affected by altitude sickness, and we now wouldn't think of staying in Breckenridge without first spending time in a lower resort. And intermediates more interested in mileage than challenges should plan to explore other resorts (covered by the lift pass) by car or bus.

THE RESORT

Breckenridge was founded in 1859 and became a booming gold-mining town. The old clapboard buildings have been well renovated and form the bottom part of Main Street. New shopping malls and buildings have been added in similar style – though they are obvious modern additions.

The town centre is lively in the evening, with over 100 restaurants and bars. Christmas lights and decorations remain throughout the season, giving the town a festive air. This is enhanced by a number of real winter festivals such as Ullr Fest – a carnival honouring the Norse God of Winter – and Ice Sculpture championships, which leave sculptures for weeks afterwards.

Hotels and condominiums are spread over a wide, wooded area and are linked by regular, free shuttle-buses (less frequent in the evening). If you stay in a condo and don't have a car, shopping at the local supermarket can be hard work – it is not in the centre of town. Although there is a lot of slope-side accommodation – more than any other Colorado resort, it is

claimed – there is also a fair amount that's inconveniently distant from Main Street and the lift base-stations. The planned new developments at the bases of Peaks 7 and 8 will increase the ski-in/ski-out options.

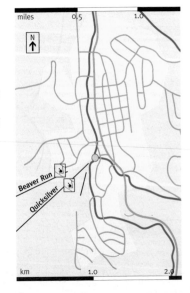

↑ Charming restored mining-era buildings form the core of the resort, but it spreads widely away from there

VAIL RESORTS, INC

KEY FACTS

Resort	2925m
	9,600ft
Slopes	2925-3915m
	9,600-12,840ft
Lifts	28
Pistes	2,208 acres
Green	15%
Blue	33%
Black	52%
Snowmaking	
	516 acres

THE MOUNTAINS

The slopes are mainly cut through the forest, with some open runs at the top. Breckenridge is in the same ownership as Vail, Beaver Creek and Keystone. A multi-day lift ticket covers all four resorts plus Arapahoe Basin. All of these resorts plus Copper Mountain are linked by regular buses (free except for the trips to Vail or Beaver Creek).

THE SLOPES
Small but fragmented
The grooming is excellent and the signposting very clear. There are free mountain tours at 9.30am daily.

There are four sectors, linked by lift and piste. Two fast chair-lifts go from the top end of town up to **Peak 9**, one accessing mainly green runs on the lower half of the hill, the other mainly blues higher up. From there you can get to **Peak 10**, which has blue and black runs served by one fast quad.

The **Peak 8** area – tough stuff at the

top, easier lower down – can be reached by a fast quad from Peak 9. The base lifts of Peak 8 at the Bergenhof can also be reached by the slow Snowflake lift from the suburbs or by the new gondola (see News). Beyond here the lower slopes of **Peak 7** are served by a single six-pack.

The higher open slopes on Peaks 7 and 8 are accessed by a T-bar reachable from either base, and now by the Imperial fast quad at the top of the Peak 8 lift network. The resort claims a top height of 3960m/13,000ft, but that involves a hike of 45m/148ft vertical from the Imperial chair.

TERRAIN-PARKS
Something for everyone
There are five terrain-parks and half-pipes. Freeway, one of the best in the US, is on Peak 8, with a series of great jumps, obstacles and an enormous championship half-pipe, which one reporter described as 'massive, steep, well kept and awesome'. Less

Breckenridge

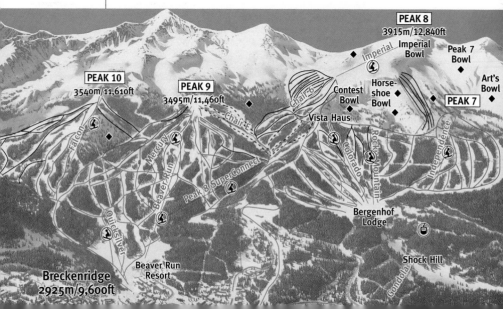

boarding

Breckenridge/ Keystone

Prices in US$

Age	1-day	6-day
under 13	39	234
13 to 64	75	450
over 65	65	390

Free under 5

Beginner included in price of lessons

Notes
Covers Breckenridge, Keystone and Arapahoe Basin, plus 3 days (on a 6-day pass) at Vail and Beaver Creek. Prices are high season rates paid in the resort. Reduced prices available if you book in advance and to international visitors who pre-book through a UK tour operator (it is not necessary to buy a complete holiday package to obtain these prices).

Breckenridge is pretty much ideal for all standards of boarder and hosts several major US snowboarding events. Beginners have ideal nursery slopes and greens to progress to. Intermediates have great cruising runs, all served by chairs. The powder bowls at the top of Peaks 7 and 8 make great riding – and access by the new Imperial quad means you can avoid the awkward T-bar, though it is still an important lift (see below). Boarders of all levels will enjoy the choice of five excellent terrain-parks and half-pipes (see 'Terrain-parks'). Nearby Arapahoe Basin is another area for hardcore boarding in steep bowls and chutes. Breckenridge pays homage to the early pioneers of the sport with a history of snowboarding display in the Vista Haus restaurant on Peak 8.

intimidating is the Gold King park on Peak 9, with jumps and railslides designed for intermediates. Trygves, on Peak 8, has gentle jumps and an introductory pipe. And Country Boy is the latest addition – medium-sized, with jumps, rails and a half-pipe. Eldorado is a mini-park on Peak 9.

SNOW RELIABILITY
Excellent
With its high altitude, Breckenridge boasts an excellent natural snow record – annual average 300 inches. That is supplemented by substantial snowmaking (used mainly early in the season to form a good base). There are a lot of east- and north-east-facing slopes, which hold snow well.

FOR EXPERTS
Lots of short but tough runs
A remarkable 52% of Breckenridge's runs are classified black – either 'most difficult' (single-black-diamond) or 'expert' (double-black-diamond) terrain. That's a higher proportion than the famous 'macho' resorts, such as Jackson Hole, Taos and Snowbird. But it's a high proportion of what is a fairly small area, and some readers find the the black classification is sometimes an exaggeration of difficulty.

There is worthwhile terrain on all the peaks, but Peaks 7 and 8 are likely to grab your attention first. The new Imperial quad rises only 285m/940ft. From this lift you can ski Imperial Bowl repeatedly, and access high terrain outside the bowl that previously involved hiking. But you still have to use the T-bar to spend time on the more extensive runs on the front face – such as Horseshoe and Contest bowls, where the snow is normally good.

On our last visit, we particularly liked the lightly wooded back bowls of Peak 8, beneath Chair 6 – picturesque and not too steep. Steep black mogul fields lead down to the junction with Peak 9. Peak 9's North Slope under Chair E is very steep – always short of snow when we have visited, but enjoyed by reporters last season.

On Peak 10, at the edge of the area, is a network of interlinking steep mogul runs. To skier's left of the chair is a lovely, lightly wooded off-piste area called The Burn.

FOR INTERMEDIATES
Nice cruising, limited extent
Breckenridge has some good blue cruising runs for all intermediates. But dedicated piste-bashers are likely to find the runs short and limited in variety. Peak 9 has the easiest slopes. It is nearly all gentle, wide, blue runs at the top and almost flat, wide, green runs at the bottom. And the ski patrol is supposed to enforce slow-speed skiing in narrow and crowded areas, though a reader last year did not see much evidence of this.

Peak 10 has a number of more challenging runs classified blue-black, such as Crystal and Centennial, which make for good fast cruising. Peaks 7 and 8 both have a choice of blues on trails cut close together in the trees. Adventurous intermediates will also like to try some of the high bowl runs. A reporter suggests the gentle Ore Bucket glades on the fringe of Peak 7 as quiet and 'great fun'.

FOR BEGINNERS
Excellent
The bottom of Peak 9 has a big, virtually flat area and some good, gentle nursery slopes. There's then a good choice of green runs to move on to. Beginners can try Peak 8 too, with another selection of green runs and a choice of trails back to town. Reporters praise the good-value beginner package which includes lessons, equipment rental and lift pass.

Breckenridge
t 453 3272

Classes
Half day (2½hr) $75
Private lessons
$365 for 3hr

CHILDREN

**Children's Center,
Peak 8**
t 453 3258
**Children's Center,
Peak 9**
t 496 7449
Complex array of
options for all-day
care from 8.30 to
4.30 for children from
age 2mnth – prior
reservation essential.

Ski school
For ages 3 to 12, 9.45
to 3.45 daily ($105
for full day, incl.
lunch).

FOR CROSS-COUNTRY
Specialist centre in woods
There are 50km/31 miles of groomed
trails in total. Breckenridge's Nordic
Center is prettily set in the woods
between the town and Peak 8 (served
by the shuttle-bus). It has 30km/19
miles of trails and 20km/12 miles of
snow-shoeing trails. A further 20km/12
miles of cross-country trails are located
at the golf course.

QUEUES
Not normally a problem
Breckenridge's nine fast chair-lifts
make light work of peak-time crowds,
and getting to Peaks 7 and 8 should
be a quicker process when the new
gondola opens. Neither we nor our
reporters have come across serious
queues, apart from at exceptional
times, such as President's Day
weekend and on powder days – when
the Quicksilver chair can get very busy
('45 minutes' says a 2006 reporter).
Surprisingly, the new Imperial chair has
come in for criticism: it has very few

chairs and therefore limited carrying
capacity, and builds long queues at
peak holiday times – as well as being
prone to closure by wind.

MOUNTAIN RESTAURANTS
Slow progress
Breckenridge has made some effort to
improve on the standard US cafeterias:
both Tenmile Station, where Peak 9
meets 10, and the Vista Haus on Peak
8 are food-court operations. But they
get very busy ('a nightmare queuing
and finding a table') and the food is
'uninspiring'. Border Burritos at Vista
Haus serves 'huge portions'.

SCHOOLS AND GUIDES
Excellent reports
Our reporters are unanimous in their
praise for the school: classes of four to
eight (sometimes smaller), doing what
the class, not the instructor, wants.
'Superb, fantastic value for money. You
can buy three days of lessons and take
them whenever you want,' says one
reporter. A 2006 visitor also received
'friendly, first-class instruction'. Special
clinics include bumps, telemark and
powder. The new Big Mountain
Experience offers guided instruction
around Imperial Bowl.

FACILITIES FOR CHILDREN
Excellent facilities
Every report on the children's school
and nursery is full of plaudits. Typical
comments: 'excellent, combining
serious coaching with lots of fun', 'our
boys loved it', 'so much more positive
than ski schools in Europe'.

Breckenridge

595

The Freeway park is
dominated by its
World Cup-calibre
super-pipe →

GETTING THERE

Air Denver 167km/
104 miles (2½hr).

ACTIVITIES

Indoor Spas, theatre, museum, ice skating, recreation centre (pool, tubs, gym, tennis, climbing wall) on the outskirts of town – accessible by bus

Outdoor Horse-drawn sleigh rides, dog-sledding, fishing, snowmobiles, snow-shoeing, ice skating, hot-air balloon rides

OUR WEBSITE

Go to our website at wtss.co.uk for resort news, links to resort sites, a build-your-own resort shortlist system and reader forums.

Phone numbers
From distant parts of the US, add the prefix 1 970.
From abroad, add the prefix +1 970.

TOURIST OFFICE

t 453 5000
breckguest@vail
resorts.com
www.breckenridge.
snow.com

STAYING THERE

HOW TO GO
Lots of choice
A lot of tour operators feature Breckenridge.
Chalets Several tour operators have very comfortable chalets.
Hotels There's a good choice of style and price range.
((((4 **Great Divide Lodge** (453 5500) Owned by Vail Resorts. Prime location, vast rooms. Pool, tubs.
((((4 **Main Street Station** (800-869-9172) Closest thing Breckenridge has to a luxury hotel. On Main Street, close to slopes. Hot-tub, outdoor pool, sauna.
((((4 **Lodge at Breckenridge** (453 9300) Stylish luxury spa resort set out of town among 32 acres, with great views. Private shuttle-bus. Pool, tubs.
((((4 **Little Mountain Lodge** (453 1969) Luxury B&B near ice rink.
((((4 **Village** (547 5725) Central 3-star. 'Good value with spacious rooms.'
(((3 **Beaver Run** (453 6000) Huge, resort complex with 520 spacious rooms. Great location, by one of the main lifts up Peak 9. Pool, hot-tubs.
(((3 **Barn on the River** (800 795 2975) B&B on Main St. Said to do one of the best breakfasts in town.
Self-catering There is a huge choice of condominiums, many set conveniently off the aptly named Four O'Clock run. There are lots of houses to rent, too .

EATING OUT
Over 100 restaurants
There's a very wide range of eating places, from typical American food to fine dining. At peak times they get busy and mostly don't take bookings. The Breckenridge Dining Guide lists the full menu of most places.

The Brewery is famous for its enormous portions of appetisers such as buffalo wings – as well as its splendid brewed-on-the-spot beers – and is still 'the liveliest spot in town'. Endorsed again in 2006. The sophisticated food at both Café Alpine ('excellent') and Pierre's Riverwalk Café have been recommended. Mi Casa (Mexican) has had good reviews as has the Kenosha steakhouse – 'specials at great prices'. The owners of previously recommended Sushi Breck have opened a new sushi place, Wasabi. Mountain Flying Fish also does sushi. The Hearthstone is said to do 'lovely food in good surroundings', the Blue River Bistro to offer 'a wide selection

of food at affordable prices', and Bubba Gump Shrimp Company to have 'good food and exceptional service'. Michael's Italian is recommended for 'extensive menu, large portions and reasonable prices'. Rasta Pasta offers pasta with a Jamaican twist. My Thai is recommended by a 2006 reporter.

APRES-SKI
The best in the area
A reporter this year notes that there is not much tea-time animation at the lift bases. Recommendations – that perhaps get more lively later – include Breckenridge Brewery, Tiffany's, Liquid Lounge, Fatty's and Sherpa & Yetti's. The Gold Pan saloon is reputedly the oldest bar west of the Mississippi. Cecilia's serves good cocktails; Gracy O'Malley's is an Irish bar; Downstairs at Eric's is a disco sports-bar.

OFF THE SLOPES
Pleasant enough
Breckenridge is a pleasant place to wander around, with plenty of souvenir and gift shops. Silverthorne (about 30 minutes away) has excellent bargain factory outlet stores: 'Well worth a visit,' writes a reporter. A visit to Buffalo Bill's grave and museum is recommended by a 2006 visitor.

STAYING DOWN THE VALLEY
Good for exploring the area
Staying in Frisco makes sense for those touring around or on a tight budget. It's a small town with decent bars and restaurants. There are cheap motels, a couple of small hotels and some B&Bs; Hotel Frisco (668 5009) is 'comfortable, spacious and friendly', says a recent reporter, who recommends the 'excellent' Backcountry Brewery for drinking and eating, the 'basic' Moose Jaw bar, 'good Italian' at Tuscato and American food at Farrellys and Silverlode.

Copper Mountain

Great terrain with reliable snow for all ability levels, above a born-again Intrawest resort

RATINGS

The slopes

Fast lifts	**
Snow	*****
Extent	**
Expert	****
Intermediate	****
Beginner	****
Convenience	****
Queues	****
Mountain restaurants	*

The rest

Scenery	***
Resort charm	**
Off-slope	*

KEY FACTS

Resort	2955m
	9,700ft
Slopes	2955-3750m
	9,700-12,300ft
Lifts	22
Pistes	2,433 acres
Green	21%
Blue	25%
Black	54%
Snowmaking	
	380 acres

SNOWPIX.COM / CHRIS GILL

The Village at Copper. The I-70 freeway is actually much less intrusive than it seems here ↓

- Convenient purpose-built resort, transformed by owners Intrawest (of Whistler fame)
- Fair-sized mountain, with good runs for all abilities
- Free lift pass offer (see News)
- Few queues on weekdays, but ...

- Can be long lift queues at weekends (avoided by Beeline Advantage pass)
- Village still limited
- Black-diamond bowls at the top offer only limited vertical
- Risk of altitude sickness
- Mediocre mountain restaurants

Copper's slopes are some of Colorado's best, and now there's a modern, purpose-built village at the base. But expect weekend crowds, and watch out for that altitude sickness; Copper's village is even higher than Breckenridge.

THE RESORT

Rather like the French resorts of the 1960s, Copper Mountain was originally high on convenience, low on charm. But new owner, Intrawest, has done a typically thorough job with the new Village at Copper, a group of wood-and-stone-clad condo buildings with shops, restaurants and car-free walkways and squares, forming the heart of the resort, set just off the I-70 freeway from Denver. There are two other bases: East Village at the foot of Copper's steeper terrain and Union Creek at the foot of the easiest runs and beginner area. Each of these is smaller than the Village but has accommodation and restaurants. A free shuttle-bus runs between them.

Keystone, Breckenridge and Arapahoe Basin are all nearby, and Vail and Winter Park a bit further.

THE MOUNTAIN

The area is medium-sized by American standards, and has great runs for all ability levels, with an attractive mix of wooded, gladed and open slopes. Guided tours are available twice daily.
Slopes The area divides into slopes below Copper Peak and below Union Peak, with fast quads towards each from the main base area. Between the two is Union Bowl. In general, as you look at the mountain the easiest runs are on the right and it gets progressively steeper the further left you go. On the back of the hill are the high Spaulding and Copper Bowls – open slopes, in contrast to the wooded lower runs.
Terrain-parks The main Catalyst park is beside the American Flyer chair and has areas for beginners, intermediates and experts, plus a super-pipe (there's a second super-pipe at the base area). At the top of the Flyer chair there's the Kidz park with a mini-pipe (open to learning adults too), and there are terrain-park zones on the High Point trail under the chair. Early season, before Catalyst opens, there's a jib park at the top of the American Eagle.

597

NEWS

For 2005/06 the free snowcat service to the tough terrain of Tucker Mountain (the far side of Copper Bowl) was extended. Two 12-person snowcats run from 10am to 1.30pm daily. The area closes at 2pm.

As for the previous two seasons, if you book a week's holiday in the resort through most UK tour operators, you will get a free lift pass, which includes the queue-busting Beeline Advantage (see 'Queues') and a day at Winter Park.

OUR WEBSITE

Go to our website at wtss.co.uk for resort news, links to resort sites, a build-your-own-shortlist system and reader forums.

Central reservations
Call 968 2882.
Toll-free number
(from within the US)
1 888 219 2441.

Phone numbers
From distant parts of the US, add the prefix 1 970.
From abroad, add the prefix +1 970.

TOURIST OFFICE

t 866 841 2481
copper-marketing@
coppercolorado.com
www.coppercolorado.
com

REPORTS WANTED

Recently we have had few reports on this resort. If you go there, please do send us a report.

The best reports earn a copy of the next edition, and can lead to free lift passes in future.

See page 12.

A free night-time jib park operates on Friday and Saturday at the base.

Snow reliability Height and extensive snowmaking give Copper an early opening date and excellent reliability. Snowfall averages 280in a year.

Experts There is a lot of good expert terrain. Spaulding and Copper bowls offer gradients ranging from moderate to seriously steep, but with limited vertical. The wooded bump runs lower down the left side of the main mountain are much longer.

Intermediates There are runs to suit everyone, from top-to-bottom greens on the right of the map through similarly long blues to challenging (usually bumpy) black runs.

Beginners The nursery slopes at Union Creek are excellent, and there are plenty of very easy green runs to graduate to.

Snowboarding There are great slopes for all abilities, plus several terrain-parks.

Cross-country There are 25km/15 miles of trails through the White River forest.

Queues On weekdays you may find no queues, but weekend visitors pour in from Denver and cause 20-minute queues. You can buy a (pricey) Beeline Advantage pass to jump the queues (it is free if you book a holiday through most UK tour operators – see News).

Mountain restaurants Not a lot on offer. There's a food court at Solitude Station, which offers 'tasty chilli'. The T-Rex Grill has only outside seating. Or head back to base.

Schools and guides The school offers a wide variety of courses and has a fine reputation, especially for children.

Facilities for children The Belly Button childcare facility takes children from two months old and ski school takes children from age three. On the mountain, there are dedicated fun trails and a special kids' map.

STAYING THERE

How to go A number of tour operators offer packages to Copper.

Hotels and condos There are no hotels but some condos are splendidly luxurious, with outdoor hot-tubs, etc.

Eating out Alexander's on the Creek does excellent sophisticated food. Blue Moose pizza, Endo's and JJ's Rocky Mountain Tavern are popular. The Imperial Palace, Creekside Pizza and Salsa Mountain Cantina were recommended by a 2005 visitor. Sleigh rides take people out to Western-style dinners in tents.

Après-ski Après-ski is lively as the lifts close. Later on, Endo's Adrenaline Cafe and JJ's Rocky Mountain Tavern (with live music) are popular. Pravda is a Russian-style vodka bar and McGillycuddy's is an Irish bar with live music. The Storm King Lounge offers cocktails, pool and sushi.

Off the slopes Ther8e's a good sports club, with a huge pool and indoor tennis, and ice skating on the lake.

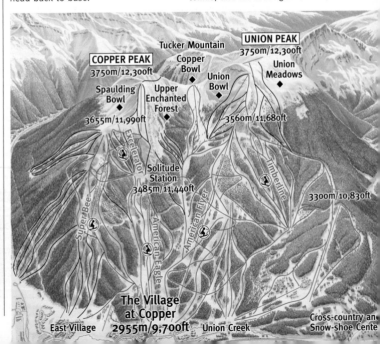

Tucker Mountain

UNION PEAK
3750m/12,300ft

COPPER PEAK
3750m/12,300ft

Copper Bowl

Union Meadows

Spaulding Bowl

Upper Enchanted Forest

Union Bowl

3655m/11,990ft

3560m/11,680ft

Solitude Station
3485m/11,440ft

3300m/10,830ft

The Village at Copper
2955m/9,700ft

East Village

Union Creek

Cross-country and Snow-shoe Centre

Keystone

A rather disappointing modern resort with plenty of comfortable lodgings, beneath a satisfying mountain with expanding cat-skiing

COSTS

① ② ③ ④ ⑤ ⑥

RATINGS

The slopes
Fast lifts	★★★★
Snow	★★★★★
Extent	★★
Expert	★★★
Intermediate	★★★★
Beginner	★★★★
Convenience	★★
Queues	★★★★
Mountain restaurants	★★★

The rest
Scenery	★★★
Resort charm	★★
Off-slope	★★

NEWS

For 2006/07 there are plans to add another 300 acres of ungroomed terrain served by snowcats.

Keystone continues to focus on terrain-park improvements: for 2005/06 a quarter-pipe was added to the main park. And there were more upgrades to snowmaking and grooming equipment.

REPORTS WANTED

Recently we have had few reports on this resort. If you go there, please do send us a report.

The best reports earn a copy of the next edition, and can lead to free lift passes in future. See page 12.

OUR WEBSITE

Go to our website at wtss.co.uk for resort news, links to resort sites, a build-your-own-shortlist system and reader forums.

➕ Good mountain with something for everyone

➕ Huge night-skiing operation

➕ Other nearby resorts on lift pass

➕ Luxurious condominiums

➖ Very scattered resort, with a lot of bussing or driving for most visitors, and no village atmosphere except in small River Run development

➖ Risk of altitude sickness for visitors coming straight from sea level

Keystone's slopes are impressive from many points of view, but there isn't a proper village at the foot of them. Luxurious condos are scattered over a wide area, and the nearest thing to a 'village' is the limited River Run development. We prefer to stay elsewhere and make day-trips to Keystone's slopes.

THE RESORT

Keystone is a sprawling resort of condominiums spread around a partly wooded valley floor. It has no clear centre and is divided into seven 'neighborhoods'. Some are little more than groups of condos, while others have shops, restaurants and bars (though no supermarkets or liquor stores – they are on the main highway).

River Run, at the base of the main gondola, is the nearest thing to a conventional ski resort village, with condo buildings, a short main street, a square and a few restaurants, bars and shops. A second lift base area half a mile to the west, Mountain House, is much less of a village. Another mile west is Lakeside Village, which is not a village at all but a hotel and condo complex, weirdly lacking animation, beside a lake – a huge natural ice rink.

Buses ('free, efficient and friendly') link all the component parts . At weekends, overflow parking lots come into operation and the bus services become overstretched.

THE MOUNTAINS

By US standards Keystone offers extensive intermediate slopes and some challenging steeper stuff, recently expanded with the opening of Erickson and Bergman Bowls. The resort is owned by Vail Resorts, and the lift pass covers Vail, Beaver Creek, Breckenridge and Arapahoe Basin (a few minutes away by road). Copper Mountain is also nearby.

Slopes Three wooded mountains form Keystone's local slopes. Lifts depart from Mountain House and River Run to the one above the resort, Dercum Mountain. The front face of the mountain has Keystone's biggest network of lifts and runs, mainly of easy and intermediate gradient. From the top you can drop over the back down to lifts up the next hill, North Peak. Or you can ride the Outpost gondola directly to the shoulder of North Peak. Beyond North Peak is the third peak, The Outback. Keystone has the biggest floodlit skiing operation in the US, covering Dercum Mountain top to bottom up to 9pm on certain nights of the week. Finding your way around is no problem say reporters: 'big coloured banners make it easy'; 'everything is clearly marked'.

Terrain-parks The A51 terrain-park is huge, with features for all levels including a super-pipe and new quarter-pipe; it has its own chair-lift and is floodlit several nights a week. The beginner's park has expanded.

Snow reliability Snow shortage is rarely a problem, and there's one of the world's biggest snowmaking systems.

Experts Keystone has a lot of steeper, ungroomed terrain. The Windows is a 60-acre area of experts-only glade runs on Dercum Mountain's back side. From The Outback there are black runs with all sorts of challenges, route-finding being one of them. You can hike to open and gladed runs in the North and South Bowls, Erickson Bowl and Bergman Bowl, or pay for snowcat access and guidance ($75 for four hours with guides from Dercum; $5 for a ride but no guide on Outback).

Intermediates Keystone has lots to offer. The front face of Dercum Mountain itself is a network of beautifully groomed blue and green

KEY FACTS

Resort	2835m
	9,300ft
Slopes	2835-3650m
	9,300-11,980ft
Lifts	19
Pistes	2,870 acres
Green	19%
Blue	32%
Black	49%
Snowmaking	
	650 acres

600

**Central reservations
phone number**
1 877 753 9786
(toll free from within
the US).
Phone numbers
From distant parts of
the US, add the prefix
1 970.
From abroad, add the
prefix +1 970.

TOURIST OFFICE

t 496 2316
keystoneinfo@
vailresorts.com
www.keystone.snow.
com

runs through the trees. The Outback
and North Peak also have easy cruising
and some steeper blues. Some of the
blacks are groomed, and are
tremendous fun early in the day.
Beginners There are good nursery
slopes at the top and bottom of
Dercum Mountain, although a reporter
found the area at the top 'a little
daunting' for novices arriving from the
gondola. There are excellent long
green runs to progress to.
Snowboarding Keystone is ideal for
beginners and intermediates, with
mainly chair-lifts and gondolas, good
beginner areas and cruising runs.
Expert riders will love The Outback.
Cross-country There are 16km/10 miles
of groomed trails and 57km/35 miles
of unprepared trails.
Queues Reporters this year are
unanimous in their praise for blissfully
quiet slopes and few queues after the
morning peak.
Mountain restaurants The table-service
Alpenglow Stube (North Peak) is a
delightfully cosseting place, and one of
our favourites in the US: the fixed-price
lunch is a bargain at about $20. The
alternatives, at the top of Dercum and
at the lift base between the two hills,
are much less appealing, but a 2006
reporter had no complaints.
Schools and guides As well as the
normal lessons, there are bumps, race
and various other advanced classes.
One reporter enjoyed 'excellent'
instruction in very small groups.
Facilities for children Excellent, with
programmes tailored to specific age
groups, dedicated children's teaching
areas and organised kids' nights out.

STAYING THERE

How to go Regular shuttles operate
from Denver airport. Most
accommodation is in condominiums.
Hotels There isn't a great choice but
they're all of a high standard.
Self-catering All the condominiums are
large and luxurious – and we've stayed
in some fabulous ones.
Eating out Disappointing: the
restaurants are scattered around the
valley, and there isn't the range of
mid-market restaurants that makes
eating out such a pleasure in many
American resorts. You can eat up the
mountain at the Summit House or
Alpenglow Stube.
Après-ski The Summit House has live
music and caters for night skiing
customers too. But this is not the
resort for late-night revellers.
Off the slopes There are plenty of
activities, including skating on the
frozen lake, tubing and indoor tennis.
Silverthorne has a leisure centre,
swimming pool and skate park, as well
as factory-outlet shopping.

Snowmass

Aspen's modern satellite – with impressively varied and extensive slopes, and a cool new Base Village under construction

COSTS

① ② ③ ④ ⑤ ⑥

RATINGS

The slopes

Fast lifts	*******
Snow	*********
Extent	********
Expert	*********
Intermediate	*********
Beginner	*********
Convenience	********
Queues	********
Mountain restaurants	*******

The rest

Scenery	********
Resort charm	******
Off-slope	*******

REPORTS WANTED

Recently we have had few reports on this resort. If you go there, please do send us a report.

OUR WEBSITE

Go to our website at wtss.co.uk for resort news, links to resort sites, a build-your-own-shortlist system and reader forums.

➕ Big, varied mountain with a vertical of 1340m/4,400ft – biggest in the US

➕ Aspen's three mountains also accessible by frequent free bus

➕ Uncrowded slopes

➕ Lots of slope-side lodgings

➖ Snowmass 'village' offers very limited shopping and nightlife, though things will improve as the new Base Village takes shape

➖ Diversions of Aspen town are a bus-ride away

The slopes of Snowmass are a key part of the attraction of nearby Aspen as a destination. As a base, Snowmass has mainly appealed to families wanting great green runs on their doorstep; but its appeal will broaden over the next few years as the range of restaurants and shops improves.

THE RESORT

Snowmass is a modern, purpose-built resort with most of the accommodation in low-rise buildings set alongside the gentle home slope. At the heart of these buildings is Snowmass Village Mall, with a small cluster of shops and restaurants. There are also lots of private homes set along roads that wind up into the lower slopes.

The Mall contains the essentials of resort life, but not much more. The new Base Village taking shape is a very welcome development. Aspen is some 12 miles away, its Highlands and Buttermilk mountains slightly less. Efficient free bus services link the resorts and mountains. The service to Aspen town runs to 2am (small charge after 4.30pm).

THE MOUNTAIN

Snowmass is big: it has 60 per cent of the area covered by the Aspen pass. It is almost 8km/5 miles across and has the biggest vertical in the US. Most of the slopes are in the forest; higher ones are open or only lightly wooded. **Slopes** Chair-lifts and a new gondola from the base go to the two extremes of the area, Elk Camp and Sam's Knob, with links higher up to the two sectors in the middle, High Alpine and Big Burn. There is also fast access from Two Creeks – much nearer to Aspen town, with free slope-side parking. **Terrain-parks** The main Pipeline park is 2.5km/1.5 miles long and incorporates a rail park, super-pipe, quarter-pipe and kicker line – all well shaped. There are separate beginner and kids' parks.

601

ELK CAMP
...m/11,320ft

HIGH ALPINE
3590m

Hanging Valley

The Cirque
3815m/12,510ft

BIG BURN
3610m/11,830ft

SAM'S KNOB
3240m/10,630ft

Cafe Suzanne

Ullrhof
3005m

Fanny Hill

Alpine Springs

Big Burn

Coney Glade

Gondola

Village

Two Creeks
247om/8,100ft

Snowmass
2565m/8,420ft

Fanny Hill, running the length of the resort, is a great beginner slope →

NEWS

A 'new Snowmass' is being created: a new Base Village is being built, linked by gondola to Village Mall, the existing resort centre. A new children's centre is due to open in 2006/07. Condos and hotels are being built, along with 11 new restaurants and bars opening over the next three years.

For 2006/07 a gondola from Base Village is expected to replace the Funnel chair-lift to Elk Camp.

For 2005/06 a six-pack replaced the Fanny Hill chair to Sam's Knob.

KEY FACTS

Resort	2565m
	8,420ft
Snowmass only	
Slopes	2470-3815m
	8,100-12,510ft
Lifts	21
Pistes	3,128 acres
Green	6%
Blue	50%
Black	44%
Snowmaking	
	185 acres

See Aspen chapter for statistics on other mountains – star rating for extent includes them all.

Phone numbers
From distant parts of the US, add the prefix 1 970.
From abroad, add the prefix +1 970.

TOURIST OFFICE

t 925 1220
intlres@skiaspen.com
www.aspensnowmass.com

Snow reliability With 300 inches a year plus snowmaking, it's good.

Experts There's great terrain. Our favourite area is around the Hanging Valley Wall and Glades – beautiful scenery and steep wooded slopes. The other seriously steep area is the Cirque. The Cirque drag-lift takes you well above the tree line to Aspen's highest point. From here, the Headwall is not terrifyingly steep, but there are also narrow, often rocky, chutes – Gowdy's is one of the steepest. All these runs funnel into a pretty, lightly wooded valley. Consider joining a guided group as an introduction to the best of Snowmass.

Intermediates Excellent – the best mountain in the Aspen area. All four sectors have lots to offer. Highlights include the top slopes on Big Burn – a huge, varied, lightly wooded area, including the Powerline Glades for the adventurous; long, top-to-bottom cruises from Elk Camp and High Alpine; regularly groomed single-black runs from Sam's Knob. Long Shot is a glorious, ungroomed, 5km/3 mile run, lost in the forest, and well worth the short hike from the top of Elk Camp.

Beginners In the heart of the resort is a broad, gentle beginners' run. An even easier slope is the wide Assay Hill, at the bottom of Elk Camp. From Sam's Knob there are long, gentle cruises leading back to the resort.

Snowboarding A great mountain, whatever your boarding style.

Cross-country Excellent trails between here and Aspen – see Aspen chapter.

Queues Snowmass has so many alternative lifts and runs that you can normally avoid problems. Some long, slow chairs can be cold in mid-winter. The home slope gets very crowded.

Mountain restaurants There are refuelling stops at several key points, but also some places worth seeking out. Gwyn's High Alpine is an elegant table-service restaurant serving above-average food. The best views are from Sam's Knob, with self-service and table-service restaurants. Cafe Suzanne on Elk Camp has a French flavour and does 'exceptionally good crêpes'.

Schools and guides A reporter last year had three rewarding days, but warns that his 'off-piste' group turned out to be just a standard class, going off-piste only if everyone wanted to.

Facilities for children We lack recent reports, but a new children's centre is due to open at Base Village this year. There are special family skiing zones.

STAYING THERE

How to go Most accommodation is self-catering.

Hotels The focal hotel is the Silvertree (923 3520) – an ocean liner parked next to the home slope and the Mall – with excellent top-floor Brothers' Grille restaurant and pools. Stonebridge Inn (923 2420) is a good-value alternative; nice restaurant, pool, hot-tub.

Self-catering Tamarack Townhouses, Terrace House and Top of the Village have been recommended by reporters.

Eating out The choice is adequate. As well as the excellent Brothers' Grille and a nearby steakhouse there are Italian, Tex-Mex, Provençal and 'pan-Asian' restaurants. Butch's Lobster Bar 'is by far the best in town', says a regular reporter. The Blue Door (see below) does Cajun food. Sno Beach Café is good for breakfast.

Après-ski The Cirque next to the home slope has live bands most days but closes at 6pm. The restaurants have bars – the Margarita keeps 30 tequilas. The Mountain Dragon is popular. The Blue Door nightclub sometimes has live music.

Off the slopes There's tubing on Assay Hill 1pm to 8pm, snow-shoe trails, nature tours, piste-basher rides, zip-wire rides and dog-sledding.

Steamboat

*The home of Champagne Powder™ makes a great place to develop
your powder skills, from a convenient slope-side base*

➕ Excellent easy runs

➕ Famed for its glade terrain

➕ Good snow record

➕ Table-service mountain restaurants

➕ Plenty of high-quality slope-side lodgings at reasonable rates

➕ Town has some Western character

➖ Town is a drive from the slopes

➖ Modern base 'village' is sprawling, with some eyesore buildings

➖ Not enough runs to amuse keen intermediates for a week

➖ Not a huge amount of challenging terrain – some of it is a hike away

Steamboat's mountain may not match some of its competitors for extent, but it's one of the best for powder fun among the trees. The lift-base village is no beauty; but it's best to stay there, and plan on just the occasional foray to the unremarkable 'cattle town' of Steamboat Springs.

THE RESORT

The resort village is a 10-minute bus-ride from the old town of Steamboat Springs. Near the gondola there are a few shop- and restaurant-lined multi-level squares, some of which are receiving a much-needed facelift over the next few years. Some lodgings are up the sides of the piste, but the resort also sprawls across the valley. The old town can be a bit of a disappointment. It may be a working cattle town, but the Wild West isn't much in evidence. The wide main street is lined with bars, hotels and shops in a mixture of styles, from old wooden buildings to concrete plazas. The free bus service is said to be 'good'. Plans to expand the regional airport should provide more flights and improve accessibility to the resort.

THE MOUNTAINS

Steamboat's slopes are prettily set among trees, with extensive views over rolling hills and the wide Yampa valley. The place is relatively isolated, but you could combine it with resorts west of Denver, from Winter Park to Vail.
Slopes The gondola from the base rises to the low peak of Thunderhead. Beyond it are lifts to Storm Peak and Sunshine Peak – the latter offering a broad area of blue runs now served by a fast quad. On the back of the hill is the Morningside Park area, with a slow chair back up to the high-point of Mt Werner, also accessing some of the top runs on the front side. Below these is an area served by the Pony Express

fast chair. Views differ on signposting; one reporter accidentally led his novice wife down a black ('there are so many signs pointing in similar directions, it is very easy to go wrong').
Terrain-parks The SoBe terrain-park includes rails, jumps, a mini-pipe and the Mavericks super-pipe, claimed to be the longest in North America. Beehive is a special park for kids. New family fun features are planned for the Sunshine area.
Snow reliability The term Champagne Powder™ was invented here, so it's no surprise to find that, despite a relatively low altitude, Steamboat has an excellent snow record. With a 10-year annual average of 335 inches, it's not far behind the Colorado leader, Winter Park. There is snowmaking from top to bottom, too.
Experts The main attraction is the challenging terrain in the glades. A great area is on Sunshine Peak below the Sundown chair. Morningside Park and the Pony Express area also have excellent gladed runs. Three steep chutes are easily accessed via the lift

Resort	2105m
	6,900ft
Slopes	2105-3220m
	6,900-10,570ft
Lifts	20
Pistes	2,965 acres
Green	13%
Blue	56%
Black	31%
Snowmaking	
	438 acres

back from Morningside, and a short hike gets you to the tree runs of Christmas Tree Bowl. For bumps, try the runs off Four Points. Many runs are of limited vertical; a 2006 reporter singles out Valley View for a longer black run to the base.

Intermediates Much of the mountain is ideal, with long cruising blue runs. Morningside Park is a great area for easy black as well as blue slopes – and 'lovely ungroomed terrain in the trees.' The Sunshine area is very gentle. Some of the black runs are regularly groomed, and 'much enjoyed' by reporters. Keen intermediates will find the mountain limited in extent, but given fresh powder it offers a great introduction to tree skiing.

Beginners There's a big nursery area at the base of the mountain, which a 2006 reporter thought 'quite steep and awkwardly cambered'. Lots of easy trails offer good progression – some of the blues are quieter and more relaxing than the greens, which include many cat-tracks with steep drops at the side. The Sunshine area is particularly suited to families skiing together.

Snowboarding There's a special learning area, gentle slopes to progress to and you can get around using chair-lifts and the gondola. For experienced riders, riding the glades in fresh powder is unbeatable.

Cross-country A free shuttle service takes you to 30km/19 miles of groomed tracks at the Touring Center.

Queues Queues form for the gondola first thing, but they move quickly (and can be avoided using chairs). The Sundown chair gets queues at peak times. The new Sunshine quad should eliminate the queues that the old slow triple caused – and should mean slightly fewer complaints from readers about the slow lifts.

Mountain restaurants There are food courts and table-service restaurants at Thunderhead and Rendezvous Saddle – better than the American fast-food norm, though peak time crowds can be a problem. Both lodges are being refurbished for 2006/07.

Schools and guides Reports are very positive. 'Very good in every respect, except that time was wasted as lessons were assembled and grouped,' writes a 2006 visitor – most guests purchase tuition on a daily basis.

Facilities for children Arrangements are exceptional, winning awards from American magazines; even evening entertainment. Kids under 12 ski free with a parent or a grandparent buying a pass for at least five days.

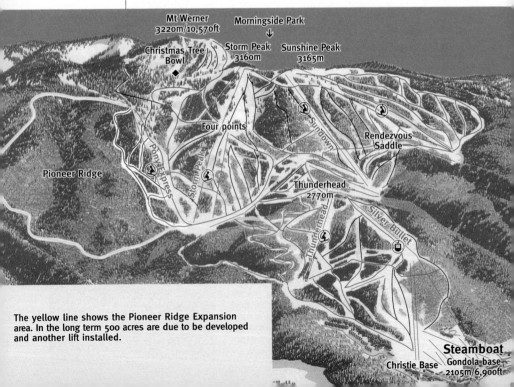

The yellow line shows the Pioneer Ridge Expansion area. In the long term 500 acres are due to be developed and another lift installed.

Mt Werner
3220m/10,570ft

Morningside Park

Christmas Tree Bowl

Storm Peak
3160m

Sunshine Peak
3165m

Four points

Rendezvous Saddle

Pony Express

Storm Peak

Sundown

Pioneer Ridge

Thunderhead
2770m

Silver Bullet

Thunderhead

Steamboat

Christie Base

Gondola base
2105m/6,900ft

OUR WEBSITE

Go to our website at
wtss.co.uk for resort
news, links to resort
sites, a build-your-
own resort shortlist
system and reader
forums.

Central reservations
phone number
1 800 922 2722
(toll free in the US).

Phone numbers
Calling long-distance,
add the prefix 1 970.
From abroad, add the
prefix +1 970.

TOURIST OFFICE

t 879 6111
info@steamboat.com
www.steamboat.com

STEAMBOAT / LARRY PIERCE

For powder among
the aspens, there are
few places better than
Steamboat ↓

STAYING THERE

How to go A fair number of UK tour
operators feature Steamboat.
Chalets There are some catered chalets
run by UK tour operators.
Hotels There are smart hotels at the
base, including the 'excellent' Steamboat
Grand (871 5050) – more characterful
ones in town. Recommendations by
reporters include: the Rabbit Ears
Motel (879 1150) and the slope-side
Ptarmigan Inn (879 1730) ('friendly,
comfortable and convenient').
Self-catering There are countless
condos, many with good pool/hot-tub
facilities, all on a free bus route. There
are plenty of good places at the lift
base. Antlers offers the best luxury ski-
in, ski-out accommodation; Eagleridge
and Canyon Creek are pretty luxurious,
too. Timber Run, The Lodge, Ski Inn
and the Rockies all offer good value.
Eating out There are over 70 bars and
restaurants. Pick up a dining guide
booklet to check out the menus. You
can dine in three restaurants up the
mountain. Recommendations at the
base area include the Tugboat Grill and
Pub ('great food, good service and
lively atmosphere'), Cafe Diva, La

Montaña (Tex-Mex) and the 'classy but
pricey' Butcher's Shop for steaks and
fish. The Wired internet cafe is good
for breakfast. In downtown Steamboat
Springs there is quite a wide range of
options. Try Antares for Asian fusion
cuisine, Old West Steakhouse, or the
Cottonwood Grill for its 'fabulously
tasty Pacific Rim cuisine'. Reporters
also recommend the 8th Street
Steakhouse with its communal
barbecue ('great fun, good food'). For
a budget meal, head for the Double Z
(pronounced Zee, of course).
Après-ski The base lodge area is livelier
than the old town in the evening. At
close of play the big Slopeside Grill is
popular. The Bear River Bar has a
comedy club, and the Tugboat has live
music and dancing. The Old Town Pub
in the town is 'great for beer and a
game of pool.' There's a new nightlife
trail map – presumably for the ultimate
bar crawl.
Off the slopes Getting to Thunderhead
restaurant complex is easy for
pedestrians. Visiting town is, too. The
Strawberry Park Hot Springs are 'a
great experience – lovely and relaxing'.
Snowmobiling and dog-sledding are
also possible.

Steamboat

605

Telluride

*Cute old town, smart new Mountain Village, slopes to suit all.
What more could you want? More terrain, that's all*

606

COSTS

① ② ③ ④ ⑤ ⑥

RATINGS

The slopes

Fast lifts	*****
Snow	****
Extent	**
Expert	****
Intermediate	***
Beginner	*****
Convenience	****
Queues	*****
Mountain restaurants	*

The rest

Scenery	****
Resort charm	****
Off-slope	**

NEWS

From 2005/06, you can rent a device that tracks the runs and amount of vertical you do in a day. Results are traced on a souvenir map. The luxurious Tempter House at 3720m/12,200ft is now available for overnight stays.

KEY FACTS

Resort	2665m	
	8,750ft	
Slopes	2665-3735m	
	8,750-12,260ft	
Lifts		16
Pistes	1,700 acres	
Green		24%
Blue		38%
Black		38%
Snowmaking		
	204 acres	

➕ Charming restored Victorian mining town with a Wild West atmosphere

➕ Slopes for all, including experts

➕ Dramatic, craggy mountain scenery – unusual for Colorado

➖ Isolated location

➖ Despite expansion, still a small area

➖ Mountain Village a little quiet

➖ Limited mountain restaurants

We love the old town of Telluride and always enjoy its scenic, varied slopes; but their limited extent makes the place difficult to recommend for a holiday except in combination with another resort – which means travelling some distance.

THE RESORT

Telluride is an isolated resort in south-west Colorado. It first boomed when gold was found – and Butch Cassidy robbed his first bank here. The town's old red-brick and timber buildings have been well restored, and it has more Wild West charm than any other resort. Shops and restaurants have gone upmarket since its 'hippy' days of a few years ago and a lot of celebrities have plush holiday-homes here now. But Telluride is still friendly and small-scale. On the slopes, the Mountain Village is a development of lavish modern condos and hotels. A gondola links the town and village and runs until midnight.

THE MOUNTAINS

There is something for everyone here.
Slopes Slow chairs and a gondola from the old town access steep wooded slopes above it and runs beyond – the easiest leading down to the Mountain Village (which can also be reached by staying on the gondola). There are also steep open slopes at the very top.
Terrain-parks The huge, 10-acre Sprite Air Garden terrain-park above the Mountain Village has a super-pipe and all the features you could dream of. The separate Pocket Park off the Ute Park lift is suitable for beginners.
Snow reliability With an average of 309 inches of snow a year and some snowmaking, reliability is good, but there have been some slow starts to recent seasons; it gets a different weather pattern to the main Colorado resorts further north.
Experts The double-black bump runs down from Giuseppe's towards town are classic tests, and there are steep gladed runs from all along the ridge

between Giuseppe's and Gold Hill. The fast Gold Hill lift accesses some truly challenging terrain, from wide open steeps to narrow chutes and gnarly wooded trails. There is also hike-to backcountry terrain in Prospect Bowl you can try with the ski school. Helitrax runs a heli-skiing operation.
Intermediates There are ideal blue cruising runs with great views from the top down to Mountain Village (including the aptly-named See Forever). The Prospect Bowl lift accesses some great intermediate terrain, with dozens of rolling pitches through the trees – a very relaxing and pretty area. More challenging are some of the bumpy double-blues from the Apex and Palmyra chairs. Some of the blacks above the town get groomed – worth catching if you can. The blue Telluride Trail back to town is a narrow catwalk ('treacherous' says a reporter). But the area is small and keen piste-bashers could get bored after a couple of days.
Beginners There are ideal runs below Mountain Village, and splendid long greens served by the Sunshine chair.
Snowboarding The lift system means it is easy to get about, and the huge terrain-park offers plenty of scope.
Cross-country The beauty of the area makes it splendid for cross-country – both in the valley and at altitude, with 30km/19 miles in total.
Queues These are rarely a problem.
Mountain restaurants Gorrono Ranch is the main on-mountain restaurant, with a big terrace, live music and a BBQ. There are a couple of snack shacks higher up, with great views.
Schools and guides As well as lessons the school offers backcountry guiding.
Facilities for children The Mountain Village Activity Centre has a nursery and ski lessons can start at age 3.

OUR WEBSITE

Go to our website at wtss.co.uk for resort news, links to resort sites, a build-your-own resort shortlist system and reader forums.

Central reservations
Call 728 7507.
Toll-free number (from within the US)
1 888 827 8050.

Phone numbers
From distant parts of the US, add the prefix 1 970.
From abroad, add the prefix +1 970.

TOURIST OFFICE

t 728 6900
info@tellurideskiresort.com
www.tellurideskiresort.com

REPORTS WANTED

Recently we have had few reports on this resort. If you go there, please do send us a report.

The best reports earn a copy of the next edition, and can lead to free lift passes in future.

See page 12.

STAYING THERE

Telluride is tricky to get to from the UK, involving two or three flights or a long 540km/335 mile drive from Denver.
How to go Packages fly into nearby Montrose or the tiny Telluride airport (prone to closure by the weather).
Hotels In town, hotel Columbia is luxurious, as is the plush yet friendly Camel's Garden Hotel and Spa. The New Sheridan is actually old – a Main Street USA classic, and comfortable too. In the Mountain Village, the Peaks Resort is enormous but has luxurious rooms, a spectacular lounge area and impressive spa facilities. A recent reporter recommends the Blue Mesa Lodge and the Inn at Lost Creek
Self-catering There are plenty of luxurious-looking condos.
Eating out The Cosmopolitan in the Hotel Columbia is renowned as the best in town. Other sophisticated options include the Marmotte and Harmon's (in the old station). Honga's Lotus Petal has sushi, curries, cocktails and a huge tea menu. Allred's, at the top of the gondola, is open for gourmet dining in the evenings. In Mountain Village try Simon Telluride at the Peaks for fine dining, or 9545 at the Inn at Lost Creek. Poacher's Pub and La Piazza del Villaggio are recommended for more relaxed dining.
Après-ski There's a lively bar-based après-ski scene in town. The West End Tavern has a popular happy hour from 4pm to 6pm. The New Sheridan has a lovely old bar dating from 1895. The Last Dollar has been recommended by locals. The Fly Me to the Moon Saloon has live music and stays open late. There's a swanky candlelit lounge called the Noir Bar attached to the Blue Point Grill. There are often concerts at the historic Sheridan Opera House. The Nugget Theatre shows latest cinema releases. Mountain Village is quieter. Try Poacher's Pub or Skier's Union at the base or, for the spectacular views, Allred's at the top of the gondola. Thrill Hill has floodlit tubing, sledding and snowbiking.
Off the slopes There's quite a lot to do around town if you are not skiing or boarding, such as dog-sledding, horse riding, snow-shoeing, ice skating, snowmobiling and glider rides. The Golden Door Spa in the Wyndham Peaks Resort was voted one of the top 10 spas in the world by *Condé Nast Traveller* readers.

Telluride

607

Vail

A vast, swanky resort with some very swanky hotels at the foot of one of the biggest (but also busiest) ski areas in the States

608

➕ One of the biggest areas in the US – great for confident intermediates, especially

➕ The Back Bowls are big areas of treeless terrain – unusual in the US

➕ Fabulous area of ungroomed, wooded slopes at Blue Sky Basin

➕ Largely traffic-free resort centres, very pleasant in parts – but ...

➖ Resort as a whole is a vast sprawl, and Lionshead is a dreary mess, though it's now being redeveloped

➖ Slopes can be crowded by American standards, with serious lift queues

➖ Inadequate mountain restaurants

➖ Blue Sky Basin and the Back Bowls may not be open in early season; warm weather can close the Bowls

➖ Expensive

We always enjoy skiing Vail; it's a big mountain with a decent vertical, and Blue Sky Basin has added hugely to its attractions. But it is far from being our favourite American mountain. In an American resort you expect the runs to be pretty much crowd-free; in any resort, these days, you expect 20-minute lift queues to be a thing of the past; and in such a swanky resort you expect lunch on the hill to be a pleasurable part of the day. In all respects, Vail disappoints.

At Vail's heart is the pseudo-Tirolean Vail Village, full of very expensive neo-Tirolean hotels – very nice if you can afford them, and if you can take this Disney-style approach to resort design. For our money, Vail can't compete with more distinctively American resorts based on old mining or cowboy towns. If we're going that far West, we like it to be a bit Wild.

THE RESORT

Standing in the centre of Vail Village, surrounded by chalets and bierkellers, you could be forgiven for thinking you were in the Tirol – which is what Vail's founder, Pete Seibert, intended back in the 1950s. But Vail Village is now just part of an enormous resort, mostly built in anonymous modern style, stretching for miles beside the I-70 freeway running west from Denver.

The vast village benefits from a free and efficient bus service – 'superb', say reporters – which makes choice of location less than crucial. But there's no denying that the most convenient –

and expensive – places to stay are in mock-Tirolean Vail Village, near the Vista Bahn fast chair, or in functional Lionshead, near the gondola – a much less attractive area that really needs the revamp it is currently getting. There is a lot of accommodation further out – the cheapest tends to be across the I-70.

Beaver Creek, 10 miles away, is covered by the lift pass and is easily reached by bus. A short drive gets you to Breckenridge and Keystone (both owned by Vail Resorts and covered by the lift pass), and Copper Mountain. Each of these resorts is covered in its own chapter in this guide.

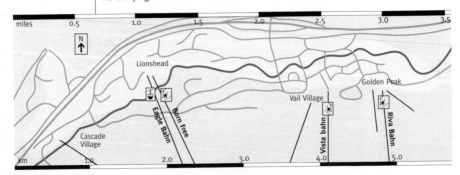

↑ The largely treeless Back Bowls are in the distance; you have to pass through them to get to Blue Sky Basin, from where this photo was taken

KEY FACTS

Resort	2500m
	8,200ft
Slopes	2475-3525m
	8,120-11,570ft
Lifts	34
Pistes	5,289 acres
Green	18%
Blue	29%
Black	53%
Snowmaking	
	390 acres

LIFT PASSES

Vail/Beaver Creek

Prices in US$

Age	1-day	6-day
under 13	49	294
13 to 64	81	486
over 65	71	426

Free under 5

Beginner included in price of lessons

Notes
Covers all Vail, Beaver Creek, Breckenridge and Keystone resorts, plus Arapahoe Basin. Prices are regular season rates paid in the resort. Reduced prices available if booked in advance and to international visitors who pre-book through a UK tour operator (it is not necessary to buy a complete holiday package to obtain these prices).

THE MOUNTAINS

Vail has one of the biggest areas of slopes in the US (only recently overtaken by Big Sky/Moonlight Basin) with immaculately groomed trails and ungroomed terrain in open bowls and among the trees. You get a real sense of travelling around the mountain – something missing in many smaller American resorts. Some of the runs (especially blacks) are overclassified. But a couple of 2006 reporters were also critical of trail signposting.

THE SLOPES
Something for everyone
The slopes above **Vail** can be accessed via three main lifts. From right next to Vail Village, the Vista Bahn fast chair goes up to the major mid-mountain focal point, Mid-Vail; from Lionshead, the Eagle Bahn gondola goes up to the Eagle's Nest complex; and from the Golden Peak base area just to the east of Vail Village, the Riva Bahn fast chair goes up towards the Two Elk area.

The front face of the mountain is largely north-facing, with well-groomed trails cut through the trees. At altitude the mountainside divides into three bowls – Mid-Vail in the centre, with

BLUE SKY BASIN

When Blue Sky Basin opened it transformed the attraction of Vail for competent skiers. The runs are not very steep, but the sector has a satisfying 'backcountry' feel that the rest of Vail lacks. There are 645 acres of terrain, served by three fast quads. There are some easy blue runs that are frequently groomed, but most of the area is left ungroomed and the runs among the trees – some widely spaced, some very tight – are delightful for strong skiers and boarders. Snow is usually much better than in the Back Bowls because of the shelter given by the trees and the generally north-facing aspect. One 2006 group was 'disappointed' by BSB, finding the runs short and the snow skied out by crowds. Well, the lifts are of respectable vertical by American standards – the biggest of the three lifts is 585m/1,920ft; and we've experienced good snow and no sign of crowds. The free daily tours are recommended, starting at 10am at the Blue Sky Basin sign at Patrol Headquarters.

Game Creek to the south-west and Northeast Bowl to the, er, north-east. Lifts reach the ridge at three points, all giving access to the **Back Bowls** (mostly ungroomed and treeless) and through them to the **Blue Sky Basin** area (mostly ungroomed and wooded).

The slopes have yellow-jacketed patrollers who stop people speeding recklessly. There's a New Technology Center where you can test equipment.

TERRAIN-PARKS
Pick your park
There are four designated freestyle areas. Two of them are aimed at novices and are great, fun areas to catch air or hit a box for the first time. Mule Skinner park is served by the Riva Bahn fast chair, and the new Hunky Dory beginner park is located off the Wildwood Express lift; it has various little boxes, rails and mini hits. Intermediates should head up the Eagle Bahn gondola to the Bwana park. Medium sized kickers and rails will prepare you to step up to the big Golden Peak park. This park and super-pipe – again served by the Riva Bahn fast chair – are home to various high-profile events and are often in top ten terrain-park lists and polls. A huge triple-jump line, a quarter-pipe, and a unique log rail park are built in nice fluid lines. The pipe boasts 5.5m/18ft walls and is 130m/425ft long.

SNOW RELIABILITY
Excellent, except in the Bowls
As well as an exceptional natural snow record, Vail has extensive snowmaking facilities, normally needed only in early season. Both the Back Bowls and Blue Sky Basin usually open later in the season than the front mountain. Blue Sky is largely north-facing (and

Vail

609

Two Elk Lodge
3420m/11,220ft

Patrol Headquarters
3430m/11,250ft

The major bottleneck that gives Vail its reputation for serious queues

Wildwood
3345m/10,98

Northeast Bowl

Northwoods

Mountaintop

Wildwood

Mid-Vail
3095m/10,150ft

Avanti

Vail's most challenging terrain, with a choice of a fast lift or a slow one, for minimum crowds on the runs

RiverBahn

Vista Bahn

FRONT SIDE

Golden Peak

Vail Village
2500m/8,200ft

Lionshead
2475m/8,120

Game Creek Bowl ←

Patrol Headquarters
3430m/11,250ft

Two Elk Lodge
3420m/11,220ft

Sun Down Bowl

Sun Up Bowl

China Bowl

Siberia Bowl

Outer Mon
Bowl

Orient Express

Inner Mongolia
Bowl

Tea Cup Bowl

Tea Cup

BACK BOWLS

3000m/9,840ft

Pete's

2865m/9,400ft

2915m/9,560ft

Skyline

Blue Sky Basin

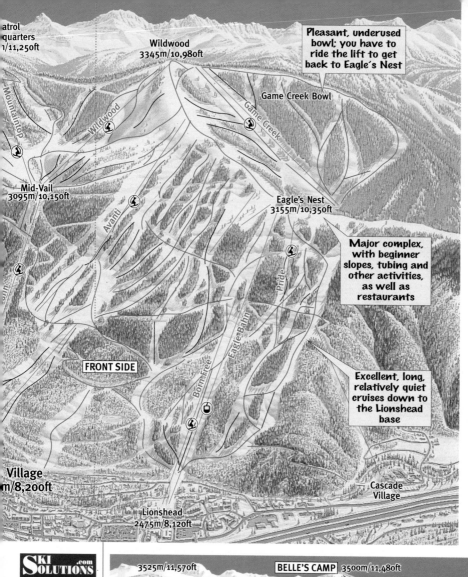

atrol
quarters
1/11,250ft

Wildwood
3345m/10,980ft

Pleasant, underused
bowl; you have to
ride the lift to get
back to Eagle's Nest

Game Creek Bowl

Mountaintop

Mid-Vail
3095m/10,150ft

Avanti

Wildwood

Game Creek

Eagle's Nest
3155m/10,350ft

Major complex,
with beginner
slopes, tubing and
other activities,
as well as
restaurants

FRONT SIDE

Pride

Eagle-Bahn

Born Free

Excellent, long,
relatively quiet
cruises down to
the Lionshead
base

Village
m/8,200ft

Cascade
Village

Lionshead
2475m/8,120ft

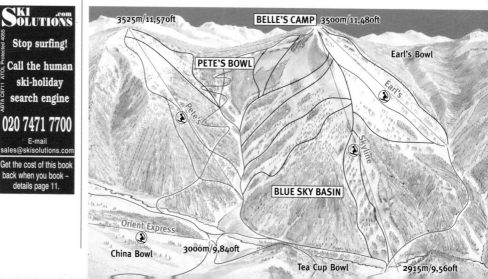

3525m/11,570ft

BELLE'S CAMP 3500m/11,480ft

PETE'S BOWL

Earl's Bowl

Earl's

Pete's

Skyline

BLUE SKY BASIN

Orient Express

China Bowl

3000m/9,840ft

Tea Cup Bowl

2915m/9,560ft

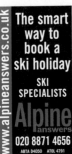

boarding

The terrain is about as big as it comes in America. Beginners will enjoy the front side's gentle groomed pistes, ideal for honing skills and serviced by fast modern chair-lifts. Beware flat areas, however, especially at the top of the Wildwood and Northwoods lifts. The back bowls will keep most riders busy for days when the snow is right. Blue Sky Basin is definitely worth checking out, with its acres of natural trails, gladed trees and cornices. Great terrain-parks, too. There is a Burton test centre at the New Technology Center at the top of the Mountaintop chair, which will help if you have any issues with your board, or want to demo the latest gear. There are plenty of specialist shops in town, as well as good snowboard school facilities, with adult-specific courses.

CHILDREN

Small World Play School
t 479 3285
Ages 2mnth to 6yr;
8am to 4.30; $92 per day; reservations essential

Ski school
Ages 3 to 12 at Golden Peak and Lionshead (full day including lift pass and lunch US$132)

SCHOOLS

Vail
t 1 800 354 5630

Classes
Full day (9.45-3.30)
$110
Private lessons
$160 for 1hr for 1 to 6 people

wooded) and keeps its snow well, but the Bowls are sunny, and in warm weather snow can deteriorate to the point where they are closed or a traverse is kept open to allow access to Blue Sky Basin – boring, for boarders especially.

FOR EXPERTS
Transformed by Blue Sky Basin
Vail's Back Bowls are vast areas, served by four chair-lifts and a short drag-lift. You can go virtually anywhere you like in the half-dozen identifiable bowls, trying the gradient and terrain of your choice. There are interesting, lightly wooded areas, as well as open slopes that dominate the area. Some 87 per cent of the runs in the Back Bowls are classified black but are not particularly steep, and they have disappointed some of our expert reporters. The snow can deteriorate rapidly in warm, sunny weather.

Blue Sky Basin has some great adventure runs in the trees – see feature panel earlier in this chapter.

On the front face there are some genuinely steep double-black-diamond runs which usually have great snow; they are often mogulled but sometimes groomed to make wonderful fast cruising. The slow Highline lift on the extreme east of the area serves three – a reporter had 'great fun' here on 'deserted' trails. Prima Cornice, served by the Northwoods Express, is one of the steepest runs on the front side.

If the snow is good, try the back-country Minturn Mile – you leave the ski area through a gate in the Game Creek area to descend a powder bowl and finish on a path by a river – ending up at the atmospheric Saloon.

FOR INTERMEDIATES
Ideal territory
The majority of Vail's front face is great intermediate territory, with easy

cruising runs. Above Lionshead, especially, there are excellent long, relatively quiet blues – Born Free and Simba both go from top to bottom. Game Creek Bowl, nearby, is excellent, too. Avanti, underneath the chair of the same name, is a nice cruiser.

As well as tackling some of the easier front-face blacks, intermediates will find plenty of interest in the Back Bowls (given good visibility). Some of the runs are groomed and several are classified blue, including Silk Road, which loops around the eastern edge, with wonderful views. Some of the unpisted slopes make the ideal introduction to powder skiing. Confident intermediates will also enjoy Blue Sky Basin's clearly marked blue runs.

FOR BEGINNERS
Good but can be crowded
There are excellent nursery slopes at resort level and at altitude, and easy longer runs to progress to. But they can be rather crowded.

FOR CROSS-COUNTRY
Some of the best
Vail's cross-country areas are at the foot of Golden Peak and at the Nordic Center on the golf course. Cross-country and telemark lessons are available at Golden Peak.

QUEUES
Can be bad
Vail has some of the longest lift lines we've hit in the US, especially at weekends because of the influx from Denver. Most of our reporters agree. Mid-Vail is a bottleneck that is difficult to avoid; 20-minute waits are common. At peak times it's possible to queue for 45 minutes here and in the Back Bowls, particularly for the slow chairs. The Lionshead gondola is not entirely queue-free, either.

GETTING THERE

Air Eagle 56km/ 35 miles (1hr); Denver 193km/ 120 miles (2½hr).

ACTIVITIES

Indoor Athletic clubs and spas, massage, ski museum

Outdoor Ice skating, fishing, snowmobiles, tubing hill, snow-shoe excursions, tobogganing, dog-sledding, horse riding

OUR WEBSITE

Go to our website at wtss.co.uk for resort news, links to resort sites, a build-your-own resort shortlist system and reader forums.

MOUNTAIN RESTAURANTS
Surprisingly poor (and pricey)

As other major American resorts are gradually improving their mountain restaurants, Vail's are slipping further behind: demand is increasing to the point where the major self-service restaurants can be unpleasantly crowded from 11am to 2pm. Basically, there are simply not enough restaurants. The ones that do exist are also expensive (especially the huge Two Elk, where a reporter said 'a hot dog, fries and coke cost £10'). One reporter recommends the Wildwood Smokehouse at the top of Wildwood lift – 'atmospheric, slightly different food and very good value'. 'Good barbecues,' says another.

There's only one table-service restaurant on the hill (with a limited menu): the Blue Moon at Eagle's Nest; this place is currently getting a makeover, which may be good news.

SCHOOLS AND GUIDES
Among the best in the world

The Vail-Beaver Creek school generates many glowing reports: 'excellent'; 'the best ski lesson I've ever had'. Class sizes are usually small. Even the one recent critical report came from a visitor who also had a satisfactory lesson with another instructor. You can sign up for lessons on the mountain.

FACILITIES FOR CHILDREN
Excellent

The comprehensive arrangements for young children look excellent, and we've had good reports on the children's school. There are splendid children's areas with adventure trails and themed play areas. There's even a special kids' cafe area at Mid Vail. The Night Owl programme gives parents an evening off and includes supervised activities and dinner at Adventure Ridge at the top of the gondola.

STAYING THERE

HOW TO GO
Package or independent

There's a big choice of packages to Vail. It's easy to organise your own visit, with regular airport shuttles.

Chalets Several UK tour operators offer catered chalets. Many are out of the centre at East Vail or West Vail or across the busy I-70 freeway.

Hotels Vail has a fair choice of hotels, though nearly all are expensive. Check online for the best deals.

((((⑤ **Vail Cascade** A resort within a resort – lots of facilities and a chair-lift right outside.

((((⑤ **Sonnenalp Bavaria Haus** Very smart and central. Large spa and splendid piano bar-lounge.

((((⑤ **Lodge at Vail** Right by the Vista Bahn. Some standard rooms small. Huge buffet breakfast. Outdoor pool. 'A real treat,' writes a reporter.

((((⑤ **Marriot Mountain Resort** Also owned by Vail Resorts, near the Eagle Bahn gondola. Impressive spa facilities.

((((⑤ **Manor Vail Resort** At Golden Peak. Suites with sitting area, fireplace, kitchen and terrace. Spa and pool. Breakfast included. 'I definitely recommend it,' says a recent visitor.

(((④ **Evergreen Lodge** Between village and Lionshead. Outdoor pool. Sports bar. 'Spacious and friendly,' says a 2006 reporter.

Self-catering The Racquet Club at East Vail has lots of amenities. Mountain Haus has high-quality condos in the centre of town. And the Pitkin Creek is recommended in 2006.

EATING OUT
Endless choice

Whatever kind of food you want, Vail has it – but most of it is pricey.

Fine-dining options include the Wildflower, in the Lodge, the Tour (modern French) – recommended

Vail

613

Central reservations phone number
Call 1 800 404 3535 (toll-free from within the US).

Phone numbers
From distant parts of the US, add the prefix 1 970.
From abroad, add the prefix +1 970.

TOURIST OFFICE

t 496 4500
vailinfo@vailresorts.com
vail.snow.com

highly by a reporter – and Ludwig's, in the Sonnenalp Bavaria Haus. Other recommendations for an Alpine ambience are the Alpenrose and Pepi's in the hotel Gramshammer.

For better value, we've found Blu's 'contemporary American' food satisfactory; a reader recommends Bagali's Kitchen for pizza; Billy's Island Grill does 'superb steaks at moderate prices'. Bart & Yeti's or Bogart's Bar and Bistro are good for local ales and no-frills, filling American food. The Lancelot at Vail Village (steaks and seafood) is a 2006 reporter's favourite. Other recommendations from readers include May Palace (Chinese) in West Vail, Sapphire (seafood), Montauk (seafood), the Bistro at the Racquet Club, Los Amigos ('decent Mexican fare'), Russell's, the Bottega, Vendetta's, Pazzo's ('good pizzas, relatively cheap') and the 'good value' Sweet Basil at Vail Village.

APRES-SKI
Fairly lively

Lionshead is said to be quiet in the evenings; but the Lions Den is popular at the end of the day, with live music. Nearby Garfinkel's has a DJ, sun deck and happy hour. The Red Lion in the village centre is 'good fun' and has live music, big-screen TVs and huge portions of food. The George tries to be an English-style pub. The Ore House serves 'mean margaritas and hot wings', but gets mixed reviews. The Tap Room in the Vista Bahn building is a relaxed woody bar – 'good range of wines by the glass'. Los Amigos and Bogart's Bar and Bistro are lively places at four o'clock.

You can have a good night out at Adventure Ridge at the top of the gondola. As well as bars and restaurants, there's lots to do on the snow – though a reporter reckons the tubing hill is no match for Keystone's.

Later on, Ski+Bar is a popular disco. 8150 is also good, with a suspended floor that moves with the dancing; the Bully Ranch at the Sonnenalp has great 'mudslide' drinks; the Semana is a snowboard hangout.

OFF THE SLOPES
A lot to do

Getting around on the free bus is easy, and there are lots of activities to try. The factory outlets at Silverthorne are a must if you can't resist a bargain.

Winter Park

Good value, great terrain, huge snowfalls, unpretentious town and about to get a world-class village at the base

NEWS

A new triple chair is planned for the back side of Parsenn Bowl. This will make the return journey to Parsenn Bowl much quicker after skiing Backside Parsenn or Vasquez Cirque.

For 2005/06 a new six-pack replaced the fast quad up Mary Jane. New gladed terrain also opened in this area, and signage was improved.

Phase one of Intrawest's multi-million dollar plan for expanding the base area is now under way and the Timberline and Sunnyside lifts are set to be replaced in the next few years.

+ The best snowfall record of all Colorado's major resorts

+ Superb beginner terrain and lots of groomed cruises

+ Lots for experts, at least when conditions are right

+ Quiet on weekdays

+ Leading resort for teaching people with disabilities to ski and ride

+ Largely free of inflated prices and ski-resort glitz, but ...

− Lacking the range of shops and restaurants you might expect

− Town is a bus-ride from the slopes, and strung-out along the main road

− 'Village' at the lift base is still very limited, and dead in the evening

− Trails tend to be either easy cruises or stiff mogul fields

− One or two slow lifts in key spots

− The nearest big resort to Denver, so can get crowded at weekends

Winter Park's ski area – developed for the recreation of the citizens of nearby Denver, and still owned by the city – is world class. Now there is the prospect of a world-class resort at the base, too: Intrawest (developers of resorts such as Whistler) is in the first phase of a massive expansion plan. The place looks set to be a construction site for a few years, but the end product should be good.

For the present, there's only a small 'village' at the base and most lodging, shops and restaurants are a bus-ride away downtown. If that doesn't matter to you, Winter Park is well worth considering. Some of our reporters rate it their favourite Colorado resort, partly because it makes such a refreshing change from the norm. Both the mountain and the old town have a distinct character.

THE RESORT

Winter Park started life around the turn of the century as a railway town, when Rio Grande railway workers climbed the slopes to ski down. One of the resort's mountains, Mary Jane, is named after a legendary 'lady of pleasure' who is said to have received the land as payment for her favours.

The railway still plays an important part in Winter Park's existence, with a station right at the foot of the slopes where trains deposit Denverites every Saturday and Sunday morning; there's apparently quite an après-ski party on the homebound leg.

Most accommodation is a shuttle-bus-ride away in spacious condos scattered around either side of US highway 40, the road through the town of Winter Park. Drive into Winter Park at night, and it seems to resemble an established ski resort town, with brightly lit shops, motels, restaurants and bars – but in the daytime it's clear that the place doesn't amount to much.

In the last few years, stylish accommodation has been developed at or near the foot of the slopes, including a car-free mini-resort known as The

Village at Winter Park Resort. But as yet it's very small without many shops, bars or restaurants and very quiet at night. Confusingly, an area between the mountain and the town is known as Old Town. Shuttle-buses run between the town and the lift base, and the hotels and condos also provide shuttles. A car simplifies getting around and allows day trips to Denver or other resorts such as Copper Mountain, Breckenridge and Keystone.

The approach road is more like the Alps than Colorado, going over the Continental Divide at Berthoud Pass (3450m/11,320ft). The resort is not the highest in Colorado but it's not far off and several reporters mention the possibility of altitude sickness.

THE MOUNTAINS

Winter Park's ski area is big by US standards, with a mix of terrain that suits all abilities – when it's all open.

THE SLOPES
Interestingly divided

There are five distinct, but well-linked, sectors. From the main base, a fast quad takes you to the peak of the

KEY FACTS

Resort	2745m
	9,000ft
Slopes	2745-3675m
	9,000-12,060ft
Lifts	24
Pistes	2,762 acres
Green	9%
Blue	34%
Black	57%
Snowmaking	
	294 acres

LIFT PASSES

Winter Park Resort

Prices in US$

Age	1-day	6-day
under 14	32	192
over 14	58	348

Free under 6; also over 70 (Mon to Thu only)

Beginner included in price of lessons

Notes
Prices quoted are advance purchase prices. Special deals for disabled skiers.

boarding

There is some great advanced and extreme boarding terrain and a high probability of fresh powder to ride. The four levels of park (see 'Terrain-parks') make Winter Park even more attractive to all levels of freestyler. The resort is also an ideal beginner and intermediate boarder area, with excellent terrain for learning. A good school provides classes for all levels, including learning to jump and ride rails.

original **Winter Park** mountain. From there, you can descend in all directions. Runs lead back towards the main base and over to the **Vasquez Ridge** area on the far right, served by the Pioneer fast quad.

You can also descend to the base of **Mary Jane** mountain, where four chairs up the front face serve tough runs; other chairs serve easier terrain on the flanks. From the top you can head up to **Parsenn Bowl**, via the slow Timberline chair, for intermediate terrain above and in the trees. This chair is exposed at the top, and can be closed for long periods in bad weather. From here, conditions permitting, you can skate or walk for up to half an hour to access the advanced and extreme slopes of **Vasquez Cirque**. From 2006/07 you should be able to

return to Parsenn Bowl by the planned new chair (see News) saving a long run-out to the Pioneer lift.

TERRAIN-PARKS
Four levels for all standards
The flagship Rail Yard park, with 30 features including big jumps, a host of variously shaped rails and a super-pipe, is enough to challenge most experts. It runs down much of the front of Winter Park mountain for 1280m/ 4,200ft. Halfway down it crosses a bridge so that those on the Cranmer Cutoff green run can cross the park safely. At the bottom are the huge features of Dark Territory, open to pass holders only (you need to pay $20, sign a waiver and watch a safety video to get one). For those who prefer

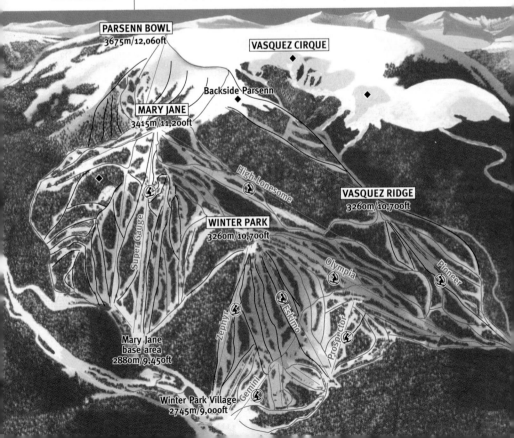

PARSENN BOWL
3675m/12,060ft

VASQUEZ CIRQUE

Backside Parsenn

MARY JANE
3415m/11,200ft

High Lonesome

VASQUEZ RIDGE
3260m/10,700ft

WINTER PARK
3260m/10,700ft

Super Gauge

Olympia

Pioneer

Zephyr

Eskimo

Prospector

Mary Jane
base area
2880m/9,450ft

Gemini

Winter Park Village
2745m/9,000ft

↑ The Village at Winter Park is small, quiet at night but convenient – and massive expansion is planned

SNOWPIX.COM / CHRIS GILL

SCHOOLS

Winter Park
t 1 800 729 7907
National Sports Center for the Disabled
t 726 1518
Special programme for disabled skiers and snowboarders.

Classes (Winter Park prices)
Half day (2½hr) $65
Private lessons
$259 for 2hr for 1 to 3 people

CHILDREN

Child Care
t 1 800 420 8093
Ages 2mnth to 6yr; $91 per day; 8am to 4pm.

Ski school
Takes ages 3 to 17 ($114 per day including lift ticket and lunch)

OUR WEBSITE

Go to our website at wtss.co.uk for resort news, links to resort sites, a build-your-own resort shortlist system and reader forums.

smaller hits, there's an intermediates' park nearby, Dog Patch. There's also a beginners' park, Kendrick, on the Jack Kendrick green run. Check them all out at www.rlyrd.com.

SNOW RELIABILITY
Among Colorado's best
Winter Park's position, close to the Continental Divide, gives it an average yearly snowfall of over 350 inches – the highest of any major Colorado resort. Snowmaking covers a lot of Winter Park mountain's runs.

FOR EXPERTS
Some hair-raising challenges
Mary Jane has some of the steepest mogul fields, chutes and hair-raising challenges in the US. On the front side are a row of long black mogul fields that are quite steep enough for most of us. There are some challenges on Winter Park mountain, too.

Some of the best terrain is open only when there is good snow and/or good weather – so it's especially unreliable early in the season. The fearsome chutes of Mary Jane's back side – all steep, narrow and bordered by rocks – are accessed by a control gate. Parsenn Bowl, served by the high, exposed Timberline chair has superb blue/black gladed runs and tougher tree skiing on the back side. Vasquez Cirque, the least reliably open area, has excellent ungroomed expert terrain with extensive views. You don't get much vertical before you hit the forest, though.

FOR INTERMEDIATES
Choose your challenge
From pretty much wherever you are on Winter Park mountain and Vasquez Ridge you can choose a run to suit your ability. Most blue runs are well groomed every night, giving you perfect early morning cruising on the

famous Colorado 'corduroy' pistes. Black runs, however, tend not to be groomed, and huge moguls form. If bumps are for you, try Mary Jane's front side. If you're learning to love them, the blue/black Sleeper enables you to dip in and out.

Parsenn Bowl has grand views and some gentle cruising pistes as well as more challenging ungroomed terrain. It's also an ideal place to try powder for the first time. When it's actually snowing, though, you are better off lower down, sticking to the edges of tree-lined runs to find the best powder and visibility.

FOR BEGINNERS
About the best we've seen
Discovery Park is a 25-acre dedicated area for beginners, reached by a high-speed quad and served by two more chairs. As well as a nursery area and longer green runs, it has an adventure trail through trees. Once out of the Park, there are easy runs back to base. And the Sorensen learning zone at the base area is good too.

FOR CROSS-COUNTRY
Lots of it
There are several different areas, all with generally excellent snow, totalling over 200km/125 miles of groomed trails, as well as backcountry tours.

QUEUES
Weekend crowds at the base
During the week the mountain is generally quiet. However, there may be a crowd waiting for the opening of the Zephyr Express from the main base and there can be queues on the slow Timberline chair up Parsenn Bowl. At weekends the Denver crowds arrive and big queues form at the base when the train gets in (though they move quickly) – 'Get up the mountain before 9am to avoid them,' says a reporter.

Winter Park

617

GETTING THERE

Air Denver 145km/ 90 miles (1½hr).

Rail Denver, Sat and Sun only. Journey time 2½hr.

ACTIVITIES

Indoor Fitness clubs, hot-tubs, museum

Outdoor Dog-sledding, ice rink, snow-shoeing, sleigh rides, tubing, snowmobiling, snowcat tours, hot air ballooning, hot springs

Central reservations Call 726 5587. Toll-free number (from within the US) 1 800 729 5813.

Phone numbers From distant parts of the US, add the prefix 1 970. From abroad, add the prefix +1 970.

TOURIST OFFICE

t 726 4118
wpinfo@skiwinterpark.com
www.skiwinterpark.com

MOUNTAIN RESTAURANTS
Some good facilities

The highlight is the Lodge at Sunspot, at the top of Winter Park mountain. This wood and glass building has a welcoming bar with a roaring log fire, a table-service restaurant and very good self-service food – but it gets very busy. Lunch Rock Cafe at the top of Mary Jane does quick snacks and has a deli counter, and there is a self-service at Snoasis, by the beginner area. Otherwise, it's down to the bases. The recently refurbished Club Car at the base of Mary Jane offers table-service and 'a good atmosphere and more varied menu' than the American norm.

SCHOOLS AND GUIDES
Very good reports

'Three people in our group had lessons, and the improvement in all their abilities was quite startling to see,' says a 2006 reporter. As well as standard classes there are ideas such as Family Private (for different abilities together) and themed lessons such as bumps and women-only clinics.

FACILITIES FOR CHILDREN
Some of the best

The Children's Center at Winter Park base area houses day-care facilities and is the meeting point for children's classes, which have their own areas, including moving carpets.

STAYING THERE

HOW TO GO
Fair choice

Several UK operators offer Winter Park.
Chalets A few are available.
Hotels There are a couple of hotel/condo complexes with pools and restaurants at Winter Park Village.
(((④ Iron Horse Resort Slope-side. 'Superb,' says a 2006 reporter.
(((④ Vintage Near resort entrance; good facilities but some poor past reports of it (and it will be converted to employee housing in a few years).
(((③ Winter Park Mountain Lodge Inconveniently positioned across the valley from the lifts; incorporates a micro-brewery; gets mixed reports.
Self-catering There are a lot of comfortable condos, including the slope-side Zephyr Mountain Lodge. 'Fantastic apartment, spacious and comfy with good views', says a 2006 reporter. Beaver Village condos, a five-minute shuttle-bus ride, were

recommended by another: 'Very high standard, but the last shuttle leaves the mountain at 5.15pm.'

EATING OUT
A fair choice

The range of options is gradually improving, but still isn't a match for that in more established 'destination' resorts. Get hold of the giveaway Grand County menu guide. In town, reporters are keen on the long-established Deno's – seafood, steaks etc (also a popular après-ski bar). In the Cooper Creek Square area the New Hong Kong ('excellent' Chinese food says a 2006 report) and the Divide Grill (for pasta, seafood and grills) are worth a look. Readers also recommend the Shed ('excellent steak and seafood, reasonably priced'), Carlos and Maria's for Tex-Mex, Hernando's for pizza/pasta and Nonna Lil's for 'good value' Italian. Gasthaus Eichler does 'very good' German-influenced food, at slightly higher prices. Try the Crooked Creek Saloon at Fraser for atmosphere and typical American food. The Lodge at Sunspot, up the mountain, is open some nights, with a 'fantastic' five-course fine-dining option on Saturday. They put gondola cabins on the chair-lift to get you up there in comfort.

APRES-SKI
If you know where to go …

At close of play, there's action at the main lift base at the Derailer Bar ('the best and cheapest' says a 2006 report) and Doc's Roadhouse, and at the base of Mary Jane the Club Car – but 2006 reporters were disappointed at how early they close. Later on, the Shed ('excellent food') and Randi's Irish Saloon can be lively. The Crooked Creek is popular with locals and the Winter Park Pub attracts the younger crowd. Buckets is a funky sports-bar and 'the liveliest in town', says a 2005 reporter.

OFF THE SLOPES
Mainly the great outdoors

Most diversions involve getting about on snow in different ways. Several reporters are enthusiastic about the floodlit tubing at Fraser. If you like shopping, you'll rapidly exhaust the local possibilities and will want to visit Silverthorne's factory outlet stores (around 90 minutes away) – but you'll need a car to do so.

Crested Butte

Crested Butte has one of the cutest old Wild West towns in Colorado. The steep, gnarly terrain enjoys cult status among experts, but there isn't enough suitable terrain for keen, mileage-hungry intermediates.

KEY FACTS

Resort	2860m
	9,380ft
Slopes	2775-3620m
	9,100-11,880ft
Lifts	15
Pistes	1,125 acres
Green	23%
Blue	57%
Black	20%
Snowmaking	
	282 acres

TOURIST OFFICE

t 970 349 2286
info@cbmr.com
www.skicb.com

THE RESORT

This small town in a remote corner of Colorado takes its name from the local mountain – an isolated peak (a butte, pronounced 'beaut') with a distinctive shape. It was a mining town in the late 1800s and is now one of the cutest resorts in the Rockies – a few narrow streets with beautifully restored wooden buildings and sidewalks and a good selection of bars and restaurants. You can stay there or at the mountain, a couple of miles away, with its modern resort 'village'.

THE MOUNTAINS

It's a small area, but it packs in an astonishing mixture of perfect beginner slopes, easy cruising runs and expert terrain. Snowfall is modest by Colorado standards – an average of 240 inches compared with over 300 for many other resorts. But for those who like steep, ungroomed terrain, if the snow is good, Crested Butte is idyllic – the 448 acres of the Extreme Limits at the top of the mountain offer seriously steep, prettily wooded terrain; but it is not unusual for it to be closed until late January to allow the snowpack to build up. To make the most of the area, take an instructor or buy the more detailed map of the area. There are also a few 'ordinary' black runs.

Good intermediates will find the area limited, with few challenging groomed trails. For early intermediates, there are lots of wide, fairly gentle, well-groomed and normally uncrowded cruising runs. There are excellent nursery slopes near the village and lots of good long runs to progress to. The ski school has an excellent reputation and there are a couple of mountain restaurants.

Short turns

619

Durango Mountain Resort

Durango Mountain Resort (not to be confused with Durango, a nearby city) is not a resort you would cross the Atlantic to visit – but if you're passing, you could do worse than give it a day or two.

KEY FACTS

Resort	2680m
	8,790ft
Slopes	2680-3300m
	8,790-10,820ft
Lifts	11
Pistes	1,200 acres
Blue	23%
Red	51%
Black	26%
Snowmaking	
	250 acres

TOURIST OFFICE

t 970 247 9000
info@durango
mountainresort.com
www.durango
mountainresort.com

THE RESORT

The heart of the resort is Purgatory Village, a modern, purpose-built affair with hotel and condo accommodation – as convenient and soulless as the many similar developments in France. Evening options in the 'village' are extremely limited. Fortunately, Hamilton's Chop House down on the roadside at The Inn at DMR is a surprisingly competent restaurant. There is tubing and snowmobiling. The city of Durango has a historic district and is worth a look. Other diversions a drive away include hot springs, Sky Ute Casino and a steam railroad.

THE MOUNTAIN

Practically all the runs are cut through dense forest. It's a small area even by US standards, and won't amuse most non-beginners for more than a day or two. Directly above the resort is a steepish slope served by a six-pack and a parallel triple, with a slow double chair off to the right serving gentle green runs. All link to the shady mountainside that forms the main part of the area, served by a row of three chairs with a vertical of not much over 350m/1,150ft. The first, a fast quad, serves a handful of pleasant blue runs. The others serve steeper terrain with some genuine blacks – including a nice little gladed area – and some very short double-diamond pitches. Snowcat skiing is said to operate from the top.

The snowfall record isn't Colorado's best, but an average of 260 inches is not bad. There are two terrain-parks with all the usual features, including a half-pipe. Amazingly, the mountain restaurants include a highly regarded table-service place, Café de los Piños.

Utah

Salt Lake City and the resorts just to the east of it got a bit of a boost to their international profile a while back, hosting the 2002 Winter Olympics. Now it's back to business as usual – playing second fiddle to Colorado on the international market, despite a marketing slogan that ought to bring in the customers in bigger numbers than it does: The Greatest Snow on Earth.

Utah's extravagant climatic claim (which features on many local car number plates) has some basis. Some Utah resorts do get huge dumps – up to twice the amount, over the season, that falls on some big-name Colorado resorts. And by Alpine standards the snow here is wonderful. If you like the steep and deep, you should at some point make the pilgrimage to Utah.

The biggest dumps are reserved for **Snowbird** and **Alta** – an average of 500 inches a year that has made these small resorts the powder capitals of the world. Recently their snow record has been matched by that of **Brighton**, in the next valley, and almost matched by that of **Solitude**, next door. And in these less well known places the snow gets tracked out less quickly, because the resorts attract far fewer experts.

Park City is the main 'destination' resort of the area, and an excellent holiday base because it has upmarket **Deer Valley** next door and **The Canyons** only a short drive away. As the crow flies these resorts are only a few miles from Alta/Snowbird (and indeed you can ski between them off-piste – see Park City chapter) but they get 'only' 300 to 350 inches of snow.

It was unknown **Snowbasin** (400 inches of snow), well to the north, that hosted the Olympic downhill events.

Separate chapters follow on these resorts. The other resort that gets a bit of international attention – not least because it's owned by Robert Redford – is **Sundance**. It gets 'only' 320 inches of snow a year, has some smart accommodation in cabins, a base lodge and a small ski area. There is more information about it in the Resort Directory at the back of the book.

Utah is the Mormon state, which means that sale and consumption of alcohol is tightly controlled. But we've never found getting a drink a problem on our visits. Provided you're over 21 and can prove it, nether should you. If you are eating, getting alcohol with your meal is no problem. But at bars and clubs that are more dedicated to drinking (ie don't feature food but do serve spirits or beer stronger than 3.2% alcohol) membership of some kind is required. This may involve one of your party handing over $4 or more – one member can introduce numerous 'guests' – or else there'll be some old guy at the bar already organised to 'sponsor' you (sign you in) for the price of a beer. A membership lasts three weeks, but a reporter points out that the system can be very expensive if you visit different resorts most days and just want a quick beer before hitting the road. Places with tavern licences serve 3.2% beer and don't operate as clubs – but you do still need to be 21.

Phone numbers
From distant parts of the US, add the prefix 1 801.
From abroad, add the prefix +1 801.

TOURIST OFFICES
Ski Utah
www.skiutah.com
Sundance
www.sundanceresort.com

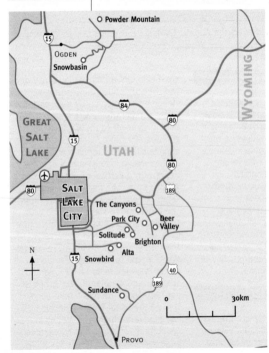

Alta

Cult powder resort linked to Snowbird but with less brutal architecture and a friendlier, old-fashioned feel

COSTS

① ② ③ ④ ⑤ ⑥

RATINGS

The slopes
Fast lifts	★★★
Snow	★★★★★
Extent	★★★
Expert	★★★★★
Intermediate	★★★
Beginner	★★★
Convenience	★★★★
Queues	★★★
Mountain restaurants	★★

The rest
Scenery	★★★
Resort charm	★★
Off-slope	★

KEY FACTS

Resort	2600m
	8,530ft

For Alta and Snowbird combined area see Snowbird

For Alta only
Slopes	2600-3200m
	8,530-10,500ft
Lifts	12
Pistes	2,200 acres
Green	25%
Blue	40%
Black	35%
Snowmaking	
	50 acres

NEWS

For 2005/06 the Watson Shelter lodge above Wildcat was replaced by a new building at the mid-station of the Collins chair, with a large cafeteria, a sun deck and a table-service restaurant.

SNOWPIX.COM / CHRIS GILL

Alta is littered with high go-anywhere bowls and chutes like this →

+ Phenomenal snow and steep terrain mean cult status among experts (but there's great beginner terrain, too)

+ Linked to Snowbird, making it one of the largest ski areas in the US

+ Ski-almost-to-the-door convenience

– 'Resort' is no more than a scattering of lodges – not much après-ski atmosphere, and few off-slope diversions

– Limited groomed runs for intermediates

Alta and Snowbird are the powder capitals of the world. The snow here is as plentiful, frequent and light as it comes. It is only five seasons ago that they agreed to link their neighbouring areas of slopes and we're delighted they did. To European eyes the link makes a lot of sense. But many locals we meet are still Alta or Snowbird devotees and never ski the other area. Madness (unless you're a boarder, in which case Snowbird is your only option – boarding is banned in Alta). On balance, we'd choose to stay in Alta – it has a friendlier feel and less brutal architecture.

THE RESORT

Alta sits at the craggy head of Little Cottonwood Canyon, 2km/1 mile beyond Snowbird and less than an hour's drive from downtown Salt Lake City. Both the resort and the approach road are prone to avalanches and closure: visitors can be confined indoors for safety. Where once there was a bustling and bawdy mining town, now there is just a strung-out handful of lodges and parking areas. Life revolves around the two separate lift base areas – Albion and Wildcat – linked by a bi-directional rope tow along the flat valley floor. There are about a dozen places to stay.

THE MOUNTAINS

Alta's slopes are lightly wooded, with some treeless slopes. Check out the Snowbird chapter for the linked slopes.
Slopes The dominant feature of Alta's terrain is the steep end of a ridge that separates the area's two basins. To the left, above Albion Base, the slopes stretch away over easy green terrain towards the blue and black runs from Point Supreme and from the top of the Sugarloaf quad (also the access lift for Snowbird). To the right, above Wildcat Base, is a more concentrated bowl with blue runs down the middle and blacks either side, now served by the fast two-stage Collins chair. The two sectors are linked at altitude, and by the flat rope tow along the valley floor.

Terrain-parks There's a park with jumps, boxes and rails above Albion Base, near the Sunnyside lift.
Snow reliability The quantity and quality of the snow and the northerly orientation put Alta in the top rank.
Experts Even without the Snowbird link Alta had cult status among local experts, who flocked to the high ridges after a fresh snowfall. There are dozens of steep slopes and chutes.
Intermediates Adventurous intermediates who are happy to try ungroomed slopes and learn to love powder should like Alta, too. There are good blue bowls in both Alta and Snowbird and not-so-tough blacks to progress to. But if it is miles of

REPORTS WANTED

Recently we have had few reports on this resort. If you go there, please do send us a report.

The best reports earn a copy of the next edition, and can lead to free lift passes in future.

See page 12.

OUR WEBSITE

Go to our website at wtss.co.uk for resort news, links to resort sites, a build-your-own-shortlist system and reader forums.

Phone numbers
From distant parts of the US, add the prefix 1 801.
From abroad, add the prefix +1 801.

TOURIST OFFICE

t 359 1078
info@alta.com
www.alta.com

perfectly groomed piste you are after, there are plenty of better resorts.

Beginners Timid intermediates and beginners will be very happy on the gentle lower slopes of the Albion side. But it's hard to recommend such a narrowly focused resort to beginners.

Snowboarding Boarding is banned (but guided snowcat boarding is available in nearby Grizzly Gulch).

Cross-country There's a 5km/3 mile groomed track and the Alta Nordic Center offers lessons and equipment.

Queues The slopes are normally uncrowded, but the fast Collins lift (new two seasons ago) is said to be increasing numbers on the Wildcat side, with 'everybody skiing top to bottom, making it impossible to load at the mid-station'.

Mountain restaurants There's one in each sector of the slopes, offering mainly fast food. Alf's on the Albion side 'serves great chilli in bread bowls'. The old Watson Shelter on the Wildcat side was replaced last season by a 'nice, light and airy' building with self-service and table-service sections. Several lodges at the base do lunch.

Schools and guides The ski school naturally specialises in powder lessons – though there are regular classes, too.

Facilities for children Day care for children over three months is available at the Children's Center at Albion Base.

STAYING THERE

How to go None of the hotels is luxurious in US terms. Most get booked up well in advance by repeat visitors. Unusually for America, most lodges (as they're called) operate half-board deals, with dinner included.

Hotels The venerable Alta Lodge (742 3500) has comfortable rooms and an atmospheric bar, and has developed a cult following in the US by serving a limited dinner menu at shared tables, in two sittings, instead of enlarging its dining room. Ingenious. Rustler Lodge (742 2200) is more luxurious, with a big outdoor pool, but impersonal. The comfortable, modern and conveniently located Goldminer's Daughter (742 2300) and the basic Peruvian Lodge (742 3000) are cheaper. The Snowpine Lodge (742 2000) is 'convenient, comfortable and friendly' but rather 'old-fashioned'.

Eating out It is possible, but eating in is the routine.

Après-ski This rarely goes beyond a few drinks in one of the hotel bars and possibly a video in your lodge. The Goldminer's Daughter has the main après-ski bar, with pool table etc.

Off the slopes There are few options other than a sightseeing trip to Salt Lake City, or the spa at Snowbird.

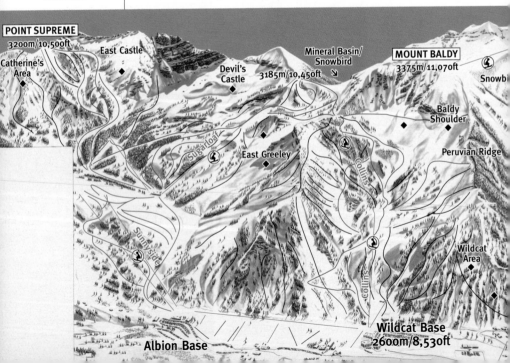

The Canyons

The fourth biggest ski area in the US and still growing, with a resort developing at the base of the slopes on the edge of Park City

RATINGS

The slopes

Fast lifts	★★★
Snow	★★★★
Extent	★★★
Experts	★★★★
Intermediate	★★★★
Beginner	★★
Convenience	★★★★
Queues	★★★★
Mountain restaurants	★★★

The rest

Scenery	★★★
Resort charm	★★
Off-slope	★★

NEWS

For 2006/07 a new quad chair is planned to the north-east of the Dreamscape area, together with an additional 200 acres of intermediate and advanced terrain. And the Silverado Lodge, a 'luxury' slope-side condo-hotel, is due to open.

For 2005/06 a second terrain-park aimed at beginners opened.

+ Extensive area of slopes for all abilities – and continuing to grow

+ Modern lift system with few queues

+ Convenient purpose-built resort village taking shape at the base

+ Very easy access to Park City and Deer Valley ski areas

+ Excellent snow in general, but ...

− Snow on the many south-facing slopes affected by sun

− Many runs are short

− Few green runs suitable for those progressing from nursery slopes

− Resort village offers limited après-ski and dining possibilities, and few off-slope diversions

The Canyons has the potential to become the most extensive ski area in the US (and already claims it is the fourth biggest). It has eight linked mountains, another lift going in this season to serve an additional 200 acres and plans to open up a ninth peak for 2007/08. Anyone having a holiday in Park City should plan to spend some time here. Whether staying in the purpose-built resort village at the lift base makes sense is another question.

THE RESORT

The Canyons has been transformed over the last decade or so. The area of the slopes has been doubled and a car-free village at the base now has a few shops, restaurants and bars as well as accommodation (though it feels like the building site it still is). Staying at the base is convenient but the village isn't a very appealing place to spend time, and we would much rather stay in the centre of Park City. Regular shuttle-buses run to the resort (but its 'a long walk from the bus stop to the access gondola', complain reporters), and there is also a car park below the village from which you get a cabriolet lift up to the village.

THE MOUNTAINS

The Canyons gets its name from the valleys between the eight mountains that make up the ski area.

Slopes Red Pine Lodge, at the heart of the slopes, is reached by an eight-seat gondola from the village. From here you can move in either direction across a series of ridges and valleys. Runs come off both sides of each ridge and generally face north or south. Most runs finish on the valley floors, with some long, relatively flat run-outs, which make the areas feel somehow poorly linked with quite short runs. The core of the lift system either side of Red Pine Lodge consists of fast quads, but the left-hand third of the

623

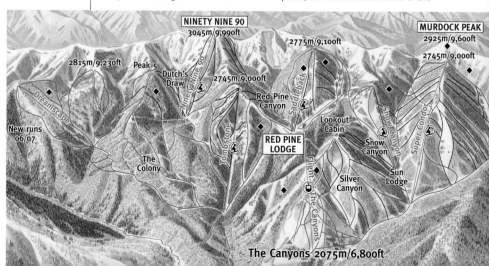

NINETY NINE 90
3045m/9,990ft

MURDOCK PEAK
2925m/9,600ft

2775m/9,100ft

2745m/9,000ft

2815m/9,230ft   Peak 5

Dutch's Draw

2745m/9,000ft

Red Pine Canyon

Dreamscape

New runs 06/07

Lookout Cabin

Snow Canyon

Super Condor

Red Pine Canyon

Tombstone

RED PINE LODGE

Flight of The Canyons

Saddleback

The Colony

Snow Canyon

Silver Canyon

Sun Lodge

The Canyons 2075m/6,800ft

The new village (in the distance) and the slopes above it are set well off the main highway into Park City →

UTAH

624

KEY FACTS

Resort	2075m
	6,800ft
Slopes	2075-3045m
	6,800-9,990ft
Lifts	16
Pistes	3,500 acres
Green	14%
Blue	44%
Black	42%
Snowmaking	
	160 acres

Central reservations
Call 1 866 604 4171 (toll-free from within the US).
Phone numbers
From distant parts of the US, add the prefix 1 435.
From abroad, add the prefix +1 435.

TOURIST OFFICE

t 649 5400
info@thecanyons.com
www.thecanyons.com

OUR WEBSITE

Go to our website at wtss.co.uk for resort news, links to resort sites, a build-your-own resort shortlist system and reader forums.

trail map has no fast lifts. Free daily mountain tours start at 10.30am.
Terrain-parks There are six natural half-pipes across the mountain (marked on the trail map). The SoBe terrain-park, which includes a super-pipe, jumps and rails, is near the Sunpeak Express. The Learning Park aimed at beginners is just above here, accessed by the fast Saddleback chair.
Snow reliability Snow is not the best in Utah. The Canyons gets as much on average as Park City (350 inches) and more than Deer Valley. But the south-facing slopes suffer in late-season sun.
Experts There is steep terrain all over the mountain. We particularly liked the north-facing runs off Ninety Nine 90, with steep double-black-diamond runs plunging down through the trees to a pretty but almost flat run-out trail. There is also lots of double-diamond terrain on Murdock Peak (a 20-minute hike from the Super Condor lift). Runs off the Peak 5 chair are more sheltered.
Intermediates There are groomed blue runs for intermediates on all the main sectors except Ninety Nine 90. Some are quite short, but you can switch from valley to valley for added interest. From the Super Condor and Tombstone fast chairs there are excellent double-blue-square runs. The Dreamscape area can be blissfully quiet, and a great area for experiments off-piste.
Beginners There are good areas with magic carpets up at Red Pine Lodge. But the run you progress to is rather short and very busy.
Snowboarding Except for the flat run-outs from many runs, it's a great area, with lots of natural hits. Canis Lupis is a mile-long, tight gully with high banked walls and numerous obstacles – like riding a bob-sleigh course.
Cross-country There are prepared trails on the Park City golf course and the Homestead Resort course.

Queues The gondola can be busy at peak times. And a 2006 reporter complained of queues for the key Tombstone fast chair.
Mountain restaurants Satisfactory, by US standards. Red Pine Lodge is a large, attractive log-and-glass building with a busy cafeteria and a table-service restaurant. Reporters found the Sun Lodge and small Dreamscape Grill 'much quieter and more relaxing, with good soup'. The Lookout Cabin has wonderful views, and we've had excellent table-service food there.
Schools and guides As well as the usual group and private lessons, there are special terrain-park clinics, telemark lessons, three-day women's clinics and teen clinics. Children's classes are for ages four to 12.
Facilities for children There's day care in the Grand Summit Hotel for children from six weeks to four years.

STAYING THERE

How to go Accommodation at the resort village is still fairly limited.
Hotels The luxurious Grand Summit is at the base of the gondola, and has a pool on the roof. Silverado Lodge is due to open for 2006/07 (see 'News').
Self-catering The Sundial Lodge condos are in the resort village, with a rooftop hot-tub and plunge pool.
Eating out The Cabin restaurant, in the Grand Summit, serves eclectic US cuisine; Smokie's in the village is more casual and Island Spice serves Jamaican food. There is a Viking yurt for 'gourmet' dining after a sleigh ride.
Après-ski The Cabin Lounge in the Grand Summit has live entertainment, and Smokie's is good for après-ski (and live music on Wed and Sat).
Off the slopes There's a factory outlet mall nearby and a fair bit going on in Salt Lake City and Park City.

Deer Valley

Deer Valley is top of the Ivy League of US ski resorts. It promises, and delivers, the best ski and gastronomic experience. We love it

COSTS

① ② ③ ④ ⑤ ⑥

RATINGS

The slopes
Fast lifts	★★★★
Snow	★★★★
Extent	★★
Expert	★★★
Intermediate	★★★★
Beginner	★★★★
Convenience	★★★★
Queues	★★★★
Mountain restaurants	★★★★

The rest
Scenery	★★★
Resort charm	★★★
Off-slope	★★

NEWS

For 2006/07 Bald Mountain will get a third fast quad (replacing the Sterling triple). And new gladed skiing will be added off the Sterling Express quad (itself new for last season).

2005/06 also saw a doubling in size of the terrain-park.

SNOWPIX.COM / CHRIS GILL

The rolling hills of Deer Valley with the slopes of Park City Mountain Resort in the distance ↓

- ➕ Immaculate piste grooming, good snow record and lots of snow-guns
- ➕ Good tree skiing
- ➕ Many fast lifts and no queues
- ➕ Good mid-mountain restaurants (and accommodation)
- ➕ Very easy access to Park City and The Canyons

- ➖ Relatively expensive
- ➖ Small area of slopes
- ➖ Mostly short runs of less than 400m/1,310ft vertical
- ➖ Deer Valley itself is quiet at night – though Park City is right next door

Deer Valley prides itself on pampering its guests, with valets to unload your skis, gourmet dining, immaculately groomed slopes, limited numbers on the mountain – and no snowboarding. But it also has has some excellent slopes, with interesting terrain for all abilities, including plenty of ungroomed stuff.

The slopes of Deer Valley and Park City are separated by nothing more than a fence which, given Deer Valley's ethos, seems likely to be permanent. Any skier visiting the area should try both; for most people, Park City is the obvious base – but there are some seductive hotels here at mid-mountain Silver Lake.

THE RESORT

Just a mile from the end of Park City's Main Street, Deer Valley is unashamedly upmarket – famed for the care and attention lavished on both slopes and guests. It's very obviously aimed at people who are used to being pampered and can pay for it. But it remains surprisingly unpretentious.

There is no village as such. The lodgings – luxurious private chalets and swanky hotels – are scattered around the fringes of the slopes, with more concentrated clusters on the valley floor near the main lift base and at Silver Lake Lodge (mid-mountain but accessible by road). For ski-town animation, head for Park City, or base yourself there. There are free buses.

THE MOUNTAINS

The slopes are varied and interesting. Deer Valley's reputation for immaculate grooming is justified, but there is also a lot of exciting tree skiing (great when snow is falling) – and some steep bump runs, too. There are free mountain tours for different standards (we were the only two on a black-diamond tour on our last visit and had a great time). **Slopes** Two fast quads take you up to Bald Eagle Mountain, just beyond which is the mid-mountain focus of Silver Lake Lodge. You can ski from here to the isolated Little Baldy Peak, served by a gondola and a quad chair-lift, with mainly easy runs to serve property developments there, and also some short black runs. But the main skiing is on three linked peaks beyond Silver Lake Lodge, all served by fast quads – Bald Mountain, Flagstaff Mountain and Empire Canyon. The top of Empire is just a few metres from the runs of the Park City ski area.
Terrain-parks The TNT (Tricks 'n' Turns) park on Empire Mountain offers rails, jumps and boxes.
Snow reliability As you'd expect in Utah, snow reliability is excellent, and there's plenty of snowmaking too.
Experts Despite the image of pampered luxury there is excellent expert terrain on all three main mountains, including fabulous glades,

625

Resort	2195m
	7,200ft
Slopes	2000-2915m
	6,570-9,570ft
Lifts	21
Pistes	1,825 acres
Green	15%
Blue	50%
Black	35%
Snowmaking	
	500 acres

OUR WEBSITE

Go to our website at wtss.co.uk for resort news, links to resort sites, a build-your-own resort shortlist system and reader forums.

Central reservations
Call 645 6528.

Phone numbers
From distant parts of the US, add 1 435. From abroad, add the prefix +1 435.

UTAH

626

TOURIST OFFICE

t 649 1000
marketing@deervalley.com
www.deervalley.com

bumps, chutes and open bowls. And the snow doesn't get skied out quickly. The Ski Utah Interconnect Tour to Alta now starts here (see Park City chapter).
Intermediates There are lots of immaculately groomed blue runs all over the mountains.
Beginners There are nursery slopes at Silver Lake Lodge as well as the base, and gentle green runs (some, like Bandana, with great views from the top) to progress to on all mountains.
Snowboarding Boarding is banned.
Cross-country There are prepared trails on the Park City and Homestead Resort golf courses and lots of scope for backcountry trips.
Queues Waiting in lift lines is not something that Deer Valley wants its guests to experience, so it limits the number of lift tickets sold. But a recent visitor found the area 'crowded compared with nearby resorts'.
Mountain restaurants There are attractive wood-and-glass self-service places at both Silver Lake and the base lodge, with free valet ski storage (you can store them free overnight, too). The food is fine (but expensive). The grill restaurant at the Empire Canyon Lodge has been consistently recommended. For a bit of a treat, try the restaurants at Stein Eriksen Lodge (including an all-you-can-eat buffet, which we thought excellent and very good value) or the Goldener Hirsch.

Schools and guides The ski school is doubtless excellent. Classes have a maximum of four pupils. Telemark lessons are now available. The Mahre Training Center (run by Olympian brothers Steve and Phil) is based here.
Facilities for children Deer Valley's Children's Center gives parents complimentary pagers. The free 'early drop' system means you can leave your kids at 8.30am.

STAYING THERE

How to go A car is useful for visiting the other nearby Utah resorts, though Deer Valley, Park City and The Canyons are all linked by regular shuttle-buses.
Hotels Stein Eriksen Lodge and the Goldener Hirsch at Silver Lake are two of the plushest hotels in any ski resort.
Self-catering There are many luxury apartments and houses to rent.
Après-ski The Lounge of the Snow Park Lodge at the base area is the main après-ski venue, with live music. Then there's Main Street in Park City.
Eating out Of the gourmet restaurants, the Mariposa is the best. The Seafood Buffet is also recommended. 'Fireside Dining' evenings at the Empire Canyon Lodge are held two days a week.
Off the slopes Park City has lots of shops, galleries etc. Salt Lake City has concerts, sights and shopping. Balloon rides and snowmobiling are popular.

SNOWPIX.COM / CHRIS GILL

Park City

Stay near the cute and lively old Main Street and visit the three local mountains plus some further afield for a varied holiday

627

COSTS

① ② ③ ④ ⑤ ⑥

RATINGS

The slopes

Fast lifts	***
Snow	****
Extent	***
Expert	****
Intermediate	****
Beginner	****
Convenience	**
Queues	****
Mountain restaurants	**

The rest

Scenery	***
Resort charm	***
Off-slope	***

NEWS

For 2006/07 a new triple chair is planned to run from the Resort Center to a blue run that takes you down to the King Con fast chair. Three new intermediate trails are also being created.

In 2005/06 a new Three Resort International Pass was launched, covering Park City, The Canyons and Deer Valley. You purchase it in advance through selected tour operators and exchange a voucher for a ticket each day.

PARK CITY MOUNTAIN RESORT

The top bowls offer excellent go-anywhere terrain for good skiers and boarders →

➕ Entertaining, historic Main Street, convenient for slopes

➕ Lots of bars and restaurants make nonsense of Utah's Mormon image

➕ Well maintained slopes, with lots of snowmaking

➕ Good lift system, with four six-packs

➕ Easy to visit other resorts – Deer Valley and The Canyons (covered by area pass) are effectively suburbs

➖ Away from Main Street, town is an enormous (still expanding) sprawl – inconvenient as well as charmless

➖ The blue and black runs tend to be rather short

➖ Most lodgings involve driving or bussing to Main Street and slopes

➖ Snowfall record comes nowhere near that of Alta, Snowbird et al

➖ Lack of spectacular scenery

Park City has clear attractions, particularly if you ignore its sprawling suburbs and stay near the centre to make the most of the lively bars and restaurants in Main Street. And it's an excellent base for touring other resorts – notably next-door Deer Valley and The Canyons, both covered by the Three Resort Pass.

Deer Valley is separated from Park City's slopes by a fence between two pistes, and by separate ownership with different objectives. They could be linked by removing the fence – but it stays in place. To European eyes, all very strange. The Canyons is only a little further away, and reached by free buses.

Then there are the famously powdery resorts of Snowbird and Alta, less than an hour away by car or bus. Even the Olympic downhill slopes of Snowbasin are within easy reach if you have a car.

THE RESORT

Park City is about 45 minutes by road from Salt Lake City. It was born with the discovery of silver in 1872. By the turn of the century the town boasted a population of 10,000, a red-light area, a Chinese quarter and 27 saloons.

Careful restoration has left the town with a splendid historic centre-piece in Main Street, now lined by a colourful selection of art galleries, boutiques, bars and restaurants, many quite smart. New buildings have been tastefully designed to blend in smoothly. But away from the centre the resort is an amorphous sprawl, still expanding. Traffic congestion can be bad, especially at weekends. And a 2006 reporter complained of being hassled by real estate salespeople trying to interest her in listening to a sales pitch in return for a free lift pass.

The Town chair-lift goes up to the slopes from Main Street, but the main lift base is on the fringes at Resort Center; there are lodgings out there.

Deer Valley, The Canyons and Park City are linked by free shuttle-buses, which also go around town and run

KEY FACTS

Resort	2105m 6,900ft
Slopes	2105-3050m 6,900-10,000ft
Lifts	14
Pistes	3,300 acres
Green	18%
Blue	44%
Black	38%
Snowmaking	475 acres

until late. A car is useful for visiting other ski areas on the good roads.

If you're not hiring a car, pick a location that's handy for Main Street and the Town chair or the free bus.

THE MOUNTAIN

Mostly the area consists of blue and black trails cut through the trees on the flanks of rounded mountain ridges, with easier runs running along the ridges and the gullies between. The more interesting terrain is in the lightly wooded bowls and ridges at the top.

THE SLOPES
Bowls above the woods

A fast six-seat chair-lift whisks you up from Resort Center, and another beyond that up to Summit House, the main mountain restaurant.

miles
0.5
1.0
1.5
2.0
Resort Center
Prospector Square
Pay Day
Town
Park City
Deer Valley
N
Silver Lake
Carpenter
Silver Lake
km
1.0
2.0
3.0

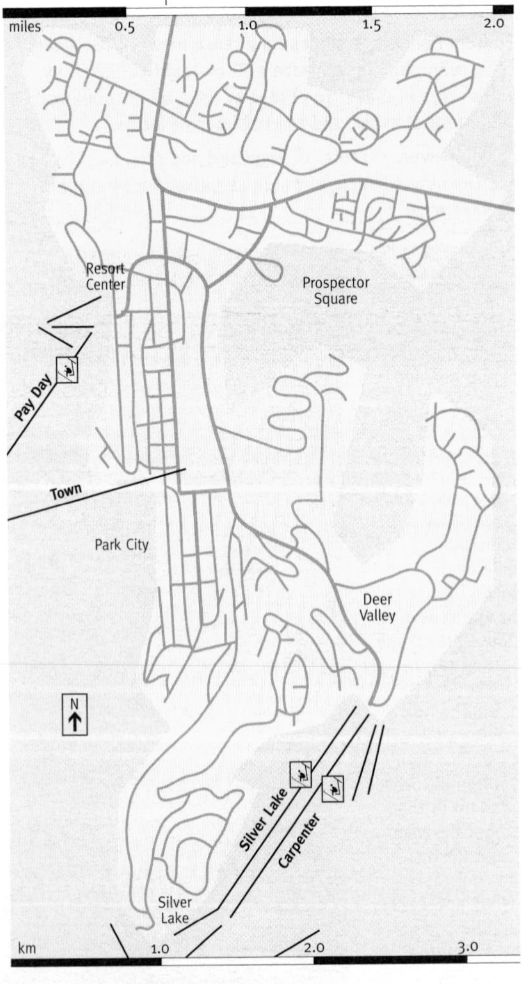

Most of the easy and intermediate runs lie between the Summit House and the base area, and spread along the sides of a series of interconnecting ridges. Virtually all the steep terrain is above Summit House in a series of ungroomed bowls, and accessed by the McConkey's six-pack and the old Jupiter double chair.

There are free, twice-daily Mountain History Tours of the slopes, looking at the area's silver mining heritage (including old mine workings). A long floodlit run and a floodlit terrain-park and half-pipe are open until 7.30pm.

TERRAIN-PARKS
Among the best in the world

There are four terrain-parks here to suit all levels. The vast number of kickers, rails and pipes are maintained daily, and rank among the best in the world. Novices start their freestyle career in Jonesy's park located under the Bonanza lift. Five mini-jumps in a row and several ride-on rails will really give you a perfect platform to get the basics right. The Pick 'N' Shovel park, accessible via the Three Kings lift, is the biggest and most frequented park. Intermediate to advanced kickers, a step-down feature, hip, a plethora of hand rails and boxes, and a wall ride are all kept pristine throughout the season, as is the Eagle super-pipe that was used for the 2002 Winter Olympics. On the northern slope overlooking the resort is the King's Crown Superpark – a slew of pro-standard jumps and rails for advanced riders only. Last but not least the Pay Day park along the Pay Day run stays open until 7.30pm with a host of lit jibs and jumps.

SNOW RELIABILITY
Not quite the greatest on Earth

Utah is famous for the quality and quantity of its snow. Park City's record doesn't match those of Snowbird and Alta, but an annual average of 350 inches is still impressive, and ahead of most Colorado figures. And snowmaking covers about 15 per cent of the terrain.

FOR EXPERTS
Lots of variety

There is a lot of excellent advanced and expert terrain at the top of the lift system. It is all marked as double-diamond on the trail map, but there are many runs that deserve only a single-diamond rating – so don't be

Park City

Prices in US$

Age	1-day	6-day
under 13	45	228
13 to 64	74	402
over 65	45	270

Free under 7

Beginner no deals

Notes
Covers all lifts in Park City Mountain Resort, with ski-bus. 6-day prices are advance purchase prices. Additional discounts if purchased in advance with lodging.

Alternative passes
Three Resort International Pass covering Park City, The Canyons and Deer Valley available through selected tour operators (around £220 for a 6 days).

boarding

It was not until 1996, when Park City won its Olympic bid, that the resort lifted its ban on snowboarding. Since then it has steamrolled ahead to attract the snowboarding community by building some of the best terrain-parks in the world. By enlisting the help and expertise of some big-name pros, namely JP Walker, Jeremy Jones and Chris Englesman, Park City has created something really special, in the form of original and varying obstacles for all levels and an incredible half-pipe. However, looking past the terrain-parks, Park City does have some great ungroomed terrain on offer as well. The higher bowls offer tree-lined powder runs, and great kicker-building spots. Beginners will have no trouble on the lower slopes, all serviced by fast chair-lifts. But beware: at weekends and during high season it can get very crowded, especially in the terrain-parks.

put off. We particularly like the prettily wooded McConkey's Bowl, served by a six-pack and offering a range of open pitches and gladed terrain. The old Jupiter lift accesses the highest bowls, which include some serious terrain – with narrow couloirs, cliffs and cornices – as well as easier wide-open slopes. The Jupiter bowl runs are under the chair, but there is a lot more terrain accessible by traversing and hiking – turn left for West Face, Pioneer Ridge and Puma Bowl, right for Scott's Bowl and the vast expanse of Pinecone Ridge, stretching literally for miles down the side of Thaynes Canyon.

Lower down, the side of Summit House ridge, serviced by the Thaynes and Motherlode chairs, has some little-used black runs, plus a few satisfying trails in the trees. There's a zone of steep runs towards town from further round the ridge. And don't miss Blueslip Bowl near Summit House – so called because in the past when it was out of bounds, ski company employees caught skiing it were fired, and were given their notice on a blue slip.

Good skiers (no snowboarders, due to some long flat run-outs) should not miss the Utah Interconnect – see feature panel. For bigger budgets, Park City Powder Guides offers heli-skiing.

FOR INTERMEDIATES
OK for a day or two
There are blue runs served by all the main lifts, apart from Jupiter (the blue Jupiter Access is worth a go though, even if you don't ride the chair, for the

Park City

629

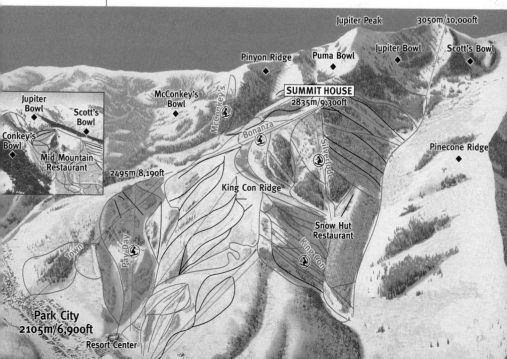

Jupiter Peak — 3050m/10,000ft

Pinyon Ridge — Puma Bowl — Jupiter Bowl — Scott's Bowl

McConkey's Bowl

SUMMIT HOUSE
2835m/9,300ft

Jupiter Bowl — Scott's Bowl

Conkey's Bowl

Mid-Mountain Restaurant
2495m/8,190ft

Pinecone Ridge

King Con Ridge

Snow Hut Restaurant

Park City
2105m/6,900ft

Resort Center

SCHOOLS
Park City
t 1 800 227 2754

Classes
1 3hr day $75
Private lessons
$120 for 1hr

CHILDREN
Little Groomers
(run by ski school)
t 1 800 227 2754
9am-3pm or 9.45-
3.45; ages 3½ to 5;
5 days $650, includes
ski tuition, lunch and
indoor activities
Guardian Angel
t 783 2662
Babysitting service

Ski school
The school offers
classes for ages 6 to
13, 9.30-3.30, $125
per day including
lunch

OUR WEBSITE
Go to our website at
wtss.co.uk for resort
news, links to resort
sites, a build-your-
own resort shortlist
system and reader
forums.

sight of people coming down the chutes). The areas around the King Con high-speed quad and Silverlode high-speed six-pack have a dense network of great (but fairly short) cruising runs. There are also more difficult trails close by, for those looking for a challenge.

But there are few long, fast cruising runs – most trails are around 1 to 2km/0.5 to 1 mile, and many have long, flat run-outs. The Pioneer and McConkey's chair-lifts are off the main drag and serve some very pleasant, often quiet runs. The runs under the Town lift have great views of the town.

Intermediates will certainly want to visit The Canyons and Deer Valley for a day or two (see separate chapters).

FOR BEGINNERS
A good chance for fast progress
Novices start on short lifts (the First Time chair is now a fast quad) and a beginners' area near the base lodge. Classes graduate up the hill quite quickly, and there's a good, gentle and wide 'easiest way down' – the three-and-a-half-mile Home Run – clearly marked all the way from Summit House. It's easy enough for most to manage after only a few lessons. The Town chair can be ridden down.

FOR CROSS-COUNTRY
Some trails; lots of backcountry
There are prepared trails on both the Park City golf course, next to the downhill area, and the Homestead Resort course, just out of town. There is lots of scope for backcountry trips.

QUEUES
Peak period crowds
Lift queues aren't normally a problem with so many six-packs. But it can get pretty crowded (on some trails as well as the lifts) at weekends and in high season, particularly on the Pay Day lift from Resort Center. With a pass for five days or more, the Fast Track system means you can jump the queues on four main lifts.

MOUNTAIN RESTAURANTS
Standard self-service stuff
The Mid-Mountain Lodge is a 19th-century mine building which was heaved up the mountain to its present location near the bottom of Pioneer chair. The food is standard self-service fare but most reporters prefer it to the alternatives. The Summit House is cafe-style – serving chilli, pizza, soup etc. The Snow Hut is a smaller log building and usually has an outdoor grill. Caffé Amante is a coffee house halfway down the Bonanza chair-lift. There are more options down at Resort Center ('a delicious salad bar and top-quality fresh fish' said a 2006 reporter).

SCHOOLS AND GUIDES
Good reports
We continue to receive positive reports of snowboard group lessons: 'Excellent,' said the daughter of a 2006 reporter, who was given a detailed record of her achievements in a small two-day class and was riding blue runs by the end.

FACILITIES FOR CHILDREN
Well organised; ideal terrain
There are a number of licensed carers who operate either at their own premises or at visitors' lodgings. The ski school takes children from the age of three and a half. Book in advance.

THE UTAH INTERCONNECT

Good skiers prepared to do some hiking should consider this excellent guided backcountry tour that runs four days a week from Deer Valley to Snowbird. (Three days a week it runs from Snowbird, but only as far as Solitude.) When we did it (a few years back, starting from Park City) we got fresh tracks in knee-deep powder practically all day. After a warm-up run to weed out weak skiers, you head up to the top chair, go through a 'closed' gate in the area boundary and ski down a deserted, prettily wooded valley to Solitude. After taking the lifts to the top of Solitude we did a short traverse/walk, then down more virgin powder towards Brighton. After more powder runs and lunch back in Solitude, it was up the lifts and a 30-minute hike up the Highway to Heaven to north-facing, tree-lined slopes and a great little gully down into Alta. How much of Alta and Snowbird you get to ski depends on how much time is left. The price ($175) includes two guides – one leading, the other at the rear – lunch, lift tickets for all the resorts you pass through and transport home.

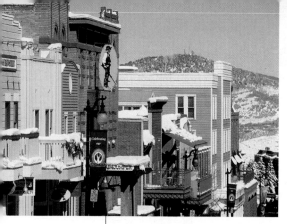

↑ The cute Main Street dates from the silver-mining boom of the 19th century

GETTING THERE

Air Salt Lake City 58km/36 miles (½hr).

ACTIVITIES

Indoor Park City Racquet Club (tennis, racquetball, swimming pool, hot-tub, gym); Silver Mountain Sports Club and Spa (pools, hot-tubs, sauna, steam room, tennis, racquetball, gym); other fitness clubs, spa treatments, museum

Outdoor Ice skating, snowmobiles, dog sledding, sleigh rides, hot-air ballooning, ski jumping, bob-sleigh track, snow-shoeing, snowtubing, winter fly fishing

Phone numbers
From distant parts of the US, add the prefix 1 435.
From abroad, add the prefix +1 435.

TOURIST OFFICE

t 649 8111
info@pcski.com
www.parkcitymountain.com
www.parkcityinfo.com

STAYING THERE

HOW TO GO
Packaged independence
Park City is the busiest and most atmospheric of the Utah resorts, and a good base for visiting the others. We prefer to stay near Main Street and its bars and restaurants, but suburbs such as Kimball Junction are convenient and cheap (but soulless) if you have a car and want to try different resorts daily.
Hotels There's a wide variety, from typical chains to individual little B&Bs.
(((((5) **Park City** (200 2000) Swanky new all-suite place on outskirts, better placed for golf than skiing.
(((((4) **Silver King** (649 5500) De luxe hotel/condo complex at base of the slopes, with indoor-outdoor pool.
((((4) **Park City Peaks** (649 5000) Excellent rooms and indoor-outdoor pool, but out of town.
((((4) **Washington School Inn** (649 3800) 'Absolutely excellent' historic inn with 'fantastic service' say reporters. In a great location near Main Street.
((((4) **Yarrow** (649 7000) Adequate, charmless base, a bearable walk from Main Street. Pool.
(((3) **Best Western Landmark Inn** (649 7300) At Kimball Junction. Pool.
((2) **Chateau Apres Lodge** (649 9372) Close to the slopes: comfortable, faded, cheap.
((2) **1904 Imperial Inn** (649 1904) Quaint B&B at the top of Main Street.
Self-catering There's a big range. The Townlift studios near Main Street and Park Avenue condos are both modern and comfortable and the latter have pool and hot-tubs. Silver Cliff Village is adjacent to the slopes and has spacious units and access to the facilities of the Silver King Hotel. Blue Church Lodge is a well-converted 19th-century Mormon church with luxury condos and rooms.

EATING OUT
Lots of choice
There are over 100 restaurants. Our favourites are Wahso (Asian fusion); 350 Main (new American); and Riverhorse – in a grand, high-ceilinged first-floor room with live music. Zoom is the old Union Pacific train depot, now a trendy restaurant owned by Robert Redford (we got mixed reports in 2006 – from 'our best meal' to 'mediocre and overpriced'). Chez Betty is small and just may have the best food in town – expensive though. Other reporter recommendations include Cisero's and Grappa (Italian), Chimayo ('south-western-with-a-twist food but service too quick and rushed'), Wasatch Brew Pub ('lively atmosphere, best value'), Bandits Grill ('good value'), Claimjumper ('really juicy steaks and enormous desserts') and Butchers Chop House ('excellent beef'). There are lots of Tex-Mex places: La Casita, Zona Rosa and El Chubasco have been recommended. The seafood buffet at Snow Park Lodge, at Deer Valley, is worth the journey.

APRES-SKI
Better than you might think
As the slopes close, Legends and the Brewhouse are the places to head for at the Resort Center. Pig Pen in the ice skating plaza was recommended by a 2006 reporter. In Main Street, the Wasatch Brew Pub makes its own ale. The Claimjumper, JB Mulligans, O'Shuck's and the scruffy Alamo are lively and there's usually live music and dancing at week-ends. Harry O's and Cisero's nightclub are good too. The Monkey Bar has DJs and pole dancing.

OFF THE SLOPES
Should be interesting
There's a factory outlet mall at Kimball Junction. Balloon flights and excursions to Nevada for gambling are popular. Backcountry snowmobiling is big around here. In January there's Robert Redford's Sundance Film Festival and in February Winterfest is a 10-day celebration of the 2002 Olympics, including concerts and snow sculpture.
There are lots of shops and galleries. The museum and old jail house are worth a visit. Salt Lake City is easily reached and has some good concerts, shopping and Mormon heritage sites.
You might like to learn to ski-jump or try the Olympic bob track at the Winter Sports Park down the road.

Park City

631

Snowbird

A powder-pig paradise linked to neighbouring Alta; with big concrete and glass base buildings that remind us of Flaine

NEWS

For 2006/07 the old Peruvian chair from the base is due to be replaced by a high-speed quad that will go almost to the top of the mountain. At the top a 175m/575ft tunnel with a moving carpet will provide access to Mineral Basin on the back of the mountain. This should ease the demand and cut queues for the cable-car.

Last season, a new day lodge, including a cafe and large terrace, opened at the base of the Gadzoom chair-lift.

+ Quantity and quality of powder snow unrivalled

+ Link to Alta makes one of the largest ski areas in the US

+ Fabulous ungroomed slopes, with steep and not-so-steep options

+ Slopes-at-the-door convenience

– Limited groomed runs for intermediates

– Tiny, claustrophobic resort 'village'

– Stark concrete Bauhaus architecture

– Frequent queues for main cable-car

– Mainly slow chair-lifts

– Very quiet at night

There can be few places where nature has combined the steep with the deep better than at Snowbird and next-door Alta, and even fewer places where there are also lifts to give you access. The two resorts' combined area is one of the top powder-pig paradises in the world and one of the US's biggest lift-linked ski areas. So it is a shame that Snowbird's concrete, purpose-built 'base village' is so lacking in charm and ski resort ambience. Snowboarders are banned from Alta's slopes, so cannot take advantage of the link.

THE RESORT

Snowbird lies 40km/25 miles from Salt Lake City in Little Cottonwood Canyon – just before Alta. The setting is rugged and rather Alpine – and both the resort and (particularly) the approach road are prone to avalanches and closure: visitors are sometimes confined indoors for safety. The resort buildings are mainly block-like – but they provide ski-in/ski-out lodging.

The resort area and the slopes are spread along the road on the south side of the narrow canyon. The focal Snowbird Center (lift base/shops/restaurants) is towards the eastern, up-canyon end. All the lodgings and restaurants are within walking distance. The main cable-car station is central and the other main Gad lifts can be reached on snow. There are shuttle-buses, with a service to Alta.

THE MOUNTAINS

Snowbird's link with Alta forms one of the largest ski areas in the US.
Slopes The north-facing slopes rear up from the edge of the resort. Six access lifts are ranged along the valley floor, the main ones being the 125-person cable-car (the Aerial Tram) to Hidden Peak, the Peruvian Express quad chair (see News) and the Gadzoom fast quad chair. To the west, in Gad Valley, there are runs ranging from very tough to nice and easy. Mineral Basin, on the

back of Hidden Peak, offers 500 acres of terrain for all abilities, but can be badly affected by sun. One of the two fast quads there forms the link with Alta. The Chickadee nursery slopes are floodlit three times a week.
Terrain-parks There are two terrain-parks, a huge one for experts and one for intermediates, plus a 114m/375ft super-pipe.
Snow reliability Snowbird and Alta average 500 inches of snowfall a year – twice as much as some Colorado resorts and around 50 per cent more than the nearby Park City area. Snowmaking ensures excellent cover in busy areas.
Experts Snowbird was created for experts; the trail map is liberally sprinkled with double-black-diamonds, and some of the gullies off the Cirque ridge – Silver Fox and Great Scott, for example – are exceptionally steep and frequently neck-deep in powder. Lower down lurk the bump runs, including Mach Schnell – a great run straight down the fall line through trees. There is wonderful ski-anywhere terrain in the bowl beneath the high Little Cloud chair, and the Gad 2 lift opens up attractive tree runs. Fantastic go-anywhere terrain under the High Baldy traverse is controlled by gates – catch the area as the ski patrol opens them after a snowfall and you're in for a real treat. A reporter rates the 'less obvious' challenges from the Baby Thunder chair. Mineral Basin has more

KEY FACTS

Resort	2470m
	8,100ft

For Snowbird and Alta combined area

Slopes	2365-3350m
	7,760-11,000ft
Lifts	23
Pistes	4,700 acres
Green	25%
Blue	37%
Black	38%
Snowmaking	
	125 acres

Snowbird only

Slopes	2365-3350m
	7,760-11,000ft
Lifts	11
Pistes	2,500 acres
Green	27%
Blue	38%
Black	35%
Snowmaking	
	75 acres

Phone numbers
From distant parts of the US, add the prefix 1 801.
From abroad, add the prefix +1 801.

TOURIST OFFICE

t 933 2222
info@snowbird.com
www.snowbird.com

expert terrain. Backcountry tours and heli-lifts are available.

Intermediates The winding Chip's Run on the Cirque ridge provides the only comfortable route down from the top. For adventurous intermediates wanting to try powder skiing, the bowl below the Little Cloud lift is a must. There are some challenging runs through the trees off the Gad 2 lift and some nice long cruises in Mineral Basin. But the groomed runs don't add up to a lot.

Beginners There is a good nursery slope next to Cliff Lodge, and the Mountain Learning area part-way up the hill. But progression to longer runs is not easy.

Snowboarding Competent free-riders will have a wild time in Snowbird's powder (though a 2006 reporter complains of 'flat sticky spots where you have to walk'). Alta bans boarders.

Cross-country No prepared trails.

Queues Every time we've visited there have been long queues ('50 minutes' complained a 2006 reporter) for the

cable-car. Hopefully these will be cut by the new Peruvian chair (see 'News').

Mountain restaurants It's the Mid-Gad Lodge self-service cafeteria or back to one of the bases.

Schools and guides The ski school offers a range of lessons and speciality clinics – such as women-only, over-50s and experts-only programmes.

Facilities for children The 'kids ski free' programme allows two children (12 and under) to ski for free ($15 a day extra for use of the Tram) with each adult.

STAYING THERE

How to go A few UK tour operators feature Snowbird.

Hotels There are several lodges, and smaller condo blocks. Cliff Lodge is a huge concrete hotel; splendid rooftop pool and renovated rooms, but generally depressing. The Lodge at Snowbird was recently renovated. Recent reporters tell of 'friendly but amateurish staff' in both places.

Eating out Cliff Lodge and Snowbird Center are the focal points. The 'fine dining' Aerie in the Cliff Lodge gets mixed reviews. Readers recommend the Steak Pit in Snowbird Center.

Après-ski Après-ski tends to be a bit muted. The Tram Club and El Chanate are lively as the slopes close. But a recent reporter complains that many places close early and 'enforce a curfew in a manner that any small dictatorship would envy'.

Off the slopes Apart from spas in the various lodges, there's a skating rink and a family tubing hill.

Snowbird

633

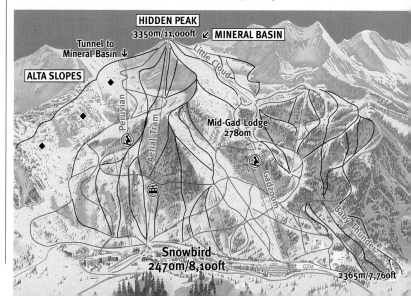

HIDDEN PEAK
3350m/11,000ft ↙ MINERAL BASIN
Tunnel to Mineral Basin ↓
Little Cloud
ALTA SLOPES
Peruvian
Aerial Tram
Mid-Gad Lodge 2780m
Gadzoom
Baby Thunder
Snowbird 2470m/8,100ft
2365m/7,760ft

Brighton/Solitude

These linked neighbours in the valley next to famous Alta and Snowbird get much the same amount of lovely powder snow. Solitude has come on a lot in recent years, and in some ways is now an attractive destination.

KEY FACTS

Resort	2490/2670m
	8,160/8,760ft
Slopes	2435-3200m
	7990-10,500ft
Lifts	15
Pistes	2,250 acres
Blue	20%
Red	50%
Black	30%
Snowmaking	
Brighton	20%
Solitude	21 runs

TOURIST OFFICE

Brighton
t 801 532 4731
info@skibrighton.com
www.skibrighton.com

Solitude
t 801 534 1400
info@skisolitude.com
www.skisolitude.com

THE RESORTS

Solitude is the obvious place to stay – a smart car-free mini-village with an ice rink in the centre and a choice of condos (some quite luxurious) or the 46-room Inn at Solitude. There are several restaurants, including one doing French gourmet cuisine and a family-friendly Italian. Brighton offers the slope-side Brighton Lodge – rooms with breakfast – and some cabins. In either resort, you're in for a quiet time.

THE MOUNTAINS

The two resorts now offer a joint lift pass. The total acreage is half that of Alta/Snowbird, but is fair by general US standards. This valley attracts fewer people – experts, in particular – so the powder doesn't get tracked out in hours, as it does over the hill.

Brighton, at the head of the canyon, has the slicker lift system, with three fast chairs, including one serving the resort's maximum vertical of 530m/1,740ft on Clayton Peak. This and the slightly lower Mt Millicent are almost all expert terrain, but other lifts serve a wide spectrum of runs.

Most (not all) of the slopes immediately above Solitude are easy or intermediate, including a wide area served by the one fast quad. But the top lift accesses lots of steeps in Honeycomb Canyon, on the back of the hill, now with a short quad to bring you back to the front face.

The resorts' boundaries are open, and there are excellent backcountry adventures to be had. The Solitude ski patrol runs guided groups of up to 10, with all necessary safety kit provided – good value at $150, including lift pass. Both resorts have terrain-parks.

Snowbasin

The 2002 Olympics put Snowbasin on the map. It's a great hill, and it gets great snow (usually). All it needs is a great village – and we don't doubt it will get one. For now, it makes a great day out from Park City, for example.

KEY FACTS

Resort	1965m
	6,450ft
Slopes	1965-2865m
	6,450-9,400ft
Lifts	11
Pistes	2,660 acres
Green	20%
Blue	50%
Black	30%
Snowmaking	
	600 acres

TOURIST OFFICE

t 801 620 1000
info@snowbasin.com
www.snowbasin.com

THE RESORT

A plush base lodge (but no accommodation) was built for the 2002 Olympics. Big investment is expected over the next few years, but for now you have to stay elsewhere – in the town of Ogden on the Salt Lake plain, or nearer the mountain in the backwater of Huntsville. The drive from Park City takes less than an hour.

THE MOUNTAIN

Snowbasin's slopes cover a lot of pleasantly varied terrain and its 11 lifts include two gondolas and a fast quad chair, all running bottom to top. There are beginner and expert terrain-parks, another planned, and a super-pipe.

This is a great mountain for experts. All the lifts serve worthwhile terrain. The Grizzly Downhill course, designed by Bernhard Russi, drops 885m/2,900ft and is already claimed to be a modern classic. Between the race course and the area boundary is a splendid area of off-piste wooded glades and gullies, served by the fast John Paul chair. This is where most experts will want to spend their time. It's good for intermediates, too. The Strawberry gondola accesses mainly long open blue runs but also leads to a lightly wooded steeper slope at the extremity of the area. Middle Bowl is great terrain for the adventurous, with a complex network of blues and blacks. There is a nursery slope, and a few green runs to progress to.

At 400 inches the average snowfall is in the usual Utah class.

There are two smart, self-service mountain restaurants. The one at the top of Middle Bowl 'serves excellent Austrian-style food' says a 2006 reporter.

Rest of the West

This section covers a variety of resorts in different parts of the great Rocky Mountain chain that stretches from Montana and Idaho down through Wyoming and Colorado to New Mexico. Each has its own unique character. Most of the resorts mentioned below get detailed coverage later in this section.

Sun Valley, Idaho, was America's first purpose-built resort, developed in the 1930s by the president of the Union Pacific Railway. It quickly became popular with the Hollywood jet set and has managed to retain its stylish image and ambience; it has one of our favourite luxury hotels.

Also in Idaho, as it happens, is America's latest purpose-built resort (and the first to be built since Beaver Creek) – **Tamarack,** at McCall (two hours north of Boise) on the shores of Cascade Lake, a large reservoir. The resort opened two seasons back with five lifts and now has seven, including three fast quads, serving 850 skiable acres and 855m/ 2,800ft vertical. Tamarack gets more snow than Sun Valley (300+ inches on average, 400+ last season) and it still gets a lot of sun. An American reader spent 12 days there two seasons back and reported: 'Tamarack skis like a mountain that has been open 20 years or more. Great top-to-bottom fall line cruising with bowls and glades at the top of the lifts. Snowmaking on the lower runs when they need it. Even with only two major lifts in [it now has a third], it skis big. Endless backcountry either north or south from a long ridge with easy access – and the runs all end at the resort or road.' There is a super-pipe and other terrain features. There are ambitious plans for a 'lively village with three distinct plazas', now under construction. Last season, hotel rooms

and condos joined the lodging options, alongside chalets, townhomes and 'cottages'.

Jackson Hole in Wyoming is a resort with an impressive snow record and equally impressive steep slopes. Jackson is the nearest there is to a town with a genuine Wild West cowboy atmosphere. A 90-minute drive (or slower excursion buses) from Jackson over the Teton pass brings you to **Grand Targhee**, which gets even more snow. The slopes are usually blissfully empty, and much easier than at Jackson. The main Fred's Mountain offers 1,500 acres and 610m/2,000ft vertical accessed from a central fast quad. One-third of smaller Peaked Mountain is accessed by a fast quad while the rest – over 1,000 acres – is used for guided snowcat skiing.

A little way north of Jackson, just inside Montana, is **Big Sky** (not to be confused with Big Mountain, away to the north), with one of the biggest verticals in the US(1280m/4,200ft). We visited the resort last winter, and were very impressed – we have now given it a full chapter. From Big Sky you might visit **Bridger Bowl**, a 90-minute drive away. It boasts broad, steep, lightly wooded slopes which offer wonderful powder descents after a fresh snowfall.

A long way south of all these resorts, **Taos** in New Mexico is the most southerly major resort in America, and because of its isolation it is largely unknown on the international market.

A small part of the amazingly quiet slopes of Big Sky, promoted to a full detailed chapter this year, following an editorial visit ➜

Big Sky

Now America's biggest linked ski area, with extraordinarily quiet slopes and a small purpose-built resort at the base

COSTS

① ② ③ ④ ⑤ ⑥

RATINGS

The slopes
Fast lifts	★★★
Snow	★★★★★
Extent	★★★★
Expert	★★★★
Intermediate	★★★★
Beginner	★★★★★
Convenience	★★★★
Queues	★★★★★
Mountain restaurants	★

The rest
Scenery	★★★
Resort charm	★
Off-slope	★★

KEY FACTS

Resort	2285m
	7,500ft
Slopes	2070-3400m
	6,800-11,150ft
Lifts	18
Pistes	3,812 acres
Green	17%
Blue	25%
Black	58%
Snowmaking	350 acres

Note: Big Sky and Moonlight Basin areas combined have 5,512 acres of slopes.

NEWS

For 2006/07, Big Sky will open another 212 acres of terrain on Lone Mountain, accessed by the Tram and to skier's right of Liberty Bowl. A new mountain restaurant is being built on Andesite, which may be open in time for 2006/07.

636

- ➕ Ski area (shared with neighbouring Moonlight Basin) is now slightly bigger than Vail, with the bonus of a big vertical by US standards
- ➕ Wide range of runs for all abilities, including great expert terrain
- ➕ By far the quietest slopes you will find in a major resort, anywhere
- ➕ Excellent snow record
- ➕ Some comfortable slope-side accommodation, but ...

- ➖ Many condos are spread widely away from the lift base
- ➖ Base area lacks charm and a village focus, though things are slowly improving
- ➖ Resort amenities are limited, with little choice of nightlife
- ➖ Tiny top lift accessing the most testing terrain is prone to queues
- ➖ Isolated location – normally needs three flights to reach it from the UK

Big Sky is renowned for its powder, steeps and big vertical, and has lots of intermediate and beginner slopes and tree skiing as well. Now that it has buried the hatchet with next-door Moonlight Basin and agreed a joint lift pass, it can boast the biggest single linked ski area in the US – taking that title from Vail. It should also be claiming the title of the ski area with most deserted slopes – on our February 2006 visit, we were astonished by the lack of people. The quality of the skiing is excellent and the resort deserves to be better known internationally.

The mountain village is not much more than three hotels, with a few shops, bars, restaurants, and an increasing number of condos and cabins extending out around them. And it is sadly lacking in charm or animation.

THE RESORT

Big Sky celebrated its 30th anniversary in 2004. At the foot of the slopes is Mountain Village Center with three hotels, a handful or bars and restaurants, a variety of shops and some slope-side condos. It is a hotchpotch of buildings in different styles (and from different eras) set vaguely around a traffic-free central Plaza and bordered by car parks and service vehicle roads. There's a French-purpose-built-resort-style underground Mountain Mall with shops and access to many of the bars and restaurants and some of the lodging. On the whole, it feels rather dreary and is crying out for the planned demolition of the oldest buildings and the building of a smart new Intrawest-style development – but no date has been fixed for that.

Some outlying condos and chalets are served by lifts to the slopes, others by free buses, but it's most convenient to stay near the main access lifts.

The resort is set amid the wide open spaces of Montana, one hour's drive from the airport town of Bozeman and it's a roundabout journey (normally involving three different flights) to get there from the UK. Bridger Bowl ski area is an easy day trip by car.

THE MOUNTAINS

Taking Big Sky and Moonlight Basin's slopes together covers a big area (5,512 acres) spread over two linked mountains, with long runs for all abilities. There is a gondola, a so-called 'Tram' (see 'The slopes') and five fast quad chairs, but many of the chairs are still old triples and doubles. There are free mountain tours available at both Big Sky and Moonlight. It is cheapest to buy tickets just for the area you are staying in and to buy a Big Sky-Moonlight Interconnect ticket (substantially more expensive) only for days you intend to ski both areas.

THE SLOPES
Deserted terrain for all abilities

Lone Mountain provides the resort's poster shot, with some seriously steep, open upper slopes. From the Village Center a gondola or parallel high-speed quad go to mid-mountain. From there you can get to the Lone Peak chair which takes you up to the Lone

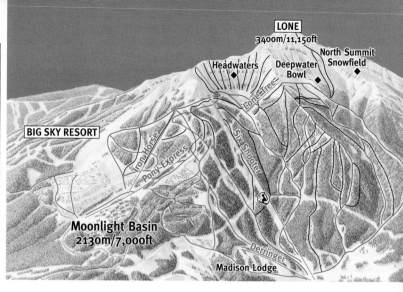

Peak Tram – really two 15-person gondolas, which are operated as if they were a cable-car. This leads to the top and fabulous 360° views (go up for the view even if you don't fancy the runs). Lone Mountain's lower slopes are wooded and varied, as are those of **Andesite Mountain**, which has less vertical, but three of the fast lifts, including one from the Village Center. From various points on Lone Mountain you can head down to the **Moonlight Basin** slopes, which start with a slow chair from Moonlight Lodge. Runs from the top of that lead to the Six Shooter fast chair which, together with the slow

Lone Tree quad near the top, serves nearly all Moonlight's wooded, largely easy intermediate terrain. The Headwaters lift at the top serves expert-only runs.

The amazing thing about the whole area is how deserted the slopes are. We skied there in February 2006 and most of the time didn't see anyone else on the runs we were on. Between them, Big Sky and Moonlight get an average of around 2,500 skiers and boarders a day on their slopes. Divided between 5,512 acres of terrain, that's over two acres each.

Big Sky

Lone Mountain has steep open slopes at the top and gentler wooded runs lower down →

SNOWPIX.COM / CHRIS GILL

TERRAIN-PARKS
Head for Andesite
There's a terrain-park on Andesite, with rails, boxes, slides and a half-pipe, served by the Ramcharger fast quad. Lone Mountain has a natural half-pipe.

SNOW RELIABILITY
No worries here
Snowfall averages 400+ inches – more than most resorts in Colorado. Grooming is good, too.

FOR EXPERTS
Enough to keep you amused
All of the terrain accessed from the Tram is single- or double-black-diamond. The steepest runs are the Big Couloir on the Big Sky side and the North Summit Snowfield on the Moonlight side. For both, you are required to have a partner to ski with, an avalanche transceiver and a shovel. We'd recommend a guide too. There are easier ways down though – Liberty Bowl is easiest (stay left for the best snow that the prevailing wind blows in). Marx and Lenin are a little steeper. Lower down, the Lone Peak Triple, Challenger and Shedhorn chairs also serve good steep terrain. There are some excellent gladed runs, especially on Andesite. In the Moonlight sector the Headwaters is the biggest challenge – but it gets windblown and you may have to pick your way through rocks at the top. The further you hike to skier's left the steeper the

couloirs. There are some good gladed runs lower down.

FOR INTERMEDIATES
Great deserted cruising
The bulk of the terrain on both mountains is of intermediate difficulty (including lots of easy blacks). The main complaint we have is that they don't seem to groom any blacks – which means that you can't hurtle down them taking advantage of the lack of people. But there is lots of excellent blue run cruising served by fast chairs with few others on the runs – Ramcharger and Thunder Wolf on Andesite, Swift Current on Lone Mountain and Six Shooter in the Moonlight sector. Several wide, gentle bowls offer a good introduction to off-piste. And there are some good easy glade runs such as Singlejack on Moonlight and The Congo on Andesite. In general the groomed blues in Moonlight are easier than those in Big Sky, especially the ones served by the Lone Tree chair. Adventurous intermediates could try Liberty Bowl from the top of the Tram; but be prepared for a rocky, windswept traverse between wooden barriers at the top to access the run.

FOR BEGINNERS
Ideal – shame Big Sky is so far
Go to Big Sky rather than Moonlight. There's a good nursery area at the base of the Explorer chair and gondola

REPORTS WANTED

Recently we have had few reports on this resort. If you go there, please do send us a report.

The best reports earn a copy of the next edition, and can lead to free lift passes in future.

See page 12.

boarding
The terrain suits boarders well. Advanced riders will enjoy the steeps and the glades, free-riders the terrain-park at Big Sky and beginners and intermediates the easy cruising runs served by boarder-friendly chair-lifts.

SCHOOLS

Big Sky
t 995 5743

Classes
Half day (2½hr) $49
Private lessons
$210 for 2 hr for 1 to 3 persons

CHILDREN

Lone Peak Playhouse
t 993 2223
Ages 6mnth to 8yr; 8.30 to 4.30; $80 per day; $126 per day incl ski school

Ski school
Ages 6 to 17; 9.00-3.30; $105 per day.

GETTING THERE

Air Bozeman 93km/ 58 miles (1hr).

ACTIVITIES

Indoor Solace Spa (massage, beauty treatments), fitness centres in hotels

Outdoor
Snowmobiles, snow-shoeing, sleigh rides, tubing, horse-riding, fly-fishing, visiting Yellowstone National Park

Central reservations
Call 1 800 548 4486 (toll-free within US).

Phone numbers
From distant parts of the US, add the prefix 1 406. From abroad, add the prefix +1 406.

TOURIST OFFICE

Big Sky
t 995 5000
info@bigskyresort.com
www.bigskyresort.com
Moonlight Basin
t 995 7716
resort@
moonlightbasin.com
www.moonlightbasin.
com

on Lone Mountain and long, deserted greens to progress to from those lifts and from the fast Southern Comfort lift on Andesite.

FOR CROSS-COUNTRY
Head for the Ranch
There are 75km/47 miles of trails at Lone Mountain Ranch, and more at West Yellowstone.

QUEUES
Only for the Tram
The tiny Tram attracts serious queues on busy days – up to 45 minutes we hear. Queues are rare otherwise – and the runs are deserted. But there are still a lot of slow lifts.

MOUNTAIN RESTAURANTS
Back to base for lunch?
The only (basic) mountain restaurant burnt down a couple of years ago. See News for replacement plans. So it might still be back to base for lunch – we had a decent lunch at the Caribiner in the Summit hotel. In Moonlight the Jackass Saloon at Madison base was OK – it does a decent buffalo burger.

SCHOOLS AND GUIDES
Good reputation
We lack recent reports but the Big Sky ski school has a good reputation.

FACILITIES FOR CHILDREN
Usual high US standard
Lone Peak Playhouse in the slope-side Snowcrest Lodge takes children from age six months to eight years and will take them to and from ski school ('perfection', says a reporter). It also operates on Thursday evening and babysitters are available with 48 hours' notice. Children 10 years and under ski free. Moonlight has its own Wranglers day and evening care programme.

STAYING THERE

HOW TO GO
Prepare for a long journey
Only North American specialist tour operators offer Big Sky.
Hotels There's not much choice at the mountain.
((((⑤ **Summit** Best in town, relatively new, central, slope-side, good rooms, outdoor hot pool with mountain views. We stayed there and enjoyed it.
((((④ **Huntley Lodge** Big Sky's original hotel, central, part of Mountain Mall, outdoor pool, hot-tubs, sauna.

Down in the valley, Buck's T-4 Lodge and Rainbow Ranch have been recommended.
Self-catering The good-value Stillwater condos have been recommended, along with Arrowhead, Beaverhead, Snowcrest Lodge, Big Horn and, way out of town, Powder Ridge Cabins.

EATING OUT
A fair choice for a small place
Locals' recommendations include: Huntley Dining Room (smart restaurant, good prime rib); The Peaks in the Summit (formal, lots of choice); The Cabin (local buffalo and elk); Bambu (Asian fusion); MR Hummers (ribs, prawns, popular with locals); Dante's Inferno (Italian); Chet's (giant burgers, sandwiches). Down in the valley we had excellent wild boar steak at Buck's T-4 and Rainbow Ranch has been highly recommended for 'fine dining'.

APRES-SKI
A few places to try
Chet's bar has live music and pool. The Carabiner in the Summit had live music when we were there. The Black Bear can be lively and the basement Alpine Lodge is popular with locals.

OFF THE SLOPES
Mainly the great outdoors
There's snowmobiling, snow-shoeing, sleigh rides, a new floodlit tubing hill, visiting Yellowstone National Park, treatments at the Solace Spa and the Huntley Lodge pool etc is open to all for a fee.

Moonlight Basin
2130m/7,000ft
There's not much at Moonlight except condos and cabins and the impressive Moonlight Lodge at the base. The Lodge is spacious and log-built with high ceilings and beams and a popular bar. But the spa was disappointing – a ridiculously small changing room, and hot-tubs without jets that you can turn on. Our condo was in shoddy condition and a complaint at the front desk failed to result in necessary repairs to the plumbing and lighting. Maybe the Cowboy Heaven Cabins are better. The bar at the Lodge was lively as the slopes closed and Timbers restaurant there gets good reviews. We had an enjoyable dinner a drive away at the Jackass Creek Saloon (good crab cakes, scallops and elk steak).

Jackson Hole

*Touristy 'Wild West' town, big, exciting slopes and a rapidly
changing base village; in some eyes, the best the US has to offer*

- ➕ Some real expert-only terrain and one of the US's biggest verticals
- ➕ Jackson town has an entertaining Wild West ambience
- ➕ Unspoiled, remote location with interesting wildlife
- ➕ Excellent snow record
- ➕ Even more snow (and empty slopes) 90 minutes away at Grand Targhee
- ➕ Some unique off-slope diversions
- ➕ The town is only 15 minutes from the airport, but ...

- ➖ The town is also 15 minutes from the slopes – though the slope-side village is an increasingly attractive alternative place to stay
- ➖ Intermediates wanting groomed runs will find the area very limited
- ➖ Low altitude and sunny orientation mean snow can deteriorate quickly
- ➖ Inadequate mountain restaurants, though changes are afoot
- ➖ Getting there from the UK involves two or three flights

With its wooden sidewalks, country-music saloons and pool halls, tiny Jackson is a determinedly Western town, designed to amuse summer visitors to Yellowstone – great fun, if you like that kind of thing.

For those who like steep slopes smothered in deep powder or plastered with big bumps, Jackson Hole is Mecca. Like many American mountains, Jackson has steeps that you can't find in Europe except by going off-piste with a guide. What marks it out is the sheer quantity of this terrain, and the almost Alpine vertical.

Of course, there is also skiing for those afraid of the black, but intermediates wanting to build up confidence should look elsewhere. This is partly because the place gets a lot of snow, and soft, fresh snow forms bumps, even on blues.

The ancient, locally revered bottom-to-top cable-car (carrying capacity an astonishing 270 people an hour) is no more. With a replacement not expected until 2008/09, the resort is installing a temporary chair-lift to access the top slopes. Queue connoisseurs will be able to stand in line there, instead.

The new cable-car will carry twice as many people as the old lift; Teton Village, at the foot of the mountain now has three distinctly smooth, upmarket hotels; a table-service mountain restaurant is about to open. Gradually, Jackson Hole is changing. Locals who identify with the resort's hardcore image will tell you the place is losing its soul, going soft, selling out. Maturing nicely, we'd say.

THE RESORT

The town of Jackson sits at the south-eastern edge of Jackson Hole – a high, flat valley surrounded by mountain ranges, in north-west Wyoming. Jackson gets many more visitors in summer than in winter, thanks to the nearby national parks. To entertain summer tourists the town strives to maintain its Wild West flavour, with traditional-style wooden buildings and sidewalks, and a couple of 'cowboy' saloons. It has lots of clothing and souvenir shops, as well as upmarket galleries appealing to second-home owners. In winter it's half-empty and accommodation prices come down. A

2006 reporter was full of praise for the friendly and helpful locals.

The slopes, a 15-minute drive or $3 bus-ride ('crowded') north-east, rise abruptly from the flat valley floor. At the lift base is Teton Village, which has expanded over the last few years to become a much more attractive base, with an increased choice of bars, restaurants and hotels – some of these notably upscale. Homes to rent are spread over quite an area.

A popular excursion by car or daily bus is over the Teton pass to the smaller resort of Grand Targhee, which gets even more snow (and keeps it better, with gentler, shadier slopes). See Rest of the West introduction.

be able to do laps on the upper slopes using just the top two chairs, which would be excellent were it not for the prospect of queues.

Alternatively you can work your way across from the gondola to **Apres Vous** mountain, with half the vertical and mostly much gentler runs, accessed from the village by the short Teewinot and the longer Apres Vous fast quad.

Snow King is a separate area right by Jackson town. There's a good choice of short, steep slopes. Locals use it at lunch-time and in the evenings (it's partly floodlit).

TERRAIN-PARKS
Getting better
There's a terrain-park by the Apres-Vous chair, with newly improved jumps and rails, music and a 137m/450ft long super-pipe. Dick's Ditch is a natural pipe and there's a mini-park for novices. But you really come to Jackson for the steeps and deeps of the free-riding.

SNOW RELIABILITY
Steep lower slopes can suffer
The claimed average of 460 inches of snow is much more than most Colorado resorts claim. But the base elevation is relatively low for the Rockies, and the slopes are quite sunny – they basically face south-east. If you're unlucky, you may find the steep lower slopes, like the Hobacks, in poor shape, or even shut. Locals claim that you can expect powder roughly half the time. Don't assume early-season conditions will be good.

FOR EXPERTS
Best for the brave
For the good skier or boarder who wants challenges without the expense of hiring a guide to go off-piste, Jackson is one of the world's best resorts – maybe even the best. Rendezvous mountain offers virtually nothing but black and very black slopes. The routes down the main Rendezvous Bowl are not particularly fearsome; but some of the alternatives are. Go down the East Ridge at least once to stare over the edge of the notorious Corbet's Couloir. It's the jump in that's special; the slope you land on is a mere 50°, they say.

Jackson Hole

641

KEY FACTS	
Resort	1925m
	6,310ft

Jackson Hole	
Slopes	1925-3185m
	6,310-10,450ft
Lifts	12
Pistes	2,500 acres
Green	10%
Blue	40%
Black	50%
Snowmaking	
	160 acres

Grand Targhee	
Slopes	2310-3050m
	7,600-10,000ft
Lifts	5
Pistes	2,000 acres
(plus 1,000 acres	
served by snowcat)	
Green	10%
Blue	70%
Black	20%
Snowmaking	none

THE MOUNTAINS

Most of the slopes are below the tree-line, but one of the attractions of the place is that most of the forest is not dense. Trail classifications are accurate: our own small map doesn't distinguish black from double-black-diamond runs, but the distinction matters – 'expert only' tends to mean just that. There are complimentary tours daily.

THE SLOPES
One big mountain, one small one
For the moment, the main lift out of Teton Village is the Bridger gondola. This goes up over a broad mountainside split by gullies, and gives speedy access to the chain of three chairs that for the moment provide access to the upper slopes of the big mountain that makes Jackson Hole famous – **Rendezvous**. The mountain provides a 1260m/4,130ft vertical – exceptional for the US. But without the cable-car, doing top-to-bottom laps will no longer be very appealing. On the other hand, you will

LIFT PASSES

Jackson Hole

Prices in US$

Age	1-day	6-day
under 15	35	195
15 to 21	56	312
22 to 64	70	390
over 65	35	195

Free under 6

Beginner ticket for Eagles Rest and Teewinot lifts ($10)

Notes
Covers all lifts in Jackson Hole. Half-day ticket available.

Alternative passes
Grand Targhee; Snow King Mountain

boarding

Jackson Hole is a cult resort for expert snowboarders, as for skiers: the steeps, cliffs and chutes make for a lot of high-adrenalin thrills for competent free-riders. It's not a bad resort for novices, with the beginner slopes served by a high-speed quad. Intermediates not wishing to venture off the groomed runs will find the resort limited. Two terrain-parks and a super-pipe provide the freestyle thrills. There are some good snowboard shops, including the Hole-in-the-Wall at Teton Village.

Below Rendezvous Bowl, the wooded flanks of Cheyenne Bowl offer serious challenges, at the extreme end of the single-black-diamond spectrum. If instead you take the ridge run that skirts this bowl to the right, you get to the Hobacks – a huge area of open and lightly wooded slopes, gentler than those higher up, but still black.

Corbet's aside, most of the seriously steep slopes are more easily reached from the slightly lower quad chairs. From Sublette, you have direct access to the short but seriously steep Alta chutes, and to the less severe Laramie Bowl beside them. Or you can track over to Tensleep Bowl – pausing to inspect Corbet's from below – and on to the less extreme (and less chute-like) Expert Chutes, and the single-black Cirque and Headwall areas. Casper Bowl (now with named routes) – accessed through gates only – is recommended for untracked powder. The Crags terrain is an area of bowls, chutes and glades – but it involves a good half-hour hike to reach it. Thunder chair serves further steep, narrow, north-facing chutes.

Again, the lower part of the mountain here offers lightly wooded single-black-diamond slopes.

The gondola serves terrain not without interest for experts. In particular, Moran Woods is a splendid, under-utilised area. And even Apres Vous itself has an area of serious single blacks in Saratoga bowl.

The gates into the backcountry access over 3,000 acres of amazing terrain, which should be explored only with guidance. You can stay out overnight at a backcountry yurt. There are some helicopter operations.

FOR INTERMEDIATES
Exciting for some
There are great cruising runs on the front face of Apres Vous, and top-to-bottom quite gentle blues from the gondola. But they don't add up to a great deal of mileage, and you shouldn't consider Jackson unless you want to tackle the blacks. It's then important to get guidance on steepness and snow conditions. The steepest single blacks are steep, intimidating when mogulled and fearsome when hard. The daily grooming map is worth consulting.

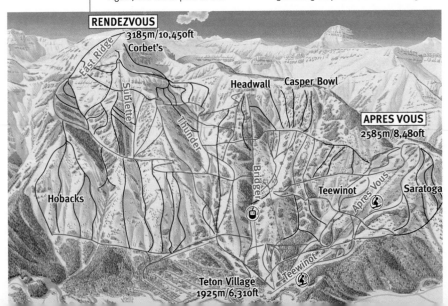

SCHOOLS

Jackson Hole
t 739 2663

Classes
Full day (5½hr) $75
Private lessons
Half day (3hr) $295

CHILDREN

Kids' Ranch
t 739 2691
Wranglers: ages
6mnth to 2yr; 8.30-
4.30; $110 per day
Rough Riders: ages 3
to 6; 9am-3.30;
includes skiing; $110
per day
Little Rippers: ages
5-6; 9am-3.15;
includes skiing; $175
per day

Ski school
Explorers: ages 7 to
14; 9.00-3.30; $110
per day.

GETTING THERE

Air Jackson 19km/
12 miles (½hr).

FOR BEGINNERS
Fine, up to a point
There are good broad, gentle beginner slopes. The progression to the blue Werner run off the Apres Vous chair is gradual enough and the mid-mountain blues on the Casper Bowl chair are now reachable via the new chair from the beginner area. But few other runs will help build confidence.

FOR CROSS-COUNTRY
Lots of possibilities
There are three centres, and one at Grand Targhee, offering varied trails. The Spring Creek Nordic Center has some good beginner terrain and moonlight tours. The Nordic Center at Teton has 20km/12 miles of trails and organises trips into the National Parks.

QUEUES
Upwardly mobile queues
The cable-car was famous for its queues. The promised substantial increase in capacity of the Bridger gondola will easily compensate for the loss of the cable-car and, more importantly, experts are now unlikely to descend to the village except at the end of the day – so there is no reason to expect queue problems at village level. But we reckon you can expect queues at altitude, because experts who were wasting time descending to the village and waiting for a cable-car will now be staying high. A recent early-season reporter was very critical of the poor information given to visitors on the slope conditions ('we were actively misled').

MOUNTAIN RESTAURANTS
They're building a second!
The restaurant at the base of the Casper chair-lift does a good range of self-service food, but gets very crowded. A new table- and self-service restaurant is expected to open at the top of the gondola for 2006/07. There are simple snack bars at four other points on the mountain.

SCHOOLS AND GUIDES
Learn to tackle the steeps
As well as the usual lessons, there are also special types – steep and deep, women-only, for example – on certain dates. Backcountry guides can be hired – Rendezvous Ski Tours is 'highly recommended' by a recent reporter who enjoyed exploring the backcountry from Teton Pass and elsewhere.

FACILITIES FOR CHILDREN
Just fine
The area may not seem to be one ideally suited to children, but in fact there are enough easy runs and the 'Kids' Ranch' care facilities are good. There are various classes catering for ages 3 to 17.

STAYING THERE

HOW TO GO
In town or by the mountain
Teton Village is convenient, while Jackson has the cowboy atmosphere – but bear in mind that some of the hotels are way out of town.
Hotels Because winter is low season, prices are low.
TETON VILLAGE
((((⑤ **Four Seasons Resort** (732 5000) Stylish luxury, with art on the walls, superb skier services, health club, an exceptional outdoor pool, perfect position just above the base.
((((④ **Teton Mountain Lodge** (734 7111) Very comfortable. Good indoor and outdoor pool and fitness centre.
(((④ **Snake River Lodge & Spa** (732 6000) Smartly welcoming and comfortable, with fine spa facilities.
(((④ **Alpenhof** (733 3242) Tirolean-style, with varied rooms. Good food. Pool, sauna, hot-tub.
((② **Hostel x** (733 3415) Basic, good value. Recommended by a reporter.
JACKSON TOWN
((((④ **Wort** (733 2190) Comfortable, central, above the lively Silver Dollar Bar. Hot-tub.
(((④ **Rusty Parrot Lodge** (733 2000) A stylish place with a rustic feel and handcrafted furniture. Hot-tub. 'Awesome' breakfasts.
(((④ **Painted Porch** (733 1981) Gorgeous B&B full of antiques.
((③ **Jackson Hole Lodge** (733 2992) Western-style place on outskirts. Comfortable mini-suite rooms, and free breakfast ('very good'). Pool, sauna, hot-tubs. Shuttle to the slopes.
((③ **Snow King Resort** (733 5200) Ski-in, ski-out hotel and condo complex at Snow King Mountain.
((③ **Forty Niner Inn and Suites** (733 7550) Central, good value. Recommended last season.
((③ **Parkway Inn** (733 3143) Friendly, family-run, central; big rooms, antique furniture, pool, hot-tubs.
((② **Trapper Inn** (733 2648) Friendly, good value, a block or two from Town Square. Hot-tubs.

↑ We love these runs in fresh snow; when they are bumped up, we spend a lot of time like these guys, thinking about it

JACKSON HOLE RESORT

ACTIVITIES

Indoor Fitness centres, swimming, tennis, library, concerts, wildlife art and other museums

Outdoor Snowmobiles, snow-shoeing, sleigh rides, dog-sledding, tubing, snowkite boarding

OUR WEBSITE

Go to our website at wtss.co.uk for resort news, links to resort sites, a build-your-own-shortlist system and reader forums.

Phone numbers
From distant parts of the US, add the prefix 1 307.
From abroad, add the prefix +1 307.

TOURIST OFFICES

Jackson Hole
t 733 2292
info@jacksonhole.com
www.jacksonhole.com

Grand Targhee
t 353 2300
info@grandtarghee.com
www.grandtarghee.com

BETWEEN THE TWO
((((⑤ **Amangani Resort** (734 7333)
Hedonistic luxury in isolated position way above the valley.
(((④ **Spring Creek Ranch** (733 8833)
Exclusive retreat; cross-country on hand. Hot-tub.
Self-catering There is lots of choice around Jackson and at Teton Village.

EATING OUT
A reasonable range of options
In classic American style, Jackson offers a good range of excellent dining options, whether you stay in town or at the base. To check out menus, get hold of the local dining guide.

Most of the best bets at Teton Village are in the hotels. One reporter enjoyed 'scallops to die for' at the Alpenhof Bistro. The Vertical (Inn at Jackson Hole) is excellent, with a short, eclectic menu and long wine list. It's rivalled by the Cascade Grillhouse and Spirits (Teton Mountain Lodge). Options at the Four Seasons include the Peak – a 'good value' casual place. The lively Mangy Moose does steaks and seafood.

In Jackson town there is more choice. The cool art-deco Cadillac Grille does good food. The Blue Lion is small and casually stylish. The 'saloons' do hearty meals and good steaks. A reporter praises Antony's Italian and 'for a treat' the Rusty Parrot Lodge. Thai Me Up does 'good value, decent food', the cute log cabin Sweetwater serves 'Greek-inspired' food and Stone Table does 'awesome' South American dishes as well as tapas. The Snake River brew-pub – not to be confused with the excellent but expensive Snake River Grill – serves 'award winning

beers and excellent pasta'. The Old Yellowstone Garage has 'superb Italian food in an elegant setting', Nani's (also Italian) is 'surprisingly inexpensive' and Rendezvous Bistro ('good food and atmosphere') is very popular.

Out of town, The Grill at Amangani has 'a supremely stylish setting, stunning food and prices lower than expected'. Calico is a much more modest spot – a large Italian place, popular with locals.

APRES-SKI
Amusing saloons
For immediate après-ski at Teton Village, the Mangy Moose is a big, happy, noisy place, often with live music ('a cool hangout,' says a snowboarder). For a quieter time head for Dietrich's bar at the Alpenhof.

In Jackson there are two famous 'saloons'. The Million Dollar Cowboy Bar features saddles as bar stools and a stuffed grizzly bear, and is usually the liveliest place in town, with live music and dancing some nights. The Silver Dollar around the corner is more subdued; there may be ragtime playing as you count the 2032 silver dollars inlaid into the counter. The Rancher is a huge pool-hall. The Shady Lady saloon sometimes has live music. The Virginian saloon is much quieter and a locals' hang-out: 'If you like beer, guns and ammo, you'll be in good company,' says one. For a night out of town, join the locals at the Stagecoach Inn at Wilson, especially Sundays for church: 'A real western and blue grass swing night with music from a band that has not missed a night since 1969.'

OFF THE SLOPES
'Great' outdoor diversions
Yellowstone National Park is 100km/ 60 miles to the north. You can tour the park by snowcat or snowmobile with a guide; numbers are now restricted to reduce pollution. Some visitors really enjoy the park; we weren't keen. The National Elk Refuge, with the largest elk herd in the US, is next to Jackson – 'you can get really close to the elk,' says one reporter – and across the road from the National Museum of Wildlife Art. Reporters recommend both. In town there are some 40 galleries and museums and a number of outlets for Western arts and crafts. Joining the Jackson Hole Ski Club ($30) is recommended – good discounts in shops, restaurants, lodgings etc.

Sun Valley

Built in the 1930s, Sun Valley was the US's first luxury, purpose-built winter resort and soon became popular with the stars. For a peaceful, relaxing time, it's hard to beat. For skiing and boarding alone, there are better resorts.

KEY FACTS

Resort	1750m
	5,750ft
Slopes	1750-2790m
	5,750-9,150ft
Lifts	14
Pistes	2,054 acres
Green	36%
Blue	42%
Black	22%
Snowmaking	73%

TOURIST OFFICE

t 208 786 8259
ski@sunvalley.com
www.sunvalley.com

THE RESORT

Sun Valley is based around the old mining village of Ketchum, and its current owner has pumped millions of dollars into the mountain to restore it to state-of-the-art luxury. The town retains its old-world charm and has atmospheric bars, restaurants and shops; you can sometimes find Clint Eastwood in the Pioneer Saloon. The stylish Sun Valley Lodge is one of our favourite ski hotels, and its corridors are lined with photos of film-star guests. Shuttle-buses link the slopes to most accommodation.

THE MOUNTAINS

The slopes of Bald Mountain (known locally as Baldy) are accessed from one of two luxurious base lodge complexes at River Run and Warm Springs. Of the lifts, seven are high-speed quads. The separate Dollar Mountain has good beginner slopes. The resort has an erratic natural snow record, but snowmaking covers over 70 per cent of the runs. There are a few tough slopes for experts, but nothing beyond single-black-diamond pitch. Most of the terrain is ideal for intermediates, with lots of runs at a consistent pitch. There are good blue bowl runs with great views from the top ridge as well as well-groomed cruisers through the trees. Dollar is the place for beginners, with gentle, green runs to progress to. Sun Valley doesn't have a snowboard culture and for years it wasn't allowed; but it is now and there's even a super-pipe. The mountain restaurants and base lodges are way ahead of most US on-slope facilities; Dollar got a new base lodge two years ago. There are 40km/25 miles of good cross-country.

Short turns

645

Taos

Set high above an arid New Mexico valley, Taos Ski Valley is the most southerly of North America's major ski areas. It offers some good expert terrain but snowboarders are banned from sampling its slopes.

KEY FACTS

Resort	2805m
	9,210ft
Slopes	2805-3600m
	9,210-11,820ft
Lifts	12
Pistes	1,294 acres
Green	24%
Blue	25%
Black	51%
Snowmaking	100%
of green/blue slopes	

TOURIST OFFICE

t 866 968 7386
tsv@skitaos.org
www.skitaos.org

THE RESORT

Taos Ski Valley, at the foot of the slopes, is tiny. It has around 1,000 beds in a handful of hotels and condos, with little room for expansion and no room for the swimming pools, ice rinks, galleries and boutiques you find in larger places. The Hotel St Bernard, Edelweiss Lodge and Snakedance condos all offer good slope-side accommodation. 18 miles down the valley, the traditional adobe town of Taos, with its art and craft galleries and shops, makes an alternative base.

THE MOUNTAINS

When you hit Taos Ski Valley the first thing you will see is Al's Run, a steep mogul-field rising sheerly out of the resort. To allay people's fears a prominent sign reads: 'Don't panic! You're looking at 1/30 of Taos Ski Valley. We have many easy runs too.' But it's good skiers who will get the most out of the resort. There are numerous long steep runs through the trees, and many of the best runs require a hike from the top lifts.

There's enough to keep intermediates happy for a few days, especially if they're willing to tackle some of the steeper runs, too. Beginners have their own dedicated area and easy green runs to progress to. And the ski school has a very high reputation. Snowfall averages over 300 inches but because it is so far south, snow can be bad here (as in 2006/07) when its good elsewhere (and vice versa); all the green and blue runs have snowmaking.

There are a couple of basic mountain restaurants but many people head back to base for lunch.

New England

You go to Utah for the deepest snow, to Colorado for the lightest powder and swankiest resorts, to California for big mountains and low prices. You go to New England for ... well, for what? Extreme cold? Rock-hard artificial snow? Mountains too limited to be of interest beyond New Jersey? Yes and no: all of these preconceptions have some basis, but they are an incomplete and unfair picture.

Yes, it can be cold: one of our reporters recorded –27°C, with wind chill producing a perceived –73°C. Early in the season, people wear face masks to prevent frostbite. It can also be warm – another reporter had a whole week of rain that washed away the early-season snow. The thing about New England weather is that it varies – rather like ours. The locals' favourite saying is: 'If you don't like the weather in New England, wait two minutes.'

New England doesn't usually get much super-light powder or deep snow to play in. But the resorts have big snowmaking installations, designed to ensure a long season and to help the slopes to 'recover' after a thaw or spell of rain. They were the pioneers of snowmaking technology; and 'farming' snow, as they put it, is an art form and a way of life – provided the weather is cold enough. Many of the resorts get impressive amounts of natural snow too – in some seasons.

The mountains are not huge in terms of trail mileage (the largest, Killington, is the smallest American resort to get its own chapter in these pages). But several have verticals of over 800m/2,620ft (on a par with Colorado resorts such as Keystone) and most have over 600m/1,970ft (matching Breckenridge), and are worth considering for a short stay, or even for a week if you like familiar runs. For more novelty, a two- or three-centre trip is the obvious solution. Most resorts suit snowboarders well, often having more than one terrain-park.

You won't lack challenge – most of the double-black-diamond runs are seriously steep. And you won't lack space: most Americans visit over weekends, which means deserted slopes on weekdays – except at peak holiday periods. It also means the resorts are keen to attract long-stay visitors, so UK package prices are low. But the big weekend and day-trip trade also means that few New England resorts have developed atmospheric resort villages – just a few condos and a hotel, maybe, with places to stay further out geared to car drivers.

New England is easy to get to from Britain – a flight to Boston, then perhaps a three- or four-hour drive to your resort. And there are some pretty towns to visit, with their clapboard houses and big churches. You might also like to consider spending a day or two in Boston – one of America's most charming cities. And you could have a shopping spree at the factory outlet stores that abound in New England.

We cover four of the most popular resorts on the UK market in the chapters that follow – a long chapter on **Killington**, a short one on **Stowe**, and Short Turns entries on **Smugglers' Notch** and **Sunday River**. But there are many other small areas, too. If you are going for a week or more, plan to rent a car and visit a few resorts.

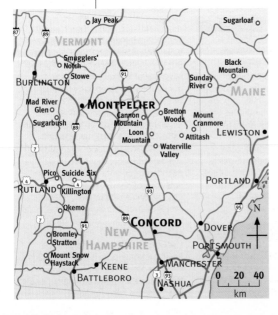

Killington

New England's leading resort, in most respects; good slopes, great après-ski, no village – but they're working on it, at last

COSTS

① ② ③ ④ ⑤ ⑥

RATINGS

The slopes

Fast lifts	**
Snow	***
Extent	**
Expert	***
Intermediate	***
Beginner	****
Convenience	*
Queues	****
Mountain restaurants	*

The rest

Scenery	***
Resort charm	*
Off-slope	*

NEWS

If all goes according to plan, the 10-year process of building Killington's new base village should begin soon: the first stage will include shops and accommodation in the Snowshed and Ramshead areas.

For 2005/06 the Bear and Ramshead day lodges were revamped; and Bear Mountain gained a new rail park.

The Killington Grand Hotel opened a new spa and wellness centre.

KEY FACTS

Resort	670m
	2,200ft
Slopes	355-1285m
	1,170-4,220ft
Lifts	33
Pistes	1,209 acres
Green	26%
Blue	36%
Black	38%
Snowmaking	
	1,850 guns

➕ The biggest mountain in the east, matching some Colorado resorts

➕ Lively après-ski, with lots of bar-restaurants offering happy hours and late-night action

➕ Excellent nursery slopes

➕ Comprehensive and very effective snowmaking

➕ Good childcare, although it's not a notably child-oriented resort

➖ No resort village yet: hotels, condos and restaurants are widely spread, mostly along the five-mile access road – a car is almost a necessity

➖ Crowds on holidays and weekends

➖ New England weather – highly changeable, and can be very cold

➖ The trail network is complex, and there are lots of trail-crossings

➖ Terminally tedious for anyone who is not a skier or boarder

It's difficult to ignore Killington. It claims to have the largest mountain, largest number of quad chairs, largest grooming fleet and longest season in the east, and the world's biggest snowmaking installation. (It tries to be the first resort in the US to open, in October, but often shuts again shortly afterwards.) It also claims to have America's longest lift and longest trail (a winding 16km/10 miles) and New England's steepest mogul slope (Outer Limits – average gradient 46 per cent).

These things may matter if your choice of destination is limited to those in the eastern US. In the general scheme of things, they count for very little. Killington is a minor resort, chiefly of interest if you find yourself within driving distance at a time when conditions look good.

THE RESORT

Killington is an extraordinary resort, especially to European eyes. Most of its hotels and restaurants are spread along a five-mile approach road. The nearest thing you'll find to a focus is the occasional set of traffic lights with a cluster of shops, though there is a concentration of buildings along a two-and-a-half mile stretch of the road. The resort caters mainly for weekend visitors who drive in from the east-coast cities. The car is king; but there's also a good 'but infrequent' free day-time shuttle-bus service around the base areas and lodgings. Beyond this it costs $2.

There are lodgings around the lift base, and plans for something like a village there have been revived, now that the resort's owners have brought in a new partner – development is planned to begin during 2006.

Staying near the start of the access road leaves you well placed for the gondola station on the main highway leading past the resort, and for outings to Pico, a separate little mountain in the same ownership, perhaps one day to be linked to Ramshead.

THE MOUNTAINS

Runs spread over a series of wooded peaks, all quite close together but giving the resort a basis for claiming to cover six mountains – or seven if you count Pico. An impressive number of runs and lifts are crammed into a modest area. To some extent the terrain on each sector suits a different ability level. But there are also areas where a mixed ability group would be happy, and there are easy runs from top to bottom of each peak.

Some runs of all levels are left to form bumps; there is half-and-half grooming on selected trails; and terrain features – ridges etc – are created. There are also Fusion Zones – thinned-out forest areas, not groomed or patrolled, where you pick your own line. They come in blue and single- and double-black-diamond grades. We found them great fun.

THE SLOPES
Complicated
The Killington Base area has chairs radiating to three of the six peaks – **Snowdon**, **Killington** (the high-point of the area) and **Skye** – the last also

LIFT PASSES

Killington Mountain Pass

Prices in US$

Age	1-day	6-day
under 13	45	224
13 to 18	54	269
19 to 64	69	344
over 65	45	224

Free under 6

Beginner included in price of lessons

Notes

Covers Killington and Pico ski areas. Prices include sales tax. Discount if you book online 14 days in advance. Special prices for lift pass, equipment and lessons combined.

OUR WEBSITE

Go to our website at wtss.co.uk for resort news, links to resort sites, a build-your-own resort shortlist system and reader forums.

boarding

A cool resort like Killington has to take boarding seriously, and it does. There are terrain features scattered around the area, with lots of interest for all levels, and parts of the mountain have been reshaped to cut out some of the unpleasant flats on green runs. There are excellent beginner slopes, and plenty of friendly (ie slow-loading) high-speed chair-lifts – and the Perfect Turn Discovery Center caters just for beginners. Several big-name board events are held here, and the terrain-parks just get bigger and better.

accessible by gondola starting beside US Highway 4. Novices and families head for the other main base area, which has two parts: Snowshed, at the foot of the main beginner slope, served by several parallel chairs; and Ramshead, just across the road up to Killington Base, where there's a Family Center at the foot of the entirely gentle **Ramshead** mountain.

The two remaining peaks are behind Skye Peak; they can be reached by trails from Killington and Skye, but each also has a lift base accessible by road. **Bear** is the experts' hill, served by two quad chairs from its mid-mountain base area. The sixth 'peak', **Sunrise**, is a slight blip on the mountainside, with a short triple chair up from the Sunrise Village condos. The result is a complex network of runs; signposting hasn't been adequate in the past, but concentrated efforts to improve matters have paid off, says a 2006 reporter – 'colour coding for each mountain and trail maps located by each lift and junction'.

There are free guided tours given by 'knowledgeable, enthusiastic and entertaining' 'ambassadors'.

TERRAIN-PARKS
Lots of possibilities

There's a good choice, including early and late season parks (plus one at Pico). Bear mountain is home to the main freestyle area, with separate sections along the Wildfire and Dreammaker trails. Features include a super-pipe, jumps, table-tops and a new urban-style rail park. There's also a boarder-cross course with berms and rollers. All suit advanced riders best. Timberline on Ramshead is better suited to intermediates, has a quarter-pipe and was recently expanded. There's a beginner mini-park and kids have their own park and pipe classes.

SNOW RELIABILITY
Good if it's cold

Killington has a good snowfall record and a huge snowmaking system – (although a recent reporter was surprised to find this little used during his peak season visit, despite low temperatures). But even that is no good if temperatures are too high to operate it. Bad weather can ruin a holiday even in mid-season. A reporter who had new powder each night on a

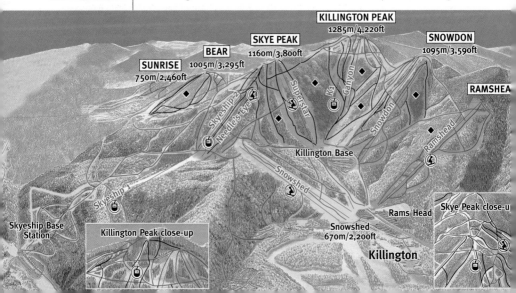

KILLINGTON PEAK
1285m/4,220ft

SKYE PEAK
1160m/3,800ft

SNOWDON
1095m/3,590ft

BEAR
1005m/3,295ft

SUNRISE
750m/2,460ft

RAMSHEA

Skyeship 2
Needle's Eye
Superstar
K1
Canyon
Snowdon
Ramshead

Killington Base

Skyeship 1

Snowshed

Skyeship Base Station

Killington Peak close-up

Rams Head

Skye Peak close-u

Snowshed
670m/2,200ft

Killington

March visit went back at the same time
the following year to find people skiing
in shorts and T-shirts on the few runs
that were open. A February visitor told
of 'everything from frostbite warnings
to pouring rain'. Grooming has been
reported to be poor, but the resort has
just bought six additional machines,
which should help.

FOR EXPERTS
Some challenges
The main areas that experts head for
are Killington Peak, where there is a
handful of genuine double-diamond
fall-line runs under the two chair-lifts,
and Bear mountain – though one
reporter did not find them very
challenging. Most of the slopes here
are single blacks but Outer Limits,
under the main quad chair, is a
double-diamond, claimed to be 'the
steepest mogul slope in the east'. We
suspect there are steeper runs at
Stowe and Smugglers' Notch. There are
two or three worthwhile blacks on
Snowdon and Skye, too. Also the
Fusion Zones on Skye, Snowdon and
Bear are well worth seeking out.

FOR INTERMEDIATES
Limited extent
There are lots of easy cruising blue
and green runs all over the slopes,
except on Bear mountain, where the
single blacks present a little more of a
challenge for intermediates. Snowdon
is a splendid area for those who like to
vary their diet, although a reporter
favoured the trails on Skye. There's a
blue-classified Fusion Zone on
Ramshead. One reporter liked Pico but
complained that the blue run down
was more difficult than some blacks.

FOR BEGINNERS
Splendid
The facilities for complete beginners
are excellent. The Snowshed slope is

one vast nursery slope served by three
chair-lifts and a very slow drag-lift.
Ramshead also has excellent gentle
slopes. The ski school runs a special,
purpose-built Discovery Center just for
first-time skiers and boarders – they
introduce you to the equipment, show
you videos and provide refreshments.

FOR CROSS-COUNTRY
Two main options
Extensive cross-country loops are
available at two specialist 'resorts' –
Mountain Meadows, down on US
Highway 4, and Mountain Top Ski
Touring, just a short drive away
at Chittenden.

QUEUES
Weekend crowds
Killington gets a lot of weekend and
holiday business, but at other times
the slopes and lifts are likely to be
quiet. One holiday visitor found long
lines for the Ramshead chair, the K1
gondola and the Bear Mountain chair.
Overcrowded slopes are more of a
problem than lift queues – the
approaches to Bear lift base were
singled out by a reporter.

MOUNTAIN RESTAURANTS
Bearable base lodges
The Killington Peak Lodge (in what
was the top station of the old gondola)
is the only real mountain restaurant;
we lack recent reports, but we've
received mixed reports in the past.
There's a warming hut at Northbrook
station on Skye Peak where you can
get soups, and areas are provided if
you wish to bring your own food. Most
people use the base lodges; those at
Bear, Ramshead and Snowshed have
all received recent improvements and
reporters comment on 'freshly cooked
food' and 'affordable prices'. But the
K-1 lodge is said to be the liveliest of
the bunch.

↑ Most of the terrain features are at Bear, including the super pipe

KILLINGTON RESORT

ACTIVITIES

Indoor Killington Grand Resort Hotel has massage, fitness centre, outdoor pool, hot-tub, sauna; theatre, cinemas, bowling, at Rutland; climbing wall at Snowshed base

Outdoor Ice rink, snow-shoeing, dog-sledding, snowmobile tours, sleigh rides

Central reservations phone number
Call 1 800 621 6867 (toll-free from within the US).

Phone numbers
From distant parts of the US, add the prefix 1 802.
From abroad, add the prefix +1 802.

TOURIST OFFICE

t 422 3333
info@killington.com
www.killington.com

SCHOOLS AND GUIDES
In search of the Perfect Turn

The philosophy of the Perfect Turn school is to build on your strengths, and it seems to work for most people. Beginners start and finish their day in a dedicated building with easy chairs, coffee, videos and help with fitting equipment. Speciality clinics include mogul weekends and park classes.

FACILITIES FOR CHILDREN
Fine in practice

There is a Family Center at the Ramshead base, which takes kids from 12 weeks and will introduce them to skiing from age two years. Classes are reported to be small.

STAYING THERE

HOW TO GO
Wide choices

There is a wide choice of places to stay. As well as hotels and condos, there are a few chalets.

Hotels There are a few places near the lifts, but most are a drive or bus-ride away, down Killington Road or on US4.
((((④ **Cortina Inn** (773 3333) 20 minutes away on US4, near Pico; pool, 'excellent food, poor soundproofing'.
((((④ **Grand Resort** (422 6888) Swanky resort-owned place at Snowshed, with outdoor pool and health club.
(((④ **Inn of the Six Mountains** (228 4676) Couple of miles down Killington Road; 'spacious rooms, good pool'.

((③ **Red Rob Inn** (422 3303) Short drive from slopes – 'good restaurant, a cut above the usual motel style'.
((③ **North Star Lodge** (422 2296) Well down Killington Road; 'good budget accommodation'.

EATING OUT
You name it

There are all sorts of restaurants spread along the Killington Road, from simple pizza or pasta through to 'fine dining' places. Many of the places in the Après-ski section serve food – be aware, though, that most bars do not allow children. The local menu guide is essential reading. Claude's, Choices, the 'excellent' Grist Mill, Hemingway's, Charity's, the Cortina Inn and Red Rob Inn have been recommended. Sugar and Spice is reported to serve good breakfasts, as does Ppeppers, which also has 'good burgers' and desserts.

APRES-SKI
The beast of the east

Killington has a well-deserved reputation for a vibrant après-ski scene; many of its short-stay visitors are clearly intent on making the most of their few days (or nights) here.

Although there are bars at the base lodges, keen après-skiers head down Killington Road to one of the lively places scattered along its 8km/5 mile length. From 3pm it's cheap drinks and free munchies, then in the early evening it's serious dining time, and later on the real action starts (and admission charges kick in).

The train-themed Casey's Caboose is said to have the best 'wings' in town. Charity's is another lively bar, with an interior apparently lifted from a late-19th-century Parisian brothel. The Wobbly Barn ('expensive' but 'very good' food) is a famous live-music place that claims to be one of the leading après-ski venues in the US. The Pickel Barrel caters for a younger crowd, with theme nights. The Outback complex has something for everyone, from pizzas and free massages to disco and live bands.

OFF THE SLOPES
Rent a car

If there is a less amusing resort in which to spend time off the slopes, we have yet to find it. Make sure you have a car, as well as a good book. Factory shopping at Manchester is recommended (45-minute drive).

Stowe

Classic charming Vermont town some miles from its small but serious – and improving – area of slopes on Mount Mansfield

COSTS

① ② ③ ④ ⑤ ⑥

RATINGS

The slopes
Fast lifts	***
Snow	***
Extent	*
Expert	***
Intermediate	****
Beginner	****
Convenience	*
Queues	****
Mountain restaurants	**

The rest
Scenery	***
Resort charm	****
Off-slope	*

NEWS

For 2006/07 a 10-person gondola is planned to link the two lift bases. Facilities at the Spruce base will move to a temporary building until work is complete.

Last season a fast quad replaced the double chair to the top of Spruce Peak.

At Mt Mansfield, the Cliff House restaurant was renovated.

STOWE MOUNTAIN RESORT
Can't have been easy, getting the town and hill into one shot ↓

- ➕ Cute tourist town in classic New England style
- ➕ Some good slopes for all abilities, including serious challenges
- ➕ Few queues
- ➕ Excellent cross-country trails
- ➕ Great children's facilities

- ➖ Slopes a bus-ride from town
- ➖ Slopes limited in extent – though two sectors now being linked
- ➖ New England weather – highly changeable, and can be very cold
- ➖ Slow chair-lifts in main sector
- ➖ Weekend queues
- ➖ No après-ski animation

Stowe is one of New England's cutest little towns, its main street lined with dinky clapboard shops and restaurants; you could find no sharper contrast to the other New England resorts we feature. Its mountain, six miles away, is another New England classic: something for everyone, but not much of it.

THE RESORT

Stowe is a picture-postcard New England town – and a popular spot for tourists year-round, with bijou shops and more 3- and 4-diamond hotels and restaurants than any other place in New England except Boston. The slopes of Mount Mansfield, Vermont's snow-capped (though mainly wooded) highest peak, are a 15-minute drive away and much of the accommodation is along the road out to it. There's a good day-time shuttle-bus service but a car is recommended for flexibility (and excursions).

THE MOUNTAIN

There are three sectors, two linked, the third a short shuttle-bus ride away. There are free daily mountain tours. **Slopes** The main sector, served by a trio of chair-lifts from Mansfield base lodge, is dominated by the famous Front Four – a row of double-black-diamond runs. But there is plenty of easier stuff, too. An eight-seat gondola serves the next sector. The third area, Spruce Peak, has the main nursery area at the bottom. A fast quad heads up to mid-mountain and another now serves the upper slopes. The old link with Smugglers' Notch, from the top of this sector over the hill, is now a backcountry route. For 2006/07 the bases of Spruce Peak and Mt Mansfield will be linked by a new gondola. Night-skiing is offered three times a week.

Terrain-parks Stowe has three terrain-parks and a half-pipe: one is for beginners, the others are best suited to advanced users.

Snow reliability This is helped by snowmaking on practically all the blue (and some black) runs of the main sectors, and on all of Spruce Peak. Grooming is reported to be 'excellent'.

Experts The 'scarily narrow' and seriously steep Front Four and their variants on the top half of the main sector present a real challenge (if they are open) – and there are others nearby. There are various gladed areas.

Intermediates The usual New England reservation applies: the terrain is limited in extent; there's also a severe shortage of ordinary black runs (as opposed to double-diamonds). The planned gondola link between the sectors will at least mean that you can get around all the slopes easily.

Beginners The nursery slopes at Spruce Peak are now excellent. Recent additions include a short chair-lift and another run. There are also splendid

long green runs to progress to in the main sector, down to Toll House base.

Snowboarding Stowe attracts many snowboarders. Beginners learn on special customised boards at the Burton Method Center on Spruce Peak. There's a snowboarder-specific resort web site: www.ridestowe.com.

Cross-country There are excellent centres scattered around (including one at the musically famous Trapp Family Lodge) – 150km/93 miles of groomed and 100km/62 miles of backcountry trails form the largest network in the eastern US.

Queues The area is largely queue-free mid-week but we've had reports of 25-minute queues at weekends – the Four Runner quad was mentioned recently. New lifts at Spruce Peak should have reduced congestion there.

Mountain restaurants The newly renovated Cliff House, at the top of the gondola, is a lofty room with table-service and good food and views – it is Vermont's highest restaurant, not surprisingly. Next-best is Midway Cafe near the base of the gondola, with a BBQ deck and table-service inside.

Schools and guides We lack recent reports. You can try out the latest equipment, with instruction, at the Stowe Toys Demo Centre. Semi-private lessons are available (maximum of three in a group).

Facilities for children Facilities are excellent and the nursery takes children from age six weeks to six years.

STAYING THERE

How to go There are hotels in and around Stowe itself and along the road to the slopes, some with Austrian or Scandinavian names and styles.

Hotels 1066 Ye Olde England Inne is recommended (despite the appalling name), as are Stowehof Inn, Green Mountain Inn and the 'pleasant' and welcoming Stowe Inn. The Golden Eagle has 'excellent breakfasts', pool and hot-tub. The smart Inn at the Mountain, at Toll House, is the only slope-side accommodation, with chair-lift access to the main sector of slopes.

Self-catering There is a reasonable range of condos available for rent.

Eating out There are restaurants of every kind. The Whip in the Green Mountain Inn, the Shed ('good ribs') and an Italian restaurant, Trattoria La Festa, have all been recommended.

Après-ski Après-ski is muted – Stowe reportedly goes to bed early. The Matterhorn, Shed and Rusty Nail on the access road are popular. There's a good cinema with new releases.

Off the slopes Stowe is a pleasant town in which to spend time off the slopes – at least if you like shopping. The Vermont Ski Museum is 'worth a visit', says a reporter; and a trip to the Burlington shopping mall and a tour (with samples) of Ben & Jerry's ice cream factory just down the road have also been recommended. There is snowmobiling and dog-sledding.

SMUGGLERS' NOTCH RESORT

Smugglers' Notch

Smuggs hits the family target squarely, with a constant round of early-evening activities, sympathetic instructors, comprehensive childcare, a generally child-friendly layout and some long, quiet, easy runs.

KEY FACTS

Resort	315m
	1,030ft
Altitude	315-1110m
	1,030-3,640ft
Lifts	8
Pistes	1,000 acres
Green	19%
Blue	50%
Black	31%
Snowmaking	60%

TOURIST OFFICE

t 644 8851
smuggs@smuggs.com
www.smuggs.com

THE RESORT

Smugglers' Notch is about the nearest thing you'll find in the US to a French-style purpose-built family resort – except that it doesn't look so bad. The resort is entirely focused on the family market, and those not afflicted with children would find the family orientation a bit overpowering. There are lots of comfortable condos on or near the slopes, but no hotels. Après-ski and eating-out options are extremely limited. Off-slope options include a pool and ice rink.

THE MOUNTAINS

Smuggs has varied and satisfying slopes, spread over three hills, with a worthwhile vertical of 800m/2,610ft. Morse is directly above the village, with a separate learning area.

Madonna and Sterling have a separate base area, linked to the village but also reachable by road. Skiing together as a family can be difficult: different levels of ability mean being on different mountains. The lifts are slow but not prone to queues – it's blissfully quiet except at weekends and holidays. There are some challenges at the top of Madonna (genuine double blacks and even one triple) as well as plenty of easy cruising. It's a great area for beginners, with dedicated slopes. Snowboarding is encouraged, with good learning facilities. There are three impressive terrain-parks to suit all abilities and an Olympic-size super-pipe. More child-friendly terrain features have been added this year. The ski school has often been voted the best in North America. The childcare and tuition arrangements are of course superb.

Short turns

653

SUNDAY RIVER SKI RESORT

Sunday River

Sunday River was one of the pioneers of snowmaking, and over 90% of its trails are served by it. So the snow should be as good here as anywhere in the east. The terrain is varied but quite limited in extent. There is no village as such.

KEY FACTS

Resort	245m
	800ft
Slopes	245-955m
	800-3,140ft
Lifts	18
Pistes	663 acres
Green	25%
Blue	35%
Black	40%
Snowmaking	
	610 acres

TOURIST OFFICE

t 824 3000
info@sundayriver.com
www.sundayriver.com

THE RESORT

There isn't really a base village yet. At present, mainly condo developments cluster beside the lower slopes at the three main lift bases at the eastern end of the mountain, the dominant feature of which is the Grand Summit hotel. 5km/3 miles away at the western end of the mountain is the Jordan Grand hotel; there are plans for major development here, but not much sign of it happening. Bethel is a small town, a 10-minute drive away; it's a pleasant place with shops, several restaurants and bars as well as lodges and motels.

THE MOUNTAINS

The slopes spread across eight peaks, each basically served by one lift, with links from one to the next. But it's a small area – and many of the runs are

either short or very gentle. You get a satisfying feeling of travel, and the western sector (Aurora, Oz and Jordan Bowl) has far fewer lifts and runs than the eastern end, where most of the lifts, as well as most of the beds, are concentrated. Only four of the chairs are fast quads, and two of these are on the lower slopes; but queues are not a problem – midweek, the resort is very quiet. Some 40 per cent of the trails are classified black, and there are challenging narrow, often mogulled double-blacks on White Cap and Barker Mountain, and excellent glade skiing elsewhere. It's good for intermediates, with a series of nice rolling blues (often deserted). There are some easy glades to tempt the bold. South Ridge is a well-organised area for beginners, with good, easy runs to progress to. There are no mountain restaurants. Cross-country is big around here.

Canada

More British skiers and snowboarders go to Canada than to the USA. In many ways it combines the best that the US has to offer – good service, a warm welcome, relatively quiet slopes, good lift systems with lots of high-speed lifts, heavy dumps of snow, great grooming and a high standard of accommodation – with more spectacular scenery and lower prices. It also has the advantage that you can get direct flights to its main airports without having to change planes and go through customs part-way through your journey. And the charter flights and direct Air Canada and British Airways flights have now been joined by the budget scheduled airline Zoom.

After an exceptionally poor year for snow in many resorts in western Canada in 2004/05, normal service was resumed last season with Whistler, for example, receiving a bumper 470 inches of snow (compared with its claimed average of 360 inches). We can vouch for Banff's best start to the season for years – we had great powder there in mid-December and even Sunshine's extreme Delirium Dive area was open (which takes a lot of snow). Good snow is one of the main attractions of western Canada: in an average year, you can expect much better snow than in the Alps. A few seasons ago we drove from Whistler to Banff, calling in at lots of smaller resorts on the way. The whole trip took two weeks and for eight consecutive days in the middle it did not stop snowing. It made driving from resort to resort

WHISTLER RESORT ASSOCIATION / PAUL MORRISON

← All the Canadian resorts except Banff and Lake Louise that have full chapters in this book have tastefully designed, traffic-free villages at the foot of the slopes

Introduction

655

tricky, as we stuck to our normal scheme of driving at night after getting in a full day on the slopes. But the skiing was spectacular – day after day of dry, light powder. We asked a local on a chair-lift whether they ever got any sunshine and he looked at us as if we were mad – 'What do you want sunshine for? It ruins the snow,' he said.

So you go to Canada for the skiing or boarding, not the sunbathing. If you prefer long lunches on sun-drenched mountain restaurant terraces, stick to March in the Alps. If you want a good chance of hitting powder, head for western Canada. The east is different: expect snow and extremes of weather more like in New England. The main attraction of Québec for us is the French culture and unique ambience; it also has the advantage of a shorter flight time.

If you really want untracked powder and are feeling flush, there is nothing to beat Canada's amazing heli-skiing and snowcat skiing operations. It is the leading country for both these activities and you can expect run after run in virgin snow. The main difference is that the former is faster paced and more expensive than the latter. You can do it by the day, but the hedonistic option is to book a few days or a week in a luxury lodge (such as the one offered by Great Northern Snowcats) and stepping out of the door each morning straight into the chopper or snowcat.

But if you resist heli-skiing or snowcat heaven, you'll find a holiday in Canada can be reasonably cheap. Package prices start at under £500 for a week to western Canada. And eating and drinking tend to be cheaper than in the US or the Alps.

One disadvantage for young people is that laws about buying and consuming alcohol are more strictly enforced than in the UK. The legal age is 18 in Alberta and Québec but 19 in British Columbia; carrying your passport as evidence of age is a good idea even if you are well over the required age. People unable to prove their age may be refused entry to bars and clubs but will usually be allowed in restaurants (though not to drink alcohol).

Another disadvantage is that, as in the US, lifts close much earlier than in Europe – as early as 3pm in some cases.

Western Canada

For international visitors to Canada, the main draw is the west. It has fabulous scenery, good snow and a wonderful sense of the great outdoors. The big names of Whistler, Banff and Lake Louise capture most of the British market but there are lots of good smaller resorts that more British skiers and boarders are now starting to explore. We recommend renting a car and combining two or more of these, with a couple of days on virgin powder served by helicopters or snowcats as well, perhaps. We've done this on several occasions but visiting seven or eight resorts on each trip; it's tiring but rewarding. Take it a bit easier than we do (we're working, of course) and you'll have the holiday of a lifetime.

The three big resorts mentioned above and seven of the smaller ones you're most likely to want to visit for a while get their own write-ups in this section of the book.

There are big differences between them, so be sure to read each one. For example, Whistler is the busiest and most developed, Kicking Horse the newest and just starting to be developed. Fernie has great steep powder terrain for experts, Big White great gentle powder terrain to learn how to ski it. Sun Peaks is a fairly new, compact, purpose-built resort with a vaguely Tirolean feel and the second-biggest (to Whistler) ski area in

British Columbia. Panorama is a longer-established, purpose-built resort undergoing a renaissance and boasting the second-biggest (to Whistler) vertical in Canada. Banff and Lake Louise are very different bases from which to ski three separate areas, which you need transport to reach. Jasper and Silver Star are of more limited interest and get shorter write-ups.

There are other resorts in the west, of course. Two of those that we were most impressed by on our 2004 tour of the west were Apex and Red Resort – and these have entries in the Resort index / directory at the back of the book – as does Kimberley.

657

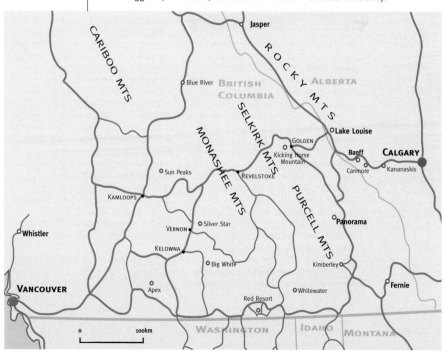

Banff

A big resort in a National Park with spectacular scenery, interesting wildlife and three varied ski areas, each a bus-ride from town

COSTS

① ② ③ ④ ⑤ ⑥

RATINGS

The slopes
Fast lifts	****
Snow	****
Extent	****
Expert	****
Intermediate	****
Beginner	***
Convenience	*
Queues	****
Mountain restaurants	***

The rest
Scenery	****
Resort charm	***
Off-slope	*****

NEWS

In Sunshine a third very steep area called Silver City opened for 2005/06. It is accessed by dropping over the ridge to skier's right on Lookout Mountain below the arrival point of the Angel Express quad or the Tee Pee Town double. As with Delirium Dive, you need a companion, avalanche transceiver and shovel to be allowed in.

Further rooms have been renovated at the Sunshine Inn.

There was also more snowmaking, and all Norquay's beginner and intermediate slopes are now covered.

➕ Spectacular high-mountain scenery – quite unlike the Colorado Rockies

➕ Some wildlife around the valley

➕ Lots of touristy shops

➕ Good-value lodging because winter is the area's low season

➕ Late season holidays

➕ Extensive slopes with excellent snow record at Sunshine, but ...

➖ Sunshine is a 20-minute drive away

➖ You'll probably want to take in Lake Louise, too – a 45-minute drive

➖ Can be very cold; most lifts have no covers and waiting for shuttle-buses can be unpleasant

➖ Banff lacks ski resort atmosphere – though it's not an unattractive town

Huge numbers of British skiers and boarders go to Banff. Price has been a key factor in getting us to make the trip, though costs are now creeping up. Most visitors are delighted with what they find, and are keen to go back.

It's not difficult to see why. The landscape is one of glaciers, jagged peaks and magnificent views, the valleys have wildlife that you'll never see in Europe (though it's much less evident than it used to be). The slopes have something for everyone, from steep couloirs to gentle cruising. The snow is some of the coldest, driest and most reliable you'll find anywhere in the world, and there's a lot of it (at Sunshine Village, at least). And there are the standard Canadian assets of people who are friendly and welcoming, and low prices for meals and other on-the-spot expenses.

For us, these factors count for more than the drawbacks. But then we, luckily, have never encountered the extremely low temperatures (–35°C is not unknown) that have left some early-season reporters feeling less convinced.

THE RESORT

Banff is a big summer resort that happens to have some nearby ski areas. Norquay is a small area of slopes overlooking the town. Sunshine Village, 20 minutes away, is a bigger mountain; despite the name, it's not a village (it has just one small hotel at mid-mountain) – nor is it notably sunny. Most visitors buy a three-area pass that means they can also spend some time at Lake Louise, 45 minutes away – covered by a separate chapter.

Banff is spectacularly set, with a few towering peaks on its outskirts. There is wildlife to see, especially elk and long-horned sheep (but the town is now trying to keep elk away and the main road to Sunshine and Lake Louise is fenced to keep wildlife off).

Banff town has grown substantially since 1990, when it became independent of the Banff National Park authority. But it still consists basically of a long main street and a small network of side roads built in grid fashion, lined with clothing and souvenir shops

(aimed mainly at summer visitors) and a few ski shops. The buildings are low-rise and some are wood-clad. The town is pleasant enough, but lacks genuine charm; it's a commercial tourist town, not another Aspen or Telluride.

Some of the Banff lodgings (even on the main Banff Avenue) are quite a distance from downtown. A car can be helpful here, especially in cold weather (it's best to splash out on a 4-wheel drive in case you hit heavy snow).

Unless you stay mid-mountain on Sunshine (see 'Staying up the mountain'), getting to the slopes means a drive or a bus-ride. Buses are free to Tri-area lift pass holders, frequent, generally reliable, and 'highly organised' – though, depending on the

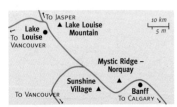

Lookout Mountain at Sunshine Village is right on the Continental Divide and gets way over twice as much snow as either Lake Louise or Norquay →

KEY FACTS

Resort	1380m
	4,530ft

Norquay, Sunshine and Lake Louise, covered by the Tri-area pass

Slopes	1630-2730m
	5,350-8,950ft
Lifts	27
Pistes	7,748 acres
Green	23%
Blue	39%
Black	38%
Snowmaking	
	1,900 acres

Norquay only

Slopes	1630-2135m
	5,350-7,000ft
Lifts	5
Pistes	190 acres
Green	20%
Blue	36%
Black	44%
Snowmaking	85%

Sunshine only

Slopes	1660-2730m
	5,440-8,950ft
Lifts	13
Pistes	3,358 acres
Green	22%
Blue	31%
Black	47%
Snowmaking	none

number of pick ups, they can take twice as long as advertised and it can be a cold wait. One reporter also complained that because skis and boards are piled up in the belly of the bus, her board was 'ruined; scratched beyond recognition'. Another suggests putting your skis/board in a bag.

Buses are also arranged to the more distant major resorts of Panorama and Kicking Horse (see separate chapters) and the smaller (and closer) resort of Nakiska, and day-trip heli-skiing and boarding can be organised, too. Banff Airporter does transfers to and from Calgary airport.

THE MOUNTAINS

The Sunshine Village slopes are set right on the Continental Divide and as a result get a lot of snow. Most of the slopes above the village are above the tree line and can be very cold and bleak during a snowfall or cold snap. Although there is a wooded sector served by the second section of the gondola and a couple of chairs, in bad weather you're better off elsewhere. It is great, however, for late-season skiing, which goes on until May.

Norquay is much smaller. But it's worth a visit, especially in bad weather or as a first day warm-up – it has a small area of wooded slopes to suit all abilities and the trails can be delightfully quiet.

THE SLOPES
Lots of variety

The main slopes of **Sunshine Village** are not visible from the base station: you ride a gondola to Sunshine Village itself, with a mid-station at the base of Goat's Eye Mountain.

Goat's Eye is served by a fast quad rising 580m/1,900ft. Although there are some blue runs, this is basically a black mountain, with some genuine double-diamonds at the extremities (including the Wild West area that opened a couple of seasons ago – which you need a companion and avalanche safety equipment to ski).

Lifts fan out in all directions from Sunshine Village, with short runs back from Mount Standish and longer ones from Lookout Mountain. Lookout is where the Continental Divide is, with the melting snow flowing in one direction to the Pacific and in the other to the Atlantic. From the top here experts can pass through a gate (you need an avalanche transceiver to get through) and hike up to the extreme terrain of Delirium Dive. The new Silver City area of extreme terrain is also on Lookout – see News.

Many people ride the gondola down at the end of the day. But the 2.5km/1.5 mile green run to the bottom is a pretty cruise. If you go down while the lifts are running you can take the Jackrabbit chair to cut out a flat section, but the run gets crowded and is much more enjoyable if you delay

LIFT PASSES

Tri-area lift pass

Prices in C$

Age	1-day	6-day
under 13	34	209
13 to 17	62	377
18 to 64	67	401
over 65	62	377

Free under 6

Beginner lift, lesson and rental package

Notes

Covers all lifts and transport between Banff, Lake Louise, Norquay and Sunshine Village. Prices include tax.

boarding

Boarders will feel at home in Banff and there is some excellent free-riding terrain. 'There are so many natural ledges, jumps and tree gaps to play with that the terrain-park seems almost unnecessary!' said a reporter. But Sunshine also has some flat areas to beware of, where scooting or walking is required (such as the green run to the base), and the blue traverse on Goat's Eye is tedious. A trip to Lake Louise's Powder Bowls is a must for free-riders. There are specialist snowboard shops in Banff: Rude Boys, Rude Girls and Unlimited Snowboards.

your descent a bit. The Canyon trail is a scenic alternative for more advanced skiers and riders. Though the lower part is marked black diamond, it's not steep – just a bit narrow in places.

The slopes at **Norquay** are served by a row of five parallel lifts and have floodlit trails on Friday nights.

TERRAIN-PARKS
Park – and ride ...
At Sunshine, the Rodgers terrain-park on Lookout Mountain has some fun

average-sized obstacles including a wall-ride, several kickers and a host of rails and boxes. Shapers tend to add more features as the season goes on.

The bigger and more advanced park at Norquay has its own reduced park pass for avid freestylers. Gap jumps, tabletops, rails and boxes litter the park, which also boasts a good-sized half-pipe. On Friday nights the park is lit for night sessions.

Then there's the Lake Louise park to try – see separate chapter.

Goat's Eye has some great steep terrain – single- and double-black-diamond runs and an extreme zone. But it's very rocky and windswept and needs a lot of snow to be enjoyable

GOAT'S EYE
2600m/8,530ft

Delir
Div

Goat's Eye

Wild West
◆◆

Wolverine

Gondola

1660m/5,440ft

2020m/6,630ft

If it's snowing hard, visibility is usually best on the easy runs in the trees around here and on the long run down to the bottom of the gondola

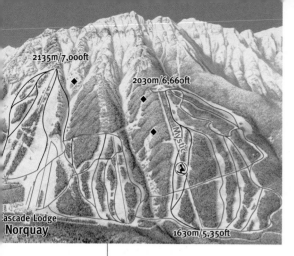

2135m/7,000ft

2030m/6,66oft

Mystic

1630m/5,35oft

ascade Lodge
Norquay

remain rocky but the blues are usually
fine. 'Three times the snow' is another
Sunshine slogan – a cryptic reference
to the fact that the average snowfall
here is 360 to 400 inches (depending
on which figures you believe) – as
good as anything in Colorado –
compared with a modest 140 inches at
Lake Louise and 120 inches on Norquay.
But we're told the Sunshine figures
relate to Lookout, and that Goat's Eye
gets less. There is snowmaking on all
green and blue pistes at Norquay. So all
in all, lack of snow is unlikely to be a
problem in a normal season and late-
season snow on Sunshine is usually
good (we've had great April snow
there on our last two visits).

SNOW RELIABILITY
Excellent
Sunshine Village claims '100 per cent
natural snow', a neat reversal of the
usual snowmaking hype. In a poor
snow season, some black runs can

FOR EXPERTS
Pure pleasure
Both Sunshine and Norquay have
satisfying terrain for good skiers
and boarders.

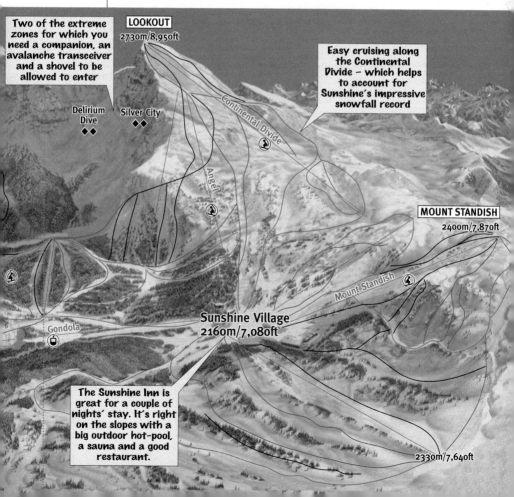

Two of the extreme
zones for which you
need a companion, an
avalanche transceiver
and a shovel to be
allowed to enter

LOOKOUT
2730m/8,95oft

Easy cruising along
the Continental
Divide – which helps
to account for
Sunshine's impressive
snowfall record

Delirium
Dive
◆◆

Silver City
◆◆

Continental Divide

Angel

MOUNT STANDISH
2400m/7,87oft

Mount Standish

Sunshine Village
2160m/7,08oft

Gondola

The Sunshine Inn is
great for a couple of
nights' stay. It's right
on the slopes with a
big outdoor hot-pool,
a sauna and a good
restaurant.

2330m/7,64oft

Sunshine has plenty of open runs of genuine black steepness above the tree line on Lookout, but Goat's Eye is much more compelling. It has a great area of expert double-black-diamond trails and chutes, both above and below the tree line. But the slopes are rocky and need good cover, and the top can be windswept.

There are short, not-too-steep black runs on Mount Standish. One more challenging novelty here is a pitch known as the Waterfall run – because you do actually ski down over a snow-covered frozen fall. But a lot of snow is needed to cover the waterfall and prevent it reverting to ice. Also try the Shoulder on Lookout Mountain; it is sheltered, tends to accumulate powder and has been deserted whenever we've been there – it's a long traverse to reach it so maybe most people don't bother.

Real experts will want to get to grips with Delirium Dive and the new Silver City on Lookout Mountain's north face and the Wild West area on Goat's Eye (with some narrow chutes and rock bands). For all three you must have a companion, an avalanche transceiver and a shovel – and a guide is recommended. ('Book in advance' and 'rent your transceiver and shovel in Banff – you can't at Sunshine' advise disappointed reporters.) We tried Delirium in a group with the ski patrol who provided equipment and the scariest part was the walk in, along a narrow, icy path with a sheer drop (protected by a flimsy-looking net).

Norquay's two main lifts give only 400m/1,300ft vertical, but both serve black slopes and the North American chair accesses a couple of double-diamond runs that justify their grading.

Heli-skiing is available from bases outside the National Park in British Columbia – roughly two hours' drive.

FOR INTERMEDIATES
Ideal runs
Half the runs on Sunshine are classified as intermediate. Wherever you look there are blues and greens – some of the greens as enjoyable (and pretty much as steep) as the blues.

We particularly like the World Cup Downhill run, from the top of Lookout to the mid-mountain base. The slow Wawa chair gives access to the Wawa Bowl and Tincan Alley. This is a good area for intermediates and offers tree-lined protection from bad weather. There's a delightful wooded area under the second stage of the gondola served by Jackrabbit and Wolverine chairs. The blue runs down Goat's Eye are good cruises too.

The Mystic Express quad at Norquay serves a handful of quite challenging tree-lined blues and a couple of sometimes-groomed blacks – great for a snowy day or a 'first day warm-up'.

FOR BEGINNERS
Pretty good terrain
Sunshine has a good area by the mid-mountain base, served by a moving carpet. And the long Meadow Park green is a great, long, easy run to progress to.

Norquay has a good small nursery area with a moving carpet and gentle greens served by the Cascade chair.

Banff is not the ideal destination for a mixed party of beginners (who may want to stay in one area) and more experienced friends (who are likely to want to visit other places).

FOR CROSS-COUNTRY
High in quality and quantity
It's a good area for cross-country. There are trails near Banff, around the Bow River, and on the Banff Springs golf course. But the best area is around Lake Louise. Altogether, there are around 80km/50 miles of groomed

SCHOOLS

Club Ski and Club Snowboard
t 760 7731

Classes
3 days guided tuition of the three areas C$250 incl. tax.

Private lessons
Half day (3hr) C$363, incl. tax.

CHILDREN

Tiny Tigers (Sunshine)
t 762 6563
Ages 19mnth to 6yr; 8.30-4.30

Kid's Place (Norquay)
t 760 7709
Ages 19mnth to 6yr; 9am to 4pm

Childcare Connection
t 760 4443
Childminding in guest accommodation

Ski school
Takes ages 6 to 12 (3 days C$250, incl. tax and lunch).

GETTING THERE

Air Calgary 122km/ 76 miles (1½hr).

---

trails within Banff National Park. Beware of the wildlife though: a few years ago a cross-country skier was killed by a mountain lion.

QUEUES
Sunshine can get busy

Half the visitors come for the day from cities such as Calgary – so it's fairly quiet during the week. But Sunshine can get busy at weekends and public holidays; a 2005 reporter found queues of up to 30 minutes on 27 December and 'gave up at lunchtime'; another in 2006 had a 30-minute wait at the base of the gondola at Easter, and there were big queues for Goat's Eye when we were there in early April, though they moved quickly and using the singles line proved a good ploy.

MOUNTAIN RESTAURANTS
Quite good

The Sunshine Inn hotel has the best food – table-service in the Chimney Corner Lounge (great buffalo stew in a bread bowl). The Day Lodge offers three different styles of food on three floors (table service in the top-floor Lookout Bistro, with great views). Mixed reports of the food. Mad Trapper's Saloon is a jolly western-style place in Old Sunshine Lodge, serving good beer and different food on its two levels (shame about the disposable plates though). At the bottom of Goat's Eye Mountain there's a temporary tent-like structure called Goat's Eye Gardens; we've had mixed reports of the food here.

At the base of Norquay, the big, stylish, timber-framed Cascade Lodge is excellent – it has great views and a table-service restaurant upstairs as well as a self-service cafeteria.

SCHOOLS AND GUIDES
Some great ideas

Both mountains have their own school. But recognising that visitors wanting lessons won't want to be confined to just one mountain, the resorts have organised an excellent Club Ski and Club Snowboard Program – three-day courses starting on Sundays and Thursdays that take you to Sunshine, Norquay and Lake Louise on different days, offering a mixture of guiding and instruction and including free video analysis, a fun race and a group photo. Reporters rave about it: 'absolutely brilliant', 'a great way to meet other people', 'learnt more in three days

---

than I did in the whole week last year'. All abilities are catered for, including beginners. One reporter recommends booking a midweek group lesson: 'Normally only one or two people; I did an excellent Black Diamond class.'

We also have a fat file full of praise for the free mountain tours by friendly local volunteer snow hosts.

FACILITIES FOR CHILDREN
Excellent

One reporter who used Sunshine, Norquay and Lake Louise said: 'I'd recommend all three.'

STAYING THERE

HOW TO GO
Superb-value packages

A huge amount of accommodation is on offer – especially hotels and self-catering, but also a few catered chalets. **Hotels** Summer is the peak season here. Prices are much lower in winter (though seem to have been creeping up in the last few years).
《《《4 Fairmont Banff Springs (762 2211) A late 19th-century, castle-style property, well outside town (and they don't run their own bus – you have to get taxis into and from town). It's virtually a town within itself – it can sleep 2,000 people, has over 40 shops, several restaurants and bars, a nightclub and a superb health club and spa (which costs extra).
《《《4 Rimrock (762 3356) Spectacularly set, out of town, with great views and a smart health club. Luxurious.
《《3 Inns of Banff (762 4581) About 20 minutes' walk from town, but it runs its own free half hourly shuttle bus to and from; praised by reporters for large rooms, comfort, room service and fitness facilities; 'very large' hot-tub.
《《3 Banff Park Lodge (762 4433) Best-quality central hotel, with hot-tub, steam room and indoor pool.
《2 Banff Caribou Lodge (762 5887) On the main street, slightly out of town. A variety of wood-clad, individually designed rooms, sauna and hot-tub and a good restaurant and bar. Repeatedly recommended by reporters.
《2 Juniper Inn (762 2281) At foot of Norquay and reachable on skis. Comfortable, good views, hot-tub. Recently renovated and expanded: 'Service is outstanding and the food exceptional,' said a 2006 reporter.
《2 Banff International (762 5666) 'Central, saving walking in the

ACTIVITIES
Indoor Film theatre, museums, galleries, swimming pools (one with water slides), gym, squash, racquetball, weight training, bowling, hot-tub, sauna, climbing wall

Outdoor Swimming in hot springs, ice rink, sleigh rides, dog-sled rides, snowmobiles, curling, ice fishing, helicopter tours, snow-shoeing

Phone numbers
From distant parts of Canada, add the prefix 1 403. From abroad, add the prefix +1 403.

TOURIST OFFICE
Banff
t 762 4754
info@SkiBig3.com
www.SkiBig3.com

evenings. Excellent, can't fault it,' said a 2005 reporter.
① **Homestead** (762 4471) Central, cheap, good-sized rooms, approved of by two 2005 reporters.
Self-catering Don't expect the choice or luxury you find in many North American resorts. But there are some decent options. The Banff Rocky Mountain Resort is set in the woods on the edge of town, with indoor pool, squash and hot-tubs. Reporters have also recommended the Douglas Fir resort for families – though it's 'a bit out of town'.

EATING OUT
Lots of choice
Banff boasts over 100 restaurants, from McDonald's to fine dining in the Fairmont Banff Springs hotel.

We enjoyed two meals in designer-cool Saltlik last season – there's a bar area you can eat in as well as the upstairs restaurant; good game, steak and fish. Reader recommendations include Earl's (burgers and ethnic dishes, very popular and lively), Magpie & Stump ('excellent, good value' Mexican, with Wild West decor and 'jars' of ale), Caramba in the Banff Ptarmigan Inn (Mediterranean, 'well worth the money'), the Keg ('quality steaks'), Wild Bill's ('the biggest and best burgers in town', dancing and live entertainment), Melissa's ('good steaks', 'excellent choice of beers', 'best value in town'), Bumpers ('big slabs of rib', 'best steaks'), Grizzly House ('fondues and fun', 'great selection of meats'), the Old Spaghetti Factory ('great for families'), the Maple Leaf ('best meal I had in Banff'), and Tommy's Neighbourhood Pub ('very informal atmosphere and good food in generous portions'). Sunday brunch at the Banff Springs hotel is highly recommended by one reporter.

APRES-SKI
Livens up later on
One of the drawbacks of the area is that tea-time après-ski is limited because the resort is a drive from the slopes. But Mad Trapper's Saloon at the top of the Sunshine gondola is popular during the close-of-play happy hour (with endless free peanuts). They also do evenings with tobogganing, a buffet, live music and dancing, followed by a gondola ride down. In town later, Wild Bill's has live country and western music and line dancing. The Rose & Crown has live music and gets crowded. The St James's Gate Irish pub has 'great atmosphere, good-value food and a wide range of beers'. Melissa's and Saltlik are popular. The Elk and Oarsman nightclub is popular. Hoodoo Lounge attracts a young lively crowd, while Aurora is for more serious clubbing.

OFF THE SLOPES
Lots to do
Banff has lots to offer: plenty of wildlife to see, lovely walks (including ice canyon walks), and you can go snow-shoeing, dog-sledding, skating and snowmobiling. There are sightseeing tours, several museums and natural hot springs to try although one reporter said they were a let-down ('you are limited to 20 minutes in a pool, and it is just that, a pool'). Reporters have enjoyed evenings in Calgary watching the Flames play ice hockey ('sit back and enjoy the fights').

STAYING UP THE MOUNTAIN
Worth considering
We loved spending a night on the slopes of Sunshine Village at the Sunshine Inn (762 6550), which is in the later stages of a complete revamp. Luggage is transported for you in the gondola while you hit the slopes. Rooms vary in size. Big outdoor hot-pool. Sauna. Good restaurant.

Big White

It's not big by Euro-resort standards, but it's certainly white. There are few places to match it if you want to learn to ski powder

NEWS

For 2006/07, what's claimed to be Canada's longest six-pack, the Snow Ghost Express, is due to open. It will run parallel to the Ridge Rocket chair and is designed to alleviate peak time queues. And a new 120m/390ft moving carpet is planned for the Happy Valley beginner area.

For 2005/06 six new intermediate runs were opened in the Gem Lake area.

KEY FACTS

Resort	1755m
	5,760ft
Slopes	1510-2320m
	4,950-7,610ft
Lifts	15
Pistes	2,765 acres
Green	18%
Blue	54%
Black	28%
Snowmaking	
	In terrain-park

+ Great for learning to ski powder

+ Extensive, varied slopes, quiet except at weekends and holidays

+ Convenient, purpose-built village with high-quality, good-value condos

+ Very friendly staff; good for families

− Visibility can be poor, especially on the upper mountain, because of snow, cloud or freezing fog

− Few off-slope diversions – and isolated without a car

− Limited après-ski

'It's the snow' says the Big White slogan. And as slogans go, it's spot on. If you want a good chance of skiing powder on reasonably easy slopes, put Big White high on the shortlist. But if you want a sun tan (or lively après-ski, or extensive steep bowls and chutes) look elsewhere. Consider combining it with another BC resort such as Sun Peaks or Silver Star for variety.

THE RESORT

Big White is a modern, rapidly growing, purpose-built resort. The village is rather piecemeal but attractive in wood and stone and much accommodation is ski-in/ski-out. Reporters remark on the large number of 'very friendly and happy' Aussie workers. Silver Star resort is under the same ownership and there are weekly day trips by bus.

THE MOUNTAINS

Much of the terrain is heavily wooded. But the trees thin out towards the summits, leading to almost open slopes in the bowls at the top. There's at least one green option from the top of each lift but the one from Gem Lake is narrow and can be tricky and busy.
Slopes Fast chairs run from points below village level to above mid-

mountain, serving the main area of wooded beginner and intermediate runs above and beside the village. Slower lifts – a T-bar and four chairs – serve the higher slopes. Quite some way across the mountainside is the Gem Lake fast chair, serving a range of long top-to-bottom runs; with its 710m/2,330ft vertical, this lift is in a different league from the others. 'Snow hosts' (highly praised by reporters) run twice-daily guided ski tours.
Terrain-parks Served by a double chair and by Big White's first snowmaking, the excellent park includes a half-pipe, super-pipe, boarder-cross and rails for all levels. It is floodlit at night and is highly praised by reporters.
Snow reliability Big White has a reputation for great powder; average snowfall is about 300 inches, which is similar to many Colorado resorts. At the top of the mountain the trees

665

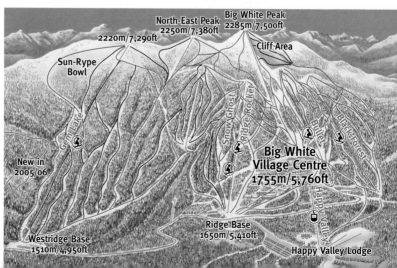

North-East Peak 2250m/7,380ft
Big White Peak 2285m/7,500ft
2220m/7,290ft
Cliff Area
Sun-Rype Bowl
New in 2005/06
Big White Village Centre 1755m/5,760ft
Ridge Base 1650m/5,410ft
Westridge Base 1510m/4,950ft
Happy Valley Lodge

WESTERN CANADA

666

Central reservations
Call 765 8888; toll-free (within Canada) 1 800 663 1772.
Phone numbers
From distant parts of Canada, add the prefix 1 250. From abroad, add +1 250.

TOURIST OFFICE
t 765 3101
bigwhite@bigwhite.com
www.bigwhite.com

usually stay white all winter and are known as snow-ghosts; they make visibility tricky in a white-out but are great fun to ski between on clear days.
Experts The Cliff area at the top right of the ski area is of serious double-black-diamond pitch; the runs are short but you can ski them repeatedly using the Cliff chair. The Sun-Rype bowl at the opposite edge of the ski area is more forgiving. There are some long blacks off the Gem Lake chair and several shorter ones off the Powder and Falcon chairs. There are glades to explore and bump runs too.
Intermediates The resort is excellent for cruisers and families, with long

blues and greens all over the hill. Good intermediates will enjoy the easier blacks and some of the gladed runs too. In general the runs get steeper from right to left as you look at the mountain. The Black Forest area has some marvellous easy skiing among the trees, while some of the blues off the Gem Lake chair are quite steep, narrow and challenging.
Beginners There's a good dedicated nursery area in the village and lots of long easy runs to progress to.
Snowboarding There's some excellent beginner and free-riding terrain with boarder-friendly lifts and few flat areas.
Cross-country Trails total 25km/16 miles.
Queues Queues are pretty rare except at weekends at the start of the day. The Snow Ghost Express, due for this season, might even eliminate those.
Mountain restaurants There aren't any – it's back to the bottom for lunch.
School and guides We receive rave reviews from reporters for both adult and children's lessons – and for the free mountain tours.
Facilities for children The excellent Kids' Centre takes children from 18 months. Evening activities are organised.

STAYING THERE

How to go There's an increasing range of packages to Big White.
Hotels The White Crystal Inn receives better reports than the Inn at Big White.
Self-catering Standards are high. We stayed at the Stonebridge condos and loved them – big, central, well-furnished, private hot-tub on the balcony. Grocery shopping has improved since the store doubled in size last year.
Eating out We had good meals in the Copper Kettle in the White Crystal Inn and the Kettle Valley Steakhouse at Happy Valley. Reporters also recommend Snowshoe Sam's ('imaginative food'), Swiss Bear in the Chateau Big White and Frank's Chinese Laundry.
Après-ski The atmospheric Snowshoe Sam's has a DJ, live entertainment and dancing; try its trademark alcoholic gunbarrel coffee if only for the show of making it in the shotgun. Raakel's in the Hopfbrauhaus has live music and dancing. The Snowghost Lounge in the White Crystal Inn has 'live music three nights a week and an impressive selection of malt whiskies'.
Off the slopes Happy Valley has ice skating, snowmobiling, tubing and snow-shoeing. There are two spas.

Fernie

Lots of snow and lots of steeps – best explored with a guide; a choice of convenient base lodging or a drive from Fernie town

COSTS

①②③④⑤⑥

RATINGS

The slopes

Fast lifts	**
Snow	*****
Extent	***
Expert	*****
Intermediate	**
Beginner	****
Convenience	****
Queues	****
Mountain restaurants	*

The rest

Scenery	***
Resort charm	**
Off-slope	**

NEWS

For 2006/07 a new cafe is expected to open at the top of Timber Bowl.

For 2005/06 terrain improvements included better access to trails in Lizard Bowl and a new groomed trail out of the bottom of Currie Bowl.

Trees were cleared to create more glades in the Currie and Timber Bowls – and this work continues.

Snowmaking was also increased.

- ✛ Good snow record, with less chance of rain than at Whistler (and less chance of Arctic temperatures than at resorts up in the Rockies)
- ✛ Great terrain for those who like it steep and deep, with lots for confident intermediates too
- ✛ Snowcat operations nearby
- ✛ Some good on-slope accommodation available, but ...

- ▬ Mountain resort is very limited
- ▬ Still too many slow, old lifts
- ▬ After a dump it can take time to make the bowls safe
- ▬ Little groomed cruising for timid or average intermediates
- ▬ Poor trail map and on-mountain signposting
- ▬ No decent mountain restaurants

Fernie has long had cult status among Alberta and British Columbia skiers for its steep gladed slopes and superb natural snow. There has been a lot of investment in the development of the village at the foot of the slopes – though it remains small, without many facilities. Some visitors would rather see more investment in the mountain, to replace slow old lifts, cut down hiking and traversing and to hasten reopening after a serious snowfall. We see their point, but most reports we get are dominated by excitement at Fernie's combination of snow and terrain – 'just like Jackson Hole' is one typical verdict. You'll enjoy Fernie most if you are a good skier or rider wanting adventure.

THE RESORT

Fernie Alpine Resort is set a little way up the mountainside from the flat Elk Valley floor and a couple of miles from the little town of Fernie. It has grown from very little in the past few years, but there's still not much there except convenient lodging and a few restaurants, bars and small shops. It is quiet at night.

The town of Fernie is named after William Fernie – a prospector who discovered coal here and triggered a boom in the early 1900s. Much of the town was destroyed by fire in 1908 but some buildings survived. It is primarily a town for locals, not tourists. There are some lively bars, decent places to eat and good outdoor shops. It is down to earth rather than charming and reporters' reactions to it vary: 'I liked the way it felt like real Canada and enjoyed staying in a town with some history,' said one; 'The flipside of being a real town is having a real

White Pass quad serves a lot of gladed terrain in Timber and Currie Bowls ➜

THE TRAIL MAP AND ON-MOUNTAIN SIGNPOSTING

Over the years we have complained about many poor trail maps and resorts with inadequate on-mountain signposting. But we have rarely come across such a dangerous combination of the two as you get at Fernie. Runs marked on the map just aren't clearly marked on the mountain, especially some of the steeper runs through the trees. For example, when we tried to find the long black Diamond Back run from the top of the White Pass quad, we failed and ended up in tight trees on a slope of triple-diamond steepness – scary.

With so much tree skiing, it's not reasonable to expect comprehensive signposting of every run; but it is reasonable to expect reliable signposting of identified runs on the map. So: what the resort needs to do is decide which runs can be properly signposted; install the necessary signs; mark those runs as lines on the map; and then mark other identifiable slopes simply with a black diamond, not a line. Where there is no line, you'd be well advised to get guidance.

highway run through it,' said another. Most stress the friendliness of the locals, though not that of seasonal 'immigrant' workers.

There are buses between the town and the mountain, which run at half-hourly intervals at peak times and cost C$3 one way (they are free in the evenings and run every half an hour until 2am). Each hotel has specific pick-up times although we have a report that the service is unreliable.

Outings to Kimberley are possible; a coach does the trip every Thursday – the drive takes about 90 minutes. (there's also a helicopter option).

THE MOUNTAINS

Fernie's 2,500 acres pack in a lot of variety, from superb green terrain at the bottom to ungroomed chutes (that will be satisfyingly steep to anyone but the extreme specialist) and huge numbers of steep runs in the trees. Quite a few runs have the quality of going directly down the fall line.

THE SLOPES
Bowl after bowl
What you see when you arrive at the lift base is a trio of impressive mogul slopes towering above you. The slow Deer chair approaches the foot of these slopes, but goes no further. You get to them by traversing and hiking from the main Lizard Bowl, on the right. **Lizard Bowl** is a broad snowfield reached by a series of lifts: the slow Elk quad; the fast Great Bear quad; and finally the short Face Lift, a dreadful rope tow which has been somewhat improved by adding buttons to the handles on the rope. It often doesn't run, because of either too little

or too much snow. This is also the main way into **Cedar Bowl** and to Snake Ridge beyond it. The only lift here is the Haul Back T-bar, which brings you out. You can still traverse into the lower parts of both Lizard and Cedar Bowls when the Face Lift isn't working. There is a mini-bowl between them, served by the Boomerang chair.

The Timber Bowl fast quad chair gives access to **Siberia Bowl** and the lower part of **Timber Bowl**. But for access to the higher slopes and to **Currie Bowl** you must take the White Pass quad. A long traverse from the top gets you to the steeper slopes on the flanks of Currie (our favourite area). From there you have to go right to the bottom (unless you head over into Lizard Bowl) and it takes quite a while to get back for another go.

There are free tours of the area in groups of different abilities for two hours twice a day, but only on blue and green runs. For the steeper, deeper stuff you need to hire a guide or join the Steep and Deep tours. Using these services to get your bearings is a good idea. Going with someone who knows the area makes it much more enjoyable – chat to the locals ('if you are a good skier, they will be delighted to show you the best runs'). We found both signs and trail map dangerously inadequate – see feature panel below.

TERRAIN-PARKS
Up to scratch
There's a terrain-park on the Falling Star trail near the top of the Timber Chair in Siberia Bowl, with berms, jumps, rollers, table top, large hip and box, a new rail jam area and boarder-cross features.

KEY FACTS

Resort	1065m	
	3,490ft	
Slopes	1065-1925m	
	3,490-6,320ft	
Lifts		10
Pistes	2,504 acres	
Green		30%
Blue		40%
Black		30%
Snowmaking		
	125 acres	

Fernie is a fine place for good boarders (and there are a lot of local experts here). Lots of natural gullies, hits and endless off-piste opportunities – including some adrenalin-pumping tree-runs and knee-deep powder bowls – will keep free-riders of all abilities grinning from ear to ear. And, as one reader commented, 'The only flat sections are at the base and coming out of Falling Star.' The main board shops, Board Stiff and Edge of the World, are in downtown Fernie, the latter with an internet connection and an indoor skate park to use while your board gets tuned. It's not a brilliant place for freestylers – the terrain-park doesn't have anything approaching a dedicated lift. And beginners and faint-hearted intermediates should stay away.

LIFT PASSES

Fernie

Prices in C$

Age	1-day	6-day
under 13	21	126
13 to 17	53	318
18 to 64	74	444
over 65	60	360

Free under 6

Beginner drag-lift only, C$21 a day

Notes

Prices include taxes. Half-day pass available from 12.30.

SNOW RELIABILITY
A key part of the appeal

Fernie has an excellent snow record – with an average of 350 inches per year, better than practically all of Colorado. But the altitude is modest – rain is not unknown, and in warmer weather the lower slopes can suffer. Too much snow can be a problem, with the high bowls prone to closure – shut all week during a 2006 reporter's visit. Snowmaking has been increased, and now covers most of the base area. Reports on piste maintenance vary. A couple of seasons ago it was said to be poor – but that was a bad season for snow. This year 'every effort was made to maintain the runs'.

Some reporters have said that, while some runs were well groomed after a snowfall, some blue runs were never groomed at all.

FOR EXPERTS
Wonderful – deep and steep

The combination of heavy snowfalls and abundant steep terrain with the shelter of trees makes this a superb mountain for good skiers. There are about a dozen identifiable faces offering genuine black or double-black slopes, each of them with several alternative ways down. Currie and Timber Bowls both have some serious double-diamonds but mainly have single-diamonds. However, as one of our regular reporters says, 'Most of the single blacks are tough. With some I don't see how you could get anything harder without falling off the mountain ... just like Jackson Hole but without the cliffs.' Even where the trail map shows trees to be sparse, expect them to be close together, and where there aren't any, expect alder bushes unless there's lots of snow. And see our warning in the feature panel about the trail map and signposting.

There are backcountry routes you can take with guidance (some include an overnight camp) and snowcat operations in other nearby mountains – see feature panel over the page. A regular reporter especially enjoyed exploring Fish Bowl, a short hike outside the resort boundary.

Fernie

669

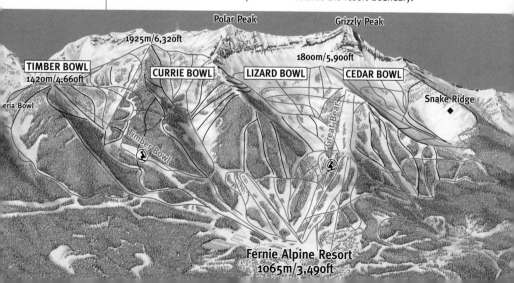

Polar Peak

Grizzly Peak

1925m/6,320ft

1800m/5,900ft

TIMBER BOWL
1420m/4,660ft

CURRIE BOWL

LIZARD BOWL

CEDAR BOWL

...eria Bowl

Snake Ridge

Timber Bowl

Great Bear

Fernie Alpine Resort
1065m/3,490ft

RIDE THE SNOWCATS – HELI-SKIING AT AN AFFORDABLE PRICE

Good skiers who relish off-piste should consider treating themselves to some cat skiing (where you ride snow-cats instead of lifts); there are several operations in this area. Island Lake Lodge (423 3700) does three- or four-day all-inclusive packages in a cosy chalet 10km/6 miles from Fernie, amid 7,000 acres of spectacular bowls and ridges. It has 36 beds, and four cats. In a day you might do eight powder runs averaging 500m/1,640ft vertical, taking in all kinds of terrain from gentle open slopes to some very Alpine adventures. We've heard they can be booked solid up to three years in advance. You can do single days on a standby basis; we managed this once and loved it, but our second attempt failed. A 2006 visitor picked up a late-season bargain with Powder Cowboy (422 8754). It has two cats accessing 6,000 acres 60km/37 miles from Fernie. 'Absolutely superb – the perfect hosts and guides. The best day's skiing we have ever had.' We've had mixed reports of Fernie Wilderness Adventures (423 6704); some readers have complained that the terrain is more testing than advertised. But the verdict from a 2006 group: 'Absolutely fantastic.'

SCHOOLS
Fernie
t 423 4655

Classes
Half day C$85 (incl. taxes)

Private lessons
C$245 (incl. taxes) for 2hr for up to 5 people

CHILDREN
Telus Resort Kids
t 423 2430
Newborn to age 6; 8.30 to 4.30

Ski school
For ages 5 to 12 (C$95, incl. taxes, per day)

FOR INTERMEDIATES
Far from ideal
Although there are intermediate runs both low down and high up, they don't add up to a lot of mileage. Most high runs are not groomed, and are quite challenging as a result. Adventurous, strong intermediates willing to give the ungroomed terrain a try will enjoy the area. But if you want miles of groomed cruising, go elsewhere.

FOR BEGINNERS
Excellent
There's a good nursery area served by two lifts (a moving carpet and a drag) and the lower mountain served by the Deer and Elk chairs has lots of wide, smooth trails to gain confidence on. But the green runs from the top of the mountain are usually cat-tracks, which nonetheless have tough parts to them.

FOR CROSS-COUNTRY
Some possibilities
There are 14km/9 miles of trails marked out in the forest adjacent to the resort, and the fairways of the Fernie golf course are accessible.

QUEUES
Not usually a problem
Unless there are weekend crowds from Calgary, or heavy snow keeps part of the mountain closed, queues are rare. The slopes are delightfully quiet too. But people do complain about the slow chair-lifts, and about frequent stoppages on one or two.

MOUNTAIN RESTAURANTS
What mountain restaurants?
Bear's Den at the top of the Elk chair is an open-air fast-food kiosk, not a mountain restaurant, so it's back to base for lunch. The ancient Day Lodge is a no-frills place serving salads and burgers ('friendly with good service') and Snow Creek is handy for the nursery slopes. But a 2006 reporter reckons the Wood on the Hill, beside the Lizard Creek Lodge, is 'easily the best option', though on Sundays you should head for brunch at the Lizard Creek ('you won't eat for the rest of the day').

A new cafe, Lost Boys, is planned for the top of the Timber Express chair-lift for 2006/07 – though it sounds like it will be another soup shack.

SCHOOLS AND GUIDES
Highly praised
Reporters praise the school, which seems to achieve rapid progress – no doubt partly because groups are often very small. A 2006 reporter enjoyed 'excellent lessons, which took us from powder novices to bump and tree skiing in three hours'. Also praised was the way in which individuals were encouraged to set their own objectives, then helped to achieve them. We've also had good reports of the Steep and Deep camps and private lessons. 'First Tracks' gets you up the mountain at 7.45am for two hours, but when we tried it the instructor didn't know which lifts were open and there was a lot of wasted time.

FACILITIES FOR CHILDREN
Good day care centre
There's a day care centre in the Cornerstone Lodge, which a reporter found 'very well run'. There are also 'Kids' Activity Nights' for children aged six to 12.

ACTIVITIES

Indoor Museum, galleries, aquatic centre, bowling, fitness centre, ice skating, cinema, curling

Outdoor Sleigh rides, snowmobiling, dog-sledding, helicopter rides, snow-shoe excursions, ice fishing

OUR WEBSITE

Go to our website at wtss.co.uk for resort news, links to resort sites, a build-your-own resort shortlist8 system and reader forums.

Central reservations phone number For all resort accommodation call 1 800 258 7669 (toll-free from within Canada).

Phone numbers From distant parts of Canada, add the prefix 1 250. From abroad, add the prefix +1 250.

TOURIST OFFICE

t 423 4655
info@skifernie.com
www.skifernie.com

STAYING THERE

HOW TO GO
More packages
Fernie is increasingly easy to find in tour operator brochures. Unless stated, accommodation listed is at the resort.
Chalets Some UK tour operators run chalets. Beavertail Lodge is run along chalet lines and has received several rave reviews from reporters: 'The best chalet I have ever stayed in, with food equal to a Michelin-starred restaurant.' Canadian Powder Tours has a chalet and includes in the price guiding by the owners, who know the mountain well: 'Food was excellent. I am a novice off-piste skier but had a brilliant time.'
Hotels and condos There's a wide choice, some impressively comfortable.
((((4) **Lizard Creek Lodge** Luxury ski-in/ski-out condo hotel. Spa, outdoor pool and hot-tub. We loved it and a recent reporter gives it '10 out of 10'.
(((3) **Snow Creek Lodge** Similar to the Lizard Creek Lodge. Recommended in 2006: 'Lovely slope-side position. Absolutely no complaints.'
(((3) **Cornerstone Lodge** Condo hotel.
(((3) **Best Western Fernie Mountain Lodge** Next to golf course near town. Recommended by reporters. Pool, hot-tub, fitness room. But a 30-minute bus-ride to the slopes.
(((3) **Griz Inn Sport Hotel** Condo-hotel with good facilities. Pool.
((2) **Wolf's Den Mountain Lodge** 'Simple but comfortable,' say reporters. Indoor hot-tub, small gym. At base of slope. Due to be refurbished for 2006/07.
((2) **Timberline Lodges** Very comfortable condos a shuttle-ride from the lifts.
((2) **Cedar Lodge Motel** on road to town. 'Comfortable and clean, but not very welcoming,' said reporters.
((2) **Alpine Lodge** B&B recommended by a reporter.

EATING OUT
Steadily improving
At the base, the Lizard Creek Lodge is recommended in 2006 for 'good sized portions and the Okanagan red wines'. Reporters highly praise the food at Beavertail Lodge (which takes outsiders if it's not full): 'worth a Michelin star' and 'superb food including wild mushroom soup, parfait de foie gras, duck confit'. The Wood on the Hill is recommended although 'it's on the pricey side for Fernie and there is limited choice'. We've had very mixed reports on Kelsey's (part of a

chain). Gabriella's does cheap and cheerful Italian, and lots of readers have enjoyed it. The Slope Side Coffee and Deli in the Cornerstone Lodge has been recommended.

In the town of Fernie, there are quite a few options, which may be a key factor in deciding where to stay. Recommendations include the pricey Old Elevator (a converted grain store with 'good grills and pasta'), Jamochas (a coffee house that does meals), the Curry Bowl (various Asian styles and 'a beer menu with 60 brews'), the Royal hotel (Australian cuisine), Rip'n Richard's Eatery (south-western food and a lively atmosphere), the Corner Pocket in the Grand Central Hotel ('terrific bison, venison and steaks'; 'refreshing basil ice-cream'), Yamagoya ('good sushi') and Mojo Rising ('good quality; huge portions'). El Guapo, in the Edge of the World board shop, does 'cheap and tasty' Mexican.

APRES-SKI
Have a beer
The Griz bar now has a sun deck and is quite lively when the lifts close – sometimes with live bands. During the week, the bars are pretty quiet later on. In town, the bars of the Royal hotel are popular with locals. Other recommendations are the Park Place Lodge Pub, the bar in the Grand Central hotel, the Central bar and the Eldorado Lounge, which sometimes has live bands for later on.

The resort offers BBQ at Bear's Den twice a week, with a torchlit descent.

OFF THE SLOPES
Get out and about
There is a heritage walking tour of historic Fernie and the old railroad station is now the Art Station. You could take in an ice-hockey game. But the main diversion is the great outdoors. There's a pool at the Aquatic Centre.

Fernie

671

Kicking Horse

Canada's newest resort: great powder high up, the country's best mountain restaurant and a fledgling village at the base

➕ Great terrain for experts and some for adventurous intermediates

➕ Big vertical served by a fast lift

➕ Splendid mountain-top restaurant

➖ Resort village still in early stages

➖ Gondola has no mid-station, so you may have to ski crud lower down

➖ Few groomed intermediate runs

In 2000/01, a tiny local hill with lifts only on the lower slopes was transformed by a new gondola rising 1150m/3,770ft to the top of high, powdery bowls and chutes. In 2002 came a new quad chair-lift (slow, sadly) serving more high slopes. Now a few lodges have opened to form the first stage of a mountain village at the lift base. The resort suits experts best and makes a good day trip from Banff or Lake Louise for them and adventurous intermediates. But it's a shame there's no gondola mid-station so that you could ski the top half repeatedly without depending on less reliably good snow below.

THE RESORT

Eight miles from the small logging town of Golden, Kicking Horse is in the early stages of development and the first phase of a resort village opened two seasons ago. By the 2006/07 season there will be six lodges, a few restaurants and bars, a ski shop and a general store. The idea is for the resort to be complete by 2010. Daily round-trip buses run from Banff and Lake Louise – C$75 including a lift pass.

Golden is a spread-out place beside the transcontinental highway. It has no real charm or centre – we'd prefer to stay at the mountain.

THE MOUNTAINS

The lower two-thirds of the hill are wooded, with trails cut in the usual style. The upper third is a mix of open and lightly wooded slopes. There's a (fenced) grizzly bear sanctuary right by a blue run at mid-mountain.

Slopes The only way up to the top part of the mountain is by the eight-seat gondola to Eagle's Eye. Despite the serious vertical of 1150m/3,770ft, this lift goes up in a single stage. The lack of a mid-station is a real drawback: unless you ride the slow chair to the slightly higher peak of Blue Heaven all the time, you have to make the full descent (and the snow conditions on the lower slopes may be poor). As well as the marked runs, there are literally hundreds of ways down through the bowls, chutes and trees. Two chair-lifts from near the base serve the lower runs that formed the original ski area. There are free mountain tours.

Terrain-park There isn't one.

Snow reliability It gets an average of 275 inches of snow a year; not enough to put it in the very top flight, but not far off. The top part of the mountain usually has light, dry powder; the lower part may have crud and thin cover.

Experts It's advanced skiers and riders who will get the most out of the area.

BLUE HEAVEN
2445m/8,030ft

EAGLE'S EYE
2345m/7,700ft

Feuz Bowl

Terminator Ridge

Bowl Over

CPR Ridge

Crystal Bowl

Redemption Ridge

Golden Eagle Express

Kicking Horse
1190m/3,900ft

↑ Not bad views huh? It includes the best mountain restaurant in Canada

KICKING HORSE RESORT

NEWS

Last season Mountaineer Lodge (a condo hotel) and Highland Lodge opened. For 2006/07 Palliser Lodge is due to open, and the resort is installing much-needed snowmaking on the lower slopes. The resort also claims to be increasing its grooming.

KEY FACTS

Resort	1190m
	3,900ft
Slopes	1190-2445m
	3,900-8,030ft
Lifts	5
Pistes	2,750 acres
Green	20%
Blue	20%
Black	60%
Snowmaking	None

Central reservations phone number
For resort accommodation call 1 250 439 5400 (toll-free from within Canada).

Phone numbers From distant parts of Canada, add the prefix 1 250. From abroad, add the prefix +1 250.

TOURIST OFFICE

t 439 5424
guestservices@kicking horseresort.com
www.kickinghorse resort.com

From CPR ridge, drop off to skier's right through trees or to skier's left through chutes – there are endless options. If it's open you can also hike to Terminator Ridge (often closed due to avalanche danger). The chair to Blue Heaven opens up easier ski-anywhere terrain down into Crystal Bowl. From the top you can also drop down into the steeper but wonderfully wide Feuz Bowl. The lower half of the mountain has fine black runs on cleared trails, some with serious moguls. There is also heli-skiing nearby.

Intermediates Adventurous intermediates will have a fine time learning to play in the powder from Blue Heaven down to Crystal Bowl. Most of it is open, but you can head off into trees if you want to. There is very little groomed cruising – though the resort claims to be increasing its grooming. The only easy, groomed way down the mountain has been a 10km/6 mile winding road called It's a Ten. Piste-bashers and timid intermediates should go elsewhere.

Beginners We can't imagine why a UK-based beginner would come here.

Snowboarding Free-riders will love this powder paradise.

Cross-country There are 14km/9 miles of trails at Dawn Mountain and a 5km/3 mile loop on the golf course.

Queues None of our reporters have experienced any large queues.

Mountain restaurants The Eagle's Eye table-service restaurant at the top of the gondola is Canada's best mountain restaurant and serves excellent food in stylish log-cabin surroundings with splendid views. The base lodge is also smartly built with logs and beams and has a small self-service restaurant. A yurt (tent) in Crystal Bowl serves snacks.

Schools and guides Two reporters booked group lessons and each was the only pupil: 'excellent' was the verdict from both. Another joined a free mountain tour and again was the

only one. Yet another took an avalanche safety course that 'was worth every penny; truly memorable'.

Facilities for children The school teaches children from the age of three.

STAYING THERE

How to go Stay at the slopes.

Hotels We were very impressed with the 10-room log-built Vagabond Lodge B&B, personally run by the owners. Huge open-plan living room with log fire, rooms with delightfully comfortable-looking beds and nice bathrooms. Steam room and outdoor hot-tub. Copper Horse Lodge next door has bigger rooms, more modern ambiance (leather bedheads, satellite TV in rooms), outdoor hot-tub. The 10-room Highland Lodge looked good as we saw it being built (big, light airy bedrooms and public rooms, outdoor hot-tubs). The Mountaineer Lodge, Glacier Lodge and (new for 2006/07) Palliser Lodge all have around 50 rooms each and are much less personal.

Self-catering The Whispering Pines town homes were 'the most luxurious ski lodgings we've had' said a reporter.

Eating out The Local Hero in Highland Lodge does modern Canadian cooking with a Scottish flavour. Corks in the Copper Horse Lodge does 'mountain bistro dining'. Kuma is a sushi bar that closed at 7pm last season. Eagle's Eye at the top of the gondola opens some nights and is well worth a visit. Extreme Peaks is a big new restaurant in Glacier Lodge that opened last year. In Golden, the Kicking Horse Grill and the out-of-town Cedar House Cafe are highly rated.

Après-ski The liveliest place as the lifts close is reportedly The Local Hero with its deck, blazing outdoor fireplace, and music. In Golden the Mad Trapper and Golden Taps are lively bars.

Off the slopes There is snowmobiling, snow-shoeing, ice-climbing, dog-sledding.

Kicking Horse

673

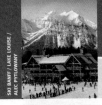

Lake Louise

Stunning views and the biggest ski area in the Banff region, with some good places to stay but no real village

COSTS

① ② ③ ④ ⑤ ⑥

RATINGS

The slopes
Fast lifts	✱✱✱
Snow	✱✱✱
Extent	✱✱✱✱
Expert	✱✱✱✱
Intermediate	✱✱✱✱
Beginner	✱✱✱
Convenience	✱
Queues	✱✱✱✱
Mountain restaurants	✱✱

The rest
Scenery	✱✱✱✱✱
Resort charm	✱✱✱
Off-slope	✱✱✱✱

NEWS

For 2005/06 the Olympic double chair on the Front Side was decommissioned. The double-black-diamond Gully No5 was opened in the Powder Bowls (the new name for what used to be called its Back Bowls, though we've rarely seen good powder there on our numerous visits).

There are longer-term plans to build a new mountain restaurant close to the top of the Grizzly Express gondola.

➕ Spectacular high-mountain scenery – the best of any North American resort

➕ Slopes are the largest in the Canadian Rockies

➕ Snowy slopes of Sunshine Village within reach (see Banff chapter)

➕ Lots of wildlife around the valley

➕ Good value for money

➖ Local slopes are a short drive away from the 'village', Banff areas further

➖ Snowfall modest by local standards

➖ Can be very cold and the chair-lifts have no covers, but the Grizzly Express gondola is warmer

➖ 'Village' is just a few hotels and shops, fairly quiet in the evening

If you care more for scenery than for après-ski action, Lake Louise is worth considering for a holiday. We've seen a few spectacular mountain views, and the view from the Fairmont Chateau Lake Louise hotel of the frozen lake and the Victoria Glacier behind it is as spectacular as they come; it is simply stunning.

Even if you prefer the more animated base of Banff, you'll want to make expeditions to Lake Louise during your holiday. It can't compete with Sunshine Village for quantity of snow, but it's a big and interesting mountain. And from the slopes you get a distant version of that view.

THE RESORT

Although it's a small place, Lake Louise is a resort of parts. First, there's the lake itself, in a spectacular setting beneath the Victoria Glacier. Tom Wilson, who discovered it in 1882, declared, 'As God is my judge, I never in all my exploration have seen such a matchless scene.' Neither have we. And it can be appreciated from many of the rooms of the vast Fairmont Chateau Lake Louise hotel on the shore. Then there's Lake Louise 'village' – a collection of a few hotels, condos, petrol station, liquor store and shops, a couple of miles away on a road junction. Finally, a mile or two across the valley is the lift base station. A car helps, especially in cold weather. Buses to the Lake Louise ski area run every half hour, but a lot less frequently to the Banff areas of Sunshine and Norquay. Bus trips to the more distant resorts of Panorama and Kicking Horse and the small resorts of

Nakiska and Fortress are possible. Day-trip heli-skiing can also be arranged. Banff Airporter do transfers from and to Calgary airport.

THE MOUNTAINS

The Lake Louise ski area is big, with a mixture of high open slopes, low trails cut through forest and gladed slopes between the two. Reporters are usually full of praise for the free guided tours given by volunteers. There has been some criticism of inconsistent piste grading and lots about cold lifts with no covers.

THE SLOPES
A wide variety
From the base area you have a choice of a fast quad to mid-mountain, followed by a six-pack to the top centre of the **Front Side** (also called the South Face), or the gondola direct to a slightly lower point on the right side of the Front Side. From both places, as elsewhere, there's a choice of green, blue or black runs (good for a group of mixed abilities who want to keep meeting up). In poor visibility, the gondola is a better option as the tree line goes almost to the top there. Or stay on the lower part of the mountain using the chairs. From mid-mountain on the left, the long Summit

To JASPER

Lake Louise ▲ Lake Louise Mountain

10 km
5 m

To VANCOUVER

Mystic Ridge – Norquay

Sunshine Village ▲ ▲ Banff

To VANCOUVER   To CALGARY

drag-lift takes you to the high-point of the area, at the shoulder of Mount Whitehorn – there's a stunning view of peaks and glaciers including Canada's Matterhorn lookalike, Mount Assiniboine.

From here or the top chair you can go over the ridge and into Lake Louise's almost treeless **Powder Bowls** (the new name for what it used to call its Back Bowls) – open, predominantly north-facing and mainly steep. From the top of the gondola, the Ptarmigan area is more wooded.

From low down in the bowls you can take the Paradise lift back to the top again or continue lower to the separate **Larch** area, served by a fast quad chair. With a lift-served vertical of 375m/1,230ft it's not huge, but it has pretty wooded runs of all grades. From the bottom you can return to the top

of the main mountain via the Ptarmigan chair or take a long green path back to the main base area.

TERRAIN-PARKS
Huge and varied

The Telus Showtime park under the Glacier lift has been divided into three separate areas to cover all levels. The Marmot park is the beginner park and has three small roller-style jumps which will ease you into being comfortable in the air. There are also several small ride-on boxes to get the feeling for sliding on steel. The Eagle Plains intermediate park has three average-sized jumps with gentle and wide transitions – these are great fun. There is a small hip as well as several rails and boxes. The expert Juniper park is situated just below and has

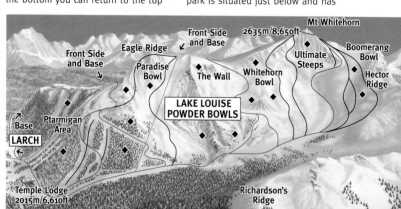

boarding

Tri-area lift pass

Prices in C$

Age	1-day
6-day	
under 13	34
209	
13 to 17	62
377	
18 to 64	67
401	
over 65	62
377	

Free under 6

Beginner lift, lesson and rental package

Notes
Covers all lifts and transport between Banff, Lake Louise, Norquay and Sunshine Village. Prices include tax.

Lake Louise is a great mountain for free-riders, with all the challenging terrain in the bowls and glades. The two sides of the mountain mean there is ample space at this sometimes very crowded resort. Get up early and head to the Powder Bowls first thing for some epic fun. Ask a local or hire a guide to get the best out of the bowls, as there is often great terrain only a short hike away. Beginners will have fun on the Front Side's blue and green runs. But there's a T-bar at the base area and beware of the vicious Summit button-lift (top left looking at the trail map). Also avoid the long, flat green run through the woods from Larch back to base. For those less into free-riding there are three terrain-parks to suit all levels.

excellent fluid lines. From kicker to hip to quarter-pipe, the park will test all aspects of your riding. The pièce de résistance is called The Cliff and is a man-made cliff drop that looms over the park and drops into a nice long landing. Various big rails and boxes will take you to the bottom of the Glacier lift for another loop.

SNOW RELIABILITY
Usually OK
Lake Louise gets around 140 inches a year on the Front Side, which by the standards of western Canada is not a lot. But it is usually enough, and there is snowmaking on 40 per cent of the pistes. The north-facing Powder Bowls and Larch hold the snow pretty well.

FOR EXPERTS
Widespread pleasure
There are plenty of steep slopes. On the Front Side, as well as a score of marked black-diamond trails in and above the trees, there is the alluring West Bowl, reached from the Summit drag – a wide open expanse of snow outside the area boundary. Because this is National Park territory, you can in theory go anywhere. But outside the boundaries there are no patrols and, of course, no avalanche control. A guide is essential. 'You get a real feel of being in the middle of nowhere. The return through thick woods with small plunges and over-hanging branches is great fun,' says a reporter.

Inside the boundaries, going over to the Powder Bowls opens up countless black mogul/powder runs. From the Summit drag, you can drop into The Ultimate Steeps (if it is open), directly behind the peak. The runs here gave our Aussie editor what she called 'some of the most exciting in-bounds skiing in North America' – a row of extreme chutes, almost 1km/0.5 mile long. You can also access lots of much tamer, wide open Powder Bowl slopes

that take you right away from all signs of lifts.

The Top of the World six-pack takes you to the very popular Paradise Bowl, served by its own triple chair – there are endless variants here. The seriously steep slope served by the Ptarmigan quad chair has great gladed terrain and is a good place to beat the crowds and find good snow. The Larch area has some steep double-diamond stuff in the trees, and open snowfields at the top for those with the energy to hike up. Heli-skiing is available from bases outside the National Park.

FOR INTERMEDIATES
Some good cruising
Almost half the runs are classified as intermediate. But from the top of the Front Side the blue runs down are little more than paths in places, and there are very few blues or greens in the Powder Bowls. Once you get part way down the Front Side the blues are much more interesting. And when groomed, the Men's and Ladies' Downhill black runs are great fast cruises on the lower half of the mountain. Juniper is a wonderful cruising run in the same area. Meadowlark is a beautiful tree-lined run to the base area – to find it from the Grizzly Express gondola, first follow Eagle Meadows. The Larch area has some short but ideal intermediate runs – and reporters have enjoyed the natural lumps and bumps of the aptly named blue, Rock Garden. The adventurous should also try the blue-classified Boomerang, which starts with a short side-step up from the top of the Summit drag, and some of the ungroomed Powder Bowls terrain.

FOR BEGINNERS
Excellent terrain
Louise has a good nursery area near the base, which has attracted praise, served by a short T-bar, which has not.

Lake Louise

677

↑ Temple Lodge,
near the bottom of
the Larch area, has
the Sawyer's Nook
table-service
restaurant as well as
a self-service option

SCHOOLS

**Club Ski and Club
Snowboard**
t 760 7731

Classes
3 days guided tuition
of the three areas
C$250 incl. tax
Private lessons
Half day (3hr) C$363,
incl. tax

CHILDREN

**Telus Play Station &
Daycare**
t 522 3555
Ages 18 days to 6yr;
8.30 to 4.30

Ski school
Takes ages 6 to 12 (3
days C$250, incl. tax
and lunch)

You progress to the gentle, wide
Wiwaxy, Pinecone Way and the slightly
more difficult Deer Run or Eagle
Meadows (all designated 'slow skiing
zones'). There are even green slow-
skiing zones round the Powder Bowls
and in the Larch area – worth trying for
the views, though some do contain
slightly steep pitches. A past reporter
lost confidence on these, and found
that people still skied fast in the slow
areas and that they were quite
crowded.

FOR CROSS-COUNTRY
High in quality and quantity
It's a very good area for cross-country,
with around 80km/50 miles of groomed
trails in the National Park. There are
excellent trails in the local area and on
Lake Louise itself. And Emerald Lake
Lodge 40km/25 miles away has some
lovely trails and has been recommended
as a place to stay for a peaceful time.

QUEUES
Not unknown
Half of the area's visitors come for the
day from nearby cities such as Calgary
– so it can have queues at weekends
and public holidays, especially for the
slow chairs on the back of the
mountain.

MOUNTAIN RESTAURANTS
Good base facilities
There's not much choice up the
mountain. Temple Lodge, near the
bottom of Larch, is built in rustic style
with a big terrace. Sawyer's Nook there
is the only table-service option on the
mountain and it continues to receive
praise from reporters; it gets busy, so
reserve a table. The Temple Lodge self-
service cafeteria can get very crowded.
Whitehorn Lodge, at mid-mountain on
the Front Side, is a cafeteria with fine
views from its balcony. At the base,
the Lodge of the Ten Peaks is a hugely
impressive, spacious, airy, modern,
log-built affair with various eating,
drinking and lounging options,
including the Great Bear Room self-
service (which is described as having
'Interactive Lunch Stations') – the
buffet breakfast here is recommended
('Good value, with as much as you
want to eat,' says a 2006 visitor). The
neighbouring Whiskeyjack building has
another self-service. The Kokanee
Kabin has BBQ food.

SCHOOLS AND GUIDES
Generally good reports
'The best teaching we've encountered'
is how a reporter described his
'bumps' lesson at Lake Louise. Another
reporter enjoyed the lessons, but said
she could not get afternoon-only
classes. And her five-year-old daughter
did not like being put in classes with
eight- to ten-year-olds. See the Banff
chapter for details on the excellent
three-day, three-mountain Club Ski and
Club Snowboard Program.

FACILITIES FOR CHILDREN
Varying reports
A reporter who used Lake Louise,
Sunshine and Norquay facilities said:
'I'd recommend all three and advise
booking in advance at Lake Louise.'

STAYING THERE

HOW TO GO
Good value accommodation
Hotels Summer is the peak season here. Prices are much lower in winter.
((((4) **Fairmont Chateau Lake Louise** (522 3511) Isolated position with stunning views over frozen Lake Louise, 500 rooms, lots of shops, pool, hot-tub, sauna.
((((4) **Post** (522 3989) Small, comfortable Relais & Châteaux place in the village, with good restaurant (huge wine list), pool, hot-tub, steam room. Avoid rooms on railway side.
((2) **Lake Louise Inn** (522 3791) Cheaper option in the village, with pool, hot-tub and sauna. 'Comfortable rooms'; 'good food'; 'staff helpful' said a 2005 reporter.
((2) **Deer Lodge** (522 3747) Charming old hotel next to the Chateau, good restaurant, rooftop hot-tub.
Self-catering Some is available but local shopping is limited. The Baker Creek Chalets (522 3761) were highly recommended by reporters on their honeymoon ('really romantic').

EATING OUT
Limited choice
We had a delicious dinner at the Post hotel in 2005, with good-value house wine. The Fairview Dining Room at the Chateau is also top notch. The Outpost Pub (part of the Post) does inexpensive pub food. The Station restaurant is in an atmospheric old station building. The bakery/ coffee shop in the village has been praised by reporters and is good for breakfast.

APRES-SKI
Lively at tea time, quiet later
There are several options at the bottom of the slopes. The Lodge of the Ten Peaks has lovely surroundings, an open fire and a relaxed atmosphere.

The Kokanee Kabin has live music on spring weekend afternoons. On Monday and Friday there's live music and dancing and a buffet dinner at the mid-mountain Whitehorn Lodge. You ski or ride there as the lifts close, and the evening ends with a torchlit descent. It is hugely popular with British visitors.

Later on, things are fairly quiet. But the Glacier Saloon, in Chateau Lake Louise, with traditional Wild West decor, often has live music until late. Explorer's Lounge, in the Lake Louise Inn, has entertainment. The Post's Outpost Pub is worth a look.

OFF THE SLOPES
Beautiful scenery
Lake Louise makes a lovely, peaceful place to stay for someone who does not intend to hit the slopes. The lake itself makes a stunning setting for walks, snow-shoeing, cross-country skiing and ice skating. You can go on ice canyon walks, sleigh rides, dog-sledding, snowmobiling, sightseeing tours and visit natural hot springs.

For a more lively day or for shopping you can visit Banff.

Lake Louise is near one of the Columbia Icefields Parkway, a three-hour drive to Jasper through National Parks, amid stunningly beautiful scenery of high peaks and glaciers – one of the world's most beautiful drives.

STAYING UP THE MOUNTAIN
Try ski touring
Skoki Lodge (522 3555) is 11km/ 7 miles on skis from Temple Lodge. Built in the 1930s, it sleeps 22 in the lodge and cabins and allegedly has 'gourmet food'. Reports welcome.

Panorama

A fast-developing purpose-built resort with an unusual mountain – not many lifts, but a sizeable area and an impressive vertical

679

COSTS

① ② ③ ④ ⑤ ⑥

RATINGS

The slopes
Fast lifts	★★★
Snow	★★★
Extent	★★
Expert	★★★★
Intermediate	★★★
Beginner	★★★★
Convenience	★★★★
Queues	★★★★★
Mountain restaurants	★

The rest
Scenery	★★★
Resort charm	★★
Off-slope	★

NEWS

For 2005/06 new runs were created in Taynton Bowl. The Elkhorn Cabin was almost doubled in size. The snowmaking and grooming fleet were expanded.

➕ Car-free village with some slope-side accommodation, plus a lower part

➕ Fair-sized ski area with big vertical

➕ Runs are usually deserted

➖ Not many easy cruising runs

➖ Snowfall record not impressive by high local standards

➖ Quiet, even lifeless village

Panorama's vertical of 1220m/4,000ft is one of the biggest in North America, and it has some excellent terrain for experts and adventurous intermediates. It's good for beginners too. But timid intermediates may find themselves confined to the rather limited lower mountain.

THE RESORT

Panorama is a small, quiet, purpose-built resort above the lakeside town of Invermere in eastern British Columbia, about two hours' scenic drive south-west of Banff. Accommodation is concentrated mainly in two car-free areas. There are attractive lodges with a hot-pool complex and a skating rink at the foot of the main slopes; with ski-in/ski-out convenience, this is the best place to stay. But a lot of lodging is in a 'lower village' which lacks character or life. This is linked to the 'upper village' and the slopes by a bucket lift that runs until 10pm. The resort runs day trips to Lake Louise and Kicking Horse (given a demand).

THE MOUNTAIN

The slopes basically follow three ridges, joined at top and bottom. Almost all of the terrain is wooded. 'Informative' free tours are available twice daily. Night-skiing and boarding is offered Thursday to Sunday.

Slopes From the upper village, a fast quad goes over gentle slopes to mid-mountain, and above it another fast quad serves both intermediate and expert slopes. Then a slow quad takes you to the summit. From here there are long blue and black runs down various ridges, and serious expert runs down Taynton bowl and the Extreme Dream zone. The trail map is twice the size it needs to be, but is certainly clear. Hand-written boards at the lifts show trail conditions.

Terrain-parks There are two: the main Showzone terrain-park, with table tops, spines, rails, fun-boxes and a half-pipe, and the Blue Park for beginner freestylers, with scaled-down rails, kickers and fun-boxes. They are both floodlit Thursday to Sunday evenings.

Snow reliability Annual snowfall is low by local standards – less than half the Fernie figure. But snowmaking covers 40 per cent of trails, and grooming is 'excellent' say reporters.

Experts There are genuine black runs scattered all over the mountain, and some expert-only areas. At the very top of the mountain and accessed through a gate is the Extreme Dream Zone – seriously steep trails with cliffs as well as tight trees. Off the back of the summit is the Taynton Bowl area, with challenging but (even though it is marked double-black-diamond on the map) less extreme terrain – hiking over to the far runs can be worth it for fresh tracks. Then there's the local heli-skiing – see Intermediates.

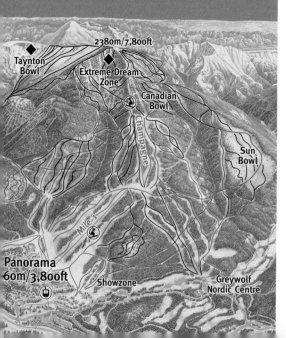

Taynton Bowl

238om/7,8ooft

Extreme Dream Zone

Canadian Bowl

Champagne

Mile-1

Sun Bowl

Panorama
60m/3,8ooft

Showzone

Greywolf Nordic Centre

KEY FACTS

Resort	1160m
	3,800ft
Slopes	1160-2380m
	3,800-7,800ft
Lifts	9
Pistes	2,847 acres
Green	20%
Blue	55%
Black	25%
Snowmaking	40%

Central reservations
1 800 663 2929 (toll-free within Canada).

Phone numbers
From distant parts of Canada, add the prefix 1 250.
From abroad, add +1 250.

TOURIST OFFICE

t 342 6941
paninfo@intrawest.com
www.skipanorama.com

OUR WEBSITE

Go to our website at wtss.co.uk for resort news, links to resort sites, a build-your-own resort shortlist system and reader forums.

Intermediates For adventurous intermediates the terrain is excellent – there are easy blacks all over the mountain, some of them regularly groomed. The black View of 1000 Peaks has fabulous views but can be a bit tricky in parts. Both this and the blue run from the top are long for North America (up to 3.5km/2 miles). Sun Bowl is a good introduction to a powder bowl and Millennium (black running into blue) is a great roller-coaster. But the less confident may find all this uncomfortably challenging. The blues in the centre of the area such as World Cup Way, Skyline and Rollercoaster are gentler but they don't add up to a lot. RK Heli-Skiing has a base right next to the village and specialises in one-day sessions for first-time heli-skiers – 'an exceptional experience', said a recent reporter.

Beginners There are a couple of nursery lifts and a moving carpet serving a quiet and gentle nursery area. Then there are good, longer runs to progress to served by the Mile 1 quad.

Snowboarding There is good steep terrain and tree runs for expert free-riders. The main lifts are all chairs and beginners have several good long green runs to practise on, but the main nursery slopes are served by drag-lifts.

Cross-country There are 30 km/19 miles of trails starting from the Nordic Centre.

Queues The lift system now seems to be queue-free, although the Sunbird triple chair is said to be prone to breakdowns. The trails are delightfully deserted except at peak times.

Mountain restaurants There are just huts offering basic refreshments – but reporters seem to like them. The Summit has daily specials and the Cappuccino has a warming tepee and does 'excellent brownies'. The Ski Tip Lodge at the base is excellent, but gets busy. The clubhouse at the Nordic Centre is quieter – 'good soups'.

Schools and guides We have mainly had glowing reports of the ski school. 'A professional but flexible approach'; 'progressed quickly'; and 'massive leap in skiing – felt great' are typical comments. There's a school TV channel with tips and videos and a new Extreme Makeover clinic. Children's classes have also been praised.

Facilities for children Wee Wascals is the childcare centre, taking children from 18 months. Snowbirds is for three- to four-year-olds, and the Adventure Club caters for kids from five to 14. Kids' nights and a teen nightclub are arranged some evenings. Evening babysitters are also available.

STAYING THERE

How to go The better places are the newer ones in the upper village.

Hotels Panorama Springs is right on the slopes with a big outdoor hot-pool and sauna facility. And the 1000 Peaks Lodge and 1000 Peaks Summit units, around a public ice rink, look good.

Self-catering There are plenty of condo blocks and town homes. The store is inadequate, so stock up in Invermere.

Eating out Eating out options are limited but improving. Earl Grey Lodge has established itself at the top of the market with excellent fixed menus. The Wildfire Grill, the Heli Plex restaurant ('great views; marvellous steaks') and the Great Hall (pasta and pizza) are recommended by reporters. The ski school organises BBQs at Elkhorn Cabin (doubled in size recently and now serving lunch), followed by a torchlight descent. There's a horse-drawn wagon ride followed by chilli around a campfire. A shuttle-bus to the restaurants in Invermere leaves at 7.15 and comes back around 9.30. A 2006 reporter enjoyed a visit to Angus McToogle's there.

Après-ski Après-ski revolves around the Crazy Horse Saloon in the Pine Inn, which sometimes has live music, and the Jackpine pub in the Horsethief Lodge. Ski Tip Lodge is popular as the lifts close. The Glacier is the nightclub.

Off the slopes The hot-pool facility, with thermal baths, a swimming pool, slides and sauna, is excellent, but gets rather taken over by kids. There are snowmobile tours, ice-fishing excursions, snow-shoeing and skating. The Wolf Education Centre ('extremely interesting') and new Bavin Glassworks ('great for gifts') are worth a visit.

Sun Peaks

Attractive car-free village at the foot of BC's second-biggest ski area, with varied slopes including some unusual easy groomed gladed runs

COSTS

① ② ③ ④ ⑤ ⑥

RATINGS

The slopes
Fast lifts	★★★
Snow	★★★★
Extent	★★★
Expert	★★★
Intermediate	★★★★
Beginner	★★★★
Convenience	★★★★
Queues	★★★★★
Mountain restaurants	★

The rest
Scenery	★★★
Resort charm	★★★
Off-slope	★★

➕ Some great terrain for all standards

➕ Excellent glades for intermediates up

➕ Slopes very quiet during the week

➕ Attractive traffic-free slope-side village – with some smart shops

➕ Good for families

➖ Village may be too small and quiet for some tastes

➖ Snow on some of the lower steep terrain can suffer from the sun

➖ Although the second largest ski area in BC, it's not big by Alpine standards

Sun Peaks has sprung from the drawing board since the mid-1990s and we have been increasingly impressed on each of three successive visits. It now has an almost complete small village and a fair amount of varied terrain. Former Olympic slalom champion Nancy Greene and husband Al Raine, who were instrumental in developing Whistler, have made Sun Peaks their new project. Al runs a hotel here and Nancy is Director of Skiing and skis with guests daily. We suggest combining it with, say, Silver Star or Big White on a multi-centre trip.

THE RESORT

Until 1993 Sun Peaks was known as Tod Mountain, a local hill for the residents of nearby Kamloops. Since then the company that bought it has overseen the development of a small, attractive resort village with low-rise pastel-coloured buildings with a vaguely Tirolean feeling to them. The traffic-free main street is lined with accommodation, restaurants and shops including a smart art gallery, great chocolate shop and good coffee bar.

THE MOUNTAINS

681

With almost 3,700 acres of skiable terrain, Sun Peaks is the second biggest ski area in British Columbia (Whistler is the biggest). There are free guided tours twice a day and at 11am and 1.30 you can ski for free with former Olympic champion and Canada's Female Athlete of the 20th Century Nancy Greene when she's in town (don't miss it – she is great fun!).
Slopes There are three distinct sectors, each served by a high-speed quad. One goes from the centre of the village to mid-mountain on Sun Peaks' original ski hill, Mt Tod. This has mainly black runs but there are easier blues and greens. A tiny snowcat offers day-long backcountry skiing here but runs are very short (100–130m/328–426ft vertical) and lots of slopes had been tracked by snowmobilers when we did it. Many of Mt Tod's steepest runs are served only by the slow Burfield quad (there's a mid-station to allow you to ski the top runs only) – a resulting bonus says a 2006 reporter is that the runs down to it are 'even quieter than the rest'. Also reached from the village centre, the Sundance area has mainly blue and green cruising runs. Both Sundance and Tod have some great gladed areas

NEWS

For 2006/07 a new fixed-grip quad chair on Mt Tod will take you from mid-mountain to near the top of the Sunburst Express, allowing advanced and expert skiers to ski some steep black and gladed runs repeatedly without returning to the bottom of the mountain. Four new blue runs will be created on Orient Ridge (mainly to access homes in the East Village area). There will be a new ski-in/ski-out Umbrella cafe near the base of Mt Morrisey. And a new Kids Ranch animated theme park with fun features designed for kids three to 12 years old will be created at the top of the beginner area.

For 2005/06 grooming and snowmaking were increased and the Children's Learning Centre was expanded and a moving carpet installed.

(12 of them marked on the trail map). Mt Morrisey is reached by a long green run from the top of Sundance and has a delightful network of easy blue runs with trees left uncut in the trails, making them effectively groomed glade runs which even early intermediates can try.

Terrain-parks There are two parks on Sundance – one for novices and an advanced park with table-tops, rails and fun-boxes – plus a half-pipe.

Snow reliability Sun Peaks gets an average snowfall of 220 inches a year; not in the top league but better than some. The snow can suffer on the lower part of Mt Tod's south-facing slopes, especially later in the season.

Experts Mt Tod has most of the steep terrain, though some of the blacks on Mt Morrisey (such as Static Cling) are long mogul runs too. You could also try the backcountry snowcat operation.

Intermediates This is great terrain for

early intermediates, with the easy groomed glades of Mt Morrisey, lovely swooping blues on Sundance and the long 5 Mile run from Mt Tod. More adventurous intermediates can tackle the easier glades (such as Cahilty) and blacks (such as Peek-A-Boo).

Beginners There are nursery slopes right in the village centre, with long easy greens to progress to.

Snowboarding Boarders can explore the whole mountain. But beware the flat greens to and from Mt Morrisey.

Cross-country There are 40km/25 miles of groomed trails.

Queues Weekdays are usually very quiet; it's only at peak weekends that you might find short queues ('6 or 7 minutes' says a 2006 reporter).

Mountain restaurants The Sunburst Lodge is the only option; its cinnamon buns are highly recommended.

Schools and guides A 2006 reporter's family had mixed experiences. She had

KEY FACTS

Resort	1255m
	4,120ft
Slopes	1200-2080m
	3,930-6,820ft
Lifts	12
Pistes	3,678 acres
Green	10%
Blue	58%
Black	32%
Snowmaking	
	40 acres

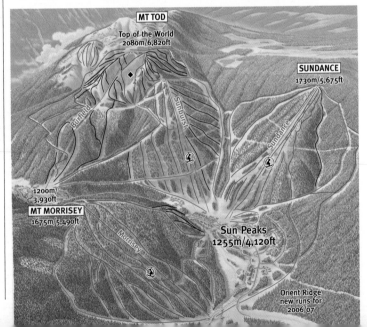

MT TOD
Top of the World
2080m/6,820ft

SUNDANCE
1730m/5,675ft

Burfield

Sunburst

Sundance

1200m/
3,930ft
MT MORRISEY
1675m/5,490ft

Morrisey

Sun Peaks
1255m/4,120ft

Orient Ridge
new runs for
2006/07

Sun Peaks is an attractive village with some good tree-lined intermediate cruising ➔

Phone numbers
From distant parts of Canada, add the prefix 1 250. From abroad, add the prefix +1 250.

a 'fantastic instructor' and was the only person in a group lesson and her kids 'were happy'. But her husband found his lesson (with five others) was 'more like a guided tour'.
Facilities for children The playschool takes kids from age 18 months and the ski school from three years.

STAYING THERE

How to go There's a lot of self-catering accommodation as well as hotels.
Hotels Nancy Greene's Cahilty Lodge is a friendly and comfortable ski-in/ski-out base and you get the chance to ski with her and husband Al Raine (former Canadian ski team coach) at 9am most days – 'Great fun skiing with Nancy and Al, good rooms, a very welcoming hotel,' says a reporter. The ski-in/ski-

out Delta Sun Peaks Resort (outdoor pool and hot-tub) in the village centre is 'impressive with friendly staff and well priced food'.
Eating out For a small resort, there's a good choice of restaurants, including Thai, Italian and, of course, North American. Macker's Bistro is popular and we had great Thai-style sea bass there. Powder Hounds does good steaks and Servus more sophisticated food.
Après-ski Bottoms, Masa's and Macker's are the main après-ski bars. At weekends MackDaddy's nightclub in The Delta can get lively. There are fondue evenings with torchlit descents, winter bonfires and tobogganing.
Off the slopes There's skating, tubing, snowmobiling, dog-sledding and snow-shoeing.

Sun Peaks

683

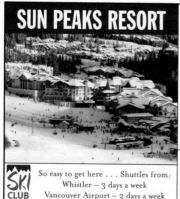

Whistler

North America's biggest mountain, with terrain to suit every standard and with a big purpose-built village to match

RATINGS

The slopes

Fast lifts	****
Snow	****
Extent	****
Expert	*****
Intermediate	*****
Beginner	***
Convenience	****
Queues	***
Mountain restaurants	**

The rest

Scenery	***
Resort charm	***
Off-slope	**

NEWS

For 2006/07 a new high-speed quad is planned near the top of Whistler Mountain. Called the Piccolo Express, it will run from the bottom of Flute Bowl to Piccolo peak. This whole area was out of bounds until a couple of seasons ago, and the new lift will access expert terrain, a new intermediate gladed area and two trails for early intermediates. It will also mean the hike to the top of Flute bowl will be around 10 minutes shorter and you will no longer have to hike out of the bottom. All in all, it looks like a very worthwhile addition.

For 2005/06 the Family Zone on Whistler Mountain was increased in size and moved to Ego Bowl, and a new Tube Park was built on Blackcomb.

+ North America's biggest, both in area and vertical (1610m/5,280ft)

+ Good slopes for most abilities, with an unrivalled combination of high open bowls and woodland trails

+ Good snow record

+ Almost Alpine scenery, unlike the rounded Rockies of Colorado

+ Attractive modern villages at the foot of the slopes with car-free centres, one with lively après-ski

+ Good range of restaurants and bars (though not enough of them)

– Proximity to the ocean means a lot of cloudy weather and when it's snowing on the mountain it's often raining at resort level

– Two separate mountains are linked only at resort level

– Lift queues and crowded runs can be a problem

– Mountain restaurants are mostly functional (and overcrowded)

– Whistler has become a victim of its own success – attracting more people than it can cope with

Whistler is unlike any other resort in North America. It's bigger, both in terms of vertical drop and skiable area. The town is big too. Combine that with hordes of people pouring in from Vancouver on powder days and weekends and you can get lengthy lift queues and crowded trails – unusual for North America. The facilities in town can get overstretched too, with tables in restaurants difficult to come by. If you want to get away from the crowds, you should go elsewhere.

But a lot of people will put up with the crowds for Whistler's other attractions. There are some fine up-market hotels and a good variety of restaurants. And the mountain is simply the best that North America has to offer. Great open bowls, steeps and deeps, tree-lined intermediate cruising and good beginner slopes. The ski schools are excellent. The lifts are generally fast and efficient. And the snow on the upper half of the mountain is as reliable and powdery as you'll find. But be prepared for rain at resort level and poor snow on the lower slopes.

Whistler will host many events during the 2010 Winter Olympics.

THE RESORT

Whistler Village sits at the foot of its two mountains, Whistler and Blackcomb, a scenic 115km/71 mile drive from Vancouver on Canada's west coast. Whistler started as a locals' ski area in 1966 with a few ramshackle buildings in what is now the revamped Whistler Creek (aka Creekside). Whistler Village, a 10-minute bus-ride away, developed in the late 1970s. And another village spread up the lower slopes of Blackcomb Mountain in the 1980s; this village, a 10-minute walk from Whistler, is now known simply as Upper Village.

The centres of all the villages are traffic-free. The architecture is varied and, for a purpose-built resort, quite tasteful. There are lots of chalet-style apartments on the hillsides. The centres have individually designed wood and concrete buildings, blended together around pedestrian streets and squares. There are no monstrous high-rise blocks – but there are a lot of large five- or six-storey buildings.

Whistler Village has most of the bars, restaurants and shops, and two

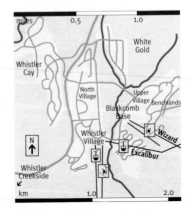

gondolas (one to each mountain). Whistler North, further from the lifts, is newer and has virtually merged with the original village, making a huge car-free area of streets lined with shops, condos and restaurants. Upper Village is smaller and quieter.

Creekside has been revamped and expanded and it will play an important role in the Olympics, with many of the alpine events finishing here.

There is a free bus between Whistler and Upper Village but it can be just as quick to walk. Some lodging is a long way from the villages and slopes and means taking (inexpensive) buses or taxis. Some hotels have free buses, which will pick you up as well as take you to restaurants and nightlife.

The most convenient place to stay is Whistler Village as you can access either mountain by gondola (though some reporters find the central area around Village Square noisy in the early hours). Creekside is quieter and though convenient for Whistler Mountain, is less so for Blackcomb.

THE MOUNTAINS

The area has acquired a formidable and well-deserved reputation among experts. But both Whistler and Blackcomb also have loads of intermediate terrain. Together they have over 200 marked trails, and form the biggest area of slopes, with the longest runs, in North America.

Many reporters enthuse about the mountain host service and the 'go slow' patrol – some find the latter 'over zealous', but crowded slopes, especially on the runs home, mean they're often needed ('They do a good job,' says a 2005 reporter).

But reporters also comment on the early closing times for lifts (3pm until end-January, 3.30 in February and 4pm thereafter). Upper lifts may close earlier. And a 2006 reporter complained about insufficient grooming of intermediate runs during the snowy period he was there, leading to mogulled blue runs.

THE SLOPES
The best in North America
Whistler Mountain is accessed from Whistler Village by a two-stage, 10-person gondola that rises over 1100m/3,610ft to Roundhouse Lodge, the main mid-mountain base. There is an alternative of two consecutive fast quads, which take you slightly lower; they are a good choice when queues for the gondola are long.

Runs back down through the trees fan out from the gondola – cruises to the Emerald and Big Red fast chairs, longer runs to the gondola mid-station.

From Roundhouse you can see the jewel in Whistler's crown – magnificent above-the-tree-line bowls, served by the fast Peak and Harmony quads and, from 2006/07, by the new Piccolo Express (see 'News'). The bowls are mostly go-anywhere terrain for experts

KEY FACTS		
Resort	675m	
	2,210ft	
Altitude	650-2285m	
	2,140-7,490ft	
Lifts		33
Pistes	8,171 acres	
Green		18%
Blue		55%
Black		27%
Snowmaking		
	565 acres	

One of our favourite runs is behind the mountain away from all the lifts on the Blackcomb glacier – over 1000m/3,280ft vertical to the Excelerator chair

BLACKCOMB

Blackcomb Glacier

Horstman Hut 2285m/7,490ft

Lovely sunny cruising above and among the trees

7th Heaven

The Nintendo terrain-park is one of North America's best – with a Highest Level section that you can enter only if you wear a helmet and sign a waiver

Horstman Glacier

Rendezvous Lodge 1860

Glacier

Crystal Hut

Jersey Cream

1645m

Solar Coaster

Glacier Creek

Excelerator

1130m

Wizard

Great blue and green cruising, but beginners should beware of some steeper sections on the greens

Excalibur

Blackcomb Base

New Piccolo Express lift for 2006/07 will make the Flute Bowl area much more accessible – with new blue runs and easy glades as well as expert terrain

Piccolo

Flute Bowl

WHISTLER MOUNTAIN
2180m/7,160ft

The classic high bowls that first gave Whistler cult status among expert skiers in the 1980s and 1990s

Symphony Bowl

Glacier Bowl

The Peak

Whistler Bowl

West Bowl

Bagel Bowl

Piccolo

Harmony

Roundhouse Lodge
1850m

Emerald

1595m

The 1500m/4,920ft vertical Peak-to-Creek runs were created two seasons ago

Big Red

1425m

Whistler Village

Garbanzo

Raven's Nest
1300m

Take the gondola from 7.15am for uncrowded fresh tracks skiing and a buffet breakfast

1005m

Fitzsimmons

Creekside

These runs are to be the 2010 Winter Olympic downhill and Super G courses – black for men and blue for women

Creekside
650m/2,140ft

**Whistler Village
675m/2,210ft**

but there are groomed trails, so anyone can appreciate the views.

A six-person gondola from Creekside also accesses Whistler Mountain.

Access to **Blackcomb** from Whistler Village is by an eight-seater gondola, followed by a fast quad (which is a bottleneck first thing). From the base of Blackcomb you take two consecutive fast quads up to the main Rendezvous restaurant. From the arrival points you can go left for great cruising terrain and the Glacier Express quad up to the Horstman Glacier area, or right for steeper slopes, the terrain-park or the 7th Heaven chair. The 1610m/5,280ft vertical from the top of 7th Heaven to the base is the largest in North America (and big even by Alpine standards). Or you can go into the glacier area. A T-bar from the Horstman Glacier brings you (with a very short hike) to the Blackcomb Glacier in the next valley – a beautiful run that takes you away from all lifts.

Fresh Tracks is a deal that allows you to ride up Whistler Mountain (at extra cost) from 7.15am, have a buffet breakfast and get to the slopes as they open – very popular with many reporters. A good tip is to hit the slopes first and breakfast after – that way you find the slopes at their quietest.

Free guided tours of each mountain are offered at 11.30am.

TERRAIN-PARKS
For high-fliers and mere mortals
There's a good rating system based on size (S, M, L, XL). Novices should begin in the Big Easy Terrain Garden on Blackcomb. This is a great area with small obstacles to get a feel for airtime and improve your control. For the S-M line hit the Habitat park by the Emerald chair on Whistler Mountain. Initiate yourself on a host of rails, boxes, medium kickers and a hip. The M-L Nintendo park is the busiest and is by the Catskinner lift on Blackcomb. Step-up jumps, hips, tabletops, rails, boxes and a super-pipe are the order of the day. This park will suit most advanced riders. Pros and very confident freestylers should hit the Highest Level Park (part of the Nintendo park). The fact that you need to sign a waiver, wear a helmet and buy a special pass indicates the size of the obstacles here. From Thursday to Saturday in the evening a super-pipe and a mini-jib park are open near the Magic Chair on Blackcomb; the same pass will get you into both. In the summer the Horstman Glacier at the top of Blackcomb hosts the Camp of Champions, which boasts the biggest summer park in North America (www.campofchampions.com); it has over 40 obstacles.

SNOW RELIABILITY
Excellent at altitude
Snow conditions at the top are usually excellent – the place gets around 360 inches of snow a year, on average. But because the resort is low and close to the Pacific, the bottom slopes can be wet, icy or unskiable. People may 'download' from the mid-stations due to poor snow, especially in late season. After the exceptionally poor season in 2004/05, when Whistler was plagued by high temperatures and rain, it had 470 inches of snow last season with a record 180 inches in January alone.

FOR EXPERTS
Few can rival it
Whistler Mountain's bowls are enough to keep experts happy for weeks. Each has endless variations, with chutes and gullies of varied steepness and width. The biggest challenges are around Flute, Glacier, Whistler and West Bowls, with runs such as The Cirque and Doom & Gloom – though you can literally go anywhere in these high,

boarding

Whistler has world-class terrain-parks as well as epic terrain for free-riders: bowls with great powder and awesome steeps, steep gullies, tree runs, and shed-loads of natural hits, wind lips and cliffs. Get up early if you fancy cutting first tracks, however. There are mellow groomed runs ideal for beginners too, and the lifts are generally snowboard-friendly; there are T-bars on the glacier, but they're not vicious and any discomfort is worth it for the powder. The resort is fast gaining as big a reputation for its summer snowboarding facilities and camps on the glacier as for its winter snowboarding. The resort's specialist school will teach riders how to ride piste, pipe, park and powder according to your level. Specialist snowboard shops include Showcase and Katmandu Boards.

↑ There are easy groomed trails as well as loads of ungroomed terrain in Whistler Mountain's high bowls

INTRAWEST / PAUL MORRISON

wide areas. The new quad from Flute Bowl (see 'News') will make that area much more easily accessible.

Blackcomb's slopes are not as extensive as Whistler's, but some are more challenging. From the top of the 7th Heaven lift, traverse to Xhiggy's Meadow, for sunny bowl runs.

If you're feeling brave, go in the opposite direction and drop into the extremely steep chutes down towards Glacier Creek, including the infamous 41° Couloir Extreme, which can have moguls the size of elephants at the top. Or try the also serious, but less frequented, steep bowls reached by hiking up Spanky's Ladder, after taking the Glacier Express lift.

Both mountains have challenging trails through trees. Two seasons ago saw the addition of the new 400 acre Peak to Creek area from below Whistler's West Bowl to Creekside.

If all this isn't enough, there's also out-of-bounds backcountry guiding (see Schools and guides), and local heli-skiing available by the day.

FOR INTERMEDIATES
Ideal and extensive terrain

Both mountains are an intermediate's paradise. In good weather, good intermediates will enjoy the less extreme variations in the bowls on both mountains.

One of our favourite intermediate runs is down the Blackcomb Glacier, from the top of the mountain to the bottom of the Excelerator chair over 1000m/3,28oft below. This 5km/3 mile run, away from all lifts, starts with a two-minute walk up from the top of the Showcase T-bar. Don't be put off by the sign that says 'Experts only'. You drop over the ridge into a wide bowl – not too suddenly or you'll get a short, sharp shock in the very steep double-diamond Blowhole. The further you traverse, the shallower the slope.

You are guaranteed good snow on the Horstman Glacier too, and typically gentle runs. The blue runs served by the 7th Heaven chair are 'heavenly on a sunny day', as a reporter put it. Lower down there are lots of perfect cruising runs through the trees – ideal when the weather is bad.

On Whistler Mountain, there are easy blue pistes in Symphony, Harmony, Glacier bowls and (new for 2006/07) in Flute bowl. Even early intermediates should try them (the first three anyway, since there's always an easy way down). The Saddle run from the top of the Harmony Express lift is a favourite with many of our reporters, though it can get busy. The blue Highway 86 path, which skirts West Bowl from the top of the Peak chair, has beautiful views over a steep valley and across to the rather phallic Black Tusk mountain. The green Burnt Stew Trail also has great views.

Lower down the mountain there is a vast choice of groomed blue runs with a series of efficient fast chairs to bring you back up to the top of the gondola. It's a cruiser's paradise – especially the aptly named Ego Bowl. A great long run is the fabulous Dave Murray Downhill all the way from mid-mountain to the finish at Creekside. Although it will be the Olympic men's downhill course and is marked black on the map, it's a wonderful fast and varied cruise when it has been groomed. There is also the new groomed blue in the Peak to Creek area to try if snow is good enough.

FOR BEGINNERS
OK if the sun shines

Whistler has excellent nursery slopes by the mid-station of the gondola, as does Blackcomb, down at the base area. Both have facilities higher up too.

The map has a guide to easy runs, and slow zones are marked. On Whistler, after progressing from the nursery slopes, there are some gentle first runs from the top of the gondola. Their downside is other people speeding past. You can return by various chairs or continue to the base area on greens. Check the latter are in good condition first, and maybe avoid them at the end of the day, when they can get very crowded.

On Blackcomb, Green Line runs from the top of the mountain to the bottom. The top part is particularly gentle, with some steeper pitches lower down. As one reporter said, 'A tentative beginner in our group found it hard to move around with confidence because of the varying steepness of green runs.'

Another reservation is – you guessed – the weather. Beginners don't get a lot out of heavy snowfalls, and might be put off by rain and unpredictable conditions.

FOR CROSS-COUNTRY
Picturesque but low

There are over 28km/17 miles of cross-country tracks around Lost Lake, starting by the river, on the path between Whistler and Blackcomb. But it is low altitude here, so conditions can be unreliable. There's a specialist school, Cross-Country Connection (905 0071) offering lessons, tours and rental. Keen cross-country merchants can catch the train to better areas.

QUEUES
An ever-increasing problem

Whistler has become a victim of its own success. Even with 16 fast lifts (including the new Piccolo) – more than any other resort in North America – the mountains are queue-prone, especially at weekends when people pour in from Vancouver. There are noticeboards displaying waiting times at different lifts, and although readers generally find them useful (though one last year found them 'unreliable'), most people would prefer shorter queues.

Some reporters have signed up with the ski school just to get lift priority. Others have visited Vancouver at the weekend to avoid the crowds.

The routes out of Whistler Village in the morning can be busy. Creekside is less of a problem. Some of the chairs higher up both mountains produce long queues – especially Harmony (where even the singles line can take ages). And we had a report of a 45-minute wait for The Peak chair on an early-January Sunday. Visiting outside peak season may not help – we found some lifts, including the gondola to Blackcomb, were kept closed in an early-December visit and readers have reported closed lifts in late season. Crowds on the slopes, especially the runs home, can be annoying too.

MOUNTAIN RESTAURANTS
Overcrowded

The main restaurants sell decent, good-value food but are charmless self-service stops with long queues. They're huge, but not huge enough. 'Seat-seekers' are employed to find spaces, but success is not guaranteed.

Past reporters have stressed the need to lunch early. But even that no longer works – 'avoid 11.15am to 1.45pm' says a recent visitor. But late lunches mean little skiing afterwards because the lifts close early; so the answer may be a big breakfast, ski through the day and eat later.

Blackcomb has the Rendezvous, mainly a big (850-seat) self-service

SCHOOLS

Whistler and Blackcomb
t 604 932 3434

Classes (incl. taxes)
3 days Ski Esprit/Ride Guides): C$249

Private lessons
Half day (3hr): C$427

GUIDES

Whistler Guides
t 604 932 3434

CHILDREN

Whistler Kids
t 1 800 766 0449
Ages 3mnth to 4yr;
from 8am; non-skiing;
C$105 per day (incl. taxes)

Ski school
Offers Adventure Camps for ages 3 to 12 and Ride Tribe programme for ages 13 to 17 (from C$578 incl. taxes for 5 days for 3 to 4 year olds)

GETTING THERE

Air Vancouver 115km/71 miles (2hr).

OUR WEBSITE

Go to our website at wtss.co.uk for resort news, links to resort sites, a build-your-own resort shortlist system and reader forums.

place but also home to Christine's, a table-service restaurant – the best on either mountain. Glacier Creek Lodge, at the bottom of the Glacier Express, is a better self-service place ('Try the breakfast croissant,' says a reader). But even this (1,496 seats) gets incredibly crowded. Whistler has the massive (1,740-seat) Roundhouse Lodge; Steeps Grill is its table-service refuge.

Reporters generally prefer the smaller places – but they're still packed unless you time it right, and may be closed early and late season. On Blackcomb, Crystal Hut at the top of the Crystal Ridge chair (great waffles, say reporters) and Horstman Hut at the mountain-top are tiny with great views.

On Whistler, Raven's Nest, at the top of the Creekside gondola, is a small and friendly deli/cafe. The Chic Pea near the top of the Garbanzo chair-lift – 'funky and rustic' but 'noisy' – does pizza and barbecue. The Harmony Hut, at the top of the Harmony chair, specialises in stews and cider. You can of course descend to the base – the table-service Dusty's at Whistler Creek has been recommended by several reporters and doesn't get too crowded. There's also a Snack-Shack on each mountain, if all you fancy is a quick drink and hot-dog.

SCHOOLS AND GUIDES
A great formula
Ski Esprit and Ride Guides programmes run for three or four days and combine instruction with showing you around the mountains – with the same instructor daily. Many of our reporters have joined these groups (usually small), and all reports are glowing: 'Big improvement in confidence and skill' is typical. 'Double-diamonds were no problem under our instructor's expert guidance,' says a 2006 reporter. There are specialist clinics and snowboard classes, too. But a 2005 reporter was disappointed that 'it wasn't possible to arrange lessons shorter than three hours' and 'we couldn't sign up for Ski Esprit as a family as our 16-year-old son was classified as too young'.

Extremely Canadian specialises in guiding and coaching adventurous advanced intermediates upwards in Whistler's steep and deep terrain. A lot of its coaches compete in free-ride and skier-cross competitions. We have been with them a few times and they really are great. As a reporter said,

'You end up skiing places that other people don't even know about – we were very impressed.' They run two-day clinics three times a week.

Backcountry day trips or overnight touring are available with the Whistler Alpine Guides Bureau.

FACILITIES FOR CHILDREN
Impressive
Blackcomb's base area has a slow-moving Magic Chair to get children part-way up the mountain. Whistler's gondola mid-station has a splendid kids-only area. A reporter found the staff 'friendly and instilled confidence'. The Children's Adventure Park on Blackcomb features a Magic Castle, terrain features and 'colourful characters'. A 2006 reporter was enthusiastic about 'climb and dine', where children can spend a few fun hours at the Great Wall climbing centre (see 'Off the slopes'), including a meal, while parents go out to eat.

STAYING THERE

HOW TO GO
High quality packages
A lot of British tour operators go to Whistler and some run catered chalets. **Hotels** There is a wide range, including a lot of top-end places.
((((5 **Fairmont Chateau Whistler** (938 8000) Well run and luxurious at the foot of Blackcomb. Excellent spa with pools and tubs. The Gold floor is expensive and especially cosseting.
((((5 **Westin Resort & Spa** (905 5000) Luxury all-suite hotel at the foot of Whistler mountain next to the lifts, with pools and hot-tubs.
((((5 **Four Seasons** (905 3300) Luxury hotel five-minutes walk from Blackcomb base but with ski valet service there. Good fitness and spa facilities.
(((4 **Pan Pacific** (905 2999) Luxury, all-suite, at Whistler Village base. Pool/sauna/hot-tub.
(((4 **Lost Lake Lodge** (932 2882) 'Excellent' place: studios and suites, out by the golf course. Pool/hot-tub.
(((4 **Crystal Lodge** (932 2221) Has been renovated. 'Comfortable, friendly, convenient', in Whistler Village. Pool/sauna/hot-tub.
(((3 **Glacier Lodge** (932 2882) In Upper Village. 'Big rooms, quiet area, recommended.' Pool/hot-tub.
Self-catering There are plenty of spacious, comfortable condominiums in both chalet and hotel-style blocks.

ACTIVITIES

Indoor Sports arena (ice rink, pool, hot-tubs), museum, art galleries, tennis, spa and health clubs, library, cinemas, climbing wall

Outdoor Flightseeing, snow-shoeing, snowmobiling, fishing, dog-sledding, sleigh rides, bungee jumping, ziptrek ecotours in the treetops on platforms and boardwalks and using harnesses and wires

Phone numbers
From distant parts of Canada, add the prefix 1 604.
From abroad, add the prefix +1 604.

TOURIST OFFICE

t 932 3434
wbres@intrawest.com
www.whistler-blackcomb.com
www.mywhistler.com

EATING OUT
High quality and plenty of choice

Reporters are enthusiastic about the range, quality and value of places to eat, but we and they find Whistler simply doesn't have enough restaurant seats to meet demand. Some cheaper places won't take bookings for small groups, meaning long waits. One way round the problem is to eat in a bar – the food is generally decent. But that may not work if you've got kids, who may not be allowed in.

At the top of the market, Il Caminetto di Umberto in Whistler Village has classy Italian cuisine. The Rimrock Café at Whistler Creek serves 'the best seafood we have ever eaten', says a reporter.

Good mid-market Whistler Village places include Araxi (Pacific), the Keg ('great value' steak and seafood), Teppan (Japanese), Mongolie (Asian) and Kypriaki Norte ('excellent duck'). We've had mixed reports on Crab Shack (seafood). Reporters also suggest La Bocca (Italian: 'excellent home-made pasta', 'inexpensive'), the Bearfoot Bistro (European: 'the best gourmet restaurant, with a stellar wine list', 'bar is out of this world') and Sushi Village ('The best Japanese I've had outside Tokyo,' says a well-travelled reporter).

In Village North: the good-value Brewhouse (steaks, burgers, beef ribs) has good microbrews and a lively atmosphere, Caramba has 'good Mediterranean food at reasonable prices'. Hy's Steakhouse has the best steaks ('melt in your mouth'). Sushi-Ya and Quattro (Italian) are good. In Upper Village, Thai One On is 'excellent', and Monk's Grill has 'very good steaks'.

There are plenty of budget places, including the après-ski bars below. Uli's Flipside at Creekside and the Old Spaghetti Factory in Whistler Village have been recommended for pasta.

APRES-SKI
Something for most tastes

Whistler is very lively. Popular at Whistler are the Longhorn, with a huge terrace, the Garibaldi Lift Company and The Dubh Linn Gate Irish pub. Citta's was a 2006 reporter's 'favourite stopping point for an après-ski drink or five'. Tapley's seems 'the nearest thing to a locals' bar'. Merlin's is the focus at Blackcomb base and 'it shows British football and rugby on TV', though readers also recommend the Monk's Grill. Dusty's is the place at Creekside – good beer, loud music.

Later on, Buffalo Bill's is lively and loud and the Amsterdam Café is worth a look. Tommy Africa's, Maxx Fish, the Savage Beagle, Garfinkel's and Moe Joe's are the main clubs. Try the Mallard bar in Chateau Whistler and the Crystal Lodge piano bar for a quieter time. Garfinkel's and the Mallard have inside smoking areas.

OFF THE SLOPES
Not ideal

Whistler is a long way to go if you don't intend to hit the slopes. Meadow Park Sports Centre has a full range of fitness facilities. There are also several luxurious spas. Reporters have recommended walks around the lake, the Great Wall Underground climbing centre and a shop where you can paint your own pottery. There's an eight-screen cinema in Whistler Village. And Ziptrek Ecotours (935 0001) offers ecological journeys using harnesses, cables and suspension bridges through the forest between Whistler and Blackcomb mountains. You can also do ATV/snowmobile trips and dog-sledding. Excursions to Squamish (famous for its eagles) are easy, as are day trips to Vancouver.

JASPER PARK LODGE

Jasper

Set in the middle of Jasper National Park, Jasper appeals more to those keen on scenery and wildlife (and cross-country skiing) rather than piste miles. A visit could be combined with a stay in Whistler, Banff or Lake Louise.

THE RESORT

Jasper is a low-key, low-rise little town. On a clear day, the three-hour drive to or from Lake Louise on the Columbia Icefields Parkway past glaciers, frozen waterfalls and lakes is simply stunning.

Most accommodation is out of town or on the outskirts and the local slopes are a 30-minute drive The Fairmont Jasper Park Lodge (852 3301) has luxurious family-friendly log cabins set 4km/2 miles out of town around a lake.

THE MOUNTAINS

The slopes are very limited in size. A high-speed quad takes you to mid-mountain, with three slow chairs and a drag above that. Snowfall is modest by North American standards and there is lots of steep terrain that needs good snow to be fun. Keen piste-bashers will cover all the groomed runs in half a day. There are excellent nursery slopes and gentle greens to progress to.

At mid-mountain there are self-service cafe and table-service options and at the base the rebuilt Caribou Chalet is attractive. There are 300km/ 186 miles of cross-country trails.

Short turns

ER STAR RESORT / DON WEIXL PHOTOGRAPHY

Silver Star

This quiet, family-friendly resort has a tiny traffic-free centre resembling a 19th-century mining town. There are slopes to suit everyone and it's easy to combine a stay here with one at Big White, which has the same owners.

THE RESORT

Silver Star is a small, recently built resort right on the slopes and with a compact car-free centre of brightly painted Victorian-style buildings with wooden sidewalks and pseudo gas lights. It's a bit Disneyesque but works surprisingly well. Big (also brightly coloured) chalets are dotted in the trees. There are several ski-in/ski-out condo-hotels, apartments and homes to let. There are a couple of decent restaurants but après-ski is quiet.

THE MOUNTAINS

The wooded mountain has three main linked faces. The south face around the village has mainly easy intermediate slopes served by a six-pack, which starts below the main village. For 2005/06 it was joined by the new Silver Woods area of north-east-facing, mainly intermediate slopes, served by a new high-speed quad.

The top of the south face links to the back (or north) side, which has lots of steep black and double-black trails, mostly with big moguls, served by a fast quad. But you can stick to easier alternatives too. There's a small atmospheric hut near the top of the quad, serving simple hot food.

There are lots of flat areas, including the link with the back side, which make life difficult for boarders. The ski school has a good reputation. Cross-country is big; they claim 'The Best Nordic Skiing in North America'.

There's a pretty natural ice rink on a lake and a nearby tubing hill.

TOURIST OFFICE

t 250 542 0224 www.skisilverstar.com

Eastern Canada

694

NEWS

For 2005/06 Le Massif opened a new terrain-park (The Zone), a new mini-park and a new day-lodge, all at the summit.

Stoneham added a new 3D Zone terrain-park, conveniently located next to the resort's fast quad. The beginners' Intro Park was doubled in size. Snowmaking was improved.

TOURIST OFFICES

Mont Blanc
www.skimontblanc.com

Mont-St-Sauveur
www.mssi.ca

Québec city
www.quebecregion.com

Mont-Ste-Anne
www.mont-sainte-anne.com

Stoneham
www.ski-stoneham.com

Le Massif
www.lemassif.com

For us the main attraction of skiing or riding in eastern Canada is the French culture and language that are predominant in the province of Québec. It really feels like a different country from the rest of Canada – as indeed many of its residents want it to become. It is relatively easy to get to – only a six-hour flight from the UK, compared with a 10-hour flight for western Canada.

Tremblant is the main destination resort and is one of the cutest purpose-built resorts we've seen (though it is now in danger of being spoiled by expansion). The other main base is Québec city, which dates from the 17th century and is full of atmosphere and Canadian history. Slopes of the main resorts are small, both in extent and in vertical drop, and the weather can be perishingly cold in early and mid-winter. But at least this means that the extensive snowmaking systems, common to all the resorts, can be effective for a long season. Be prepared for variable snow conditions and don't go expecting light, dry powder – if that's what you want, head west.

There are lots of ski and snowboard areas in Ontario – Canada's most populated province – but most of them are tiny and cater just for locals. For people heading on holiday for a week or more, eastern Canada really means the province of Québec. The province and its capital, Québec city, are heavily dominated by the French culture and language. Notices, menus, trail maps and so on are usually printed in both French and English. Many ski area workers are bilingual or just French-speaking. And French cuisine abounds. The Frenchness of it is one of the big attractions for us.

The weather is very variable, rather like New England's – but it can get even colder. Hence the snow, though pretty much guaranteed by snowmaking, can vary enormously in quality. When we were there one April we were slush skiing in Tremblant one day and rattling along on a rock-hard surface in Mont-Ste-Anne the next. One reporter who visited Mont-Ste-Anne, Stoneham and Le Massif in late January experienced mild temperatures and several perfect blue-sky days.

The main destination resort is **Tremblant** (see separate chapter following this introduction), about 90 minutes' drive from Montreal. Other areas near here that are popular with locals include **Mont Blanc** (with only 300m/980ft of vertical, hardly a competitor to the Franco-Italian version) and the **St-Sauveur** valley (five areas, each with around 200m/660ft of vertical and with

interchangeable lift passes).

The other main place to stay for easy access to several ski resorts is **Québec city**. Old Québec, at the city's heart, is North America's only walled city and is a World Heritage site. Within the city walls are narrow, winding streets and 17th- and 18th-century houses. It is situated right on the banks of the St Lawrence river. In January/February there is a famous two-week carnival, with an ice castle, snow sculptures, dog-sled and canoe races, night parades and grand balls. But most of the winter is low season for Québec city, with good-value rooms available in big hotels. Because of this, the area is popular with British school groups, especially in late season. Non-skiers, or those who like the option to do other activities, won't be bored, whatever time of year they go.

There are several ski and snowboard areas close to Québec city, and a Carte Blanche pass which covers the three main areas: a total of 106 runs, 26 lifts and Canada's largest night skiing area. A car is handy, but there are buses to some areas.

The biggest and most varied area is **Mont-Ste-Anne**, 30 minutes from Québec and with some accommodation of its own. It extends to only 430 acres – easily skied in a day by a good skier – but has a respectable vertical of 625m/2,050ft. A gondola takes you to the top, and slopes lead down the front (south) and back (north) sides. The views from the front over the ice floes of the St Lawrence river are

spectacular. Among its 68km/42 miles of trails are intermediate cruising runs on both sides and some steep blacks (including World Cup runs) through the trees on the front. These include double-diamonds down the lift lines, and the Black Forest, a gladed area offering single- and double-diamond runs. There are some easy top-to-bottom runs and good nursery slopes at the base. There are restaurants at the summit and the north side base, as well as the main base lodge. In spring you can stop by the Sugar Shack and try fresh maple toffee. The resort has three terrain-parks, a beginners' half-pipe and a 600m/ 1,970ft boarder-cross course. Floodlighting covers 17 trails until 10pm seven nights a week (five in January and February). Over 80 per cent of the runs are covered by snowmaking. It also has the largest cross-country centre in Canada, with 223km/139 miles of trails.

Stoneham is the closest resort to Québec city, around 20 minutes away. It also has its own small village with accommodation and an impressive base lodge with bar, restaurant and big wooden deck. Après-ski in the lodge can be lively, and there is often live music. It is a small area, with 815 acres of terrain spread across three linked peaks and a vertical of 420m/1,380ft. But it is very sheltered in a sunny setting protected from wind. It suits families well, with mainly

intermediate and beginner terrain, and has a special beginner area equipped with a moving carpet. Snowboarders, freestylers and freeskiers are attracted to the area by the resort's impressive four terrain-parks with countless rails and table-tops, a 1000m/3,280ft boarder-cross course and a super-pipe with 5m/17ft walls. Stoneham also has the biggest night skiing operation in Canada – 16 runs – with two of the three faces lit top to bottom. Some 86 per cent of the area has snowmaking.

Le Massif is around an hour away from Québec city and is a cult area with locals. It is in a UNESCO World Biosphere Reserve and is just metres from the St Lawrence river. The views of the ice floes are stunning, and you feel you are heading straight down into them when you are on the pretty, tree-lined trails. The area of slopes, though small, has the largest vertical in the east – 770m/2,525ft. There are a couple of steep double-black-diamond runs and some good, well-groomed black and blue cruising runs, including a run designed to meet World Cup standards. The three fast quad chairs include Québec's longest. Guided tours are available all day. Snowmaking covers 54 per cent of its trails. The owners of Le Massif have grand long-term plans for expansion of the terrain by 30 per cent and the creation of a base village, to attract international business.

Introduction

695

STONEHAM / JEAN VAUDREUIL
Stoneham: terrain-parks on the left, steep stuff on the right, a bit of everything in the middle ↓

Tremblant

Traffic-free village – purpose-built but cute – at the foot of a small area of slopes (half the size of Killington, in New England)

COSTS

① ② ③ ④ ⑤ ⑥

RATINGS

The slopes

Fast lifts	****
Snow	****
Extent	*
Expert	**
Intermediate	***
Beginner	****
Convenience	****
Queues	***
Mountain restaurants	**

The rest

Scenery	***
Resort charm	****
Off-slope	***

NEWS

For 2005/06 the Versant Nord Chalet gained a new terrace. The Nansen green trail was improved, and a new restaurant opened in town.

696

+ Charming purpose-built core village
+ Good snow reliability with extensive artificial back-up
+ Some good runs for all abilities

− Very limited area for piste-bashers
− Can be perishingly cold in midwinter
− Weekend queues and overcrowding
− Rapid expansion planned

Tremblant is eastern Canada's main destination resort and attracts quite a lot of Brits. But for keen piste-bashers the limited slopes don't really match the appeal of the cute and lively little core village, built in traditional style and with typical thoroughness by Intrawest.

THE RESORT

Tremblant has been transformed from a local's hill to being eastern Canada's leading destination ski resort. Intrawest (which also owns Whistler and several other North American resorts) developed a purpose-built village in the style of old Québec. Buildings in vibrant colours line narrow, cobbled, traffic-free streets and squares, and it has a very French feel to it. Recent expansion on the edge is not so cute. There's a regular, free ski-bus and a local town service for C$1.

THE MOUNTAIN

In its small area, Tremblant has a good variety of pleasantly wooded terrain.
Slopes A heated gondola takes you to the top, from where there are good views over the village and a 14km/9 mile lake on the so-called South Side, and over National Park wilderness on the North Side (which is really north-east facing and gets the morning sun). A high-speed quad brings you back and there are two other chairs to play on. The slow Edge lift accesses another summit, serving mainly expert terrain. On the South Side (really south-west facing and so good for the pm sun) you can go right back to town on blue or green runs, or use two high-speed quads to explore the top and bottom halves. The Versant Soleil area is more directly south-facing and has one top-to-bottom blue run, all the rest being black runs and tree runs. Free mountain tours go twice daily.
Terrain-parks The excellent 18-acre Gravité terrain-park plus a super-pipe is on the top half of the North Side. There's a mini Gravité park here, too, and a third park on the South Side. The school now offers freestyle classes.
Snow reliability Canada's east coast doesn't get as much snow as the west, but over 75% of the trails are covered by snowmaking. Grooming is excellent.

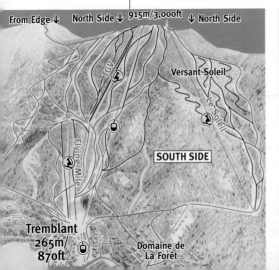

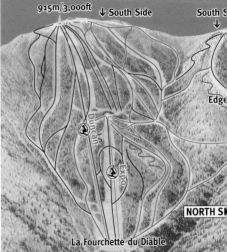

KEY FACTS

Resort	265m
	870ft
Slopes	230-875m
	750-2,870ft
Lifts	13
Pistes	628 acres
Green	17%
Blue	33%
Black	50%
Snowmaking	
	885 guns

Central reservations phone number
Call 425 8681.

Phone numbers
From distant parts of Canada, add the prefix 1 819.
From abroad, add the prefix +1 819.

TOURIST OFFICE

t 681 2000
info_tremblant@
intrawest.com
www.tremblant.ca

Experts Half the runs are classified as suitable for advanced skiers and riders. But we found many of the blacks did not deserve their grading. There are steep top-to-bottom bump runs on the North Side and great gladed tree runs off the Edge lift. The Versant Soleil area has more black runs and some tough runs in the trees. However, the gladed runs really need decent snow, preferably fresh, to be much fun.

Intermediates Both North and South Sides have good cruising and we found the North Side less crowded. There are blue-classified runs in the trees as well as on groomed trails.

Beginners The 2-acre beginner area is excellent, and there are long, easy, top-to-bottom green runs to progress to.

Snowboarding The slopes are good for beginners, but better boarders can't count on fresh natural snow to play in. A specialist shop, Adrénaline, runs a Burton learn-to-ride programme. And there are good terrain-parks.

Cross-country There are around 65km/40 miles of trails, some at the top of the mountain, with great views.

Queues At weekends there can be queues, but they tend to move quickly. We found crowds on the main run back to the village more of a problem.

Mountain restaurants The main Grand Manitou restaurant has good views and decent food but can get crowded.

Many people go back to town for lunch.

Schools and guides Reporters praise the school: 'good instructors and both children made progress', 'excellent – a 4-year-old was skiing greens in a week'.

Facilities for children The Kid's Club offers day care from age 1 to 6 years, until 4.30pm. There's a children's adventure area on the Nansen trail.

STAYING THERE

How to go There's no shortage of packages from the UK.

Hotels and condos The luxurious Fairmont Tremblant and the condos in the Place St Bernard, the Tour des Voyagers and the Chouette have been recommended. But the nearest supermarket is a car- or bus-ride away and there can be long waits between buses.

Eating out Try the Forge, Ya'ooo Pizza Bar, Shack, Casey's and the Loup Garou at the Fairmont. Fat Mardi's (steaks and seafood) is new, has a kids' menu and live jazz music Friday and Saturday evenings. Plus Minus, Spag & Co, Windigo and Restaurant U were recommended by a recent reporter.

Après-ski Octobar Rock is popular with Brits, the Forge is good as the slopes close, the Shack brews its own beer. Or you can chill out in the N'Ice bar – new at the ice hotel last season. There is often live music and a good atmosphere in the main square. There are floodlit slopes some nights.

Off the slopes The Aquaclub La Source pool complex resembles a lake set in a forest, but reporters complain it's pricey (C$13 for three hours). For adults only, the 'excellent' Spa Scandinavie offers sauna, steam room, outdoor hot-tubs and waterfalls. You can also go hiking, ice-climbing, horse-riding, ice skating, snow-shoeing, tubing, snowmobiling, dog-sledding and swimming – and visit Montreal ('highly recommended').

Tremblant

697

Spain

These days it's dangerous to generalise about Spanish resorts – which is why we don't provide the lists of ➕ and ➖ points that we do for other second-division countries. There are now some well-equipped Pyrenean resorts with fine, snow-sure slopes that compare favourably with mid-sized places in the Alps. Two resorts are certainly not downmarket – Sierra Nevada and Baqueira-Beret (see next chapter) are both frequented by the King of Spain. Winter sports are becoming more popular with the prosperous Spanish themselves, and as a result many of the smaller resorts are continually improving.

The general ambience of Spanish resorts is attractive – not unlike that of Italy, with eating, posing and partying taken seriously.

Sierra Nevada (2100m/6,890ft) is in the extreme south of Spain, near Granada (a must-see, and much quieter than in summer), with views from the top to the Atlas mountains in Morocco.

The hub of the resort is Pradollano, a stylish modern development with shops and a few restaurants and bars set around traffic-free open spaces.

Most of the accommodation is in older, less smart buildings set along a road winding up the steep hillside. A two-stage chair-lift also goes up the hillside, with red runs back down to the main lift stations at Pradollano. Choose your location with care.

From Pradollano an old four-person gondola and a newer 14-person one go up to Borreguiles, at the heart of the 84km/52 miles of slopes. Here there are excellent nursery slopes, and lifts going up to the broad upper slopes beneath the peak of Veleta. There are three identifiable sectors, well linked, with a good range of intermediate and easy runs. It is not a big area, and there is not a lot for experts.

Queues can develop at Pradollano and higher up there are quite a lot of slow old lifts that cause queues at peak times. The chair up the village slope gets the biggest queues of all. Most chairs have singles lines, though. The home run can get crowded.

Sierra Nevada's weather is unrelated to that in the Alps. In 1990, when the Alps were famously snowless, Sierra Nevada had the best conditions in Europe. But the World Championships scheduled to be held here in the mid-1990s had to be postponed. Most slopes face north-west, but some get the full force of the afternoon sun. And

when the wind blows, as it does, the slopes close; there are no trees.

There is a group of worthwhile resorts in the western Pyrenees, between Pau and Huesca.

Formigal is only the third-largest ski area in the Spanish Pyrenees (83km/52 miles of runs) but is a favourite with experts for its 22 blacks runs (though many of them could be red). The village, of solidly built oblong apartment blocks, is on the east side of the Tena valley, while all the skiing is on the west side, spreading over a series of side-valleys with north- and south-facing treeless slopes served by 23 lifts. So ski-in/ski-out this is not. The whole thing is really set up for motorists, who can park at one of four lift bases. Sextas, the first and the nearest to the village, has been a mess for some time, but full facilities and a new lift there are promised for 2006/7. Although the top station is only 2,250m/7,380ft, Formigal has a justified reputation for wind. If it gets too bad you can slip down to **Panticosa**, only 10km/6 miles away, where the 34km/21 miles of runs offer something for everybody in a slightly more protected environment.

Candanchu and nearby **Astún**, with almost 100km/62 miles of pistes between them, are popular on the Spanish market. They offer a wide range of lodging set in some of the Pyrenees' most stunning scenery. Candanchu has some tough runs.

The other main group of Spanish resorts is just east of Andorra. The 50km/31 miles of runs at **La Molina** and its purpose-built satellite Supermolina (1700m/5,580ft) are now linked to those of **Masella**, over the mountain, via a gondola and six-pack. The whole area, called Alp 2500, now offers 110km/68 miles of slopes.

698

TOURIST OFFICES

Sierra Nevada
www.sierranevadaski.com

Formigal
www.formigal.com

Candanchu
www.candanchu.com

Astún
www.astun.com

La Molina
www.lamolina.com

REPORTS WANTED

We would welcome more reports on Spanish resorts. If you go there, please do send us a report.

The best reports earn a copy of the next edition, and can lead to free lift passes in future.

See page 12.

Baqueira-Beret

*Spain's leading winter resort, with high, extensive, north-facing
slopes; for Spanish animation, though, stay down the valley*

COSTS

①②③④⑤⑥

RATINGS

The slopes
Fast lifts	**
Snow	***
Extent	**
Expert	***
Intermediate	****
Beginner	**
Convenience	***
Queues	****
Mountain restaurants	**

The rest
Scenery	***
Resort charm	**
Off-slope	*

OUR WEBSITE

Go to our website at
wtss.co.uk for resort
news, links to resort
sites, a build-your-
own resort shortlist
system and reader
forums.

BAQUEIRA TOURIST OFFICE

Tasteful development
spreads up the hill
from 1500 to 1700 ↓

➕	Compact modern resort
➕	Reasonable snow reliability
➕	Some good off-piste potential
➕	Lots of good intermediate slopes
➕	Friendly, helpful locals

➖	Drab blocks dominate the main village, which lacks atmosphere
➖	Resort is not cleverly laid out, and traffic intrudes
➖	Still lots of old, slow lifts

**Baqueira is in a different league from other resorts in the Spanish Pyrenees – a
smart, family-oriented resort with a wide area of slopes that gives a real feeling
of travel. It attracts an almost entirely Spanish clientele (which regularly
includes their royal family), so don't count on English being spoken.**

THE RESORT

Baqueira was purpose-built in the
1960s and has its fair share of drab,
high-rise blocks; these are clustered
below the road that runs through to
the high pass of Port de la Bonaigua,
while the main lift base is just above
it. But up the steep hill from the main
base are some newer, smaller-scale
stone-clad developments. At the very
top is an alternative chair-lift into the
slopes. The most convenient base is
close to the main lifts, but the village
is small enough for location not to be
too much of an issue. There is a lot of
accommodation spread down the
valley, and a big car park with road-
train shuttle up to the lift base.

THE MOUNTAINS

There is an extensive area of long,
mainly intermediate, runs, practically
all of them on open, treeless slopes
and facing roughly west.
Slopes The slopes are split into three
distinct but well-connected areas –
Baqueira, Beret and Bonaigua. From
the base station at Baqueira, a fast
quad which you ride with skis off and
a new parallel gondola take you up to
the nursery slopes at 1800m/5,910ft.
Fast chairs go on up to Cap de
Baqueira. From here there is a wide
variety of long runs, served by chairs
and drags – including a long black
down to Orri. From several points you
can descend into the Bonaigua sector,
leading over to the summit of the
Bonaigua pass. You can ride a chair
from the pass to get to an expanding
area of slopes descending to the east
of the pass and served by a fast quad.
   From the opposite extremity of the
Baqueira sector at Orri a triple chair
takes you off to the Beret sector,
where a series of more-or-less parallel
chairs serve mainly blue and red runs.
A fast quad from Beret accesses a
fourth sector at Blanhiblar, with red
and blue pistes and an itinerary. All
main lift bases are accessible by road.
Terrain-parks There's a terrain-park
with half-pipe in the Bonaigua area.
Snow reliability Most of the slopes are
above 1800m/5,910ft and there is
extensive snowmaking, but afternoon
sun is a problem in spring. We've had
mixed reports of the grooming.
Experts Experts will find few on-piste
challenges, but there are extensive off-
piste opportunities all over the area.
And there are four ungroomed itinerary

699

NEWS

A new gondola out of the village to the main beginner area, opened for 2005/06. A lower stage will now be added, starting at the Val de Ruda complex.

Snowmaking was also increased.

KEY FACTS

Resort	1500m
	4,920ft
Slopes	1500-2510m
	4,920-8,230ft
Lifts	30
Pistes	104km
	65 miles
Green	7%
Blue	51%
Red	34%
Black	8%
Snowmaking	37km
	23 miles

Phone numbers
From abroad use the prefix +34.

TOURIST OFFICE

t 973 639010
baqueira@baqueira.es
www.baqueira.es

runs including the steep and narrow Escornacrabes, from the top of Cap de Baqueira. Cheap heli-lifts are available.
Intermediates It's excellent, with lots of good long runs such as the 4km/2 mile blue from Tuc deth Dossau and some classic reds such as Muntanyo down to Port de la Bonaigua and Mirador above town. Less daring intermediates will enjoy the Beret and Bonaigua areas best.
Beginners There are good nursery runs above Baqueira, recently improved. Some of the longer blues can be a bit tough. Beret has an excellent nursery slope and gentler blues.
Snowboarding The main nursery slopes are served by a drag-lift and moving carpets. Experienced free-riders have plenty of chair-served off-piste.
Cross-country There are 7km/4 miles of trails between Orri and Beret.
Queues Weekdays are quiet and weekend queues seem to have been removed by the new gondola. The Blanhiblar sector is always quiet.
Mountain restaurants All run by the lift company, the huts are said to be 'lacking in number and variety, and very smoky'. Another reader recommends the self-service places at Beret, and the table-service place at 1800m. You can also get table-service at Cap del Port (at the Bonaigua pass), at Baqueira 2200 and at Beret.
Schools and guides The school gets

good reports – some spoken English. Ski Miquel organises lessons with British instructors.
Facilities for children The kindergarten takes very young children but lack of spoken English is a problem. Ski school classes start from age four and there are snow gardens in each sector.

STAYING THERE

How to go There is a reasonable choice of hotels and apartments locally. Ski Miquel has a catered chalet.
Hotels In the main village recommendations include the 4-star Montarto (973 639001) with 'pool and wonderful food' and the 5-star Rafael La Pleta (973 645550), just above the village – 'outstanding rooms and service', 'excellent food'. The Parador (973 640801) down the valley in Arties and the 2-star Husa Vielha (973 640275) in Vielha, 15km/9 miles away, have been recommended.
Eating out The more interesting restaurants are down the valley in Salardu, Arties and Vielha. Reporters have enjoyed the local tapas bars.
Après-ski There are pubs and discos down the valley. Pacha, in the main village, gets going late.
Off the slopes Pool and spa facilities are available in some hotels. Vielha has a sports centre and ice rink.

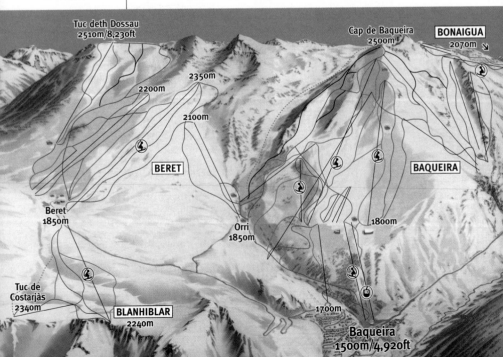

Tuc deth Dossau
2510m/8,230ft

Cap de Baqueira
2500m

BONAIGUA
2070m

2350m

2200m

2100m

BERET

BAQUEIRA

Beret
1850m

Orri
1850m

1800m

Tuc de
Costarjàs
2340m

BLANHIBLAR
2240m

1700m

Baqueira
1500m/4,920ft

Finland

NEWS

In Ruka, for 2005/06 a fast six-seat chair replaced several T-bars on Ruka East. There are more plans to replace T-bars with chairs for the 2006/07 season.

➕ Peace, quiet and Lapp charm

➕ Ideal terrain for cross-country and gentle downhilling

➕ Reliable late snow

➕ Jolly outings

➖ Cold

➖ Small ski areas

➖ Quite expensive

➖ Uninspiring food

For skiers with no appetite for the hustle and hassle of Alpine resorts in high season – perhaps especially for families – escape to the white silence of Lapland may be an attractive alternative. Finland has the lion's share of Lapland and has successfully marketed it, not only for day-trip visits to Santa but also for ski holidays to resorts with limited downhill slopes but limitless cross-country. Of the resorts covered here, only Ruka and Iso-Syöte are south of the Arctic Circle.

The Arctic landscape of flat and gently rolling forest punctuated by many lakes and the occasional treeless hill is a paradise for cross-country skiing. Weather permitting, it also offers good beginner and intermediate downhilling, albeit on a small scale.

The resorts usually open a few runs in late November. For two months in midwinter the sun does not rise – at least, not at ground level. Most areas have floodlit runs. The mountains do not open fully until mid-February, when a normal skiing day is possible and Finnish schools have holidays that usually coincide with ours – a busy time. Finland comes into its own at the end of the season, with friendlier temperatures and long daylight hours. Understandably, Easter is extremely popular, and the slopes are crowded.

Conditions are usually hard-packed powder or fresh snow from the start of the season to the end (early May).

The temperature can be extremely variable, yo-yoing between zero and minus 30°C several times in a week. Fine days are the coldest, but usually the best for skiing: it may be 10 to 15 degrees warmer on the slopes than at valley level. 'Mild' days of cloud and wind are much worse, and face masks are widely sold.

The staple Finnish lift is the T-bar. Ruka has some chairs, and Levi has Finland's only gondola. Pistes are wide, uncomplicated and well maintained, with good nursery slopes. The Finns are great boarders and consider their terrain-parks far superior to those in the Alps; super-pipes are increasingly common.

None of the areas has significant vertical by alpine standards, and in some cases it is seriously limited. The runs are so short that there is no need for mountain restaurants – you are never far from the base, with its shops and self-service restaurant. The ski areas also have shelters or 'kotas' – log-built teepees with an open fire and a smoke hole – where you can eat a snack or grill some food.

Ski school is good, with English widely spoken. All ski areas have indoor playrooms for small children, but they may be closed at weekends.

Excursions are common – husky-sledding, snowmobile safaris, a reindeer sleigh ride and tea with the Lapp drivers in their tent. 'The whole experience is wonderful,' says a typically enthusiastic participant.

Hotels are self-contained resorts, large and practical rather than stylish, typically with a shop, a cafe, a bar with dance floor, and a pool and sauna with outdoor cooling-off area. Hotel supper is typically served no later than seven, sometimes followed by a children's disco or dancing to a live band.

Finns usually prefer to stay in cabins, and tour operators offer the compromise of staying in a cabin but taking half-board at a nearby hotel. Cabins vary, but are mostly spacious and well equipped, with a sauna and heated drying cupboard as standard.

The main resorts are Levi and Ylläs, respectively 17km/10 miles north and 50km/31 miles west of Kittilä, which has direct charter flights from Britain.

Ylläs mountain has two gateways, both 4km/2 miles from the mountain. The minor one is Ylläsjärvi, the major one Äkäslompolo – a traditional

Phone numbers
From abroad use the prefix +358 and omit the initial '0' of the phone number.

TOURIST OFFICES

Levi
www.levi.fi
Ylläs
www.yllas.fi
Ruka
www.ruka.fi
Pyhä
www.pyha.fi
Iso-Syöte
www.isosyote.fi

OUR WEBSITE

Go to our website at wtss.co.uk for resort news, links to resort sites, a build-your-own resort shortlist system and reader forums.

lakeside Lapp settlement. Cross-country skiing makes sense of a resort such as Äkäslompolo, which has 320km/200 miles of trails, transforming it from awkward sprawl to doorstep ski resort of limitless scope. From the lift base trails fan out around the mountain, across the frozen lake and away through the endless forest.

Ylläs is the largest downhill ski area in Finland with 463m/1,520ft vertical. Having lifts and pistes on two broad flanks of the mountain gives plenty of scope for skiers just off the nursery slopes. Second- and third-week skiers will rapidly conquer the benign black runs. Ylläs has a welcoming, snow-encrusted mountain-top restaurant – the highest in the country at 718m/2,360ft.

The Hillankukka log cabins at Äkäslompolo are exceptionally good, but the 10-minute walk to and from meals at the Äkäs hotel (016 553000) is not to be underestimated. A reporter praises the hotel itself – 'beautiful hotel, excellent hydrotherapy pool'.

Levi is a purpose-built village of hotels and cabins at the foot of its slopes: 47 runs served by 26 lifts, including 23 red and five black slopes – one of which hosted a women's World Cup event in 2004. It claims Finland's biggest terrain-park. The daughter of a 2005 reporter loved the resort and 'her skiing improved'. Levi has 230km/143 miles of cross-country trails. Its biggest hotel, Levitunturi (016 646301), was rated 'great' by a recent reporter, with 'excellent' facilities – a pool, tennis, and a children's activity centre. Of the 30 or so restaurants, readers recommend the Steak House, Myllyn Aija ('good value'), Arran and (for a treat) the White Reindeer; and of the bars, Panimo (a microbrewery), Crazy Reindeer (karaoke), Arran ('more sophisticated').

Ruka lies 80km/50 miles south of the Arctic Circle, close to Kuusamo airport and the Russian border, in a region known for abundant and enduring snow. The ski area, on two sides of a single low hill (Ruka East and Ruka West), has a mixture of open and forest terrain, 18 lifts (including one six-pack and four other chairs), and 20km/12 miles of pistes, most covered by floodlighting and snowmaking. There are runs of all colours, but none is steep. A 2006 reporter rates it 'excellent for beginners and intermediates looking for a relaxed atmosphere and blissfully

uncrowded slopes'. But be warned: the vertical is a very modest 200m/660ft. There are of course terrain-parks.

Our reporter was very happy with the ski school, despite having to join a class below his standard.

The cross-country scope is vast: they advertise 500km/310 miles, of which 40km/25 miles are floodlit.

The atmosphere at the resort and on the slopes is upbeat – with live music in the Wunderbar and sun terraces outside the Piste, very popular in spring. Hotels include the Rukahovi (08 85910), only 50m/160ft from the slopes, and the Royal Ruka (08 868 6000), the resort's flagship property. The best accommodation is in cabins. Most of it requires use of the ski-bus service. Good restaurants include Riipinen, which offers capercaillie, bear and boar, Vanha Karhu, and Kalakeidas – an intimate little place doing 'a range of traditional Finnish food, all freshly cooked'. There's lots to do off the slopes, including ice karting and various excursions.

Pyhä, 150km/93 miles north-east of Rovaniemi, has seven lifts (including two chairs) and 10 runs on a mountain, much of which is a National Park. The vertical is only 280m/920ft and there is no steep terrain, but it has good off-piste. The best powder runs are on both sides of a long T-bar on the north slope. The Hotel Pyhätunturi (016 856111) is at mid-mountain.

Iso-Syöte, 150km/93 miles south of the Arctic Circle and 140km/87 miles from Oulu airport, is Finland's southernmost fell region – but it receives the most snow in the country. Catering mainly for families, it suits beginners and intermediates since, of its 12 pistes (covering 20km/12 miles), five are easy and five are intermediate, and there are only two black runs. However, there is a free-ride area among the trees. The runs are short, with the longest 1200m/3940ft and a maximum vertical of less than 200m/660 feet. Seven runs are floodlit at night. There's a terrain-park with boxes and rails plus a super-pipe and quarter pipe, a snow-tubing area and a sledging hill. Cross-country is big here, with 120km/75 miles of trails.

Accommodation is mainly hotels and log cabins, including the Iso-Syöte hotel (0201 476400) at the top of the slopes, with a pool and sauna. You can try snowmobiling, husky safaris, snow-shoeing and reindeer driving.

Norway

COSTS

NEWS

In Hafjell, the ski area north of Lillehammer, massive development is planned for 2006/07. A new eight-seat gondola, a new chair and new pistes are due to be built.

In Geilo for 2005/06 a new spa and fitness centre offering swimming, massage and exercise programmes opened. Snowmaking was increased too.

For 2006/07 an eight-seat chair-lift is planned for the Fageråsen area of Trysil. And a Minipark (children's fun-park), which was started in 2005/06, should be completed this year.

REPORTS WANTED

We would welcome more reports on Norwegian resorts. If you go there, please do send us a report.

The best reports earn a copy of the next edition, and can lead to free lift passes in future. See page 12.

➕ One of the best places in Europe for serious cross-country skiing

➕ The home of telemark – plenty of opportunities to learn and practise

➕ Complete freedom from the glitz and ill-mannered lift queues of the Alps

➕ Impressive snowboard parks

➕ Usually reliable snow conditions throughout a long season

➖ Very limited downhill areas

➖ Very basic mountain restaurants

➖ Booze is prohibitively taxed

➖ Unremarkable resort scenery

➖ Après-ski that is either deadly dull or irritatingly rowdy

➖ Short daylight hours in midwinter

➖ Highly changeable weather

➖ Limited off-slope activities

Norway and its resorts are very different from the Alps, or indeed the Rockies. Some people find the place very much to their taste. For downhillers who dislike the usual ski-resort trappings and prefer a simpler approach to winter holidays, it could be just the place. For families with young children, in particular, the drawbacks are less pronounced than for others; you'll have no trouble finding junk food to please the kids – the mountain restaurants serve little else.

Speaking for ourselves, any one of the first three ➖ points we've listed above would probably be enough to put us off. Combine these in a single destination – then add in the other non-trivial negative points – and you can count us out.

There is a traditional friendship between Norway and Britain, and English is widely spoken.

For the Norwegians and Swedes, skiing is a weekend rather than a special holiday activity, and not an occasion for extravagance. So at lunchtime they tend to haul sandwiches out of their backpacks as we might while walking the Pennine Way, and in the evening they cook in their apartments. Don't expect a tempting choice of restaurants.

The Norwegians have a problem with alcohol. Walk into an après-ski bar at 5pm on a Saturday and you may find young men already inebriated – not merry, but incoherent. And this is despite – or, some say, because of – prohibitively high taxes on booze. Restaurant prices for wine are ludicrous, and shop prices may be irrelevant – Hemsedal has no liquor store. Our one attempt at self-catering there was an unusually sober affair as a result. Other prices are generally not high by Alpine standards.

Cross-country skiing comes as naturally to Norwegians as walking; and even if you're not very keen, the fact that cross-country is normal, and not a wimp's alternative to 'real' skiing, gives Norway a special appeal. Here, cross-country is both a way of

getting about the valleys and a way of exploring the hills. What distinguishes Norway for the keen cross-country skier is the network of long trails across the gentle uplands, with refuges along the way where backpackers can pause for refreshment or stay overnight.

More and more Norwegians are taking to telemarking, and snowboarding is very popular – local youths fill the impressive terrain-parks at weekends.

For downhill skiing, the country isn't nearly so attractive. Despite the fact that it is able to hold downhill races, Norway's Alpine areas are of limited appeal. The most rewarding resort is **Hemsedal**, covered in the next chapter.

Just 20 minutes from the centre of Oslo on an extension of the underground system is **Tryvann** (150m/490ft), a small area popular with the locals. The slopes are near the top station (525m/1720ft) on Holmenkollen. The main slopes – with a vertical of 380m/1,250ft – are served by two drags and two chairs, one of them fast. Two drags serve a separate nursery slope. There's a good terrain-park and a half-pipe. The whole area has snowmaking and can offer good conditions even when downtown Oslo has no snow in the streets. The slopes are floodlit until 10pm most evenings –

Phone numbers
From abroad use the
prefix +47.

and are busier then than in the day.

The site of the 1994 Olympics, the little lakeside town of **Lillehammer**, is not actually a downhill resort at all. The Olympic slalom events were held 15km/9 miles north at Hafjell (230m/ 750ft). This is a worthwhile little area with a vertical of 830m/2,720ft, 13 lifts, including a new eight-person gondola planned for 2006/07, plus a new chair and pistes. At the moment pistes total 33km/21 miles. The downhill and super-G races went to Kvitfjell, about 35km/22 miles further north, developed specially for the purpose. It's steeper but smaller – 18km/11 miles of pistes.

Norway's other internationally known resort is **Geilo** (800m/2,620ft). This is a small, quiet, unspoiled community on the railway line from Bergen, on the coast, to Oslo. It provides all the basics of a resort – a handful of cafes and shops around the railway station, a dozen hotels more widely spread around the wide valley, children's facilities and a sports centre.

Geilo is a superb cross-country resort. As the Bergen-Oslo railway runs through the town it is possible to go for long tours and return by train.

Geilo is very limited for downhillers, but it does claim to have Scandinavia's only super-pipe. The 32km/20 miles of piste are spread over two small hills – one, Geilolia, a bus-ride away from Geilo, with a good, informal hotel, a restaurant at its foot and a pizzeria on the mountain. This area was extended two seasons ago by a six-pack link to the family beginners' zone. None of the runs is really difficult.

Clearly the best hotel, and one of the attractions of staying in Geilo, is the Dr Holms Hotel (call central reservations on 320 95940) – smartly white-painted outside, beautifully furnished and spacious inside. This is the centre for après-ski, but prices are steep. The resort is quiet at the end of

the day, but the main hotels provide live entertainment.

On the edge of the beautiful Jotunheimen National Park, about 225km/140 miles north-west of Oslo, lies the small resort of **Beitostølen** (750m/2,460ft). The 12 slopes are best suited to beginners and early intermediates. Confident intermediates and experts will find more of a challenge at the Alpine Centre, 6km/ 4 miles away, where they will find blacks, moguls and off-piste. There are 150km/93 miles of cross-country, some in the national park.

A long way north of the other resorts is **Oppdal** (550m/1,800ft), with more downhill runs than any of its rivals (55km/34 miles). The total vertical is 790m/2,590ft, but this is misleading – most runs are short.

There are slightly more extensive slopes at **Trysil** (460m/1,510ft), off to the east, on the border with Sweden, and the runs are longer (up to 4km/ 2 miles and 685m/2,250ft vertical). Well suited to families, it has a fast lift to the nursery area and gentle runs to progress to, and a new eight-seat chair is planned for this year (see 'News'). The runs here are all around the conical Trysilfjellet, some way from Trysil itself – though there is some accommodation at the hill.

In complete contrast to all of these resorts is **Voss** (50m/160ft), a sizeable lakeside town quite close to the sea, which a 2006 reporter says is 'friendly, child friendly and has high standards of accommodation'. A cable-car links the town to the slopes on Hangur and Slettafjell, with a total of 40km/25 miles of 'impeccably maintained' pistes and 'no queues'. The ski school is reportedly 'brilliant', with small classes. There are 11km/9 miles of cross-country trails. There are plenty of excursion possibilities, in particular the spectacular Flåm railway.

Hemsedal

The best place for Alpine skiing in Norway (though we prefer the Alps) with the slopes an awkward distance from Hemsedal village

COSTS

① ② ③ ④ ⑤ ⑥

RATINGS

The slopes
Fast lifts	**
Snow	****
Extent	*
Expert	**
Intermediate	****
Beginner	***
Convenience	**
Queues	****
Mountain restaurants	*

The rest
Scenery	**
Resort charm	**
Off-slope	*

NEWS

In the children's area, a new fun-park, tobogganing area and barbecue area were built for 2005/06 and terrain-park improvements included a half-pipe for the beginner park. Snowmaking was increased with more planned for 2006/07.

For 2006/07 a new drag-lift and slope are planned for the children's area.

OUR WEBSITE

Go to our website at wtss.co.uk for resort news, links to resort sites, a build-your-own resort shortlist system and reader forums.

➕ Impressive snow reliability because of northerly location

➕ Increasing amounts of convenient slope-side accommodation

➕ Extensive cross-country trails compared to the Alps

➕ Some quite challenging slopes, and mountains with a slightly Alpine feel

➖ Not much of a village

➖ Limited slopes

➖ Exposed upper mountain prone to closure because of bad weather

➖ Weekend queues

➖ One abysmal mountain restaurant

➖ No liquor store for miles

➖ Après-ski limited during the week and rowdy at weekends

Hemsedal's craggy terrain is reminiscent of a small-but-serious Alpine resort. Most people not resident in Scandinavia would be better advised to go for the real thing, but if you like the sound of Norway, Hemsedal is the place for downhill skiing. Go after the February school holidays, if possible.

THE RESORT

Hemsedal is both an unspoiled valley and a village, also referred to as Trøym and Sentrum ('Centre'), which amounts to very little – a couple of apartment/hotel buildings, a few shops, a bank and a petrol station (but, note, no liquor store and a 2006 visitor advises getting money from the two ATMs at lunchtime as they tend to have emptied by evening). Though there has been talk of a lift from Trøym to the slopes, for now the lift base is a mile or two away, across the valley.

There are self-catering apartments and houses beside the slopes (more were built for 2005/06 and even more are planned for 2006/07) in the Skarsnuten area, which is linked to the main network by its own lift and red piste – and in a pleasantly woody separate cluster a walkable distance down the hill from the lifts.

A ski-bus links these points and others in the valley (but a 2006 visitor says it is 'busy, irregular and not suitable for a child's buggy'). It's a 'good 20 minutes walk along a busy road or an expensive taxi-ride into Hemsedal town'. The place is geared to weekenders arriving by car or coach.

THE MOUNTAINS

Hemsedal's slopes pack a lot of variety into a small space. They are shaded in midwinter, and can be very cold.
Slopes With no fewer than four fast

chairs to play on, you can pack a lot of runs into the day. And there's night skiing until 9pm, Tuesdays to Fridays. The lift pass also covers smaller Solheisen, a few miles up the valley. A small supplement is required to ski at Geilo, an hour away.
Terrain-parks There are two terrain-parks ('absolutely fantastic' says a 2006 reporter). The main one has separate sections for advanced and expert jibbers, a half- and two quarter-pipes plus a big jump, rails and boxes. The beginner park was upgraded for 2005/06 and also has a half- and quarter-pipe, jumps, rails and tabletops.
Snow reliability The combination of latitude, altitude and orientation makes for impressive snow reliability – and there's extensive snowmaking.
Experts There is quite a bit to amuse experts – several black pistes of 450m/1,480ft vertical served by a fast eight-seat chair (or the adjacent 'very steep and very bumpy' T-bar) from the

REPORTS WANTED

Recently we have had few reports on this resort. If you go there, please do send us a report.

The best reports earn a copy of the next edition, and can lead to free lift passes in future.

See page 12.

Phone numbers
From abroad use the prefix +47.

TOURIST OFFICE

t 320 55030
info@hemsedal.com
www.hemsedal.com

base (one left as a mogul slope) – and wide areas of gentler off-piste terrain served by drags above the tree line.
Intermediates Mileage-hungry piste-bashers will find Hemsedal's runs very limited. There are quite a few red and blue runs to play on, but the difference in difficulty is slight.
Beginners There's a gentle nursery area for absolute beginners. And there are splendid long green runs – but they get a lot of traffic, some of it irresponsibly fast. Some long blues and reds also suit near-beginners.
Snowboarding There is plenty of free-riding terrain, and some pistes are suitable for carving. The parks are popular and there's a boarder-cross.
Cross-country By Alpine standards there is lots to do – 130km/80 miles of prepared trails in the valley and forest and (later in the season) 80km/50 miles at altitude. There is a special trail map. Most of the trails are a few miles down the valley at the Gravset centre and 12km/7 miles of them are floodlit.
Queues Hemsedal is only a three-hour drive from Oslo, the capital. Good weekend weather fills the car parks, leading to queues for the main access lifts after mid-morning, and possibly for others. But during the week it is quiet. The upper lifts are very exposed, and are easily closed by bad weather, producing crowds lower down.
Mountain restaurants There is one functional self-service mountain restaurant doing dreary fast food, plus two or three kiosks with benches.

Schools and guides Our most recent reporter was greatly impressed: 'Lots of one-to-one, very encouraging.'
Facilities for children The facilities at the lift base are good, with day care for children over three months. But a 2006 reporter complains that 'you can't book in advance and parents are expected to check on their children hourly and provide all snacks and meals'. The kids' nursery slope is admirably gentle.

STAYING THERE

How to go Most of the accommodation is in apartments, varying widely in convenience. Catered chalets are available through certain UK operators.
Hotels The best hotel is the Skogstad (320 55000) in central Hemsedal – comfortable, but noisy at weekends. Other hotels along the valley are used by UK tour operators. The hotel Skarsnuten, on the mountain, is stylishly modern (with no smoking).
Self-catering The Alpin apartments, a walk from the lift base, are satisfactory if you don't fill all the beds. The adjacent Tinden ones are quite smart.
Eating out The Oxon restaurant and bar and Pepe's pizza were recommended by a 2006 reporter.
Après-ski It's minimal in the week, rowdy at weekends and holidays.
Off the slopes Diversions include dog-sledding, tobogganing and snowmobiling. The hotel Skogstad pool is open to the public.

Sweden

NEWS

In the Vemdalsskalet area of Vemdalen for 2005/06 a new skiing area opened with a six-pack, four slopes ranging from expert to beginner and a large terrain-park.

For 2006/07 at Björkliden cat-skiing is planned to take skiers and snowboarders to off-piste areas that would previously have taken four hours' touring.

+ Snow-sure from December to May
+ Unspoiled, beautiful landscape
+ Uncrowded pistes and lifts
+ Vibrant (but regimented) après-ski
+ Excellent cross-country and good range of non-skiing activities

- Limited challenging downhill terrain
- Small areas by Alpine standards
- Lacks the dramatic peaks and vista of the Alps
- Short days during the early season

Sweden's landscape of forests and lakes and miles of unspoiled wilderness is entirely different from the Alps' grandeur and traffic-choked roads. Standards of accommodation, food and service are good and the people welcoming, lively and friendly. There are plenty of off-slope activities, but most of the downhill areas are limited in size and challenge. Sweden is likely to appeal most to those who want an all-round winter holiday in a different environment and culture.

Holidaying in Sweden is a completely different experience, culturally as well as physically, from a holiday in the Alps. The language is generally incomprehensible to us and, although virtually everyone speaks good English, the menus and signs are often written only in Swedish. The food is delightful, especially if you like fish and venison. And resorts are very family-friendly.

Sweden is significantly cheaper than neighbouring Norway, but reporters still complain that beer is £5 a pint, wine £15 a bottle and traditional Swedish restaurants very expensive.

One myth about Swedish skiing is that it is dark. It is true that the days are very short in December and early January. But from early February the lifts generally work from 9am to 4.30 and by March it is light until 8.30. Most resorts have some floodlit pistes.

On the downside, downhill slopes are generally limited in both challenge and extent and the lift systems tend to be dominated by T-bars. But there is lots of cross-country and backcountry skiing. Snowboarding is also popular, with parks and pipes in most resorts.

Après-ski is taken very seriously – with live bands from mid- to late-afternoon. But it stops suddenly, dinner is served and then the nightlife starts. There is plenty to do off the slopes: snowmobile safaris, ice fishing, dog-sled rides, ice-climbing, and saunas galore. You can also visit a local Sami village.

The main resort is **Åre** (see separate chapter). **Sälen** is Scandinavia's largest winter sports area – and is made up of four separate sets of slopes totalling 144km/89 miles of piste. Most slopes are very gentle, suiting beginners and early or timid intermediates best.

Vemdalen has two main areas of slopes 18km/11 miles apart by road. **Björnrike** is great for families, beginners and early intermediates, with nine lifts and 15km/9 miles of mainly gentle pistes. There is a hotel right on the slopes, built in modern style. **Vemdalsskalet** has more advanced intermediate terrain, 11 lifts, 20km/12miles of pistes and a terrain-park. The Högfjällshotell at the base is large and prides itself on its lively après-ski.

Riksgränsen, above the Arctic Circle, is an area of jagged mountain peaks and narrow fjords. The season starts in mid-February and ends in June – when you can ski under the midnight sun.

Björkliden, also above the Arctic Circle, is famous for its subterranean skiing inside Scandinavia's largest cave system. You need to go with a guide.

Ramundberget is a small, quiet, ski-in/ski-out family resort. It gets lots of snow and has 22km/14 miles of pistes.

707

Åre

Sweden's best slopes, strung out along a frozen lake above a small but charming town and with lots of non-skiing activities to try

COSTS

①②③④⑤⑥

RATINGS

The slopes

Fast lifts	**
Snow	***
Extent	**
Expert	**
Intermediate	****
Beginner	****
Convenience	***
Queues	****
Mountain restaurants	***

The rest

Scenery	***
Resort charm	***
Off-slope	***

NEWS

For 2006/07 the Olympia fast chair is due to be replaced by a new 'chondola' with eight-seat chairs and eight-seat gondolas.

The Tott hotel is being renovated with new apartments.

New restaurants and shops are planned for the marketplace.

708

+	Cute little town centre	–	Lots of T-bars
+	Good snow reliability	–	Exposed upper mountain prone to closure because of bad weather
+	Good intermediate and beginner runs		
+	Extensive cross-country trails	–	High winds detrimental to snow conditions
+	Excellent children's facilities		
+	Lively après-ski scene	–	Few expert challenges
+	Lots of off-slope diversions	–	High season and weekend queues

Åre has the biggest area of linked slopes in Sweden and some of its most challenging terrain. But it suits beginners, intermediates and families best. It has a dinky little town centre and a long area of slopes set along a frozen lake.

THE RESORT

Åre is a small town made up of old, pretty, coloured wooden buildings and some larger, modern additions. When we were there the main square had a roaring open fire to warm up by. As well as accommodation in town, there is lots spread out along the valley, with a concentration in the Duved area. All the slopes and accommodation are set on the shore of a huge, long lake, frozen in the winter months.

THE MOUNTAINS

The terrain is mainly beginner and intermediate tree-lined slopes, with a couple of windswept bowls above.
Slopes There are two main areas (linked by an efficient ski bus). The largest is accessed by a funicular from the centre of town or by a six-pack or cable-car a short climb above it. This takes you to the hub of a network of

runs and (mainly) T-bars that stretches for 10km/6 miles from end to end. The cable-car is often shut because it goes to the top of the above-the-tree-line slopes (known as the 'high zone'), which often suffers from howling gales. A gondola also accesses the high zone from a different point. You can get back on-piste right into the town square. A separate area of slopes is above Duved and served by a high-speed chair. There are four floodlit slopes, each open on a different night. A reporter who had suffered altitude problems in the Alps particularly liked the low altitude of the slopes.
Terrain-parks There's a boarder-cross course, a half-pipe and a big terrain-park, plus two parks for novices.
Snow reliability Snow reliability is good from November to May. But high winds can blow fresh snow away. They also mean that artificial snow is often made wet so that it doesn't blow away and it compacts to a hard, icy surface.

REPORTS WANTED

Recently we have had few reports on this resort. If you go there, please do send us a report.

The best reports earn a copy of the next edition, and can lead to free lift passes in future.

See page 12.

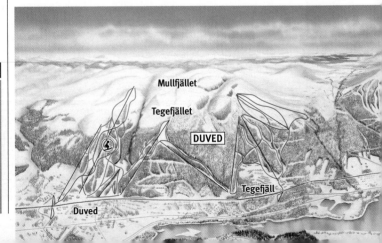

KEY FACTS

Resort	380m
	1,250ft
Slopes	380-1275m
	1,250-4,180ft
Lifts	40
Pistes	97km
	60 miles
Green	12%
Blue	39%
Red	39%
Black	10%
Snowmaking	
	23 pistes

Central reservations phone number
For all resort accommodation call 17700.

Phone numbers
From elsewhere in Sweden add the prefix 0647.
From abroad use the prefix +46 647.

TOURIST OFFICE

t 17720
info@areresort.se
www.skistar.com

OUR WEBSITE

Go to our website at wtss.co.uk for resort news, links to resort sites, a build-your-own resort shortlist system and reader forums.

Experts Experts will find Åre's slopes limited, especially if the 'high zone' is closed. If it is open, there is a lot of off-piste available, including an 8km/ 5 mile run over the back, accessed by a snowcat service in high season. On the main lower area the steepest (and iciest when we were there) pistes are in the Olympia area. There are also steep black and red runs back to town.
Intermediates The slopes are ideal for most intermediates, with pretty blue runs through the trees. Because they tend to be more sheltered, the blue runs also often have the best snow. You can get a real sense of travelling from hill to hill on the main area.
Beginners There are good facilities, both on the main area and at Duved.
Snowboarding There's good varied terrain for boarders, plus three terrain-parks (see above). But there are a lot of drag-lifts (31 out of a total of 40).
Cross-country There's an amazing 300km/185 miles of cross-country trails, both on prepared tracks and unprepared trails marked with red crosses. Some trails are floodlit.
Queues In high season there can be queues for some lifts, especially in the central area immediately above Åre.

Mountain restaurants There are some good ones. Our favourite was the rustic Buustamons, tucked away in the woods near Rödkulleomradret.
Schools and guides The ski school has a good reputation and a 2006 reporter was impressed with his private lesson.
Facilities for children There are special children's areas and under eight-year-olds get free lift passes if wearing helmets. There's a kindergarten that takes children from the age of two.

STAYING THERE

How to go Neilson is the only big UK tour operator to offer packages to Åre.
Hotels The main central hotels are the charming old Åregarden and the simpler Diplomat Ski Lodge. The slope-side Tott has good spa facilities and is being renovated for this year. The Renen in Duved is popular with families and 'well organised with good meals'.
Self-catering There are plenty of cabins and apartments; reporters have recommended the ones at Åre Fjällby.
Eating out The Bistro is good and there are plenty of alternatives, but a 2004 reporter found traditional Swedish restaurants expensive.
Après-ski Après-ski is amazingly lively. The Diplomat is packed from 3pm and has live bands. Later on, the Country Club and Bygget also have live bands and there are plenty of bars for a quiet drink. Reporters recommended the concerts held in igloos by the 'awe inspiring' Tannforsen frozen waterfall .
Off the slopes Lots to do, including dog- or reindeer-sled rides, skating, ice fishing, tobogganing, ice-driving, ice-climbing, snowmobiling (with amazing views) and paragliding. The Holiday Club's facilities are open to non-residents.

Åre

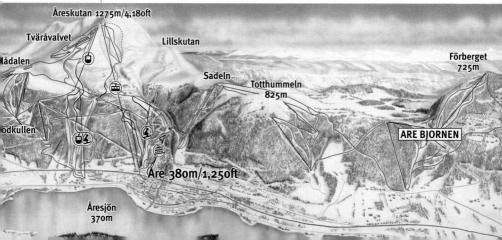

Bulgaria

Bulgaria has traditionally attracted beginners and early intermediates looking for a jolly time on a tight budget. Despite low prices for packages and on the spot, in the past we've found it difficult to recommend the place, because standards were so low. But Bansko, launched on the international scene a couple of seasons ago, has set new standards for Bulgarian resorts (see separate chapter). The long-established resorts of Borovets and Pamporovo are supposedly investing to compete. To judge by reports from readers, they face a struggle to improve not only the infrastructure but also the ambience and the food. There's not a lot they can do about their terrain, and even here Bansko has the edge. What's more, recent visitors have found prices higher than expected – higher than at home, even.

Pamporovo is strictly for beginners and very unadventurous intermediates, with mostly easy runs. Others are likely to find the limited area of short runs inadequate, despite recent expansion. The slopes are pretty and sheltered, with pistes starting at a high point of 1925m/6,320ft and cutting through pine forest. The ski schools are repeatedly praised by reporters – instructors are patient, enthusiastic and speak good English, and class sizes are usually quite small.

The main hotels are in a purpose-built village in an attractively wooded setting slightly away from the slopes – there is a shuttle-bus. The hotel Pamporovo gets the best reports, but the food is reportedly 'very poor'. A new 5-star, the Orlovetz, opened in 2005/06. There is a handful of lively bars and discos, but very few restaurants.

Borovets has more to offer intermediates. The resort is a collection of large, modern hotels in a beautiful wooded setting, with bars, restaurants and shops housed within them. There is a small selection of quirkier bars, shops and eating places.

A long gondola rises over 1000m/ 3,280ft to reach both the small, high, easy slopes of Markoudjika and the longer, steepish Yastrebets pistes. The runs are best for good intermediates. There are no challenges for experts. The slopes are not ideal for novices; nursery slopes are overcrowded, and the step from the Markoudjika blue runs to testing reds is a big one.

Queues for the gondola can be bad once novices are ready to go up the mountain. Grooming is erratic and signing poor. The gondola is said to be prone to closure by wind.

Mountain restaurants are mostly basic but serve decent steaks.

Instructors are generally praised by reporters, but classes can be large.

Most reporters stay at the Rila or the Samokov hotels – both huge and impersonal but with 'good, clean rooms'. Meals at the latter seem to have improved of late, but a 2005 visitor to the Rila chose to eat out at Katy's Steak Pub instead. There are lively bars catering well to an '18-30' type crowd. Tour operator reps organise pub crawls, folklore evenings etc. Excursions to the Rila monastery or Sofia by coach are interesting.

Bansko

Small area of beginner and intermediate slopes served by modern lift system above a rapidly growing resort town and base

COSTS

① ② ③ ④ ⑤ ⑥

RATINGS

The slopes

Fast lifts	****
Snow	***
Extent	*
Expert	**
Intermediate	****
Beginner	**
Convenience	**
Queues	****
Mountain restaurants	***

The rest

Scenery	***
Resort charm	**
Off-slope	*

NEWS

For 2006/07 snowmaking is being extended and there will be a new, much bigger ski hire shop at the base of the gondola to handle the higher visitor numbers Bansko is now attracting. Some existing pistes have been widened for the same reason.

In the longer term more lifts (and hopefully pistes) are planned.

KEY FACTS

Resort	935m
	3.070ft
Slopes	935-2560m
	3,070-8.400ft
Lifts	19
Pistes	65km
	40 miles
Blue	35%
Red	40%
Black	25%
Snowmaking	80 guns

+ Bulgaria's best mountain
+ Efficient lifts with few queues
+ Picturesque town at the base
+ Smart new or renovated hotels
+ Low prices
+ Friendly, helpful locals
+ Cheap and very cheerful traditional restaurants all over the town, but ...

- You may find you want to eat out in those restaurants even if you've bought a half-board package
- Long gondola-ride from the town to the main lift base
- Limited slopes by Alpine standards
- Long airport transfers on poor roads
- Few off-slope diversions

Bansko completed its first season in full operation in 2004/05 and has shown what eastern Europe can offer the skiing world, given a decent level of investment – more than £20 million spent on smart new lifts, snowmaking and even a hands-free lift pass system. Readers are impressed: 'Bansko for us next year,' says one of several highly satisfied reporters – in sharp contrast to reports on the rest of Bulgaria. But the bed-base is expanding rapidly, with many apartments being sold to Brits – let's hope it doesn't become too busy.

THE RESORT

Bansko, set on a flat valley floor circled by spectacular peaks, looks like a giant goods yard on the outskirts – more of an industrial town than a tourist destination. But around the central square the town has a quiet and charming heart, with architecture straight out of Disney's *Beauty And The Beast*. There are few outward signs of commercial tourism here except for hotels, which nestle between homes, shops, restaurants and churches. But a new hub with apartments and hotels is developing rapidly near the gondola base.

For visitors, life in the town revolves around the dozens of mehanas (traditional inns) selling traditional Bulgarian food very cheaply and providing entertainment in the shape of live traditional music. There are lots of little shops, well stocked.

THE MOUNTAINS

Until 2003/04, the drag-lifts and pistes in the Pirin National Park were accessible only by army jeeps and minibuses up a tortuous 12km/7 mile road. Now an eight-seater gondola ferries skiers to the main lift base at Bunderishka. There is a blue piste back to the town, now with snowmaking.
Slopes From Bunderishka two successive fast quad chairs take you up mainly north-facing slopes to the high point of the area. From there you can ski down reds or blues to Shiligarnika, or a red followed by a black (called Alberto Tomba, after the famous Italian racer who opened the revamped ski area) to Bunderishka. There are also a few slopes near the mid-station of the gondola. As we went to press, it was uncertain when the third area with one red run and one chair above Bunderishka was reopening.

Terrain-parks There's meant to be a half-pipe at mid-mountain and a terrain-park near the top, but one reporter questions their existence.

Snow reliability A claimed 80 per cent of the pistes are covered by snowmaking. Together with good grooming (by Bulgarian standards) and north-facing slopes, this means more reliable snow than the Bulgarian norm.

Experts There are no challenging pistes – the one black ought to be red – but there is some good tree skiing.

Intermediates Good medium-to-difficult reds come straight down the face from the top, and varied blues go round to

skiers' right. All in all, there are four or five ways down the 900m/2,950ft vertical of the main area.

Beginners The nursery slopes near the top of the gondola are good, with little through traffic. There are blue runs served by drag-lifts at the top of the mountain and the long ski road back from top to bottom of the gondola is gentle and easy if the snow is good.

Queues 2006 reporters complained of some queues for the main gondola on Sunday mornings – otherwise, no problems. Alongside all the new chairs there are still some old drag-lifts, which can break down.

Mountain restaurants A fair sprinkling, including some modern ones with outdoor bars. The char-grills they serve are 'delicious and cheap'. The Platoto near the top is reporters' favourite.

Schools and guides The main Ulen school gets good reports: 'Love the ski school here,' says a 2006 reporter, but another said her 10- to 13-year-old children could 'wander freely out of lessons and were put in classes with four- to five-year-olds'.

Facilities for children There is a kindergarten at mid-mountain, with a rope tow outside and satellite TV.

STAYING THERE

How to go Several UK operators feature Bansko.

Hotels There is a growing cluster of new hotels around the gondola station, including the swanky but traditional-style Grand Arena, the more modern Perun and the 'spacious' Lion. Refurbished places include the 'excellent' Pirin, near the town square and the 'wonderful' Strazhite, near the gondola. All these hotels have pools and some spa/fitness facilities. Most central hotels run a shuttle-bus service to the gondola.

Eating out Reporters enthuse about the town's scores of authentic mehanas with roaring fires, attentive waiters, real Bulgarian food and good wine.

Après-ski There are lively bars at the gondola base and new ones keep opening. The Lion pub, B4 and Amigos are popular with reporters, as is the bowling alley at the hotel Strazhite. The nightclub Amnesia is 'good' on some nights, 'empty' on others.

Off the slopes Excursions to the Rila monastery and trips across the border into Greece are possible. The spa at the Grand Arena got a rave review.

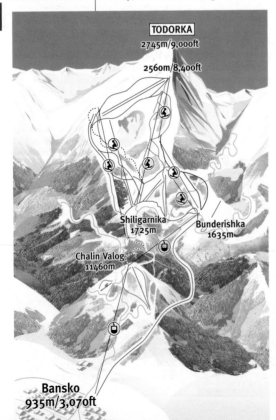

TODORKA
2745m/9,000ft

256om/8,400ft

Shiligarnika
1725m

Bunderishka
1635m

Chalin Valog
1146om

Bansko
935m/3,070ft

Romania

➕ Cheap packages, and extremely low prices on the spot

➕ Interesting excursions and friendly local people

➕ Good tuition, enthusiastic instructors

➖ Primitive facilities – especially mountain restaurants and toilets

➖ Uninspiring food

➖ Very limited slopes – of no interest to anyone other than novices

Romania sells mainly on price. On-the-spot prices, in particular, are very low. Provided you don't have unreasonably high expectations, you'll probably come back from Poiana Brasov content. The real appeal of the place is that it allows complete beginners to try a ski holiday at the absolute minimum cost, and to have a jolly time in the evenings without adding substantially to that cost. Reporters have commented on the friendliness of the people, and most recommend exploring beyond the confines of the resorts.

Romania's main resort – and now the only one featuring regularly in UK package programmes – is **Poiana Brasov** (1030m/3,380ft). It is a short drive above the city of Brasov in the Carpathian mountains, about 120km/75 miles (on alarmingly rough, slow roads) north-west of the capital and arrival airport, Bucharest.

Poiana Brasov is purpose-built, but not designed for convenience: the hotels are scattered about a pretty, wooded plateau, served by regular buses and cheap taxis. The place has the air of a spacious holiday camp, but one that incorporates some serious-sized hotels – some right by the lifts.

The slopes are extremely limited – approximately 12km/7 miles of pistes in total. They consist of decent intermediate tree-lined runs of about 750m/2,460ft vertical, roughly following the line of the main cable-car and gondola, plus an open nursery area at the top. There are also some nursery lifts at village level, which are used when snow permits. There's a terrain-park and half-pipe. Night skiing is also now available. The resort gets weekend crowds from Brasov and Bucharest, and queues can result, but during the week there are few problems.

A key part of the resort's appeal is the friendly and effective instructions.

Hotel standards are higher than you might expect. The linked Bradul (0268 262252) and Sport (0268 262252) hotels are handy for the lower nursery slopes and for one of the cable-cars, and look smart after refurbishment. Guests in both have use of the Sport's sauna/hot-tub/fitness room. The resort's first five-star, the Heraldic Club, opened last season, along with a clutch of four-stars.

Après-ski revolves around the hotel bars, night clubs and discos – supplemented by carnivorous outings to rustic barns with gypsy music. With cheap beer and very cheap spirits on tap, things can be quite lively. Off-slope facilities are limited; there is a good-sized pool, and bowling. Outings to the bars and restaurants of Brasov are recommended. An excursion to nearby Bran Castle (Count Dracula's home) is also popular.

713

Phone numbers
From abroad use the prefix +40 and omit the initial '0' of the phone number.

Slovenia

714

+ Good value for money
+ Beautiful scenery
+ Good beginners' slopes and lessons

− Limited, easy slopes on the whole
− Mainly slow, antiquated lifts
− Uninspiring food, but improving

Slovenia offers good value for money 'on the sunny side of the Alps'. The main resorts are popular with economy-minded British and Dutch visitors and with visitors from neighbouring Italy and Austria, giving quite a cosmopolitan feel.

Slovenia is a small country bordering Italy to the west and Austria to the north. The first state to break away from Yugoslavia, it managed to escape the turmoil that engulfed the Balkans. There is a positive feel to the resorts – along with a warm and hospitable welcome. Prices are low: our latest reporters say drinks are under £1.

The main resorts are within two-and-a-half hours' bus-ride of the capital, Ljubljana. The ski areas are small, with fairly antiquated lifts but few queues. Ski schools are of a high standard and cheap, reputedly with good English. Hotel star ratings tend to be a trifle generous, but standards of service and hygiene are high.

Kranjska Gora (810m/2,660ft) is the best-known resort, a pretty village not far from the Austrian and the Italian borders and dominated by the majestic Julian Alps. The Lek, Kompas and Larix hotels – with pools – are the best placed for slope-side convenience. A reporter enjoyed varied food and 'amazing breakfasts' at the Larix.

There are 30km/19 miles of mainly intermediate slopes, rising up to 1570m/5,150ft. Challenges are largely confined to the World Cup slalom run. Snow reliability is not good, despite snowmaking and a northerly exposure. The lift system is rather antiquated (17

of the 22 lifts are T-bars), but at least queues are rare, except at New Year and on local holidays. There are 40km/25 miles of cross-country trails. Although it is family orientated, there is a selection of bars and discos.

Vogel (1535m/5,040ft), in the beautiful **Bohinj** basin, has the best slopes and conditions in the area. The 18km/11 miles of slopes are reached by a cable-car up from the valley. There's a collection of small hotels and restaurants at the base. Pistes of varying difficulty run from the high point at 1800m/5,910ft back into a central bowl with a small beginner area. When conditions permit, there is a long run to the bottom cable-car station. For a change of scene, **Kobla**, with 23km/14 miles of wooded runs, is a short bus-ride away.

Bled, with its beautiful lake and fairly lively nightlife, is an attractive base. Its local slopes are very limited, but free buses run to Vogel (about 20km/12 miles) and Kobla (a bit nearer).

Slovenia's second city, **Maribor** (265m/870ft), in the north-east, is 6km/4 miles from its local slopes – the biggest ski area in the country, with 64km/40 miles of runs, 28km/17 miles of cross-country and 21 lifts. There are several atmospheric old inns serving good, Hungarian-influenced food.

Scotland

NEWS

The erratic snowfall that is the bane of Scottish skiing has been particularly in evidence in recent years. Last season, a barren start was followed by a bumper period in March-April.

One or two of the lift companies have been through financial crises in recent years, but as far as we can tell all five are likely to operate next season.

- ✚ Easy to get to from northern Britain
- ✚ It is possible to experience perfect snow and stirring skiing
- ✚ Decent, cheap accommodation and good-value packages are on offer
- ✚ Mid-week it's rarely crowded
- ✚ Extensive ski-touring possibilities
- ✚ Lots to do off the slopes

- ▬ Weather is extremely changeable and sometimes vicious
- ▬ Snowfall is erratic, to say the least, and pistes can be closed through lack of snow
- ▬ Slopes are limited; runs mainly short
- ▬ Queueing can be a problem
- ▬ Little ski village ambience and few memorable mountain restaurants

Conditions in Scotland are unpredictable, to say the least. If you live nearby and can go at short notice when things look good, the several ski areas are a tremendous asset. But booking a holiday here as a replacement for your usual week in the Alps is just too risky.

FURTHER INFORMATION

The VisitScotland organisation runs an excellent website at:
ski.visitscotland.com

t 0845 22 55 121
info@visitscotland.com

For novices who are really keen to learn, Scotland could make sense, especially if you live nearby. You can book instruction via one of the excellent outdoor centres, many of which also provide accommodation and a wide range of other activities. The ski schools at the resorts themselves are also very good.

Most of the slopes in most of the areas fall around the intermediate level. But all apart from The Lecht offer one or two tough or very tough slopes.

Snowboarding is popular and most of the resorts have some special terrain features, but maintaining these facilities in good nick is problematic. The natural terrain is good for free-riding when the conditions are right.

Cairngorm is the best-known resort, with 16 lifts and 37km/23 miles of runs. Aviemore is the main centre (with a shuttle-bus to the slopes), but you can stay in other villages in the Spey valley. The slopes are accessed by a funicular from the main car park up to Ptarmigan at 1100m/3,610ft.

Nevis Range opened in 1989 and is the highest Scottish resort. It has 11 lifts in addition to the long six-seat gondola accessing the slopes, and 35km/22 miles of runs on the north-facing slopes of Aonach Mor – Britain's eighth-highest peak. There are many B&Bs and hotels in and around Fort William, 10 minutes away by shuttle.

Glenshee boasts 23 lifts and 40km/25 miles of runs, spread out over three minor parallel valleys. Glenshee remains primarily a venue for day-trippers, though there are hotels, hostels and B&Bs in the area.

Glencoe's more limited slopes (seven lifts, 20km/12 miles of runs) lie just east of moody Glen Coe itself. You have to ride a double chair-lift and a button lift to get to the main slopes, including the nursery area. The isolated Kings House Hotel is 2km/1 mile away.

The Lecht is largely a novices' area, with 12 lifts and 20km/12 miles of runs on the gentle slopes beside a high road pass, with a series of parallel lifts and runs just above the car parks. With a maximum vertical of only 200m/660ft, runs are short. There's extensive snowmaking. And there's a new day lodge at the base. The village of Tomintoul is 10km/6 miles away.

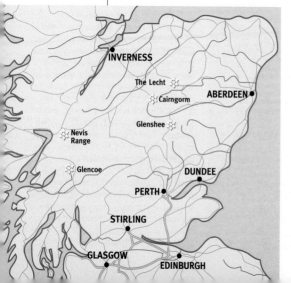

INVERNESS

The Lecht

Cairngorm

ABERDEEN

Glenshee

Nevis Range

Glencoe

DUNDEE

PERTH

STIRLING

GLASGOW

EDINBURGH

Japan

- ➕ Reliable deep powder snow in Hokkaido resorts, lift-served
- ➕ Exotic atmosphere, fabulous food
- ➕ Polite and gracious locals
- ➕ Extremely inexpensive alcohol
- ➕ Night skiing is the norm, allowing a long ski day if you want one

- ➖ The language barrier
- ➖ Expensive – you could get a very indulgent holiday in the Alps for the same cost
- ➖ Lack of off-slope diversions
- ➖ Snowfall can go on for weeks in Hokkaido resorts

Although it is roughly the same size as the British Isles, Japan has hundreds of ski resorts. This season, not for the first time, UK tour operators are showing an interest, going to a couple on the northern island of Hokkaido that have developed something like cult status with keen skiers and riders from Australia, in particular. The reason? Snow – huge and reliable falls of powder snow.

In these remote parts of Japan, hardly anything is written in English and no English-language media are available. Going independently sounds like hard work; but presumably going with a tour operator is not.

There are lots of resorts on the main island of Honshu; only the better-known ones are shown on our map. But the best snow is on Hokkaido ↓

Crystal and Inghams are both offering holidays in two resorts on Japan's northernmost island, Hokkaido: Niseko, the largest resort on the island, and smaller but smoother Rusutsu. You fly in to Sapporo, about two hours by bus from Rusutsu and three hours from Niseko, via Tokyo or Osaka.

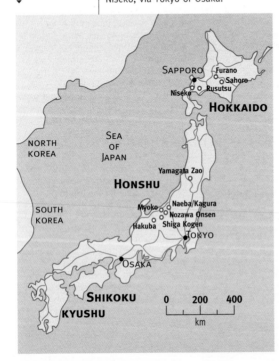

Niseko is made up of three areas of slopes – Grand Hirafu (Hirafu and Hanazono), Annupuri and Higashiyama – with a total of 37 lifts covered by a single pass. The three are linked, but not as efficiently as you might wish. There are modern lifts, but also some old single chairs on upper slopes.

The most popular and easily accessible area, Grand Hirafu, is open from 8.30am to 9pm thanks to what is one of the world's largest – and most heavily used – night skiing operations.

Niseko has a well-deserved reputation for powder snow, which falls almost constantly from December to the end of February. Skiing waist-deep powder is an everyday occurrence. Clearly, this will suit some holiday skiers and not others. Niseko does offer groomed runs, but you can get those closer to home, and get a tan while you ski them. The snow does stop sometimes, and when it does the powder gets tracked out quickly. But it's usually not too long before another snowstorm marches in across the Sea of Japan from Siberia, and the powder returns. The terrain is not steep, disappointing some experts.

The lack of sun has not proved a deterrent to Australians, who now come in their thousands (and, it must be said, are not an entirely welcome presence). For them, guaranteed powder and reasonable costs is an unbeatable combination. For UK-based

No, the skiing doesn't take place on the volcano; the 500-room hotel Prince is at the foot of Niseko's Higashiyama slopes →

TRAVELPLAN AUSTRALIA

KEY FACTS

Niseko
Grand Hirafu (Hirafu and Hanazono), Annupuri and Higashiyama

Vertical	920m	
	3,020ft	
Lifts	37	
Pistes	40km	
	25 miles	
Longest run	5.6km	
	3.5 miles	
Green	30%	
Blue	44%	
Black	26%	

Rusutsu

Vertical	610m	
	2,000ft	
Lifts	25	
Pistes	42km	
	26 miles	
Green	30%	
Blue	40%	
Black	30%	

More information
To really get to grips with the resorts on offer in Japan, spend some time delving into this site:
www.snowjapan.com

TOURIST OFFICES

Hirafu
0136 22 0109
www.niseko-tokyu.co.jp

Higashiyama
0136 44 1111
www.princehotels.co.jp/niseko

Annupuri
0136 58 2080

Rusutsu
0136 46 3331
www.rusutsu.co.jp

travellers, the cost is higher: £1,000 to £1,700 for a week's half-board.

There are several modern ski-in/ski-out hotels at the bases, which is what the UK operators are majoring on. Independent travellers can also stay in the atmospheric potato farming town of Hirafu; the lift bases are well serviced by shuttle-buses. The Australian influx means that Hirafu has developed considerably with many new restaurants, more menus in English and a busier vibe. In the last two years impressive new modern apartments have gone up beside traditional pensions and lodges, raising accommodation standards well above the norm for the simple country town. Demand for accommodation is suddenly so high it has prompted the formation of an Australian company, Harmony Resorts, with a plan to build an 800-bed village at a base area just over the hill from Hirafu.

While there isn't a lot to do outside of ski, eat and drink in Hirafu, the charming little town makes up for its lack of sophistication with a vibrant nightlife and plenty of variety in the way of bars, restaurants and tiny underground-style clubs. There are now a few very upmarket restaurants in town and several chic bars. It is so cold that an igloo-style Ice Bar is dug out of a snowdrift each year, complete with icicles on the roof and a real bar selling all manner of cocktails.

Rusutsu is about an hour from Niseko, and makes a viable day trip from the larger resort. But it also makes an attractive base: the pivotal, self-contained Rusutsu Resort Hotel complex offers a wide choice of good restaurants plus all sorts of other facilities – bars, shopping mall, swimming and wave pool, spas and a fun-park with roller coaster. The snow here can be as good as in Niseko, and it doesn't get tracked out so quickly. The slopes are more limited, but offer slightly more challenge.

One of the main alternatives to these two on Hokkaido is **Furano** – one of the more famous resorts within Japan, capable of hosting World Cup events and offering a tad more vertical than Niseko, at 950m/3,120ft.

The largest ski area in Japan is on the main island of Honshu: **Shiga Kogen**, comprising 21 interlinked resorts and a huge diversity of terrain covered by one lift ticket. It was the site of several major events in the 1998 Winter Olympics.

Hakuba is also handy to reach via train if you find yourself in Tokyo and don't have time for the trip to Hokkaido. It is a group of 10 resorts accessing more than 200 runs amid the rugged peaks of Japan's 'Alps'.

Introduction

717

THE ONSEN EXPERIENCE

Onsen are complexes of hot baths to soak in, showers and communal volcanic thermal pools; they are a key part of Japanese culture and a major part of après-ski. All onsen are basically set up in the same way: men and women shower and bathe in their separate areas. Then, if they wish, they can congregate to soak and drink beer in a communal thermal pool, which more often than not will be outside and surrounded by snow.

Australia

- ✚ Offers skiing and boarding during the European summer
- ✚ In one holiday you can also take in a visit to tropical northern Australia
- ✚ Some of the resorts offer upmarket slope-side accommodation

- ▬ It's a long way from Britain
- ▬ Mountains are rather low, and lift/trail networks are small by Alpine standards
- ▬ Day lift passes are very expensive – up to £38 per day

Even more than New Zealand, Australia offers resorts that are basically of local interest, but which might amuse people with other reasons to travel there – catching up with those long-lost relatives, say. Skiing among snow-laden gum trees is also a unique experience for northern hemisphere skiers, plus there is often the chance to see kangaroos, emus, echidnas and wombats.

The major resorts are concentrated in the populous south-east corner of the country, between Sydney and Melbourne, with the largest in New South Wales (NSW) – in the National Park centred on Australia's highest mountain, Mt Kosciusko (2230m/ 7,320ft), about six hours' drive from Sydney. Skiing has been going on here since the early 1900s – as in the next-door state of Victoria.

The Australian ski season generally runs from early June to mid-October. Traditionally the big snows rarely arrive before late July. In the last few years it has dumped in June, but August and September are the most reliable months. A major hydroelectric company has started a cloud-seeding programme that some people claim was responsible for the bumper falls enjoyed in recent seasons.

Thredbo, established in 1957, is a sophisticated, upmarket Alpine-style village in NSW. It hosted the only World Cup race event held in Australia, thanks to a vertical of 670m/2,200ft.

Thredbo is rather like a small French purpose-built resort – user-friendly, and mostly made up of modern apartments, many new luxury ski-in/ski-out chalets and lodges run by clubs. Originally it had an Austrian flavour but this has now given way to lively, modern, casual-elegant bars and restaurants and increasing numbers of very smart architect-designed apartments. It's a steep place, with stiff climbs to get around from one part to another. Road access is easy, but it costs A$27 a day just to enter the Kosciusko National Park in which the NSW resorts lie.

The slopes, prettily wooded with gum trees, rise up across the valley from the village, served by a regular shuttle-bus through the resort. The runs are many and varied. The dozen lifts include three fast quad chairs, and the trails include Australia's highest (2037m/ 6,680ft) and longest (6km/4 miles). While the blacks are not difficult – except for one called Funnelweb, after Australia's most poisonous spider – on the higher lifts there are off-piste variants, including a beautiful guided backcountry tour to Dead Horse Gap, with transport back to the resort provided. Thredbo's slopes are now dotted with terrain features. New for 2006 is night skiing and a big snowmaking system on the sometimes problematic lower slopes.

There is an attractive pedestrian mall with good shopping and some high-class restaurants – Segreto and Credo are top favourites – both on and off the mountain. There is also an impressive sports training complex open to the public, with an Olympic-size pool. The 700m/2,300ft public bob-sleigh track is popular.

On the other side of the mountain range is the large **Perisher Blue** resort complex, with a pass covering 51 lifts – more than anywhere else in Australia – but a vertical of less than 400m/1,310ft. The main area is Perisher/Smiggins, where lifts and runs – practically all easy or intermediate – range over three lightly wooded sectors. The resort is reachable by road, or by the Skitube, a rack railway that tunnels up from Bullocks Flat and goes on to the second area, **Blue Cow/Guthega**, where the slopes offer more challenges.

Perisher Blue is doing its best to catch up with Thredbo by upgrading hotels and building more facilities. The resort is very spread out and has no central focus, and while a sophisticated pedestrian village has been widely talked about, the project has stalled. Perisher has more ski-in- ski-out accommodation than Thredbo, although it does appeal more to the masses, with its shopping-mall-style village centre filled with every manner of shop, bar and fast food restaurant. Its main advantage over Thredbo is its snow, thanks to its position further within the mountain ranges and its higher altitude. There is a super-sized terrain-park at Blue Cow.

Many on a budget choose to stay in the apartments or hotels in the lakeside town of Jindabyne, a half-hour drive from both Thredbo and Perisher, with a lively youth-oriented nightlife scene. There are also some rather upmarket chalets along the Alpine Way, which leads to Thredbo, the most popular being Lake Crackenback Village next door to the Skitube.

From Perisher, a snowcat can take you on an 8km/5 mile ride to the isolated chalets of Australia's highest resort, **Charlotte Pass** (1760m/5,770ft), with five lifts but only 200m/660ft vertical. People visit the Pass more for its charm than for the skiing. The major hotel is the historic and turreted Kosciusko Chalet, a good spot for romantic weekends. Mt Kosciusko, Australia's highest point, is easily reached on cross-country skis.

If you want to learn to ski among the gum trees at the most affordable price, **Selwyn Snowfields** is your choice. It has 12 lifts, snowtubing and tobogganing and is about an hour from Cooma, near Jindabyne.

In Victoria, resorts are not as high as in NSW but many have good snow. **Mount Hotham** has a justified reputation for good snow and bills itself 'the powder capital of Australia'. An airport just 20 minutes' drive from the ski field makes it the most accessible resort in Australia, with seven 85-minute flights a week from Sydney alone and two from Melbourne. There's an emphasis on attracting the professional Sydney crowd, so there are concierges at the airport to arrange everything during your stay, and some of Australia's most exclusive hotels are now being constructed. The resort's 13 lifts serve a complete range of runs,

with plenty of variety. The longest run is 2.5km/1.5 miles and there is more consistently steep terrain here than at any other area in Australia. A free snowcat service tows skiers out to nearby backcountry slopes. The village is built along the top of a ridge, with the slopes below it. The focus of the village is Mount Hotham Central, with apartments, shops, a few excellent restaurants and now the new White Mountain Spa. Hotham Heights Chalets is a nest of upscale architect-designed multi-storey buildings. You can also stay 15 minutes' drive away at Dinner Plain – stunning architect-designed chalets set prettily among gum trees. There are also a number of restaurants and bars here, and cross-country trails.

There is a six-minute helicopter link from Mount Hotham to another resort nearby (and covered by the same lift pass), **Falls Creek**, that costs all of A$99 return. Falls Creek is the most Alpine of Australia's resorts, completely snow-bound in winter (there are snowcats from the car park). There are 18 lifts, though the area is smaller than Mount Hotham's and the runs are mostly intermediate. There are extensive terrain-park features. Falls Creek has also built a lavish spa to rival Mt Hotham's, called the Huski.

For some, the big attraction at Falls Creek is being able to access Australia's steepest skiing on the adjacent **Mt McKay** – 365m/1,200ft vertical of true black-diamond terrain. Guided snowcat trips take place twice a day. It's well worth the trip.

The other Victorian resort of note is the isolated peak of **Mt Buller**. Only a two-hour drive from Melbourne, this place is a magnet for old money, which has financed a proper sophisticated resort village with a luxury hotel, a pampering spa, Australia's highest cinema complex and even a university campus. Draped around the mountain are 25 lifts – the largest network in Victoria, including 13 chair-lifts. There's a hefty resort entry fee of A$30 and then A$6 to park overnight.

Mt Buffalo is worth visiting, mainly to stay in the historic Mt Buffalo Chalet, with its dramatic views over the craggy Victorian alps. The Chalet, done up in true 1930s style, offers gourmet dining and is improving under new ownership. The slopes, a short drive away, are in an Alpine basin surrounded by boulders, with five lifts almost purely for beginners.

TOURIST OFFICES

Thredbo
www.thredbo.com.au
Perisher Blue
(for Perisher, Smiggins, Blue Cow, Guthega)
www.perisherblue.com.au
Charlotte Pass
www.charlottepass.com.au
Selwyn Snowfields
www.selwynsnow.com.au
Mount Hotham
www.hotham.com.au
Falls Creek
(for Falls Creek and Mt McKay)
www.fallscreek.com.au
Mt Buller
www.mtbuller.com.au
Mt Buffalo
www.mtbuffalochalet.com.au

New Zealand

- ➕ For Europeans, more interesting than summer skiing on glaciers
- ➖ It's a long way from anywhere except Australia
- ➕ For Australians, conveniently close, with flights from Sydney
- ➖ Limited on-mountain restaurants – though these are being upgraded
- ➕ Huge areas of off-piste terrain accessible by helicopter
- ➖ Half-hour-plus drives from accommodation up to the ski areas
- ➕ Some spectacular scenery, as seen in *The Lord of the Rings* movies
- ➖ Highly changeable weather
- ➖ No trees

The number of keen Kiwi skiers and boarders kicking around the Alps gives a clue that there must be some decent slopes back home – and indeed there are. The resorts are different from those of the Alps or the Rockies – generally, you don't stay near the slopes. The networks of lifts and runs are rather limited. But the heli-skiing around the Mt Cook region on the South Island is definitely worth writing home about. For Europeans already spending a lot to travel to New Zealand, the extra cost of a day or two's heli-drops around the Methven area is well worth while.

There are resorts on both North Island and South Island. The main concentration on South Island is around the scenic lakeside resort of Queenstown – see next chapter.

As in the northern hemisphere, the season doesn't really get under way until midwinter – mid or late June; it runs until some time in October. Mount Hutt aims to open first, in mid-May, and disputes the longest-season title with Whakapapa, generally open until mid-November and again in December for Christmas skiing.

Skiing at almost every New Zealand ski resort involves at least a half-hour drive from a nearby town – usually below the snowline – to the ski field itself. Coach transfers from the hotels and towns to the ski fields are generally well organised. The ski field will have a base lodge, usually with a restaurant and a cafeteria, equipment rental and one or two shops, as well as the main lifts. The only on-snow accommodation is in smart apartments at Cardrona on the South Island, and some private lodges at the base of Whakapapa on the North Island.

In what follows, we describe the most prominent resorts (apart from Queenstown and its mountains), but there are other possibilities.

Any of the major resorts is worth a day or two of your time if you're in the area and the conditions are right. But

if your credit card is also in good condition, don't miss the heli-skiing; even if you're no expert off-piste, with powder skis it's a doddle, and tremendously satisfying.

Methven Heliski or Wilderness Heliski (03 302 8108) offer the longest and most spectacular runs. Both are operated by the same company, Alpine Guides (based at Mt Cook), but fly to different regions. The cost for about five runs is around NZ$795. There are several other companies operating on South Island. Harris Mountain Heliskiing (03 442 6722), operating out of Queenstown and Wanaka, caters mainly for the large Japanese market, and the three-run days are generally very easy skiing, with long waits between lifts. New two seasons ago was Alpine Heliski (03 441 2300), based in Queenstown, started by a breakaway group from the major Queenstown operation, Southern Lakes Heli-Ski (03 442 6222). Alpine's prices start at NZ$680 for three runs; Southern charges NZ$880 for six runs, or four runs in exciting glacial terrain. Both these companies are more amenable to exciting skiing. Try to leave the arrangements loose, to cope with the changeable weather.

An alternative adventure is to fly by plane to ski down the Tasman Glacier. For two gentle 10km/6 mile schusses down the length of the glacier the cost

Phone numbers
From abroad use the
prefix +64 and omit
the initial '0' of the
phone number.

KEY FACTS

Whakapapa

Altitude	1630-2300m
	5,350-7,550ft
Lifts	14
Pistes	550 hectares
	1,360 acres
Blue	25%
Red	50%
Black	25%
Snowmaking	some

Mount Hutt

Altitude	1405-2075m
	4,610-6,810ft
Lifts	9
Pistes	365 hectares
	900 acres
Green	25%
Blue	50%
Black	25%
Snowmaking	
	42 hectares
	104 acres

Treble Cone

Altitude	1200-1860m
	3,940-6,100ft
Lifts	5
Pistes	550 hectares
	1,360 acres
Green	15%
Blue	45%
Black	40%
Snowmaking	
	50 hectares
	125 acres

Cardrona

Altitude	1670-2060m
	5,480-6,760ft
Lifts	8
Pistes	320 hectares
	791 acres
Green	25%
Blue	55%
Black	20%
Snowmaking	none

is high – about NZ$700 for the day. The main draw is the immense grandeur of the place, along with the flights over stunning blue ice floes. If you're a good skier, you will find the Clarke Glacier four-run day out of Queenstown more satisfying, though priced at $NZ880.

Snowboarding is very popular in New Zealand, and most of the major resorts have special terrain-parks.

Whakapapa (pronounced Fukapapa) is on the slopes of the active volcano Mt Ruapehu, which has occasionally erupted in recent years, leaving the slopes black with volcanic ash. Until the late 1990s the volcano had not caused havoc since the 1950s, when an eruption carried away a bridge.

Mt Ruapehu is in the middle of the North Island and within four hours' drive of both Auckland and Wellington. Whakapapa, New Zealand's largest ski field, is located on the north-facing slopes, with a vertical of 670m/2,200ft served by 14 lifts including one fast quad. Current plans include two new fast lifts for the 2007 season. Terrain is typified by large, wide open cruisers plus challenging off-piste. Next to the base lodge is an extensive beginners' area, Happy Valley, with half-a-dozen rope tows, a chair-lift and snowmaking that allows this particular section to open early in the season. The resort's lifts and runs range across craggy terrain made especially interesting because of the twists, turns and drops of the solidified lava on which it sits. There is a mix of deep gullies, superb natural half-pipes for snowboarders

and narrow chutes. There is a handful of mountain restaurants.

Accommodation is mostly 6km/4 miles away at Whakapapa village, with the best middle-of-the-road property being a motel named the Skotel. There is on-snow accommodation at the base. A complete anomaly in this area of rustic lodges is the Chateau, a hotel in the grand style of the 1920s, with overly high ceilings, sweeping drapes over picture windows, a marble foyer and formal dining room with grand piano. It has just undergone major renovations and extensions.

Worth knowing about is the hike to Mt Ruapehu's fizzing Crater Lake. Ask a ski patrol for directions or, better, talk them into taking you on a guided trip. This involves about a half-hour (500m/1,640ft) hike up from the top of the highest T-bar, and then a long traverse across a large flat tundra-like area. A few lefts and rights and you are staring into the mouth of a volcano. Awesome views and neighbouring volcanos give this area an other-worldly feel.

On the south-western slope of Mt Ruapehu is **Turoa** – now under the same ownership as Whakapapa. You can ski both on the same ticket, which cost NZ$76 last season, the cheapest deal in NZ skiing. Turoa is a fraction smaller, but with an impressive 722m/2,370ft vertical – the biggest in Australasia. The longest run is 4km/2.5 miles. A new fast lift is planned here, too. There's plenty of off-piste scope away from the gentle intermediate runs, plus the chance to ski on the Mangaehuehu Glacier. Accommodation

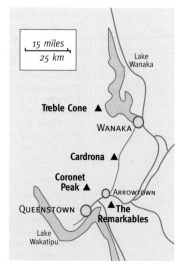

Phone numbers
From abroad use the prefix +64 and omit the initial '0' of the phone number.

TOURIST OFFICES

Whakapapa
t 07 892 3738
info@mtruapehu.com
www.mtruapehu.com

Mount Hutt
t 03 302 8811
service@mthutt.co.nz
www.nzski.com

Treble Cone
t 03 443 7443
tcinfo@treblecone.com
www.treblecone.co.nz

Cardrona
t 03 443 7341
info@cardrona.com
www.cardrona.com

Snow Park
t 03 443 9991
info@snowparknz.com

Waiorau Snow Farm
t 03 443 0300
info@snowfarmnz.com

is 20 minutes away in the funky and lively town of Ohakune, which is well worth a visit.

The South Island has 15 ski areas, including five club fields. **Mt Hutt**, an hour west of Christchurch in the northern part of the island, has a 670m/2,200ft vertical and some of the country's most impressive, consistently steep, wide-open terrain – all within view of the Pacific Ocean. On a clear day you can even see the sandy beaches in the distance beyond the patchwork Canterbury plains – in fact it often snows on the beaches here. The lift system is half the size of Whakapapa's but recently it was totally upgraded and rearranged. The main area is an open bowl with gentle terrain in the centre and the steeper terrain up higher, ringing the skifield.

Mt Hutt has an impressive modern base lodge, including a spacious, welcoming cafe and brasserie with a glorious outdoor terrace, plus a well-stocked rental shop.

Mt Hutt Helicopters (03 302 8401) offers six-run days in the mountains beyond for about NZ$795, or one run on a peak just behind Mt Hutt for NZ$155, with extra runs for NZ$90. The helicopter departs from the heli-pad right in the car park – just wander up to the heli-hut and book in.

There is no accommodation on-mountain – most people stay in the little town of **Methven**, where there are several comfortable up-market B&Bs as well as motels. The very British South Island capital of Christchurch, 90 minutes away, is also an option.

About six hours' drive south of Christchurch is the quiet lakeside town of Wanaka, which is also 90 minutes from Queenstown, and there are two resorts accessible from here.

Treble Cone, 20km/12 miles from Wanaka, has more advanced slopes than any other NZ ski area, plus the advantage of a better lift system. In area, the ski-field comes second only to the North Island fields. Three new runs were added in 2006. There are backcountry ski tours, the only ones out of a resort in NZ, offering powder runs in Treble's back bowls. Back on the ski field, there are two well-maintained intermediate trails, one 3.5km/2 miles, the other 2km/1.2 miles. Both on the main flank and off to the side in Saddle Basin there are long natural half-pipes which are great fun when snow is good, as well as smooth,

wide runs for cruising. Treble Cone is reached by a long and winding dirt track that adds to the excitement, although the new owners are planning to install a gondola from the valley floor. The ski field offers stunning views across Lake Wanaka, with snowcapped Alpine-style peaks in the distance. There's a cosmopolitan cafe at the lift base. An enormous sun deck sharing that view was added in 2004. The food here and at Cardrona is generally better than at other resorts.

Cardrona, 34km/21 miles from Wanaka, is famous for its dry snow and is popular with families due to its superior childcare and teaching facilities. The terrain is noted for its well-groomed, flattering cruisers. But there are some serious if short chutes, and the middle basin, Arcadia, hosts the New Zealand Extreme Skiing Championships. The total vertical is a modest 390m/1,280ft. Millions have been poured into the resort by its family owners over the past few years, resulting in a large base area focused around an odd clock tower. Cardrona is unique in that it has a 1.2km/0.75 mile long terrain-park – the largest in the Southern Hemisphere, with four half-pipes – and right beside it a park for intermediates/learners.

There's a bar and brasserie-style restaurant, a new ski-in/ski-out noodle bar with sun deck overlooking the nursery slopes, large rental facility and a licensed childcare centre, plus 10 modern apartments at the base (but bring all your own supplies). Five of the apartments were new in 2006. Learners are looked after well, with three moving carpets.

Snow Park – a dedicated terrain-park on the South Island dead opposite Cardrona – is really making waves and attracting the cream of international free-ride skiers and snowboarders. Snow Park is in its fourth season and provides world-class kickers, table-tops, rails, slides and the rest. A proper restaurant and bar have now been built.

Nearby, at a height of 1500m/4,920ft, is New Zealand's only cross-country ski area, the **Waiorau Snow Farm**, a beautiful place with 55km/34 miles of what the owners claim are the best-prepared trails in the world. There are classic and skating lanes on all trails, designed for all levels. Accommodation is in the older-style Snow Farm Alpine Lodge.

Queenstown

A lively lakeside year-round resort, famous for its adrenalin-rush activities and well placed for a range of South Island resorts

➕ For Europeans, more interesting than summer skiing on glaciers

➕ Huge areas of off-piste terrain accessible by helicopters

➕ Lots to do off the slopes, especially for adrenalin junkies

➕ Lively town, with lots going on and good restaurants

➕ Grand views locally, and the spectacular 'fjord' country nearby

➖ Slopes (in two separate areas locally) are a drive from town

➖ Limited lift-served slopes in each area

➖ It's a long way from anywhere except Australia

➖ Highly changeable weather

➖ No trees, so skiing in bad weather is virtually impossible

If you want a single destination in New Zealand – as opposed to visiting a few different mountains on your travels – Queenstown is probably it, especially if you can cope with the cost of a few heli-drops. Although the resorts of North Island are impressive, the Southern Alps are, in the end, more compelling – and their resorts are free of volcanic interruptions. From Queenstown you have a choice of the two local ski areas – Coronet Peak and The Remarkables – plus the option of an outing to Treble Cone – the mountain to visit if you are an advanced-to-expert skier – and Cardrona, perhaps with a few nights in Wanaka. There are direct flights to Queenstown from Sydney, Brisbane and Melbourne.

THE RESORT

Queenstown is a winter-and-summer resort on the shore of Lake Wakatipu. (There is a map of the area in the introductory chapter on New Zealand.) Although the setting is splendid, with views to the peaks of the aptly named Remarkables range beyond the lake, the town itself is no great beauty – it has grown up to meet tourists' needs, and has a very commercial feel. Shopping is good, of course, as are the many wineries and cheese factories that are well worth a visit.

In recent years much effort has been put into smartening up the town, with such additions as the classy Steamer Wharf; the many new lakeside luxury apartments and hotels include the boutique Spire Hotel and the Sofitel Queenstown. It has a lively, relaxed feel, and makes a satisfactory base, with more than 160 licensed bars and cafes, some good restaurants, and lots of touristy clothes shops. There are no less than 173 activity operators in town; it's the base for every kind of adventure activity, offering bungee jumping, jet boating, river surfing, horse-trekking.

There are four lift-served mountains – all small by Alpine standards – that

you can get to from Queenstown. The two described here – Coronet Peak and The Remarkables – are close by (about a 30-minute drive). The others – Treble Cone and Cardrona – are at least 90 minutes away, near Wanaka – a much quieter town in another beautiful lakeside setting with accommodation. See NZ introduction.

THE MOUNTAINS

At each base area you'll find a mini-resort – a ski school, a ski rental shop, a functional self-service restaurant, but no accommodation except at Cardrona.

All the areas have something for all abilities of skier or boarder, with off-piste opportunities as well as prepared and patrolled trails. They use the American green/blue/black convention for run classification. New last season were the Burton Learn To Ride systems at both The Remarkables and Coronet Peak, designed to turn beginners into life-time skiers and riders.

THE SLOPES
Not the height of convenience – but getting there
The Remarkables, true to their name, are a dramatic range of craggy peaks visible across the lake from some parts

Resort	310m
	1,020ft

The Remarkables

Slopes	1580-1935m
	5,180-6,350ft
Lifts	5
Pistes	220 hectares
	545 acres
Green	30%
Blue	40%
Black	30%
Snowmaking	
	25 acres

Coronet Peak

Slopes	1230-1650m
	4,040-5,410ft
Lifts	6
Pistes	280 hectares
	690 acres
Green	20%
Blue	45%
Black	35%
Snowmaking	
	200 acres

boarding

Boarding is popular in New Zealand, and although the two mountains close to Queenstown don't seem to have quite such a hold on the boarding market as Cardrona (see New Zealand introduction), they have everything you need, including equipment and tuition. You needn't go anywhere near a drag-lift, and there are no flats to worry about except on the lowest green at The Remarkables.

of Queenstown. The slopes are tucked in a bowl right behind the largest visible peak, a 45-minute drive from town. This resort is fine for families and beginners, (though there is limited extreme skiing for experts), with the emphasis on taking it easy and enjoying entertainment on the restaurant's sun decks during the week. Children under 10 ski for free at The Remarkables. The addition of new terrain-parks for both experts and beginners have brought a younger vibe to the mountain in recent years.

Two chairs go up from the base, a fast quad serving easy runs and the Sugar Bowl chair, which accesses mainly long, easy runs plus a couple of black chutes. The terrain-parks have transformed the resort and attracted a whole new market of jibbers. The Shadow Basin chair leads to steeper terrain, including three hike-accessed, expert-only chutes that drop down to Lake Alta, and the Homeward Run – a broad, fairly gentle, unprepared slope down to the resort access road, where a shuttle-truck takes you back to the base.

Coronet Peak, about 25 minutes' drive from Queenstown, is a far more satisfying resort, especially for

intermediates and above. There is some seriously steep terrain for experts. Again, there are three main chair-lifts, including a fast quad that accesses practically all the runs, and new in the 2005 season was a six-seater that opened up more terrain and improved the resort dramatically. A novice trail was added a few seasons ago to appeal to beginner skiers and boarders. The main mountainside is a pleasantly varied intermediate slope, full of highly enjoyable rolling terrain that snowboarders adore, though it steepens near the bottom. A fourth lift, a T-bar, serves another intermediate area to one side. There are also drags for beginners. Night skiing runs from July to September on Fridays and Saturdays only. A couple of seasons ago the resort added 30 new guns on the 1.8km/1.1 mile main trail.

TERRAIN-PARKS
Coronet rules
Coronet Peak has two half-pipes and The Remarkables recently became a competitor in the park market with its super-pipe plus two enormous terrain-parks, new for the 2005 season, one aimed at beginners and the other for intermediate/advanced.

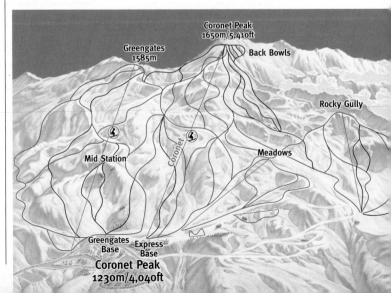

SNOW RELIABILITY
Good overall, but unpredictable
The New Zealand weather is highly variable, so it's difficult to be confident about snow conditions – though the mountains certainly get oodles of snow. The South Island resorts are at the same sort of latitude as the Alps, but are much more influenced by the ocean; fortunately, their ocean is a lot colder than ours. Coronet tends to receive sleet and/or rain even when it's snowing in The Remarkables. But Coronet Peak has snowmaking on practically all its intermediate terrain, from top to bottom of the mountain.

FOR EXPERTS
Challenges exist
Both areas have quite a choice of genuinely black slopes. Coronet's Back Bowls is a seriously steep experts-only area, and there are other black slopes scattered around the mountain. The main enjoyment comes from venturing off-piste all over the place. The Remarkables' Shadow Basin chair serves some excellent slopes. And The Remarkables' hike-up expert chutes are truly world-class.

FOR INTERMEDIATES
Fine, within limits
There's some very enjoyable intermediate skiing in both areas – appreciably more at Coronet, where there are also easy blacks to go on to. But remember: these are very small areas by Alpine standards.

FOR BEGINNERS
Excellent
There are gentle slopes at both areas, served by rope tows, and longer green runs served by chairs. And many other diversions if you decide it's a drag.

FOR CROSS-COUNTRY
Limited
There is a short loop around a lake in the middle of The Remarkables area, but the only serious cross-country area is the elevated plateau of Waiorau Snow Farm, near Cardrona. This is an impressive dedicated cross-country facility with 50km/31 miles of trails.

QUEUES
It depends
Coronet and The Remarkables can suffer a little from high-season crowds – there are certainly enough beds locally to lead to queues at peak times. But these aren't normally a major worry.

MOUNTAIN RESTAURANTS
Er, what mountain restaurants?
Both areas have a simple cafeteria at the base, and Coronet has a brasserie facing the slopes, but nothing up the mountain. The Remarkables cafeteria has a big sunny deck, often visited by the large local mountain parrots, called keas, and entertainment most days.

SCHOOLS AND GUIDES
All the usual classes
The schools are well organised, with a wide range of options, including 'guaranteed' beginner classes.

FACILITIES FOR CHILDREN
Look good
Childcare looked okay to us. At both resorts there is a nursery for children aged from two to five years old. Coronet Peak has a Skiwiland Club for children aged four to six. The Remarkables has Skiwiland for four and five year olds. There's also a wide range of kid's activities on offer each day. The Queenstown nursery can take younger children all day.

STAYING THERE

HOW TO GO
Sheer luxury?
There are lots of big, luxury hotels – all either new or refurbished – built to meet the big summer demand for beds in this popular lakeside resort.
Hotels Some hotels are quite some way from central Queenstown – inconvenient for après-ski unless there's a shuttle-bus. In town they range from the very simple to the glossily pretentious Millennium (03 441 8888) and The Spire (03) 441 0004 – a chic new spot. Azur is the newest high-end luxury lodge with swanky rooms overlooking the lake. Two of the best places to stay are the Heritage Hotel (03 442 4988) or the Mercure Grand Hotel St Moritz (03 442 4990).

EATING OUT
Lots of choice
We're told there are now over 160 bars and restaurants – a quite astonishing figure. Restaurants include Chinese, Italian, Malaysian, Japanese – you name it, Queenstown has it. The Boardwalk in the Steamer Wharf complex overlooking the lake is the place to go for seafood, especially the Wai. Breakfast at Joe's Garage is a must. You might see the famous actor Sam Neil, who's a local. A dining experience with a difference is the Bath House, located in a 1911 Victorian bath house right on the lake shore. Solero Vino has delicious Mediterranean food and a rustic bar, and Dux Deluxe (formerly McNeill's) is an excellent brew-pub with a range of tasty beers, housed in a stone cottage. The Bunker does excellent local cuisine such as Bluff oysters and lamb. Gantley's, in a historic home a little way out of town, is a classic restaurant with the most expensive wine list in the area. At the other end of the scale, pizza-lovers crowd into The Cow, a cosy barn-like place where you sit on logs around a fire waiting for tables or takeaways. Lone Star offers satisfying American-style food.

APRES-SKI
Lively little town
Queenstown has a good range of bars and clubs that stay open late, with disco or live music. Winnebagos is very lively and has a roof that slides back to the night sky to allow the hot and sweaty dance floor a blast of fresh air and even fresh snow. There's a small upmarket casino in the plush Steamer Wharf, which also contains a classy cigar bar and good duty-free shopping.

OFF THE SLOPES
Scare yourself silly
There are lots of scary things to do – see the feature box below. To the west is the spectacularly scenic 'fjord country', and you can go on independent or guided walks. The sightseeing flights by plane or helicopter are to be preferred to the slow bus-ride – weather permitting. A marvellous thing to do is to take the Skyline gondola 400m/1,310ft above Queenstown for the great view; try a spin down the public go-cart track, too. Cruise the lake on an historic steamship or go wine tasting. Arrowtown is interesting for a quick visit – it's a cute, touristy old mining town where you can kit yourself out to go panning for gold. The Winter Festival, in early July, is an annual 'action-packed week of mayhem'.

Phone numbers
From abroad use the prefix +64 and omit the initial '0' of the phone number.

TOURIST OFFICES
The Remarkables
t 03 442 4615
service@theremarkables.co.nz
www.nzski.com

Coronet Peak
t 03 442 4620
service@coronetpeak.co.nz
www.nzski.com

GET THAT ADRENALIN RUSH

The streets of Queenstown are lined by no less than 173 activity operators offering various artificial thrills. We've sampled just a few.

AJ Hackett's bungee jump at Kawarau Bridge is where this crazy activity got off the ground – you plunge towards the icy river, but are pulled up short by your bungee cord and lowered into an inflatable boat. The Shotover Jet Boat experience is less demanding. You get chauffeured at high speed along the rocky river in a boat that can get along in very shallow water, execute high-speed 360° turns and pass very close to cliffs and trees. Fly By Wire, where you swing through a canyon on a cable propelled by a fan engine on your rear, is new and unusual.

The whitewater rafting is genuinely thrilling – and not as uncomfortable as you'd expect, thanks to the full wetsuit, helmet, boots and gloves, and to the exertion involved. The rivers have some exciting rapids. One route even passes through a tunnel excavated in the gold-mining days.

Argentina

- ➕ Varied terrain and excellent off-piste
- ➕ High octane Argentinian buzz
- ➕ Comfortable hotels, good restaurants
- ➕ Favourable exchange rate

- ➖ Remote and inaccessible, even from Buenos Aires
- ➖ Very little English spoken
- ➖ Unpredictable weather, prone to high winds and fierce storms

Although most of South America was colonised by Spain, the invaders' lifestyle only survives in its purest form in Argentina. For preference, Argentinians rise late, drift through the day, dine at 10pm and gamble or party till dawn. The main mountain resorts indulge their taste for luxury hotels, gourmet restaurants and casinos. Music booms out of the bars over the slopes, competing with high-speed conversation and unrestrained laughter. As a bonus, their resort terrain includes some of the most radical in the Southern Hemisphere.

Argentina lies on the eastern, rain-shadowed side of the Andes, a recipe for dry, light powder at high altitudes throughout a season that lasts from June to October.

The premier resort is **Las Leñas**, built by Frenchmen in the 1980s when pyramid architecture ruled. It dominates a white wilderness, miles from civilisation. When it's good, it's as good as it gets, but gales and blizzards can close it down for days, especially during late July and August. A dozen lifts serve well-groomed slopes for all levels, and freestylers can rip it up in the terrain-park and half-pipe. But the attraction for experts is an antiquated double chair called El Marte which, allegedly, accesses more extreme terrain than any other lift on the planet. When the sun shines after a storm, the Argentinians and the Brazilians may still be sleeping, but the American bums are out in force, queuing to make first tracks in the tangle of gullies, drop-offs and bowls in the 1.5km/1 mile long double chute beneath the chair line. Before you go under the rope (this is all out of bounds) you have to sign out. The more adventurous can go east or west along the ridge, for ever more daring routes, or tackle the face of Las Leñas, with a choice of 40 daunting chutes. The smartest hotel at the base is the 5-star Pisces, with a pool, hot tub, sauna and gym. Escorpio is a 4-star option. Late night fun is guaranteed in the Corona Club and the Casino.

San Carlos de Bariloche has almost nothing in common with Las Leñas, except it is Argentina's only other international winter sports option. Founded in 1903 by Swiss and German immigrants on the shores of Lake Nahuel Huapi, it is a substantial resort town with a cheerful lifestyle and is still influenced by the Swiss-German culture – one of the local specialities is chocolate, produced, eaten and drunk in massive quantities. The smart Llao Llao Resort and Spa, on a bluff above the lake, has a pool, sauna and fitness centre, plus free tango, salsa and yoga lessons. The Edelweiss offers top quality facilities in the town centre.

The slopes are at Gran Catedral, 20 minutes away by regular shuttle-bus. They are well below the tree line, and good quality snow cannot be guaranteed. The runs, which are cut through the forest, face east to protect them from the prevailing westerlies and are best for intermediates, though there is some good off-piste. There's a terrain-park and half-pipe. Best avoid August, the Argentinian society choice and therefore prone to long queues.

Cerro Castor, the most southerly city in the world, is a remote outpost just 195m/640ft above sea level. The Beagle Strait off Tierra del Fuego is famously windy, but winter is the calmest period and conditions are often surprisingly good. It has a small ski area with 19 runs but a vertical drop of 770m/2,530ft. The British and other ski teams were well satisfied with the facilities when they trained here in the run-up to the Turin Winter Olympics: where the racers lead, others will surely follow.

Chile

➕ One of the most varied options for the European summer

➕ The Andes are truly spectacular

➕ Good snow records

➕ Good local food and wine

➖ It's a long way from Britain

➖ By Alpine standards, the ski areas are small and resorts lack character

➖ Nightlife is limited

Skiing in the Andes is well worth the long journey. You may plan it as a once-in-a-lifetime experience, but beware: it could become an addiction. Even compared with the Alps, the mountains are outstanding – row upon row of magnificent peaks towering over Chile's narrow coastal plain. There's lots of off-piste and heli-skiing as well as pistes and at least three worthwhile resorts to visit.

Lying in the path of the prevailing winds off the Pacific, the Chilean Andes are ideally located to catch all the snow that's going, resulting in truly dramatic falls in good years. In such a long narrow country, conditions vary considerably from north to south. In general, the season starts in mid-June and finishes in early October, though it can be longer in the south. The ski areas are small in comparison with big Alpine resorts (a keen piste-basher could ski all the pistes in an area in a day) but there's a lot of off-piste available. Adventurous skiers and boarders should sign on for the well-run heli-ski operations, both for the spectacular flights over 5000m/16,400ft peaks and the remote powder fields. We'd recommend visiting two or three ski areas as you are travelling so far.

Valle Nevado (just 60km/37 miles from Santiago), La Parva and El Colorado form the biggest area of linked pistes. **La Parva** is condoville for the capital's elite, a collection of apartments occupied mostly at weekends, while **El Colorado** offers a scattering of accommodation around a shabby base station. Both are linked to **Valle Nevado**, a high-rise, wood-clad tourist development in the mode of Les Arcs, not surprisingly as it was designed by the Chilean architect Eduardo Stern after he'd studied in France in the 1980s. The complex includes restaurants, shops and three hotels arranged around a central sun deck with a circular heated pool surrounded by a glass screen. Although the hotels are of different standards, residents in any of them can use the facilities in the other two and attend free daily entertainment,

ranging from wine tasting to indoor football. The basic packages are half-board and guests can eat in six restaurants, of which the best are La Fourchette d'Or and Don Giovanni.

Valle Nevado is ski-in/ski-out and has a network of well-groomed, mainly intermediate pistes served by 11 lifts including the Andes Express fast quad, the starting point for expeditions to La Parva and El Colorado.

Portillo, 164km/102 miles from Santiago, is the grand dame of Andean skiing, in action since the late 19th century when Norwegian engineers surveyed the Uspallata Pass for the first rail link with Argentina.

The Portillo hotel, an ocean liner of a building that stands alone above the Laguna del Inca, was built in 1949 and is a startling chrome yellow. It attracts a loyal crowd of guests, many of whom return year after year. Its American owner, Henry Purcell, came to work for his Uncle Bob, who'd just bought it, in 1961. Now in his mid-70s, Henry still runs it with his son and wife.

In Portillo, what you see is what you get: no shops, no bars, no restaurants – just a hotel that takes a maximum of 450 guests on a full-board basis. The traditional public rooms are handsomely furnished with polished wood and deep sofas.

Portillo means 'narrow valley', an accurate description of the terrain, which determines the nature of the lift system. The hotel and lake stand between two unconnected areas. Turn right for the El Plateau double chair to Tio Bob's, the only mountain restaurant. Then drop into the rocky jaws of Garganta, the challenging black run back to base, or sweep down the

friendly blue. The Laguna quad chair, on the other side of the hotel, accesses the Juncalillo piste, the longest in the resort. But to stick to the groomers is to miss the point. Portillo has famously radical terrain on both sides of the mountain, but the first challenge is the Va et Vient slingshot lift, Portillo's unique method of scaling the heights. Skiers ride on linked buttons four or five abreast, blasting upwards at high speed to a treacherously steep landing point. From the top of Roca Jack, the longer of the two slingshots, a high traverse, leads to a series of testing chutes. When the lake is frozen, skiers can take the steep powder slopes down to the shore and skate back to the hotel. Then custom dictates a dip in the heated open-air pool, followed by a roll in the massive snow banks around it.

Termas de Chillán is Chile's leading ski and spa resort, in a forested setting and with a small network of lifts under twin volcanoes, one of them still active. It is around 80km/50 miles from the railway station at Chillán, a small town four hours by train to the south of Santiago (or you can fly to Concepcion 195km/121 miles away). You can ski all day and then enjoy a relaxing soak in a thermal pool and a spa treatment to get rid of the aches and pains.

There are three contrasting hotels, all ski-in/ski-out in the right conditions. The opulent 5-star Gran has 120 rooms, two restaurants, a pub, three thermal swimming pools, a spa and a gym. The more easy-going 3-star, Pirigallo, has a thermal pool and a spa, log fires, a restaurant, a pub and a games room. The Pirimahuida is the newest, sleeping 80 guests. In addition to this there are six apartment

buildings, a shop and a clubhouse.

The ski area boasts South America's longest run – 13km/8 miles – and an impressive 1100m/3,610ft vertical. There are blue and red versions of this, which take you well away from the lift system. As well as 33 pistes, there is a lot of off-piste available, including heli-skiing. For freestylers, there's a terrain-park with half- and quarter-pipes, jumps and a fun-box.

The Don Otto double chair, the longest in South America, opens up some short steep descents. And a couple of T-bars that you can reach from it offer more gentle cruising. The El Fresco T-bar to the top accesses the long Tres Marias and Golf cruisers down to the valley floor.

As well as downhill skiing there is cross-country, snowmobiling and dog-sledding.

Like Termas de Chillán, **Pucón**, on the eastern shore of Lake Villarrica, was developed as a summer resort. Skiing began on the Villarrica Volcano in 1948, but the present lift system was installed between 1988 and 1990 on a safer part of the mountain and serves limited terrain for all standards. The climb up to the crater, which requires skins and crampons, takes between two and four hours from the top of the lifts, but it's worth it for the awesome close-up of molten lava. The Gran Hotel Pucón, built in 1934 on the lake shore, is the best place to stay.

Cerro Mirador is Chile's most southerly snow-zone, located 8km/5 miles outside Punta Arenas in the Magellanes National Reserve. It has wooded runs and dramatic views over the Magellan Straits. But it is tiny, with just 11 pistes accessed by a double chair and a T-bar. There is no on-mountain accommodation.

Introduction

729

Reference
section

A classified listing of the names, numbers and addresses you are likely to need.

Tour operator directory 732

Most people still prefer the convenience of a package holiday, which is what most of the companies listed are set up to provide. But note that we've also included some operators that offer accommodation without travel arrangements.

Ski business directory 738

Resort directory / index 745

TOUR OPERATOR DIRECTORY

This is a list of all the UK-based companies we know of that offer ski holidays – mainly but not exclusively package holidays including travel as well as accommodation. Lists of which operators go where are given in the Resort directory / Index right at the back of the book.

360 Sun and Ski
Family holidays in Les Carroz
Tel 0870 068 3180
info@360sunandski.com
www.360sunandski.co.uk

Airtours
Mainstream operator
Tel 0870 241 8964
www.airtoursski.co.uk

Albus Travel
St Anton specialist
Tel 01449 711952
info@albustravel.com
www.albustravel.com

Alpine Action
Chalets in Les Trois Vallées
Tel 01273 597940
sales@alpineaction.co.uk
www.alpineaction.co.uk

Alpine Answers Select
Tailor-made holidays
Tel 020 8871 4656
select@alpineanswers.co.uk
www.alpineanswers.co.uk

Alpine Club
Chalet in St-Martin-de-Belleville
Tel 07977 465285
info@thealpineclub.co.uk
www.thealpineclub.co.uk

Alpine Events
Corporate ski specialist
Tel 0207 622 2265
ski@offsiteevents.com
www.alpineevents.co.uk

Alpine Tours
Group and schools holidays
Tel 01628 826699
sales@alpinetours.co.uk
www.alpinetours.co.uk

Alpine Weekends
Weekends in the Alps
Tel 020 8944 9762
info@alpineweekends.com
www.alpineweekends.com

Alps Accommodation
In Samoëns and Les Carroz
Tel 00 33 688 655070
whereto@alpsaccommodation.com
www.alpsaccommodation.com

Altitude Holidays
Catered chalet in the Alps
Tel 0870 870 7669
info@altitudeholidays.com
www.altitudeholidays.com

AmeriCan Ski
Hotels and apartments in France and North America
Tel 01892 511894
ian@awwt.co.uk
www.awwt.co.uk

American Ski Classics
Holidays in major North American resorts
Tel 0870 242 0623
sales@holidayworld.ltd.uk
www.americanskiclassics.com

Aravis Alpine Retreat
Chalet in St Jean-de-Sixt (La Clusaz)
Tel 020 8282 1650
info@business-retreats.co.uk
www.business-retreats.co.uk

Balkan Holidays
Holidays in Bulgaria, Slovenia, Romania and Serbia
Tel 0845 130 1114
res@balkanholidays.co.uk
www.balkanholidays.co.uk

Barrelli Ski
Chalets in Champagny, Chamonix and Les Houches
Tel 0870 220 1500
chalets@barrelliski.co.uk
www.barrelliski.co.uk

Belvedere Chalets
Specialist luxury chalet operator in Méribel
Tel 01264 738 257
info@belvedereproperties.net
www.belvedereproperties.net

Bigfoot Travel
Variety of holidays in the Chamonix valley
Tel 0870 300 5874
sales@bigfoot-travel.co.uk
www.bigfoot-chamonix.com

Bladon Lines
Chalet arm of Inghams
Tel 020 8780 8800
bladonlines@inghams.co.uk
www.inghams.co.uk

BoardnLodge
Catered snowboarding holidays
Tel 020 7419 0722
info@boardnlodge.com
www.boardnlodge.com

Bonne Neige Ski Holidays
Catered chalets in Méribel
Tel 01270 256966
ukoffice@bonne-neige-ski.com
www.bonne-neige-ski.com

Borderline
Specialist in Barèges
Tel 00 33 562 926895
info@borderlinehols.com
www.borderlinehols.com

Canadian Powder Tours Chalet Holidays
Chalet holidays in Western Canada
Tel 001 250 423 3019
cdnpowder@elkvalley.net
www.canadianpowdertours.com

Canterbury Travel
Holidays in Finland
Tel 01923 457017
reservations@laplandmagic.com
www.laplandmagic.com

Catered Ski Chalets
Catered chalets worldwide
Tel 020 30800200
info@catered-ski-chalets.co.uk
www.catered-ski-chalets.co.uk

Chalet Chocolat
Chalet in Morzine
Tel 01872 580814
info@chalet-chocolat.co.uk
www.skiretreatmorzine.com

The Chalet Company
Catered chalets in Morzine and Ardent (Avoriaz)
Tel 0871 717 4208 /
00 33 450 796840
moran@thechaletco.com
www.thechaletco.com

The Chalet Group
Chalet holidays in Europe and Canada
katie@chaletgroup.com
www.chaletgroup.com

Chalet Gueret
Luxury chalet in Morzine
Tel 01884 256542
info@chaletgueret.com
www.chaletgueret.com

Chalet Kiana
Chalet in Les Contamines
Tel 00 33 450 915518
info@chaletkiana.com
www.chaletkiana.com

Chalet Number One
Chalet in Ste-Foy
Tel 00 33 479 069533
info@chn1.co.uk
www.chn1.co.uk

alpineaction.co.uk
Meribel & La Tania
Chambery flights • Superior chalets with hot-tubs, sauna's and jacuzzi baths • Great locations
01273 597940

Les Chalets de St Martin
Catered and self-catered chalets in St-Martin
Tel 00 33 479 089177
les.chalets@virgin.net
www.leschalets.co.uk

Chalet Snowboard
Snowboard holidays in Morzine
Tel 0870 800 4020
info@chaletsnowboard.co.uk
www.chaletsnowboard.co.uk

Chalet World Ski
Chalets in big-name resorts
Tel 01743 231199
sales@chaletworldski.co.uk
www.chaletworldski.co.uk

Challenge Activ
Chalets and apartments in Morzine
Tel 0871 717 4113
info@challenge-activ.com
www.challenge-activ.com

Chamonix.uk.com
Apartment holidays in central Chamonix
Tel 028 9042 4662
sales@chamonix.uk.com
www.chamonix.uk.com

Chamonix Backcountry
Backcountry skiing in the Chamonix valley
Tel 00 44 1 274 530 313 /
00 33 450 542284
s@mcnab.co.uk
www.ChamonixBackcountry.
com

Le Chardon Mountain Lodges
Val d'Isère
Upmarket chalets in Val-d'Isère
Tel 0845 092 0350
sales@lechardonvaldisere.com
www.lechardonvaldisere.com

Chez Jay Ski Chalets
Chalet in Villaroger (Les Arcs) and Montchavin (La Plagne)
ski@chezjayski.com
www.chezjayski.com

Chill Chalet
Apartments in Bourg-St-Maurice and Morzine
Tel 07931 967861
chris@chillchalet.com
www.chillchalet.com

Classic Ski Limited
Holidays for 'mature' skiers/beginners
Tel 01590 623400
info@classicski.co.uk
www.classicski.co.uk

Club Europe Schools Skiing
Schools trips to Europe
Tel 0800 496 4996
ski@club-europe.co.uk
www.club-europe.co.uk

Club Med
All-inclusive holidays in 'ski villages'
Tel 0845 3676767
admin.uk@clubmed.com
www.clubmed.co.uk

Club Pavilion/Concept Holidays
Budget ski holidays
Tel 0870 241 0427
info@conceptholidays.co.uk
www.conceptholidays.co.uk

Cold Comforts Lodging
Accommodation in Whistler
Tel 0800 404 9297
info@cold-comforts.com
www.cold-comforts.com

Collineige
Chamonix valley specialist
Tel 01276 24262
sales@collineige.com
www.collineige.com

Connick Ski
Chalet in Châtel
Tel 00 33 450 732212
nick@connickski.com
www.connickski.com

Contiki Holidays
Coach-travel holidays for 18-35s
Tel 020 8290 6422
travel@contiki.co.uk
www.contiki.com

Cooltip Mountain Holidays
Chalets in Méribel
Tel 01964 563563
ski@cooltip.com
www.cooltip.com

The Corporate Ski Company
Corporate specialists
Tel 020 8542 8555
ski@vantagepoint.co.uk
www.thecorporateskicompany.
co.uk

Crystal
Major mainstream operator
Tel 0870 160 6040
skires@crystalholidays.co.uk
www.crystalski.co.uk

Crystal Finest
Ski holidays to Europe and North America
Tel 020 8939 0842
info@crystalfinest.co.uk
www.crystalfinest.co.uk

When you book with Equity Ski, please add all these extras: Lunch, drinks. All-in ski holidays. Direct. **www.equityski.co.uk** **01273 298 298** ABTA V5376 · ATOL 2680

CV Travel
Holidays in upmarket resorts
Tel 0870 0623425
cvski@cvtravel.co.uk
www.cvtravel.co.uk

Descent International
Luxury chalets in France and Switzerland
Tel 020 7384 3854
sales@descent.co.uk
www.descent.co.uk

Directski.com
Holidays in Austria, France, Italy and Andorra
Tel 0800 587 0945
sales@directski.com
www.directski.com

Elegant Resorts
Luxury ski holidays
Tel 01244 897333
enquiries@elegantresorts.
co.uk
www.elegantresorts.co.uk

Elevation Holidays
Holidays in the Austrian Alps
Tel 0845 644 3578
info@elevationholidays.com
www.elevationholidays.com

Equity Ski
All-in holidays
Tel 01273 298298
travel@equity.co.uk
www.equityski.co.uk

Erna Low
Hotel and self-catering holidays in the Alps and North America
Tel 0870 750 6820
info@ernalow.co.uk
www.ernalow.co.uk

Esprit Ski
Families specialist in Europe and North America
Tel 01252 618300
www.esprit-holidays.co.uk

The Family Ski Company
Family holidays in France
Tel 01684 540333
enquiries@familyski.co.uk
www.familyski.co.uk

Ferme de Montagne
Chalet in Les Gets
Tel 00 33 450 753679
enquiries@fermedemontagne.
com
www.fermedemontagne.com

Finlays
Mainly chalets in France
Tel 01573 226611
info@finlayski.com
www.finlayski.com

First Choice Holidays and Flghts
Major mainstream operator
Tel 0870 754 3477
sales@fcski.co.uk
www.firstchoice.co.uk/ski

Flexiski
Flexible breaks in chalets and hotels in Europe
Tel 0870 909 0754
reservations@flexiski.com
www.flexiski.com

Friendship Travel
Holidays for singles 25 to 60
Tel 028 9446 2211
sales@friendshiptravel.com
www.friendshiptravel.com

Frontier Ski
Holidays in Canada and Alaska
Tel 020 8776 8709
info@frontier-travel.co.uk
www.frontier-ski.co.uk

Frozenplanet.co.uk
Chalets and apartments, mostly in the Alps
Tel 07947 331606
contact@frozenplanet.co.uk
www.frozenplanet.co.uk

Haig Ski
Hotels with guiding in Châtel and Morzine
Tel 00 33 450 811947
sales@haigski.com
www.haigski.com

Hannibals
Holidays in Serre-Chevalier
Tel 01233 813105
sales@hannibals.co.uk
www.hannibals.co.uk

Headwater Holidays
Cross-country skiing holidays
Tel 01606 720199
info@headwater.com
www.headwater.com

High Mountain Holidays
*Holidays in Les Praz
(Chamonix)*
Tel 01993 775540
info@highmountain.co.uk
www.highmountain.co.uk

Hucksters
Lodges in the French Alps
Tel 01208 821100
info@hucksterslodge.com
www.hucksterslodge.com

Independent Ski Links
*Tailor-made holidays in Europe
and N America*
Tel 01964 533905
info@ski-links.com
www.ski-links.com

Inghams
Major mainstream operator
Tel 020 8780 4433
reservations@inghams.co.uk
www.inghams.co.uk

Inntravel
Cross-country skiing holidays
Tel 01653 617920
winter@inntravel.co.uk
www.inntravel.co.uk

Inspired to Ski
Holidays with tuition in France
Tel 0208 877 5775
sally@inspiredtoski.com
www.inspiredtoski.com

Interhome
*Apartments and chalets in
Europe*
Tel 020 8891 1294
info@interhome.co.uk
www.interhome.co.uk

Interski
*Group holidays with tuition in
Italy*
Tel 01623 456333
email@interski.co.uk
www.interski.co.uk

Italian Safaris
*Italian ski specialists and
multi-resort safaris*
Tel +39 0347 348 5757
info@italiansafaris.com
www.italiansafaris.com

James Orr Heli-ski
*Heli-skiing packages in
Canada*
Tel 01799 516964
james.orr@btinternet.com
www.heliski.co.uk

Jeffersons Private Jet Holidays
Private jet holidays
Tel 0870 850 8181
info@jeffersons.com
www.jeffersons.com

Just Slovenia
Accommodation in Slovenia
Tel 01373 814230
justslovenia@planos.co.uk
www.justslovenia.co.uk

Kaluma Ski
Holidays in the Alps
Tel 0870 442 8044
enquiries@kalumatravel.co.uk
www.kalumatravel.co.uk

Kuoni
Holidays in Switzerland
Tel 01306 747000
switzerland.sales@kuoni.co.uk
www.kuoni.co.uk

Lagrange Holidays
Ski holidays in Europe
Tel 020 7371 6111
info@lagrange-holidays.co.uk
www.lagrange-holidays.co.uk

The Last Resort
*Chalet and apartments in St
Jean-de-Sixt*
Tel 0800 652 3977
info@lastresort.info
www.lastresort.info

Le Ski
*Chalets in Courchevel, Val-
d'Isère and La Tania*
Tel 0870 754 4444
email@leski.com
www.leski.com

Made to Measure Holidays
*Wide variety of tailor-made
holidays*
Tel 01243 533333
sales@mtmhols.co.uk
www.mtmhols.co.uk

Mark Warner
*Chalet-hotel holidays in big-
name resorts*
Tel 0870 899 8813
sales@markwarner.co.uk
www.markwarner.co.uk

MasterSki
Christian holidays
Tel 020 8942 9442
holidays@mastersun.co.uk
www.masterski.co.uk

McNab Snowboarding
*Snowboarding holidays
worldwide*
Tel 01546 830243
info@mcnabsnowboarding.
com
www.mcnabsnowboarding.
com

Meriski
Chalet specialist in Méribel
Tel 01285 648510
sales@meriski.co.uk
www.meriski.co.uk

MGS Ski Limited
Apartments in Val-Cenis
Tel 01799 525984
skimajor@aol.com
www.mgsski.com

Momentum Ski
Tailor-made specialists
Tel 020 7371 9111
sales@momentumski.com
www.momentumski.com

Moswin Tours
Small German programme
Tel 08700 625040
germany@moswin.com
www.moswin.com

Mountain Heaven
*Self-catered accommodation in
La Plagne*
Tel 0151 625 1921
info@mountainheaven.co.uk
www.mountainheaven.co.uk

Mountain Beds
*Tailor-made holidays, mainly
in Verbier*
Tel 020 7924 2650
info@mountainbeds.com
www.mountainbeds.com

Mountainsun Ltd
Chalets in Europe
Tel 07941 196517
mail@mountainsunltd.com
www.mountainsunltd.com

Mountain Tracks
*Ski safaris in Europe and
North America*
Tel 020 8877 5773
info@mountaintracks.co.uk
www.mountaintracks.co.uk

Neilson
Major mainstream operator
Tel 0870 333 3347
sales@neilson.com
www.neilson.com

Optimum Ski
Chalet in Villaroger (Les Arcs)
Tel 08702 406198
info@optimumski.com
www.optimumski.com

The Oxford Ski Company
*Chalets in France and
Switzerland*
Tel 0870 787 1785
rupert@oxfordski.com
www.oxfordski.com

Panorama Holidays
*Budget-oriented holidays in
Europe*
Tel 08707 582518
panorama@phg.co.uk
www.panoramaski.co.uk

Parklife
*Summer boarding camps in
Les Deux-Alpes*
Tel 0208 1334180
info@myparklife.com
www.myparklife.com

Peak Leisure
*Chalets and ski safaris in
France*
Tel 0870 760 5610
info@peak-leisure.co.uk
www.peak-leisure.co.uk

Peak Retreats
*Holidays to the lesser-known
Alpine resorts*
Tel 0870 770 0408
bonjour@peakretreats.co.uk
www.peakretreats.co.uk

Peak Ski
Chalets in Verbier
Tel 01442 832629
peakski@which.net
www.peakski.co.uk

PGL Ski Europe
Specialist in school group holidays
Tel 0870 143 0143
ski@pgl.co.uk
www.pgl.co.uk

PGL Travel
Holidays for teenagers
Tel 08700 507507
holidays@pgl.co.uk
www.pgl.co.uk

Piste Artiste Ltd
Self-catered chalets in Champéry
reserve@pisteartiste.com
www.pisteartiste.com

Powder Byrne
Small programme of luxury hotel holidays in Europe
Tel 020 8246 5300
enquiries@powderbyrne.co.uk
www.powderbyrne.com

Powder Skiing in North America Limited
Heli-skiing holidays in Canada
Tel 020 7736 8191
info@psna.co.uk

Powder White
Chalets in Courchevel, Verbier, Méribel and Val-d'Isère
Tel 020 8355 8836
info@powderwhite.co.uk
www.powderwhite.co.uk

Première Neige
Catered and self catered holidays in Ste-Foy
Tel 0870 383 1000
snow@premiere-neige.com
www.premiere-neige.com

Purple Ski
Chalet holidays in Méribel
Tel 01494 488633
michael@purpleski.com
www.purpleski.com

Pyrenees Ski Experience
Catered chalet holidays in the Pyrenees
Tel 00 33 468 041879
info@pyrenees-ski-experience.com
www.pyrenees-ski-experience.com

Ramblers Holidays
Mostly cross-country holidays
Tel 01707 331133
info@ramblersholidays.co.uk
www.ramblersholidays.co.uk

Re-lax Holidays
Hotel holidays in Switzerland
Tel 020 8367 6633
sarah@re-laxholidays.co.uk
www.re-laxholidays.co.uk

Rocketski
All-in holidays online
Tel 01273 262626
info@rocketski.com
www.rocketski.com

Scott Dunn Latin America
Tailor-made holidays to South America
Tel 020 8682 5030
latin@scottdunn.com
www.scottdunn.com

Scott Dunn Ski
Upmarket holidays
Tel 020 8682 5050
ski@scottdunn.com
www.scottdunn.com

Silver Ski
Chalet holidays in France
Tel 01622 735544
karen@silverski.co.uk
www.silverski.co.uk

Simon Butler Skiing
Holidays with instruction in Megève
Tel 0870 873 0001
info@simonbutlerskiing.co.uk
www.simonbutlerskiing.co.uk

Ski 2
Monterosa specialists
Tel 01962 713330
info@ski-2.com
www.ski-2.com

Ski4you
Accommodation in Europe
Tel 0870 192 1621
enquiries@ski4you.co.uk
www.ski4you.co.uk

Ski Activity
Holidays in big-name resorts
Tel 01738 840888
sales@skiactivity.com
www.skiactivity.com

Ski Addiction
Chalets and hotels in Châtel, Chapelle d'Abondance and Monterosa Ski
Tel 01580 819354
sales@skiaddiction.co.uk
www.skiaddiction.co.uk

Ski à la Carte
Luxury chalet in Alpe-d'Huez
Tel 020 8542 5559
info@skialacarte.co.uk
www.skialacarte.co.uk

Ski All America
US, Canadian and S American holidays
Tel 08701 676 676
sales@skiallamerica.com
www.skiallamerica.com

Skialot
Chalet in Châtel
Tel 020 8363 8326
stuey@skialot.com
www.skialot.com

Ski The American Dream
Major operator to America and Canada
Tel 0870 350 7547
holidays@skidream.com
www.skidream.com

Ski Amis
Catered chalet and self-catered holidays in the French Alps
Tel 020 7692 0850
info@skiamis.com
www.skiamis.com

Ski Balkantours
Holidays in Eastern Europe
Tel 028 9024 6795
mail@balkan.co.uk
www.balkan.co.uk

Ski Barrett-Boyce
Chalet in Megève with tuition
Tel 01737 831184
info@skibb.com
www.skibb.com

Ski Basics
Chalets in Méribel
Tel 01225 444143
sales@skibasics.co.uk
www.skibasics.co.uk

Ski Beat
Chalets in the French Alps
Tel 01243 780405
Ski@skibeat.co.uk
www.skibeat.co.uk

Tour operator directory

Ski Blanc
Chalet holidays in Méribel
Tel 020 8502 9082
sales@skiblanc.co.uk
www.skiblanc.co.uk

Ski Bon
Chalets in Méribel
Tel 07711 008357
sales@skibon.com
www.skibon.com

SkiBound
Schools division of First Choice
Tel 0870 754 3477
sales@skibound.co.uk
www.skibound.co.uk

Ski Chamois
Holidays in Morzine
Tel 01302 369006
sales@skichamois.co.uk
www.skichamois.co.uk

Ski Cuisine
Chalets in Méribel
Tel 01702 589543
info@skicuisine.co.uk
www.skicuisine.co.uk

Ski Deep
Chalets in La Tania and Le
Praz
Tel 01483 722706 /
00 33 479 081905
ferg@skideep.net
www.skideep.net

Ski Etoile
Chalets and hotels in
Montgenèvre
Tel 01588 640442
info@skietoile.co.uk
www.skietoile.co.uk

Ski Expectations
Mainly hotels and chalets in
Europe
Tel 01799 531888
ski.expectations@virgin.net
www.skiexpectations.com

Ski Famille
Family holidays in Les Gets
and Morzine
Tel 0845 644 3764
info@skifamille.co.uk
www.skifamille.co.uk

Ski France
Chalets and catered
apartments in France
Tel 0870 787 3402
ski@skifrance.co.uk
www.skifrance.co.uk

Skifrance4less
Self-catered
apartments/chalets in the
French Alps
Tel 01724 290660
info@french-freedom.co.uk
www.french-freedom.co.uk

Ski Freshtracks
Holidays for Ski Club of GB
members
Tel 0845 458 0784/0208 8410
2022
holidays@skifreshtracks.co.uk
www.skifreshtracks.co.uk /
www.skiclub.co.uk

SkiGower
School trips to Switzerland
Tel 01527 851411
peter@gowstrav.demon.co.uk
www.gowertours.com

Ski Hame
Catered chalets in the Three
Valleys
Tel 01875 320157
powderpigs@skihame.co.uk
www.skihame.co.uk

Ski High Days
Holidays in Italy and France
Tel 0117 955 1814
john@high-days.co.uk
www.skihighdays.com

Ski Hillwood
Austrian, French and Canadian
family holidays
Tel 01923 290700
sales@hillwood-holidays.co.uk
www.hillwood-holidays.co.uk

Ski Hiver
Chalets in Peisey (Paradiski)
Tel 01329 847788
skihiver@wanadoo.fr
www.skihiver.co.uk

Skiholidayextras
Accommodation in France
Tel 0870 787 3402
admin@skiholidayextras.com
www.skiholidayextras.com

Ski Independence
USA and Canada; self-drive to
France and Switzerland
Tel 0845 310 3030
ski@ski-i.com
www.ski-i.com

Ski La Cote
Catered chalet holidays in the
Portes du Soleil
Tel 01482 668357
adrian@ski-la-cote.karoo.co.uk
www.ski-la-cote.karoo.net

Ski Leisure Direction
Mainly self-catering in France
Tel 0870 442 9842
ski@leisuredirection.co.uk
www.leisuredirection.co.uk

Ski Line
Chalet holidays in Europe and
North America
Tel 0870 950 4420
angus@skiline.co.uk
www.skiline.co.uk

Ski Link
Holidays in Courchevel
Tel 0871 218 0174
enquiries@ski-link.com
www.ski-link.co.uk

Ski McNeill
Tailor-made to the US and
European weekends
Tel 02890 666699
contact@skimcneill.com
www.skimcneill.com

Ski Miquel
Small but eclectic programme
Tel 01457 821200
ski@miquelhols.co.uk
www.miquelhols.co.uk

Ski-Monterosa Ltd
Monterosa (Alagna) specialist
Tel richard@ski-monterosa.com
www.ski-monterosa.com

Ski Morgins Holidays
Chalet holidays in Morgins
Tel 01568 770681
info@skimorgins.com
www.skimorgins.com

Ski Morzine
Holiday accommodation in
Morzine
Tel 0845 370 1104
info@skimorzine.com
www.skimorzine.com

Ski 'n' Action
Chalet holidays in Arosa
Tel 00 33 (0) 630 855691
courchevelonions@hotmail.
com
www.ski-n-action.com

Ski Olympic
Chalet holidays in France
Tel 01302 328820
info@skiolympic.co.uk
www.skiolympic.co.uk

Ski Peak
Specialist in Vaujany
Tel 01428 608070
info@skipeak.com
www.skipeak.com

SkiPlan Travel Service
Schools programme
Tel 01273 774778
sales@sts-skiplan.co.uk
www.skiplan.co.uk

Ski Power
Chalets in La Tania and
Courchevel 1650
Tel 01737 823232
info@skipower.co.uk
www.skipower.co.uk

Ski Rosie
Luxury catered chalet in
Morgins and self-catered
apartments in Châtel
Tel 00 33 450813100
rosie@skirosie.com
www.skirosie.com

Ski Safari
Canadian/US specialist, but
also Chile
Tel 01273 224060
info@skisafari.com
www.skisafari.com

Ski Scott James
Chalets in Argentière
Tel 01845 501139
jamie@skiscottjames.co.uk
www.skiscottjames.co.uk

Ski Solutions
Tailor-made holidays
Tel 020 7471 7777
alc@skisolutions.com
www.skisolutions.com

Ski St Anton
St Anton specialist
Tel 01276 61072 /
0871 666 1259
office@skistanton.net
www.skistanton.net

Ski Supreme
Coach and self-drive holidays
to France
Tel 01355 260547
info@skisupreme.co.uk
www.skisupreme.co.uk

Skitopia
Holidays to the southern
French Alps
Tel 01872 272767
jc@tjmtravel.com
www.skitopia.co.uk

Ski Tracer
Holidays in Europe, Canada
and America
Tel 0870 420 5782
info@skitracer.com
www.skitracer.com

Ski-Val
Holidays in France and Austria
Tel 0870 746 3030
reservations@skival.co.uk
www.skival.co.uk

Ski Verbier
Specialists in Verbier
Tel 020 7385 8050
info@skiverbier.com
www.skiverbier.com

Ski Weekend
Weekend and ten-day holidays
Tel 0870 060 0615
sales@skiweekend.com
www.skiweekend.com

Ski Weekends & Board Breaks
Three- and six-day holidays to France
Tel 0870 4423400
sales@skiweekends.com
www.skiweekends.com

Ski Wild
Holidays in Europe and North America; specialise in Austria
Tel 0870 746 9668
info@llgroup.co.uk
www.skiwild.co.uk

Ski with Julia
Hotels and catered chalets in Verbier
Tel 01386 584478
julia@skijulia.co.uk
www.skijulia.co.uk

Skiworld
European and North American programme
Tel 0870 241 6723
sales@skiworld.ltd.uk
www.skiworld.ltd.uk

Ski Yogi
Holidays in Italy
Tel 01799 531886
ski.expectations@virgin.net
www.skiexpectations.com

Sloping Off
Schools holidays by coach
Tel 01273 886888
info@sloping-off.co.uk
www.sloping-off.co.uk

Snowbizz
Holidays in Puy-St-Vincent
Tel 01778 341455
wendy@snowbizz.co.uk
www.snowbizz.co.uk

Snowcoach
Holidays to Austria and France
Tel 01727 866177
info@snowcoach.co.uk
www.snowcoach.co.uk

SnowCrazy
Chalets in La Rosière
Tel 01342 302910
gosnowcrazy@aol.com
www.snowcrazy.co.uk

Snowebb
Catered chalets in Canada
Tel 020 8123 5861/
001 250 765 9058
david@snowebb.com
www.snowebb.com

Snowfocus
Chalet in Châtel
Tel 01392 479555 / 00 33
450 732863
action@snowfocus.com
www.snowfocus.com

Snowgums
Apartments in Briançon (Serre-Chevalier)
Tel 00 33 492 245647
www.alpsholiday.com

Snowlife
Catered chalet in La Clusaz
Tel 01534 863630
info@snowlife.co.uk
www.snowlife.co.uk

Snowline
Chalet holidays in France
Tel 08701 123118
ski@snowlineVIP.com
www.snowline.co.uk

Snow Monkey Chalets
Chalets in Les Arcs, La Plagne and Paradiski
Tel 00 33 611 42 21 61
enquiries@
snowmonkeychalets.co.uk
www.snowmonkeychalets.
co.uk

Snoworks
Holidays with tuition
Tel 0870 1225549
philsmith@snoworks.co.uk
www.snoworks.co.uk

Snowscape
Flexible trips to Austria
Tel 08453 708570
skiandboard@snowscape.
co.uk
www.snowscape.co.uk

Snowstar Holidays
Catered chalets in Tignes
Tel 0870 068 6611
info@snowstar.co.uk
www.snowstar.co.uk

SnowYourWay.com
In Valfréjus (Maurienne) with transport provided
Tel 0870 760 6448
info@snowyourway.com
www.snowyourway.com

Snowy Pockets
Chalet holidays in Arosa
Tel 0247 611 1126
info@snowypockets.com
www.snowypockets.com

Solo's
Singles' holidays, ages 25 to 69
Tel 08700 720700
travel@solosholidays.co.uk
www.solosholidays.co.uk

La Source
Accommodation in Villard-Reculas (Alpe-d'Huez)
Tel 01707 655988
lasourcefrance@aol.com
www.lasource.org.uk

Stanford Skiing
Megève specialist
Tel 01603 477471
info@stanfordskiing.co.uk
www.stanfordskiing.co.uk

St Anton Ski Company
Hotels and chalets in St Anton
Tel 00 43 676 495 3438
jonathanstanton@mac.com
www.atlas.co.uk/ski

Supertravel
Upmarket European and North American holidays
Tel 020 7962 9933
ski@lotusgroup.co.uk
www.supertravel.co.uk

Susie Ward Alpine Holidays
Flexible-length holidays to Châtel
Tel 01872 553055
susie@susieward.com
www.susieward.com

Swiss Travel Service
Hotels in Switzerland
Tel 0870 191 7175
swiss@bridge-travel.co.uk
www.swisstravel.co.uk

Switzerland Travel Centre
Specialists in Swiss resorts
Tel 020 7420 4900
sales@stc.co.uk
www.stc.co.uk

Ted Bentley Chalet Holidays
Chalet holidays in Nendaz
Tel 01934 820854
www.tedbentley.co.uk

Thomson Ski
Major mainstream operator
Tel 0870 606 1470
info@thomson-ski.com
www.thomson-ski.co.uk

Tops Ski Chalets and Hotels
Chalets and hotels in French and Austrian resorts
Tel 0870 240 1133
sales@topstravel.co.uk
www.topstravel.co.uk

Total
Chalet holidays in Europe
Tel 08701 633633
www.skitotal.com

Trail Alpine
Chalet in Morzine
Tel 0870 750 6560
info@trailalpine.co.uk
www.trailalpine.co.uk

Trailfinders
North American programme
Tel 0845 050 5900
www.trailfinders.com

UCPA
Budget trips to France
www.ucpa.com/en

United Vacations Ski USA & Canada
US and Canada programme
Tel 0870 606 1006
info@unitedvacations.com
www.unitedvacations.co.uk

Val d'Isère A La Carte
Specialists in Val-d'Isère hotels and self-catering holidays
Tel 01481 236800
skialacarte@aol.com
www.skivaldisere.co.uk

Vanilla Ski
Chalet in Seez (near La Rosière and Les Arcs)
Tel 01932 860696
sam@vanillaski.com
www.vanillaski.com

VIP
Chalets in Val-d'Isère, Méribel and Zermatt
Tel 08701 123119
ski@vip-chalets.com
www.vip-chalets.com

Virgin Snow
Holidays to America
Tel 0870 220 2707
customerrelations@
virginholidays.co.uk
www.virgin.com/Holidays

Waymark Holidays
Cross-country skiing holidays
Tel 0870 950 9800
enquiries@waymarkholidays.
com
www.waymarkholidays.com

Weekends in Val d'Isère
Weekends – and not just in Val-d'Isère
Tel 020 8944 9762
info@alpineweekends.com
www.alpineweekends.com

White Heat Skiing
Swiss/Austrian trips and tuition
Tel 020 7193 4793
info@whiteheatski.biz
www.whiteheatski.biz

White Roc
Weekends and tailor-made hotel holidays
Tel 020 7792 1188
ski@whiteroc.co.uk
www.whiteroc.co.uk

YSE
Variety of holidays in Val d'Isère
Tel 0845 122 1414
sales@yseski.co.uk
www.yseski.co.uk

SKI BUSINESS DIRECTORY

This is a list of companies and organisations providing goods and services you might find helpful in organising a holiday, grouped under a dozen headings. Tour operators are listed separately, in the previous section, starting on page 732.

AIRLINES

Air Canada
Tel 0871 220 1111
www.aircanada.ca

Air France
Tel 0870 142 4343
www.airfrance.com/uk

Air New Zealand
Tel 0800 028 4149
www.airnewzealand.com

Alitalia
Tel 0870 544 8259
www.alitalia.co.uk

American Airlines
08547 789789 outside London
Tel 0800 435 7300
www.aa.com

Austrian Airlines
Tel 0870 124 2625
www.austrianairlines.co.uk

Bmibaby
Tel 0871 224 0224
www.bmibaby.com

British Airways
Flight enquiries:
0870 55 111 55
Tel 0870 850 9850
www.britishairways.com

Continental Airlines
Tel 0800 231 0856
www.continental.com

Delta Airlines
Tel 0845 600 0950
www.delta.com

EasyJet
Tel 0870 6 000 000
www.easyjet.com

Flybe
Tel 0871 700 0535
www.flybe.com

Helvetic
Tel 0207 026 3464
www.helvetic.com

Jet2.com
Tel 0871 226 1737
www.jet2.com

KLM
Tel 08705 074074
www.klmuk.co.uk

Lufthansa
Tel 0208 750 3460
www.lufthansa.com

Qantas
Tel 0208 222 9199
www.qantas.com.au

Ryanair
Tel 0906 270 5656
www.ryanair.com

Swiss International Air Lines
Tel 0845 601 0956
www.swiss.com

Thomsonfly
Tel 0870 190 0737
www.thomsonfly.com

United Airlines
Tel 0845 844 4777
www.unitedairlines.co.uk

Virgin Atlantic Airways
Flight information 0871
2223767
Tel 08705 747 747
www.virgin-atlantic.com

Zoom Airlines
Flights to Canada
Tel 0870 240 0055
www.flyzoom.com

AIRPORTS

Aberdeen Airport Ltd
Tel 0870 040 0006
www.baa.co.uk

Belfast International Airport
Tel 028 9448 4035
info.desk@bial.co.uk
www.bial.co.uk

Birmingham International Airport
Tel 08707 335511
info@bhx.co.uk
www.bhx.co.uk

Bournemouth International Airport
Tel 01202 364000
feedback@
bournemouthairport.co.uk
www.flybournemouth.com

Bristol International Airport
Tel 0870 121 2747
feedback@bristolairport.com
www.bristolairport.co.uk

Cardiff International Airport
Tel 0800 0199 796
infodesk@cwl.aero
www.cial.co.uk

Dublin Airport
Tel +353 1 814 1111
information@
dublinairport.com
www.dublin-airport.com

Durham Tees Valley Airport
Tel 01325 332811
information@
durhamteesvalleyairport.com
www.durhamteesvalleyairport.com

Edinburgh Airport
Tel 0870 040 0007
www.baa.co.uk

Exeter International Airport
Tel 01392 367433
marketing@exeter-airport.co.uk
www.exeter-airport.co.uk

Glasgow Airport
Tel 0870 040 0008
www.baa.co.uk

Leeds Bradford International Airport
Tel 0113 250 9696
www.lbia.co.uk

London Gatwick Airport
Tel 0870 000 2468
www.baa.com

London Heathrow Airport
Tel 0870 000 0123
www.baa.co.uk/main/airports/heathrow/

London Luton Airport
Tel 01582 405100
info@ltn.aero
www.london-luton.com

London Stansted Airport
Tel 0870 000 0303
www.baa.co.uk

Manchester Airport
Tel 0161 489 3000
www.manchesterairport.co.uk

Newcastle International Airport Ltd
Tel 0870 122 1488
Callctr@
newcastleinternational.co.uk
www.newcastleairport.com

Nottingham East Midlands Airport
Tel 0871 919 9000
enquiries@
nottinghamema.com
www.eastmidlandsairport.com

Southampton Airport
Tel 0870 040 0009
www.baa.co.uk

AIRPORT TRANSFERS

Airport Transfer Service
Tel +33 450 536397
sales@a-t-s.net
www.a-t-s.net

AlpineCab
Tel 00 33 450 731938
info@alpinecab.com
www.alpinecab.com

Flytransfer
Tel 028 9042 4662
info@flytransfer.com
www.flytransfer.com

BREAKDOWN INSURANCE

AA Five Star Europe
Tel 0870 600 0371
customer.services@theAA.com
www.theAA.com

Autohome
Tel 0800 371 280
www.autohome.co.uk

Direct Line Rescue
Tel 0845 246 8702
www.directline.com/rescue

Europ Assistance
Tel 0870 737 5720
customerservices@europ-
assistance.co.uk
www.europ-assistance.co.uk

Green Flag Motoring Assistance
Tel 0845 246 1557
european-
sales@greenflag.com
www.greenflag.com

Leisurecare Insurance Services
Tel 01793 750150

Mondial Assistance UK
Tel 0208 681 2525
enquiries@mondial-
assistance.co.uk
www.mondial-assistance.co.uk

RAC Travel Services
Tel 08705 722 722
traveladmin@rac.co.uk
www.rac.co.uk

CAR HIRE

Alamo Rent A Car
Tel 0870 400 4562
international@goalamo.com
www.alamo.co.uk

Avis Rent A Car
Tel 08700 100 287
customer.service@avis.co.uk
www.avis.co.uk

Budget Car and Van Rental
Tel 0353 906627711
reservations@budget-uk.com
www.budget-uk.com

Europcar UK
Tel 0870 607 5000
reservationsuk@mail.europcar.
com
www.europcar.co.uk

Hertz UK Ltd
Tel 08708 448844
www.hertz.co.uk

Holiday Autos International Ltd
Tel 0870 400 4447
www.holidayautos.com

Suncars
Tel 0870 500 5566
customerservices@
suncars.com
www.suncars.co.uk

CAR WINTER EQUIPMENT

Brindley Chains Ltd
Pewag snowchains
Tel 01925 825555
enquiries@brindley-
chains.co.uk
www.brindley-chains.co.uk

GT Towing Ltd
Ski boxes and snowchains
Tel 01707 287287
sales@gttowing.co.uk
www.gttowing.co.uk

Lakeland Roof Box Centre
Roof boxes, snowchains
Tel 08700 766326
www.roofbox.co.uk

Latchmere Motor Spares
Snowchains, roof bars, ski clamps, boxes
Tel 020 7228 3907

Motor Traveller / Carbox
Thule racks and boxes; Milz snowchains
Tel 01753 833442
info@carbox.freeserve.co.uk
www.carbox.co.uk

The Roof Box Company
Tel 08700 766326
www.roofbox.co.uk

RUD Chains Ltd
Snowchains
Tel 01227 276611
sales@rud.co.uk
www.rud.co.uk

skidrive.co.uk
Thule roof systems, Karrite boxes, Skandibox, Konig snowchains
Tel 01223 323488
skidrive@dapcambridge.co.uk
www.skidrive.co.uk

Snowchains Ltd
Thule ski boxes, roof bars and ski racks; Weissenfels snowchains
Tel 01732 884408
info@snowchains.co.uk
www.snowchains.co.uk

Spikes Spider
Tel 01706 819365
pparkinson@ndirect.co.uk
www.spikesspider.com

Thule Ltd
Tel 01275 340404
www.thule.co.uk

CROSS-CHANNEL TRAVEL

Brittany Ferries
Portsmouth-Caen
Tel 08703 665 333
reservations@brittany-
ferries.com
www.brittanyferries.co.uk

Eurotunnel
Folkestone-Calais/Coquelles via the Channel Tunnel
Tel 08705 35 35 35
www.eurotunnel.com

LD Line
Portsmouth-Le Havre
www.ldline.co.uk

Norfolkline
Dover-Dunkerque
Tel 0870 870 1020
doverpax@norfolkline.com
www.norfolkline.com

P&O Ferries
Dover-Calais; Portsmouth-Le Havre; Hull Rotterdam Zeebrugge
Tel 08705 980 333
customer.services@posl.com
www.poferries.com

SeaFrance
Dover-Calais
Tel 08705 711 711
enquiries@seafrance.com
www.seafrance.com

SpeedFerries
Dover-Boulogne
Tel 0870 220 0570
mail@speedferries.com
www.speedferries.com

Stena Line
Harwich-Hook of Holland
Tel 08705 707070
www.stenaline.co.uk

DRY SKI SLOPES

SOUTH-WEST ENGLAND

Avon Ski Centre
Lyncombe Lodge, Churchill,
North Somerset
Tel 01934 852335
info@highaction.co.uk
www.highaction.co.uk

Christchurch Ski Centre
Matchams Lane, Hurn,
Christchurch, Dorset
Tel 01202 499155
info@christchurch-
skicentre.com
www.newforest-
online.co.uk/christchurch_ski

Exeter and District Ski Club
Clifton Hill Sports Ground,
Belmont Road, Exeter
Tel 01392 211422

John Nike Leisuresport – Plymouth
Plymouth Ski Centre, Alpine
Park, Marsh Mills, Plymouth
Tel 01752 600220
www.jnll.co.uk

Torquay Alpine Ski Club
Barton Hall, Kingskerswell
Road, Torquay, Devon
Tel 01803 313350
info@skitorquay.co.uk
www.skitorquay.co.uk

Warmwell Ski Centre
Warmwell, Dorchester, Dorset
Tel 01305 853245

Yeovil Ski Centre
Addlewell Lane, Nine Springs,
Yeovil, Somerset
Tel 01935 421702

SOUTH-EAST ENGLAND

Alpine Snowsports Aldershot
Gallwey Road, Aldershot,
Hants
Tel 01252 325889
info@alpinesnowsports.co.uk
www.alpinesnowsports.co.uk

Bowles Outdoor Centre
Eridge Green, Tunbridge Wells
Tel 01892 665665
admin@bowles.ac
www.bowles.ac

Bromley Ski Centre
Sandy Lane, St Paul's Cray,
Orpington, Kent
Tel 01689 876812
management@
bromleyski.co.uk
www.c-v-s.co.uk/bromleyski/

Calshot Activities Centre
Calshot Spit, Fawley,
Southampton
Tel 023 8089 2077
calshot.ac@hants.gov.uk
www.hants.gov.uk/calshot

Christ's College Ski Club
Larch Avenue, Guildford,
Surrey
Tel 01483 504988
www.ccski.co.uk

Folkestone Sports Centre Ski Slope
Radnor Park Avenue,
Folkestone, Kent
Tel 01303 850333
www.folkestonesports.ndo.
co.uk/swimski.html

John Nike Leisuresport - Bracknell
Bracknell Ski Centre, Amen
Corner, Bracknell, Berkshire
Tel 01344 789000
www.jnll.co.uk

John Nike Leisuresport - Chatham
Chatham Ski and Snowboard
Centre, Alpine Park, Capstone
Road, Gillingham, Kent
Tel 01634 827979
www.jnll.co.uk

Plas y Brenin
Capel Curig, Conwy
Tel 01690 720214
info@pyb.co.uk
www.pyb.co.uk

Sandown Ski Centre
More Lane, Esher, Surrey
Tel 01372 467132
sandown@sandownsports.co.
uk
www.sandownsports.co.uk

Southampton Alpine Centre
The Sports Centre, Bassett,
Southampton
Tel 0870 040 0009
info@southampton-alpine-
centre.co.uk
www.southampton-alpine-
centre.co.uk

Wycombe Summit
Abbey Barn Lane, High
Wycombe, Bucks
Tel 01494 474711
info@wycombesummit.co.uk
www.wycombesummit.co.uk

MIDDLE ENGLAND

The Ackers
Golden Hillock Road, Small
Heath, Birmingham
Tel 0121 772 5111
www.ackers-adventure.co.uk

Gloucester Ski and Snowboard Centre
Jarvis International Hotel and
Country Club, Robinswood
Hill, Matson Lane, Gloucester
Tel 08702 400375
www.gloucesterski.com

John Nike Leisuresport - Swadlincote
Swadlincote Ski Centre, Hill
Street, Swadlincote,
Derbyshire
Tel 01283 217200
www.jnll.co.uk

Kidsgrove Ski Centre
Bathpool Park, Kidsgrove,
Stoke-on-Trent
Tel 01782 784908
info@ski-kidsgrove.co.uk
www.ski-kidsgrove.co.uk

Stoke Ski Centre
Festival Park, Stoke-on-Trent
Tel 01782 204159
wilsonpb@postmaster.co.uk
www.stokeskicentre.co.uk

Tallington Ski and Snowboard Centre
Tallington Lakes Leisure Park,
Barholm Road, Tallington,
Stamford, Lincs
Tel 01778 344990
sales@waspdirect.com
www.waspdirect.com

Tamworth Snowdome
Leisure Island, River Drive,
Tamworth, Staffordshire
Tel 08705 000011
info@snowdome.co.uk
www.snowdome.co.uk

Telford Ski Centre
Court Street, Madeley, Telford,
Shropshire
Tel 01952 586862
madeleyskicentre@
telford.gov.uk
www.telford.gov.uk/FreeTime/
Sports/
LeisureAndSportCentres.htm

Xscape Milton Keynes
602 Marlborough Gate,
Central Milton Keynes
Tel 0871 200 3220
www.xscape.co.uk

EASTERN ENGLAND

Brentwood Park Ski and Snowboard Centre
Warley Gap, Brentwood, Essex
Tel 01277 211994
info@
brentwoodskicentre.co.uk
www.brentwoodskicentre.
co.uk

Gosling Ski Centre
Stanborough Road, Welwyn
Garden City, Hertfordshire
Tel 01707 331056
info@goslingsports.co.uk
www.goslingsports.co.uk

Hemel Ski Centre
St Albans Hill, Hemel
Hempstead, Herts
Tel 01442 241321
communicate@hemel-ski.co.uk
www.hemel-ski.co.uk

Norfolk Ski Club
Whitlingham Lane, Trowse,
Norwich, Norfolk
Tel 01603 662781
info@norfolkskiclub.co.uk
www.norfolkskiclub.com

Suffolk Ski Centre
Bourne Hill, Wherstead,
Ipswich
Tel 01473 602347
enquiries@
suffolkskicentre.co.uk
www.suffolkskicentre.co.uk

NORTHERN ENGLAND

Alston Training and Adventure Centre
High Plains Lodge, Alston,
Cumbria
Tel 01434 381886
alstontraining@btconnect.com
www.alstontraining.co.uk

Halifax Ski and Snowboard Centre
Ploughcroft Lane, Halifax
Tel 01422 340760
skislope@ridehalifax.co.uk
www.ridehalifax.co.uk

Kendal Ski Club
Canal Head North, Kendal,
Cumbria
Tel 01695 624199
sec@kendalski.co.uk
www.kendalski.co.uk

Pendle Ski Club
Clitheroe Road, Sabden,
Clitheroe, Lancs
Tel 01200 425222
info@pendleskiclub.org.uk
www.pendleskiclub.org.uk

Runcorn Ski and Snowboard Centre
Town Park, Palace Fields,
Runcorn, Cheshire
Tel 01928 701965
info@runcornskicentre.co.uk
www.runcornskicentre.co.uk

Sheffield Ski Village
Vale Road, Parkwood Springs,
Sheffield
Tel 0114 276 9459
www.sheffieldskivillage.co.uk

Ski Rossendale
Haslingden Old Road,
Rawtenstall, Rossendale,
Lancashire
Tel 01706 226457
ski-rossendale@rltrust.co.uk
www.rltrust.co.uk/
ski_rossendale

Whickham Thorns Outdoor Centre
Market Lane, Dunston
Tel 0191 433 5767
whickhamthorns@
leisure.gatesheadmbc.gov.uk
www.gateshead.gov.uk/
leisserv/whickhamthorns.htm

Xscape Castleford
Colorado Way,
Glasshoughton, Castleford,
West Yorkshire
Tel 0871 200 3221
enquiriescastleford@
xscape.co.uk
www.xscape.co.uk

WALES

Cardiff Ski & Snowboard Centre
Fairwater Park, Fairwater Rd,
Cardiff
Tel 029 2056 1793
info@skicardiff.com
www.skicardiff.com

Dan-yr-Ogof Ski Slopes
Glyn Tawe, Abercraf, West
Glamorgan
Tel 01639 730284
www.showcaves.co.uk

John Nike Leisuresport – Llandudno
Wyddfyd Road, Great Orme,
Llandudno
Tel 01492 874707
www.jnll.co.uk

Pontypool Ski Centre
Pontypool Leisure Park,
Pontypool, Gwent
Tel 01495 756955

Ski Pembrey
Pembrey Country Park, Burry
Port, Llanelli, Dyfed
Tel 01554 834443

SCOTLAND

Alford Ski Centre
Greystone Road, Alford,
Aberdeenshire
Tel 01975 563024
keith.morris@
aberdeenshire.gov.uk
www.aberdeenshire.gov.uk/
recreation

Ancrum Outdoor Education Resource Centre
10 Ancrum Road, Dundee,
Tayside
Tel 01382 435911
ancrum.centre@
dundeecity.gov.uk
www.ancrum.com

Bearsden Ski & Board
Stockiemuir Road, Bearsden,
Glasgow
Tel 0141 943 1500
info@skibearsden.co.uk
www.skibearsden.co.uk

Firpark Ski Centre
Tillicoultry, Clackmannanshire
Tel 01259 751772
www.clacksweb.org.uk/culture/
sport/

Glasgow Ski & Snowboard Centre
Bellahouston Park, 16
Dumbreck Road, Glasgow
Tel 0141 427 4991
info@ski-glasgow.org
www.ski-glasgow.org

Glenmore Lodge
Scottish National Sports
Centre, Aviemore, Inverness-
shire
Tel 01479 861256
enquiries@
glenmorelodge.org.uk
www.glenmorelodge.org.uk

Loch Insh Watersports and Ski Centre
Kincraig, Kingussie,
Invernesshire
Tel 01540 651272
enquiries@lochinsh.com
www.lochinsh.com

Midlothian Snowsports Centre
Hillend, Near Edinburgh,
Midlothian
Tel 0131 445 4433
ski@midlothian.gov.uk
ski.midlothian.gov.uk

Neptune Ski and Snowboard Club
The Sports Drome, HMNB
Clyde, Helensburgh
Tel 01436 674 321 ext 6966
neptune.skiboard@virgin.net

Polmonthill Ski Centre
Polmont, Falkirk
Tel 01324 503835
ski@
polmonthill.freeserve.co.uk

Xscape Braehead
Kings Inch Road , Braehead,
Renfrew
Tel 0871 200 3221
www.xscape.co.uk

NORTHERN IRELAND

Craigavon Golf and Ski Centre
Turmoyra Lane, Silverwood,
Lurgan, Co Armagh
Tel 028 3832 6606
golf.ski@craigavon.gov.uk
www.craigavon.gov.uk

INSURANCE COMPANIES

Atlas Insurance
Tel 0870 811 1700
sales@travel-insurance.co.uk
www.atlasdirect.net

AUL
Tel 01206 577770
enquiries@aul.co.uk
www.aul.co.uk

Best Ski Insurance
Tel 0870 458 2985
sales@best-ski-
insurance.co.uk
www.best-ski-insurance.co.uk

CGNU
Tel 0800 0150 362
support@norwich-union.co.uk
www.norwichunion.co.uk

Direct Line Travel Insurance
Tel 0845 246 8704
www.directline.com/travel

Direct Travel Insurance
Tel 0845 605 2700
info@direct-travel.co.uk
www.direct-travel.co.uk

Douglas Cox Tyrie
Tel 01708 385969

Matthew Gerard Travel Insurance Ltd
Tel 01483 730900
sales@mgtis.easynet.co.uk

P J Hayman & Company
Tel 023 9241 9050
travel.insurance@
pjhayman.com
www.pjhayman.com

Preferential
Tel 0870 428 4399
www.preferential.co.uk

Primary Insurance Group
Tel 0870 220 0634
customersupport@primaryinsu
rance.co.uk
www.primaryinsurance.co.uk

Select Travel Insurance
Tel 0870 737 0870
select@inter-group.co.uk
www.select-insurance.co.uk

Skicoverdirect
www.skicoverdirect.co.uk

ski-insurance.co.uk
Tel 0870 755 6101
info@ski-insurance.co.uk
www.ski-insurance.co.uk

Skisure.com
Tel 0845 2220020
info@skisure.com
www.skisure.com

Snowcard Insurance Services Ltd
Tel 01327 262805
enquiries@snowcard.co.uk
www.snowcard.co.uk

Sportscover Direct Ltd
Tel 0845 120 6400
contact@sportscover.co.uk
www.sportscover.co.uk

Travel Insurance Direct
Tel 01603 464123
info@insurance.uk.com
www.travelcover.co.uk

WorldCover Direct
Tel 0800 365 121
world.cover@gecapital.com

WorldSki
Tel 0870 428 8706
info@worldski.co.uk
www.worldski.co.uk

Worldwide Travel Insurance Services Ltd
Tel 0870 112 8100
sales@worldwideinsure.com
www.worldwideinsure.com

NATIONAL TOURIST OFFICES

Andorran Embassy
Tel 020 8874 4806

Argentine Embassy
Tel 0800 999 5000
info@turismo.gov.ar
www.turismo.gov.ar

Australian Tourist Commission
Tel 09068 633235
www.australia.com

Austrian National Tourist Office
*Correspondence and phone
calls only*
Tel 0845 101 1818
holiday@austria.info
www.austria.info/uk

Canadian Tourism Commission
Tel 0906 871 5000
visitcanada@dial.pipex.com
www.travelcanada.ca

Chile – Consulate General
Tel 020 7580 6392
cglonduk@
congechileuk.demon.co.uk
www.echileuk.demon.co.uk

Czech Tourism
info-uk@czechtourism.com
www.czechtourism.com

Finnish Tourist Board
Tel 020 7365 2512
finlandinfo.lon@mek.fi
www.finland-tourism.com

French Government Tourist Office
Tel 09068 244123
info.uk@franceguide.com
www.franceguide.com

German National Tourist Office
Tel 020 7317 0908
gntolon@d-z-t.com
www.germany-tourism.co.uk

Italian State Tourist Office
Brochure line: 09065 508925
Tel 020 7408 1254
italy@italiantouristboard.co.uk
www.italiantouristboard.co.uk

Japan National Tourist Organisation
Tel 020 7734 9638
info@jnto.co.uk
www.seejapan.co.uk

Norwegian Tourist Board
Tel 0906 302 2003
infouk@ntr.no
www.visitnorway.com

Romanian Tourist Office
Tel 020 7224 3692
infouk@RomaniaTourism.com
www.romaniatourism.com

Scottish Tourist Board
ski.visitscotland.com

Slovenian Tourist Office
Tel 0870 225 5305
info@slovenian-tourism.co.uk
www.slovenia-tourism.si

Spanish Tourist Office
Tel 020 7486 8077
tourspain@latestinfo.co.uk
www.tourspain.co.uk

Swedish Travel and Tourism Council
Tel 0207 108 6168
info@swetourism.org.uk
www.visit-sweden.com

Switzerland Tourism
Tel 00800 100 200 30
info.uk@myswitzerland.com
www.MySwitzerland.com

Tourism New Zealand
Tel 0906 601 3601
www.newzealand.com

Turkish Tourist Board
Tel 020 78397778
info@gototurkey.co.uk
www.gototurkey.co.uk

Visit USA Association
Tel 0870 777 2213
www.visitusa.org.uk

RAILWAYS

Deutsche Bahn AG
Tel 0870 243 5363
sales@bahn.co.uk
www.deutsche-bahn.co.uk

Eurostar
Tel 08705 186 186
new.comments@
eurostar.co.uk
www.eurostar.com

Rail Europe
Tel 08708 30 20 08
reservations@raileurope.co.uk
www.raileurope.co.uk

Swiss Federal Railways
Tel 00800 100 200 30
(Switzerland Tourism)
info.uk@switzerland.com
www.rail.ch

RETAILERS
SOUTH-WEST ENGLAND

Devon Ski Centre
Oak Place, Newton Abbot, Devon
Tel 01626 351278
www.devonski.co.uk
/www.skisuk.com

Kidski
Tel 01202 631222
help@kidski.co.uk
www.kidski.co.uk

Mission Adventure Ltd
1 Bank Lane, Brixham, Devon
Tel 0870 1430 689
www.missionadventure.co.uk

Noahs Ark
London Road, Chalford, Stroud, Gloucestershire
Tel 01453 884738
www.noahsark.co.uk

Penrose Outdoors
Town Quay, Truro, Cornwall
Tel 01872 272116
www.penroseoutdoors.co.uk

Skate and Ski
104 High Street, Staple Hill, Bristol
Tel 0117 970 1356

Snow & Rock
Units 1-3 Shield Retail Centre, Link Road, Filton, Bristol
Tel 0117 914 3000
www.snowandrock.com

Snow Togs
6 St Michaels Road, Bournemouth, Dorset
Tel 01202 557690
www.skishops.co.uk

Snowtrax
Matchams Lane, Hurn, Christchurch, Dorset
Tel 01202 499155
www.snowtrax.eu

Team Ski
37 High East Street, Dorchester, Dorset
Tel 01305 268035
www.teamski.co.uk

Westsports
Market House, Marlborough Road, Old Town, Swindon
Tel 01793 532588
www.skishops.co.uk

SOUTH-EAST ENGLAND

Activ (Folkestone)
145 Sandgate Road, Folkestone, Kent
Tel 01303 240110
www.activfolkestone.com

Bartletts
1-2 Rosslyn Parade, Uxbridge Road, Hillingdon, Middlesex
Tel 020 8848 0040
www.skibartlett.com

Captain's Cabin
93 High Street, Chatham, Kent
Tel 01634 819777
www.captainscabin.com

Captain's Cabin
14 St George's Walk, Croydon
Tel 020 8680 6968
www.captainscabin.com

Captain's Cabin
19 Wincheap, Canterbury, Kent
Tel 01227 457906
www.captainscabin.com

Captain's Cabin
93b High Street, Chatham, Kent
Tel 01634 819777
www.captainscabin.com

John Pollock
157 High Road, Loughton, Essex
Tel 020 8508 6626
www.johnpollock.co.uk

John Pollock
67 High Street, Barnet
Tel 020 8440 3994
www.johnpollock.co.uk

Mountain High
41 Reading Road, Pangbourne, Berkshire
Tel 0118-984 1851

Outdoor Life
3 High Street, Old Town, Eastbourne, East Sussex
Tel 01323 725372

Snow & Rock
188 Kensington High Street, London
Tel 0207 937 0872
www.snowandrock.com

Snow & Rock
4 Mercer Street, Covent Garden, London
Tel 0207 420 1444
www.snowandrock.com

Snow & Rock
150 Holborn, Corner of Grays Inn Road, London
Tel 0207 831 6900
www.snowandrock.com

Snow & Rock
Sporting Club, 38-42 King's Road, London
Tel 0207 589 5418
www.snowandrock.com

Snow & Rock
99 Fordwater Road, Chertsey, Surrey
Tel 01932 566886
www.snowandrock.com

Snow & Rock
The Boardwalk, Port Solent, Portsmouth, Hampshire
Tel 023 9220 5388
www.snowandrock.co.uk

Snow Togs
431 Millbrook Road, Southampton, Hampshire
Tel 023 8077 3925
www.skishops.co.uk

Active Outdoor & Ski
Active Clothing Ltd, 77 Castle Quay, Banbury, Oxfordshire
Tel 01295 273700
www.aosbanbury.com

MIDDLE ENGLAND

Beans
86 Sheep Street, Bicester, Oxfordshire
Tel 01869 246451
www.beansonline.co.uk

BestBuys
Nene Court, 27-31 The Embankment, Wellingborough, Northamptonshire
Tel 01933 272699
www.best-buys.co.uk

Force
26 Bakers Lane, Lichfield, Staffordshire
Tel 01543 411249
www.ski-force.co.uk

Force
Guildhall Shopping Centre, Stafford
Tel 01785 225737
www.skiforce.co.uk

Fox's
1 London Road, Amersham
Tel 01494 431431
www.foxsoutdoor.co.uk

Lockwoods Ski Shop
125-129 Rugby Road, Leamington Spa, Warwickshire
Tel 01926 339388
www.lockwoods.com

Noahs Ark
London Road, Chalford, Stroud, Gloucestershire
Tel 01453 884738
www.noahsark.co.uk

Snow & Rock
14 Priory Queensway, Birmingham
Tel 0121 236 8280
www.snowandrock.com

Sporting Triangle
18 West Street, Hereford
Tel 01432 271500
www.sportingtriangle.com

EASTERN ENGLAND

Revolutionz
21 Lower Goat Lane, Norwich
Tel 01603 629313
www.revolutionz.co.uk

Snow & Rock
Hemel Ski Centre, St Albans Hill, Hemel Hempstead, Hertfordshire
Tel 01422 235305
www.snowandrock.com

SnowFit
2 Cucumber Lane, Brundall, Norwich
Tel 01603 716655
www.snowfit.co.uk

NORTHERN ENGLAND

BAC Outdoor Leisure
Central Hall, Coronation Street, Elland, Halifax, West Yorkshire
Tel 01422 371146
www.bac-e.com

Sayers
66 High Street, Yarm, Cleveland
Tel 01642 785423
www.skiwearhire.com

Severn Sports / Mountain Adventures
80 Town Street, Armley, Leeds, West Yorkshire
Tel 0113 279 1618
www.severnsports.co.uk

Severn Sports Mountain Adventures Ltd
5-7 Church Lane, Crossgates, Leeds
Tel 0113 2643847

Snow & Rock
Metro Park West, Gibside Way, Gateshead
Tel 0191 493 3680
www.snowandrock.com

Snow & Rock
Sheffield Ski Centre, Vale Road, Parkwood Springs, Sheffield
Tel 0114 275 1700
www.snowandrock.com

Snow & Rock
Unti 1 Eastham Point, New Chester Road, Eastham, Wirral
Tel 0151 328 5500
www.snowandrock.com

Snow & Rock
Princess Parkway, Princess Park, Didsbury, Manchester
Tel 0161 448 4444
www.snowandrock.com

SCOTLAND

Craigdon Mountain Sports
Advertising House, Burghmuir Circle, Inverurie, Highland
Tel 01467 624900
www.craigdonmountainsports.com

Craigdon Mountain Sports
5 St Andrew's Street, Aberdeen
Tel 01224 624333
www.craigdonmountainsports.com

Craigdon Mountain Sports
25-29 Kinnoull Street, Perth
Tel 01738 831006
www.craigdonmountainsports.com

NORTHERN IRELAND

Macski
140 Lisburn Road, Belfast
Tel 028 9066 5525
www.macski.com

REPUBLIC OF IRELAND

The Great Outdoors
Chatham Street, Dublin 2, Ireland
Tel 00 353 1679 4293
www.greatoutdoors.ie

Bunac / Gap Canada
Tel 020 7251 3472
enquiries@bunac.org.uk
www.bunac.org

Free Radicals
Tel 07968 183848
enquiries@freeradicals.co.uk
www.freeradicals.co.uk

Just Jobs 4 Students
www.justjobs4students.co.uk

Natives
Tel 08700 463377
info@natives.co.uk
www.natives.co.uk

Season Workers
Tel 01383 723344
www.seasonworkers.com

Ski Connection
amanda@skiconnection.co.uk
www.skiconnection.co.uk

Voovs.com
Tel 01707 396511 or 0207 442 3456
info@voovs.com
www.voovs.com

British Association of Snowsport Instructors (BASI)
Tel 01479 861717
basi@basi.org.uk
www.basi.org.uk

British Ski Club for the Disabled
BSCDWeb@hotmail.com
www.bscd.org.uk

Disability Snowsport UK
Ski organisation and ski school for people with disabilities
Tel 01479 861272
info@uphillskiclub.co.uk
www.disabilitysnowsport.org.uk

Ski Club of Great Britain
Tel 020 8410 2000
skiers@skiclub.co.uk
www.skiclub.co.uk

Snowboard Club UK (SCUK)
Tel 01273 687788
www.SnowboardClub.co.uk

Snowsport England
Tel 0121 501 2314
admin@englishski.org
www.snowsportengland.org.uk

SnowsportGB
Tel 0131 445 7676
info@snowsportgb.com
www.snowsportgb.com

Snowsport Scotland
Tel 0131 445 4151
info@snowsportscotland.org
www.snsc.demon.co.uk

Snowsport Wales
Tel 029 2056 1904
admin.snowsportwales@virgin.net
www.snowsportwales.net

Ski business directory

744

SKI TRAVEL AGENTS

Alpine Answers
Tel 020 8871 4656
ski@alpineanswers.co.uk
www.alpineanswers.co.uk

Catered Ski Chalets
Tel 020 7835 0635
info@catered-ski-chalets.co.uk
www.catered-ski-chalets.co.uk

Iglu.com
Tel 020 8542 6658
enquiries@iglu.com
www.iglu.com

Independent Ski Links
Tel 01964 533905
info@ski-links.com
www.ski-links.com

Kwik Ski
Tel 0870 499 3114
ski@kwiktravel.co.uk
www.kwik-ski.co.uk

Ski & Surf
Tel 0208 731 2111
janm@skisurf.com
www.skisurf.com

Ski-direct.co.uk
Tel 08700 171935
www.ski-direct.co.uk

Ski Expectations
Tel 01799 531888
ski.expectations@virgin.net

Ski Line
Tel 0870 950 4420
angus@skiline.co.uk
www.skiline.co.uk

Ski McNeill
Tel 0870 600 1359
contact@skimcneill.com
www.skimcneill.com

Skis and Tees
Tel 0870 240 7416
enquiries@skisandtees.co.uk
www.skisandtees.co.uk

Ski Solutions
A La Carte department:
020 7471 7777
Tel 020 7471 7700
www.skisolutions.com

Ski Tracer
Tel 0870 420 5782
sales@skitracer.com
www.skitracer.com

Ski Travel Centre
Tel 0141 649 9696
snow@skitravelcentre.com
www.ski-travel-centre.co.uk

Snow Finders
Tel 01858 466888
sales@snowfinders.com
www.snowfinders.com

Snow Hounds
Tel 01243 788487
www.snowhounds.co.uk

Snow Line
Tel 0870 050 7025
sales@snow-line.co.uk
www.snow-line.co.uk

RESORT DIRECTORY / INDEX

This is an index to the resort chapters in the book; you'll find page references for about 400 resorts that are described in those chapters. But you'll also find brief descriptions here of another 700 resorts, most of them smaller than those we've covered in full. We also list the companies offering package holidays to each resort. To get in touch with one of these tour operators, look them up in the list starting on page 732.

Key

⬓ Lifts
⬧ Pistes
✉ UK tour operators

49 Degrees North USA
Inland area with best snow in Washington State; 120-acre bowl reserved for powder weekends.
1195m; slopes 1195–1760m
⬓ 5 ⬧ 780 acres

Abetone Italy
Resort in the exposed Appennines, less than two hours from Florence and Pisa.
1390m; slopes 1390–1900m
⬓ 25 ⬧ 50km
✉ Erna Low

Abtenau Austria
Sizeable village in Dachstein-West region near Salzburg, on large plain ideal for cross-country.
710m; slopes 710–1260m
⬓ 6 ⬧ 10km

Achenkirch Austria
Unspoilt, low-altitude Tirolean village close to Niederau and Alpbach. Beautiful setting overlooking a lake.
930m; slopes 930–1800m
⬓ 7 ⬧ 25km
✉ Ramblers Holidays

Adelboden 492
✉ Crystal, Interhome, Kuoni, Swiss Travel Service, Switzerland Travel Centre, Thomson

Les Aillons France
Traditional village near Chambéry. Sheltered slopes.
1000m; slopes 1000–1900m
⬓ 22 ⬧ 40km

Alagna 450
Small resort on the western fringe of Monterosa Ski area.
✉ Alpine Answers, Italian Safaris, Mountain Tracks, Ski 2, Ski Freshtracks, Ski Weekend

Alba Italy
Picturesque Trentino village with a small, quiet area; access to the Sella Ronda at nearby Canazei.
1515m; slopes 1515–2440m
⬓ 5 ⬧ 10km

Albiez-Montrond France
Authentic old French village in Maurienne valley with panoramic views.
1500m; slopes 1500–2200m
⬓ 12 ⬧ 40km
✉ Lagrange Holidays

Alleghe Italy
Dolomite village near Cortina in a pretty lakeside setting close to numerous areas.
980m
⬓ 24 ⬧ 80km
✉ Interhome

Les Allues 319
Rustic village on the road up to Méribel, close to the mid-station of the gondola up from Brides-les-Bains.

Alpbach 127
✉ Crystal, Inghams, Interhome, Made to Measure Holidays

Alpe-d'Huez 241
✉ Airtours, Alpine Answers, Catered Ski Chalets, Chalet World Ski, Club Med, Club Pavilion, Crystal, Equity Ski, Erna Low, First Choice Ski, Friendship Travel, Independent Ski Links, Inghams, Interhome, La Source, Lagrange Holidays, Made to Measure Holidays, Mark Warner, Neilson, Rocketski, Ski à la Carte, Ski Expectations, Ski France, Ski Freshtracks, Ski Independence, Ski Leisure Direction, Ski Line, Ski Miquel, Ski Solutions, Ski Supreme, Ski Tracer, Ski4you, Skifrance4less, Skiworld, Thomson, Tops Ski Chalets and Club Hotels

Alpe-du-Grand-Serre France
Tiny resort near Alpe-d'Huez and Les Deux-Alpes. Good for bad-weather days.
1400m; slopes 1400–2200m
⬓ 20 ⬧ 55km

Alpendorf 234
Outpost of St Johann im Pongau, at one end of an extensive three-valley lift network linking via Wagrain to Flachau – all part of the Salzburger Sportwelt area.

Alpenglow USA
Alaskan ski resort.
762m; slopes 2500–3900m
⬓ 4 ⬧ 320 acres

Alpine Meadows 580

Alps Resort South Korea
Korea's most northerly, snow-reliable resort, about five hours from Seoul. ⬓ 5

Alta 621
✉ AmeriCan Ski, Mountain Tracks, Ski All America, Ski Independence, Ski The American Dream, Ski Tracer

Alta Badia 461

Altenmarkt Austria
Unspoiled village, well placed just off the Salzburg-Villach autobahn for numerous resorts including snow-sure Obertauern and those in the Salzburger Sportwelt.
855m; slopes 855–2130m
⬓ 23 ⬧ 150km

Alto Campoo Spain
Barren, desolate place with undistinguished slopes, but with magnificent wilderness views.
1650m; slopes 1650–2170m ⬓ 11

Alt St Johann Switzerland
Old cross-country village with Alpine slopes connecting into Unterwasser area near Liechtenstein.
900m; slopes 900–2260m
⬓ 21 ⬧ 50km

Alyeska USA
Alaskan area 60km/37 miles from Anchorage, with luxury hotel. 'Spectacular views – a very special place,' enthuses a 2004 visitor.
75m; slopes 75–1200m
⬓ 9 ⬧ 785 acres
✉ Frontier Ski, Ski All America

Aminona 501
Purpose-built resort on the eastern side of the Crans-Montana network.
✉ Lagrange Holidays

Andalo 478
Trentino village not far from Madonna.
✉ Equity Ski, Rocketski, Ski Supreme

Andermatt 494
✉ Mountain Tracks, Ski Freshtracks, Ski Weekend, Switzerland Travel Centre

Andorra la Vella 108
✉ Lagrange Holidays

Angel Fire USA
Intermediate area near Taos, New Mexico. Height usually ensures good snow.
2620m; slopes 2620–3255m
⬓ 5 ⬧ 455 acres

Les Angles France
Attractive resort with one of the best ski areas in the Pyrenees. Pretty, tree-lined, mostly easy skiing.
1650m; slopes 1650–2400m
⬓ 24 ⬧ 40km
✉ Lagrange Holidays, Pyrenees Ski Experience

Annaberg-Lungötz Austria
Peaceful village in a pretty setting, sharing a sizeable area with Gosau. Close to Filzmoos.
775m; slopes 775–1620m
⬓ 33 ⬧ 65km

Anthony Lakes USA
Ski resort in Oregon, 300 miles east of Portland.
slopes 2165–2435m
⬓ 2 ⬧ 23 trails

Anzère Switzerland
Sympathetically designed modern resort on a sunny balcony near Crans-Montana, with slopes suited to leisurely intermediates.
1500m; slopes 1500–2460m
⬓ 13 ⬧ 40km
✉ Alpine Tours, Interhome, Lagrange Holidays

Aosta Italy
Historic working valley town with a gondola up to the mountain resort of Pila.
1800m; slopes 1550–2710m
⬓ 13 ⬧ 70km

Apex Canada
Small, friendly, rather isolated modern village. Well worth stopping off here on a tour of western BC resorts.
1575m; slopes 1575–2180m
⬓ 4 ⬧ 1,112 acres
✉ AmeriCan Ski, Frontier Ski, Ski Independence, Ski Safari, Ski The American Dream

Aprica Italy
Ugly, straggling village between Lake Como and the Brenta Dolomites, with bland slopes and limited facilities.
1180m; slopes 1180–2310m
⬓ 24 ⬧ 40km

Arabba 461
✉ Independent Ski Links, Inghams, Momentum Ski, Neilson, Ski Yogi

Aragnouet-Piau France
Purpose-built mid-mountain satellite of St-Lary, best suited to families, beginners and early intermediates.
1850m; slopes 1420–2500m
⬓ 32 ⬧ 80km

Arapahoe Basin USA
Small, exceptionally high day-skiing area near Keystone with excellent snowfall record and very long season. Lifts to good mix of open and wooded runs of every standard, plus serious steeps reached by hiking.
3285m; slopes 3285–3795m
⬓ 6 ⬧ 890 acres

Belle-Plagne 343
High-altitude satellite of La Plagne.
1955m; slopes 1900–2900m
⛷ 32 🚠 90km

Bellwald Switzerland
Traditional Rhône valley resort near Fiesch, Riederalp and Bettmeralp.
slopes 1600–2560m
⛷ 5 🚠 31km

Ben Lomond Australia
Small intermediate/beginner area in Ben Lomond National Park, Tasmania, 260km/162 miles from Hobart.
1450m; slopes 1460–1570m
⛷ 6 🚠 14 hectares

Berchtesgaden Germany
Pleasant old town close to Salzburg, known for its Nordic skiing but with several little Alpine areas nearby.
550m
✉ Moswin Tours

Bergün Switzerland
Traditional, quiet, unspoiled, virtually traffic-free little family resort on the rail route between Davos and St Moritz. 5km/3 mile toboggan run.
1375m; slopes 1400–2550m
⛷ 5 🚠 25km

Berkshire East USA
Resort in Massachusetts, southern New England, near the Mohawk Trail.
slopes 165–525m
⛷ 5 🚠 200 acres

Berthoud Pass 615
Powder heaven on the drive to Winter Park.

Berwang Austria
Unspoiled village nestling in a spacious valley, close to Lermoos.
1335m; slopes 1335–1740m
⛷ 12 🚠 40km
✉ Lagrange Holidays

Bessans France
Old cross-country village near Modane. Well placed for touring Maurienne valley resorts such as Val-Cenis.
1710m; slopes 1740–2200m
⛷ 4 🚠 5km

Besse France
Charming old village built out of lava, with purpose-built slope-side satellite Super-Besse. Beautiful extinct-volcano scenery.
1050m; slopes 1300–1850m
⛷ 22 🚠 45km
✉ Lagrange Holidays

Bethel USA
Pleasant, historic town very close to Sunday River, Maine. Attractive alternative to staying in the slope-side resort.

Le Bettex 311
Small base above St-Gervais, with links to Megève.

Bettmeralp Switzerland
Central village of the sizeable Aletsch area near Brig, perched high above the Rhône valley, amid spectacular glacial scenery.

1955m; slopes 1900–2900m
⛷ 32 🚠 90km

Beuil-les-Launes France
Alpes-Maritimes resort closest to Nice. Shares area with Valberg.
1400m; slopes 1400–2100m
⛷ 26 🚠 90km

Bezau Austria
No slopes of its own, but the main village in Bregenzerwald region north-west of Lech.
650m; slopes 1210–1650m ⛷ 2
✉ Inntravel

Biberwier Austria
Limited little village with a small area of its own. Quiet base to access the Zugspitz area.
1000m; slopes 1000–1790m
⛷ 6 🚠 8km

Bichlbach Austria
Smallest of the Zugspitz villages with very limited slopes of its own.
1070m; slopes 1070–1620m
⛷ 3 🚠 7km

Bielmonte Italy
Popular with day-trippers from Milan. Worthwhile on a bad-weather day.
1200m; slopes 1200–1620m
⛷ 13 🚠 20km

Big Mountain USA
Impressive ski area close to Canadian border and to Montana's Glacier National Park. Good snow and a fun town.
1370m; slopes 1370–2135m
⛷ 10 🚠 3,000 acres
✉ AmeriCan Ski, Ski Activity, Ski All America, Ski The American Dream

Big Powderhorn USA
Area with the most 'resort' facilities in south Lake Superior region. The area suffers from winds.
370m; slopes 370–560m
⛷ 10 🚠 250 acres

Big Sky 636
✉ AmeriCan Ski, Ski Independence, Ski Safari, Ski The American Dream

Big White 665
✉ AmeriCan Ski, American Ski Classics, Frontier Ski, Independent Ski Links, Made to Measure Holidays, Ski Activity, Ski All America, Ski Independence, Ski Line, Ski Safari, Ski The American Dream, Snowebb

Bischofshofen Austria
Working town and mountain resort near St Johann im Pongau, with very limited local runs.
545m; slopes 545–1000m
⛷ 1 🚠 2km

Bivio Switzerland
Quiet village near St Moritz with easy slopes opened up by a few lifts.
1775m; slopes 1780–2600m
⛷ 4 🚠 40km

Bizau Austria
One of two main areas in the low Bregenzerwald region north-west of Lech.
680m; slopes 680–1700m
⛷ 6 🚠 24km

Björkliden 707

Björnrike 707

Blackcomb 684
Smaller and quieter than neighbouring Whistler.
✉ Frontier Ski

Black Mountain USA
New Hampshire area with lodging in nearby Jackson.
⛷ 4 🚠 143 acres

Blatten Switzerland
Mountainside hamlet above Naters, beside the Rhône near Brig. Small but tall area in stunning glacial scenery, with larger Aletsch area nearby.
1320m; slopes 1320–3100m
⛷ 9 🚠 60km

Bled 714
✉ Alpine Tours, Balkan Holidays, Crystal, Directski.com, Just Slovenia, Thomson, Waymark Holidays

Blue Cow 718

Blue Mountain Canada
Largest area in Ontario, with glorious views of Lake Huron. High-capacity lift system and 100% snowmaking.
230m; slopes 230–450m
⛷ 15 🚠 275 acres

Blue River Canada
Base of world-famous Mike Wiegele heli-ski operation in Cariboo and Monashee mountains.

Bluewood USA
Particularly remote area even by north-west American standards. Worth a visit if you're in Walla Walla.
1355m; slopes 1355–1725m
⛷ 3 🚠 530 acres

Bogus Basin USA
Sizeable area overlooking Idaho's attractive, interesting capital, Boise.
1760m; slopes 1760–2310m
⛷ 8 🚠 2,600 acres

Bohinj 714
✉ Balkan Holidays, Directski.com, Just Slovenia, Thomson

Bois-d'Amont France
One of four resorts that make up Les Rousses area in Jura region.
1050m; slopes 1120–1680m
⛷ 40 🚠 40km
✉ Lagrange Holidays

Boi Taull Spain
A typical Pyrenean resort set high above the Boi Valley, close to the stunning Aigues Tortes National Park. Good intermediate terrain.
slopes 2020–2750m
⛷ 16 🚠 43km
✉ Alpine Tours

Bolognola Italy
Tiny area in Macerata region near the Adriatic Riviera.
1070m; slopes 1070–1845m
⛷ 7 🚠 5km

Bolton Valley USA
Resort near Stowe with mostly intermediate slopes.
465m; slopes 465–960m
⛷ 6 🚠 155 acres

Bonneval-sur-Arc France
Unspoiled, remote old village in the Haute Maurienne valley with many of its slopes at high altitude. Pass to neighbouring Val-d'Isère is closed in winter.
1800m; slopes 1800–3000m
⛷ 10 🚠 25km

Bons 294
Rustic, unspoiled old hamlet linked to Les Deux-Alpes' skiing.

Boreal USA
Closest area to north Lake Tahoe town, Truckee..
2195m; slopes 2195–2375m
⛷ 9 🚠 380 acres

Bormio 426
✉ Equity Ski, Interhome, Italian Safaris, Rocketski

Borovets 710
✉ Airtours, Balkan Holidays, Crystal, Directski.com, First Choice Ski, Inghams, Neilson, Panorama Holidays, Ski Balkantours, Thomson

Bosco Chiesanuova Italy
Weekend day-trippers' place near Verona.
1105m; slopes 1105–1805m
⛷ 18 🚠 20km

Bosco Gurin Switzerland
Highest ski area in Ticino. The only German speaking village in the Italian canton.
1500m; slopes 1500–2400m
⛷ 6 🚠 30km

Les Bottieres 377
Hamlet inconveniently set on fringes of Les Sybelles area.

La Bourboule France
Spa and cross-country village with the Alpine slopes of Le Mont-Dore nearby.
850m; slopes 1050–1850m
⛷ 41 🚠 80km
✉ Lagrange Holidays

Bourg-d'Oisans France
Pleasant valley town on main Grenoble-Briançon road. Cheap base for visits to Alpe-d'Huez and Les Deux-Alpes.

Bourg-St-Maurice 250
French valley town with a funicular to Les Arcs.
✉ Interhome, Ski Freshtracks

Bovec Slovenia
Town near Kanin ski area, a few miles from the Italian border.
✉ BoardnLodge, Just Slovenia

Boyne Highlands USA
Area with impressive, high-capacity lift system for weekend Detroit crowds. Fierce winds off Lake Michigan.
225m; slopes 225–390m
⛷ 10 🚠 240 acres

Boyne Mountain USA
Resort popular with weekend Detroit crowds. Not as windy as sister resort Boyne Highlands.
190m; slopes 190–340m
📏 12 ➚ 115 *acres*

Bozel France
Small town that, in good snow conditions, you can ski down to off-piste from Courchevel and catch a bus back. *860m*

Bramans France
Old cross-country village near Modane. Well placed for touring numerous nearby resorts such as Val-Cenis and Valloire.
1230m 📏 1

Bramberg Austria
Village near Pass Thurn (Kitzbühel area). Shares odd area with Neukirchen – the only valley lift is in Neukirchen.
820m; slopes 820–900m 📏 2

Brand Austria
Family resort, less popular now, perhaps because it lacks the charm to compensate for its small, low area.
1050m; slopes 1050–1920m
📏 13 ➚ 50km
✉ *Ski Wild*

Les Brasses France
Collective name for six traditional hamlets with some of the closest slopes to Geneva, but best for cross-country.
900m; slopes 900–1600m
📏 17 ➚ 50km

Braunwald Switzerland
Sunny but limited area, a funicular ride above Linthal.
1300m; slopes 1300–1910m
📏 8 ➚ 32km

Breckenridge 592
✉ *AmeriCan Ski, American Ski Classics, Catered Ski Chalets, Chalet World Ski, Crystal, Crystal Finest, Erna Low, Independent Ski Links, Inghams, Made to Measure Holidays, Neilson, Ski Activity, Ski All America, Ski Expectations, Ski Independence, Ski Line, Ski Safari, Ski Solutions, Ski The American Dream, Ski Tracer, Ski Wild, Skiworld, Supertravel, Thomson, Trailfinders, United Vacations, Virgin Snow*

Brentonico Italy
Little resort just off Verona-Trento motorway.
1160m; slopes 1160–1520m 📏 16

La Bresse France
Largest resort in the northerly Vosges mountains.
900m; slopes 900–1350m
📏 21 ➚ 62km

Bretton Woods USA
Area with best snowfall record in New Hampshire, and one of several small resorts scattered along the Interstate 93 highway. Mostly easy slopes. Attractive base lodge, good views.
480m; slopes 480–940m
📏 9 ➚ 435 *acres*

✉ *Equity Ski, Waymark Holidays*

Briançon 364
Part of the Grand Serre Chevalier region, but with own ski area.
✉ *BoardnLodge, Lagrange Holidays, Snowgums*

Brian Head USA
Utah area south of Salt Lake City, too far from Park City for a day trip.
2925m; slopes 2925–3445m
📏 10 ➚ 500 *acres*

Brides-les-Bains 319
Quiet spa town in valley below Méribel.
✉ *AmeriCan Ski, Crystal, Directski.com, Erna Low, First Choice Ski, Lagrange Holidays, Peak Retreats, Ramblers Holidays, Ski Leisure Direction, Ski Weekends, Ski4you, Snowcoach*

Bridger Bowl USA
Modest-sized day-trip resort (just a shop and fast-food restaurant at the base) and an interesting excursion from Big Sky.
1855m; slopes 1855–2460m
📏 6 ➚ 1,200 *acres*

Brigels-Andiast Switzerland
In the same valley as Flims-Laax. Access from two sunny villages.
1300m; slopes 1300–2415m
📏 7 ➚ 75km

Brighton 634
✉ *AmeriCan Ski, Equity Ski*

Brixen 202
Best equipped of Grossraum villages, with gondola access to slopes shared with Söll/Ellmau.

Brodie Mountain USA
Largest Massachusetts area. 100% snowmaking and mostly easy slopes.
440m; slopes 440–820m
📏 6 ➚ 250 *acres*

Bromley USA
New York City weekend retreat, reputedly the warmest place to ski in chilly Vermont.
595m; slopes 595–1000m
📏 9 ➚ 300 *acres*

Bromont Canada
Purpose-built resort an hour east of Montreal.
slopes 405–575m
📏 6 ➚ 135 *acres*
✉ *AmeriCan Ski*

Bruck am Grossglockner Austria
Low beginners' resort, but could suit intermediates looking for a small, quiet base from which to visit nearby Zell am See.
760m

Brundage Mountain USA
Remote, uncrowded Idaho area with glorious views across the lake towards Hell's Canyon. Mostly intermediate slopes.
1760m; slopes 1760–2320m
📏 5 ➚ 1,300 *acres*

Bruneck Italy
German name for Brunico.

Brunico Italy
Town with gondola link into the Plan de Corones/Kronplatz area.
📏 8 ➚ 20km

Bruson 532
Relaxing respite from Verbier's crowds, on the other side of Le Châble. Well placed for car trips to Chamonix and Champéry.

Les Bugnenets-Savagnieres Switzerland
Very small area in the Jura mountains, north of Neuchatel. Short runs served by drag lifts.
slopes 1090–1440m
📏 7 ➚ 30km

Burke Mountain USA
Uncrowded, isolated family resort in Vermont with mostly intermediate slopes.
385m; slopes 385–995m
📏 4 ➚ 130 *acres*

Bürserberg Austria
Undistinguished valley town near Brand.
900m; slopes 1035–1850m
📏 13 ➚ 50km

Cairngorm 715

Caldirola Italy
Genoese weekend day-tripper spot in a remote region off the motorway to Turin.
1010m; slopes 1010–1460m
📏 3 ➚ 5km

Cambre-d'Aze France
Quiet ski area in the Pyrenees with few British visitors. Good beginner and intermediate terrain.
1640m; slopes 1640–2400m
📏 17 ➚ 35km
✉ *Pyrenees Ski Experience*

Camigliatello Italy
Tiny area on the foot of the Italian 'boot' near Cosenza. Weekend/day-trip spot.
1270m; slopes 1270–1750m
📏 4 ➚ 6km

Campitello 478
✉ *First Choice Ski, Neilson*

Campitello Matese Italy
The only slopes near Naples. Surprisingly large area when snowcover is complete. Weekend crowds.
1440m; slopes 1440–2100m
📏 8 ➚ 40km

Campo di Giove Italy
Highest slopes in L'Aquila region east of Rome.
1070m 📏 6 ➚ 23km

Campodolcino Italy
Valley town with new funicular up to Madesimo's slopes.
1070m; slopes 1545–2880m
📏 6 ➚ 8km

Campo Felice Italy
Easiest resort to reach from Rome, off Aquila motorway. One of the better lift systems in the vicinity.
1410m; slopes 1520–2065m
📏 14 ➚ 40km

Campo Imperatore Italy
One of the best of many little areas east of Rome in L'Aquila region.

1980m
📏 8 ➚ 20km

Canazei 478
✉ *Crystal, Equity Ski, First Choice Ski, Inghams, Interhome, Neilson, Ski Wild*

Candanchu/Astún 698

Canillo 115
Small, quiet town, with good sports facilities and newly developed lifts and slopes, linked to Soldeu.

Canmore Canada
Old frontier town on the way to Nakiska/Fortress, an attractive alternative to staying in Banff.

Cannon USA
One of several small New Hampshire resorts scattered along the Interstate 93 highway; a ski area and nothing more.
605m; slopes 605–1260m
📏 9 ➚ 165 *acres*
✉ *Equity Ski*

The Canyons 623
✉ *AmeriCan Ski, Ski All America, Ski Independence, Ski Safari, Ski The American Dream, Ski Tracer, Skiworld, United Vacations*

Cardrona 720

Les Carroz-d'Arâches 300
An attractive, spacious village on the road up to Flaine.
✉ *360 Sun and Ski, Alps Accommodation, AmeriCan Ski, Erna Low, Lagrange Holidays, Peak Retreats, Ski Independence, Ski Leisure Direction, Ski4you*

Caspoggio Italy
Attractive, unspoiled village north-east of Lake Como, with easy slopes; more at Chiesa.
1100m; slopes 1100–2155m
📏 8 ➚ 22km

Castelrotto Italy
Picturesque village west of Sella Ronda circuit with small sunny Alpine area and good cross-country trails. *1060m*

Castel S Angelo Italy
Tiny area in Macerata region near Adriatic Riviera.
805m 📏 4 ➚ 2km

Castle Mountain Canada
Remote resort south of Calgary. Good proportion of intermediate and advanced terrain.
1410m; slopes 1410–2270m
📏 5 ➚ 250 *acres*

Cauterets 418
✉ *Lagrange Holidays, Ski Leisure Direction*

Cavalese Italy
Unspoiled medieval town in Val di Fiemme with pretty slopes at Alpe Cermis.
1000m; slopes 975–2265m
📏 9 ➚ 70km
✉ *Thomson*

Caviahue Argentina
Mountain village at the foot of the Copahue Volcano, 357km from Neuquén City.

1645m; slopes 1645–2045m
🚡 8 ⬆ 3716km

The Cedars Lebanon
The largest of Lebanon's ski areas, 130km/80 miles inland from Beirut.
1850m; slopes 2100–2700m 🚡 5

Ceillac France
Tight cluster of rustic old buildings near Serre-Chevalier.
1600m; slopes 1600–2400m

Celerina 526
Quiet, unpretentious village, with links up to St Moritz's Corviglia sector.

Cerkno Slovenia
Modern, family resort 50km/31 miles from Ljubljana.
1935m; slopes 1935–1290m
🚡 8 ⬆ 70 hectares

Cerler Spain
Very limited, purpose-built resort with a compact ski area similar to nearby Andorra's Arinsal.
1500m; slopes 1500–2630m
🚡 16 ⬆ 45km

Le Cernix France
Hamlet near Megève where Les Saisies' slopes link to those of Crest-Voland. Uncrowded retreat.
1250m; slopes 1150–1950m
🚡 41 ⬆ 80km

Cerrato Lago Italy
Very limited area near the coastal town of La Spezia.
1270m; slopes 1270–1890m
🚡 5 ⬆ 3km

Cerro Bayo Argentina
Limited area amid stunning scenery 10km/6 miles from La Angostura, and 90km/56 miles from San Carlos de Bariloche.
slopes 1050–1780m
🚡 11 ⬆ 200 hectares
✉ Snoworks

Cerro Castor 727

Cerro Catedral (Bariloche) 727
✉ Scott Dunn Latin America, Ski All America

Cerro Mirador 728

Cervinia 428
✉ Alpine Answers, Club Med, Crystal, Elegant Resorts, First Choice Ski, Independent Ski Links, Inghams, Interhome, Momentum Ski, Ski Solutions, Ski Supreme, Ski Tracer, Ski Weekend, Ski4you, Thomson

Cesana Torinese 330
Little Italian village in the Milky Way.

Le Châble 532
Small village below Verbier, linked by gondola.

Chacaltaya Bolivia
Highest lift-served ski area in the world and the only ski area in Bolivia.
5190m; slopes 5220–5420m
🚡 1 ⬆ 2km
✉ Scott Dunn Latin America

Chaillol France
Cross-country base on the edge of the Ecrins National Park..
1600m; slopes 1450–2000m 🚡 11

Chamois Italy
Small area above Buisson, a few miles down the road from Valtournenche (near Cervinia).
1815m; slopes 1815–2270m
🚡 9 ⬆ 20km

Chamonix 264
✉ Alpine Answers, Alpine Weekends, Barrelli Ski, Bigfoot Travel, BoardnLodge, Catered Ski Chalets, Chalet Group, Chalet World Ski, Chamonix.uk.com, Club Med, Club Pavilion, Collineige, Corporate Ski Company, Crystal, Directski.com, Erna Low, Esprit Ski, Flexiski, High Mountain Holidays, Independent Ski Links, Inghams, Interhome, Lagrange Holidays, Made to Measure Holidays, McNab Snowboarding, Momentum Ski, Mountain Tracks, Neilson, Oxford Ski Company, Peak Retreats, Ski Expectations, Ski France, Ski Freshtracks, Ski Independence, Ski Leisure Direction, Ski Line, Ski Solutions, Ski Tracer, Ski Weekend, Ski Weekends, Ski4you, Skifrance4less, Skitopia, Thomson, Total, White Roc

Champagny-en-Vanoise 343
Charming village linking to the La Plagne network.
✉ Barrelli Ski, Erna Low, Independent Ski Links, Lagrange Holidays, Made to Measure Holidays, Peak Retreats, Ski Independence, Skitopia

Champéry 499
✉ Alpine Answers, Chalet Group, Corporate Ski Company, Made to Measure Holidays, Piste Artiste Ltd, Ski Tracer, Ski Weekend, White Roc

Champex Switzerland
Lakeside hamlet, a nice quiet, unspoiled base from which to visit Verbier's area.
1470m; slopes 1470–2220m
🚡 4 ⬆ 8km

Champfér 526
Lakeside hamlet between St Moritz and Silvaplana.

Champoluc 450
Unspoiled village at one end of the Monterosa Ski area.
✉ Alpine Answers, Catered Ski Chalets, Crystal, CV Travel, Momentum Ski, Mountain Tracks, Ski 2, Ski Tracer, Ski Yogi, Skitopia

Champorcher Italy
Small village south of Aosta valley with tall but narrow ski area, mostly red runs on open slopes, with one black through the trees..
1430m; slopes 1430–2500m
🚡 5 ⬆ 21km

Champoussin 499
Quiet mountainside village in the Champéry area.

Chamrousse France
Functional family resort near Grenoble, with sheltered slopes.
1650m; slopes 1400–2255m
🚡 26 ⬆ 77km
✉ Erna Low, Lagrange Holidays, Ski4you

Chandolin Switzerland
Picturesque, unspoiled village in the Val d'Anniviers off the Valais, with high, easy open slopes (shared with St Luc).
1935m; slopes 1660–3025m
🚡 16 ⬆ 75km

Chantemerle 364
Valley village with direct access to Serre-Chevalier's slopes.

Chapa Verde Chile
60km/37 miles north-east of Rancagua and 145km/90 miles from Santiago.
1200m; slopes 1200–2500m
🚡 4 ⬆ 1200 hectares

Chapelco Argentina
Small ski area with full infrastructure of services 19km/12 miles from sizeable town of San Martin de Los Andes.
slopes 1250–1980m
🚡 10 ⬆ 140 hectares
✉ Ski All America, Snoworks

La Chapelle-d'Abondance 274
Unspoiled village 5km/3 miles down the valley from Châtel.
✉ Ski Addiction, Ski La Cote

Charlotte Pass 718

Château d'Oex Switzerland
Pleasant little valley town that is the main French-speaking component of the shared lift-pass area around Gstaad.
970m; slopes 890–3000m
🚡 67 ⬆ 250km
✉ Alpine Tours

Châtel 274
✉ Catered Ski Chalets, Chalet Group, Connick Ski, Equity Ski, Haig Ski, Interhome, Lagrange Holidays, Peak Retreats, Rocketski, Ski Addiction, Ski Independence, Ski Leisure Direction, Ski Line, Ski Rosie, Ski Tracer, Skialot, Snowfocus, Susie Ward Alpine Holidays, Tops Ski Chalets and Club Hotels

Le Chatelard France
Small resort in remote Parc des Bauges between Lake Annecy and Chambéry.

Chiesa Italy
Attractive beginners' resort with a fairly high plateau of easy runs above the resort.
1000m; slopes 1700–2335m
🚡 16 ⬆ 50km

Le Chinaillon 279
Modern, chalet-style village above Le Grand-Bornand.

Chiomonte Italy
Tiny resort on the main road east of Bardonecchia and Sauze d'Oulx.
745m; slopes 745–2210m
🚡 6 ⬆ 10km

Chsea Algeria
Largest of Algeria's skiable areas, 135km/84 miles south-east of coastal town of Alger in the Djur Djur mountains.
1860m; slopes 1860–2510m 🚡 2

Chur-Brambruesch Switzerland
Chur's local ski area.
slopes 1200–2175m
🚡 7 ⬆ 25km

Churwalden Switzerland
Hamlet on fringe of Lenzerheide-Valbella area.
1230m; slopes 1230–2865m
🚡 35 ⬆ 155km

Claviere 330
Small Italian village linked to Montgenèvre (in France)
✉ Crystal, Equity Ski, First Choice Ski, Rocketski, Ski4you

La Clusaz 279
✉ Aravis Alpine Retreat, Classic Ski Limited, Crystal, Interhome, Lagrange Holidays, Last Resort, Made to Measure Holidays, Ski Activity, Ski Tracer, Ski Weekend, Skitopia, Snowlife

Les Coches 343
Small, purpose-built village, linked to the La Plagne ski area.
✉ Catered Ski Chalets, Erna Low, Family Ski Company, Finlays, Independent Ski Links, Lagrange Holidays, Mountainsun, Ski Independence, Ski Leisure Direction, Ski Line, Ski4you

Cogne Italy
One of Aosta valley's larger villages near Pila.
1530m; slopes 1530–2245m
🚡 5 ⬆ 8km

Colfosco 461
Small but sprawling village that makes up part of the Sella Ronda circuit.

Colle di Tenda Italy
Dour, modern resort that shares a good area with much nicer Limone. Not far from Nice.
1400m; slopes 1120–2040m
🚡 33 ⬆ 80km

Colle Isarco Italy
Brenner Pass area – and the bargain-shopping town of Vipiteno is nearby.
1095m; slopes 1095–2720m
🚡 5 ⬆ 15km

Le Collet-d'Allevard France
Ski area of sizeable summer spa Allevard-les-Bains in remote region east of Chambéry.
1450m; slopes 1450–2100m
🚡 13 ⬆ 35km

Collio Italy
Tiny area of short runs in a remote spot between lakes Garda and d'Iseo.
840m; slopes 840–1715m 🚡 14

Les Collons 532
A collection of roadside chalets, including bars/restaurants, below purpose-built Thyon 2000.
✉ Alpine Tours

Eaglecrest USA
Close to famous Yukon gold
rush town Skagway. Family
resort famous for its ski school.
365m; slopes 365–790m
⛰ 3 ⛷ 640 acres

Eaux-Bonnes-Gourette France
Most snow-sure resort in the
French Pyrenees. Very popular
with local families, so best
avoided at weekends.
1400m; slopes 1400–2400m
⛰ 23 ⛷ 30km

Eben im Pongau Austria
Part of Salzburger Sportwelt
Amadé area that includes nearby
St Johann, Wagrain, Flachau and
Zauchensee.
855m; slopes 855–2185m
⛰ 100 ⛷ 350km
⊠ *Solo's*

Ehrwald Austria
Friendly, relaxed, pretty village
with several nicely varied areas,
notably the Zugspitz glacier.
1000m; slopes 1000–3000m
⛰ 11 ⛷ 45km
⊠ *Lagrange Holidays*

El Colorado/Farellones 728
Area connected to the Valle
Nevado ski area.
slopes 2430–3335m
⛰ 19 ⛷ 40km

Eldora Mountain USA
Day-visitor resort with varied
terrain (including plenty of steep
stuff) close to Denver Boulder.
All forest trails, but with some
good glade areas.
2795m; slopes 2805–3230m
⛰ 12 ⛷ 680 acres

Elk Meadows USA
Area south of Salt Lake City, a
day trip from Park City.
2775m; slopes 2745–3170m
⛰ 6 ⛷ 1,400 acres

Ellmau 135
⊠ *Crystal, Inghams, Interhome,
Neilson, Ramblers Holidays, Ski
Line, Ski Tracer, Ski Wild,
Thomson*

Elm Switzerland
One hour from Zurich, at the
head of a quiet valley.
1000m; slopes 1000–2100m
⛰ 6 ⛷ 40km

Encamp 108

Enego Italy
Limited weekend day-trippers'
area near Vicenza and Trento.
1300m; slopes 1300–1445m
⛰ 7 ⛷ 30km

Engelberg 560
⊠ *Alpine Answers, Corporate
Ski Company, Crystal,
Independent Ski Links,
Inntravel, Interhome, Kuoni,
Made to Measure Holidays,
Momentum Ski, Ski Freshtracks,
Ski Solutions, Ski Tracer, Ski
Weekend, Swiss Travel Service,
Switzerland Travel Centre,
Waymark Holidays, White Roc*

Entrèves 439
Hotels at the base of the lift up
to Courmayeur's slopes.

Escaldes Andorra
Central valley town, effectively
part of Andorra la Vella.

Etna Italy
Scenic, uncrowded, short-season
area on the volcano's flank, 20
minutes from Nickolossi.
1800m; slopes 1800–2350m
⛷ 5km

Evolène Switzerland
Charming rustic village with own
little area in unspoiled,
attractive setting south of Sion.
1380m; slopes 1300–3330m
⛰ 100 ⛷ 400km

Faak am See Austria
Limited area, one of five
overlooking town of Villach.
560m; slopes 560–800m
⛰ 1 ⛷ 2km

Fai della Paganella Italy
Trentino village near Madonna
that shares its slopes with
Andalo.

Fairmont Hot Springs Canada
Major luxury spa complex ideal
for a relaxing holiday with some
gentle skiing thrown in.
⛰ 2 ⛷ 60 acres

Faistenau Austria
Cross-country area close to
Salzburg and St Wolfgang.
Limited Alpine slopes.
785m; slopes 785–1000m
⛰ 5 ⛷ 3km

Falcade Italy
Trentino village south of the
Sella Ronda with lifts up to
slopes at San Pellegrino.
1145m; slopes 1145–2170m
⛰ 11 ⛷ 39km
⊠ *Alpine Tours*

Falera 509
Small village with access to ski
area shared by Flims and Laax.

Le Falgoux France
One of the most beautiful old
villages in France, set in the very
scenic Volcano National Park.
Several ski areas nearby.
930m; slopes 930–1350m

Falkertsee Austria
Base area rather than a village,
with bleak, open slopes in
contrast to nearby
Badkleinkirchheim.
1690m; slopes 1690–2385m
⛰ 5 ⛷ 15km

Falls Creek 718

La Feclaz France
One of several little resorts in
the remote Parc des Bauges.

Fernie 667
⊠ *Alpine Answers, AmeriCan
Ski, American Ski Classics,
Canadian Powder Tours,
Catered Ski Chalets, Chalet
Group, Crystal, Frontier Ski,
Independent Ski Links,
Inghams, Made to Measure
Holidays, Neilson, Ski Activity,
Ski All America, Ski Freshtracks,
Ski Independence, Ski Safari,
Ski The American Dream, Ski
Tracer, Skitopia, Skiworld,
Snoworks, Virgin Snow*

Fieberbrunn 234
⊠ *Snowscape, Thomson*

Fiesch Switzerland
Traditional Rhône valley resort
close to Brig, with a lift up to
Fiescheralp.
1060m; slopes 1900–2900m
⛰ 50 ⛷ 100km

Fiescheralp Switzerland
Mountain outpost of Fiesch,
down in the Rhône valley.
2220m; slopes 1900–2900m
⛰ 32 ⛷ 90km

Filzmoos Austria
Charming, unspoiled, friendly
village with leisurely slopes that
are ideal for novices. Good snow
record for its height.
1055m; slopes 1055–1645m
⛰ 12 ⛷ 32km ⊠ *Inghams*

Finkenberg 172
Between Mayrhofen and
Hintertux.
⊠ *Crystal*

Fiss 234
Traditional village sharing an
extensive area with Serfaus.
⊠ *Alpine Tours, Interhome*

Flachau 234
Quiet, spacious village linking
via Wagrain to Alpendorf.
⊠ *Interhome, Made to Measure
Holidays*

Flachauwinkl Austria
Tiny ski station beside Tauern
autobahn, at the centre of an
extensive three-valley lift
network linking Kleinarl to
Zauchensee.
930m; slopes 800–2185m
⛰ 59 ⛷ 200km

Flaine 300
⊠ *Alpine Answers, Altitude
Holidays, Classic Ski Limited,
Crystal, Erna Low, Independent
Ski Links, Inghams, Lagrange
Holidays, Neilson, Ski
Freshtracks, Ski Independence,
Ski Leisure Direction, Ski
Tracer, Ski Weekend, Ski4you,
Skifrance4less, Thomson*

Flims 509
⊠ *Alpine Answers, Corporate
Ski Company, Interhome, Made
to Measure Holidays,
Momentum Ski, Powder Byrne,
Ski Tracer, Ski Weekend, Swiss
Travel Service, Switzerland
Travel Centre, White Heat
Skiing, White Roc*

Flumet France
Surprisingly large traditional
village, the main place from
which to ski the sizeable Val
d'Arly ski area.
1000m; slopes 1000–1600m
⛰ 10 ⛷ 40km

Flumserberg Switzerland
Collective name for the villages
sharing a varied area an hour
south-east of Zürich.
1220m; slopes 1220–2220m
⛰ 42 ⛷ 142km

Folgaria Italy
Largest of several resorts east of
Trento. Old lift system.

Fieberbrunn *1165m; slopes 1185–2005m*
⛰ 38 ⛷ 70km
⊠ *Alpine Tours, Ski Wild*

Folgarida 448
Small Dolomite village, with
links to Madonna di Campiglio
⊠ *Alpine Tours, Equity Ski,
Rocketski*

Foncine-le-Haut France
Major cross-country village in
the Jura Mountains with
extensive trails.
⊠ *Lagrange Holidays*

Fonni Gennaragentu Italy
Sardinia's only 'ski area' – and
it's tiny.
⛰ 1 ⛷ 5km

Font-Romeu 418
⊠ *Lagrange Holidays, Pyrenees
Ski Experience, Solo's,
Waymark Holidays*

Foppolo Italy
Relatively unattractive but user-
friendly village, a short transfer
from Bergamo.
1510m; slopes 1610–2160m
⛰ 9 ⛷ 47km
⊠ *Equity Ski*

Forca Canapine Italy
Limited area near the Adriatic
and Ascoli Piceno. Popular with
weekend day-trippers.
1450m; slopes 1450–1690m
⛰ 11 ⛷ 20km

Formazza Italy
Cross-country base with some
downhill slopes.
1280m; slopes 1275–1755m
⛷ 8km

Formigal 698
⊠ *White Roc*

Formigueres Spain
Small downhill and cross-
country area in the Neiges
Catalanes.
slopes 1700–2350m
⛰ 8 ⛷ 19km
⊠ *Pyrenees Ski Experience*

Le Fornet 398
Rustic, old hamlet 3km/2 miles
down the valley from Val-d'Isère.

Forstau Austria
Secluded hamlet above
Radstadt-Schladming road. Very
limited area with old lifts.
930m; slopes 930–1885m
⛰ 7 ⛷ 14km

La Foux-d'Allos France
Purpose-built resort that shares
intermediate area with Pra-Loup.
1800m; slopes 1800–2600m
⛰ 52 ⛷ 167km
⊠ *Lagrange Holidays, Ski4you*

Frabosa Soprana Italy
One of numerous little areas
south of Turin, well placed for
combining winter sports with
Riviera sightseeing.
850m; slopes 860–1740m
⛰ 7 ⛷ 40km

Frisco 592
Small town based on a Victorian
settlement, down the valley from
Breckenridge.
⊠ *AmeriCan Ski*

Frontignano   Italy
Best lift system in the Macerata region, near the Adriatic Riviera.
1340m; slopes 1340–2000m
⛷ 8 🚡 10km

Fügen   Austria
Unspoiled Zillertal village with limited area best suited to beginners.
550m; slopes 550–2400m
⛷ 19 🚡 48km
✉ *Lagrange Holidays, Ski Wild*

Fulpmes   **221**
✉ *Crystal*

Furano   Japan
Small resort on snowy northern island of Hokkaido, two hours from Sapporo.
235m; slopes 235–1065m ⛷ 13

Fusch   Austria
Cheaper, quiet place to stay when visiting Zell am See.
805m; slopes 805–1050m
⛷ 2 🚡 5km

Fuschl am See   Austria
Attractive, unspoiled, lakeside village close to St Wolfgang and Salzburg, 30 minutes from its slopes. *670m*

Gålå   Norway
Base for downhill and cross-country skiing, an hour's drive north of Lillehammer.
930m; slopes 830–1150m
⛷ 7 🚡 20km ✉ *Inntravel*

Gallio   Italy
One of several low resorts near Vicenza and Trento. Popular with weekend day-trippers.
1100m; slopes 1100–1550m
⛷ 11 🚡 50km

Galtür   **150**
Charming village near Ischgl.
✉ *Directski.com, Inghams, Made to Measure Holidays*

Gambarie d'Aspromonte Italy
Italy's second most southerly ski area (after Mt Etna). On the 'toe' of the Italian 'boot' near Reggio di Calabria.
1310m; slopes 1310–1650m ⛷ 3

Gargellen   **177**
Quiet village tucked up a side valley in the Montafon area.
✉ *Interhome, Made to Measure Holidays*

Garmisch-Partenkirchen
  Germany
Twin classic old-fashioned winter sports resorts; unspoiled, traditional Partenkirchen much the prettier. Superb main area of wooded runs when the unreliable snow-cover allows.
720m; slopes 720–2830m
⛷ 38 🚡 71km
✉ *Moswin Tours*

Gaschurn   **177**
Village in the Montafon area,
✉ *Made to Measure Holidays*

Gaustablikk   Norway
Small snow-sure Alpine area on Mt Gausta in southern Norway.
🚡 15km
✉ *Waymark Holidays*

Gavarnie   France
Traditional village and fair-sized ski area, with the longest green run in the Pyrenees. Grand views of the Cirque de Gavarnie.
1400m; slopes 1850–2400m
⛷ 11 🚡 45km

Geilo   **703**
✉ *Crystal, Headwater Holidays, Inntravel, Neilson*

Gérardmer   France
Sizeable lakeside resort in the northerly Vosges mountains near Strasbourg, with plenty of amenities. Limited downhill slopes nearby include one of almost 4km/2.5 miles.
665m; slopes 750–1150m
⛷ 20 🚡 40km
✉ *Lagrange Holidays*

Gerlitzen Alpe   Austria
A gondola ride above Villach and with good views.
500m; slopes 1003–1911m
⛷ 14 🚡 20km

Gerlos   Austria
One of Austria's few inexpensive but fairly snow-sure resorts, linked to Zell im Zillertal and Königsleiten.
1250m; slopes 1250–2300m
⛷ 40 🚡 115km ✉ *Interhome*

Gerlosplatte   Austria
Inexpensive but fairly snow-sure area linked to Königsleiten, Gerlos and Zell am Ziller.

Les Gets   **307**
✉ *Alpine Answers, AmeriCan Ski, Catered Ski Chalets, Chalet Group, Descent International, Esprit Ski, Ferme de Montagne, First Choice Ski, Haig Ski, Independent Ski Links, Lagrange Holidays, Made to Measure Holidays, Oxford Ski Company, Peak Retreats, Rocketski, Ski Activity, Ski Expectations, Ski Famille, Ski Hillwood, Ski Independence, Ski Tracer, Ski Weekend, Total Resort, Thomson*

La Giettaz   **311**
Tiny rural village between La Clusaz and Megève.

Gitschtal/Weissbriach Austria
One of many little ski areas near Hermagor in eastern Austria..
690m; slopes 690–1400m
⛷ 4 🚡 5km

Glaris   Switzerland
Hamlet base station for the uncrowded Rinerhorn section of the Davos ski area.
1455m; slopes 1455–2490m
⛷ 5 🚡 30km

Glencoe   **715**

Glenshee   **715**

Going   **135**
Small local ski area near Ellmau,. ✉ *Solo's*

Goldegg   Austria
Year-round resort famous for its lakeside castle. Limited slopes but Wagrain (Salzburger Sportwelt) is nearby.
825m; slopes 825–1250m
⛷ 4 🚡 12km

Golden   Canada
Small logging town, the place to stay when visiting Kicking Horse resort 15 minutes away.

Golte   Slovenia
Ski area in the East Karavante mountains, above Mozirje.
⛷ 4 🚡 18km

Gore Mountain   USA
One of the better areas in New York State. Near Lake Placid, sufficiently far north to avoid worst weekend crowds.
455m; slopes 455–1095m
⛷ 9 🚡 290 acres

Göriach   Austria
Hamlet with trail connecting into one of the longest, snow-sure cross-country areas in Europe.
1250m

Gosau   Austria
Straggling village with plenty of pretty, if low, runs. Snow-sure Obertauern and Schladming are within reach.
755m; slopes 755–1800m
⛷ 37 🚡 80km

Götzens   Austria
Valley village base for Axamer Lizum slopes.
870m ⛷ 1
✉ *Lagrange Holidays*

Grächen   Switzerland
Charming chalet-village reached by tricky access road off the approach to Zermatt. A small area of open slopes, mainly above the trees and of red-run difficulty.
1615m; slopes 1615–2890m
⛷ 13 🚡 40km
✉ *Interhome*

Le Grand-Bornand   France
Pleasant, atmospheric village with a pretty, extensive, varied intermediate area close to La Clusaz and a quieter base.
1000m; slopes 1000–2100m
⛷ 39 🚡 90km
✉ *Lagrange Holidays, Last Resort, Thomson*

Grand Targhee   **640**
Powder skiing paradise an hour from Jackson Hole.
✉ *AmeriCan Ski, Ski Safari*

Grangesises   Italy
Small satellite of Sestriere, with lifts up to the main slopes.

Granite Peak   USA
One of the oldest areas in the Great Lakes region..
⛷ 7 🚡 400 acres

Grau Roig   **113**
Mini-resort at foot of Pas de la Casa's only woodland runs, with one smart hotel and abundant day-tripper parking.

La Grave   **309**
✉ *Alpine Answers, AmeriCan Ski, Interhome, Lagrange Holidays, Mountain Tracks, Peak Retreats, Ski Freshtracks, Ski Weekend*

Great Divide   USA
Area near Helena, Montana, best for experts. Mostly bowls; plus near-extreme Rawhide Gulch.
1765m; slopes 1765–2195m
⛷ 6 🚡 720 acres

Gresse-en-Vercors   France
Resort south of Grenoble. Sheltered slopes worth noting for bad-weather days.
1250m; slopes 1600–1800m
⛷ 16 🚡 18km
✉ *Interhome, Lagrange Holidays*

Gressoney-la-Trinité   **450**
Village in the Monterosa Ski area.
✉ *Alpine Answers, Crystal, Inspired to Ski, Momentum Ski, Mountain Tracks, Ski Addiction, Ski Freshtracks, Ski Tracer, Ski Yogi, Snoworks*

Gressoney-St-Jean   **450**
LVillage in the Monterosa Ski area.
✉ *Alpine Answers, Italian Safaris*

Grimentz   Switzerland
Exceptionally cute, unspoiled rustic village with high, varied runs. In the Val d'Anniviers.
1670m; slopes 1570–2900m
⛷ 12 🚡 50km
✉ *Mountain Tracks, Ski Freshtracks*

Grindelwald   **511**
✉ *Corporate Ski Company, Crystal, Elegant Resorts, Independent Ski Links, Inghams, Interhome, Kuoni, Lagrange Holidays, Made to Measure Holidays, Momentum Ski, Powder Byrne, Ski Freshtracks, Solo's, Swiss Travel Service, Switzerland Travel Centre, Thomson, White Roc*

Grossarl   **129**
Secluded village in the Gastein valley.

Grouse Mountain   Canada
The Vancouver area with the largest lift capacity. Superb city views from mostly easy slopes.
880m; slopes 880–1245m
⛷ 11 🚡 120 acres
✉ *AmeriCan Ski*

Grünau   Austria
Spacious riverside village in a lovely lake-filled part of eastern Austria. Nicely varied area
525m; slopes 600–1600m
⛷ 14 🚡 40km

Gryon   **543**
Village below Villars, with which it shares a ski area.

Gstaad   **560**
✉ *Alpine Answers, Corporate Ski Company, Interhome, Made to Measure Holidays, Momentum Ski, Ski Weekend, Switzerland Travel Centre, White Roc*

Gunstock USA
One of the New Hampshire resorts closest to Boston, popular with families. Primarily easy slopes. Gorgeous Lake Winnisquam views.
275m; slopes 275–700m
⬛8 🚠 220 acres

Guthega 718

Guzet France
A charming cluster of chalets set among a pine forest at Guzet 1400. Three main sectors offer slopes for all levels.
1400m; slopes 1100–2100m
⬛14 🚠 40km

Hafjell Norway
Main ski area for Lillehammer.
⬛12 🚠 33km

Hakuba Happo One Japan
European-style resort four hours from Tokyo. One of Japan's more challenging areas.
750m; slopes 750–1830m ⬛33

Harper Mountain Canada
Small, family-friendly resort in Kamloops, British Colombia.
1100m; slopes 1100–1525m
⬛3 🚠 400 acres

Harrachov Czech Republic
Closest resort to Prague, with enough terrain to justify a day trip. No beginner area.
650m; slopes 650–1020m
⬛15 🚠 8runs

Hasliberg Switzerland
Four rustic hamlets on a sunny plateau overlooking Meiringen and Lake Brienz. Two of them are the bottom stations of a varied intermediate area.
1055m; slopes 600–2435m
⬛16 🚠 60km

Haus 195
Village next to Schladming.

Haystack USA
Minor satellite of Mount Snow, in Vermont, but with a bit more steep skiing.
580m; slopes 580–1095m
⬛26 🚠 540 acres

Heavenly 568
✉ AmeriCan Ski, American Ski Classics, Crystal, Directski.com, Equity Ski, Erna Low, Independent Ski Links, Ski Activity, Ski All America, Ski Independence, Ski Line, Ski Safari, Ski The American Dream, Ski Tracer, Skiworld, Trailfinders, United Vacations

Hebalm Austria
One of many small areas in Austria's easternmost ski region near Slovenian border.
1350m; slopes 1350–1400m
⬛6 🚠 11km

Heiligenblut Austria
Picturesque village in beautiful surroundings with mostly high terrain..
1300m; slopes 1300–2910m
⬛14 🚠 55km

Hemlock Resort Canada
Area 89km/55 miles east of Vancouver towards Sun Peaks. Mostly intermediate terrain and with snowfall of 600 inches a year.
1000m; slopes 1000–1375m
⬛4 🚠 350 acres

Hemsedal 705
✉ Crystal, Neilson

Heremence Switzerland
Quiet village in unspoiled attractive setting south of Sion. Verbier's slopes are accessed a few minutes' drive away at Les Masses. *1250m*

Hermagor Austria
Main village base for the Nassfeld ski area in Carinthia.
600m; slopes 610–2000m
⬛30 🚠 100km

Hintermoos 143
Village in the Hochkönig area.
✉ Elevation Holidays

Hintersee Austria
Easy slopes very close to Salzburg. Several long top-to-bottom runs and lifts means the size of the area is greatly reduced if the snowline is high.
745m; slopes 750–1470m
⬛9 🚠 40km

Hinterstoder Austria
Quiet, unspoiled traditional village, 80km/50 miles east of Salzburg, with a good snow record for its height.
600m; slopes 600–1860m
⬛10 🚠 35km

Hinterthal 143
Village in the Hochkönig area.
✉ Elevation Holidays

Hintertux/Tux valley 138
✉ Ski Tracer, Snoworks

Hippach 172
Hamlet near a crowd-free lift into Mayrhofen's main area.

Hochgurgl 182
Quiet village with connection to Obergurgl's slopes.
✉ Inghams, Neilson, Ski Expectations, Thomson

Hochkönig 143

Hochpillberg Austria
Peaceful, virtually traffic-free hamlet with fabulous views towards Innsbruck and a lift into varied terrain above Schwaz.
1000m; slopes 1000–2030m
⬛6 🚠 10km

Hochsölden 199
Satellite above Sölden.

Hoch-Ybrig Switzerland
Purpose-built complex only 64km/40 miles south-east of Zürich, with facilities for families.
1050m; slopes 1050–2200m
⬛16 🚠 50km

Hohuanshan Taiwan
Limited ski area with short season in high, wild, inaccessible Miitaku mountains. Also known as Mt Hehuan.
3275m ⬛1

Holiday Valley USA
Family resort in New York State, south-east of Buffalo.
slopes 485–685m
⬛12 🚠 270 acres

Hollersbach Austria
Hamlet near Mittersill, over Pass Thurn from Kitzbühel, with a gondola up to the Resterhöhe above Pass Thurn.
805m; slopes 805–1000m
⬛2 🚠 5km

Homewood 566

Hoodoo Ski Bowl USA
Typical Oregon area with sizeable but short runs. Snow record isn't as good as its competitors near Portland.
1420m; slopes 1420–1740m
⬛5 🚠 800 acres

Hopfgarten 202
Small chalet village with lift link into extensive Ski Welt area.
✉ Contiki, First Choice Ski

Horseshoe Resort Canada
Toronto region resort with high-capacity lift system and 100% snowmaking. The second mountain – The Heights – is open to members only.
310m; slopes 310–405m
⬛7 🚠 60 acres

Hospental 494
Small village connected to Andermatt by road and rail.

Les Houches 419
✉ AmeriCan Ski, Barrelli Ski, Bigfoot Travel, Club Pavilion, Erna Low, Lagrange Holidays, Peak Retreats, Ski Expectations, Ski France, Ski Leisure Direction, Ski4you

Hovden Norway
Big, modern luxury lakeside hotel in wilderness midway between Oslo and Bergen. Cross-country venue with some Alpine slopes.
820m; slopes 820–1175m
⬛5 🚠 14km

La Hoya Argentina
Small uncrowded resort 15km/9 miles from the small town of Esquel.
slopes 1350–2150m
⬛6 🚠 22km

Huez 241
Charming old hamlet on the road up to Alpe-d'Huez.

Hunter Mountain USA
Popular New Yorkers' area so it gets very crowded at weekends.
485m; slopes 485–975m
⬛14 🚠 230 acres

Hüttschlag Austria
Hamlet in a dead-end valley with lifts into the Gastein area at nearby Grossarl.
1020m; slopes 1020–1220m ⬛1

Hyundai Sungwoo Resort South Korea
Modern high-rise resort, 140km/87 miles from Seoul. Own English-language web site at www.hdsungwoo.co.kr. ⬛9

Idre Fjäll Sweden
Collective name for four areas 490km/300 miles north-west of Stockholm.
slopes 590–890m
⬛30 🚠 28km

Igls 146
✉ Inghams, Lagrange Holidays, Made to Measure Holidays

Iizuna Japan
Tiny area 2.5 hours from Tokyo. ⬛6

Incline Village USA
Large village on northern edge of Lake Tahoe – a reasonable stop-off if you are touring.

Indianhead USA
South Lake Superior area with the most snowfall in the region.
395m; slopes 395–585m
⬛12 🚠 195 acres

Inneralpbach 127
Small satellite of Alpbach, 3km/2 miles up the valley.

Innerarosa 496
The prettiest part of Arosa.

Innichen Italy
German name for San Candido.

Innsbruck 146
✉ Corporate Ski Company, Directski.com, Lagrange Holidays

Interlaken 545
Lakeside summer resort near Wengen/Grindelwald/Mürren.
✉ Crystal, Kuoni, Swiss Travel Service

Ischgl 150
✉ Alpine Answers, Crystal, First Choice Ski, Inghams, Made to Measure Holidays, Momentum Ski, Ski Freshtracks, Ski Solutions, Ski Tracer, Ski Wild

Ishiuchi Maruyama-Gala-Yuzawa Kogen Japan
Three resorts with a shared lift pass 90 minutes from Tokyo by bullet train and offering the largest ski area in the central Honshu region.
255m; slopes 255–920m ⬛52

Isola 2000 419
✉ Club Pavilion, Crystal, Erna Low, Lagrange Holidays, Ski France, Ski Leisure Direction, Ski4you, Skifrance4less

Iso Syöte 701
✉ Crystal, Thomson

Itter 202
Next to Söll.

Jackson USA
Classic New England village, and a minor cross-country base. A lovely place from which to ski New Hampshire's Alpine areas.

Jackson Hole 640
⊠ *Alpine Answers, AmeriCan Ski, American Ski Classics, Crystal, Inghams, Momentum Ski, Mountain Tracks, Ski Activity, Ski All America, Ski Freshtracks, Ski Independence, Ski Line, Ski Safari, Ski The American Dream, Ski Tracer, Skiworld, Supertravel, Trailfinders, United Vacations, Virgin Snow*

Jasná Slovakia
Largest area in the Low Tatras mountains, linked to Chopok, which has an additional 11 lifts covering 11 km/7 miles.
slopes 1240–2005m
▲13 ☂ 21km
⊠ *Club Pavilion*

Jasper 693
⊠ *AmeriCan Ski, Crystal, Elegant Resorts, Frontier Ski, Inghams, Made to Measure Holidays, Neilson, Ski Activity, Ski All America, Ski Independence, Ski Safari, Ski The American Dream, Skiworld, Virgin Snow*

Jay Peak USA
Vermont resort near Canadian border with best snowfall record in the east. Tree-lined intermediate/advanced slopes – as many classified black as blue.
550m; slopes 550–1205m
▲8 ☂ 385 acres

Jochberg 156
Straggling village, 8km/5 miles from Kitzbühel.

La Joue-du-Loup France
Slightly stylish little purpose-built ski-in/ski-out family resort a few km north-west of Gap. Shares a fair-sized intermediate area with Superdévoluy.
1500m; slopes 1500–2510m
▲32 ☂ 100km
⊠ *Lagrange Holidays, Ski France*

Jouvenceaux 456
Less boisterous base from which to ski Sauze d'Oulx's terrain.

Jukkasjärvi Sweden
Centuries-old cross-country resort with unique ice hotel rebuilt every December.

June Mountain USA
Small area a half-hour drive from Mammoth and in same ownership. Empty slopes except on peak weekends.
2300m; slopes 2300–3090m
▲8 ☂ 500 acres

Juns 138
Small village between Lanersbach and Hintertux.

Kals am Grossglockner Austria
Village in a remote valley north of Lienz.
1325m; slopes 1325–2305m
▲7 ☂ 28km

Kaltenbach Austria
One of the larger, quieter Zillertal areas, with plenty of high-altitude slopes, mostly above the tree line. 'Superb area with lots of potential for off piste,' says a 2006 reporter.
560m; slopes 560–2300m
▲16 ☂ 145km

Kananaskis Canada
Small area near Calgary, nicely set in woods, with slopes at Nakiska and Fortress Mountain.
slopes 1525–2465m
▲12 ☂ 605 acres
⊠ *Frontier Ski*

Kandersteg Switzerland
Good cross-country base set amid beautiful scenery near Interlaken.
1175m; slopes 1175–2000m
▲7 ☂ 13km
⊠ *Headwater Holidays, Inghams, Inntravel, Kuoni, Swiss Travel Service, Switzerland Travel Centre, Waymark Holidays*

Kanin Slovakia
Small area near Bovec, 17km/11 miles from the Italian border, with plans to link with Sella Nevea in Italy.
slopes 1600–2300m
☂ 15km

Kappl 150
Small village down-valley from Ischgl.

Kaprun 229
Classic Austrian village near Zell am See.
⊠ *Airtours, Catered Ski Chalets, Crystal, Directski.com, Esprit Ski, Neilson, Ski Line, Ski Wild, Thomson*

Les Karellis France
Resort with slopes that are more scenic, challenging and snow-sure than those of better-known Valloire, nearby.
1600m; slopes 1600–2550m
▲19 ☂ 60km

Kastelruth Italy
German name for Castelrotto.
⊠ *Inntravel*

Kasurila Finland
Siilinjarvi ski area popular with boarders. ▲5

Katschberg Austria
Cute hamlet on the road pass from Styria to Carinthia. Good area of intermediate slopes.
1140m; slopes 1075–2220m
▲16 ☂ 60km
⊠ *Neilson*

Keystone 599
⊠ *AmeriCan Ski, American Ski Classics, Crystal, Erna Low, Ski Activity, Ski All America, Ski Independence, Ski Safari, Ski The American Dream, Ski Tracer, Thomson, United Vacations*

Kicking Horse 672
⊠ *AmeriCan Ski, Canadian Powder Tours, Crystal, Frontier Ski, Made to Measure Holidays, Ski All America, Ski Freshtracks, Ski Independence, Ski Safari, Ski The American Dream, Ski Tracer, Skiworld*

Killington 647
⊠ *American Ski Classics, Crystal, Directski.com, Equity Ski, Independent Ski Links, Inghams, Ski Activity, Ski All America, Ski Independence, Ski Line, Ski Safari, Ski The American Dream, Ski Tracer, Thomson, Trailfinders, Virgin Snow*

Kimberley Canada
New mountain village at the foot of limited slopes a few miles from the Bavarian/mock Tudor resort, and in a beautiful setting two hours from Banff.
1230m; slopes 1230–1980m
▲10 ☂ 1,800 acres
⊠ *AmeriCan Ski, Frontier Ski, Inghams, Ski Activity, Ski All America, Ski Safari, Ski The American Dream*

Kirchberg 156
Lively little town close to Kitzbühel.
⊠ *Airtours, Club Pavilion, Directski.com, First Choice Ski, Interhome, Lagrange Holidays, Made to Measure Holidays, Snowscape, Thomson*

Kirchdorf 219
Attractive village a bus-ride from St Johann in Tirol, with good local beginner slopes.
⊠ *Snowcoach, Thomson*

Kirkwood 580

Kitzbühel 156
⊠ *Airtours, Alpine Answers, Alpine Weekends, Catered Ski Chalets, Corporate Ski Company, Crystal, Crystal Finest, Directski.com, Elegant Resorts, First Choice Ski, Independent Ski Links, Inghams, Interhome, Lagrange Holidays, Made to Measure Holidays, Momentum Ski, Neilson, Panorama Holidays, Ski Freshtracks, Ski Line, Ski Solutions, Ski Tracer, Ski Wild, Snowscape, Thomson*

Kleinarl Austria
Secluded traditional village up a pretty side valley from Wagrain, at one end of a three-valley lift network linking it via Flachauwinkl to Zauchensee – all part of the Salzburger Sportwelt ski pass area that our figures relate to.
1015m; slopes 800–2185m
▲59 ☂ 200km

Klippitztörl Austria
One of many little areas in Austria's easternmost ski region near Slovenian border.
1550m; slopes 1460–1820m
▲6 ☂ 25km

Klösten Austria
Valley village at the base of the Sonnenkopf ski area a few km west of the Arlberg pass – covered by the Arlberg ski pass.
1100m; slopes 1100–2300m
▲10 ☂ 39km

Klosters 515
⊠ *Alpine Answers, Descent International, Flexiski, Inghams, Kuoni, Made to Measure Holidays, Momentum Ski, Oxford Ski Company, Powder Byrne, Ski Freshtracks, Ski Solutions, Ski Weekend, Swiss Travel Service, Switzerland Travel Centre, White Heat Skiing, White Roc*

Kobla 714

Kolsass-Weer Austria
Pair of Inn-side villages with low, inconvenient and limited slopes.
555m; slopes 555–1010m
▲3 ☂ 14km

Königsleiten Austria
Quiet, high resort sharing fairly snow-sure area with Gerlos, and linked to Zell im Zillertal to form a fair-sized area. 'Two excellent blacks for high-speed carving runs,' enthuses a 2006 reporter.
1600m; slopes 1245–2300m
▲55 ☂ 155km

Kopaonik Serbia
Modern, sympathetically designed family resort in a pretty setting.
1770m; slopes 1110–2015m
▲21 ☂ 57km
⊠ *Balkan Holidays, Crystal, Thomson*

Koralpe Austria
Largest and steepest of the gentle little areas in Austria's easternmost ski region near the Slovenian border.
1550m; slopes 1550–2050m
▲10 ☂ 25km

Kössen Austria
Village near St Johann in Tirol with low, scattered and limited local slopes.
600m; slopes 600–1700m
▲9 ☂ 25km

Kötschach-Mauthen Austria
One of many little areas near Hermagor in eastern Austria, close to the Italian border.
710m; slopes 710–1300m
▲4 ☂ 7km

Kranjska Gora 714
⊠ *Alpine Tours, Balkan Holidays, Crystal, Directski.com, Erna Low, First Choice Ski, Inghams, Just Slovenia, Panorama Holidays, Solo's, Thomson*

Krimml Austria
Sunny area, high enough to have good snow usually. Shares regional pass with Wildkogel resorts (Neukirchen).
1075m; slopes 1640–2040m
▲9 ☂ 33km

Krispl-Gaissau Austria
Easy slopes very close to Salzburg. Several long top-to-bottom lifts mean the size of the area is greatly reduced if the snowline is high.
925m; slopes 750–1570m
▲11 ☂ 40km

Kronplatz Italy
Charming Dolomite village with a delightful, sizeable area well covered by snow-guns. See entry under its Italian name, San Vigilio.
☒ *Momentum Ski, Neilson*

Krvavec Slovenia
Slopes spread across Kalska mountain. Lifts include a new gondola.
1450m; slopes 1450–1970m
⬈ 11 ⬈ 24km
☒ *Just Slovenia*

Kühtai 146
☒ *Crystal, Inghams*

Kusatsu Kokusai Japan
Attractive spa village with hot springs, three hours from Tokyo. ⬈ 13

Laax 509
Old farming community linked to Flims.
☒ *Alpine Answers, Switzerland Travel Centre*

Le Lac Blanc France
Mini-resort about to install the first six-pack in the northerly Vosges mountains near Strasbourg. Extensive ski de fond trails.
830m; slopes 830–1235m
⬈ 9 ⬈ 14km

Lachtal Austria
Second largest ski resort in the styrian region NE of Salzburg.
1600m; slopes 1600–2100m
⬈ 8 ⬈ 29km

Ladis Austria
Smaller alternative to Serfaus and Fiss, with lifts that connect into the same varied ski area.
1200m; slopes 1200–2540m
⬈ 42 ⬈ 160km

Lagunillas Chile
83km SE of Santiago.
⬈ 494 acres

Le Laisinant 398
Tiny hamlet with a short bus-ride down the valley from Val-d'Isère.

Lake Louise 674
☒ *Alpine Answers, AmeriCan Ski, Crystal, Crystal Finest, CV Travel, Elegant Resorts, Equity Ski, Frontier Ski, Independent Ski Links, Inghams, Made to Measure Holidays, Neilson, Ski Activity, Ski All America, Ski Independence, Ski Line, Ski Safari, Ski The American Dream, Ski Tracer, Skiworld, Solo's, Supertravel, Thomson, Trailfinders, United Vacations, Virgin Snow*

Lake Tahoe USA
Collection of 14 ski areas spectacularly set on California-Nevada border – Heavenly and Squaw Valley best known in Britain.
☒ *AmeriCan Ski, Independent Ski Links, Ski Activity, Skiworld, Supertravel, Thomson, United Vacations, Virgin Snow*

Lamoura France
One of four villages that make up the Jura's Les Rousses area.
1120m; slopes 1120–1680m
☒ *Headwater Holidays*

Landeck-Zams Austria
Small ski area in the Tirol region
816m; slopes 816–2210m
⬈ 7 ⬈ 22km
☒ *Alpine Tours*

Lanersbach 138
Attractive village near Hintertux.

Lans-en-Vercors France
Village close to Villard-de-Lans and 30km/19 miles from Grenoble. Highest slopes in the region; few snowmakers.
1020m; slopes 1400–1805m
⬈ 16 ⬈ 24km

Lanslebourg 419
One of the villages that makes up Val-Cenis.
1005m; slopes 1005–2250m
⬈ 9 ⬈ 30km
☒ *Lagrange Holidays*

Lanslevillard 419
One of the villages that makes up Val-Cenis.

Laturns-Gapfohl Austria
900m; slopes 900–1785m
⬈ 6 ⬈ 27km

Lauterbrunnen 517
Valley town in the Jungfrau region.
☒ *Re-lax Holidays, Ski Miquel*

Le Lavancher 264
Quiet village between Chamonix and Argentière.

Lavarone Italy
One of several areas east of Trento, good for a weekend day trip.
1195m; slopes 1075–1555m
⬈ 13 ⬈ 12km

Leadville USA
Old mining town full of historic buildings. Own easy area (Ski Cooper) plus snowcat operation. Picturesque inexpensive base for visiting Copper Mountain, Vail and Beaver Creek.

Lech 163
☒ *Alpine Answers, Alpine Weekends, Catered Ski Chalets, Corporate Ski Company, Crystal, CV Travel, Elegant Resorts, Erna Low, Flexiski, Independent Ski Links, Inghams, Made to Measure Holidays, Momentum Ski, Oxford Ski Company, Ski Expectations, Ski Freshtracks, Ski Solutions, Ski Tracer, Ski Weekend, Skiworld, Total, White Roc*

The Lecht 715

Lélex France
Family resort with pretty wooded slopes between Dijon and Geneva.
900m; slopes 900–1680m
⬈ 29 ⬈ 50km

Las Leñas 727
☒ *AmeriCan Ski, Scott Dunn Latin America, Ski All America*

Lenggries-Brauneck Germany
Bavarian resort south of Munich.

Lincoln USA
Sprawling New Hampshire town from which to visit Loon mountain.

Lindvallen-Högfjället Sweden
Two of the mountains that make up the ski areas of Sälen.
800m; slopes 590–890m
⬈ 46 ⬈ 85km

Le Lioran France
Auvergne village near Aurillac with a purpose-built satellite above. Spectacular volcanic scenery.
1160m; slopes 1160–1850m
⬈ 24 ⬈ 60km

Livigno 444
☒ *Airtours, Directski.com, Equity Ski, Independent Ski Links, Inghams, Interhome, Italian Safaris, Neilson, Panorama Holidays, Ramblers Holidays, Ski Tracer*

Lizzola Italy
Small base development in remote region north of Bergamo. Several other little areas nearby.
1250m; slopes 1250–2070m
⬈ 9 ⬈ 30km

Llaima Chile
Exotic area in central Chile, around and below a mildly active volcano.
1500m ⬈ 5

Loch Lomond Canada
Steep, narrow, challenging slopes near Thunder Bay on the shores of Lake Superior. Candy Mountain is nearby.
215m; slopes 215–440m
⬈ 3 ⬈ 90 acres

Lofer Austria
Quiet, traditional village in a pretty setting north of Saalbach with a small area of its own. Waidring's relatively snow-sure Steinplatte nearby.
640m; slopes 640–1745m
⬈ 14 ⬈ 46km
☒ *Ski Line, Ski Wild*

Longchamp 409
Dreary purpose-built resort that shares slopes with Valmorel.

Loon Mountain USA
Small, smart, modern resort just outside Lincoln, New Hampshire; mostly intermediate, though some fall-line runs merit their black grading.
290m; slopes 290–910m
⬈ 10 ⬈ 275 acres
☒ *Equity Ski, Virgin Snow*

Lost Trail USA
Remote Montana area, open only Thursday to Sunday and holidays. Mostly intermediate slopes.
2005m; slopes 2005–2370m
⬈ 6 ⬈ 800 acres

Loveland USA
Exceptionally high and snowy slopes right next to highway I70, just east of the Continental Divide, easily reached from other Colorado resorts.
3230m; slopes 3230–3870m
⬈ 9 ⬈ 1,265 acres

Lenk Switzerland
Traditional village that shares a sizeable area with Adelboden.
1070m; slopes 1070–2355m
⬈ 56 ⬈ 170km
☒ *Swiss Travel Service*

Lenzerheide 560
☒ *Interhome, Kuoni, Made to Measure Holidays, Switzerland Travel Centre*

Leogang 189
Quiet village with link to Saalbach-Hinterglemm.
☒ *Inntravel*

Lermoos Austria
Focal resort of the Zugspitze area: a pleasant little village with a small area of shady intermediate slopes.

Lessach Austria
Hamlet with trail connecting into one of longest, most snow-sure cross-country networks in Europe.
1210m ⬈ 1

Leukerbad Switzerland
Major spa resort of Roman origin, recently revamped.

Leutasch Austria
Traditional cross-country village with limited slopes but a pleasant day trip from nearby Seefeld or Innsbruck.
1130m; slopes 1130–1605m
⬈ 3 ⬈ 6km
☒ *Headwater Holidays, Inntravel*

Levi 701
☒ *Bladon Lines, First Choice Ski, Inghams*

Leysin Switzerland
Large spread-out village near Aigle, with a good range of facilities, but low, sunny terrain.
1300m; slopes 1300–2205m
⬈ 19 ⬈ 60km
☒ *Crystal, Lagrange Holidays, Mountain Tracks, Switzerland Travel Centre*

Lienz Austria
Pleasant town in pretty surroundings.
675m; slopes 730–2290m
⬈ 17 ⬈ 41km

Lillehammer 703
☒ *Crystal, Directski.com, Waymark Holidays*

Limone Italy
Pleasant old town not far from Turin, with a pretty area, but far from snow-sure.
1010m; slopes 1030–2050m
⬈ 25 ⬈ 80km

Lenk Switzerland
680m; slopes 700–1700m
⬈ 21 ⬈ 34km
☒ *Moswin Tours*

Lenk Switzerland

Luchon France
Sizeable village with plenty of amenities, with gondola (eight minutes) to its ski area at purpose-built Superbagnères.
630m; slopes 1440–2260m
⛷ *16* 🚠 *35km*
✉ *Lagrange Holidays, Ski Leisure Direction*

Lurisia Italy
Sizeable spa resort, a good base for visits to surrounding little ski areas and to Nice.
750m; slopes 800–1800m
⛷ *8* 🚠 *35km*

Lutsen Mountains USA
Largest ski area in between Vermont and Colorado, with panoramic views of Lake Superior, only 3km/2 miles away. Four small linked hills with 95% snowmaking offer surprisingly good and extensive terrain, with something for everyone. Moose Mountain has the biggest vertical (250m/820ft), with cruisers or bumps top to bottom, great views of the lake, and backcountry glade runs. Small slope-side village. Good cross-country, snow-shoeing and snowmobiling nearby.
80m; slopes 80–335m
⛷ *9* 🚠 *1,000 acres*

Luz-Ardiden France
Spa village below its ski area. Cauterets and Barèges nearby.
710m; slopes 1730–2450m
⛷ *15* 🚠 *60km*

Macugnaga 483
✉ *Neilson*

Madesimo 483
✉ *Inghams, Italian Safaris*

Madonna di Campiglio 448
✉ *Crystal, Directski.com, Equity Ski, First Choice Ski, Inghams, Interhome, Italian Safaris, Rocketski, Ski Wild, Ski Yogi, Solo's*

Mad River Glen USA
Cult resort, co-operatively owned, with some tough ungroomed terrain, a few well-groomed intermediate trails and antique lifts. Snowboarding is banned.

La Magdelaine Italy
Close to Cervinia, and good on bad-weather days.
1645m; slopes 1645–1870m
⛷ *4* 🚠 *4km*

Maishofen Austria
Cheaper place to stay for Saalbach and Zell am See.
765m

Malbun Liechtenstein
Quaint user-friendly little family resort, 16km/10 miles from the capital, Vaduz.
1600m; slopes 1595–2100m
⛷ *6* 🚠 *21km*

Malcesine Italy
Large summer resort on Lake Garda with a fair area of slopes.
1430m; slopes 1430–1830m
⛷ *8* 🚠 *12km*

Malga Ciapela Italy
Resort at the foot of the Marmolada glacier massif, with a link into the Sella Ronda.
1445m; slopes 1445–3270m
⛷ *8* 🚠 *18km*

Mallnitz Austria
Village in a pretty valley close to Slovenia, with two varied areas providing a fine mix of wooded and open runs.
1200m; slopes 1300–2650m
⛷ *5* 🚠 *30km*

Mammoth Mountain 573
✉ *AmeriCan Ski, American Ski Classics, Independent Ski Links, Made to Measure Holidays, Ski Activity, Ski All America, Ski Independence, Ski Line, Ski Safari, Ski The American Dream, Ski Tracer, United Vacations, Virgin Snow*

Manigod France
Small valley village over the Col de la Croix-Fry from La Clusaz.

Marble Mountain Canada
Tiny area in the Humber Valley on the island of Newfoundland. Good snow record by east coast standards.
85m; slopes 10–545m
⛷ *5* 🚠 *175 acres*
✉ *Club Pavilion, Frontier Ski*

Les Marecottes Switzerland
Small area near Martigny. Valid with the Valais Ski Card.
1100m; slopes 1100–2200m
⛷ *5* 🚠 *25km*

Maria Alm 143
Charming unspoiled village at one end of the Hochkönig area.
✉ *Elevation Holidays, Equity Ski, Tops Ski Chalets and Club Hotels*

Mariapfarr Austria
Village in one of the longest, most snow-reliable cross-country networks in Europe.
1120m ⛷ *5* 🚠 *30km*

Mariazell Austria
Traditional Styria village with an impressive basilica. Limited slopes.
870m; slopes 870–1265m
⛷ *5* 🚠 *11km*

Maribor 714

Marilleva 448
Small resort with direct links to Madonna di Campiglio's extensive intermediate slopes.
✉ *Alpine Tours, Interhome, Interhome*

Le Markstein France
Long-standing small resort in the northerly Vosges mountains near Strasbourg, which has hosted World Cup slalom races. Extensive ski de fond trails.
slopes 770–1270m ⛷ *10*

Masella Spain
Pyrenean village linked with slopes of La Molina to form the Alp 2500 area.
1600m; slopes 1600–2535m
⛷ *20* 🚠 *100km*

La Massana 108
✉ *Directski.com*

Le Massif 694
✉ *AmeriCan Ski, Frontier Ski, Ski All America, Ski Safari, Ski The American Dream, Virgin Snow*

Matrei in Osttirol Austria
Large market village south of Felbertauern tunnel. Mostly high slopes.
1000m; slopes 1000–2400m
⛷ *7* 🚠 *33km*

Maurienne Valley France
A great curving trench with over 20 winter resorts, ranging from pleasant old valley villages to convenience resorts purpose-built in the 1960s.

Mauterndorf Austria
Village near Obertauern with tremendous snow record.
1120m; slopes 1075–2360m
⛷ *10* 🚠 *35km*
✉ *Equity Ski*

Maverick Mountain USA
Montana resort with plenty of terrain accessed by few lifts. Cowboy Winter Games venue – rodeo one day, ski races the next.
2155m; slopes 2155–2800m
⛷ *2* 🚠 *500 acres*

Mayens de Riddes 532
Tiny hamlet next to La Tzoumaz with its links up to Savoleyres and the Verbier network.
✉ *Interhome*

Mayens-de-Sion 532
Tranquil hamlet off the road up to Les Collons – part of the Verbier area.

Mayrhofen 172
✉ *Crystal, Equity Ski, First Choice Ski, Independent Ski Links, Inghams, Interhome, Neilson, Rocketski, Ski Line, Ski Tracer, Ski Wild, Snowcoach, Thomson*

Méaudre France
Small resort near Grenoble with good snowmaking to make up for its low altitude.
1000m; slopes 1000–1600m
⛷ *10* 🚠 *18km*

Megève 311
✉ *Alpine Answers, AmeriCan Ski, Classic Ski Limited, Corporate Ski Company, Erna Low, Flexiski, Interhome, Lagrange Holidays, Made to Measure Holidays, Momentum Ski, Oxford Ski Company, Peak Retreats, Simon Butler Skiing, Ski Barrett-Boyce, Ski Expectations, Ski Independence, Ski Solutions, Ski Tracer, Ski Weekend, Stanford Skiing, White Roc*

Meiringen Switzerland
Varied terrain, a good outing from the nearby Jungfrau resorts or Interlaken. Particularly suitable for beginners. New high-speed gondola in 2003/04.
600m; slopes 600–2435m
⛷ *20* 🚠 *80km*

Melchsee-Frutt Switzerland
Limited, but high and snow-sure bowl above a car-free village. Family-friendly.
1080m; slopes 1080–2255m
⛷ *11* 🚠 *32km*

Les Menuires 317
✉ *Club Med, Club Pavilion, Crystal, Directski.com, Erna Low, Family Ski Company, First Choice Ski, Independent Ski Links, Interhome, Lagrange Holidays, Neilson, Ski France, Ski Independence, Ski Leisure Direction, Ski Olympic, Ski Supreme, Ski Tracer, Ski4you, Skitopia*

Merano Italy
Purpose-built base on a high plateau near Bolzano.
2000m; slopes 2000–2240m
⛷ *18* 🚠 *28km*

Méribel 319
✉ *Airtours, Alpine Action, Alpine Answers, Belvedere Chalets, Bladon Lines, Bonne Neige Ski Holidays, Catered Ski Chalets, Chalet Group, Chalet World Ski, Club Med, Club Pavilion, Cooltip Mountain Holidays, Corporate Ski Company, Crystal, Crystal Finest, Descent International, Directski.com, Elegant Resorts, Erna Low, First Choice Ski, Flexiski, Independent Ski Links, Inghams, Inspired to Ski, Interhome, Kaluma Ski, Lagrange Holidays, Made to Measure Holidays, Mark Warner, Meriski, Momentum Ski, Mountain Tracks, Neilson, Oxford Ski Company, Powder White, Purple Ski, Scott Dunn Ski, Silver Ski, Ski Activity, Ski Amis, Ski Basics, Ski Beat, Ski Blanc, Ski Bon, Ski Cuisine, Ski Expectations, Ski France, Ski Hame, Ski Independence, Ski Leisure Direction, Ski Line, Ski Olympic, Ski Solutions, Ski Supreme, Ski Tracer, Ski Weekend, Ski4you, Skifrance4less, Skiworld, Snowline, Snoworks, Supertravel, Thomson, Total, VIP, White Roc*

Métabief-Mont-d'Or France
Twin villages in the Jura region, not far from Geneva.
900m; slopes 880–1460m
⛷ *22* 🚠 *42km*

Methven 720
Nearest town/accommodation to Mt Hutt.

Mieders 221

Mijoux France
Pretty wooded slopes between Dijon and Geneva. Lélex nearby.
1000m; slopes 900–1680m
⛷ *29* 🚠 *50km*
✉ *Lagrange Holidays*

Mission Ridge USA
Area in dry region that gets higher-quality snow than other Seattle resorts but less of it.
1390m; slopes 1390–2065m
⛷ *6* 🚠 *300 acres*

Mount Hood Meadows USA
One of several sizeable areas amid magnificent Oregon scenery.
1375m; slopes 1375–2535m
⛡ 12 ⛡ 2,150 acres

Mount Hood Ski Bowl USA
Sizeable area set amid magnificent Oregon scenery. Weather can be damp.
1095m; slopes 1095–1540m
⛡ 9 ⛡ 960 acres

Mount Hotham 718

Mount Hutt 720

Mount Lemmon USA
Southernmost area in North America, close to famous Old West town Tombstone, Arizona. Reasonable snowfall.
2500m; slopes 2500–2790m
⛡ 3 ⛡ 70 acres

Mount McKay 718

Mount Pilio Greece
Pleasant slopes cut out of dense forest, only 15km/9 miles from the holiday resort of Portaria above town of Volos.
1500m ⛡ 3

Mount Rose 566

Mount Shasta Ski Park USA
Californian resort 300 miles N of San Francisco.
⛡ 4 ⛡ 425 acres

Mount Snow USA
Minor peak with a fair amount of accommodation around the base, and reputedly excellent terrain-parks.
580m; slopes 580–1095m
⛡ 26 ⛡ 540 acres

Mount Spokane USA
Little intermediate area outside Spokane (Washington State).
1160m; slopes 1160–1795m
⛡ 5 ⛡ 350 acres

Mount St Louis / Moonstone Canada
Premier area in Toronto region, spread over three peaks. Very high-capacity lift system and 100% snowmaking.
⛡ 13 ⛡ 175

Mount Sunapee USA
Area in New Hampshire closest to Boston; primarily intermediate terrain.
375m; slopes 375–835m
⛡ 10 ⛡ 230 acres

Mount Vermio Greece
Oldest ski base in Greece. Two areas in central Macedonia 60km/37 miles from Thessaloniki. Barren but interesting slopes.
slopes 1420–2000m ⛡ 4

Mount Washington Resort Canada
Scenic area on Vancouver Island with lodging in the base village.
1110m; slopes 1110–1590m
⛡ 6 ⛡ 970 acres
✉ *AmeriCan Ski, Frontier Ski, Ski Safari*

Mt Falakro Greece
Area two hours' drive from Salonica in northern Greece; almost as big as Parnassos, uncrowded and with good views.
1720m ⛡ 2

Mount Waterman USA
Small Los Angeles area where children ski free. The lack of much snowmaking is a drawback.
2135m; slopes 2135–2440m
⛡ 3 ⛡ 210 acres

Mühlbach 143
Village in the Hochkönig area.

Mühltal Austria
Small village halfway between Niederau and Auffach in the Wildschönau..
780m; slopes 830–1900m
⛡ 29 ⛡ 42km

Muhr Austria
Village by Katschberg tunnel well placed for visiting St Michael, Badkleinkirchheim, Flachau and Obertauern.
1110m

Muju Resort South Korea
Largest area in Korea and with a fair amount of lodging. Though it is the furthest resort from Seoul (four hours south) it is still overcrowded. ⛡ 14

Mürren 517
✉ *Inghams, Kuoni, Made to Measure Holidays, Ski Freshtracks, Ski Line, Ski Solutions, Swiss Travel Service, Switzerland Travel Centre*

Mutters 146

Myoko Suginohara Kokusai Japan
A series of small resorts two or three hours from Tokyo, which together make up an area of extensive slopes with longer, wider runs than normal for Japan. ⛡ 15

Naeba Japan
Fashionable resort with lots of accommodation two hours north of Tokyo. Crowded slopes.
900m; slopes 900–1800m ⛡ 28

Nakiska Canada
Small area of wooded runs between Banff and Calgary, with emphasis on downhill speed. Unreliable snow, but state-of-the-art snowmaking and pancake-flat grooming.
1524m; slopes 1525–2215m
⛡ 4 ⛡ 230 acres

Nasserein 208
Quiet suburb of St Anton, a short bus-ride from the lifts.

Nassfeld Austria
Fair-sized, scenic area on the sunny side of the Alps, right on the Italian border. Accommodation is in the tiny valley village of Tröpolach, at the bottom of the access gondola, or the bigger village of Hermagor, 10km/6 miles to the east.

1500m; slopes 610–2195m
⛡ 30 ⛡ 110km
✉ *Crystal, Equity Ski, Ski Line, Ski Wild, Thomson*

Nauders/Reschenpass 180

Nax Switzerland
Quiet, sunny village in a balcony setting overlooking the Rhône valley. Own little area and only a short drive from Veysonnaz.
1300m

Nendaz 532
Quiet alternative to Verbier.
✉ *Interhome, Ted Bentley Chalet Holidays*

Neukirchen Austria
Quiet, pretty beginners' resort with a fairly snow-sure plateau at the top of its mountain.
855m; slopes 855–2150m
⛡ 14 ⛡ 35km
✉ *Crystal*

Neustift 221
✉ *Alpine Tours, Catered Ski Chalets, Crystal, Esprit Ski, Interhome, Made to Measure Holidays*

Nevegal Italy
Weekend place near Belluno, south of Cortina.
1030m; slopes 1030–1650m
⛡ 14 ⛡ 30km

Nevis Range 715

Niederau 225
Amorphous chalet-style village in the Wildschönau region.
✉ *Airtours, Directski.com, First Choice Ski, Inghams, Neilson, Panorama Holidays, Thomson*

Niseko 716
✉ *Crystal, Inghams*

Nockberge Innerkrems Austria
Area just south of Katschberg tunnel.
1500m; slopes 1500–2300m
⛡ 10 ⛡ 33km

Nordseter Norway
Cluster of hotels in deep forest north of Lillehammer. Some Alpine facilities but best for cross-country.
850m; slopes 1000–1090m
⛡ 2 ⛡ 2km

Norefjell Norway
Norway's toughest run, a very steep 600m/1,970ft drop. 120km/75 miles north-west of Oslo. *185m; slopes 185–1185m*
⛡ 10 ⛡ 23km

La Norma France
Traffic-free, purpose-built resort near Modane and Val-Cenis, with mostly easy terrain.
1350m; slopes 1350–2750m
⛡ 18 ⛡ 65km
✉ *AmeriCan Ski, Erna Low, Interhome, Lagrange Holidays, Peak Retreats, Ski Leisure Direction*

Norquay 658
Banff's quiet local hill – worth a visit, especially in bad weather.

North Conway USA
Attractive factory-outlet-shopping town in New Hampshire close to Attitash and Cranmore ski areas.
✉ *Virgin Snow*

Northstar-at-Tahoe 580
✉ *Ski The American Dream, United Vacations*

Nôtre-Dame-de-Bellecombe France
Pleasant village spoiled by the busy road. Inexpensive base from which to visit Megève. 'Very French,' says a 2006 reporter.
1130m; slopes 1130–2070m ⛡ 18
✉ *AmeriCan Ski, Peak Retreats*

Nova Levante Italy
Village close to Bozen/Bolzano with lifts up to small network around Passo di Costalunga.
1180m; slopes 1180–2200m
⛡ 14 ⛡ 20km

Nozawa Onsen Japan
Spa village with good hot springs three hours from Tokyo. The runs are cut out of heavy vegetation.
500m; slopes 500–1650m ⛡ 24

Nub's Nob USA
One of the most sheltered Great Lakes ski areas (many suffer fierce winds). 100% snowmaking; weekend crowds from Detroit. Wooded slopes suitable for all abilities.
275m; slopes 275–405m
⛡ 8 ⛡ 245 acres

Oberau 225
Pretty village in the Wildschönau region.
✉ *Inghams*

Obereggen Italy
Tiny resort close to Bozen/Bolzano with modest area of slopes also accessible from Predazzo in Val di Fiemme.
1550m; slopes 1550–2200m
⛡ 6 ⛡ 10km

Obergurgl 182
✉ *Airtours, Catered Ski Chalets, Corporate Ski Company, Crystal, Crystal Finest, Directski.com, Esprit Ski, First Choice Ski, Independent Ski Links, Inghams, Made to Measure Holidays, Neilson, Ski Expectations, Ski Freshtracks, Ski Solutions, Ski Tracer, Thomson*

Oberjoch-Hindelang Germany
Small, low-altitude resort, particularly good for beginners.
850m; slopes 1140–1520m
⛡ 12 ⛡ 32km

Oberlech 163
Car- and crowd-free family resort alternative to Lech.
✉ *Elegant Resorts, Kaluma Ski*

Oberndorf 219
Quiet hamlet with beginners' area and a chair connecting it to St Johann's ski area.
✉ *Lagrange Holidays*

Peyragudes-Peyresourde
France
Small Pyrenean resort with its
ski area starting high above.
1000m; slopes 1600–2400m
🎿 15 🚡 37km
✉ *Lagrange Holidays, Ski
France, Ski4you*

Pfunds
Austria
Picturesque valley village with
no slopes but quick access to
several resorts in Switzerland
and Italy, as well as Austria.
970m

Phoenix Park
South Korea
Golf complex with 12 trails in
winter. Two hours (140km/87
miles) from Seoul.
slopes 650–1050m 🎿 8

Piancavallo
Italy
Uninspiring yet curiously trendy
purpose-built village, an easy
drive from Venice.
1270m; slopes 1270–1830m
🎿 17 🚡 45km ✉ *Equity Ski*

Piani delle Betulle
Italy
One of several little areas near
the east coast of Lake Como.
730m; slopes 730–1850m
🎿 6 🚡 10km

Piani di Artavaggio
Italy
Small base complex rather than
a village. One of several little
areas near Lake Como.
875m; slopes 875–1875m
🎿 7 🚡 15km

Piani di Bobbio
Italy
Largest of several tiny resorts
above Lake Como.
770m; slopes 770–1855m
🎿 10 🚡 20km

Piani di Erna
Italy
Small base development – no
village. One of several little
areas above Lake Como.
600m; slopes 600–1635m
🎿 5 🚡 9km

Piau-Engaly
France
User-friendly St-Lary satellite in
one of the best Pyrenean areas.
1850m; slopes 1700–2500m
🎿 20 🚡 40km
✉ *Lagrange Holidays*

Piazzatorre
Italy
One of many little areas in the
Bergamo region.
870m; slopes 870–2000m
🎿 5 🚡 25km

Pichl
195
In Dachstein-Tauern region,
close to Schladming.

Pico
647
Low-key little family area (no
resort) close to Killington.

Pievepelago
Italy
Much the smallest and most
limited of the Appennine ski
resorts. Less than two hours
from Florence and Pisa.
1115m; slopes 1115–1410m
🎿 7 🚡 8km

Pila
483
✉ *Crystal, Independent Ski
Links, Interhome, Interski, Ski
Supreme, Thomson*

Pinzolo
478
Trentino resort near Madonna.

Pitztal
Austria
Long valley with good glacier
area at its head, accessed by
underground funicular.
1250m; slopes 880–3440m
🎿 19 🚡 87km

Pla-d'Adet
France
Limited purpose-built complex at
the foot of the St-Lary ski area
(the original village is further
down the mountain).
1680m; slopes 1420–2450m
🎿 32 🚡 80km
✉ *Lagrange Holidays*

La Plagne
343
✉ *Airtours, Alpine Answers,
Catered Ski Chalets, Chalet
Group, Chalet World Ski, Chez
Jay Ski Chalets, Club Med,
Crystal, Equity Ski, Erna Low,
Esprit Ski, Finlays, First Choice
Ski, Independent Ski Links,
Inghams, Interhome, Lagrange
Holidays, Made to Measure
Holidays, Mark Warner,
MasterSki, Mountain Heaven,
Neilson, Rocketski, Silver Ski,
Ski Activity, Ski Amis, Ski Beat,
Ski Expectations, Ski France,
Ski Freshtracks, Ski
Independence, Ski Leisure
Direction, Ski Line, Ski Olympic,
Ski Solutions, Ski Supreme, Ski
Tracer, Ski4you, Skifrance4less,
Skiworld, Snow Monkey
Chalets, Thomson*

Plan-Peisey
250
Small development with link to
Les Arcs.

Plose
Italy
Varied area with the longest run
in South Tirol (9km/6 miles). In
Dolomiti Superski region.
560m; slopes 1065–2500m
🎿 11 🚡 40km

Poiana Brasov
713
✉ *Airtours, Balkan Holidays,
Inghams, Neilson, Solo's,
Thomson*

PontediLegno
Italy
Attractive sheltered alternative
to bleak, ugly neighbour Passo
Tonale. Linked by piste and bus.
1255m; slopes 1255–1920m
🎿 5 🚡 15km

Pontresina
Switzerland
Small, sedate sunny village
linked to nearby St Moritz by
road, with extensive cross-
country trails. *1805m*
✉ *Made to Measure Holidays,
Switzerland Travel Centre*

Port-Ainé
Spain
Small but high intermediate area
in the Spanish Pyrenees near
Andorra.
1975m; slopes 1650–2440m
🎿 8 🚡 44km

Port del Comte
Spain
High resort in the forested
region of Lleida, north-west of
Barcelona. *slopes 1730–2110m*
🎿 15 🚡 40km

Porté-Puymorens
France
Little-known Pyrenean area close
to Pas de la Casa in Andorra.
Plans to link the two are moving
forward with the opening in
2005 of the first lift on the
French side of Pas de la Casa.
slopes 1600–1900m
🎿 13 🚡 45km
✉ *Pyrenees Ski Experience*

Porter Heights
New Zealand
Closest skiing to Christchurch.
Open, sunny bowl offering
mostly intermediate skiing –
with back bowls for powder.
1340m; slopes 1340–1950m
🎿 5 🚡 200 acres

Portes du Soleil
353
✉ *Waymark Holidays*

Portillo
728
✉ *AmeriCan Ski, Crystal,
Momentum Ski, Scott Dunn
Latin America, Ski All America,
Ski Safari*

Powderhorn
USA
Area in west Colorado perched
on the world's highest flat-top
mountain, Grand Mesa. Day trip
from Aspen. Sensational views.
2490m; slopes 2490–2975m
🎿 4 🚡 300 acres

Powder King
Canada
Remote resort in British
Columbia, between Prince
George and Dawson City. As its
name suggests, it has great
powder. Plenty of lodging.
880m; slopes 880–1520m
🎿 3 🚡 160 acres

Powder Mountain
USA
Sizeable Utah area, a feasible
day out from Park City,
renowned for bowls of fluffy
virgin powder. Snowcat
operation too.
2100m; slopes 2100–2740m
🎿 7 🚡 5,500 acres

Pozza di Fassa
Italy
Pretty Dolomite village with its
own slopes, three other small
areas close by and access to
Sella Ronda at Campitello.
1340m; slopes 1340–2155m
🎿 6 🚡 20km

Pragelato
Italy
Inexpensive base, a short drive
east of Sestriere. Its own area is
worth a try for half a day.
1535m; slopes 1535–2700m
🎿 6 🚡 50km

Prägraten am Grossvenediger
Austria
Traditional mountaineering/ski
touring village in lovely setting
south of Felbertauern tunnel.
Matrei's slopes are nearby.
1310m; slopes 1310–1490m
🎿 2 🚡 30km

Prali
Italy
Tiny resort east of Sestriere – a
worthwhile half-day trip.
1450m; slopes 1450–2500m
🎿 7 🚡 25km

Pralognan-la-Vanoise
France
Unspoiled traditional village
overlooked by spectacular
peaks. Champagny (La Plagne)
and Courchevel are close by.
1410m; slopes 1410–2355m
🎿 14 🚡 30km
✉ *Erna Low, Lagrange
Holidays, Ski Independence*

Pra-Loup
France
Convenient, purpose-built family
resort with an extensive, varied
intermediate area linked to La
Foux-d'Allos.
1500m; slopes 1500–2600m
🎿 32 🚡 83km
✉ *Club Pavilion, Lagrange
Holidays*

Prati di Tivo
Italy
Weekend day-trip place east of
Rome and near the town of
Teramo. A sizeable resort by
southern Italy standards.
1450m; slopes 1450–1800m
🎿 6 🚡 16km

Prato Nevoso
Italy
Purpose-built resort with rather
bland slopes. Part of Mondolé
ski area with Artesina.
1500m; slopes 1500–1950m
🎿 25 🚡 90km
✉ *Equity Ski, Rocketski,
Thomson*

Prato Selva
Italy
Tiny base development (no
village) east of Rome near
Teramo. Weekend day-trip place.
1370m; slopes 1370–1800m
🎿 4 🚡 10km

Praz-de-Lys
France
Little-known snow-pocket area
near Lake Geneva that can have
good snow when nearby resorts
(eg La Clusaz) do not.
1500m; slopes 1200–2000m
🎿 23 🚡 60km
✉ *Lagrange Holidays, Ski4you*

Le Praz
283
The lowest and most attractive
of the Courchevel resorts.
✉ *Ski Deep*

Les Praz
264
Quiet hamlet 4km/2 miles from
Chamonix.
✉ *Bigfoot Travel*

Praz-sur-Arly
France
Traditional village in a pretty,
wooded setting just down the
road from Megève, with its own
varied slopes.
1035m; slopes 1035–2000m
🎿 14 🚡 60km
✉ *Lagrange Holidays, Ski
France, Ski Leisure Direction*

Le Pré
250
Hamlet with lifts up to Arc 2000.

Predazzo
Italy
Small, quiet place between
Cavalese and the Sella Ronda
resorts.
995m; slopes 995–2205m 🎿 8 🚡 17km

Premanon
France
One of four resorts that make
up the Jura area Les Rousses.
1050m; slopes 1120–1680m 🎿 40
✉ *Lagrange Holidays*

Serrada Italy
Very limited area near Trento.
slopes 1250–1605m ⛷ *5*
⊠ *Equity Ski*

Serre-Chevalier 364
⊠ *Alpine Answers, AmeriCan Ski, Bladon Lines, BoardnLodge, Catered Ski Chalets, Chalet Group, Chill Chalet, Club Med, Club Pavilion, Crystal, Equity Ski, Erna Low, First Choice Ski, Hannibals, Independent Ski Links, Inghams, Interhome, Lagrange Holidays, Neilson, Peak Retreats, Rocketski, Ski Expectations, Ski France, Ski Independence, Ski Leisure Direction, Ski Miquel, Ski Tracer, Ski4you, Skifrance4less, Skitopia, Skiworld, Thomson, Tops Ski Chalets and Club Hotels*

Sesto Italy
Dolomite village on the road to Cortina, surrounded by pretty little areas.
1310m ⛷ *31* ⛷ *50km*

Sestola Italy
Appennine village a short drive from Florence with its pistes almost completely equipped with snowmakers.
900m; slopes 1280–1975m
⛷ *23* ⛷ *50km*

Sestriere 474
⊠ *Alpine Answers, Club Med, Crystal, Equity Ski, First Choice Ski, Independent Ski Links, Inghams, Interhome, Momentum Ski, Neilson, Rocketski, Ski Tracer, Ski Weekend, Ski4you, Thomson*

Sexten Italy
German name for Sesto.

Shames Mountain Canada
Remote spot inland from Prince Rupert, with impressive snow record. Deep powder.
670m; slopes 670–1195m
⛷ *3* ⛷ *183 acres*

Shawnee Peak USA
Small area near Bethel and Sunday River renowned for its night skiing. Spectacular views. Mostly groomed cruising.
185m; slopes 185–580m
⛷ *5* ⛷ *225 acres*

Shemshak Iran
Most popular of the three mountain resorts within easy reach of Tehran (60km/37 miles).
3600m; slopes 2550–3050m ⛷ *7*

Shiga Kogen 716
Largest area in Japan.
930m; slopes 1220–2300m
⛷ *73* ⛷ *130km*

Showdown USA
Intermediate area in Montana cut out of forest north of Bozeman. 50km/30 miles to the nearest hotel.
2065m; slopes 2065–2490m
⛷ *4* ⛷ *640 acres*

Sierra-at-Tahoe 580

Sierra Nevada 698
⊠ *Independent Ski Links, Thomson*

Sierra Summit USA
Sierra Nevada area accessible only from the west..
2160m; slopes 2160–2645m
⛷ *8* ⛷ *250 acres*

Silbertal 177
Low secluded village in the Montafon area.

Sillian Austria
A gondola and two fast quads serve this varied area in Austria's Hochpustertal region.
1100m ⛷ *6* ⛷ *45km*

Sils Maria 526
Pretty lakeside village, linked to the St Moritz Corvatsch slopes.
⊠ *Interhome*

Silvaplana 526
Pretty lakeside village near St Moritz.
⊠ *Interhome, Switzerland Travel Centre*

Silver Star 693
⊠ *AmeriCan Ski, American Ski Classics, Chalet Group, Frontier Ski, Made to Measure Holidays, Ski Activity, Ski All America, Ski Independence, Ski Line, Ski Safari, Ski The American Dream, Snowebb*

Silverthorne USA
Factory outlet town on main road close to Keystone and Breckenridge. Good budget base for skiing those resorts plus Vail and Beaver Creek.
⊠ *AmeriCan Ski*

Silverton USA
Expert-only area in southern Colorado that used to be heli-ski country. Served by one lift. Avalanche transceiver, shovel and probe compulsory.
3170m; slopes 3170–3750m ⛷ *1*

Sinaia Romania
Depressed and depressing main-road town with a modest area.
795m; slopes 795–2030m
⛷ *10* ⛷ *20km*

Sipapu USA
Great little New Mexico area, with mostly tree-lined runs. Snow unreliable, but 70% snowmaking.
slopes 2500–2765m
⛷ *4* ⛷ *70 acres*

Siusi 468
Village west of the Sella Ronda circuit; Seis in German.
⊠ *Equity Ski, Rocketski*

Siviez 532
A quieter and cheaper base for Verbier's Four Valleys circuit.
⊠ *Interhome*

Sixt-Fer-a-Cheval 300
Traditional village near Samoëns.
⊠ *AmeriCan Ski, Lagrange Holidays, Peak Retreats*

Sjusjøen Norway
Cluster of hotels in deep forest close to Lillehammer. Some Alpine facilities but better for cross-country.
885m; slopes 1000–1090m
⛷ *2* ⛷ *2km*
⊠ *Inntravel, Waymark Holidays*

Ski Apache USA
Apache-owned area south of Albuquerque noted for groomed steeps. Panoramic views. Nearest lodging in Ruidoso.
2925m; slopes 2925–3505m
⛷ *11* ⛷ *750 acres*

Ski Cooper USA
Small area close to historic Old West town of Leadville. Good ski/sightseeing day out from nearby Vail, Beaver Creek and Copper Mountain.
slopes 3200–3565m ⛷ *4*

Ski Windham USA
Two hours from New York City and second only to Hunter for weekend crowds. Decent slopes by eastern standards.
485m; slopes 485–940m
⛷ *7* ⛷ *230 acres*

Smokovec Slovakia
Spa town with small modern centre near Poprad, with three small areas known collectively as High Tatras. Funicular railway and snowmaking facilities.
1480m; slopes 1000–1500m
⛷ *6* ⛷ *4km*

Smugglers' Notch 653

Snowbasin 634

Snowbird 632
⊠ *AmeriCan Ski, American Ski Classics, Ski All America, Ski Independence, Ski The American Dream, Ski Tracer, Skiworld, United Vacations*

Snowbowl (Arizona) USA
One of America's oldest areas, near Flagstaff, Arizona, atop an extinct volcano and with stunning desert views. Good snowfall record.
2805m; slopes 2805–3505m
⛷ *5* ⛷ *135 acres*

Snowbowl (Montana) USA
Montana area renowned for powder, outside lively town of Missoula. Intermediate pistes plus 700 acres of extreme slopes. Grizzly Chute is the ultimate challenge.
1520m; slopes 1520–2315m
⛷ *4* ⛷ *1400 acres*

Snowmass 601
⊠ *Alpine Answers, AmeriCan Ski, Ski All America, Ski Independence, Ski The American Dream, United Vacations*

Snow Park 720

Snow Summit USA
San Bernardino National Forest ski area near Palm Springs. Lovely lake views. High-capacity lift system for weekend crowds.
2135m; slopes 2135–2500m
⛷ *12* ⛷ *230 acres*

Snow Valley USA
Area quite near Palm Springs. Fine desert views.
2040m; slopes 2040–2390m
⛷ *11* ⛷ *230 acres*

Solda – Sulden Italy
The other side of the Stelvio Pass from Bormio. Very long airport transfers.
1905m; slopes 1905–2625m
⛷ *10* ⛷ *40km*

Sölden 199
⊠ *Airtours, Crystal, Crystal Finest, Neilson, Ski Wild*

Soldeu 115
⊠ *Airtours, Club Pavilion, Crystal, Directski.com, First Choice Ski, Independent Ski Links, Inghams, Lagrange Holidays, Neilson, Panorama Holidays, Ski Tracer, Ski Wild, Thomson*

Soldier Mountain USA
Family resort in Central Idaho; backcountry snowcat tours.
slopes 1770–2195m
⛷ *4* ⛷ *670 acres*

Solitude 634
⊠ *AmeriCan Ski*

Söll 202
⊠ *Airtours, Catered Ski Chalets, Crystal, Directski.com, First Choice Ski, Independent Ski Links, Inghams, Neilson, Panorama Holidays, Ski Hillwood, Ski Line, Ski Tracer, Ski Wild, Thomson*

Solvista USA
Child-oriented resort close to Winter Park. Low snowfall record for Colorado.
2490m; slopes 2490–2795m
⛷ *5* ⛷ *250 acres*

Sommand France
Purpose-built base that shares area with Praz-de-Lys.
1420m; slopes 1200–1800m
⛷ *22* ⛷ *50km*

Sonnenkopf Austria
Ski area above Klösterle a few km west of the Arlberg pass – covered by the Arlberg ski pass.
slopes 1100–2300m
⛷ *10* ⛷ *39km*

Sorenberg Switzerland
Popular weekend retreat between Berne and Lucerne, with a high proportion of steep, low runs.
1165m; slopes 1165–2350m
⛷ *18* ⛷ *50km*

South Lake Tahoe USA
Tacky base for skiing Heavenly, with cheap lodging, traffic and gambling.

Spindleruv Mlyn Czech Republic
Largest Giant Mountains region resort but with few facilities serving several little low areas.
715m; slopes 750–1310m
⛷ *23* ⛷ *25km*

Thollon-les-Mémises   France
Attractive base for a relaxed
holiday. Own little area and
close to Portes du Soleil.
1000m; slopes 1600–2000m
⛷ 19 ⛏ 50km
✉ *Lagrange Holidays*

Thredbo   718

The Three Valleys   386

La Thuile   476
✉ *Alpine Answers, Crystal, First
Choice Ski, Independent Ski
Links, Inghams, Interski,
Neilson, Ski Tracer, Thomson*

Thyon 2000   532
Extremely limited ski-from-the-
door mid-mountain resort above
Veysonnaz in the Verbier ski
area.

Tignes   388
✉ *Alpine Answers, Catered Ski
Chalets, Chalet Group, Chalet
World Ski, Club Med, Corporate
Ski Company, Crystal, Crystal
Finest, Directski.com, Erna Low,
Esprit Ski, First Choice Ski,
Hucksters, Independent Ski
Links, Inghams, Inspired to Ski,
Interhome, Lagrange Holidays,
Made to Measure Holidays,
Mark Warner, MasterSki,
Mountain Tracks, Mountainsun,
Neilson, Peak Leisure, Ski
Activity, Ski Amis, Ski
Expectations, Ski France, Ski
Freshtracks, Ski Independence,
Ski Leisure Direction, Ski Line,
Ski Olympic, Ski Solutions, Ski
Supreme, Ski Tracer, Ski
Weekend, Ski4you, Skitopia,
Skiworld, Snoworks, Snowball
Holidays, Thomson, Total,
White Roc*

Timberline (Palmer Snowfield)
USA
East of Portland, Oregon, and
the only lift-served summer
skiing in the US: winter snow is
maintained by spreading vast
amounts of salt to harden it.
slopes 1830–2600m
⛷ 6 ⛏ 2,500 acres

Toblach   Italy
German name for Dobbiaco.

Togari   Japan
One of several areas close to
the 1998 Olympic site Nagano,
2.5 hours from Tokyo. ⛷ 10

Torgnon   Italy
Small village off the road up to
Cervinia, good for bad-weather
days. Some good cross-country
loops.
1500m; slopes 1500–1965m
⛷ 7 ⛏ 6km

Torgon   Switzerland
Old village in a pretty wooded
setting, with a connection to the
Portes du Soleil. 'Appalling lifts,'
says a recent reporter.
1150m; slopes 975–2275m
⛷ 219 ⛏ 650km
✉ *Interhome*

Le Tour   264
Charming, unspoiled hamlet at
the head of the Chamonix valley.

La Toussuire   377
✉ *Equity Ski, Erna Low,
Interhome, Lagrange Holidays*

Trafoi   Italy
Quiet, traditional (Austrian-style)
village near Bormio, worth a day
trip if snow is good at low
levels.
1570m; slopes 1570–2550m
⛷ 6 ⛏ 10km

Treble Cone   720

Tremblant   696
✉ *American Ski Classics,
Crystal, CV Travel, Elegant
Resorts, Equity Ski, Erna Low,
Frontier Ski, Inghams, Neilson,
Ski All America, Ski
Independence, Ski Safari, Ski
The American Dream, Ski
Tracer, Ski Wild, Skiworld,
Thomson, Trailfinders, United
Vacations, Virgin Snow*

Trentino   478

Troodos   Cyprus
Ski area on Mt Olympus, a 70-
minute drive from Nicosia.
Pretty, wooded slopes and fine
views.
⛷ 4 ⛏ 5km

Tröpolach   Austria
Small village at base of access
gondola for Nassfeld ski area.
610m; slopes 610–2195m
⛷ 30 ⛏ 100km

Trysil   703

Tryvann   703

Tschagguns   177
Village with a varied little area
of its own; part of the Montafon
valley area.

Tsugaike Kogen   Japan
Sizeable resort four hours from
Tokyo, three hours from Osaka.
Helicopter service to the top
station.
800m; slopes 800–1700m ⛷ 28

Tulfes   146

Turoa   720
On the south-western slopes of
Mt Ruapeha, with NZ's biggest
vertical. Mainly open, gentle
runs, with steeper runs at the
edges of the area. Plenty of
scope for off-piste.

Turracherhöhe   Austria
Tiny, unspoiled resort on a
mountain shelf, with varied
intermediate slopes above and
below it. A good outing from
Bad Kleinkirchheim.
1765m; slopes 1400–2200m
⛷ 11 ⛏ 30km
✉ *Alpine Tours*

Tyax Mountain Lake Resort
Canada
Heli-skiing operation in the
Chilcotin mountains – transfers
from Whistler or Vancouver.

Uludag   Turkey
Surprisingly suave, laid-back,
well-equipped, purpose-built
resort near Bursa, south of
Istanbul.
1750m; slopes 1750–2322m
⛷ 14 ⛏ 15km

Unken   Austria
Traditional village hidden in a
side valley. Closest slopes to
Salzburg.
565m; slopes 1000–1500m
⛷ 4 ⛏ 8km

Untergurgl   182
Valley-floor alternative to staying
in more expensive Hochgurgl or
Obergurgl.

Unternberg   Austria
Riverside village with trail
connecting into one of the
longest, most snow-sure cross-
country networks in Europe. St
Margarethen downill slopes
close by.
1030m

Unterwasser   Switzerland
Old but not especially attractive
resort 90 minutes from Zürich.
Fabulous lake and mountain
views. The more challenging half
of the area shared with
Wildhaus.
910m; slopes 900–2260m
⛷ 21 ⛏ 50km

Uttendorf-Weiss-See   Austria
Astute alternative to crowded
Kaprun when the snowline is
high.
805m; slopes 1485–2600m
⛷ 9 ⛏ 18km

Vail   608
✉ *Alpine Answers, AmeriCan
Ski, American Ski Classics,
Catered Ski Chalets, Chalet
World Ski, Crystal, Crystal
Finest, CV Travel, Elegant
Resorts, Erna Low, Independent
Ski Links, Inghams, Made to
Measure Holidays, Momentum
Ski, Ski Activity, Ski All
America, Ski Expectations, Ski
Freshtracks, Ski Independence,
Ski Line, Ski Safari, Ski
Solutions, Ski The American
Dream, Ski Tracer, Ski Wild,
Skiworld, Supertravel,
Thomson, Trailfinders, United
Vacations, Virgin Snow*

Valbella   Switzerland
Convenient but ordinary village
sharing large intermediate
Lenzerheide area.
1540m; slopes 1470–2865m
⛷ 39 ⛏ 155km

Valberg   France
Large Alpes-Maritimes resort
(bigger than better-known Isola
2000) close to Nice.
1650m; slopes 1430–2100m
⛷ 26 ⛏ 90km
✉ *Club Pavilion*

Val-Cenis   419
✉ *AmeriCan Ski, Crystal, Erna
Low, Lagrange Holidays, MGS
Ski, Peak Retreats, Ski Leisure
Direction, Ski4you, Snowcoach*

Val di Fassa   478
✉ *Directski.com, Thomson*

Val d'Illiez   Switzerland
Peaceful, unspoiled village a few
minutes below Champoussin.
Open-air thermal baths. Good
views of impressive Dents du
Midi. *950m*

Val-d'Isère   398
✉ *Airtours, Alpine Answers,
Alpine Weekends, Bladon Lines,
Catered Ski Chalets, Chalet
Group, Chalet World Ski,
Chardon Mountain Lodges, Club
Med, Corporate Ski Company,
Crystal, Crystal Finest, CV
Travel, Descent International,
Directski.com, Elegant Resorts,
Erna Low, Esprit Ski, Finlays,
First Choice Ski, Flexiski,
Independent Ski Links,
Inghams, Inspired to Ski,
Interhome, Lagrange Holidays,
Le Ski, Made to Measure
Holidays, Mark Warner,
Momentum Ski, Mountain
Tracks, Neilson, Oxford Ski
Company, Powder White, Scott
Dunn Ski, Silver Ski, Ski
Activity, Ski Amis, Ski Beat, Ski
Expectations, Ski France, Ski
Freshtracks, Ski Independence,
Ski Leisure Direction, Ski Line,
Ski Olympic, Ski Solutions, Ski
Supreme, Ski Tracer, Ski
Weekend, Ski-Val, Ski4you,
Skifrance4less, Skiworld,
Snowline, Snoworks,
Supertravel, Thomson, Total,
Val d'Isère A La Carte, VIP,
Weekends in Val d'Isère, White
Roc, YSE*

Val Ferret   Switzerland
Old climbing village near
Martigny, with spectacular views.
Own tiny area.
1600m ⛷ 4

Valfrejus   419
✉ *AmeriCan Ski, Erna Low,
Lagrange Holidays, Peak
Retreats*

Val Gardena   468

Vallandry   250
Family-friendly satellite of Les
Arcs with direct access to the
Paradiski area. For package
holidays see Peisey-Vallandry.
✉ *Ski Independence*

Valle Nevado   728
✉ *AmeriCan Ski, Crystal,
Momentum Ski, Scott Dunn
Latin America, Ski All America,
Ski Safari*

Valloire   419
✉ *Airtours, AmeriCan Ski, Club
Pavilion, Crystal, Erna Low,
Lagrange Holidays, Peak
Retreats, Ski France, Ski
Independence, Ski Leisure
Direction, Ski4you, Snowcoach*

Vallter 2000   Spain
Small resort on the far eastern
fringes of the Pyrenees, close to
the Costa Brava.
slopes 1950–2535m
⛷ 8 ⛏ 420 acres

Valmeinier   419
✉ *Airtours, Crystal, Erna Low,
Lagrange Holidays, Ski France,
Ski Independence, Ski Leisure
Direction, Ski4you,
Skifrance4less, Snowcoach*

Valmorel 409
⊠ Alpine Answers, Catered Ski Chalets, Crystal, Erna Low, Independent Ski Links, Lagrange Holidays, Neilson, Ski Amis, Ski Independence, Ski Leisure Direction, Ski Supreme, Ski Tracer, Ski4you

Val Senales Italy
Top-of-the-mountain hotel, the highest in the Alps, in the Dolomites near Merano.
3210m; slopes 2110–3210m
🛗 12 🚡 35km
⊠ Inntravel

Val-Thorens 411
⊠ Airtours, Catered Ski Chalets, Chalet World Ski, Club Med, Crystal, Directski.com, Erna Low, First Choice Ski, Flexiski, Independent Ski Links, Inghams, Interhome, Lagrange Holidays, Made to Measure Holidays, Neilson, Silver Ski, Ski Activity, Ski Amis, Ski Expectations, Ski France, Ski Freshtracks, Ski Independence, Ski Leisure Direction, Ski Line, Ski Solutions, Ski Supreme, Ski Tracer, Ski Weekend, Ski4you, Skifrance4less, Skiworld, Thomson, Total

Valtournenche 428
Cheaper alternative to Cervinia, with genuine Italian atmosphere, and access to the extensive area.

Vandans 177
Sizeable working village well placed for visiting all the Montafon areas.

Vars 357
Large, convenient purpose-built resort linked to Risoul.
⊠ Catered Ski Chalets, Crystal, Equity Ski, Erna Low, Interhome, Lagrange Holidays, Rocketski, Tops Ski Chalets and Club Hotels

Vasilitsa Greece
Resort in northern Greece, in the Pindos range, offering 'very good intermediate skiing,' according to reports.
1750m 🛗 2

Vaujany 241
Tiny, rustic village with lift accessing the heart of the Alpe-d'Huez ski area.
⊠ AmeriCan Ski, Erna Low, Peak Retreats, Ski Independence, Ski Leisure Direction, Ski Peak

Vegas Resort USA
Area formerly known as Lee Canyon, cut from forest only 50 minutes' drive from Las Vegas. Height and snowmaking gives fairly reliable snow. Night skiing.
2590m; slopes 2590–2840m
🛗 3 🚡 200 acres

Velka-Race Slovakia
600m; slopes 600–1050m
🛗 4 🚡 15km

Vemdalen 707
⊠ Neilson

Vemdalsskalet 707

Venosc France
Captivating tiny village of cobbled streets, ancient church and craft shops.

Vent Austria
High, remote Oztal village known mainly as a touring base, with just enough lift-served skiing to warrant a day trip from nearby Obergurgl.
1900m; slopes 1900–2680m
🛗 4 🚡 15km

Ventron France
Small village near La Bresse in the northerly Vosges mountains near Strasbourg, with more ski de fond than downhill terrain.
630m; slopes 900–1110m
🛗 8 🚡 15km

Verbier 532
⊠ Alpine Answers, Alpine Weekends, Bladon Lines, Catered Ski Chalets, Chalet World Ski, Corporate Ski Company, Crystal, Crystal Finest, Descent International, Elegant Resorts, Erna Low, First Choice Ski, Flexiski, Independent Ski Links, Inghams, Interhome, Jeffersons, Kaluma Ski, Made to Measure Holidays, Momentum Ski, Mountain Beds, Mountain Tracks, Oxford Ski Company, Peak Ski, Powder White, Ski Activity, Ski Expectations, Ski Freshtracks, Ski Independence, Ski Line, Ski Solutions, Ski Tracer, Ski Verbier, Ski Weekend, Ski with Julia, Skiworld, Supertravel, Swiss Travel Service, Thomson, Total, White Heat Skiing, White Roc

Vercorin Switzerland
Cluster of picture-postcard chalets on a shelf overlooking the Valais, reached by roundabout road or cable-car from near Chalais. Valley pass also covers Zinal, Grimentz and St Luc/Chandolin.
1330m; slopes 1330–2400m
🛗 9 🚡 35km

Verditz Austria
One of several small, mostly mountain-top areas overlooking the town of Villach.
675m; slopes 675–2165m
🛗 5 🚡 17km

Vex Switzerland
Major village in unspoiled, attractive setting south of Sion. Verbier slopes accessed nearby at Mayens-de-l'Ours.
900m

Veysonnaz 532
Little, old village within Verbier's Four Valleys network.

Vichères-Liddes Switzerland
Limited area near to Martigny. Valid with the Valais ski card.
1350m; slopes 1350–2270m
🛗 4 🚡 15km

Vic-sur-Cère France
Charming village with fine architecture, beneath Super-Lioran ski area. Beautiful extinct-volcano scenery.
680m; slopes 1250–1850m
🛗 24 🚡 60km
⊠ Lagrange Holidays

Viehhofen Austria
Cheaper place to stay when visiting Saalbach. It is 3km/2 miles from the Schönleiten gondola, and there is a run back to the village from the Asitz section.
860m 🛗 1

Vigo di Fassa Italy
Best base for the Fassa valley, with Sella Ronda access via nearby Campitello.
1430m; slopes 1465–2060m
🛗 8 🚡 25km

La Villa 461
Quiet Sella Ronda village in pretty setting, surrounded by mostly very easy skiing.

Villach-Dobratsch Austria
One of several small, mostly mountain-top areas overlooking the town of Villach.
900m; slopes 980–2165m
🛗 8 🚡 15km
⊠ Equity Ski

Villar-d'Arêne France
Tiny area on main road between La Grave and Serre-Chevalier. Empty, immaculately groomed, short easy runs, plus a couple of hotels.
1650m

Villard-de-Lans France
Unspoiled, lively, traditional village west of Grenoble. Snow-sure, thanks to snowmaking.
1050m; slopes 1160–2170m
🛗 29 🚡 130km
⊠ AmeriCan Ski, Lagrange Holidays

Villard-Reculas 241
Rustic village on periphery of Alpe-d'Huez ski area, with few local amenities.

Villaroger 250
Rustic hamlet with direct links up to Arc 2000 and excellent runs back down.
⊠ Chez Jay Ski Chalets

Villars 543
⊠ Club Med, Corporate Ski Company, Crystal, Inghams, Interhome, Kuoni, Lagrange Holidays, Made to Measure Holidays, Momentum Ski, Ski Independence, Ski Line, Ski Solutions, Ski Tracer, Ski Weekend, Swiss Travel Service, Switzerland Travel Centre, Thomson

Vipiteno Italy
Bargain-shopping town close to Brenner Pass.
960m; slopes 960–2100m
🛗 12 🚡 25km

Virgen Austria
Traditional village in a beautiful valley south of the Felbertauern tunnel. Slopes at Matrei. 1200m

Vitosha Bulgaria
Limited area of slopes and a few widely scattered hotels, 22 km/14 miles from Sofia, leading to crowds at weekends. The slopes are north-facing and have a decent snow record.
1810m; slopes 1515–2290m
🛗 8 🚡 29km

Vogel 714

Vorderlanersbach 138
Small, satellite village of pretty Lanersbach, with access to Mayrhofen ski area.

Voss 703
⊠ Alpine Tours, Crystal, Inghams

Vuokatti Finland
Small mountain in a remarkable setting, surrounded on three sides by lots of little lakes. Good activity base. 🛗 8

Wagrain 234

Waidring Austria
Quiet valley village north of Kitzbühel, with nursery slopes on the doorstep and a powerful gondola (with big car parks) on the outskirts going up to Steinplatte – an area of mainly gentle open slopes which is also accessible from Germany. Impressive lift system with two six-packs and four quads, but still prone to weekend queues. Slopes face north, and there is extensive snowmaking.
780m; slopes 1230–1860m
🛗 8 🚡 25km
⊠ Thomson

Waiorau Snow Farm 720

Wald im Pinzgau Austria
Cross-country village surrounded by Alpine areas – Gerlos, Krimml and Neukirchen – and with Pass Thurn also nearby.
885m
🛗 55 🚡 155km

Wanaka 720
Quiet, diffuse village in beautiful lakeside mountain setting, with two ski areas each half an hour away.

Waterville Valley USA
Popular New Hampshire area with spread-out village built in pleasing wooden low-rise style. There are a couple of genuine double-black-diamond mogul fields, but most of the slopes are intermediate.
600m; slopes 600–1215m
🛗 12 🚡 255 acres

Weinebene Austria
One of many gentle little areas in Austria's easternmost ski region near the Slovenian border. No major resorts in the vicinity.
1560m; slopes 1560–1835m
🛗 5 🚡 12km

Weissbach bei Lofer Austria
Traditional resort between Lofer
and Saalfelden. It has no slopes
of its own, but it's well placed
for touring the Tirol. Kitzbühel,
Saalbach, St Johann and Zell am
See are nearby.
665m

Weissensee Naggeralm
Austria
Little area in eastern Austria and
the location of Europe's largest
frozen lake, used for all kinds of
ice sports, including ice-golf.
930m; slopes 930–1400m
⬆5 ⬆ 6km

Weisspriach Austria
Hamlet on snowy pass near
Obertauern that shares its area
with Mauterndorf and St
Michael.
1115m; slopes 1115–2050m
⬆5 ⬆ 30km

Wengen 545
☒ Club Med, Crystal,
Independent Ski Links,
Inghams, Kuoni, Made to
Measure Holidays, Re-lax
Holidays, Ski Freshtracks, Ski
Line, Ski Solutions, Swiss
Travel Service, Switzerland
Travel Centre, Thomson

Wentworth Canada
Long-established Nova Scotia
area with largest accessible
acreage in the Maritime
Provinces. Harsh climate ensures
good snow-cover despite low
altitude.
55m; slopes 55–300m
⬆6 ⬆ 150 acres

Werfen Austria
Traditional village spoiled by the
Tauern autobahn, which runs
between it and the slopes. Good
touring to the Dachstein West
region.
620m

Werfenweng Austria
Hamlet with the advantage over
the main village of Werfen of
being away from the autobahn
and close to the slopes. Best for
novices.
1000m; slopes 1000–1835m
⬆10 ⬆ 25km
☒ Thomson

Westendorf 223
☒ Inghams, Thomson

Whakapapa 720

Whistler 684
☒ Alpine Answers, AmeriCan
Ski, American Ski Classics,
Catered Ski Chalets, Chalet
World Ski, Cold Comforts
Lodging, Crystal, Crystal Finest,
CV Travel, Directski.com,
Elegant Resorts, Equity Ski,
Erna Low, Frontier Ski,
Independent Ski Links,
Inghams, Kaluma Ski, Made to
Measure Holidays, MasterSki,
M-----entum Ski, Neilson, Ski
--y, Ski All America, Ski
---ations, Ski Freshtracks,
-ependence, Ski Line, Ski
Ski Safari, Ski

Solutions, Ski The American
Dream, Ski Tracer, Ski Wild,
Skitopia, Skiworld, Solo's,
Supertravel, Thomson,
Trailfinders, United Vacations,
Virgin Snow

Whitecap Mountains Resort
USA
Largest, snowiest area in
Wisconsin, close enough to Lake
Superior and Minneapolis to
ensure winds and weekend
crowds.
435m; slopes 435–555m
⬆7 ⬆ 500 acres

Whiteface Mountain USA
Varied area in New York State
15km/10 miles from attractive
lakeside resort of Lake Placid.
93% snowmaking ensures good
snowcover. Plenty to do off the
slopes.
365m; slopes 365–1345m
⬆10 ⬆ 211 acres

White Pass Village USA
Closest area to Mt St Helens.
Remote and uncrowded with a
good snowfall record. Mostly
intermediate cruising.
1370m; slopes 1370–1825m
⬆6 ⬆ 635 acres

Whitewater Canada
Renowned for powder (40% off-
piste), food ('Excellent day
lodge,' says a 2006 reporter)
and weekend party atmosphere.
Accommodation in the historic
town of Nelson or a great day
out from nearby Red Resort.
1640m; slopes 1640–2040m ⬆3
☒ Frontier Ski, Ski Safari, Ski
The American Dream

Wildcat Mountain USA
New Hampshire area infamous
for bad weather, but one of the
best areas on a nice day.
Lodging in nearby Jackson and
North Conway.
slopes 600–1250m
⬆4 ⬆ 225 acres

Wildhaus Switzerland
Undeveloped farming community
in stunning scenery near
Liechtenstein; popular with
families and serious
snowboarders.
1100m; slopes 1100–2075m
⬆9 ⬆ 50km

Wildschönau 225
☒ Interhome

Lauchernalp Switzerland
Main village in secluded,
picturesque dead-end
Lötschental, north of Rhône
valley, with small but tall slopes
reached by cable-car.
1420m; slopes 1420–2700m
⬆7 ⬆ 33km

Willamette Pass USA
US speed skiing training base in
national forest near beautiful
Crater Lake, Oregon. Small but
varied slopes popular with
weekenders.
1560m; slopes 1560–2035m
⬆7 ⬆ 550 acres

Williams USA
Tiny area above the main place
to stay for the Grand Canyon.
slopes 2010–2270m
⬆2 ⬆ 50 acres

Windischgarsten Austria
Large working village in Upper
Austria with cross-country trails
around and downhill slopes at
nearby Hinterstoder and Spital
am Pyrhn. *600m*

Winter Park 615
☒ Alpine Answers, AmeriCan
Ski, American Ski Classics,
Catered Ski Chalets, Crystal,
Equity Ski, Erna Low,
Independent Ski Links, Neilson,
Ski All America, Ski
Independence, Ski Safari, Ski
Solutions, Ski The American
Dream, Ski Tracer, Skiworld,
Supertravel, Thomson, United
Vacations, Virgin Snow

Wolf Creek USA
Remote area on a pass of the
same name, with 'the most
snow' in Colorado.
3140m; slopes 3140–3630m
⬆6 ⬆ 1,600 acres
☒ AmeriCan Ski

Wolf Mountain USA
Utah cross-country area close to
Salt Lake City. Powder Mountain
and Snowbasin are nearby
Alpine areas.
⬆3 ⬆ 100 acres

Xonrupt France
Cross-country venue only 3km/2
miles from nearest Alpine slopes
at Gérardmer.
715m
☒ Lagrange Holidays

Yangji Resort South Korea
Modern resort an hour (60km/37
miles) south of Seoul, with runs
cut out of dense forest. Gets
very crowded. ⬆6

Ylläs 701
☒ Bladon Lines, First Choice
Ski, Inghams, Inntravel

Yong Pyong Resort
South Korea
Aka Dragon Valley. 200km/125
miles east of Seoul, close to the
east coast. Self-contained
purpose-built resort village.
750m; slopes 750–1460m
⬆15 ⬆ 20km

Zakopane Poland
An interesting old town
100km/62 miles south of Kraków
on the Slovakian border. Mostly
intermediate slopes.
830m; slopes 1000–1960m
⬆20 ⬆ 10km
☒ Ramblers Holidays

Zao Japan
Big area with unpredictable
weather, four hours from Tokyo
by train. Known for 'chouoh' –
pines frozen into weird shapes.
780m; slopes 780–1660m ⬆42

Zauchensee Austria
Purpose-built resort at the head
of its valley, at one end of
three-valley lift network linking
it via Flachauwinkl to Kleinarl.

855m; slopes 800–2185m
⬆59 ⬆ 200km
☒ Ski Hillwood

Zell am See 229
☒ Airtours, Catered Ski
Chalets, Chalet Group, Crystal,
Directski.com, Erna Low, First
Choice Ski, Independent Ski
Links, Inghams, Interhome,
Lagrange Holidays, Neilson,
PGL Travel, Ski Freshtracks, Ski
Line, Ski Tracer, Ski Wild,
Snowscape, Thomson

Zell im Zillertal Austria
Sprawling valley town with
slopes on two nearby
mountains. Now linked to higher
Gerlos and Königsleiten to form
a fair-sized area. 'Some of the
best wide motorway skiing,'
reports a 2004 visitor.
580m; slopes 930–2410m
⬆40 ⬆ 115km
☒ Neilson

Zermatt 550
☒ Alpine Answers, Alpine
Weekends, Bladon Lines,
Catered Ski Chalets, Chalet
World Ski, Corporate Ski
Company, Crystal, Crystal
Finest, CV Travel, Descent
International, Elegant Resorts,
Independent Ski Links,
Inghams, Interhome, Kuoni,
Lagrange Holidays, Lagrange
Holidays, Made to Measure
Holidays, Momentum Ski,
Mountain Beds, Mountain
Tracks, Oxford Ski Company,
Powder Byrne, Scott Dunn Ski,
Ski Expectations, Ski
Freshtracks, Ski Independence,
Ski Line, Ski Solutions, Ski
Tracer, Ski with Julia,
Supertravel, Swiss Travel
Service, Switzerland Travel
Centre, Thomson, Total, VIP,
White Roc

Zillertal Austria
Valley of ten ski resorts, of
which the most well known is
Mayrhofen.

Zinal Switzerland
Pretty, rustic village with some
modern development, near the
head of the Val d'Anniviers.
1680m; slopes 1680–2895m
⬆9 ⬆ 70km ☒ Interhome

Zug 163
Tiny village in scenic location
with Lech's toughest skiing on
its doorstep.

Zürs 163
High, smart but soulless village
on road to Lech.
☒ Alpine Answers, Corporate
Ski Company, Crystal, Elegant
Resorts, Inghams, Made to
Measure Holidays, Oxford Ski
Company, Powder Byrne

Zweisimmen Switzerland
Limited but inexpensive base for
slopes around Gstaad, with its
own delightful easy area too.
965m; slopes 950–3000m
⬆67 ⬆ 250km